KU-007-554

Contents at a Glance

Alessandro Del Sole

Visual Basic® 2015

UNLEASHED

SAMS | 800 East 96th Street, Indianapolis, Indiana 46240 USA

Visual Basic® 2015 Unleashed

ISBN-13: 978-0-672-33450-4

ISBN-10: 0-672-33450-X

Library of Congress Control Number: 2015906633

Printed in the United States of America

First Printing July 2015

Trademarks

All terms mentioned in this book that are known to be trademarks or service marks have been appropriately capitalized. Sams Publishing cannot attest to the accuracy of this information. Use of a term in this book should not be regarded as affecting the validity of any trademark or service mark.

Warning and Disclaimer

Every effort has been made to make this book as complete and as accurate as possible, but no warranty or fitness is implied. The information provided is on an "as is" basis. The author and the publisher shall have neither liability nor responsibility to any person or entity with respect to any loss or damages arising from the information contained in this book.

Special Sales

For information about buying this title in bulk quantities, or for special sales opportunities (which may include electronic versions; custom cover designs; and content particular to your business, training goals, marketing focus, or branding interests), please contact our corporate sales department at corpsales@pearsoned.com or (800) 382-3419.

For government sales inquiries, please contact governmentsales@pearsoned.com.

For questions about sales outside the U.S., please contact international@pearsoned.com.

Editor-in-Chief
Greg Wiegand

Acquisitions Editor
Joan Murray

Development Editor
Mark Renfrow

Managing Editor
Kristy Hart

Senior Project Editor
Betsy Gratner

Indexer
Tim Wright

Proofreader
Katie Matejka

Technical Editors
Anthony D. Green
Lucian Wischik

Publishing Coordinator
Cindy Teeters

Cover Designer
Mark Shirar

Senior Compositor
Gloria Schurick

> **NOTE**
>
> In order to accommodate maximum page count for a print book and still be the exhaustive reference on Visual Basic, Chapters 52 and 53 are only available online. To access them, register your book at www.informit.com/title/9780672334504. Click the *Register Your Product* link. You will be prompted to sign in or create an account. When asked for the ISBN, enter 9780672334504. This *print book* ISBN must be entered even if you have a digital copy of the book. From there, click *Access Bonus Content* in the "Registered Products" section of your account page.

Table of Contents

Online-Only Chapters

52   Advanced IDE Features

53   Testing Code with Unit Tests and Test-Driven Development

---
NOTE

In order to accommodate maximum page count for a print book and still be the exhaustive reference on Visual Basic, Chapters 52 and 53 are only available online. To access them, register your book at www.informit.com/title/9780672334504. Click the *Register Your Product* link. You will be prompted to sign in or create an account. When asked for the ISBN, enter 9780672334504. This *print book* ISBN must be entered even if you have a digital copy of the book. From there, click *Access Bonus Content* in the "Registered Products" section of your account page.

Foreword

Back in 2013 Alessandro Del Sole reached out to the Visual Basic team to let us know that the VB Tips & Tricks user group in Italy had reached a 15-year milestone and that what would make it even more special would be to have a team member come out and celebrate with them. Being asked by the leader of one of our longest-running user groups boasting a membership of 40,000+ strong, it was a no-brainer. I knew I had to go. So I hopped on a 12-hour flight to Milan to give a 1-hour talk, a 10-minute speech, turned around, and flew back home (another 12 hours)—and it was totally worth it!

I joined the Visual Basic team in 2010 and in the entire time that I've known him since then, Alessandro has been an invaluable member of the VB community. He has consistently exemplified the qualities of an MVP, demonstrating technical leadership in the community, subject matter expertise, and receiving ongoing nominations and recognition by his peers as MVP of the Year.

Being familiar with Alessandro's VB books, I've always admired the comprehensiveness of his writing style. So many books approach development from just the language, or just a few libraries, but Alessandro covers the end-to-end—from language to library to IDE, in keeping with the Visual Basic spirit. And that style continues in this new edition. Here in Redmond, we're all very proud of the tremendous value we've added for VB developers in Visual Studio 2015, including a new ecosystem of Roslyn-powered diagnostic analyzers, refactoring (for the first time), great productivity language features, and a brand new experience for developing universal Windows 10 apps that run on PCs, Windows Phone, Xbox One, Microsoft Band, and HoloLens! True to form, Alessandro has taken the time to revisit everything new; each of his chapters in this edition highlights those enhancements, leaving nothing out. And personally, as the PM for the Roslyn APIs and a VB language designer for the last five years, I was especially thrilled to see him take up the topic of authoring code analysis tools with Roslyn (with his usual technical fervor) in the "Code Analysis" chapter.

So if you're looking for one-stop shopping to get the big picture (and get developing) in .NET and Visual Studio for VB developers in 2015, then this is the book for you. You'll be glued to it for a week integrating all the little enhancements into your day-to-day. And then after you've caught your breath, you'll keep coming back to it again and again as you explore whole new technologies over time. Much like those 24 hours of flying back in 2013, this book is totally worth it!

Anthony D. Green

Program Manager, Visual Basic, Microsoft

About the Author

Alessandro Del Sole, a Microsoft Most Valuable Professional (MVP) for .NET and Visual Basic since 2008, is well known throughout the global VB community. He is a community leader on the Italian Visual Basic Tips and Tricks website (http://www.visual-basic.it), which serves more than 46,000 VB developers, as well as a frequent contributor to the MSDN Visual Studio Developer Center. He has been awarded MVP of the Year five times (2009, 2010, 2011, 2012, 2014) and enjoys writing articles on .NET development both in English and Italian. He also writes blog posts and produces instructional videos as well as Windows Store apps. You can find him online in forums and you can follow him on Twitter at @progalex.

Dedication

Acknowledgments

First, I would like to thank Joan Murray, Betsy Gratner, Kitty Wilson, Mark Renfrow, and everyone else at Sams Publishing for trusting me enough to write the third edition of this book about Visual Basic. Writing books like this is hard work not only for the author but also for all the people involved in the reviews and in the production process. Working with these guys made the process much more pleasant. Thank you!

Very special thanks to Lucian Wischik and Anthony D. Green from the Managed Languages Team at Microsoft, who have been the technical editors for this book. They did an incredible job walking through every single sentence and every single line of code. As the people who best know the Visual Basic language in the world, their suggestions and corrections were invaluable to me and definitely contributed to creating excellent and precise content. Thank you so much.

Great thanks also to the guys from the Italian subsidiary of Microsoft, Roberto Andreoli, Lorenzo Barbieri, Erica Barone, and Matteo Pagani, for their continuous support and encouragement for my activities. My deep thanks and appreciation for their passionate work with communities and with MVPs to Alessandro Teglia, Cristina Gonzalez Herrero (my MVP lead), and Marjorie di Clemente.

I would like to thank my everyday friends who are always ready to encourage me even if they are not developers and will never read my books. Most importantly, these people always support me when I need their help. So my deep thanks to Nadia Paloschi, Roberto Bianchi, Alessandro Ardovini, Michela Santini, Leonardo Amici, and Karin Meier. You are in my heart.

As a community leader in the Italian Visual Basic Tips and Tricks community (www.visual-basic.it), I would like to thank all those guys who are the stimulus for making things better every day; all those people who visited my blog at least once or who read even one article of mine; and all those people who visit our website and follow us on forums, videos, articles, and blogs. Special thanks to my MVP colleagues Diego Cattaruzza, Antonio Catucci, Renato Marzaro, and Raffaele Rialdi for their great support and valuable suggestions. Thanks to Marco Notari for his continuous support and encouragement.

We Want to Hear from You!

As the reader of this book, *you* are our most important critic and commentator. We value your opinion and want to know what we're doing right, what we could do better, what areas you'd like to see us publish in, and any other words of wisdom you're willing to pass our way.

We welcome your comments. You can email or write to let us know what you did or didn't like about this book—as well as what we can do to make our books better.

Please note that we cannot help you with technical problems related to the topic of this book.

When you write, please be sure to include this book's title and author as well as your name and email address. We will carefully review your comments and share them with the author and editors who worked on the book.

Email: consumer@samspublishing.com

Mail: Sams Publishing
         ATTN: Reader Feedback
         800 East 96th Street
         Indianapolis, IN 46240 USA

Reader Services

Visit our website and register this book at informit.com/register for convenient access to any updates, downloads, or errata that might be available for this book.

Introduction

A new era is coming for Microsoft. From Windows 10, to embracing open source, to opening to third-party platforms and operating systems, to the cloud first/mobile first vision, to the release of Visual Studio 2015, it is really an exciting time to be a software developer working with Microsoft products and technologies. From a developer perspective, Visual Studio 2015 marks a very important milestone because it is the state of the art in representing Redmond's new vision and because it is the most productive version ever. Both the Visual Basic and C# compilers have been open sourced, together with a tiny, modular subset of the .NET Framework called .NET Core, which is intended for cross-platform development. There are many new features, many new tools, and many new development opportunities with Visual Studio 2015 and the Visual Basic language that certainly open up amazing new scenarios but that also require some changes in how to approach building applications, especially with regard to mobile devices. As an experienced developer working with Visual Basic for many years and as a community person who daily connects with developers worldwide, I know very well what programmers using Visual Basic need to face in the real world, what they expect from developer tools and learning resources, and what they need to get the most out of their code and skills in order to build high-quality, rich applications and to get appropriate information to look at the future.

This book has two main goals: the first goal is to walk through the Visual Basic programming language deeply, explaining all the available language features, object-oriented programming, common patterns, and everything you need to know to really master the language. The second goal is to show what you can do with Visual Basic in practice; for instance, you can build Windows applications for the desktop, and you can also build apps for Windows 10 (which is a brand-new topic), as well as applications for the web, the cloud, and other platforms. Describing the VB language and what you can do with it is a tradition retaken from previous editions; but technology evolves, and so does the *Visual Basic Unleashed* book. With updated content and chapters that describe in details all the new language features, this new edition also focuses on the latest tools and platforms. As a couple of significant examples, *Visual Basic 2015 Unleashed* explains how to build universal Windows apps for Windows 10 and how to leverage the new compiler APIs from the .NET Compiler Platform to write custom domain-specific live code analysis rules. In addition, the book explains how to get the maximum out of the Visual Studio's development environment so that you can be more productive than ever. But there is a lot more; this book embraces all the possible development areas available to Visual Basic today. A new era is coming for Microsoft, and it's coming for you, too.

Code Samples and Software Requirements

Good explanations often require effective code examples. The companion source code for this book can be downloaded from www.informit.com/title/9780672334504. Code samples are organized by chapter so that it is easy to find the code you need. In order to load, compile, and test the source code, you need Microsoft Visual Studio 2015. If you are not an MSDN subscriber or you did not purchase one of the paid editions, you can download Visual Studio 2015 Community, which is available for free and is enough to run the sample code. You can download Visual Studio 2015 Community (as well as a trial of the Enterprise edition) from https://www.visualstudio.com/downloads/visual-studio-2015-downloads-vs. You are also encouraged to download and install the Visual Studio 2015 Software Development Kit (SDK), which is a requirement in some chapters and is available from the same location as the free download.

Code-Continuation Arrows

When a line of code is too long to fit on the page of the printed book, a code-continuation arrow (➥) appears to mark the continuation. Here is an example:

```
        somePeople.Add(New Person With {.FirstName = "First Name: " &
➥i.ToString,
```

CHAPTER 1

Introducing .NET 2015

As a Visual Basic 2015 developer, you need to understand the concepts and technology that empower your applications. Microsoft .NET is the technology that provides the infrastructure for building next-generation applications for the desktop, the web, and the cloud—that run on the most recent operating systems. Although covering every aspect of .NET is not possible, in this chapter you learn the basics of its architecture, as well as the Base Class Library and tools. This chapter also introduces important concepts and terminology that are used throughout the rest of the book. If you have already had experience with .NET, in this chapter you will learn about the revolutionary changes in how Microsoft is offering .NET today.

.NET 2015: A New Vision for Development

Generally speaking, applications you develop need an execution environment that offers services, tools, and libraries. For many years, for applications built with Microsoft Visual Basic, the execution environment has been the Microsoft .NET Framework. In previous releases, the .NET Framework was a unique environment for building a variety of applications, including desktop applications, web applications, and apps for mobile devices. With the new release, Microsoft has taken some steps forward: It has kept the full .NET Framework, now in version **4.6**, for desktop applications, and it has created **.NET Core 5**, a new open source, modular framework for creating cross-platform applications and Windows 10 applications. Both frameworks share a number of major components, such as compilers, some libraries, and the garbage collector. Both frameworks are part of the new .NET vision called **.NET 2015**. Figure 1.1 shows a high-level diagram of .NET 2015.

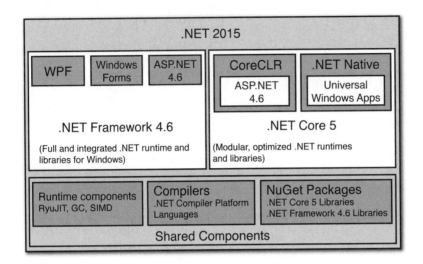

FIGURE 1.1   Components of .NET 2015.

Actually, .NET 2015 is not a specific development platform. Rather, it is an umbrella for a group of platforms, a convenient way to highlight and summarize what is new in this release. This chapter provides information about both .NET Framework 4.6 and .NET Core 5 to give you a more precise idea about new directions for developing using .NET.

THE FOCUS OF THIS BOOK

Most concepts you learn in this book apply to both .NET Framework 4.6 and .NET Core 5. However, some topics are specific to each platform. Specifically, Parts I, "Learning the Basics of VB," II, "Object-Oriented Programming with Visual Basic 2015," III, "Advanced Language Features," IV, "Data Access with ADO.NET and LINQ," and X, "Code Analysis with VB 2015," apply to both .NET Framework 4.6 and .NET Core 5. For the most part, Parts V, "Building Windows Desktop Applications," VI, "Building Web and Mobile Applications," VII, "Networking and Exposing Data Through Networks," VIII, "Advanced .NET Framework with VB 2015," and IX, "Applications Deployment," apply to the .NET Framework 4.6; however, Chapter 36, "Building Universal Apps for Windows 10," applies to .NET Core 5, and Chapters 41, "Parallel Programming and Parallel LINQ," and 42, "Asynchronous Programming," apply to both .NET Framework 4.6 and .NET Core 5.

Because you will work with the .NET Framework 4.6 for building desktop applications and because .NET Core 5 has limited support for Visual Basic today, a more thorough discussion will be provided for .NET Framework 4.6, but of course, many concepts will be valid for .NET Core 5 as well.

The .NET Framework 4.6 for Desktop

Microsoft .NET Framework 4.6 for Desktop is a complex technology that provides the infrastructure for building, running, and managing Windows and web applications. In a layered representation, the .NET Framework is a layer positioned between the Microsoft Windows operating system and your applications. .NET Framework 4.6 is composed of several parts, including libraries, executable tools, and relationships, and it integrates with the Windows operating system. Microsoft Visual Studio 2015 relies on the new version of the .NET Framework 4.6. Visual Basic 2015, C# 6.0, and F# 4.0 are .NET languages that can build applications for the .NET Framework 4.6. The new version of this technology introduces important new features that will be described later. In this chapter you get an overview of the most important features of the .NET Framework so that you will know how applications built with Visual Basic 2015 can run and how they can be built. From a developer's perspective, with .NET Framework 4.6 you can build the following kinds of applications:

▶ Web applications with the ASP.NET 4.6 platform.

▶ Windows desktop applications with the Windows Presentation Foundation (WPF) platform.

▶ Windows desktop applications with the Windows Forms platform. Windows Forms is still supported by Microsoft, but it is an obsolete platform and should only be used for maintaining existing programs. (The latest update to Windows Forms was in 2010.) You should never use Windows Forms on new projects but should use WPF instead.

▶ Distributed services for exchanging data through networks with Windows Communication Foundation (WCF) services (server side only) and WebAPI services.

.NET Core 5 targets other kinds of applications, as described in the next section.

Where Is the .NET Framework?

When you install Microsoft Visual Studio 2015, the setup process installs.NET Framework 4.6 into a folder named %windir%\Microsoft.NET\Framework\4.0.30319. (See the section "Differences Between .NET 4.6 and 4.5," later in this chapter, for details about versioning.) If you open this folder with Windows Explorer, you see many DLL libraries that constitute the Base Class Library, which exposes types that you use in your applications. The Base Class Library is discussed in more detail later in this chapter. The .NET Framework also provides several command-line tools, such as MSBuild (the build engine for Visual Studio), but in most scenarios you will not need to invoke them manually because you will work with the Microsoft Visual Studio 2015 IDE, which invokes the appropriate tools when needed. Information on these and other .NET tools invoked by Visual Studio is provided throughout this book.

MSBUILD IS OPEN SOURCE

The MSBuild tool has been recently released as an open source project, available at https://github.com/microsoft/msbuild.

The Architecture of the .NET Framework 4.6

To better understand the structure of the .NET Framework 4.6, think about it as a layered architecture. Figure 1.2 shows a high-level representation of the .NET Framework 4.6 architecture. The first level of the representation is the Windows operating system; the .NET Framework's layer is located between the system and applications. The second level is the *Common Language Runtime* (*CLR*), which is the part of the .NET Framework that does the most work. We discuss the CLR later in this chapter. The next level is the *Base Class Library* (*BCL*), which provides all .NET objects that can be used both in your code and by Visual Basic when creating applications. The BCL also provides the infrastructure of several .NET technologies that you use in building applications, such as WPF, Windows Forms, and ASP.NET. The last level is applications that rely on the other layers.

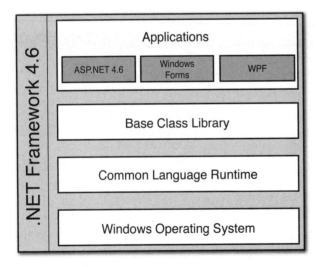

FIGURE 1.2   The layered architecture of the .NET Framework 4.6.

THE SILVERLIGHT STORY

If you have read previous editions of this book, one difference you will notice is that this edition does not discuss Silverlight. For years, Silverlight was a great companion for building rich-client applications running in the browser. However, Microsoft stopped working on Silverlight a few years ago. Microsoft still supports Silverlight, but it will not make any new versions available. Instead of talking about Silverlight, this edition provides information on more modern development platforms, such as universal Windows apps.

Differences Between .NET 4.6 and 4.5

The .NET Framework 4.6 is an in-place update for .NET Framework 4.0, 4.5, 4.5.1, and 4.5.2. If you try to install the .NET Framework 4.6 on a machine that already has .NET 4.5 installed, you will simply overwrite that version in the same directory and add new assemblies specific to the new version. As a result, applications that you created with Visual Studio 2010 (including the Express editions), Visual Studio 2012, and Visual Studio 2013 will still run with no problems, but they will not take advantage of the new version's features. As another result, migrating a project from Visual Studio 2010, 2012, and 2013 to Visual Studio 2015 should be painless. Of course, version 4.6 provides a lot of changes and improvements at the architecture level, so installing the new version will update existing core assemblies of.NET 4.x (if any) with more recent files and will also update the architectural infrastructure of the CLR.

An important difference between .NET 4.6 and previous .NET 4.x versions is that with .NET 4.6, the %windir%\Microsoft.NET\Framework\4.0.30319 folder contains assemblies of the Base Class Library for all versions from 4.0 up to 4.6, but it no longer contains compilers and the MSBuild tool. In .NET 4.6, these are instead located in C:\Program Files (x86)\MSBuild\14.0\Bin. Tools and compilers you still see in %windir%\Microsoft.NET\Framework\4.0.30319 are from previous versions of .NET.

APIS AND RUNTIME DIFFERENCES

If you are interested in what APIs and runtime tools have been improved or changed in the .NET Framework 4.6 compared to .NET 4.5, 4.5.1, and 4.5.2, visit http://msdn.microsoft.com/en-us/library/ms171868(v=vs.110).aspx.

Understanding that .NET Framework 4.6 is an update of previous versions is also important for another reason: When browsing the MSDN documentation, you might find pages about specific programming topics that still refer to Visual Studio 2013 and 2012. In such a case, you might think that the MSDN documentation is not up to date, but it is actually presenting topics that are still valid in the 2015 version.

The Common Language Runtime

As its name implies, the Common Language Runtime provides an infrastructure that is common to all.NET languages. This infrastructure is responsible for taking control of an application's execution and manages tasks such as memory management, access to system resources, security services, and so on. This kind of common infrastructure bridges the gap that exists between different Win32 programming languages because all .NET languages have the same possibilities. Moreover, the CLR enables applications to run inside a managed environment. The word *managed* is fundamental in the .NET development, as explained in the next section.

Writing Managed Code

When talking about Visual Basic 2015 development and, more generally, about .NET development, you often hear about writing managed code. Before the first version of .NET (or still with non-.NET development environments), the developer was the only person responsible for interacting with system resources and the operating system. The developer had to consider tasks such as taking care of accessing parts of the operating system and managing memory allocation for objects. In other words, the applications could interact directly with the system. However, as you can easily understand, this approach has some big limitations both because of security issues and because damages could be dangerous. The .NET Framework provides instead a managed environment. This means that the application communicates with the .NET Framework instead of with the operating system, and the .NET Runtime is responsible for managing the application execution, including memory management, resource management, and access to system resources. For example, the Common Language Runtime can prevent an application from accessing particular system resources if it is not considered fully trusted according to the .NET security zones.

SPEAKING WITH THE SYSTEM

You can still interact directly with the operating system, such as to invoke Windows APIs (also known as Platform Invoke, or P/Invoke for short). This technique is known as writing unmanaged code, and it should be used only when strictly required. This topic is discussed in Chapter 46, "Platform Invokes and Interoperability with the COM Architecture."

Managed code and the CLR also affect how applications are produced by compilers.

Assemblies in .NET Framework 4.6 for Desktop

In classic Win32 development environments, such as Visual Basic 6 or Visual C++, source code is parsed by compilers that produce binary executable files that can be immediately loaded and run by the operating system. This affects both standalone applications and dynamic/type libraries. Actually, Win32 applications, built with Visual Basic 6 and C++, used a runtime, but if you had applications developed with different programming languages, you also had to install the appropriate runtimes. In .NET development, things are quite different. Whatever .NET language you create applications with, compilers generate an *assembly*, which is a file containing .NET executable code and is composed essentially of two kinds of elements: CIL code and metadata.

CIL (formerly known as MSIL) stands for Common Intermediate Language and is a high-level assembly programming language that is also object oriented and provides a set of instructions that are CPU independent (rather than building executables that implement CPU-dependent sets of instructions). CIL is a common language in the sense that the same programming tasks written with different .NET languages produce the same IL code. Metadata, on the other hand, is a set of information related to the types implemented in the code. Such information can contain signatures, functions and procedures, members in types, and members in externally referenced types. Basically, the purpose of metadata is to describe the code to the .NET Framework.

Obviously, although an assembly can have an .exe extension, due to the described structure, it cannot be directly executed by the operating system. In fact, when you run a .NET application, the operating system can recognize it as a .NET assembly (because between .NET and Windows there is a strict cooperation) and invoke the just-in-time (JIT) compiler. When you launch an assembly for execution, the .NET Framework packages all the information and translates it into an executable that the operating system can understand and run. This task is the responsibility of the JIT compiler, which compiles code on-the-fly just before its execution and keeps the compiled code ready for execution. It acts at the method level. This means that it first searches for and compiles the application's entry point (typically the Sub Main), loads types used in the entry point, and then compiles other procedures or functions (*methods* in .NET terminology). If you have some code defined inside external assemblies, just before the method is executed, the JIT compiler loads the assembly in memory and then compiles the code. Of course, loading an external assembly in memory could require some time and affect performance, but it can be a good idea to place seldom-used methods inside external assemblies, just as it could be a good idea to place seldom-used code inside separated methods.

The .NET Framework 4.6 introduces important enhancements to the JIT compiler for 64-bit processors, which provide significant improvements to performances. The new JIT compiler, called **RyuJIT**, is the default compiler on 64-bit machines.

CONSIDERATIONS ABOUT WINDOWS 10 APPS

While what you have read in this section is true in the .NET Framework 4.6 for desktop, things are different when you build apps for Windows 10. The section "The .NET Native Technology," later in this chapter, provides more information about these differences.

IL Disassembler

The .NET Framework 4.6, as well as its predecessor, offers the IL Disassembler tool, also known as ILDasm, which allows you to investigate the intermediate language for the specified assembly. This tool is available in the C:\Program Files (x86)\MSBuild\14.0\ Bin folder and is named ILDasm.exe. You can launch this tool and select the assembly you want to investigate via a convenient user interface. For an example of using IL Disassembler, see Chapter 44, "Reflection."

The Base Class Library

The .NET Framework Base Class Library (BCL) provides thousands of reusable types that you can use in your code and that cover all the .NET technologies, such as WPF, ASP. NET 4.6, LINQ, and so on. Types defined in the BCL enable you to do millions of things without requiring you to call unmanaged code and Windows APIs and, often, without using external components. A type is something that states what an object must represent. For example, String and Integer are types, and you might have a variable of type String (that is, a text message) or a variable of type Integer (a number). Note that a *type* is not the same as a *class*. In fact, types can be of two kinds—reference types and value types—and a class is a reference type. This topic is the subject of Chapter 4, "Data Types and Expressions."

Types in the BCL are organized within namespaces, which act as containers for types; the name of each namespace is strictly related to the technology it refers to. For example, the `System.Windows.Controls` namespace implements types for drawing controls in Windows Presentation Foundation applications, whereas `System.Web` implements types for working with web applications. You will get a more detailed introduction to namespaces in Chapter 3, "The Anatomy of a Visual Basic Project," and Chapter 9, "Organizing Types Within Namespaces." Basically each namespace name that begins with `System` is part of the BCL. There are also some namespaces whose names begin with `Microsoft` that are also part of the BCL. These namespaces are typically used by the Visual Studio development environment and by the Visual Basic compiler, although you can also use them in your code in some particular scenarios (such as code generation or interaction with the Windows registry). The BCL is composed of several assemblies. One of the most important is MsCorlib.dll (Microsoft Core Library), which is part of the .NET Framework and will always be required in your projects. Other assemblies can often be related to specific technologies; for example, the System.ServiceModel.dll assembly integrates the BCL with the WCF main infrastructure. Also, some namespaces don't provide the infrastructure for other technologies and are used only in particular scenarios; therefore, they are defined in assemblies external to MsCorlib (Microsoft Core Library). All these assemblies and namespaces are described in the appropriate chapters.

Introducing .NET Core 5

.NET Core 5 is an open source, general-purpose, and modular subset of the .NET Framework that is designed to be portable across platforms, with the goal of maximizing code reuse and sharing. .NET Core 5 is modular because it is offered in smaller assembly packages with mostly no dependencies rather than one large assembly that contains most of the core functionality. This is important for two reasons: Microsoft can update .NET Core 5 with an agile development model, while you as a developer can simply choose the functionality pieces that you actually need for your apps and libraries. Instead of adding assembly references, as you are used to doing if you have existing experience with Visual Studio, when developing for .NET Core 5, you get packages via the NuGet Package Manager, an integrated tool in Visual Studio 2015 that makes it easy to download and include libraries in your projects. It is used several times throughout the book and is discussed more thoroughly in Chapter 52, "Advanced IDE Features."

Today, with .NET Core 5, you can build the following kinds of applications:

▶ Universal apps for Windows 10 (see Chapter 36)

▶ Cross-platform web applications with ASP.NET 5

▶ Portable class libraries

▶ Portable Console applications (currently available only for ASP.NET 5 Core)

The promise is that .NET Core 5 will run on Windows, Mac OSX, and Linux systems, which is a revolutionary change for Microsoft. For this reason, .NET Core 5 could be your primary choice in the future if you plan to build cross-platform web applications and apps for mobile devices. .NET Core 5 has two major components:

▶ **A small Runtime that is built from the same code base as the .NET Framework CLR (CoreCLR)**—The .NET Core Runtime includes the same garbage collector and just-in-time compiler (RyuJIT), but it does not include features like application domains or code access security. The Runtime is delivered via NuGet and is currently represented by the Microsoft.CoreCLR package.

▶ **Base class libraries**—These libraries offer almost the same code as the full .NET Framework BCL, but they have been refactored to remove dependencies, so that it is easier to enable a smaller set of libraries.

Applications you build with .NET Core 5 run in an isolated environment. Visual Studio 2015 packages the CoreCLR, the application package, and libraries used by your application all into one local package. With this approach, your applications are not affected by machine-wide versions of the full .NET Framework, and, most importantly, they have no dependencies on the operating system. And because .NET Core 5 could run on Windows, Mac OSX, and Linux, it provides a shared implementation of APIs exposed by each operating system so that you can write the same code, regardless of the platform the application will run on. With regard to Windows 10 apps, .NET Core 5 provides the core runtime, but applications are compiled with **.NET Native**, a new compiler that compiles managed code into native code. .NET Native compilation starts with the VB (and C#, too) compiler generating IL code, then it generates C++, and finally it compiles into native machine code. .NET Native makes the startup time for a Windows 10 app up to 60% faster, and it optimizes memory usage. Figure 1.3 provides a representation of the .NET Core 5 architecture.

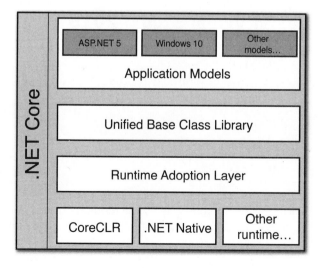

FIGURE 1.3 The .NET Core 5 layered architecture.

You'll see an example of building apps on .NET Core 5 in Chapter 36, which provides information on building a universal app for Windows 10. This book does not provide any examples of building ASP.NET Core applications because Visual Studio 2015 does not include any project templates for Visual Basic 2015, at least at this writing. (This chapter was written using the Release Candidate of Visual Studio 2015.) If you are interested in walking through the source code for .NET Core, you can visit https://github.com/dotnet/coreclr. The source code for ASP.NET Core is available at https://github.com/aspnet/Home.

What Is Open Source Today?

Most of the major components in .NET Core 5 are open source. In particular, the following is a list of open source layers:

▶ CoreCLR

▶ ASP.NET Core 5

▶ .NET Core 5 libraries

▶ Runtime components

▶ Compilers (see "The .NET Compiler Platform" section, later in this chapter)

▶ WCF client

At the moment, the Universal Windows Platform (UWP) is not open source. The .NET Foundation (www.dotnetfoundation.org) is an organization created by Microsoft to foster open development and collaboration around the .NET development platforms. Visit its website to find a full list of open source projects managed by Microsoft, including the aforementioned .NET Core 5 components.

Programming Languages in Visual Studio 2015

With Visual Studio 2015, you can develop applications with the following integrated programming languages:

▶ Visual Basic 14

▶ C# 6

▶ F# 4

▶ C++ 11/14/17

Depending on where you look, you may see the latest version of Visual Basic described as either Visual Basic 2015 or Visual Basic 14. For the most part, these terms are interchangeable, though this book uses the name Visual Basic 2015. Officially, 14 is the version number of the Visual Basic language—the syntax and semantics accepted as valid Visual Basic programs. Visual Basic 14 is an open source language with a freely available language specification that anyone may use to implement a Visual Basic compiler (such as Mono). Visual Basic 2015 is the product name for the collection of features, including code editing features like IntelliSense and refactorings, debugging features like Edit and Continue, and all other tooling to support the Visual Basic language in Visual Studio 2015. This convention is the same for the other Visual Studio languages, but only Visual Basic is still called "Visual," even when just talking about the language, due to its strong affiliation with Visual Studio. That is also why the Visual Basic language always shares the same version number as its corresponding version Visual Studio (in this case, 14).

There are also several third-party implementations of famous programming languages for .NET, such as Fortran, Forth, or Pascal, and several non-.NET languages supported by Visual Studio, such as Python, JavaScript, and TypeScript. However, these languages are beyond the scope of this book. It is, however, important to know that all these languages can take advantage of the .NET Framework BCL and infrastructure, the same as VB and C#. This is possible because of Common Language Runtime offers a common infrastructure for all .NET programming languages.

What's New with Compilers

With .NET 2015, Microsoft brings revolutionary changes to compilers, including the Visual Basic compiler. With the .NET Compiler Platform, Microsoft has rewritten compilers entirely in .NET and made them available as open source projects. In addition, Microsoft introduces the .NET Native technology, which optimizes the compilation process for Windows 10 apps. Both are described in this section.

The .NET Compiler Platform

Over the past five years, Microsoft has been working hard on rewriting the Visual Basic and C# compilers entirely in managed code. Visual Studio 2015 with .NET Framework 4.6 relies on this new implementation, known as the .NET Compiler Platform (formerly known as "Project Roslyn"). This is a revolutionary innovation for many reasons, including (but not limited to) the following:

▶ .NET now offers *compilers-as-a-service*. Compilers can generate assemblies, but they also expose APIs to developers. Such APIs focus on syntax analysis, semantic analysis, dynamic compilation to intermediate language, and code emission.

▶ Developers can take advantage of APIs exposed by compilers to create tools that easily integrate with Visual Studio, such as custom code analyzers.

▶ Visual Basic and C# compilers are now offered as an open source project, available at https://github.com/dotnet/roslyn. Microsoft is accepting contributions from the developer community.

▶ Compilers written in managed code can leverage all the power of the .NET Framework.

▶ Visual Studio 2015 has many integrated tools, such as new code editor features, powered by the .NET Compiler Platform, which dramatically enhance the coding experience, increasing the developer's productivity and code quality. In addition, in Visual Studio 2015, many integrated tools (including many tool windows) have been completely rewritten on the .NET Compiler Platform, providing a more reliable and efficient infrastructure.

From a language and syntactical perspective, you will not notice any changes (except for the new features, of course). You use the Visual Basic language (and C# as well) the usual way, and you will be able to take advantage of powerful coding tools as always. For these reasons, and because this book focuses on the Visual Basic language rather than on how the compiler is architected, we do not dive deeply into the .NET Compiler Platform. However, in Chapter 51, "Code Analysis: The .NET Compiler Platform and Tools," you will learn how to take advantage of the APIs exposed by the .NET Compiler Platform to create live code analyzers. For additional and more detailed information about it, see the "Project Roslyn" home page, at https://github.com/dotnet/roslyn.

The .NET Native Technology

.NET Native is a pre-compilation technology included in .NET Core 5 that allows you to compile Windows 10 universal apps written in managed code into native code directly. In the typical .NET Framework compilation process, your projects are first compiled into intermediate language (IL), and the just-in-time compiler translates IL into native code on-the-fly. In contrast, .NET Native compiles a Windows Store app directly into native code. This has the following advantages:

▶ Apps provide the superior performance of native code.

▶ You, as a developer, can still write Visual Basic code as you are used to doing.

▶ You can still take advantage of .NET resources such as garbage collection, exception handling, reflection, serialization, and memory management.

In addition, apps compiled with .NET Native offer a number of advantages for your users, such as faster execution time, faster startup time, and optimized memory usage. All these advantages make perceived performance very much better. Behind the scenes, .NET Native is more than just compiling into native code. In fact, .NET Native really changes the way that .NET apps are built and executed. Following is a list of changes in the build and execution process introduced by .NET Native:

▶ .NET Native statically links required portions of the .NET Framework into your app. This allows you to deploy an app with local packages, following the philosophy of .NET Core 5.

▶ .NET Native is optimized for static compilation, and it therefore offers superior performance.

▶ .NET Native uses the same backend as the C++ compiler, which is optimized for static compilation scenarios.

.NET Native is included in the Windows 10 Developer Tools for Visual Studio 2015. You can find an example in Chapter 36.

The Windows Software Development Kit

When you install Visual Studio 2015 with the .NET Framework and the development environment, the setup process also installs the Windows SDK on your machine. This SDK provides additional tools and libraries that are useful for developing applications for the .NET Framework. Microsoft released the Windows SDK, which provides tools for building both managed and unmanaged applications. The Windows SDK is installed in the C:\ Program Files (x86)\Windows Kits10 folder. It includes several additional tools also used by Microsoft Visual Studio for tasks different from building assemblies, such as deployment and code analysis, and for generating proxy classes for WCF projects. You do not typically need to invoke these tools manually because Visual Studio does that work for you. You can find information on the Windows SDK tools throughout this book.

Summary

Understanding the .NET technology is of primary importance in developing applications with Visual Basic 2015 because you will build applications for the .NET Framework. This chapter presented a high-level overview of the new .NET 2015 vision, showing how you can build applications for the desktop with .NET Framework 4.6 and introducing .NET Core 5, the new modular framework for building cross-platform applications. The chapter also explained key concepts such as the Common Language Runtime, the Base Class Library, and the .NET Compiler Platform. It also explained how an application is compiled and executed, including the new .NET Native technology for Windows 10 apps. You even got an overview of the most important command-line tools and the .NET languages.

CHAPTER 2

The Visual Studio 2015 IDE for Visual Basic

You develop Visual Basic applications by using the Visual Studio 2015 Integrated Development Environment (IDE), which is where you will spend most of your developer life. Before diving deep into the Visual Basic language, you need to know what instruments you need in order to develop applications. Although the Visual Studio IDE is a complex environment, this chapter provides an overview of the most common tasks you will perform from within Visual Studio 2015 and the most important tools you will utilize so that you can feel at home within the IDE. You'll get an introduction to some of the new features in the new version of the IDE that you'll use throughout this book. You'll learn more about some advanced IDE features in Part X, "Code Analysis with VB 2015," and the online chapters.

It is worth mentioning that many IDE features have been completely rebuilt on the .NET Compiler Platform. Therefore, the migration of some tools might be incomplete in Visual Studio 2015; the Call Hierarchy tool window described at the end of the chapter provides one example. This chapter tells you where there are differences between migrated tools and their previous versions.

What's New in Visual Studio 2015

The Visual Studio 2015 IDE is an evolution of Visual Studio 2013, which heavily relies on the .NET Compiler Platform and brings many improvements in different areas of the IDE.

As with Visual Studio 2013, the goal in the Visual Studio 2015 IDE is to help developers focus on writing code or on designing the application rather than on the development environment. So the environment now has fewer modal dialogs, more floating tool windows that do not block other activities, and, in general, many more productivity improvements. This chapter gives you an overview of the tools you most commonly need for developing Visual Basic applications, and it includes tips about getting help with code and libraries. (More details on advanced IDE features are provided in Part X.)

Status Bar and Start Page

When you first run Visual Studio 2015, you notice the Start Page, shown in Figure 2.1. This page has been improved to provide additional learning resources. Also, its content is automatically resized every time you resize Visual Studio. The parts of the Start Page are described in the following subsections.

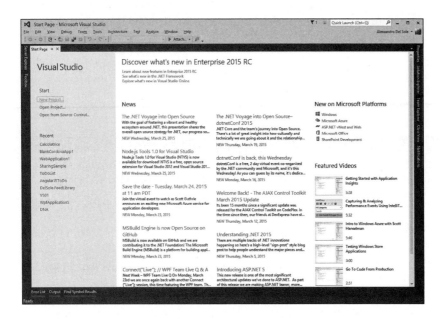

FIGURE 2.1   The Start Page in Visual Studio 2015.

In the Start Page, note that the color of the status bar changes according to the particular task Visual Studio is running. These are the possible colors for the status bar (see Figure 2.2):

▶ **Violet**—This is the color of the status bar when Visual Studio is ready (for example, at startup).

▶ **Light blue**—This is the color of the status bar at development time—that is, during coding, designing of the user interface, or any other task you complete before compiling the code and running the application.

▶ **Blue**—This is the color of the status bar when Visual Studio 2015 is building the solution and compiling the code.

▶ **Orange**—This is the color of the status bar when you are running the application in debugging mode (that is, by pressing **F5**).

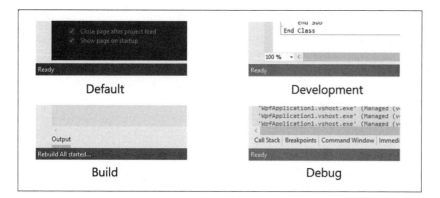

FIGURE 2.2   The status bar colors.

THEMES FOR VISUAL STUDIO 2015

Visual Studio 2015 ships with three themes: Blue, Light, and Dark. This book uses the Blue theme, but feel free to use a different theme. The Light theme is based on light gray tones. The Dark theme reproduces the look of Microsoft Expression Blend and it uses black and other dark tones. You can change the theme by going to Tools, Options and then selecting a different theme in the Color Theme drop-down box in the Environment tab.

The Start Page is a central point in the IDE. It organizes the most common tasks, based on area of interest. On the left side of the screen you can find links for creating new projects and opening existing projects, as well as the list of recently opened projects. You can easily remove recent projects by right-clicking a project name and then selecting **Delete**.

Note that the Start Page relies on the Windows Presentation Foundation (WPF) technology and is completely written in XAML code. This means that it can be customized according to your needs. Customizing the Start Page is beyond the scope of this chapter. However, the following sections discuss the default settings, which you absolutely need to be familiar with.

The News Section

The News section (refer to Figure 2.1) provides hyperlink to news, articles, and blog posts about product releases and updates. It helps you stay informed about new tools and Microsoft events such as conferences.

The Discover What's New Section

The Discover What's New in Visual Studio 2015 section provides a number of links to MSDN documentation about what's new in the IDE, in the .NET Framework, and in Team Foundation Server/Visual Studio Online. This section is very useful for getting further details about new features and libraries in .NET 2015.

The What's New on Microsoft Platforms Section

The What's New on Microsoft Platforms section (refer to Figure 2.1) offers links to MSDN developer centers for several development platforms, such as Windows, Microsoft Azure, Microsoft Office, and SharePoint.

The Featured Videos Section

The Featured Videos section shows a list of instructional videos created by Microsoft, each related to a specific feature in the IDE. These videos are very useful for becoming familiar with interesting tools and functionalities of the development environment. Typically, these videos are available online only, and Visual Studio 2015 allows you to stream them.

Working with Projects and Solutions

Each time you want to develop an application, you create a project. A *project* is a collection of files, such as code files, resources, data, and all the other files you need to build your final assembly. A Visual Basic project is represented by a .vbproj file, which is an *Extensible Markup Language (XML)* file that contains all the information required by Visual Studio to manage files that constitute your project.

Projects are organized into solutions. A *solution* is basically a container for projects. In fact, solutions can contain infinite projects of different kinds, such as Visual Basic projects, projects produced with programming languages other than Visual Basic, class libraries, projects for Windows client applications, Windows Communication Foundation services, and so on. In other words, a solution can include each kind of project you can create with Visual Studio 2015. Solutions also can contain external files, such as documents or help files. A solution is an .sln file that has an XML structure and stores the information required to manage all the projects contained in the solution. Visual Studio 2015 can also open solutions created with previous versions of the IDE.

PROJECT UPGRADES AND "ROUND-TRIPPING"

You can upgrade previous versions of your solutions by simply opening them in Visual Studio 2015. The new version of the IDE supports project *round-tripping*, which means you can use Visual Studio 2015 to open a solution created with Visual Studio 2013, Visual Studio 2012, or Visual Studio 2010 with Service Pack 1, with no upgrades; then you can open the same solution back in the Visual Studio version you created the project with. For solutions created with other versions, the Upgrade Wizard can guide you through the upgrade process in a few steps. There are some exceptions to project round-tripping, which you can read about at http://msdn.microsoft.com/en-us/library/hh266747(v=vs.120).aspx.

Typically you manage your projects and solutions by using the Solution Explorer window, which is discussed later in this chapter.

Creating Visual Basic Projects

Creating a new Visual Basic project is a simple task. You can select either **File, New Project** or click the **New Project** link on the Start Page. In either case, Visual Studio shows the New Project window, as shown in Figure 2.3.

FIGURE 2.3   The Visual Basic New Project window.

To understand what kind of Visual Basic applications you can create, you simply need to select the **Visual Basic** node on the left side of the window. Under this node, you see a lot of different kinds of applications you can create with Visual Basic 2015, such as Windows applications, web applications, Office customizations, Windows Communication Foundation services, Windows Store apps for Windows 8.1 and Windows Phone 8.1, and so on.

AVAILABLE PROJECT TEMPLATES

The list of installed project templates in the New Project window can vary depending on either the Visual Studio 2015 edition or additional items that are installed (for example, from the Visual Studio Gallery).

The main part of the New Project window shows a variety of available templates. Each kind of application is represented by a specific project template, which provides a skeleton of a project for that particular kind of application, including all the references and the basic code files required. For example, the WPF Application project template provides a skeleton of a project for creating a Windows application using WPF technology; it includes references to the WindowsBase.dll assembly, specific `Imports` directives, and WPF objects represented by the appropriate code files. Moreover, when you select this template, Visual Studio automatically enables the WPF designer. When you select a template in the New Project window, you see a detailed description for the template on the right side of the window.

NOTE

Part II, "Object-Oriented Programming with Visual Basic 2015," discusses several kinds of applications you can build with Visual Basic 2015. At the moment, you don't need to worry about all the details, but if you want a quick description, just look at the right side of the New Project window. Note that this first part of the book uses the Console Application project template.

When you create a new project, Visual Studio usually creates a solution containing that project. If you plan to add other projects to the solution, it can be a good idea to create a directory for the solution. This allows you to better organize your projects because one directory can contain the solution file, and that directory can then contain subdirectories, each of them related to a specific project. To create a director for a solution, in the New Project window, ensure that the Create Directory for Solution check box is selected.

The New Project window also allows you to do the following: .NET Framework multi-targeting, search through templates, manage templates, and find samples on the Internet. The following sections discuss these features.

Multi-targeting

In Visual Studio 2015, as in other recent versions, you can choose which version of the .NET Framework an application targets. This can be useful if you plan to develop applications with high compatibility levels but still want to take advantage of the new features of the IDE and some new language features that do not require assemblies from the higher version. You can choose from the following:

- .NET Framework 4.6 (the default)
- .NET Framework 4.5.1
- .NET Framework 4.5
- .NET Framework 4.0
- .NET Framework 3.5
- .NET Framework 3.0
- .NET Framework 2.0

You simply select the appropriate version from the combo box at the top of the window, as shown in Figure 2.4.

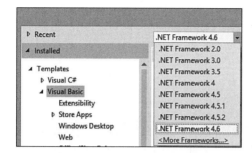

FIGURE 2.4   Choosing the .NET Framework version for your application.

> **NOTE**
>
> Remember that, depending on the version of the .NET Framework you choose, you might not be able to use some libraries or technologies. For example, if you choose .NET Framework 3.0 as the target version, you cannot use LINQ, which is available only in .NET Framework 3.5 and higher. So keep in mind these limitations when developing your applications on previous .NET Framework versions.

Accessing Recent and Online Templates

Visual Studio 2015 allows you to access the most recently used templates and install additional templates from the Internet. You can easily access the most recently used project templates by selecting **Recent, Templates** on the left side of the New Project window. You then see a list of the recently used project templates, as shown in Figure 2.5. You can also find additional online templates and install them to the local system. To accomplish this, you select **Online, Templates** the New Project window. Visual Studio checks for online templates and shows a list of all the ones that are available (see Figure 2.6).

As you can see in Figure 2.6, Visual Studio lists all the online templates for both Visual Basic and Visual C#. It shows a description of each template, information about the author, and a small picture with ratings, when available. To download and install a template, simply double-click its name. After a few seconds, you are prompted to agree to the installation. You get a warning message if the new extension for Visual Studio does not contain a digital signature. If you trust the publisher and want to continue, click **Install**. After a few seconds, you see the newly installed project template available among the other ones.

As in the previous versions of Visual Studio, you can still export projects as reusable project templates. We discuss this process in Chapter 52, "Advanced IDE Features."

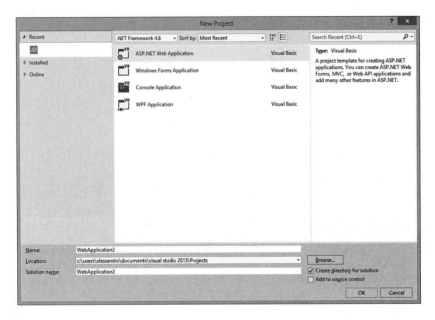

FIGURE 2.5   Accessing the most recently used projects templates.

FIGURE 2.6   Additional online templates you can add to Visual Studio 2015.

Searching for Installed Templates

Visual Studio 2015 provides lots of default project templates, and as you saw earlier, you can add your own custom ones, too. When you have a lot of available templates, finding the necessary one at a certain moment can be difficult. Therefore, the New Project window provides a search box, in the upper-right corner (see Figure 2.7). Just begin typing the name of the project template you are looking for, and the New Project window shows all the project templates that match. Each time you type a character, the window updates to show results that more closely match your search string. For example, in Figure 2.7, Visual Studio shows all the project templates whose names match the search string *excel*.

> **NOTE**
>
> Remember that the search functionality can retrieve all project templates related to a search string. This means that the search results may contain not only Visual Basic projects but also templates for other programs, such as Visual C#, Visual F#, and so on.

FIGURE 2.7   Searching for installed project templates by using the search feature.

Finding Code Samples on the Internet

Visual Studio 2015 enables you to search for sample code on the Internet directly from the New Project dialog box. Visual Studio performs this search inside the MSDN Code Gallery (http://code.msdn.microsoft.com), a website where developers can publish sample code they want to share with others. To find code samples, click **Online, Samples** on the left side of the New Project dialog box (refer to Figure 2.6). Then you can browse the Code Gallery from within the dialog box. For example, if you search for a specified language, you will then be able to discover samples of the language based on various technologies (such as Windows, Web, Cloud, Windows Phone, and so on). For each of these categories, you will find additional subcategories where samples are divided by framework (for instance, Windows development samples divided into WPF, Windows Forms, Windows Runtime, and so on). Figure 2.8 shows what it looks like to browse samples online from Visual Studio 2015.

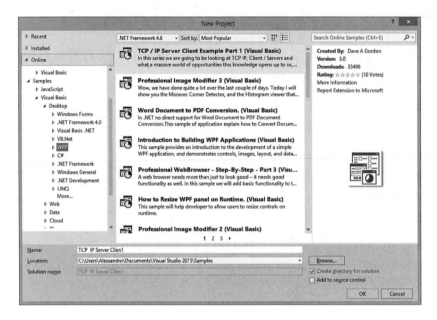

FIGURE 2.8   Browsing online code samples from Visual Studio 2015.

You can select a sample from the list and then click **OK** or simply double-click the sample. Visual Studio 2015 then downloads the sample to your hard disk and asks you to accept the license agreement that the developer who published the code added to the sample. After it's downloaded, the sample is opened as a normal project. This is possible because, before a sample can be uploaded to the gallery, the developer must supply a full project (or an entire solution) in order to enable other developers to reuse the code with ease.

Creating Reusable Projects and Items Templates

As in previous versions, in Visual Studio 2015 you can create custom projects and item templates and then export them to disk and make them available within the IDE. (This topic is discussed in Chapter 52.)

Creating Your First Visual Basic 2015 Project

Now that you have seen the main new features for project creation, you are ready to create your first Visual Basic project. This section shows how easily you can create a Visual Basic 2015 application. You can create a new project for the Console by following these steps:

1. Select **File, New Project** or click the **New Project** link on the Start Page to open the New Project window.

2. In the New Project window, select the **Console Application** project template.

> **NOTE**
>
> Until Part IV, "Data Access with ADO.NET and LINQ," all code examples, listings, and code snippets are based on Console applications, so remember to create a Visual Basic project for the Console when testing the code.

3. Name the new project **MyFirst2015Program** and then click **OK** (see Figure 2.9).

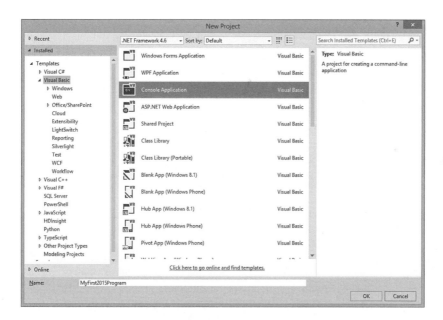

FIGURE 2.9   Creating your first VB 2015 application.

After a few seconds, Visual Studio creates the new project and makes it available to be edited as shown in Figure 2.10.

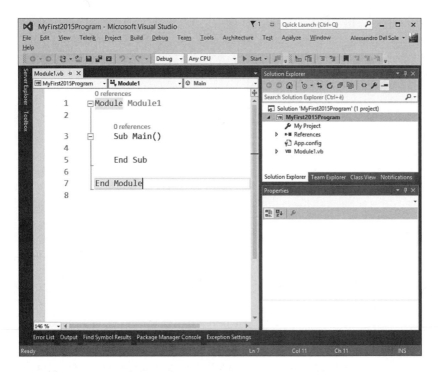

FIGURE 2.10   Your first VB 2015 project.

If you already have experience with Visual Studio, you will feel at home with the new version of the environment. For example, you can access the Solution Explorer, Properties, and Error List windows exactly as you did in earlier versions of Visual Studio.

TIPS ABOUT THE NAVIGATION BAR

In Figure 2.10, at the top of the code editor window, you can see the navigation bar, which is divided into three parts. If you hover over each part with the mouse pointer, you get a ToolTip describing it. In particular, the first part shows a list of projects in the solution and is new in Visual Studio 2015; it allows you to change the active project, in case you are editing a linked file or a file inside a shared project, and the file is consumed by two or more projects in your solution. The second part allows you to select objects in the active code file, including events. When you select an object, the third part of the bar shows members and event handlers for the selected object. You can click on any member, and the code editor immediately brings the cursor to the member definition. If the member has not been implemented yet, as in the case of event handlers, a member skeleton is generated for you. If you do not see the navigation bar, select **Tools, Options, Text Editor, All Languages,** and enable the **Navigation Bar** option.

An interesting feature in the code editor is that by pressing **Ctrl** and moving the mouse wheel up and down, you can zoom in and out within the code editor, without needing to change the font settings each time the Visual Studio options changes. For testing purposes, you could add a couple lines of code to the `Main` method, which is the entry point for a Console application. Listing 2.1 shows the complete code for creating a simple VB 2015 application.

LISTING 2.1　Creating a Simple VB 2015 Application

```
Module Module1
    Sub Main()
        Console.WriteLine("Hello Visual Basic 2015!")
        Console.ReadLine()
    End Sub
End Module
```

WHAT IS A CONSOLE?

In a Console application, the `System.Console` class is the main object for working with the Windows Console. Such a class provides methods for reading and writing from and to the Console and for performing operations against the Console itself.

This code simply shows a message in the Console window and waits for the user to press a key. This is obviously a very basic application, but it will help you understand other topics in this chapter.

Finding Visual Basic Projects

By default, Visual Studio 2015 (like previous versions) stores its information in a user-level folder called **Visual Studio 2015** that resides inside the My Documents folder. Here you can find settings, add-ins, code snippets, and projects. By default, your projects are located in C:\Users*UserName*\Documents\Visual Studio 2015\Projects, where *UserName* is the name of the user who is logged in to Windows. Of course, you can change the default projects directory by opening the Options window (by selecting **Tools, Options**), selecting the **Projects and Solutions** item on the left side, and replacing the value for the Projects Location text box.

Working with the Code Editor

As a developer, you'll spend most of your Visual Studio time in the code editor, along with the designers. Knowing how to get the best out of the code editor is very important. In this chapter you'll see just a few code editor features; you'll learn about others—ones that are related to specific topics—in later chapters. The following sections focus on features that are available in any project you are working on and that will help you be more productive. Some of these features were introduced in Visual Studio 2013, and others are new in Visual Studio 2015.

Zooming the Code

You can zoom the code editor in and out by simply pressing the **Ctrl** key and moving the mouse wheel up and down. This is a useful feature particularly when you are presenting technical speeches because you can enlarge the code without modifying Visual Studio settings in the Options window. Figure 2.11 shows an example of this feature in use; notice that the font for the code is larger than the default settings, and the zoom percentage is visible in the bottom-left corner.

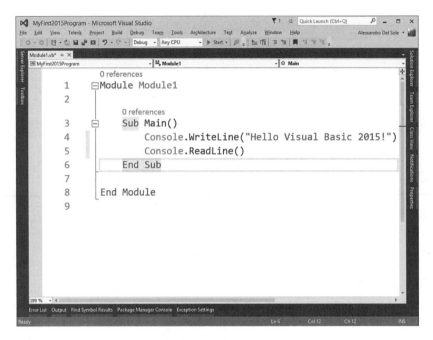

FIGURE 2.11   The code editor zoom feature enables you to enlarge and reduce the font size of the code in real time without changing settings in Visual Studio.

If you used this feature in Visual Studio 2010, you might remember that the scroll bar on the right also changed size according to the zoom. This was fixed in Visual Studio 2012, and since then, the bar size has always been the same and independent from the zoom.

IntelliSense Technology

IntelliSense is one of the most important technologies in the coding experience with Visual Studio. IntelliSense is a pop-up window that appears in the code editor each time you begin typing a keyword or an identifier; it shows options for auto-completing words. Figure 2.12 shows IntelliSense in action as a new instruction is being added to code.

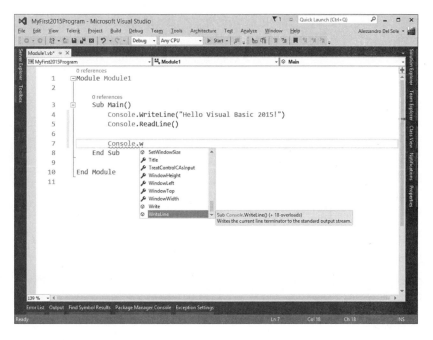

FIGURE 2.12   IntelliSense in action.

To auto-complete your code typing, you have the following options:

▶ **Tab**—Pressing Tab selects the highlighted auto-completion option and enables you to write other code.

▶ **Spacebar**—Pressing the spacebar selects the highlighted auto-completion option, adds a blank space at the end, and enables you to write other code.

▶ **Enter**—Pressing Enter selects the highlighted auto-completion option, adds a pair of empty parentheses at the end, and positions the cursor on a new line. You should use this technique when you need to invoke a method that does not require arguments.

▶ **Left parenthesis**—Pressing (selects the highlighted auto-completion option, adds a left parenthesis at the end, and enables you to supply arguments.

▶ **Ctrl+spacebar**—Pressing Ctrl+spacebar brings up the full list of IntelliSense options.

IntelliSense is activated when you type one character, and it even works with Visual Basic reserved words. Moreover, it remembers the last member you supplied to an object if you invoke that particular object more than once. For example, say that you use IntelliSense to provide the `WriteLine` method to the `Console` object as follows:

```
Console.WriteLine()
```

Then when you try to invoke IntelliSense on the `Console` object again, it proposes as the first alternative the `WriteLine` method you supplied the first time.

IntelliSense is important because it lets you write code more quickly and provides suggestions about which members to add to your code. Microsoft has also improved IntelliSense in Visual Studio 2013 and Visual Studio 2015 in the XAML code editor, as you'll discover in Chapters 28 to 33.

Touch Improvements

The code editor in Visual Studio 2015 has been improved to offer better support for common touch gestures, including the following:

▶ **Pinch and zoom**—You can zoom the code editor in and out by using this gesture, which commonly is accomplished with the thumb and index fingers.

▶ **Scroll**—You can use your fingers to scroll the code editor in a very responsive way.

▶ **Word selection**—You can easily select any identifier by using a double-tap gesture.

▶ **Line selection**—You can easily select a line of code with a single touch on the left border of the code editor.

▶ **Context menu gesture**—You can easily open a context menu (which you usually open by right-clicking) by simply keeping your finger pressed until the menu appears.

You will find these improvements very useful on any touch screen.

> **NOTE**
>
> The Visual Studio 2015 IDE introduces light bulbs for quick actions, which give you an integrated and unobtrusive way to fix common code issues, including errors and refactoring. Light bulbs are discussed in more detail in Chapter 6, "Errors, Exceptions, and Code Refactoring."

Peek Definition

The Peek Definition option, introduced in Visual Studio 2013, is a feature that enables you to open a type definition in the active code editor window. For example, suppose you have a large project with a dozen code files, and you need to find and edit a class definition. If you right-click the type name and then select Peek Definition from the context menu, you can edit the type in a convenient pop-up inside the active window, as shown in Figure 2.13.

The Peek Definition pop-up shows the name of the code file where the type is defined and is a fully-functional code editor, so you can make changes and see them immediately reflected to the code. When you're done, you simply click the x button in the upper-right corner by the code filename.

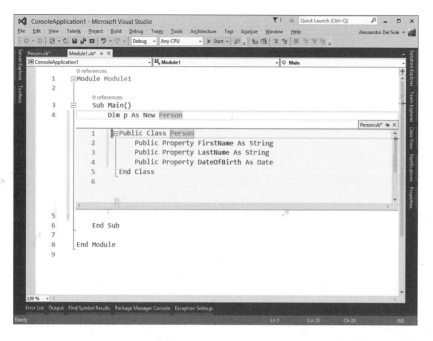

FIGURE 2.13   Using Peek Definition to edit a type definition in the active window.

Enhanced Scroll Bar

The enhanced scroll bar, also known as the map-mode scroll bar, is another feature that was introduced with Visual Studio 2013. It provides an easy way to move within long code files, showing a preview of the code while you hover with the mouse pointer. To understand how it works, in the code editor right-click the scroll bar and select **Scroll Bar Options**. In the Options window that appears (see Figure 2.14), you can enable the **Use Map Mode for Vertical Scroll Bar** option and select one of the available Source Overview settings. Try the **Wide** option and then click **OK**.

At this point, the scroll bar in the code editor shows a small preview of the code, and when you pass the mouse pointer over the scroll bar, a magnifier shows a larger preview of the code at that specific location, as you can see in Figure 2.15.

This feature can be very useful in some situations. However, you will not use it in this book, so if you switched to it, be sure to revert back to the original scroll bar by enabling the **Use Bar Mode for Vertical Scroll Bar** option in Options window.

Navigate To

Navigate To, which is inherited from Visual Studio 2013, provides an easy way to search for a type definition. To use this feature, place the cursor on a type name (like the Person class you saw in Figure 2.13) and then press **Ctrl+,**. The code editor shows a pop-up that contains the full list of types matching the name of the selected type, including type definitions contained in projects created in different programming languages, such as C#. Figure 2.16 shows an example.

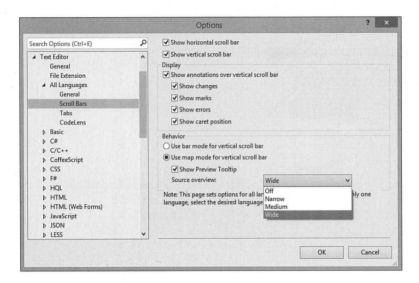

FIGURE 2.14   Enabling the map-mode scroll bar.

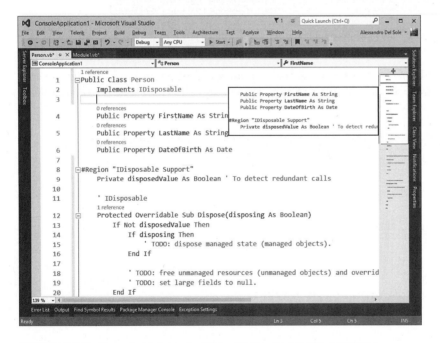

FIGURE 2.15   Browsing long code files with the map-mode scroll bar.

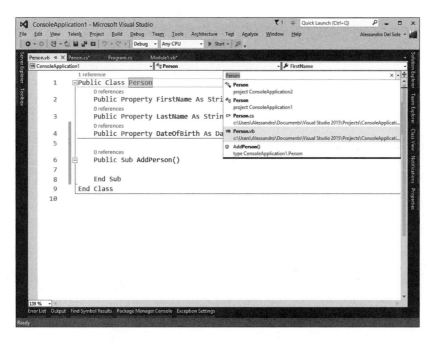

FIGURE 2.16   Using Navigate To for finding type definitions.

The pop-up also shows a list of projects that contain the type name and code files. As you move between items in the list, Visual Studio automatically opens a code editor window for the selected item.

HINTS ABOUT CODELENS

The Enterprise edition of Visual Studio 2015 includes a feature known as CodeLens, which allows you to see how many references a type or member has within a solution. In addition, CodeLens integrates with Team Foundation Server and can show who in a development team made edits, and what they were, in a portion of code. You can't assume that all readers have the Enterprise edition, but you can find further information at http://msdn.microsoft.com/en-us/library/dn269218.aspx.

Working with Tool Windows

As in the previous versions of Visual Studio, lots of the tools in Visual Studio 2015 are provided via *tool windows*. *Tool windows* are floating windows that can be docked to the IDE interface and are responsible for various tasks. As a general rule, you find the tool windows provided by Visual Studio 2015 in the View menu. However, you find the test tool windows and the analysis tool windows in the Test and Analyze menus, respectively, and tool windows specific for debugging are available in the Debug menu. (See Chapter 5, "Debugging Visual Basic 2015 Applications.")

NOTE

This book utilizes several tool windows, and this chapter provides an overview of the ones that are most frequently used. In particular, this chapter focuses on the Solution Explorer, Error List, Properties, and Output windows. These are the tool windows you will use in each of your projects. You'll learn about less commonly used tool windows in other chapters, as their use crops up.

To dock a tool window to the desired position in the IDE, you just move that window onto the most appropriate arrow in the cross shown in Figure 2.17 and then release.

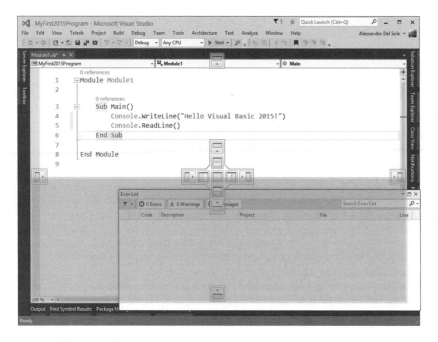

FIGURE 2.17   Docking a floating tool window to the IDE's interface.

Visual Studio 2015 automatically positions some tool windows in specific places in the IDE, but you can rearrange tool windows as you like. The following sections discuss the tool windows you'll use most frequently.

The Solution Explorer Window

Solution Explorer is a special window that enables you to manage solutions, projects, and files. It provides a complete view of the files in a project, and it enables you to add or remove files and to organize files into subfolders. Figure 2.18 shows how a WPF project looks inside Solution Explorer.

Back button   Show All Files button

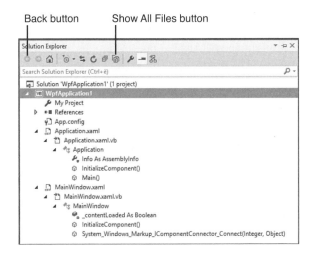

FIGURE 2.18   An example of the Solution Explorer window.

As you can see, the project is at the root level. Nested under it are code files and subfolders containing pictures, data, and documents. You can also get a list of all the references in the project. You use Solution Explorer to add and manage items in projects as well as to see which files constitute a project. By default, Solution Explorer shows only the items that compose the project. If you need a complete view of references and auto-generated code files, you can click the **Show All Files** button located on the upper-left portion of the window.

In Solution Explorer you can see a list of types and members that a code file defines by expanding the name of the code file. For instance, Figure 2.18 shows that the MainWindow.xaml.vb code file defines a class called `MainWindow`, which exposes a field called `_contentLoaded` of type `Boolean`, and two methods, `InitializeComponent` and `System_Windows_Markup_IComponentConnector_Connect`. When you double-click a member, you are automatically redirected to its definition in the code file.

The Solution Explorer window also shows arguments and their type. This is useful when you have hundreds of files and need to know which types are defined within a file but don't want to search inside all the others. Also, Solution Explorer has a useful search box in which you can type a search key to have the IDE search for all the items in the solution that contain the specified word(s). Another interesting feature of the new Solution Explorer is that you can discover the following for members defined in code:

▶ Calls that the member makes

▶ Members that are calling the selected member

▶ Members that are using the selected member

You can simply right-click a member defined inside a code file and then select the desired commands, which are Calls, Called By, and Used By, respectively. At that point, Solution Explorer shows the list of members that are invoked by, are calling, or are using the selected member. To go back to the full list, you simply use the Back button in the toolbar (see Figure 2.18). The new Solution Explorer also provides interaction with Team Foundation Server and allows you to generate a visual representation of the object graph for the selected node. To manage your project's items, you just need to right-click the project name and select the most appropriate command from the context menu that appears. Figure 2.19 shows this context menu.

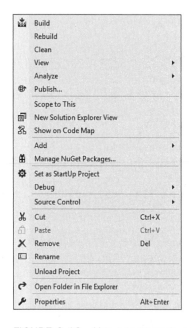

FIGURE 2.19   You can manage solution items in Solution Explorer by using the context menu.

As you can see from Figure 2.19, the pop-up menu shows several tasks you can perform on your projects or solutions. You can easily add new items by selecting the **Add** command. You also can perform tasks against specific files if you right-click items in the solution instead of right-clicking the project's name.

ADDING ITEMS TO PROJECTS

Throughout this book you will need to add many new items to projects and solutions. Keep in mind that you can accomplish this by right-clicking the project name in Solution Explorer and then selecting **Add, New Item** from the context menu.

You can easily find Solution Explorer by pressing **Ctrl+Alt+L** if it is not open yet in the IDE.

The Error List Window

The Error List window shows a list of all messages, including warnings and information, generated by Visual Studio during the development of an application. Figure 2.20 shows the Error List window.

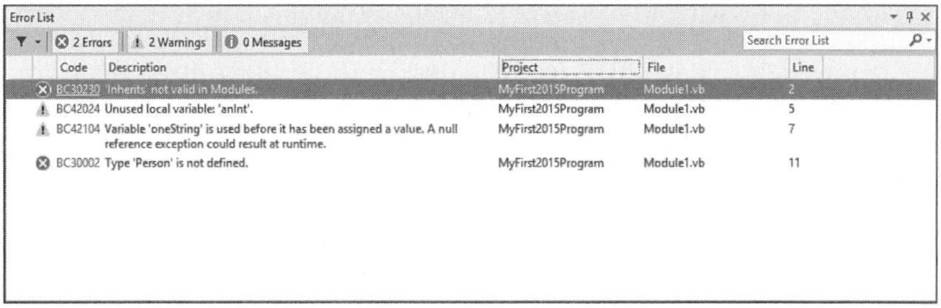

FIGURE 2.20   The Error List window.

Typically, the Error List window shows three kinds of messages:

▶ Error messages

▶ Warning messages

▶ Information messages

Errors listed in the Error List window are underlined in the code editor with *squiggles*, or wavy lines that appear under code issues. Squiggles are red for errors and green for warnings. Error messages are related to errors that prevent your application from running, such as if your code cannot compile successfully. Errors include any problems that Visual Studio or the background compiler encounters during the development process, such as attempting to use an object that has not been declared, corrupted auto-generated WPF files that must be edited in the Visual Studio designer, or corrupted Visual Studio files in situations that report error messages you can see in the Error List window.

Another kind of message is a warning. Warnings are related to situations that will not necessarily prevent your code from being successfully compiled or your application from running. It's good practice to try to solve the problems that caused these messages. For example, you can run the Code Analysis tool to get a report on warnings about code that is not compliant with Microsoft guidelines. With warnings, an application will probably work, but something in that code should be improved.

In both error and warning messages, you can go right to the code that caused the message by double-clicking the message itself. You can also get help about the message by right-clicking it and then selecting the **Show Error Help** command or by pressing **F1**.

Information messages just provide information. You can usually ignore them with regard to the code, although they could be useful for understanding what the IDE wants to tell you.

In Visual Studio 2015, the Error List window has been improved and provides the following additional features:

▶ For each message, an error code is provided in the form of a hyperlink. If you click such a hyperlink, Visual Studio opens your default web browser and provides information about the error code.

▶ There used to be a limit of 100 messages for the Error List window. However, that limit has been removed, and now the Error List window shows the full list of errors, warnings, and informational messages.

▶ Columns have a filter button so that you can filter messages by error code, project, and code files.

▶ You can filter error messages by selecting the current project, the active code file, or all open files.

You can open the Error List window by pressing **Ctrl+** or **Ctrl+E**.

The Properties Window

In.NET development, everything has *properties*, which are the characteristics of a particular item. Classes can have properties, files can have properties, and so on. For example, the filename is a property of a file. You often need to set properties for your code, for .NET objects you use in your code, and for your files. To make things easier, Visual Studio provides the Properties window, which is a graphical tool for setting the properties of items. Figure 2.21 shows the Properties window for a button in WPF.

The Properties window is structured as a two-column table, in which the left column specifies a property and the right column gets or sets the value for each property. Although you often need to set properties in code, the Properties window provides a graphical way to perform this assignment, and it can be particularly useful when you're designing a user interface or need to specify how a file must be packaged into the executable assembly. You open the Properties window by pressing **F4**.

The Output Window

Visual Studio often uses external tools to perform actions. For example, when you compile a project, Visual Studio invokes the Visual Basic command-line compiler; the IDE captures the output of the tools it utilizes and redirects the output to the Output window. The purpose of the Output window is to show results of actions that Visual Studio has to perform or that you need Visual Studio to perform. So when you compile your projects, the Output window shows the results of the build process. In Figure 2.22, the Output window contains the results of the build process for a Visual Basic project.

The Output window is interactive. For example, if you're compiling a program, if the compiler reports any errors, the Output window shows them.

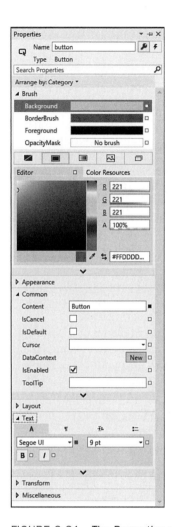

FIGURE 2.21   The Properties window.

FIGURE 2.22   The Output window, showing results of a build process.

COMMAND NAMES

You can hover over buttons and controls in the Error List window with your mouse to open up a ToolTip that shows the name for each of the commands described in the next paragraph.

You can click the **Go to Next Message** button or **Go to Previous Message** button to navigate error messages. When you do this, the current error message is highlighted. Each time you move to another error message, you are redirected to the code that caused the error. The Output window can capture the output not only of the compiler but also of other tools that Visual Studio needs to use, such as the debugger. You can get a list of the available outputs by clicking the **Show Output From** combo box.

The My Project Window

My Project is a special window that allows you to set project properties. You open the My Project window by double-clicking the **My Project** item in Solution Explorer or by selecting **Project**, *ProjectName* **Properties**(where *ProjectName* is the current project name). Figure 2.23 shows how My Project looks for the sample application you created earlier in this chapter.

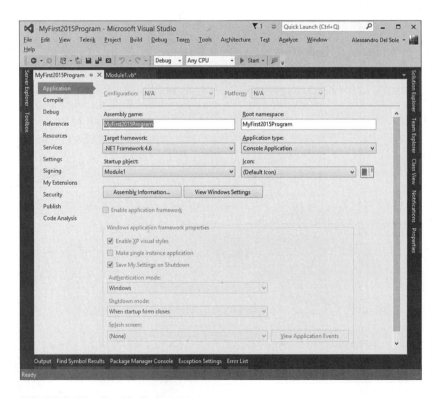

FIGURE 2.23   The My Project window.

My Project is organized into tabs, and each tab represents a specific area of the project, such as application-level properties, external references, deployment options, compile options, and debugging options. For now, you don't need to learn all the tabs of the My Project window; you'll have plenty of time for that throughout this book. At this point, here's what you need to do:

▶ Understand what My Project is.

▶ Remember how to open it.

▶ Learn about the Application tab, which is discussed in the following section.

UNDERSTANDING MY PROJECT

Understanding My Project is important because this window provides most of the infra-structure for the `My` namespace that is discussed in Chapter 19, "The `My` Namespace." Most of settings you can specify in the My Project window are then accessible by invoking `My`. Chapter 3, "The Anatomy of a Visual Basic Project," describes the structure of My Project.

Specifying Application Settings in the Application Tab

Each application has some settings, such as the executable's name, icon, or metadata that will be grabbed by the operating system, such as the program version, copyright informa-tion, and so on. The Application tab of the My Project windows allows you to edit these kinds of settings. The Application tab is shown by default when you first open My Project (see Figure 2.23). Some settings here are common to every kind of Visual Basic project, whereas other ones are related to specific project types. This chapter provides an overview of the common settings, and other settings are discussed in the following chapters.

Assembly Name

You use the Assembly Name field to set the name of the compiled assembly (that is, your executable). By default, Visual Studio assigns this setting based on the project name, but you can replace it as needed.

Root Namespace

You use the Root Namespace field to set the root-level namespace identifier. (Namespaces are discussed later in this book, particularly in Chapter 9, "Organizing Types Within Namespaces.") You can think of the root namespace as the object that stores everything that your project implements. According to Microsoft specifications, the root namespace should be formed as follows: *CompanyName.ProductName.Version*. This convention is optimal when developing class libraries or components but might not be necessary when developing standalone executables. By default, Visual Studio sets the root namespace based on the project name.

Application Type

The Application Type text box specifies the application type (for example, Console application, class library, Windows Forms application) and is automatically set by Visual Studio. You should not change the default setting in this box.

Icon

The Icon field allows you to set an icon for the executable file. You can browse the disk and select an existing .ico file as the executable icon.

ASSIGNING ICONS

Assigning an icon to the executable file does not automatically assign icons to Windows Forms windows or WPF windows when you're developing client applications. In such scenarios, you need to explicitly assign icons for each window because the Icon item in the Application tab just sets the icon for the executable.

Startup Object

You use the Startup Object field to specify which object will be executed first when your application runs. For example, say that you have a WPF application with more than one window. You might want to decide which window must be the application's main window. You specify your choice in the Startup Object field. Notice that the startup object changes based on the project type. For example, in a WPF application, the startup object is a `Window` object, whereas in a Console application, the default startup object is a `Module` object in which the `Sub Main` method is located. The name of this field also changes based on the project type. In a Console application, it is called Startup Object, whereas in a WPF application, it is called Startup URI.

CHANGING THE STARTUP OBJECT

Please be careful when changing the Startup Object field. A wrong choice could cause errors in your application and prevent it from running.

Assembly Information

Clicking the Assembly Information button gives you access to the Assembly Information window, as shown in Figure 2.24.

In this window you can specify several properties for your executable that will be visible both to the .NET Framework and to the Windows operating system. Table 2.1 explains each property.

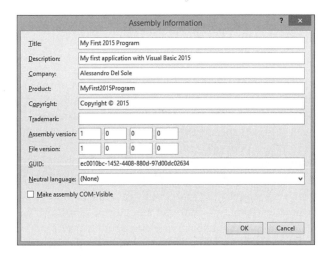

FIGURE 2.24   The Assembly Information window.

TABLE 2.1   Assembly Information Explained

Property	Description
Title	The title for your application (for example, "My First 2015 Program")
Description	The description for your application (for example, "My first application with Visual Basic 2015")
Company	The company name
Product	The product name (for example, "Suite of My New 2015 Applications")
Copyright	Copyright information
Trademark	Trademark information
Assembly version	The version number for the assembly, in the format *Major.Minor.Build.Revision*, which identifies the assembly for the .NET Framework
File version	The version number for the executable, in the format *Major.Minor.Build.Revision*, which is visible to the Windows operating system
GUID	A globally unique identifier assigned to the assembly that you can replace with a new one or leave as the GUID provided by the IDE
Neutral language	The local culture that is used as the neutral language
Make assembly COM-Visible	The ability to expose .NET assemblies can be to COM

The Assembly Information window is important because it enables you to specify settings that you want to be visible to your customers and other settings needed by the .NET

Framework. Behind the scenes, all this information is translated into Visual Basic code, which is discussed more in Chapter 3.

View Windows Settings

With Windows Vista, Microsoft introduced to the Windows operating system an important component known as User Account Control (UAC). When enabled, this mechanism requires the user to explicitly grant elevated permissions to applications that are being run. With Visual Studio 2008 and newer, you can specify the permissions level your application will require for the UAC. For example, if your application needs to write to the Program Files folder (this is just an example and is rarely a good idea), you should require elevated permissions to the UAC. You can specify UAC settings for an application by clicking the **View Windows Settings** button. At this point, Visual Studio generates a new XML manifest that will be packaged into your executable and that you can edit within the IDE. This file contains information for UAC settings and for specifying the operating systems that the application is designed to work for (see the `supportedOS` node). Listing 2.2 shows an excerpt of the default content of the manifest, related to the UAC settings.

LISTING 2.2   The UAC Manifest Content

```
<?xml version="1.0" encoding="utf-8"?>
<asmv1:assembly manifestVersion="1.0" xmlns="urn:schemas-microsoft-com:asm.v1"
xmlns:asmv1="urn:schemas-microsoft-com:asm.v1" xmlns:asmv2="urn:schemas-microsoft-
com:asm.v2" xmlns:xsi="http://www.w3.org/2001/XMLSchema-instance">
  <assemblyIdentity version="1.0.0.0" name="MyApplication.app"/>
  <trustInfo xmlns="urn:schemas-microsoft-com:asm.v2">
    <security>
      <requestedPrivileges xmlns="urn:schemas-microsoft-com:asm.v3">
        <!-- UAC Manifest Options
            If you want to change the Windows User Account Control
            level replace the
requestedExecutionLevel node with one of the following.
            <requestedExecutionLevel  level="asInvoker" uiAccess="false" />
            <requestedExecutionLevel  level="requireAdministrator" uiAccess="false" />
            <requestedExecutionLevel  level="highestAvailable" uiAccess="false" />
            Specifying requestedExecutionLevel node will
            disable file and registry virtualization.
            If you want to utilize File and Registry Virtualization for backward
            compatibility then delete the requestedExecutionLevel node.
        -->
        <requestedExecutionLevel level="asInvoker" uiAccess="false" />
      </requestedPrivileges>
    </security>
  </trustInfo>
  <compatibility xmlns="urn:schemas-microsoft-com:compatibility.v1">
    <application>
      <!-- A list of all Windows versions that this application is designed
```

```
            to work with.
      Windows will automatically select the most compatible environment.-->
      <!-- If your application is designed to work with Windows Vista,
            uncomment the following supportedOS node-->
      <!--<supportedOS Id="{e2011457-1546-43c5-a5fe-008deee3d3f0}"/>-->
      <!-- If your application is designed to work with Windows 7, uncomment the
            following supportedOS node-->
      <!--<supportedOS Id="{35138b9a-5d96-4fbd-8e2d-a2440225f93a}"/>-->
      <!-- If your application is designed to work with Windows 8, uncomment the
            following supportedOS node-->
      <!--<supportedOS Id="{4a2f28e3-53b9-4441-ba9c-d69d4a4a6e38}"/>-->
    </application>
  </compatibility>
  <!-- Enable themes for Windows common controls and
        dialogs (Windows XP and later) -->
  <!-- <dependency>
    <dependentAssembly>
      <assemblyIdentity
          type="win32"
          name="Microsoft.Windows.Common-Controls"
          version="6.0.0.0"
          processorArchitecture="*"
          publicKeyToken="6595b64144ccf1df"
          language="*"
        />
    </dependentAssembly>
  </dependency>-->
</asmv1:assembly>
```

Notice that a huge number of comments in this listing help you understand the file content and how to manage the behavior of your application according to the Windows version that your application is going to target. The `requestedExecutionLevel` element enables you to specify which permission level must be requested to the UAC. You have three possibilities, as explained in Table 2.2.

TABLE 2.2   UAC Settings

Setting	Description
asInvoker	Runs the application with the privileges related to the current user. If the current user is a standard user, the application will be launched with standard privileges. If the current user is an administrator, the application will be launched with administrative privileges. This is the default selection in the manifest.
requireAdministrator	Requires administrative privileges.
highestAvailable	Requires the highest privilege level possible for the current user.

To specify a privilege level, you just uncomment the line of XML code that corresponds to the desired level. You can also delete the `requestedExecutionLevel` node if you want to use file and registry virtualization for backward compatibility with older versions of the Windows operating system.

PAY ATTENTION TO UAC REQUIREMENTS

Be careful about the combination of activities that you need to execute on the target machine and the user privileges because bad UAC settings could cause big problems. A good practice is to select the `asInvoker` level and architect your application so that it will work on user-level folders and resources. In some situations, you will need deeper control of the target machine and administrator privileges, but these should be considered exceptions to the rule.

The Application Framework

In the lower part of the Application tab of the My Project window is the Enable Application Framework group, which allows you to execute special tasks at the beginning and end of the application lifetime. For Console applications, it is not available, but it is relevant to other kinds of applications; for instance, in the Windows Forms application, it enables you to set a splash screen or establish which form is the main application form. (The application framework is discussed in Chapter 19.)

Target Framework

From the Target Framework combo box on the Applications tab, you can select the version of the .NET Framework that your application will target. You also see this combo box when you create a new project, but in this case, you can target the .NET Framework Client Profile for versions 4.0, 3.5 Service Pack 1, and 3.5 Server Core. The .NET Framework Client Profile is a subset of the .NET Framework that provides the infrastructure for client applications and that can be included in your deployments instead of the full version. Microsoft removed the .NET Framework Client Profile in version 4.5.

FOR VISUAL STUDIO 2010 USERS

Now the Target Framework option is available in the Application tab of the My Project window, but in Visual Studio 2010 and earlier, it is available in the Advanced Compile Options dialog box.

Compiling Projects

Compiling a project (or *building*, in Visual Studio terminology) is the process that produces a .NET assembly starting from the project and source code (see Chapter 1, "Introducing .NET 2015"). An assembly can be a standalone application (an .exe assembly) or a .NET class library (a .dll assembly). To compile a project into an assembly, you need to click

Build, Build *ProjectName*, where *ProjectName* is the name of your project. When you invoke this command, Visual Studio launches the Visual Basic command-line compiler (Vbc.exe) and provides this tool all the necessary command-line options. For solutions that contain different kinds of projects, Visual Studio launches MSBuild.exe, a command-line utility that can compile entire solutions containing several projects written in different languages and of different types. At the end of the build process, Visual Studio shows a log inside the Output window. Figure 2.25 shows the output log of the build process for the MyFirst2015Program sample application.

FIGURE 2.25   The Output window shows the compilation process results.

The compilation log shows useful messages that help you understand what happened. In this case, there were no errors, but in situations in which the compilation process fails because of some errors in the code, you are notified of the errors that the compiler found. The Error List window shows a complete list of error messages and warnings and enables you to easily understand where the errors happened by double-clicking the error message. This operation redirects you to the code that generated the error. The executable (or executables, if the solution contains more than one project) will be put in a subfolder within the project's directory, called Bin\Debug or Bin\Release, depending on the output configuration you chose. Configurations are discussed next.

Debug and Release Configurations

Visual Studio provides two default possibilities for compiling your projects. Both of these possibilities are represented by *configurations*. By default, Visual Studio offers two built-in configurations:

▶ **Debug**—When the Debug configuration is active, the Visual Basic compiler generates debug symbols that the Visual Studio debugger can process. Without these symbols, you cannot debug your applications with the Visual Studio debugger.

▶ **Release**—The Release configuration basically excludes debug symbols from the build process. It is the configuration you use when building the final version of your application—that is, the executable you will release to your customers. To set the current configuration, you have two possibilities: You can use the combo box located on the Visual Studio toolbar or you can use the Compile tab of the My Project window (see Figure 2.26).

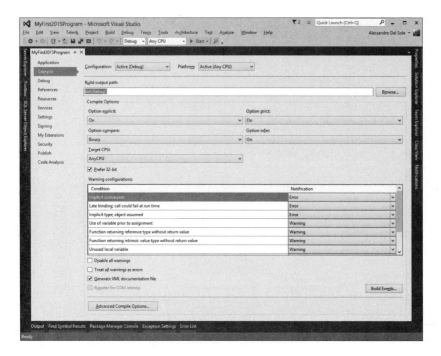

FIGURE 2.26   Compile options in the My Project window.

At the top of the window is a Configuration combo box from which you can select the most appropriate configuration. By default, Visual Studio 2015 is set to the Debug configuration. You can also consider building a custom configuration, as discussed next. (However, you can also customize both Debug and Release instead of making new configurations.) For now, you can leave the Debug configuration selected because you will be studying the Visual Studio debugging features in depth.

Creating Custom Configurations with Configuration Manager

You might have situations in which both the Debug and Release configurations are not enough for your needs. In such cases, you can create a custom configuration. To accomplish this, you need to access the Configuration Manager window (see Figure 2.27) by selecting **Build, Configuration Manager**. You can use this window to edit an existing configuration or create a new one.

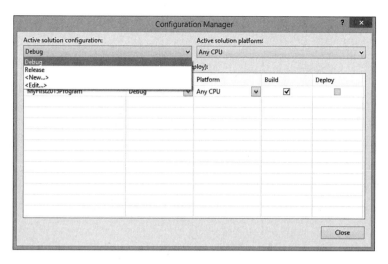

FIGURE 2.27   The Configuration Manager.

To create a new custom configuration, perform the following steps:

1. From the Active Solution Configuration combo box, select the **New** option.

2. In the New Solution Configuration window that appears, specify a name for the new configuration and select an existing configuration (such as Debug) from which settings will be copied. Figure 2.28 shows an example. When you're done with this window, click **OK**.

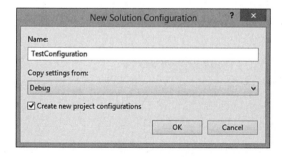

FIGURE 2.28   Creating a custom configuration that imports settings from an existing one.

3. Back in the Configuration Manager window, click **Close**.

4. Click the **Advanced Compiler Options** button in the Compile tab of the My Project window and specify which compile options must affect the new configuration. For example, if you decide to affect just compilations against 64-bit processors, you need to change the value in the Target CPU combo box. At this point, you can modify your real configuration settings and how your project should be built.

The modifications you make to the new configuration influence just the new configuration. Moreover, if you decide to use the new configuration, you will have a new Bin*CustomConfiguration* subfolder (in this case, Bin\TestConfiguration) in your project's main folder that will contain the output of the build process made with that configuration. For the MyFirst2015Program sample, the project folder is named MyFirst2015Program and contains the Bin subfolder, which also contains the default Debug and Release subfolders. With your custom configuration, a new TestConfiguration subfolder will be available under Bin.

Background Compiler

Visual Basic 2015 offers a great feature, the background compiler, which is more powerful than ever before due to the reimplementation provided by the .NET compiler platform. While you write your code, the IDE invokes the Visual Basic compiler, which immediately compiles the code and notifies you about errors that occur by showing messages in the Error List window. This is possible because the Visual Basic compiler can compile your code on-the-fly while you type. This feature means you do not necessarily need to build your project each time to determine whether your code can be successfully compiled.

You are most likely to see the background compiler in action when your see error messages in the Error List window while you're typing code (refer to Figure 2.20). In this window, you can double-click an error message to be redirected to the line of code that caused the error. Also, the IDE underlines code containing errors with squiggly lines so that it is easier to understand where the problem is.

> **ABOUT SQUIGGLES**
>
> In previous versions of Visual Basic, you had to click outside the current line to let squiggle appears. In Visual Basic 2015, squiggles appear immediately as you type.

Other Compile Options

Visual Studio 2015 enables you to get strong control over the build process. For example, you can control compile options that are specific to the Visual Basic language. Table 2.3 lists them in detail.

TABLE 2.3   Visual Basic Compile Options

Option	Description
Option Explicit	When this is set to On, you must declare an object before using it in code.
Option Strict	When this is set to On, you must specify the type when declaring objects. In other words, Object is not automatically assigned as the default type. Moreover, Option Strict On disallows late binding and conversions from one type to another where there is a loss of precision or data. You should always set Option Strict On unless required—for instance when you need to work with late binding techniques.

Option	Description
Option Compare	This option determines which method must be used when comparing strings (Binary or Text). The Binary option enables the compiler to compare strings based on a binary representation of the characters, while the Text option enables string comparisons based on textual sorting, according to the local system's international settings.
Option Infer	When this is set to On, it enables local type inference (which is discussed in Chapter 20, "Advanced Language Features").

Option Strict On

By default, Option Strict is set to Off. You can set it to On each time you create a new project, but you can also change the default setting by selecting **Tools, Options**. Then in the Options dialog box, you expand the Projects and Solutions node, select **VB Defaults**, and change the default setting for the Option Strict combo box.

The background compiler also considers the options listed in Table 2.3, and it notifies you immediately if your code does not match these requirements.

Target CPU

You can specify the CPU architecture that your applications will target. You can choose among 32-bit architectures (x86), 64-bit architectures (x64), ARM (in the case of Windows Store apps), or any architecture (AnyCPU). The default configuration is AnyCPU, with the Prefer 32-bit option enabled. When Prefer 32-bit is enabled, the process works as follows:

▶ If it runs on a 32-bit Windows system, it runs as a 32-bit process, and the intermediate language is compiled to x86 machine code.

▶ If it runs on a 64-bit Windows system, it runs as a 32-bit process, and the intermediate language is compiled to x86 machine code.

▶ If it runs on an ARM Windows system, it runs as a 32-bit process, but the intermediate language is compiled to ARM machine code.

In Visual Studio 2010 and earlier, these settings were available in the Advanced Compile Options dialog box.

Warning Configurations

Warning configurations state how the Visual Basic compiler should notify a developer of some particular errors: by sending either warning messages (which do not prevent VB from compiling the project) or error messages (which prevent VB from completing the build process).

DO NOT IGNORE WARNING MESSAGES

Even if warning messages will not prevent the completion of the build process, you should never blindly ignore them. They could be suggestions of potential exceptions at runtime. You should always accurately determine why a warning message is reported and, possibly, solve the issue that caused the warning. You can ignore warnings in very limited situations, such as when running code analysis on code that does not need to be compliant with Microsoft specifications (for example, the user interface side of a WPF application). In all other situations, you should be careful about warnings.

Depending on how you set the Visual Basic compile options just discussed, Visual Studio will propose some default scenarios for sending notifications (and, consequently, influencing the build process). Table 2.4 lists the available warning conditions.

TABLE 2.4   Warning Conditions

Condition	Description

Implicit conversion	Checked when trying to assign an object of one type to an object of another type. For example, the following code causes the condition to be checked (implicit conversion from `Object` to `String`):
	`Dim anObject As Object = "Hi!"`
	`Dim aString As String = anObject`

Late binding	Checked when trying to assign at runtime a typed object to another one of type `Object`.
Implicit type	Checked when not specifying the type for an object declaration. If `Option Infers` is on, this condition is checked only for declarations at the class level. For example, the following class-level declaration would cause the condition to be checked: `Private Something` This condition is determined by `Option Strict On`.

Use of variable prior of assignment	Checked when attempting to use a variable that doesn't have a value yet. This is typical with instance variables. The following code causes this condition to be checked:
	`Dim p As Process`
	`Console.WriteLine(`
	`p.ProcessName.ToString)`
	In this case, `p` must get an instance of the `Process` object before attempting to use it.

Function/operator without return value	Checked when a `Function` method or an operator definition performs actions without returning a value.
Unused local variable	Checked when a variable is declared but not used. It's a good practice to remove unused variables both for cleaner code and for memory allocation.

Condition	Description
Instance variable accesses shared members	Checked when trying to invoke a member from an instance object that is instead a shared member.
Recursive operator or property access	Checked when trying to use a member (properties or operators) inside the code block that defines the member itself.
Duplicate or overlapping catch blocks	Checked when a `Catch` clause inside a `Try..Catch..End Try` code block is not reached because of inheritance. The following code causes the condition to be checked because `FileNotFoundException` inherits from `Exception` and therefore should be caught before the base class; otherwise, `Exception` would be always caught before derived ones:

```
Try
Catch ex As Exception
Catch ex As FileNotFoundException
End Try
```

You can also change single notifications; just select the most appropriate notification mode for your needs. Based on the explanations provided in Table 2.4, be careful about the consequences that this operation could cause. If you are not sure about consequences, it's best to leave the default options unchanged. Three other compile options that are listed at the bottom of the Compile tab are described in Table 2.5.

TABLE 2.5   Additional Compile Options

Option	Description
Disable All Warnings	The Visual Basic compiler will not produce warning messages.
Treat All Warnings As Errors	The Visual Basic compiler will treat all warning messages as if they were errors.
Generate XML Documentation File	When this option is selected, Visual Studio generates an XML file for documenting the source code. If XML comments are included in the code, this file also contains descriptions and detailed documentation for the code. This is useful when you need to automate the documentation process for class libraries.

Advanced Compile Options

You can specify advanced settings for the build process. To accomplish this, you need to click the **Advanced Compile Options** button in the Compile tab to open the Advanced Compiler Settings window (see Figure 2.29).

COMPILER SETTINGS AND CONFIGURATIONS

Advanced compiler settings occur at the configuration level. This means the Debug configuration has its own advanced settings, the Release configuration has its own settings,
and your custom configurations have their own settings. Please remember this when
providing advanced settings.

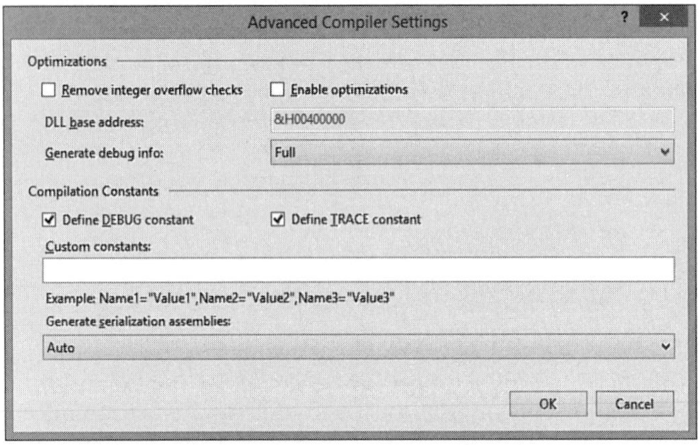

FIGURE 2.29   The Advanced Compiler Settings window.

You use the Advanced Compiler Settings window to set compiler options that drive the
build process. The following sections discuss these options in detail.

Optimizations

The Optimizations section of the Advanced Compiler Settings window offers options that
can potentially lead to building a smaller and faster executable. This section provides four
options:

▶ **Remove Integer Overflow Checks**—When you make calculations in your code
against `Integer` or `Integer`-style data types, the Visual Basic compiler checks that
the result of the calculation falls within the range of that particular data type. By
default, this option is turned off so that the compiler can do this kind of check. If
you select this check box, the compiler does not check for such overflows, and the
application execution might occur faster. Be careful about this choice, especially if
your code implements calculations.

▶ **Enable Optimizations**—When this check box is selected, the compiler basically removes some opcodes that are required for interacting with the debugger.
Moreover, the just-in-time compilation is optimized because the Runtime knows that
a debugger will not be attached. On the other hand, this can result in major difficulties when debugging applications. For example, you might not use breakpoints at
specific lines of code and, consequently, you might perform debugging tasks even
though the optimization process could produce a smaller and faster executable.

- ▶ **DLL Base Address**—This option, which is available when you're developing class libraries and user controls, provides the ability to specify the base address for the assembly. The *base address* is the location in memory where a .dll file is loaded. By default, Visual Studio assigns a base address in hexadecimal format. If you need to provide a custom base address, this is where you can do it.

- ▶ **Generate Debug Information**—Generating debug information when building a project allows you to use the debugger against your application. By default, this option is set to Full, which means that full debug information is generated so that the debugger can be fully used to debug an application. (This is the case with the Debug configuration.) If you set this option to None, no debug information will be generated; if you set this option to pdb-only, the compiler will produce just a .pdb file that contains debug symbols and project state information.

Compilation Constants

You can use compilation constants to conditionally compile blocks of code. Conditional compilation relies on the evaluation to `True` of constants that will be included in the final assembly. The Visual Basic compiler defines some default constants you can evaluate within your code; you can also declare custom constants. In the Advanced Compiler Settings window, you can specify whether the compiler needs to include the DEBUG and TRACE constants. The DEBUG constant enables you to understand whether the application is running in debug mode (that is, if the application has been compiled using the Debug configuration). The TRACE constant is also related to debugging tasks; in particular, the .NET Framework exposes the `Trace` class, which is used in debugging and can send the tracing output to the Output window when the TRACE constant is defined. If TRACE is not used, no output is generated because invocations against the `Trace` class are ignored.

For a full list of built-in constants, head to the MSDN Library, at http://msdn.microsoft.com/en-us/library/dy7yth1w(v=vs.120).aspx. Evaluating constants in code is simple. You can use the #If, #Else, #ElseIf, and #EndIf directives. For example, if you want to evaluate whenever an application has been compiled with the Debug configuration, you could use the following code:

```
#If DEBUG Then
        Console.WriteLine("You are in Debug configuration")
#Else
        Console.WriteLine("You are not in Debug configuration")
#End If
```

This essentially verifies whether the constant is defined and takes some action at that point. In our example, if the DEBUG constant is defined in the assembly, this means that it has been built via the Debug configuration.

Custom Constants

You can define custom constants in two different ways. The first is to add custom constants in the appropriate field of the Advanced compiler settings window. Each constant must have the form of *Name="Value"*, and constants are separated by commas.

The second way is to add a `#Const` directive in your code. For example, the following line of code

```
#Const TestConstant = True
```

defines a constant named `TestConstant` whose value is set to `True`. The big difference in using a `#Const` directive is that it defines just private constants that are visible within the code file that defines them. Custom constants are also very useful with shared projects, where you can use `#if` directives to detect which project is running the shared code. (See Chapter 17, "Working with Objects: Visual Tools and Code Sharing," for more details.)

Generating Serialization Assemblies

As you'll learn in Chapter 39, "Serialization," serialization in .NET development is a technique that allows you to persist the state of an object. Among several alternatives, this can be accomplished using a class called `XmlSerializer`. In such situations, the Visual Basic compiler can optimize applications that use the `XmlSerializer` class, generating additional assemblies for better performances. By default, this option is set to **Auto** so that Visual Studio generates serialization assemblies only if you are effectively using XML serialization in your code. Other options are `On` and `Off`.

Debugging Overview

This section provides an overview of the debugging features in Visual Studio 2015 for Visual Basic applications. Although the debugger and debugging techniques are detailed in Chapter 5, this chapter provides information on the most common debugging tasks, which you need to know about in this first part of your journey through the Visual Basic programming language.

Debugging an Application

To debug a Visual Basic application, you basically need to perform two steps:

1. Enable the Debug configuration in the compile options.

2. Press F5 to start debugging. Visual Studio runs your application and attaches an instance of the debugger to the application.

Because the Visual Studio debugger needs the debug symbols in order to proceed, if you do not choose the Debug configuration, you cannot debug your applications. The instance of the debugger detaches when you shut down your application.

TIP

As an alternative, you can click the **Start** button on the Visual Studio standard toolbar. If the Debug configuration is selected, this action does the same thing as pressing **F5**. If the Release configuration is selected, selecting **Start** does the same thing as launching the application with **Ctrl+F5**.

The debugger monitors your application's execution and notifies you of runtime errors; it allows you to take control over the execution flow as well. Figure 2.30 shows our sample application running with the Visual Studio debugger attached.

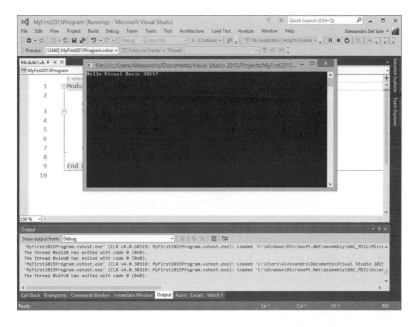

FIGURE 2.30   Our sample application running with an attached instance of the Visual Studio debugger.

In the bottom area of the IDE, notice that some tabs are available, such as Locals, Watch 1, Watch 2, Call Stack, Breakpoints, Command Window, Immediate Window, and Output. Each tab represents a tool window that has specific debugging purposes. Also, notice that the status bar becomes orange, and an orange border is placed around the IDE, to remind you that the IDE is running in debugging mode.

The Visual Studio debugger is a powerful tool. Next, you'll learn the most important tasks in debugging applications. Before you learn about the tools, though, you need to modify the source code of our test application so that it can intentionally cause some errors and you can see the debugger in action. The `Sub Main` method's code could be rewritten as shown in Listing 2.3.

LISTING 2.3   Modifying `Sub Main` for Debugging Purposes

```
Sub Main()
    'A text message
    Dim message As String = "Hello Visual Basic 2015!"
    Console.WriteLine(message)
    'Attempt to read a file that does not exist
    Dim getSomeText As String =
```

```
                    My.Computer.FileSystem.ReadAllText("FakeFile.txt")
        Console.WriteLine(getSomeText)
        Console.ReadLine()
End Sub
```

This code simply declares a message object of type `String`, which contains a text message. This message is then shown in the Console window. This is useful for understanding breakpoints and other features in the code editor. The second part of the code tries to open a text file, which effectively does not exist, and store its content in a variable called `getSomeText` of type `String`. This will help you understand how the debugger catches errors at runtime.

Breakpoints and Data Tips

Breakpoints enable you to control the execution flow of an application. A breakpoint breaks the execution of the application at the point where the breakpoint itself is placed so that you can take required actions (a situation known as *break mode*). You can then resume the application execution. To place a breakpoint on a specific line of code, you just place the cursor on the line of code you want to debug and then press **F9**.

A breakpoint is easily recognizable because it highlights in red the selected line of code (see Figure 2.31).

To see how breakpoints work, you can run the sample application by pressing **F5**. When the debugger encounters a breakpoint, it breaks the execution and highlights in yellow the line of code that is being debugged, as shown in Figure 2.32, before the code is executed.

In Figure 2.32, if you pass the mouse pointer over the message variable, IntelliSense shows the content of the variable itself, which at the moment contains no value (in fact, it is set to `Nothing`). This feature, known as DataTips, is useful if you need to know the content of a variable or of another object in a particular moment of the application execution.

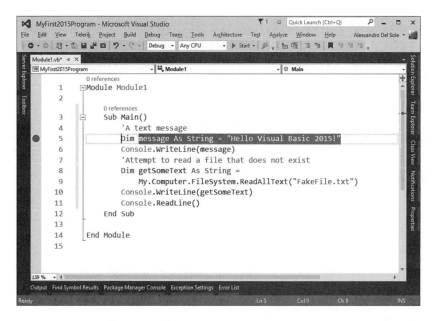

FIGURE 2.31   Placing a breakpoint in the code editor.

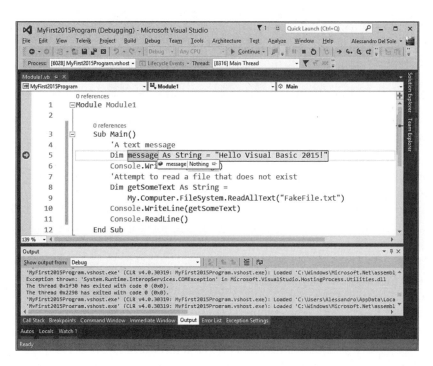

FIGURE 2.32   When it encounters a breakpoint, Visual Studio highlights the line of code that is currently debugged.

You can then execute just one line of code at a time by pressing **F11** (which is a shortcut for the Step Into command from the Debug menu). For example, if you want to check whether the message variable is correctly initialized at runtime, you can press **F11**. The line of code where the breakpoint is placed is now executed, and Visual Studio highlights the next line of code. At this point, you can still pass the mouse pointer over the variable to see the assignment result, as shown in Figure 2.33.

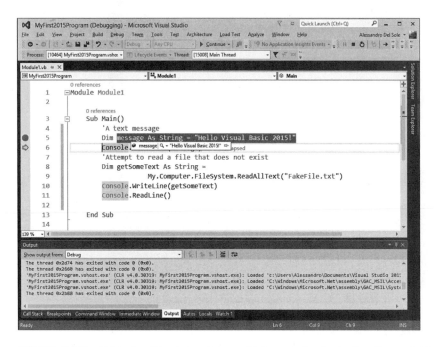

FIGURE 2.33   Using the Step Into command lets you check whether the variable has been assigned correctly.

When you finish checking the assignments, you can resume the execution by pressing **F5**. The execution of the application continues to another breakpoint or until a runtime error is encountered.

Runtime Errors

A runtime error is an error that occurs during application execution. These errors are not predictable and occur due to programming errors that are not visible at compile time. An example of a runtime error is creating an application and giving users the ability to specify a filename, but then the file is not found on disk; another example is needing to access a database and passing an incorrect SQL query string. Obviously, in real-life applications, you should predict such possibilities and implement the appropriate error-handling routines (discussed in Chapter 6), but for the purpose of learning about the debugger, you need some code that voluntarily causes an error. If you continue with the debugging you began in the previous section, the application's execution resumption causes a runtime error because the code is searching for a file that does not exist. When the error is raised, Visual Studio breaks the execution, as shown in Figure 2.34.

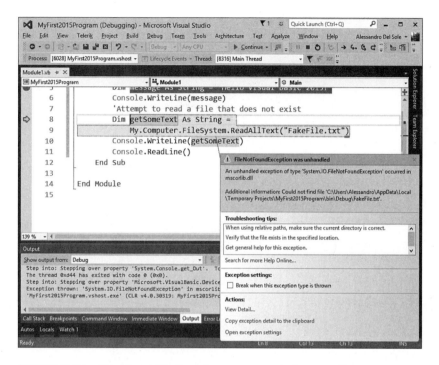

FIGURE 2.34   The Visual Studio debugger encountering a runtime error.

As you can see, the line of code that caused the error appears highlighted. You can also see a pop-up window that shows some information about the error. In this case, the code searched for a file that does not exist, so a `FileNotFoundException` error was thrown and was not handled by error-handling routines; therefore, the execution of the application was broken. Visual Studio also shows a description of the error message. (In this example, it communicates that the code could not find the FakeFile.txt file.) Visual Studio also shows some suggestions. For example, the Troubleshooting Tips section suggest some tasks you could perform at this point, such as verifying that the file exists in the specified location, checking the pathname, and getting general help about the error. If you click a tip, you are redirected to the MSDN documentation about the error. This can be useful when you don't exactly know what an error message means.

There are also options in the Actions group of the error message. The most important is View Detail, which enables you to open the View Detail window, shown in Figure 2.35. Notice how the `StackTrace` item shows the hierarchy of calls to classes and methods that effectively produced the error. Another interesting item is `InnerException`. In our example it is set to `Nothing`, but it's not unusual for this item to show an exceptions tree that enables you to better understand what actually caused an error. For example, think of working with data. You might want to connect to SQL Server and fetch data from a database. If you do not have sufficient rights to access the database, the Runtime might return a data access exception that does not allow you to immediately understand what the problem is. Browsing the `InnerException` can help you understand that the problem was caused by insufficient rights. You need to go back to the code to fix it, and this is where the Edit and Continue features, discussed next, come in.

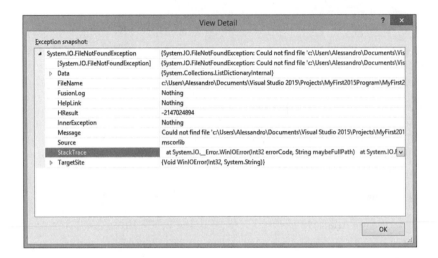

FIGURE 2.35   The View Detail window enables you to examine what caused an exception.

Edit and Continue

The Edit and Continue features enable you to fix bad code and resume the application execution from the point where it was broken, without having to restart the application. You just need to run the application by pressing **F5**; and then you can break its execution by pressing **Ctrl+Alt+Break** or either selecting **Debug, Break All** or clicking **Pause** on the Debug toolbar.

AVAILABILITY OF EDIT AND CONTINUE

Generally, you can use the Edit and Continue features, but there are situations in which you can't. For example, if fixing your code might influence the general application behavior, you need to restart the application. It is worth mentioning that Visual Studio 2015 introduces support for Edit and Continue against lambda expressions.

In the current example, you need to fix the code that searches for a file that doesn't exist. You can replace the line of code with this one:

```
Dim getSomeText As String = "Fixed code"
```

This replaces the search of a file with a text message. At this point, you can press **F5** (or **F11** if you want to just execute the line of code and debug the next one) to resume the execution. Figure 2.36 shows the application now running correctly. (Remember that debugging features in Visual Studio are covered in detail in Chapter 6.)

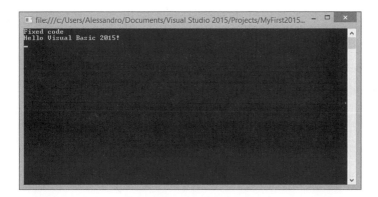

FIGURE 2.36   The sample application running correctly after you fix the errors.

After this brief overview of the debugging features in Visual Studio 2015, it's time to talk about another important topic that will help you feel at home in the Visual Studio 2015 IDE when developing applications: getting help and documentation.

Browsing the Visual Basic and .NET Documentation

The *.NET Framework Base Class Library* is very large, and it's not likely that you'll be able to remember all the objects you can use in your applications (or the ones the .NET Framework relies on). Instead of memorizing the library, you just need to know where and how to search for information. You have different tools available to browse the .NET Framework and its documentation—and for Visual Basic, too. The goal of this chapter is to provide information on the primary tools you need for developing Visual Basic applications, and getting help with the language and its tools is absolutely one of the primary necessities.

Online Help and the MSDN Library

Visual Studio 2015 ships with the MSDN Library, which is where you can find documentation for Visual Basic 2015 and the .NET Framework 4.6. There are basically two ways to access the MSDN Library: offline and online. To access the MSDN Library offline, you have the following alternatives:

▶ Select **Help**, **View Help** in Visual Studio.

▶ Press **F1** from wherever you are in Visual Studio.

If you are writing code or performing a particular task on a tool within the IDE, pressing **F1** is the best choice because you will be redirected to the help page related to the instruction, code statement, or tool you're dealing with. If you are instead searching for information about a particular technology or framework, such as WPF or the Office Developer Tools, you could consider the other choice. To access the MSDN Library online, you need an Internet connection, and you need to specify to always use the online help by selecting **Help, Set Help Preference** and then clicking **Launch in Browser or Launch Help Viewer**. Alternatively, you can manually open one of the following websites, which are the main points of interest for a Visual Basic developer:

► The MSDN Library portal at http://msdn.microsoft.com/en-us/library/default.aspx

► The .NET Framework reference at http://msdn.microsoft.com/en-us/library/w0x726c2(VS.110).aspx

► The Visual Basic page on the Visual Studio Developer Center at http://msdn.microsoft.com/en-us/vstudio/hh388573

You can also quickly find information on particular objects by using built-in tools such as the Object Browser.

MANAGING HELP CONTENTS

You can download additional documentation or remove documentation that is already on your system by selecting **Help, Add or Remove Help Content**.

Object Browser Window

The Object Browser is a special tool window that enables you to browse the .NET Framework class library, including .NET for Windows Store apps, as well as any referenced libraries and types defined in your projects. You can get a hierarchical view of the Base Class Library and of all the types defined in your solution, including types defined in referenced external assemblies. You activate the Object Browser by pressing **Ctrl+Alt+J**. The Object Browser is useful because it helps you understand how a type is defined, which members it exposes, which interfaces it implements, and which other classes it derives from. If the types are documented, you can get a description for each object or member.

Figure 2.37 provides an example of the Object Browser showing members of the `System.Windows.ContentElement` class.

The right side of the window lists methods and properties exposed by the selected object. When you click on a method or on a member of the object in the left side of the window, a short description of the object appears on the bottom-right side of the Object Browser. If the description is not useful enough for you to understand the meaning of an object or of one of its members, you can press **F1**, and Visual Studio shows the online help (if available) for the object or member. The Object Browser also provides links to objects used by the object you are exploring. In Figure 2.37, you can see the description of a method, and you can also click the parameters' identifiers to be redirected to the definition of the parameter.

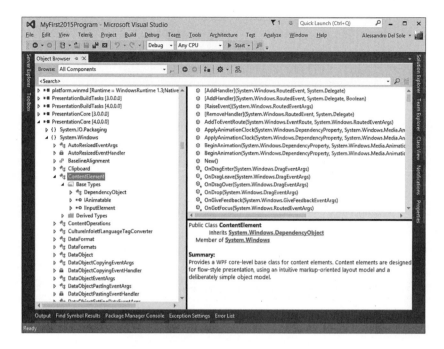

FIGURE 2.37   The Object Browser enables you to explore .NET objects showing information.

Inspecting Built-in Types

In previous versions of Visual Studio, you could enable the Object Browser window by right-clicking a type in the code editor and then selecting **Go to Definition** from the context menu. In Visual Studio 2015, Go to Definition is still available, but it now opens the type definition in the code editor itself. This means you can see the source code of built-in .NET types. This feature is also known as Metadata as Source. Figure 2.38 shows, as an example, the source code for the `String` class, which has been reached by right-clicking the `String` type in the code editor and then selecting Go to Definition.

For your own types, Go to Definition works as in previous versions, redirecting to the proper code. The new feature is very interesting and brings parity with Visual C#, where it has been available since previous versions.

Quick Launch Tool

Visual Studio 2015 provides a tool called Quick Launch, which makes it easy to find commands, options, and recently opened files. The tool is available through a search box located in the upper-right corner of the IDE. For example, imagine that you need to launch the SQL Server Object Explorer window but do not remember where the command for launching such a window is, and you don't want to waste time browsing every menu. If you type **SQL** in the Quick Launch search box, Visual Studio shows all menu commands, options, and recently opened files (if any) that contain the **SQL** word. As you can see in Figure 2.39, SQL Server Object Explorer is the first search result, so you can simply click it to open that tool.

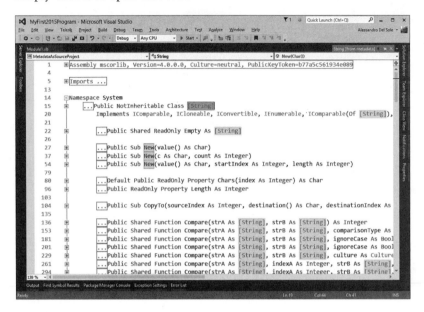

FIGURE 2.38   Inspecting .NET built-in types.

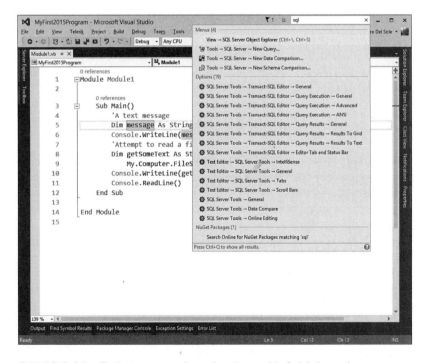

FIGURE 2.39   Finding commands and options with Quick Launch.

To understand how Quick Launch works, repeat the search and select the SQL Server Tools -> General option from the list. You then see how Visual Studio opens the Options dialog box and points to the requested setting. This useful tool can save you a lot of time finding the necessary tools, including NuGet packages.

Showing the Hierarchy of Method Calls

Visual Studio 2015 offers a window named Call Hierarchy. As its name implies, Call Hierarchy enables you to see the hierarchy of calls to one or more methods. To understand how it works, consider the following code:

```
Module Module1
  Sub Main()
    DoSomething()
  End Sub
  Sub DoSomething()
    DoSomethingElse()
  End Sub
  Sub DoSomethingElse()
    DoNothing()
  End Sub
  Sub DoNothing()
    '
  End Sub
End Module
```

This code defines some method, without performing any particular tasks, but it demonstrates a nested hierarchy of method calls. If you right-click the name of one of the methods and then select View Call Hierarchy from the context menu, you can see the method call hierarchy, as shown in Figure 2.40.

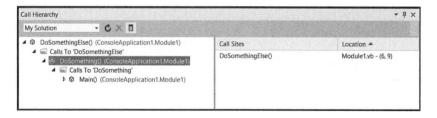

FIGURE 2.40   Analyzing method calls with Call Hierarchy.

As you can see in Figure 2.40, the tool shows the first-level hierarchy, but you can also expand method names to see the full hierarchy, including nested method calls. On the right side of the window is the line number in the code file where the selected method is defined. Also, if you double-click a method name in the Call Hierarchy window, the code editor automatically focuses on the method definition.

CALL HIERARCHY DIFFERENCES IN VISUAL STUDIO 2015

If you have had experience with Visual Studio versions 2010 up to 2013, you might notice that in the new release, the tool window does not show calls *from* methods. The reason is that the Call Hierarchy window is another tool rebuilt on the .NET Compiler Platform, and the migration has not been totally completed yet. Because of this, in Visual Studio 2015, you only have calls to methods, but not from methods. It is reasonable to expect that this will be fixed in future versions.

Summary

As a Visual Basic developer, you need to feel at home in the Visual Studio 2015 Integrated Development Environment. Tasks such as creating projects, compiling projects, debugging applications, and searching for documentation and tools are the most common in a developer's life, and this chapter offers a fast way to understand all the primary tools you need for building applications with Visual Basic 2015. You've also seen some productivity tools like Quick Launch and Call Hierarchy in this chapter. Now that you know how you can move inside the IDE, it's time to begin working with the Visual Basic programming language.

CHAPTER 3

The Anatomy of a Visual Basic Project

You can create lots of kinds of projects both for Windows and the web with Visual Basic 2015. However, regardless of the type of project, you need a common set of files for each project. In this chapter you'll learn which files give the structure to a project and how these files influence the building of an application. You'll also get an overview of references, namespaces, classes, modules, and Visual Basic keywords.

Brief Overview of Types and Members

Part II, "Object-Oriented Programming with Visual Basic 2015," discusses important topics related to object-oriented programming with Visual Basic 2015 and explores features such as types, classes, modules, namespaces, interfaces, and class members. At this point, you need a more basic overview of classes, modules, namespaces, and class members because you will find these objects in code examples and in Visual Basic features that are shown prior to Part II.

IF SOMETHING IS NOT CLEAR

This chapter provides only a brief overview of some important topics. Don't worry if any of concepts you learn about here are unclear. Starting in Chapter 4, "Data Types and Expressions," and continuing through Part II of this book, all these concepts are discussed in detail.

Comments

Describing what a piece of code does is an important programming practice. It helps other developers understand your code, and it also helps you when go back to work on your own code sometime later. You can comment a piece of code by typing the comment symbol ' and then writing your comments. The compiler simply ignores comments, so they do not affect performances at all. You can write comments on multiple lines, each starting with the comment symbol. The following code provides an example:

```
'The following code writes something
'to the Console window
Sub DoSomething()
    Console.WriteLine("Doing something")
End Sub
```

DIFFERENT TYPES OF COMMENTS

You can use the REM keyword for commenting code, instead of the ' comment symbol, but that is not recommended as it is really just maintained for backward compatibility with older versions of the language. Visual Basic 2015 introduces support for comments after the implicit line continuation, described shortly, which basically allows you to add comments in scenarios like LINQ queries or array literals.

Classes

Classes in .NET development represent objects whose declaration is enclosed within Class..End Class blocks. The following is an example of a class declaration:

```
Class Person
End Class
```

Classes are *reference types* (explained further in Chapter 4), and a class can expose members that influence the object's behavior, such as properties *and* methods. Classes can implement interfaces; they can also be static (or shared, in VB terminology) and can provide support for inheritance.

Properties

Properties are characteristics of a type. For example, the previously shown class Person could have two properties, such as the first name and the last name:

```
Class Person
  Property FirstName As String
  Property LastName As String
End Class
```

READ-ONLY AUTO-IMPLEMENTED PROPERTIES

Visual Basic 2015 introduces *auto-implemented read-only properties*, which no longer require you to specify the `Get` method explicitly. This enhancement to auto-implemented properties, introduced with Visual Basic 2015, is discussed further in Chapter 7, "Class Fundamentals."

Methods

Methods represent actions and are the .NET equivalent of what in other programming environments are called functions and procedures. A method can be a member of classes, structures, and modules. Methods that return a value are represented by `Function..End Function` blocks, such as the following:

```
Function DoSomething() As String
     Return "A text message"
End Function
```

Methods that do not return a value are represented by `Sub..End Sub` blocks, such as the following:

```
Sub DoSomething()
'write your code here
End Sub
```

Methods can receive parameters that can be processed within code blocks. Such parameters are called, in .NET terminology, *arguments*. The following code block shows an example of an argument named `message`:

```
Sub DoSomething(message As String)
    Console.Writeline(message)
End Sub
```

Modules

Modules are defined within a `Module..End Module` code block. Modules are basically `Shared` classes, but unlike classes, they cannot implement interfaces or use inheritance. The following is an example of a module:

```
Module Module1
    Sub DoSomething()
        'Code goes here
    End Sub
End Module
```

Members defined inside modules don't require the name of the module when invoked. Visual Basic 2015 introduces partial modules, which allow you to split a module definition across multiple files. Partial modules are discussed in greater detail in Chapter 10, "Modules."

Structures

Structures are .NET objects that are represented by a `Structure..End Structure` code block. Structures are *value types*, and they are described in more detail in Chapter 4. For classes, structures can expose properties, methods, and so on. The following is an example of a structure declaration:

```
Structure SomeValues
    Property FirstValue As Boolean
    Property SecondValue As Integer
    Sub DoSomething()
    End Sub
End Structure
```

Inheritance

Inheritance is one of the most important features of the .NET Framework. A class can inherit or derive from another class, which means that the new class can have all of its properties, methods, and members exposed by the first class, which is called the *base class*. The new class can then define its members. Inherited members can then be over-ridden to adapt their behavior to the new class's context. The .NET Framework provides single-level inheritance, which means a class can inherit from one other class at a time.

Each class derives implicitly from `System.Object`, and the `Inherits` keyword is used to inherit classes. The following code provides an example of a base class named `Person` and a derived class named `Customer`:

```
Public Class Person
    Public Property FirstName As String
    Public Property LastName As String
    'A new definition of System.Object.ToString
    Public Overrides Function ToString() As String
        Return String.Concat(FirstName, " ", LastName)
    End Function
End Class
Public Class Customer
    Inherits Person
    Public Property CompanyName As String
    Public Overrides Function ToString() As String
        Return CompanyName
    End Function
End Class
```

In this example, the `Person` class overrides (that is, provides a new definition of) the `System.Object.ToString` method. The `Customer` class exposes a new `CompanyName` property; also, via inheritance, it exposes the `FirstName` and `LastName` properties. Finally, the class overrides the `Person.ToString` method. Inheritance is discussed in Chapter 12, "Inheritance."

Namespaces

A *namespace* is basically a container of types. This means that one namespace can contain multiple classes, multiple modules, multiple interfaces, multiple structures, and so on. The following is an example of a namespace exposing two classes, one module, one structure, and one interface:

```
Namespace Test
    Class Person
        Property FirstName As String
        Property LastName As String
    End Class
    Class Employee
        Inherits Person
        Property EmployeeID As Integer
    End Class
    Module Module1
        Sub DoSomething()
        End Sub
    End Module
    Interface ITest
        Sub TakeATest()
    End Interface
    Structure SomeValues
        Property FirstValue As Boolean
        Property SecondValue As Integer
    End Structure
End Namespace
```

Namespaces are important for better organizing types, but they are important for another reason, too. Say that you have two classes with the same name (for example, `Employee`) but with different properties. You can use namespaces to avoid conflicts in such scenarios. You can access types exposed by a namespace by writing its identifier followed by a dot and then the type name. For example, if you want to invoke the method `DoSomething` in Module1, you can write the following line of code:

```
Test.Module1.DoSomething()
```

Namespaces are described in detail in Chapter 9, "Organizing Types Within Namespaces."

Accessing Members

Unless you declare shared objects, you need to instantiate classes and structures before you can use members and store information within those objects. You instantiate a class by declaring a variable and using the New keyword, as in the following line of code:

```
Dim testPerson As New Person
```

Then you can set properties for the new instance or eventually invoke other members, such as methods. For example, you could initialize testPerson's properties as follows:

```
testPerson.FirstName = "Alessandro"
testPerson.LastName = "Del Sole"
```

When you need to invoke a member of a class, you type the name of the instance (in this example, testPerson) followed by a dot and the name of the member. For shared members, you just write the name of the class or structure followed by a dot and the name of the member.

INITIALIZING MEMBERS

Since version 2008, Visual Basic has offered an alternative way to initialize members' values when instantiating classes: using object initializers. Object initializers are discussed in Chapter 7.

Imports **Directives**

As you saw earlier in this chapter, namespaces can expose objects that expose members. Moreover, namespaces can expose nested namespaces, which expose objects, and so on. You often need to access members of objects exposed by nested namespaces. To avoid needing to type the entire names of long (or nested) namespaces and write long lines of code, the Visual Basic language offers the Imports directive. For example, consider the following lines of code that open a file on disk:

```
Dim myFile As New System.IO.FileStream("C:\test.bin",
                                    IO.FileMode.Open)
myFile.Close()
```

The FileStream class is exposed by the IO namespace, which is exposed by the System namespace. You could place the following directive at the beginning of the code:

```
Imports System.IO
```

At this point, the first line of code could be rewritten as follows:

```
Dim myFile As New FileStream("C:\test.bin", FileMode.Open)
```

Because you might be using long namespaces, Visual Basic offers a feature known as *namespace aliasing*, which allows you to define a custom identifier to represent the namespace. The following line demonstrates how to define a `GZip` identifier to import the `System.IO.Compression` namespace:

```
Imports GZip = System.IO.Compression
```

This is useful when you need to invoke members of the namespace in code, as in the following example:

```
'Instead of using System.IO.Compression.GZipStream,
'you can use a shortened format with namespace aliasing
Dim archive As GZip.GZipStream
```

`Imports` directives are useful because they help make code much clearer. Just remember that such directives must be the first lines of each code file. The only exceptions are the `Option` clause, which must precede the `Imports` directives and, of course, comments.

Region **Directives**

Visual Basic provides an efficient way of organizing your code within regions. A *region* is a collapsible area of the code editor that can contain any code and that takes advantage of the outlining feature of Visual Studio 2015. You define a region with `#Region..#End Region` directives. The following code snippet shows how to define a region:

```
#Region "Private Members"
    Private firstItem As String
    Private secondItem As Integer
#End Region
```

The `#Region` directive requires you to specify a descriptive caption. After you declare regions, you can then collapse them by clicking the - (minus) symbol on the left of the `#Region` directive. When it is collapsed, the region shows just the descriptive caption; you can expand it by clicking the + (plus) symbol. Also notice that the Visual Studio 2015 IDE allows you to collapse a region by double-clicking anywhere on the `#Region..#End Region` connector line on the left side of the code window. Such directives are not compiled and do not affect performance at all.

Visual Basic 2015 improves the way you can use regions. In fact, in previous versions of the language, `#Region` directives could not appear inside a method body, nor could they begin in one block and end in another one. In Visual Basic 2015, such directives can appear inside a method and span block boundaries, which means you can start and end regions anywhere in your code. For example, the following region definition is now allowed:

```
    Sub DoSomething()
#Region "A new support for regions"
        Console.WriteLine("Doing something")
    End Sub
```

```
    Sub DoSomethingElse()
        Console.WriteLine("Doing something else")
#End Region
    End Sub
```

This improvement means you can customize the organization of your code in a better way.

Attributes

Attributes are classes derived from the `System.Attribute` class. They give declarative information to objects or members they are applied to, providing the capability to change their behavior. Applying an attribute is also known as *decorating* or *marking* a member.

Attributes are basically class instances. You can apply attributes by enclosing their names within < > symbols. Moreover, they can receive arguments. The following are examples of decorating members with attributes:

```
<Serializable()> Class Test
End Class
<CLSCompliant(True)> Class Test
End Class
```

In these snippets, the `Serializable` attribute creates a new instance of the `System.SerializableAttribute` class, which indicates to the compiler that the decorated class can take advantage of the serialization process. The `CLSCompliant` attribute, whose value is `True`, means that the decorated class is compliant with Microsoft's Common Language Specification. Attributes are discussed in Chapter 45, "Coding Attributes," and you'll also see many examples in this book of code being decorated with attributes.

Implicit Line Continuation

In older versions of Visual Basic, if you needed to split a long line of code into more brief and readable lines of code in the editor, you had to add an underscore (_) character. Starting with Visual Basic 2010, this is no longer necessary due to a feature called *implicit line continuation*, which makes the underscore unnecessary. You can press Enter when you need to split a line of code, and the compiler will automatically recognize a line continuation, depending on the type of code you are writing.

In some situations, implicit line continuation is not allowed. It is allowed in the following situations:

- ▶ Within LINQ queries
- ▶ Within embedded expressions in LINQ-to-XML queries
- ▶ After dots
- ▶ After commas
- ▶ After brackets

▶ When decorating members with attributes

▶ Before an assignment

Let's see how implicit line continuation works. The following code snippet shows a LINQ query:

```
Dim query = From proc In Process.GetProcesses.AsEnumerable
            Where (proc.ProcessName.StartsWith("A"))
            Select proc
```

Before Visual Basic 2010, you needed to add an underscore after the first and second lines of code. Fortunately, this is no longer necessary. The following code snippet shows a LINQ-to-XML query with embedded expressions, without underscores:

```
Dim doc = <?xml version="1.0"?>
          <Processes>
            <%= From proc In query
              Select <Process>
                        <Name <%= proc.ProcessName %>/>
                     </Process>
            %>
          </Processes>
```

The following code snippet shows both commas and brackets, without underscores:

```
Dim p As New List(Of Integer) From {
                                     1,
                                     2,
                                     3,
                                     4}
```

The following code snippet is about dots. In this case, implicit line continuation can be useful when invoking methods or properties:

```
Dim appDataDir As String = My.Computer.FileSystem.
SpecialDirectories.AllUsersApplicationData()
```

The following code snippet shows implicit line continuation with attributes:

```
<CLSCompliant(True)>
Class Test
End Class
```

The following code snippet demonstrates how you can use implicit line continuation before an assignment:

```
Dim aValue As Integer
aValue =
        10
```

All the preceding code snippets are now perfectly legal. In all cases other than the preceding examples, implicit line continuation is not allowed. For example, you still must add an underscore after the `Handles` clause when handling events, as shown here:

```
Private Sub AnEventHandler(sender As Object, e As EventArgs) _
                        Handles anObject.Disposed

End Sub
```

Of course, implicit line continuation is not mandatory: If you still prefer using the underscore when writing code, you can certainly do that. It is also worth mentioning that, in Visual Studio 2015, the IDE will pretty-list away redundant explicit line continuation.

Visual Basic 2015 now allows comments after implicit line continuation. For instance, the following comments are now allowed:

```
Dim processes =
From proc In Process.GetProcesses        'query the list of processes
Where proc.ProcessName.StartsWith("A")   'filter by process name
Select proc
```

This definitely allows you to write much cleaner code.

Visual Basic 2015 Reserved Keywords

When writing code, you often define types or declare variables. Types and variables are recognizable via *identifiers*. An *identifier* is essentially the name of a type or of a variable and not necessarily a word that makes sense, although it is a good practice to assign human-readable identifiers. For example, an identifier such as *DoSomething* is much better than *DoSmt*. There are some words in the Visual Basic lexical grammar that you cannot use as identifiers for your variables because they are reserved for the language.

NAMING CONVENTIONS FOR IDENTIFIERS

.NET programming principles establish some rules that identifiers must abide by when you're writing code. For example, the Common Language Specification talks about some naming conventions, which are covered in Chapter 20, "Advanced Language Features." For now, keep in mind the best practice of making identifiers human readable. Later in the book you'll learn more specifics about how to name identifiers.

Although the code editor is smart enough to tell you when you are attempting to use a reserved keyword as an identifier, having a reference is practical. Therefore, Table 3.1 lists the Visual Basic 2015 reserved words.

TABLE 3.1   Visual Basic 2015 Reserved Keywords

AddHandler	AddressOf	Alias	And
AndAlso	As	Boolean	ByRef
Byte	ByVal	Call	Case
Catch	CBool	CByte	CChar
CDate	CDbl	CDec	Char
CInt	Class	CLng	CObj
Const	Continue	CSByte	CShort
CSng	CStr	CType	CUInt
CULng	CUShort	Date	Decimal
Declare	Default	Delegate	Dim
DirectCast	Do	Double	Each
Else	ElseIf	End	EndIf
Enum	Erase	Error	Event
Exit	False	Finally	For
Friend	Function	Get	GetType
GetXmlNamespace	Global	GoSub	GoTo
Handles	If	Implements	Imports
In	Inherits	Integer	Interface
Is	IsNot	Let	Lib
Like	Long	Loop	Me
Mod	Module	MustInherit	MustOverride
MyBase	MyClass	NameOf	Namespace
Narrowing	New	Next	Not
Nothing	NotInheritable	Object	Of
On	Operator	Option	Optional
Or	OrElse	Overloads	Overridable
Overrides	ParamArray	Partial	Private
Property	Protected	Public	RaiseEvent
ReadOnly	ReDim	REM	RemoveHandler
Resume	Return	SByte	Select
Set	Shadows	Shared	Short
Single	Static	Step	Stop
String	Structure	Sub	SyncLock
Then	Throw	To	True
Try	TryCast	TypeOf	UInteger
ULong	UShort	Using	Variant
Wend	When	While	Widening
With	WithEvents	WriteOnly	Xor

3

USING RESERVED WORDS AS IDENTIFIERS

You can use reserved words as identifiers if you enclose them in a pair of square brackets. For example, `New` is a reserved word and cannot be used, but `[New]` is an acceptable identifier name. Although this practice is allowed, however, you should use it only in particular cases because it could lead to confusion, especially if you are not an experienced developer.

Visual Basic has a number of *unreserved keywords* that are basically words you can use as identifiers but that the programming language keeps for its own usage in particular contexts—usually before or after another keyword. Table 3.2 provides a full list of unreserved keywords. It's a good idea to always avoid using unreserved keywords as identifiers for your objects or variables.

TABLE 3.2   Visual Basic 2015 Unreserved Keywords

Aggregate	Ansi	Assembly	Async
Auto	Await	Binary	Compare
Custom	Distinct	Equals	Explicit
From	Group By	Group Join	Into
IsFalse	IsTrue	Iterator	Join
Key	Mid	Off	Order By
Preserve	Skip	Skip While	Strict
Take	Take While	Text	Unicode
Until	Where	Yield	#Region
#ExternalSource	#Disable	#Enable	

VISUAL BASIC IS CASE-INSENSITIVE

When writing code, remember that Visual Basic is a case-insensitive programming language. This means that, unlike in C# or C++, in Visual Basic, writing Hello is the same of writing HELLO or hello or heLLo. It's important to remember this when you're assigning identifier names.

Understanding Project Files

Each Visual Basic project is composed of several code files. Some of them are by default visible to you, and they are the ones you need to edit to create your application. In addition, some other files (which are hidden by default but can be made visible manually) can be considered as support files. To understand the kind of support that these files offer, consider that most of the settings you can provide to your applications via the My Project window are represented with Visual Basic code. Particularly, Visual Basic translates into code the content of the Application, Resources, Settings, and My Extensions tabs. The following sections provide a detailed description of the files that represent the Application tab in My Project; then it provides an overview of files that represent other tabs. Although you seldom edit these code files manually because all of them have design time support from My Project (as detailed in Chapter 19, "The My Namespace"), there may be some situations in which you need to manually edit them. Thus, it's important to know something about them.

Before you continue, you need to click the **Show All Files** button in the Solution Explorer. This makes visible several code files that are hidden by default and that provide the main infrastructure for each Visual Basic project.

> **NOTE**
>
> Windows Store app projects for Windows 8.x applications have a slightly different structure; because the focus of this book is not Windows 8.x development, except for what the book explains in Chapter 36, "Building Universal Apps for Windows 10," in this chapter you'll learn about the composition of Visual Basic projects for general purposes.

Dissecting My Project

Chapter 2, "The Visual Studio 2015 IDE for Visual Basic," introduces the My Project window and its graphical tools for specifying some settings when developing applications, such as application information and compile options. My Project also provides the infrastructure of the My namespace, which allows you to specify important settings, as discussed in Chapter 19. For now, you need to know that My Project offers a graphical representation of information stored in some code files.

In the Solution Explorer you can see an element named My Project. When you double-click this element, you are redirected to the My Project window. Then, when you enable the All Files view, you can see that the My Project element can be expanded. Within this element (which is a folder physically stored inside the project's folder and that contains all files described in this section), several files are packaged into the assembly's metadata when you build the project. The following sections discuss these files and how they work.

> **THE VERSATILITY OF MY PROJECT**
>
> Depending on the kind of application you develop, My Project can implement additional tabs or remove some. For example, if you develop an ASP.NET web application, you can find tabs in My Project that are specific to that platform, such as Package/Publish Web. These platform-specific tabs are discussed in the appropriate chapters throughout this book.

Application.myapp

The Application.myapp file is an XML representation of the project's main properties. Listing 3.1 shows the content of this file, which becomes available when you create a new Console application.

LISTING 3.1   The Content of Application.myapp

```
<?xml version="1.0" encoding="utf-8"?>
<MyApplicationData xmlns:xsi="http://www.w3.org/2001/XMLSchema-instance"
xmlns:xsd="http://www.w3.org/2001/XMLSchema">
  <MySubMain>false</MySubMain>
  <SingleInstance>false</SingleInstance>
  <ShutdownMode>0</ShutdownMode>
  <EnableVisualStyles>true</EnableVisualStyles>
  <AuthenticationMode>0</AuthenticationMode>
  <ApplicationType>2</ApplicationType>
  <SaveMySettingsOnExit>true</SaveMySettingsOnExit>
</MyApplicationData>
```

The XML elements in this file are self-explanatory, and you might notice that each of them represents a particular item on the Application tab. The Application.myapp file is the brother of another file, named Application.Designer.vb. That file stores information related to Windows Forms applications, such as the authentication mode and the shutdown mode. It is the complement to those application options that you can see in the Windows Application Framework Properties group in the Application tab. Listing 3.2 shows the content of the Application.Designer.vb file as it is generated for a Windows Forms application.

WINDOWS FORMS COMPATIBILITY

Windows Forms is not covered in this book because it is an obsolete presentation technology. However, this section includes some reference to Windows Forms for compatibility with existing applications and to provide a way to get a deeper knowledge of what you have developed in the past (or that you are currently building with that platform).

LISTING 3.2   The Content of Application.Designer.vb

```
Partial Friend Class MyApplication
        Public Sub New()
            MyBase.New(Global.Microsoft.VisualBasic.ApplicationServices.
    AuthenticationMode.Windows)
            Me.IsSingleInstance = false
            Me.EnableVisualStyles = true
            Me.SaveMySettingsOnExit = true
            Me.ShutDownStyle = Global.Microsoft.VisualBasic.ApplicationServices.
    ShutdownMode.AfterMainFormCloses
        End Sub
        Protected Overrides Sub OnCreateMainForm()
            Me.MainForm = Global.WindowsApplication1.Form1
        End Sub
End Class
```

For the sake of simplicity, the preceding code omits some attributes that Visual Studio adds to class members and that are related to the debugger interaction. As you can see by examining Listing 3.2, items in the Application tab of My Project have been mapped to Visual Basic properties. The `Me` identifier represents the instance of the current application. The `OnCreateMainForm` method establishes which window must be the startup one. In this case, `Form1` is the default name that Visual Studio assigns to the main window when a new project is created.

If you also examine the code inside the IDE, you can see that some comments in the code advise that the code itself is auto-generated and that you should not edit it manually because you can use the My Project designer to automatically map changes to the Visual Basic code. You might need to set custom actions for application events (such as startup or shutdown, which are usually handled in the ApplicationEvents.vb file), and Application. Designer.vb is the place for these changes.

AssemblyInfo.vb

Chapter 2 discusses the Assembly Information dialog box and talks about how to use it to specify information about applications. All that information is stored in a file named AssemblyInfo.vb. Listing 3.3 shows the content of this file as it is available when you create a new project.

Listing 3.3 contains several items whose identifiers begin with the word *Assembly*, such as `AssemblyTitle`, `AssemblyCompany`, and so on. Each of these items is in relationship with fields of the Assembly Information dialog box. Such items are marked with an attribute named `Assembly`. Attributes are discussed in Chapter 45.

It is useful to know about the AssemblyInfo.vb file because sometimes you need to edit this file manually. For example, you may need to edit it when you're dealing with localization of WPF applications or when marking an assembly as compliant with *Microsoft's Common Language Specification*.

LISTING 3.3   AssemblyInfo.vb Content

```
Imports System
Imports System.Reflection
Imports System.Runtime.InteropServices
' General Information about an assembly is controlled through the following
' set of attributes. Change these attribute values to modify the information
' associated with an assembly.
' Review the values of the assembly attributes
<Assembly: AssemblyTitle("WindowsApplication1")>
<Assembly: AssemblyDescription("")>
<Assembly: AssemblyCompany("")>
<Assembly: AssemblyProduct("WindowsApplication1")>
<Assembly: AssemblyCopyright("Copyright © 2015")>
<Assembly: AssemblyTrademark("")>
<Assembly: ComVisible(False)>
```

```
'The following GUID is for the ID of the typelib if this project is exposed to COM
<Assembly: Guid("5572d199-a7ca-48c3-98d3-56533cd6ba86")>
' Version information for an assembly consists of the following four values:
'
'        Major Version
'        Minor Version
'        Build Number
'        Revision
'
' You can specify all the values or you can default the Build and Revision Numbers
' by using the '*' as shown below:
' <Assembly: AssemblyVersion("1.0.*")>
<Assembly: AssemblyVersion("1.0.0.0")>
<Assembly: AssemblyFileVersion("1.0.0.0")>
```

Resources and the Resources.resx File

Visual Studio 2015 enables you to define resources that you can embed in your assembly's metadata and use within your applications. Resources can include strings, icons, picture files, audio files, and so on. My Project offers a tab named Resources that provides a visual way to define project-level resources.

PRACTICAL USE OF RESOURCES

Although they are available in several kinds of projects, resources have to be used to fit particular scenarios. For example, resources can be successfully used in Windows applications such as the Console and Windows Forms, but they are not the best choice for XAML-based platforms such as Windows Presentation Foundation or Windows 8.x Store applications. So you need to pay attention when using resources and note the particular situations.

Figure 3.1 shows the Resources tab of My Project, with the definition of a `String` resource named `TextMessage` that has a value and a description. The book revisits the Resources tab in Chapter 19, where it discusses the `My` namespace, but if you are curious, you can play with the designer to see what types of resources you can add.

Resources are supported by two files stored inside the My Project folder: Resources.resx and Resources.designer.vb. The first one is basically an XML schema that Visual Studio uses for working with resources. Listing 3.4 shows the content of this schema.

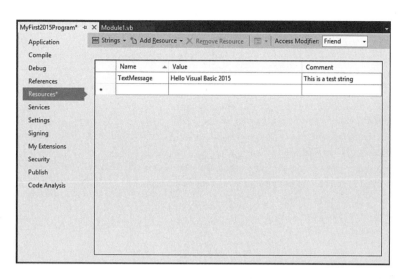

FIGURE 3.1   The My Resources tab of My Project.

LISTING 3.4   The Content of Resources.resx

```
<root>
  <xsd:schema id="root" xmlns="" xmlns:xsd="http://www.w3.org/2001/XMLSchema"
  xmlns:msdata="urn:schemas-microsoft-com:xml-msdata">
    <xsd:import namespace="http://www.w3.org/XML/1998/namespace" />
    <xsd:element name="root" msdata:IsDataSet="true">
      <xsd:complexType>
        <xsd:choice maxOccurs="unbounded">
          <xsd:element name="metadata">
            <xsd:complexType>
              <xsd:sequence>
                <xsd:element name="value" type="xsd:string" minOccurs="0" />
              </xsd:sequence>
              <xsd:attribute name="name" use="required" type="xsd:string" />
              <xsd:attribute name="type" type="xsd:string" />
              <xsd:attribute name="mimetype" type="xsd:string" />
              <xsd:attribute ref="xml:space" />
            </xsd:complexType>
          </xsd:element>
          <xsd:element name="assembly">
            <xsd:complexType>
              <xsd:attribute name="alias" type="xsd:string" />
              <xsd:attribute name="name" type="xsd:string" />
            </xsd:complexType>
          </xsd:element>
          <xsd:element name="data">
```

```
              <xsd:complexType>
                <xsd:sequence>
                  <xsd:element name="value" type="xsd:string" minOccurs="0"
➥msdata:Ordinal="1" />
                  <xsd:element name="comment" type="xsd:string" minOccurs="0"
➥msdata:Ordinal="2" />
                </xsd:sequence>
                <xsd:attribute name="name" type="xsd:string" use="required"
➥msdata:Ordinal="1" />
                <xsd:attribute name="type" type="xsd:string" msdata:Ordinal="3" />
                <xsd:attribute name="mimetype" type="xsd:string"
                    msdata:Ordinal="4" />
                <xsd:attribute ref="xml:space" />
              </xsd:complexType>
            </xsd:element>
            <xsd:element name="resheader">
              <xsd:complexType>
                <xsd:sequence>
                  <xsd:element name="value" type="xsd:string" minOccurs="0"
➥msdata:Ordinal="1" />
                </xsd:sequence>
                <xsd:attribute name="name" type="xsd:string" use="required" />
              </xsd:complexType>
            </xsd:element>
          </xsd:choice>
        </xsd:complexType>
      </xsd:element>
    </xsd:schema>
    <resheader name="resmimetype">
      <value>text/microsoft-resx</value>
    </resheader>
    <resheader name="version">
      <value>2.0</value>
    </resheader>
    <resheader name="reader">
      <value>System.Resources.ResXResourceReader, System.Windows.Forms,
        Version=4.0.0.0, Culture=neutral, PublicKeyToken=b77a5c561934e089</value>
    </resheader>
    <resheader name="writer">
      <value>System.Resources.ResXResourceWriter, System.Windows.Forms,
➥Version=4.0.0.0, Culture=neutral, PublicKeyToken=b77a5c561934e089</value>
    </resheader>
    <data name="TextMessage" xml:space="preserve">
      <value>Hello Visual Basic 2015</value>
      <comment>This is a test string</comment>
    </data>
  </root>
```

This schema establishes how a resource is defined, with names, values, comments, and a MIME (Multipurpose Internet Mail Extensions) type that identifies the file type. At the end of the XML markup code, you can see how resources are stored. You can see the name of the resource (inside the data element), its value, and the description provided via the designer. Visual Studio uses this schema for design-time purposes.

To work with resources in the applications, Visual Studio also needs to provide Visual Basic code support for resources. A code file named Resources.designer.vb is involved in this. This file handles a reference to a .NET object called `ResourceManager` that is responsible for managing resources in code. Listing 3.5 shows the content of Resources.designer.vb.

NOTE

For the sake of simplicity, auto-generated attributes are not covered here.

LISTING 3.5 Content of Resources.designer.vb

```vb
Friend Module Resources
        Private resourceMan As Global.System.Resources.ResourceManager
        Private resourceCulture As Global.System.Globalization.CultureInfo
        Friend ReadOnly Property ResourceManager() As
    Global.System.Resources.ResourceManager
            Get
                If Object.ReferenceEquals(resourceMan, Nothing) Then
                    Dim temp As Global.System.Resources.ResourceManager =
    New Global.System.Resources.ResourceManager("MyFirst2012Program.Resources",
    GetType(Resources).Assembly)
                    resourceMan = temp
                End If
                Return resourceMan
            End Get
        End Property
        Friend Property Culture() As Global.System.Globalization.CultureInfo
            Get
                Return resourceCulture
            End Get
            Set(value As Global.System.Globalization.CultureInfo)
                resourceCulture = value
            End Set
        End Property
        Friend ReadOnly Property TextMessage() As String
            Get
                Return ResourceManager.GetString("TextMessage", resourceCulture)
            End Get
        End Property
    End Module
```

At this point in the book, you don't really need to know what each type used in code refers to, although it is useful to know about the ResourceManager property, which points to the project resources. (See the declaration of the temp variable.) This handles a reference to the application-level ResourceManager that enables access to resources.

Another property, named Culture, is of type System.Globalization.CultureInfo. This property sets or returns the current localization for resources.

The last property in the code, named TextMessage, is the Visual Basic representation of the string resource defined in My Project. This is a read-only property that you cannot change in code (you can change it only via designer); it returns a localized version of the resource invoking the GetString method of the ResourceManager class. GetString requires an object of type CultureInfo (in our code, it's resourceCulture) that represents the culture to which the resource must be localized. The following line of code shows how you can access the preceding defined resource, which is discussed further in Chapter 19:

```
Dim myString As String = My.Resources.TextMessage
```

When you access resources, as discussed in Chapter 19, you do not need to manually invoke this background code, but you need to know how it is structured to better understand what's happening behind the scenes.

Resources are not the only feature in My Project that is supported by Visual Basic code for design-time features. Settings are another of these features, as discussed next.

Application Settings

Settings in Visual Basic development are particular objects that provide a managed way of manipulating applications and user-level settings. For example, you could provide users with the ability to customize options in the user interface of your application. To save and read such customizations to and from disk, you can use .NET settings. My Project provides a tab named Settings that enables you to specify information at the application or user level (see Figure 3.2).

As you can see in Figure 3.2, you can specify an identifier for each setting, a type (which you'll understand better after you read Chapter 4), the scope, and the value. For the scope, User means that only the user who runs the application can use the setting. Application means that the setting is available at the application level, independently from the user who logged in to Windows (and therefore is available to all users). Like resources, settings are also described in detail in Chapter 19. Settings are represented by a simple XML file, named Settings.settings. Listing 3.6 shows the content of Settings.settings after the addition of the sample setting.

VIEWING THE SETTINGS.SETTINGS FILE WITH THE XML EDITOR

To view the XML content for the Settings.settings file, right-click the filename in Solution Explorer, select **Open With**, and select **Xml (Text) Editor** in the Open With dialog box.

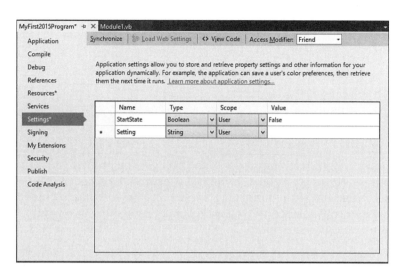

FIGURE 3.2   The Settings tab in My Project.

LISTING 3.6   Settings.settings Content

```
<?xml version='1.0' encoding='utf-8'?>
<SettingsFile xmlns="http://schemas.microsoft.com/VisualStudio/2004/01/settings"
CurrentProfile="(Default)" GeneratedClassNamespace="My" GeneratedClass-
Name="MySettings" UseMySettingsClassName="true">
  <Profiles />
  <Settings>
    <Setting Name="StartState" Type="System.Boolean" Scope="User">
      <Value Profile="(Default)">True</Value>
    </Setting>
  </Settings>
</SettingsFile>
```

In this XML markup, you can see the presence of a Settings node that stores as many Setting elements and as many settings as you specify in My Project. In our example there is just one Setting element that contains the name of the setting, the data type, the scope, and the default value (which means the value you specify in My Project).

The Settings.settings file also has Visual Basic support, which is represented by another file, named Settings.designer.vb. You do not need to examine all the content of this file as just a couple parts of the code are interesting. First, this file implements a property named Settings that is accessible via the My namespace, as detailed in Chapter 19. Listing 3.7 shows the definition of this property.

LISTING 3.7   Definition of the `Settings` Property

```
Friend ReadOnly Property Settings() As
      Global.MyFirst2015Program.My.MySettings
   Get
      Return Global.MyFirst2015Program.My.MySettings.Default
   End Get
End Property
```

The `Settings` property represents the active instance of the `Settings` object that you can use in your applications. How the active instance is defined is beyond the scope of this chapter, but now you know that the Settings tab in My Project also has a counterpart in two support files. Just for your convenience, the following line of code shows how you can access settings and how you set them before:

```
Dim currentValue As Boolean = My.Settings.StartState
```

The value stored in the `StartState` setting will be assigned to a variable named `currentValue`. Examining the `My` namespace in Chapter 19 can clarify how you use settings and resources, as well as many other interesting features.

Understanding References

The Base Class Library (BCL) exposes types through several assemblies that are part of the .NET Framework, and you will often need to invoke types from those assemblies. Moreover, although it is very rich, the BCL cannot define types covering every aspect of application development. This means you will often need to use types exposed by other assemblies, such as other projects in the same solution or external compiled assemblies.

> **NOTE**
>
> Each time you create a new Windows client project (via Windows Forms, WPF, Console), Visual Studio automatically adds references to some .NET assemblies (such as System.dll and System.Core.dll) that are necessary for each kind of application and that expose the BCL's core part. In Visual Studio 2015, this changes for ASP.NET Core and for Universal Windows apps for Windows 10, where the IDE downloads and references only the necessary libraries instead of requiring the full .NET Framework.

To use types defined in external assemblies, you need to add to your project a reference to the desired assembly. To accomplish this, right-click the project name in Solution Explorer and click the **Add Reference** command from the context menu or select the References tab in My Project and click **Add**. Either way, you open the Reference Manager dialog box, as shown in Figure 3.3.

You can select all the assemblies you want to reference; multiple selections are allowed by clicking the check box near the assembly name or by pressing **Ctrl** and then clicking the name of the required assembly. The Reference Manager dialog box is divided into several tabs. The default tab, Assemblies, shows a list of all the available assemblies in the global assembly cache through a group called Framework, and it shows a list of available assemblies exposed by installed extensions for Visual Studio through a group called Extensions.

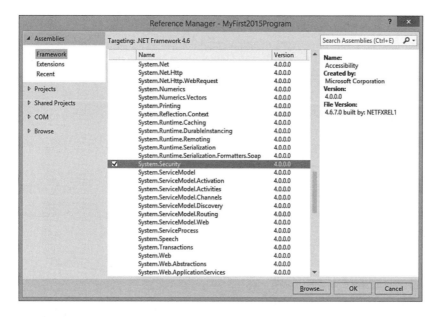

FIGURE 3.3   The Reference Manager dialog box.

WHAT IS THE GLOBAL ASSEMBLY CACHE?

The global assembly cache (GAC) can be described as a repository for information and locations on installed assemblies. The .NET Framework knows where assemblies can be found by browsing the GAC, which also can distinguish between different versions of an assembly. The GAC is discussed in detail in Chapter 48, "Understanding the Global Assembly Cache."

The Reference Manager dialog box shows the version numbers of assemblies; this is useful because you can have different versions of an assembly with the same name. When you add a reference to an assembly, Solution Explorer updates the References node. For example, to add security features to your applications, you need to add a reference to the System.Security.dll assembly (refer to Figure 3.3), which is part of the BCL. When this is added, Solution Explorer looks as shown in Figure 3.4.

You can use the code types that are exposed by the specified assemblies that have public visibility. New in Visual Basic 2015 is the automatic availability of the References node in Solution Explorer; you can simply expand this node to see a list of currently referenced assemblies or projects. In earlier versions of VB, you had to enable the All Files view to get this result.

FIGURE 3.4   Solution Explorer is updated with the new reference.

The Reference Manager dialog box also provides other tabs and groups:

▶ The Recent group in the Assemblies tab shows a list of all the most recently used assemblies for faster reuse.

▶ The Browse tab enables you to search for assemblies that are not registered in the GAC.

▶ The Solution tab enables you to add references to other projects in the solution. This is typically the case when you have a class library that exposes types you want to use inside a client application.

▶ A new tab called Shared Projects allows you to add references to Shared Projects, a new feature in Visual Basic 2015 that allows you to share code between different project types (see Chapter 17, "Working with Objects: Visual Tools and Code Sharing").

▶ The COM tab lets you add references to COM-type libraries, as discussed next.

Adding References to COM Libraries

In some situations you might be required to use COM-type libraries in your .NET applications, a scenario also known as COM Interop. This should be rare, though, because .NET and COM are very different architectures, and they were not made to work together. However, Visual Studio 2015 enables you to add references to old libraries. To accomplish this, you need to select the COM tab in the Reference Manager dialog box. All the registered COM-type libraries are shown in the dialog box, and you can select the needed components (see Figure 3.5).

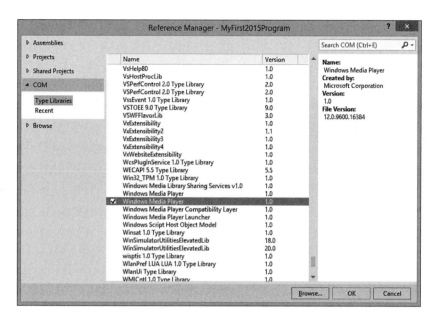

FIGURE 3.5   Adding a reference to a COM component.

For example, say that you want to include Windows Media Player functionalities in your application. To do this, you can select the **Windows Media Player** component and then click **OK** (see Figure 3.5). Visual Studio then shows a reference named WMPLib.dll in Solution Explorer and generates an assembly named Interop.WMPLib.dll. This assembly is a managed wrapper for the Windows Media Player component, and it provides managed access to types exposed by the type library.

More generally, Visual Studio generates an Interop.*AssemblyName*.dll assembly (where *AssemblyName* is the original name of the assembly) for each referenced type library. These are known as primary interoperability assemblies (PIAs), and they allow interoperation between .NET and COM architectures.

Unlike in previous versions of .NET Framework and Visual Studio, by default you no longer see the wrapper assemblies included in your build output because of a feature called Deploy Without PIAs, discussed next.

Deploy Without PIAs

When deploying applications that reference a COM library, you must include in your distribution the PIAs. In our example, the PIA is Interop.WMPLib.dll. You can avoid including PIAs in your distributions, although you need to reference those assemblies. This is possible because Visual Studio can embed in your executable only the types that you effectively use from the referenced assembly. This prevents you from needing to include the assembly itself in the build output and, consequently, in the deployment process. For our sample scenario about including the Windows Media Player component, you could write a small application that has the name of a media file provided by the user and that then launches WMP. Listing 3.8 accomplishes this.

LISTING 3.8   Using a COM Component in Code

```
Module Module1
    Sub Main()
        Console.WriteLine("Type the name of a media file:")
        Dim fileName As String = Console.ReadLine
        Dim wmp As New WMPLib.WindowsMediaPlayer
        wmp.openPlayer(fileName)
    End Sub
End Module
```

In the preceding code, take a look at this simple line:

```
Dim wmp As New WMPLib.WindowsMediaPlayer
```

Declaring an instance of the `WMPLib.WindowsMediaPlayer` class is sufficient for Visual Studio to embed the definition of the `WindowsMediaPlayer` object inside the executable so that it will not need to include the entire Interop.WMPLib.dll assembly in the build output. As you can imagine, this is a great feature because, if you have a large type library and you need to use only a few types, you can use this feature to save space and preserve performance.

The Deploy Without PIAs feature is enabled by default. If you instead prefer to avoid embedding types within your executable and including the PIAs in your build output, you need to right-click the referenced assembly in Solution Explorer and then click **Properties**. Continuing with our example, you would then need to select **WMPLib.dll** in Solution Explorer. The Properties window then shows a property called `Embed Interop Types` that is set to `True` by default (see Figure 3.6).

If you change the value to `False`, types will no longer be embedded in your executable, and the PIAs will be included in the build output.

VERIFYING TYPES EMBEDDING

If you are an experienced developer, you can easily verify whether types have been embedded in your executable via the Deploy Without PIAs feature by opening executables with tools such as Reflector or IL Disassembler.

Final Considerations

The first three chapters of this book provide a necessary overview of tools and features that you must understand before moving on. Now that you have completed these introductory steps, you are ready to get your hands dirty on the core of the Visual Basic 2015 programming language.

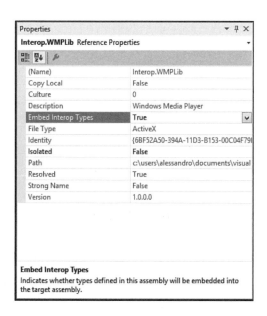

FIGURE 3.6   Enabling the Deploy Without PIAs feature and setting the `Embed Interop Types` property.

Summary

This chapter provides an overview of some important language features. It also presents a complete list of the Visual Basic 2015 reserved words that you cannot use as identifiers for your variables. Another important topic discussed is how a Visual Basic project is structured and which files compose a Visual Basic project. Finally, you got an overview of references and why they are important in developing applications. In this discussion, you learned about some new features in Visual Basic 2015: comments after implicit line continuation and a more flexible support for `#Region..#End Region` directives.

CHAPTER 4

Data Types and Expressions

Every programming task manipulates data. Data can be of different kinds; you will often work with strings, dates and time, numbers, files, and custom data. Each of them is represented by a data type. The .NET Framework 4.6 (but also the .NET Core runtime) provides tons of built-in data types and enables developers to easily create their own custom data types. In this chapter you will learn how the .NET Framework handles data types and how you can work with *value types* and *reference types*. When you understand data types, you can learn how to use them with special Visual Basic language constraints such as loops, iterations, and special statements. This is a fundamental chapter, and you should pay particular attention to the concepts here; you need to understand them before you get into object-oriented programming with Visual Basic 2015.

Introducing the Common Type System

The .NET Framework provides a special way of manipulating data types, called the *Common Type System*. In its name, the word *Common* has two particular meanings. First, the Common Type System provides a unified model for exposing data types so that all the .NET languages, such as Visual Basic, Visual C#, and Visual F#, can consume the same data types. For example, a 32-bit integer is represented by the System.Int32 data type, and all the .NET languages can invoke the System.Int32 object for declaring integers because this type is provided by the .NET Framework and is language independent. Second, each data type is an object that inherits from the System.Object class, as we discuss next.

Everything Is an Object

In.NET development, you might hear that everything is an object. This is because all the types in the .NET Framework, including built-in and custom types, inherit from the `System.Object` class. Inheritance is an important concept in object-oriented programming and is discussed in Chapter 12, "Inheritance." For now, we can define *inheritance* as a way of reusing and extending data types so developers can create their hierarchy of types. `System.Object` provides the primary infrastructure that all .NET types must have. The .NET Framework ships with thousands of built-in data types that all derive from `System.Object`. But why is this class so important in the Common Type System? The answer is simple: The Common Type System ensures that all .NET types inherit from `System.Object`; in particular, both *value types* and *reference types* inherit from `System.Object`. The following section provides an overview of value types and reference types, and then we delve into both categories.

Introducing Value Types and Reference Types

Value types are data types that store data directly. Examples of value types are integers (`System.Int32`), Booleans (`System.Boolean`), and bytes (`System.Byte`). Value types are stored in a memory area called the *stack*. They are represented by (and defined via) structures that are enclosed in `Structure..End Structure` code blocks. The following is an example of a value type that contains a value:

```
Dim anInteger As System.Int32 = 5
```

Reference types are data types that, as their name implies, just reference the actual data. In other words, reference types store the address of their data in the stack, whereas the actual data is stored in the managed heap. Reference types are represented by classes. The following is an example of a reference type:

```
Class Person
    Property FirstName As String
    Property LastName As String
End Class
```

DON'T BE AFRAID OF MEMORY LOCATIONS

If you've never heard about the stack and the managed heap, don't worry. You'll learn more later in this chapter, in the section "Memory Allocation."

Reference types inherit directly from `System.Object` or from other classes that derive from `Object`. This is because `System.Object` is a reference type. So the question you will probably ask now is, "If both value types and reference types have to inherit from `System.Object`, how can value types inherit from `System.Object` if it is a reference type?" The answer is that in the case of value types, an intermediate type named `System.ValueType` inherits from `System.Object` and ensures that all deriving objects are treated as value types. This is possible because the Common Language Runtime (CLR) can distinguish how types are defined and consequently can distinguish between value types and reference types.

NAMING `System.Object`

Object is also a reserved word of the Visual Basic programming language and is the representation of `System.Object`. Because of this, we refer indistinctly to `Object` as `System.Object`.

`System.Object` and `System.ValueType`

At this point, it is necessary to provide an overview of both `System.Object` and `System.ValueType`. Instead of showing a diagram of inheritance, it is a good idea to offer a Visual Studio–oriented view so you can better understand what happens in the development environment. This can be accomplished via the Object Browser tool window introduced in Chapter 2, "The Visual Studio 2015 IDE for Visual Basic." You can browse for both classes by just typing their names in the search box. Figure 4.1 shows how `System.Object` is defined, which members it exposes, and a full description.

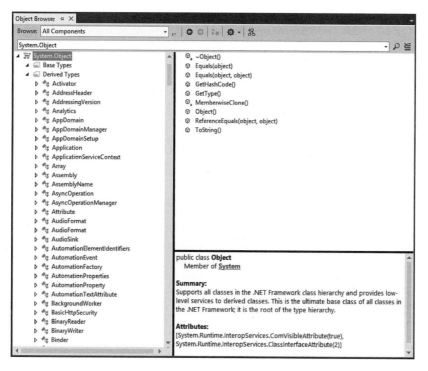

FIGURE 4.1   `System.Object` shown in detail in the Object Browser window.

Several things are worth mentioning. First, consider the class description. As you can see, `System.Object` is defined as the root of the type hierarchy, and all other classes within the .NET Framework derive from `System.Object`. This means that custom classes automatically inherit from `Object`. This class provides the infrastructure for all derived classes and exposes some methods. Because `System.Object` is important and because you will often invoke methods inherited from `Object`, it's convenient to get a simple reference for each method. Table 4.1 describes methods exposed by `System.Object`.

TABLE 4.1   Methods Exposed by `System.Object`

Method	Description
`Equals`	Compares two objects for equality.
`Finalize`	Attempts to free up some resources during the object lifetime.
`New`	Creates a new instance of the `Object` class.
`GetHashCode`	Returns a hash code for the given object.
`GetType`	Retrieves the qualified data type for the specified object.
`MemberwiseClone`	Creates a shallow copy of the current `Object` instance.
`ReferenceEquals`	Returns `true` if both of the specified `Object` instances refer to the same instance.
`ToString`	Provides a string representation of the `Object`.

Methods listed in Table 4.1 are covered several times during the rest of the book, so don't be afraid if something is not clear at the moment. If you now refer to Figure 4.1, you can see that the `Object` class has no base types. This is because, as mentioned earlier, `Object` is the root in the type hierarchy. If you try to expand the Derived Types node in the Object Browser, you see a list of hundreds of .NET Framework built-in classes that derive from `Object`. One of these classes is `System.ValueType`. Figure 4.2 shows how this class is represented in the Object Browser.

You should focus on the description first. As you can see, `System.ValueType` is the base class for all value types. It is declared as `MustInherit`, or `abstract` in C# (discussed in detail in Chapter 12), which means it must necessarily be inherited and that it can't work as a standalone object, and it provides the base infrastructure for derived value types. If you expand the Base Types node, you see that `ValueType` is a derived class from `Object`. If you then try to expand the Derived Types node, you get a long list of types that inherit from `ValueType`, such as `Boolean`, `Byte`, and other primitive data types. As mentioned earlier, the CLR can determine that a type deriving from `System.ValueType` must be treated as a value type and not as a reference type.

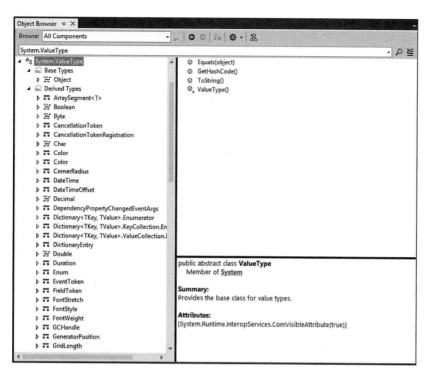

FIGURE 4.2   `System.ValueType` shown in detail in the Object Browser.

Understanding Value Types

Value types are data types that directly store data that they define. For example, a `System.Int32` object represents a value type that can store an integer number, as in the following line of code:

```
Dim anInteger As System.Int32 = 5
```

The most common value types are numeric types that enable, for example, performing math operations or implementing counters or just storing numeric values. Value types enable you to choose the best data type for a particular scenario. As mentioned at the beginning of this chapter, value types are `Structure` objects. The .NET Framework provides several built-in value types that cover most needs in your development process, although you can create custom data types. In this section you'll learn about the most common built-in value types and about building your own structures, including how value types are declared and used and how they are stored in memory.

.NET Framework Primitive Value Types

The .NET Framework Base Class Library provides lots of built-in value types that you can use according to your needs. Each value type is a structure exposed by the Base Class Library.

Visual Basic 2015 provides reserved words that are counterparts of the most common value type names. For example, the `System.Int32` value type has an alias in the `Integer` reserved word. The following two lines of code are perfectly equivalent:

```
Dim anInteger As System.Int32 = 0
Dim anInteger As Integer = 0
```

You can use the .NET names and the Visual Basic reserved words interchangeably when referring to built-in value types.

NAMING CONVENTIONS

Although you are allowed to invoke value types with both .NET names and the Visual Basic counterparts' keywords, it's a best practice to choose the .NET names when developing reusable class libraries, according to the Microsoft Common Language Specification. For example, the `System.Convert.ToInt32` method would not be named `ToInt` or `ToInteger`. (We discuss this topic later in this chapter.) In such a scenario, it is a good practice to use the .NET names because you should avoid language-dependent features and practices when developing assemblies that are bound to also work with other .NET languages; using a .NET-oriented approach instead of a language-oriented one will not change the results, but it will make your code cleaner.

Table 4.2 lists the most common value types in the .NET Framework, along with a description of each and the Visual Basic–related keywords.

TABLE 4.2   The Most Common Value Types in the .NET Framework 4.6

Value Type	Description	Visual Basic Reserved Keyword
System.Int16	Represents a numeric value with a range between –32768 and 32767.	Short
System.Int32	Represents a numeric value with a range between –2147483648 and 2147483647.	Integer
System.Int64	Represents a numeric value with a range between –9223372036854775808 and 9223372036854775807.	Long
System.Single	Represents a floating-point number with a range from –3.4028235E+38 to 3.4028235E+38.	Single
System.Double	Represents a large floating-point number (double precision) with a range from –1.79769313486232e308 to 1.79769313486232e308.	Double
System.Boolean	Accepts True or False values.	Boolean
System.Char	Represents a single Unicode character.	Char

Value Type	Description	Visual Basic Reserved Keyword
System.IntPtr	Represents a pointer to an address in memory.	-
System.DateTime	Represents dates, times, or both in different supported formats (see the following paragraphs).	Date
System.Numerics. BigInteger	Represents an arbitrarily large integer with no maximum and minimum values.	-
System.Byte	Represents an unsigned byte, with a range from 0 to 255.	Byte
System.SByte	Represents a signed byte, with a range from −128 to 127.	SByte
System.UInt16	Represents a numeric positive value with a range between 0 and 65535.	UShort
System.UInt32	Represents a numeric positive value with a range between 0 and 4294967295.	UInteger
System.UInt64	Represents a numeric positive value with a range between 0 and 18446744073709551615.	ULong
System.Decimal	Represents a decimal number in financial and scientific calculations with large numbers, in a range between −79228162514264337593543950335 and 79228162514264337593543950335.	Decimal
System.TimeSpan	Represents an interval of time, in a range between −10675199.02:48:05.4775808 and 10675199.02:48:05.4775807 ticks.	
System.TimeZone	Represents time information according to a particular time zone.	
System.Guid	Allows the generation of *globally unique identifiers*.	

UPGRADING FROM VISUAL BASIC 6

If you are upgrading from Visual Basic 6, keep in mind that VB 6's Long is an Integer in .NET and that VB 6's Integer is Short in .NET.

As you might notice in Table 4.2, most built-in value types are exposed by the System namespace. However, the BigInteger type is instead exposed by the System.Numerics namespace.

MEMORY REQUIREMENTS

You might wonder what influences your choice when working with value types. The answer is that it depends. Of course, you should take care of memory allocation. If you know that you need to work with a small number, you will probably do best if you choose a `Byte` instead of a `Short`. Consider that `Byte` requires 8 bits, `Short` requires 16 bits, `Integer` and `Single` require 32 bits, `Long` and `Double` require 64 bits, and `Decimal` requires 128 bits. The CLR is optimized for 32-bit integers, so `Integer` is of course a better choice than `Short`, but in cases where size in memory or on disk is paramount (such as in a database), you should choose smaller data types like `Byte` (1 byte) instead of `Integer` (4 bytes) for representing smaller ranges of values.

Using Value Types

To learn to use value types, it is a good idea to create a new Visual Basic project for the Console (see Chapter 2 for details). Listing 4.1 shows how you can declare variables that store value types. For learning purposes, you can put this code inside the `Main` method of your project.

LISTING 4.1   Using Value Types

```
Sub Main()
    'Declares an Integer
    Dim anInteger As Integer = 2
    'Declares a double and stores the result of a calculation
    Dim calculation As Double = 74.6 * 834.1
    'Declares one byte storing a hexadecimal value
    Dim oneByte As Byte = &H0
    'Declares a single character
    Dim oneCharacter As Char = "a"c
    'Declares a decimal number
    Dim sampleDecimal As Decimal = 8743341.353531135D
    'Declares a Boolean variable
    Dim isTrueOrFalse As Boolean = True
    'Declares a BigInteger
    Dim arbitraryInteger As New System.Numerics.BigInteger(800000)
    Console.WriteLine(anInteger)
    Console.WriteLine(calculation)
    Console.WriteLine(oneByte)
    Console.WriteLine(oneCharacter)
    Console.WriteLine(isTrueOrFalse)
    Console.WriteLine(arbitraryInteger)
    Console.ReadLine()
End Sub
```

You can declare variables of the desired value types by using the Dim keyword followed by the identifier of the variable and the As clause, which then requires the type specification.

NOTES ABOUT Dim AND As

Dim is the most important keyword for declaring variables, and it is commonly used in local code blocks. It is also worth mentioning that in the .NET Framework, you can declare different kinds of objects both with Dim and with other keywords, depending on the scope of the objects (such as fields, properties, and classes). This is discussed in Chapter 7, "Class Fundamentals." Then in Chapter 20, "Advanced Language Features," you'll learn about another important feature in the .NET Framework, local type inference, which prevents you from needing to add the As clause in particular scenarios such as data access with LINQ.

You can also declare more than one variable within the same Dim statement by writing something like this:

```
Dim anInteger As Integer = 2, calculation As Double = 3.14,
    TrueOrFalse As Boolean = True
```

You can also declare more than one variable of the same type just by specifying such a type once, as in the following line of code:

```
'Three integers
Dim anInteger, secondInteger, thirdInteger As Integer
```

If you upgrade from Visual Basic 6, this is a great change because in a declaration like the preceding one, VB 6 automatically assigns Variant instead of the appropriate data type. Generally, you do not need to specify the constructor (the New keyword) when declaring value types. This is because in such situations, the constructor addition is implicit and provided by the compiler behind the scenes. An exception to this general rule is the BigInteger type, which instead allows the constructor to be explicit but also allows inline initialization. Listing 4.1 also shows how you can get the value stored in value types. In this example, values are written to the Console window, but you can use values in other ways, as appropriate to your situation. Figure 4.3 shows the result of the code in Listing 4.1.

Pay attention when using Char and String data types. Because both types require their content to be enclosed within quotes, the value of a Char must be followed by the c letter, which tells the compiler to treat that value as a single character (if you are using Option Strict On). The Decimal data type also has similar behavior. When you declare a decimal value (see Listing 4.1), you must ensure that the value is followed by the uppercase D character; otherwise, the compiler treats the number as a Double and raises an error. Identifiers like c and D are also known as *literal type characters* and are available for a number of primitive types, as summarized in Table 4.3.

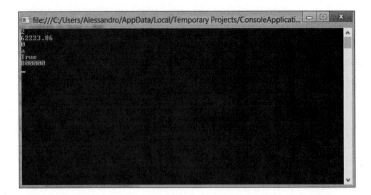

FIGURE 4.3   Using value types in the sample code produces this result.

TABLE 4.3   Literal Type Characters

Character	Type	Example
C	Char	oneChar = "s"c
D	Decimal	oneDec = 87.2D
F	Single	oneSingle = 87.2F
I	Integer	anInt = 18I
L	Long	oneLong = 1324L
R	Double	oneDouble = 1234R
S	Short	oneShort = 18S
UI	UInteger	anInt = 18UI
UL	ULong	oneLong = 1324UL
US	UShort	oneShort = 18US

Literal type characters are not available for the following types:

▶ Boolean

▶ Byte

▶ Date

▶ Object

▶ SByte

▶ String

Assigning Value Types

At the beginning of the section, we mentioned that value types directly store the data to which they refer. This can be easily verified with assignments. Consider the following code:

```
Sub DoAssignments()
    Dim anInteger As Integer = 10
    Dim anotherInteger As Integer = anInteger
    Console.WriteLine(anInteger)
    Console.WriteLine(anotherInteger)
    Console.ReadLine()
End Sub
```

This code produces the following output:

```
10
10
```

This is because the value of anInteger has been assigned to another variable of type Integer, named anotherInteger. anotherInteger is a copy of the first variable and lives its own life, independent from anInteger. If you now write the following line of code after the anotherInteger assignment:

```
anotherInteger = 5
```

the code produces the following output:

```
10
5
```

So you changed the value of anotherInteger while you left unchanged the value of anInteger because they are two different objects with separate lives. Although this can appear obvious, it is important because it is the basis for understanding the different behaviors in reference types. You might also use assignments in situations in which you need to get a result without knowing values that produce the result itself, such as in calculations that require input from the user. For example, consider the following code:

```
Dim firstNumber As Double = 567.43
Dim secondNumber As Double = 321.52
Dim result As Double = firstNumber * secondNumber
Console.WriteLine(result)
Console.ReadLine()
```

In this code, you get the result of the multiplication of two numbers. In real scenarios, the two numbers would be provided by the user, and the result variable would store the result of the calculation. Such calculations are performed not on numbers but on the values of variables that store numbers. This means that you do not need to know in advance the numbers; you just work on variables and assignments.

NOTE

You could probably expect a code example in which the input should be provided by the user. Reference types, conversion operators, and parsing methods have not been discussed yet but will be later in this book. At this point, the goal is to avoid confusion because user input is provided as `String` objects. There will be appropriate code examples when needed, as in the next paragraph.

Analyzing the Content of Value Types

In most cases, you will require users to enter an input that you will then need to elaborate. Or you could simply read the content of a text file and then convert such content into the appropriate .NET value type. Typically, user input is provided as strings; you also get strings when reading text files. In business applications, you need to implement validation rules on the user input, but it is worth mentioning that value types offer common methods for analyzing the contents of a string and checking whether such content matches a particular value type. Even though we have not discussed the `String` object (which is a reference type) yet, the following code samples are easy to understand. For example, this code declares some strings:

```
Dim firstValue As String = "1000"
Dim secondValue As String = "True"
Dim thirdValue As String = "123.456"
```

The content of each string is a representation of a particular value type: `firstValue` content represents an integer, `secondValue` represents a Boolean, and `thirdValue` represents a `Double`. You could parse the content of each string and transform it into the appropriate value type as follows:

```
Dim anInteger As Integer = Integer.Parse(firstValue)
Dim aBoolean As Boolean = Boolean.Parse(secondValue)
Dim aDouble As Double = Double.Parse(thirdValue)
```

As you can see, value types expose a method called `Parse` that converts the string representation of a numeric or logical value into the corresponding value type. For example, `Integer.Parse` converts the `"1000"` string into a 1000 integer. If the method cannot perform the conversion, a `FormatException` error is thrown and the application execution is broken. To avoid possible errors, you could use another method, `TryParse`, that returns `True` if the conversion succeeds or `False` if it fails. For example, consider the following code:

```
Dim testInteger As Integer
Dim result = Integer.TryParse(secondValue, testInteger)
```

This code attempts to convert a string that contains the representation of a Boolean value into an `Integer`. Because this is not possible, `TryParse` returns `False`. Notice that in this particular case, you don't perform an assignment to another variable (as in the case of `Parse`) because `TryParse` requires the variable that will store the value as the second argument, passed by reference. (A more detailed explanation on passing arguments by reference is provided in Chapter 7.)

VALUE TYPE METHODS

The purpose of this book is to examine the Visual Basic 2015 language features, and examining all the .NET Framework available types and members isn't possible. Therefore, this book describes only methods common to all value types. Methods and members specific to some value types are left to you for future study. Always remember that when you do not know an object member, IntelliSense and the Object Browser together with the MSDN documentation can be your best friends, providing useful information.

Value types (including `System.Char` and `System.DateTime`) also expose two properties named `MinValue` and `MaxValue` that contain the minimum accepted value and the maximum accepted value for each type, respectively. For example, the following line of code produces –2147483648 as the result:

```
Console.WriteLine(Integer.MinValue)
```

The following line of code produces the ? character as the result:

```
Console.WriteLine(Char.MaxValue)
```

Finally, the following line of code produces 12/31/9999 11:59:59PM as the result:

```
Console.WriteLine(Date.MaxValue)
```

`MinValue` and `MaxValue` can be useful in two situations: The first situation is times when you don't remember the minimum and maximum values accepted by a particular value type. The second situation involves comparisons, when you might need to check whether a value or a number is in the range of accepted values by a particular data type.

Now we have completed a general overview of value types. Next, we focus on optimizations and on using special value types such as `System.DateTime`.

Optimization Considerations

When working with value types, you should always choose the best type for your needs. For example, if you need to work with a number composed in the `Integer` range, you should not use a `Long` type. Moreover, the Visual Basic compiler (and, behind the scenes, the CLR) provides optimizations for the `System.Int32` and `System.Double` types, so you should always use these types when possible. For example, you should use an `Int32` instead of an `Int16`, even though the number you work with is composed in the range of the `Int16`. Other considerations about unsigned value types are related to compliance with the Microsoft Common Language Specification, which is discussed later in this chapter.

NULLABLE TYPES

Sometimes you need to assign null values to value types, such as when mapping SQL Server data types to .NET data types for fetching data. To accomplish this, the .NET Framework provides support for nullable types. Nullable types have the same syntax as generic objects, as discussed in Chapter 14, "Generics and Nullable Types."

Working with `BigInteger`

`System.Numerics.BigInteger` is a value type exposed by the `System.Numerics` namespace that requires a reference to the System.Numerics.dll assembly. It represents a signed, arbitrarily large integer number. This means it doesn't have minimum and maximum values, unlike value types such as `Integer` and `Long`. Instantiating a `BigInteger` is easy, as you can see from the following line of code:

```
Dim sampleBigInteger As New System.Numerics.BigInteger
```

You can assign any signed number to a `BigInteger` because it has no minimum and maximum values, as demonstrated by the following code snippet:

```
'Neither minimum nor maximum values
sampleBigInteger = Byte.MinValue
sampleBigInteger = Long.MaxValue
```

`Byte` and `Long` are the smallest and the biggest acceptable signed integers, respectively. `BigInteger` directly supports integer types such as `SByte`, `Byte`, `UInteger`, `Integer`, `UShort`, `Short`, `ULong`, and `Long`. You can also assign to a `BigInteger` values of type `Double`, `Single`, and `Decimal`, but you do need to accomplish this by passing the value as an argument to the constructor or performing an explicit conversion using `CType` (assuming that `Option Strict` is `On`). The following code demonstrates both situations:

```
'The constructor can receive arguments, Double is accepted
Dim sampleBigInteger2 As New   _
                    System.Numerics.BigInteger(123456.789)
'Single is accepted but with explicit conversion
Dim singleValue As Single = CSng(1234.56)
Dim sampleBigInteger3 As New System.Numerics.BigInteger
sampleBigInteger3 = CType(singleValue, _
                    Numerics.BigInteger)
```

Notice that rounding occurs when you convert floating types to `BigInteger`. In addition, there are shared methods for performing arithmetic operations. You can add, subtract, divide, and multiply with `BigInteger`, as in the following code:

```
'Assumes an Imports System.Numerics directive
'Sum
Dim sum As BigInteger =
    BigInteger.Add(sampleBigInteger, sampleBigInteger2)
'Subtract
Dim subtraction As BigInteger =
    BigInteger.Subtract(sampleBigInteger, sampleBigInteger2)
'Division
Dim division As BigInteger =
    BigInteger.Divide(sampleBigInteger, sampleBigInteger3)
```

```
'Multiplication
Dim multiplication As BigInteger =
    BigInteger.Multiply(sampleBigInteger2, sampleBigInteger3)
```

You can also perform complex operations, such as exponentiation and logarithm calculations, as demonstrated here:

```
'Power
Dim powerBI As BigInteger = BigInteger.Pow(sampleBigInteger2, 2)
'10 base logarithm
Dim log10 As Double = BigInteger.Log10(sampleBigInteger3)
'natural base logarithm
Dim natLog As Double = BigInteger.Log(sampleBigInteger, 2)
```

As usual, IntelliSense can be very useful when you're exploring methods from `BigInteger`. It can help you understand what other math calculations you can perform.

Building Custom Value Types

You can build custom value types by creating *structures*. Creating structures can be a complex task, and it is thoroughly discussed in Chapter 11, "Structures and Enumerations."

Understanding Reference Types

Reference types are represented by classes. Classes are probably the most important items in modern programming languages and are the basis of object-oriented programming. Reference types have one big difference from value types. Variables that declare a reference type do not store the data of the type itself; they just store an address to the data. In other words, they are just pointers to the data. To better explain (and understand) this fundamental concept, let's look at an example. Consider the following class, `Person`, which exposes two simple properties:

```
Class Person
    Property FirstName As String
    Property LastName As String
End Class
```

You need to create an instance of such a class so that you can store data (in this case, setting properties) and then manipulate the same data. You can do this by using the following lines of code:

```
Dim onePerson As New Person
onePerson.FirstName = "Alessandro"
onePerson.LastName = "Del Sole"
```

STRONGLY TYPED OBJECTS

In .NET development, you often encounter the term *strongly typed*. To understand this term, let's look at an example. The `onePerson` object in the preceding code is strongly typed because it is of a certain type, `Person`. This means that `onePerson` can accept an assignment only from compliant objects, such as other `Person` objects. Such restriction is important because it prevents errors and problems. Moreover, the compiler knows how to treat such a specialized object. A variable of type `Object` is not strongly typed because it is just of the root type and is not specialized. `Object` can accept anything, but without restrictions, the use of non-strongly typed objects could lead to significant problems. Chapter 14 discusses generics, and at that point, you'll get a more thorough understanding of strongly typed objects.

Now you have an instance of the `Person` class, named `onePerson`. Consider the following line of code:

```
Dim secondPerson As Person = onePerson
```

A new object of type `Person` (`secondPerson`) is declared and is assigned with the `onePerson` object. Because of the equality operator, you would probably expect `secondPerson` to be an exact copy of `onePerson`. You could consider at this point some edits to the `secondPerson` object; for example, we could modify the first name:

```
secondPerson.FirstName = "Alex"
```

You can try to check the result of the previous operations by simply writing the output to the Console window. Try writing the result of `secondPerson`, like so:

```
Console.WriteLine(secondPerson.FirstName)
Console.WriteLine(secondPerson.LastName)
Console.ReadLine()
```

As you might correctly expect, the preceding code produces the following result:

```
Alex
Del Sole
```

Now you can simply write the result for `onePerson` to the Console window:

```
Console.WriteLine(onePerson.FirstName)
Console.WriteLine(onePerson.LastName)
Console.ReadLine()
```

This code produces the following result:

```
Alex
Del Sole
```

As you can see, editing the first name in `secondPerson` also affected `onePerson`. This means that `secondPerson` is not a copy of `onePerson`. It is instead *a copy of the reference* to the actual data. Now you should have a better understanding of reference types.

As their name implies, reference types have an address in memory where data is stored, and variables declaring and instantiating reference types just hold a reference to that data. To get a real copy of data, you can write something like this:

```
Dim secondPerson As New Person
secondPerson.FirstName = onePerson.FirstName
secondPerson.LastName = onePerson.LastName
```

Then you can edit `secondPerson`'s properties, ensuring that this will not affect the `onePerson` object. This kind of technique for creating a clone for a reference type is good with objects exposing only a few properties, but fortunately there are more interesting techniques for cloning more complex objects. These are discussed in the "Deep Copy and Shallow Copy" section, later in this chapter.

STRING TYPE IN THE .NET FRAMEWORK

In the .NET Framework, `String` is a reference type, but it's actually treated as a value type, as explained shortly.

.NET Framework Primitive Reference Types

The .NET Framework 4.6 ships with tons of reference types that are exposed by the Base Class Library and that cover most needs. However, you will often use several reference types in the development process that many other reference types derive from. Table 4.4 lists the most common reference types.

TABLE 4.4   The Most Common Built-in Reference Types in the .NET Framework

Type	Description
System.Object	The root class in the object hierarchy.
System.String	Represents a string.
System.Array	Represents an array of objects.
System.Exception	Represents an error occurring during application execution.
System.IO.Stream	The base class for accessing other resources such as files or in-memory data.

You can use a number of reference types when developing real-life applications, and most of them are discussed in subsequent chapters; however, the ones listed in Table 4.4 provide the basis for working with reference types. Most of them are the base infrastructure for other important derived classes. We previously discussed `System.Object`, so we will not do it again. It is instead worth mentioning that `System.String` is a reference type, although it seems natural to think about it as a value type. System.String, or simply String, is used as a value type, which makes it easy to build strings. By the way, strings are immutable (which means "read-only"), so each time you edit a string, the runtime creates a new instance of the String class and passes in the edited string. Because of this, editing strings using System.String can cause unnecessary memory usage. To solve this problem, the .NET Framework provides more efficient ways, as you will see in the sections "Working with Strings," "Working with Dates," and "Working with Arrays," later in this chapter.

Differences Between Value Types and Reference Types

Value types and reference types differ in several ways. In the previous sections you saw how they differ in assignment and how a value type can directly store data, whereas a reference type stores only the address to the actual data. Next you'll learn about such implementation and other differences between value and reference types.

Memory Allocation

Value types and reference types are allocated differently in memory. Value types are allocated in the stack. The *stack* is a memory area where methods are executed in the *last-in, first-out* manner. The first method *pushed* to the stack is the application entry point—that is, the Main method. When Main invokes other methods, the CLR creates a sort of restore point and pushes those methods to the stack. When the method needs to be executed, data required by that method is also pushed to the stack. When a method completes, the CLR removes (*pops*) it from the stack together with its data and restores the previous state. Because of this ordered behavior, the stack is efficient, and the CLR can easily handle it. Consider the following line of code, which declares a variable of type Integer and therefore a value type:

```
Dim anInteger As Integer = 5
```

Figure 4.4 shows how the anInteger variable is allocated in the stack.

Reference types are allocated in a memory area called the *managed heap*. Unlike how objects are treated in the stack, objects in the managed heap are allocated and deallocated randomly. This provides fast allocation but requires more work for the CLR. To keep things ordered, the CLR needs two instruments: the *garbage collector* and the *memory manager*. We provide details about this architecture in Chapter 8, "Managing an Object's Lifetime." At the moment you just need to understand how reference types and their data are allocated. Consider the following lines of code, which declare a new version of the Person class and an instance of this class:

```
Class Person
    Property Name As String
    Property Age As Integer
End Class
```

```
Dim onePerson As New Person
onePerson.Name = "Alessandro Del Sole"
onePerson.Age = 37
```

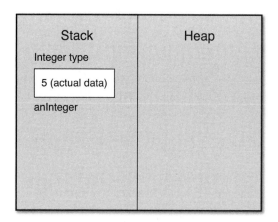

FIGURE 4.4   Value types are allocated in the stack.

As you can see, there is now a property in this class (Age) that is a value type. The instance of the class will be allocated in the heap, and its reference (onePerson) will be allocated in the stack. Figure 4.5 provides a visual representation of this scenario.

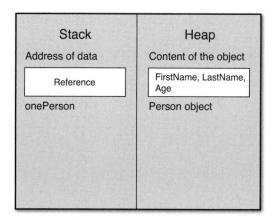

FIGURE 4.5   Reference types are allocated in the heap, whereas their addresses reside in the stack.

The Person class handles a value type in one of its properties, and such value types stay in the stack. Figure 4.6 completes this overview of value and reference types. In Part II, "Object-Oriented Programming with Visual Basic 2015," you will have more opportunities to explore reference types and memory management when discussing the object's lifetime.

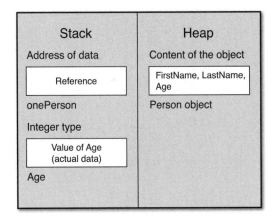

FIGURE 4.6   Complete overview of memory allocation for value and reference types.

Object-Oriented Differences

Object-oriented programming is based on some unique principles. These principles are discussed in detail in Part II, but here we need to get a brief introduction to them.

Inheritance

An important principle of object-oriented programming is inheritance, which is covered in Chapter 12. Classes (that is, reference types) support inheritance, whereas structures (value types) do not. Consider the following code:

```
Class Person
    Property FirstName As String
    Property LastName As String
End Class
Class Developer
    Inherits Person
    Property UsedProgrammingLanguage As String
    Public Overrides Function ToString() As String
        Return Me.LastName
    End Function
End Class
```

In this example, the Person class is the base class and provides the basic properties for representing a hypothetical person. The Developer class inherits from Person (note the Inherits keyword), and this means that the Developer class will expose both the FirstName and LastName properties plus the new one, named UsedProgrammingLanguage. It also redefines the behavior of the default ToString method so that it can return a more significant name for the object.

In Visual Basic 2015, a class can inherit from only one object at a time. Thus, `Developer` can inherit only from `Person` and not from any other object. If you need multiple-level inheritance, you should architect your object's framework so that a second class can inherit from the first one, a third one from the second one, and so on. Structures do not support inheritance at all, except for the fact that they inherit by nature from `System.ValueType`.

Implementation of Interfaces

Both classes and structures provide support for implementation of interfaces. For example, you could implement the `IComparable` interface with both classes and structures, as shown here:

```
Class Person
    Implements IComparable
    Property FirstName As String
    Property LastName As String
    Public Function CompareTo(obj As Object) As Integer Implements
            System.IComparable.CompareTo
        'Write your code here
    End Function
End Class
Structure Dimension
    Implements IComparable
    Public Function CompareTo(obj As Object) As Integer Implements
            System.IComparable.CompareTo
        'Write your code here
    End Function
    Property X As Integer
    Property Y As Integer
    Property Z As Integer
End Structure
```

Inheritance and interfaces are discussed in Part II, so don't worry if something in this section is not clear at this point.

Constructors

When you declare a reference type, you need an instance before you can use it (except with shared classes, which are discussed in Chapter 7). You create an instance by invoking the *constructor* via the `New` keyword. When you declare a value type, the new variable is automatically initialized to a default value; this is usually zero for numbers and `False` for Booleans. Because of this, a value type does not need to have a default constructor invoked. The Visual Basic compiler still accepts declaring a value type and invoking the constructor, which also initializes the type with the default value. However, in this case, you cannot initialize the value. The following code snippet demonstrates this:

```
'Declares an Integer and sets the value to zero
Dim anInt As New Integer
'Initialization not allowed with New
Dim anotherInt As New Integer = 1
'Allowed
Dim aThirdInt As Integer = 1
```

Finalizers

Finalizers are related to an object's lifetime and are discussed thoroughly in Chapter 8. By the way, as it was for constructors, it's convenient having a small reference for finalizers here. We previously said that when methods using value types complete their execution, they are automatically removed from the stack together with the data. This is managed by the CLR, and because of this ordered behavior, value types do not need to be finalized. In contrast, reference types are allocated on the heap and have different behavior. Deallocation from memory is handled by the garbage collector, which needs finalizers on the reference type's side to complete its work.

Performance Differences

A lot of times value types store data directly, whereas reference types store only the address of the data. Although you can create and consume types according to your needs, there are some concerns with performance, particularly regarding methods. Methods can accept parameters, also known as *arguments*. Arguments can be value types or reference types. If you pass a value type to a method, you pass to that method all the data contained in the value type, which could be time-consuming and cause performance overhead. Passing a reference type passes only the address to the data, so it could be faster and more efficient. There could be situations in which you need to pass one or more value types to methods. What you pass depends on your needs. Generally, the performance difference in such a scenario is not relevant, but it depends on the size of the value type. If your method receives a large value type as an argument but is invoked only once, performance should not be affected. But if your method is invoked many times, perhaps passing a reference type would be better. Just be aware of this when implementing your methods.

What Custom Type Should I Choose?

Answering this question is not simple. It depends. If you need to implement a custom type that will act similarly to a value type (for example, a type that works with numbers), you should choose a Structure. If you need to implement an object for storing a large amount of data, it could be a good idea to choose a class. Such considerations are not mandatory, and their purpose is simply to let you think a little bit more about what you are going to implement and what your needs are.

Converting Between Value Types and Reference Types

In your life as a developer, you'll often need to convert one data type into another in different types of situations. For example, you might need to convert a value type into another type or just convert an instance of type `Object` into a strongly typed object. In this section, you'll learn how to convert between data types and about conversion operators, beginning with basic but important concepts, such as implicit conversions, boxing, and unboxing.

Understanding Implicit Conversions

Previously we discussed the `System.Object` class. As you might remember, this class is the root in the class hierarchy. That said, you can assign both reference types and value types to an `Object` instance because they both inherit from `System.Object`. Consider the following lines of code:

```
Dim anInt As Object = 10
Dim onePerson As Object = New Person
```

The first line assigns a value type (`Integer`) to an `Object`, and the second one assigns an instance of the `Person` class to an `Object`. Visual Basic 2015 always enables such assignments because they are always safe. However, it is unsafe to try to assign an `Object` to a strongly typed instance, such as an instance of the `Person` class. This is quite obvious because `Object` can represent any type, and the compiler cannot be sure if that type is a `Person`, which can cause errors. Consider the following line of code:

```
Dim onePerson As Person = New Object
```

This code is trying to assign an instance of the `Object` class to an instance of `Person`. The Visual Basic compiler can handle such situations in two different ways, depending on how `Option Strict` (which is discussed in Chapter 2) is set. If `Option Strict` is set to `On`, the preceding line of code causes an error. The Visual Basic compiler does not allow an implicit conversion from `Object` to a strongly typed object, and it reports an error message that you can see in the code editor, as shown in Figure 4.7.

This is useful because it prevents type conversion errors. If you want to perform an assignment of this kind, you need to explicitly convert `Object` into the appropriate data type. You can do this, for example, by using the `CType` conversion operator, as in the following line of code:

```
Dim onePerson As Person = CType(New Object, Person)
```

A conversion operator provides another advantage: It communicates whether the conversion is possible; if it's not, you can handle the situation, particularly at runtime. The code editor also simplifies the addition of a `CType` conversion by offering a convenient correction pop-up that you enable by hovering the red squiggle that appears under the bad object and then clicking the light bulb symbol. You then see possible fixes, including an option to perform the conversion into the appropriate type (see Figure 4.8 for an example). Note that CType will work without throwing an exception only if the target type for the conversion is the correct type.

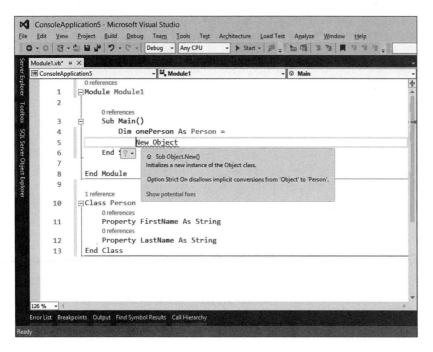

FIGURE 4.7   With Option Strict set to On, the Visual Basic compiler disallows implicit conversions.

FIXING CODE ISSUES WITH THE LIGHT BULB

Visual Studio 2015 introduces a brand-new way of fixing code issues via the light bulb shown in Figure 4.8. You will use the light bulb many times to fix code issues. The light bulb is discussed in more detail in Chapter 6, "Errors, Exceptions, and Code Refactoring."

By the way, the Visual Basic compiler provides a way to allow implicit conversions and avoid error messages. To accomplish this, you need to set Option Strict to Off. You can write the following line of code before all the other code and Imports directives:

```
Option Strict Off
```

You can also adjust Option Strict settings in the Compiler tab of the My Project window, as discussed in Chapter 2. Assigning an Object to a Person, as you did earlier, is perfectly legal. But please be careful: If you do not need to perform such assignments, avoid Option Strict Off and instead use Option Strict On. This can ensure fewer runtime and compile-time errors and enable you to write more efficient code.

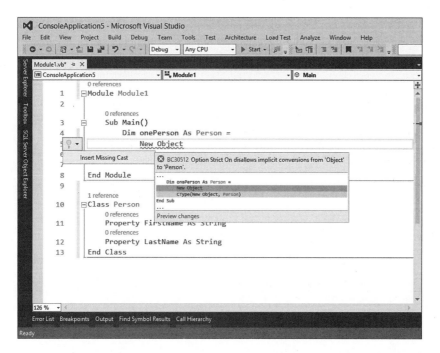

FIGURE 4.8   Using the error correction options to easily add CType.

Boxing and Unboxing

The common type system enables implicit conversions. It also enables conversions between reference types and value types—and vice versa—because both inherit from System.Object. You often need to work with two techniques, boxing and unboxing, when you have methods that receive arguments of type Object.

Boxing

Boxing occurs when you convert a value type to a reference type. In other words, boxing happens when you assign a value type to an Object. The following lines of code demonstrate boxing:

```
Dim calculation As Double = 14.4 + 32.12
Dim result As Object = calculation
```

In this example, the `calculation` variable, which stores a value deriving from the sum of two numbers, is a `Double` value type. The `result` variable, which is of type `Object` and therefore a reference type, is allocated in the heap and boxes the original value of calculation so that you now have two copies of the value: one in the stack and one in the heap. Figure 4.9 shows how boxing causes memory allocation.

Boxing requires performance overhead. This will be clearer when you read the next section.

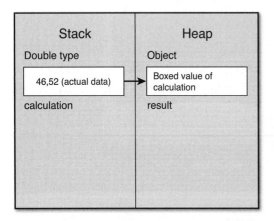

FIGURE 4.9   Boxing causes both stack and heap allocation.

Unboxing

Unboxing occurs when you convert a reference type to a value type. You perform unboxing when converting an `Object` into a value type. Continuing with the previous example, the following line of code demonstrates unboxing:

```
Dim convertedResult As Double = CType(result, Double)
```

Unboxing can cause another copy of the original value (the same value stored in the `calculation` variable) to be created and allocated in the stack. Figure 4.10 shows a representation of what happens with unboxing of a value.

Boxing and unboxing cause performance overhead, so you should avoid them if they're not truly needed. This is because value types directly store the data they refer to and therefore create three copies of the data, which can consume more resources than necessary. If the value types that you box and unbox are small, performance might not be influenced (or, better, you might not see the difference). But if the value types store a large amount of data, the loss of performance could be significant.

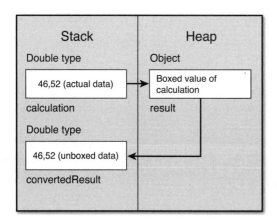

FIGURE 4.10   Unboxing causes a third copy of the original value to be created.

AVOIDING BOXING AND UNBOXING

Boxing and unboxing can be necessary if you have methods that receive arguments of type `Object`. There are a couple of best practices that you can observe when implementing methods, such as using generics and implementing overloads of methods that can accept multiple strongly typed arguments. Generics and generic method overloads are discussed in Chapter 14.

EARLY BINDING AND LATE BINDING

An important topic related to reference types is early binding and late binding. Although this might be the right place to discuss them, I postpone their discussion until Chapter 44. This way, you can get a complete overview of reference types before you get real examples of the late binding technique.

Deep Copy and Shallow Copy

In the "Understanding Reference Types" section, earlier in this chapter, you saw how reference type assignments differ from value type assignments and how assignments are not enough to create a copy of a reference type. You also saw one basic solution to this problem, which involved creating a new instance of a specified reference type and then assigning each property of the target instance with values coming from the original one. But this is not enough, both because it is not complete and because it can be good only with small classes.

To create a complete clone of a reference type, in.NET development, you can take advantage of two techniques: *deep copy* and *shallow copy*. Both of these techniques require implementation of the `ICloneable` interface. Although we discuss interfaces later, the concepts presented here are easy to understand. The `ICloneable` interface provides a unique method named `Clone` that enables you to know what classes can be easily cloned. For example, consider the following implementation of the `Person` class that also implements the `ICloneable` interface:

```
Class Person
    Implements ICloneable
    Property FirstName As String
    Property LastName As String
    Property Work As Job
    Public Function Clone() As Object Implements System.ICloneable.Clone
        Return Me.MemberwiseClone
    End Function
End Class
```

The most interesting thing in the code is the `Clone` method required by the `ICloneable` interface. In the method body, you write code that performs the real copy of the reference type. Fortunately, the `Object` class provides a method named `MemberwiseClone` that automatically returns a shallow copy of your reference type. The keyword `Me` indicates the current instance of the class. Because `Clone` must work with all possible types, it returns `Object`. (You'll see later in this chapter how to convert this result.) The class exposes two `String` properties, `FirstName` and `LastName`. You might remember that although `String` is a reference type behind the scenes, you actually treat it as a value type. The class also exposes another property, named `Work`, of type `Job`. This is a new reference type representing a person's occupation. `Job` is implemented as follows:

```
Class Job
    Property CompanyName As String
    Property Position As String
End Class
```

Given this implementation, you can simply create a shallow copy.

Shallow Copy

When you create a *shallow copy*, you create a new instance of the current object and copy values of members of the original to the new one but do not create copies of children (referenced) objects.

Let's continue the example from the preceding section. `Clone` creates a copy of the `Person` class into a new instance and copies members' values that are value types or `Strings`. Because `Job` is a pure reference type, the shallow copy provided by `Clone` will not also create a clone of `Job`. (Remember that a shallow copy creates a copy only of the specified instance but not of children objects.) You can easily verify these assertions by writing the following code:

```
Sub Main()
    'The original person
    Dim firstPerson As New Person
    firstPerson.FirstName = "Alessandro"
```

```
            firstPerson.LastName = "Del Sole"
            'Defines a work for the above person
            Dim randomJob As New Job
            randomJob.CompanyName = "Del Sole Ltd."
            randomJob.Position = "CEO"
            'Assignment of the new job
            firstPerson.Work = randomJob
            'Gets a shallow copy of the firstPerson object
            Dim secondPerson As Person = CType(firstPerson.Clone, Person)
            'Check if they are the same instances
            'returns False, 2 different instances:
            Console.WriteLine(firstPerson.FirstName Is secondPerson.FirstName)
            'returns True (still same instance of Job!):
            Console.WriteLine(firstPerson.Work Is secondPerson.Work)
            Console.ReadLine()
      End Sub
```

This code first gets a new instance of the `Person` class and sets some properties such as a new instance of the `Job` class, too. Notice how the result of the `Clone` method, which is of type `Object`, is converted into a `Person` instance, using `CType`. At this point, you can check what happened. The `Is` operator enables you to compare two instances of reference types and returns `True` if they are related to the same instance. For the `FirstName` property, the comparison returns `False` because the shallow copy creates a new, standalone instance of the `Person` class. But if you do the same check on the `Work` property, which is a child reference type of the `Person` class, the comparison returns `True`. This means that `firstPerson.Work` refers to the same instance of the `Job` class as in `secondPerson.Work`. And this also means that a shallow copy did not create a new copy of the `Job` class to be assigned to the `secondPerson` object. This is where the *deep copy* comes in.

Deep Copy

Creating a deep copy is a complex way to create a perfect copy of an entire object's graph. If you need to perform a deep copy, you have some alternatives. The easiest way is to perform a shallow copy of the main object and then manually copy the other properties of child reference types. Later in this chapter, you'll instead learn about an alternative technique related to serialization, which is discussed in Chapter 39, "Serialization." At the moment you can focus on editing the previous implementation of the `Clone` method for performing a simple deep copy. You can also implement the `ICloneable` interface in the `Job` class, as follows:

```
Class Job
    Implements ICloneable
    Property CompanyName As String
    Property Position As String
    Public Function Clone() As Object Implements System.ICloneable.Clone
        Return Me.MemberwiseClone
    End Function
End Class
```

Now you can modify the `Clone` implementation inside the `Person` class, as follows:

```
Class Person
    Implements ICloneable
    Property FirstName As String
    Property LastName As String
    Property Work As Job
    Public Function Clone() As Object Implements System.ICloneable.Clone
        Dim tempPerson As Person = CType(Me.MemberwiseClone, Person)
        tempPerson.Work = CType(Me.Work.Clone, Job)
        Return tempPerson
    End Function
End Class
```

IMPLEMENTING `ICloneable`

Implementing `ICloneable` in referenced classes is not the only way of providing deep copies. You could also generate a new instance of the `Job` class and manually assign values read from the original instance. But because we are discussing `ICloneable` and `Clone`, the preceding example is completed this way.

The code first obtains a shallow copy of the current instance of the `Person` class and then gets a shallow copy of the child instance of the `Job` class.

RECURSIVE CLONING

Cloning objects with recursive calls to the `Clone` method could lead to a stack overflow if the hierarchy of objects is particularly complex. Because of this, the previous implementation goes well with small classes and small object graphs. In other situations, you should instead use serialization.

If you now try to run the same check again, comparing the instances of `firstPerson` and `secondPerson`, the output will be as follows:

```
False
False
```

This is because now the instances are different. You have two completely standalone instances of the `Person` class.

The `GetType` Keyword

Each time you create an instance of a class, the .NET runtime creates an instance behind the scenes of the `System.Type` class that represents your object. In.NET development you have the ability to inspect instances of the `System.Type` class (known as reflection) at runtime and to get a reference to that `System.Type`. The Visual Basic programming language offers the `GetType` keyword, which enables you to accomplish both tasks. The

GetType keyword has two different behaviors: First, it is an operator, and second, it is a method. GetType is typically used to compare two instances of an object or to access metadata of a type at runtime. To understand GetType, we'll look at a few examples. Consider this first code snippet:

```
'GetType here is related to the type
Dim testType As Type = GetType(Integer)
For Each method As System.Reflection.MethodInfo
            In testType.GetMethods
    Console.WriteLine(method.Name)
Next
Console.ReadLine()
```

Basically, the preceding code retrieves all the information and metadata related to the System.Int32 type. Then it shows a list of all the methods exposed by that type, using reflection. (MethodInfo is an object representing the method's information.) This is useful if you need to retrieve information on a particular data type. If you instead need to retrieve information about metadata of a specific instance of a data type, you can use the GetType method, as shown in the following code:

```
'GetType here is related to an instance
Dim testInt As Integer = 123456
Dim testType As Type = testInt.GetType
For Each method As System.Reflection.MethodInfo
            In testType.GetMethods
    Console.WriteLine(method.Name)
Next
Console.ReadLine()
```

In this particular situation, you retrieve information on an instance of the System.Int32 type and not on the type.

You can also use GetType to compare two types for equality:

```
'Comparing two types
If testInt.GetType Is GetType(Integer) Then
    Console.WriteLine("TestInt is of type Integer")
End If
```

Understanding Conversion Operators

In the previous section we discussed converting between value types and reference types. These kinds of conversions are not the only ones allowed by the .NET Framework. You often need to perform conversions between two value types or two reference types. For example, imagine that you want to represent a number as a text message. In such a case, you need to convert an Integer into a String; you could also have an Integer value that must be passed to a method that instead receives an argument of type Double.

Another common scenario is when you work with user controls in the user interface. Some controls, such as `ListBox` and `DataGridView` on the Windows side or the `DataGrid` on the web side can store any kind of object. If you show a list of `Person` objects inside a `ListBox`, the control stores a list of `Object`, so you need to perform an explicit conversion from `Object` to `Person` each time you need to retrieve information on a single `Person`. In this section we show how conversions between types can be performed.

Widening and Narrowing Conversions

With the exception of boxing and unboxing, conversions are of two kinds: *widening* conversions and *narrowing* conversions. Their type depends on whether the conversion is explicit or implicit, as explained in the following sections.

Widening Conversions

Widening conversions occur when you try to convert a type into another one that can include all values of the original type. A typical example of a widening conversion is converting from an `Integer` into a `Double`, as in the following lines of code:

```
'Widening conversion
Dim i As Integer = 1
Dim d As Double = i
```

As you might remember from Table 4.2, `Integer` represents a numeric value, whereas `Double` represents a large floating-point number. Therefore, `Double` is greater than `Integer` and can accept conversions from `Integer` without loss of precision. Widening conversions do not need an explicit conversion operator, which instead happens for narrowing conversions.

Narrowing Conversions

The opposite of widening conversions, *narrowing conversions* occur when you attempt to convert a type into another that is smaller or with a loss of precision. For example, converting a `Double` into an `Integer` can cause a loss of precision because `Double` is a large floating-point number, and `Integer` is just a numeric value, which is also smaller than `Double`. There are several ways to perform narrowing conversions, depending on how the types you need to convert are implemented. Visual Basic 2015, continuing what was already available in previous versions of the language, provides an easy way to perform conversions between base types wrapped by Visual Basic keywords. For example, if you need to convert a `Double` into an `Integer`, you could write the following lines of code:

```
Dim d As Double = 12345.678
Dim i As Integer = CInt(d)
```

The `CInt` function converts the specified `Object` into an `Integer`. In this particular case, the value of `i` becomes `12346` because the conversion caused a loss of precision, and the Visual Basic compiler produced an integer number that is the closest to the original value.

Another example is when you need to convert a number into a string representation of the number itself. This can be accomplished with the following line of code:

```
Dim s As String = CStr(i)
```

The CStr function converts the specified Object into a string. With particular regard to string conversions, all .NET objects expose a method named ToString that performs a conversion of the original data into a new String. The last line of code could be rewritten as follows:

```
Dim s As String = i.ToString()
```

ToString is also useful because you can format the output. For example, consider the following code:

```
Dim i As Integer = 123456
Dim s As String = i.ToString("##,##.00")
```

The ToString method enables you to specify how the string should be formatted. On my machine, the code produces the following output:

```
123,456.00
```

The output depends on regional settings for your system, such as the separator settings.

USING Tostring INSTEAD OF CStr

Because it enables you to format the result, ToString should be preferred to CStr. You can override the standard implementation of ToString (provided by the Object class) so that you can provide your own conversion logic. This is discussed later in Chapter 12.

Table 4.5 shows the complete list of conversion functions provided by the Visual Basic grammar.

TABLE 4.5   Visual Basic Conversion Functions

Operator	Description
CInt	Converts an object into an Integer.
CLng	Converts an object into a Long.
CShort	Converts an object into a Short.
CSng	Converts an object into a Single.
CDbl	Converts an object into a Double.
CBool	Converts an object into a Boolean.
CByte	Converts an object into a Byte.
CChar	Converts an object into a Char.
CStr	Converts an object into a String.

Operator	Description
CObj	Converts an object into an instance of `Object`.
CDate	Converts an object into a `Date`.
CUInt	Converts an object into a `UInteger`.
CULong	Converts an object into a `ULong`.
CUShort	Converts an object into a `UShort`.
CSByte	Converts an object into a `SByte`.

REMEMBERING THE LOSS OF PRECISION

Always take care when performing narrowing conversions because of the loss of precision, particularly with numeric values. Another particular case is when converting from `String` to `Char`. Such conversions retrieve only the first character of the specified string.

When narrowing conversions fail, an `InvalidCastException` is thrown by the .NET Runtime. An example of this situation occurs when you attempt to convert a `String` into an `Integer`. Because `String` is a valid object expression, you do not get an error at compile time, but the conversion would fail at runtime. Because of this, you should always enclose conversions within error-handling code blocks (see Chapter 6 for details). There are also alternatives provided by the .NET Framework that are independent of the Visual Basic language. One alternative is to use the `System.Convert` class that is available on objects that implement the `IConvertible` interface. `Convert` exposes a lot of methods, each for converting into a particular data type. For example, the following line of code converts a string representation of a number into an integer:

```
Dim c As Integer = System.Convert.ToInt32("1234")
```

If the string contains an invalid number, a `FormatException` is thrown. Methods exposed by the `Convert` class are well implemented because they accept not only `Object` expressions but also specific types, such as `Integer`, `Boolean`, `String`, and so on. IntelliSense can help you understand which types are supported. Table 4.6 provides an overview of the most common conversion methods exposed by `System.Convert`.

TABLE 4.6 The Most Commonly Used `System.Convert` Methods

Method	Description
ToBool	Converts the specified type into a `Boolean`.
ToByte	Converts the specified type into a `Byte`.
ToChar	Converts the specified type into a `Char`.
ToDateTime	Converts the specified type into a `Date`.
ToDecimal	Converts the specified type into a `Decimal`.
ToDouble	Converts the specified type into a `Double`.

Method	Description
ToInt16	Converts the specified type into a Short.
ToInt32	Converts the specified type into an Integer.
ToInt64	Converts the specified type into a Long.
ToSByte	Converts the specified type into a SByte.
ToSingle	Converts the specified type into a Single.
ToString	Converts the specified type into a String.
ToUInt16	Converts the specified type into an UShort.
ToUInt32	Converts the specified type into a UInteger.
ToUInt64	Converts the specified type into an ULong.

Notice that System.Convert also provides other methods that are not discussed here because they are related to particular situations that assume you have a deep knowledge of specific .NET topics and are beyond the scope of this general discussion.

CType, DirectCast, and TryCast

The Visual Basic programming language offers some other conversion operators that are commonly used because of their flexibility. The first one is CType. It converts from one type to another; if no valid conversion exists, the Visual Basic compiler reports an error. If the conversion fails at runtime, an exception is thrown. The good news is that conversions that can never succeed are immediately detected by the background compiler, so if the target type's range exceeds the source one, you are immediately notified of the problem. For example, the compiler knows that converting a Date into an Integer is not possible, so in such a scenario, you are immediately notified. If the conversion is legal (and therefore can compile), but types are populated at runtime with data that cannot be converted, an InvalidCastException is thrown. For example, the following code converts an Integer into a Short:

```
Dim i As Integer = 123456
Dim s As Short = CType(i, Short)
```

CType is also useful in unboxing. The following code converts from an Object that contains an Integer into a pure Integer:

```
Dim p As Object = 1
Dim result As Integer = CType(p, Integer)
```

Of course, it can also be used for converting between reference types:

```
Dim p As Object = New Person
Dim result As Person = CType(p, Person)
```

CType is specific to the Visual Basic runtime and enables widening and narrowing conversions from one type into another type. For example, a Double can be converted to an Integer, although with loss of precision. Another couple of important operators,

`DirectCast` and `TryCast`, can be used the same way, but they have different behavior. Both operators enable conversions when there is an inheritance or implementation relationship between the two types. For example, consider the following lines of code:

```
Dim d As Double = 123.456
Dim s As Short = CType(d, Short)
```

Converting from `Double` to `Short` using `CType` succeeds. Now consider the usage of `DirectCast` in the same scenario:

```
Dim d As Double = 123.456
Dim s As Short = DirectCast(d, Short)
```

This conversion fails because `Short` does not inherit from `Double` and no implementation relationship exists between the two types. You are notified of a conversion failure via a compile-time error indicating that such conversion cannot be done.

You should use `DirectCast` only when you are sure that the inheritance or implementation conditions between types are satisfied. `DirectCast` conversions are also checked by the background compiler, so you are immediately notified if conversions fail via the Error List window. `DirectCast` works with both value and reference types. The difference between `CType` and `DirectCast` is that `CType` can perform both user-defined conversions (see Chapter 11) and intrinsic conversions defined by the Visual Basic language (such as between Integer and Short), whereas `DirectCast` cannot. `DirectCast` can perform conversions only if the runtime type of the object being converted is the same as the target type or is derived from the target type through either inheritance or interface implementation.

However, using `DirectCast` has some advantages in terms of performance because it relies directly on the .NET Runtime. In most cases where either `CType` or `DirectCast` can be used, the performance is the same because the compiler emits the same instructions. The one exception to this is when converting from a value of type `Object` to any of the built-in Visual Basic types, such as `Integer`, `Date`, and `String`. In this specific case, the compiler emits a call to helper methods defined in the Visual Basic Runtime. This is because the Visual Basic language defines more extensive conversions than .NET between primitive types. For example, if a value of type `Object` contains a boxed `Short`, using `DirectCast` to convert to `Long` will fail with an `InvalidCastException` at runtime because `Short` does not derive from `Long`; however, using `CType` will succeed because the Visual Basic Runtime will first unbox the `Short` and then widen it to `Long`. This makes `CType` generally more powerful, but there is a tiny performance overhead in this one specific scenario. In the vast majority of applications, this overhead is unnoticeable. When you want to perform conversions between reference types, it's a best practice to check whether the two types are compliant so you can reduce the risks of errors:

```
'In this example P is of type Object but stores a Person
If TypeOf (p) Is Person Then
    Dim result As Person = DirectCast(p, Person)
End If
```

The `TypeOf..Is..` operator compares an object reference variable to a data type and returns `True` if the object variable is compatible with the given type. As of VB 2015, you can use the `TypeOf..IsNot..` operator to detect when an object variable is not compatible with a given type. As you might imagine, such checks can involve performance overhead. Another operator that works only with reference types is `TryCast`. This one works exactly like `DirectCast`, but instead of throwing an `InvalidCastException` in the case of conversion failure, it returns a null object (`Nothing`). This can be useful because you can avoid implementing an exceptions check, which simplifies your code (because it will only need to check for a null value) and reduces performance overhead. The preceding code snippet could be rewritten as follows:

```
'In this example P is of type Object but stores a Person
Dim result As Person = TryCast(p, Person)
```

If the conversion fails, `TryCast` returns `Nothing`, so you just need to check such a result.

Working with .NET Fundamental Types

You will often work with some special objects, such as strings, dates and times, and arrays. Although you will often work with collections, too (see Chapter 16, "Working with Collections and Iterators"), understanding how such objects work is an important objective. The .NET Framework 4.6 simplifies your developer life because objects provide methods to perform the most common operations on data.

EXTENSION METHODS

This section describes built-in methods from value and reference types. Because of the .NET infrastructure, all types provide the ability to invoke extension methods that could potentially be used for accomplishing some of the tasks proposed in this section. They are not described here because the goal of this chapter is to describe built-in members; you need to understand extension methods, though, so be sure to read Chapter 20.

Working with Strings

Working with strings is one of the most common developer activities. In the .NET common type system, `System.String` is a reference type. This might be surprising because strings actually behave like value types. The `String` class cannot be inherited, so you can't create a custom class derived from it. In addition, `string` objects are immutable, like value types. What does this mean? It means that when you create a new `String`, you cannot change it. Although you are allowed to edit a string's content, behind the scenes, the CLR does not edit the existing string; it instead creates a new instance of the `String` object that contains your edits. The CLR then stores such `String` objects in the heap and returns a reference to them. We discuss how to approach strings in a more efficient way later in this chapter; at the moment, you need to understand how to work with them.

The `System.String` class provides lots of methods for working with strings without the need to write custom code. If you understand the previous section related to reference types, you can learn how to manipulate strings using the most common `System.String` methods.

`System.String` METHODS

`System.String` provides several methods for performing operations on strings. We discuss the most important of them in this chapter. Each method comes with several overloads. Discussing every overload is not possible, so you'll learn how methods work, and you can use IntelliSense, the Object Browser, and the documentation for further information.

Comparing Strings

Comparing the content of two strings is an easy task. The most common way to compare strings is taking advantage of the equality (=) operator, which checks whether two strings have the same value. The following is an example of comparing strings for equality:

```
Dim stringOne As String = "Hi guys"
Dim stringTwo As String = "How are you?"
Dim stringThree As String = "Hi guys"
'Returns False
Dim result1 As Boolean = (stringOne = stringTwo)
'Returns True
Dim result2 As Boolean = (stringOne = stringThree)
```

You can also use the equality operator inside conditional blocks, as in the following snippet:

```
If stringOne = stringTwo Then
    'Do something if the two strings are equal
End If
```

You check for strings' inequality by using the inequality operator (<>).

THE VISUAL BASIC COMPILER AND THE EQUALITY OPERATOR

When you use the equality operator for string comparisons, the Visual Basic compiler works differently from other managed languages. Behind the scenes, it makes a call to the `Microsoft.VisualBasic.CompilerServices.Operators.CompareString` method, whereas other languages, such as C#, make an invocation to `System.String.Equals`. The difference is that `CompareString` considers two null strings to be equal, and it also considers a null string and an empty string to be equal; on the other hand, `String.Equals` considers these not equal.

The `String` class also exposes other interesting methods for comparing strings: `Equals`, `Compare`, `CompareTo`, and `CompareOrdinal`. `Equals` checks for string equality and returns a Boolean value of `True` if the strings are equal or `False` if they are not (which is exactly like the equality operator). The following code compares two strings and returns `False` because they are not equal:

```
Dim firstString As String = "Test string"
Dim secondString As String = "Comparison Test"
Dim areEqual As Boolean = String.Equals(firstString, secondString)
```

`Equals` has several signatures that allow deep control of the comparison. For example, you could check whether two strings are equal according to the local system culture and without being case-sensitive:

```
Dim areCaseEqual As Boolean =
    String.Equals(firstString, secondString,
    StringComparison.CurrentCultureIgnoreCase)
```

The `StringComparison` object provides a way to specify comparison settings. IntelliSense provides a description for each available option. Then there is the `Compare` method. It checks whether the first string is less than, equal to, or greater than the second and returns an `Integer` value representing the result of the comparison. If the first string is less than the second, it returns `-1`; if it is equal to the second one, the method returns `0`; if the first string is greater than the second, it returns `1`. The following code snippet demonstrates this kind of comparison:

```
Dim firstString As String = "Test string"
Dim secondString As String = "Comparison Test"
Dim result As Integer = String.Compare(firstString, secondString)
```

In this case, `Compare` returns `1` because the second string is greater than the first one. `Compare` enables you to specify several comparison options. For example, you could perform the comparison based on case-sensitive strings. The following code demonstrates this:

```
Dim caseComparisonResult As Integer =
    String.Compare(firstString, secondString, True)
```

For `Equals`, `Compare` also enables a comparison based on other options, such as the culture information of your system. The next method is `String.CompareTo`, whose return values are the same as those for `String.Compare`; however, `String.CompareTo` is an instance method. You use it as shown in the following code:

```
Dim firstString As String = "Test string"
Dim secondString As String = "Comparison Test"
Dim result As Integer = firstString.CompareTo(secondString)
```

The last valuable method is `String.CompareOrdinal`, which checks for case differences via ordinal comparison rules, which means comparing the numeric values of the corresponding `Char` objects that the string is composed of. The following is an example:

```
Dim firstString As String = "test"
Dim secondString As String = "TeSt"
'Returns:
'0 if the first string is equal to the second
'< 0 if the first string is less than the second
'> 0 if the first string is greater than the second
Dim result As Integer = String.CompareOrdinal(firstString, secondString)
```

Checking for Empty or Null Strings

The `System.String` class provides a method named `IsNullOrEmpty` that easily enables you to check whether a string is null or whether it does not contain any characters. You use it as follows:

```
If String.IsNullOrEmpty(stringToCheck) = False Then
    'The string is neither null nor empty
Else
    'The string is either null or empty
End If
```

Of course, you could also perform your check against `True` instead of `False`. In such situations, both conditions (null or empty) are evaluated. This can be useful because you often need to validate strings to check whether they are valid. There could be situations in which you need to just ensure that a string is null or not empty. In this case, you should use the usual syntax:

```
If stringToCheck Is Nothing Then
    'String is null
End If
If stringToCheck = "" Then
    'String is empty
End If
```

You could also use the new null conditional operator `?`, which is discussed later in this chapter.

Formatting Strings

Often you need to send output strings in a particular format, such as currency, percentage, or decimal numbers. The `System.String` class offers a useful method named `Format` that enables you to easily format text, plus a new strongly typed way called *string interpolation*. The following code is an example of the classic way. Pay particular attention to the comments:

```
'Returns "The cost for traveling to Europe is $1,000.00
Console.WriteLine(String.Format("The cost for traveling to Europe is {0:C}
                                 dollars", 1000))
'Returns "You are eligible for a 15.50% discount"
```

```
Console.WriteLine(String.Format("You are eligible for a {0:P} discount",
                    15.55F))
'Returns "Hex counterpart for 10 is A"
Console.WriteLine(String.Format("Hex counterpart for 10 is {0:X}", 10))
```

The first thing to notice is how you present your strings; `Format` accepts a number of values to be formatted and then embedded in the main string, which are referenced with the number enclosed in brackets. For example, {0} is the second argument of `Format`, {1} is the third one, and so on. Symbols enable the format; for example, `c` stands for currency, `P` stands for percentage, and `x` stands for hexadecimal. Visual Basic 2015 offers the symbols listed in Table 4.7.

TABLE 4.7   Acceptable Format Symbols

Symbol	Description
C or c	Currency
D or d	Decimal
E or e	Scientific
F or f	Fixed point
G or g	General
N or n	Number
P or p	Percentage
R or r	Roundtrip
X or x	Hexadecimal

ROUNDTRIP

Roundtrip ensures that conversions from floating point to `string` and then back are allowed.

You can format multiple strings in one line of code, as in the following example:

```
Console.Writeline(String.Format("The traveling cost is" &
            " {0:C}. Hex for {1} is '{1,5:X}'", 1000, 10))
```

The preceding code produces the following result:

```
The traveling cost is $1,000.00. Hex for 10 is '    A'
```

As you can see, you can specify a number of white spaces before the next value. This is accomplished by typing the number of spaces you want to add followed by a : symbol and then the desired format symbol. `string.Format` also enables the use of custom formats. Custom formats are based on the symbols shown in Table 4.8.

TABLE 4.8   Acceptable Symbols for Custom Formats

Symbol	Description
0	A numeric placeholder showing 0
#	A digit placeholder
%	Percentage symbol
.	Decimal dot
,	Thousands separator
;	Section separator
"ABC" or 'ABC'	String literals
\	Escape
E or e combined with + or -	Scientific

According to Table 4.8, you could write a custom percentage representation like this:

```
'Returns "Custom percentage %1,550"
Console.WriteLine(String.Format("Custom percentage {0:%##,###.##} ", 15.50))
```

Or you might want to write a custom currency representation. For example, if you live in Great Britain, you could write the following line to represent the sterling currency:

```
Console.WriteLine(String.Format("Custom currency {0:£#,###.00} ", 987654))
```

Another interesting feature in customizing output is the ability to provide different formats according to the input value. For example, you might decide to format a number depending on whether it is positive, negative, or zero. For example, consider the following code:

```
Dim number As Decimal = 1000
Console.WriteLine(String.
            Format("Custom currency formatting:
            {0:£#,##0.00;*£#,##0.00*;Zero}",
            number))
```

Here you specify three different formats, separated by semicolons. The first format affects positive numbers (such as the value of the number variable), the second one affects negative numbers, and the third one affects a zero value. The preceding example therefore produces the following output:

```
Custom currency formatting: £1,000.00
```

If you try to change the value of the number to -1000, the code produces the following output:

```
Custom currency formatting: *£1,000.00*
```

Finally, if you assign number = 0, the code produces the following output:

```
Custom currency formatting: Zero
```

As mentioned at the beginning of this section, Visual Basic 2015 introduces a new way of formatting strings, called *string interpolation*. This is basically an easier way of writing strings that contain expressions. With string interpolation, you no longer need to use the positional placeholders, and you have full IntelliSense support, with colorization. To understand how it works, consider the following simple Person class:

```
Class Person
    Property FirstName As String
    Property LastName As String
    Property Height As Double
End Class
```

Now suppose you have an instance of this Person class that you create like this:

```
Dim onePerson As New Person
onePerson.FirstName = "Alessandro"
onePerson.LastName = "Del Sole"
onePerson.Height = 175D
```

At this point, you want to format a string containing the person's information, as shown in the following example:

```
        Dim formatted As String =
              String.Format("Hello, I'm {0} {1} and I'm {2:0.00} centimeters tall",
onePerson.FirstName, onePerson.LastName, onePerson.Height)
```

This code produce the following result:

```
Hello, I'm Alessandro Del Sole and I'm 175,00 centimeters tall
```

With string interpolation, you can rewrite the preceding code as follows:

```
        Dim formatted As String =
              $"Hello, I'm {onePerson.FirstName}
➡{onePerson.LastName} and I'm {onePerson.Height:0.00}
➡centimeters tall"
```

You use the dollar symbol ($) before quotes to tell the compiler that the string is using interpolation. As you can see, you no longer need to use positional placeholders, like {0} and {1}, or place values after the closing quotes. You instead use the object and members directly; this means you end up writing cleaner code, being able to use IntelliSense, and saving time. String interpolation allows you to invoke methods other than properties, as they are objects' members. Say that the Person class is extended with the following method:

```
Function FullName() As String
    Return Me.FirstName & " " & " " + Me.LastName
End Function
```

You could rewrite the string with interpolation as follows:

```
Dim formatted As String =
        $"Hello, I'm {onePerson.FullName()} and I'm
{onePerson.Height:0.00} centimeters tall"
```

String interpolation is also very useful with strings generated programmatically, especially with values supplied by the user. The following examples demonstrates this:

```
'Generate a programmatic string (e.g. user input)
Dim formattedFile As String = $"{filePath}\{fileName}.{fileExtension}"

'Generate a web URL programmatically
Dim protocol As String = "http"
Dim webSite As String = "www.visual-basic.it"
Dim page As String = "videos.aspx"
Dim formattedUrl As String = $"{protocol}://{webSite}/{page}"
```

Behind the scenes, string interpolation is shorthand for `String.Format`. For this reason, by default it uses the current culture. If you are building a string that includes values with special formatting requirements, such as floating-point numbers, you should use the `InvariantCulture` culture. To accomplish this, you can create a helper function that takes an argument of type `System.FormattableString`, which implements the `IFormattable` interface and allows you to invoke its `ToString` method by passing the `InvariantCulture` object. The following code demonstrates this:

```
Function InvariantFormat(stringToFormat As FormattableString) As String
    Return stringToFormat.ToString(Globalization.CultureInfo.InvariantCulture)
End Function

Sub DoWork()
    'This string is formatted using the InvariantCulture culture
    Dim invariantText =
    InvariantFormat($"Hello, I'm
{onePerson.FullName()} and I'm
{onePerson.Height:0.00} centimeters tall")
    End Sub
```

Also, string interpolation does not produce a constant. It actually invokes `String.Format` behind the scenes. Because of this implicit invocation, the compiler is able to optimize string interpolation performance if it can predict how `String.Format` will behave. If you need to use curly braces in a formatted string, you simply use double curly braces, as you would do with quotation marks:

```
'Returns Hello, I'm {Alessandro Del Sole}
Dim formatted As String =
    $"Hello, I'm {{onePerson.FullName}} "
```

String interpolation is definitely an amazing new feature that helps you write cleaner code and save time.

Creating Copies of Strings

Strings in .NET are reference types. Because of this, assigning a string object to another string to perform a copy will just copy the reference to the actual string. Fortunately, the System.String class provides two useful methods for copying strings: Copy and CopyTo. The first one creates a copy of an entire string:

```
Dim sourceString As String = "Alessandro Del Sole"
Dim targetString As String = String.Copy(sourceString)
```

Copy is a shared method and can create a new instance of String and then put into this instance the content of the original string. If you instead need to create a copy of only a subset of the original string, you can invoke the instance method CopyTo. This method works a little differently from Copy because it returns an array of Char. The following code provides an example:

```
Dim sourceString As String = "Alessandro Del Sole"
Dim charArray(sourceString.Length) As Char
sourceString.CopyTo(11, charArray, 0, 3)
Console.WriteLine(charArray)
```

You need to declare an array of Char, and in this case it should be as long as the string length. The first argument of CopyTo is the start position in the original string; the second is the target array. The third one is the start position in the target array, and the fourth one is the number of characters to copy. In the end, such code produces Del as the output.

Clone METHOD

The String class also offers a method named Clone. You should not confuse this method with Copy and CopyTo because it just returns a reference to the original string and not a real copy.

Inspecting Strings

When you work with strings, you often need to inspect or evaluate their content. The System.String class provides both methods and properties for inspecting strings. Imagine that you have the following string:

```
Dim testString As String = "This is a string to inspect"
```

You can retrieve the string's length via its `Length` property:

```
'Returns 27
Dim length As Integer = testString.Length
```

Another interesting method is `Contains`, which enables you to determine whether a string contains the specified substring or array of `Char`. `Contains` returns a Boolean value, as you can see in the following code snippet:

```
'Returns True
Dim contains As Boolean = testString.Contains("inspect")
'Returns False
Dim contains1 As Boolean = testString.Contains("Inspect")
```

Just remember that evaluation is case-sensitive.

In some situations, you might need to check whether a string begins or ends with a specified substring. You can verify both situations by using `StartsWith` and `EndsWith` methods:

```
'Returns False, the string starts with "T"
Dim startsWith As Boolean = testString.StartsWith("Uh")
'Returns True
Dim endsWith As Boolean = testString.EndsWith("pect")
```

Often you might also need to get the position of a specified substring within a string. To accomplish this, you can use the `IndexOf` method. For example, you could retrieve the start position of the first `"is"` substring as follows:

```
'Returns 2
Dim index As Integer = testString.IndexOf("is")
```

This code returns 2 because the start index is zero-based and refers to the `"is"` substring of the `"This"` word. You do not need to start your search from the beginning of the string; you can specify a start index or specify how the comparison must be performed via the `StringComparison` enumeration. Both situations are summarized in the following code:

```
'Returns 5
Dim index1 As Integer = testString.IndexOf("is", 3,
                    StringComparison.InvariantCultureIgnoreCase)
```

`StringComparison` ENUMERATION

For further details on the `StringComparison` enumeration options, you can refer to IntelliSense. The options are self-explanatory, and for the sake of brevity, all options cannot be shown here.

`IndexOf` performs a search on the exact substring. You might also need to search for the position of just one character in a set of characters. This can be accomplished using the `IndexOfAny` method, as follows:

```
'Returns 1
Dim index2 As Integer = testString.
                    IndexOfAny(New Char() {"h"c, "s"c, "i"c})
```

The preceding code has an array of `Char` storing three characters, all available in the main string. Because the first character in the array is found first, `IndexOfAny` returns its position. Generally, `IndexOfAny` returns the position of the character that is found first. There are counterparts to both `IndexOf` and `IndexOfAny`: `LastIndexOf` and `LastIndexOfAny`. The first two methods perform a search starting from the beginning of a string, whereas the last two perform a search starting from the end of a string. This is an example:

```
'Returns 5
Dim lastIndex As Integer = testString.LastIndexOf("is")
'Returns 22
Dim lastIndex1 As Integer = testString.LastIndexOfAny(New Char()
                        {"h"c, "s"c, "i"c})
```

Notice how `LastIndexOf` returns the second occurrence of the `"is"` substring if you consider the main string from the beginning. Indexing is useful, but this only stores the position of a substring. If you need to retrieve the text of a substring, you can use the `SubString` method, which works as follows:

```
'Returns "is a string"
Dim subString As String = testString.Substring(5, 11)
```

You can also just specify the start index if you need the entire substring, starting from a particular point.

Editing Strings

The `System.String` class provides members for editing strings. The first method, named `Insert`, enables you to add a substring into a string at the specified index. Consider the following example:

```
Dim testString As String = "This is a test string"
'Returns
'"This is a test,for demo purposes only,string"
Dim result As String = testString.Insert(14, ",for demo purposes only,")
```

As you can see from the comment in the code, `Insert` adds the specified substring from the specified index but does not append or replace anything. `Insert`'s counterpart is `Remove`, which enables you to remove a substring starting from the specified index or a piece of substring from the specified index and for the specified number of characters. This is an example:

```
'Returns "This is a test string"
Dim removedString As String = testString.Remove(14)
```

Remember that you always need to assign the result of a method call that makes an edit to a string because of the immutability of string types. In this case, invoking Remove does not change the content of testString, so you need to assign the result of the method call to a variable (new or existing).

Another common task is replacing a substring within a string with another string. For example, say that you want to replace the "test" substring with the "demo" substring within the testString instance. This can be accomplished by using the Replace method, as follows:

```
'Returns
'"This is a demo string"
Dim replacedString As String = testString.Replace("test", "demo")
```

The result of Replace must be assigned to another string to get the desired result. (See "Performance Tips" at the end of this section.) Editing strings also contain splitting techniques. You often need to split one string into multiple strings, especially when the string contains substrings separated by a symbol. For example, consider the following code, in which a string contains substrings separated by commas, as in CSV files:

```
Dim stringToSplit As String = "Name,Last Name,Age"
```

You might want to extract the three substrings Name, Last Name, and Age and store them as unique strings. To accomplish this, you can use the Split method, which can receive as an argument the separator character:

```
Dim result() As String = stringToSplit.Split(","c)
For Each item As String In result
    Console.WriteLine(item)
Next
```

The preceding code retrieves three strings that are stored in an array of String and then produces the following output:

```
Name
Last Name
Age
```

Split has several overloads that you can inspect with IntelliSense. One of these enables you to specify the maximum number of substrings to extract and split options, such as normal splitting or splitting if substrings are not empty:

```
Dim result() As String = stringToSplit.Split(New Char() {","c}, 2,
            StringSplitOptions.RemoveEmptyEntries)
```

In this overload, you explicitly specify an array of `Char`; in this case, there is just a one-dimensional array that contains the split symbol. Such code produces the following output because only two substrings are accepted:

```
Name
Last Name, Age
```

In addition to `Split`, there is also a `Join` method that enables you to join substrings into a unique string. Substrings are passed as an array of `String` and are separated by the specified character. The following code shows an example:

```
'Returns "Name, Last Name, Age"
Dim result As String = String.Join(",",
                    New String() {"Name", "Last Name", "Age"})
```

Another way to edit strings is to trim them. Say that you have a string containing white spaces at the end of the string or at the beginning of the string, or both. You might want to remove white spaces from the main string. The `System.String` class provides three methods, `Trim`, `TrimStart`, and `TrimEnd`, that enable you to accomplish this task, as shown in the following code (see comments):

```
Dim stringWithSpaces As String = "    Test with spaces    "
'Returns "Test with spaces"
Dim result1 As String = stringWithSpaces.Trim
'Returns "Test with spaces    "
Dim result2 As String = stringWithSpaces.TrimStart
'Returns "    Test with spaces"
Dim result3 As String = stringWithSpaces.TrimEnd
```

All three methods provide overloads for specifying characters that are different from white spaces. (Imagine that you want to remove an asterisk.) Another method, `System.String`, exposes `PadLeft` and `PadRight`. Let's look at a practical example. Consider the following code:

```
Dim padResult As String = testString.PadLeft(30, "*"c)
```

It produces the following result:

```
*********This is a test string
```

`PadLeft` creates a new string, whose length is the one specified as the first argument of the method and includes the original string with the addition of a number of symbols that is equal to the difference from the length you specified and the length of the original string. In this case, the original string is 21 characters long, even though you specified 30 as the new length. So there are 9 asterisks. `PadRight` does the same, but symbols are added on the right side, as in the following example:

```
Dim padResult As String = testString.PadRight(30, "*"c)
```

This code produces the following result:

```
This is a test string*********
```

Both of these methods are useful if you need to add symbols to the left or to the right of a string.

PERFORMANCE TIPS

Each time you edit a string, you are not actually editing the string. Instead, you are creating a new instance of the `System.String` class. As you might imagine, this could lead to performance issues. That said, although `System.String` is fundamental to knowing how to edit strings, you should prefer the `StringBuilder` object when concatenating a huge number of strings, such as inside loops. `StringBuilder` is discussed later in this chapter.

Multiline Strings

Visual Basic 2015 simplifies the way you manipulate multiline strings. Before Visual Basic 2015, to create a multiline string, you had to use the `System.Environment.NewLine` object like this:

```
Dim multiLine As String = "Hello, " & Environment.NewLine &
                          "my name is " & Environment.NewLine &
                          "Alessandro Del Sole"


Console.WriteLine(multiLine)
Console.Read()
```

This code produces the following output:

```
Hello,
my name is
Alessandro Del Sole
```

Now you can obtain the same result by simply pressing Enter every time you want a new line, without needing underscores and other objects:

```
        Dim multiLine As String =
            "Hello,
my name is
Alessandro Del Sole"
```

This feature is referred to as *multiline string literals*. Notice that when you go on a new line, text is aligned to the border of the code editor. If you add any spaces, they will be added to the output result. So, for example, attempting to indent the previous string like this:

```
Dim multiLine As String =
    "Hello,
    my name is
    Alessandro Del Sole"
```

Would produce the following output:

```
Hello,
            my name is
            Alessandro Del Sole
```

The reason for this is that you are actually adding spaces between words in a string.

So even if it's not very good looking, you have to leave words or phrases near the border of the code editor to get the correct alignment.

Concatenating Strings

Concatenation is perhaps the most common task that developers need to perform on strings. Visual Basic 2015 provides have some alternatives. First, you can use the addition operator:

```
Dim firstString As String = "Hello! My name is "
Dim secondString As String = "Alessandro Del Sole"
Dim result As String = firstString & secondString
```

Another, better, approach is the `String.Concat` method:

```
Dim concatResult As String =
                    String.Concat(firstString, secondString)
```

Both ways produce the same result (`&` invokes `String.Concat` behind the scenes), but both ways have a big limitation: Because strings are immutable, the CLR needs to create a new instance of the `String` class each time you perform a concatenation. This scenario can lead to a significant loss of performance. If you need to concatenate 10 strings, the CLR creates 10 instances of the `String` class; this might not be significant, but things change if strings grow into the thousands. Fortunately, the .NET Framework provides a more efficient tool for concatenating strings: the `StringBuilder` object.

The `StringBuilder` Object

The `System.Text.StringBuilder` class provides an efficient way to concatenate strings. You should not use `StringBuilder` every time, but it is very useful with large string concatenations, such as in loops. The difference with `String.Concat` is that `StringBuilder` can create a buffer that grows along with the real needs of storing text. (The default constructor creates a 16-byte buffer.) Using the `StringBuilder` class is straightforward. To understand the difference, consider the following code, where a loop concatenates 500,000 strings using the `&` operator (thus `String.Concat`):

```
Sub ConcatenatingStringsWithoutStringBuilder()
    Dim start As Date = Date.Now
    Dim x As String = ""
    For i As Integer = 0 To 500000
        x = x & "!"
    Next
    Dim finish = Date.Now
    Console.WriteLine($"Time taken {finish - start})")
    Console.ReadLine()
End Sub
```

If you execute this code, you will see that it takes about one minute. Now rewrite the code as follows:

```
Sub ConcatenatingStringsWithStringBuilder()
    Dim start As Date = Date.Now
    Dim x As New StringBuilder
    For i As Integer = 0 To 500000
        x.Append("!")
    Next
    Debug.WriteLine(x.ToString)
    Dim finish = Date.Now
    Console.WriteLine($"Time taken {finish - start})")
    Console.ReadLine()
End Sub
```

Concatenating 500,000 strings using StringBuilder takes less than one second. This difference is huge, but using this object makes sense only in some kinds of situations.

To use StringBuilder, you simply create an instance using the New keyword and then invoke the Append method that receives as an argument the string that must be concatenated. In the end, you need to explicitly convert the StringBuilder to a String that invokes the ToString method. This class is powerful and provides several methods for working with strings, such as AppendLine (which appends an empty line with a carriage return), AppendFormat (which enables you to format the appended string), and Replace (which enables you to replace all occurrences of the specified string with another string). The EnsureCapacity method ensures that the StringBuilder instance can contain at least the specified number of characters. You can find in the StringBuilder class the same methods provided by the String class (Replace, Insert, Remove, and so on), so working with StringBuilder should be familiar and straightforward. Also, it is worth mentioning that String.Format uses StringBuilder behind the scenes, which means you can use string interpolation instead of coding StringBuilder explicitly, with the same benefits.

The NameOf Operator

Visual Basic 2015 introduces a new operator called NameOf. It produces a string for the name of the specified type or member. The purpose of NameOf is to make it easier to embed string literals that refer to names of objects or members in your code with

IntelliSense support, thus avoiding the risk of typos. To understand how `NameOf` works and what benefit it provides, consider the following `Person` class, which implements `System.ComponentModel.INotifyPropertyChanged` in order to raise change notifications:

```
Class Person
    Implements INotifyPropertyChanged

    Private _firstName As String
    Private _lastName As String

    Property FirstName As String
        Get
            Return _firstName
        End Get
        Set(value As String)
            _firstName = value
            RaiseEvent PropertyChanged(Me,
            New PropertyChangedEventArgs("FirstName"))
        End Set
    End Property
    Property LastName As String
        Get
            Return _lastName
        End Get
        Set(value As String)
            _lastName = value
            RaiseEvent PropertyChanged(Me,
            New PropertyChangedEventArgs("LastName"))
        End Set
    End Property
    Public Event PropertyChanged As PropertyChangedEventHandler _
            Implements INotifyPropertyChanged.PropertyChanged
End Class
```

Consider both of the `RaiseEvent` statements. In both of them, the constructor of the `PropertyChangedEventArgs` class takes an argument of type `String`, representing the exact name of the property that raises the change notification. Property names are string literals, which means you can accidentally make typos and cause your code to not work correctly. With `NameOf`, you can rewrite the code as follows:

```
Property FirstName As String
    Get
        Return _firstName
    End Get
    Set(value As String)
        _firstName = value
        RaiseEvent PropertyChanged(Me, New
```

```
                   PropertyChangedEventArgs(NameOf(FirstName)))
    End Set
End Property
Property LastName As String
    Get
        Return _lastName
    End Get
    Set(value As String)
        _lastName = value
        RaiseEvent PropertyChanged(Me, New
                  PropertyChangedEventArgs(NameOf(LastName)))
    End Set
End Property
```

NameOf can take expressions as an argument, where an expression can be an object name, a namespace name, a member name, and so on. It generates a compile-time constant, which represents your object's name without the risk of any typos. When using NameOf, you get full IntelliSense support, and you can refer to any object's name without writing it manually. Another example might be useful. Imagine that you rename the LastName property as Surname, but you forget to change the property name in the RaiseEvent statement, as in the following code:

```
Property Surname As String
    Get
        Return _lastName
    End Get
    Set(value As String)
        _lastName = value
        RaiseEvent PropertyChanged(Me,
        New PropertyChangedEventArgs("LastName"))
    End Set
End Property
```

This code would definitely compile, but it would not work correctly at runtime because the property raises a change notification with a bad name. If you instead use NameOf, the operator argument is also renamed automatically. In other words, if you use NameOf in the preceding code, the code editor automatically renames LastName to Surname:

```
Property Surname As String
    Get
        Return _lastName
    End Get
    Set(value As String)
        _lastName = value
        RaiseEvent PropertyChanged(Me,
        New PropertyChangedEventArgs(NameOf(Surname)))
    End Set
End Property
```

There are many other situations in which you might want to refer to an object's name in code. For example, the following method takes an argument that cannot be null and throws an error via the `ArgumentNullException` exception if it is:

```
Sub ManipulateFile(fileName As String)
    If String.IsNullOrEmpty(fileName) Then
        Throw New ArgumentNullException("fileName")
    End If
End Sub
```

The `ArgumentNullException` exception takes an argument of type `String`, which contains the name of the null parameter. Such an argument is a string literal that represents the actual parameter name. With `NameOf`, you can rewrite the preceding code as follows:

```
Sub ManipulateFile(fileName As String)
    If String.IsNullOrEmpty(fileName) Then
        Throw New ArgumentNullException(NameOf(fileName))
    Else
        'Not null, perform your tasks here
        '...
    End If
End Sub
```

In this way, you will avoid typos, and you will get IntelliSense support, ensuring that caller code will get the correct name of the null parameter. In summary, you can use `NameOf` every time you need to reference the name of an object/member in your code.

Working with Dates

In addition to using strings, you often need to handle dates and moments in time. To accomplish this, the .NET Framework 4.6 provides the `System.DateTime` value type.

MinValue AND MaxValue

Being a value type, `System.DateTime` has two shared fields: `MinValue` and `MaxValue`. These store the minimum accepted date and the maximum date, respectively. The minimum date is 01/01/0001 00:00:00 a.m., and maximum date is 12/31/9999 11:59:59 p.m.

Creating Dates

The Visual Basic grammar offers the `Date` keyword, which is a lexical representation of the `System.DateTime` object, so you can use either `Date` or `System.DateTime`. For consistency, we use the `Date` reserved keyword, but keep in mind that this keyword creates (or gets a reference to) an instance of the `System.DateTime` type. Working with dates is an easy task. You can create a new date by creating an instance of the `DateTime` class:

```
Dim myBirthDate As New Date(1977, 5, 10)
```

The constructor has several overloads, but the most common is the preceding one, where you can specify year, month, and day. For example, such values could be written by the user and then converted into a `DateTime` object. Another common situation in which you need to create a date is for storing the current system clock date and time. This can be easily accomplished using the `DateTime.Now` property, as follows:

```
Dim currentDate As Date = Date.Now
```

Such code produces the following sample result:

```
12/26/2014 11:35:35 PM
```

When you get an instance of a `DateTime`, you can retrieve a lot of information about it. For example, consider the following code and especially pay attention to the comments:

```
'Creates a new date; May 10th 1977, 8.30 pm
Dim myBirthDate As New Date(1977, 5, 10,
                            20, 30, 0)
'In 1977, May 10th was Tuesday
Console.WriteLine(myBirthDate.DayOfWeek.
                ToString)
'8.30 pm
Console.WriteLine("Hour: {0}, Minutes: {1}",
                myBirthDate.Hour,
                myBirthDate.Minute)
'Is the date included within the Day Light Saving Time period?
Console.WriteLine("Is Day light saving time: {0}",
                myBirthDate.IsDaylightSavingTime.
                ToString)
'Is leap year
Console.WriteLine("Is leap: {0}",
                Date.IsLeapYear(myBirthDate.Year).
                ToString)
```

The code first creates the following date, representing my birth date: 5/10/1977 8:30:00 p.m. Then it retrieves some information, such as the name of the day of the week (represented by the `DayOfWeek` enumeration), the hours, the minutes (via the `Hour` and `Minute` integer properties), and the specified date within Daylight Saving Time. The `DateTime` object also exposes a shared method named `IsLeapYear` that can establish whether the specified year is a leap year. In our example, the year is not passed directly but is provided via the `Year` property of the `myBirthDate` instance. The following is the result of the code:

```
Tuesday
Hour: 20, Minutes: 30
Is Day light saving time: True
Is leap: False
```

Finally, you can declare dates with the *date literals*. The following is an example of how you can customize the date format:

```
Dim customDate As Date = #5/25/2015 8:00:00 PM#
```

Visual Basic 2015 adds support for these *year-first date literals*, which allow you to use the year as the first part of a date. Because of this addition, you can now create a date like this:

```
Dim customDate As Date = #2015/12/26 11:00:00 PM#
```

You can also create a date literal based on a 24-hour clock, like this:

```
Dim customDate As Date = #2015/12/26 23:00:00 #
```

Converting Strings into Dates

It is not unusual to ask a user to provide a date within an application. Typically, this is accomplished via the user interface and, if you do not provide a specific user control (such as the WPF `DatePicker` or the Win Forms `DateTimePicker`) for selecting dates in a graphical fashion, such input is provided in the form of a string. Because of this, you need a way of converting the string into a date, so that you can then manipulate the user input as an effective `DateTime` object (unless the string is invalid; then you need validation). To accomplish this kind of conversion, the `System.DateTime` class provides two methods that you already saw when we discussed value types: `Parse` and `TryParse`. For example, consider the following code, which receives an input by the user and attempts to convert the input into a `DateTime` object:

```
Sub ParsingDates()
    Console.WriteLine("Please specify a date:")
    Dim inputDate As Date
    Dim result As Boolean = Date.TryParse(Console.ReadLine, inputDate)
    If result = False Then
        Console.WriteLine("You entered an invalid date")
    Else
        Console.WriteLine(inputDate.DayOfWeek.ToString)
    End If
End Sub
```

The `TryParse` method receives the string to convert as the first argument (which in this case is obtained by the Console window) and the output object passed by reference (`inputDate`); it returns `True` if the conversion succeeds or `False` if it fails. The conversion succeeds if the input string format is accepted and recognized by the `DateTime` type. If you run this code and enter a string in the format `1977/05/10`, the conversion succeeds because this format is accepted by `DateTime`. You can then manipulate the new date as you like. (In the preceding example, the code shows the day of the week for the specified date, which in my example is Tuesday.)

> **TIP**
>
> In many cases you work with data from a database. The ADO.NET engine and layered technologies, such as LINQ, map dates from databases directly into a `System.DateTime` object so that you will be able to work with and manipulate such objects from and to data sources.

Formatting Dates

You need to present dates for several scenarios, and you might be required to perform this task in different ways. Fortunately, `System.DateTime` provides many ways of formatting dates. The easiest way is to invoke the `ToString` method, which accepts an argument that enables you to specify how a date must be presented. For example, consider the following code snippet, which writes the current date in both the extended (D) and short (d) date formats:

```
Console.WriteLine(DateTime.Now.ToString("D"))
Console.WriteLine(DateTime.Now.ToString("d"))
```

This code produces the following output:

```
Saturday, December 27, 2014
12/27/2014
```

The result is based on the regional and culture settings of your system. Table 4.9 summarizes symbols you can use with the `ToString` method.

TABLE 4.9   Date Formatting Symbols with `ToString`

Symbol	Preview
D	Saturday, December 27, 2014
d	12/27/2014
T	10:02:35 PM
t	10:02 PM
F	Saturday, December 27, 2014 10:02:35 PM
f	Saturday, December 27, 2014 10:02 PM
G	12/27/2014 10:02:35 PM
g	12/27/2014 10:02 PM
s	2014-12-27T22:2:35
U	Saturday, December 27, 2014 10:02:35 PM
u	2014-12-27 22:2:35Z

`ToString` also recognizes date literals. The following is an example of how you can customize and write a date:

```
Console.WriteLine(Date.Today.ToString("dd/MM/yyyy"))
```

This code prints the current date in the day/month/year format. `System.DateTime` provides a plethora of other useful methods you can use for formatting dates. Such methods also return different data types, depending on the scenario in which they are used. Table 4.10 summarizes the most important methods, and you can inspect them at any time with IntelliSense and the Object Browser.

TABLE 4.10   Useful Methods for `System.DateTime`

Method	Description	Type Returned
`ToLocalTime`	Returns the full date representation according to regional settings.	`Date (System.DateTime)`
`ToLongDateString`	Returns a long-format date (without time).	`String`
`ToLongDateString`	Returns a long-format date (without time).	`String`
`ToShortDateString`	Returns a short-format date (without time).	`String`
`ToLongTimeString`	Returns a long-format time (without date).	`String`
`ToShortTimeString`	Returns a short-format time (without date).	`String`
`ToUniversalTime`	Returns a full date representation according to the Coordinated Universal Time specifications.	`Date (System.DateTime)`
`ToOADate`	Returns an OLE automation date format.	`Double`
`ToFileTime`	Returns the Windows file time representation of a date.	`Long`
`ToFileTimeUtc`	Returns the Windows file time representation of a date, according to the Coordinated Universal Time specifications.	`Long`

The following code snippet uses all the preceding methods to demonstrate how the output differs depending on the method:

```
Console.WriteLine("Local time: {0}", Date.Now.ToLocalTime)
Console.WriteLine("Long date: {0}", Date.Now.ToLongDateString)
Console.WriteLine("Short date: {0}", Date.Now.ToShortDateString)
Console.WriteLine("Long time: {0}", Date.Now.ToLongTimeString)
Console.WriteLine("Short time: {0}", Date.Now.ToShortTimeString)
Console.WriteLine("Universal time: {0}", Date.Now.
                 ToUniversalTime.ToString)
Console.WriteLine("File time: {0}", Date.Now.
                 ToFileTime.ToString)
Console.WriteLine("File time UTC: {0}", Date.Now.
```

```
                ToFileTimeUtc.ToString)
Console.WriteLine("OLE Automation date: {0}", Date.Now.
                ToOADate.ToString)
```

The preceding code produces the following result, which you can compare with the methods described in Table 4.9:

```
Local time: 05/28/2012 19:27:22

Local time: 12/27/2014 18:46:50
Long date: Saturday, December 27, 2014
Short date: 27/12/2014
Long time: 18:46:50
Short time: 18:46
Universal time: 27/12/2014 17:46:50
File time: 130641760107079387
File time UTC: 130641760107089384
OLE Automation date: 42000,7825313542
```

Subtracting Dates and Adding Time to Time

It's not unusual to need to know the amount of time spent between two dates. The System.DateTime enables you to find this by invoking a Subtract method, which returns a System.TimeSpan value. For example, consider the following code, which subtracts one date from another one:

```
Dim birthDate As Date = New Date(1977, 5, 10, 20, 30, 0)
Dim secondDate As Date = New Date(1990, 5, 11, 20, 10, 0)
Dim result As System.TimeSpan = secondDate.Subtract(birthDate)
'In days
Console.WriteLine(result.Days)
'In "ticks"
Console.WriteLine(result.Ticks)
```

You can subtract two DateTime objects and get a result of type TimeSpan (discussed next). You can then get information on the result, such as the number of days that represent the difference between the two dates or the number of ticks. The previous code produces the following result:

```
4748
4103124000000000
```

You can also add values to a date. For example, you can edit a date by adding days, hours, minutes, seconds, or ticks or by incrementing the year. Consider the following code snippet:

```
Dim editedDate As Date = birthDate.AddDays(3)
editedDate = editedDate.AddHours(2)
editedDate = editedDate.AddYears(1)
Console.WriteLine(editedDate)
```

This code adds three days and two hours to the date and increments the year by one unit. In the end, it produces the following output:

```
5/13/1978 10:30:00 PM
```

You can use negative numbers to subtract values from a single date, and you end up with a `Date` object instead of `TimeSpan`, as with `Subtract`. For instance, the following code subtracts a day from the date represented by the `birthDate` variable:

```
'Returns 05/09/1977
Dim result As Date = birthDate.AddDays(-1)
```

Dates are important and, although they allow you to work with time, too, the .NET Framework provides an important structure that is specific for representing pieces of time: `System.TimeSpan`.

OPERATORS

You can use standard operators such as the addition and subtraction operators when working with both `DateTime` and `TimeSpan` objects. This is possible because both objects overload the standard operators. Overloading operators is discussed in Chapter 11.

The `DateTimeOffset` Structure

The .NET Framework exposes another structure for working with dates: `System.DateTimeOffset`. This object behaves like `System.DateTime`, but it is all about the Coordinated Universal Time (UTC) standard. The `DateTimeOffset` object has almost the same members of the `DateTime` class, except that it does not expose methods for conversions to different date/time formats. This is because the purpose of `DateTimeOffset` is to record the exact date, time, and time zone when an event occurred. Following are examples of this structure:

```
Dim dateOffset As DateTimeOffset = DateTimeOffset.Now
'Print the specified date in the UTC standard's format
Console.WriteLine(dateOffset.UtcDateTime)
'Print the hh:mm:ss:mmss time in the current instance
Console.WriteLine(dateOffset.TimeOfDay.ToString)

'Create a new DateTimeOffset
Dim myDate As New DateTimeOffset(2015, 1, 18, 10, 0, 0, Nothing)
```

To understand where using `DateTimeOffset` is a more appropriate choice, you can refer to the following summary:

▶ If your business logic needs to record the time and date and time zone (or at least the time zone offset) at which an event occurred, then you should use `DateTimeOffset`.

▶ If your business logic needs to record the time and date but does not need to record the time zone, then `DateTime` is a perfectly fine choice.

▶ If every date and time in your business logic is in UTC, then you could invoke the `DateTime.ToUniversalTime` method on a date; this records exactly the same information as if you had a `DateTimeOffset` with its `Offset` set to 0h00.

The `DateTimeOffset` object is also very important when building Windows Store apps because built-in user controls that work with dates require objects of type `DateTimeOffset` instead of `DateTime`. The structure exposes a property called `Date`, which returns a `DateTime` representation of the current instance. `DateTimeOffset` is not new in the .NET Framework 4.6, but this version adds support to conversions to Unix time representation via the `ToUnixTimeMilliseconds` and `ToUnixTimeSeconds` methods.

Working with Time

You often need to represent intervals of time in your applications, especially in conjunction with dates. The .NET Framework provides a structure for this: a value type named `System.TimeSpan`. This structure can represent time from a minimum value (one tick) until a maximum value (one day). A *tick* is the smallest unit for time representations and is equal to 100 nanoseconds. `TimeSpan` represents a summed amount of time between two given time values, and the time portion of a `Date` object represents a single specific moment in time.

MINIMUM AND MAXIMUM VALUES

As for other value types, `System.TimeSpan` also provides two shared properties named `MinValue` and `MaxValue`. `MinValue` returns `-10675199.02:48:05.4775808`, and `MaxValue` returns `10675199.02:48:05.4775807`. For the sake of clarity, these values are equal to, respectively, `System.Int64.MinValue` and `System.Int64.MaxValue`.

You can find other cases in which `TimeSpan` is needed for something other than simply working with dates. For example, you might want to create performance benchmarks by using the `StopWatch` object, which returns a `TimeSpan`. Or you might need such structure when working with animations in WPF applications. The following code example simulates a performance test; a `System.StopWatch` object is started, an intensive loop is performed, and then the `StopWatch` is stopped. The `StopWatch` class offers an `Elapsed` property that is of type `TimeSpan` and can be useful for analyzing the amount of elapsed time:

```
Dim watch As New Stopwatch
watch.Start()
For i = 0 To 10000
    'Simulates intensive processing
    System.Threading.Thread.SpinWait(800000)
Next
watch.Stop()
Console.WriteLine(watch.Elapsed.Seconds)
Console.WriteLine(watch.Elapsed.Milliseconds)
Console.WriteLine(watch.Elapsed.Ticks)
```

The preceding code produced the following result on my machine, but it will be different on yours, depending on your hardware:

```
35
480
354800566
```

The `TimeSpan` structure is similar to the area of the `DateTime` type that is related to time. Notice that `TimeSpan` offers several similar properties, such as `Days`; `Hours`, `Minutes`, `Seconds`, and `Milliseconds`, and methods, such as `AddDays`, `AddHours`, `AddMinute`, and `Subtract`. `TimeSpan` is all about time; this means that although there are similarities, as mentioned before, with the time-related `DateTime` members, you cannot (obviously) work with dates. The following code provides an example of creating a `TimeSpan` instance starting from an existing date:

```
Sub TimeSpanInstance()
    Dim currentDate As Date = Date.Now
    'Because the System namespace is imported at project
    'level, we do not need an Imports directive
    Dim intervalOfTime As TimeSpan = currentDate.TimeOfDay
    Console.WriteLine("My friend, in the current date " &
                     "there are {0} days; time is {1}:{2}:{3}",
            intervalOfTime.Days,
            intervalOfTime.Hours,
            intervalOfTime.Minutes,
            intervalOfTime.Seconds)
End Sub
```

The preceding code produces the following result:

```
My friend, in the current date there are 0 days; time is 8:30
```

In the specified interval, there is only the current day, so the first argument returns zero. Take a look back at the section "Subtracting Dates and Adding Time to Time" to see an example of using `TimeSpan` for an interval of time retrieved by subtracting two dates.

Working with `TimeZone` and `TimeZoneInfo`

You might often wonder what people are doing on the other side of world when in your country it's a particular time of the day. Working with time zones can also be important for your business if you need to contact people who live in other countries. The .NET Framework provides two types, `TimeZone` and `TimeZoneInfo`, that enable you to retrieve information on time zones. Both types are exposed by the `System` namespace. For example, say that you want to retrieve information on the time zone of your country. This can be accomplished as follows (assuming that regional settings on your machine are effectively related to your country):

```
Dim zone As TimeZone = TimeZone.CurrentTimeZone
```

`TimeZone` is a reference type, and through its `CurrentTimeZone` property, it provides a lot of information, such as the name of the time zone or the Daylight Saving Time period, as demonstrated here:

```
Console.WriteLine(zone.DaylightName)
Console.WriteLine(zone.StandardName)
Console.WriteLine(zone.IsDaylightSavingTime(Date.Now))
```

This code produces the following result on my machine:

```
W. Europe Daylight Time
W. Europe Standard Time
True
```

The official MSDN documentation states that using the `TimeZoneInfo` class should be preferred over using `TimeZone`. This is because `TimeZoneInfo` also provides the ability to create custom time zones. The following code shows how you can retrieve current time zone information by using `TimeZoneInfo`:

```
Dim tz As TimeZoneInfo = TimeZoneInfo.Local
'Shows the current time zone Identifier
Console.WriteLine(tz.Id)
```

Creating a custom time zone is also a simple task, and you accomplish it by using the following code:

```
Dim customZone As TimeZoneInfo = TimeZoneInfo.
    CreateCustomTimeZone("CustomTimeZone",
    Date.UtcNow.Subtract(Date.Now),
    "Custom Zone", "Custom Zone")
```

You just need to specify a custom identifier, the difference between the UTC time span and the local time span, a daylight identifier, and a standard identifier. `TimeZoneInfo` also provides another useful method for enumerating time zones recognized by the system, named `GetSystemTimeZones`; you use it like this:

```
For Each timez As TimeZoneInfo In TimeZoneInfo.GetSystemTimeZones
    Console.WriteLine(timez.DisplayName)
Next
```

The following is an excerpt of the output provided by this simple iteration:

```
(UTC-12:00) International Date Line West
(UTC-11:00) Midway Island, Samoa
(UTC-10:00) Hawaii
(UTC-09:00) Alaska
(UTC-08:00) Pacific Time (US & Canada)
(UTC-08:00) Tijuana, Baja California
(UTC-07:00) Arizona
(UTC-07:00) Chihuahua, La Paz, Mazatlan
(UTC-07:00) Mountain Time (US & Canada)
(UTC-06:00) Central America
(UTC-06:00) Central Time (US & Canada)
(UTC-05:00) Eastern Time (US & Canada)
(UTC-05:00) Indiana (East)
(UTC-04:30) Caracas
(UTC-04:00) Santiago
(UTC-03:30) Newfoundland
(UTC-01:00) Cape Verde Is.
(UTC) Casablanca
(UTC) Coordinated Universal Time
(UTC) Dublin, Edinburgh, Lisbon, London
(UTC) Monrovia, Reykjavik
(UTC+01:00) Amsterdam, Berlin, Bern, Rome, Stockholm, Vienna
(UTC+02:00) Windhoek
(UTC+03:00) Baghdad
(UTC+03:00) Kuwait, Riyadh
(UTC+03:00) Moscow, St. Petersburg, Volgograd
(UTC+03:00) Nairobi
(UTC+06:00) Almaty, Novosibirsk
(UTC+06:00) Astana, Dhaka
(UTC+06:30) Yangon (Rangoon)
(UTC+07:00) Krasnoyarsk
(UTC+08:00) Beijing, Chongqing, Hong Kong, Urumqi
(UTC+08:00) Perth
(UTC+08:00) Taipei
(UTC+09:00) Yakutsk
(UTC+09:30) Adelaide
(UTC+10:00) Vladivostok
(UTC+11:00) Magadan, Solomon Is., New Caledonia
(UTC+12:00) Auckland, Wellington
(UTC+12:00) Fiji, Kamchatka, Marshall Is.
(UTC+13:00) Nuku'alofa
```

4

Thanks to this information, you could use the `TimeZoneInfo` class to convert between time zones. The following code demonstrates how to calculate the time difference, in hours, between Italy and Redmond, Washington:

```
'Redmond time; requires specifying the Time Zone ID
Dim RedmondTime As Date = TimeZoneInfo.
    ConvertTimeBySystemTimeZoneId(DateTime.Now, "Pacific Standard Time")
Console.WriteLine("In Italy now is {0} while in Redmond it is {1}",
                Date.Now.Hour,RedmondTime.Hour)
```

By invoking the `ConvertTimeBySystemZoneId` method, you can convert between your local system time and another time, based on the zone ID. If you don't know zone IDs, just replace the previous iterations for showing the content of the `timez.Id` property instead of `DisplayName`.

Working with GUIDs

How many times do you need to represent something with a unique identifier? Probably very often. Examples are items with the same name but different characteristics. The .NET Framework enables you to create unique identifiers via the `System.Guid` structure (which is a value type). This lets you generate a unique 128-bit string as an identifier. To generate a unique identifier, you invoke the `Guid.NewGuid` method, which works as follows:

```
'Declaring a Guid
Dim uniqueIdentifier As Guid
'A unique identifier
uniqueIdentifier = Guid.NewGuid
Console.WriteLine(uniqueIdentifier.ToString)
'Another unique identifier,
'although to the same variable
uniqueIdentifier = Guid.NewGuid
Console.WriteLine(uniqueIdentifier.ToString)
```

If you run the preceding code, you notice that each time you invoke the `NewGuid` method, a new GUID is generated, although you assign such a value to the same variable. This makes sense because you use the GUID each time you need a unique identifier. On my machine, the preceding code produces the following result:

```
46e0daca-db56-45b1-923e-f76cf1636019
6fd3a61d-ec17-4b6a-adec-6acfa9a0cb00
```

EXAMPLES OF GUIDS

The Windows operating system makes huge usage of GUIDs. If you try to inspect the Windows Registry, you'll find lots of examples.

The `Guid.NewGuid` method provides auto-generated GUIDs. If you need to provide your own GUID, you can use the `New` constructor followed by the desired identifier:

```
'Specifying a Guid
uniqueIdentifier = New Guid("f578c96b-5918-4f79-b690-6c463ffb2c3e")
```

The constructor has several overloads, which enable you to generate GUIDs also based on byte arrays and integers. Generally, you use GUIDs each time you need to represent something as unique. Several .NET types accept GUIDs, so you need to know how you can create them in code, although this is not the only way.

Creating GUIDs with the Visual Studio Instrumentation
The Visual Studio IDE provides a graphical tool for generating GUIDs. You can run this tool by selecting the Create GUID command from the Tools menu. Figure 4.11 shows the Create GUID window.

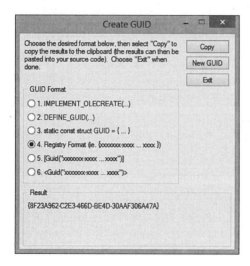

FIGURE 4.11   The Create GUID tool from Visual Studio.

You can choose the format you need for your GUID, such as Windows-like GUIDs. When you get your GUID, you can copy it to the clipboard and then reuse it in your code.

Working with Arrays
As a developer, you know what arrays are. And you know that you can use an array to store a set of items, generally of the same type. In the .NET Framework 4.6 (as in older versions), arrays are reference types all deriving from the `System.Array` class and can be both one-dimensional and multidimensional.

ARRAYS VERSUS COLLECTIONS

Collections, especially generic ones, are more efficient than arrays. I recommend working with collections instead of arrays, except when strictly needed. (For example, you might need jagged arrays.)

You can either declare an array and use it later in your code or declare it and assign it with objects. The following is an example of declaring an array of `String` objects, which means it can store only objects of type `String`:

```
Dim anArrayOfString() As String
```

This line of code declares an array of `String`. This array has no predefined bounds, so it is flexible and useful if you cannot predict how many items it needs to store. There is also an alternative syntax, which allows you to place parentheses at the end of the type, as follows:

```
'Alternative syntax
Dim anArrayOfString As String()
```

You are free to use either syntax. For the sake of consistency, the first one is used in this book.

IS `Option Strict` ON?

The preceding code examples and the following ones assume that `Option Strict` is set to `On`. If it is `Off`, adding instances of `System.Object` is also allowed but might cause errors at runtime. It is recommended that you set `Option Strict` to `On` to avoid implicit conversion, and this is one of those cases.

You can initialize arrays directly when declaring them, as in the following code, which declares an array of strings and stores three instances of the `System.String` class:

```
'Inline initialization with implicit bounds
Dim anArrayOfThreeStrings() As String = New String() {"One", "Two", "Three"}
```

Notice that you assign an array by using the `New` keyword followed by the type name and a couple parentheses. Brackets contain the items to store. The declared array has no bounds limits, but actually, after the assignment, its upper bound is 2, so its bounds are determined by the number of values it is initialized with.

ARRAYS BASE

Arrays are zero based. This means that an array with an upper bound of 2 can store three items (index of zero, index of one, and index of two). This also means that the upper bound will always be one less than the `Length` property of the array.

This approach works with arrays of other .NET types, too, as in the following code, which uses `Char` and `Byte`:

```
Dim anArrayOfChar() As Char = New Char() {"a"c, "b"c, "c"c}
Dim anArrayOfByte() As Byte = New Byte() {1, 2, 3}
```

If you already know how many items the array can store, you can specify the bounds limits. For example, say that you want to store three instances of `System.Byte` in an array of `Byte`. This can be accomplished via the following code:

```
Dim anExplicitBoundArrayOfByte(2) As Byte
anExplicitBoundArrayOfByte(0) = 1
anExplicitBoundArrayOfByte(1) = 2
anExplicitBoundArrayOfByte(2) = 3
```

INLINE INITIALIZATION WITH EXPLICIT BOUNDS

Inline initialization is not allowed against arrays declared with explicit bounds. In such situations, the only allowed syntax is that shown in the previous code snippet.

The upper limit is enclosed in parentheses. Storing items is accomplished through indices. (The first one is always zero.) As with assignment, you can retrieve the content of a particular item by using indices:

```
'Outputs 2
Console.WriteLine(anExplicitBoundArrayOfByte(1).ToString)
```

You can also perform tasks on each element in the array by using a `For Each` loop, as in the following code snippet, which works the same on an array of `Byte` and on array of `String`:

```
For Each value As Byte In anExplicitBoundArrayOfByte
    Console.WriteLine(value)
Next
For Each value As String In anArrayOfThreeStrings
    Console.WriteLine(value)
Next
```

Another important task you should perform when working with arrays that are not explicitly bound is to check whether they contain something. You can accomplish this by checking whether the array is `Nothing`:

```
If anArrayOfString Is Nothing Then
    'The array is not initialized
End If
```

This works because attempting to access a null array causes the Runtime to throw an exception.

The ReDim Keyword

In some situations, you need to increase the capacity of an array that you previously declared with explicit bounds. Let's look again one of the previous arrays:

```
Dim anExplicitBoundArrayOfByte(2) As Byte
anExplicitBoundArrayOfByte(0) = 1
anExplicitBoundArrayOfByte(1) = 2
anExplicitBoundArrayOfByte(2) = 3
```

At runtime you might need to store an additional `Byte`, and in this case, you should first increase the array's size. To accomplish this, the Visual Basic grammar provides a special keyword, `ReDim`. `ReDim` redeclares an array of the same type with new bounds. But this keyword also cleans all the previously stored items. So what if you just need to add a new item to an existing list, without clearing? Fortunately, the Visual Basic grammar provides another keyword, `Preserve`, that is the best friend of `ReDim` in such situations and enables you to maintain the previously stored values and prevent cleaning. The following code redeclares the preceding array without cleaning previous values:

```
ReDim Preserve anExplicitBoundArrayOfByte(3)
```

At this point, you can add a new item by using the new available index:

```
anExplicitBoundArrayOfByte(3) = 4
```

Notice that you do not specify again the type of the array when using `ReDim`.

Multidimensional Arrays

Arrays can have multiple dimensions. Two-dimensional (also known as *rectangular*) and three-dimensional arrays are the most common situations. The following code declares a two-dimensional array with four values but with no explicit dimensions specified:

```
Dim multiArray(,) As Integer = {{1, 2}, {3, 4}}
```

You can also specify dimensions as follows:

```
Dim multiArrayWithExplicitBounds(5, 1) As Integer
```

You cannot initialize arrays inline in the case of multidimensional arrays. You can then access indices as follows:

```
multiArrayWithExplicitBounds(1, 0) = 1
multiArrayWithExplicitBounds(2, 0) = 2
multiArrayWithExplicitBounds(1, 1) = 3
```

ARRAY LITERALS

Visual Basic offers a specific feature for working with both multidimensional arrays and jagged arrays (discussed next): array literals. This feature enables the compiler to infer the appropriate type for arrays. Because you need to be familiar with local type inference to understand array literals, array literals are discussed in Chapter 20.

Jagged Arrays

Jagged arrays are arrays of arrays and are similar to multidimensional arrays. However, they differ because each item of a dimension is an array. Here you see examples of jagged arrays of `Integer`. To declare a jagged array, you can use the following syntax:

```
'A 9-entry array on the left and
'an unbound array on the right
Dim firstJaggedArray(8)() As Integer
```

As you can see, a jagged array declaration is characterized by a double pair of parentheses. You can also declare a jagged array that is not explicitly bound, as in the following code snippet:

```
Dim unboundJaggedArray()() As Integer
```

Although you can perform inline initializations, this coding technique could become difficult with complex arrays. Therefore, it could be more convenient to declare the array and then assign its indices as follows:

```
Dim oneIntArray() As Integer = {1, 2, 3}
Dim twoIntArray() As Integer = {4, 5, 6}
unboundJaggedArray = {oneIntArray, twoIntArray}
```

By the way, the following initialization is perfectly legal:

```
Dim unboundJaggedArray()() As Integer _
    = {New Integer() {1, 2, 3}, New Integer() {4, 5, 6}}
```

As I explain in Chapter 20, array literals make inline initialization easier. You can then normally access arrays (that is, items) in a jagged array, for example, to perform a `For..Each` loop:

```
'Returns 1 2 3 4 5 6
        For Each arr As Integer() In unboundJaggedArray
            For Each item As Integer In arr
                Console.WriteLine(item.ToString)
            Next
        Next
```

Sorting, Creating, Copying, and Inspecting Arrays with the `System.Array` Class

As mentioned at the beginning of this section, all arrays derive from the `System.Array` class and therefore are reference types. This is an important consideration because you have to know how to manipulate them. `System.Array` provides several static and instance members for performing tasks on arrays. This section discusses the most important members and method overloads; they should be self-explanatory. IntelliSense can help by showing the necessary information. First, here's an example of an array of `Byte`:

```
Dim anArrayOfByte() As Byte = New Byte() {1, 2, 3}
```

In this array, bounds are not explicit. Particularly at runtime, you might need to access array indices. To avoid `IndexOutOfRange` exceptions, though, you need to know at least the upper bound. Just for clarification, say that you want to perform a `For..Next` loop against an array. To accomplish this, you first need to know the bounds. The `GetLowerBound` and `GetUpperBound` methods enable you to retrieve the lower and upper bounds of an array, as shown in the following code:

```
'Returns 0 and 2
Console.WriteLine($"Lower bound {anArrayOfByte.
GetLowerBound(0)},
upper bound {anArrayOfByte.GetUpperBound(0)}")
```

Both methods receive the dimension of the array as an argument. This is because they can work on both one-dimensional arrays and multidimensional arrays. A zero dimension means that you are working with a one-dimensional array or with the first dimension of a multidimensional array.

Another common task is sorting arrays. There are two methods you can use for this, `Sort` and `Reverse`. `Sort` performs an ordering of arrays in an ascending way, whereas `Reverse` performs the ordering in a descending way. Starting from the `anArrayOfByte` array, the following code reverses the order:

```
'Array now contains 3, 2, 1
Array.Reverse(anArrayOfByte)
```

To sort the array back, you can simply invoke the `Sort` method:

```
Array.Sort(anArrayOfByte)
```

Both methods perform ordering according to the `IComparable(Of T)` interface. You can also search for a particular item within an array. You can use two methods for this purpose: `IndexOf` and `BinarySearch`. Both return the index of the specified item, but the first one just stops searching when the first occurrence is found; the second one searches through the entire array, but only if the array is sorted according to the implementation of the `IComparable` interface. Their usage is very straightforward:

```
'A conversion to Byte is required
'Both return 1
Dim position As Integer = Array.IndexOf(anArrayOfByte, CByte(2))
Dim position2 As Integer = Array.BinarySearch(anArrayOfByte, CByte(2))
```

Both methods receive an `Object` as the second argument. But you have an array of `Byte`. Because just writing `2` tells the compiler to recognize such a number as an `Integer`, you need to explicitly convert it to `Byte`.

System.Array METHODS

System.Array also provides methods that take a lambda expression as arguments. Lambdas are discussed in Chapter 20, so this chapter does not explain how to apply them to arrays. A quick recap is done for your convenience in the appropriate place.

Another common task with arrays is copying. Because arrays are reference types, assigning an array to another just copies the reference. To create a real copy of an array, you can take advantage of the shared Copy method and the instance CopyTo method. First, you need to declare a target array. Continuing the example about the anArrayOfByte array, you could declare the new one as follows:

```
'Declares an array to copy to,
'with bounds equals to the source array
Dim targetArray(anArrayOfByte.GetUpperBound(0)) As Byte
```

To ensure that the upper bound is the same as in the original array, you invoke the GetUpperBound method. Next, you can copy the array:

```
'Copies the original array into the target,
'using the original length
Array.Copy(anArrayOfByte, targetArray, anArrayOfByte.Length)
```

Array.Copy needs you to pass the source array, the target array, and the total number of items you want to copy. If you want to perform a complete copy of the source array, you can just pass its length. The alternative is to invoke the instance method CopyTo:

```
anArrayOfByte.CopyTo(targetArray, 0)
```

The method receives the target array as the first argument and the index where copying must begin as the second argument. A third way to copy an array is to invoke the Clone method, which is inherited from System.Object. Note that Copy and CopyTo provide more granularity and control over the copy process. The last scenario creates arrays on-the-fly. You might need to perform such a task at runtime, given a number of items of a specified type—for example, when you receive several strings as user input. The System.Array class provides a shared method named CreateInstance, which creates a new instance of the System.Array class. It receives two arguments: the System.Type for the array and the upper bound. For example, the following code creates a new array of String that can store three elements:

```
Dim runTimeArray As Array = Array.CreateInstance(GetType(String), 2)
```

PAYING ATTENTION TO CreateInstance

You should use CreateInstance with care because you can write code that is correctly compiled but that can cause runtime errors (for example, with regard to array bounds).

Because the first argument is the representation of the `System.Type` you want to assign to the array, you must use the `GetType` keyword to retrieve information about the type. You can assign items to each index by invoking the `SetValue` method, which is an instance method. The following line of code assigns a string to the zero index of the previous array:

```
runTimeArray.SetValue(CStr("Test string"), 0)
```

If you want to retrieve your items, simply invoke the `GetValue` method, specifying the index:

```
'Returns "Test string"
Console.WriteLine(runTimeArray.GetValue(0))
```

Common Operators

When working with data types, there are several tasks you often need to perform on them. Depending on which type you work with, the Visual Basic programming language offers different kinds of operators, such as arithmetic operators, logical and bitwise operators, and shift operators. In this section you'll learn about Visual Basic operators and how you can use them in your own code. Let's begin by discussing arithmetic operators, which are probably the operators you will use most frequently.

Arithmetic Operators

Visual Basic 2015 provides some arithmetic operators, listed in Table 4.11.

TABLE 4.11   Arithmetic Operators

Operator	Description
+	Addition operator
–	Subtraction operator
*	Multiplication operator
/	Division operator
\	Integer division operator
^	Exponentiation operator
Mod	Integer division remainder

The first three operators are self-explanatory, so I would like to focus on the other ones. As shown in Table 4.11, Visual Basic offers two symbols, the slash (/) and backslash (\), for division. The first one can be used in divisions between floating-point numbers (such as `Double` and `Single` types), and the second can be used only in divisions between integer numbers. Using the backslash is fast when you're working with integers and truncates the result in case it is a floating-point number. The backslash accepts and returns just integers. To understand this concept, consider the following division between `Doubles`:

```
'Division between double: returns 2.5
Dim dblResult As Double = 10 / 4
```

The result of this calculation is 2.5. Now consider the following one:

```
'Division between integers: returns 2
Dim intResult As Integer = 10 \ 4
```

The result of this calculation is 2. This is because the \ operator truncates the result, due to its integer nature. If you try to use such operators in a division involving floating-point numbers, the Visual Basic compiler reports an error, which is useful for avoiding subtle logic errors. By the way, such an error is reported only with Option Strict On, which you should always set as your default choice.

SUPPORTED TYPES

The integer division operator supports the SByte, Byte, Short, UShort, Integer, UInteger, Long, and ULong data types, which are all numeric types that do not support floating-point numbers.

For divisions between floating-point numbers, it's worth mentioning that divisions between Single and Double are also allowed but cause the compiler to perform some implicit conversions that should be avoided. In such situations, you should just perform an explicit conversion, as in the following code:

```
'Division between Single and Double
Dim singleValue As Single = 987.654
Dim doubleValue As Double = 654.321
Dim division As Single = singleValue / CSng(doubleValue)
```

The next interesting operator is the exponentiation operator (^). A simple example follows:

```
Dim result As Double = 2 ^ 4  'returns 16
```

The exponentiation operator returns a Double value. Because of this, even if operands are other types (such as Integer or Long), they will always be converted to Double. Behind the scenes, the ^ operator invokes the Pow method exposed by the System.Math class. So you could also rewrite the preceding line of code as follows:

```
Dim result As Double = System.Math.Pow(2,4)  'returns 16
```

The last built-in operator is Mod (which stands for *modulus*), and it returns the remainder of a division between numbers. The following lines of code show an example:

```
'Mod: returns 0
Dim remainder As Integer = 10 Mod 2
'Mod: returns 1
Dim remainder As Integer = 9 Mod 2
```

A typical usage of Mod is for determining whether a number is odd or even. To accomplish this, you could create a function like the following:

```
Function IsOdd(number As Integer) As Boolean
  Return (number Mod 2) <> 0
End Function
```

If the remainder is different from zero, the number is odd and therefore returns True. Mod supports all numeric types, including unsigned types and floating-point ones. The .NET Framework offers another method for retrieving the remainder of a division, System.Math. IEEERemainnder, which works as follows:

```
'Double remainder
Dim dblRemainder As Double = System.Math.IEEERemainder(10.42, 5.12)
```

Although both Mod and IEEERemainder return the remainder of a division between numbers, they use different formulas behind the scenes. Thus, the results can differ. According to the MSDN documentation, this is the formula for the IEEERemainder method:

```
IEEERemainder = dividend - (divisor * Math.Round(dividend / divisor))
```

This is the formula for the modulus operator:

```
Modulus = (Math.Abs(dividend) - (Math.Abs(divisor) *
          (Math.Floor(Math.Abs(dividend) / Math.Abs(divisor))))) *
          Math.Sign(dividend)
```

You can see how calculations work differently, especially where modulus gets the absolute value for dividend and divisor.

System.Math CLASS

This section provides an overview of the arithmetic operators that are built in to the Visual Basic 2015 programming language. The System.Math class provides lots of additional methods for performing complex calculations, but they are beyond the scope of this chapter.

Assignment Operators

You can use the operators shown in the preceding section for incremental operations. Consider the following code:

```
Dim value As Double = 1
value += 1 'Same as value = value + 1
value -= 1 'Same as value = value - 1
value *= 2 'Same as value = value * 2
value /= 2 'Same as value = value / 2
```

```
value ^= 2 'Same as value = value ^ 2
Dim test As String = "This is"
test &= " a string" 'same as test = test & " a string"
```

You can abbreviate your code by using this particular form when performing operations or concatenations. Also note that that += assignment operator works on strings as well.

Logical, Bitwise, and Shift Operators

Visual Basic 2015 offers logical, bitwise, and shift operators. Logical operators are special operators that enable comparisons between Boolean values and return Boolean values. Bitwise and shift operators enable performing operations bit by bit. Next let's discuss both logical and bitwise operators.

Logical Operators

Visual Basic 2015 has eight logical/bitwise operators: Not, And, Or, Xor, AndAlso, OrElse, IsFalse, and IsTrue. In this section you'll learn about the first four; the other ones are covered in the next section. The first operator, Not, returns the opposite of the actual Boolean value. For example, the following lines of code return False because, although the 43 number is greater than 10, Not returns the opposite:

```
'Returns False
Dim result As Boolean = (Not 43 > 10)
```

Logical operators can also be used with reference types. For example, you can return the opposite of the result of a comparison between objects (see the section "Comparison Operators" for details):

```
Dim firstPerson As New Person
Dim secondPerson As New Person
'Returns True
result = (Not firstPerson Is secondPerson)
```

This code returns True; the comparison between firstPerson and secondPerson returns False because they point to two different instances of the Person class, but Not returns the opposite. The next operator is And, which compares two Boolean values or expressions and returns True if both values or expressions are True; otherwise, if at least one value is False, And returns False. Here is an example of And:

```
'Returns False
result = 10 > 15 And 30 > 15
'Returns True
result = 20 > 15 And 30 > 15
'Returns True
result = 20 > 15 And 15 = 15
```

And is also useful for comparing Boolean properties of objects or expressions that return a Boolean value. For example, say that you want to check whether the current operating system is Windows 8.1 Update 1 and the available physical memory is more than 3 giga-bytes, You could use the following code:

```
If My.Computer.Info.OSVersion = "6.3.9600" And
    My.Computer.Info.AvailablePhysicalMemory > 3072000000 Then
      'And evaluates *both* conditions
End If
```

Remember that And evaluates all conditions, so it returns True if all conditions return True; otherwise, it returns False. If you used AndAlso instead of And, the second condition is evaluated only if the first one is True; otherwise, the code returns False without evaluating the second condition. The next operator is Or. This operator works as follows: If expressions or values are True, it returns True; if both are False, it returns False; and if one of the two expressions is True, it returns True. The following code demonstrates this scenario:

```
'Returns True
result = 10 > 15 Or 30 > 15
'Returns True
result = 10 < 15 Or 30 > 15
'Returns False
result = 10 > 15 Or 30 < 15
```

Or, like And, evaluates all the conditions. OrElse, on the other hand, evaluates one condition at a time. The last operator is Xor (which stands for *exclusive or*). This operator compares two Boolean expressions (or values) and returns True only if one of the two expressions is True; in all other cases, it returns False. Continuing the first example, Xor returns the values described inside comments:

```
'Returns True
result = 10 > 15 Xor 30 > 15
'Returns False
result = 20 > 15 Xor 30 > 15
'Returns False
result = 20 > 15 Xor 15 = 15
```

Short-Circuiting Operators

Sometimes you do not need to perform the evaluation of the second expression in a Boolean comparison because evaluating the first one provides the result you need. In such scenarios, you can use two *short-circuiting operators,* AndAlso and OrElse. *Short-circuiting* means that code execution is shorter and performance is improved. Such operators are particularly useful when you need to invoke an external method from within an If..Then code block. Consider the following example, which checks whether a file exists and deter-mines its size, with the And operator:

```
If My.Computer.FileSystem.FileExists("C:\MyFile.txt") = True And
    My.Computer.FileSystem.ReadAllText("C:\MyFile.txt").Length > 0 Then
        'Valid file
End If
```

The Visual Basic compiler performs both evaluations. What happens if the file does not exist? It throws a `FileNotFoundException` when the `ReadAllText` method is invoked because the `And` operator requires both expressions to be evaluated. You should implement error-handling routines for such code, but this example is related just to operators. You can prevent your code from encountering the previously described problem by using `AndAlso`. You need to replace `And` with `AndAlso`, as in the following code:

```
If My.Computer.FileSystem.FileExists("C:\MyFile.txt") = True AndAlso
My.Computer.FileSystem.ReadAllText("C:\MyFile.txt").Length > 0 Then
        'Valid file
    End If
```

`AndAlso` evaluates the first expression; if this returns `False`, the second expression is not evaluated at all. In this case, if the file does not exist, the code exits from the `If` block. `AndAlso`'s counterpart is `OrElse`, which evaluates the second expression only when the first one is `False`. Finally, Visual Basic has two other operators, named `IsTrue` and `IsFalse`. The first one works in conjunction with the `OrElse` operator, while the second works with `AndAlso`. You cannot explicitly invoke these operators in your code because it is the job of the Visual Basic compiler to invoke them within an evaluation expression. This means that the types you want to be evaluated via `OrElse` or `AndAlso` must expose both of them. The following is a simple example:

```
Public Structure myType
    Public Shared Operator IsFalse(value As myType) As Boolean
        Dim result As Boolean
        ' Insert code to calculate IsFalse of value.
        Return result
    End Operator
    Public Shared Operator IsTrue(value As myType) As Boolean
        Dim result As Boolean
        ' Insert code to calculate IsTrue of value.
        Return result
    End Operator
End Structure
```

Bitwise Operators

Performing bitwise operations means performing operations with two binary numbers, bit by bit. The problem here is that Visual Basic does not allow you to work directly with binary numbers, so you need to write code against decimal or hexadecimal numbers that the Visual Basic compiler will actually treat, behind the scenes, in their binary representation. However, you still need to write them in a comprehensible way.

CONVERTING BETWEEN DECIMAL AND BINARY

You can use the Windows Calculator in scientific mode to perform conversions between decimal/hexadecimal and binary numbers.

The bitwise operators in Visual Basic are still And, Or, Not, and Xor. Unlike logical operations, though, in which the operators evaluate expressions, bitwise operations are related to bit manipulations. You might wonder why you would need to perform bitwise operations in the era of WPF, Universal apps, and other high-level technologies. You could get multiple answers to this question, but the most useful one is probably that some applications interact with hardware devices in a bit-by-bit fashion. Another common situation in Visual Basic is the combination of Enum flags. Let's look at some examples. The And operator combines two operands into a result. Inside such a result, it places a 1 value where both operands have 1 in a particular position; otherwise, it places a 0. For example, consider the following code:

```
Dim result As Integer = 152 And 312
```

The binary counterpart of 152 is 10011000, whereas the binary counterpart of 312 is 100111000. The result variable's value is 24, whose binary counterpart is 11000. Observe the following representation:

```
 10011000
100111000
    11000
```

Notice that the third line, which represents the result of the And operation, contains 1 only in positions in which both operands have 1. If you then convert the result back to a decimal number, you get 24. The Or operator works similarly: It combines two operands into a result; inside such a result, it places a 1 value if at least one of the operands has a 1 value in a particular position. Consider this code:

```
Dim result As Integer = 152 Or 312
```

Both the 152 and 312 binary counterparts are the same as in the previous example. The Or operator produces 110111000 as a binary output, and the decimal counterpart is 440. To understand this step, take a look at this comparison:

```
 10011000
100111000
110111000
```

It's easy to see that the result contains 1 where at least one of the operands contains 1 in a particular position. The Xor operator combines two operands into a result; inside the result, it places a 1 value if at least one of the operands has a 1 value in a particular position, but not if both have 1 in that position. (In such a case, it places 0.) Consider this bitwise operation:

```
Dim result As Integer = 152 Xor 312
```

The 152 and 312 binary counterparts are the same as in the preceding example. But this line of code returns `416`, whose binary counterpart is 110100000. So let's see what happened:

```
 10011000
100111000
110100000
```

As you can see, `Xor` placed `1` where at least one of the operands has 1 in a particular position, but where both operands have 1, it placed `0`. The `Not` operator is probably the easiest to understand. It just reverses the bits of an operand into a result value. For example, consider this line of code:

```
Dim result As Integer = Not 312
```

In the following comparison, the second line is the result of the preceding negation:

```
100111000
011000111
```

This result has -313 as its decimal counterpart.

BINARY NUMBERS

This book does not teach binary numbers, so the code shown in this section and in the following one assumes that you are already familiar with binary representations of decimal numbers.

Shift Operators

Like bitwise operators, shift operators also make more sense with binary numbers than with decimal or hexadecimal numbers, although you need to provide them via their decimal representations. With shift operators, you can move (that is, shift) a binary representation left or right the specified number of positions. The left-shift operator is `<<`, and the right-shift operator is `>>`. For example, consider the following `Integer`:

```
'Binary counterpart is
'101000100
Dim firstValue As Integer = 324
```

The binary representation for 324 is 101000100. At this point, suppose you want to left-shift the binary by four positions. The following code accomplishes this:

```
'Returns 5184, which is
'1010001000000
Dim leftValue As Integer = firstValue << 4
```

With the left-shifting by four positions, the number 101000100 produces 1010001000000 as a result. This binary representation is the equivalent of the 5184 decimal number, which is the actual value of the `leftValue` variable. The right-shift operator works the same but moves positions on the right:

```
'Returns 20, which is
'10100
Dim rightValue As Integer = firstValue >> 4
```

This code moves 101000100 for four positions to the right, so the binary result is 10100. Its decimal equivalent is then 20, which is the actual value of the `rightValue` variable.

SUPPORTED TYPES

Shift operators support `Byte`, `Short`, `Integer`, `Long`, `SByte`, `UShort`, `UInteger`, and `ULong` data types. When you use shift operators with unsigned types, there is no sign bit to propagate; therefore, the vacated positions are set to zero.

The Ternary `If` Operator

The ternary `If` operator allows you to evaluate conditions on-the-fly. With this operator, you can evaluate a condition and return the desired value either in case the condition is `True` or if it is `False`. The `If` operator allows evaluations over three operands or two operands. Let's start by looking at evaluations over three operands. Imagine that you have a `Person` class exposing both `FirstName` and `LastName` string properties and that you want to verify that an instance of the `Person` class is not `Nothing` and, subsequently, that its `LastName` properties are initialized. The following code shows how you can accomplish the first task (see the comments):

```
Sub EvaluatePerson(p As Person)
    'Check if p (a Person instance) is Nothing
    'If it is Nothing, returns False else True
    'The result is returned as a delegate
    Dim checkIfNull = If(p Is Nothing, False, True)

    'If False, p is Nothing, therefore
    'throws an exception
    If checkIfNull = False Then
        Throw New ArgumentNullException("testPerson")
    End If

End Sub
```

As you can see, the `If` operator receives three arguments: The first one is the condition to evaluate; the second is the result to return if the condition is `True`; the third is the result to return if the condition is `False`. In this specific example, if the `Person` instance is null, the code returns `False`; otherwise, it returns `True`. The result of this code is assigned to a Boolean variable (`checkIfNull`) that contains the result of the evaluation. If the result is

`False`, the code throws an `ArgumentNullException`. You could write the preceding code in a simpler way, as follows:

```
If p Is Nothing Then
    'do something
Else
    Throw New ArgumentNullException
End If
```

The difference is that, with the ternary operator, you can perform inline evaluations. Now it's time to check whether the `LastName` property was initialized. The following code snippet shows an example that returns a `String` instead of a `Boolean` value:

```
Dim executeTest = If(String.IsNullOrEmpty(p.LastName) = True,
                    "LastName property is empty",
                    "LastName property is initialized")
```

The explanation is simple: If the `LastName` property is an empty string or a null string, the code returns a message saying that the property is empty. Otherwise, it returns a message saying that the property has been correctly initialized. You could rewrite the code in the classic fashion, as follows:

```
If String.IsNullOrEmpty(p.LastName) = True Then
    'LastName property is empty
Else
    'LastName property is initialized
End If
```

The following lines show how you can test the preceding code:

```
'Throws an ArgumentNullException
EvaluatePerson(Nothing)
'A message says that the LastName property is initialized
Dim p1 As New Person
p1.LastName = "Del Sole"
EvaluatePerson(p1)
```

The `If` operator also allows evaluations over two operands. In this scenario, the first operand is an expression that is evaluated to determine whether it is `Nothing` or not (either a reference type or nullable type). If it is not `Nothing`, the expression is simply returned as the result of the evaluation. If it is `Nothing`, `If` returns the expression in the second operand. The following code demonstrates how to check whether an instance of a `Person` class is `Nothing` and, if so, how to return a new instance:

```
Dim p As Person 'p has value of Nothing
'The following evaluates that "p" has value of Nothing
'then returns the result of New Person
Dim check As Person = If(p, New Person)
```

The ternary `If` operator is very useful for inline evaluations, and you will use it many times with LINQ queries and lambda expressions, as described in Chapter 20.

Concatenation Operators

As in the previous versions, Visual Basic 2015 still offers concatenation operators: the `+` and `&` symbols. The main difference between them is that the `+` symbol is intended for numeric additions, although it can also work with strings; the `&` symbol is defined only for strings, and it should be preferred when concatenating strings so that you can avoid possible errors. Listing 4.2 shows an example of concatenation.

LISTING 4.2   Concatenation Operators

```
Module ConcatenationOperators
    Sub ConcatenationDemo()
        Dim firstString As String = "Alessandro"
        Dim secondString As String = "Del Sole"
        Dim completeString As String = firstString & secondString
        'The following still works but should be avoided
        'Dim completeString As String = firstString + secondString
    End Sub
End Module
```

Using the `&` operator for string concatenation is very important, especially with interoperation with other languages, such as C#. For example, consider the following concatenation in C#:

```
string s = "One = " + 1;
```

In C#, `+` implicitly converts the integer `1` to the string `"1"` and concatenates. In Visual Basic, here is the same concatenation:

```
Dim s As String = "One = " + 1
```

In this case, the compiler tries to convert the string `"One = "` to an integer and fails at runtime, forcing you to manually convert the integer `1` to a string by either calling `ToString` or using the `CStr` operator. If you use `&`, you get the C# behavior where the integer operand is converted to a string.

Comparison Operators

Like its predecessors, Visual Basic 2015 still defines some comparison operators. Typically, comparison operators are of three kinds: numeric operators, string operators, and object operators. Let's see these operators in detail.

Numeric Comparison Operators

You can compare numeric values by using the operators listed in Table 4.12.

TABLE 4.12   Numeric Comparison Operators

Operator	Description
=	Equality operator
<>	Inequality operator
<	Less than
>	Greater than
<=	Less than or equal to
>=	Greater than or equal to

These operators return a Boolean value that is `True` or `False`. The following code snippet shows an example (comments within the code contain the Boolean value returned):

```
Sub NumericOperators()
    Dim firstNumber As Double = 3
    Dim secondNumber As Double = 4
    Dim comparisonResult As Boolean = False
    'False
    comparisonResult = (firstNumber = secondNumber)
    'True
    comparisonResult = (secondNumber > firstNumber)
    'False
    comparisonResult = (secondNumber <= firstNumber)
    'True
    comparisonResult = (secondNumber <> firstNumber)
End Sub
```

String Comparison Operators

String comparison is discussed in the section "Working with Strings," earlier in this chapter.

Objects Comparison Operators: `Is`, `IsNot`, and `TypeOf`

You can compare two or more objects to understand whether they point to the same instance or what type of object you are working with. The three operators for comparing objects are `Is`, `IsNot`, and `TypeOf`. `Is` and `IsNot` are used to understand whether two objects point to the same instance. Consider the following code:

```
Dim firstPerson As New Person
Dim secondPerson As New Person
'Returns True, not same instance
If firstPerson IsNot secondPerson Then
```

```
End If
'Returns False, not same instance
If firstPerson Is secondPerson Then
End If
'Returns True, same instance
Dim onePerson As Person = secondPerson
If secondPerson Is onePerson Then
End If
```

`firstPerson` and `secondPerson` are two different instances of the `Person` class. In the first comparison, `IsNot` returns `True` because they are two different instances. In the second comparison, `Is` returns `False` because they are still two different instances. In the third comparison, the result is `True` because you might remember that simply assigning a reference type just copies the reference to an object. In this case, both `secondPerson` and `onePerson` point to the same instance. The last example is related to the `TypeOf` operator. Typically, you use it to understand whether a particular object has inheritance relationships with another one. Consider the following code snippet:

```
'Returns True
Dim anotherPerson As Object = New Person
If TypeOf anotherPerson Is Person Then
End If
```

Here there is an `anotherPerson` object of type `Object`, assigned with a new instance of the `Person` class. (This is possible because `Object` can be assigned with any .NET type.) The `TypeOf` comparison returns `True` because `anotherPerson` is effectively an instance of `Person` (and not simply `Object`). `TypeOf` is useful if you need to check for the data type of a Windows Forms or WPF control. For example, a `System.Windows.Controls.Button` control in WPF inherits from `System.Windows.Controls.FrameworkElement`, and then `TypeOf x is FrameworkElement` and returns `True`. In Visual Basic 2015, `TypeOf` supports the `IsNot` operand. In the new version of the language, you are finally allowed to write a construct like this:

```
If TypeOf anotherPerson IsNot Person Then
End If
```

The previous versions allowed only this form:

```
If Not TypeOf anotherPerson Is Person Then
End If
```

This is definitely a nice addition that helps you write code in a more logical way.

OPERATOR PRECEDENCE ORDER

Visual Basic operators have a precedence order. For further information, refer to the MSDN Library, at http://msdn.microsoft.com/en-us/library/fw84t893(v=vs.120).aspx.

The Null-Conditional Operator: A First Look

Visual Basic 2015 introduces a new important language feature: the null-conditional operator. It gives you a more elegant and efficient way to check for null values (Nothing) before using an object. Due to its importance and to the different types of objects you can use it with, the null-conditional operator is discussed in many chapters of this book. This chapter provides an introduction to this operator. Other examples and explanations will be provided after you get the knowledge you need about specific topics, such as nullable types, to understand how you can use the new operator with value types. With plain types, it is represented by the ?. symbols. To get a taste of how it works, consider the following code:

```
Public Class Person
    Public Property FirstName As String
    Public Property LastName As String
    Public Property Address As PhysicalAddress
End Class

Public Class PhysicalAddress
    Public Property Country As String
    Public Property ZipCode As String
    Public Property City As String
End Class
```

This is a very basic implementation of the Person class, whose Address property is of type PhysicalAddress, another simple class that stores information about the place that a person lives. Now suppose you have the following instances:

```
Dim onePerson As New Person
onePerson.FirstName = "Alessandro"
onePerson.LastName = "Del Sole"

Dim address As New PhysicalAddress
address.ZipCode = "26100"
address.City = "Cremona"

onePerson.Address = address
```

The code for assigning the PhysicalAddress.Country property is intentionally missing, so it is therefore a null string. Say that you want to check whether the value of this property is null. Before Visual Basic 2015, you could use an If..IsNot Nothing construct like this:

```
If onePerson.Address.Country IsNot Nothing Then
    Dim country = onePerson.Address.Country
End If
```

Alternatively, you could use the `If` operator to check for a condition inline, as shown in the following code, which returns a default string if the checked property is null or the property value if it is not null:

```
Dim country As String = If(onePerson.Address.Country Is Nothing,
                        "Country is missing",
                        onePerson.Address.Country)
```

Again, you can use the two-operand `If` version, where the second operand is evaluated if the first one has a value of `Nothing`:

```
Dim country As String = If(onePerson.Address.Country, "Country is missing")
```

In Visual Basic 2015, you can simply write this:

```
Dim country As String = onePerson.Address?.Country
```

So the `?.` operator simplifies the way you can check for nulls. It basically checks whether the object placed before the question mark is null.

Before we look at details about its internals, let's go with another example. `?.` can work in a sequence, which makes it easier to check for nulls on objects and their members. The preceding code is very simple and assumes that an instance of `PhysicalAddress` is created and assigned to `onePerson.Address`. Now consider the following definition, where `onePerson.Address` is not assigned and therefore is `Nothing`:

```
Dim onePerson As New Person
onePerson.FirstName = "Alessandro"
onePerson.LastName = "Del Sole"
```

The correct approach here is to first check that `onePerson` is not null and then check that `onePerson.Address` is not null and use its members if they are not null. In previous versions of the language, you had to write a nested check like this:

```
If onePerson IsNot Nothing Then
    If onePerson.Address IsNot Nothing Then
        If onePerson.Address.Country IsNot Nothing Then
            Dim country As String = onePerson.Address.Country
        End If
    End If
End If
```

Or, with the `If` operator, you could use this:

```
'check if onePerson is null. If so, create a new one
Dim newPerson = If(onePerson Is Nothing,
    New Person With {.FirstName = "Alessandro",
    .LastName = "Del Sole"}, onePerson)
```

```
'Assuming you do some work with newPerson here...

'Check if Address if null. If so, assign a string
Dim country As String = If(newPerson.Address Is Nothing,
                           "Country is missing",
     newPerson.Address.Country)
```

Now, in Visual Basic 2015, you can use a sequence of ?. operators as follows:

```
Dim country As String = onePerson?.Address?.Country
```

This code tells the compiler the following: "Check whether onePerson is null. If it is null, just return Nothing. Then check whether Address is null. If it is null, just return Nothing. If it is not null, check whether Address.Country is null. If it is null, just return Nothing. If it is not null, assign its value to the country variable." If the ?. operator encounters a null object, it simply returns Nothing for reference types. For value types, the behavior is different (as described in Chapter 14).

> **NOTE**
>
> When the ?. operator is used to check for multiple null values over a sequence (such as onePerson?.Address?.Country), it is also referred to as a null-propagating operator, because the null check propagates over the sequence. You will find many references to the null-propagating name in the next chapter, so this is important to clarify.

This operator actually performs a short-circuiting operation, where it returns if the first condition (the check for null) is True. Notice that any null values used by the ?. operator return Nothing, while any null values used by the . operator throw a NullReferenceException, which is the normal behavior. You can also use the ?. operator with conditional code blocks; these are discussed in more detail in the next section, but the sample code is very easy. For instance, the following code takes the city name only if it starts with the letter *C*:

```
If onePerson?.Address?.City?.StartsWith("C") Then
    Dim city As String = onePerson.Address.City
End If
```

In this sequence, the ?. operator first checks whether onePerson is not null. If it is not null, it then checks whether Address is not null. If it is not, it then checks whether City is not null. Finally, if City is not null, it checks whether its name starts with *C*. If any objects are null, the ?. operator returns Nothing. This operator also works with method invocations. For example, in the following code, the GetType method is invoked only if both onePerson and Address are not Nothing:

```
'Invokes GetType only if both onePerson and Address
'are not null
Dim actualType As Type = onePerson?.Address?.GetType()
```

If either `onePerson` or `Address` (or both) is null, the operator returns `Nothing`. The null-conditional operator also works with arrays. For instance, the following code returns the first item from an array of strings only if it is not null:

```
'Returns the first item in the array
'only if it is not null
Dim firstItem As String = anArray?(0)
```

When working with arrays, you use the `?(x)` syntax, without the dot, where `x` is the index. More generally, you use this syntax with any object that supports indexing, including collections (described in Chapter 16). This is a very an important addition to the Visual Basic language that will definitely help you write much cleaner and more elegant code.

Iterations, Loops, and Conditional Code Blocks

Hundreds of programming techniques are based on loops and iterations. Both loops and iterations enable the repetition of some actions for a specific number of times or when a particular condition is `True` or `False`. All these cases are discussed next.

Iterations

Iterations in Visual Basic 2015 are performed via the `For..Next` and `For Each` loops. Let's analyze them more in detail.

For..Next

A `For..Next` loop enables you to repeat the same action (or group of actions) a finite number of times. The following code shows an example in which the same action (writing to the Console window) is performed 10 times:

```
For i As Integer = 1 To 10
    Console.WriteLine("This action has been repeated {0} times", i)
Next
```

In such loops, you need to define a variable of a numeric type (`i` in the preceding example) that acts as a counter.

TIP

You can also assign the variable with another variable of the same type instead of assigning a numeric value.

The previous code produces the following result:

```
This action has been repeated 1 times
This action has been repeated 2 times
This action has been repeated 3 times
This action has been repeated 4 times
```

```
This action has been repeated 5 times
This action has been repeated 6 times
This action has been repeated 7 times
This action has been repeated 8 times
This action has been repeated 9 times
This action has been repeated 10 times
```

Note that you can also initialize the counter with zero or with any other numeric value.

> **TIP**
>
> You can use the `Integer` or `UInteger` variables as counters in `For..Next` loops. This is because these data types are optimized for the Visual Basic compiler. Other numeric types are also supported but are not optimized, so you are encouraged to always use `Integer` or `UInteger`.

You can also decide how a counter must be incremented. For example, you could decide to increment a counter by two units instead of one (as in the previous example). This can be accomplished via the `Step` keyword:

```
For i As Integer = 1 To 10 Step 2
    Console.WriteLine("Current value is {0}", i)
Next
```

This code produces the following output:

```
Current value is 1
Current value is 3
Current value is 5
Current value is 7
Current value is 9
```

`Step` can also work with negative numbers and lets you perform a going-back loop:

```
For i As Integer = 10 To 1 Step -2
    Console.WriteLine("Current value is {0}", i)
Next
```

You can also decide to break a `For` loop when a particular condition is satisfied and you do not need to continue performing the iteration. This can be accomplished with the `Exit For` statement, as shown in the following example:

```
For i As Integer = 1 To 10
    Console.WriteLine("Current value is {0}", i)
    If i = 4 Then Exit For
Next
```

In the preceding example, when the counter reaches 4, the For loop is interrupted, and control is returned to the code that immediately follows the Next keyword. There is another way to control a For loop that you use, for example, when you need to pass control directly to the next iteration of the loop when a particular condition is satisfied (which is the opposite of Exit For). This can be accomplished with the Continue For statement, as shown in the following code snippet:

```
For i As Integer = 1 To 10
    If i = 4 Then  'Ignore the 4 value
        i += 1 'Increments to 5
        Continue For  'Continues from next value, that is 6
    End If
    Console.WriteLine("Current value is  {0}", i)
Next
```

In this example, you are doing some edits on the counter. Notice that each time you invoke a Continue For, the counter is incremented one unit.

For Each

A For Each loop allows you to perform an action or a group of actions on each item from an array or a collection. Although collections are discussed in Chapter 16, I provide a code example with them here because this is the typical usage of a For Each loop:

```
'A collection of Process objects
Dim procList As List(Of Process) = Process.GetProcesses.ToList
For Each proc As Process In procList
    Console.WriteLine(proc.ProcessName)
    Console.WriteLine("      " & proc.Id)
Next
```

This code snippet contains references to all the running processes on the machine. Each process is represented by an instance of the System.Diagnostics.Process class; therefore, List(Of Process) is a collection of processes. If you want to retrieve some information for each process, such as the name and the identification number, you can iterate the collection by using a For Each statement. You need to specify a variable (also known as a *control variable*) that is the same type as the item you are investigating. In the preceding code, you are just performing reading operations, but you can also edit items' properties. For example, you might have a collection of Person objects and could retrieve and edit information for each Person in the collection, as in the following code:

```
'A collection of Person objects
Dim people As New List(Of Person)
'Populate the collection here..
'....
For Each p As Person In people
    p.LastName = "Dr. " & p.LastName
    Console.WriteLine(p.LastName)
Next
```

This code will add the `Dr.` prefix to the `LastName` property of each `Person` instance.

For Each AVAILABILITY

Behind the scenes, `For Each` can be used against objects that implement the `IEnumerable` or `IEnumerable(Of T)` interfaces. Such objects expose the enumerator that provides support for `Each` iterations.

You can still use `Exit For` when you need to break out from a `For Each` statement. A `For Each` loop has better performance with collections than with arrays, but you can use it in both scenarios.

ITERATORS

Visual Basic 2015 has a feature called *iterators*. With iterators, you can return elements from a collection or an array to the caller code while the iteration is still in progress; then those elements can be used by the caller without having to wait for the iteration to be completed. Iterators are typically used with collections, so this feature is discussed in Chapter 16.

Loops

As in the previous versions of the language, Visual Basic 2015 offers two kinds of loops: `Do..Loop` and `While..End While`. This section describes them both.

Do..Loop

The `Do..Loop` is the most frequently used loop in Visual Basic, and it's also the most flexible. This loop can have two behaviors: repeating a set of actions until a condition is false and repeating a set of actions until a condition is true. The first scenario is accomplished by using a `Do While` statement, as demonstrated in Listing 4.3.

LISTING 4.3   Performing a `Do While` Loop

```
Sub LoopWhileDemo()
    Dim max As Integer = 0
    Do While max < Integer.MaxValue
        max += 1
        'Do something else here
        If max = 7000000 Then Exit Do
    Loop
    Console.WriteLine("Done: " & max.ToString)
End Sub
```

The code is quite easy to understand: Whereas the value of `max` is less than the maximum value of the `Integer` type, the code increments `max` by one unit. `Do While` evaluates a `False` condition. (The loop goes on because `max` is less than `Integer.MaxValue`.) The code also demonstrates how you can exit a loop by using an `Exit Do` statement. This passes the control to the next statement after the `Loop` keyword. The other scenario is when you need to evaluate a `True` condition. This can be accomplished via a `Do Until` loop. Listing 4.4 demonstrates this.

LISTING 4.4   Demonstrating a `Do..Until` Loop

```
Sub LoopUntilDemo()
    Dim max As Integer = 0
    Do Until max = Integer.MaxValue
        max += 1
        If max = 7000000 Then Exit Do
    Loop
    Console.WriteLine("Done: " & max.ToString)
End Sub
```

The difference here is that the loop ends when the condition is `True`—that is, when the value of `max` equals the value of `Integer.MaxValue`. As before, `Exit Do` can end the loop. The interesting thing in both cases is that you can evaluate the condition on the `Loop` side instead of the `Do` side. Listing 4.5 shows how you could rewrite both examples.

LISTING 4.5   Evaluating Conditions on the Loop Line

```
'Loop is executed at least once
Sub LoopUntilBottomDemo()
    Dim max As Integer = 0
    Do
        max += 1
        If max = 7000000 Then Exit Do
    Loop Until max = Integer.MaxValue
    Console.WriteLine("Done: " & max.ToString)
End Sub
'Loop is executed at least once
Sub LoopWhileBottomDemo()
    Dim max As Integer = 0
    Do
        max += 1
        If max = 7000000 Then Exit Do
    Loop While max < Integer.MaxValue
    Console.WriteLine("Done: " & max.ToString)
End Sub
```

Both loops behave the same way as previous ones, with one important difference: Here the loop is executed at least once.

While..End While

A `While..End While` loop performs actions when a condition is `False`. Listing 4.6 shows an example.

LISTING 4.6 `While..End While` Loop

```
Sub WhileEndWhileDemo()
    Dim max As Integer = 0
    While max < Integer.MaxValue
        max += 1
        If max = 7000000 Then Exit While
    End While
    Console.WriteLine("Done: " & max.ToString)
End Sub
```

The loop behaves the same as `Do While` because both evaluate the same condition.

Conditional Code Blocks

If..Then..Else

`If..Then..Else` is the most classical block for conditionally executing actions. An `If` evaluates an expression as `True` or `False` and, according to this, allows you to specify actions that should take place. Listing 4.7 shows an example.

LISTING 4.7 Demonstrating the `If..Then..Else` Block

```
Sub IfThenElseDemo()
    Console.WriteLine("Type a number")
    'Assumes users type a valid number
    Dim number As Double = CDbl(Console.ReadLine)
    If number >= 100 Then
        Console.WriteLine("Your number is greater than 100")
    ElseIf number < 100 AndAlso number > 50 Then
        Console.WriteLine("Your number is less than 100 and greater than 50")
    Else
        'General action
        Console.WriteLine("Your number is: {0}", number)
    End If
End Sub
```

`If` checks whether the condition is `True`; if it is, `If` takes the specified action. You can also specify to evaluate a condition for `False` (for example, `If something = False Then`). You can also use an `ElseIf` to delimit the condition evaluation. If no expression satisfies the condition, the `Else` statement provides an action that will be executed in such a situation.

> **CODING TIP**
>
> The Visual Studio IDE offers a useful feature known as *code block delimiters selection*. Because you can nest different `If..Then` blocks or can have a long code file, when you place the cursor near either the `If` or `Then` keyword or the `End If` statement, the IDE highlights the related delimiter (`End If`, if you place the cursor on an `If`, and vice versa).

Notice that the code uses an `AndAlso` operator to evaluate the condition. You can use other operators such as logical and short-circuit operators as well. Another typical example is checking whether a condition is `False` by using the `Not` operator. The following is an example:

```
If Not number >= 100 Then
    'Number is False
End If
```

`Not` also requires the same syntax when working with reference types, but in this case, you can also use the `IsNot` operator. The following example checks whether the instance of the `Person` class is not null:

```
Dim p As Person  'p is actually null
'You can check with IsNot
If p IsNot Nothing Then
    'p is not null
Else
    'p is null
End If
```

`IsNot` is not available with value types.

Select Case **Statements**

`Select Case` is a statement that allows you to evaluate an expression against a series of values. Generally, `Select Case` is used to check whether an expression matches a particular value in situations evaluated as `True`. Listing 4.8 provides an example.

LISTING 4.8   Using the `Select Case` Statement to Evaluate Expressions

```
Sub SelectCaseDemo()
    Console.WriteLine("Type a file extension (without dot):")
    Dim fileExtension As String = Console.ReadLine
    Select Case fileExtension.ToLower
        Case Is = "txt"
            Console.WriteLine("Is a text file")
        Case Is = "exe"
            Console.WriteLine("Is an executable")
        Case Is = "doc"
            Console.WriteLine("Is a Microsoft Word document")
        Case Else
```

```
                Console.WriteLine("Is something else")
        End Select
End Sub
```

The code in Listing 4.8 simply compares the string provided by the user with a series of values. If no value matches the string, a `Case Else` is used to provide a general result. Comparison is performed with the `Is` operator and the equality operator. The following syntax is also accepted:

```
Case "txt"
```

IntelliSense adds the `Is =` symbology by default. You can also break from a `Select Case` statement at any moment by using an `Exit Select` statement. `Select..Case` also offers another syntax to apply when you want to check whether a value falls within a particular range: You can use the `To` keyword instead of the `Is =` operators, as in the following code, which waits for the user to enter a number and then checks what range the number falls in:

```
Console.WriteLine("Enter a number from 1 to 50:")
Dim result As Integer = CInt(Console.ReadLine)
Select Case result
    'The user entered a number in the range from 1 to 25
    Case 1 To 25
        Console.WriteLine("You entered {0} which is a small number",
                          result.ToString)
        'The user entered a number in the range from 26 to 50
    Case 26 To 50
        Console.WriteLine("You entered {0} which is a high number",
                          result.ToString)
        'The user entered a number < 1 or > 50
    Case Else
        Console.WriteLine("You entered a number which is out of range")
End Select
```

In other words, in this preceding example, `Case 1 To 25` means that if the value to check is in the range between the left value (1) and the right value (25), take the nested action. You can also check for multiple items not ranged with the following syntax:

```
Select Case result
    'The user entered 1 or a value between 5 and 10 or 12
    'All other values are excluded
    Case Is = 1, 5 To 10, 12
        '...
End Select
```

CODING TIP

For the `If..End If` block, the code blocks delimiters selection feature is also available for `Select..End Select` blocks.

PERFORMANCE TIPS

The Visual Basic compiler evaluates expressions as a sequence. Because of this, in `Select Case` statements, it evaluates all conditions until the one that matches the value is found. Consequently, the first `Case` instructions in the sequence should be related to expressions that are evaluated the most frequently.

Constants

Constants provide a way to represent an immutable value with an identifier. There could be situations in which your applications need to use the same value (which can be of any .NET type); therefore, it can be convenient to define an easy-to-remember identifier instead of a value. What would happen if such a value were a `Long` number? You declare constants as follows:

```
Const defaultIntegerValue As Integer = 123456789
Const aConstantString As String = "Same value along the application"
```

Constants are read-only fields that can be declared only at the module and class level or within a method and must be assigned with a value when declared. Constants within methods have public visibility by default, whereas constants at the module and class levels can have one of the .NET scopes, as in the following lines:

```
Private Const defaultIntegerValue As Integer = 123456789
Public Const aConstantString As String= "Same value along the application"
```

The reason constants must be assigned when declared is that the expression is evaluated at compile time. Starting from Visual Basic 2008, there are a couple of things to consider. Look at the following line of code:

```
Private Const Test = "Test message"
```

The type for the `Test` variable is not specified. Until Visual Basic 2005, with `Option Strict Off`, such a declaration would assign `Object`. In later versions of the language, if `Option Infer` is `On`, the compiler assigns `String`; if it is `Off`, the compiler goes back to assigning `Object`.

`With..End With` Statements

Visual Basic provides an alternative way of invoking object members, the `With..End With` statement. Consider the following code block, in which a new `Person` class is instantiated and then properties are assigned while methods are invoked:

```
Dim p As New People.Person
p.FirstName = "Alessandro"
p.LastName = "Del Sole"
Dim fullName As String = p.ToString
```

Using a `With..End With` statement, you just need to specify the name of the class once and then type a dot so that IntelliSense shows members you can use, as follows:

```
Dim p As New People.Person
With p
    .FirstName = "Alessandro"
    .LastName = "Del Sole"
    Dim fullName As String = .ToString
End With
```

There is no difference between these two coding techniques, so feel free to use the one you like most. `With..End With` offers the advantage of speeding up code writing a little, and it can be useful if you have a lot of members to invoke or assign at one time.

Summary

Every development environment relies on data types. The .NET Framework relies on two kinds of data types: value types and reference types. Both kinds of types are managed by the common type system, which provides a common infrastructure to .NET languages for working with types. In this chapter, you've learned the important basics of.NET development and the Visual Basic language, which can be summarized as follows:

▶ Common type system

▶ Value types and reference types

▶ `System.Object` and inheritance levels in value types and reference types

▶ Memory allocation of both value types and reference types

▶ Converting between types and conversion operators

▶ The most common value types and reference types

▶ Common operators, including the new null conditional operator

You often need to work with and analyze data types. Visual Basic 2015 provides several ways to perform work on types and the data they store. To accomplish this, you can use:

▶ Iterations, such as `For..Next` and `For..Each`

▶ Loops, such as `Do..Loop`

▶ Conditional code blocks, such as `If..End If` and `Select Case..End Select`

It's important to understand all the preceding features because they often recur in your developer life; these features appear extensively in the rest of the book. But you also might encounter errors when working with types. The next two chapters discuss two fundamental topics in.NET development with Visual Basic: debugging and handling errors.

CHAPTER 5

Debugging Visual Basic 2015 Applications

Debugging is one of the most important tasks in your developer life. Debugging enables you to investigate for errors and analyze the application's execution flow over an object's state. Visual Studio 2015 offers powerful tools for making debugging an easier task. In this chapter you get details about the Visual Studio instrumentation and learn how to make your code interact better with the debugger. Microsoft introduced some specific enhancements to the debugger in Visual Studio 2015; as described in this chapter, these enhancements affect application performance. In this chapter you also find information regarding the generality of Visual Basic applications. Chapter 2, "The Visual Studio 2015 IDE for Visual Basic," provides an overview of the most common debugging tasks, but in this chapter you learn about more advanced debugging tools and techniques available in the IDE. Be sure you read Chapter 2 before continuing on with this one.

Preparing an Example

Most debugging features illustrated in this chapter require some code before you can use them. At the moment, it's more important that you understand the Visual Studio 2015 instrumentation than see complex code, so we start with a simple code example that is a good base for understanding how the debugger works. You can create a new Visual Basic project for the Console and then type the code, as shown in Listing 5.1.

LISTING 5.1   Preparing the Base for the Debugger

```
Module Module1
    Sub Main()
        Console.WriteLine("Enter a valid string:")
        Dim lineRead As String = Console.ReadLine()
        Dim result As Boolean = Test(lineRead)
        Console.WriteLine("Is a valid string: " & result.ToString)
        Console.ReadLine()
    End Sub
    Function Test(name As String) As Boolean
        If String.IsNullOrEmpty(name) = False Then
            Return True
        Else
            Return False
        End If
    End Function
End Module
```

The code is quite simple. The application just asks the user to enter a string and then returns False if the string is null or is empty; it returns True if the string is valid. With such simple code, you can now begin learning the advanced debugging instrumentation available in Visual Studio 2015.

Debugging Instrumentation

The Visual Studio 2015 IDE offers several powerful tools for deeply debugging applications. These tools are part of the development environment instrumentation and are discussed in this section. Remember that when you debug an application, the status bar and the border of Visual Studio 2015 become orange.

Debugging in Steps

When the application execution breaks, such as when the debugger finds a breakpoint, you can usually continue to execute the application running just one line of code per time or a small set of lines of code per time. In Chapter 2, you learned about the Step Into command; this section discusses other similar commands that cause different debugger behaviors.

HOW CAN I EXECUTE SUCH TECHNIQUES?

The debugging techniques described in this section can be accomplished by invoking commands available in the Debug menu of Visual Studio 2015. In the meantime, shortcuts are available for invoking the same commands using the keyboard. These are provided when discussing each command.

Step Into

The Step Into command executes one instruction per time. It is similar to Step Over, but if the instruction to be executed is a method, the method is executed one instruction per time and, when finished, the execution goes back to the caller. You can invoke Step Into by pressing **F11**.

NOTE ON KEYBOARD SHORTCUTS

The keyboard shortcuts in this chapter assume that you are using the default keyboard layout provided by Visual Studio's general settings and can vary depending on the IDE configuration settings. The Debug menu shows the appropriate keyboard shortcuts for your active configuration.

Step Over

Similarly to Step Into, Step Over executes one instruction per time. The difference is that if the instruction to be executed is a method, the debugger does not enter the method and completes its execution before going back to the caller. You can invoke Step Over by pressing **F10**. This can be useful when you need to debug a portion of code that invokes several methods you already tested and that you do not need to delve into each time.

Step Out

Step Out works only within methods and enables executing all lines of code next to the current one, until the method completes. If you consider the code shown in Listing 5.1 and place a breakpoint on the `If` statement inside the `Test` method definition, invoking Step Out can cause the debugger to execute all the lines of code next to the If, completing the execution of the method. In this example, after Step Out completes, the control is returned to the second `Console.Writeline` statement in `Sub Main`. You can invoke Step Out by pressing **Shift+F11**.

Run to Cursor

You can place the cursor on a line of code, right-click the line of code, and tell the debugger to execute all the code until the selected line. This can be accomplished by selecting the **Run to Cursor** command on the pop-up menu.

Set Next Statement

Within a code block, you can set the next statement to be executed when resuming the application execution after a breakpoint or stop. Continuing the previous code example, if you place a breakpoint on the first `Console.Writeline` statement, inside the `Main` method, the application stops the execution at that point. Now imagine you want the debugger to resume debugging from the second `Console.Writeline` statement (therefore skipping the debugging of the `Test` method invocation) and execute the lines of code before. You can right-click the `Console.Writeline` statement and select **Set Next Statement** from the pop-up menu, and this line will be the first that you can step through. As an alternative, you can drag the yellow arrow in the IDE to the desired line.

Show Next Statement

This command moves the cursor to the next executable statement. This can be useful if you have long code files and breakpoints are not immediately visible. You can invoke it simply by right-clicking the code editor and selecting the **Show Next Statement** command from the pop-up menu.

Mixed Mode Debugging

You can debug Visual Basic applications built on both managed and native code with the Mixed Mode feature, which is available for both 32-bit and 64-bit applications. To enable mixed-mode debugging, follow these steps:

1. In Solution Explorer, select the project you want to debug.

2. Open My Project and select the **Debug** tab.

3. Select the **Enable Native Code Debugging** check box.

"Just My Code" Debugging

You might remember from Chapter 2 and Chapter 3, "The Anatomy of a Visual Basic Project," that every time you create a Visual Basic application the IDE generates some background code. Moreover, your code often invokes system code that you do not necessarily need to investigate. In Visual Basic the IDE offers the capability of debugging just your own code, excluding system and auto-generated code. This feature is also known as Just My Code debugging. This is useful because you can focus on your code. Just My Code is enabled by default in Visual Studio 2015. To disable it or enable it, open the Options window, select the **Debugging** node on the left, and then flag or unflag the **Enable Just My Code (Managed Only)** check box, as shown in Figure 5.1.

Behind the scenes, Just My Code adds (or removes) some .NET attributes to auto-generated code that can influence the debugger behavior. To see a simple example, open or create a project and then click the **Show All Files** button in Solution Explorer. After doing this, go to the Settings.designer.vb code file. Listing 5.2 shows the content of the My namespace definition inside the file.

LISTING 5.2   Understanding Just My Code Behind the Scenes

```
Namespace My
    <Global.Microsoft.VisualBasic.HideModuleNameAttribute(), _
     Global.System.Diagnostics.DebuggerNonUserCodeAttribute(), _
     Global.System.Runtime.CompilerServices.CompilerGeneratedAttribute()> _
    Friend Module MySettingsProperty
        <Global.System.ComponentModel.
         Design.HelpKeywordAttribute("My.Settings")> _
        Friend ReadOnly Property Settings() As
        Global.DebuggingFeatures.My.MySettings
            Get
                Return Global.DebuggingFeatures.My.MySettings.Default
```

```
            End Get
        End Property
    End Module
End Namespace
```

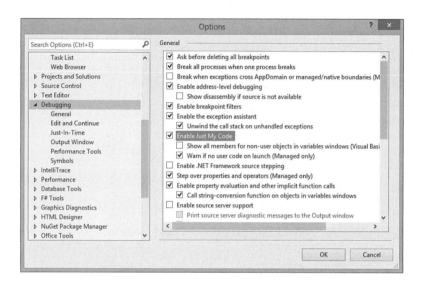

FIGURE 5.1   Enabling/disabling Just My Code debugging.

You can notice that the module `MySettingsProperty` is decorated with a particular attribute named `System.Diagnostics.DebuggerNonUserCodeAttribute`. This attribute indicates to the debugger that the code is not your code (user code) and that it will not be
debugged when Just My Code is on. Three attributes influence the debugger's behavior in
this feature. Table 5.1 shows the complete list.

TABLE 5.1   Just My Code Attributes

Attribute	Description
DebuggerNonUserCode	Indicates to the debugger that the code is not user code and therefore is treated as system code
DebuggerHidden	Indicates to the debugger that code will not be visible at all to the debugger and therefore will be excluded from debugging
DebuggerStepThrough	Indicates to the debugger that the Step Into procedure is not allowed

Of course, you can use attributes of your own so that you can influence the behavior of
the debugger when Just My Code is disabled.

Working with Breakpoints, Conditions and Actions

In Chapter 2 you learned about breakpoints and how to break application execution before some statements are executed. You now learn some interesting features of breakpoints when debugging Visual Basic applications. This section also describes a new breakpoint experience in Visual Studio 2015.

The Breakpoints Window

Using the Breakpoints window, you can manage all breakpoints in your solution. You can open such a window by pressing **Ctrl+Alt+B**. If you placed three breakpoints in the sample application, Figure 5.2 shows how the Breakpoints window would look.

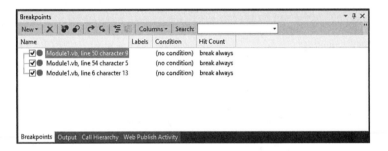

FIGURE 5.2   The Breakpoints window.

In the Breakpoints window, you can easily manage your breakpoints. For example, you could delete, temporarily disable, or enable again the breakpoints. You can also specify the behavior for each breakpoint, such as Hit count, Filter, and other functionalities that are described next. Also, you can easily switch to the source code in which the breakpoint is located or to the disassembly view. (See Figure 5.12 in the "Call Stack Window" section later in this chapter.) An important opportunity is exporting and importing breakpoints; Visual Studio 2015, as well as its predecessor, can export to XML files the list of breakpoints or import a list from an XML file. If you have lots of breakpoints, you can search breakpoints according to specific criteria using the Label feature, which this section focuses on next. The Breakpoints window provides a graphical unified instrument for performing operations on breakpoints.

Editing Breakpoints Labels

You can add labels to breakpoints. Labels are a kind of identifier that can identify more than one breakpoint, and their purpose is categorizing breakpoints so that you can easily find and manage them within the Edit Breakpoint Label window. You can add a label to a breakpoint by right-clicking the red ball (also referred to as the *red glyph*) on the left of the desired breakpoint in the code editor and then selecting the **Edit Labels** command from the pop-up menu. The Edit Breakpoint Labels window appears (see Figure 5.3).

FIGURE 5.3   The Edit Breakpoint Labels window enables categorizing breakpoints.

You need to specify labels and click **Add**. When you finish, select the label you want from the list and click **OK** so that the label is assigned to the breakpoint. You can assign the same label to multiple breakpoints performing the same steps, or you can assign multiple labels to a single breakpoint. Assigning labels to breakpoints can be reflected into the **Breakpoints** window in which you can search for breakpoints specifying labels in the search box.

Configuring Breakpoint Settings: Conditions and Actions

If you have experience with previous versions of Microsoft Visual Studio, you already know that you can configure some special breakpoint settings. You might be surprised to see that Visual Studio 2015 provides a totally new experience in configuring breakpoint settings. You can still decide when breakpoints should condition the application execution, but Visual Studio 2015 allows you to accomplish this in a more logical way and, most importantly, without the need for modal dialogs. In particular, for each breakpoint, you can specify conditions and actions. *Conditions* determine when the debugger should break the application execution when it encounters a breakpoint, whereas *actions* allow special tasks to occur when a breakpoint is hit. Conditions and actions can definitely work together. In order to configure a breakpoint's settings, you hover over the red glyph and click the Settings button available on the small toolbar that appears over the glyph (see Figure 5.4).

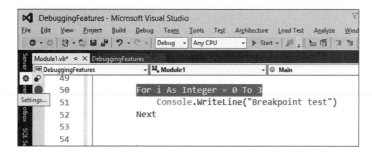

FIGURE 5.4   Invoking breakpoint settings.

After you click Settings, Visual Studio 2015 opens a *peek window* (see Figure 5.5), which is very similar to the Peek Definition window you saw in Chapter 2. This is different from the past editions of Visual Studio, where you used modal dialogs that would block your activity. Here you can still focus on your code and never leave the active editor window. In a peek window you can configure both conditions and actions.

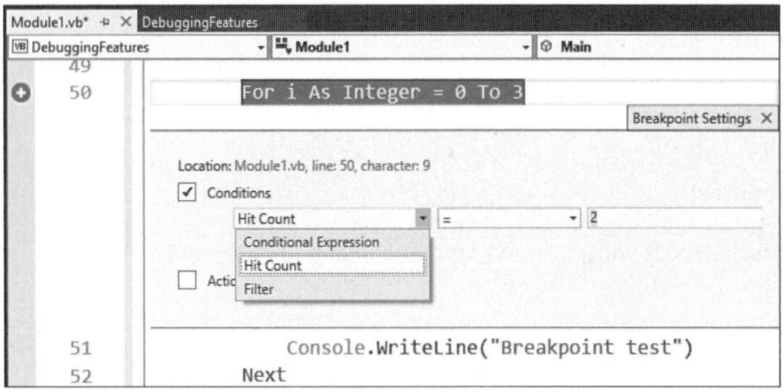

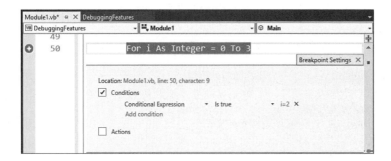

FIGURE 5.5 Configuring breakpoint settings in a peek window.

Conditions determine whether the debugger should break the application execution when it encounters a breakpoint. As shown in Figure 5.5, the options for conditions in this case are Conditional Expressions, Hit Count, and Filter. The Conditional Expressions option allows the application execution to break when the specified expression evaluates to `True` or when the expression changes. For example, consider the following code snippet and say that you have a breakpoint on the `Console.WriteLine` statement:

```
For i As Integer = 0 To 3
    Console.WriteLine("Breakpoint test")
Next
```

Now suppose you want to break the application execution only when the value of the `i` variable is `2`. The condition you apply at this point requires the `Is true` evaluation and the `i = 2` expression, as shown in Figure 5.6.

FIGURE 5.6 Setting a breakpoint condition.

You can take advantage of IntelliSense while writing the expression.

The next option is Hit Count. With the *hit* term we mean each time a breakpoint is encountered and therefore the application execution should stop. You can control the hit's behavior. For example, imagine you have a cyclic code that contains a breakpoint, but you need to break the execution only when the cycle arrives at a particular point. By using the Hit Count option, you can specify when the debugger must break the application. For example, consider the `For` loop in the previous code snippet.

Imagine that you place a breakpoint on the `Console.WriteLine` statement and that you want the debugger to break only starting from the second iteration. You can specify this condition by selecting the **Hit Count** option. If you do not explicitly specify a Hit Count condition, the default setting is always break, which means that the debugger breaks the execution each time a breakpoint is encountered. Possible options are = (equal to), **Is a multiple of**, and >= (greater than or equal to). For example, if you set the condition to >= with value of **2**, (see Figure 5.7), the previous code breaks starting from the second iteration. This option can be convenient when you need to debug your code only from a certain point.

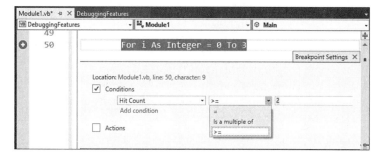

FIGURE 5.7   Specifying a Hit Count condition.

The last option, Filter, allows the application to break execution when the breakpoint is hit on a particular thread, process, or machine. You simply specify the process name, thread ID, or machine name.

> **TIP**
>
> You can add multiple conditions by clicking **Add Condition**. Also, you can easily remove conditions by clicking the closing symbol (x) near each one.

It is now time to talk about actions. In previous versions of Visual Studio, actions were known as *tracepoints*. An *action* basically allows you to write the specified information to the Output window.

You can set one of the built-in expressions to build a kind of log message that will be written to the Output window. For example, Figure 5.8 shows how to send the call stack to the Output window by using a function called $CALLSTACK.

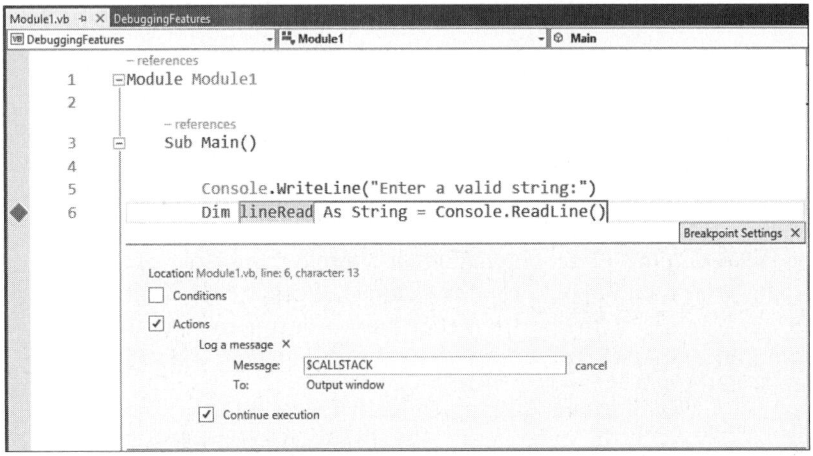

FIGURE 5.8   Specifying an action.

IntelliSense shows the list of available functions when you type the $ symbol. Also, you can write custom expressions. For more information on custom expressions, see this blog post from the Visual Studio team: http://blogs.msdn.com/b/visualstudioalm/archive/2014/10/06/new-breakpoint-configuration-experience.aspx.

PerfTips: Investigating Code Performance

Visual Studio 2015 introduces a new debugging tool called **PerfTips**, which stands for Performance ToolTips. PerfTips allows you to measure how long it takes to execute a specific code block, and it shows the elapsed time near the code. This feature is very useful for understanding the behavior of your code over long-running operations, such as CPU-intensive work. To understand how PerfTips works, consider the following code, which simply downloads the content of the RSS feed from my blog, using the System.Net.WebClient class and its DownloadString method:

```
Using client As New WebClient
    client.DownloadString (
        New Uri("http://community.visual-basic.it/Alessandro/rss.aspx"))
End Using
```

Place a breakpoint on the second line of this code and then press **F5**. The application execution breaks before the code downloads the RSS content. At this point, press **F11** for a Step Into execution. As you can see in Figure 5.9, Visual Studio shows the elapsed time for the code execution (up to 80 milliseconds in this case) via an informational ToolTip.

FIGURE 5.9   PerfTips displays elapsed time for your code.

PerfTips is a very useful feature because it gives you a good idea of how your code behaves. However, it is worth mentioning that values are approximate. In fact, the debugger adds some overhead to the execution, plus there are situations in which the execution time does not depend on how good your code is but rather depends on conditions such as your network's latency for operations that require an Internet connection. Regardless, this is definitely a very interesting addition to the debugging toolbox.

NEW PERFORMANCE AND DIAGNOSTIC TOOLS

In addition to PerfTips, Visual Studio 2015 introduces some other great new tools that are useful for analyzing how an application consumes memory and CPU. In fact, when you press F5 to start debugging a client application, you see a new integrated window called Diagnostic Tools. This advanced diagnostic tool is discussed fully in Chapter 51, "Code Analysis: The .NET Compiler Platform and Tools." In that chapter you will learn about all kinds of advanced analysis tools, including IntelliTrace. You need to understand how the different kinds of .NET applications are constructed before being you can analyze their performance issues.

Locals Window

The Locals window shows the active local variables and their values. Considering the example in Listing 5.1, when stepping into the `Main` method the Locals window shows information about `lineRead` and `result` variables, as shown in Figure 5.10.

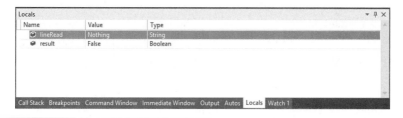

FIGURE 5.10   The Locals window shows information on local variables.

As you can see, the window shows names of the local variables, their types (in our example `Boolean` and `String`), and their actual values. When a variable is not initialized yet, the window shows the default value (for example, `Nothing` for reference types and zero for `Integers`). Moreover, if a variable represents an object such as a class or a collection, the variable can be expanded to show members and their values. You can also change variables' values by double-clicking each one. Some variables cannot be viewed without executing code, such as in-memory queries (they can be still viewed, though the IDE will run the code in memory to be able to display the results).

Command Window

The Command window enables evaluating expressions or running functions without running the application or continuing the debug. It also allows you to execute menu commands and commands that do not appear in any menu. Figure 5.11 shows the Command window evaluating an `Integer.Parse` statement and an invocation to our `Test` method.

FIGURE 5.11   The Command window enables evaluating expressions and functions.

This can be useful because you do not need to run our application to see whether a method works, and you could also evaluate complex expressions before writing code. Just remember that only functions are allowed; procedures are not supported. Expressions can be constituted by several .NET objects and Visual Basic keywords, but not all of them are supported. You can get a complete list of supported keywords and expressions from the related MSDN web page available at http://msdn.microsoft.com/en-us/library/099a40t6(v=vs.120).aspx. To evaluate an expression or test a function, you need to first write a question mark (?) symbol. Using a double question mark (??) causes the debugger to open a Quick Watch window, which is discussed later in this chapter. It is worth mentioning that the ? symbol works when either in debug mode or not, while the ?? symbol requires the IDE to be already in debug mode.

Call Stack Window

The Call Stack window shows the method calls stack frame. In other words, you can see how method calls run in the stack. The window can show the programming language that the method is written with and can display calls to external code. By default, the Call Stack window shows information about Just My Code. To understand method calls, press **F11** to step into the code. Figure 5.12 shows the Call Stack window related to Listing 5.1.

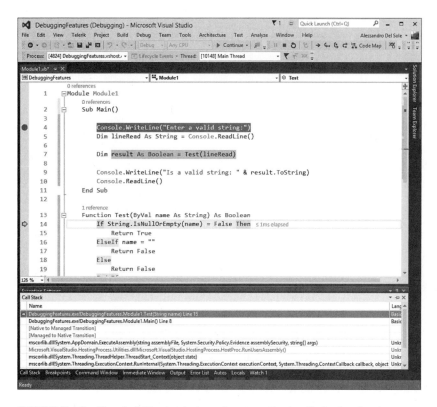

FIGURE 5.12 The Call Stack window shows method calls in the Stack.

The window shows the names of methods being executed and the programming language with which they were written. Calls to .NET Framework system methods are also shown. Another interesting feature is that you can see the assembly code for code execution. Right-click the window and select the **Go to Disassembly** command from the pop-up menu. As shown in Figure 5.13, you can see Visual Basic lines of code and the related underlying assembly code that you can step into by pressing **F11**.

You can also customize the type of information you want to visualize by expanding the View Options control. This feature provides great granularity on what's happening behind the scenes and allows understanding if method calls are executed correctly. You can invoke the Call Stack window by pressing **Ctrl+Alt+C**.

THREADS AND CALL STACK

The Call Stack window can show information only on the current thread. Therefore, method calls on other threads are ignored by the window.

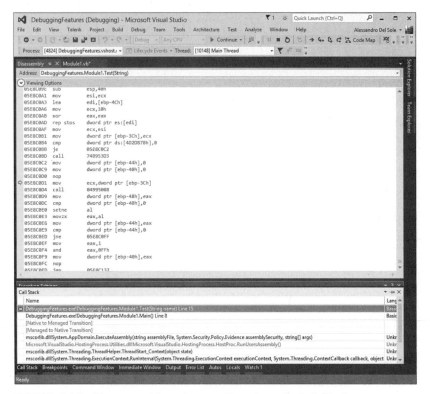

FIGURE 5.13   The assembly code execution shows in Call Stack.

Watch Windows

Watch windows enable monitoring object variables or expressions so that you can track what a variable is doing. There are four Watch windows available, enabling you to track different objects or expressions. To add items to a Watch window, when in break mode right-click the object in the code editor and then select the **Add Watch** command from the pop-up menu. Continuing our example of Listing 5.1, imagine you want to keep track of the `Test` method state. Run the application in Step Into mode by pressing **F11**. When the debugger breaks the application execution, right-click the `Test` method definition and then click **Add Watch**. The method is considered as an expression. The first available Watch window is shown and contains the `Test` item but advertises that no argument has been supplied, as shown in Figure 5.14.

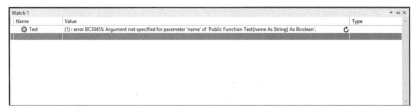

FIGURE 5.14   Adding an expression to a Watch window.

If you continue stepping into the code, you notice that when the debugger begins stepping into the `Test` method, the expression is first evaluated as `False`. (This is the default value for Boolean.) When the code completes the execution, the Watch window contains the actual evaluation of the expression; in our example, if the user writes a valid string in the Console window, the expression is evaluated as `True`, as shown in Figure 5.15.

In this way you can control whether your variables or methods are correctly executed.

FIGURE 5.15   Evaluation of the expression is completed within the Watch window.

DEBUGGING LAMBDA EXPRESSIONS

Visual Studio 2015 introduces support for debugging lambda expressions and LINQ queries in the Watch and Immediate windows. Since this scenario requires knowledge of lambda expressions, this new feature is described in Chapter 20, "Advanced Language Features."

Quick Watch Window

The Quick Watch window is an additional Watch window that enables quickly evaluating one expression or variable per time, choosing between items you previously added to Watch windows or right-clicking an object in the code editor and then selecting the **Quick Watch** command. In this scenario, the expression or variable is evaluated considering its state at the moment you request the Quick Watch to appear. Figure 5.16 shows the Quick Watch window.

You can pick an expression from the Expression combo box. When you choose the expression, you can click **Reevaluate** to run the evaluation. Just remember that this dialog box is a modal dialog box, so you need to close it before you can go back to Visual Studio.

Threads Window

.NET applications can run multiple threads. This can happen with your applications, too. You can get a view of the running threads and debugging threads within the Threads window, which you can enable by pressing **Ctrl+Alt+H**. Figure 5.17 shows the Threads window open when the sample application is in break mode.

FIGURE 5.16   The Quick Watch window.

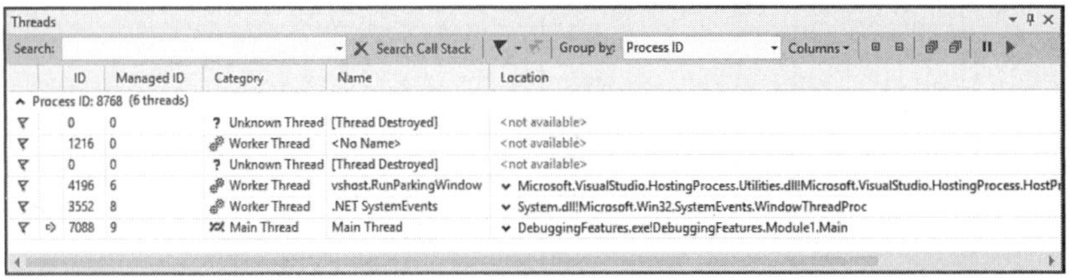

FIGURE 5.17   The Threads window.

The window shows a list of running threads and enables stepping into the Call Stack for the various threads. If the source code is available for threads other than the current one, you can step into this code. In our example, the main thread is the Console application. You can also organize and filter the view, search within the Call Stack, and get information on the thread's priority. The Threads window is particularly useful with multi-threaded applications. For applications that use the Task Parallel Library and the Async/Await pattern, the Visual Studio 2015 debugger provides other tools, which are described in Chapters 41, "Parallel Programming and Parallel LINQ," and 42, "Asynchronous Programming."

CALL STACK

You can get the method call stack per thread by passing the mouse pointer over each thread in the window. The list of method calls is offered under the form of a tooltip.

Autos Window

The Autos window shows the variables used by the current statement and by the previous three and next three statements. Figure 5.18 shows an example of the Autos window.

FIGURE 5.18   The Autos window.

For the Autos window, you can change variables' values by double-clicking each one.

64-BIT SUPPORT

The Visual Studio 2015 debugger supports the mixed mode with 64-bit application debugging.

Inspecting Object Details with Debugger Visualizers

Debugger visualizers are built-in tools that enable viewing information on objects, controls, members, and variables (generally complex data) in a particular format. For example, if you place a breakpoint on the following line of code of the sample project

```
Dim result As Boolean = Test(lineRead)
```

you can then open the Locals window and select the lineRead variable. In the Value column, notice the small magnifying glass you can click. From there, you can choose how you want to visualize information on the lineRead variable, such as Text format, XML format, and HTML format. Of course, trying to view the content of plain text as XML content does not provide any benefits, but if you have a string representing XML data or HTML code, you could get an appropriate representation to understand what's happening. Visualizers are also useful when you have a large multiline string and you need to see how it is formatted. In our example, Figure 5.19 shows the Text visualizer for the lineRead variable.

The visualizers' purpose is to provide a graphical tool for analyzing what's happening on expressions.

CUSTOM DEBUGGER VISUALIZERS

Visual Studio 2015 offers default debugger visualizers that are useful in common situations, but you might need custom visualizers. You can build custom visualizers, but this is beyond the scope of this chapter. Information on creating custom visualizers is available in the MSDN documentation at http://msdn.microsoft.com/en-us/library/e2zc529c(v=vs.120).aspx.

FIGURE 5.19   Viewing information with debugger visualizers.

Debugging in Code

The .NET Framework offers the ability to interact with the debugger via managed code. You can use two classes, System.Diagnostics.Debug and System.Diagnostics.Trace, to verify conditions and evaluations that can be useful to provide feedback about your code if it is working correctly. Information generated by these classes can eventually be added to the application.

Debug AND Trace ARE SHARED
Both Debug and Trace classes are zero-instance shared classes and therefore expose only shared members.

The Debug Class

The Debug class, exposed by the System.Diagnostics namespace, provides interaction with the Visual Studio debugger and lets you know whether your code is working correctly via instrumentation that evaluates conditions at a certain point of your code. The Debug class exposes only shared methods and can display contents into the Output window so that you can programmatically interact with the debugger without the need to set breakpoints. Table 5.2 provides an overview of Debug methods.

TABLE 5.2   Debug Class Methods

Method	Description
Assert	Checks for a condition and shows a message if the condition is False
Close	Empties the buffer and releases trace listeners
Fail	Generates an error message
Flush	Empties the buffer and forces data to be written to underlying trace listeners
Indent	When writing to the Output window, increases the text indentation
Print	Writes the specified message to the listeners; supports text formatting
Unindent	When writing to the Output window, decreases the text indentation
Write	Writes the specified message to the listeners without a line terminator; supports text formatting
WriteIf	Writes the specified message to the listeners without a line terminator if the supplied condition is True; supports text formatting
WriteLine	Writes the specified message to the listeners with a line terminator; supports text formatting
WriteLineIf	Writes the specified message to the listeners with a line terminator if the supplied condition is True; supports text formatting

DEBUG OUTPUT

Saying that the Debug class can display contents to the Output window is true only in part. Developers can use other built-in outputs known as *trace listeners* to redirect the output. This chapter provides an overview of trace listeners.

Unlike in previous editions, in Visual Studio 2015, before you use the Debug (and Trace) class, you have to perform some manual steps. In fact, Visual Studio 2015 is automatically set up to send information to a text file on disk rather than to the Output window. (This will be clearer shortly, when we talk about trace listeners.) That said, in Solution Explorer, double-click the App.config file, which also contains information about debugging options. When the file content appears, locate the following section:

```
<trace autoflush="true">
  <listeners>
    <add name="DemoTestWriter"
     type="System.Diagnostics.TextWriterTraceListener"
        initializeData="output.txt"/>
    <!-- If you want to disable the DefaultTraceListener-->
    <remove name="Default"/>
  </listeners>
</trace>
```

You should comment both lines inside the `<listeners>` node like this:

```
<trace autoflush="true">
  <listeners>
    <!--<add name="DemoTestWriter"
         type="System.Diagnostics.TextWriterTraceListener"
         initializeData="output.txt"/>-->
    <!-- If you want to disable the DefaultTraceListener-->
    <!--<remove name="Default"/>-->
  </listeners>
</trace>
```

Now you are ready to use the `Debug` class. Continuing the code example in Listing 5.1, try to add the following lines of code after the declaration and assignment of the `result` variable within the `Main` method:

```
Debug.WriteLine("Value of result is " & result.ToString)
Debug.WriteLineIf(result = True, "Result is valid because = True")
'If you type an empty or null string,
'then the condition "result=True" is False therefore
'shows an error message
Debug.Assert(result = True, "Needed a valid string")
```

Now run the application and type in a valid (nonempty) string. Figure 5.20 shows how the Output window appears when the runtime encounters the Debug methods.

FIGURE 5.20   Writing debug information to the Output window.

The first line shows the Boolean value of the `result` variable. The `WriteLine` method can be useful if you need to monitor objects' values without breaking the application. This method also adds a line terminator so that a new line can begin. The `Write` method does the same but does not add a line terminator. The `WriteLineIf` (and `WriteIf`) writes a message only if the specified condition is evaluated as `True`. If you enter a valid string, the `WriteLineIf` method writes a message. Notice that there is an invocation to the `Assert` method. This method causes the runtime to show a message box containing the specified message that is shown only if the specified expression is evaluated as `False`. According to this, if you enter a valid string in the sample application, the expression is evaluated as `True`; therefore, no message is shown. If you instead enter an empty string (that is, press **Enter**), the runtime shows the dialog box represented in Figure 5.21.

FIGURE 5.21   The Assertion dialog box.

The `Fail` method, which is not shown in the example, shows a similar dialog box but without evaluating any condition. In Table 5.2, method descriptions mention trace listeners. You now get an overview of the `Trace` class and then an overview of the particular objects.

The `Trace` Class

The `Trace` class, which is also exposed by the `System.Diagnostics` namespace, works exactly like the `Debug` class. One important difference influences the building process. The output of the `Debug` class is included in the build output only if the `DEBUG` constant is defined, but the `Trace` class's output is included in the build output only if the `TRACE` constant is defined. When you build your applications with the Debug configuration active, both constants are defined, so both outputs are included. The Release configuration defines only the `TRACE` constant, so it includes only this output.

Understanding Trace Listeners

In the preceding examples related to the `Debug` class (and consequently related to the `Trace` class, too), you saw how to send the output of the debugger to the Output window. The .NET Framework enables sending the output to other targets, known as *trace listeners*. A trace listener is an object that "listens" to what is happening at debugging time and then collects information under various forms. For example, you could collect information as XML files or just send such information to the Output window. Both the `Debug` and `Trace` classes expose a property named `Listeners` that represents a set of built-in listeners. Table 5.3 groups the .NET Framework built-in listeners.

TABLE 5.3   .NET Built-In Trace Listeners

Listener	Description
`DefaultTraceListener`	Redirects the output to the Output window.
`TextWriterTraceListener`	Redirects the output to a text file.
`XmlWriterTraceListener`	Redirects the output to an XML file.
`EventLogTraceListener`	Redirects the output to the operating system's events log.
`DelimitedListTraceListener`	Redirects the output to a text file. Information is separated by a symbol.
`EventSchemaTraceListener`	Redirects the output to an XML schema that is formed on the supplied arguments.
`ConsoleTraceListener`	Redirects the output to the Console window.

`System.Diagnostics` NAMESPACE REQUIRED

All listeners listed in Table 5.3 are exposed by the `System.Diagnostics` namespace, which is not mentioned for the sake of brevity. Usually this namespace is imported by default, according to the options set within My Project. If the background compiler advises that classes are not defined, you should add an `Imports System.Diagnostics` directive to your code.

When you invoke members from the `Debug` and `Trace` classes, and after you make the edits described in the previous section, by default the output is redirected to the output window. This is because the `DefaultTraceListener` is attached to the application by the debugger. Now suppose you want to redirect the output to a text file. This can be accomplished by writing the following lines of code:

```
Trace.Listeners.Clear()
Trace.Listeners.Add(New
    TextWriterTraceListener
    ("C:\users\alessandro\desktop\TraceOutput.txt"))
'This will ensure the file is closed when
'the debugger shuts down
Trace.AutoFlush = True
Trace.WriteLineIf(result = True, "You entered a valid string")
```

LISTENERS DO NOT OVERWRITE FILES

All built-in trace listeners that redirect output to a file do not overwrite the file itself if it already exists. They just append information to an existing file. If you need to create a new file each time from scratch, remember to remove the previous version (for example, invoking the `File.Delete` method).

The `Trace.Listener.Clear` method ensures that all previous information from other listeners gets cleared. You need to add a new instance of the `TextWriterTraceListener` class to listeners' collection. At this point you need to supply the name of the output file as an argument. If you add the preceding code after the declaration and assignment of the `result` variable within the `Main` method of our main example, the output is redirected to a text file, as shown in Figure 5.22.

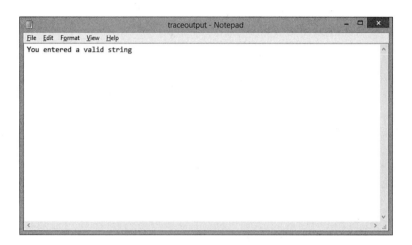

FIGURE 5.22   The debugging output has been redirected to a text file.

The `AutoFlush` property set as `True` ensures that the text file is correctly closed when the debugger shuts down. In the end, you write evaluations as you would do when sending output to the Output window (see `WriteLineIf` method). A class named `DelimitedListTraceListener` inherits from `TextWriterTraceListener` and enables writing information to a file using a delimitation symbol. By default, this symbol is a comma (output files are Comma Separated Value [CSV] files that can be opened with Microsoft Excel), but you can set the `Delimiter` property value with another symbol. The usage remains the same as its base class. You also might want to redirect output to an XML file. This can be accomplished adding an instance of the `XmlWriterTraceListener` class, as shown in the following code:

```
Trace.Listeners.Clear()
Trace.Listeners.Add(New
        XmlWriterTraceListener
        ("C:\users\alessandro\desktop\TraceOutput.xml"))
'This will ensure the file is closed when
'the debugger shuts down
Trace.AutoFlush = True
Trace.WriteLineIf(result = True, "You entered a valid string")
```

The usage is the same as in the `TextWriterTraceListener` example. If you try to run the preceding code, you can obtain a well-formed XML document, as shown in Figure 5.23.

FIGURE 5.23   The output produced by the `XmlWriterTraceListener` class.

As you should understand, writing the output to an XML document is a more powerful
task because of the amount of information collected. All the information persisted to the
XML document is reflected by properties of the instance of the `XmlWriterTraceListener`
class. Each property is named as the related information in the XML document. For
example, the `Computer` property represents the name of the computer running the
debugger, the `ProcessName` property represents the name of the process that the debugger is attached to, the `ProcessID` property represents the process identification number
of the process, and the `ThreadID` property represents the thread identification number
of the process. Another listener that you can use for producing XML files is named
`EventSchemaTraceListener`. This object creates an XML schema starting from debugging
information; the `EventSchemaTraceListener` constructor has several overloads that enable
specifying how the schema will be formed. The following code shows an example:

```
Trace.Listeners.Add(New
        EventSchemaTraceListener("Test.xsd",
        "My listener",
        32768,
        TraceLogRetentionOption.LimitedCircularFiles,
        65536, 10))
```

Explaining this class in detail is beyond the scope of this book. If you would like to read further details on this class, you can read the official MSDN documentation at http://msdn.microsoft.com/en-us/library/system.diagnostics.eventschematracelistener (v=vs.110).aspx. The `EventLogTraceListener` class works similarly to the previous ones. The following lines of code attach a new instance of the class to the debugger, and the debug output is redirected to the Windows Event Log:

```
Trace.Listeners.Clear()
Trace.Listeners.Add(New EventLogTraceListener
                    ("Chapter 5 - Debugging applications"))
'This will ensure the log resources are released when
'the debugger shuts down
Trace.AutoFlush = True
Trace.WriteLineIf(result = True, "You entered a valid string")
```

APPLICATION LOG REQUIRES ADMINISTRATOR

Writing to the application log requires administrative privileges. If you run Windows 7 or Windows 8.x and you have the User Account Control active on your system, you should also run Visual Studio 2015 as an administrator.

The preceding code creates a new entry in the application log of the operating system. Figure 5.24 shows the content of the application log, which is reachable via the Event viewer shortcut of the Administrative tools menu.

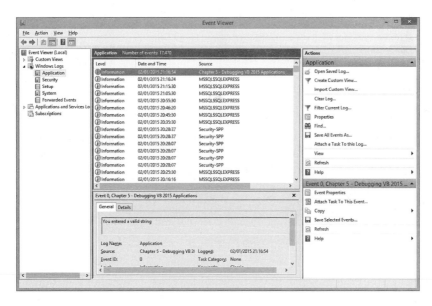

FIGURE 5.24   Windows's Event viewer shows the application log containing our debug output.

My.Application.Log

Visual Basic 2015 offers an alternative to the `EventLogTraceListener` that is provided by the `My` namespace. As you see in Chapter 19, "The `My` Namespace," an object named `My.Application.Log` provides a simpler way for writing the trace output to the application log.

The last listener object is named `ConsoleTraceListener` and enables sending messages to the Console window. You use this object as the previous ones. At this point we should focus on an important feature of listeners: Hard-coding listeners in Visual Basic code is not mandatory. The good news is that you can add listeners to a configuration file that can be manually edited externally from Visual Studio.

Setting Listeners in Configuration Files

To set listeners to a configuration file, first you need one. Visual Studio 2015 should automatically add a configuration file, but in case it is not available, in the Solution Explorer, right-click the project name and then select the **Add New Item** command from the pop-up menu. When the Add New Item dialog box appears, you can search for the Application Configuration File template using the search box, as shown in Figure 5.25.

FIGURE 5.25   Adding a new configuration file to the project.

If you now double-click the configuration file in Solution Explorer, you notice a section that is named `System.Diagnostics`, as in the following snippet:

```
<system.diagnostics>
    <sources>
        <source name="DefaultSource" switchName="DefaultSwitch">
            <listeners>
                <add name="FileLog"/>
            </listeners>
        </source>
    </sources>
    <switches>
        <add name="DefaultSwitch" value="Information" />
    </switches>
</system.diagnostics>
```

This section represents the same-named namespace and offers the capability to specify trace listeners. By default, a `DefaultTraceListener` is added. This can be understood examining the preceding code snippet. You might also add other listeners, such as a `TextWriterTraceListener` or an `XmlWriterTraceListener`. The following code snippet shows how you can add a `TextWriterTraceListener` to the App.config file, remembering that it must be nested into the `System.Diagnostics` node:

```
<trace autoflush="true">
  <listeners>
    <add name="DemoTestWriter"
         type="System.Diagnostics.TextWriterTraceListener"
         initializeData="output.txt"/>
    <!-- If you want to disable the DefaultTraceListener-->
    <remove name="Default"/>
  </listeners>
</trace>
```

As you can see, you need to supply a name, the type (that is, the class name), and the output file. The following code snippet shows instead how you can add an `XmlWriterTraceListener`:

```
<trace autoflush="true">
  <listeners>v
    <add name="DemoTestWriter"
         type="System.Diagnostics.XmlWriterTraceListener"
         initializeData="output.xml"/>
    <!-- If you want to disable the DefaultTraceListener-->
    <remove name="Default"/>
  </listeners>
</trace>
```

Of course, using configuration file is optional. This could be a good choice if another person who cannot edit your source code should change how the debugger information is collected because the configuration file can be edited externally from Visual Studio.

Using Debug Attributes in Your Code

The section "'Just My Code' Debugging" explains how some attributes can influence the debugger's behavior versus autogenerated code and that you can use that versus your own code. The .NET Framework also provides other attributes you can use to decorate your code for deciding how the debugger should behave versus such code. Table 5.4 lists other attributes that complete the list in Table 5.1.

TABLE 5.4   Debug Attributes

Attribute	Description
DebuggerVisualizer	Indicates to the IDE that the code implements a custom debugger visualizer.
DebuggerStepperBoundary	When a DebuggerNonUserCode attribute is also specified, this causes the debugger to run the code instead of stepping through.
DebuggerBrowsable	Establishes how data should be shown in the Data Tips windows.
DebuggerDisplay	Allows customizing strings and messages in Data Tips.
DebuggerTypeProxy	Allows overriding how DataTips are shown for a particular type.

As previously described in this chapter, discussing custom debugger visualizers is beyond the scope of this book, so the DebuggerVisualizer attribute is not discussed here.

NOTE ON DEBUG ATTRIBUTES

The previous attributes are effectively used and useful when debugging the application from within Visual Studio. When you compile the application in Release mode, debug attributes are ignored and do not affect your code at runtime.

DebuggerStepperBoundary

This attribute is used only in multithreading scenarios and has effects only when a DebuggerNonUserCode is also specified. It is used to run code instead of stepping through it when you are stepping into user code that does not actually relate to the thread you were debugging. Due to its particular nature, this attribute is not discussed in detail. The MSDN Library provides additional information at this address: http://msdn.microsoft.com/en-us/library/system.diagnostics.debuggerstepperboundaryattribute(v=vs.110).aspx.

DebuggerBrowsable

You can use the DebuggerBrowsable attribute to establish how an item should be visualized in Data Tips or debugging windows by specifying one of the following arguments exposed by the System.Diagnostics.DebuggerBrowsableState enumeration:

▶ Collapsed, which establishes that an item is collapsed and that you have to click the + symbol to expand it and see its children elements

▶ `Never`, which causes the specified item to never be visible in windows such as Autos and Locals

▶ `RootHidden`, which forces the debugger to show just the children elements of the specified item

For example, consider the following code snippet that retrieves an array of processes (each represented by an instance of the `System.Diagnostics.Process` class):

```
<DebuggerBrowsable(DebuggerBrowsableState.RootHidden)>
Private ProcessesList As Process()
Sub ShowProcesses()
    ProcessesList = Process.GetProcesses
End Sub
```

The preceding code causes the debugger to show only the children element of the array, excluding the root (`ProcessesList`), as shown in Figure 5.26.

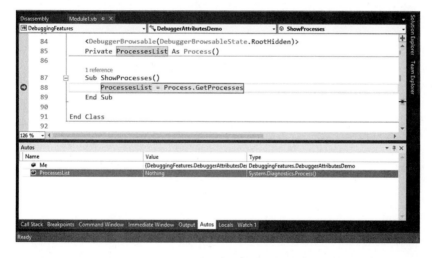

FIGURE 5.26   By using `DebuggerBrowsable`, you can establish how an object can be shown in debugger windows.

DebuggerDisplay

The `DebuggerDisplay` attribute also enables you to establish how an item should be shown inside Data Tips. With this attribute, you can replace Visual Studio default strings and customize the description for an object within Data Tips. For example, imagine you have the code shown in Listing 5.3, in which a `Person` class and code creates a list of people.

LISTING 5.3   Using the `DebuggerDisplay` Attribute

```vb
Module Module1
    Sub Main()
        Dim p As New List(Of Person)
        p.Add(New Person With {.FirstName = "Alessandro", .LastName = "Del Sole"})
        p.Add(New Person With {.FirstName = "MyFantasyName",
                               .LastName = "MyFantasyLastName"})
        Console.ReadLine()
    End Sub
End Module
<DebuggerDisplay("This person is {FirstName} {LastName}")>
Class Person
    Property FirstName As String
    Property LastName As String
End Class
```

At this point, it's not important to focus on how collections of objects are created. However, it's interesting to understand what the `DebuggerDisplay` attribute does. Now place a breakpoint on the `Console.ReadLine` statement and then run the application. If you pass the mouse pointer over the p object, Data Tips for this object will be activated. The debugger then displays data formatted the way described in the `DebuggerDisplay` attribute. Figure 5.27 shows the result of our customization.

FIGURE 5.27   The `DebuggerDisplay` attribute enables customizing Data Tips messages.

DebuggerTypeProxy

As its name implies, the `DebuggerTypeProxy` enables you to override how debug information for a specific data type is shown within Data Tips. Listing 5.4 shows how you can implement such an attribute.

LISTING 5.4   Using the `DebuggerTypeProxy` Attribute

```
Module Module1
    Sub Main()
        Dim p As New List(Of Person)
        p.Add(New Person With {.FirstName = "Alessandro", .LastName = "Del Sole"})
        p.Add(New Person With {.FirstName = "MyFantasyName",
                                .LastName = "MyFantasyLastName"})
        Console.ReadLine()
    End Sub
End Module
<DebuggerTypeProxy(GetType(PersonProxy))>
Class Person
    Property FirstName As String
    Property LastName As String
End Class
Class PersonProxy
    Dim myProxy As Person
    Sub New(ByVal OnePerson As Person)
        myProxy = OnePerson
    End Sub
    ReadOnly Property Length As Integer
        Get
            Return String.Concat(myProxy.FirstName, " ", myProxy.LastName).Length
        End Get
    End Property
End Class
```

The `PersonProxy` class gets the instance of the `Person` class being debugged, reads the information from such instance, and returns via the `Length` property the length of the string composed by the `FirstName` and `LastName` properties. The `Length` property here is a basic example, but it is useful to understand where the real proxy is. To activate the proxy, you need to decorate the `Person` class with the `DebuggerTypeProxy` attribute whose argument is the Type representation of what you need to debug. This type is retrieved using a `GetType` keyword. If you now try to run the application, you can see that the debugger can display the new Length information, as shown in Figure 5.28.

So you now have a powerful way to customize debug information.

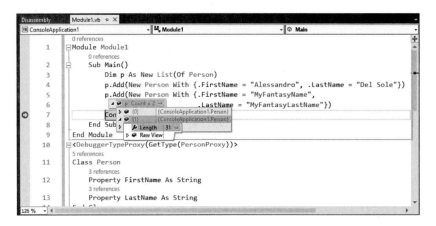

FIGURE 5.28   The DebuggerTypeProxy enables customizing the debug information.

Summary

Debugging is a primary task in developing applications. The Visual Studio 2015 IDE offers lots of useful tools that can enhance the debugging experience. This chapter introduced Just My Code, breakpoints, conditions, and actions, and also debugging in steps. You also saw the debugger windows in action, enabling deep control over variables and objects. In the end, you learned how to customize your own code to take advantage of the Visual Studio debugging tools by decorating your code with debug attributes. But debugging is just one part in the development process that fights against errors. Exceptions are the other part, and they are discussed in Chapter 6, "Errors, Exceptions, and Code Refactoring."

Errors, Exceptions, and Code Refactoring

Every application might encounter errors during its execution, even when you spend several nights on testing the application and all the possible execution scenarios. Runtime errors are especially unpredictable because the application execution is conditioned by user actions. Because of this, error handling is a fundamental practice that, as a developer, you need to know in depth. In this chapter you learn how the .NET Framework enables handling errors and how to get information to solve problems deriving such errors. In other words, you learn about .NET exceptions. In addition, in this chapter you also learn about new tools in Visual Basic 2015 for refactoring your code. Refactoring is definitely a best practice for keeping your code well organized and clean, especially after you have run many tests in handling errors.

Introducing Exceptions

In development environments other than .NET, programming languages can handle errors occurring during the application execution in different ways. For example, the Windows native APIs return a 32-bit HRESULT number in case an error occurs. Visual Basic 6 uses the On Error statements, whereas other languages have their own error-handling infrastructures. As you can imagine, such differences cannot be allowed in the .NET Framework because all languages rely on the Common Language Runtime (CLR), so all of them must intercept and handle errors the same way. With that said, the .NET Framework identifies errors as *exceptions*. An exception is an instance of the System. Exception class (or of a class derived from it) and provides deep information on the error that occurred.

Such an approach provides a unified way for intercepting and handling errors. Exceptions are *thrown* during the application execution. Errors (and warnings) can also be *reported* by the Visual Basic compiler at compile time or by the background compiler when typing code. Errors occurring when designing the user interface of an application or when working within the Visual Studio 2015 IDE are typically called exceptions. This is because such tasks (and most of the Visual Studio IDE) are powered by the .NET Framework. Chapter 2, "The Visual Studio 2015 IDE for Visual Basic," introduced the Visual Studio debugger and saw how it can be used for analyzing error messages provided by exceptions (see the "Runtime Errors" section in Chapter 2). In that case, you did not implement any error-handling routine because that chapter was just introducing the debugging features of Visual Studio during the development process. But what if an error occurs at runtime when the application has been deployed to your customer without implementing appropriate error-handling code? Imagine an application that attempts to read a file that does not exist and in which the developer did not implement error checks. Figure 6.1 shows an example of what could happen and what should never happen in a real application.

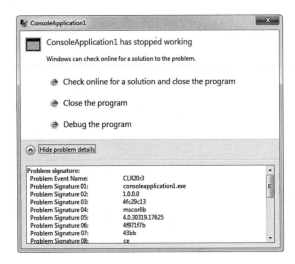

FIGURE 6.1   Without handling exceptions, solving errors is difficult.

As you can see from Figure 6.1, in case of an error the application stops its execution and no resume is possible. Moreover, identifying the type of error occurred can also be difficult. Because of this, as a developer it is your responsibility to implement code for intercepting exceptions and take the best actions possible to solve the problem, while keeping your users' choices in mind. The best way to understand exceptions is to begin to write some code that causes an error, so this is what you do in the next section.

Handling Exceptions

Visual Basic 2015 enables deep control over exceptions. With regard to this, an important concept is that you not only can check for occurring exceptions, but can also conditionally manage solutions to exceptions and raise exceptions when needed. This section discusses all these topics, providing information on how you can intercept and manage exceptions in your application.

Tips for Visual Basic 6 Migration

One of the (very few) commonalities between Visual Basic 6 and Visual Basic .NET and higher is the syntax approach. This should help a little more in migrating from Visual Basic 6 to 2015. Although Visual Basic 2015 (more precisely, VB.NET from 2002 to 2015) still enables the usage of the `On Error Goto` and `On Error Resume` statements, when developing .NET applications with Visual Basic, you should never use such statements for two reasons. First, exceptions are the only thing that enables interoperation with other .NET languages such as Visual C# and Visual F#. This is fundamental when developing class libraries or components that could potentially be reused from other languages than Visual Basic. The second reason is that the old-fashioned way for handling errors is not as efficient as handling .NET exceptions. If you decided to migrate, you should completely forget `On Error` and exclusively use exceptions.

`System.Exception`, Naming Conventions, and Specialization

`System.Exception` is the most general exception and can represent all kinds of errors occurring in applications. It is also the base class for derived exceptions, which are specific to situations you encounter. For example, the `System.IOException` derives from `System.Exception`, is thrown when the application encounters input/output errors when accessing the disk, and can be handled only for this particular situation. On the other hand, `System.Exception` can handle not only this situation, but also any other occurring errors. You can think of `System.Exception` as the root in the exceptions hierarchy. The hierarchy of exception handling is explained later in this chapter. Classes representing exceptions always end with the word `Exception`. You encounter exceptions such as `FileNotFoundException`, `IndexOutOfRangeException`, `FormatException`, and so on. This is not mandatory, but a recommended naming convention. Generally, .NET built-in exceptions inherit from `System.Exception`, but because they are reference types, you find several exceptions inheriting from a derived exception.

Handling Exceptions with `Try..Catch..Finally` Blocks

You perform exception handling by writing a `Try..Catch..Finally` code block. The logic is that you say to the compiler, "Try to execute the code; if you encounter an exception, take the specified actions; whenever the code execution succeeds or it fails due to an exception, execute the final code." The most basic code for controlling the execution flow regarding exceptions is the following:

```
Try
    'Code to be executed
Catch ex As Exception
    'Code to handle the exception
End Try
```

IntelliSense does a great job here. When you type the `Try` keyword and then press **Enter**, it automatically adds the `Catch` statement and the `End Try` terminator. The `ex` variable gets the instance of the `System.Exception` that is caught, and that provides important information so that you can best handle the exception. To see what happens, consider the following code snippet:

```
Try
    Dim myArray() As String = {"1", "2", "3", "4"}
    Console.WriteLine(myArray(4))
Catch ex As Exception
    Console.WriteLine(ex.Message)
End Try
```

Here you have an array of strings in which the upper range of the array is 3. The `Try` block tries to execute code that attempts writing the content of the fourth index to the Console window. Unfortunately, such an index does not exist, but because the code is formally legal, it will be correctly compiled. When the application runs and the runtime encounters this situation, it throws an exception to communicate the error occurrence. So the `Catch` statement intercepts the exception and enables deciding which actions must be taken. In our example, the action to handle the exception is to write the complete error message of the exception. If the code within `Try` succeeds, the execution passes to the first code after the `End Try` terminator. In our example, the control transfers to the `Catch` block that contains code that writes to the Console window the actual error message that looks like the following:

```
Index was outside the bounds of the array
```

The runtime never throws a generic `System.Exception` exception. There are specific exceptions for the most common scenarios (and it is worth mentioning that you can create custom exceptions as discussed in Chapter 12, "Inheritance") that are helpful to identify what happened instead of inspecting a generic exception. Continuing our example, the runtime throws an `IndexOutOfRangeException` that means the code attempted to access and index greater or smaller than allowed. Based on these considerations, the code could be rewritten as follows:

```
Try
    Dim myArray() As String = {"1", "2", "3", "4"}
    Console.WriteLine(myArray(4))
Catch ex As IndexOutOfRangeException
    Console.WriteLine("There is a problem: probably you are "
            & Environment.NewLine &
```

```
                " attempting to access an index that does not exist")
    Catch ex As Exception
        Console.WriteLine(ex.Message)
    End Try
```

As you can see, the most specific exception needs to be caught before the most generic one. This is quite obvious because, if you first catch the `System.Exception`, all other exceptions will be ignored. Intercepting specific exceptions can also be useful because you can both communicate the user detailed information and decide which actions must be taken to solve the problem. Anyway, always adding a `Catch` block for a generic `System.Exception` is a best practice. This enables you to provide a general error-handling code in case exceptions you do not specifically intercept will occur. You could also need to perform some actions independently from the result of your code execution. The `Finally` statement enables executing some code either if the `Try` succeeds or if it fails, passing control to `Catch`. For example, you might want to clean up resources used by the array:

```
Dim myArray() As String = {"1", "2", "3", "4"}
Try
    Console.WriteLine(myArray(4))
Catch ex As IndexOutOfRangeException
    Console.WriteLine("There is a problem: probably you are "
            & Environment.NewLine &
            " attempting to access an index that does not exists")
Catch ex As Exception
    Console.WriteLine(ex.Message)
Finally
    myArray = Nothing
End Try
```

Notice how objects referred within the `Finally` block must be declared outside the `Try..End Try` block because of visibility. The code within `Finally` will be executed no matter what the result of the `Try` block will be. This is important; for example, think about files. You might open a file and then try to perform some actions on the file that for any reason can fail. In this situation you would need to close the file, and `Finally` ensures you can do that if the file access is successful and even if it fails (throwing an exception). An example of this scenario is represented in Listing 6.1.

LISTING 6.1   Using `Finally` to Ensure Resources Are Freed Up and Unlocked

```
Imports System.IO
Module Module1
    Sub Main()
        Console.WriteLine("Specify a file name:")
        Dim fileName As String = Console.ReadLine
        Dim myFile As FileStream = Nothing
        Try
            myFile = New FileStream(fileName, FileMode.Open)
```

```
        'Seek a specific position in the file.
        'Just for example
        myFile.Seek(5, SeekOrigin.Begin)
    Catch ex As FileNotFoundException
        Console.WriteLine("File not found.")
    Catch ex As Exception
        Console.WriteLine("An unidentified error occurred.")
    Finally
        myFile?.Close()
    End Try
    Console.ReadLine()
End Sub
End Module
```

The code in Listing 6.1 is quite simple. First, it asks the user to specify a filename to be accessed. Accessing files is accomplished with a `FileStream` object. Notice that the `myFile` object is declared outside the `Try..End Try` block so that it can be visible within `Finally`. Moreover, its value is set to `Nothing` so that it has a default value, although it's null. If you did not assign this default value, `myFile` would just be declared but not yet assigned, so the Visual Basic compiler would report a warning message. By the way, setting the default value to `Nothing` will not prevent a `NullReferenceException` at runtime unless the variable gets a value. The `Try` block attempts accessing the specified file. The `FileStream.Seek` method here is just used as an example needed to perform an operation on the file. When accessing files, there could be different problems, resulting in various kinds of exceptions. In our example, if the specified file does not exist, a `FileNotFoundException` is thrown by the runtime and the `Catch` block takes control over the execution. Within the block, the code just communicates that the specified file was not found. If, instead, the file exists, the code performs a search. In both cases, the `Finally` block ensures that the file gets closed, independently on what happened before. This is fundamental because if you leave a file open, other problems would occur.

Exceptions Hierarchy

In Listing 6.1, you saw how you can catch a specific exception, such as `FileNotFoundException`, and then the general `System.Exception`. By the way, `FileNotFoundException` does not directly derive from `System.Exception`; instead, it derives from `System.IO.IOException`, which is related to general input/output problems. Although you are not obliged to also catch an `IOException` when working with files, adding it could be a good practice because you can separate error handling for disk input/output errors from other errors. In such situations, the rule is that you have to catch exceptions from the most specific to the most general. Continuing the previous example, Listing 6.2 shows how you can implement exceptions hierarchy.

LISTING 6.2   Understanding Exceptions Hierarchy

```vb
Imports System.IO
Module Module1
    Sub Main()
        Console.WriteLine("Specify a file name:")
        Dim fileName As String = Console.ReadLine
        Dim myFile As FileStream = Nothing
        Try
            myFile = New FileStream(fileName, FileMode.Open)
            'Seek a specific position in the file.
            'Just for example
            myFile.Seek(5, SeekOrigin.Begin)
        Catch ex As FileNotFoundException
            Console.WriteLine("File not found.")
        Catch ex As IOException
            Console.WriteLine("A general input/output error occurred")
        Catch ex As Exception
            Console.WriteLine("An unidentified error occurred.")
        Finally
            If myFile IsNot Nothing Then
                myFile.Close()
            End If
        End Try
        Console.ReadLine()
    End Sub
End Module
```

FileNotFoundException is the most specific exception, so it must be caught first. It derives from IOException, which is intercepted second. System.Exception is instead the base class for all exceptions and therefore must be caught last.

System.Exception Properties

The System.Exception class exposes some properties that are useful for investigating exceptions and then understanding what the real problem is. Particularly when you catch specialized exceptions, it could happen that such exception is just the last ring of a chain and that the problem causing the exception itself derives from other problems. System.Exception's properties enable a better navigation of exceptions. Table 6.1 lists the available properties.

TABLE 6.1   System.Exception's Properties

Property	Description
Message	Gets the complete error message generated from the exception
Source	Represents the name of the application or the object that threw the exception
TargetSite	Retrieves the method that actually throws the exception
Data	Stores a sequence of key/value pairs containing additional information on the exception
Help	Allows specifying or retrieving the name of the help file associated with the exception
InnerException	Gets the instance of the exception object that actually caused the current exception
StackTrace	Retrieves the method calls hierarchy in the call stack when the exception occurred

Listing 6.3 shows how you can retrieve deep information on the exception. In the example, information is retrieved for the System.IO.FileNotFoundException, but you can use these properties for any exception you like.

LISTING 6.3   Investigating Exceptions Properties

```
Imports System.IO
Module Module1
    Sub Main()
        Console.WriteLine("Specify a file name:")
        Dim fileName As String = Console.ReadLine
        Dim myFile As FileStream = Nothing
        Try
            myFile = New FileStream(fileName, FileMode.Open)
            'Seek a specific position in the file.
            'Just for example
            myFile.Seek(5, SeekOrigin.Begin)
        Catch ex As FileNotFoundException
            Console.WriteLine()
            Console.WriteLine("Error message: " & ex.Message
                    & Environment.NewLine)
            Console.WriteLine("Object causing the exception: "
                        & ex.Source & Environment.NewLine)
            Console.WriteLine("Method where the exception is thrown; "
                        & ex.TargetSite.ToString & Environment.NewLine)
            Console.WriteLine("Call stack:" & ex.StackTrace & Environment.NewLine)
            Console.WriteLine("Other useful info:")
            For Each k As KeyValuePair(Of String, String) In ex.Data
                Console.WriteLine(k.Key & " " & k.Value)
```

```
        Next
    Catch ex As IOException
        Console.WriteLine("A general input/output error occurred")
    Catch ex As Exception
        Console.WriteLine(ex.Message)
    Finally
        If myFile IsNot Nothing Then
            myFile.Close()
        End If
    End Try
    Console.ReadLine()
End Sub
End Module
```

If you run this code and specify a filename that does not exist, you can retrieve a lot of useful information. Figure 6.2 shows the result of the code.

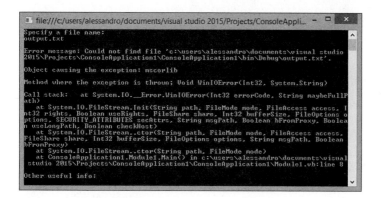

FIGURE 6.2   Getting information on the exception.

As you can see from Figure 6.2, the `Message` property contains the full error message. In production environments, this can be a useful way to provide customers a user-friendly error message. The `Source` property shows the application or object causing the exception. In our example, it retrieves Mscorlib, meaning that the exception was thrown by the CLR. The `Target` property retrieves the method in which the exception was thrown. It is worth mentioning that this property retrieves the native method that caused the error, meaning that the method was invoked by the CLR. This is clearer if you take a look at the content of the `Stack` property. You can see the hierarchy of method calls in descending order: the `.ctor` method is the constructor of the `FileStream` class, invoked within the `Main` method; the next method, named `Init`, attempts to initialize a `FileStream` and is invoked behind the scenes by the CLR. `Init` then invokes the native `WinIOError` function because accessing the file was unsuccessful. Analyzing such properties can be useful to understand what happened. Because there is no other useful information, iterating the `Data` property produced no result. By the way, if you just need to report a detailed message about the exception, you can collect most of the properties' content by invoking the `ToString` method of the `Exception` class. For example, you could replace the entire `Catch ex as FileNotFoundException` block as follows:

```
Catch ex As FileNotFoundException
    Console.WriteLine(ex.ToString)
```

This edit produces the result shown in Figure 6.3. As you can see, the result is a little different from the previous one. You can find a lot of useful information, such as the name of the exception, complete error message, filename, call stack hierarchy, and line of code that caused the exception.

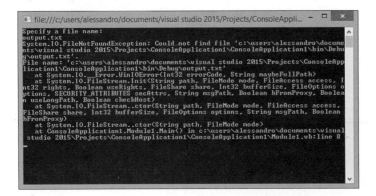

FIGURE 6.3   Invoking the `Exception.ToString` method offers detailed information.

Typically, you use `ToString` just to show information, whereas you use properties to analyze exception information.

NOTE ABOUT PERFORMANCE

Catching exceptions is necessary but is also performance consuming. Sometimes you could simply check the value of an object instead of catching exceptions. For example, you could check with an `If..Then` statement whether an object is null instead of catching a `NullReferenceException` (when possible, of course). Exceptions are best left to handling "exceptional" situations that occur in code, so you should limit the use of them when possible.

Catching and Ignoring Exceptions

You can also ignore exceptions by simply not writing anything inside a `Catch` block. For instance, the following code catches a `FileNotFoundException` and prevents an undesired stop in the application execution but takes no action:

```
Try
    testFile = New FileStream(FileName, FileMode.Open)
Catch ex As FileNotFoundException
End Try
```

Nested `Try..Catch..Finally` Blocks

You also have the ability to nest `Try..Catch..Finally` code blocks. Nested blocks are useful when you have to try the execution of code onto the result of another `Try..Catch` block. Consider the following code that shows the creation time of all files in a given directory:

```
Try
    Dim allFiles As String() =
        Directory.GetFiles("C:\TestDirectory")
    Try
        For Each f As String In allFiles
            Console.WriteLine(File.GetCreationTime(f).ToString())
        Next
    Catch ex As IOException
    Catch ex As Exception
    End Try
Catch ex As DirectoryNotFoundException
Catch ex As Exception
End Try
```

The first `Try..Catch` attempts reading the list of files from a specified directory. Because you can encounter directory errors, a `DirectoryNotFoundException` is caught. The result (being an array of `String`) is then iterated within a nested `Try..Catch` block. This is because the code is now working on files and then specific errors might be encountered.

`Exit Try` Statements

You can exit from within a `Try..Catch..Finally` block at any moment using an `Exit Try` statement. If a `Finally` block exists, `Exit Try` pulls the execution into `Finally` that otherwise resumes the execution at the first line of code after `End Try`. The following code snippet shows an example:

```
Try
    'Your code goes here
    Exit Try
    'The following line will not be considered
    Console.WriteLine("End of Try block")
Catch ex As Exception
End Try
'Resume the execution here
```

The `Throw` Keyword

In some situations you need to programmatically throw exceptions or you catch exceptions but do not want to handle them in the `Catch` block that intercepted exceptions. Programmatically throwing exceptions can be accomplished via the `Throw` keyword. For instance, the following line of code throws an `ArgumentNullException` that usually occurs when a method receives a null argument:

```
Throw New ArgumentNullException
```

You often need to manually throw exceptions when they should be handled by another portion of code, also in another application. A typical example is when you develop class libraries. A class library must be as abstract as possible, so you cannot decide which actions to take when an exception is caught; this is the responsibility of the developer who creates the application that references your class library. If both developers are the same person, this remains a best practice because you should always separate the logic of class implementations from the client logic (such as the user interface). To provide a clearer example, a class library cannot show a graphical message box or a text message into the Console window. It instead needs to send the code the exception caught to the caller, and this is accomplished via the `Throw` keyword. A code example is now provided. In Visual Studio 2015, create a new blank solution and then add a new Class Library project that you could name, for example, `TestThrow`. Listing 6.4 shows the content of the class.

LISTING 6.4   Throwing Back Exceptions to Caller Code

```
Imports System.IO
Public Class TestThrow
    Public Sub TestAccessFile(ByVal FileName As String)
        If String.IsNullOrEmpty(FileName) Then
            Throw New ArgumentNullException("FileName",
                    "You passed an invalid file name")
        End If
        Dim testFile As FileStream = Nothing
        Try
            testFile = New FileStream(FileName, FileMode.Open)
        Catch ex As FileNotFoundException
            Throw New FileNotFoundException("The supplied file name was not found")
        Catch ex As Exception
            Throw
        Finally
            If testFile IsNot Nothing Then
                testFile.Close()
            End If
        End Try
    End Function
End Class
```

The TestThrow class's purpose is just attempting to access a file. This is accomplished by invoking the TestAccess method that receives a FileName argument of type String. The first check is on the argument: If it is null, the code throws back to the caller an ArgumentNullException that provides the argument name and a description. In this scenario, the method catches but does not handle the exception. This is thrown back to the caller code, which is responsible to handle the exception (for example, asking the user to specify a valid filename). The second check is on the file access. The Try..Catch.. Finally block implements code that tries to access the specified file and, if the file is not found, it throws back the FileNotFoundException describing what happened. In this way the caller code is responsible for handling the exception; for example, asking the user to specify another filename. Also notice how a generic System.Exception is caught and thrown back to the caller by simply invoking the Throw statement without arguments. This enables the method to throw back to the caller the complete exception information. Remember that you can also use the NameOf operator, described in Chapter 4, "Data Types and Expressions," to refer to argument names in a strongly typed way. With NameOf, the first Throw statement in Listing 6.4 could be rewritten as follows:

```
Throw New ArgumentNullException(NameOf(FileName),
        "You passed an invalid file name")
```

RETHROWING EXCEPTIONS

Throwing back an exception to the caller code is also known as the *rethrow technique*.

Now you can create an application that can reference the TestThrow class library and handle exceptions on the client side. Add to the solution a new Visual Basic project for the Console and add a reference to the TestThrow class library by selecting **Project, Add Reference**. Adding a reference to another assembly enables you to use types exposed publicly from such an assembly. Finally, write the code shown in Listing 6.5.

LISTING 6.5   Handling Exceptions on the Client Side

```
Imports System.IO
Module Module1
    Sub Main()
        Console.WriteLine("Specify the file name:")
        Dim name As String = Console.ReadLine
        Dim throwTest As New TestThrow.TestThrow
        Try
            throwTest.TestAccessFile(name)
        Catch ex As ArgumentNullException
            Console.WriteLine(ex.ToString & Environment.NewLine &
                    "You passed an invalid argument")
        Catch ex As FileNotFoundException
            Console.WriteLine(ex.Message)
        Catch ex As Exception
```

```
        Console.WriteLine(ex.ToString)
    Finally
        Console.ReadLine()
    End Try
End Sub
End Module
```

The code in Listing 6.5 first asks the user to specify a filename to access. If you press **Enter** without specifying any filename, the `TestAccessFile` method is invoked passing an empty string, so the method throws an `ArgumentNullException`, as shown in Figure 6.4.

FIGURE 6.4   Passing an empty string as an argument causes an `ArgumentNullException`.

If this situation happened inside a Windows application, you could provide a `MessageBox` showing the error message. With this approach, you maintain logics separately. If you instead specify a filename that does not exist, the caller code needs to handle the `FileNotFoundException`; the result is shown in Figure 6.5.

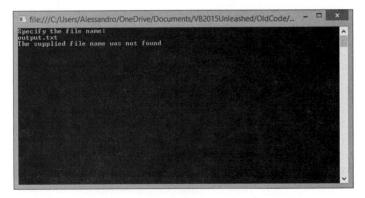

FIGURE 6.5   The caller code handles the `FileNotFoundException` and shows a user-friendly message.

The caller code writes the content of the `ex.Message` property to the Console window, which is populated with the error message provided by the `Thrown` statement from the class library. If any other kinds of exceptions occur, a generic `System.Exception` is handled and its content is shown to the user.

CATCHING TASK-SPECIFIC EXCEPTIONS

Depending on which tasks you perform within a `Try..Catch` block, always catch exceptions specific for those tasks. For example, if your code works with files, don't limit it to catch a `FileNotFoundException`. Consider file-related and disk-related exceptions, too. To get a listing of the exceptions that a class was designed to throw, you can read the MSDN documentation related to that class. The documentation describes in detail which exceptions are related to the desired object.

Performance Overhead

Invoking the `Throw` keyword causes the runtime to search through all the code hierarchy until it finds the caller code that can handle the exception. Continuing our previous example, the Console application is not necessarily the first caller code. There could be another class library that could rethrow the exception to another class that could then rethrow the exception to the main caller code. Obviously, going through the callers' hierarchy is a task that could cause performance overhead, so you should take care about how many callers are in your code to reduce the overhead. In the end, if the caller code is missing a `Catch` block, the result will be the same as what is shown in Figure 6.1, which should always be avoided.

The `When` Keyword

Sometimes you might need to catch an exception only when a particular condition exists. You can conditionally control the exception handling using the `When` keyword, which enables taking specific actions when a particular condition is evaluated as `True`. Continuing the example of the previous paragraph, the `TestThrow` class throws an `ArgumentNullException` in two different situations (although similar). The first one is if the string passed to the `TestAccessFile` method is empty; the second one is if the string passed to the method is a null value (`Nothing`). So it could be useful to decide which actions to take depending on what actually caused the exception. According to this, you could rewrite the code shown in Listing 6.5 as what is shown in Listing 6.6.

LISTING 6.6   Conditional Exception Handling with the `When` Keyword

```
Imports System.IO
Module Module1
    Sub Main()
        Console.WriteLine("Specify the file name:")
        Dim name As String = Console.ReadLine
        Dim throwTest As New TestThrow.TestThrow
        Try
            throwTest.TestAccessFile(name)
```

```
        Catch ex As ArgumentNullException When name Is Nothing
            Console.WriteLine("You provided a null parameter")
        Catch ex As ArgumentNullException When name Is String.Empty
            Console.WriteLine("You provided an empty string")
        Catch ex As FileNotFoundException
            Console.WriteLine(ex.Message)
        Catch ex As Exception
            Console.WriteLine(ex.ToString)
        Finally
            Console.ReadLine()
        End Try
    End Sub
End Module
```

As you can see from Listing 6.6, by using the When keyword you can conditionally handle exceptions depending if the expression on the right is evaluated as True. In this case, when handling the ArgumentNullException, the condition is evaluating the name variable. If name is equal to Nothing, the exception is handled showing a message saying that the string is null. If name is instead an empty string (which is different from a null string), another kind of message is shown. When can be applied only to Catch statements and works only with expressions. Of course, you can use the When keyword also with value types; for example, you might have a counter that you increment during the execution of your code and, in case of exceptions, you might decide which actions to take based on the value of your counter. The following code demonstrates:

```
Dim oneValue As Integer = 0
Try
    'perform some operations
    'on oneValue
Catch ex As Exception When oneValue = 1
Catch ex As Exception When oneValue = 2
Catch ex As Exception When oneValue = 3
End Try
```

Catching Exceptions Without a Variable

You do not always need to specify a variable in the Catch block. This can be the case in which you want to take the same action independently from the exception that occurred. For example, consider the following code:

```
Try
    Dim result As String =
        My.Computer.FileSystem.ReadAllText("C:\MyFile.txt")
Catch ex As Exception
    Console.WriteLine("A general error occurred")
End Try
```

The ex variable is not being used and no specific exceptions are handled. So the preceding code can be rewritten as follows, without the ex variable:

```
Try
    Dim result As String =
        My.Computer.FileSystem.ReadAllText("C:\MyFile.txt")
Catch
    Console.WriteLine("A general error occurred")
End Try
```

Whichever exception occurs, the code shows the specified message. This also works with regard to the rethrow technique. The following code simply rethrows the proper exception to the caller:

```
Try
    Dim result As String =
        My.Computer.FileSystem.ReadAllText("C:\MyFile.txt")
Catch
    Throw
End Try
```

Handling Warnings

As you learned in Chapter 2, the Visual Basic compiler reports warning messages when it finds some specific code issues that do not prevent the application from running. The following code shows two common situations, where a variable is declared but never used and where another variable is assigned but an object instance does not exist:

```
'Unused local variable: 'anInt'
Dim anInt As Integer

'Variable myFile is used before it has been assigned a value
'A null reference exception could result at runtime
Dim myFile As FileInfo
myFile.Delete()
```

Of course, you should not ignore either warning, but especially not the second one. However, there are situations in which you need to write code this way. Because in such situations warning messages could be annoying, in Visual Basic 2015 you can use the #Disable Warning and #Enable Warning directives to disable and enable warning messages, respectively. Both take the warning code as an argument. You can see the warning code in the Error List window. For example, you can disable the first warning in the example with the following code:

```
#Disable Warning BC42024
        'Unused local variable: 'anInt'
        Dim anInt As Integer

        'Additional code here...
#Enable Warning BC420204
```

This code suppresses the warning message for a specific code block and then re-enables the warning message at the end of the block. However, you can also disable (and enable) warning messages at the class/module level or at the code file level. For example, the following directive suppresses the warning message for the current module:

```
Module Module1
#Disable Warning BC42024
    Sub Main()

        'Unused local variable: 'anInt'
        Dim anInt As Integer

        'Nested directives are ignored
        'The next declaration is not highlighted
#Enable Warning BC420204
        Dim anotherInt As Integer

    End Sub
End Module
```

Notice that #Enable Warning directives are ignored if they appear inside an object at a lower level; the same is true with #Disable Warning directives. The following code demonstrates how to disable a warning message for the current code file:

```
#Disable Warning BC42024
Module Module1

    Sub Main()
        Dim anInt As Integer
    End Sub
End Module

Class Foo
    Sub New()
        Dim anInt As Integer
    End Sub
End Class
```

Neither the `anInt` variable in the module nor the `anInt` variable in the `Foo` class will be highlighted with warning messages. You can disable or enable multiple warnings by placing a comma after each warning code as a separator.

Refactoring Your Code: Light Bulbs and Quick Actions

One of the benefits provided by the .NET Compiler Platform is live static code analysis, which means that compilers use grammar and semantic rules to analyze your code as you type. Managed compilers provide a built-in set of *code analyzers*, which send to the code editor information for immediately highlighting errors and code issues, suggesting fixes, and allowing reorganization of the code in a better way, using refactoring techniques. Visual Basic 2015 takes strong advantages of all these new functionalities, providing the best coding experience ever. You can now fix and improve your code without ever losing your focus on the code editor.

CODE ANALYZERS AND CUSTOM REFACTORING

Chapter 51, "Code Analysis: The .NET Compiler Platform and Tools," explains how to create custom code analyzers and provides further information about this topic.

Specifically, every time the Visual Basic compiler detects code that has errors or other issues, the IDE shows a light bulb icon, as shown in Figure 6.6.

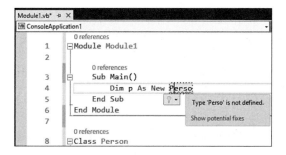

FIGURE 6.6   The light bulb icon.

The light bulb is a container of *quick actions*, or possible fixes or suggestions for the current code issue. Light bulbs and quick actions can provide error fixes as well as suggestions on how to refactor your code. In fact, Visual Basic 2015 finally provides support for built-in refactoring techniques, which is something that C# has had since ancient times; this is described shortly. The light bulb icon appears every time you hover over error squiggles; you can also open it manually by pressing **Ctrl+.** (dot).

> **TIP**
>
> You can also invoke the light bulb icon by right-clicking anywhere in your code and then selecting **Quick Actions** from the pop-up menu. Which suggestions or refactoring tools are available depends on where you invoked the light bulb.

In the next sections, you learn how to use the light bulb to both fix errors and refactor your code, and you need to prepare an example for the practicing you'll do. Simply create a new Console application and add the following simple `Person` class definition:

```
Class Person
    Property FirstName As String
    Property LastName As String
    Property DateOfBirth As Date
End Class
```

This is enough to simulate some interesting scenarios for the light bulb.

Fixing Errors and Code Issues

The light bulb and quick actions can help you fix errors and code issues very quickly, without needing to leave the active code editor window. To understand more about this feature, consider the following line of code, which attempts to declare an object of type `Perso` that obviously does not exist:

```
Dim p As New Perso
```

The compiler detects that the `Perso` object does not exist, and so it shows a red error squiggle. At this point, hover over the `Perso` object with your mouse, and when the light bulb appears, click the arrow to expand the available quick actions or click **Show Potential Fixes**. As you can see in Figure 6.7, Visual Basic shows a number of possible solutions. For each solution, it also shows a preview where the code highlighted in green is the code that will be added, and code highlighted in red is the code that will be removed. Also, the compiler is intelligent enough to understand that your error is probably just a typo and then suggests, as a possible solution, to replace `Perso` with `Person`.

If you are satisfied with what the preview shows, simply click the current selection. You also have an option to see a more detailed preview of changes by clicking **Preview Changes** in the preview box. Figure 6.8 shows the Preview Changes dialog that appears at this point.

The Preview Changes dialog highlights the code that will be changed and shows the list of code files and child objects affected by changes. If you are fine with replacing `Perso` with `Person`, you can simply apply this solution.

Now let's consider another example, where you simulate a missing implementation of an interface. Under the `Person` class declaration, type the following directive without pressing Enter:

```
Implements INotifyPropertyChanged
```

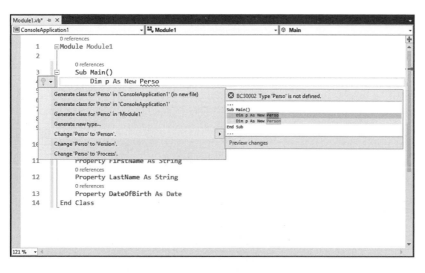

FIGURE 6.7   The light bulb shows potential fixes for your code, with a preview.

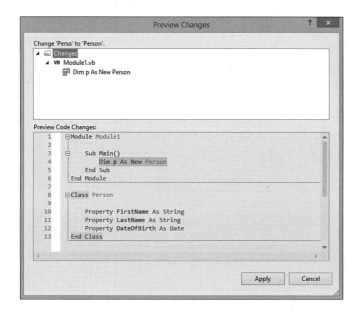

FIGURE 6.8   A more detailed preview of changes to your code.

When the error squiggle appears, enable the light bulb. As you can see from Figure 6.9, the compiler detects that your code is missing an `Imports System.ComponentModel` directive and provides appropriate suggestions. For the sake of clarity, choose the first one from the list.

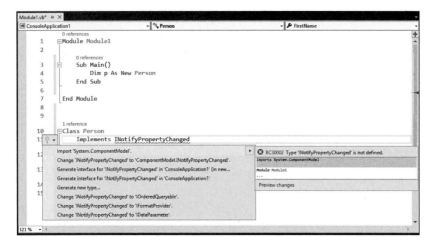

FIGURE 6.9   Detecting and fixing missing Imports directives.

At this point, the error is not completely solved because you still need to implement the interface. The light bulb can provide an appropriate solution called Implement Interface, as shown in Figure 6.10.

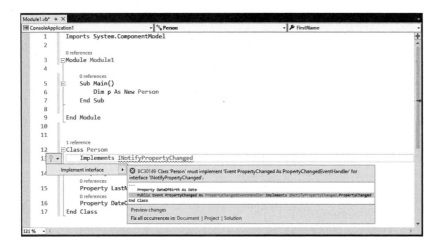

FIGURE 6.10   Implementing an interface.

Notice that you have an option of applying changes to all the possible `Person` class definitions in the current code file and also in the entire project or solution. The live static code analysis is also powerful for another reason: Compilers can suggest fixes according to the behaviors of specific objects. For example, remove the `INotifyPropertyChanged` interface implementation and then add the following directive, still without pressing Enter:

```
Implements IDisposable
```

You get detailed information about the `IDisposable` interface in Chapter 8, "Managing an Object's Lifetime," so I will not spend additional time on it here. But note that the light bulb suggests quick actions that are specific to this interface; for example, in Figure 6.11 you can see the possible solutions Implement Interface and Implement Interface with Dispose Pattern. The preview shows different interface implementations, depending on what solution you choose.

FIGURE 6.11   Getting possible solutions that are specific to an object's behavior.

Figure 6.12 shows how the Preview Changes dialog appears in this scenario. It provides a full code preview and helps you understand more easily how changes affect your code, including the list of files involved in changes.

In this section you got three examples of how to fix code issues with the light bulb and quick actions; these simple examples are enough to put you on the right path to successfully using the new tools with any error you encounter when writing code. Without a doubt, this new way of solving code issues is one of the most powerful and interesting new features in Visual Basic 2015. Furthermore, you can extend it by writing custom code analyzers (see Chapter 51).

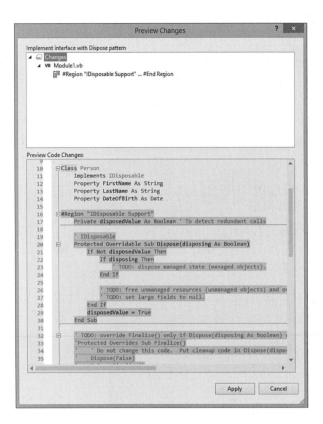

FIGURE 6.12   Getting a full preview of changes in your code.

Improving Code Quality: Refactoring

For the first time in the history of Visual Basic .NET, Visual Basic 2015 introduces support for built-in refactoring techniques. Refactoring allows you to reorganize portions of your code a better and cleaner way, without changing its original behavior. Visual Basic 2015 makes it easier to refactor your code via special tools offered by the light bulb. In this section you learn about the most common refactoring techniques.

Extract Interface

Refactoring allows you to extract an interface from a class. Consider Listing 6.7, which shows an extended definition of the `Person` class discussed above.

WHY `StringBuilder`?

You might argue that the code would be better if it simply used methods from the `String` class instead of the `StringBuilder` class. This might be correct, but here this object is used because it is also the basis for another refactoring technique described later in this section.

LISTING 6.7   Preparing a Class for Refactoring

```
Imports System.Text
Class Person
    Property FirstName As String
    Property LastName As String
    Property DateOfBirth As Date

    Public Function FullName() As String
        Dim name As New StringBuilder
        name.Append(Me.FirstName)
        name.Append(" ")
        name.Append(Me.LastName)
        name.Append(" ")
        name.Append("born on ")
        name.Append(Me.DateOfBirth.ToShortDateString)
        Return name.ToString
    End Function
End Class
```

When you're ready, right-click the `Person` identifier and select **Quick Actions** from the pop-up menu. A quick action called **Extract Interface** appears, and when you click it, the Extract Interface dialog shows up (see Figure 6.13.)

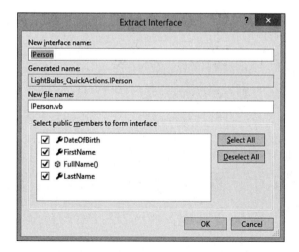

FIGURE 6.13   The Extract Interface dialog.

As you can see, the IDE allows you to select members that you want to wrap into a new interface, and it gives you an opportunity to change the interface's code filename. If you click OK, Visual Studio generates the following interface:

```
Interface IPerson
    Property DateOfBirth As Date
    Property FirstName As String
    Property LastName As String
    Function FullName() As String
End Interface
```

In addition, Visual Studio has automatically changed the original `Person` class to implement the `IPerson` interface, as follows:

```
Class Person
    Implements IPerson
    Property FirstName As String Implements IPerson.FirstName
    Property LastName As String Implements IPerson.LastName
    Property DateOfBirth As Date Implements IPerson.DateOfBirth

    Public Function FullName() As String Implements IPerson.FullName
        Dim name As New StringBuilder
        name.Append(Me.FirstName)
        name.Append(" ")
        name.Append(Me.LastName)
        name.Append(" ")
        name.Append("born on ")
        name.Append(Me.DateOfBirth.ToShortDateString)
        Return name.ToString
    End Function
End Class
```

This is a very useful technique if you want to make your code more object oriented. You'll learn more about this in Part II, "Object-Oriented Programming with Visual Basic 2015."

Extract Method

You can easily refactor portions of code into separate methods for better reusability. In fact, doing so is a best practice. For example, consider the following code, which calculates the area of a circle, given its radius:

```
Module Module1

    Sub Main()

        Dim radius As Double = 3
        Dim circleArea As Double = radius * radius * Math.PI
    End Sub

End Module
```

It would be nice to have a reusable method to perform the same operation in different places. You can accomplish this by using Extract Method refactoring. Notice that this is available only when you explicitly select one or more lines of code. In this case, you can select the `radius * radius * Math.PI` code and enable the light bulb, which is also available under the Refactor command in the code editor's pop-up menu. Figure 6.14 shows how Extract Method appears at this point.

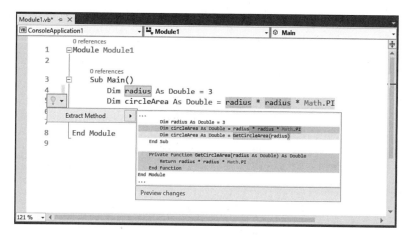

FIGURE 6.14   Extracting code into a separate method.

As you can see, the light bulb shows the usual preview and automatically suggests a method name based on the local variable name. If you accept the suggested changes, the code then looks like this:

```
Sub Main()
    Dim radius As Double = 3
    Dim circleArea As Double = GetCircleArea(radius)
End Sub

Private Function GetCircleArea(radius As Double) As Double
    Return radius * radius * Math.PI
End Function
```

With this feature, you can easily separate code blocks into logical units, which improves code reusability and readability. When the new method is created, Visual Studio gives you an opportunity to rename the method, as discussed in the next section.

Inline Rename

Renaming objects and their members is a common task. In previous versions of Visual Studio, in order to rename an identifier, you had to use a modal dialog. In Visual Studio 2015, renaming an identifier happens directly in the active editor window. This new approach is known as Inline Rename, and it is definitely more powerful than in the renaming available in previous versions of the IDE. To understand all this power, add a comment and a `Console.WriteLine` statement to the previous code, like this:

```
Sub Main()
    Dim radius As Double = 3
    Console.WriteLine("Invoking GetCircleArea...")
    Dim circleArea As Double = GetCircleArea(radius)
End Sub


'GetCircleArea calculates the area of a circle
Private Function GetCircleArea(radius As Double) As Double
    Return radius * radius * Math.PI
End Function
```

Right-click the `GetCircleArea` method name and then select **Rename**. Visual Studio highlights in green all the occurrences of the specified identifier, and it shows a pop-up inside the active editor window where you can specify additional options (see Figure 6.15).

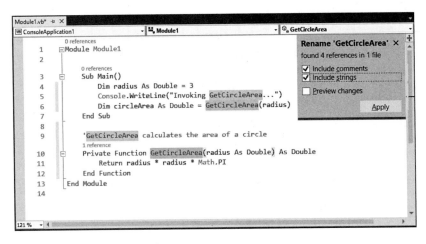

FIGURE 6.15   Enabling Inline Rename.

To rename the identifier, simply type the new name. If you select the **Include Comments** and/or **Include Strings** options, Visual Studio also renames occurrences of the specified identifier that appears inside comments and string literals. Figure 6.16 demonstrates this.

When you are satisfied with your changes, simply click **Apply** in the pop-up or press **Enter**. You can also preview your changes by selecting the **Preview Changes** option and then clicking **Apply**.

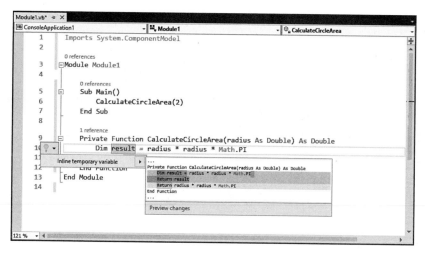

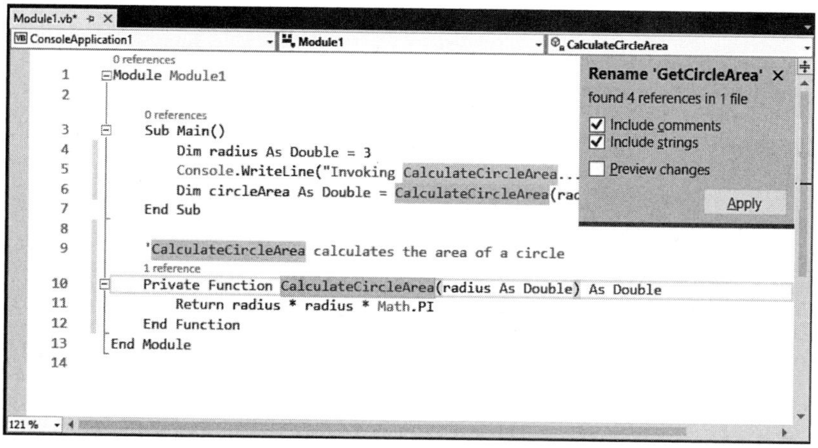

(Screenshot of Visual Studio showing Module1.vb with a "Rename 'GetCircleArea'" dialog)

```
Module1.vb* ≠ ×
ConsoleApplication1                    Module1                    CalculateCircleArea
           0 references
 1    ⊟Module Module1                          Rename 'GetCircleArea'  ×
 2                                              found 4 references in 1 file
           0 references
 3    ⊟    Sub Main()                           ☑ Include comments
 4            Dim radius As Double = 3          ☑ Include strings
 5            Console.WriteLine("Invoking CalculateCircleArea...  ☐ Preview changes
 6            Dim circleArea As Double = CalculateCircleArea(rad
 7        End Sub                                                    Apply
 8
 9        'CalculateCircleArea calculates the area of a circle
           1 reference
10    ⊟    Private Function CalculateCircleArea(radius As Double) As Double
11            Return radius * radius * Math.PI
12        End Function
13    ⊡End Module
14
121 %
```

FIGURE 6.16   Renaming an identifier, as well as occurrences in comments and string literals.

Introduce Temporary Variable

Introduce Temporary Variable is a new refactoring technique for both Visual Basic and C# that allows you to remove unnecessary variable declarations. To understand how it works, consider the following definition of the `CalculateCircleArea` method:

```
Private Function CalculateCircleArea(radius As Double) As Double
    Dim result = radius * radius * Math.PI
    Return result
End Function
```

If you right-click the result variable and enable the light bulb, Visual Studio suggests removing the variable declaration and returning the result directly (see Figure 6.17).

```
Module1.vb* ≠ ×
ConsoleApplication1                    Module1                    CalculateCircleArea
 1        Imports System.ComponentModel
 2
           0 references
 3    ⊟Module Module1
 4
           0 references
 5    ⊟    Sub Main()
 6            CalculateCircleArea(2)
 7        End Sub
 8
           1 reference
 9    ⊟    Private Function CalculateCircleArea(radius As Double) As Double
10 �▾     Dim result = radius * radius * Math.PI
11
12  Inline temporary variable    ▸    ...
13                                     Private Function CalculateCircleArea(radius As Double) As Double
    ⊡End Module                           Dim result = radius * radius * Math.PI
14                                         Return result
                                           Return radius * radius * Math.PI
                                       End Function
                                       ...

                                     Preview changes
121 %
```

FIGURE 6.17   Introducing a temporary variable.

If you accept the suggestion, the code then looks like this:

```
Private Function CalculateCircleArea(radius As Double) As Double
    Return radius * radius * Math.PI
End Function
```

This is a cleaner way of writing the same code, with one line fewer.

Introduce Local Variable

Introduce Local Variable is another new refactoring technique for Visual Basic and C#. It allows you to simplify complex code by adding local variables. Consider this new version of the `CalculateCircleArea` function, which takes an argument of type `Object` and performs the proper conversion to `Double`:

```
Private Function CalculateCircleArea(radius As Object) As Double
    Dim circleArea As Double =
    Convert.ToDouble(radius) * Convert.ToDouble(radius) * Math.PI
    Return circleArea
End Function
```

If you select the first `Convert.ToDouble(radius)` invocation and enable the light bulb, two refactoring options become available: **Introduce Local for Convert.ToDouble(radius)** and **Introduce Local for all Occurrences of 'Convert.ToDouble(radius)'**. The first option fixes the code only on the selected occurrence, whereas the second option fixes the code on all occurrences of the method invocation. As shown in Figure 6.18, the preview is useful for understanding possible fixes.

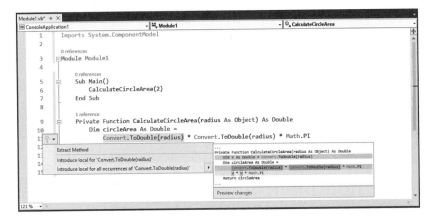

FIGURE 6.18   Introducing a local variable.

If you select the second option, your code then looks like this:

```
Private Function CalculateCircleArea(radius As Object) As Double
    Dim v As Double = Convert.ToDouble(radius)
    Dim circleArea As Double =
    v * v * Math.PI
    Return circleArea
End Function
```

In this case, you have simplified a complex expression into a more readable block. When you apply for a local variable, Inline Rename is automatically invoked, and you can choose a different name for the local variable.

Encapsulate Field

Visual Basic 2015 offers a convenient way to refactor fields into properties. For instance, suppose you have the following field in the `Person` class you defined earlier:

```
Private phoneNumber As String
```

If you right-click the field's name and enable the light bulb, two possible quick actions are suggested: **Encapsulate Field *'fieldname'* (Usages Reference Field)** and **Encapsulate Field: *'fieldname'*,** where *fieldname* stands for the field name. The first option refactors the field into a property and changes all code referencing the field to match the new property, whereas the second option encapsulates the field into a new property without changing any existing references. Figure 6.19 shows an example, including a preview.

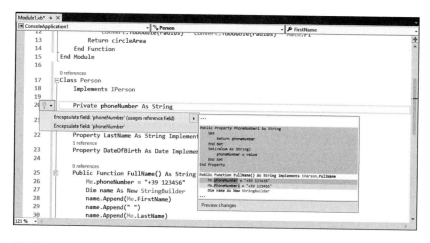

FIGURE 6.19   Encapsulating a field into a property.

If you select the first fix, for example, your code is then changed to the following:

```
Public Property PhoneNumber1 As String
    Get
        Return phoneNumber
    End Get
    Set(value As String)
        phoneNumber = value
    End Set
End Property

Public Function FullName() As String Implements IPerson.FullName
    Me.PhoneNumber1 = "+39 123456"
...
End Function
```

This is a useful refactoring, but it probably needs some manual edits. For instance, you might want to use the typical Visual Basic conventions and rename the field's identifier so that it includes an underscore, or you might want to simply change the added property into an auto-implemented property.

Introduce Constant

Visual Basic 2015 offers the Introduce Constant and Introduce Local Constant refactoring options. Both allow you to replace hard-coded values with constants, which can be at the class level (Introduce Constant) or within a method body (Introduce Local Constant). To understand how this feature works, consider the following code:

```
Module Module1
    Sub Main()
        Dim result = CalculateCircleArea(1.5)
    End Sub

    Private Function CalculateCircleArea(radius As Double) As Double
        Return radius * radius * Math.PI
    End Function
End Module
```

Here you have an invocation of the `CalculateCircleArea` method, which passes a numeric value as an argument. If you select such a numeric value and enable the light bulb, you get the following options (see Figure 6.20 for a sample preview):

► Introduce Constant for '1.5'

► Introduce Constant for All Occurrences of '1.5'

► Introduce Local Constant for '1.5'

► Introduce Local Constant for All Occurrences of '1.5'

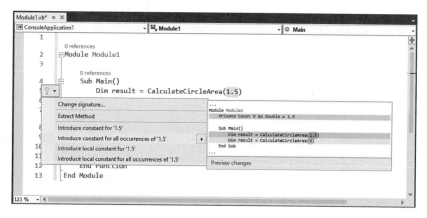

FIGURE 6.20   Introducing a constant.

The first and second options, respectively, introduce a constant at the class level for the selected occurrence and for all occurrences of the numeric value. The third and fourth options, respectively, introduce a constant within the method body for the selected occurrence and for all occurrences of the numeric value. The following code demonstrates the result of selecting the first option:

```
Module Module1
    Private Const V As Double = 1.5

    Sub Main()
        Dim result = CalculateCircleArea(V)
    End Sub

    Private Function CalculateCircleArea(radius As Double) As Double
        Return radius * radius * Math.PI
    End Function
End Module
```

Notice that when you apply the refactoring, Inline Rename appears and allows you to specify a different name for the constant.

Organizing Imports and Redundant Code

Visual Basic 2015 provides an easy way to manage the Imports directive and remove redundant code. Consider Listing 6.8, which extends the Person class definition shown in Listing 6.7 by adding a method that writes the full name to disk and some Imports directives.

LISTING 6.8   Preparing an Example with Redundant Code

```
Imports System.Linq
Imports System.Math
Imports System.Text
Imports System.IO
Class Person
    Property FirstName As String
    Property LastName As String
    Property DateOfBirth As Date

    Public Function FullName() As String
        Dim name As New StringBuilder
        name.Append(Me.FirstName)
        name.Append(" ")
        name.Append(Me.LastName)
        name.Append(" ")
        name.Append("born on ")
        name.Append(Me.DateOfBirth.ToShortDateString)
        Return name.ToString
    End Function

    Public Sub WriteFullNameToDisk()
        Using fs As New StreamWriter("C:\Temp\Fullname.txt")
            fs.WriteLine(FullName)
        End Using
    End Sub
End Class
```

In this code, only the System.Text and System.IO namespaces are required. The first is used to invoke the StringBuilder class, whereas the second one is required to use the StreamWriter class. The Visual Basic compiler automatically detects that the System.Linq and System.Math namespaces are unnecessary and so grays them out. If you hover over the Imports directives and enable the light bulb, you see the option Remove Unnecessary Imports, as shown in Figure 6.21. In addition, if you right-click any Imports directive, you see a new submenu called Organize Imports, which offers the following options (see Figure 6.22):

▶ **Remove Unnecessary Imports**—This is the same option you get in the light bulb.

▶ **Sort Imports**—This allows you to sort directives alphabetically but does not remove unnecessary ones.

▶ **Remove and Sort Imports**—This option removes unnecessary directives and sorts the remaining Imports alphabetically.

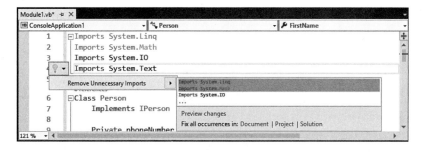

FIGURE 6.21   Removing unnecessary `Imports`.

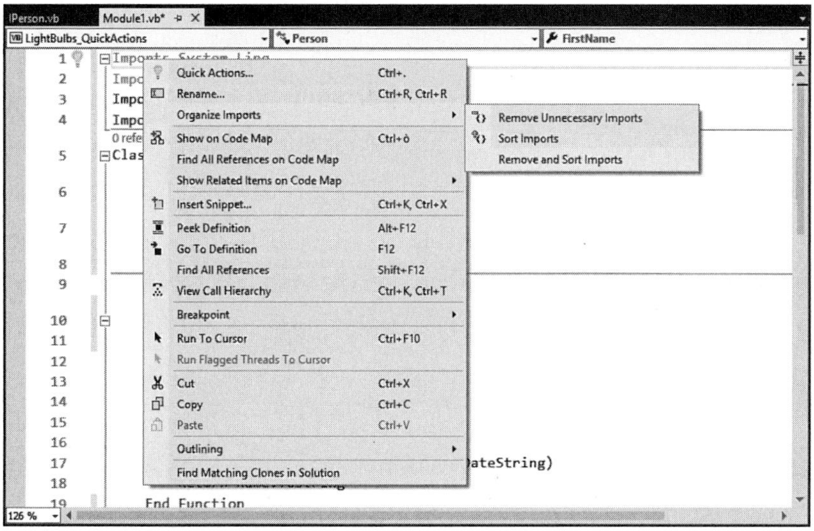

FIGURE 6.22   Organizing `Imports`.

For instance, if you select the **Remove and Sort Imports** options, `Imports` directives in the sample code now appear as follows:

```
Imports System.IO
Imports System.Text
```

This means that Visual Basic has removed the unnecessary `System.Linq` and `System.Math` imports and has sorted the valid ones alphabetically. More generally, the Visual Basic compiler is able to detect any redundant code, not just `Imports` directives. When it detects unnecessary code, it grays it out. This feature is referred to as *faded redundant code*. For example, you can see in Figure 6.23 that the `Me` qualification is faded in the `Person` class. As you can also see in Figure 6.23, if you enable the `light bulb`, you get the option Remove 'Me' Qualification.

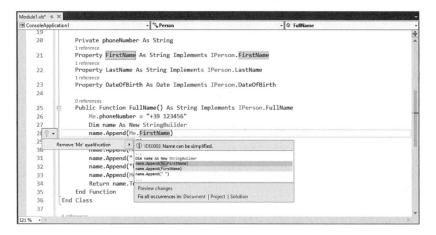

FIGURE 6.23   Removing redundant code.

Of course, redundant `Imports` directives and other code do not prevent the application from running and are not errors. However, they make for messy code. The features described in this section help you keep your code as clean and well organized as possible.

TIP

If you write custom code analyzers, you can integrate the light bulb and quick actions with your custom analysis rules. This is possible because the light bulb's architecture is extensible.

Summary

Managing errors is something that every developer needs to take into consideration. The .NET Framework provides a unified system for managing errors, which is the exception handling. `System.Exception` is the root class in the exceptions hierarchy, and exceptions are handled using a `Try..Catch..Finally` block. You can create nested `Try..Catch..Finally` blocks and check exceptions conditionally using the `When` keyword. In the end, you can programmatically generate exceptions using the `Throw` keyword that is particularly useful in class libraries development. This chapter provided a high-level overview of exceptions; now you can decide which kinds of exceptions you need to handle for your code and how to take actions to solve errors. The second part of the chapter introduced new interesting things in Visual Basic 2015, like the possibility of suppressing warning messages and how to use the light bulb and quick actions to write better and cleaner code.

CHAPTER 7

Class Fundamentals

In your everyday life, you perform all sorts of activities using objects. You use a fork to eat; you drive your car to reach your office; and you spend money to buy things. Each of these objects has its own characteristics. There are hundreds of car models; they have different colors, different engines, and different accessories, but they all are cars. *Object-oriented programming (OOP)* is similar to this view of life. In fact, OOP relies on objects; for example, you can have an object that enables working on files or another object that enables managing pictures. In .NET, development of an object is typically represented by a class. Structures are also objects, but their purpose is to represent a value more than to take actions. For car characteristics, objects have their own characteristics known as *properties*. But they also have some members that enable taking actions, known as *methods*. In this chapter you learn how classes in .NET development are structured and how to create your own classes, implementing all members that the .NET Framework enables in the context.

Declaring Classes

Classes in Visual Basic 2015 are declared with `Class..End Class` statements. Classes support the following visibility modifiers: `Public`, `Protected`, `Friend`, `Private`, and `Protected Friend`. Classes with `Public` can be reached from other assemblies, whereas classes with `Friend` visibility can be reached from within the assembly that defines them. Both modifiers are the only valid ones for nonnested classes, as you will see later in this chapter.

The following are the only acceptable class declarations:

```
Public Class Test

End Class
Friend Class Test

End Class
```

If you omit the qualifier (that is, `Public` or `Friend` keyword), the Visual Basic compiler assigns `Friend` by default. Classes can define members, such as fields, properties, and methods (all covered in this chapter), but also other classes and structures. The next section covers members that can be defined within classes so that you can have a complete overview about creating your custom classes.

CLASS LIBRARIES

You can define classes in whatever code file you like. Usually developers assign a single code file to one class. If you plan to develop a reusable assembly, exposing classes or types' definitions only, you can use the Class Library project template that enables you to build a .dll assembly that can be referenced by other projects and applications, which is particularly useful for the modular development. Also, Visual Studio 2015 offers the Portable Class Library project template that enables you to create class libraries that can be successfully reused across multiple platforms such as .NET Framework and Windows Store apps. The Portable Class Library template is discussed later in Chapter 17, "Working with Objects: Visual Tools and Code Sharing," because it requires a deeper knowledge of concepts about OOP.

Nested Classes

You can organize classes within other classes. The following code snippet shows how you can define a nested class:

```
Public Class Test

    Friend Class NestedClass

    End Class

End Class
```

Nested classes can also be marked as `Private`, and this is the only situation in which the qualifier is enabled. If you make a class private, you cannot use that class outside the class that defines it. Continuing with the preceding example, if the `NestedClass` class were marked as `Private`, you could use it only within the `Test` class. If a nested class is not private, you can invoke it the usual way; you need to write the full name of the class as follows:

```
Dim nc As New Test.NestedClass
```

Typically, classes are organized within namespaces (as described in Chapter 9, "Organizing Types Within Namespaces"), but there can be situations in which you need to organize small frameworks of classes, and then nested classes are useless without the parent class.

Fields

Fields are the places in which you store information to and read information from. They are declared in the form of class-level variables and differ from local variables in that they are declared at the method or property level. The following code shows how simple it is to declare fields:

```
Class FieldsDemo

    'a private field
    Private counter As Integer

    'a public field
    Public publicCounter As Integer

    Public Sub DoSomething()

        'a local variable
        Dim localVariable As Integer = 0
    End Sub
End Class
```

Fields can be reachable from within the class and its members, and if you specify one of the appropriate qualifiers (such as `Public`), they can also be reached from the external world. Inside fields, you store the actual information your custom objects need.

You can also provide inline initialization of fields, as in the following snippet:

```
Private counter As Integer = 2

'With reference types
Public inlineDemo As Person = New Person
```

Assigning a field inline or not is something that depends exclusively on your needs. Probably you will initialize fields at runtime when you receive an input from the user or with a value received from the constructor, whereas you might prefer inline initialization when you need to start from a certain value. Fields can also be read-only. When you need to provide a field with an immutable value, you can use read-only fields as follows:

```
'read-only fields
Private ReadOnly counter As Integer = 3
Private ReadOnly testReference As Person = New Person
```

A read-only field can be initialized inline. If you do not initialize a field, zero will be assigned to value types, and Nothing will be assigned to reference types. Also, fields can be initialized in the object's constructor. Read-only fields work similarly to constants with one big difference: Constants are evaluated at compile time; in contrast, read-only fields are evaluated at runtime, meaning that their initial value can be the result of a method call or value coming from some other runtime derived object.

SCOPE

Fields, as much as properties, have scope. To understand how you can limit or grant access to fields and properties using the appropriate qualifiers, see the "Types and Members Visibility: Scope" section in this chapter.

Avoiding Ambiguities with Local Variables

As previously mentioned, fields are at class level, unlike local variables which are at the method/property level. There could be situations in which a local variable has the same name of a field. For example, consider the following code in which two items are named counter: a class-level field and a local variable:

```
Public Class AvoidingAmbiguities
    Private counter As Integer

    Public Sub DoSomething()

        'a local variable
        Dim counter As Integer

        counter = CInt(Console.ReadLine)
    End Sub
End Class
```

The code will be correctly compiled; no conflict exists between the two counter members because the second one is enclosed within a method and has no external visibility. This also means that the assignment performed within the DoSomething method will not affect the counter private field. If you instead need to assign such a field, you need to use the Me keyword as follows:

```
Public Sub DoSomething()

    'a local variable
    Dim counter As Integer

    'Will assign the class level field
    Me.counter = CInt(Console.ReadLine)
End Sub
```

Storing Information with Properties

Properties are the public way that callers have to access data stored within fields. With properties, you decide the type of permissions users can have to read and write the actual information. Properties are typically used as fields, but they act as methods. Starting from Visual Basic 2010, properties have been completely revisited; in fact, until Visual Basic 2010, a typical property was implemented as follows:

```
Private _firstName As String

Public Property FirstName As String
    Get
        Return _firstName
    End Get
    Set(ByVal value As String)
        _firstName = value
    End Set
End Poperty
```

You had a private field in which you stored an incoming value and whose value you returned to the callers. Starting from Visual Basic 2010, the same property can be defined as follows:

```
Public Property FirstName As String
```

This feature is known as *auto-implemented properties*. You just need to specify the name and the type for the property. The Visual Basic compiler handles read-and-write operations for you. The resulting code is much cleaner, and you can avoid the need of writing several lines of code. If you had 10 properties, until Visual Basic 2010 you had to write 10 of the previously shown code blocks. Now, though, you need to write 10 lines of code-defining properties. Auto-implemented properties and fields might sound similar, but actually properties are definitely more robust and can be used in data-binding scenarios, while fields cannot. An interesting thing is that if you try to define a private field as in the old code and then an auto-implemented property, you receive this code:

```
'Error: field matching implicit
'auto-generated identifier
Private _firstName As String
Public Property FirstName As String
```

The Visual Basic compiler reports an error because, behind the scenes, it creates a private field with the same name for handling read/write operations on the property. Of course, you can change the identifier if you need a private field for your purposes.

AUTO-IMPLEMENTED PROPERTIES IN THIS BOOK

Except when specifically needed, you should always use auto-implemented properties when providing code examples that require properties. This is because they provide a much cleaner way for writing code; moreover, code samples seldom need customizations of the read/write actions.

Auto-implemented properties are useful if you need a default behavior for your properties that store and return a value. In some situations you need to perform manipulations over a value before you return it; you store a value provided by the user (property Setter) and then return the value with some edits (property Getter). In this case, you cannot use auto-implemented properties, but you can still write properties the old-fashioned way. The following code snippet shows an example:

```
Public Class Woman

    Private Const Prefix As String = "Mrs."

    Private _firstName As String
    Public Property FirstName As String
        Get
            Return Prefix & Me._firstName
        End Get
        Set(ByVal value As String)
            Me._firstName = value
        End Set
    End Property
End Class
```

In the preceding code, the value stored by the property is edited before it is returned by adding a prefix. Because the default Visual Studio's behavior is all about auto-implemented properties, you do not gain a great advantage from IntelliSense in this scenario. To write code faster, if you do not need auto-implemented properties, follow these steps:

1. Write an auto-implemented property.

2. On the following line of code, type the Get keyword and press **Enter**. Visual Studio automatically adds the Get and Set method definitions, plus the End Property delimiter.

As an alternative, you can type Property and then press **Tab** so that Visual Studio will add a property stub using a predefined code snippet. Visual Basic 2015 introduces read-only auto-implemented properties, as discussed in the next section.

Read-Only Properties

It's not unusual to give a class the capability of exposing data but not of modifying such data. Continuing the example of the Person class, imagine you want to expose the

FirstName and LastName properties plus a FullName property that returns the full name of the person. This property should be marked as read-only because only the FirstName and LastName properties should be editable and FullName is the result of the concatenation of these two properties. You can therefore define a read-only property as follows:

```
Public Class Person
    Public Property FirstName As String
    Public Property LastName As String

    Public ReadOnly Property FullName As String
        Get
            Return Me.FirstName & " " & Me.LastName
        End Get
    End Property
End Class
```

The ReadOnly keyword marks properties as read-only. Visual Basic 2015 introduces a new feature known as *read-only auto-implemented properties*, which are simpler read-only properties that return a value provided on initialization. Continuing the example of the Person class, suppose you want to add a read-only property that returns the date of birth for a person. You can now write it as follows:

```
Public ReadOnly Property DateOfBirth As Date
```

Of course, you need to initialize the property's value in some way; otherwise, this new syntax is useless. One way is inline initialization:

```
Public ReadOnly Property DateOfBirth As Date = New Date(1977, 5, 10)
```

This is fine if you want to assign the property a value you already know. The second way is to assign the property's value from the class's constructor, as follows:

```
Public ReadOnly Property DateOfBirth As Date
Public Sub New(firstName As String, lastName As String, dateOfBirth As Date)
    Me.FirstName = firstName
    Me.LastName = lastName

    Me.DateOfBirth = dateOfBirth
End Sub
```

A read-only property can never be assigned a value, but for auto-implemented ones, the only (and necessary) exception is when you assign a value from a type's constructor.

In summary, read-only auto-implemented properties are useful when you know in advance their value or when you initialize them from the constructor; in other cases, you should use the classic syntax with the Get method, where you can perform custom manipulations. With auto-implemented properties, the compiler implicitly creates and hides a private field, which it uses for storing the property value, which in the current example is:

```
Private _DateOfBirth As Date
```

You can see this in action by writing it explicitly. You will then see that the compiler reports an error, saying that the field conflicts with an implicit member declared for the DateOfBirth property.

Write-Only Properties

Opposite to read-only properties, you can also implement write-only properties. In real-life applications, write-only properties are uncommon, so you will probably never implement such members. It makes much more sense to provide read-only members than members that you can only write to but not read from. Anyway, you can implement write-only properties marking your properties with the WriteOnly keyword as demonstrated in the following code snippet:

```
Private _fictitiousCounter As Integer

Public WriteOnly Property FictitiousCounter As Integer
    Set(ByVal value As Integer)
        _fictitiousCounter = value
    End Set
End Property
```

You have different options here; one is storing the value received by the setter within a field that you can then eventually reutilize. Otherwise, you can perform some tasks directly within the setter.

Exposing Custom Types

Properties can expose both reference and value types, and they are not limited to built-in .NET types. Thus, you can expose your custom classes and structures through properties. The following code shows an Order class that exposes a property of type Customer; such type is another custom class representing a fictitious customer of your company:

```
Public Class Customer
    Public Property CompanyName As String
    Public Property ContactName As String
End Class

Public Class Order
    Public Property CustomerInstance As Customer
    Public Property OrderID As Integer
End Class
```

You can use the same technique for exposing custom structures. After all, you do nothing different from when you expose strings and integers. Remember that if you do not initialize properties with values, value types returned by properties will have a default value while reference types could result in null references causing runtime errors.

Accessing Properties

Accessing properties is a simple task. You access properties for both reading and writing information that a type needs. The following code demonstrates this:

```
Dim p As New Person

'Properties assignment (write)
p.FirstName = "Alessandro"
p.LastName = "Del Sole"

'Properties reading
If p.LastName.ToLower = "del sole" Then
    Console.WriteLine(p.LastName)
End If
```

Default Properties

Visual Basic language enables defining default properties. A *default property* is a property marked with the Default keyword that enables assignments to the objects defining the property without the need of invoking the property itself. Default properties are strictly related to data arrays and collections of objects because they provide the ability of managing an index. For example, imagine you have an array of strings defined within a class as follows:

```
Private listOfNames() As String = _
    {"Alessandro", "Del Sole", "VB 2015 Unleashed"}
```

A default property enables easy access to such an array, both for reading and writing. The following code demonstrates how you can implement a default property:

```
Default Public Property GetName(ByVal index As Integer) As String
    Get
        Return listOfNames(index)
    End Get
    Set(ByVal value As String)
        listOfNames(index) = value
    End Set
End Property
```

PARAMETER TYPES

The preceding example shows the most common use of default properties, where they accept a numeric index. By the way, default properties can accept any data type as the parameter, not only numeric types. The only rule is actually that the default property must have a parameter.

Notice the Default keyword and how the property accesses the array taking advantage of the index argument to return the desired item in the array. Supposing the preceding definition was contained within a class named TestDataAccess, the following code demonstrates how you can access the default property:

```
Dim t As New TestDataAccess
t(2) = "Visual Basic 2015 Unleashed"
Console.WriteLine(t(1))
Console.WriteLine(t(2))
```

As you can see, you do not need to specify the property name when performing assignments or invocations. The preceding code would produce the following result:

```
Del Sole
Visual Basic 2015 Unleashed
```

INDEXERS

Visual Basic default properties are exposed to Visual C# as *indexers* and vice versa. It's important to know this terminology because you will often hear about indexers.

Types and Members Visibility: Scope

All .NET types and their members have *scope*, which represents the level of visibility and accessibility that a type or its members can have. For example, the *public* scope enables members of classes or structure within a class library to be reachable by other classes or assemblies. On the other hand, the *private* scope can prevent members of classes or structures to be reached from outside the class or structure in which they are defined. You assign scope to your objects or members via *qualifiers*, which are special keywords or combination of keywords that establish how an object or its members can be reached from outside the object. Table 7.1 summarizes scope levels in Visual Basic 2015.

TABLE 7.1   Scope Levels in Visual Basic 2015

Qualifier	Description
Public	Allows types and members to be accessed from anywhere, also from external assemblies. It assigns no access restrictions.
Private	Types and members are visible only within the object in which they are defined.

Qualifier	Description
Friend	Types and members are visible within the assembly that contains declarations.
Protected	Types and members are visible within the objects they are defined in and from derived classes.
Protected Friend	Types and members are visible within the assembly, within the objects they are defined in, and from derived classes.

The following code snippet gives you an alternative view of scope:

```
'The class is visible to other
'external assemblies.
Public Class ScopeDemo

    'This field is visible only
    'within the class
    Private counter As Integer

    'Visible within this assembly, this class,
    'derived classes, other assemblies: no restrictions
    Public Property FirstName As String
    Public Property LastName As String

    'Only within this class and derived classes
    Protected Property Age As Integer

    'Within this assembly
    Friend Property ReservedInformation As String

    'Within this assembly, this class and derived classes
    Protected Friend Function ReturnSomeInformation() As String
        Return FirstName & " " & LastName
    End Function

End Class
```

`Public` and `Private` qualifiers are self-explanatory, so you probably need some more information about the other ones. To make things easier, let's create a new class that derives from the preceding `ScopeDemo`, as in the following code snippet:

```
Public Class InheritedScopeDemo
    Inherits ScopeDemo

End Class
```

If you try to reach the base class's members, you notice that only the ones marked with Friend, Protected Friend, and Protected are visible to the new class (other than Public, of course). But this happens until you are working with one assembly—more precisely, with the assembly that defines all the preceding members. What about another assembly referencing the first one? If you have created a Visual Basic solution for testing the preceding code, add a new Visual Basic project to the solution, and to the new project add a reference to the previous one. In the new project, write the following code:

```
Dim testScope As New Scope.InheritedScopeDemo
```

If you try to invoke members of the testScope object, you can see only the FirstName and LastName properties because they were marked as Public. This qualifier is the only one allowing members to be reached from external assemblies. As you might imagine, establishing the appropriate scope is fundamental. For example, you might need a field for storing some data that you do not want to share with the external world; marking a field as Private prevents derived classes from reaching the field. So you should instead mark it as Protected or Protected Friend according to the access level you want to grant. Particularly when working with inheritance, scope is important.

Executing Actions with Methods

A *method* is a member that performs an operation. Methods are of two kinds: Sub (which does not return values) and Function (which returns a value). The following are minimal examples of methods:

```
Sub DoSomething()
    If IO.File.Exists("C:\SomeFile.txt") = False Then
        Throw New IO.FileNotFoundException
    Else
        Console.WriteLine("The file exists")
    End If

End Sub


Function DoSomethingElse() As Boolean

    Dim result As Boolean = IO.File.Exists("C:\SomeFile.txt")
    Return result
End Function
```

This book makes intensive use of methods, so detailed descriptions on implementations are provided across chapters.

SCOPE

Methods' visibility within types can be assigned using one of the qualifiers listed in Table 7.1. If no qualifier is specified, Public is assigned by default.

Invoking Methods

To invoke a method, you call its name. Continuing with the preceding example, you can invoke the DoSomething method by typing the following line:

```
DoSomething()
```

If the method is a Function, you should assign the invocation to a variable as follows:

```
Dim targetOfInvocation As Boolean = DoSomethingElse()
```

This is important if you need to evaluate the value returned by the method. If you do not need to evaluate the result, you can invoke Function as if it were Sub:

```
'Allowed
DoSomethingElse()
```

You can invoke functions anywhere you need a value. Continuing with the preceding example, the following code is acceptable:

```
Console.WriteLine(DoSomethingElse())
```

In the preceding examples, the code acts as if the method were defined within a module. If the method is exposed by a class, you need to add a dot symbol after the class name and then type the name of the method, as follows:

```
Public Class Person

    Public Sub DoSomething()

    End Sub
End Class

Dim p As New Person
p.DoSomething()
```

The Visual Basic grammar also provides the Call keyword, which enables you to invoke methods. You can use it as follows:

```
Call DoSomething()
```

You should typically avoid using this keyword, though, because it is obsolete. However, there are some particular situations in which Call is still useful. For instance, you can use Call in a statement like the following one:

```
Call Async Sub()
        'Do you async task here...
End Sub.Invoke()
```

Because you cannot start a statement with the `Async` keyword, with `Call` you can solve this problem. As another example, because you cannot start a statement with parentheses, with `Call` you can write code like the following:

```
Call (1 + 2).ToString()
```

Method Arguments: `ByVal` and `ByRef`

Methods can receive parameters and can then work with data provided by arguments. In the .NET terminology, parameters are objects that methods accept and that you write when you declare a method (or lambdas). Arguments are the expressions you pass to a method when you invoke it, and each one satisfies a method's parameter. The following code shows a simple sample of a method definition receiving an argument and subsequent invocation of that method passing an argument; the method declaration defines a parameter called `stringToPrint` and then the method body passes an argument to the `Console.Writeline` method:

```
Public Sub PrintString(ByVal stringToPrint As String)
    Console.WriteLine(stringToPrint)
End Sub


Sub RunTest()
    PrintString("Visual Basic 2015 Unleashed")
End Sub
```

Arguments can be passed by value and by reference. Arguments are passed by value by adding the `ByVal` keyword, whereas they are passed by reference by specifying the `ByRef` keyword. In the previous versions of Visual Basic, if you did not specify either keyword, the code editor automatically added a `ByVal` keyword passing arguments by value as a default. Starting with Visual Basic 2012, if you do not specify either `ByVal` or `ByRef`, the code editor does not add any keyword but the compiler assumes `ByVal` by default. So in Visual Basic 2015, the `PrintString` method of the preceding code snippet can be rewritten as follows:

```
Public Sub PrintString(stringToPrint As String)
    Console.WriteLine(stringToPrint)
End Sub
```

So, in this code the compiler assumes that the `stringToPrint` argument is passed by value. This book uses both syntaxes. This will be useful to avoid confusion in case you have existing code that you want to analyze while reading this book. There are differences between passing arguments by value and by reference. Before providing code examples for a better understanding, these differences are all related to the variables you pass as arguments and can be summarized as follows:

▶ If you pass a value type by value, the compiler creates a copy of the original value so changes made to the argument are not reflected to the original data. If you pass a value type by reference, changes made to the object referenced by the argument are reflected to the original data because, in this case, the argument is the memory address of the data.

▶ If you pass a reference type by reference, the compiler passes in the memory address. If you pass a reference type by value, the compiler passes a copy of the memory pointer. In both cases, the original object will be modified regardless of how the parameter is passed. The difference is that when you pass a reference type variable by reference, the called method can change what object the variable refers to by replacing its content with a memory pointer to a different object.

Listing 7.1 shows how value types can be passed by value and by reference.

LISTING 7.1   Passing Arguments by Value

```
Module ByValByRefDemo

    Dim testInt As Integer = 10

    'Creates a copy of the original value(testInt)
    'and does not change it. Outputs 10
    Sub ByValTest(ByVal anInt As Integer)
        anInt = 20
        Console.WriteLine(testInt)
    End Sub

    'Gets the reference of the original value (testInt)
    'and changes it. Outputs 20
    Sub ByRefTest(ByRef anInt As Integer)
        anInt = 20
        Console.WriteLine(testInt)
    End Sub

    Sub Main()
        ByValTest(testInt)
        ByRefTest(testInt)
        Console.ReadLine()
    End Sub

End Module
```

Both the ByValTest and ByRefTest methods receive an argument of type Integer. Such an argument is the testInt variable. In the ByValTest method, the argument is passed by value, so the compiler creates a copy of the original data and changes made to the argument variable are not reflected to the original one—in fact, the code returns 10, which is the original value for the testInt variable. In the ByRefTest method, the argument is passed by reference. Thus, the compiler gets the memory address of the original value and changes made to the argument variable are also reflected to the original data—in fact, this code returns 20, which is the new value for the `testInt` variable. Now consider the following code that provides a similar demonstration for passing reference type both by value and by reference:

```
Dim testString As String = "Visual Basic 2015"
Sub ByValStringTest(ByVal aString As String)
    aString = "Visual Basic 2015 Unleashed"
    Console.WriteLine(testString)
End Sub

Sub ByRefStringTest(ByRef aString As String)
    aString = "Visual Basic 2015 Unleashed"
    Console.WriteLine(testString)
End Sub
```

Invoking the `ByValStringTest` method, passing the `testString` variable as an argument will not change the original value for the reasons previously explained. Invoking the `ByRefStringTest` method, still passing the `testString` variable as an argument, will also change the original value of the `testString` variable that now becomes `Visual Basic 2015 Unleashed`.

PASSING ARRAYS

When passing arrays as arguments, these will be affected by any modifications to their members, because they are reference types, regardless of whether you pass the array by value or by reference. As for other reference types, the most important thing to care about is that when you set the variable's reference in the method to `Nothing`, the original reference is not destroyed if the array is passed by value, whereas it might be destroyed if the array is passed by reference and no other references to that object exist.

`ParamArray` Arguments

Another way of supplying arguments to a method is the `ParamArray` keyword. As its name implies, the keyword enables specifying an array of a given type to be accepted by the method. Each item in the array is then treated as a single argument. The following example shows how to implement `ParamArray` arguments:

```
Sub ParamArrayTest(ByVal ParamArray names() As String)
    'Each item in the array is an
    'argument that you can manipulate
    'as you need
    For Each name As String In names
        Console.WriteLine(name)
    Next
End Sub
```

You can then invoke the method as follows:

```
ParamArrayTest("Alessandro", "Del Sole", "Visual Basic 2015 Unleashed")
```

This method produces the following result, considering that each string is an argument:

```
Alessandro
Del Sole
Visual Basic 2015 Unleashed
```

`ParamArray` arguments are always the last argument of a method definition and are always passed by value, and because they are real arrays, they are reference types. So in reality, arrays are passed by reference (and changes to the array values will persist). You can first declare an array and then pass it to the method invocation, like so:

```
Dim args() As String = {"Alessandro", "Del Sole",
        "Visual Basic 2015 Unleashed"}
ParamArrayTest(args)
```

Because of being arrays, you can perform any other operations that these objects support. You can pass to methods an array as an argument or an arbitrary number of single arguments that, behind the scenes, are turned into an array. Finally, remember that you cannot pass an array with empty fields. The following code will not be compiled:

```
ParamArrayTest("Alessandro", , "Visual Basic 2015 Unleashed")
```

The Visual Basic background compiler shows an error message saying `Omitted Argument Cannot Match ParamArray Argument`.

Optional Arguments

Methods can receive optional arguments. Therefore, methods modify their behavior according to the number of arguments they received. Optional arguments are defined with the `Optional` keyword. The following code snippet shows how you can define optional arguments:

```
'Returns the full name of a person
Function FullName(ByVal FirstName As String,
        Optional ByVal LastName As String = "",
        Optional ByVal Title As String = "") As String

    'Assumes that the optional Title parameter
    'was not passed by comparing the default value
    If Title = "" Then Title = "Mr. "

    Dim result As New System.Text.StringBuilder
    result.Append(Title)
```

```
    result.Append(LastName)
    result.Append(FirstName)

    Return result.ToString
End Function
```

The purpose of the preceding `FullName` method is simple (and simplified). It should return the full name of a person, but the `LastName` and `Title` arguments are optional, meaning that the caller must provide at least the `FirstName`. Optional arguments must be assigned with a default value; in the preceding code, the default value is an empty string.

DEFAULT VALUES

Default values for optional arguments must be constant expressions. This is the reason I did not assign a `String.Empty` object but assigned a = "" value. The compiler provides the appropriate warnings if the default value is not good.

Default values are important for at least one reason: there are no other ways for understanding whether an optional argument were passed. A default value is therefore needed for comparison. Moreover, there could be situations in which a default value would be necessary—for example, for object initializations. In the preceding code, to check whether the optional `Title` parameter were passed, a comparison is performed against the `Title`'s value. If its value equals the default value, you can assume that the argument was not supplied. This example provides a custom value in case the argument was not passed. If you write the following invocation

```
Console.WriteLine(FullName("Alessandro"))
```

you would get the following result: `Mr. Alessandro`. Behind the scenes, the Visual Basic compiler generates a new invocation that includes all optional parameters with a default value, as follows: `FullName("Alessandro","","")`. Although useful, optional arguments are not always the best choice, and we do not recommend their usage. This is because other .NET languages implement them differently and so they are not compliant with Microsoft's Common Language Specifications. So if you produce class libraries, you should be aware of this. Instead, the .NET Framework provides a cleaner way for handling methods with different arguments and signatures that is powerful; it's known as *overloading* and is discussed next.

Optional Nullable Arguments

Visual Basic 2015 allows passing nullable types as optional arguments. The following code demonstrates this:

```
Sub NullableDemo(ByVal firstArgument As String,
        Optional ByVal secondArgument As _
        Nullable(Of Integer) = Nothing)
```

```
    If secondArgument Is Nothing Then
      'You can assume that the
      'optional argument was not supplied
    End If
End Sub
```

As you can see, nullable arguments are supported, but you are still required to provide a default value, which can also be null. Remember that optional nullable arguments can only go after nonoptional ones in the argument list. They are particularly useful when dealing with scenarios like Microsoft Office automation, where optional arguments are common.

Overloading Methods

One of the most powerful features in the object-oriented development with the .NET Framework is the capability of overloading methods. *Overloading* means providing multiple signatures of the same method, in which signature is the number and types of arguments a method can receive. The following code snippet demonstrates overloading:

```
Private Function ReturnFullName(ByVal firstName As String,
        ByVal lastName As String) As String
    Return firstName & " " & lastName
End Function


Private Function ReturnFullName(ByVal firstName As String,
      ByVal lastName As String,
      ByVal Age As Integer) As String
    Return firstName & " " & lastName & " of age " & Age.ToString
End Function


Private Function ReturnFullName(ByVal title As String,
      ByVal firstName As String,
      ByVal lastName As String) As String
    Return title & " " & firstName & " " & lastName
End Function


Private Function ReturnFullName(ByVal title As String,
      ByVal firstName As String,
      ByVal lastName As String,
      ByVal Age As Integer) As String
    Return title & " " & firstName & " " & lastName & _
      " of age " & Age.ToString
End Function
```

As you can see, there are four different implementations of one method named `ReturnFullName`. Each implementation differs from the others in that it receives a different number of arguments. The preceding example is simple, and the arguments are self-explanatory; each implementation returns the concatenation of the supplied arguments. You might wonder why you would need overloading and to provide four different implementations of a single method when you would obtain the same result with optional arguments. The answer is that this approach is the only accepted method by the Microsoft Common Language Specification and ensures that every .NET language can use the different implementations, whereas optional arguments are not supported from other .NET languages. Another good reason for using overloads is that you can return strongly typed results from methods. If you need to work with specific data types, you can use overloaded signatures instead of providing one signature that returns `Object`. The Visual Basic grammar defines an `Overloads` keyword as one that can be used to define overloaded signatures; the following example is an excerpt of the previous one, now using `Overloads`:

```
Private Overloads Function ReturnFullName(ByVal firstName As String,
        ByVal lastName As String) As String
    Return firstName & " " & lastName
End Function

Private Overloads Function ReturnFullName(ByVal firstName As String,
          ByVal lastName As String,
          ByVal Age As Integer) As String
    Return firstName & " " & lastName & " of age " & Age.ToString
End Function
```

There's no difference in using the `Overloads` keywords. If you decide to use it, you must decorate it with all other definitions. To support overloading, signatures must differ from each other in some points:

▶ Signatures cannot differ only in `ByVal` or `ByRef` arguments. If two signatures have two arguments of the same type, the arguments cannot differ only in `ByVal`/`ByRef` even though they consist of different types.

▶ In the case of `Function`, overloaded implementations can return the same type or different types. If they return different types but have exactly the same parameters, the code cannot be compiled. This means that different implementations must have different arguments.

You invoke methods defined in this way as you would normally with other methods. Moreover, IntelliSense provides a great help on finding the most appropriate overload for your needs, as shown in Figure 7.1.

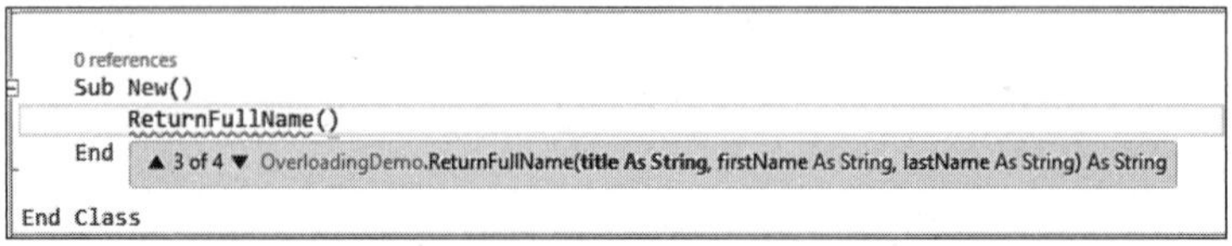

```
    0 references
    Sub New()
        ReturnFullName()
    End    ▲ 3 of 4 ▼  OverloadingDemo.ReturnFullName(title As String, firstName As String, lastName As String) As String

End Class
```

FIGURE 7.1   IntelliSense helps you choose among overloads.

Coercion

It can happen that an invocation to an overloaded method supplies a compliant type but not the same type established in the signature. Consider the following overloaded method:

```
Private Sub CoercionDemo(ByVal anArgument As Double)
    Debug.WriteLine("Floating point")
End Sub

Private Sub CoercionDemo(ByVal anArgument As Integer)
    Debug.WriteLine("Integer")
End Sub
```

The Visual Basic compiler can decide which signature is the most appropriate according to the argument passed. This is particularly important when working with numeric types. Moreover, the compiler can also handle coercion, meaning that it can perform conversion when there's no loss of precision. Consider the following code:

```
Dim testValue As Byte = 123
CoercionDemo(testValue)
```

The `CoercionDemo` overloads do not support `Byte`—only `Double` and `Integer`. Because `Byte` is basically an integer type, the Visual Basic compiler converts the object into an `Integer` type because this expansion conversion will always be successful. The compiler can also decide the best overload to fit the scenario.

Overload Resolution

Visual Basic 2015 has specific rules for managing the precedence of the invocation of generic methods' overloads, where the generic type is an `IEnumerable(Of T)`.

WHAT ARE GENERICS?

Generic types are .NET types that can adapt their behavior to different kinds of objects without the need of defining a separate version of the type. Generics are discussed further in Chapter 14, "Generics and Nullable Types." If you already have experience with Visual Basic (since version 2005), you might already know about them. What you need to know about them here is that they are types that can represent a lot of other types.

For example, consider the following code:

```
Sub Demo()
    Dim x As New List(Of Integer)
    x.Add(1)
    x.Add(2)
    x.Add(3)
    Calculate(x.AsEnumerable)
End Sub
```

```
Sub Calculate(Of T)(x As T)
    'Perform your calculation here
End Sub

Sub Calculate(Of T)(x As IEnumerable(Of T))
    'Perform your calculation here
End Sub
```

The `Calculate` method has two overloads, and both can accept an `IEnumerable(Of T)` as the generic type. In this case, then, the compiler must be intelligent enough to understand which of the two overloads must be invoked from the `Demo` method. Until Visual Basic 2010, such a situation would cause some conflicts. Now the compiler automatically invokes the overload where the generic parameter is more deeply nested; in this case it invokes the second overload (the one with a generic parameter of type `IEnumerable(Of T)`). You can easily verify this by placing a breakpoint on the second overload of the `Calculate` method and stepping into the code by pressing F11. Actually, this is one of those improvements required to make the compiler work better with the asynchronous programming patterns, but it is important that it exists.

Declaring Optional Parameter Overloads

You can define optional arguments for method overloads. The following code provides an example:

```
Sub MyMethod(x As Integer)
End Sub

Sub MyMethod(x As Integer, Optional y As Integer = 0)
End Sub
```

You can specify an optional parameter inside a method overload; this solves a previous conflict that caused the second method to be exactly like the first one if the second argument were not passed. To make sure the correct method is selected, you add the comma for the optional parameter but provide no value.

Overloading Properties

Now that you know what overloading is, you need to know that the technique is not limited to methods but can also be applied to properties. The following code snippet shows an example:

```
Property Test(ByVal age As Integer) As Integer
    Get

    End Get
    Set(ByVal value As Integer)

    End Set
End Property
```

```
Property Test(ByVal name As String) As String
    Get

    End Get
    Set(ByVal va=-lue As String)

    End Set
End Property
```

Because of their different implementations, in this scenario you cannot use auto-implemented properties, mainly because overloads cannot differ only because of their return type. To provide overloaded properties, you need to remember the same limitations listed for methods.

Exit from Methods

Methods execution typically completes when the `End Sub` or `End Function` statements are encountered. You often need to break methods execution before the execution completes. In the case of `Sub` methods, you can accomplish this using the `Exit Sub` statement. The following example checks the value of an integer and immediately breaks if the value is greater than 10. If not, it loops until the value is 10 and then breaks:

```
Sub TestingValues(ByVal anInteger As Integer)
    If anInteger > 10 Then
     Exit Sub
    ElseIf anInteger < 10 Then
     Do Until anInteger = 10
        anInteger += 1
     Loop
     Exit Sub
    End If
End Sub
```

You can also use the `Return` keyword without a value instead of `Exit Sub`. For Function methods, things are a little different because they return a value. When the methods execution completes regularly, you return a value via the `Return` keyword. Until now, you found several examples of methods returning values.

AVOID VISUAL BASIC 6 STYLE

If you migrate from Visual Basic 6, you probably return values from functions assigning the result to the name of the function itself. In .NET development, this is deprecated, although it will be compiled. The `Return` keyword is optimized for returning values and all .NET languages have a specific keyword, so you should always use this approach.

When you instead need to break the method execution, you can use the `Exit Function` statement, as shown in the following code snippet:

```
Function TestingValue(ByVal anInteger As Integer) As Boolean

    Dim result As Boolean

    If anInteger < 10 Then
      Do Until anInteger = 10
        anInteger += 1
      Loop
      result = True
      'Returns False
    ElseIf anInteger = 10 Then
    Exit Function
  Else
        result = False
    End If
    Return result
End Function
```

Keep in mind that Function methods always have to return something. Because of this, `Exit Function` returns the current value of the implicit return type. In the preceding example, the method returns `Boolean`, so `Exit Function` returns `False`. If the method returned `Integer` or another numeric type, `Exit Function` would return zero. If the method returned a reference type, `Exit Function` would return `Nothing`. Another best practice in returning value is to assign the result of the evaluation to a variable (result in the preceding example) and then provide a single invocation to the `Return` instruction because this can optimize the compilation process, as well as make coding easier.

Organizing Code with Partial Classes

You can split the definition of a class across multiple parts using the *partial classes* feature. You do not actually create different classes; you create one class implemented within multiple parts, typically across multiple files. This feature was first introduced in Visual Basic 2005 for separating Visual Studio's auto-generated code from developer's code, but it is useful in various scenarios. To see a practical implementation of partial classes, create a new Windows Forms project. Then click the **Show All Files** button in Solution Explorer, expand the Form1.vb item, and double-click the **Form1.designer.vb** file. Inside this file you can find the definition of the Form1 class, as shown in Listing 7.2.

LISTING 7.2   Visual Studio Auto-Generated Partial Class

```
Partial Class Form1
    Inherits System.Windows.Forms.Form

    'Form overrides dispose to clean up the component list.
    <System.Diagnostics.DebuggerNonUserCode()> _
    Protected Overrides Sub Dispose(ByVal disposing As Boolean)
```

```
        Try
      If disposing AndAlso components IsNot Nothing Then
        components.Dispose()
      End If
        Finally
      MyBase.Dispose(disposing)
      End Try
    End Sub


    'Required by the Windows Form Designer
    Private components As System.ComponentModel.IContainer

    'NOTE: The following procedure is required by the Windows Form Designer
    'It can be modified using the Windows Form Designer.
    'Do not modify it using the code editor.
    <System.Diagnostics.DebuggerStepThrough()> _
    Private Sub InitializeComponent()
        components = New System.ComponentModel.Container()
        Me.AutoScaleMode = System.Windows.Forms.AutoScaleMode.Font
        Me.Text = "Form1"
    End Sub
End Class
```

As you can see, the class definition includes the `Partial` keyword. This indicates to the compiler that elsewhere in the project another piece of the class is defined within a different code file. In this case, the other piece is the Form1.vb file whose code is simple when you create a new project:

```
Public Class Form1

End Class
```

Both files implement one class. By the way, this approach makes your code much cleaner. In this example, partial classes help developers to concentrate on their own code, ensuring that auto-generated code will not be confusing. The Visual Studio IDE makes a huge usage of partial classes; LINQ to SQL and ADO.NET Entity Framework are just a couple examples. Following is a custom example of partial classes. Imagine you have this implementation of the `Person` class within a code file named Person.vb:

```
Public Class Person

    Public Property FirstName As String
    Public Property LastName As String
    Public Property Age As Integer
```

```
    Public Overrides Function ToString() As String
        Return String.Concat(FirstName, " ", LastName)
    End Function

    Public Sub New(ByVal Name As String, ByVal SurName As String,
            ByVal Age As Integer)
      Me.FirstName = Name
      Me.LastName = SurName
      Me.Age = Age
    End Sub
End Class
```

Then you decide to implement the ICloneable interface to provide a custom implementation of the Clone method, but you want to separate the implementation from the rest of the class code. At this point, you can add a new code file to the project and write the following:

```
Partial Public Class Person
    Implements ICloneable

    Public Function Clone() As Object Implements System.ICloneable.Clone
        Return Me.MemberwiseClone
    End Function
End Class
```

This last code will be still part of the Person class; it has been defined in another place.

PARTIAL CLASSES TIPS

You can split your classes within multiple files. Generally, you create partial classes within just two files, but you have to know that you are allowed to create them within two or more files. Partial classes also take whatever scope you define in one of the partial class definitions.

Also notice how IntelliSense can improve your coding experience by showing a list of the partial classes you can complete (see Figure 7.2).

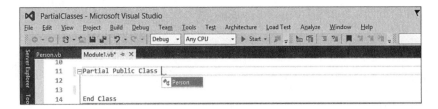

FIGURE 7.2   IntelliSense helps choose the available partial classes.

A partial approach can also be applied to Structures as follows:

```
Partial Structure Test

End Structure
```

PARTIAL CLASSES HOW-TO

Partial classes can be split across multiple parts—parts, not files. This is because one Visual Basic code file can contain the implementation of theoretically infinite types, so you can split a class definition within the same code file using partial classes. You can, but you probably will not. Partial classes are particularly useful for splitting definitions across multiple files, which is covered when discussing LINQ to SQL and the ADO.NET Entity Framework.

Partial classes indeed have a limitation: You cannot define them within other classes. For example, the following code will correctly be compiled, but it does not implement partial classes even though it creates two different classes:

```
Class TestPartial

    'Compiles, but creates a new partial class
    'instead of extending the previous Person
    Partial Class Person

    End Class
End Class
```

Splitting Method Definitions with Partial Methods

Another interesting feature is partial methods. The concept behind this feature is the same as for partial classes: Method implementations can be split across multiple parts. Partial methods have three particular characteristics: They must be `Private` methods, they cannot return values (that is, only `Sub` methods are allowed), and their bodies must be empty in the class in which methods are defined. Consider the following code, in which a class named `Contact` is split across partial classes and a partial method is defined:

```
Public Class Contact

    Public Property FirstName As String
    Public Property LastName As String
    Public Property EmailAddress As String

    Public Sub New(ByVal Name As String,
        ByVal LastName As String, ByVal Email As String)
      Me.FirstName = Name
```

```
    Me.LastName = LastName
    Me.EmailAddress = Email
  End Sub


  Partial Private Sub Validate(ByVal Email As String)
  End Sub

End Class
```

A partial method is marked with the `Partial` keyword. It has a `Private` scope, it returns no value, and its definition's body is empty. Suppose you want to implement the actual code for your method. For example, you could verify whether the Email address provided by the user is a valid address; to accomplish this, you can use regular expressions.

ABOUT REGULAR EXPRESSIONS

Regular expressions are an advanced way to work with text. The .NET Framework provides the `System.Text.RegularExpression` namespace that exposes classes for managing regular expressions with .NET languages.

The following code shows how you can implement a partial class in which the actual code for a partial method is provided:

```
Partial Public Class Contact

  Private Sub Validate(ByVal Email As String)

    Dim validateMail As String = _
    "^([\w-\.]+)@((\[[0-9]{1,3}\." &
    "[0-9]{1,3}\.)|(([\w-]+\.)+))" &
    "([a-zA-z]{2,4}|[0-9]{1,3})(\]?)$"

    If Text.RegularExpressions.
      Regex.IsMatch(Email, validateMail) _
      = False Then
      Throw New _
      InvalidOperationException _
      ("The specified mail address is not valid")
    End If
  End Sub
End Class
```

When you effectively implement the partial method, you do not need to mark it again as `Partial`. This qualifier must be added only in the empty method definition. The preceding code checks whether the specified email address is valid; if it is not, it throws an `InvalidOperationException`.

PRACTICAL IMPLEMENTATIONS

Partial methods are mentioned when discussing LINQ to SQL so that you can get an overview of practical implementations of partial methods, which are particularly useful when you need to provide custom validation techniques.

To describe partial methods in another way, the concept is "to accomplish this particular task, you do need this particular method. But the implementation of the method is left to your choice."

Instantiating Objects with Constructors

A constructor is a method you invoke to create a new instance of a class that is represented by the New keyword in Visual Basic. For instance, if you have the following Contact class,

```
Public Class Contact

    Public Property FirstName As String
    Public Property LastName As String
    Public Property Email As String
    Public Property Address As String

    Public Sub New()

    End Sub
End Class
```

you can then create a new instance of the Contact class as follows:

```
'First syntax
Dim aContact As Contact
aContact = New Contact

'Second syntax
Dim aContact As New Contact

'Third syntax
Dim aContact As Contact = New Contact
```

All the three preceding syntaxes are enabled, so you can use the one you prefer. (I use the second one for better readability.) In other words, creating an instance means giving life to a new copy of the object so you can use it for your purposes, such as storing data or performing tasks. All classes must have a constructor. If you do not provide a constructor, Visual Basic provides one for you. The default constructor is hidden in the code editor, but it has public visibility and contains no code; it serves just for instantiating the object.

If you want to make it visible, click the **Member** combo box in the code editor and select the **New** method, as shown in Figure 7.3.

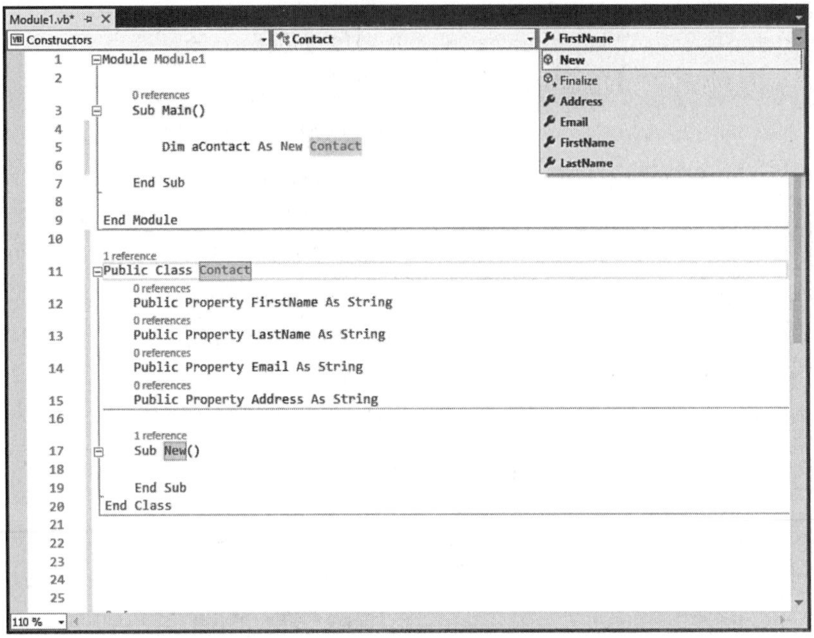

FIGURE 7.3   Making the default constructor visible.

Constructors are useful for initializing objects' members. Because of this, and because constructors are basically methods, they can receive arguments. For example, you could implement the constructor in a way that receives appropriate arguments for initializing the Contact class's properties:

```
Public Sub New(ByVal name As String,
        ByVal surName As String,
        ByVal emailAddress As String,
        ByVal homeAddress As String)

    Me.FirstName = name
    Me.LastName = surName
    Me.Email = emailAddress
    Me.Address = homeAddress
End Sub
```

In this way you can easily assign members of the class. You invoke the parameterized constructor as follows:

```
Dim aContact As New Contact("Alessandro",
        "Del Sole",
        "alessandro.delsole@visual-basic.it",
        "5Th street")
```

At this point, your object is ready to be used and is populated with data. You might also want to add simple validations for arguments received by the constructor. This is important because, if you need data initialization, you also need valid data. You can throw an ArgumentException if arguments are invalid, as shown here:

```
Public Sub New(ByVal name As String,
        ByVal surName As String,
        ByVal emailAddress As String,
        ByVal homeAddress As String)

    If surName = "" Then _
      Throw New ArgumentException("surName")
    Me.FirstName = name
    Me.LastName = surName
    Me.Email = emailAddress
    Me.Address = homeAddress
End Sub
```

Continuing the discussion about members' initialization, you might have members (typically fields) with inline initialization. In this scenario, when you invoke the constructor, members' initialization is also performed even if the constructor contains no code about initialization. This is demonstrated by the following code snippet:

```
Public Class Contact

    Private ReadOnly InitializationDemo As Integer = 100

'Just for demo purposes!
    Public Sub New()
        Console.WriteLine(InitializationDemo.ToString)
        Console.ReadLine()
    End Sub
End Class
```

The constructor does not perform any initialization, but when the class gets instantiated, the value is assigned. The preceding code produces 100 as the output. Another interesting thing is that constructors are the only place in which you can initialize read-only fields. You can rewrite the preceding code as follows:

```
Public Class Contact

    Private ReadOnly InitializationDemo As Integer

    'Just for demo purposes!
    Public Sub New()
        InitializationDemo = 100
        Console.WriteLine(InitializationDemo.ToString)
        Console.ReadLine()
    End Sub
```

Notice that the code is correctly compiled and the produced output is 100. This technique is important if you plan to expose read-only members in your classes.

Overloading Constructors

Because constructors are effectively methods, they support the overloading feature. You can therefore provide multiple implementations of the New method, taking care of the limitations described for methods. You cannot use the Overloads keyword; the compiler does not need it. Continuing the example of the Contact class, you can provide different implementations of the constructor as follows:

```
Public Sub New()
    Me.FirstName = "Assigned later"
    Me.LastName = "Assigned later"
    Me.Email = "Assigned later"
    Me.Address = "Assigned later"
End Sub

Public Sub New(ByVal surName As String)
    If String.IsNullOrEmpty(surName) Then _
        Throw New ArgumentException("surName")

    Me.LastName = surName

    'Will be assigned later
    Me.FirstName = ""
    Me.Email = ""
    Me.Address = ""
End Sub

Public Sub New(ByVal name As String,
        ByVal surName As String,
        ByVal emailAddress As String,
        ByVal homeAddress As String)
```

```
    If surName = "" Then _
       Throw New ArgumentException("surName")
    Me.FirstName = name
    Me.LastName = surName
    Me.Email = emailAddress
    Me.Address = homeAddress
End Sub
```

The first overload receives no arguments and provides a default members' initialization. The second overload receives just an argument, initializing other members with empty strings. The last overload is the most complete and provides initialization features for all the properties exposed by the class.

Nested Invocations

Overloads are useful, but when working with constructors, you might want to consider a common place for initializing members. To accomplish this, you can invoke constructors' overloads from another overload. Consider the following code snippet:

```
Public Sub New(ByVal LastName As String)
    Me.New(LastName, "")
End Sub

Public Sub New(ByVal LastName As String, ByVal Email As String)
    Me.LastName = LastName
    Me.Email = Email
End Sub
```

The first overload can invoke the second overload, passing required arguments. In the preceding example, only an empty string is passed, but according to your scenario you could make a different elaboration before passing the argument. The good news in this technique is that you need to provide initialization code only once (in this case, in the second overload). By the way, take care about the hierarchical calls; the first overload can invoke the second one because this receives more arguments, but not vice versa. This kind of approach can be used because both overloads have an argument in common. For instance, say you instead had a ContactID property of type Integer that you wanted to initialize via the constructor and you had the following overloads:

```
Public Sub New(ByVal LastName As String)

End Sub

Public Sub New(ByVal ContactID As Integer)

End Sub
```

In this case the two overloads have no arguments in common; because of this, if you want to provide a common place for initializations, you need to implement a private constructor as follows:

```
Private Sub New()
    'Replace with your
    'initialization code
    Me.ContactID = 0
    Me.LastName = "Del Sole"
End Sub
```

Then you can redirect both preceding overloads to invoke a private constructor:

```
Public Sub New(ByVal LastName As String)
    Me.New()
    Me.LastName = LastName
End Sub

Public Sub New(ByVal ContactID As Integer)
    Me.New()
    Me.ContactID = ContactID
End Sub
```

PRIVATE CONSTRUCTORS

There is a little bit more to say about private constructors that is discussed later in this chapter in the section "Shared Members." At the moment, you need to remember that if you place a private constructor, you *must* remove the public one with the same signature. For example, if you have a `Private Sub New()`, you cannot also have a `Public Sub New()`.

Object Initializers

Object initializers enable inline initialization of objects' members when creating an instance, without the need of providing specific constructors' overloads. For a better understanding, let's provide a practical example. The `Contact` class could be implemented without a constructor overload that receives any arguments for initialization:

```
Public Class Contact

    Public Property FirstName As String
    Public Property LastName As String
    Public Property Email As String
    Public Property Address As String

End Class
```

To instantiate the class and initialize its members, according to the classical, old-fashioned syntax, you should write the following code:

```
Dim aContact As New Contact
With aContact
    .FirstName = "Alessandro"
    .LastName = "Del Sole"
    .Email = "alessandro.delsole@visual-basic.it"
    .Address = "5Th street"
End With
```

The recent Visual Basic syntax instead enables the object initializers way, which works as in the following snippet:

```
Dim aContact As New Contact With {.LastName = "Del Sole",
    .FirstName = "Alessandro",
    .Email = "alessandro.delsole@visual-basic.it",
    .Address = "5Th street"}
```

You add the `With` keyword after the instance declaration. The keyword is followed by a couple of brackets. Within the brackets, you can easily assign members by writing members' names preceded by a dot symbol and separated by commas. This code demonstrates how you can provide inline initialization of members even if no constructor's overloads receive an appropriate number of arguments for the purpose of initialization. I will often write code using object initializers; this feature is important for advanced language features, which are covered in the next part of the book.

WHY OBJECT INITIALIZERS?

You might wonder why this feature exists in .NET languages, considering that there were already several ways for providing initialization. The reason is LINQ. As you see later in the book, object initializers provide a way for initializing objects within queries; another important feature known as *anonymous types* takes advantage of object initializers. Chapter 20, "Advanced Language Features," discusses anonymous types.

Shared Members

Classes can expose instance and shared members. Until now, all discussions used instance members for examples. It's important to understand the difference between instance and shared members because you can successfully use both of them in your classes. When you create a new instance of a class, you create a copy of that class with its own life and its own data. On the other hand, with shared members, you work with only one copy of a class and of its data. Classes can support different situations, such as all shared members or just a few shared members. For example, if you have a class exposing only shared members, you work with exactly one copy of the class. If you have only a few shared members within a class, all instances of that class access only one copy of the data marked as shared.

SHARED/STATIC

In Visual Basic we talk about *shared* members. This is because these members are marked with the `Shared` keyword. In other programming languages, such behavior is represented by the "static" definition; *shared* and *static* mean the same thing. Typically, the static definition is better when talking about interoperability with other .NET languages; both definitions refer to the same thing and the shared definition is used for consistency.

You expose only shared members in two main circumstances: with mere methods libraries or with classes that can exist in only one copy (known as *singleton*), such as the `Application` class in Windows Forms applications. Now you learn how to implement shared members within classes.

Shared Classes

Visual Basic, different from other .NET languages such as Visual C#, does not provide the capability of creating shared classes. To accomplish this, you have two alternatives: You can create a class the usual way and mark all members as shared, or you can create a module. Modules are a specific Visual Basic feature that work almost as shared classes (see Chapter 10, "Modules").

Shared Fields

Shared fields are useful to store information that is common to all instances of a class. For example, imagine you have a class named `Document` that represents a text document. You could implement a shared field acting as a counter of all the documents opened in your application:

```
Public Class Document

    Private Shared _documentCounter As Integer

    Public Sub New()
    _documentCounter += 1
    End Sub

End Class
```

The code in the example increments the counter each time a new instance is created. The `documentCounter` field is common to all instances of the Document class because it is marked with the Shared keyword.

Shared Properties

In an object-oriented approach, fields should be wrapped by properties that gain access to fields. This also happens with shared members. A shared property can be implemented either as an auto-implemented property or explicitly. For instance, continuing with the preceding example, a shared property could be implemented as follows:

```
Public Shared Property DocumentCounter As Integer
```

You can still write shared properties the old-fashioned way for further manipulations, like this:

```
Private Shared _documentCounter As Integer

Public Shared Property DocumentCounter As Integer
    Get
        Return _documentCounter
    End Get
    Set(value As Integer)
        _documentCounter = value
    End Set
End Property
```

You can also write shared read-only properties. The following is an example:

```
Public Class Document

    Private Shared _documentCounter As Integer

    Public Shared ReadOnly Property DocumentCounter As Integer
        Get
            Return _documentCounter
        End Get
    End Property


    Public Sub New()
        _documentCounter += 1
    End Sub
End Class
```

In this case, the property's value is incremented only when a new instance of the class is created, passing through the related field. The new read-only auto-implemented properties in Visual Basic 2015 can also be applied to shared properties. The preceding code could be rewritten as follows:

```
Public Class Document
    Public Shared ReadOnly Property DocumentCounter As Integer

    Public Sub New()
        _documentCounter += 1
    End Sub
End Class
```

In this case, you directly assign the implicit backing field, as you would do with the explicit field when using the extended syntax.

Shared Methods

Shared methods can be invoked without the need of creating an instance of the class that defines them. As in the previous members, shared methods are decorated with the Shared keyword. A common use of shared methods is within class libraries that act as helper repositories of functions. For example, you can have a class that provides methods for compressing and decompressing files using the System.IO.Compression namespace. In such a scenario, you do not need to create an instance of the class; in fact, shared methods just need to point to some files and not to instance data. The following code snippet provides an example of shared methods:

```
Public Class CompressionHelper

    Public Shared Sub Compress(ByVal fileName As String,
            ByVal target As String)
        'Code for compressing files here
    End Sub

    Public Shared Sub Decompress(ByVal fileName As String,
            ByVal uncompressed As String)
        'Code for decompressing files here
    End Sub
End Class
Sub Test()

    CompressionHelper.Compress("Sourcefile.txt", "Compressedfile.gz")

    CompressionHelper.Decompress("Compressedfile.gz", "Sourcefile.txt")

End Sub
```

As you can see, you invoke shared methods by writing the name of the class instead of creating an instance and invoking methods onto the instance. This approach is useful for organizing functions in libraries according to their purpose (established via the class name). If you try to invoke shared methods from an instance, the Visual Basic compiler reports a warning message advising that such invocation might be ambiguous and will offer an autocorrect option to change the instance name to the class name, removing the potential ambiguity. Of course, you can remove such warnings by editing the **Instance Variable Accesses Shared Member** option in the Compiler tab within My Project. You should leave the default setting unchanged because it can help you avoid ambiguous code. Shared methods also support overloading, so you can take advantage of this feature if necessary. When implementing shared methods, you should be aware of some considerations. First, you cannot work with instance members from within shared methods. For instance, the following code reports a compilation error:

```
'Instance field
Private instanceField As Integer

'Cannot refer to an instance member
Public Shared Function testSharedInstance() As Integer
    Return instanceField
End Function
```

To solve this error, you should mark as `Shared` the member you are working with (`instanceField` in the preceding example):

```
'Shared field
Private Shared sharedField As Integer

'Correct
Public Shared Function testSharedInstance() As Integer
    Return sharedField
End Function
```

The alternative is to change the method from shared to instance, removing the `Shared` keyword from the method definition. But this is not a game. You need to evaluate how your methods will behave and how they will use members exposed by your classes. According to this, you can decide whether methods can be shared or must be instance ones. Another consideration is related to classes exposing only shared methods. Because in this scenario the class does not need to be instantiated, a private empty constructor must be supplied as follows:

```
Private Sub New()
    'No code
End Sub
```

This constructor contains no code (but it could for initialization purposes) and is just necessary to prevent instance creation.

Shared Sub Main

In all code examples shown to this point, you saw how Console applications provide a module containing the entry point for applications, which is the `Sub Main`. Because modules are basically shared classes, you can supply a class containing shared members with a `Shared Sub Main` that works as in modules. Although modules are suggested instead of shared classes, because they cause less confusion and are a Visual Basic-specific feature, you need to know how to implement the `Shared Sub Main` within classes. If you ever use conversion tools from Visual C# to VB (or if you get code examples translated into VB by Visual C# folks), you will typically find a class named Program containing the previously mentioned shared entry point.

Shared Constructors

Classes can implement shared constructors, as shown in the following code:

```
'Private visibility
Shared Sub New()
    'Initialization of shared
    'members
    sharedField = 10
End Sub
```

Shared constructors are particularly useful for initializing shared members or for loading data that is common to all instances of a class. A shared constructor is invoked immediately before the normal constructor that creates a new instance of the class. With that said, the following code is appropriate and accepted by the compiler:

```
Shared Sub New()
    'Initialization of shared
    'members
    sharedField = 10
End Sub

Sub New()

End Sub
```

Another important thing to take care of is that shared constructors have `Private` visibility, and they are the only point in the class in which you can initialize a read-only field.

Common Language Specification

One of the most important features of the .NET Framework is the CLR, which offers a common infrastructure for various .NET languages. You might also remember from Chapter 1, "Introducing .NET 2015," that all .NET compilers produce Intermediate Language (IL) code. Because of this, .NET languages can interoperate: An assembly produced with Visual Basic can be used by an application written in Visual C#, and vice versa. But different languages have, of course, different characteristics; so if developers use specific features of a language, the risk is that another language cannot use that produced assembly because they might encounter several errors. This can occur when companies produce reusable components, such as class libraries or user controls that you should be able to use from whatever .NET application written in whatever language you want without problems. To provide a common set of rules that developers should follow to ensure interoperability, Microsoft wrote the Common Language Specification (CLS) that are a set of rules that every developer has to follow to produce reusable assemblies. This chapter provides an overview of the CLS and gives you information about applying such rules to the topics discussed in this chapter. Each time a new topic is covered, tips for making code CLS-compliant are provided.

COMMON LANGUAGE SPECIFICATION WEBSITE

Microsoft offers a dedicated page to CLS on the MSDN portal that you should look at: http://msdn.microsoft.com/en-us/library/12a7a7h3(v=vs.110).aspx

---

Where Do I Need to Apply?

CLS is important when producing reusable components, such as class libraries or user controls. Because only public classes and public members from public classes can be used from other applications also written in different languages, the CLS applies only to

▶ Public classes

▶ Public members exposed by public classes, such as methods or properties, and members that can be inherited

▶ Objects used by public members, such as types passed as arguments to methods

In all other cases, such as private members, applying CLS is ignored by the compiler. Another situation when you do not need to apply CLS is when you do not produce reusable components. For example, the UI side of a Windows application (Win Forms or WPF) is not required to be CLS-compliant because external applications will not invoke the UI.

Marking Assemblies and Types as CLS Compliant

Chapter 2, "The Visual Studio 2015 IDE for Visual Basic," and Chapter 3, "The Anatomy of a Visual Basic Project," offer an overview of assemblies. When you produce a reusable component such as a class library or a user control such as a .dll assembly, you need to ensure that it is CLS-compliant. You can add the following attribute to the assembly definition:

```
<Assembly: CLSCompliant(True)>
```

This attribute tells the compiler to check whether a type used in your code is CLS-compliant. If the compiler finds a non–CLS-compliant type, it reports a warning message. Assembly members should also be marked as CLS-compliant if you plan that they will be. A class is defined CLS-compliant as follows:

```
<CLSCompliant(True)> Public Class Person
```

You might wonder why you should add this attribute at the class level if you specified one at the assembly level. The reason is that you might implement non–CLS-compliant classes (therefore assigning `False` to the `CLSCompliant` attribute). This is useful for communicating to both the compiler and code analysis tools that a non–CLS-compliant class should not be checked.

CODE ANALYSIS

There are different code analysis tools for checking whether code is CLS-compliant. The first one is the well-known Microsoft FxCop. The second one is the code analysis instrumentation available in Visual Studio 2015, which is covered in Chapter 51, "Code Analysis: The .NET Compiler Platform and Tools." Both are important for finding errors about CLS compliance of your code.

Naming Conventions

Assigning comprehensible identifiers to types and members is a best practice in every development environment. This becomes a rule in .NET development, especially if you want your code to be CLS-compliant. To understand this, you need to first know that the Common Language Specification enables only two notations, Pascal and camel. If you are an old Visual Basic 6 or Visual C++ developer, you might be familiar with the Hungarian notation that is not supported by .NET rules. An identifier is Pascal-cased when the first letter of each word composing the identifier is uppercase. The following identifier is Pascal-case: `FirstName`. An identifier is instead defined as camel-case when the first character of the first word composing the identifier is lowercase. The following identifier is camel-cased: `firstName`. It's important to know this difference to understand where and when you should use one notation or the other one. You use the Pascal notation in the following situations:

▶ Namespaces' identifiers

▶ Identifiers of all public members within an assembly, such as classes, properties, methods, and custom types

Instead, use the camel notation in the following situations:

▶ Identifiers of all private members within an assembly, such as fields, methods, and so on. This is not actually a requirement (because private members are not affected by CLS in terms of naming conventions), but it's a good programming practice.

▶ Arguments' names for methods, both public and private.

No other naming notation is enabled in the Common Language Specification.

USING AN UNDERSCORE WITH PRIVATE VARIABLES

As a commonly accepted convention, often the name of private variables starts with an underscore (_). This is useful when you declare properties the extended way and need a backing field that holds the property value. Different from Visual C#, which is case-sensitive, in Visual Basic you cannot have two identifiers with the same name but with different casing, so an underscore at the beginning of the private variable's name solves the problem and is a standardized practice.

Obviously, if you do not plan to write CLS-compliant code, you can use any notation you like. However, using a .NET-oriented notation is certainly preferable. Another important rule about naming conventions is in methods' names. You should first place the name of the verb and then the target of the action. For example, `CompressFile` is correct, whereas `FileCompress` is not. The following code shows an example of a well-formed class:

```
'Public members of an assembly
'are pascal cased
Public Class NamingConventionsDemo

    'private fields are camel-cased
    Private documentCounter As Integer = 0

    'public properties are pascal-cased
    Public Property FirstName As String

    'public methods are pascal-cased
    'arguments are camel-cased
    Public Function CompressFile(ByVal sourceFile As String,
            ByVal targetFile As String) As Boolean

    End Function

    'private methods are camel-cased
    'arguments are camel-cased
    Private Sub checkForFileExistance(ByVal fileName As String)

    End Sub

End Class
```

Because of their importance, this book follows the preceding naming conventions, even for CLS-incompliant code.

Rules About Classes

The CLS influences classes' implementation with basically a few rules. The most rules are related to inheritance as much is for methods. Because inheritance hasn't been covered yet (discussed in Chapter 12, "Inheritance"), the only rule mentioned here is that if a class exposes only shared members, it must have an empty private constructor and must be marked as NotInheritable, as follows:

```
<CLSCompliant(True)> Public NotInheritable Class GzipCompress
    'Empty private constructor
    Private Sub New()

    End Sub

    Public Shared Sub Compress(ByVal fileName As String,
            ByVal target As String)

    End Sub

    Public Shared Sub Decompress(ByVal fileName As String,
            ByVal source As String)

    End Sub
End Class
```

The other rules about classes are described in Chapter 12.

Rules About Properties

The CLS provides a couple of rules about properties implementation:

- ▶ All properties exposed by a class must have the same access level, meaning that they must be all instance properties or all shared properties or all virtual properties. Virtual properties (that is, marked with the MustOverride keyword) are described in Chapter 12.

- ▶ Get, Set, and the property itself must return and receive the same type; the type must also be CLS-compliant. If the property returns String, both Get and Set must handle String, too. The type must be passed by value and not by reference.

Rules About Methods

CLS influences methods both for inheritance implementations and for declarations. You need to know that arguments with a nonfixed length must be specified only with the ParamArray keyword.

Rules About Arrays

For arrays, CLS rules are simple:

- ▶ Items within arrays must be CLS-compliant types.

- ▶ Arrays' dimensions must have a lower bound of zero.

- ▶ Arrays must be zero-based. (This is mostly a rule for compilers.)

Summary

In this chapter, you learned several important concepts about object-oriented programming with Visual Basic 2015. You saw how classes are the most important item in the object-oriented programming; you also learned how to declare classes and how to expose members from classes, such as methods, properties, and fields. Summarizing these features, you might remember that fields are the real state of objects and properties are a way for ruling access to fields from the external world. You can also remember that methods are procedures that take actions. Methods are flexible due to the overloading technique that enables implementing different signatures of the same method. A special method known as constructor creates an instance of a class and gives the class the real life. Each time you create an instance of a class, you create a new copy of an object with its own life and data. But there are situations in which you need only one copy of an object and data, and that is where shared members come in. You also took a tour of interesting features such as partial classes and partial methods that enable a better organization of your classes' infrastructure. But as in all fantastic worlds, the risk of doing something wrong is always there, especially if you consider the CLR infrastructure that enables .NET languages to interoperate. Because of this, a set of rules named the Common Language Specification has been created to ensure that all classes and their members can be used from all .NET languages with the minimum risk of errors. After this overview of classes, it's time to understand how they live within memory.

CHAPTER 8

Managing an Object's Lifetime

Real life is often a great place to get programming examples. Think of life: Humans are born; they grow up; they live their lives; they do tons of things; and, at a certain point, they die. Managing objects in programming environments works similarly. You give life to an object by creating an instance; then you use it in your own application while it is effectively useful to the application. But there is a point at which you do not need an object anymore, so you need to destroy it to free up memory and other resources, bringing an object to "death." Understanding how object lifetimes work in .NET programming is fundamental because it gives you the ability to write better code—code that can take advantage of system resources, to consume resources the appropriate way or return unused resources to the system.

Understanding Memory Allocation

Chapter 4, "Data Types and Expressions," discusses value types and reference types, describing how both of them are allocated in memory. Value types reside in the stack, whereas reference types are allocated on the managed heap. When you create a new instance of a reference type, via the New keyword, the .NET Framework reserves some memory in the managed heap for the new object instance. Understanding memory allocation is fundamental, but an important practice is to also release objects and resources when they are unused or unnecessary. This returns free memory and provides better performance. For value types, the problem has an easy solution: Being allocated on the stack, they are simply removed from memory when you assign the default zero value. The real problem is about reference types—you need to destroy the instance of an object. To accomplish this, you assign `Nothing` to the instance of a reference type.

When you perform this operation, the .NET Framework marks the object reference as no longer used and marks the memory used by the object as unavailable to the application. However, it does not immediately free up the Heap, and the runtime cannot immediately reuse such memory. Memory previously used by no-longer-referenced objects can be released by the .NET Framework after some time because the .NET Framework knows when it is the best moment for releasing resources. Such a mechanism is complex, but fortunately it is the job of the *garbage collector*.

Understanding Garbage Collection

In your applications, you often create object instances or allocate memory for resources. When you perform these operations, .NET Framework checks for available memory in the Heap. If available memory is not enough, .NET Framework launches a mechanism known as *garbage collection*, powered by an internal tool named *garbage collector*. The garbage collector can also be controlled by invoking members of the `System.GC` class, but the advantage is leaving the .NET Framework the job of handling the process automatically for you. The garbage collector first checks for all objects that have references from your applications, including objects referenced from other objects, enabling object graphs to be kept alive. Objects having any references are considered as used and alive, so the garbage collector marks them as in use and therefore will not clean them up. Any other objects in the Heap are considered as unused, and therefore the garbage collector removes these objects and references to them. After this, it compresses the Heap and returns free memory space that can be reallocated for other, new objects or resources. In all this sequence of operations, you do nothing. The garbage collector takes care of everything required. You can, however, decide to release objects when you do not need them anymore; you set their references to `Nothing` to free up some memory. The following snippet shows how you can logically destroy an instance of the `Person` class:

```
Dim p As New Person
p.FirstName = "Alessandro"
p.LastName = "Del Sole"
p = Nothing
```

When you assign an object reference with `Nothing`, the Common Language Runtime (CLR) automatically invokes the destructor (the `Finalize` method is covered in the next section) that any class exposes because the most basic implementation is provided by `System.Object`. At this point, there is a problem. The garbage collection behavior is known as *nondeterministic*, meaning that no one can predict the moment when the garbage collector is invoked. In other words, after you set an object reference to `Nothing`, you cannot know when the object will be effectively released. There can be a small delay, such as seconds, but there can also be a long delay, such as minutes or hours. This can depend on several factors; for example, if no additional memory is required during your application's lifetime, an object could be released at the application shutdown. This can be a problem of limited importance if you have only in-memory objects that do not access to external resources, such as files or the network. You do not have to worry about free memory because, when required, the garbage collector will kick in. Anyway, you can force a garbage collection process by invoking the System.GC.Collect method. The following is an example:

```
p = Nothing
'Forces the garbage collector
'so that the object is effectively
'cleaned up
System.GC.Collect()
```

Forcing the garbage collection process is not a good idea. As you can imagine, frequently invoking a mechanism of this type can cause performance overhead and significantly slow down your application performances. When you work with in-memory objects that do not access external resources, such as the Person class, leave the .NET Framework the job of performing a garbage collection only when required. The real problem is when you have objects accessing to external resources, such as files, databases, and network connections, which you want to be free as soon as possible when you set your object to Nothing and therefore you cannot wait for the garbage collection process to kick in. In this particular scenario, you can take advantage of two methods that have very similar behaviors: Finalize and Dispose.

OUT-OF-SCOPE OBJECTS

Objects that go out of scope will also be marked for garbage collection if they have no external reference to them, even if you don't set them explicitly to Nothing.

Understanding the `Finalize` Method

The Finalize method can be considered as a destructor that executes code just before an object is effectively destroyed, that is when memory should be effectively released. This method is inherited from System.Object; therefore any class can implement the method by declaring it as Protected Overrides, as follows:

```
Protected Overrides Sub Finalize()
    'Write your code here for releasing
    'such as closing db connections,
    'closing network connections,
    'and other resources that VB cannot understand

    MyBase.Finalize() 'this is just the base implementation
End Sub
```

If you need to destroy an object that simply uses memory, do not invoke Finalize. You need to invoke it when your object has a reference to something that Visual Basic cannot understand because the garbage collector does not know how to release that reference.

Thus, you need to instruct it by providing code for explicitly releasing resources. Another situation is when you have references to something that is out of the scope of the object, such as unmanaged resources, network connections, and file references different from .NET streams. If an object explicitly provides a `Finalize` implementation, the CLR *automatically* invokes such a method just before removing the object from the Heap. This means that you *do not* need to invoke it manually. Notice that `Finalize` is not invoked immediately when you assign `Nothing` to the object instance you want to remove. Although `Finalize` enables you to control how resources must be released, it does not enable you to control when they are effectively released. This is due to the nondeterministic behavior of the garbage collector that frees up resources in the most appropriate moment, meaning that minutes or hours can be spent between the `Finalize` invocations and when resources are effectively released. However, invoking `Finalize` marks the object as no longer available. You could force the garbage collection process and wait for all finalizers to be completed, if you wanted to ensure that objects are logically and physically destroyed. Although this is not a good practice, because manually forcing a garbage collection causes performance overhead and loss of .NET Framework optimizations, you can write the following code:

```
'Object here is just for demo purposes
Dim c As New Object
c = Nothing
GC.Collect()
GC.WaitForPendingFinalizers()
```

Here are a few considerations on what `Finalize` should contain within its body:

▶ Do not throw exceptions within `Finalize` because the application cannot handle them and will crash.

▶ Invoke only shared methods except when the application is closing; this will avoid invocations on instance members from objects that can be logically destroyed.

▶ Continuing the previous point, do not access external objects from within `Final`.

To complete the discussion, it is worth mentioning that destruction of objects that explicitly provide `Finalize` require more than one garbage collection process. The reason destroyed objects are removed from the Heap at least at the second garbage collection is that `Finalize` could contain code that assigns the current object to a variable, keeping a reference still alive during the first garbage collection. This is known as *object resurrection* and is discussed in the section called "Restoring Objects with Object Resurrection." As a consequence, implementing `Finalize` can negatively impact performance and should be used only when strictly required.

Understanding `Dispose` and the `IDisposable` Interface

One of the issues of the `Finalize` destructor is that you cannot determine whether resources will be freed up and when an object will be physically destroyed from memory. This is because of the nondeterministic nature of the garbage collector—unused references will still remain in memory until the garbage collector kicks in, which is not a good idea. A better approach is to provide clients the ability to immediately release resources (such as network connections, data connections, or system resources) just before the object is destroyed, setting it to `Nothing`. The .NET Framework provides a way for releasing resources immediately and under your control, which is the `Dispose` method. Implementing `Dispose` avoids the need of waiting for the next garbage collection and enables you to clean up resources immediately, right before the object is destroyed. In contrast to `Finalize`, `Dispose` must be invoked manually. To provide a `Dispose` implementation, your class must implement the `IDisposable` interface. Visual Studio 2015 provides a skeleton of `IDisposable` implementation when you add the `Implements` directive (see Figure 8.1.) The code in Listing 8.1 shows the implementation.

FIGURE 8.1   IntelliSense speeds up implementing the `IDisposable` interface providing a skeleton of required `members`.

LISTING 8.1   Implementing the IDisposable Interface

```vb
Class DoSomething
    Implements IDisposable

#Region "IDisposable Support"
    Private disposedValue As Boolean ' To detect redundant calls

    ' IDisposable
    Protected Overridable Sub Dispose(disposing As Boolean)
        If Not Me.disposedValue Then
            If disposing Then
                ' TODO: dispose managed state (managed objects).
            End If

            ' TODO: free unmanaged resources (unmanaged objects) and
            ' override Finalize() below.
            ' TODO: set large fields to null.
        End If
        Me.disposedValue = True
    End Sub

    ' TODO: override Finalize() only if Dispose(disposing As Boolean) above
    'has code to free unmanaged resources.
    'Protected Overrides Sub Finalize()
    'Do not change this code.  Put cleanup
    'code in Dispose(disposing As Boolean) above.
    '    Dispose(False)
    '    MyBase.Finalize()
    'End Sub

    ' This code added by Visual Basic to correctly
    ' implement the disposable pattern.
    Public Sub Dispose() Implements IDisposable.Dispose
        ' Do not change this code.  Put cleanup
        'code in Dispose(disposing As Boolean) above.
        Dispose(True)
        GC.SuppressFinalize(Me)
    End Sub
#End Region
End Class
```

Notice how Dispose is declared as Overridable so that you can provide different implementations in derived classes. Visual Studio is polite enough to provide comments showing you the right places for writing code that release managed or unmanaged resources. Also notice the implementation of `Finalize` that is enclosed in comments and is therefore inactive. Such a destructor should be provided only if you have to release unmanaged resources. You invoke the `Dispose` method before setting your object reference to nothing, as demonstrated here:

```
Dim dp As New DoSomething
'Do your work here...

dp.Dispose()
dp = Nothing
```

As an alternative, you can take advantage of the `Using..End Using` statement covered in the next section. When implementing the `Dispose` pattern, in custom classes you need to remember to invoke the `Dispose` method of objects they use within their bodies so they can correctly free up resources. Another important thing to take care of is checking whether an object has already been disposed when `Dispose` is invoked, but the auto-generated code for the `Dispose` method already keeps track of this for you.

`Dispose` AND INHERITANCE

When you define a class deriving from another class that implements `IDisposable`, you do not need to override `Dispose` unless you need to release additional resources in the derived class.

`Using..End Using` Statement

As an alternative to directly invoking `Dispose`, you can take advantage of the `Using..End Using` statement. This code block automatically releases and removes from memory the object that it points to, invoking `Dispose` behind the scenes for you. The following code shows how you can open a stream for writing a file and ensure that the stream will be released even if you do not explicitly close it:

```
Using dp As New IO.StreamWriter("C:\TestFile.txt", False)
    dp.WriteLine("This is a demo text")
End Using
```

Notice how you simply create an instance of the object via the `Using` keyword. The `End Using` statement causes `Dispose` to be invoked on the previously mentioned instance. The advantage of `Using..End Using` is that the resource is automatically released in cases of unhandled exceptions, and this can be useful.

Putting `Dispose` and `Finalize` Together

Implementing `Dispose` and `Finalize` cannot necessarily be required. It depends only on what kind of work your objects perform. Table 8.1 summarizes what and when you should implement.

TABLE 8.1   Implementing Destructors

What	When
No destructor	Objects that just work in memory and that reference other .NET in memory objects.
Finalize	Executing some code before the object gets finalized. The limitation is that you cannot predict when the garbage collector comes in.
Dispose	Your objects access external resources that you need to free up as soon as possible when destroying the object.
Finalize and Dispose	Your objects access unmanaged resources that you need to free up as soon as possible when destroying the object.

You already have seen examples about Finalize and Dispose, so here you get an example of their combination. Before you see the code, you have to know that you will see invocations to Win32 unmanaged APIs that you do not need in real applications, but these kinds of functions are useful to understand to know how to release unmanaged resources. Now take a look at Listing 8.2.

LISTING 8.2   Implementing Dispose and Finalize

```
Imports System.Runtime.InteropServices

Public Class ProperCleanup
    Implements IDisposable

    Private disposedValue As Boolean ' To detect redundant calls

    'A managed resource
    Private managedStream As IO.MemoryStream

    'Unmanaged resources
    <DllImport("winspool.drv")>
    Shared Function OpenPrinter(deviceName As String,
                                deviceHandle As Integer,
                                printerDefault As Object) _
                                As Integer
    End Function
    <DllImport("winspool.drv")>
    Shared Function _
    ClosePrinter(deviceHandle As Integer) _
            As Integer
    End Function

    Private printerHandle As Integer
```

```vb
'Initializes managed and unmanaged resources
Public Sub New()
    managedStream = New IO.MemoryStream
    OpenPrinter("MyDevice", printerHandle, &H0)
End Sub


'Just a sample method that does nothing
'particular except for checking if the object
'has been already disposed
Public Function FormatString(myString As String) As String
    If disposedValue = True Then
        Throw New ObjectDisposedException("ProperCleanup")
    Else
        Return "You entered: " & myString
    End If
End Function


' IDisposable
Protected Overridable Sub Dispose(disposing As Boolean)
    If Not Me.disposedValue Then
        If disposing Then
            ' TODO: dispose managed state (managed objects).
            managedStream.Dispose()
        End If

        ' TODO: free unmanaged resources (unmanaged objects)
        ' and override Finalize() below.
        ' TODO: set large fields to null.
        ClosePrinter(printerHandle)
    End If
    Me.disposedValue = True
End Sub


' TODO: override Finalize() only if Dispose(disposing As Boolean)
' above has code to free unmanaged resources.
Protected Overrides Sub Finalize()
    ' Do not change this code.  Put cleanup code in
    ' Dispose(disposing As Boolean) above.
    Dispose(False)
    MyBase.Finalize()
End Sub


' This code added by Visual Basic to correctly
' implement the disposable pattern.
Public Sub Dispose() Implements IDisposable.Dispose
    ' Do not change this code.  Put cleanup code
```

```
            ' in Dispose(disposing As Boolean) above.
            Dispose(True)
            GC.SuppressFinalize(Me)
        End Sub
End Class
```

The code in Listing 8.2 has some interesting points. First, notice how both managed resources (a `System.IO.MemoryStream`) and unmanaged resources (`OpenPrinter` and `ClosePrinter` API functions) are declared. Second, notice how the constructor creates instances of the previous resources. Because there are unmanaged resources, you need to override the `Finalize` method. Visual Basic is polite enough to show you comments describing this necessity, so you simply uncomment the `Finalize` block definition. This method invokes the `Dispose` one passing `False` as an argument; this can ensure that `Dispose` will clean up unmanaged resources as you can understand examining the conditional code block within the method overload that accepts a Boolean argument. Finally, notice how the other `Dispose` overload, the one accepting no arguments, invokes the other overload passing `True` (therefore requiring managed resources to be released); then it invokes the `GC.SuppressFinalize` method to ensure that `Finalize` is not invoked. There are no unmanaged resources to release at this point because `Finalize` was previously invoked to clean up unmanaged resources.

Restoring Objects with Object Resurrection

With the *object resurrection* phrase, we describe the scenario in which an object is restored after its reference was removed, although the object was not removed yet from memory. This is an advanced technique, but it is not very useful and Microsoft strongly discourages you from using it in your applications. It is helpful to understand something more about objects' lifetime. An object being finalized can store a self-reference to a global variable, and this can keep the object alive. In simpler words, a reference to a "died" object is restored when within the `Finalize` method the current object is assigned (using the `Me` keyword) to a class-level or module-level variable. Here's a small code example for demonstrating object resurrection. Keep in mind that the code is simple to focus on the concept more than on the code difficulty, but you can use this technique with more and more complex objects. You add this code to a module:

```
Public resurrected As ResurrectionDemo
Sub TestResurrection()
    Dim r As New ResurrectionDemo
    'This marks the object to be collectible
    'so that Finalize gets run on it when GC next happens
    r = Nothing
End Sub
```

The resurrected variable is of type `ResurrectionDemo`, a class that will be implemented next. This variable holds the actual reference to the finalizing object so that it can keep it alive. The `TestResurrection` method creates an instance of the class and sets it to

Nothing, causing the CLR to invoke `Finalize`. Now notice the implementation of the `ResurrectionDemo` class and specifically the Finalize implementation:

```
Class ResurrectionDemo
    Protected Overrides Sub Finalize()
        'The object is resurrected here
        resurrected = Me
        GC.ReRegisterForFinalize(Me)
    End Sub
End Class
```

Notice how `Finalize`'s body assigns the current object to the resurrected variable, which holds the reference. When an object is resurrected, `Finalize` cannot be invoked a second time because the garbage collector removed the object from the finalization queue. This is the reason the `GC.ReRegisterForFinalize` method is invoked. As a consequence, multiple garbage collections are required for a resurrected object to be cleaned up. At this point, just think of how many system resources this can require. Moreover, when an object is resurrected, previously referenced objects are also resurrected. This can result in application faults because you cannot know whether objects' finalizations already occurred. As mentioned at the beginning of this section, the object resurrection technique rarely takes place in real-life application because of its implications and because it can be successfully used only in scenarios in which you need to create pools of objects whose frequent creation and destruction could be time-consuming.

Advanced Garbage Collection

The garbage collection is a complex mechanism, and in most cases you do not need to interact with the garbage collector because, in such cases, you must be extremely sure that what you are doing is correct. The .NET Framework automatically takes care of what the CLR needs. Understanding advanced features of the garbage collector can provide a better view of objects' lifetime. The goal of this section is therefore to show such advanced features.

Interacting with the Garbage Collector

The `System.GC` class provides several methods for manually interacting with the garbage collector. In this chapter you already learned some of them. Remember these methods:

▶ `Collect`, which enables you to force a garbage collection

▶ `WaitForPendingFinalizers`, which enables you to wait for all `Finalize` methods to be completed before cleaning up resources

▶ `ReRegisterForFinalize`, which puts an object back to the finalization queue in object resurrection

▶ `SuppressFinalize`, which is used in the `Dispose` pattern for avoiding unnecessary finalizations

There are other interesting members; for example, you can get an approximate amount of allocated memory as follows:

```
Dim bytes As Long = System.GC.GetTotalMemory(False)
```

You pass `False` if you do not want a garbage collection to be completed before returning the result. Another method is `KeepAlive` that adds a reference to the specified object preventing the garbage collector from destroying it:

```
GC.KeepAlive(anObject)
```

You can then tell the garbage collector that a huge amount of unmanaged memory should be considered within a garbage collection process; you accomplish this by invoking the `AddMemoryPressure` method. It requires the amount of memory as an argument. Next, you can tell the garbage collector that an amount of unmanaged memory has been released by invoking the `RemoveMemoryPressure` method. Other interesting members enable garbage collector interaction; these are covered in the next section for their relationship with the specific topic.

Understanding Generations and Operation Modes

The garbage collector is based on *generations* that are basically a counter representing how many times an object survived the garbage collection. The .NET Framework supports three generations. The first one is named `gen0` and is when the object is at its pure state. The second generation is named `gen1` and is when the object survived one garbage collection; the last generation is named `gen2` and is when the object survived two or more garbage collections. This is a good mechanism for figuring the garbage collector's performance because it first tries to remove objects at `gen2` instead of searching for all live references. The garbage collection process is available in two modes: server and workstation. The first one is intended for server applications, whereas the second mode is typically intended for standalone machines. The garbage collection can be executed on multiple threads, and this is known as *concurrent* garbage collection. Until .NET Framework 3.5 SP 1, concurrent garbage collection could perform collections on both `gen0` and `gen1` concurrently or most of a `gen2` without pausing managed code, but never `gen2` concurrently with the other ones. In .NET Framework 4.0, a new feature named *Background GC* was introduced and replaced concurrent garbage collection; this enables collecting all generations together and also enables allocating memory while collecting.

The good news is that you can also take advantage of a feature that enables subscribing to garbage collection events, so that you can be notified once the `gen2` completes. The code in Listing 8.3 demonstrates this (read comments for explanations).

LISTING 8.3   Registering for Garbage Collection Events

```
Sub Main()
    Try
        'Registers for notification about gen2 (1st arg) and
        'large objects on the Heap (2nd arg)
```

```vb
        GC.RegisterForFullGCNotification(10, 10)

        'Notifications are handled via a separate thread
        Dim thWaitForFullGC As New Thread(New _
                                    ThreadStart(AddressOf WaitForFullGCProc))
        thWaitForFullGC.Start()

    Catch ex As InvalidOperationException

        'Probably concurrent GC is enabled
        Console.WriteLine(ex.Message)
    End Try
End Sub

Public Shared Sub WaitForFullGCProc()
    While True
        'Notification status
        Dim s As GCNotificationStatus

        'Register for an event advising
        'that a GC is imminent
        s = GC.WaitForFullGCApproach()

        If s = GCNotificationStatus.Succeeded Then
            'A garbage collection is imminent

        End If

        'Register for an event advising
        'that a GC was completed
        s = GC.WaitForFullGCComplete()
        If s = GCNotificationStatus.Succeeded Then

            'A garbage collection is completed
        End If
    End While
End Sub
```

You can easily subscribe for garbage collection events by invoking WaitForFullGCComplete and WaitForFullApproach.

Summary

Understanding how memory and resources are released after object usage is fundamental in every development environment. In .NET, this is accomplished by the garbage collector, a complex mechanism that works after you set an object reference to Nothing or when you attempt to create new instances of objects but don't have any more memory available. You can also implement explicit destructors, such as Finalize or Dispose, according to specific scenarios in which you do need to release external or unmanaged resources before destroying an object.

CHAPTER 9

Organizing Types Within Namespaces

The .NET Framework ships with many built-in types. Such an enormous quantity necessarily needs a hierarchical organization in which types must be divided into their areas of interest (data access, file manipulation, communications, and so on). Moreover, the .NET Framework provides an extensible platform, and companies can also build their own custom components exposing types that could have the same name of existing built-in types in .NET Framework. To avoid naming conflicts and to enable a hierarchical organization of the code, Visual Basic offers the *namespaces* feature discussed in this chapter.

Understanding Namespaces

Namespaces provide a way for a better organization of the code and avoiding conflicts between types with the same name. Consider a complex hierarchical framework of objects (such as the .NET Framework or Windows Runtime) in which you have the need to expose more than one type with a particular identifier. The typical example is when software companies produce class libraries; different companies could need to provide their own implementation of the `Person` class, or the same company could provide different implementations of the `Person` class within the same assembly, so there could be ambiguities for developers when invoking a particular implementation of the `Person` class. To solve this coding problem, programming languages in the .NET family offer the capability of organizing types within namespaces. For example, imagine using assemblies from two companies, `Company1` and `Company2`, with both produced assemblies exposing their own implementation of the `Person` class. You would need to use one of the two implementations, but you would still need to reference both assemblies in your project. The following code

```
Dim p As New Person
```

can cause the Visual Basic compiler to report an error because it does not know which of the two implementations you want to invoke. By using namespaces, you can avoid this ambiguity as follows:

```
Dim p1 As New Company1.Person
Dim p2 As New Company2.Person
```

In this code example, `Company1` and `Company2` are namespaces that virtually encapsulate lots of types, whereas both `Company1.Person` and `Company2.Person` represent the full name of the `Person` class. The .NET Framework Base Class Library (BCL) relies heavily on namespaces. The main namespace in the BCL is `System`, which is the root in the BCL hierarchy. `System` exposes dozens of other namespaces, such as `System.Xml`, `System.Data`, `System.Linq`, and so on. Each of these namespaces exposes types and other nested namespaces, and in this way a hierarchical framework is more maintainable. Namespaces solve a coding problem and an object implementation problem. This is because namespaces are all about coding. The Common Language Runtime (CLR) does not recognize namespaces, but it does recognize only full class names, such as `Company2.Person` in the previous example or `System.Object` or `System.Console`. Namespaces are just a logical feature that helps developers write better-organized and reusable code. The CLR never encounters conflicts because it recognizes only full class names, but as you learn later in this chapter, as a developer you might encounter such conflicts. So, having some help in writing and organizing code will be necessary, especially when working with long named classes (see the "`Imports` Directives" section).

Organizing Types Within Namespaces

Namespaces are defined within `Namespace..End Namespace` blocks. Every namespace can expose the following types and members:

▶ Classes

▶ Structures

▶ Enumerations

▶ Modules

▶ Interfaces

▶ Delegates

▶ Nested namespaces

Listing 9.1 shows an example of a namespace exposing most of the preceding listed members.

LISTING 9.1   Organizing Types Within a Namespace

```vbnet
Namespace People

    Public Interface IContactable
        ReadOnly Property HasEmailAddress As Boolean
    End Interface

    Public MustInherit Class Person
        Public Property FirstName As String
        Public Property LastName As String

        Public Overrides Function ToString() As String
            Return FirstName & " " & LastName
        End Function
    End Class

    Public Enum PersonType
        Work = 0
        Personal = 1
    End Enum

    Public Class Contact
        Inherits Person
        Implements IContactable

        Public Property EmailAddress As String

        Public Overrides Function ToString() As String
            Return MyBase.ToString()
        End Function

        Public ReadOnly Property HasEmailAddress As Boolean _
                        Implements IContactable.HasEmailAddress
            Get
                If String.IsNullOrEmpty(Me.EmailAddress) Then
                    Return False
                Else
                    Return True
                End If
            End Get
        End Property
    End Class

    Public Class Employee
        Inherits Person
```

6

```vb
        Public Property Title As String

        Public Overrides Function ToString() As String
            Return Me.Title & " " & Me.FirstName & " " & Me.LastName
        End Function
    End Class


    Public Class Customer
        Inherits Person

        Public Property CompanyName As String
        Public Overrides Function ToString() As String
            Return Me.LastName & " from " & Me.CompanyName
        End Function

    End Class


    Module GlobalDeclarations
        Public Data As Object
    End Module


    Public Structure PersonInformation
        Public Property PersonCategory As PersonType
        Public Property HasEmailAddress As Boolean
    End Structure
End Namespace
```

As you can see in Listing 9.1, you can organize your custom objects within a namespace. The code implements an abstract class (Person), three derived classes (Contact, Employee, and Customer), an interface (which is then implemented by the Contact class), an enumeration (PersonType), a structure (PersonInformation), and a module (GlobalDeclarations). The namespace becomes part of the full name of a type. For example, the full name for the Contact class is People.Contact. Therefore, if you need to access a type defined within a namespace, you need to refer to it by writing the full name, as in the following line of code:

```vb
Dim firstContact As New People.Contact
```

ADDING IMPORTS

Later on, this chapter discusses the Imports directives, which can prevent the need to add the namespace identifier to the full type name every time.

Namespaces can also expose partial classes. This is a common situation within .NET Framework built-in namespaces.

Why Are Namespaces So Useful?

The purpose of namespaces is to enable a better organization of types. In some situations, an object's hierarchy could expose two different types with different behaviors, but with the same name. For example, imagine you have two `Person` classes; the first one should represent business contacts, and the second one should represent your friends. Of course, you cannot create two classes with the same name within one namespace. Because of this, you can organize such types in different namespaces and thus avoid conflicts. The code in Listing 9.2 shows how you can define two `Person` classes within two different namespaces.

LISTING 9.2   Avoiding Conflicts with Different Namespaces

```
Namespace People

    Public Class Person
        Public Property FirstName As String
        Public Property LastName As String

        Public Overrides Function ToString() As String
            Return FirstName & " " & LastName
        End Function
    End Class
End Namespace


Namespace MyFriends
    'Will not conflict with People.Person
    Public Class Person
        Public Property FirstName As String
        Public Property LastName As String
        Public Property Sibling As String

        Public Overrides Function ToString() As String
            Return FirstName & " " & LastName & ": " & Sibling
        End Function
    End Class
End Namespace
```

This is the way two classes with the same name can coexist within the same assembly. To access both of them, you just need to invoke their full names, as follows:

```
Dim aFriend As New MyFriends.Person
Dim aContact As New People.Person
```

> **NOTE**
>
> The `Person` class is just an example. You can refer to inheritance as in Listing 9.1 instead of providing different namespaces, but the `Person` class is the simplest example for demonstrating topics, which is the reason to continue to use such a class.

Nested Namespaces

You can nest namespaces within namespaces to create a complex hierarchy of namespaces. However, you should be careful in creating complex hierarchies of namespaces because this can lead to particular complexity in your code that can cause difficulties in maintainability and reuse. You nest a namespace within another one by adding a new `Namespace..End Namespace` block. For example, in Listing 9.1 there are two different kinds of people: personal contact and business people (which includes `Customer` and `Employee`). You could then consider defining a new namespace for your business objects and one for your personal objects. Listing 9.3 shows a shorter version of the first example, in which nested namespaces expose the two kinds of classes.

LISTING 9.3   Implementing Nested Namespaces

```
Namespace People

    Public Interface IContactable
        ReadOnly Property HasEmailAddress As Boolean
    End Interface

    Public MustInherit Class Person
        Public Property FirstName As String
        Public Property LastName As String

        Public Overrides Function ToString() As String
            Return FirstName & " " & LastName
        End Function
    End Class
    Namespace Work
        Public Class Customer
            Inherits Person

            Public Property CompanyName As String
            Public Overrides Function ToString() As String
                Return Me.LastName & " from " & Me.CompanyName
            End Function

        End Class
```

```vbnet
        Public Class Employee
            Inherits Person

            Public Property Title As String

            Public Overrides Function ToString() As String
                Return Me.Title & " " & Me.FirstName & " " & Me.LastName
            End Function
        End Class
    End Namespace

    Namespace Personal
        Public Class Contact
            Inherits Person
            Implements IContactable

            Public Property EmailAddress As String

            Public Overrides Function ToString() As String
                Return MyBase.ToString()
            End Function

            Public ReadOnly Property HasEmailAddress As Boolean _
                        Implements IContactable.HasEmailAddress
                Get
                    If String.IsNullOrEmpty(Me.EmailAddress) Then
                        Return False
                    Else
                        Return True
                    End If
                End Get
            End Property
        End Class
    End Namespace
End Namespace
```

As you can see from Listing 9.3, nesting namespaces is an easy task. Creating complex hierarchies can lead to problems in code readability because of several possible indentations. Luckily, Visual Basic enables an alternative syntax for defining nested namespaces without writing indented code. Listing 9.4 shows how you can create nested namespace with the alternative syntax.

LISTING 9.4   Nesting Namespace Without Indented Code

```
Namespace People

    Public Interface IContactable
        ReadOnly Property HasEmailAddress As Boolean
    End Interface

    Public MustInherit Class Person
        Public Property FirstName As String
        Public Property LastName As String

        Public Overrides Function ToString() As String
            Return FirstName & " " & LastName
        End Function
    End Class
End Namespace

Namespace People.Work
    Public Class Employee
        Inherits Person

        Public Property Title As String

        Public Overrides Function ToString() As String
            Return Me.Title & " " & Me.FirstName & " " & Me.LastName
        End Function
    End Class

    Public Class Customer
        Inherits Person

        Public Property CompanyName As String
        Public Overrides Function ToString() As String
            Return Me.LastName & " from " & Me.CompanyName
        End Function
    End Class
End Namespace

Namespace People.Personal
    Public Class Contact
        Inherits Person
        Implements IContactable

        Public Property EmailAddress As String
```

```
        Public Overrides Function ToString() As String
            Return MyBase.ToString()
        End Function

        Public ReadOnly Property HasEmailAddress As Boolean _
                    Implements IContactable.HasEmailAddress
            Get
                If String.IsNullOrEmpty(Me.EmailAddress) Then
                    Return False
                Else
                    Return True
                End If
            End Get
        End Property
    End Class
End Namespace
```

As you can see from Listing 9.4, you can nest namespaces by adding a dot after the parent namespace and then specifying the child namespace name without having to nest namespaces on the code side. This produces the same result, but your code is more readable. By the way, you are free to use both methodologies.

Scope

Namespaces have scope of visibility. As a rule, namespaces have public visibility because they can be recognized within the project, from other projects that reference the project defining the namespace and from external assemblies. Because of this behavior, namespace declarations can be adorned neither with qualifiers nor with attributes. Members defined within namespaces can only be `Friend` or `Public`. If you do not want the external world to use some members defined within a namespace, you need to mark such members as `Friend`. By default, Visual Basic considers members within namespaces as `Friend`. If you want them to be of public access, you need to explicitly mark them as `Public`.

Root Namespace

Each application has a root namespace that contains all types defined in the application. When you create a new project, Visual Studio automatically assigns the root namespace (also known as the *first-level namespace*) with the name of the project. This is important to understand, for several reasons. First, if you develop class libraries or reusable components, the root namespace must follow the naming conventions of the Common Language Specification (CLS). Second, you must know how your types and auto-generated code are organized within your project. For example, the project containing the code of this chapter is named `OrganizingTypesWithinNamespaces`. By default, Visual Studio assigned the root namespace identifier with the `OrganizingTypesWithinNamespaces` identifier. Continuing the previous example, you access the `People` namespace in this way:

`OrganizingTypesWithinNamespaces.People.` You then get access to `People`'s objects as follows:

`OrganizingTypesWithinNamespaces.People.Person`

To replace the identifier for your root namespace, you need to open the My Project window and open the Application tab. You find a text box named Root namespace, which is represented in Figure 9.1.

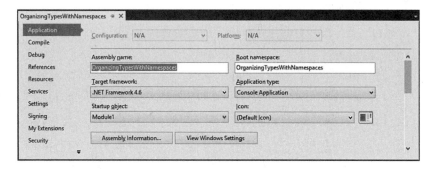

FIGURE 9.1   Checking and editing the root namespace.

Here you can change the root namespace. If you develop class libraries, the root namespace should have the following form: `CompanyName.ProductName` (for this particular scenario, you should also consider the Global namespace feature discussed at the end of this chapter).

ROOT NAMESPACE

When invoking a member defined inside the root namespace, you do not need to include the name of the namespace. This is the only exception when invoking members. For example, if you need to access the `People` namespace defined in the code example, type `People` and not `OrganizingTypesWithinNamespaces.People`.

Imports Directives

It often happens that you need to invoke types defined within long-named, nested namespaces. To invoke types, you need to write the full name of the type, which includes the identifier of the namespace that defines a particular type, as in the following code:

```
Dim aFile As New System.IO.FileStream("C:\test.txt",
               System.IO.FileMode.Open)
Dim onePerson As New ImportsDirectives.People.Work.Customer
```

Although IntelliSense has been highly improved from previous versions and it helps in writing code, it can result quite annoyingly in typing long-named namespaces. To help developers write code faster, Visual Basic enables the usage of Imports directives. Such directives enable developers to avoid having to write the full namespace identifier preceding the types' names. The preceding code can be rewritten as follows:

```
Imports System.IO
Imports ImportsDirectives.People.Work

...

        Dim aFile As New FileStream("C:\test.txt", FileMode.Open)
        Dim onePerson As New Customer
```

POSITION IN CODE OF Imports DIRECTIVES

Imports directives can be added to each code file you need. They *must* be the first lines of code, preceding any other code except comments, the Option Strict, Option Compare, Option Explicit, and Option Infer directives that are the only lines of code always on the top.

You can now invoke types exposed by the System.IO namespace without having to write the namespace identifier each time. In this particular code example, there were just two invocations of members from the namespace, but in an application that manipulates files, you could have hundreds of invocations with a single Imports directive. You do not need to write the namespace identifier before the types' names each time. System.IO is a .NET built-in namespace, but the same applies to your own namespaces (in our example, the ImportsDirectives.People.Work). You can also take advantage of another technique that enables assigning an identifier to a long namespace so that invocations can be smarter (a feature known as *namespace alias*):

```
Imports work = ImportsDirectives.People.Work

...

        Dim onePerson As New work.Customer
```

IMPORTING XML NAMESPACES

Starting from Visual Basic 2008, Imports directives also enable importing XML namespaces. This feature is discussed in Chapter 27, "Manipulating XML Documents with LINQ and XML Literals," for LINQ to XML.

Imports directives also enable importing class names. This enables invoking only shared members without the need of writing the full class name. Consider the following code, which deletes a file from disk:

```
System.IO.File.Delete("C:\text.txt")
```

Delete is a shared method exposed by the System.IO.File class. You can rewrite the previous code as follows:

```
Imports System.IO.File
...
        Delete("C:\text.txt")
```

This can be useful if you need to invoke lots of shared members from a particular class.

Project-Level Default Imports

By default, Visual Studio 2015 adds some auto-generated Imports directives each time you create a new Visual Basic project, so you do not need to manually add such statements. Default Imports are specific to the project type, so if you create a Console application, there will be Imports related to these kinds of applications. If you create a web application, there will be Imports related to the most common namespaces for web applications and so on. You can easily add project-level namespaces via the My Project window. In the References tab, you can find a group box named Imported namespaces, as shown in Figure 9.2.

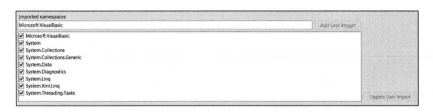

FIGURE 9.2   Setting project-level namespaces.

You can click the check box corresponding to each available namespace to add project-level Imports directives. This avoids the need of manually typing such Imports.

Additionally, if a particular namespace is not available in the list, you can manually enter its name and it will be added.

> **TIP**
>
> You can add a namespace alias in the Imported namespaces list. For example, if you want to import the System.Windows.Forms namespace, you can type something like F = System.Windows.Forms and then access namespace members as if you wrote the alias in the code (for example, F.TextBox).

Organizing Imports

More often than not, you will add many Imports directives to your code files. As the number of directives grows, it is helpful to keep them organized and remove unnecessary ones. Visual Basic 2015 offers convenient ways to organize your Imports directives via refactoring commands. To understand how you can accomplish this, consider the following simple code, which gets the list of running processes on your machine and writes the list to a text file:

```
Imports System.Text
Imports System.Linq
Imports System.IO
Imports Microsoft.Win32

Module Module1

    Sub Main()
        Dim proc = From prox In Process.GetProcesses
                   Select prox

        Dim stringContent As New StringBuilder

        For Each item In proc
            stringContent.AppendLine(item.ProcessName)
        Next

        Using fs As New StreamWriter("C:\temp\processes.txt")
            fs.WriteLine(stringContent.ToString)
        End Using
    End Sub

End Module
```

The code is very simple, and even if you might not yet be used to LINQ queries, now your focus must be on the `Imports` directives. First, the IDE detects that `System.Linq` and `Microsoft.Win32` are not necessary; in fact, `System.Linq` is included in the default imported namespaces. Second, you are not using any object from the `Microsoft.Win32` namespace. Because of this, both directives are grayed out, which means they are redundant code. The code is instead using objects from the `System.Text` and `System.IO` namespaces and the `StringBuilder` and `StreamWriter` classes. You could definitely reorganize the `Imports` directive a better way. Right-click the code editor and select **Organize Imports** (see Figure 9.3). You have three options:

▶ **Remove Unnecessary Imports**—This option removes redundant directives.

▶ **Sort Imports**—This option sorts directives alphabetically.

▶ **Remove and Sort Imports**—This option removes redundant directives and sorts alphabetically.

For instance, if you select the third option, the unnecessary directives will be removed, and the remaining directives will be sorted so that the `System.IO` directive appears before `System.Text`. As an alternative, you could use the light bulb to fix redundant code, but it does not provide an option for sorting directives.

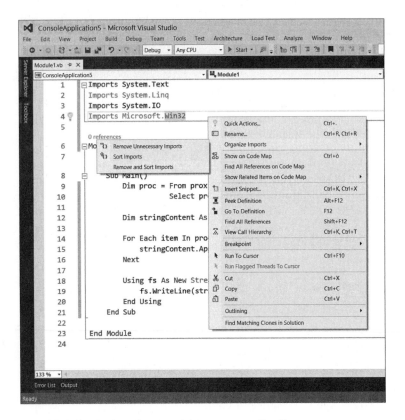

FIGURE 9.3   Options for organizing `Imports` directives.

Avoiding Ambiguities

You might have situations in which you need to access objects with the same name, coming from different namespaces. For example, both Windows Forms and Windows Presentation Foundation technologies provide a `MessageBox` class. In interoperability scenarios, where you have both references to Windows Forms and WPF assemblies, invoking such objects could result in ambiguities. Consider the following code:

```
Imports System.Windows.Forms
'The following is a project-level Imports and only added for demo purposes
Imports System.Windows
Class Window1
    Public Sub MyMethod()
        MessageBox.Show("")
    End Sub
End Class
```

Both `System.Windows` and `System.Windows.Forms` namespaces expose a `MessageBox` class, but you need those Imports for working with other classes. In such situations, adding `Imports` directives can cause the background compiler to report an error. This is because the code is ambiguous in invoking the `MessageBox` class, since it is not clear which of the two classes the runtime should invoke. In this case, you can avoid ambiguities by writing the full name of the class:

```
'Invokes the WPF MessageBox
System.Windows.MessageBox.Show("")
```

You could also solve this ambiguity by using namespace aliasing. Another example is the one provided by Listing 9.2. There you have two different implementations of the `Person` class, so adding an `Imports` directive would lead to ambiguities. Thus, in that case, you have to invoke members with their full names. Generally, when you have multiple namespaces defining classes with the same name, you should write the full class name including the namespace. This is probably one of the best examples for understanding why namespaces are so useful. In this kind of situation, the Visual Studio 2015 IDE shows a light bulb, which helps you fix your code by providing fully qualified names, as shown in Figure 9.4.

FIGURE 9.4   Fixing ambiguities with a light bulb and quick actions.

Smart Name Resolution

A new feature in Visual Basic 2015 is called Smart Name Resolution. This feature makes it easier to invoke objects exposed by namespaces with the same name, typically nested inside other namespaces. To understand how it works, suppose you have a WPF application that contains the following lines of code:

```
'Resolves to System.Threading
Threading.Thread.Sleep(1000)

'Resolves to System.Windows.Threading
Threading.Dispatcher.CurrentDispatcher.BeginInvoke(Sub()
                                          '...
                            End Sub)
```

The first line of code uses the `Thread` class, from the `System.Threading` namespace. The second line uses the `Dispatcher` class, from the `System.Windows.Threading` namespace. Smart Name Resolution merges namespaces together until it finds a match. It works closely with IntelliSense so that you can choose members as you type and disregard what the actual namespace is; it is the compiler's job to find the appropriate namespace, you only have to choose the object(s) you need to work with. You can see this if you type the code above manually; you will see that IntelliSense shows just one `Threading` namespace but allows you to choose objects from both `System.Threading` and `System.Windows.Threading`.

Namespaces and the Common Language Specification

The Common Language Specification provides a couple of simple rules about namespaces. The first rule is that namespaces identifiers must be Pascal-cased. For example, `MyCustomTypes` is a well-formed namespace identifier. The second rule establishes that to be CLS-compliant, a namespace must expose at least five types (classes, structures, enumerations, delegates, and so on). If this is not your case, you should prefer single classes or modules or consider merging types within another namespace already containing other types.

Global Namespaces and the `Global` Keyword

A common scenario in .NET development is creating class libraries that will be reused in other projects or given (or sold) to other developers. In these situations, it is convenient defining one or more first-level namespaces that can expose types or other namespaces. However, when you create a new project, Visual Basic also defines the root namespace (refer to Figure 9.1 for an example). This implies that defining a custom namespace like this:

```
Namespace MyUtilities
   Public Class Utility1
      'Your implementation goes here...
   End Class
End Namespace
```

causes the Visual Basic compiler to include the new namespace inside the root one whose name is, by default, the same as the project name (unless you change it

manually). Continuing the example, the full name for the new namespace becomes
`OrganizingTypesWithinNamespaces.MyUtilities`, which can be easily verified through the
Object Browser window, as represented in Figure 9.5.

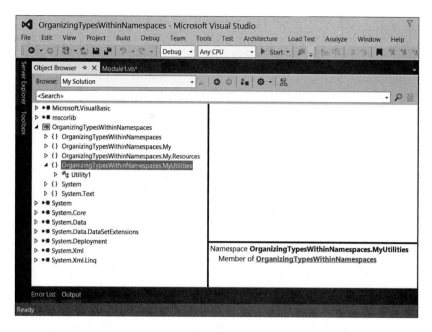

FIGURE 9.5   New namespaces are nested in the root namespace by default.

So the need at this point is abstracting custom namespaces from the root namespace, so
that custom namespaces can be at the first-level like the root one. To accomplish this,
you use a feature known as **Global Namespaces**, which allows you to bring custom
namespaces to the same level of the root namespace by using the `Global` keyword. You
place the `Global` keyword before the name of the namespace as follows:

```
Namespace Global.MyUtilities
  Public Class Utility1
    'Your implementation goes here...
  End Class
End Namespace
```

In this way, you can define standalone namespaces that are independent from the project's root namespace, as you can easily verify again via the Object Browser (see Figure 9.6).

6

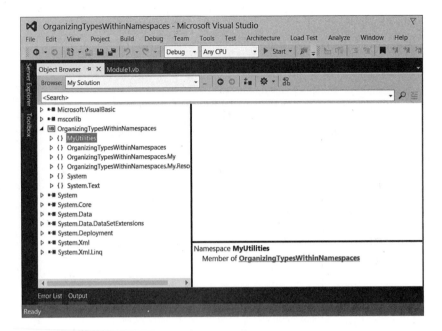

FIGURE 9.6   Global namespaces are at the same level as the root namespace.

This should also make it easy to understand that this technique allows extending the .NET Framework's namespaces from others without having the source code. The following code demonstrates how to extend the internal `System.String` type with a new extension method, passing through the `Global` namespace:

```
Imports System.Runtime.CompilerServices
Namespace Global.System
  'You can also use the following syntax:
  'Namespace Global
  '    Namespace System
  Public Module Extensions
    <Extension()>
    Public Function Parse(element As String) As String
      Return element + " is made of " + CStr(element.Length) + " characters"
    End Function
  End Module
End Namespace
```

Extension methods are discussed in more detail in Chapter 20, "Advanced Language Features," but the code should make you understand how an internal type in .NET is extended. The suggestion is therefore to always specify the full name of the namespace to avoid confusion. The following code demonstrates how to extend another namespace, more precisely `System.Text`, with a new class:

```
Namespace Global.System.Text
  Public Class CustomStringBuilder
    Private _builder As StringBuilder
    Public ReadOnly Property Builder As StringBuilder
      Get
        Return _builder
      End Get
    End Property

    'Storing the original string into a new string builder
    'This is just for demo
    Public Sub New(startString As String)
      Me._builder.AppendLine(startString)
    End Sub

  End Class
End Namespace
```

The purpose of the code is just to show how to extend a namespace, so it is very simple. The new type is being added to the `System.Text` namespace via the namespace declaration and demonstrating this is easy:

```
Sub Demo()
  'Using the new class from the extended namespace
  Dim txt As New System.Text.CustomStringBuilder("Starting string")
  Console.WriteLine(txt.Builder.ToString)
End Sub
```

In summary, the `Global` namespace allows abstracting custom namespaces from the project's root namespace and extending existing namespaces.

Summary

.NET Framework Base Class Library ships with many built-in types that are organized within namespaces. As a developer, you can build your custom types; therefore, you can organize them in namespaces. Namespaces are also a way to have different implementations of objects with the same name within a complex framework hierarchy. Because they are visible to other projects or assemblies, namespaces have a `Public` or `Friend` scope. Namespaces are also flexible; you can implement complex hierarchies nesting namespaces, and you can use whatever identifier you like. Finally, you saw the `Global` namespace and the usage of the `Global` keyword. You have to deal with namespaces many times in object-oriented programming, so this chapter gives you the basis for feeling at home with this important feature of the .NET Framework.

CHAPTER 10
Modules

Visual Basic programming language provides a simplified way for working with shared classes. Modules have been a part of Visual Basic since the beginning, so it is the real reason why Visual Basic .NET has modules versus C# which has shared classes. In this brief chapter you learn about the module feature.

Modules Overview

Modules are a specific feature of the Visual Basic programming language. You can think of modules as classes exposing only shared members; each module is defined within a `Module..End Module` code block. The following code provides an example of a module:

```
Module Module1

    Sub Main()
        'DoSomething is a method defined elsewhere
        DoSomething()
    End Sub

End Module
```

Differently from Visual C#, Visual Basic does not directly support shared classes; it provides support for classes with only shared members. According to this, the preceding module is the Visual Basic representation of the following class:

```
Class Program
    Shared Sub Main()
        'DoSomething is a method defined elsewhere
```

```
        DoSomething()
    End Sub
End Class
```

If you had any other member in this class, it should be marked as `Shared`. Modules are particularly useful when you want to implement objects and members that can be easily shared across your application and that do not need an instance.

Multiple modules can be defined in one code file, or multiple code files can define one or more modules as well. The following module defines a field and a property that you can reach from anywhere in your project:

```
'From anywhere in your project you'll be able
'to reach the two objects
Module Declarations

    Friend myFirstField As String
    Friend Property myFirstProperty As Integer

End Module
```

Because you cannot create an instance of a module, you have just one copy in memory of both the field and the property. The following example instead defines a method that assigns variables defined inside a different module:

```
Module Methods
    Friend Sub DoSomething()
        myFirstField = "A string"
        myFirstProperty = 0
    End Sub
End Module
```

It is worth mentioning that, different from classes, you do not need to invoke methods by writing first the name of the class that defines methods. For example, if the `DoSomething` method were defined within a class named Program, you should use the following syntax:

```
Program.DoSomething()
```

With modules, this is not necessary—you simply need to invoke the method name:

```
DoSomething()
```

This is true unless a conflict exists with the method name and a local method of the same name.

Partial Modules

Visual Basic 2015 introduces partial modules. Similarly to what you learned about partial classes, with partial modules you can split a module definition across multiple code files.

For example, you could extend the definition of the `Methods` sample module by adding a new code file and then adding a partial module, like this:

```
Partial Module Methods
    Friend Sub DoSomethingElse()
        Console.WriteLine("Hey, I live in a partial module!")
    End Sub
End Module
```

You use the `Partial` keyword here as you do for classes. When you type `Partial Module`, IntelliSense helps you choose one of the available modules in your project. Partial modules are helpful when you have long module definitions and you want to provide better organization inside your project.

Scope

Typically, modules are required within a project and are not exposed to the external world. Because of this, the default scope qualifier for modules is `Friend`. But because of their particular nature, modules are also allowed to be `Public`—but neither `Private` nor `Protected`/`Protected Friend`. Members defined within modules can be also marked as `Private`.

ABOUT PUBLIC MODULES

There is a particular exception to the previous discussion: creating a custom extension methods library. Because in Visual Basic you define extension methods within modules, if you want to export such methods, you need to mark them as `Public`. Extension methods are discussed in Chapter 20, "Advanced Language Features."

Differences Between Modules and Classes

There are some differences between modules and classes. This brief section looks at those differences.

No Constructor

As previously mentioned, modules can be considered as shared classes, although Visual Basic provides support for classes with only shared members and not direct support for shared classes. Because of their shared nature, as a general rule modules do not support the constructor (`Sub New`). An exception is that you can declare a `Sub New` in a module that will be private and any code in the private constructor will be executed the first time any call to the module is made.

No Inheritance Support

Modules cannot inherit from other modules or classes or be inherited. Therefore, the `Inherits`, `NotInheritable`, and `MustInherit` keywords are not supported by modules.

INHERITANCE AND SHARED MEMBERS

Although it is not a good programming practice, it is legal to create a `NotInheritable` `Class` that exposes only shared members.

No Interface Implementation

Modules cannot implement interfaces. If you need to implement interfaces, you should consider developing a class with shared members instead of a module.

Summary

Modules are an alternative for working with shared members and data. Although they have some limitations compared to classes, they are useful for exchanging information across the project. In this chapter you got an overview of modules and saw the differences between modules and classes.

CHAPTER 11

Structures and Enumerations

So far, many important concepts about .NET development with Visual Basic have been discussed. Just to mention some key topics, the book has covered class fundamentals, object lifetimes, type organization, and exception handling. All these concepts have been applied to reference types (classes). But in your developer life, you will often work with value types, both built-in and custom ones. In Chapter 4, "Data Types and Expressions," you started with the most important built-in value types in the .NET Framework. To complete your skills, though, you now need to know how to implement your own value types. In this chapter you get this information. You first understand structures and how to create them. Then you learn how to extend structures with custom versions of operators. Finally, you learn about enumerations, another kind of value type in the .NET Framework. This is not just a simple illustration because you also gain information on memory allocation to get a complete overview of this development area.

Understanding Structures

Structures in .NET development are the way to create custom value types. You find a lot of similarities between classes and structures, although this section explains some important differences. Also, Visual Basic 2015 has some improvements from previous versions with regard to structures. You create structures using a `Structure..End Structure` block. The following code provides an example of a structure representing a fictitious order received by your company:

```
Public Structure Order

    Public Property OrderID As Integer
    Public Property OrderDate As Date
    Public Property ShippedDate As Date
    Public Property CustomerID As Integer
    Public Property EmployeeID As Integer
    End Structure
```

Structure can expose several members, such as fields, properties, and methods, as it happens for classes. One important difference has to do with constructors. First, to create an instance of a structure, you aren't required to use the New keyword as you are for classes. The following code shows how you can instantiate a structure:

```
Dim o As Order
Dim o1 As New Order
```

Both syntaxes are legal. The only difference is that if you don't use the New keyword, the variable will be marked as unused until you assign a value and the VB compiler will show a warning message about this. Then you can assign (or invoke) members of the structure by typing the name followed by a dot:

```
o.OrderDate = Date.Now
o.OrderID = 1
'Other assignments..
```

Notice that, when you declare a structure without assigning its members, the compiler assigns the structure members a default value (which is usually zero for value types and Nothing for reference types). You can also utilize the object initializers feature discussed in Chapter 7, "Class Fundamentals," to initialize members of a structure. The following syntax is allowed but requires the specification of the New keyword:

```
Dim o As New Order With {.OrderID = 1, .OrderDate = Date.Now,
    .ShippedDate = Date.Now.AddDays(1), .CustomerID = 1,
    .EmployeeID = 1}
```

Visual Basic 2015 automatically provides an implicit constructor with no parameters, and you cannot explicitly provide a constructor that receives no parameters; if you try to do so, the Visual Basic compiler reports an error. Instead, you can provide a constructor that receives arguments, as follows:

```
Public Sub New(Id As Integer,
               OrderDate As Date,
               ShippedDate As Date,
               CustomerId As Integer,
               EmployeeId As Integer)
```

```
        Me.OrderID = Id
        Me.OrderDate = OrderDate
        Me.ShippedDate = ShippedDate
        Me.CustomerID = CustomerId
        Me.EmployeeID = EmployeeId
    End Sub
```

As previously stated, structures can expose methods and fields but also shared members. Consider the following new implementation of the structure:

```
Public Structure Order

    Private Shared orderCount As Integer

    Public Property OrderID As Integer
    Public Property OrderDate As Date
    Public Property ShippedDate As Date
    Public Property CustomerID As Integer
    Public Property EmployeeID As Integer

    Public Sub New(ByVal Id As Integer,
                   ByVal OrderDate As Date,
                   ByVal ShippedDate As Date,
                   ByVal CustomerId As Integer,
                   ByVal EmployeeId As Integer)

        Me.OrderID = Id
        Me.OrderDate = OrderDate
        Me.ShippedDate = ShippedDate
        Me.CustomerID = CustomerId
        Me.EmployeeID = EmployeeId

        orderCount += 1
    End Sub

    Public Shared Function Count() As Integer
        Return orderCount
    End Function
End Structure
```

As you can see, now a private shared field exists that provides a counter for the instances of the type. Moreover, a shared method named Count returns the number of instances of the structure. The following code snippet demonstrates how the method works:

```
Dim firstOrder As New Order(1, Date.Now, Date.Now, 1, 1)
Dim secondOrder As New Order(2, Date.Now, Date.Now, 1, 1)
'Returns 2
Console.WriteLine(Order.Count)
```

The preceding code returns 2 because there are two active instances of the structure. Notice that the code would not work if you initialized the structure using object initializers because the `orderCount` field is incremented in the parameterized constructor. Regarding shared members, it is worth mentioning that auto-implemented properties contained in structures cannot have initializers unless they are marked as `Shared`.

Assigning Structures to Variables

Because structures are value types, assigning an instance of a structure to a variable declared as of that type creates a full copy of the data. The following brief code demonstrates this:

```
'Creates a real copy of firstOrder
Dim thirdOrder As Order
thirdOrder = firstOrder
```

In the preceding code, `thirdOrder` is a full copy of `firstOrder`. You can easily check this by using the DataTips feature of the Visual Studio Debugger or adding the variable to a Watch window.

Passing Structures to Methods

Structures can be passed to methods as arguments. For example, consider the following method that simulates an order process taking an instance of the previously shown `Order` structure:

```
Private Sub ShowOrderInfo(ByVal orderInstance As Order)
    Console.WriteLine("Order info:")
    Console.WriteLine("ID: {0}, Date received: {1}",
                      orderInstance.OrderID,
                      orderInstance.OrderDate)
    Console.ReadLine()
End Sub
```

You can then invoke the method, passing the desired instance as follows:

```
Dim firstOrder As New Order(1, Date.Now, Date.Now, 1, 1)
ShowOrderInfo(firstOrder)
```

The preceding code produces an output that looks like this:

```
ID: 1, Date received: 12/23/2015 08:47:11
```

Members' Visibility

Structures' members require you to specify a scope qualifier. Structures accept only the `Private`, `Public`, and `Friend` qualifiers. If no qualifier is specified, `Public` is provided by default. Only fields can be declared using the `Dim` keyword, and they are equivalent to `Public`. The following line demonstrates this:

```
Public Structure Order
'Means Public:
    Dim orderCount As Integer
```

Inheritance Limitations and Interface Implementation

As for other built-in value types, structures implicitly inherit from the `System.ValueType` type that inherits from `System.Object`. This is the only inheritance level allowed for structures. This means that, different from reference types (classes), structures can neither inherit nor derive from other structures. Therefore, the `Inherits` keyword is not allowed within structures. Because structures derive from `System.Object`, they inherit only from classes such as the `Equals`, `GetHashCode`, and `ToString` methods that can also be overridden within structures. Chapter 12, "Inheritance," provides detailed information on inheritance and overriding. Structures can instead implement interfaces; therefore, the `Implements` keyword is enabled. Chapter 13, "Interfaces," discusses interfaces.

Memory Allocation

Structures are value types. This means they are allocated in the stack. Such behavior provides great efficiency to structures because when they are no longer necessary, the Common Language Runtime (CLR) removes them from the stack and avoids the need of invoking the garbage collector as happens for reference types. But this is just a general rule. Structures' members can expose any kind of .NET type and therefore reference types, too. The following revisited implementation of the `Order` structure provides an example, exposing an `OrderDescription` property of type `String` that is a reference type:

```
Public Structure Order

    Public Property OrderID As Integer
    Public Property OrderDate As Date
    Public Property ShippedDate As Date
    Public Property CustomerID As Integer
    Public Property EmployeeID As Integer

    Public Property OrderDescription As String
End Structure
```

In this scenario, the garbage collection process is invoked to free up memory space when the `OrderDescription` is released and causes an increase in performance overhead. With that said, value types are faster and more efficient than reference types only if they do not expose members that are reference types. Another important consideration is that when you pass or assign a structure to a method or variable, the actual value and data of the structure are passed (or copied in assignments) unless you pass the structure to a method by reference. If the data you want to represent is large, you should consider reference types.

Organizing Structures

You can optimize structures' efficiency with a little bit of work. This work is related to the order in which you implement members within a structure. For example, consider the following code:

```
Public Structure VariousMembers
    Public Property anInteger As Integer
    Public Property aByte As Byte
    Public Property aShort As Short
End Structure
```

Notice in which order the members are exposed. Because of their memory allocation in bytes, it's preferable to expose members in the order of bytes they require. This is a revisited, more efficient version of the structure:

```
Public Structure VariousMembers
    Public Property aByte As Byte
    Public Property aShort As Short
    Public Property anInteger As Integer
End Structure
```

If you are in doubt, don't worry. The .NET Framework offers an interesting attribute named `StructLayout`, exposed by the `System.Runtime.InteropServices` namespaces, which tells the compiler to organize a structure in the most appropriate way and that you can use as follows:

```
'Requires
'Imports System.Runtime.InteropServices
<StructLayout(LayoutKind.Auto)>
Public Structure VariousMembers
    Public Property aByte As Byte
    Public Property aShort As Short
    Public Property anInteger As Integer
End Structure
```

IMPORTANT NOTE

Remember that if you use the `StructLayout` attribute and you want to pass your structure to unmanaged code such as Windows APIs, you need to use the `LayoutKind.Sequential` value. This is because the Windows APIs expect members to be presented in a predefined order and not reorganized at compile time.

Overloading Operators

In Chapter 4 you learned about operators offered by the Visual Basic grammar. Although Visual Basic does not enable creating new custom operators, it offers the possibility of *overloading* existing operators. In other words, you have the ability to extend existing operators with custom versions. You might wonder when and why this could be necessary. You get an answer to this question with the following code. Consider the simple structure that represents a three-dimensional coordinate:

```
Public Structure ThreePoint

    Public Property X As Integer
    Public Property Y As Integer
    Public Property Z As Integer

    Public Sub New(valueX As Integer, valueY As Integer,
                    valueZ As Integer)
        Me.X = valueX
        Me.Y = valueY
        Me.Z = valueZ
    End Sub
End Structure
```

Now imagine that, for any reason, you want to sum two instances of the structure using the + operator. If you try to write the following code:

```
'Won't compile, reports an error
Dim result As ThreePoint = t1 + t2
```

the Visual Basic compiler reports an error saying that the + operator is not defined for the `ThreePoint` structure. You should begin understanding why operator overloading can be a good friend. The same situation is for other operators. In Visual Basic, you overload operators using a `Public Shared Operator` statement within your type definition. The following code overloads the + and - operators:

```
Public Shared Operator +( firstValue As ThreePoint,
                        secondValue As ThreePoint) As ThreePoint
    Return New ThreePoint With {.X = firstValue.X + secondValue.X,
                                .Y = firstValue.Y + secondValue.Y,
                                .Z = firstValue.Z + secondValue.Z}
End Operator

Public Shared Operator -( firstValue As ThreePoint,
                        secondValue As ThreePoint) As ThreePoint
    Return New ThreePoint With {.X = firstValue.X - secondValue.X,
                                .Y = firstValue.Y - secondValue.Y,
                                .Z = firstValue.Z - secondValue.Z}
End Operator
```

Of course, this is just an example, and you might want to perform different calculations. Both overloads return a `ThreePoint` structure whose members have been populated with the sum and the difference between the x, y, and z properties, respectively, from both initial instances. When overloading operators, you need to remember that some of them require you to also overload the negation counterpart. For example, the equality = operator cannot be overloaded alone but requires the overloading of the inequality <> operator. You will be informed by the Visual Basic background compiler when an operator can't be overloaded alone. The following code shows an overloading example of equality and inequality operators for the ThreePoint structure:

```
Public Shared Operator =( firstValue As ThreePoint,
                          secondValue As ThreePoint) As Boolean
    Return (firstValue.X = secondValue.X) _
           AndAlso (firstValue.Y = secondValue.Y) _
           AndAlso (firstValue.Z = secondValue.Z)
End Operator

Public Shared Operator <>( firstValue As ThreePoint,
                           secondValue As ThreePoint) As Boolean
    Return (firstValue.X <> secondValue.X) _
           OrElse (firstValue.Y <> secondValue.Y) _
           OrElse (firstValue.Z <> secondValue.Z)
End Operator
```

IntelliSense can help you understand which operators can be overloaded. For your convenience, a list of operators that can be overloaded is provided in Table 11.1.

TABLE 11.1   Operators That Can Be Overloaded

Operator	Type
+	Unary/binary
-	Unary/binary
Not	Unary
IsTrue	Unary
IsFalse	Unary
*	Binary
/	Binary
\	Binary
&	Binary
^	Binary
Mod	Binary
Like	Binary
CType	Unary
=	Logical
<>	Logical

Operator	Type
`>, >=`	Logical
`<, =<`	Logical
`And/Or/Xor`	Logical
`<<`	Shift
`>>`	Shift

OPERATORS CONTEXT

Overloading operators is discussed in this chapter because operators such as sum and subtraction make more sense with value types. However, this technique is also allowed with classes—for example, for comparison operators. You can certainly overload operators within reference types, too.

Overloading `CType`

The `CType` operator also can be overloaded to provide appropriate mechanisms for converting to and from a custom type. The interesting thing in overloading `CType` is that you have to consider both situations studied in Chapter 4, known as *widening* and *narrowing* conversions (see that topic for further details). Continuing the previous example of the `ThreePoint` structure, the following code snippet offers a special implementation of `CType`, enabling conversions to and from an array of integers:

```
'From ThreePoint to Array of Integer
Public Shared Narrowing Operator CType(instance As ThreePoint) _
                                As Integer()
    Return New Integer() {instance.X,
                        instance.Y,
                        instance.Z}
End Operator


'From Integer() to ThreePoint
Public Shared Widening Operator CType(instance As Integer()) _
                                As ThreePoint
    If instance.Count < 3 Then
        Throw New ArgumentException("Array is out of bounds",
                            "instance")
    Else
        Return New ThreePoint With {.X = instance(0),
                            .Y = instance(1),
                            .Z = instance(2)}
    End If
End Operator
```

The code is quite simple. Notice how you must specify a keyword corresponding to the effective kind of conversion (`Widening` and `Narrowing`) and how, within the `Widening` definition, the code performs a basic validation ensuring that the array of integers contains at least three items.

CType CONVENTIONS

As a convention, your type should implement an overload of `CType` that converts from a `String` into the custom type. Such conversion should also be offered implementing two methods conventionally named as `Parse` and `TryParse` that you saw in action in Chapter 4 with several primitive types.

Structures and Common Language Specification

The Common Language Specification (CLS) has established specific rules for structures. If you want your structure to be CLS-compliant, you need to overload the equality and inequality operators and redefine the behavior of the `Equals` and `GetHashCode` methods inherited from `Object`. Listing 11.1 shows an example of a CLS-compliant structure.

LISTING 11.1   Building a CLS-Compliant Structure

```
<CLSCompliant(True)>
Public Structure CLSCompliantStructure

    Public Shared Operator =( obj1 As CLSCompliantStructure,
                              obj2 As CLSCompliantStructure) As Boolean
        Return obj1.Equals(obj2)
    End Operator

    Public Shared Operator <>( obj1 As CLSCompliantStructure,
                              obj2 As CLSCompliantStructure) As Boolean
        Return Not obj1.Equals(obj2)
    End Operator

    Public Overrides Function Equals(obj As Object) As Boolean
        Return Object.Equals(Me, obj)
    End Function

    Public Overrides Function GetHashCode() As Integer
        Return Me.GetHashCode
    End Function
End Structure
```

If you are not already familiar with overriding, you can read the next chapter and then take a look back at the preceding code.

Grouping Constants with Enumerations

Enumerations are another kind of value type available in the .NET Framework. They represent a group of constants enclosed within an `Enum..End Enum` code block. An enumeration derives from `System.Enum`, which derives from `System.ValueType`. The following is an example of enumeration:

```
'These are all Integers
Public Enum Sports
    Biking        '0
    Climbing      '1
    Swimming      '2
    Running       '3
    Skiing        '4
End Enum
```

By default, enumerations are sets of integer values. The preceding code defines a `Sports` enumeration of type `Integer`, which stores a set of integer constants. The Visual Basic compiler can also automatically assign an integer value to each member within an enumeration, starting from zero, as indicated in comments. You can eventually manually assign custom values, but you should avoid this when possible because the standard behavior ensures that other types can use your enumeration with no errors. The following code shows how you can change the result type of an enumeration instead:

```
Public Enum LongSports As Long
    Biking
    Climbing
    'and so on...
End Enum
```

IntelliSense can help you understand that enumerations support only numeric types, such as `Byte`, `Short`, `Integer`, `Long`, `UShort`, `UInteger`, `ULong`, and `SByte`. Notice that enumerations can be made of mixed numeric data types if assigned with values of different numeric types.

WRITING ENUMERATIONS

Enumerations are easy to use and fast to implement. They are essentially read-only groups of read-only constants. Because of this, use them when you are sure that those values need no modifications; otherwise, consider implementing a structure instead.

Using Enumerations

You use enumerations as any other .NET type. For example, consider the following method that receives the `Sports` enumeration as an argument and returns a response depending on which value has been passed:

```
Private Sub AnalyzeSports(ByVal sportsList As Sports)
    Select Case sportsList
        Case Is = Sports.Biking
            Console.WriteLine("So, do you really like biking my friend?")
        Case Is = Sports.Climbing
            Console.WriteLine("I do not like climbing like you!")
        Case Else
            Console.WriteLine("Every sport is good!")
    End Select
End Sub
```

The following code snippet then declares a variable of type `Sports`, assigns a value, and then invokes the method by passing the variable:

```
Dim mySport As Sports = Sports.Climbing
AnalyzeSports(mySport)
```

Notice how IntelliSense comes in when you need to specify a value whose type is an enumeration. Figure 11.1 shows the IntelliSense pop-up window related to our custom enumeration.

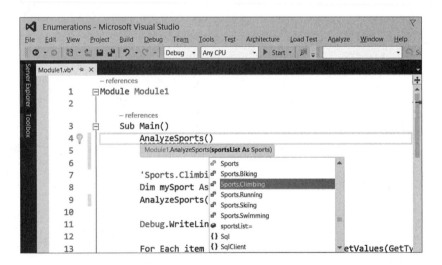

FIGURE 11.1   IntelliSense provides flexibility in choosing and assigning enumerations.

Useful Methods from `System.Enum`

As mentioned at the beginning of this section, all enumerations derive from the `System.Enum` class. Such a type exposes some shared methods that enable performing operations on enumerations. This subsection explains how you can take advantage of methods for working on enumerations.

`GetValues` and `GetNames`

The first two methods described are `GetValues` and `GetNames`. Both enable retrieving an array of items stored within an enumeration, but `GetValues` gets an array of integers corresponding to the numeric values of enumerations' items, whereas `GetNames` retrieves an array of strings storing the names of the enumerations' items. Continuing the example of the `Sports` enumeration, consider the following code:

```
For Each item As Integer In System.Enum.GetValues(GetType(Sports))
    Console.WriteLine(item)
Next
```

This code's output is the following list:

```
0
1
2
3
4
```

`GetNames` works similarly except that it returns an array of strings:

```
For Each item As String In System.Enum.GetNames(GetType(Sports))
    Console.WriteLine(item)
Next
```

And this code produces the following output:

```
Biking
Climbing
Swimming
Running
Skiing
```

Notice how both methods require a `System.Type` argument instead of a `System.Enum`; therefore, you must invoke the `GetType` operator. Another interesting thing about the syntax is that the `System.Enum` class full name for invoking its methods is used here because the `Enum` class is exposed by the `System` namespace that is always imported at project level. Technically, you could just write invocations as follows: `Enum.GetNames`. But this is not allowed in Visual Basic because of conflicts with the `Enum` reserved keyword. To use the simplified syntax, you can enclose the `Enum` work within square brackets as follows:

```
[Enum].GetNames(GetType(Sports))
```

The Visual Basic compiler enables this syntax perfectly equivalent to the previous one. Notice that the IDE will add the square brackets for you when typing `Enum`. Now, let's discover other useful methods.

GetName

GetName works similarly to GetNames, except that it returns just a single name for a constant. Consider the following code:

```
'Returns Climbing
Console.WriteLine(System.Enum.GetName(GetType(Sports), 1))
```

You need to pass the type instance and the value in the enumeration whose name you want to retrieve.

IsDefined

IsDefined checks whether the specified constant exists within an enumeration and returns a Boolean value. The following code looks first for an existing value and then for a nonexisting one:

```
'Returns True
Console.WriteLine(System.Enum.IsDefined(GetType(Sports), "Climbing"))
'Returns False
Console.WriteLine(System.Enum.IsDefined(GetType(Sports), "Soccer"))
```

ToString and Parse

System.Enum also provides two methods for converting to and from string. The ToString method is inherited from System.Object and is redefined so that it can provide a string representation of the specified value. Consider the following code snippet:

```
'Sports.Climbing
Dim mySport As Sports = CType(1, Sports)
Console.WriteLine(mySport.ToString)
```

Such code returns Climbing, which is the string representation of the specified constant value. Also notice how, if Option Strict is On, you must explicitly convert the value into a Sports enumeration using CType. Parse is the opposite of ToString and gets the corresponding numeric value within an enumeration depending on the specified string. The following code provides an example:

```
Console.WriteLine("Enter your favorite sport:")
Dim sport As String = Console.ReadLine
Dim result As Sports = CType(System.Enum.Parse(GetType(Sports),
                       sport, True), Sports)
'Returns 2
Console.WriteLine("The constant in the enumeration for {0} is {1}",
                  sport.ToString, CInt(result))
Console.ReadLine()
```

The previous code requires the input from the user, who has to enter a sport name. Using Parse, the code obtains the element in the enumeration corresponding to the entered string. For example, if you enter Swimming, the code produces the following output:

```
The constant in the enumeration for Swimming is 2
```

Notice how `Parse` can receive a third argument of type Boolean that enables specifying if the string comparison must ignore casing.

ASSIGNING ENUMS TO INTEGERS

You can assign an enumeration variable to an `Integer` type without a conversion operator.

Using Enums As Return Values from Methods

A common usage of enumerations is representing different results from methods that return a numeric value, as often happens for methods that return a number for communicating the result of the code. Consider the following code, which defines an enumeration that a method uses to communicate the result of a simple elaboration on a file:

```
Public Enum Result
    Success = 0
    Failed = 1
    FileNotFound = 2
End Enum

Public Function ElaborateFile(ByVal fileName As String) As Result
    Try
        Dim text As String = My.Computer.FileSystem.ReadAllText(fileName)

        'Do some work here on your string

        Return Result.Success

    Catch ex As IO.FileNotFoundException
        Return Result.FileNotFound
    Catch ex As Exception
        Return Result.Failed
    End Try
End Function
```

Each `Return` statement returns an `Integer` value from 0 to 2 depending on the method result, but using an enumeration provides a more convenient way for understanding the result, as demonstrated in the following code:

```
Sub OpenFile()
    Dim res As Result = ElaborateFile("myfile.txt")
    'Success = 0
    If res = Result.Success Then
        Console.WriteLine("Success")
        'FileNotFound = 2
    ElseIf res = Result.FileNotFound Then
```

```
        Console.WriteLine("File not found")
        'Failed = 1
    ElseIf res = Result.Failed Then
        Console.WriteLine("The elaboration failed")
    End If
End Sub
```

Enum Values As Bit Flags

Enumerations can be designed for supporting bitwise operations by marking them with the `Flags` attribute. This allows combining enumeration values with bitwise operators such as `And` and `Or`. Consider the following implementation of the `Sports` enumeration that was described previously:

```
<Flags>
Public Enum Sports
    None = 0
    Biking = 1
    Climbing = 2
    Swimming = 4
    Running = 8
End Enum
```

When you apply the `Flags` attribute, enumeration values are treated as a set of bit fields. It is important to define enumeration constants in powers of two (1, 2, 4, 8, and so on) so that individual flags in combined enumeration constants do not overlap.

When you `Flags`, values are evaluated in binary and can be combined with bitwise operators. For example, `Swimming` has the `00000100` binary representation, whereas `Running` has the `00001000` binary representation.

Combining all values with the `Or` operator will result in a `11111111` binary value. For example, you could perform an evaluation like the following:

```
'sportsTest is 000111
Dim sportsTest As Sports =
    Sports.Biking Or Sports.Climbing Or Sports.Swimming
```

This kind of approach is useful when you want to be able to perform bitwise operations and comparisons.

Enumerations and the Common Language Specification

When introducing enumerations, you learned that they support only numeric types. There is another limitation if you plan to implement CLS-compliant enumerations. Only CLS-compliant types can characterize CLS-compliant enumerations; therefore, the `SByte`, `UShort`, `UInteger`, and `ULong` types cannot be used within CLS-compliant enumerations. The following is an example of a CLS-compliant enumeration:

```
<Flags()> Public Enum ClsCompliantEnum As Byte
    FirstValue = 0
    SecondValue = 1
    ThirdValue = 2
End Enum
```

> **NOTE**
>
> In CLS-compliant enumerations, decorating an `Enum` with the `Flag` attribute indicates to the compiler that the enumeration has to be considered as a set of bit fields instead of a group of constants.

Summary

In this chapter you saw another important part of .NET development with Visual Basic, which is related to creating custom value types. Structures are the .NET way of building custom value types and can expose methods, properties, and fields. There are several similarities with classes, but structures are value types allocated in the stack and cannot inherit or derive from other structures but can implement interfaces. Because of their nature, structures are susceptible to operations. This requires, in certain situations, the need for specific operators. The .NET Framework enables overloading operators to provide custom implementations of unary, binary, and logical operators, a technique that is allowed for classes. Another kind of value types is enumeration, which represent a group of read-only constants and that are optimized for `Integer` values, offering several shared methods for performing operations on constants composing the enumeration. An overview of how Common Language Specification rules the implementation of structures and enumerations completed the chapter.

CHAPTER 12

Inheritance

Inheritance is the feature that enables you to design classes that *derive* from simpler classes, known as *base classes*. Derived classes implement members defined within the base class and have the possibility of defining new members or of redefining inherited members. Members that a derived class inherits from the base one can be methods, properties, and fields, but such members must have `Public`, `Protected`, `Friend`, or `Protected Friend` scope. (See Chapter 7, "Class Fundamentals," for details about scopes.) In .NET development, inheritance represents a typical *"is-a"* relationship. For a better understanding, let's consider real life. When you say "person," you identify a general individual. Every one of us is a person, with a first name and a last name. But a person also has a gender, either man or woman. In such a situation, a single person is the base class and a woman is a derived class because it inherits the name and last name attributes from the person but also offers a gender attribute. But this is only the first layer. Each man and each woman can have a job, and jobs are made of roles. So a woman can be employed by a company; therefore, as an employee she will have an identification number, a phone number, and an office room number. In this representation there is a deeper inheritance; because a person can be compared to a base class, a woman can be compared to an intermediate base class (also deriving from the person), and the employee is the highest level in the inheritance hierarchy. If you want to go on, you could still define other roles, such as lawyer, program manager, law clerk, pharmacist, and so on. Each of these roles could be represented by a class that derives from the employee role. As you can see, this articulate representation is something that in a development environment such as the .NET Framework enables defining a complex but powerful framework of objects. In this chapter you get a complete overview of the inheritance features in .NET Framework with Visual Basic 2015, and you will learn how you can take advantage of inheritance for both building hierarchical frameworks of custom objects and more easily reusing your code.

Applying Inheritance

Before explaining how inheritance is applied in code, a graphical representation can be useful. Figure 12.1 shows how you can create robust hierarchies of custom objects with inheritance.

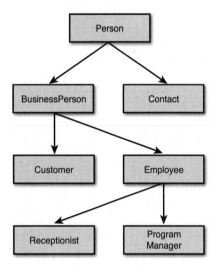

FIGURE 12.1   A graphical representation of a custom framework of objects using inheritance.

You derive a class from a base class using the `Inherits` keyword. For example, consider the following implementation of the `Person` class that exposes some basic properties:

```
Public Class Person

    Public Property FirstName As String
    Public Property LastName As String

    'A simplified implementation
    Public Function FullName() As String
        If FirstName = "" And LastName = "" Then
          Throw New _
          InvalidOperationException("Both FirstName and LastName are empty")
        Else
            Return String.Concat(FirstName, " ", LastName)
```

```
        End If
    End Function
End Class
```

Inherits System.Object

In the .NET Framework development, every class inherits from `System.Object`. Due to this, there is no need to add an inherits directive each time you implement a custom type because the Visual Basic compiler will do this for you behind the scenes.

The class also offers a `FullName` method that returns the concatenation of the two `FirstName` and `LastName` properties, providing a simplified and basic validation that is here for demonstration purposes. Now you can design a new class that inherits from `Person`, and in this scenario `Person` is the *base class*. The new class is named `Contact` and represents a personal contact in our everyday life:

```
Public Class Contact
    Inherits Person

    Public Property Email As String
    Public Property Phone As String
    Public Property BirthDate As Date
    Public Property Address As String

End Class
```

Contact is the *derived class*. It receives all public members from `Person` (in this example both the `FirstName` and `LastName` properties and the `FullName` method) and provides implementation of custom members. This is a typical application of .NET inheritance, in which one derived class inherits from the base class. The .NET Framework does not enable inheriting from multiple classes. You can create a derived class from only a base class. But in some situations multiple levels of inheritance would be required. Continuing the example of the `Person` class, you will meet several kinds of people in your life, such as customers, employees of your company, and personal contacts. All these people will have common properties, such as the first name and the last name; therefore, the `Person` class can be the base class for each of them, providing a common infrastructure that can then be inherited and customized. But if you consider a customer and an employee, both people will have other common properties, such as a title, a business phone number, and an email address. They will differ in the end because of the proper characteristics of their roles. For this purpose, you can implement intermediate classes that are derived classes from a first base class and base classes for other and more specific ones. For example, you could implement an intermediate infrastructure for both customers and employees. The following code snippet provides a class named `BusinessPerson` that inherits from `Person`:

```
Public Class BusinessPerson
    Inherits Person
```

12

```
      Public Property Email As String
      Public Property Title As String
      Public Property BusinessPhone As String

End Class
```

This class inherits the `FirstName` and `LastName` properties from `Person` (other than methods such as `ToString` and other public methods exposed by `System.Object`) and exposes other common properties for classes with a different scope. For example, both a customer and an employee would need the preceding properties, but each of them needs its own properties. Because of this, the `BusinessPerson` class is the intermediate derived class in the hierarchic framework of inheritance. Now consider the following classes, `Customer` and `Employee`:

```
Public Class Customer
      Inherits BusinessPerson

      Public Property CustomerID As Integer
      Public Property CompanyName As String
      Public Property Address As String
      Public Property ContactPerson As String
End Class
Public Class Employee
      Inherits BusinessPerson

      Public Property EmployeeID As Integer
      Public Property HomePhone As String
      Public Property MobilePhone As String
      Public Property HireDate As Date
End Class
```

Both classes receive the public properties from `BusinessPerson`, and both implement their custom properties according to the particular person they intend to represent. The situation can be summarized as follows:

`Customer` exposes the following properties:

▶ `FirstName` and `LastName`, provided at a higher level by `Person`

▶ `Email`, `Title`, and `BusinessPhone` provided by `BusinessPerson`

▶ `CustomerID`, `CompanyName`, `Address`, and `ContactPerson` provided by its implementation

`Employee` exposes the following properties:

- ▶ `FirstName` and `LastName`, provided at a higher level by `Person`
- ▶ `Email`, `Title`, and `BusinessPhone` provided by `BusinessPerson`
- ▶ `EmployeeID`, `HomePhone`, `MobilePhone`, and `HireDate` provided by its implementation

At a higher level, both classes also expose a method named `FullName`, which has public visibility, so this method is also visible from derived classes.

MEMBERS' SCOPE AND INHERITANCE

Remember that only the `Public`, `Protected`, `Friend`, and `Protected Friend` members can be inherited within derived classes.

When available, you can use derived classes the same way as you would do with any other class, even if you do not know at all that a class derives from another one. The following, simple code demonstrates this:

```
'Employee inherits from BusinessPerson
'which inherits from Person
Dim emp As New Employee With {.EmployeeID = 1,
    .Title = "Dr.",
    .LastName = "Del Sole",
    .FirstName = "Alessandro",
    .Email = "alessandro.delsole@visual-basic.it",
    .BusinessPhone = "000-000-000000",
    .HomePhone = "000-000-000000",
    .MobilePhone = "000-000-000000",
    .HireDate = New Date(5 / 30 / 2015)}
```

Until now, you've seen only properties in an inheritance demonstration. Methods are also influenced by inheritance and by interesting features that make them powerful.

INHERITANCE AND THE COMMON LANGUAGE SPECIFICATION

The Common Language Specification (CLS) establishes that a CLS-compliant class must inherit only from another CLS-compliant class; otherwise, it will not be CLS-compliant.

Illustrating `System.Object` in Detail

As you should remember from Chapter 4, "Data Types and Expressions," in.NET development all types implicitly derive from `System.Object`, considering both reference and value types. Because of the inheritance relationship, custom types also inherit some methods, so you have to know them. Table 12.1 summarizes inherited methods.

TABLE 12.1 `System.Object` Methods

Member	Description
`Finalize`	Performs cleanup operations; already described in Chapter 8, "Managing an Object's Lifetime"
`GetType`	Returns the `System. Type` object related to the instance of the class
`GetHashCode`	Returns the hash code for the current instance
`New`	Creates an instance of the class
`Equals`	Checks for equality between instances of the class
`MemberwiseClone`	Provides a shallow copy of a class instance
`ReferenceEquals`	Checks whether the two specified instances are the same instance
`ToString`	Provides a string representation of the current object

You need to understand which members are exposed by `System.Object` because they will all be inherited by your custom classes and by all built-in classes in the .NET Framework. Chapter 4 and Chapter 8 discuss the `GetType` and `Finalize` methods, respectively. Such methods are inherited by all .NET types. The `GetHashCode` method returns the hash that is assigned at runtime by the CLR to a class instance. The following code provides an example:

```
Dim p As New Object

Dim hashCode As Integer = p.GetHashCode
Console.WriteLine(hashCode.ToString)
```

On my machine the code produces the following result: `33156464`. This is useful to uniquely identify a class's instance. `New` is the constructor, as described in Chapter 7. When creating custom classes, a constructor is inherited and implicitly defined within classes and constitutes the default constructor. `Object` also exposes two shared members, `Equals` and `ReferenceEquals`, which return a Boolean value. It's worth mentioning that shared methods are also inherited by derived classes, but they cannot be overridden (as described in more detail in the next section). For example, the following code establishes whether both specified objects are considered the same instance:

```
'Two different instances
Dim firstObject As New Object
Dim secondObject As New Object

'Returns False
Dim test As Boolean = Object.ReferenceEquals(firstObject, secondObject)
```

Next, the code instead checks whether two instances are considered equal by the compiler:

```
'Returns False
Dim test As Boolean = Object.Equals(firstObject, secondObject)
```

There is also an overload of the `Equals` method that is instead an instance method. The following code shows an example of instance comparisons using `Equals`:

```
'Returns False
Console.WriteLine(firstObject.Equals(secondObject))
'Copies the reference to the instance
Dim testObject As Object = firstObject
'Returns True
Console.WriteLine(testObject.Equals(firstObject))
```

For assignments, you can always assign any type to an `Object` instance, as demonstrated here:

```
Dim aPerson As New Person
Dim anObject As Object = aPerson
```

Because `Object` is the mother of all classes, it can receive any assignment. The last method in `System.Object` (that you will often use) is `ToString`. This method provides a string representation of the object. Because `System.Object` is the root in the class hierarchy, this method just returns the pure name of the class. Therefore, the following line of code returns `System.Object`:

```
Console.WriteLine(firstObject.ToString)
```

But this is not appropriate for value types, in which you need a string representation of a number, or for custom classes, in which you need a custom representation. Taking the example of the famous `Person` class, it would be more useful to get a string composed by the last name and the first name instead of the name of the class. Fortunately, the .NET Framework inheritance mechanism provides the capability to change the behavior of inherited members as it is exposed by base classes; this is known as *overriding*.

Introducing Polymorphism

Polymorphism is another key concept in object-oriented programming (OOP). As its name implies, polymorphism enables an object to assume different forms. In .NET development, it means you can treat an object as another one, due to the implementation of common members. A first form of polymorphism is when you assign base classes with derived classes. For example, both `Contact` and `Customer` classes are derived of the `Person` class. Now consider the following code:

```
Dim c As New Contact
Dim cs As New Customer

'C is of type Contact
Dim p As Person = c
```

The new instance of the `Person` class receives an assignment from an instance of the `Contact` class. This is always possible because `Person` is the parent of `Contact` (in which base is the parent of derived). Therefore, you might also have the following assignment:

```
'Cs is of type Customer
Dim p As Person = cs
```

In this scenario, `Person` is polymorphic in that it can "impersonate" multiple classes that derive from itself.

RETRIEVING THE ACTUAL TYPE

Use the `TypeOf` operator, discussed in Chapter 4, to check whether the polymorphic base class is representing a derived one.

Polymorphism is useful when you need to work with different kinds of objects using one common infrastructure that works the same way with all of them. Now let's continue with the preceding example. The `Person` class exposes the usual `FirstName` and `LastName` properties also common to `Contact` and `Customer`. At this point, you can remember how our previous implementations of the `Person` class offered a method named `FullName` that returns the concatenation of both the `LastName` and `FirstName` properties. For the current discussion, consider the following simplified version of the `FullName` method, as part of the `Person` class:

```
Public Function FullName() As String
    Return String.Concat(FirstName, " ", LastName)
End Function
```

All classes deriving from `Person` inherit this method. All deriving classes do need a method of this kind for representing the full name of a person, but they would need different implementations. For example, the full name for a customer should include the company name, whereas the full name for a personal contact should include the title. This means that all classes deriving from `Person` will still need the `FullName` method (which is part of the commonalities mentioned at the beginning of this section) but with a custom implementation fitting the particular need. For this, the .NET Framework enables realizing polymorphism by *overriding* members, as the next section describes.

NOTE ON POLYMORPHISM

Overriding is the most important part of polymorphism in .NET development, but interfaces also play a role. Chapter 13, "Interfaces," explains how interfaces complete polymorphism.

Overriding Members

When a class derives from another one, it inherits members and the members behave as they are defined in the base class. (For this purpose, remember the scope.) As for other .NET languages, Visual Basic enables redefining inherited methods and properties so that you can change their behavior. This technique is known as *overriding* and requires a little work on both the base class and the derived class. If you want to provide the ability of overriding a member, in the base class you have to mark the member as `Overridable`. Let's continue the example of the `Person` class, defined as follows:

```
Public Class Person

    Public Property FirstName As String
    Public Property LastName As String

    'Simplified version, with no validation
    Public Function FullName() As String
        Return String.Concat(LastName, " ",
                          FirstName)

    End Function
End Class
```

The goal is providing derived classes the capability of overriding the `FullName` method so that they can provide a custom and more appropriate version. The method definition must be rewritten as follows:

```
Public Overridable Function FullName() As String
```

At this point, you could write a simplified version of the `Contact` class, inheriting from `Person`. Such implementation will override the `FullName` method to provide a custom result. Let's begin with the following code:

```
Public Class Contact
    Inherits Person

    Public Property Email As String

    Public Overrides Function FullName() As String
        'By default returns the base class'
        'implementation
        Return MyBase.FullName()
    End Function
End Class
```

Two things are important here. First, the `Overrides` keyword enables you to redefine the behavior of a member that has been marked as Overridable in the base class. Second,

Visual Studio automatically provides an implementation that is the behavior established in the base class, due to the MyBase keyword, which is discussed later. IntelliSense is powerful in this situation, too, because when you type the Overrides keyword, it shows all overridable members, making it easier to choose what you have to override (see Figure 12.2).

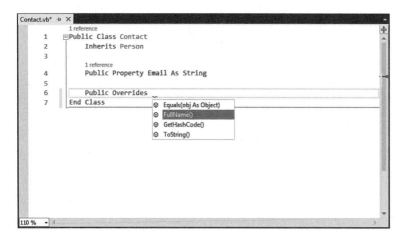

FIGURE 12.2   IntelliSense helps you choose overridable members.

Figure 12.2 can also help you understand which members from System. Object are overridable. The instance overload of Equals, GetHashCode, and ToString are methods you can redefine. You cannot instead override (neither mark as Overridable) shared members, and this is demonstrated by the fact that the shared overload of Equals and ReferenceEquals are not available in the IntelliSense pop-up window. At this point, you could write a new implementation of the FullName method specific for the Contact class:

```
Public Overrides Function FullName() As String
    'A simplified implementation
    'with no validation
    Dim result As New Text.StringBuilder
    result.Append(Me.FirstName)
    result.Append(" ")
    result.Append(Me.LastName)
    result.Append(", Email:")
    result.Append(Me.Email)

    Return result.ToString
End Function
```

Now you can create a new instance of the Contact class and invoke the FullName method to understand how overriding changed its behavior:

```
Dim testContact As New Contact With _
    {.FirstName = "Alessandro",
     .LastName = "Del Sole",
      .Email = "Alessandro.delsole@visual-basic.it"}
Console.WriteLine(testContact.FullName)
```

The preceding code produces the following result:

```
Alessandro Del Sole, Email:Alessandro.delsole@visual-basic.it
```

Such a result is, of course, more meaningful if related to the specific kind of class. Another common situation is redefining the behavior of the `ToString` method that is inherited from `Object` and that is marked as `Overridable`. For example, in the `Contact` class you could override `ToString` as follows:

```
Public Overrides Function ToString() As String
    Dim result As New Text.StringBuilder
    result.Append(Me.FirstName)
    result.Append(" ")
    result.Append(Me.LastName)
    result.Append(", Email:")
    result.Append(Me.Email)

    Return result.ToString
End Function
```

You can then invoke this method as follows:

```
Console.WriteLine(testContact.ToString)
```

Typically, overriding `ToString` is more appropriate if you need to return a string representation of a class, as in the preceding example. The `FullName` method is just an example of how you can override a custom method that is defined in a base class and that is not inherited from `System.Object`.

OVERRIDDEN IS OVERRIDABLE

When a member is overridden using the `Overrides` keyword, the member is also implicitly `Overridable`. Because of this, you cannot use the `Overridable` keyword on a member marked with `Overrides`; the compiler would report an error message, requiring you to remove the `Overridable` keyword.

NotOverridable **Keyword**

You can mark an overridden method or property as `NotOverridable` so that derived classes cannot override them again. The `NotOverridable` keyword cannot be used versus methods or properties that do not override a base member. Continuing the example of the `Contact` class previously defined, the `NotOverridable` keyword can be used as follows:

```
Public NotOverridable Overrides Function FullName() As String
    Return String.Concat(MyBase.FullName(), ": ", Email)
End Function
```

In this way the `FullName` method within the `Contact` class overrides the base class, but derived classes cannot override it again. `NotOverridable` is used only within derived classes that override the base class's members because in a base class the default behavior for members is that they cannot be overridden unless you explicitly mark them as `Overridable`.

Overloading Derived Members

You can use the overloading technique described in Chapter 7 within derived classes, with a few differences. You saw in Chapter 7 how overloaded members must not be marked with the `Overloads` keyword within a class. Instead, a derived class using the `Overloads` keyword is mandatory if you implement a new overload of a member with a different signature. The following code provides an example of overloading the `FullName` method within the `Contact` class you previously saw:

```
Public Overloads Function FullName(Age As Integer)
    Return MyBase.FullName & " of age: " & Age.ToString
End Function
```

If another signature of the member is available within the derived class, the `Overloads` keyword is required; otherwise, the compiler reports a warning message saying that another signature is declared as `Overrides` or `Overloads`. If, instead, no other signatures are available within the derived class, the `Overloads` keyword is required to prevent from shadowing the base class's member. Shadowing is discussed at the end of this chapter, in the section "Shadowing." With regard to overriding members, it is worth mentioning that the code generation for `Overrides` has been changed to imply `Overloads`. Thanks to this change, VB developers no longer need to write both `Overrides` and `Overloads` to make sure C# users of a library written in VB get the correct overload resolution.

Conditioning Inheritance

Inheritance is an important feature in OOP with .NET. You might have situations in which inheritance is not a good option, for example, when you want to prevent others from accessing members in the base class. Or there could be custom frameworks implementations in which a high-level class should not be used directly, and therefore it should be always inherited. The Visual Basic language enables accomplishing both scenarios via special keywords, as discussed in the next section.

NotInheritable **Keyword**

There are situations in which you might want to prevent inheritance from your classes. This can be useful if you do not want a client to modify in any way the base object's behavior and its members. To accomplish this, you simply need to mark a class with the NotInheritable keyword. The following code shows an example of a class that cannot be derived:

```
Public NotInheritable Class BusinessPerson
    Inherits Person

    Public Property Email As String
    Public Property Title As String
    Public Property BusinessPhone As String
End Class
```

As you can see, the BusinessPerson class is marked as NotInheritable and cannot be derived by other classes. It can still inherit from other classes but, obviously, members cannot be marked as Overridable because they are not inheritable. Another typical example of classes that cannot be inheritable is when you have a class exposing only shared members, as shown in the following code:

```
<CLSCompliant(True)>
Public NotInheritable Class CompressionHelper
    Private Sub New()

    End Sub

    Public Shared Sub CompressFile(source As String,
                                   target As String)
        'Your code goes here
    End Sub

    Public Shared Sub DecompressFile(compressed As String,
                                     original As String)
        'Your code goes here
    End Sub
End Class
```

The class is also decorated with the CLSCompliant attribute because such a situation is explicitly established by the Common Language Specification. NotInheritable is the Visual Basic counterpart of the sealed keyword in Visual C#. It's important to know the C# representation because in .NET terminology not-inheritable classes are defined as sealed and many analysis tools use this last word. NotInheritable classes provide better performance; the compiler can optimize the usage of this type of classes, but you cannot blindly use classes that cannot be inherited only to avoid a small overhead. You should always design classes that fit your needs.

`MustInherit` and `MustOverride` Keywords

Inheritance is powerful because it enables building custom objects' frameworks. In this
context, an object can represent the base infrastructure for different kinds of classes.
You saw how the `Person` class is the base infrastructure for the `Customer`, `Employee`, and
`Contact` derived classes. Because of its implementation, the `Person` class does nothing
special. It has a generic behavior, and you will probably never create instances of that
class; it is more likely that you will create instances of its derived classes. In this scenario,
therefore, when you have a general-purpose base class that acts just as a basic infrastructure for derived classes, you can force a class to be inherited so it cannot be used directly.
To accomplish this, Visual Basic provides the `MustInherit` keyword that states that a class
will work only as a base class and cannot be used directly unless you create a derived class.

ABSTRACT CLASSES

In .NET terminology, classes marked as `MustInherit` are also known as *abstract* classes.
This is important to remember because you will often encounter this term within the documentation and in several analysis tools.

The following code shows a new implementation of the `Person` class:

```
Public MustInherit Class Person

    Public Property FirstName As String
    Public Property LastName As String
End Class
```

Now you can derive classes only from `Person`. Another interesting feature is the capability to force members to be overridden. This can be accomplished using the `MustOverride`
keyword on methods and properties. Continuing with the example of the `Person` class,
the `FullName` method definition could be rewritten as follows:

```
Public MustOverride Function FullName() As String
```

When you mark a method with `MustOverride`, the method has no body. This makes sense
because, if it must be redefined within a derived class, it would not be very helpful providing a base implementation. The same thing happens with properties, meaning that you
will have only a declaration.

Inheriting from an Abstract Class

When you create a class that inherits from an abstract class (that is, marked as MustInherit), the only thing you need to pay particular attention to is overriding members. To help developers in such a scenario, the Visual Studio IDE automatically generates members' stubs for methods and properties marked as MustOverride in the base abstract class. So, if you create a new implementation of the Contact class, when you press **Enter** after typing the Inherits line of code, Visual Studio generates an empty stub for the FullName method as follows:

```
Public Class Contacts
    Inherits Person

    Public Overrides Function FullName() As String

    End Function
End Class
```

Now you can be sure that all MustOverride members have an implementation. In our example you might want to complete the code by adding the implementation shown in the "Overriding Members" section in this chapter.

Abstract Classes and Common Language Specification

The Common Language Specification contains a small rule regarding abstract classes. This rule establishes that to be CLS-compliant, members in abstract classes must explicitly be marked as CLSCompliant. The following code provides an example:

```
<CLSCompliant(True)>
Public MustInherit Class Person

    <CLSCompliant(True)> Public Property FirstName As String
    <CLSCompliant(True)> Public Property LastName As String

    <CLSCompliant(True)> Public MustOverride Function FullName() As String

End Class
```

Accessing Base Classes Members

Sometimes you need to access the base classes' members from derived classes. There are several reasons for doing this, so you need to know how. Visual Basic provides two special keywords for invoking base members, MyBase and MyClass. Both are discussed in this section.

MyBase Keyword

When you need to get a reference to the base class of the derived class you are working on, you can invoke the MyBase keyword. This keyword represents an instance of the base class and enables you to work on members as they are exposed by the base class, instead of the ones exposed by the derived class. Consider the following implementation of the Person class, in which a FullInformation method provides a representation of all the information supplied to the class:

```
Public Class Person

    Public Property FirstName As String
    Public Property LastName As String
    Public Property Age As Integer

    Public Overridable Function FullInformation() As String
        Dim info As New Text.StringBuilder

        info.Append("Name: ")
        info.Append(Me.FirstName)
        info.Append(" Last name: ")
        info.Append(Me.LastName)
        info.Append(" Age: ")
        info.Append(Me.Age.ToString)
        Return info.ToString
    End Function
End Class
```

Now you can create a new implementation of the Contact class, inheriting from Person. A new class needs to override the FullInformation method from the base class. When you type the Overrides keyword, Visual Studio generates a default implementation that looks like the following:

```
Public Overrides Function FullInformation() As String
    Return MyBase.FullInformation
End Function
```

The code returns the result offered by the FullInformation method as it is implemented in the base class, which is accomplished via the MyBase keyword. Following is the complete code for the Contact class:

```
Public Class Contact
    Inherits Person

    Public Property Title As String

    Public Overrides Function FullInformation() As String
        Dim firstInfo As String = MyBase.FullInformation

        Dim newInfo As New Text.StringBuilder
        newInfo.Append(firstInfo)
```

```
        newInfo.Append(" Title: ")
        newInfo.Append(Me.Title)
        Return newInfo.ToString
    End Function
End Class
```

Notice that the overridden method does not perform a complete string concatenation while it invokes first the MyBase. FullInformation method. This is a best practice because one of inheritance's purposes is favoring code reusability; therefore, this invocation is better than rewriting the code from scratch. The following code snippet shows how you can interact with both base class and derived class properties, assuming that FirstName and LastName have been declared as Overridable in the base class and overridden within the derived class:

```
Public Sub New(name As String,
               surName As String,
               age As Integer,
               title As String)

    'Goes to the base class properties
    MyBase.FirstName = name
    MyBase.LastName = surName

    'Current instance properties
    Me.Age = age
    Me.Title = title
End Sub
```

Me AND MyBase

The Me keyword refers to the instance of the current class, whereas MyBase refers to the base class from which the current class derives. This difference is evident when a member is overridden, but if members are not redefined, both keywords refer to the same code.

The next section details a few things you need to know about constructors within derived classes.

MyClass Keyword

Another way of accessing the base classes' members is the MyClass keyword. Imagine you have a base class exposing some overridable members, such as properties or methods; then you have a derived class that overrides those members. The MyClass keyword avoids the application of overriding and invokes members on the derived class as if they were NotOverridable on the base class. In other words, MyClass enables executing members of a base class in the context of a derived class, ensuring that the member version is the one in the base class. Listing 12.1 shows an example.

LISTING 12.1   Demonstrating the `MyClass` Keyword

```
Public Class BaseClassDemo

    Public Overridable ReadOnly Property Test As String
        Get
            Return "This is a test in the base class"
        End Get
    End Property

    Public Function DoSomething() As String
        Return MyClass.Test
    End Function
End Class

Public Class DerivedClassDemo
    Inherits BaseClassDemo

    Public Overrides ReadOnly Property Test As String
        Get
            Return "This is a test in the derived class"
        End Get
    End Property
End Class
Module Module1
    Sub Main()

        Dim derived As New DerivedClassDemo

        'Invokes the member within the derived
        'class but as if it was not overridden
        Dim result As String = derived.DoSomething
    End Sub
End Module
```

The `BaseClassDemo` base class exposes an overridable property that returns a text message, for demo purposes. It also exposes a public method that just shows the text stored within the `Test` property. Within the derived `DerivedClassDemo`, the `Test` property is overridden but the `DoSomething` method is not. This method is still available when you create an instance of the `DerivedClassDemo` class. Because the method is defined within the base class and then is executed within the derived class's context, if you implemented the method as follows:

```
Public Function DoSomething() As String
    Return Me.Test
End Function
```

it would return the content of the derived `Test` property. In some situations, though, you might want to ensure that only base class members are used within other members that are not overridden; this can be accomplished using the `MyClass` keyword. If you run the code shown in Listing 12.1, the result variable contains the string `"This is a test in the base class"`, although the `DoSomething` method has been invoked on an instance of the derived class. You can still use the overridden `Test` property for other purposes in your derived class. `MyClass` is similar to `Me` in that both get a reference to the instance of the current class, but `MyClass` behaves as if members in the base class were marked as `NotOverridable` and therefore as if they were not overridden in the derived class.

Constructors' Inheritance

The previous section discussed the `MyBase` keyword and how it can be used to access members from a base class. The keyword also has another important purpose when it comes to constructors. Consider the following constructor, which is implemented within the `Person` class (that is, the base class) shown in the previous section:

```
Public Sub New(firstName As String,
               lastName As String,
               age As Integer)

    Me.FirstName = firstName
    Me.LastName = lastName
    Me.Age = age
End Sub
```

The problem now is in derived classes. The rule is that if you have a constructor receiving arguments in the base class, you do need to provide a constructor receiving arguments also within a derived class, and the constructor needs to invoke the base class. The following code shows how a constructor needs to be implemented within the `Contact` class:

```
Public Sub New(name As String,
               surName As String,
               age As Integer,
               title As String)

    MyBase.New(name, surName, age)
    Me.Title = title
End Sub
```

As you can see from the preceding code snippet, the first line of code is an invocation to the constructor of the base class, and this is a rule that you *must* follow. After that line of code, you can provide any other initialization code. This particular requirement is necessary if you plan to provide a constructor that receives arguments within the base class, although it's not necessary if you implement a constructor that does not receive arguments or if you do not provide any constructor (which is implicitly provided by the Visual Basic compiler).

Shadowing

The beginning of this chapter explained that classes can inherit from base classes exposed by class libraries such as .dll assemblies and that you do not necessarily need the source code. You could create a class deriving from another class exposed by a compiled assembly and implement a new member. In addition, the publisher of the compiled base class could release a new version of the class, providing a member with the same name of your custom member. In this case, you would not be able to edit the base class because you wouldn't have the source code. Visual Basic 2015 provides an interesting way of dealing with such a situation known as *shadowing*. Although the Visual Basic compiler still enables compiling (it reports warning messages), your class needs to "shadow" the member with the same name of your custom one. This is accomplished using the `Shadows` keyword. Consider this particular implementation of the `Person` class, exposing a `Title` property, of type `String`:

```
Public Class Person

    Public Property FirstName As String
    Public Property LastName As String
    Public Property Title As String

End Class
```

Now consider the following implementation of the `Contact` class, which requires a value defined within the `Titles` enumeration:

```
Public Class Contact
    Inherits Person

    Public Property Title As Titles
End Class

Public Enum Titles
    Dr
    Mr
    Mrs
End Enum
```

The `Contact` class exposes a `Title` property, but its base class already has a `Title` property; therefore, the Visual Basic compiler shows a warning message related to this situation. If you want your code to use the derived `Title` property, you need to mark your member with `Shadows` as follows:

```
Public Class Contact
    Inherits Person

    Public Shadows Property Title As Titles
End Class
```

You can accomplish the same result by marking the property within the derived class as `Overloads`:

```
Public Overloads Property Title As Titles
```

Auto-implemented properties can be used in this particular example. If the property within the derived class returned the same type of the one within the base class, it would make more sense using old-fashioned properties so that you have the ability to customize the behavior.

BE VERY CAREFUL WHEN SHADOWING

If you have a derived class that shadows some property or method (like `Contact` in the example above), and you pass an instance to a method that accepts an argument of the base class type (like `Person`), if the method makes calls to something that was shadowed, it will take the base implementation, even though you passed in the derived type. This can lead to unexpected results, so be very careful when shadowing.

Overriding Shared Members

Shared members cannot be overridden. This means that you can only use them as they have been inherited from the base class or provide a shadowing implementation for creating a new definition from scratch. For example, consider this simplified implementation of the `Person` class, which exposes a shared `Counter` property:

```
Public Class Person

    Public Shared Property Counter As Integer
End Class
```

If you now create a `Contact` class that inherits from `Person`, you can use the `Counter` property as previously implemented, or you can shadow the base definition as follows:

```
Public Class Contact
    Inherits Person

    Public Shared Shadows Property Counter As Integer
End Class
```

If you intend to provide an overloaded member with a different signature, you can use overloading as follows:

```
Public Shared Shadows Property Counter As Integer
Public Shared Shadows Property Counter(maximum As Integer) As Integer
    Get
```

```
    End Get
    Set(value As Integer)

    End Set
End Property
```

Another limitation of shared members is that you cannot invoke the `MyBase` and `MyClass` keywords within them. Moreover, you cannot invoke shared members using the `MyBase` keyword. So, if you were to assign the `Counter` shared property defined in the person class, you would have to write `Person.Counter = 0` instead of `MyBase.Counter = 0`.

Practical Inheritance: Building Custom Exceptions

In Chapter 6, "Errors, Exceptions, and Code Refactoring," you learned about exceptions in .NET development; you saw what exceptions are and how you can intercept them at runtime to create well-formed applications that can handle errors. The .NET Framework ships with hundreds of exceptions related to many aspects of .NET development. You might encounter a situation where you need to implement custom exceptions. You can build custom exceptions due to inheritance. A custom exception can inherit from the root `System.Exception` class or from another exception (such as `System.IO.IOException`) that necessarily inherits from `System.Exception`. Custom exceptions should always be CLS-compliant. Let's look at the `Person` class implementation again, adding a method that returns the full name of the person and that requires at least the last name:

```
Public Class Person

    Public Property FirstName As String
    Public Property LastName As String

    Public Function FullName() As String

        If String.IsNullOrEmpty(Me.LastName) Then
            Throw New MissingLastNameException("Last name not specified")
        Else
            Return String.Concat(LastName, " ", FirstName)
        End If
    End Function
End Class
```

As you can see, if the `LastName` property contains an empty or null string, the code throws a `MissingLastNameException`. This exception is custom and must be implemented.

NAMING CONVENTIONS

Remember that every exception class's identifier should end with the `Exception` word. Microsoft naming convention rules require this.

The MissingLastNameException is implemented as follows:

```vb
<Serializable()>
Public Class MissingLastNameException
    Inherits Exception

    Public Sub New()
        MyBase.New()
    End Sub

    Public Sub New(message As String)
        MyBase.New(message)
    End Sub

    Public Sub New(message As String, inner As Exception)
        MyBase.New(message, inner)
    End Sub

    Protected Sub New(info As Runtime.Serialization.SerializationInfo,
                      context As _
                      Runtime.Serialization.StreamingContext)
        MyBase.New(info, context)
    End Sub
End Class
```

There is a series of considerations:

▶ As a custom exception, it inherits from System. Exception.

▶ The class is decorated with the Serializable attribute; this is one of the CLS establishments, and it enables developers to persist the state of the exception to disk (see Chapter 39, "Serialization").

▶ Custom exceptions expose three overloads of the base constructors plus one overload marked as Protected that is therefore available to eventually derive classes and that receives information on serialization.

▶ Custom exceptions are caught exactly as any other built-in exception.

When you have your custom exception, you can treat it as other ones:

```vb
Try
    Dim p As New Person
    'Will cause an error because
    'the LastName was not specified
    Console.WriteLine(p.FullName)
Catch ex As MissingLastNameException
    Console.WriteLine("ERROR: please specify at least the last name")
```

```
Catch ex As Exception
    Console.WriteLine("Generic error")
    Console.WriteLine(ex.ToString)
Finally
    Console.ReadLine()
End Try
```

The preceding code intentionally causes an exception to demonstrate how the
`MissingLastNameException` works, by not assigning the `LastName` property in the `Person`
class instance.

AVOID COMPLEX INHERITANCE CHAINS

Building a complex inheritance chain is something that should be carefully considered
because as the chain grows, the child classes will be tied and rely on the base classes
not changing, at risk of disrupting the inheritance chain.

Summary

Inheritance is a key topic in the object-oriented programming with Visual Basic and
the .NET Framework. In this chapter, you learned lots of important concepts. First, you
learned what inheritance is and how you can take advantage of it for creating frameworks of custom objects. Then you saw how to derive classes from base classes using the
`Inherits` keyword and how your derived classes automatically inherit some members
from `System. Object`, which is the root in the class hierarchy. When deriving classes, you
need to consider how constructors and shared members behave; the chapter also provided
an overview. But inheritance would be of less use without polymorphism. You learned
how polymorphism requires implementing one common infrastructure for multiple
objects, taking advantage of the capability to redefine inherited members' behavior. For
this purpose, the .NET Framework enables the overriding technique that you can use to
modify the behavior of derived members. Additionally, with shadowing you can override a member from a class of which you do not have the source code. You often want
to condition inheritance, establishing when classes should be sealed (`NotInheritable`) or
abstract (`MustInherit`). In inheritance scenarios, you also often need to have access to base
class members; therefore, you need the `MyBase` and `MyClass` keywords. But you seldom
work with theories. Because of this, the chapter closed with a practical demonstration of
inheritance, showing how you can build custom exceptions to use in your applications.

CHAPTER 13
Interfaces

Most people have a car. Cars have an engine, four wheels, several gears, and other instrumentation. A lot of different companies produce cars, and each company makes several models. All companies have to build car models adhering to some particular specifications established by the law, and such specifications provide information on what minimal components will compose cars, including a list of those components that are therefore common to every car. In .NET development you can compare interfaces to the previously described law specifications. Interfaces provide a list of members that an object must implement to accomplish particular tasks in a standardized way. They are also known as *contracts* because they rule how an object must behave to reach some objectives. You saw an example in Chapter 8, "Managing an Object's Lifetime," for the IDisposable interface that must be implemented if an object wants to provide the capability to release resources that are not only in-memory objects, according to a standardized way. This means that the .NET Framework knows that the Dispose method from IDisposable is required to free up resources. In this chapter you first learn how to define and implement custom interfaces; then you get an overview of the most common interfaces in .NET Framework. You also learn why interfaces are important because you will surely wonder why you should use them.

Defining Interfaces

An *interface* is a reference type defined within an Interface..End Interface block. Interfaces define only signatures for members that classes will then expose and are a set of the members' definitions. Imagine you want to create an interface that defines members for working with documents. This is accomplished with the following code:

```
Public Interface IDocument

    Property Content As String
    Sub Load(ByVal fileName As String)
    Sub Save(ByVal fileName As String)


End Interface
```

The interface is marked as `Public` because the default scope for interfaces is `Friend`. Assigning public visibility ensures that external assemblies use the interface (which is a common scenario).

INTERFACES SCOPE

Interfaces can be declared `Private`, `Protected`, or `Protected Friend` only if they are defined within a type such as a class.

As a convention, interface identifiers begin with a capital `I`. This is not mandatory (except when creating interfaces that are compliant with the Common Language Specification), but following the convention is strongly recommend. The most important consideration is that the interface definition contains only members' definitions with no body. For both the `Load` and `Save` methods' definitions, there is only a signature but not the method body and implementation, which are left to classes that implement the interface. Members defined within interfaces cannot be marked with one of the scope qualifiers, such as `Public`, `Friend`, and so on. By default, members defined by interfaces are `Public`. Finally, being reference types, interfaces need to be treated as such. See Chapter 4, "Data Types and Expressions," for further information on reference types.

NESTED CLASSES

Interfaces can define classes. A class defined within an interface is a typical `Class..End Class` block, as you would normally define one. This is an uncommon scenario and can be useful when you want to avoid naming conflicts with other classes, but you have to know that it is possible.

Implementing and Accessing Interfaces

Implementing interfaces means telling a class that it needs to expose all members defined within the interface. You do this by using the `Implements` keyword followed by the name of the interface. IntelliSense will offer a list of available interfaces, as demonstrated in Figure 13.1. The following code snippet shows how to implement the `IDocument` interface within a `Document` class:

```
Public Class Document
    Implements IDocument

    Public Property Content As String Implements IDocument.Content

    Public Sub Load(fileName As String) Implements IDocument.Load
    End Sub

    Public Sub Save(fileName As String) Implements IDocument.Save
    End Sub

End Class
```

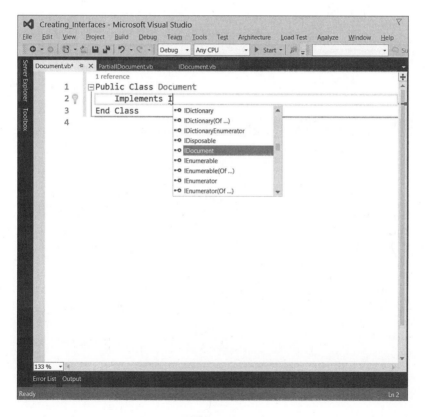

FIGURE 13.1   Choosing from available interfaces.

You'll notice that, when pressing Enter, the Visual Studio IDE automatically generates members' templates for you, as represented in Figure 13.2.

This is useful because it saves you from having to waste your time writing members' signatures. You'll also notice that when a member is defined within a class because of the interface implementation, the `Implements` keyword is also added at the end of the member followed by the related element in the interface.

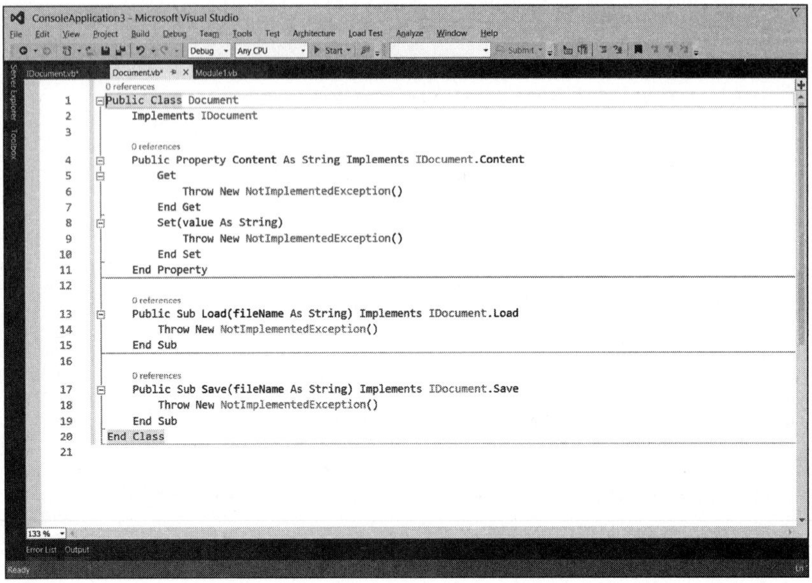

FIGURE 13.2   Visual Studio generates a skeleton for members based on the interface.

MULTIPLE IMPLEMENTATIONS

Different from inheritance, classes and structures can implement more than one interface. You see an example later in the chapter when discussing `IEnumerable` and `IEnumerator`.

The `Document` class is basic and is for demo purposes only. To complete the implementation example, you can write code to populate methods for performing operations established in the interface, as shown in Listing 13.1.

LISTING 13.1   Implementing Interfaces

```
Public Class Document
    Implements IDocument

    Public Property Content As String Implements IDocument.Content

    'Gets the content of a text document
    Public Sub Load(fileName As String) Implements IDocument.Load
        Try
            Content = My.Computer.FileSystem.ReadAllText(fileName)
        Catch ex As Exception
```

```
        Throw
    End Try
End Sub
'Saves a text document to file
Public Sub Save(fileName As String) Implements IDocument.Save
    Try
        My.Computer.FileSystem.WriteAllText(fileName,
                                    Content, False)
    Catch ex As Exception
        Throw
    End Try
End Sub

End Class
```

13

When you implement interfaces, you need to populate members' templates with your own code. This can ensure that your object is respecting the contract established by the interface. When a class implements an interface, it also needs to access members it defines. You have two alternatives for this purpose. The first one is simple and intuitive and consists of creating an instance of the class that implements the interface. Continuing with the example of the Document class shown in Listing 13.1, the following code shows how you can accomplish this:

```
Dim myDocument As New Document
myDocument.Load("SomeDocument.txt")

Console.WriteLine(myDocument.Content)
```

The code invokes instance members of the class with no differences for normal classes' implementations. The second alternative is declaring an *interface variable*. You declare a variable whose type is the interface; the variable receives the result of an explicit conversion from the class that implements the interface to the interface itself. More than words, code can provide a good explanation:

```
Dim myDocument As IDocument = CType(New Document, IDocument)
myDocument.Load("SomeDocument.txt")

Console.WriteLine(myDocument.Content)
```

The result is the same. You often find code that makes use of interface variables, so spend a little time becoming familiar with this approach. After this discussion, you will probably wonder why you need to define and implement interfaces because you just need to write code as you would do without them. The answer is *polymorphism*.

New Behaviors in Visual Basic 2015

Visual Basic 2015 has some new behaviors for interface implementation. For example, consider this interface, which exposes a read-only property and a class that implements the interface:

```
Public Interface ITest
    ReadOnly Property SomeInformation As String

    Sub DoSomething()
End Interface


Class Test
    Implements ITest

    Public ReadOnly Property SomeInformation As String
            Implements ITest.SomeInformation
        Get
            '...
        End Get
    End Property

    Public Sub DoSomething() Implements ITest.DoSomething
        '...
    End Sub
End Class
```

As you can see, the read-only property in the interface is then implemented by a read-only property in the class. Visual Basic 2015 allows the following syntax:

```
Class Test
    Implements ITest

    Public Property SomeInformation As String Implements ITest.SomeInformation

    Public Sub DoSomething() Implements ITest.DoSomething
        '...
    End Sub
End Class
```

As you can see, the class implements the member with a read/write property, so Visual Basic 2015 removes the limitation of implementing a read-only property from an interface with a read-only property in a class. The same concept applies to structure as well.

Passing Interfaces as Method Arguments

One of the most powerful features when working with interfaces is that methods can receive interfaces as parameters. This means that you can pass in any object as these parameters so long as it implements the given interface. The following example shows a method that accepts an argument of type IList, meaning that any object implementing the IList interface can be accepted:

```
'Interfaces as parameters
Public Class WorkWithLists
    Public Function Elaborate(items As IList) As Integer
        'Just for demo, returns 0 if the list contains something
        If items.Count > 0 Then
            Return 0
        Else
            'if not, adds a new object to the list
            Dim item As New Object
            items.Add(item)
            Return -1
        End If
    End Function

End Class
```

This is with no doubt one of the most important features in programming by contracts with interfaces.

Partial Interfaces

Visual Basic 2015 introduces partial interfaces, which work exactly like partial classes and partial modules, meaning that you can split the definition of a single interface into two or more code files. This helps keep your code organized in case of very long interface definitions. To define a partial interface, you use the Partial keyword. For example, suppose you have a separate code file with the following partial definition, which extends the IDocument interface with a VersionNumber property of type System.Version:

```
Partial Public Interface IDocument
    Property VersionNumber As Version
End Interface
```

As usual, IntelliSense helps you pick up one of the interfaces that you can extend. When you use the Implements keyword in a class and then press **Enter**, Visual Studio automatically provides a basic implementation, including members from all partial definitions. As for classes, you do not actually create multiple interfaces, you just create one interface whose definition is split across multiple places.

Interfaces and Polymorphism

Chapter 12, "Inheritance," discusses polymorphism, which offers a common infrastructure to different types of objects. In the discussion, interfaces find their natural habitat. They provide a common set of members that classes need to implement if they need to perform a particular series of tasks. A typical example is the `IDisposable` interface that you met in Chapter 8. All classes that need to provide a mechanism for releasing resources implement that interface, which exposes a set of common members. Another example is the `ICloneable` interface that defines a `Clone` method that classes can implement to provide the capability to copy a class instance. You can easily understand that interfaces are generic; they are not specific to any class but are instead as generic as possible so that the widest variety of classes can implement them. To provide a code example, let's reexamine the `IDocument` interface proposed in the previous section. This interface was implemented by a `Document` class. But the same interface can be implemented in other kinds of classes. For example, you can define an `Invoice` class that can implement the same `IDocument` interface because it exposes a common set of members that can be easily used within the `Invoice` class. Then the new class can provide new members specific to its particular needs and behavior. The following code demonstrates this:

```
Public Class Invoice
    Implements IDocument

    Public Property Content As String Implements IDocument.Content

    Public Sub Load(fileName As String) Implements IDocument.Load

    End Sub

    Public Sub Save(fileName As String) Implements IDocument.Save

    End Sub

    Public Property InvoiceNumber As Integer

    Public Function CalculateDiscount(price As Decimal,
                                percent As Single) As Decimal

    End Function

End Class
```

As you can see, the `IDocument` interface can serve the `Invoice` class with its members; then the class defines new members (`InvoiceNumber` and `CalculateDiscount`) strictly related to its behavior. By the way, the `IDocument` interface provides polymorphic code that can be used in different situations and objects with a common infrastructure.

Interfaces Inheritance

Two situations are related to both inheritance and interfaces. The first scenario occurs when you create a class that derives from another one that implements an interface. In such a scenario, the derived class also inherits members implemented through an interface and does not need to implement the interface again. Moreover, if the base class contains members that are marked as overridable and implemented via an interface, the derived class can override such members if not private. The second scenario is a pure interface inheritance, in which an interface can inherit from another one. Continuing the previous examples, you can consider creating an IInvoice interface that inherits from IDocument and provides some more specific members to represent an invoice. The following code demonstrates this:

```
Public Interface IInvoice
    Inherits IDocument

    'New members
    Property InvoiceNumber As Integer
    Function CalculateDiscount(price As Decimal,
                               percent As Single) As Decimal

End Interface
```

As you can see, the Inherits keyword is used also for interface inheritance. In this example, the new interface inherits all members' definitions from the IDocument interface and adds two new members, the InvoiceNumber property and the CalculateDiscount method. After this, you could rewrite the Invoice class as follows:

```
Public Class Invoice
    Implements IInvoice

    Public Property Content As String Implements IInvoice.Content

    Public Sub Load(fileName As String) Implements IInvoice.Load

    End Sub

    Public Sub Save(fileName As String) Implements IInvoice.Save

    End Sub

    Public Property InvoiceNumber As Integer Implements IInvoice.InvoiceNumber
    Public Function CalculateDiscount(price As Decimal,
                                      percent As Single) As Decimal Implements
IInvoice.CalculateDiscount

    End Function
End Class
```

It is worth mentioning that, due to inheritance, members exposed by the base interface can be implemented using the name of the base interface, instead of the derived one. For example, in the previous code snippet the Content property is implemented like this:

```
Public Property Content As String Implements IInvoice.Content
```

Because this property is exposed by the IDocument interface and inherited by IInvoice, the compiler also accepts the following implementation:

```
Public Property Content As String Implements IDocument.Content
```

Defining CLS-Compliant Interfaces

The Common Language Specification (CLS) also provides rules for interfaces. The first rule is that if you mark an interface as CLS-compliant, you cannot use CLS-noncompliant types within signatures. The following interface is not correct because it is marked as CLSCompliant but uses a noncompliant type:

```
'Incorrect: UInteger is not CLS compliant
<CLSCompliant(True)> Public Interface ITest
    Property Counter As UInteger

End Interface
```

The second rule is that a CLS-compliant interface cannot define shared members. The last rule is that all members must be explicitly marked with the CLSCompliant attribute. The following is an example of a CLS-compliant interface:

```
<CLSCompliant(True)> Public Interface IClsCompliant

    <CLSCompliant(True)> Property Counter As Integer
    <CLSCompliant(True)> Function DoSomething() As Boolean

End Interface
```

NAMING CONVENTIONS

It is an implicit rule that identifiers for all CLS-compliant interfaces *must* begin with a capital I. IDocument is a correct identifier, whereas MyDocumentInterface is not. Identifiers cannot contain the underscore character (_) and are written according to the Pascal-casing conventions.

Most Common .NET Interfaces

Because of their importance in polymorphism, the .NET Framework defines a large quantity of interfaces implemented by most types within the Framework. You need to understand the most common built-in interfaces because they provide great flexibility in your code, and in several situations you need to implement such interfaces in your objects that need to perform particular tasks. Table 13.1 summarizes the most common .NET interfaces.

TABLE 13.1   Most Common Interfaces

Interface	Description
ICloneable	Its purpose is to provide methods for cloning objects.
IDisposable	It's implemented when a class needs to provide methods for releasing resources.
IEnumerable	It's implemented to provide the enumerator, which enables objects to be iterated.
IComparable	When an object wants to provide the capability of sorting, it must implement this interface.
IConvertible	To be implemented if an object enables conversion.
IFormattable	It provides support for formatting data.

The ICloneable interface is discussed in Chapter 4, and the IDisposable interface is discussed in Chapter 8. This chapter therefore does not revisit these interfaces. Instead, you'll learn how you can implement the other ones in your code.

The IEnumerable Interface

You implement the IEnumerable interface each time you want your class to support For.. Each loops. Each time you iterate an object (typically a collection) using For Each, it is because that object implements IEnumerable. The .NET Framework offers lots of collections (including generic ones) and enables you to create custom collections inheriting from built-in ones; therefore, implementing IEnumerable will probably be spared for you. It's important to understand how the interface works, especially for its intensive usage when working with LINQ. IEnumerable provides one method, named GetEnumerator, which generally is implemented as follows:

```
Public Function GetEnumerator() As System.Collections.IEnumerator _
    Implements System.Collections.IEnumerable.GetEnumerator
    Return CType(Me, IEnumerator)

End Function
```

As you can see, the method returns the result of the conversion of the class instance to an IEnumerator object; this means that IEnumerable must be implemented together with another interface. It's named IEnumerator and offers methods and properties for moving between items in a collection and for providing information on the current item. To provide an example, imagine you have a class named Contacts that acts as a repository of items of type Contact and that implements IEnumerable to provide iteration capabilities. Listing 13.2 shows how this is accomplished in code, including a sample loop performed invoking For..Each.

LISTING 13.2   Implementing IEnumerable and IEnumerator

```vb
Public Class Contacts
    Implements IEnumerable, IEnumerator

    Public Function GetEnumerator() As System.Collections.IEnumerator _
        Implements System.Collections.IEnumerable.GetEnumerator
        Return CType(Me, IEnumerator)
    End Function


    Private position As Integer = -1


    Public ReadOnly Property Current As Object _
        Implements System.Collections.IEnumerator.Current
        Get
            Return Items(position)
        End Get
    End Property
    Public Function MoveNext() As Boolean _
        Implements System.Collections.IEnumerator.MoveNext
        position += 1
        Return (position < Items.Length)
    End Function


    Public Sub Reset() Implements System.Collections.IEnumerator.Reset
        position = -1
    End Sub


    Private Items() As Contact = New Contact() {New Contact With _
                                               {.FirstName = "Alessandro",
                                               .LastName = "Del Sole",
                                               .Email = "alessandro.delsole" & _
                                                     "@visual-basic.it",
                                               .PhoneNumber = "000-0000-00"},
                                               New Contact With _
                                               {.FirstName = "Robert",
                                               .LastName = "Green",
                                               .Email = "email@something.com",
                                               .PhoneNumber = "000-0000-00"} _
                                               }


End Class

Public Class Contact

    Public Property FirstName As String
    Public Property LastName As String
```

```
        Public Property Email As String
        Public Property PhoneNumber As String

End Class
Module Module1

    Sub Main()

        Dim c As New Contacts
        'Returns "Del Sole", "Green"
        For Each Cont As Contact In c
            Console.WriteLine(Cont.LastName)
        Next

        Console.ReadLine()
    End Sub
End Module
```

The `Contacts` class stores an array of `Contact` objects and provides a private field, position, which is used for returning information. The `Current` property returns the item in the array corresponding to the current position, whereas the `MoveNext` method increments the position variable and returns `True` if the position number is still less than the upper bound in the array. In the end, `Reset` just restores the initial value for position. You also notice how, within the `Sub Main` in `Module1`, a simple `For..Each` loop is given for demonstration purposes. If you run the code, you see that it correctly returns last names for both actual contacts within the `Contacts` class.

IEnumerable(Of T)

As for other interfaces, a generic version of `IEnumerable` supports specific types. Because Chapter 15, "Delegates and Events," discusses generics, this chapter shows the non-generic version that works the same, except that it is related to `Object`.

The `IComparable` Interface

You implement the `IComparable` interface when you want to offer custom comparison instrumentation to your objects. `IComparable` requires you to implement a `CompareTo` method that returns an `Integer` value that is less than zero if the instance is less than the compared object, is zero if the instance equals the compared object, and is greater than zero if the instance is greater than the compared object. For example, imagine you want to provide a comparison to the `Person` class based on the length of the `LastName` property. Listing 13.3 shows how you can accomplish this.

LISTING 13.3   Implementing the `IComparable` Interface

```
Public Class Person
    Implements IComparable

    Public Property FirstName As String
    Public Property LastName As String
    Public Property Email As String

    Public Function CompareTo(ByVal obj As Object) As Integer Implements
System.IComparable.CompareTo
        If Not TypeOf (obj) Is Person Then
            Throw New ArgumentException
        Else

            Dim tempPerson As Person = DirectCast(obj, Person)

            If Me.LastName.Length < tempPerson.LastName.Length Then
                Return -1
            ElseIf Me.LastName.Length = tempPerson.LastName.Length Then
                Return 0
            Else
                Return 1
            End If

        End If
    End Function
End Class
Module Module1

    Sub Main()
        Dim p1 As New Person With {.LastName = "Del Sole",
                                   .FirstName = "Alessandro"}
        Dim p2 As New Person With {.LastName = "AnotherLastName",
                                   .FirstName = "AnotherFirstName"}

        Dim c As New ComparableHelper(p1)
        Console.WriteLine(c.CompareTo(p2))
        Console.ReadLine()
    End Sub

End Module
```

You might notice that a first check is performed on the object type, which must be `Person`. If not, the code throws an `ArgumentException` (meaning that the argument is not valid). The comparison is accomplished in a simple way using unary operators. Next, to perform the comparison, you just need to create an instance of the `Person` class and then invoke its `CompareTo` method, passing the `Person` you want to compare to the current instance.

`IComparer` INTERFACE

If you want to provide custom sorting for arrays, you need to implement the `IComparer` interface. The following article in the Microsoft Knowledge Base provides a good example that is extensible to Visual Basic 2015: http://support.microsoft.com/kb/321292/en-us

Utilizing the Generic `IComparable(Of T)`

Although Chapter 14, "Generics and Nullable Types," discusses generics, this is a good point for showing something interesting about them. Many interfaces within the .NET Framework have a generic counterpart. For example, there is an `IEnumerable(Of T)` or `IComparable(Of T)`, in which `T` is a specific .NET type instead of `Object`, which would require conversions and, therefore, performance overhead. The `Person` class shown in Listing 13.3 could be rewritten using the `IComparable(Of T)` interface to provide support for `Person` objects. This is accomplished with the following code:

```
Public Class Person
    Implements IComparable(Of Person)

    Public Property FirstName As String
    Public Property LastName As String
    Public Property Email As String

    Public Function CompareTo(ByVal other As Person) As Integer _
            Implements System.IComparable(Of Person).CompareTo
        If Me.LastName.Length < other.LastName.Length Then
            Return -1
        ElseIf Me.LastName.Length = other.LastName.Length Then
            Return 0
        Else
            Return 1
        End If
    End Function

End Class
```

You will soon notice how `DirectCast` conversions disappear and how the `CompareTo` method receives an argument of type `Person` instead of `Object`. This means less code and more precision. In Chapter 14 and Chapter 16, "Working with Collections and Iterators," you gain detailed information about generics and generic collections.

The `IConvertible` Interface

Objects implementing the `IConvertible` interface expose a series of ToXXX methods exactly as the `Convert` class does so that such objects can easily be converted into another type. This example uses a structure instead of a class, for the sake of simplicity. Listing 13.4 shows how the `IConvertible` interface can be implemented.

LISTING 13.4   Implementing the `IConvertible` Interface

```
Public Structure ThreePoint
    Implements IConvertible

    Public Function GetTypeCode() As System.TypeCode Implements _
        System.IConvertible.GetTypeCode

        Return TypeCode.Object
    End Function

    'Just a custom return value
    Public Function ToBoolean(provider As System.IFormatProvider) _
        As Boolean Implements System.IConvertible.ToBoolean
        Return X > Y
    End Function

    Public Function ToByte(provider As System.IFormatProvider) _
        As Byte Implements System.IConvertible.ToByte
        Return Convert.ToByte(SumPoints)
    End Function

    Public Function ToChar(provider As System.IFormatProvider) _
        As Char Implements System.IConvertible.ToChar
        Return Convert.ToChar(SumPoints)
    End Function

    Public Function ToDateTime(provider As System.IFormatProvider) _
        As Date Implements System.IConvertible.ToDateTime
        Return Convert.ToDateTime(SumPoints)
    End Function

    Public Function ToDecimal(provider As System.IFormatProvider) _
        As Decimal Implements System.IConvertible.ToDecimal
        Return Convert.ToDecimal(SumPoints)
    End Function

    Public Function ToDouble(provider As System.IFormatProvider) _
        As Double Implements System.IConvertible.ToDouble
        Return Convert.ToDouble(SumPoints)
    End Function
```

```vbnet
Public Function ToInt16(provider As System.IFormatProvider) _
    As Short Implements System.IConvertible.ToInt16
    Return Convert.ToInt16(SumPoints)
End Function


Public Function ToInt32(provider As System.IFormatProvider) _
    As Integer Implements System.IConvertible.ToInt32
    Return SumPoints()
End Function


Public Function ToInt64(provider As System.IFormatProvider) _
    As Long Implements System.IConvertible.ToInt64
    Return Convert.ToInt64(SumPoints)
End Function


Public Function ToSByte(provider As System.IFormatProvider) _
    As SByte Implements System.IConvertible.ToSByte
    Return Convert.ToSByte(SumPoints)
End Function


Public Function ToSingle(provider As System.IFormatProvider) _
    As Single Implements System.IConvertible.ToSingle
    Return Convert.ToSingle(SumPoints)
End Function


'Required "Overloads"
Public Overloads Function ToString(provider As System.IFormatProvider) _
    As String Implements System.IConvertible.ToString
    Return String.Format("{0}, {1}, {2}", Me.X, Me.Y, Me.Z)
End Function


Public Function ToType(conversionType As System.Type,
                       provider As System.IFormatProvider) _
                       As Object Implements System.IConvertible.ToType
    Return Convert.ChangeType(SumPoints, conversionType)
End Function


Public Function ToUInt16(provider As System.IFormatProvider) _
    As UShort Implements System.IConvertible.ToUInt16

    Return Convert.ToUInt16(SumPoints)
End Function


Public Function ToUInt32(provider As System.IFormatProvider) _
    As UInteger Implements System.IConvertible.ToUInt32
    Return Convert.ToUInt32(SumPoints)
End Function
```

13

```
    Public Function ToUInt64(provider As System.IFormatProvider) _
        As ULong Implements System.IConvertible.ToUInt64
        Return Convert.ToUInt64(SumPoints)
    End Function

    Public Property X As Integer
    Public Property Y As Integer
    Public Property Z As Integer

    Public Sub New(valueX As Integer,
                   valueY As Integer,
                   valueZ As Integer)
        Me.X = valueX
        Me.Y = valueY
        Me.Z = valueZ
    End Sub
    Public Function SumPoints() As Integer
        Return (Me.X + Me.Y + Me.Z)
    End Function
End Structure
```

The `ThreePoint` structure is simple; it exposes three integer properties (x, y, and z) whose sums are returned via a `SumPoints` method. The goal of the `IConvertible` implementation is therefore to enable returning the result of the method converted into different types. Each conversion method invokes the corresponding one of the `Convert` class, with some exceptions. The first one is the `ToBoolean` method, which returns a customized result depending on the value of x and y, but this is just for demonstration purposes. (You can invoke the `Convert. ToBoolean` as well.) The second exception is the `ToString` method. When you implement an interface that provides a method already existing in the class (even because of inheritance), Visual Studio renames the interface's method by adding a 1 in the end. For example, every class exposes `ToString` because it is inherited from `System. Object`. Thus, the `ToString` version provided by the interface is automatically renamed to `ToString1`. But this is not elegant. A better technique is overloading because the method is marked with `Overloads` and named correctly.

IMPORTANT NOTICE

`IConvertible` does not adhere to the CLS because it makes use of CLS-incompliant types, such as `UInt16`, `UInt32`, and so on. You should be aware of this if you plan to develop objects that need to be CLS-compliant.

The `IFormattable` Interface

The `IFormattable` interface enables implementing a new overload of the `ToString` method to provide customized string formatting with deep control over the process, also defining custom qualifiers. Listing 13.5 shows how you can implement the `IFormattable` interface.

LISTING 13.5   Implementing the `IFormattable` Interface
```vb
Imports System.Globalization

Public Class Person
    Implements IFormattable

    Public Property FirstName As String
    Public Property LastName As String
    Public Property Email As String

    Public Overloads Function ToString(format As String,
                            formatProvider As System.IFormatProvider) _
                         As String Implements System.IFormattable.ToString
        If String.IsNullOrEmpty(format) Then format = "G"
        If formatProvider Is Nothing Then formatProvider = _
                                    CultureInfo.CurrentCulture

        Select Case format
            'General specifier. Must be implemented
            Case Is = "G"
                Return String.Format("{0} {1}, {2}",
                        Me.FirstName, Me.LastName, Me.Email)
            Case Is = "F"
                Return FirstName
            Case Is = "L"
                Return LastName
            Case Is = "LF"
                Return String.Format("{0} {1}", Me.LastName, Me.FirstName)
            Case Else
                Throw New FormatException
        End Select
    End Function
End Class

Module Module1
    Sub Main()
        Dim p As New Person With {.FirstName = "Alessandro",
            .LastName = "Del Sole",
            .Email = "alessandro.delsole@visual-basic.it"}

        Console.WriteLine("{0:G}", p)
        Console.WriteLine("{0:L}", p)
        Console.WriteLine("{0:F}", p)
        Console.WriteLine("{0:LF}", p)
        Console.ReadLine()
```

```
        End Sub
End Module
```

Listing 13.5 shows a particular implementation of the `Person` class, which exposes the `FirstName`, `LastName`, and `Email` properties. It implements the `IFormattable` interface that offers a new overload of the `ToString` method. This method receives two arguments; the first one, format, represents the qualifier. For example, in standard formatting, the letter *c* represents currency. Here you can specify your own qualifiers. Because of this, the first check is whether the format is null or empty. In such case, a `G` qualifier is assigned by default. `G` stands for `General` and is the only qualifier that *must* be implemented. When you provide `G`, you can create your own qualifiers. The next check is on `formatProvider` that represents the culture for string formatting. If it's null, the code assigns the local system culture. The subsequent `Select..End Select` block takes into consideration some identifiers as custom qualifiers. `L` stands for `LastName`, `F` stands for `FirstName`, and `LF` stands for `LastName + FirstName`. You can change or extend this code by intercepting your custom identifiers within this block. Running the code shown in Listing 13.5 produces the following result:

```
Alessandro Del Sole, alessandro.delsole@visual-basic.it
Del Sole
Alessandro

Del Sole Alessandro
```

You can easily compare the output result with the code and understand how custom formatting works. `IFormattable` is also important for string interpolation, discussed in Chapter 4, because it provides the infrastructure that the compiler uses to format strings.

Summary

This chapter focused on interfaces, another key topic in the object-oriented programming. Interfaces, which are defined within `Interface..End Interface` blocks, provide signatures of sets of members that an object must implement to accomplish specific tasks. You might remember the example of the `IDisposable` interface that must be implemented by objects that need to provide methods for freeing up resources. You saw how to create and implement custom interfaces in your code via the `Implements` keyword and then how to invoke objects that implement interfaces both by creating class instances and via interface variables. You found out why interfaces are important and why the .NET Framework makes an intensive usage of interfaces, talking about polymorphism and how interfaces can contribute to provide standardized infrastructures for multiple objects. It's important to adhere to the Common Language Specification when defining interfaces, so you got information about this. Finally, code examples have been provided for the most common .NET built-in interfaces, to provide a deeper understanding of how things happen behind the scenes and to reuse those interfaces in your code.

CHAPTER 14

Generics and Nullable Types

When you organize your home, you probably place things according to their type. For example, you have a place for food that is different from the place where you put clothes. But foods are also different. You do not treat fish like candy or pizza and so on. So you need safe places for each kind of food, avoiding the risks derived from treating all foods the same way; the same is true for clothes and any other item in your home. The .NET development would be similar without Generics. Consider groups of .NET objects of different types, all grouped into a collection of Object. How can you be sure to treat an item in the collection as you should if the collection stores different types that you identify as Object? What if you want to create just a collection of strings? Generics solve this problem. In this chapter you learn what Generics are. In Chapter 16, "Working with Collections and Iterators," you learn about generic collections and see why Generics are so useful. This chapter also introduces nullable types, which are generic on their own.

Introducing Generics

Generic types are .NET types that can adapt their behavior to different types of objects without the need of defining a separate version of the type. In other words, you can implement a generic type to work with integers, strings, custom reference types, and any other .NET type with a single implementation. Generics offer several advantages:

▶ **Strongly typed programming techniques**—Generic objects can hold only the specified type and avoid accidents of handling objects of different types within the same group.

▶ **Better performances**—Because Generics enable you to handle only the specified type, they avoid the need of boxing and unboxing from and to `System.Object`, and this retains for performance overhead.

▶ **Code reuse**—As you will see in a few moments, Generics enable you to create objects that behave the same way and that have the same infrastructure whatever kind of .NET type you pass them.

▶ **The ability of writing better code**—Avoiding working with nongeneric `System.Object`, you not only get all IntelliSense features for the specified type, but also can take advantages from not using late-binding techniques.

Generally, the use of Generics is related to the creation of strongly typed collections for storing groups of items of the same type. Because of this, there are two considerations: the first one is that you should check whether the .NET Framework provides a built-in generic collection suiting your needs before creating custom ones (see Chapter 16); the second consideration is that code examples shown in this chapter will be related to creating a generic collection so you know how to create one if .NET built-in Generics are not sufficient for you.

Creating and Consuming Generics

You can define the following types as generics: classes, interfaces, delegates, structures, and methods. Creating a generic type is accomplished by providing a parameterized type definition. The following is an example:

```
Class CustomType(Of T)

End Class
```

The `Of` keyword is followed by the type that the new object can handle. `T` is the *type parameter* and represents the .NET type you want to be held by your generic type. The type parameter's name is left to your own choosing, but `T` is often used as a common name in the .NET Framework Base Class Library (BCL). At this point, you must write code to manipulate the `T` type in a way that will be convenient for possibly every .NET type. Now imagine you want to build a custom collection that you want to reuse with any .NET type. Listing 14.1 shows how to accomplish this.

LISTING 14.1   Building a Custom Generic Type

```
Public Class CustomType(Of T)

    Private items() As T

    Public Sub New(upperBound As Integer)
        ReDim items(upperBound - 1)
    End Sub
```

```
    Private _count As Integer = 0
    'Cannot provide auto-implemented properties when read-only
    Public ReadOnly Property Count As Integer
        Get
            Return _count
        End Get
    End Property

    Public Sub Add(newItem As T)
        If newItem IsNot Nothing Then
            Me.items(Me._count) = newItem
            Me._count += 1
        End If
    End Sub

    Default Public ReadOnly Property Item(index As Integer) As T
        Get
            If index < 0 OrElse index >= Me.
                Count Then Throw New IndexOutOfRangeException
            Return items(index)
        End Get
    End Property
End Class
```

WHY ARRAYS?

You notice that the code in Listing 14.1 uses arrays to store objects. Arrays do not support removing objects or, at least, this cannot be done easily. This is the reason you only find an Add method. By the way, in this particular case you do not need to focus on how to add and remove items (Chapter 16 covers this), but you need to understand how to handle the generic type parameter.

The code shows how simple it is to manage the type parameter. It can represent any .NET type but, as in the previous example, an array can be of that type and store objects of that type. Because arrays cannot be empty, the constructor receives the upper bound that is then used by ReDim. The Add method equally receives an argument of type T whose value is pushed into the array. This introduces another important concept: generic methods. In generic methods, methods can accept generic parameters (named *type argument*). Notice how a Count property returns the number of items in the array. In this particular scenario, auto-implemented properties cannot be used because a read-only property needs an explicit Get block. Finally, the Item property enables retrieving the specified object in the array at the given index. The new class therefore can handle different types with the same infrastructure.

Consuming Generic Types

To instantiate and consume generic types, you pass to the constructor the type you want to be handled. For example, the following code creates a new instance of the CustomType class, enabling it to handle only integers or types that are converted to Integer via a widening conversion:

```
Dim integerCollection As New CustomType(Of Integer)(2)
integerCollection.Add(0)
integerCollection.Add(1)
'Writes 1
Console.WriteLine(integerCollection(1).ToString)
```

You pass the desired type to the constructor after the Of keyword. When invoking the Add method, you can notice how IntelliSense tells you that the method can receive only Integer (see Figure 14.1).

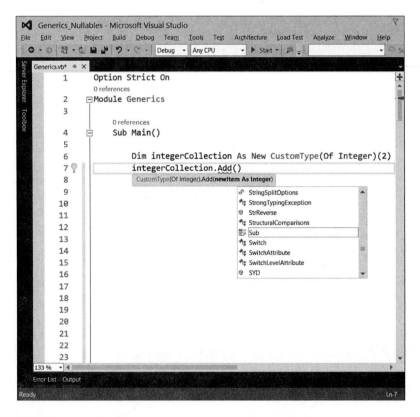

FIGURE 14.1   IntelliSense shows what type is accepted by the generic method.

If you pass a different type, you get an error message. But this does not work only with .NET common types. You can use this technique with custom types, too. For example, you can create a generic collection of `Person` objects (supposing you have defined a `Person` class in your code) as follows:

```
Dim onePerson As New Person
onePerson.FirstName = "Alessandro"
onePerson.LastName = "Del Sole"

Dim secondPerson As New Person
secondPerson.FirstName = "Robert"
secondPerson.LastName = "White"

Dim personCollection As New CustomType(Of Person)(2)
personCollection.Add(onePerson)
personCollection.Add(secondPerson)
'Returns 2

Console.WriteLine("How many people are there?")
Console.WriteLine("The answer is {0}", personCollection.Count)
```

This code produces the result shown in Figure 14.2.

FIGURE 14.2   Demonstrating the usage of custom generic types.

Generics' purpose should be clearer now. Their purpose is to provide reusable infrastructures for different types, avoiding mixed groups of objects in favor of strongly typed objects.

Implementing Generic Methods

In Listing 14.1 you saw how to implement a method that receives a generic type parameter. Generic methods are something more. You can add the `of` keyword to a generic method to parameterize the method, other than getting generic-type parameters. The following code provides an example, where two arrays of integers are swapped:

```
'Arrays are passed by reference in this case
Public Sub Swap(Of T1)(ByRef array1() As T1, ByRef array2() As T1)
    Dim temp() As T1
    temp = array1
    array1 = array2
    array2 = temp

End Sub
```

You could even rewrite the preceding code snippet in a more abstract way, as follows, which still works well with arrays:

```
Public Sub Swap(Of T1)(ByRef x As T1, ByRef y As T2)
    Dim temp As T1
    temp = x
    x = y
    y = temp

End Sub
```

Continuing the executive code shown in the "Consuming Generic Types" section, the following snippet shows how you can invoke the previous generic method to swap the content of two arrays of integers:

```
Dim arr1() As Integer = {1, 2, 3}
Dim arr2() As Integer = {4, 5, 6}
integerCollection.Swap(Of Integer)(arr1, arr2)

'Demonstrates that arr2 now
'contains values previously
'stored in arr1
For Each item In arr2
    Console.WriteLine(item)
Next
```

Similarly, you could have arrays of `Person` objects and invoke the `Swap` method on the `personCollection` class, demonstrating how generic methods can work with different types. For instance, the following code creates a new instance of the `Person` class continuing the previous example and defines two arrays of `Person`. Next, it invokes `Swap(Of Person)` on the `personCollection` class:

```
Dim thirdPerson As New Person
thirdPerson.FirstName = "Neil"
thirdPerson.LastName = "Rowe"

Dim personArray1() As Person = {onePerson, secondPerson}
Dim personArray2() As Person = {thirdPerson}
personCollection.Swap(Of Person)(personArray1,
                                 personArray2)
```

This demonstrates how different types can be targeted with generic methods.

Understanding Constraints

With constraints, you can control the behavior of generics and provide additional functionalities and limit the implementation to specific data types. Let's begin by understanding constraints on methods.

Methods Constraints

Imagine you want the ability to compare two items within an array. To accomplish this, you need to take advantage of the IComparable interface, and because of this, you want to require that the type argument implements the IComparable interface. The following code demonstrates this:

```
Public Function CompareItems(Of T As IComparable)(sourceArray() As T,
                                                  index1 As Integer,
                                                  index2 As Integer)
                                                  As Integer

    Dim result As Integer = _
                  sourceArray(index1).CompareTo(sourceArray(index2))

    Return result
End Function
```

Notice how the As clause in the method argument requires the type to implement the IComparable interface. If the type does not implement the interface, the generic method cannot be used. This simplifies how objects can be compared, in that you can directly invoke the CompareTo method on the first item in the array. This approach is useful for another reason: If you did not specify the IComparable constraint, you could attempt a conversion from T to IComparable at runtime, but this would throw an InvalidCastException if the object does not implement the interface. Therefore, by using constraints you can ensure that your objects suit your needs.

Type Constraints

At a higher level, you can apply constraints to generic objects' definitions. For example, you can require the type parameter to implement the IComparable interface as follows:

```
Public Class CustomType(Of T As IComparable)

End Class
```

You can specify which interfaces the object must implement or which class it has to inherit from. This is an example that accepts types deriving from `System.IO.Stream`:

```
Public Class CustomType(Of T As System.IO.Stream)

End Class
```

In this example, acceptable types would be `StreamWriter`, `StreamReader`, `BinaryWriter`, and `BinaryReader` objects.

New Constraints

You can combine the `As New` keywords to require the type argument to expose an explicit parameterless constructor. This is accomplished by the following definition:

```
Public Class CustomType(Of T As New)
    Public Sub TestInstance()
        Dim instance As New T
    End Sub
End Class
```

The `TestInstance` method is an example of how you can instantiate the `T` type. This approach gives you the ability to create new instances of the type and prevents the type from being an interface or an abstract (`MustInherit`) class.

Providing Multiple Constraints

You can combine multiple constraints to provide a series of requirements in your generic types. Multiple constraints are enclosed in curly braces and separated by commas. The following code defines a generic type accepting only reference types that implement the `ICloneable` interface and an explicit parameterless constructor:

```
Public Class CustomType(Of T As {Class, ICloneable, New})

End Class
```

INHERITANCE CONSTRAINT

You can also provide inheritance constraints other than interfaces constraint, as described at the beginning of this section. You provide the name of the abstract or base class you require to be inherited in the type parameter.

The `Class` keyword in the constraint indicates that only reference types are accepted. You use the `Structure` keyword if you want to accept only value types, keeping in mind that in such a scenario you cannot combine it with the `New` keyword. This is because the `Structure` constraint implies `New` and does not let you write it since doing so would be redundant. The following code demonstrates how you can directly access the `Clone` method because of the `ICloneable` implementation constraint:

```
Public Sub TestConstraint()
    Dim newObj As New T
    Dim clonedObj As Object = newObj.Clone()
End Sub
```

NESTED TYPES

The type parameter can be used only within the body of the generic type. Nested types can still take advantage of the type parameter as well, so you can create complex infrastructures in your generic types.

Overloading Type Parameters

You can overload generic definitions providing different signatures for the type parameter, similar to what happens in method overloads. The following code provides an example:

```
Public Class CustomType

End Class


Public Class CustomType(Of T1, T2)

End Class


Public Class CustomType(Of T As {Class, ICloneable, New})

End Class
```

It is worth mentioning that providing a nongeneric version of your class is not necessary. You can provide different implementations for your generic types. Now consider the following overloading attempt:

```
Class CustomType(Of T1, T2)

End Class


'Fails at compile time

Class CustomType(Of T1 As IComparable, T2 As ICloneable)

End Class
```

This code is not compiled because, although in the second definition some constraints are defined, the type implementation is considered by the compiler with the same, identical signature. Similarly, you can provide overloaded methods using techniques learned in Chapter 7, "Class Fundamentals," but against generic methods as demonstrated in the following code:

```
Sub DoSomething(Of T1, T2)(argument1 As T1, argument2 As T2)


End Sub


Sub DoSomething(Of T)(argument As T)


End Sub
```

Overloading provides great granularity over Generics implementation, and you will often see examples in built-in generic collections.

Introducing Nullable Types

As you read in the discussion of value types and reference types, value types have a default value that is zero, whereas reference types have a default value that is a null reference and is represented in VB by the Nothing language literal. This is because a reference type can store null values, but value types cannot. Attempting to assign a null value to a value type would result in resetting to the default value for that type. This is a limitation because there are situations in which you need to store null values in value types, such as when fetching data from a SQL Server database. You can have a hypothetical Orders table where the Ship date column enables null values. SQL Server has its own data types, one of which is the DBNull that enables null values. Because Visual Basic 2015 enables mapping SQL Server data types to .NET data types, as you see in Part IV, "Data Access with ADO.NET and LINQ," it could be a problem trying to map a NULL type in SQL Server into a DateTime type in VB. To avoid such problems, starting from .NET Framework 2.0, Microsoft introduced the *Nullable types*.

WHY NULLABLE TYPES IN THIS CHAPTER?

Nullable types are covered in this chapter because they are generic types and are required in the next chapters.

Nullable types differ from other types because they can have both a value and have a null value. Nullable types are generic types, and variables are declared as Nullable(Of T) or by adding a question mark just after the type name. You declare a nullable value type as follows:

```
Dim nullInt As Nullable(Of Integer)
```

The following syntax is also supported:

```
Dim nullInt as Integer?
```

You can also add inline initialization:

```
Dim nullInt As Nullable(Of Integer) = Nothing
```

Nullable types expose two properties, HasValue and Value. The first one is of type Boolean and allows understanding if a variable stores a value so that you can avoid using it if it is null. The second one returns the actual value of the type. For example, the following code checks whether the preceding declared nullInt variable has a value and shows its value if it has one:

```
'Has no value, so WriteLine is not executed
If nullInt.HasValue Then
    Console.WriteLine(nullInt.Value)
End If
```

Because you assigned Nothing, HasValue is False. The next example declares a Boolean nullable and demonstrates how you can use the value (the alternative syntax with the question mark is used):

```
Dim nullBool As Boolean? = False
If nullBool.HasValue Then
    Console.WriteLine(nullBool.Value)
End If
```

IsNot Nothing AND HasValue

On nullable types, checking the value with IsNot Nothing or with HasValue has the same effect. In fact, behind the scenes, the compiler emits a check based on HasValue for both.

Nullable types also expose a method called GetValueOrDefault, which returns the current value for the type instance if the HasValue property is True. If HasValue is False, the method returns the default value for the type or the specified default value. The following code describes how you use GetValueOrDefault:

```
Dim anInt As Integer? = 10
'HasValue is True, so returns 10
Dim anotherInt As Integer = anInt.GetValueOrDefault

Dim anInt As Integer?
'HasValue is False, so returns 0
'which is the default Value for Integer
Dim anotherInt As Integer = anInt.GetValueOrDefault

Dim anInt As Integer?
'HasValue is False, so returns the default value
'specified as the method argument
Dim anotherInt As Integer = anInt.GetValueOrDefault(10)
```

```
Dim anInt As Integer? = 5
'HasValue is True, so returns the current value
'while the method argument is ignored
Dim anotherInt As Integer = anInt.GetValueOrDefault(10)
```

Using nullables will make your life easier in lots of scenarios.

The Null-Propagating Operator and Value Types

Chapter 4, "Data Types and Expressions," introduced the null-propagating operator and you saw how you can use it against reference types to check whether an object is null before you use it. With value types, things are different. In fact, as you may recall, value types do not return Nothing but instead return a default value. For instance, the default value for the Integer type is 0. For this reason, you do not need to use the null-propagating operator against a value type directly. However, the null-propagating operator is very useful when you want to check whether an object exposing a property as a value type is not null. To better understand this, consider the following Person class, which exposes the Age and DateOfBirth properties, which are value types:

```
Public Class Person
    Public Property FirstName As String
    Public Property LastName As String
    Public Property Age As Integer
    Public Property DateOfBirth As Date
End Class
```

Suppose you want to get the person's age and birth date only if an instance of the Person class is not null. You can accomplish this with the following code:

```
'onePerson is null
Dim onePerson As Person = Nothing

'The ?. operator returns nullable types
Dim age As Integer? = onePerson?.Age
Dim [date] As Date? = onePerson?.DateOfBirth
```

In this code, onePerson is of type Person and is null because it is set to Nothing. This is useful for demonstrating the behavior of the ?. operator. In the preceding code, the ?. operator returns the value of Age and DateOfBirth only if the Person instance is not null. If it is null, as in the example, it returns Nothing. And because it returns a null value, the variable that receives the assignment must be a nullable type. Say that you wrote the following assignments:

```
Dim age As Integer = onePerson?.Age
Dim [date] As Date = onePerson?.DateOfBirth
```

The compiler would report an error (assuming that you have `Option Strict On` set) because the `?.` operator returns `Nullable(Of Integer)` for the first line and `Nullable(Of Date)` for the second line, so there is a type mismatch.

You can also use the null-propagating operator for additional short-circuiting operations, as in the following code, which returns the person's age only if the `Person` instance is not null and only if the age is greater than 35:

```
If onePerson?.Age > 35 Then
    'Take the age only if onePerson
    'is not null and Age is > 35
    Dim age As Integer = onePerson.Age
End If
```

If the object is null, the code simply ignores the `If` block. As for reference types, the `?.` operator also works well with method invocations that return value types. For example, in the following code, the `First` method returns the first character of `FirstName` but only if both `onePerson` and `FirstName` are note null:

```
Dim firstChar As Char? = onePerson?.FirstName?.First
```

Here the `?.` operator returns a `Nullable(Of Char)`, which makes sense because `Char` is a value type. Using the null-propagating operator with value types requires knowledge of nullable types, so now you understand why this particular topic has been discussed in this chapter. It is also possible to use the null-propagating operator with a nullable type itself. For example, the following code would result in an `InvalidOperationException` because `Value` is null:

```
Dim x As Date? = Nothing
Dim y = x.Value.Day
```

You can rewrite the preceding code with the `?.` operator, without calling `Value`, directly against the nullable type:

```
Dim x As Date? = Nothing
Dim y = x?.Day
```

This code assigns `y` with `Nothing`, but because it does not invoke a null object, it does not throw an exception.

Summary

Generics are a great benefit in the .NET development with Visual Basic 2015. Generics are .NET types that can adapt their behavior to different kinds of objects without the need of defining a separate version of the type. So, you can implement a generic type to work with integers, strings, custom reference types, and any other .NET type with a single implementation. They provide several benefits, including strongly typed programming, IntelliSense support, and better performance. Generics require the `of` keyword to specify the type parameter that you can manipulate in your object body.

Within Generics definition, you can implement your own custom methods both in the usual fashion and as generic methods, which still require the `of` keyword followed by the type specification. Generics are also very flexible thanks to the constraints feature. It allows them to accept only types that adhere to the specified requirements, such as interfaces implementation, inheritance, or the presence of an explicit constructor. Nullable types are special generic types that allow null values for value types. They work like other types but expose a `HasValue` property for checking whether the object is null or populated. Having knowledge of nullable types is also important for understanding the usage of the null-propagating operator against value types because this operator returns nullable types. During the rest of the book, you will find hundreds of Generics usages, especially after Chapter 16, where collections and generic collections will be covered.

CHAPTER 15

Delegates and Events

So far, you have seen how to create and manipulate your objects, working with the result of operations performed onto object instances or shared members. All the work up to now does not provide a way for understanding the moment when a particular thing happens or for being notified of a happening. In .NET development, as with many other programming environments, getting notifications for occurrences and knowing the moment when something happens is accomplished by handling *events*. Events are information that an object sends to the caller, such as the user interface or a thread, about its state so that the caller can make decisions according to the occurred event. Events in .NET programming are powerful and provide great granularity about controlling each happening. This granularity can take place because of another feature named *delegates*, which provide the real infrastructure for event-based programming. Because of this, delegates are discussed first before we get into the events discussion.

Understanding Delegates

Delegates are *type-safe* function pointers. The main difference between classic function pointers (such as C++ pointers) and delegates is that function pointers can point anywhere, which can be dangerous. Delegates, on the other hand, can point only to those methods that respect delegates' signatures. Delegates hold a reference to a procedure (its address) and enable applications to invoke different methods at runtime, but such methods must adhere to the delegate signature. Delegates also enable you to invoke a method from another object. This is important according to the main purpose of delegates, which is offering an infrastructure for handling events.

WHERE ARE DELEGATES USED?

Delegates are used in event-handling architectures, but they are powerful and can be used in other advanced techniques. You find examples of delegates being used in multithreading or in LINQ expressions. In Chapter 20, "Advanced Language Features," you learn about lambda expressions that enable implementing delegates on-the-fly.

Delegates are reference types deriving from `System.Delegate`. Because of this, they can also be defined at namespace level, as you might recall from Chapter 9, "Organizing Types Within Namespaces." They can also be defined at the class and module level. In the next section, you learn to define delegates. Pay attention to this topic because delegates have a particular syntax for being defined and that can be a little bit confusing.

Declaring Delegates

A delegate is defined via the `Delegate` keyword followed by the method signature it needs to implement. Such a signature can be referred to as a `Sub` or as a `Function` and might or might not receive arguments. The following code defines a delegate that can handle a reference to methods able to check an email address, providing the same signature of the delegate:

```
Public Delegate Function IsValidMailAddress(ByVal emailAddress _
                                        As String) As Boolean
```

DELEGATES SUPPORT GENERICS

Delegates support generics, meaning that you can define a `Delegate Function DelegateName(Of T)` or `Delegate Sub DelegateName(Of T)`.

Notice that `IsValidMailAddress` is a type and not a method as the syntax might imply. `emailAddress` is a variable containing the email address to check while any methods respecting the signature return a Boolean value depending on the check result. To use a delegate, you need to create an instance of it. The delegate's constructor requires you to specify an `AddressOf` clause pointing to the actual method that accomplishes the required job. After you get the instance, the delegate points to the desired method that you can call using the `Invoke` method. The following code demonstrates the described steps:

```
'The method's signature is the same as the delegate: correct
Function CheckMailAddress(ByVal emailAddress As String) As Boolean

    'Validates emails via regular expressions, according to the
    'following pattern
    Dim validateMail As String = "^([\w-\.]+)@((\[[0-9]{1,3}\." & _
        "[0-9]{1,3}\.)|(([\w-]+\.)+))([a-zA-z]{2,4}|[0-9]{1,3})(\]?)$"

    Return Text.RegularExpressions.Regex.IsMatch(emailAddress,
                                            validateMail)
```

```
End Function

Sub Main()
    'Creates an instance of the delegate and points to
    'the specified method
    Dim mailCheck As New IsValidMailAddress(AddressOf CheckMailAddress)

    'You invoke a delegate via the Invoke method
    Dim result As Boolean = mailCheck.
                        Invoke("alessandro.delsole@visual-basic.it")
    Console.WriteLine("Is valid: {0}", result)
End Sub
```

At this point, you might wonder why delegates are so interesting if they require so much code just for a simple invocation. The first reason is that you can provide as many methods as you like that respect the delegate signature and decide which of the available methods to invoke. For example, the following code provides an alternative (and much simplified) version of the `CheckMailAddress` method, named `CheckMailAddressBasic`:

```
Function CheckMailAddressBasic(ByVal emailAddress As String) As Boolean
    Return emailAddress.Contains("@")

End Function
```

Although different, the method still respects the delegate signature. Now you can invoke the new method by changing the `AddressOf` clause, without changing code that calls `Invoke` for calling the method:

```
'Alternative syntax: if you already declared
'an instance, you can  do this assignment
mailCheck = AddressOf CheckMailAddressBasic

'No changes here!
Dim result As Boolean = mailCheck.
                    Invoke("alessandro.delsole@visual-basic.it")
Console.WriteLine("Is valid: {0}", result)
```

If you still wonder why all this can be useful, consider a scenario in which you have hundreds of invocations to the same method. Instead of replacing all the invocations, you can change what the delegate is pointing to. `Invoke` is also the default member for the `Delegate` class, so you can rewrite the previous invocation as follows:

```
Dim result As Boolean = mailCheck("alessandro.delsole@visual-basic.it")
```

This also works against methods that do not require arguments.

15

ADVANCED DELEGATES TECHNIQUES

Starting with Visual Basic 2008, the .NET Framework introduced new language features such as lambda expressions and relaxed delegates. Both are intended to work with delegates (and in the case of lambda expressions, to replace them in some circumstances), but because of their strict relationship with LINQ, they are discussed in Chapter 20, which is preparatory for the famous data access technology.

Combining Delegates: Multicast Delegates

A delegate can hold a reference (that is, the address) to a method. It is possible to create delegates holding references to more than one method by creating multicast delegates. A multicast delegate is the combination of two or more delegates into a single delegate, providing the delegate the capability to make multiple invocations. The following code demonstrates how to create a multicast delegate, having two instances of the same delegate pointing to two different methods:

```vb
'The delegate is defined at namespace level
Public Delegate Sub WriteTextMessage(ByVal textMessage As String)


'....
Private textWriter As New WriteTextMessage(AddressOf WriteSomething)
Private complexWriter As New WriteTextMessage(AddressOf _
                                            WriteSomethingMoreComplex)


Private Sub WriteSomething(ByVal text As String)
    Console.WriteLine(" report your text: {0}", text)
End Sub

Private Sub WriteSomethingMoreComplex(ByVal text As String)
    Console.WriteLine("Today is {0} and you wrote {1}",
                    Date.Today.ToShortDateString, text)
End Sub

'Because Combine returns System.Delegate, with Option Strict On
'an explicit conversion is required.
Private CombinedDelegate As WriteTextMessage = CType(System.Delegate.
                                            Combine(textWriter,
                                            complexWriter),
                                            WriteTextMessage)


'....
CombinedDelegate.Invoke("Test message")
```

In this scenario, you have two methods that behave differently, but both respect the delegate signature. A new delegate (`CombinedDelegate`) is created invoking the `System.Delegate.Combine` method that receives the series of delegates to be combined as arguments. It is worth mentioning that `Combine` returns a `System.Delegate`; therefore, an explicit conversion via `CType` is required with `Option Strict On`. With a single call to `CombinedDelegate.Invoke`, you can call both `WriteSomething` and `WriteSomethingMoreComplex`. The preceding code produces the following output:

```
report your text: Test message
Today is 12/23/2015 and you wrote Test message
```

> **Delegate KEYWORD AND `System.Delegate`**
>
> `Delegate` is a reserved keyword in Visual Basic. Because of this, to invoke the `System.Delegate.Combine` shared method, the full name of the class has been utilized. You can still take advantage of the shortened syntax including `Delegate` within square brackets. In other words, you can write something like this: `[Delegate].Combine(params())`. This works because the `System` namespace is imported by default, and square brackets make the compiler consider the enclosed word as the identifier of a class exposed by one of the imported namespaces, instead of a reserved keyword.

Handling Events

Events are members that enable objects to send information on their state to the caller. When something occurs, an event tells the caller that something occurred so that the caller can make decisions on what actions to take. You handle events in UI-based applications, although not always. The .NET Framework takes a huge advantage from delegates to create event infrastructures, and this is what you can do in creating your custom events. In this section you first learn how to catch existing events, and then you get information on creating your own events. This approach is good because it provides a way to understand how delegates are used in event handling.

Registering for Events: `AddHandler` and `RemoveHandler`

To provide your applications the capability of intercepting events raised from any object, you need to register for events. Registering means giving your code a chance to receive notifications and to take actions when it is notified that an event was raised from an object. To register for an event notification, you use the `AddHandler` keyword that requires two arguments: The first one is the event exposed by the desired object, and the second is a delegate pointing to a method executed when your code is notified of an event occurring. The code in Listing 15.1 shows an example using a `System.Timers.Timer` object.

LISTING 15.1   Registering and Catching Events

```
Public Class EventsDemo
    'Declares a Timer
    Private myTimer As Timers.Timer

    'A simple counter
    Private counter As Integer
```

```
    'Interval is the amount of time in ticks
    Public Sub New(ByVal interval As Double)
        'Register for notifications about the Elapsed event
        AddHandler myTimer.Elapsed, AddressOf increaseCounter
        'Assigns the Timer.Interval property
        Me.myTimer.Interval = interval
        Me.myTimer.Enabled = True
    End Sub

    'Method that adheres to the delegate signature and that is
    'executed each time our class gets notifications about
    'the Elapsed event occurring
    Private Sub increaseCounter(ByVal sender As Object,
                                ByVal e As Timers.ElapsedEventArgs)
        counter += 1
    End Sub
End Class
```

Comments within Listing 15.1 should clarify the code. Notice how the `AddHandler` instruction tells the runtime which event from the `Timer` object must be intercepted (`Elapsed`). Also notice how, via the `AddressOf` keyword, you specify a method that performs some action when the event is intercepted. `AddHandler` at this particular point requires the method to respect the `ElapsedEventHandler` delegate signature. With this approach, the `increaseCounter` method is executed every time the `System.Timers.Timer.Elapsed` event is intercepted. `AddHandler` provides great granularity on controlling events because it enables controlling shared events and works within a member body, too. The `AddHandler` counterpart is `RemoveHandler`, which enables deregistering from getting notifications. For example, you might want to deregister before a method completes its execution. Continuing with the example shown in Listing 15.1, you can deregister before you stop the timer:

```
RemoveHandler myTimer.Elapsed, AddressOf increaseCounter
Me.myTimer.Enabled = False
```

As you see in the next section, this is not the only way to catch events in Visual Basic.

Declaring Objects with the `WithEvents` Keyword

By default, when you declare a variable for an object that exposes events, Visual Basic cannot see those events. This is also the case with the previous section's example, where you declare a `Timer` and then need to explicitly register for event handling. A solution to this scenario is to declare an object with the `WithEvents` keyword, which makes events visible to Visual Basic. Thanks to `WithEvents`, you do not need to register for events and can take advantage of the `Handles` clause to specify the event a method is going to handle.

The code in Listing 15.2 demonstrates this, providing a revisited version of the EventsDemo class.

LISTING 15.2   Catching Events with WithEvents and Handles

```
Public Class WithEventsDemo

    Private WithEvents myTimer As Timers.Timer

    Private counter As Integer

    Public Sub New(ByVal interval As Double)
        Me.myTimer.Interval = interval
        Me.myTimer.Enabled = True
    End Sub

    Private Sub increaseCounter(ByVal sender As Object,
                               ByVal e As Timers.ElapsedEventArgs) _
                               Handles myTimer.Elapsed
        counter += 1
    End Sub
End Class
```

Notice that if you do not specify a Handles clause, the code cannot handle the event, although it respects the appropriate delegate's signature. It is worth mentioning that languages such as Visual C# do not have a WithEvents counterpart, so you might prefer using AddHandler and RemoveHandler if you plan to write code that will be translated into or compared to other .NET languages.

PLATFORM EXCEPTIONS

Exceptions to the last sentence are Windows Presentation Foundation (WPF), Silverlight, and the Windows Runtime (WinRT). Because of the particular events' infrastructure based on routed events, the runtime can catch events even if you do not explicitly provide a Handles clause. Of course, take care in this situation.

Offering Events to the External World

In the previous section, you learned how to handle existing events. Now it's time to get your hands dirty on implementing and raising custom events within your own objects. Visual Basic provides two ways for implementing events: the Event keyword and custom events. Let's examine both of them.

Raising Events

You declare your own events by using the Event keyword. This keyword requires you to specify the event name and eventually a delegate signature. Although not mandatory (Event allows specifying no arguments), specifying a delegate signature is useful so that you can take advantage of AddHandler for subsequently intercepting events. The code in Listing 15.3 shows an alternative implementation of the Person class in which an event is raised each time the LastName property is modified.

LISTING 15.3   Implementing and Raising Events

```
Public Class Person
    Public Event LastNameChanged(ByVal sender As Object,
                                 ByVal e As EventArgs)

    Public Property FirstName As String

    Private _lastName As String
    Public Property LastName As String

        Get
            Return _lastName
        End Get
        Set(ByVal value As String)
            If value <> _lastName Then
                _lastName = value
                RaiseEvent LastNameChanged(Me, EventArgs.Empty)
            End If
        End Set
    End Property

End Class
```

Notice that in this particular case you need to implement the LastName property the old-fashioned way, so you can perform subsequent manipulations. The code checks that the property value changes; then the LastNameChanged event is raised. This is accomplished via the RaiseEvent keyword. Also notice how the LastNameChanged event definition adheres to the EventHandler delegate signature. This can be considered as the most general delegate for the events infrastructure. The delegate defines two arguments: The first one, which is named sender, is of type Object and represents the object that raised the event. The second is an argument, named e, of type System.EventArgs that is the base type for classes containing events information. You get a deeper example in the next section. At this point, intercepting the event is simple. You just need to register for event notifications or create an instance of the Person class with WithEvents. The following code demonstrates this:

```
Sub TestEvent()
    Dim p As New Person
    AddHandler p.LastNameChanged,
            AddressOf personEventHandler
    p.LastName = "Del Sole"
    Console.ReadLine()
End Sub


Private Sub personEventHandler(ByVal sender As Object,
                        ByVal e As EventArgs)
    Console.WriteLine("LastName property was changed")
End Sub
```

Now every time you change the value of the LastName property, you can intercept the edit.

PROPERTY CHANGE NOTIFICATION IN THE REAL WORLD

The .NET Framework provides the INotifyPropertyChanged interface, which is used to send notifications to the caller when the value of a property changes, by raising the PropertyChanged event exposed by the interface. The current example shows a different technique because it is useful to make you understand how events work at a more general level.

Passing Event Information

In the previous code example, you got a basic idea about passing event information via the base System.EventArgs class. In the .NET Framework, you can find hundreds of classes that inherit from System.EventArgs and that enable passing custom event information to callers. This is useful whenever you need additional information on what happened during the event handling. Continuing with the previous example, imagine you want to check whether the LastName property value contains blank spaces while you raise the LastNameChanged event, sending this information to callers. This can be accomplished by creating a new class that inherits from System.EventArgs. Listing 15.4 shows how you can implement the class and how you can take advantage of it in the Person class.

LISTING 15.4   Providing Custom Event Information

```
Public Class LastNameChangedEventArgs
    Inherits EventArgs

    Private _lastName As String
    Public ReadOnly Property LastName As String
        Get
            Return _lastName
        End Get
    End Property
```

```
    Public ReadOnly Property ContainsBlank As Boolean
        Get
            Return Me.LastName.Contains(" ")
        End Get
    End Property


    Public Sub New(ByVal lastName As String)
        Me._lastName = lastName
    End Sub
End Class


Public Class Person
    Private _lastName As String
    Public Property LastName As String
        Get
            Return _lastName
        End Get
        Set(ByVal value As String)
            If value <> _lastName Then
                _lastName = value
                Dim e As New LastNameChangedEventArgs(value)
                RaiseEvent LastNameChanged(Me, e)
            End If
        End Set
    End Property


    Public Event LastNameChanged(ByVal sender As Object,
                        ByVal e As LastNameChangedEventArgs)

End Class
```

Notice how the `LastNameChangedEventArgs` class exposes the public properties representing information you want to return to the caller. You could definitely consider the option of using a read-only auto-implemented property in this situation; the extended form is used for consistency. When raising the event in the `Person` class, you create a new instance of the `LastNameChangedEventArgs` and pass the required information elaborated by the instance. Now you can change the event handler described in the previous section as follows:

```
Private Sub personEventHandler(ByVal sender As Object,
                        ByVal e As LastNameChangedEventArgs)
    Console.WriteLine("LastName property was changed")
    Console.WriteLine("Last name contains blank spaces: " &
                    e.ContainsBlank)
End Sub
```

In this way, you can easily handle additional event information. Finally, it is important to understand how you can get the instance of the object that raised the event because it is something that you will often use in your applications. You accomplish this by converting the sender into the appropriate type. The following code shows how to get the instance of the Person class that raised the previous LastNameChanged event:

```
Dim raisingPerson As Person = DirectCast(sender, Person)
```

Creating Custom Events

You can define your own events by implementing the *custom events*. Custom events are useful because they provide a kind of relationship with a delegate. They are also useful in multithreaded applications. You declare a custom event via the Custom Event keywords combination, supplying the event name and signature as follows:

```
Public Custom Event AnEvent As EventHandler
    AddHandler(ByVal value As EventHandler)

    End AddHandler

    RemoveHandler(ByVal value As EventHandler)

    End RemoveHandler

    RaiseEvent(ByVal sender As Object, ByVal e As System.EventArgs)

    End RaiseEvent
End Event
```

IntelliSense is very cool here because, when you type the event declaration and press Enter, it adds a skeleton for the custom event that is constituted by three members (see Figure 15.1): AddHandler is triggered when the caller subscribes for an event with the AddHandler instruction; RemoveHandler is triggered when the caller removes an event registration; and RaiseEvent is triggered when the event is raised. In this basic example, the new event is of the type EventHandler, which is a delegate that represents an event storing no information and that is the most general delegate.

Now take a look at the following example that demonstrates how to implement a custom event that can affect all instances of the Person class:

```
Public Delegate Sub FirstNameChangedHandler(ByVal info As String)

Dim handlersList As New List(Of FirstNameChangedHandler)

Public Custom Event FirstNameChanged As FirstNameChangedHandler
    AddHandler(ByVal value As FirstNameChangedHandler)
        handlersList.Add(value)
        Debug.WriteLine("AddHandler invoked")
```

15

```
        End AddHandler

        RemoveHandler(ByVal value As FirstNameChangedHandler)
            If handlersList.Contains(value) Then
                handlersList.Remove(value)
                Debug.WriteLine("RemoveHandler invoked")
            End If
        End RemoveHandler

        RaiseEvent(ByVal info As String)
            'Performs the same action on all instances
            'of the Person class
            For Each del As FirstNameChangedHandler In handlersList
                If del IsNot Nothing Then
                    'del.Invoke(info ......
                End If
            Next
        End RaiseEvent
End Event
```

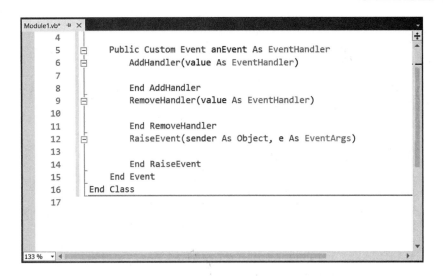

FIGURE 15.1   IntelliSense generates a skeleton for all members of custom events.

This code provides an infrastructure for handling changes on the FirstName property in the Person class. In this case, the code builds a list of delegates that is populated when the caller registers with AddHandler. When the caller invokes RemoveHandler, the delegate is popped from the list. The essence of this resides in the RaiseEvent stuff, which implements a loop for performing the same operation on all instances of the delegate and therefore of the `Person` class. To raise custom events, you use the `RaiseEvent` keyword. For this, you need to edit the `FirstName` property implementation in the `Person` class as follows:

```
Private _firstName As String
Public Property FirstName As String

    Get
        Return _firstName
    End Get
    Set(ByVal value As String)
        If value <> _firstName Then
            _firstName = value
            RaiseEvent FirstNameChanged(FirstName)
        End If
    End Set
End Property
```

You raise the event the same way for non-custom events, with the difference that custom events provide deep control over what is happening when the caller registers, deregisters, or raises the event.

Summary

Delegates are type-safe function pointers that store the address of a `Sub` or `Function`, enabling different methods to be invoked at runtime. Delegates are reference types declared via the `Delegate` keyword; they enable invoking methods via the `Invoke` method. They can be used in different programming techniques, but the most important scenario where you use delegates is within event-based programming. Events take advantage of delegates in that the objects require their signature to be respected. Coding events is something that can be divided into main areas, such as catching events and exposing events from your objects. To catch events, you can register and deregister via the `AddHandler` and `RemoveHandler` keywords, or you can declare objects by exposing events via the `WithEvents` reserved word. Then you can provide event handlers respecting the appropriate delegate signature and adding the `Handles` clause. You instead define your own events in two ways: via the `Event` keyword or with custom events. The advantage of providing custom events is that you can have deep control over the event phases, such as registering and deregistering. In this discussion, it is important to remember that you can provide custom event information by creating classes that inherit from `System.EventArgs` where you can store information useful to the caller.

CHAPTER 16

Working with Collections and Iterators

Applications often require working with data. Until now you got information on how to store data within classes and structures, but it is common to need to create groups of data. In .NET development, this is accomplished using special classes known as *collections*, which enable storing a set of objects within one class. The .NET Framework provides a lot of collections, each one specific to a particular need or scenario. The main distinction is between nongeneric collections and generic collections, but all of them can store a set of objects. Collections are not merely groups of data. They are the backend infrastructure for engines such as the ADO.NET Entity Framework and LINQ, so understanding collections is an important task. At a higher level, collections' infrastructure is offered by the `System.Collections` namespace and by some interfaces that bring polymorphism to collections. After you have stored data in collections, it is not uncommon for you to analyze the content of such collections; this task is often performed via (but not limited to) `For..Each` or `For.. Next` loops. You can also take advantage of iterators, which allow you to return a sequence of items one at a time and in a deferred manner. This is useful when prepopulating an entire collection in memory before returning to the caller would be too time-consuming, would take up too much memory (such as with large sequences), or would be impossible (as with infinite sequences). In this chapter you learn about the .NET Framework's collections, both nongeneric and generic ones. You also learn how to create and consume custom collections, and you get an overview of concurrent collections. Finally, you learn about iterators in Visual Basic 2015.

Understanding Collections Architecture

Collections are special classes that can store sets of objects; the .NET Framework offers both nongeneric and generic collections. Whatever kind of collection you work on, collections implement some interfaces. The first one is ICollection that derives from IEnumerable and provides both the enumerator (which enables For..Each iterations) and special members, such as Count (which returns the number of items within a collection) and CopyTo (which copies a collection to an array). Collections also implement IList or IDictionary; both inherit from ICollection and expose members that enable adding, editing, and removing items from a collection. The difference is that IDictionary works with key/value pairs instead of single objects as IList. The previously mentioned interfaces are about nongeneric collections. If you work with generic collections, the collections implement the generic counterpart of those interfaces such as ICollection(Of T), IList(Of T), and IDictionary(Of TKey, TValue). It's important to understand this implementation because this provides similarities between collections so that you can learn members from one collection and be able to reuse them against other kinds of collections.

USE THE OBJECT BROWSER

Remember that the Object Browser tool can provide thorough information on objects' architecture, meaning that if you don't remember which members are exposed by a collection, this tool can be your best friend. As you know, in Visual Basic 2015, the IDE can show the code that defines an object in the .NET Framework. However, the Object Browser provides a graphical, hierarchical representation of objects that can be more helpful in situations like this.

Working with Nongeneric Collections

The System.Collections namespace defines several nongeneric collections. The namespace also defines interfaces mentioned in the previous section. Here you learn to work with nongeneric collections so that in the next section you can easily understand why generic ones are more efficient.

The ArrayList Collection

System.Collections.ArrayList is the most common nongeneric collection in the .NET Framework and represents an ordered set of items. By *ordered*, we mean that you add items to the collection one after the other, which is different from sorting. ArrayList collections can store any .NET type because, at a higher level, it accepts items of type Object. The following code shows how you can create a new ArrayList and can set the number of items it can contain by setting the Capacity property:

```
Dim mixedCollection As New ArrayList
mixedCollection.Capacity = 10
```

Adding new items to an `ArrayList` is a simple task. To do this, you invoke the `Add` method that receives as an argument the object you want to add, as demonstrated by the following snippet:

```
mixedCollection.Add(35)
mixedCollection.Add("35")
mixedCollection.Add("Alessandro")
mixedCollection.Add(Date.Today)
```

The preceding code adds an `Integer`, two `Strings`, and a `Date`. Of course, you can also add composite custom types. Always be careful when using an `ArrayLists`. The first two items' value is 35, but the first one is an `Integer` whereas the second is a `String`. If you want to compare such items or iterate them, you should explicitly convert from `String` to `Integer`, or vice versa. This would require boxing/unboxing operations. You work with collections of a single type, so a better approach is avoiding nongeneric collections in favor of generic ones. For example, if you have to work with a set of strings, you should use the `List (Of String)`. The second part of this chapter discusses generic collections.

WHY YOU SHOULD PREFER GENERICS

The second part of this chapter is about generic collections. You should use this kind of collection for two reasons; the first is that generic collections are strongly typed and prevent the possibility of errors that can be caused when working with items of type `Object`. The second reason is that each time you add a value type to a nongeneric collection, the type is first subject to boxing (that was discussed in Chapter 4, "Data Types and Expressions"), which can cause performance overhead and does not provide the best object management.

You can also add a block of items in a single invocation using the `AddRange` method. The following code shows how you can add an array of strings to the existing collection:

```
Dim anArray() As String = {"First", "Second", "Third"}
mixedCollection.AddRange(anArray)
```

`Add` and `AddRange` add items after the last existing item. You might want to add items at a specified position. This can be accomplished via the `Insert` and `InsertRange` methods whose first argument is the position; the second one is the object. The following code demonstrates this:

```
mixedCollection.Insert(3, "New item")
mixedCollection.InsertRange(3, anArray)
```

You can remove items from the collection using one of two methods. `Remove` enables you to remove a specific object, and `RemoveAt` enables you to remove the object at the specified position:

```
'Removes the string "35"
mixedCollection.RemoveAt(1)
'Removes 35

mixedCollection.Remove(35)
```

One interesting method is `TrimToSize`; it enables you to resize the collection based on the number of items effectively stored. For example, consider the following code:

```
Dim mixedCollection As New ArrayList
mixedCollection.Capacity = 10

mixedCollection.Add(32)
mixedCollection.Add("32")
mixedCollection.Add("Alessandro")
mixedCollection.Add(Date.Today)

mixedCollection.TrimToSize()
```

When created, the `ArrayList` can store up to 10 items. After the `TrimToSize` invocation, `Capacity`'s value is 4, which is the number of items effectively stored. If you have a large collection, the `ArrayList` provides a `BinarySearch` method that enables searching the collection for a specified item, returning the index of the item itself:

```
'Returns 2
Dim index As Integer = mixedCollection.BinarySearch("Alessandro")
```

If the item is not found within the collection, the return value is a negative number. If the collection contains more than one item matching the search criteria, `BinarySearch` returns only one item, which is not necessarily the first one. This collection also exposes other interesting members that are summarized in Table 16.1.

TABLE 16.1   `ArrayList` Members

Member	Description
Count	Returns the number of items within the collection.
CopyTo	Copies the `ArrayList` instance into an array.
Contains	Returns `True` if the specified item exists within the collection.
ToArray	Copies the content of the `ArrayList` into an array of `Object`.
IndexOf	Returns the zero base index of the specified item.
GetRange	Creates a new `ArrayList` that is just a subset of the initial one, based on the specified criteria.
Sort	Performs a sorting operation over the collection.
Reverse	Performs a descending sorting operation over the collection.
Item	Property that gets or sets an item at the specified index. This is the default property of the `ArrayList` class.
Clear	Removes all items from the collection.

You can access an item from the `ArrayList` using the index as follows:

```
Dim anItem As Object = mixedCollection(0)
```

You need to perform a conversion into the appropriate type, which is something you can accomplish inline if you already know the type:

```
Dim anItem As Integer = CInt(mixedCollection(0))
```

If the conversion fails, an `InvalidCastException` is thrown. The `ArrayList` implements the `IList` interface and thus can take advantage of the enumerator; therefore, you can iterate it via a `For..Each` loop as follows:

```
For Each item As Object In mixedCollection
    Console.WriteLine(item.ToString)

Next
```

You just need to pay attention to the fact that each item is treated as an `Object`, so you must be aware of conversions. The `ArrayList` collection provides members that you find in other kinds of collections. This is the reason the most common members are discussed here.

The `Queue` Collection

The `System.Collections.Queue` collection works according to the FIFO (First-In, First-Out) paradigm, meaning that the first item you add to the collection is the first pulled out of the collection. `Queue` exposes two methods: `Enqueue` adds a new item to the collection, and `Dequeue` removes an item from the collection. Both methods receive an argument of type `Object`. The following code provides an example:

```
Sub QueueDemo()

    Dim q As New Queue
    q.Enqueue(1)
    q.Enqueue(2)

    'Returns
    '1
    '2
    Console.WriteLine(q.Dequeue)
    Console.WriteLine(q.Dequeue)

End Sub
```

You just need to invoke the `Dequeue` method to consume and automatically remove an item from the collection. You can also invoke the `Peek` method, which returns the first item from the collection without removing it. Be careful when adding items to a queue because you are working in a fashion that is not strongly typed. If you plan to work with objects of a specified type (for example, you need a collection of `Integer`), consider using a `Queue(Of T)` that behaves the same way except that it is strongly typed. The collection also exposes a `Count` property that returns the number of items in the collection. The constructor provides an overload that enables specifying the capacity for the collection.

The `Stack` Collection

The `System.Collections.Stack` collection mimics the same-named memory area and works according to the LIFO (Last-In, First-Out) paradigm, meaning that the last item you add to the collection is the first that is pulled out from the collection. `Stack` exposes three important methods: `Push` adds an item to the collection, `Pop` enables the consuming of and removing of an item from the collection, and `Peek` returns the top item in the collection without removing it. The following is an example:

```
Dim s As New Stack

s.Push(1)
s.Push(2)

'Returns 2 and leaves it in the collection
Console.WriteLine(s.Peek)
'Returns 2 and removes it
Console.WriteLine(s.Pop)
'Returns 1 and removes it
Console.WriteLine(s.Pop)
```

As for `Queue`, here you work with `Object` items. Although this enables pushing different kinds of objects to the collection, it is not a good idea. You should use the generic counterpart (`Stack(Of T)`) that enables you to work with a single type in a strongly typed fashion. The `Stack` collection also exposes the `Count` property, which returns the number of objects that it stores.

The `HashTable` Collection

The `System.Collections.HashTable` collection can store items according to a key/value pair, where both key and value are of type `Object`. The `HashTable` peculiarity is that its items are organized based on the hash code of the key. The following code provides an example:

```
Dim ht As New Hashtable
ht.Add("Alessandro", "Del Sole")
ht.Add("A string", 35)
ht.Add(3.14, New Person)

'Number of items
Console.WriteLine(ht.Count)
'Removes an item based on the key
ht.Remove("Alessandro")
```

Items within a `HashTable` can be accessed by the key, as shown in the last line of code in the preceding example. It also offers two methods named `ContainsKey` and `ContainsValue` that check whether a key or a value exists within the collection, as demonstrated here:

```
'Checks if a key/value exists
Dim checkKey As Boolean = ht.ContainsKey("A string")
Dim checkValue As Boolean = ht.ContainsValue(32)
```

Note that if you do not check whether a key already exists, as in the preceding example, and attempt to add a key that already exists, then an `ArgumentException` is thrown. This is because keys must be unique. A single item within the collection is of type `DictionaryEntry` that exposed two properties, `Key` and `Value`. For example, you can iterate a `HashTable` as follows:

```
'iterate items
For Each item As DictionaryEntry In ht
    Console.WriteLine("{0} {1}", item.Key, item.Value)
Next
```

`HashTable` also offers two other properties named `Keys` and `Values` that return an `ICollection` containing keys in the key/value pair and values in the same pair, respectively. This is demonstrated here:

```
'iterate keys
For Each key As Object In ht.Keys
    Console.WriteLine(key)
Next
```

It is recommended that you use a strongly typed `Dictionary(Of T, T)` that provides more efficiency. (And this suggestion is appropriate when discussing other dictionaries.)

The `ListDictionary` Collection

The `System.Collections.Specialized.ListDictionary` collection works exactly like `HashTable` but differs in that it is more efficient until it stores up to 10 items. It is not preferred after the item count exceeds 10.

The `OrderedDictionary` Collection

The `System.Collections.Specialized.OrderedDictionary` collection works like `HashTable` but differs in that items can be accessed via either the key or the index, as demonstrated by the following code:

```
Dim od As New OrderedDictionary
od.Add("a", 1)

'Access via index
Dim item As DictionaryEntry = CType(od(0), DictionaryEntry)
Console.WriteLine(item.Value)
```

16

The `SortedList` Collection

The `System.Collections.SortedList` collection works like `HashTable` but differs in that items can be accessed via the key or the index items are automatically sorted based on the key. For example, look at the following code:

```
Dim sl As New SortedList
sl.Add("Del Sole", 2)
sl.Add("Alessandro", 1)

For Each item As String In sl.Keys
    Console.WriteLine(item)
Next
```

It sorts items based on the key; therefore, it produces the following result:

```
Alessandro
Del Sole
```

The `HybridDictionary` Collection

The `System.Collections.Specialized.HybridDictionary` collection is a dynamic class in that it implements a `ListDictionary` until the number of items is small and then switches to `HashTable` if the number of items grows large. Technically, it works like `HashTable`.

The `StringCollection` Collection

The `System.Collections.Specialized.StringCollection` is similar to the `ArrayList` collection except that it is limited to accepting only strings. The following code provides an example:

```
Dim stringDemo As New StringCollection

stringDemo.Add("Alessandro")
stringDemo.Add("Del Sole")

'Returns True
Dim containsString As Boolean = stringDemo.Contains("Del Sole")

stringDemo.Remove("Alessandro")
```

You can use the same members of `ArrayList` and perform the same operations.

The `StringDictionary` Collection

The `System.Collections.Specialized.StringDictionary` collection works like the `HashTable` collection but differs in that it accepts only key/value pairs of type `String`, meaning that both keys and values must be `String`. The following is a small example:

```
Dim stringDemo As New StringDictionary

stringDemo.Add("Key1", "Value1")
stringDemo.Add("Alessandro", "Del Sole")

'Simple iteration
For Each value As String In stringDemo.Values
    Console.WriteLine(value)
Next
```

You can recall the `HashTable` collection for a full member listing.

The `NameValueCollection` Collection

The `NameValueCollection` behaves similarly to the `StringDictionary` collection, but it differs in that `NameValueCollection` enables accessing items via either the key or the index. The following code snippet provides a brief demonstration:

```
Dim nv As New NameValueCollection

nv.Add("First string", "Second string")

Dim item As String = nv(0)
```

The `Add` method also provides an overload accepting another `NameValueCollection` as an argument.

The `BitArray` Collection

The `System.Collections.BitArray` collection enables storing bit values represented by Boolean values. A `True` value indicates that a bit is on (1), whereas a `False` value indicates that a bit is off (0). You can pass to the `BitArray` arrays of `Integer` numbers or Boolean values, as demonstrated by the following code:

```
Dim byteArray() As Byte = New Byte() {1, 2, 3}
'Length in zero base
Dim ba As New BitArray(byteArray)

For Each item As Object In ba
    Console.WriteLine(item.ToString)
Next
```

This code produces the output shown in Figure 16.1, which is a human-readable representation of the bits in the collection.

The constructor also accepts a length argument that enables specifying how large the collection must be.

FIGURE 16.1   Human-readable representation of bits in a `BitArray` collection.

The `Bitvector32` Collection

`System.Collections.Specialized.BitVector32` has the same purpose of `BitArray` but
differs in two important elements; the first one is that `BitVector32` is a structure that is a
value type and therefore can take advantage of a faster memory allocation. On the other
hand, the collection manages only 32-bit integers. All data is stored as 32-bit integers
that are affected by changes when you edit the collection. The most important (shared)
method is `CreateMask` that enables creating a mask of bits. The method can create an
empty mask (which is typically for the first bit) or create subsequent masks pointing to
the previous bit. When done, you can set the bit on or off by passing a Boolean value. The
following code provides an example:

```
'Passing zero to the constructor
'ensures that all bits are clear
Dim bv As New BitVector32(0)

Dim bitOne As Integer = BitVector32.CreateMask
Dim bitTwo As Integer = BitVector32.CreateMask(bitOne)
Dim bitThree As Integer = BitVector32.CreateMask(bitTwo)

bv(bitOne) = True
bv(bitTwo) = False
bv(bitThree) = True
```

The `Data` property stores the actual value of the collection, as demonstrated here:

```
'Returns 5 (the first bit + the second bit = the third bit)
Console.WriteLine(bv.Data)
```

If you instead want to get the binary representation of the data, you can use the name of the instance. The following code demonstrates this:

```
Console.WriteLine(bv)
```

This code produces the following result:

```
BitVector32{00000000000000000000000000000101}
```

MEMBERS AND EXTENSION METHODS

Collections provide special members, such as properties and methods, and are extended by most of the built-in extension methods. Providing a thorough discussion on each member is not possible; IntelliSense can point you in the right direction to provide explanations for each member. Each member has a self-explanatory identifier; therefore, it is easy to understand what a member does when you understand the high-level logic. In this chapter you are introduced to the most important members from collections so that you can perform the most common operations.

Working with Generic Collections

The .NET Framework offers generic counterparts of the collections described in the previous section. Moreover, it offers generic collections that are specific to particular technologies such as WPF. In this section, you learn to work with generic built-in collections and how you can take advantage of a strongly typed fashion. Generic collections are exposed by the `System.Collections.Generic` namespace, but a different namespace is explained.

The `List(Of T)` Collection

The `System.Collections.Generic.List(Of T)` collection is a generic ordered list of items. It is a strongly typed collection, meaning that it can accept only members of the specified type. It is useful because it provides support for adding, editing, and removing items within the collection. For example, imagine you need to store a series of `Person` objects to a collection. This can be accomplished as follows:

```
Dim person1 As New Person With {.FirstName = "Alessandro",
                                .LastName = "Del Sole",
                                .Age = 37}
Dim person2 As New Person With {.FirstName = "XXXXX",
                                .LastName = "ZZZZZZZ",
                                .Age = 44}
```

```
Dim person3 As New Person With {.FirstName = "YYYYY",
                                .LastName = "DDDDDDDD",
                                .Age = 18}

Dim personList As New List(Of Person)
personList.Add(person1)
personList.Add(person2)
personList.Add(person3)
```

You notice that the `List(Of T)` has lots of members in common with its nongeneric counterpart, the `ArrayList`. This is because the first one implements the `IList(Of T)` interface, whereas the second one implements `IList`. The following code shows how you can access an item within the collection using the `IndexOf` method and how you can remove an item invoking the `Remove` method, passing the desired instance of the `Person` class:

```
'Returns the index for Person2
Dim specificPersonIndex As Integer = personList.IndexOf(person2)


'Removes person3
personList.Remove(person3)
```

The `List(Of T)` still provides members such as `Capacity`, `AddRange`, `Insert`, and `InsertRange`, but it exposes a method named `TrimExcess` that works like the `ArrayList`.
`TrimToSize`. Because the `List(Of T)` implements the `IEnumerable(Of T)` interface, you can then iterate the collection using a classic `For..Each` loop, but each item is strongly typed, as demonstrated here:

```
For Each p As Person In personList
    Console.WriteLine(p.LastName)
Next
```

If you need to remove all items from a collection, you can invoke the `Clear` method, and when you do not need the collection anymore, you assign it to `Nothing`:

```
personList.Clear()
personList = Nothing
```

In this case, the code simply assigns `Nothing` to the list because this does not implement the `IDisposable` interface. If it did, you have to be sure to invoke the `Dispose` method before clearing and destroying the collection to avoid locking resources. There are also other interesting ways to interact with a collection, such as special extension methods. Extension methods are discussed in Chapter 20, "Advanced Language Features." For now, you need to know that they are special methods provided by the `IEnumerable(Of T)` interface that enables performing particular operations against a collection. For example, the Single method enables retrieving the unique instance of a type that matches the specified criteria:

```
'Returns a unique Person whose LastName
'property is Del Sole
Dim specificPerson As Person = personList.Single(Function(p) _
                               p.LastName = "Del Sole")
```

This method receives a lambda expression as an argument that specifies the criteria. Lambda expressions are also discussed in Chapter 20. Another interesting method is `FindAll`, which enables the generation of a new `List(Of T)` containing all the type instances that match a particular criteria. The following snippet retrieves all the `Person` instances whose `LastName` property starts with the letter *D*:

```
'Returns a new List(Of Person) storing
'all Person instances whose LastName starts
'with "D"
Dim specificPeople = personList.FindAll(Function(p) _
                               p.LastName.StartsWith("D"))
```

As usual, IntelliSense can be your best friend in situations such as this. Because all members from each collection cannot be described here, that technology can help you understand the meaning and the usage of previously mentioned members whose names are always self-explanatory.

INVESTIGATING COLLECTIONS AT DEBUG TIME

Chapter 5, "Debugging Visual Basic 2015 Applications," discussed the DataTips features of the Visual Studio debugger. They are useful if you need to investigate the content of collections while debugging, especially if you need to get information on how collections and their items are populated.

Working with Collection Initializers

The Visual Basic language implements a feature known as *collection initializers*. This feature works like the object initializers, except that it is specific for instantiating and populating collections inline. To take advantage of collection initializers, you need to use the `From` reserved keyword enclosing items within brackets, as demonstrated in the following code:

```
'With primitive types
Dim listOfIntegers As New List(Of Integer) From {1, 2, 3, 4}
```

The preceding code produces the same result as the following:

```
Dim listOfIntegers As New List(Of Integer)

listOfIntegers.Add(1)
listOfIntegers.Add(2)
listOfIntegers.Add(3)
listOfIntegers.Add(4)
```

You can easily understand how collection initializers enable writing less code that's more clear. This feature can also be used with any other .NET type. The following code snippet shows how you can instantiate inline a `List(Of Person)`:

```
'With custom types
Dim person1 As New Person With {.FirstName = "Alessandro",
                                .LastName = "Del Sole",
                                .Age = 37}
Dim person2 As New Person With {.FirstName = "XXXXX",
                                .LastName = "ZZZZZZZZ",
                                .Age = 44}
Dim person3 As New Person With {.FirstName = "YYYYY",
                                .LastName = "DDDDDDDD",
                                .Age = 18}


Dim people As New List(Of Person) From {person1,
                                        person2,
                                        person3}
```

The code also shows how you can take advantage of implicit line continuation if you have long lines for initializations. When you have an instance of the new collection, you can normally manipulate it. Of course, this feature works with any other collection type.

NONGENERIC COLLECTIONS

Collection initializers are also supported by nongeneric collections using the same syntax.

The `ReadOnlyCollection(Of T)` Collection

The `System.Collections.ObjectModel.ReadOnlyCollection(Of T)` is the read-only counterpart of the `List(Of T)` class. Being read-only, you can add items to the collection only when you create an instance, but then you cannot change it. The constructor requires an argument of type `IList(Of T)` so that the new collection will be generated starting from an existing one. The following code demonstrates how you can instantiate a new `ReadonlyCollection`:

```
Dim person1 As New Person With {.FirstName = "Alessandro",
                                .LastName = "Del Sole",
                                .Age = 37}
Dim person2 As New Person With {.FirstName = "XXXXX",
                                .LastName = "ZZZZZZZZ",
                                .Age = 44}
Dim person3 As New Person With {.FirstName = "YYYYY",
                                .LastName = "DDDDDDDD",
                                .Age = 18}
```

```
Dim people As New List(Of Person) From {person1, person2, person3}

Dim readonlyPeople As New ReadOnlyCollection(Of Person)(people)
```

As an alternative, you can create a `ReadonlyCollection` invoking the `List(Of T).AsReadOnly` method, as shown in the following code:

```
'Same as above
Dim readonly As ReadOnlyCollection(Of Person) = people.AsReadOnly
```

Invoking `AsReadOnly` produces the same result of creating an explicit instance.

The `Dictionary(Of TKey, TValue)` Collection

The `System.Collections.Generic.Dictionary(Of TKey, TValue)` collection is the generic counterpart for the `HashTable`. Each item within a `Dictionary` is a key/value pair; therefore, the constructor requires two arguments (`TKey` and `TValue`) where the first one is the key and the second one is the value. The following code shows instantiating a `Dictionary(Of String, Integer)` in which the `String` argument contains a person's name and the `Integer` argument contains the person's age:

```
Dim peopleDictionary As New Dictionary(Of String, Integer)
peopleDictionary.Add("Alessandro", 37)
peopleDictionary.Add("Stephen", 27)

peopleDictionary.Add("Rod", 44)
```

A single item in the collection is of type `KeyValuePair(Of TKey, TValue)`, and both arguments reflect the collection's ones. For a better explanation, take a look at the following iteration that performs an action on each `KeyValuePair`:

```
For Each item As KeyValuePair(Of String, Integer) In peopleDictionary
    Console.WriteLine(item.Key & " of age " & item.Value.ToString)

Next
```

The previous code will produce the following output:

```
Alessandro of age 37
Stephen of age 27
Rod of age 44
```

Each `KeyValuePair` object has two properties, `Key` and `Value`, which enable separated access to parts composing the object. You can then manipulate the `Dictionary` like you would other collections.

16

The `SortedDictionary(Of TKey, TValue)` Collection

The `System.Collections.Generic.SortedDictionary(Of TKey, TValue)` works exactly like the `Dictionary` collection, except that items are automatically sorted each time you perform a modification. You can rewrite the code shown in the section about the `Dictionary(Of TKey, TValue)` collection as follows:

```
Dim peopleDictionary As New SortedDictionary(Of String, Integer)

peopleDictionary.Add("Alessandro", 37)
peopleDictionary.Add("Stephen", 27)
peopleDictionary.Add("Rod", 44)

For Each item As KeyValuePair(Of String, Integer) In peopleDictionary
    Console.WriteLine(item.Key & " of age " & item.Value.ToString)

Next
```

This code will produce the following result:

```
Alessandro of age 37
Rod of age 44
Stephen of age 27
```

Notice that the result has a different order than you used to add items to the collection. In fact, items are sorted alphabetically. This collection performs sorting based on the `Key` part.

The `ObservableCollection(Of T)` Collection

The `System.Collections.ObjectModel.ObservableCollection(Of T)` is a special collection that is typically used in WPF, Windows 8.x Store, and Windows Phone applications. Its main feature is that it implements the `INotifyPropertyChanged` interface and can therefore raise an event each time its items are affected by any changes, such as adding, replacing, or removing. Thanks to this mechanism, the `ObservableCollection` is the most appropriate collection for the WPF and, more generally, XAML data-binding because it provides support for two-way data-binding in which the user interface gets notification of changes on the collection and is automatically refreshed to reflect those changes. Although a practical example of this scenario is offered in the chapters about WPF, this section shows you how the collection works. The `ObservableCollection` is exposed by the `System.Collections.ObjectModel` namespace, meaning that you need to add an `Imports` directive for this namespace. Notice that back in the .NET Framework 4.5, the `ObservableCollection` has been moved to the System.dll assembly from the WindowsBase.dll assembly. This makes it usable not only in WPF applications, but also in other kinds of applications (and this is why you do not need to add any reference manually as you would do in previous versions). Now consider the following code snippet:

```
Dim people As New ObservableCollection(Of Person)
AddHandler people.CollectionChanged, AddressOf CollectionChangedEventHandler
```

The people variable represents an instance of the collection, and its purpose is to store a set of Person class instances. Because the collection exposes a CollectionChanged event, which enables intercepting changes to items in the collection, you need an event handler to understand what is happening. The following code shows an example of event handler implementation:

```
Private Sub CollectionChangedEventHandler(sender As Object,
                        e As Specialized.
                        NotifyCollectionChangedEventArgs)

    Select Case e.Action
        Case Is = Specialized.NotifyCollectionChangedAction.Add
            Console.WriteLine("Added the following items:")
            For Each item As Person In e.NewItems
                Console.WriteLine(item.LastName)
            Next
        Case Is = Specialized.NotifyCollectionChangedAction.Remove
            Console.WriteLine("Removed or moved the following items:")
            For Each item As Person In e.OldItems
                Console.WriteLine(item.LastName)
            Next
    End Select
End Sub
```

The System.Collections.Specialized.NotifyCollectionChangedEventArgs type exposes some interesting properties for investigating changes on the collection. For example, the Action property enables you to understand if an item was added, moved, replaced, or removed by the collection via the NotifyCollectionChangedAction enumeration. Next, the collection exposes other interesting properties such as NewItems, which returns an IList object containing the list of items that were added, and OldItems, which returns an IList object containing the list of items that were removed/moved/replaced. The NewStartingIndex and the OldStartingIndex provide information on the position where changes (adding and removing/replacing/moving, respectively) occurred. Now consider the following code, which declares three new instances of the Person class and then adds them to the collection and finally removes one:

```
Dim person1 As New Person With {.FirstName = "Alessandro",
                                .LastName = "Del Sole",
                                .Age = 37}
Dim person2 As New Person With {.FirstName = "XXXXX",
                                .LastName = "ZZZZZZZZ",
                                .Age = 44}
```

```
Dim person3 As New Person With {.FirstName = "YYYYY",
                                .LastName = "DDDDDDDD",
                                .Age = 18}
```

```
people.Add(person1)
people.Add(person2)
people.Add(person3)
people.Remove(person1)
```

The `ObservableCollection` works like the List one; therefore, it exposes methods such as `Add`, `Remove`, `RemoveAt`, and so on and supports extension methods. The good news is that each time a new item is added or an item is removed, the `CollectionChanged` event is raised and subsequently handled. Because of our previous implementation, if you run the code, you get the following output:

```
Added the following items:
Del Sole
Added the following items:
ZZZZZZZZ
Added the following items:
DDDDDDDD
Removed or moved the following items:
Del Sole
```

Because of its particularity, the `ObservableCollection(Of T)` can also be useful in scenarios different from WPF and WinRT, though they remain the best places where you can use it.

The `ReadonlyObservableCollection(Of T)` Collection

As for the `List(Of T)` and also for the `ObservableCollection(Of T)`, there is a read-only counterpart named `ReadonlyObservableCollection(Of T)` that works like the `ReadonlyCollection(Of T)` plus the implementation of the `CollectionChanged` event. The collection is also exposed by the `System.Collections.ObjectModel` namespace.

The `LinkedList(Of T)` Collection

Think of the `System.Collections.Generic.LinkedList(Of T)` collection as a chain in which each ring is an item in the collection that is linked to the others. In other words, an item is linked to the previous one and the next one and points to them. Each item in the collection is considered as a `LinkedListNode(Of T)`, so if you decide to create a `LinkedList(Of Person)`, each `Person` instance will be represented by a `LinkedListNode(Of Person)`. Table 16.2 summarizes the most common methods and properties for the collection over the ones that you already know (derived from `IList(Of T)`).

TABLE 16.2 `LinkedList` Members

Member	Type	Description
AddFirst	Method	Adds a new item as the first in the collection
AddLast	Method	Adds a new item as the last in the collection
AddBefore	Method	Adds a new item before the specified node
AddAfter	Method	Adds a new item after the specified node
Clear	Method	Clears all items in the collection
Contains	Method	Checks if the specified item exists in the collection
CopyTo	Method	Copies the collection into an array
Count	Property	Returns the number of items in the collection
First	Property	Returns the first node in the collection
Last	Property	Returns the last node in the collection
Remove	Method	Removes the specified item from the collection
RemoveFirst	Method	Removes the first item from the collection
RemoveLast	Method	Removes the last item from the collection

The following code provides an example of creating and consuming a `LinkedList(Of Person)` collection (see comments for explanations):

```
Dim person1 As New Person With {.FirstName = "Alessandro",
                                .LastName = "Del Sole",
                                .Age = 37}
Dim person2 As New Person With {.FirstName = "XXXXX",
                                .LastName = "ZZZZZZZZ",
                                .Age = 44}
Dim person3 As New Person With {.FirstName = "YYYYY",
                                .LastName = "DDDDDDDD",
                                .Age = 18}


'Creates a new LinkedList
Dim linkedPeople As New LinkedList(Of Person)

'Creates a series of nodes
Dim node1 As New LinkedListNode(Of Person)(person1)
Dim node2 As New LinkedListNode(Of Person)(person2)
Dim node3 As New LinkedListNode(Of Person)(person3)

'The first item in the collection
linkedPeople.AddFirst(node1)

'The last one
linkedPeople.AddLast(node3)
```

16

```
'Add a new item before the last one and after
'the first one
linkedPeople.AddBefore(node3, node2)

'Removes the last item
linkedPeople.RemoveLast()
'Gets the instance of the last item
'(person2 in this case)
Dim lastPerson As Person = linkedPeople.Last.Value

'Determines if person1 is within the collection
Dim isPerson1Available As Boolean = linkedPeople.Contains(person1)
```

The most important difference between this collection and the other ones is that items are linked. This is demonstrated by an `Enumerator` structure exposed by every instance of the collection that enables moving between items, as demonstrated in the following code snippet:

```
Dim peopleEnumerator As LinkedList(Of Person).
    Enumerator = linkedPeople.GetEnumerator

Do While peopleEnumerator.MoveNext
    'Current is a property that is of type T
    '(Person in this example)
    Console.WriteLine(peopleEnumerator.Current.LastName)
Loop
```

This code demonstrates that items in the collections are linked and that each one points to the next one (see Figure 16.2).

FIGURE 16.2   Demonstrating linked items in a `LinkedList` collection.

The `Queue(Of T)` and `Stack(Of T)` Collections

The .NET Framework offers generic versions of the `Queue` and `Stack` collections, known as `System.Collections.Generic.Queue(Of T)` and `System.Collections.Generic.Stack(Of T)`. Their behavior is the same as nongeneric version, except that they are strongly typed;

also, in the .NET Framework 4.6, they implement the `IReadonlyCollection(Of T)` interface. Because of this, you already know how to work with generic versions, so they are not
discussed here.

The Null-Conditional Operator and Collections

In Chapter 4, "Data Types and Expressions," and in Chapter 14, "Generics and Nullable
Types," you learn a little about the new null-conditional operator. Visual Basic 2015
allows you to use this operator against collections, too. You can definitely use the `?.` operator to check whether a collection is null before using it, but you can also take advantage
of a special syntax that supports indexing. For example, the following code demonstrates
how to retrieve the first item from a list of integers only if the collection is not null:

```
Function GetList() As List(Of Integer)
    Return New List(Of Integer) From {1, 2, 3}
End Function


Sub NullCheckDemo()
    Dim x As List(Of Integer) = GetList()
    'Return the first item in the collection
    'only if x is not Nothing
    Dim item1 As Integer? = x?(0)
End Sub
```

With collections, the null-conditional operator syntax is `?(n)` where *n* is the index of the
desired item. In this case, the code first checks whether the x collection is not null; if it
is not null, the code returns the item in the list at the specified index, which is 1 in this
example. Say that you change the `GetList` method body so that it just returns `Nothing`,
like this:

```
Function GetList() As List(Of Integer)
    Return Nothing
End Function
```

The null-conditional operator in the `NullCheckDemo` method will assign `Nothing` to
the `item1` variable after it detects that x is null. It is important to understand that this
operator only protects against the collection being null, but it does not protect against
`IndexOutOfRangeExceptions` if the index provided is invalid.

The null-conditional operator also offers a special syntax for the `Dictionary` collection.
More specifically, it gives you an easy way to retrieve the value from the key/value pair of
a specific item in a dictionary after checking that it is not null. The following code snippet
provides an example:

```
Function GetDictionary() As Dictionary(Of String, Integer)
    Dim testDict As New Dictionary(Of String, Integer)
    testDict.Add("Alessandro", 37)
    testDict.Add("Robert", 40)
```

16

```
    Return testDict
End Function

Sub NullDictCheckDemo()
    Dim x As Dictionary(Of String, Integer) = GetDictionary()
    'Return the Value part for the
    'Key/value pair Alessandro/37
    Dim value As Integer? = x?!Alessandro
End Sub
```

In the case of a `Dictionary`, the null-conditional operator syntax is `?!`*name*, where *name* is the item's key you want to retrieve, without quotes. In the preceding example, the null-conditional operator first checks whether the `x` dictionary is not null. If it is not null, the code returns the corresponding value for the specified key. In this case, the `value` variable is assigned with `37`. If it is null, the operator returns `Nothing`. This is why you must use a nullable type to assign the result. Support for indexing in the null-conditional operator is very useful and makes it easier to avoid exceptions at runtime.

Building Custom Collections

Built-in collections are good for most scenarios. In some situations you might need to implement custom collections. You have two options: creating a collection from scratch or recur to inheritance. The first choice can be hard. You create a class implementing the `ICollection(Of T)` and `IList(Of T)` (or `IDictionary`) interfaces, but you need to manually write code for performing the most basic actions onto items. The other choice is inheriting from an existing collection. This is a good choice for another reason: You can create your custom base class for other collections. Imagine you want to create a custom collection that stores sets of `FileInfo` objects, each one representing a file on disk. It would not be useful to reinvent the wheel, so inheriting from `List(Of T)` is a good option. The following code inherits from `List(Of FileInfo)` and extends the collection implementing a new `ToObservableCollection` method, which converts the current instance into an `ObservableCollection(Of FileInfo)` and overrides `ToString` to return a customized version of the method:

```
Public Class FileInfoCollection
    Inherits List(Of FileInfo)


    Public Overridable Function ToObservableCollection() As _
            ObservableCollection(Of FileInfo)
        Return New ObservableCollection(Of FileInfo)(Me)
    End Function

    Public Overrides Function ToString() As String
        Dim content As New StringBuilder
```

```
        For Each item As FileInfo In Me
            content.Append(item.Name)
        Next
        Return content.ToString
    End Function
End Class
```

Now you have a strongly typed collection working with `FileInfo` objects. Plus, you extended the collection with custom members.

Concurrent Collections

The .NET Framework 4.6 includes the Task Parallel Library (TPL), which offers support for multicore CPU architectures. The library exposes specific generic collections, via the `System.Collections.Concurrent` namespace that was introduced by .NET 4.0. Table 16.3 gives you a list of the new classes.

TABLE 16.3   Concurrent Collections

Name	Description
ConcurrentStack(Of T)	A thread-safe stack collection
ConcurrentQueue(Of T)	A thread-safe queue collection
ConcurrentDictionary(Of TKey, TValue)	A thread-safe strongly typed dictionary of key/value pairs
ConcurrentBag(Of T)	A thread-safe list of objects
ConcurredLinkedList(Of T)	A thread-safe collection in which items are linked to one another

You get an overview of these collections in the appropriate chapters, but for completeness, you now have a full list of available collections.

Immutable Collections

Immutable collections were introduced with .NET Framework 4.5. They do the following purposes:

▶ Making it easier to share a collection that will never change so that the collection consumers know about its immutable state

▶ Providing implicit thread safety because no locks are required to access an immutable collection

▶ Allowing you to modify a collection during enumeration while ensuring that the original collection does not change

▶ Providing support for functional programming practices

Immutable collections can be used with desktop applications, portable libraries, and Windows Store apps. However, they are not included in the core class library distributed with the .NET Framework and must be downloaded via NuGet. (For details about NuGet, see Chapter 52, "Advanced IDE Features.") In summary, to use immutable collections, you need to select **Project, Manage NuGet Packages**, and then in the NuGet Package Manager window, you have to search for the `Microsoft.Immutable.Collections` package. Once it is installed, you can consume immutable collection objects, which are exposed by the `System.Collections.Immutable` namespace. Their names recall collections already discussed in this chapter, so they are not covered again in detail; just keep in mind that each has the characteristics listed at the beginning of this section. The following immutable collections are available today:

▶ `ImmutableArray(Of T)` (This is widely used in developing with the .NET Compiler Platform.)

▶ `ImmutableDictionary(Of TKey, TValue)`

▶ `ImmutableSortedDictionary(Of TKey, TValue)`

▶ `ImmutableHashSet(Of T)`

▶ `ImmutableList(Of T)`

▶ `ImmutableQueue(Of T)`

▶ `ImmutableSortedSet(Of T)`

▶ `ImmutableStack(Of T)`

In Chapter 51, "Code Analysis: The .NET Compiler Platform and Tools," you will see some examples of immutable collections in action.

Iterators

Technically speaking, iterators are used to step through a collection and iterator functions perform custom iterations over a collection. They can have only an `IEnumerable`, `IEnumerable(Of T)`, `IEnumerator`, or `IEnumerator(Of T)` as their return type. Iterators use the new `Yield` keyword to return the item that is currently iterated to the caller code; then the iteration stops at that point. After `Yield` executes, the iteration restarts from that point. With this kind of approach, an iteration over a collection is more responsive and makes items in the collection immediately available to the caller code right after they have been returned. If this technical explanation can seem difficult, let's provide an easier one. Imagine you have a `For..Each` loop that iterates through a collection and returns a list of elements; such a loop is invoked from within a method that needs to make further elaborations over the list of elements returned by the loop. This is a common situation, and the caller method needs to wait until the `For..Each` loop completes the iteration and populates the list of elements before it can use it. If the collection that `For..Each` is iterating is very large, this task can take a lot of time and the caller code will need to wait a while. With iterators, things change for the better; in fact, if you use iterators to loop through a collection, every item in the collection will be immediately sent to the caller via Yield so that the caller can start its elaboration, while the loop is still in progress and goes to completion. In this way an application is faster and more responsive. In the next paragraphs you get more detailed explanations about iterators via some code examples. In addition to providing iterator functions, Visual Basic allows the definition of iterator properties, where the Get accessor can be defined in terms of Yield statements.

ITERATOR FUNCTIONS' SCOPE

Because they are methods, iterator functions can have the same scope of methods. So they can be Private, Public, Friend, Protected, or Protected Friend (except for when they are implemented in Module, where they can be Private, Friend, or Public).

Understanding the Benefits of Iterators in Code

Iterators have plenty of usages, and this chapter describes them all in detail. Before studying the many ways iterators can be useful, though, a better idea is understanding why they allow you to write better and more responsive code. Imagine that you have a collection of items of type Person and a method that iterates through the collection the way you know. Listing 16.1 demonstrates how to reproduce this simple scenario in code.

LISTING 16.1   Iterating Through a Collection the Usual Way

```
Public Class Person
    Public Property FirstName As String
    Public Property LastName As String
    Public Property Age As Integer
End Class


Public Class People
    Inherits List(Of Person)



End Class

Module Module1
    Dim somePeople As New People

    Sub Main()
        'Populates the collection with a million items, for demo purposes
        For i As Integer = 1 To 1000000
            somePeople.Add(New Person With {.FirstName = "First Name: " &
➥i.ToString,

                                            .LastName = "Last Name: " & i.ToString,
                                            .Age = i})
        Next
```

```
    For Each item As Person In GetPeople()
        Console.WriteLine("{0}, {1} of age: {2}", item.FirstName,
                          item.LastName, item.Age.ToString)
    Next
    Console.ReadLine()
End Sub


Function GetPeople() As IEnumerable(Of Person)
    Dim p As New People
    For Each item As Person In somePeople
        p.Add(item)
        Threading.Thread.Sleep(10)
    Next
    Return p
End Function
End Module
```

Notice how a sample collection called People is created and populated with a million items for demo purposes. The GetPeople method iterates through the People collection and returns the result to the caller code (the Main method in this example). The code execution is delayed for 10 milliseconds (via Threading.Thread.Sleep) to force a small delay and provide a demonstration of performance improvement with iterators (in-memory collections are faster than other collections such as database tables, where you could instead face long running query operations). If you run this code, you will see that GetPeople needs to populate the local p collection before returning it as a result to the caller, so you will have to wait for this before being able to iterate the result and see the list of elements in the Console window. You can now rewrite the GetPeople method using iterators, as follows:

```
Iterator Function GetPeople() As IEnumerable(Of Person)
    For Each item As Person In somePeople
        Yield item
        Threading.Thread.Sleep(10)
    Next
End Function
```

This is an iterator function. It requires the Iterator modifier in its definition and returns an object of type IEnumerable(Of T), where T is now Person. If you run the edited code, you will see how every item of type Person is returned from GetPeople immediately and made available to the caller code for further elaborations, while the iteration continues its progress. Figure 16.3 shows a moment of the operation progress. In other words, you will not have to wait for all the iteration to complete before elaborating items that it stores. As a consequence, the whole process is faster and the application is more responsive.

MEASURING PERFORMANCE

You can add a `System.Diagnostics.StopWatch` object to the code and use its `Start` and `Stop` method to measure how much time the process takes and make comparisons between both implementations of `GetPeople`.

Now that you have understood the benefits of iterators, it is time to discuss them in more detail.

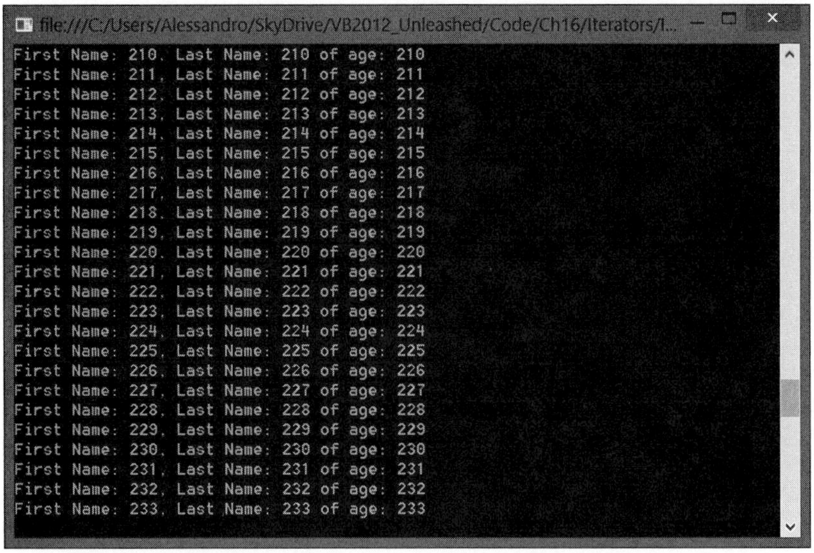

FIGURE 16.3 Iterators return items while the loop is still in progress.

Simple Iterators

You can return elements from iterator functions with multiple `Yield` invocations. The following code demonstrates how to perform a loop over an iterator that returns a collection of strings:

```
Iterator Function StringSeries() As IEnumerable(Of String)
    Yield "First string"
    Yield "Second string"
    Yield "Third string"
    '...
End Function

Sub Main()
    For Each item As String In StringSeries()
        Console.WriteLine(item)
    Next
```

```
        Console.ReadLine()
End Sub
```

You can also use a single `Yield` statement inside a `For..Each` or `For..Next` loop. The following code demonstrates how to retrieve the list of odd numbers in a sequence of integers:

```
Iterator Function OddNumbers(first As Integer,
                  last As Integer) As IEnumerable(Of Integer)
    For number As Integer = first To last
        If number Mod 2 <> 0 Then
            'is odd
            Yield number
        End If
    Next
End Function

Sub Main()
    'Prints 1, 3, 5, 7, 9
    For Each number As Integer In OddNumbers(1, 10)
        Console.WriteLine(number)
    Next

    Console.ReadLine()
End Sub
```

In this case the caller code in the `Sub Main` will not need to wait for a collection of integers to be populated before the iteration occurs; instead, each number that comes from the `Yield` invocation is immediately printed to the Console window.

Exiting from Iterators

You can break the execution of an iterator by using either an `Exit Function` or a `Return` statement. The following snippet demonstrates how to exit from an iterator function:

```
Iterator Function StringSeries() As IEnumerable(Of String)
    Yield "First string"
    Yield "Second string"
    Exit Function 'Return is also accepted
    Yield "Third string"
    '...
End Function
```

Iterators with `Try..Catch..Finally`

Unlike Visual C#, in Visual Basic the `Yield` statement can be executed from within a `Try` statement of a `Try..Catch..Finally` block. The following code demonstrates how to rewrite the `OddNumbers` iterator function including error handling:

```vb
Iterator Function OddNumbers(first As Integer,
                last As Integer) As IEnumerable(Of Integer)
    Try
        For number As Integer = first To last
            If number Mod 2 <> 0 Then
                'is odd
                Yield number
            End If
        Next
    Catch ex As Exception
        Console.WriteLine(ex.Message)
    Finally
        Console.WriteLine("Loop completed.")
    End Try
End Function
```

As you can see, the `Yield` statement is allowed inside the `Try` block.

Anonymous Iterators

Iterators can also be implemented as anonymous methods. These are discussed in more detail in Chapter 20, but for now all you need to know is that they are methods with no name and are defined on-the-fly inside a code block. The following code snippet demonstrates how to implement the previous iterator as an anonymous method:

```vb
'Type of oddSequence is inferred by the compiler
Dim oddSequence = Iterator Function(first As Integer,
                        last As Integer) As IEnumerable(Of Integer)
                Try
                    For number As Integer = first To last
                        If number Mod 2 <> 0 Then
                            'is odd
                            Yield number
                        End If
                    Next
                Catch ex As Exception
                    Console.WriteLine(ex.Message)
                Finally
                    Console.WriteLine("Loop completed.")
                End Try
            End Function
```

```
For Each number As Integer In oddSequence(1, 10)
    Console.WriteLine(number)
Next
```

As you can see, the iterator is defined as an in-line method without an explicit name and its result is assigned to a variable whose type is inferred by the compiler (in this case `IEnumerable(Of Integer)`).

Implementing an Iterator Class

Iterators can be useful in creating classes that act like lists. By implementing the `IEnumerable` interface and the `GetEnumerator` method of this interface, you can write efficient code that takes advantage of iterator functions to yield the content of a list. Listing 16.2 demonstrates how to create a class called `BottlesOfWine` that stores a list of bottles of wine given a name and a color of the wine (red or white). Internally it uses a `List(Of BottleOfWine)` instance, but instead of invoking the usual `GetEnumerator` method of the `List` class (provided by the `IEnumerable` interface that the `List` implements), it returns the list of bottles via an iterator function. It also returns a list of bottles based on their color.

LISTING 16.2   Implementing a Collection Class That Uses Iterators

```
Public Class BottleOfWine
    Property Brand As String
    Property Color As WineColor
End Class


Public Enum WineColor
    Red
    White
End Enum


Public Class BottlesOfWine
    Implements IEnumerable(Of BottleOfWine)


    Private _bottles As New List(Of BottleOfWine)


    Public Function GetEnumerator1() As IEnumerator Implements
➥IEnumerable.GetEnumerator
        Return Me._bottles.GetEnumerator
    End Function


    Public Iterator Function GetEnumerator() As IEnumerator(Of BottleOfWine)
➥Implements IEnumerable.GetEnumerator(Of BottleOfWine)


        'Use Yield instead of List.GetEnumerator
        For Each bottle As BottleOfWine In Me._bottles
```

```
            Yield bottle
        Next
    End Function


    Private Iterator Function BottlesByColor(color As WineColor) As
➥IEnumerable _
            (Of BottleOfWine)
        For Each bottle As BottleOfWine In Me._bottles
            If bottle.Color = color Then
                Yield bottle
            End If
        Next
    End Function


    Public ReadOnly Property RedBottles As IEnumerable(Of BottleOfWine)
        Get
            Return BottlesByColor(WineColor.Red)
        End Get
    End Property


    Public ReadOnly Property WhiteBottles As IEnumerable(Of BottleOfWine)
        Get
            Return BottlesByColor(WineColor.White)
        End Get
    End Property


    Public Sub AddRedBottle(name As String)
        Me._bottles.Add(New BottleOfWine With {.Brand = name, .Color =
➥WineColor.Red})
    End Sub


    Public Sub AddWhiteBottle(name As String)
        Me._bottles.Add(New BottleOfWine With {.Brand = name, .Color =
➥WineColor.White})
    End Sub
End Class
```

By returning with `Yield` the result of both the `GetEnumerator` and of `BottlesByColor` methods, the code is more responsive. You can then use the code easily. For example, you can create a list of bottles of red wine and then iterate the list in a way that is efficient because the result takes advantage of iterators, as in the following code:

```
Dim bottles As New BottlesOfWine
bottles.AddRedBottle("Chianti")
bottles.AddRedBottle("Cabernet")
```

```
'Result is returned via an iterator function
For Each bottle As BottleOfWine In bottles
    Console.WriteLine(bottle.Brand)
Next
```

ITERATORS ARE AN OPPORTUNITY, NOT THE RULE

Iterators provide an additional opportunity to write efficient code, but of course they are not necessary everywhere. You typically use iterators with large collections of objects and over long-running operations. So, they are not a new rule for iterating collections. For this reason, in this book you will find code examples for collections that are not based on iterators, which is instead the general rule. In particular circumstances, samples based on iterators are offered.

Summary

Applications often require data access. You store data within classes and structures, but often you need to group a set of data and collections to help you in this task. The .NET Framework offers both nongeneric collections (such as `ArrayList`, `Queue`, `Stack`, and `HashTable`) and generic ones (such as `List(Of T)`, `ObservableCollection(Of T)`, `Dictionary(Of TKey, TValue)`, `Queue(Of T)`, and `Stack(Of T)`). In both cases you can add, remove, and edit items within collections using the same members (due to the interfaces implementations). Moreover, with the feature of *collection initializers*, you can instantiate and populate collections inline. Although you typically use collections for manipulating data, the .NET Framework provides some special read-only collections, such as `ReadonlyCollection(Of T)`. You learned to create custom collections, which is not an uncommon scenario, and finally you learned a new efficient way to iterate over collections via iterator functions and the `Yield` keyword.

CHAPTER 17

Working with Objects: Visual Tools and Code Sharing

Visual Studio 2015 is the best version ever of the premier developer tool from Microsoft. It offers a powerful code editor with the presence of IntelliSense that dramatically simplifies your coding experience. Writing code and architecting objects before writing code have the same importance, and for this reason Visual Studio lets you reach both objectives easily. On one side, it enables you to graphically design objects for your applications and contextually write code related to such objects. The built-in tool that enables you to perform this task is known as *Class Designer*, and in this chapter you get a high-level overview of it. On the other side, it is not uncommon for you as a developer to realize that you need to implement new objects on-the-fly, such as objects that you did not previously consider but that later become necessary or existing objects that must be extended. In this chapter, you also learn how to use this instrumentation and get the most out of its capabilities. Finally, Visual Studio 2015 has many enhancements that make it easier to share the same code across multiple platforms, which is very important in this world of different kinds of applications and frameworks needing to communicate with one another. So, in this chapter you also learn how to create portable code with portable class libraries and shared projects.

Visual Studio Class Designer

Visual Studio 2015 offers an instrument known as Visual Studio Class Designer that you should already know if you have experience with previous versions. You can design objects in a visual way by taking advantage of a graphical tool. You design objects; Visual Studio generates code. In this chapter, you learn how to design objects according to object-oriented principles using the Class Designer to create a new implementation of the `Person` class and of a couple of derived classes. Before continuing to read, create a new, empty VB project for the Console. This is the base for your subsequent work.

Enabling the Class Designer

To enable the Visual Studio Class Designer, you need to right-click the project name in Solution Explorer and then select **View, View Class Diagram**. When ready, the Class Designer appears as a new window within the IDE and shows a graphical representation of the main application module, including the definition of the `Main` method. All tasks you can perform on the Class Designer can be accomplished by invoking commands exposed by the context menu that you get when right-clicking the designer's surface. Figure 17.1 shows the previously mentioned representation of `Module1` and the available commands.

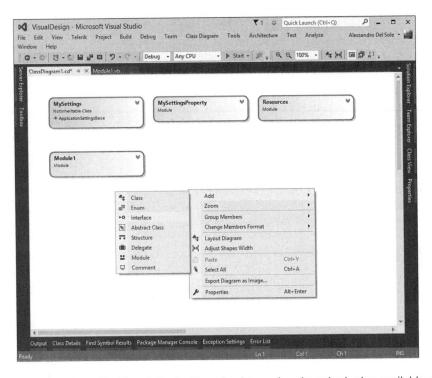

FIGURE 17.1   The Visual Studio Class Designer when launched, plus available commands for design operations.

Figure 17.1 also shows the Add command expanded; it provides a list of available objects that you can add to the diagram. Such objects include classes, enumerations, interfaces, structures, delegates, and modules. You can also select the **Comment** command to add sticky notes on the designer's surface. Table 17.1 summarizes the goal of other commands in the context menu.

TABLE 17.1   Commands List for the Class Designer

Command	Description
Add	Provides subcommands for adding objects to the designer's surface.
Zoom	Enables you to zoom the designer surface for a better visualization.
Group Members	Establishes how objects' members must be grouped. By Kind means that members are divided in types groups (for example, properties, methods, and so on). By Access means that members are grouped according to their scope (for example, all public members, all private members, and so on). Sorted Alphabetically means that objects' members are listed in alphabetical order with no grouping options.
Change Members Format	Sets how members' names appear.
Layout Diagram	Rearranges items on the designer's surface for a better view.
Adjust Shapes Width	Automatically adapts objects' width so that their members' names are more readable.
Export Diagram as Image	Enables you to export the generated diagram as an image, in different formats such as .bmp, .jpg, .png, and .tiff.

CLASS DIAGRAMS FILES

Class diagrams generated with the Visual Studio Class Designer are stored within a .cd file that becomes part of the solution. By default, the file is named ClassDiagram1.cd, but you can rename it as you like via Solution Explorer.

Now it's time to use the Class Designer. Your goal is to design an IPerson interface that an abstract class named Person can implement and that will also be the base class for two other derived classes, Customer and Contact, both created with this interesting graphical tool.

Adding and Designing Objects

The first step to perform is creating an interface. To accomplish this, follow these steps:

1. Right-click the designer surface (see Figure 17.1) and select the **Add, Interface** command.

2. When the New Interface dialog box appears, specify the IPerson name and leave all other options unchanged, which are self-explanatory. Figure 17.2 shows the dialog box. This adds a new item on the designer, representing an interface.

FIGURE 17.2   The New Interface dialog box enables you to specify the name of the new interface and other settings as the access level and the filename.

3. Right-click the new interface and select the **Add, Property** command. For each object type, the context menu provides specific commands related to members the particular object can contain. Figure 17.3 shows how you can accomplish this. When the new property is added to the interface, it is focused and highlighted for renaming, so rename it `FirstName`. Notice that the default type for members is `Integer`; therefore, you need to open the Properties window (by pressing **F4**) and write the appropriate type in the Type field.

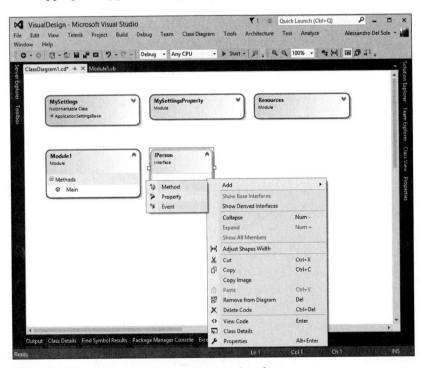

FIGURE 17.3   Adding members to the new interface.

4. Repeat the previous step to add a new `LastName` property and a `FullName` method, both of type `String` The Class Designer implements `Sub` methods by default that are switched to `Function` when you specify a return type via the Properties window. This step is shown in Figure 17.4.

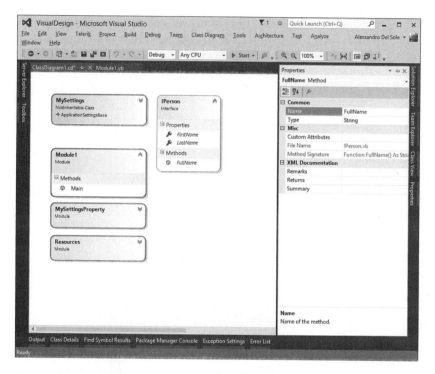

FIGURE 17.4   Specifying a return type for methods and the new completed interface.

If you now double-click the new interface, Visual Studio 2015 shows the code that it generated behind the scenes, as shown in Listing 17.1.

LISTING 17.1   IPerson Interface with Code Generated by Visual Studio

```
Public Interface IPerson
    Property LastName As String
    Property FirstName As String
    Function FullName() As String
End Interface
```

The next step is to add an abstract class named `Person`, which serves as the base class for subsequent classes. To accomplish this, right-click the designer and select the **Add, Abstract Class** command. Name the new class `Person` and, when ready, notice within the designer that is marked as `MustInherit`. Next, double-click the new class and add an

Implements IPerson statement below the class declaration. This ensures that the new class is going to implement the IPerson interface. As you know, when you implement an interface that exposes properties, the code editor provides the full property implementation, so for the sake of clarity, you can change the property implementation to auto-implemented properties. Creating the class and implementing the interface is reflected in the class diagram and confirmed by the appearance of properties and methods defined within the interface inside the new class and by a rounded symbol that identifies an interface relationship. Figure 17.5 shows the result of the preceding operations. Listing 17.2 shows the full code for the Person class.

LISTING 17.2 Code for an Abstract Class

```
Public MustInherit Class Person
    Implements IPerson
    Public Property FirstName As String Implements IPerson.FirstName
    Public MustOverride Function FullName() As String Implements IPerson.FullName
    Public Property LastName As String Implements IPerson.LastName
End Class
```

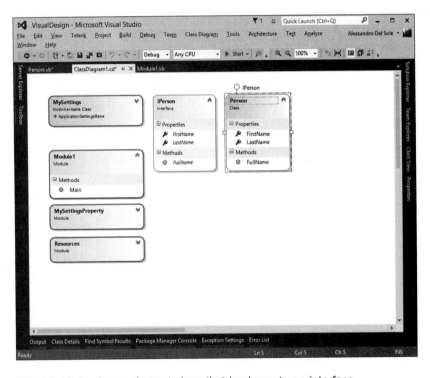

FIGURE 17.5 A new abstract class that implements an interface.

The `FullName` method must be declared as `MustOverride`. The Properties window offers deep control to classes. Table 17.2 summarizes the most important properties except those related to filenames and locations.

TABLE 17.2   Class Control Properties

Property	Description
Access	Used to set class's scope
Name	The class name
Custom attributes	Used to decorate the class with attributes
Inheritance modifiers	Set to MustInherit for an abstract class, to NotInheritable for a sealed class, or to None for a general implementation

The Properties window also offers the Remarks and Summary fields that enable you to specify descriptions under the form of XML comments. This feature is available for all members, not just classes. Also, the Properties window shows the Generic, Implements, and Inherits fields, which are disabled by design.

Implementing Derived Classes

The Class Designer is powerful enough to provide support for class inheritance. Suppose you want to create two classes deriving from `Person`—for example, `Contact` and `Customer`. To create a `Contact` class that inherits from `Person`, follow these steps:

1. Right-click the designer surface and select the **Add, Class** command. When the New Class dialog box appears, specify the class name and leave the other properties unchanged.

2. When the new class is added to the designer's surface, select Inheritance from the Toolbox and connect a line between the `Person` class and the new class. This establishes an inheritance relationship between the two classes. You notice that the designer does not show inherited properties while it is limited to show overridden methods (`FullName` in our example).

3. Add two new properties, `Age` of type `Integer` and `Email` of type `String`, using skills gained in the previous subsection. The result of this implementation is shown in Figure 17.6.

17

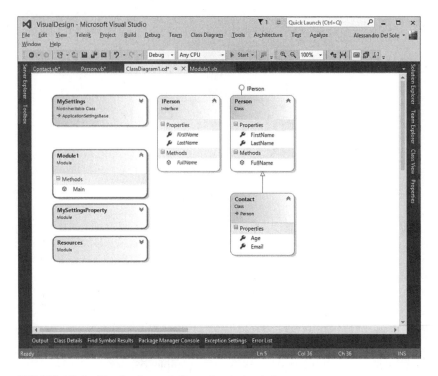

FIGURE 17.6   The implementation of a derived class.

Now create a new Customer class that still inherits from Person following the previous listed steps, adding two new properties: CompanyName of type String and CustomerID of type Integer. The result of this new implementation is shown in Figure 17.7.

To understand how Visual Studio interpreted your operations, click both the Customer and Contact classes. For your convenience, the code of both classes is shown in Listing 17.3.

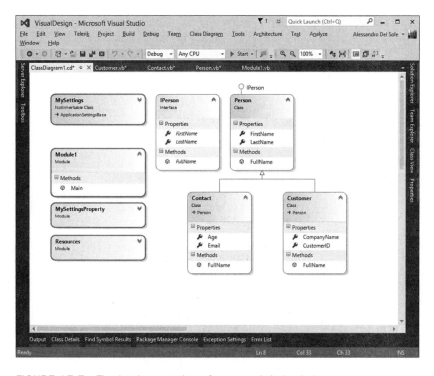

FIGURE 17.7 The implementation of a second derived class.

LISTING 17.3 Code for Derived Classes Generated by the IDE

```
Public Class Contact
    Inherits Person

    Public Property Age As Integer
    Public Property Email As String

    Public Overrides Function FullName() As String
      Throw New NotImplementedException
    End Function
End Class
Public Class Customer
    Inherits Person

    Public Property CustomerID As Integer
    Public Property CompanyName As String
    Public Overrides Function FullName() As String
      Throw New NotImplementedException
    End Function
End Class
```

It's worth noticing how the IDE correctly wrote inheritance code and marked as `Overrides` the `FullName` method in both classes. The generated code can be considered as a mere template; therefore, you have to populate it your own way. To complete your work, you need to write the methods body for `FullName` in both classes. The following is an example related to the `Contact` class:

```
Public Overrides Function FullName() As String
    Return String.Format("{0} {1}, of age: {2}",
                         Me.LastName,
                         Me.FirstName,
                         Me.Age.ToString)
End Function
```

On the other hand, the following is the implementation for the `Customer` class:

```
Public Overrides Function FullName() As String
    Return String.Format("Customer {0} is {1}",
                         Me.CustomerID,
                         Me.CompanyName)
End Function
```

You could also definitely use string interpolation to format strings. Here `String.Format` is used for consistency with previous versions of Visual Basic. In this section you have seen an alternative way for designing classes in Visual Basic 2015. That is important, particularly to get a hierarchical representation. Most of all, such work has been completed with a few mouse clicks.

Creating Multiple Diagrams

You are not limited to creating one diagram. You can add multiple class diagrams to your project so that you can have a graphical representation of a complex hierarchical object's structure. To add diagrams to your project, right-click the project name in Solution Explorer and select the **Add New Item** command. When the Add New Item dialog box appears, select the **Class Diagram** item in the Common Items list (see Figure 17.8).

This can be useful if you have to graphically represent complex frameworks, and if you need large design surfaces.

Exporting the Diagram

As a respectable graphical tool, the Class Designer can export diagrams as images. The tool supports the following image formats:

▶ Windows Bitmap (24 bit)

▶ Portable Network Graphics (.png)

▶ JPEG

▶ Tag Image File Format (.tiff)

▶ Graphics Interchange Format (.gif)

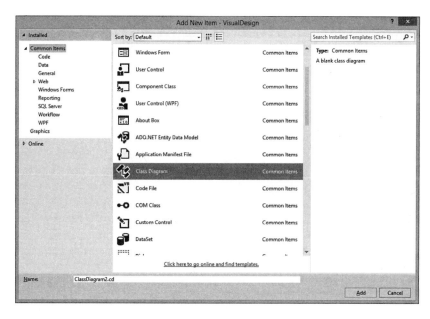

FIGURE 17.8   Adding a new class diagram to the project.

To export diagrams to images, right-click the designer's surface and select the **Export Diagram as Image** command. Figure 17.9 shows the Export Diagram as Image dialog box.

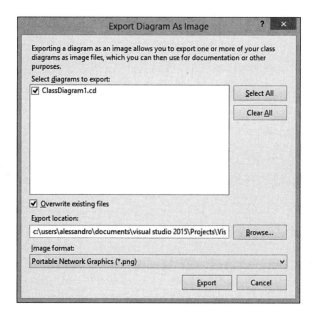

FIGURE 17.9   Exporting diagrams to images.

You can select multiple diagrams if available. You need to select the location, which by default points to the project's folder. The combo box at the bottom of the dialog box enables you to choose the image format.

Class View Window

Since the previous versions of Visual Studio, the IDE offers another graphical tool for managing objects, known as the Class View window. To enable this tool, you can press **Ctrl+Shift+C** if it's not already available as a floating window. It's a browsing tool that shows a graphical representation of the objects' hierarchy in your solution and enables you to search for specific members or get information about types being part of your project, including base types. Figure 17.10 shows this tool window in action, pointing to the same project used in the previous section.

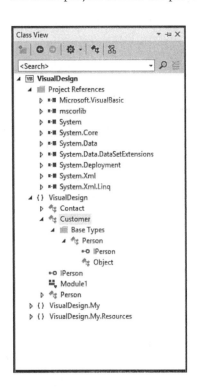

FIGURE 17.10   The Class View tool window.

As you can see in Figure 17.10, the Class View enables you to browse custom objects in your projects (including base types such as interfaces) and built-in objects invoked by your project. Moreover, you can browse references to assemblies and expand them so that you can still get information on members for your custom objects. The Class View window also provides a Settings command that enables you to specify which kind of objects will be shown. (For example, you can decide if the view must include base types.)

Creating Types with Generate from Usage

One great feature in the code editor that Visual Studio 2015 inherits from its predecessors is the ability to generate on-the-fly objects that do not exist yet. This feature is known as Generate from Usage, and now it is integrated within light bulbs and quick actions, described in Chapter 6, "Errors, Exceptions, and Code Refactoring." To understand how it works, create a new Console application named GenerateFromUsage and, within the `Main` method, type the following code:

```
Sub Main()
    Dim p As New Person

End Sub
```

Because the `Person` class has not been implemented, the Visual Basic compiler throws an exception, but if you enable the light bulb, it will suggest possible solutions, as shown in Figure 17.11.

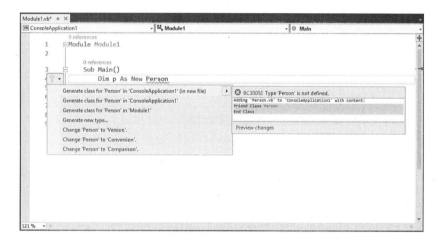

FIGURE 17.11   Suggestions on how to create the Person class.

As you can see in Figure 17.11, the IDE enables you to generate the `Person` class directly when writing code, and it offers several alternatives. More generally, the IDE provides the following possibilities:

▶ The new type is generated inside a separate code file in the current project. In this case, the option is **Generate Class for 'Person' in 'GenerateFromUsage' (in new file)**.

▶ The new type is generated in the current code file. In this case, the option is **Generate Class for 'Person' in 'GenerateFromUsage'**.

▶ The new type is generated in the current container, such as a module or class (not a structure). In this case, the option is **Generate Class for 'Person' in 'Module1'**.

For each possible solution, the light bulb shows a preview. There is also another option, **Generate new type**, which allows you to generate any type in a more detailed way; it is discussed later in this chapter. Now focus on the first choice and click the **Generate Class for Person in 'GenerateFromUsage'** option. Visual Studio creates a new code file named Person.vb that you can find in Solution Explorer as part of the project. This code file contains a basic definition for the Person class that is declared as follows:

```
Friend Class Person
End Class
```

DEFAULT ACCESSIBILITY

When generating objects on-the-fly, Visual Studio assigns the default visibility to both objects and members. If you want to provide a different scope, you need to do it by writing qualifiers manually or by selecting the Generate Other command.

Now go back to the Main method; you notice that the error message disappeared. Type the following assignment:

```
p.LastName = "Del Sole"
```

Because the LastName property is not exposed by the Person class, the Visual Basic compiler throws a new error still offering solutions, as shown in Figure 17.12.

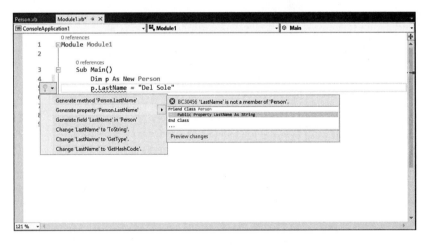

FIGURE 17.12   Generating members on-the-fly.

The IDE correctly recognizes the assignment and proposes adding a new method, property, or field in the Person class. Click the Generate property Person.LastName to add a new property that is implemented in the Person class as follows:

```
Friend Class Person
    Public Property LastName As String
```

The IDE also correctly specifies the data type to the property (`String` in the preceding example) based on the assignment content. Repeat this last step to add a second property named `FirstName` of type `String` using your first name for convenience. My code looks like the following:

```
p.LastName = "Del Sole"
p.FirstName = "Alessandro"
```

Now you should provide a method that returns the full name for the person. Generating a method stub is also an easy task. Write the following:

```
Dim fullName As String = p.FullName
```

Now the IDE offers two solutions, as shown in Figure 17.13. You can choose to generate a method or a property. The IDE can distinguish which kind of solutions it can propose in that particular coding scenario. Click the **Generate Method 'Person.FullName'** option, and Visual Studio implements the `FullName` method as follows:

```
Friend Function FullName() As String
    Throw New NotImplementedException
End Function
```

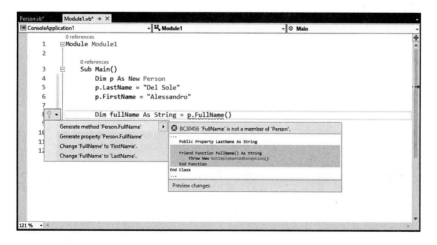

FIGURE 17.13   Generating a new method stub.

The new method throws a `NotImplementedException`; therefore, you need to replace it with code such as the following:

```
Friend Function FullName() As String
    Return $"{LastName} {FirstName}"
End Function
```

Now you have generated your definitely working `Person` class without exiting from the code editor. This is the most basic approach to the new feature, but this tooling is powerful and enables you to define different kinds of objects according to the context in which you are writing code. This is what the next sections discuss.

Generating Shared Members

Visual Studio is intelligent enough to understand whenever you try to define a shared member. For example, imagine you want to implement a method that returns the number of active instances of the `Person` class. If you type the following code:

```
Person.ReturnInstanceCount()
```

and then select the **Generate Method 'Person.ReturnInstanceCount'** correction option, Visual Studio generates the following code:

```
Friend Shared Sub ReturnInstanceCount()
    Throw New NotImplementedException
End Sub
```

For other members, you will be able to see a preview in the light bulb.

On-the-Fly Code and Object Initializers

You might often use object initializers to create objects instances in line; generating code on-the-fly is powerful. Consider the following declaration:

```
Dim p As New Person With {.FirstName = "Alessandro",
                          .LastName = "Del Sole"}
```

When you write this code, the `Person` class and its `FirstName` and `LastName` properties do not exist. At this point, you can open the correction options and select the Generate Class command. Visual Studio automatically associates the previous assignments with the class that is initialized in line and generates the appropriate members. Code generation for the previous code snippet produces the following result:

```
Class Person
    Property LastName As String
    Property FirstName As String


End Class
```

With a single mouse click, you have accomplished a task that would normally require a couple more steps, as described in the previous section.

Generating Complex Objects

You can now generate new objects on-the-fly by using default solutions proposed by Visual Studio. You are not limited to generating previously described classes and members. Visual Studio enables you to generate the following types:

- ▶ Classes
- ▶ Structures
- ▶ Interfaces
- ▶ Delegates
- ▶ Enumerations

The following is instead the list of members you can generate for the preceding types:

- ▶ Methods
- ▶ Properties
- ▶ Fields

You can generate objects on-the-fly by running the Generate Type dialog box, which you can activate by choosing **Generate New Type** instead of Generate Class. For example, imagine you want to generate a new structure on-the-fly. First, type the following line of code:

```
Dim threeDim As New ThreePoint
```

Because the `ThreePoint` type does not exist, Visual Studio 2015 throws an error proposing fixes. At this point, click the **Generate New Type** solution, as shown in Figure 17.14.

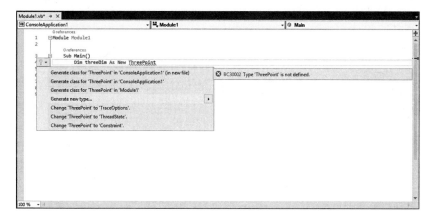

FIGURE 17.14   Selecting the Generate New Type command for constructing different types.

17

The Generate Type window displays, which enables you to get deeper control over the type generation, as shown in Figure 17.15.

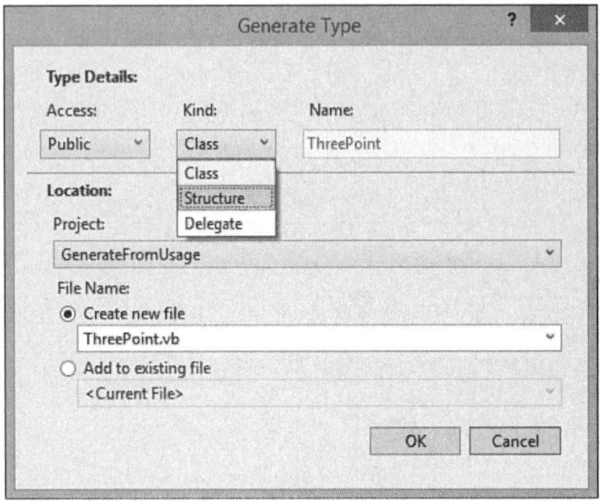

FIGURE 17.15   The Generate Type dialog box.

Several options are available for generating a new type. First, the Access combo box enables you to specify the accessibility level that can be Public, Friend, or the default level for the selected type. The Kind combo box enables you to specify which type you intend to generate. Figure 17.15 also shows a list of available types. For our example, select **Public visibility**. In the lower part of the dialog box, you can establish where the type must be declared and in which file. You can select which project (if the solution contains more than one project) defines the new type and which code file declares the new type.

Here it's worth mentioning that you can decide to create a new file or add the code to an existing one using the Add to Existing File control box (default choice). When you click **OK**, the new type is created. Visual Studio generates the following structure declaration:

```
Public Structure ThreePoint

End Structure
```

Now you can repeat the steps you performed when you added members to the `Person` class in the first section of this chapter. For example, first write the following code:

```
ThreePoint.X = 10
ThreePoint.Y = 20
ThreePoint.Z = 30
```

None of the X, Y, and Z properties has been implemented yet within the `ThreePoint` structure; therefore, you can add them via the correction options. (Refer to Figure 17.12 for a recap.)

Interfaces Additions

The Visual Studio 2015 IDE offers default solutions according to naming conventions it finds in your code. This is particularly true if you want to generate interfaces instead of other types. For example, if you type

```
Dim interfaceVariable as ITestInterface
```

The IDE notices that `ITestInterface`'s identifier begins with the letter *I* and is followed by another capital letter; therefore, it assumes you want to generate an interface (if the second letter is not capital, it would offer to generate a class). Because of this, the default solution in the correction options will not be Generate Class, but Generate Interface. The stub for the new interface is the following:

```
Friend Interface ITestInterface
End Interface
```

If you want to change the accessibility level for the new interface, you need to generate it invoking the Generate New Type window or writing the appropriate qualifier manually.

Creating Portable Classes

Throughout the years, a number of platforms have built on subsets of the .NET Framework have been produced, such as (but not limited to) Windows Phone, the Windows Runtime for Windows 8.x, and the upcoming Windows 10. Because of this, one of the biggest concerns for developers is creating class libraries that can share the same code across multiple platforms. So far, developers have had to remember which assemblies and what kind of types were supported in each of those platforms and then manually create and arrange class library projects to make them reusable. Fortunately, Visual Studio 2015 helps Visual Basic developers solve this problem by providing a project template called Portable Class Library. This project template enables you to create portable libraries that only reference assemblies that are common to the following platforms:

▶ .NET Framework 4.5.x

▶ Silverlight 5

▶ Windows Phone Silverlight 8 and Windows Phone Silverlight 8.1

▶ Windows 8 and Windows 8.1 Store apps

▶ Windows Phone 8.1

ADDITIONAL TARGETS

This list of targets refers to Visual Studio 2015 Release Candidate, which is the latest release used to write this chapter. Visual Studio 2015 RTM might possibly add other targets, such as .NET 4.6, .NET Core, and Windows 10.

You will not be able to take advantage of all the types and members offered by a specific platform, but you will be sure that what you have available in a portable class library will run on all the aforementioned platforms with no effort. You create a portable class library by selecting **File**, **New**, **Project** and then selecting the Portable Class Library project template in the Add New Project dialog box, as demonstrated in Figure 17.16.

FIGURE 17.16   Creating a new portable class library.

After specifying a name for the project and clicking **OK**, Visual Studio will ask you to select the target platforms. By default, the project will target .NET 4.5, Windows 8, Windows Phone Silverlight 8, and Windows Phone 8.1, as represented in Figure 17.17.

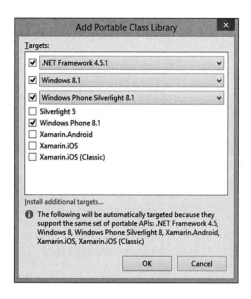

FIGURE 17.17   Specifying platforms that the portable library will target.

You can easily see which assemblies and namespaces are part of a portable library by expanding the References node in Solution Explorer and then double-clicking the **.NET** item, which will be opened in the Object Browser (see Figure 17.18) with the name .NET Portable Subset.

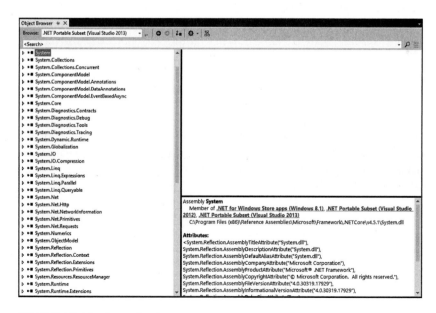

FIGURE 17.18   Investigating the portable assemblies' subset.

Of course, not all the assemblies are supported on all the platforms. You can get a full comparison between platforms and supported assemblies by visiting http://msdn. microsoft.com/en-us/library/gg597391(v=vs.110).aspx. Visual Studio 2015 adds references only to assemblies that are supported by all the selected platforms. If you try to add a reference to an assembly that is not supported by all the selected platforms, then you will get a warning.

Creating a Sample Portable Library

WHAT THIS SECTION ASSUMES ABOUT YOU

The sample demonstrated in this section assumes you already have experience with either WPF or Windows Store apps (or both), and the reason is that this section explains concepts such as the MVVM pattern that requires existing knowledge of how the data-binding works in XAML code, of what a command is in those technologies, and knowledge of other concepts specific to WPF and Windows 8.1 that it is not possible to summarize in a short chapter. Part V, "Building Windows Desktop Applications," provides guidance about WPF, so turn there if you first want to learn more about this particular platform.

Even if having an opportunity of sharing the same code across multiple platforms is obviously a great benefit at a more general level, the Portable Class Library template has a couple of specific purposes: making interaction with Windows Communication Foundation (WCF) services easier and providing portable implementations of the Model-View-ViewModel (MVVM) pattern. This pattern is very popular among developers using XAML-based platforms like WPF, Silverlight, Windows Phone, and Windows 8 because it enables them to achieve a high level of separation between data business objects (the model), the business logic (view models), and the user interface (the view) built upon XAML. So, even though you can create portable libraries for different purposes, the most common is making MVVM-based objects as reusable as possible. The MVVM pattern is not typically intended for beginners, so this section shows an example that is intended for an intermediate audience with existing experience on the WPF or Windows 8.x platforms. That said, create a new project based on the Portable Class Library template and name it ContactLibrary. The goal of the library is exposing a simplified contact management framework. When creating the project, ensure that you are targeting the following platforms: .NET 4.5, Windows 8.1, and Windows Phone 8.1. This will make the project incompatible with Visual Studio 2010, but that is fine at this point because you are working with Visual Studio 2015. The reason you are also adding support for Windows Phone 8.1, even if the sample solution will not contain a project targeting this platform, is that Windows Phone 8.1 and Windows 8.1 share the same Runtime, and so the same code could be easily reused in a Windows Phone application.

The Model

When the project is ready in Visual Studio 2015, add a new class called Contact; see the code in Listing 17.4.

LISTING 17.4   Defining the Model: A Contact Class

```
Public Class Contact
    Public Property ContactID() As Integer
    Public Property FirstName() As String
    Public Property LastName As String
    Public Property EmailAddress As String
    Public Property PhysicalAddress As String
    Public Property Phone() As String
End Class
```

The class is a simplified business object to represent a contact. Next, add a class called Contacts, which is a collection of Contact objects. The code shown in Listing 17.5 demonstrates its implementation.

LISTING 17.5   Defining the Model: A Collection of Contacts

```
Public Class Contacts
    Private _contacts As ObservableCollection(Of Contact)

    Public Sub New()
        Me._contacts = New ObservableCollection(Of Contact)
        'Create some sample data
        Me._contacts.Add(New Contact With {.ContactID = 1, .FirstName =
"Alessandro",
                                    .LastName = "Del Sole",
                                    .EmailAddress = _
                                    "alessandro.delsole@visual-basic.it",
                                    .Phone = "111-111-111",
                                    .PhysicalAddress = "Cremona"})

        Me._contacts.Add(New Contact With {.ContactID = 2, .FirstName = "Renato",
                                    .LastName = "Marzaro",
                                    .EmailAddress = _
                                    "renato.marzaro@visual-basic.it",
                                    .Phone = "222-111-111",
                                    .PhysicalAddress = "Varese"})

        Me._contacts.Add(New Contact With {.ContactID = 3, .FirstName = "Diego",
                                    .LastName = "Cattaruzza",
                                    .EmailAddress = _
                                    "dcattaruzza@visual-basic.it",
                                    .Phone = "222-222-111",
                                    .PhysicalAddress = "Trieste"})
```

```
      Me._contacts.Add(New Contact With {.ContactID = 4, .FirstName = "Antonio",
                                          .LastName = "Catucci",
                                          .EmailAddress = _
                                          "antonio.catucci@visual-basic.it",
                                          .Phone = "222-111-222",
                                          .PhysicalAddress = "Milan"})


    End Sub

    Public Function GetContacts() As ObservableCollection(Of Contact)
        Return Me._contacts
    End Function

End Class
```

The code in Listing 17.5 creates some sample contacts in the constructor and populates a collection of type `ObservableCollection(Of Contact)`. Assuming you already have experience with WPF or Windows 8.x, you might know that this is the most appropriate collection for binding data to the user interface because it supports change notification. Both the `Contact` and `Contacts` class represent our data, so they are the *Model* in the MVVM implementation. In a typical MVVM implementation, you need to add a class called `RelayCommand` (by convention), which implements the `ICommand` interface. Such an interface is typical in WPF and Windows 8.x and enables you to implement commands— that is, actions that can be executed in the desired circumstance. Implementing `ICommand` requires exposing a method called `Execute` (which represents the action to take when the command is invoked) and another method called `CanExecute` (which returns `Boolean` and establishes whether the command can be executed). With the `RelayCommand` class, the code relays the command logic by implementing a generic handler that will launch the action required by every command in the library. The code in Listing 17.6 demonstrates how to implement the `RelayCommand` class.

LISTING 17.6   Relaying the Command Logic

```
Imports System.Windows.Input

Public Class RelayCommand
    Implements ICommand

    Private _isEnabled As Boolean
    Private ReadOnly _handler As Action

    Public Sub New(handler As Action)
        _handler = handler
    End Sub

    Public Event CanExecuteChanged As EventHandler
```

```
Implements ICommand.CanExecuteChanged

    Public Property IsEnabled() As Boolean
        Get
            Return _isEnabled
        End Get
        Set(value As Boolean)
            If (value <> _isEnabled) Then
                _isEnabled = value
                RaiseEvent CanExecuteChanged(Me, EventArgs.Empty)
            End If
        End Set
    End Property

    Public Function CanExecute(parameter As Object) As Boolean Implements
ICommand.CanExecute
        Return IsEnabled
    End Function

    Public Sub Execute(parameter As Object) Implements ICommand.Execute
        _handler()
    End Sub

End Class
```

Notice how the CanExecute method returns a Boolean value that is set by the caller code. Finally, notice how Execute invokes a generic handler under the form of an instance of the Action class—that is, the actual command.

View Models

You now need an intermediate layer that contains the business logic and that exposes data and commands to the user interface. The goal is in fact separating the business logic from the user interface so that the latter will not interact directly with the data. The reason for this separation is making data and business logic abstracted from the UI and, therefore, reusable. By convention, you create a ViewModelBase class that is the base class for all other view models. The code in Listing 17.7 demonstrates how to create the ViewModelBase class and how to create a derived view model specific for the Contacts collection, which exposes data and commands (see comments in the code for explanations).

LISTING 17.7   Defining View Models

```
Imports System.ComponentModel
Imports System.Collections.ObjectModel

'Generic View Model
```

```vb
Public MustInherit Class ViewModelBase
    Implements INotifyPropertyChanged

    Public Event PropertyChanged As PropertyChangedEventHandler Implements
INotifyPropertyChanged.PropertyChanged

    'Raise a property change notification
    Protected Overridable Sub OnPropertyChanged(propname As String)
        RaiseEvent PropertyChanged(Me, New PropertyChangedEventArgs(propname))
    End Sub
End Class

Public Class ContactViewModel
    Inherits ViewModelBase

    Private _currentContact As Contact
    Private _contactList As Contacts

    Public Sub New()
        Me._contactList = New Contacts
        Me._contacts = Me._contactList.GetContacts

        SetupCommands()
    End Sub

    'Set up commands by creating instances of RelayCommand
    'and passing the appropriate delegate
    Private Sub SetupCommands()
        AddContactCommand = New RelayCommand(AddressOf AddContact)
        AddContactCommand.IsEnabled = True      End Sub

    'Expose the command
    Public Property AddContactCommand() As RelayCommand

    'Expose the list of contact
    Public Property Contacts() As ObservableCollection(Of Contact)

    'Represents the currently selected contact
    'Raise a property change notification
    'Enable the command
    Public Property CurrentContact() As Contact
        Get
            Return _currentContact
        End Get
        Set(value As Contact)
            _currentContact = value
```

```
            OnPropertyChanged("CurrentContact")
              DeleteContactCommand.IsEnabled = True
        End Set
    End Property

    'Add a new contact. In the real world, accept values
    'from the user input
    Public Sub AddContact()
        Me.Contacts.Add(New Contact With {.FirstName = "Robert",
                          .LastName = "White",
                          .EmailAddress = "robert.white@something.com",
                          .PhysicalAddress = "Rome",
                          .Phone = "123-456-789", .ContactID = 10})
    End Sub
End Class
```

It is important to remember that a good view model exposes collections of data only via
`ObservableCollection(Of T)` objects.

The View

The View represents the user interface in a client application and is typically based on
XAML code, which means WPF or Windows Store applications. The goal of the example
is to demonstrate how two different clients can share not only the same implementation
of the model and view model, but also the same XAML code. For a better understanding, add a WPF project and a Blank App project for Windows 8.1 to the current solution,
both for Visual Basic. In both projects, add a reference to the ContactsLibrary project
(for the Silverlight project the reference must be added to the client project, not the web
one). Both applications will show a data grid and a button that will enable you to delete
the selected contact in the data grid. In the WPF project, the XAML code for the main
window is represented in Listing 17.8.

LISTING 17.8   Defining a View in WPF

```
<Window x:Class="MainWindow"
    xmlns="http://schemas.microsoft.com/winfx/2006/xaml/presentation"
    xmlns:x="http://schemas.microsoft.com/winfx/2006/xaml"
    Title="MainWindow" Height="350" Width="525">
    <Grid>
        <Grid.RowDefinitions>
            <RowDefinition/>
            <RowDefinition Height="40"/>
        </Grid.RowDefinitions>
        <DataGrid Name="ContactsDataGrid" ItemsSource="{Binding Contacts}"
                AutoGenerateColumns="True" SelectedItem="{Binding
➥CurrentContact}"/>
        <Button Name="AddButton" Command="{Binding AddContactCommand}"
```

```
                    Width="100" Height="30" Grid.Row="1"
                    Content="Add"/>
        </Grid>
</Window>
```

The `DataGrid` control is data-bound to the `Contacts` collection of the view model, and the `SelectedItem` property is bound to the `CurrentContact` property of the same view model. The `Button` control does not work with a `Click` event; instead it is bound to the `AddContactCommand` command. This makes it so the user interface does not have to work directly against the data. Listing 17.9 shows the user interface in the Windows 8.1 client.

LISTING 17.9   Defining a View in Windows 8.1

```
<Page
    x:Class="App1.MainPage"
    xmlns="http://schemas.microsoft.com/winfx/2006/xaml/presentation"
    xmlns:x="http://schemas.microsoft.com/winfx/2006/xaml"
    xmlns:local="using:App1"
    xmlns:d="http://schemas.microsoft.com/expression/blend/2008"
    xmlns:mc="http://schemas.openxmlformats.org/markup-compatibility/2006"
    mc:Ignorable="d">

    <Grid Background="{ThemeResource ApplicationPageBackgroundThemeBrush}">
        <GridView Name="ContactsView" ItemsSource="{Binding Contacts}"
                  SelectedItem="{Binding CurrentContact}">
            <GridView.ItemTemplate>
                <DataTemplate>
                    <StackPanel Orientation="Vertical">
                        <TextBlock Text="{Binding FirstName}"/>
                        <TextBlock Text="{Binding LastName}"/>
                        <TextBlock Text="{Binding EmailAddress}"/>
                        <TextBlock Text="{Binding Phone}"/>
                    </StackPanel>
                </DataTemplate>
            </GridView.ItemTemplate>
        </GridView>
    </Grid>
    <Page.BottomAppBar>
        <CommandBar>
            <CommandBar.PrimaryCommands>
                <AppBarButton Command="{Binding AddContactCommand}"
                              Icon="Add" Name="AddButton" Label="Add"/>
            </CommandBar.PrimaryCommands>
        </CommandBar>
    </Page.BottomAppBar>
</Page>
```

The final step is creating an instance of the view model in the code-behind. The following code shows how to implement the constructor in the WPF project:

```
Public Sub New()

    ' This call is required by the designer.
    InitializeComponent()

    ' Add any initialization after the InitializeComponent() call.
    Me.DataContext = New ContactLibrary.ContactViewModel

End Sub
```

In Windows Store apps, instead of assigning an instance of the view model to the page's constructor, a better approach is to perform this task in the `OnNavigatedTo` method, which is invoked every time the user opens this page using navigation controls in your app:

```
Protected Overrides Sub OnNavigatedTo(e As NavigationEventArgs)
    DataContext = New ContactViewModel
End Sub
```

If you now run both the applications, you will see how they show a similar user interface and how they are able to perform exactly the same operations against the data collection, which has been possible due to the portable class library and the MVVM pattern. Figure 17.19 shows the WPF application in action, whereas Figure 17.20 shows the Windows 8.1 one, running inside the Windows Simulator.

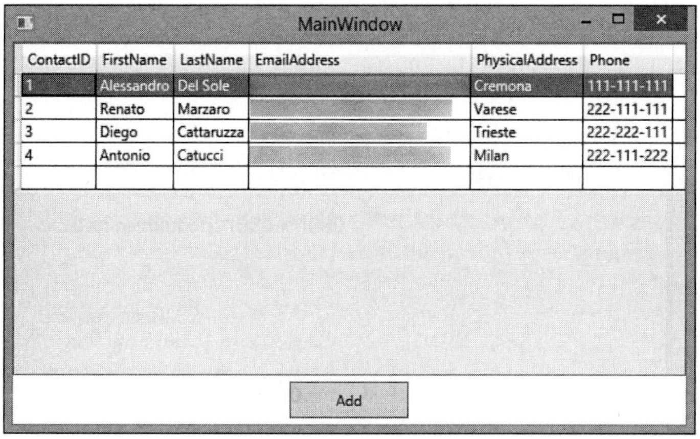

FIGURE 17.19   The WPF client in action.

FIGURE 17.20   The Windows 8.1 client in action.

You might now understand why it is so important to have an opportunity to share code across different platforms and how the Portable Class Library project template makes it easy in Visual Studio 2015. It is worth mentioning that Visual Studio 2015 has support for portable libraries targeting only Windows 8.1 and Windows Phone 8.1. This option, first introduced with Visual Studio 2013 Update 2, makes a portable library incompatible with Visual Studio 2012 and earlier. However, this particular scenario provides a common way to build the so-called universal Windows apps and allows you to conveniently share code, XAML resources, and assets across Windows and Windows Phone apps. For more about universal Windows apps, see http://msdn.microsoft.com/en-us/library/windows/apps/dn609832.aspx.

THE STORY OF UNIVERSAL APPS AND WINDOWS 10

At this writing, Windows 10 is currently under development and available to the general public as a Technical Preview that you can try as part of the Windows Insider program. Windows 10 reimagines the way developers build Windows Store apps, and this affects portable libraries as well. From a Windows 10 perspective, portable libraries will target *universal Windows apps*. These are true universal, meaning that you have one single project and a single application that runs on Windows 10 for mobile or for desktop; this is different from Windows 8.1/Phone 8.1, where you have two different binaries. In Windows 10, if you want to write a portable library that can be consumed by both Windows 10 for mobile and for desktop, you simply create a Class Library (Windows Universal). If you want to write a library that can be consumed by both Windows Phone 8.1 and Windows 10 for mobile, you need to create a Windows Phone 8.1 class library.

Deploying Portable Libraries

To deploy portable libraries, you need to add libraries as dependencies in the setup procedure you create. Visual Studio 2015 enables you to deploy applications via InstallShield Limited Edition and ClickOnce, as described in Chapter 49, "Setup and Deployment Projects with InstallShield for Visual Studio," and Chapter 50, "Deploying Applications with ClickOnce." You can find information on adding dependencies in those chapters as well as in the MSDN documentation, which also explains some hints for Silverlight clients and is available at http://msdn.microsoft.com/en-us/library/gg597391(v=vs.110).aspx.

Shared Projects

Shared projects are new project templates that easily allow you to share code, resources, and assets across multiple project types. Shared projects were introduced for the first time with Visual Studio 2013 Update 2, but they were intended for supporting universal Windows apps development only, and they were not available in Visual Basic. In Visual Studio 2015, shared projects come to Visual Basic, too, and they can be consumed by the following project types:

- ▶ Windows Presentation Foundation, Windows Forms, and Console apps
- ▶ Windows 8.1 and Windows Phone 8.1 apps
- ▶ Windows Phone 8.0 and 8.1 Silverlight apps
- ▶ Portable class libraries

WHAT THIS SECTION ASSUMES ABOUT YOU

This section assumes that you already have some experience with XAML-based development platforms. Even if shared projects are not strictly related to XAML and could definitely also be used to share code between two or more Windows Forms projects, sharing XAML is one of their biggest benefits and a common scenario, so this chapter provides an example about this situation.

Shared projects differ from portable class libraries in that they do not generate any .dll assembly, and they do not target any specific .NET subset. They simply are loose assortments of files that are added to whichever projects reference them, as if they were linked files. Then, when compiling your solution, the MSBuild tool executes against shared projects with the same rules as for linked files. The great benefit of shared projects is that they provide an easy opportunity way to share code files, assets such as images, and also resources like XAML templates.

TARGETING VISUAL BASIC AND C#

Shared projects are language specific. This means that a shared project created with Visual Basic cannot be consumed by a C# application and vice versa.

Before diving any further into shared projects, you need to create a new sample solution, so follow these steps:

1. Select **File, New Project**.

2. In the New Project dialog, expand the **Other Project Types, Visual Studio Solutions** node.

3. Select the **Blank Solution** template.

4. Create a new solution called Contacts.

The goal of the sample solution is to replicate the portable library example but with a different approach that also demonstrates how to share XAML resources.

Creating Shared Projects

Shared projects are available through specific templates. To open one, select **File, Add, New Project** and in the New Project dialog select the **Shared Project** template, as shown in Figure 17.21.

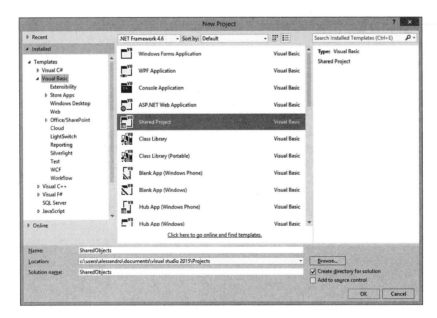

FIGURE 17.21   Creating a shared project.

Call the new project **SharedObjects** and click **OK**. When the project is ready, you can see in Solution Explorer that the project icon is different from other project types. It also has no references and, more generally, no child elements (see Figure 17.22).

FIGURE 17.22   The new shared project as it appears in Solution Explorer.

The project file for a shared project has the .shproj extension and contains the MSBuild rules used for compilation. Another file with the .projitems extension contains the list of files to share. Commonly, items you want to share are organized into subfolders. If you want to share some Visual Basic code, plus a XAML template and an image, you should create three subfolders called Code, Resources, and Assets. Then you can add some code that will be consumed by different client applications.

Sharing Code

In order to share code, your code needs to be supported by the project types that will reference shared projects. For instance, all classes and objects created in the previous ContactsLibrary sample are supported. Therefore, to the Code subfolder you should add all the code from Listings 17.4 through 17.7. Of course, you could create additional subfolders for the model and view models, but keep it simple for now.

Note that you have to add the required `Imports` directives manually because shared projects do not target any specific .NET subsets. For instance, you need an `Imports System. Collections.ObjectModel` directive in order to use the `ObservableCollection` class. After you have performed such additions, your shared project should look as shown in Figure 17.23.

17

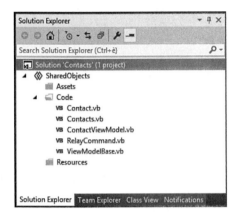

FIGURE 17.23   The shared project now has some code to share.

Sharing XAML Resources

One of the most important reasons to use shared projects is that it means you can share XAML resources such as styles, control templates, and data templates. The shared project example you're working with has the purpose of sharing a data template, for presenting data to other clients. The best way of sharing XAML resources is to use a resource dictionary. To do this, right-click the **Resources** subfolder in Solution Explorer and then select **Add, New Item**. Select the Resource Dictionary template (see Figure 17.24). You can leave the default name unchanged and click **OK**.

FIGURE 17.24   A resource dictionary allows you to share XAML resources.

The resource dictionary includes the following directive, which is specific to Windows Store and Windows Phone apps:

```
xmlns:local="using:SharedObjects"
```

If the sample project will be consumed by a WPF and a Windows Store app, you must remove this directive. You also need to add a `DataTemplate` object that provides a way to present information from each contact in the `Contacts` collection. Listing 17.10 shows the full code for the resource dictionary.

LISTING 17.10   Sharing a Data Template with a Resource Dictionary

```xml
<ResourceDictionary
    xmlns="http://schemas.microsoft.com/winfx/2006/xaml/presentation"
    xmlns:x="http://schemas.microsoft.com/winfx/2006/xaml">
  <DataTemplate x:Key="ContactTemplate">
    <StackPanel Orientation="Vertical" Margin="5">
        <TextBlock Text="{Binding FirstName}"/>
        <TextBlock Text="{Binding LastName}"/>
        <TextBlock Text="{Binding EmailAddress}"/>
        <TextBlock Text="{Binding Phone}"/>
    </StackPanel>
  </DataTemplate>
</ResourceDictionary>
```

By using this approach, you can write a data template, style, or control template once, and it will then be available to all clients that reference the shared project.

Sharing Assets

Assets are general-purpose files that an application might need, such as images, text files, and videos, among many others. Sharing assets with shared projects is an easy task. For example, suppose you want to share an image between two projects. Right-click the **Assets** folder in Solution Explorer and then select **Add Existing Item** and add an image file of your choice in one of the supported formats, such as .jpg, .png, or .gif. To share the selected image with a WPF project, to make the image usable, you must open the Properties window and change the value of **Copy to Output Directory** from **Do Not Copy** to **Copy if Newer**.

Now you have done everything you need to do in the shared project, and you are ready to see how to use it from client applications.

Consuming Shared Projects

You enable client applications to consume shared projects by simply adding a reference. Let's start with a WPF project. By following the same steps you follow with portable libraries, add a new WPF project to the current solution and give it any name you like. You must add a reference to the shared project. When you right-click **References** in Solution Explorer and then select **Add Reference**, the Reference Manager shows up, offering a new node called Shared Projects, as you can see in Figure 17.25.

17

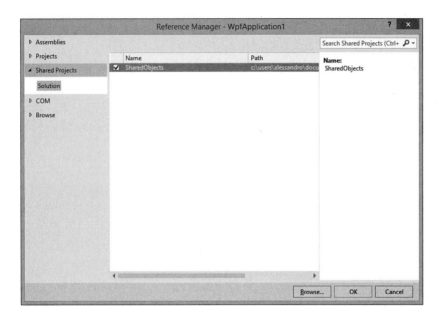

FIGURE 17.25   Adding a reference to a shared project.

Because a shared project does not produce an external assembly, you can only add references to shared projects in the current solution. The first thing you need to do at this point is add a reference to the resource dictionary in the shared project. You can do this in the Application.xaml file, as shown in Listing 17.11.

LISTING 17.11   Referencing a Resource Dictionary

```
<Application x:Class="Application"
    xmlns="http://schemas.microsoft.com/winfx/2006/xaml/presentation"
    xmlns:x="http://schemas.microsoft.com/winfx/2006/xaml"
    xmlns:local="clr-namespace:WpfApplication1"
    StartupUri="MainWindow.xaml">
    <Application.Resources>
        <ResourceDictionary>
            <ResourceDictionary.MergedDictionaries>
                <ResourceDictionary Source="/Resources/Dictionary1.xaml"/>
            </ResourceDictionary.MergedDictionaries>
        </ResourceDictionary>
    </Application.Resources>
</Application>
```

As you know, any resource dictionaries must be merged into one resource dictionary inside the Application.Resources node, taking advantage of the ResourceDictionary.

`MergedDictionaries` collection. The next step is to prepare the user interface. Listing 17.12 shows how you define the UI for the WPF application.

LISTING 17.12   The UI for the WPF Application

```
<Window x:Class="MainWindow"
        xmlns="http://schemas.microsoft.com/winfx/2006/xaml/presentation"
        xmlns:x="http://schemas.microsoft.com/winfx/2006/xaml"
        xmlns:d="http://schemas.microsoft.com/expression/blend/2008"
        xmlns:mc="http://schemas.openxmlformats.org/markup-compatibility/2006"
        xmlns:local="clr-namespace:WpfApplication1"
        mc:Ignorable="d"
        Title="MainWindow" Height="350" Width="525">
    <Grid>
        <Grid.RowDefinitions>
            <RowDefinition Height="90"/>
            <RowDefinition/>
            <RowDefinition Height="40"/>
        </Grid.RowDefinitions>
        <Image Name="BannerImage" Source="../SharedObjects/Assets/People.png"/>
        <ListBox Name="ContactsBox" Grid.Row="1"
                ItemsSource="{Binding Contacts}"
                ItemTemplate="{StaticResource ContactTemplate}"/>
        <Button Name="AddButton" Width="120" Height="30"
                Command="{Binding AddContactCommand}"
                Grid.Row="2" Content="Add"/>
    </Grid>
</Window>
```

Notice that the `Image.Source` property points to the image in the Assets folder of the shared project. Also notice that the `ListBox.ItemTemplate` points to the data template defined in the shared resource dictionary. On the XAML side, the WPF application is consuming assets and XAML resources. The only `Button` control still uses the command defined in the view model. The Visual Basic code for the main window is very simple. It just assigns an instance of the `ContactViewModel` class to the `Window.DataContext` property:

```
Public Sub New()

    ' This call is required by the designer.
    InitializeComponent()

    ' Add any initialization after the InitializeComponent() call.
    Me.DataContext = New ContactViewModel()
End Sub
```

If you now run the sample WPF application, you see that it correctly consumes all objects from the shared project, including code, assets, and XAML resources. Figure 17.26 shows the application running.

FIGURE 17.26   The WPF application is running, consuming objects from the shared project.

Now you should add a new Windows 8.1 project to the current solution, using the Blank App template (the same way you added a portable library earlier in this chapter). When the project is ready, you need to add a reference to the shared project (refer to Figure 17.25.) The first thing you need to do is edit the App.xaml file by adding the `Application.Resources` node and all its content, shown in Listing 17.11. Next, you prepare the user interface, which is a little bit different from what you did with the WPF project because you must use the Windows app bar, and you work with pages instead of windows. Listing 17.13 shows the XAML code.

LISTING 17.13   The UI for the Windows Store App

```
<Page
    x:Class="App1.MainPage"
    xmlns="http://schemas.microsoft.com/winfx/2006/xaml/presentation"
    xmlns:x="http://schemas.microsoft.com/winfx/2006/xaml"
    xmlns:local="using:App1"
    xmlns:d="http://schemas.microsoft.com/expression/blend/2008"
```

```
        xmlns:mc="http://schemas.openxmlformats.org/markup-compatibility/2006"
        mc:Ignorable="d">

        <Grid Background="{ThemeResource ApplicationPageBackgroundThemeBrush}">
            <Grid.RowDefinitions>
                <RowDefinition Height="90"/>
                <RowDefinition/>
            </Grid.RowDefinitions>
            <Image Name="BannerImage" Source="Assets/People.png"/>
            <ListView Name="ContactsBox" Grid.Row="1"
                        ItemsSource="{Binding Contacts}"
                        ItemTemplate="{StaticResource ContactTemplate}"/>
        </Grid>
        <Page.BottomAppBar>
            <CommandBar>
                <CommandBar.PrimaryCommands>
                    <AppBarButton Name="AddButton" Icon="Add" Label="Add"
                                    Command="{Binding AddContactCommand}"/>
                </CommandBar.PrimaryCommands>
            </CommandBar>
        </Page.BottomAppBar>
</Page>
```

The XAML code is still using a shared image, but the way WPF and Windows Store apps handle this is different. In fact, you can see a different packed URI for the Image.Source property, but the image is always the same. The Properties window will definitely help you pick up an image, and then the code editor will automatically write the proper packed URI for you. The ListView.ItemTemplate property is pointing to the shared data template, while the only AppBarButton points to the command in the view model. The following is the code-behind for the application's main page:

```
Protected Overrides Sub OnNavigatedTo(e As NavigationEventArgs)
    Me.DataContext = New ContactViewModel()
End Sub
```

This code simply assigns an instance of the ContactViewModel class to the Page.DataContext property. (You learned why you use the OnNavigateTo method earlier in this chapter, in the section "Creating Portable Classes.") If you now run the sample application, you can see how it is consuming code, assets, and XAML resources from the shared project, exactly as the WPF project did. This is demonstrated in Figure 17.27.

FIGURE 17.27   The sample Windows 8.1 app is running and consuming objects from the shared project.

Shared projects provide a convenient way to share a number of objects between projects of different types, assuming that the projects support objects you want to share.

Summary

In this chapter you saw how to design objects for your application using the built-in Visual Studio tool known as Visual Studio Class Designer. This tool enables you to design objects via a specific designer that offers support for adding all kinds of .NET objects, such as classes, structures, interfaces, delegates, enumerations, and modules. Behind the scenes, this tool generates code related to design operations. You saw how easily you can implement interfaces, abstract classes, and derive classes by learning steps that you will be required to perform for other objects. Completing the topic, the chapter provided information on creating multiple diagrams and exporting diagrams to images.

An overview about one of the most important IDE features in Visual Studio 2015, known as Generate from Usage, was also presented. You learned how you can generate objects on-the-fly, first writing code and then generating objects that you invoke with just a couple of mouse clicks. You also saw how you can generate customized objects running the Generate Type dialog box that provides deep control over types to be generated on-the-fly. You then learned how Visual Studio 2015 offers the perfect environment in which to create objects that can be shared across multiple platforms via the Portable Class Library addition, with an advanced example based on the Model-View-ViewModel pattern that was useful to demonstrate how the same code can run on WPF and Windows 8.1. Finally, you got details about a new feature in Visual Basic 2015: shared projects. With a shared project, you can easily share code, assets, and XAML resources across projects of different types, without needing to create an external assembly that targets a specific .NET subset.

CHAPTER 18

Manipulating Files and Streams

Manipulating files, directories, drives, and pathnames has always been one of the most common requirements for every role in IT for home users. Since MS-DOS, you have probably had this necessity tons of times. In application development for the .NET Framework with Visual Basic 2015, manipulating files is even more straightforward because you have two opportunities: accessing system resources with the usual ease due to self-explanatory classes and members and because of the Common Language Runtime (CLR) as a supervisor. In this chapter, you learn how to manipulate files, directories, and drives by using specific .NET classes. Moreover, you learn about transporting such simplicity into more general data exchange objects, known as streams.

Manipulating Directories and Pathnames

The .NET Framework makes it easier to work with directories and pathnames, providing the `System.IO.Directory` and `System.IO.Path` classes. These classes offer shared methods for accessing directories and directory names, enabling deep manipulation of folders and names. To be honest, `System.IO.Path` also provides members for working against filenames, and due to its nature, it is included in this section. In some situations, you need to work against single directories as instances of .NET objects, and this is where the `System.IO.DirectoryInfo` class comes in. In this section, you learn to get the most from these classes for directory manipulation.

> **TIP**
>
> All the code examples provided in this chapter require an `Imports System.IO` directive to shorten lines of code.

The `System.IO.Path` Class

Often you need to work with pathnames, directory names, and filenames. The .NET Framework provides the `System.IO.Path` class, offering shared members that enable you to manipulate pathnames. For example, you might want to extract the filename from a pathname. This is accomplished by invoking the `GetFileName` method as follows:

```
'Returns "TextFile.txt"
Dim fileName As String = Path.GetFileName("C:\TextFile.txt")
```

The `GetExtension` method returns instead only the file extension and is used as follows:

```
'Returns ".txt"
Dim extension As String = Path.GetExtension("C:\TextFile.txt")
```

To ensure that a filename has an extension, you can also invoke the `HasExtension` method that returns `True` if the filename has one. In some situations you need to extract the filename without considering its extension. The `GetFileNameWithoutExtension` accomplishes this:

```
'Returns "TextFile"
Dim noExtension As String = Path.
                    GetFileNameWithoutExtension("C:\TextFile.txt")
```

Another common situation is retrieving the directory name from a full pathname that includes a filename, too. The `GetDirectoryName` method enables you to perform this:

```
'Returns "C:\Users\Alessandro\My Documents"
Dim dirName As String =

    Path.GetDirectoryName("C:\Users\Alessandro\My Documents\Document.txt")
```

When working with filenames, you might want to replace the extension. This is accomplished by invoking the `ChangeExtension` method as follows:

```
'Returns "MyFile.Doc"
Dim extReplaced As String = Path.ChangeExtension("MyFile.Txt", ".doc")
```

Notice that such a method returns a string that contains the required modification but does not rename the file on disk (which is covered later). Path is also useful when you need to create temporary files or to store files in the Windows temporary folder. You invoke the `GetTempFileName` method to get a unique temporary file:

```
Dim temporaryFile As String = Path.GetTempFileName
```

The method returns the filename of the temporary file so that you can easily access it and treat it like any other file, being sure that its name is unique. If you instead need to access Windows temporary folder, you can invoke the `GetTempPath` method as follows:

```
Dim temporaryWinFolder As String = Path.GetTempPath
```

You could combine both temporary folder name and temporary filename to create a temporary file in the temporary folder. Combining pathnames is accomplished by invoking the `Combine` method, which takes two arguments such as the first pathname and the second one, or a parameter array containing strings representing pathnames. You can also generate a random filename invoking the `GetRandomFileName` method:

```
Dim randomFile As String = Path.GetRandomFileName
```

The difference with `GetTempFileName` is that this one also creates a physical file on disk, returning the full path. `System.IO.Path` offers two other interesting methods: `GetInvalidFileNameChars` and `GetInvalidPathChars`. These both return an array of `Char` storing unaccepted characters within filenames and within directory names, respectively. They are useful if you generate a string that will then be used as a filename or folder name.

The `System.IO.Directory` Class

To access directories, you use the `System.IO.Directory` class that offers shared members that enable you to perform common operations on folders. All members should be self-explanatory. For example, you can check whether a directory already exists and, if not, create a new one as follows:

```
If Not Directory.Exists("C:\Test") Then
    Directory.CreateDirectory("C:\Test")
End If
```

The `Move` method enables you to move a directory from one location to another; it takes two arguments, the source directory name and the target name:

```
Directory.Move("C:\Test", "C:\Demo")
```

If the target directory already exists, an `IOException` is thrown. You can easily get or set attribute information for directories by invoking special methods. For example, you can get the directory creation time by invoking the `GetCreationTime` method that returns a `Date` type or the `SetCreationTime` that requires a date specification, to modify the creation time:

```
Dim createdDate As Date = Directory.GetCreationTime("C:\Demo")
Directory.SetCreationTime("C:\Demo", New Date(2015, 3, 12))
```

Table 18.1 summarizes members for getting/setting attributes.

18

TABLE 18.1   Members for Getting/Setting Attributes

Method	Description
`GetAccessControl/SetAccessControl`	Gets/sets the ACL entries for the specified directory via a `System.Security.AccessControl.DirectorySecurity` object
`GetCreationTime/SetCreationTime`	Gets/sets the creation time for the directory
`GetCreationTimeUtc/SetCreationTimeUtc`	Gets/sets the directory creation time in the Coordinated Universal Time format
`GetLastAccessTime/SetLastAccessTime`	Gets/sets the directory last access time
`GetLastAccessTimeUtc/SetLastAccessTimeUtc`	Gets/sets the directory last access time in the Coordinated Universal Time format
`GetLastWriteTime/SetLastWriteTime`	Gets/sets the directory last write time
`GetLastWriteTimeUtc/SetLastWriteTimeUtc`	Gets/sets the directory last write time in the Coordinated Universal Time format

You can easily get other information, such as the list of files available within the desired directory. You can get the list of files from a directory by invoking the `GetFiles` method, returning an array of string (each one is a filename), which works like this:

```
'Second argument is optional, specifies a pattern for search
Dim filesArray() As String = Directory.GetFiles("C:\", "*.exe")
```

As an alternative, you can invoke the `EnumerateFiles` that returns an `IEnumerable(Of String)` and that works like this:

```
'get files
Dim filesEnumerable As IEnumerable(Of String) = _
                    Directory.EnumerateFiles("C:\", "*.exe")

For Each item In filesEnumerable
    Console.WriteLine("File name: {0}", item)
Next
```

This difference probably does not make much sense at this particular point of the book, but you learn later that `IEnumerable` objects are LINQ-enabled; therefore, you can write LINQ queries against sequences of this type. Similarly to `GetFiles` and `EnumerateFiles`, you invoke `GetDirectories` and `EnumerateDirectories` to retrieve a list of all subdirectories' names within the specified directory. Next, the `GetFiles` and `EnumerateFiles` return a list of all filenames and subdirectory names within the specified directory. Actually there is another difference between `GetXxx` and `EnumerateXxx` methods, which is about performance: The latter starts enumerating as the Framework is still gathering files/directories, making things faster and more efficient.

To delete a directory, you invoke the `Delete` method. It works only if a directory is empty and requires the directory name:

```
'Must be empty
Directory.Delete("C:\Demo")
```

If the folder is not empty, an `IOException` is thrown. `Delete` has an overload that accepts a Boolean value if you want to delete empty subdirectories, too. The `Directory` class also provides the capability of retrieving a list of available drives on your machine. This is accomplished by invoking the `GetLogicalDrives` method that returns an array of `String`, which you can then iterate:

```
Dim drivesOnMyMachine() As String = Directory.
                            GetLogicalDrives
For Each drive In drivesOnMyMachine
    Console.WriteLine(drive)

Next
```

On my machine the preceding code produces the output shown in Figure 18.1.

FIGURE 18.1   Enumerating the list of drives on the current system.

The last example is about retrieving the current directory, which is accomplished by invoking the `GetCurrentDirectory` method:

```
Dim currentFolder As String = Directory.GetCurrentDirectory
```

You can also set the current folder by invoking the shared `SetCurrentDirectory` method, passing the folder name as an argument. Accessing directories via the `Directory` class is straightforward, but in some circumstances you have no access to specific information. For this, a more flexible class that enables you to work on specific directories is `DirectoryInfo`.

The `System.IO.DirectoryInfo` Class

The `System.IO.DirectoryInfo` class represents a single directory. More precisely, an instance of the `DirectoryInfo` class handles information about the specified directory. It inherits from `System.IO.FileSystemInfo`, which is a base class that provides the basic infrastructure for representing directories or files. You create an instance of the `DirectoryInfo` class by passing the desired directory name as an argument to the constructor:

```
Dim di As New DirectoryInfo("C:\Demo")
```

You have the same members that you already learned about for the `Directory` class, with some differences. First, now members are instance members and not shared. Second, methods summarized in Table 18.1 are now properties. Third, members are invoked directly on the instance that represents the directory; therefore, you do not need to pass the directory name as an argument. For example, you remove an empty directory by invoking the instance method `Delete` as follows:

```
di.Delete()
```

An interesting property is `DirectoryInfo.Attributes`, which enables you to specify values from the `System.IO.FileAttributes` enumeration and that determine directory behavior. For example, you can make a directory hidden and read-only setting bitwise flags as follows:

```
di.Attributes = FileAttributes.Hidden Or FileAttributes.ReadOnly
```

When you specify values from such enumeration, IntelliSense can help you understand what the value is about; it's worth mentioning that such values are self-explanatory. Sometimes you do not programmatically create instances of `DirectoryInfo`; instead you receive an instance from some other objects. For example, the `Directory.CreateDirectory` shared method returns a `DirectoryInfo` object. In such cases, you can get further information as the directory name invoking the `FullName` property, which returns the full pathname of the folder, or the `Name` property that just returns the name without path. Both work like this:

```
Dim directoryFullName As String = di.FullName
Dim directoryName As String = di.Name
```

Use the `DirectoryInfo` class each time you need to store information for specific directories—for example, within collections.

The `System.IO.DriveInfo` Class

Similarly to `System.IO.DirectoryInfo`, `System.IO.DriveInfo` provides access to the drive's information. Using this class is straightforward; it provides information on the disk type, disk space (free and total), volume label, and other self-explanatory properties that you can discover with IntelliSense. The following example shows how you can create an instance of the class and retrieve information on the specified drive:

```
Sub DriveInfoDemo()
    Dim dr As New DriveInfo("C:\")

    Console.WriteLine("Drive type: {0}", dr.DriveType.ToString)
    Console.WriteLine("Volume label: {0}", dr.VolumeLabel)
    Console.WriteLine("Total disk space: {0}", dr.TotalSize.ToString)
    Console.WriteLine("Available space: {0}",
                      dr.AvailableFreeSpace.ToString)
    dr = Nothing
End Sub
```

Handling Exceptions for Directories and Pathnames

When working with directories and pathnames, encountering exceptions is not so uncommon. Table 18.2 summarizes directory-related exceptions.

TABLE 18.2   Directory-Related Exceptions

Method	Description
IOException	General exception that happens when operations on directories fail (such as creating existing directories, deleting nonempty directories, and so on)
DirectoryNotFoundException	Thrown when the directory is not found
PathTooLongException	Thrown when the pathname exceeds the size of 248 characters for folders and 260 for filenames
UnauthorizedAccessException	Thrown if the caller code doesn't have sufficient rights to access the directory
ArgumentNullException	Thrown when the supplied argument is Nothing
ArgumentException	Thrown when the supplied argument is invalid

It is important to implement `Try..Catch` blocks for handling the previously described exceptions and provide the user the ability to escape from such situations.

Manipulating Files

Manipulating files is a daily task for every developer. Luckily, the .NET Framework provides an easy infrastructure for working with files. In this section, you learn about the `System.IO.File` and `System.IO.FileInfo` classes that also represent some important concepts before you go into streams.

The `System.IO.File` Class

The `System.IO.File` class provides access to files on disk exposing special shared members. For example, you can easily create a text file invoking two methods: `WriteAllText` and `WriteAllLines`. Both create a new text file, put into the file the given text, and then close the file; however, the second one enables you to write the content of an array of strings into multiple lines. The following code provides an example:

```
File.WriteAllText("C:\Temp\OneFile.txt", "Test message")


Dim lines() As String = {"First", "Second", "Third"}
File.WriteAllLines("C:\Temp\OneFile.txt", lines)
```

Such methods are useful because they avoid the need to manually close files on disk when you perform the writing operation. You can also easily create binary files by invoking the `WriteAllBytes` method that works like the previous ones but requires the specification of an array of byte instead of text. The following is a small example:

```
File.WriteAllBytes("C:\Temp\OneFile.bin", New Byte() {1, 2, 3, 4})
```

Reading files' content is also easy. There are reading counterparts of the previously described method. `ReadAllText` and `ReadAllLines` enable you to retrieve content from a text file; the first one returns all content as a `String`, whereas the second one returns the content line-by-line by putting in an array of `string`. This is an example:

```
Dim text As String = File.ReadAllText("C:\Temp\OneFile.txt")
Dim fileLines() As String = File.ReadAllLines("C:\Temp\OneFile.txt")
```

Similarly you can read data from binary files invoking `ReadAllBytes`, which returns an array of `Byte`, as follows:

```
Dim bytes() As Byte = File.ReadAllBytes("C:\Temp\OneFile.bin")
```

For text files, you can also append text to an existing file. You accomplish this by invoking `AppendAllText` if you want to put an entire string or `AppendAllLines` if you have a sequence of strings. This is an example:

```
Dim lines As IEnumerable(Of String) = _
            New String() {"First", "Second", "Third"}.AsEnumerable
File.AppendAllLines("C:\Temporary\Test.txt", lines)
File.AppendAllText("C:\Temporary\Text.txt",
                "All text is stored within a string")
```

Notice how an array of strings is converted into an `IEnumerable(Of String)` invoking the `AsEnumerable` extension method, which is discussed in Chapters 20, "Advanced

Language Features," and 23, "LINQ to Objects." `AppendAllLines` takes an `IEnumerable(Of String)` as a parameter, but you can also pass an array of strings because arrays are actually enumerable. After reading and writing, copying is also important. The `Copy` method enables you to create copies of files, accepting two arguments: the source file and the target file. This is an example:

```
File.Copy("C:\OneFolder\Source.txt", "C:\AnotherFolder\Target.txt")
```

You can also move a file from a location to another by invoking `Move`. Such a method is also used to rename a file and can be used as follows:

```
File.Move("C:\OneFolder\Source.txt", "C:\AnotherFolder\Target.txt")
```

Another useful method is `Replace`. It enables you to replace the content of a file with the content of another file, making a backup of the first file. You use it as follows:

```
File.Replace("C:\Source.Txt", "C:\Target.txt", "C:\Backup.txt")
```

You are not limited to text files. The `File` class offers two important methods that provide a basic encryption service, `Encrypt` and `Decrypt`. `Encrypt` makes a file accessible only by the user who is currently logged into Windows. You invoke it as follows:

```
File.Encrypt("C:\Temp\OneFile.txt")
```

If you try to log off from the system and then log on with another user profile, the encrypted file will not be accessible. You need to log on again with the user profile that encrypted the file. To reverse the result, invoke `Decrypt`:

```
File.Decrypt("C:\Temp\OneFile.txt")
```

Finally, you can easily delete a file from disk. This is accomplished with the simple `Delete` method:

```
File.Delete("C:\Temp\OneFile.txt")
```

The `File` class also has members similar to the `Directory` class. Consider the summarization made in Table 18.1 about the `Directory` class's members. The `File` class exposes the same members with the same meaning; the only difference is that such members now affect files. Those members are not covered again because they behave the same on files.

MEMBERS RETURNING STREAMS

The `System.IO.File` class exposes methods that return or require streams, such as `Create` and `Open`. Such members are not covered here for two reasons: The first one is that the streams discussion will be offered later in this chapter; the second one is that streams provide their own members for working against files that do the same as file members and therefore a more appropriate discussion is related to streams.

The `System.IO.FileInfo` Class

Similarly to what you learned about the `System.IO.DirectoryInfo` class, there is also a `System.IO.FileInfo` counterpart for the `System.IO.File` class. An instance of the `FileInfo` class is therefore a representation of a single file, providing members that enable you to perform operations on that particular file or get/set information. Because `FileInfo` inherits from `System.IO.FileSystemInfo` like `DirectoryInfo`, you can find the same members. You create an instance of the `FileInfo` class by passing the filename to the constructor, as demonstrated here:

```
Dim fi As New FileInfo("C:\MyFile.txt")
```

You can set attributes for the specified file assigning the `Attributes` property, which receives a value from the `System.IO.FileAttributes` enumeration:

```
fi.Attributes = FileAttributes.System Or FileAttributes.Hidden
```

You can still perform operations by invoking instance members that do not require the filename specification, such as `CopyTo`, `Delete`, `Encrypt`, `Decrypt`, or `MoveTo`: the `FileInfo`, such as `Length` (of type `Long`) that returns the file size in bytes; `Name` (of type `String`) that returns the filename and that is useful when you receive a `FileInfo` instance from somewhere else; `FullName` that is the same as `Name` but also includes the full path; `Exists` that determines if the file exists; and `IsReadOnly` that determines if the file is read-only. Using `FileInfo` can be useful if you need to create collections of objects, each representing a file on disk. Consider the following custom collections that stores series of `FileInfo` objects:

```
Class MyFileList
    Inherits List(Of FileInfo)

End Class
```

Now consider the following code that retrieves the list of executable filenames in the specified folder and creates an instance of the `FileInfo` class for each file, pushing it into the collection:

```
Module FileInfoDemo

    Sub FileInfoDemo()

        'An instance of the collection
        Dim customList As New MyFileList

        'Create a FileInfo for each .exe file
        'in the specified directory
        For Each itemName As String In _
            Directory.EnumerateFiles("C:\", "*.exe")

            Dim fileReference As New FileInfo(itemName)
```

```
            customList.Add(fileReference)
        Next

        'Iterate the collection
        For Each item In customList
            Console.WriteLine("File: {0}, length: {1}, created on: {2}",
                            item.Name, item.Length, item.CreationTime)
        Next
    End Sub
End Module
```

In this particular case enclosing the code within a module is just for demonstration purposes. Notice how you can access properties for each file that you could not know in advance. Just like `DirectoryInfo`, `FileInfo` also exposes properties that are counterparts for methods summarized in Table 18.1 and that this time are related to files. Refer to that table for further information.

Handling File Exceptions

Refer to Table 18.2 for exceptions that can occur when working with files. Other than those exceptions, you may encounter a `FileNotFoundException` if the specified file does not exist.

Understanding Permissions

The .NET Framework provides a high-level security mechanism over system resources, so it can happen that you attempt to access, in both reading or writing, directories or files but you do not have the required rights. To prevent your code from failing at runtime, you can check whether you have permissions. When working with files and directories, you need to check the availability of the `System.Security.FileIOPermission` object. For example, the following code asks the system (`Demand` method) if it has permissions to read local files:

```
Dim fp As New FileIOPermission(PermissionState.None)
fp.AllLocalFiles = FileIOPermissionAccess.Read
Try
    fp.Demand()
Catch ex As Security.SecurityException
    Console.WriteLine("You have no permission for local files")
Catch ex As Exception
End Try
```

If your code has no sufficient permissions, a `SecurityException` is thrown. Checking for permission is absolutely a best practice and should be applied where possible. In Chapter 43, "Working with Assemblies," you get some more information about the security model in the .NET Framework.

Introducing Streams

Streams are sequences of bytes exchanged with some kind of sources, such as files, memory, and network. A stream is represented by the abstract `System.IO.Stream` class that is the base class for different kinds of streams and that implements the `IDisposable` interface. The `Stream` class exposes some common members that you find in all other streams. Table 18.3 summarizes the most important common members.

TABLE 18.3   Streams Common Members

Member	Description
Close	Closes the stream and releases associated resources
Write	Writes the specified sequence of bytes to the stream
WriteByte	Writes the specified byte to the stream
Read	Reads the specified number of bytes from the stream
ReadByte	Reads a byte from the stream
Length	Returns the stream's dimension (property)
Seek	Moves to the specified position in the stream
Position	Returns the current position (property)
CanRead	Determines if the stream supports reading (property)
CanWrite	Determines if the stream supports writing (property)
CanSeek	Determines if the stream supports seeking (property)
BeginRead	Starts an asynchronous reading operation
BeginWrite	Starts an asynchronous writing operation
EndRead	Waits for an asynchronous operation to be completed

Now that you have a summarization of common members, you are ready to discover specific kinds of streams that inherit from `Stream`.

Reading and Writing Text Files

You create text files by instantiating the `StreamWriter` class, which is a specific stream implementation for writing to text files. The following code, which will be explained, provides an example:

```
Dim ts As New StreamWriter("C:\Temporary\OneFile.txt",
                        False, System.Text.Encoding.UTF8)

ts.WriteLine("This is a text file")
ts.WriteLine("with multi-line example")
ts.Close()
```

The constructor provides several overloads. The one used in the code receives the file name to be created; a Boolean value indicated whether the text must be appended if the file already exists and how the text is encoded. `WriteLine` is a method that writes a string and then puts a line terminator character. When you are done, you must close the stream invoking `Close`. You can also invoke `Write` to put in just one character. The reading counterpart is the `StreamReader` that works in a similar way, as demonstrated here:

```
Dim rf As New StreamReader("C:\Temporary\OneFile.txt",
                              System.Text.Encoding.UTF8)
Dim readALine As String = rf.ReadLine
Dim allContent As String = rf.ReadToEnd

rf.Close()
```

`StreamReader` provides the ability to read one line (`ReadLine` method), one character per time (`Read` method), or all the content of the stream (`ReadToEnd` method) putting such content into a variable of type `String`. In both `StreamWriter` and `StreamReader`, the constructor can receive an existing stream instead of a string. This is exemplified by the following code:

```
Dim fs As New FileStream("C:\Temporary\OneFile.txt", FileMode.Create)
Dim ts As New StreamWriter(fs)

'Work on your file here..
ts.Close()

fs.Close()
```

First, you need an instance of the `FileStream` class, which enables you to open a communication with the specified file and with the mode specified by a value of the `FileMode` enumeration (such as `Create`, `Append`, `CreateNew`, `Open`, and `OpenOrTruncate`). This class provides support for both synchronous and asynchronous operations. Then you point to the `FileStream` instance in the constructor of the `StreamWriter`/`StreamReader` class. Remember to close both streams when you are done.

Reading and Writing Binary Files

You can read and write data to binary files using the `BinaryReader` and `BinaryWriter` classes. Both require a `FileStream` instance and enable you to read and write arrays of bytes. The following is an example of creating a binary stream:

```
Dim fs As New FileStream("C:\Temporary\OneFile.bin", FileMode.CreateNew)
Dim bs As New BinaryWriter(fs)

Dim bytesToWrite() As Byte = New Byte() {128, 64, 32, 16}

bs.Write(bytesToWrite)
bs.Close()
fs.Close()
```

The `Write` method enables you to write information as binary, but it also accepts base .NET types such as integers and strings, all written as binary. It provides several overloads so that you can also specify the offset and the number of bytes to be written. To read a binary file, you instantiate the `BinaryReader` class. The following example retrieves information from a file utilizing a `Using..End Using` block to ensure that resources are correctly freed up when no longer necessary:

```
fs = New FileStream("C:\Temporary\OneFile.bin", FileMode.Open)
Using br As New BinaryReader(fs)
    If fs IsNot Nothing AndAlso fs.Length > 0 Then
        Dim buffer() As Byte = br.ReadBytes(CInt(fs.Length))
    End If
End Using
fs.Close()
```

In this case the `ReadBytes` method, which is used to retrieve data, reads a number of bytes corresponding to the file length. Because binary data can have different forms, `ReadBytes` is just one of a series of methods for reading .NET types such as `ReadChar`, `ReadInt32`, `ReadString`, `ReadDouble`, and so on.

ASYNCHRONOUS PROGRAMMING

The .NET Framework 4.5 introduced a pattern for asynchronous programming techniques based on the Async/Await keywords. This pattern has some features for working with streams asynchronously as well. Because you first need to know how this pattern works, examples on asynchronous operations over streams will be provided in Chapter 42, "Asynchronous Programming."

Using Memory Streams

Memory streams are special objects that act like file streams but that work in memory, providing the ability to manipulate binary data. The following code creates a `MemoryStream` with 2 Kbytes capacity and puts in a string:

```
Dim ms As New MemoryStream(2048)

Dim bs As New BinaryWriter(ms)
bs.Write("Some text written as binary")
bs.Close()
ms.Close()
```

To retrieve data, you use a `BinaryReader` pointing to the `MemoryStream` as you saw in the paragraph for binary files. So, in this example, you can invoke `ReadString` as follows:

```
'The stream must be still open
Using br As New BinaryReader(ms)
    If ms IsNot Nothing AndAlso ms.Length > 0 Then
```

```
            Dim data As String = br.ReadString

      End If
End Using
ms.Close()
```

Using Streams with Strings

Although not often utilized, you can use StringReader and StringWriter for manipulating strings. The following example generates a new StringBuilder and associates it to
a new StringWriter. Then it retrieves the list of filenames in the C:\ directory and puts
each string into the writer. You notice that because of the association between the two
objects, changes are reflected to the StringBuilder. Try this:

```
Dim sBuilder As New Text.StringBuilder
Dim sWriter As New StringWriter(sBuilder)

For Each name As String In Directory.GetFiles("C:\")
    sWriter.WriteLine(name)
Next
sWriter.Close()

Console.WriteLine(sBuilder.ToString)
```

To read strings, you can use the StringReader object, whose constructor requires a string
to be read. To continue with the example, you can write code that reads the previously
created StringBuilder line-by-line:

```
Dim sReader As New StringReader(sBuilder.ToString)
Do Until sReader.Peek = -1
    Console.WriteLine(sReader.ReadLine)

Loop
```

You notice lots of similarities between string streams and StreamWriter/StreamReader
because both work with text.

Compressing Data with Streams

One of the most interesting features of streams is the ability to compress and decompress
data utilizing the GZipStream and DeflateStream objects. Both are exposed by the System.
IO.Compression namespace, and they both compress data using the GZip algorithm.
The only difference is that the GZipStream writes a small header to compressed data. The
interesting thing is that they work similarly to other streams, and when you write or read
data into the stream, data is automatically compressed or decompressed by the runtime.
The good news is that you are not limited to compressing files, but any other kind of
stream. Compressing and decompressing data is quite a simple task. In some situations

you need more attention according to the kind of data you need to access for files. To make comprehension easier, take a look at the code example provided in Listing 18.1 that contains comments that explain how such streams work. The purpose of the example is to provide the ability to compress and decompress files that is a common requirement in applications. You are encouraged to read comments within the code that can help you get started with the GZipStream.

LISTING 18.1   Compressing and Decompressing Streams

```
Imports System.IO
Imports System.IO.Compression

Module Compression

    Sub TestCompress()
        Try
            Compress("C:\Temp\Source.Txt",
                    "C:\Temp\Compressed.gzp")
        Catch ex As FileNotFoundException
            Console.WriteLine("File not found!")
        Catch ex As IOException
            Console.WriteLine("An input/output error has occurred:")
            Console.WriteLine(ex.Message)
        Catch ex As Exception
            Console.WriteLine(ex.Message)
        End Try
    End Sub

    Sub TestDecompress()
        Try
            Decompress("C:\Temp\Compressed.gzp",
                    "C:\Temp\Original.txt")

        Catch ex As FileNotFoundException
            Console.WriteLine("File not found!")
        Catch ex As IOException
            Console.WriteLine("An input/output error has occurred:")
            Console.WriteLine(ex.Message)
        Catch ex As Exception
            Console.WriteLine(ex.Message)
        End Try
    End Sub

    Public Sub Compress(inputName As String, outputName As String)

        'Instantiates a new FileStream
```

```vbnet
Dim infile As FileStream

Try
    'The Stream points to the specified input file
    infile = New FileStream(inputName, FileMode.Open, FileAccess.Read,
                        FileShare.Read)

    'Stores the file length in a buffer
    Dim buffer(CInt(infile.Length - 1)) As Byte

    'Checks if the file can be read and assigns to the "count"
    'variable the result of reading the file
    Dim count As Integer = infile.Read(buffer, 0, buffer.Length)

    'If the number of read byte is different from the file length
    'throws an exception
    If count <> buffer.Length Then
        infile.Close()
        Throw New IOException
    End If
    'closes the stream
    infile.Close()
    infile = Nothing

    'Creates a new stream pointing to the output file
    Dim ms As New FileStream(outputName, FileMode.CreateNew,
                        FileAccess.Write)

    'Creates a new GZipStream for compressing, pointing to
    'the output stream above leaving it open
    Dim compressedzipStream As New GZipStream(ms,
                                        CompressionMode.Compress,
                                        True)
    'Puts the buffer into the new stream, which is
    'automatically compressed
    compressedzipStream.Write(buffer, 0, buffer.Length)

    compressedzipStream.Close()
    ms.Close()
    Exit Sub
Catch ex As IO.FileNotFoundException
    Throw
Catch ex As IOException
    Throw
Catch ex As Exception
    Throw
```

18

```vbnet
    End Try
End Sub

Public Sub Decompress(fileName As String, originalName As String)

    Dim inputFile As FileStream

    'Defining the stream for decompression
    Dim compressedZipStream As GZipStream

    'Defining a variable for storing compressed file size
    Dim compressedFileSize As Integer

    Try

        'Reads the input file
        inputFile = New FileStream(fileName,
                                FileMode.Open,
                                FileAccess.Read,
                                FileShare.Read)

        'Reads input file's size
         compressedFileSize = CInt(inputFile.Length)

        'Creates a new GZipStream in Decompress mode
        compressedZipStream = New GZipStream(inputFile,
                                            CompressionMode.Decompress)

        'In compressed data the first 100 bytes store the original
        'data size, so let's get it
        Dim offset As Integer = 0
        Dim totalBytes As Integer = 0

        Dim SmallBuffer(100) As Byte

        'Reads until there are available bytes in the first 100
        'and increments variables that we'll need for sizing
        'the buffer that will store the decompressed file
        Do While True

            Dim bytesRead As Integer = compressedZipStream.
                                        Read(SmallBuffer, 0, 100)
            If bytesRead = 0 Then
                Exit Do
            End If
```

```
            offset += bytesRead
            totalBytes += bytesRead
        Loop

        compressedZipStream.Close()
        compressedZipStream = Nothing

        'Creates a new FileStream for reading the input file
        inputFile = New FileStream(fileName,
                            FileMode.Open,
                            FileAccess.Read,
                            FileShare.Read)

        'and decompress its content
        compressedZipStream = New GZipStream(inputFile,
                                    CompressionMode.Decompress)

        'Declares the buffer that will store uncompressed data
        Dim buffer(totalBytes) As Byte

        'Reads from the source file the number of bytes
        'representing the buffer length, taking advantage
        'of the original size
        compressedZipStream.Read(buffer, 0, totalBytes)

        compressedZipStream.Close()
        compressedZipStream = Nothing

        'Creates a new file for putting uncompressed
        'data
        Dim ms As New FileStream(originalName,
                            FileMode.Create,
                            FileAccess.Write)

        'Writes uncompressed data to file
        ms.Write(buffer, 0, buffer.Length)
        ms.Close()
        ms = Nothing
        Exit Sub

        'General IO error
    Catch ex As IOException
        Throw
    Catch ex As Exception
        Throw
        Exit Try
```

```
        End Try
    End Sub
End Module
```

> **TIP**
>
> You use `GZipStream` and `DeflateStream` the identical way. The only difference is about the header in the compressed stream. If you need further information on the difference, here is the official MSDN page: http://msdn.microsoft.com/en-us/library/system.io.compression.deflatestream(VS.110).aspx.

Notice how, at a higher level, you just instantiate the stream the same way in both compression and decompression tasks. The difference is the `CompressionMode` enumeration value that determines whether a stream is for compression or decompression. With this technique, you can invoke just the two custom methods for compressing and decompressing files, meaning that you could apply it to other kinds of data, too.

Working with Zip Archives

The .NET Framework 4.6 allows you to work with classic Zip archives. You can add a reference to the System.IO.Compression.FileSystem.dll assembly. This extends the `System.IO.Compression` namespace with new types that will be described shortly. The real thing you have to take care about is that the new features offer basic ways for working with Zip archives and so there could be some situations in which you might need more advanced libraries, such as the famous DotNetZip (http://dotnetzip.codeplex.com) or SharpZipLib (http://sharpziplib.com) available for free on the Internet. For example, currently the new classes do not enable you to enter passwords when extracting archives or specify one to protect archives. Also, full compatibility is not always guaranteed. Notice that these new types are not available for Windows Store apps, where you will still use streams described previously. In the full .NET Framework, you can now use the `ZipFile` class, which exposes two shared methods, `CreateFromDirectory` and `ExtractToDirectory`. The first method creates a Zip archive containing all files in the specified directory, whereas the second one extracts the content of a Zip archive into the specified directory. The following example demonstrates how to create and extract a Zip archive:

```
ZipFile.CreateFromDirectory("C:\temp", "C:\ZippedTemp.zip",
        CompressionLevel.Optimal, True)
ZipFile.ExtractToDirectory("C:\ZippedDemo.zip", "C:\temp")
```

In the previous example, `CreateFromDirectory` generates a compressed archive called ZippedTemp.zip, which stores the content of a folder called C:\Temp. The third argument (called `compressionLevel`) represents the compression level and requires one value from the `CompressionLevel` enumeration. You choose among `Optimal`, `NoCompression`, and `Fastest`. The fourth argument (called `includeBaseDirectory`) is instead a Boolean value that, when `True`, enables you to include the base directory in the archive. Using

`ExtractToDirectory` is even simpler because you just specify the archive to decompress and the target directory. Both methods have an overload that provides an argument called `entryNameEncoding` of type `System.Text.Encoding` which enables you to specify the encoding to use with file entries for compatibility with Zip archives that do not support UTF-8. The `System.IO.Compression` namespace also offers the `ZipArchive` and `ZipArchiveEntry` classes, representing a Zip archive and one entry inside the compressed archive, respectively. These classes provide better control over Zip files. The following code demonstrates how to show the list of files inside a Zip archive:

```
Using zipArc As ZipArchive = ZipFile.Open("C:\temp\Northwind.zip",
➥ZipArchiveMode.Read)
    For Each item As ZipArchiveEntry In zipArc.Entries
        Console.WriteLine("{0}, Compressed size: {1}, ",
                        item.FullName,
                        item.CompressedLength.ToString)
    Next
End Using
```

Because the `ZipArchive` class implements the `IDisposable` interface, it can be convenient to enclose the code within a `Using..End Using` block. Notice that the `ZipArchive` instance receives the result of another method from the `ZipFile` class, `Open`. Every item in the archive is an instance of the `ZipArchiveEntry` class; a collection called `Entries`, of type `ReadOnlyCollection(Of ZipArchiveEntry)`, can be iterated to get the list of items that are stored inside the Zip archive. It is also easy to create a new Zip file with `ZipArchive` and `ZipFile.Open`. The following code demonstrates this:

```
Using zipArc As ZipArchive = ZipFile.Open("C:\Temp\NewZipped.zip",
                    ZipArchiveMode.Create)
    zipArc.CreateEntry("C:\Temp\Northwind.sdf", CompressionLevel.NoCompression)
End Using
```

Here you use the `ZipArchiveMode.Create` mode for opening the Zip file, since you want to create a new one. Then you use the `CreateEntry` instance method of the `ZipArchive` class to add entries to the zipped archive. Notice that the entry is actually added to the archive when the `Using` block gets finalized. You can also update an existing archive by adding or deleting entries. The following code demonstrates how to add an entry to an existing archive and how to remove an existing entry:

```
Using zipArc As ZipArchive = ZipFile.Open("C:\Temp\NewZipped.zip",
                    ZipArchiveMode.Update)
    zipArc.CreateEntry("C:\Temp\AnotherFile.txt", CompressionLevel.Fastest)
    'Get the specified entry
    Dim entry As ZipArchiveEntry = zipArc.GetEntry("Northwind.sdf")
    'Delete the entry from the archive
    entry.Delete()
End Using
```

18

You use GetEntry to get the instance of the ZipArchiveEntry that you want to remove, by specifying the name. Then you invoke the Delete method on the retrieved instance.

Networking with Streams

The .NET Framework provides functionalities for data exchange through networks using streams; in particular, it exposes the System.Net.Sockets.NetworkStream class. Reading and writing data via a NetworkStream instance passes through a System.Net.Sockets.TcpClient class's instance. Code in Listing 18.2 shows how you can both write and read data in such a scenario. See comments in code for explanations.

LISTING 18.2   Networking with NetworkStream

```vb
Imports System.Net.Sockets
Imports System.Text

Module Network

    Sub NetStreamDemo()
        'Instantiating TcpClient and NetworkStream
        Dim customTcpClient As New TcpClient()
        Dim customNetworkStream As NetworkStream

        Try
            'Attempt to connect to socket
            '127.0.0.1 is the local machine address
            customTcpClient.Connect("127.0.0.1", 587) 'Port
            'Gets the instance of the stream for
            'data exchange
            customNetworkStream = customTcpClient.GetStream()

            'The port is not available
        Catch ex As ArgumentOutOfRangeException
            Console.WriteLine(ex.Message)
            'Connection problem
        Catch ex As SocketException
            Console.WriteLine(ex.Message)
        End Try

        'Gets an array of byte from a value, which is
        'encoded via System.Text.Encoding.Ascii.GetBytes
        Dim bytesToWrite() As Byte = _
            Encoding.ASCII.GetBytes("Something to exchange via TCP")
```

```
        'Gets the stream instance
        customNetworkStream = customTcpClient.GetStream()
        'Writes the bytes to the stream; this
        'means sending data to the network
        customNetworkStream.Write(bytesToWrite, 0,
                            bytesToWrite.Length)

        'Establishes the buffer size for receiving data
        Dim bufferSize As Integer = customTcpClient.
                            ReceiveBufferSize
        Dim bufferForReceivedBytes(bufferSize) As Byte

        'Gets data from the stream, meaning by the network
        customNetworkStream.Read(bufferForReceivedBytes, 0,
                            bufferSize)

        Dim result As String = Encoding.ASCII.GetString(bufferForReceivedBytes,
                            0, bufferSize)
    End Sub
End Module
```

There are several ways for data exchange, and this is probably one of the most basic ones in the era of Windows Communication Foundation. This topic is related to streams, so an overview was necessary.

Summary

Working with files, directories, and drives is a common requirement for each application. The .NET Framework provides two main classes for working with directories: `System.IO.Directory` and `System.IO.Path`. The first one enables you to perform operations such as creating, moving, renaming, and investigating for filenames. The second one is about directory and filename manipulation other than gaining access to Windows temporary folder. Similar to `Directory`, the `System.IO.DirectoryInfo` class provides access to directory operations and information, but the difference is that an instance of such a class represents a single directory. If you instead need to get information on physical drives on your machine, create an instance of the `System.IO.DriveInfo` class. Similar to `Directory` and `DirectoryInfo`, the `System.IO.File` and `System.IO.FileInfo` classes provide access to files on disk, and their members are the same as for directory classes except that they enable you to work with files. The last part of the chapter is about streams. Streams are sequences of bytes that enable you to exchange different kinds of data. All stream classes inherit from `System.IO.Stream`. `StreamReader` and `StreamWriter` enable you to read and write text files. `BinaryReader` and `BinaryWriter` enable you to read and write binary files. `MemoryStream` enables you to read and write in-memory binary data. `StringReader` and

18

`StringWriter` enable you to manage in-memory strings. `GZipStream` and `DeflateStream` enable you to compress data according to the `GZip` algorithm (you saw features in .NET 4.6 about Zip compression). `NetworkStream` enables you to exchange data through a network. Writing and reading data can often require several lines of code. Luckily the Visual Basic language offers an important alternative known as the `My` namespace that is covered in the next chapter.

CHAPTER 19

The My Namespace

The great debate is always the same: which is better, Visual Basic or Visual C#? Because of the .NET Framework, the Common Language Runtime (CLR), and the IL language, the languages' evolution brought both VB and C# to do the same things. Of course, there are some differences, and one language has some features that the other one does not have. One example is async and await in `try..catch` blocks in C#, which aren't available in VB yet, or VB's XML literals that C# does not have. Differences are obvious. One of the Visual Basic features that does not have commonalities with other managed languages is the My namespace, belonging to VB starting from Visual Basic 2005. This chapter examines the My namespace, which can help you write code more efficiently, in keeping with the philosophy "less code, more productivity." Keep in mind that what you learn in this chapter does not apply to Windows Store apps; in fact, even if the My namespace still exists in that platform, it does not expose anything. This is an important clarification and will no longer be repeated through the chapter.

Introducing the My Namespace

The My namespace provides shortcuts for accessing several common objects in .NET development. My exposes classes that wrap existing built-in objects and offers them again in a way that's easier to use. By using My, you can access lots of development areas and write less code than you would if you used traditional techniques. At a higher level My exposes the following members:

▶ `My.Application`, a property exposing members that allows access to other properties of the current application

▶ `My.Computer`, a property exposing members that provides shortcuts to common operations with your machine, such as the file system or the Registry

▶ `My.Settings`, a property that provides code support for the Settings tab in My Project and that also enables the use of settings from your application

▶ `My.Resources`, a namespace that defines several objects providing support for the Resources tab in My Project and allowing handling resources in code

▶ `My.User`, a property providing members for getting or setting information about the current user that logged into the operating system

▶ `My.WebServices`, a property that enables the retrieval of information on web services consumed by your application

The preceding listed `My` members are the most general, and you can find them in every kind of Visual Basic application (except for Store apps, as stated at the beginning of the chapter). There are also specific extensions for the `My` namespace related to specific applications, such as WPF. (A description is provided at the end of this chapter.) `My` is interesting because it can be also be extended with custom members providing great flexibility to your applications. If something within `My` does not satisfy you, you can change it. After all, `My` is a namespace, meaning that it is implemented in code.

`My` IS A RESERVED KEYWORD

Due to its particular role within the Visual Basic programming language, although it just refers to a namespace, `My` is also a reserved word in Visual Basic.

My.Application

The `My.Application` properties expose members for retrieving information on the running instance of the application. This information can be divided into three major groups: application information at assembly level, culture for localization and deployment, and environment information. Let's examine all these features.

APPLICATION FRAMEWORK

In specific kinds of applications, such as Windows Forms and WPF applications, `My.Application` also provides support for the application framework and application events. This is discussed in the last section of this chapter.

Retrieving Assembly Information

My.Application maps the same-named tab within My Project. Because of this, it provides the ability of investigating in-code assemblies' information. This can be accomplished via the My.Application.Info property (of type Microsoft.VisualBasic. ApplicationServices.AssemblyInfo) that retrieves information about the current assembly, such as the name, version, company name, copyright, and so on. The following code shows how you can accomplish this:

```
'Assembly information
Console.WriteLine("Assembly name: {0}",
                  My.Application.Info.AssemblyName)
Console.WriteLine("Assembly version: {0}",
                  My.Application.Info.Version)
Console.WriteLine("Company name: {0}",
                  My.Application.Info.CompanyName)
'Returns the directory where the application is running from
Console.WriteLine("Running from: {0}",
                  My.Application.Info.DirectoryPath)
```

Another interesting feature is that you can get information on all referenced assemblies, as shown in the following iteration:

```
Console.WriteLine("References:")
For Each item In My.Application.Info.LoadedAssemblies
    Console.WriteLine(item)
Next
```

The LoadedAssemblies property is of type ReadonlyCollection(Of System.Reflection. AssemblyInfo), so you become more skilled after reading Chapter 44, "Reflection."

Working with Cultures

In Chapter 33, "Localizing Applications," you get more information about localizing applications, but at this particular point of the book, you can get an interesting taste using My. Two cultures are settable for your application: the thread's culture, which is about string manipulation and formatting, and the user interface culture, which is about adapting resources to the desired culture. You can get information on both by invoking the Culture and UICulture properties from My.Application; then you can set different cultures for both the main culture and UI culture by invoking the ChangeCulture and ChangeUICulture methods. The following code demonstrates this:

```
Dim culture As CultureInfo = My.Application.Culture
Console.WriteLine("Current culture: {0}", culture.Name)

Dim UICulture As CultureInfo = My.Application.UICulture
Console.WriteLine("Current UI culture: {0}", UICulture.Name)
```

19

```
My.Application.ChangeCulture("it-IT")
My.Application.ChangeUICulture("it-IT")

Console.WriteLine("New settings: {0}, {1}",
                  My.Application.Culture.Name,
                  My.Application.UICulture.Name)
```

First, the code retrieves information about cultures. Such information is of type `System.Globalization.CultureInfo`. This object provides lots of information on cultures, but in this case the code uses `Name` that returns the culture name. Notice how you can change cultures by invoking `ChangeCulture` and `ChangeUICulture` just by passing a string representing the culture's name. On my machine the preceding code produces the following result:

```
Current culture: en-US
Current UI culture: en-US
New settings: it-IT, it-IT
```

If you need to pass a custom culture, you should create a new `CultureInfo` object and then pass the name of the new culture. Typically, you will not remember each culture name, so if you want to investigate available cultures, you can write a simple iteration taking advantage of the shared `GetCultureInfo` method:

```
For Each c In CultureInfo.GetCultures(CultureTypes.AllCultures)
    Console.WriteLine(c.Name)
Next
```

Deployment and Environment Information

The `My.Application` property allows managing the following environment information:

- ▶ Getting information on the ClickOnce deployment for the current application

- ▶ Retrieving environment variables

- ▶ Writing entries to the Windows Applications log

- ▶ Retrieving command line arguments

Next you see in detail how you can get/set such information using `My.Application`.

Deployment Information

It can be useful to get information on the state of the deployment if your application has been installed via the ClickOnce technology (discussed in detail in Chapter 50, "Deploying Applications with ClickOnce"). You might want to provide the ability of downloading files on-demand or to implement additional behaviors according to the updates status. You can use the `IsNetworkDeployed` property to know if an application has been deployed to a network via ClickOnce and the `My.Application.Deployment` property (which wraps `System.Deployment.Application.ApplicationDeployment`) to make other decisions. The following code shows information on the deployment status only if the application has been deployed to a network:

```
'Deployment and environment information
If My.Application.IsNetworkDeployed = True Then
    Console.
    WriteLine("Application deployed to a network via ClickOnce")

    Console.WriteLine("Current deployment version: {0}",
            My.Application.Deployment.CurrentVersion)
    Console.WriteLine("The application runs from: {0}",
            My.Application.Deployment.ActivationUri)
    Console.WriteLine("Is first time run: {0}",
            My.Application.Deployment.IsFirstRun)
End If
```

The CurrentVersion property is useful to understand the current *deployment* version, while ActivationUri is the address from which the application manifest is invoked. You can also programmatically check for updates invoking specific methods, such as CheckForUpdate, CheckForUpdateAsync, and CheckForUpdateAsyncCancel. The following is an example:

```
My.Application.Deployment.CheckForUpdate()
```

Luckily, My.Application.Deployment members' names are self-explanatory, and with the help of IntelliSense and a little bit of curiosity, you have in your hands all the power of such an object.

Retrieving Environment Variables

There are situations where you need to retrieve the content of the operating system's environment variables. This can be accomplished by invoking the GetEnvironmentVariable that receives the name of the variable as an argument. The following code shows how to retrieve the content of the PATH environment variable:

```
Dim PathEnvironmentVariable As String = My.Application.
                                 GetEnvironmentVariable("PATH")
```

Writing Entries to the Windows' Applications Log

The .NET Framework provides several ways of interacting with the operating system logs, but the My namespace offers an easy way to write information to the Windows application log. My.Application offers a Log property, of type Microsoft.VisualBasic.Logging.Log, which exposes members for writing information. The following code snippet shows how you can write a message to the application log invoking the WriteEntry method:

```
My.Application.Log.WriteEntry("Demonstrating My.Application.Log",
                    TraceEventType.Information)
```

The first argument is the message, and the second one is a member of the `TraceEventType` enumeration whose members are self-explanatory, thanks to IntelliSense, and allow specifying the level of your message. Alternatively, you can write the content of an entire exception invoking the `WriteException` method:

```
Try

Catch ex As Exception
    My.Application.Log.WriteException(ex)
End Try
```

You can also get control over the listeners and the file used by the .NET Framework by utilizing the `TraceSource` and `DefaultFileLogWriter`.

Retrieving Command-Line Arguments

If you need to retrieve command-line arguments for your application, `My.Application` offers a convenient way. To complete the following demonstration, go to the Debug tab of My Project and set whatever command-line arguments you like in the Command Line Arguments text box. `My.Application` offers a `CommandLineArgs` property, which is a `ReadOnlyCollection(Of String)` that stores such arguments. Each item in the collection represents a command-line argument. The following code shows how you can iterate such collection and check for available command-line arguments:

```
For Each argument As String In My.Application.CommandLineArgs
    Console.WriteLine(argument)
Next
```

My.Computer

`My.Computer` provides lots of shortcuts for accessing features on the local system, starting from the clipboard arriving at the Registry, passing through audio capabilities. This is a class exposing several properties, each one related to a computer area. This is a list of `My.Computer` properties:

▶ `FileSystem` provides members for accessing files, directories, and other objects on disk

▶ `Clipboard` provides members for setting data to and getting data from the system clipboard

▶ `Audio` allows playing audio files

▶ `Mouse` allows retrieving information on the installed mouse

▶ `Keyboard` provides members for getting information on the state of keys in the keyboard

▶ `Registry` provides members for getting and setting information to Windows Registry

- ▶ `Network` offers members for performing operations within the network that the computer is connected to

- ▶ `Ports` allows retrieving information on the computer's serial ports

- ▶ `Screen` allows retrieving information on the screen properties (Windows Forms only)

- ▶ `Info` provides a series of information about the running machine

As usual, IntelliSense provides detailed information on each member from the preceding properties. In the next section you learn to access your machine information with `My.Computer`, but providing examples for each member is not possible. Because of this, members for the biggest areas are summarized and code examples for the most important members are provided.

Working with the File System

`My.Computer` provides lots of shortcuts for performing most common operations on files and directories via the `FileSystem` property. Members are self-explanatory and easy to understand, so you can always take advantage of IntelliSense. To demonstrate how easy it is to work with the file system, let's go through some examples. The following code copies a directory into another one, then it creates a new directory, and finally it retrieves the current directory:

```
My.Computer.FileSystem.CopyDirectory("C:\Source", "C:\Target")
My.Computer.FileSystem.CreateDirectory("C:\Temp")
Dim currentDir As String = My.Computer.FileSystem.CurrentDirectory
```

You can also get information on Windows' special directories via the `SpecialDirectories` property as follows:

```
'Gets My Pictures path
Dim picturesFolder As String =
    My.Computer.FileSystem.SpecialDirectories.MyPictures
```

Working with files is also easy. For example, you can read or create a text file in one line of code:

```
'Read the content of a text file
Dim content As String =
    My.Computer.FileSystem.ReadAllText("C:\ADocument.txt")

'Creates a new text file
My.Computer.FileSystem.WriteAllText("C:\ADocument.txt", "File content",
                                    append:=False)
```

This can be useful if you do not need to create a text file dynamically, for example, line by line. For files, you can iterate a directory to get an array of strings storing all filenames as follows:

19

```
For Each item As String In My.Computer.FileSystem.GetFiles("C:\")
    'Do something here
Next
```

This last example allows extracting the filename of a full path name:

```
'Returns MyFile.txt
Dim parsedString As String =
    My.Computer.FileSystem.GetName("C:\Temp\MyFile.txt")
```

`My.Computer.FileSystem` is powerful and simplifies access to the file system resources avoiding the need to write lots of lines of code.

Working with the Clipboard

The `My.Computer.Clipboard` property provides members for working with the system clipboard. Table 19.1 summarizes the members.

TABLE 19.1   `My.Computer.Clipboard` Members

Member	Description
Clear	Clears the clipboard content
ContainsAudio	Checks if the clipboard contains an audio file
ContainsData	Checks if the clipboard contains data according to the specified format
ContainsFileDropList	Checks if the clipboard contains a file drop-down list
ContainsImage	Checks if the clipboard contains an image
ContainsText	Checks if the clipboard contains some text
GetAudioStream	Gets an audio file from the clipboard as a stream
GetData	Gets data from the clipboard according to the specified format
GetDataObject	Gets data from the clipboard as `IDataObject`
GetImage	Retrieves an image from the clipboard
GetFileDropDownList	Retrieves a file drop-down list from the clipboard
GetText	Retrieves text from the clipboard
SetAudio	Copies the specified audio to the clipboard
SetData	Copies the specified custom data to the clipboard
SetDataObject	Copies the specified `System.Windows.Forms.DataObject` to the clipboard
SetImage	Copies the specified image to the clipboard
SetText	Copies the specified text to the clipboard

The following code shows how you can clear the clipboard and then copy some text; in the end the code checks if some text is available and, if so, returns the text:

```
My.Computer.Clipboard.Clear()
My.Computer.Clipboard.SetText("This is some text")

If My.Computer.Clipboard.ContainsText Then
    Console.WriteLine(My.Computer.Clipboard.GetText)
End If
```

Playing Audio Files

`My.Computer.Audio` provides three methods for audio files reproduction. The first one is `Play`, which can play a .Wav file. The following is an example:

```
My.Computer.Audio.Play("C:\MySound.Wav", AudioPlayMode.WaitToComplete)
```

You need to pass at least the filename as the first argument; as an alternative, you can pass the .wav file as a byte array or a `FileStream`. The `AudioPlayMode` enumeration enables you to specify how the audio file needs to be played. `WaitToComplete` means that no other code will be executed until the reproduction ends; `Background`, which is the default setting, means that the audio is reproduced asynchronously; last, `BackgroundLoop` means that the audio file is reproduced in the loop until you explicitly invoke the `Stop` method as follows:

```
My.Computer.Audio.Play("C:\MySound.Wav",
                    AudioPlayMode.BackgroundLoop)
'Other code...
My.Computer.Audio.Stop()
```

The last method is `PlaySystemSound`, whose first argument is the system sound to reproduce, which works like this:

```
My.Computer.Audio.PlaySystemSound(Media.SystemSounds.Exclamation)
```

Sounds examples other than `Exclamation` are `Asterisk`, `Beep`, `Hand`, and `Question`.

Managing the Keyboard

You can check for the state of some keyboard keys. `My.Computer.Keyboard` lets you accomplish this via six properties. Three are about the Caps-lock, Num-lock, and Scroll-lock keys, whereas the other three let you get the state (pressed or not) of Alt, Shift, and Ctrl. The following code provides a complete example:

```
'All Boolean values
Console.WriteLine(My.Computer.Keyboard.AltKeyDown)
Console.WriteLine(My.Computer.Keyboard.CtrlKeyDown)
Console.WriteLine(My.Computer.Keyboard.ShiftKeyDown)
Console.WriteLine(My.Computer.Keyboard.CapsLock)
Console.WriteLine(My.Computer.Keyboard.NumLock)
Console.WriteLine(My.Computer.Keyboard.ScrollLock)
```

Working with the Registry

My.Computer provides fast access to Windows Registry. It exposes a Registry property wrapping lots of functionalities of Microsoft.Win32.Registry class for faster work. My.Computer.Registry offers some properties, of type Microsoft.Win32.RegistryKey, representing the most important areas of the Registry, such as HKEY_LOCAL_MACHINE (wrapped by the LocalMachine property), HKEY_ USERS (wrapped by Users), HKEY_CURRENT_USER (wrapped by CurrentUser), and HKEY_CLASSES_ROOT (wrapped by ClassesRoot). All of them provide methods for creating subkeys, querying, deleting, and setting values within subkeys. For example, the following code (which requires an Imports Microsoft.Win32 directive) creates a subkey in the HKEY_CURRENT_USER\Software key, providing a company name and the application name. The code also sets permissions for writing/reading the key and its eventual subkeys:

```
Dim regKey As RegistryKey = My.Computer.Registry.
            CurrentUser.CreateSubKey("Software\DelSole\MyApplication",
            RegistryKeyPermissionCheck.ReadWriteSubTree,
            RegistryOptions.None)
```

Because the CreateSubKey returns a RegistryKey object, you can invoke instance members from this type. For example, you can add values to the new key by invoking the SetValue method as follows:

```
'Value-name, actual value
regKey.SetValue("MyValue", 1)
```

You get the value of the desired subkey by invoking the GetValue method as follows:

```
'Returns "1"
Dim value As String = CStr(My.Computer.Registry.
    GetValue("HKEY_CURRENT_USER\Software\DelSole\MyApplication",
                                    "MyValue",
                                    Nothing))
```

Remember that GetValue returns Object, so you need to perform an explicit conversion according to the value type you expect. You also have the ability to determine what kind of value is associated to a value name. This can be accomplished by getting a RegistryValueKind value, such as DWord, Binary, String, and QWord (which is an enumeration from Microsoft.Win32) via the GetValueKind method so that you can also be more precise when requiring values:

```
'Returns DWORD
Dim valueKind As RegistryValueKind = regKey.GetValueKind("MyValue")

If valueKind = RegistryValueKind.DWord Then
        Dim value2 As Integer = _
            CInt(My.Computer.
            Registry.
```

```
        GetValue("HKEY_CURRENT_USER\Software\DelSole\MyApplication",
                    "MyValue", Nothing))
End If
```

In addition, a `GetNames` method returns an array of strings, each representing a value in the specified subkey if more than one value is stored within the subkey. The following code instead removes the previously created value:

```
regKey.DeleteValue("MyValue")
```

Remember to close (and dispose) the Registry key when you do not use it anymore:

```
regKey.Close()
regKey.Dispose()
```

Finally, you can delete a subkey by invoking the `DeleteSubKey` as follows:

```
My.Computer.Registry.
    CurrentUser.DeleteSubKey("Software\DelSole\MyApplication",
    True)
```

Other than the mentioned properties about Registry areas, `My.Computer.Registry` exposes just two interesting methods, `SetValue` and `GetValue`, which require you to specify long strings and that usually can be replaced by the same-named methods of the instance of `RegistryKey`. By the way, with `My.Computer.Registry` you can perform lots of tasks onto the system Registry writing code easier and faster.

Accessing the Network

If your machine is connected to a network, you can use the `My.Computer.Network` property that wraps some functionalities of the `System.Net` namespace. The most interesting members are the `IsNetworkAvailable` property that returns `True` if the machine is connected, the `DownloadFile` method that allows downloading a file from the network, `UploadFile` that allows uploading a file to the specified target on the network, and `Ping` that sends a ping to the specified address. The following code checks first for network availability, then sends a ping to my English language blog, and in the end attempts to download a file from the Italian VB Tips & Tricks community (where I'm a team member) passing credentials as strings:

```
    If My.Computer.Network.IsAvailable Then
        Try

            '2000 is the timeout
            Dim available As Boolean = My.Computer.
                                        Network.
Ping("http://community.visual-basic.it/AlessandroEnglish",
                        2000)
```

19

```
                    My.Computer.Network.DownloadFile("http://www.visual-
➥basic.it/scarica.asp?ID=1016",

                                        "C:\WpfDemo.zip",
                                        "MyUserName",
                                        "MyPassword")

          Catch ex As System.Net.WebException

          Catch ex As Exception

          End Try
      End If
```

Notice how a `System.Net.WebException` is caught in case there are any network problems, especially with the `DownloadFile` method. The `DownloadFile` requires you to specify the source as the first argument and the target file as the second one. You can also specify the source as a `System.Uri`; the method can also download html contents. `UploadFile` works similarly, in that it requires the name of the file to be uploaded and the address, also allowing credentials specifications. Both methods offer several overloads that IntelliSense explains in detail. About `Ping`, the methods returns `True` if the website is reachable.

Getting Computer Information

`My.Computer` provides the ability of retrieving information on the current machine. The first information is the machine name, which is available from `My.Computer.Name`, a property of type `String`. Second is the `My.Computer.Info` property of type `Microsoft.VisualBasic.Devices.ComputerInfo`, which collects information such as the total and available memory, both physical and virtual or the name, platform, and version of the operating system. The following code shows how you can get some information on the system:

```
Console.WriteLine("Computer name {0}: ", My.Computer.Name)
Console.WriteLine("Total physical memory {0}: ",
                  My.Computer.Info.TotalPhysicalMemory)
Console.WriteLine("Available physical memory {0}: ",
                  My.Computer.Info.AvailablePhysicalMemory)
Console.WriteLine("Operating system full name {0}: ",
                  My.Computer.Info.OSFullName)
Console.WriteLine("Operating system version: {0}",
                  My.Computer.Info.OSVersion)
Console.WriteLine("Installed User Interface culture: {0}",
                  My.Computer.Info.InstalledUICulture.Name)
```

`My.Computer` also exposes a `Clock` property that offers three subproperties: `GmtTime` that returns the local date and time expressed as GMT, `LocalTime` that returns the local date and time, and `TickCount` that returns the number of ticks considering the machine timer. This is how you can use it:

```
Console.WriteLine("GMT Time for local machine: {0}",
                My.Computer.Clock.GmtTime.ToString)
```

You can interact with system hardware with two other properties, `Mouse` and `Screen`. The first one allows knowing if your mouse has a wheel, if buttons' functionalities are swapped, or how many lines the scroll will be each time you move the wheel. This is an example:

```
Console.WriteLine("Mouse buttons are swapped: {0}",
                My.Computer.Mouse.ButtonsSwapped.ToString)
Console.WriteLine("Mouse has wheel: {0}",
                My.Computer.Mouse.WheelExists.ToString)
```

`Screen` is also interesting because it enables the retrieval of information on your display, such as the resolution, the device name, or the actual working area, but it is only available for Windows Forms applications. The following is an example, assuming you have a form with three `Label` controls:

```
Private Sub Form1_Load(sender As Object, e As EventArgs) Handles MyBase.Load
    Me.Label1.Text = "Screen resolution: " &
        My.Computer.Screen.Bounds.Width.ToString & _
        " x " & My.Computer.Screen.Bounds.Height.ToString
    Me.Label2.Text = "Bits per pixel: " & _
        My.Computer.Screen.BitsPerPixel.ToString
    Me.Label3.Text = "Working area: " &
        My.Computer.Screen.WorkingArea.Width.ToString & _
        " x " & My.Computer.Screen.WorkingArea.Height.ToString
End Sub
```

Figure 19.1 shows the global result of the preceding code running on my machine.

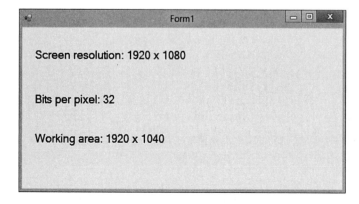

FIGURE 19.1   Information on the local machine using `My.Computer`.

You can obtain detailed information about both the computer and the operating system, including localization properties. `My.Computer` members for retrieving information are always self-explanatory, but you can always take advantage of IntelliSense and the Object Browser tool.

My.Settings

One of the most common requirements for applications is providing the ability of storing user preferences, such as the graphic theme, personal folders, options, and so on. Generally, there are two kinds of settings that the .NET Framework lets you save within the application configuration file: application-level settings and user-level settings. Application-level settings are related to the general behavior of the application, and users will not have the ability of providing modifications. User-level settings are related to each user profile that runs the applications and allows storing and editing preferences. `My` namespace provides a class named `My.Settings`, which offers members that easily allow working with settings at both levels, but only user-level settings can be written. At a higher level `My.Settings` is the code representation of the Settings tab in My Project. Therefore, this discussion about `My.Settings` starts by with the Settings designer and then how to work with settings in code.

Create a new Console project (if not yet done) and open My Project; then click the **Settings** tab. Figure 19.2 shows the Settings designer.

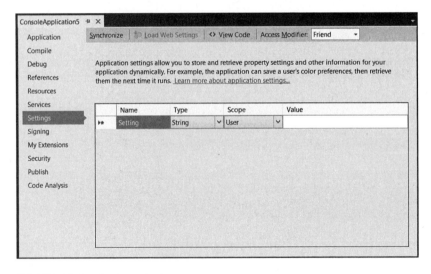

FIGURE 19.2   Settings designer.

Each setting is represented by a variable that can be of any .NET type (as long as it is marked as serializable) storing the desired value. This variable can be provided at both application level and user level, with the condition that only user-level variables can be also written. You now learn how to design settings and then how to use them in code.

Imagine you want to provide a simple way for checking if the application is running for the first time. In the Name column replace the default Settings identifier with IsFirstTimeRun. In the Type column choose the Boolean type from the combo box, and in the Scope column ensure that User is selected. In the Value column choose True from the combo box.

Notice that Visual Studio can provide appropriate values depending on the setting type; for Boolean values, it offers True and False. After this sequence, your Settings Designer looks like Figure 19.3.

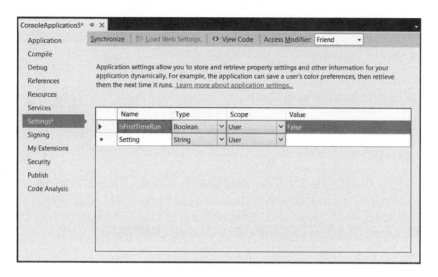

FIGURE 19.3   Providing a Boolean user-level setting.

You can now write some code to check if the application is running for the first time and, if so, set the IsFirstTimeRun setting to False as follows:

```
Sub UserSettingsDemo()

    If My.Settings.IsFirstTimeRun = True Then
        Console.WriteLine("The application is running for the first time")
            My.Settings.IsFirstTimeRun = False
            My.Settings.Save()
    Else
        Console.
        WriteLine("The application is already familiar with your system!")
    End If

End Sub
```

19

When you first launch the application, you get the following result:

```
The application is running for the first time
```

The code also changed the `IsFirstTimeRun` setting from `True` to `False`; this is possible because it is a user-level setting. If it were an application-level setting, it would be offered as a read-only property.

APPLICATION-LEVEL ONLY SETTINGS

With the Settings Designer you can define different kinds of settings, both at application level and user level. Among these settings, Connection Strings and Web Services URL are only available at application level to avoid modifications in code. In this way, only the appropriate personnel can make the right modifications if needed.

Notice also that you have to invoke the `Save` method; otherwise changes will not be saved. To check that everything works, rerun the application; you should now get the following message:

```
The application is already familiar with your system!
```

With the same technique you can easily define other settings of different types. You are not limited to types shown in the default combo box. You can choose any other .NET type that supports serialization by clicking the **Browse** command at the bottom of the combo box. This displays the Select a Type window (see Figure 19.4) where you can make your choice.

Settings definitions and default values are stored within the application configuration (app.config) file as XML definition. If your project does not already contain a configuration file, Visual Studio 2015 adds one.

User-level settings are defined within a section named `userSettings`. The following is an excerpt from the app.config file for the demo project showing the definition of the previously described `IsFirstTimeRun` setting:

```
<userSettings>
    <MyNamespace.My.MySettings>
        <setting name="IsFirstTimeRun" serializeAs="String">
            <value>True</value>
        </setting>
    </MyNamespace.My.MySettings>
</userSettings>
```

FIGURE 19.4   Selecting a nondefault .NET type for designing settings.

Notice how each setting is defined by a setting node that also defines the setting's name and way of serialization. (Although serialized as a string, based on its value, the .NET Framework can recognize the setting as Boolean.) Each setting node has a child node named value that stores the default value for the setting.

CONFIGURATION FILE NAMING

Your application configuration file is named app.config as long as it is included in your project folder. When the application is built in to the target folder (such as the default Debug and Release subfolders), the configuration file takes the complete name of the executable (for example, MyApplication.exe) plus the .config extension (for example, MyApplication.exe.config).

Similarly, application-level settings are stored within a section named `application-Settings`. The following is the excerpt related to the test setting previously shown:

```
<applicationSettings>
    <MyNamespace.My.MySettings>
        <setting name="Setting" serializeAs="String">
            <value>test</value>
        </setting>
    </MyNamespace.My.MySettings>
</applicationSettings>
```

Settings also have a Visual Basic code counterpart. Each setting is mapped to a Visual Basic property. To understand this, click the **Show All Files** button in Solution Explorer and then expand the My Project folder; double-click the **Settings.designer.vb** file under Settings.Settings. Among the code that defines `My.Settings`, you can also find the definition for your custom settings. The `IsFirstTimeRun` setting defined in the previous example is mapped to a VB property as follows:

```
<Global.System.Configuration.UserScopedSettingAttribute(), _
 Global.System.Diagnostics.DebuggerNonUserCodeAttribute(), _
 Global.System.Configuration.DefaultSettingValueAttribute("True")> _
Public Property IsFirstTimeRun() As Boolean
    Get
        Return CType(Me("IsFirstTimeRun"), Boolean)
    End Get
    Set(value As Boolean)
        Me("IsFirstTimeRun") = Value
    End Set
End Property
```

The `System.Configuration.UserScopedSettingAttribute` tells the compiler that the setting has user-level scope, whereas the `System.Configuration.DefaultSettingValueAttribute` tells the compiler that the default value for the property is `True`. Notice how an explicit conversion with `CType` is performed to avoid any problems when deserializing. Now you know how and where settings are defined, but you still probably do not know where they are actually stored when you run the application outside Visual Studio (for example, in production environments). The .NET Framework creates a folder for the application within the AppData\Local folder in Windows, which has user-level scope. If you consider the current example, named MyNamespace on my machine, the .NET Framework created the following folders structure (on Windows 8.x, Windows 7, and Windows Vista): C:\Users\Alessandro\AppData\Local\MyNamespace\MyNamespace.vshost.exe_Url_wizb0ypr4ultyjhh1g1o352espg4ehdd\1.0.0.0. This auto-generated folder contains a file named user.config that contains the following, simple markup:

```
<?xml version="1.0" encoding="utf-8"?>
<configuration>
    <userSettings>
        <MyNamespace.My.MySettings>
            <setting name="IsFirstTimeRun" serializeAs="String">
                <value>False</value>
            </setting>
        </MyNamespace.My.MySettings>
    </userSettings>
</configuration>
```

As you can see, it is the same piece of XML code that was originally defined within the application configuration file, but now it stays as a single file within a user-level folder. This file is the place where changes to an application's settings are effectively saved. Visual Studio provides a convenient way for restoring such files to the default settings' value by just clicking the **Synchronize** button in the Settings Designer.

BRINGING SETTINGS FORWARD TO NEW VERSIONS

It is worth noting that the live applications need to have the `Upgrade` method called to bring settings forward to new versions. Otherwise each new version will use the default settings again. The flaw is that you only want to call `Upgrade` when needed to avoid migrating the settings each time, and the best workaround is to set a Boolean setting called, for example, `NeedsUpgrade` with a default of `True`, and on startup, when that is true call `Upgrade` and then set `NeedsUpgrade` to `False`. It will only then be true again on the next new version of the assembly.

My.Settings Events

`My.Settings` provides some interesting events that allow understanding of what is happening behind the scenes. Here are the following four events:

▶ `SettingChanging`, which is raised just before a setting value is changed

▶ `PropertyChanged`, which is raised just after a setting value has been changed

▶ `SettingsLoaded`, which is raised just after settings values are loaded

▶ `SettingsSaving`, which is raised just before settings values are persisted to disk

To handle such events you need to double-click the **Settings.Designer.vb** file in Solution Explorer.

For example, imagine you want to validate a setting before changes are saved. To accomplish this, add a new `String` setting in the Settings Designer and name the setting as `ValidationTest`. The goal is to avoid saving the string value if it is null. The following code accomplishes this:

```
Private Sub MySettings_SettingsSaving(sender As Object,
                                      e As
                    System.ComponentModel.CancelEventArgs) _
                                Handles Me.SettingsSaving


    If My.Settings.ValidationTest Is Nothing Then
        Throw New NullReferenceException("Cannot save a null string")
        e.Cancel = True
    End If
End Sub
```

The SettingsSaving event allows performing some checks before values are saved.

The e variable of type System.ComponentModel.CancelEventArgs provides a Cancel property that cancels saving when set to True. The following example shows instead how you can handle the SettingChanging event that is raised before a setting value gets changed:

```
Private Sub MySettings_SettingChanging(sender As Object,
                                       e As _
                                       System.Configuration.
                                       SettingChangingEventArgs) _
                                       Handles Me.SettingChanging
    Console.WriteLine("About to change the settings values")
    'Waits for one second
    System.Threading.Thread.Sleep(1000)
End Sub
```

My.Settings provides a convenient way for managing user settings in a strongly typed way offering a modern infrastructure that is more efficient than older .ini files.

My.Resources

Visual Studio and the .NET Framework enable you to include resources within your application. Resources are different kinds of information that would usually be available from external files, such as sounds, images, and text. You can embed in your application all resources you want using My.Resources and the Resources Designer.

WPF RESOURCES

Things behave a little differently in XAML-based platforms like WPF and Windows Store apps. Because of their particular infrastructures, embedding resources using the Resources Designer is a practice that you must avoid. To understand how WPF resources work, take a look at the official page in the MSDN Library: http://msdn.microsoft.com/en-us/library/ms750613(VS.110).aspx. This chapter describes resources with Console and Windows Forms applications for backward compatibility with existing code you might have written in the past.

Differently from other My members, My.Resources is a namespace defining subsequent members that can wrap in code resources that you define in the designer. At this point, you need to open **My Project** and then select the **Resources** tab. Figure 19.5 shows the Resources Designer.

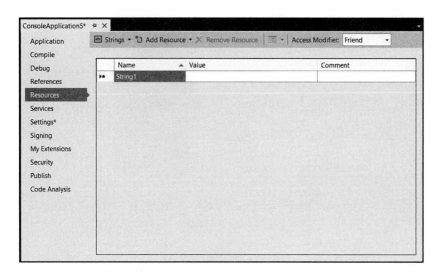

FIGURE 19.5   The Resources Designer.

Each time you add a new resource, Visual Studio generates a .NET property that provides managed access to the resource itself. For example, in the Name column replace the String1 default identifier with TestString and type **Resources demonstration** in the Value column. If you like, you can also provide a comment. Visual Studio generates a TestString property of type String and Friend visibility that you can access like any other property, as in the following code:

```
Console.WriteLine(My.Resources.TestString)
```

The interesting thing is that the Visual Basic compiler will try to format the string according to the current culture settings. By clicking the **Add Resource** button, you will be prompted with a series of file types to add as resources. If you add a text file, the file will be represented by a String property. You can add both existing or new files. For example, click the **Add Resource** button and select the **New Image, JPEG Image...** command. After you specify the new image name, Visual Studio 2015 shows the image editor where you can leverage your drawing ability. Figure 19.6 shows an editor in action.

19

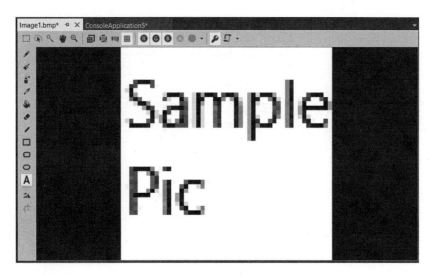

FIGURE 19.6   The Visual Studio 2015's built-in image editor.

After you create your image, or even if you add an existing one from disk, the IDE generates a property of type System.Drawing.Bitmap pointing to the image. If you have a
Windows Forms application, you could recall your image as follows:

```
'PictureBox1 is a Windows Forms "PictureBox" control
'MyCustomImage is the name of the new custom image
Me.PictureBox1.Image = My.Resources.MyCustomImage
```

You can then pick images from resources if you need to populate a PictureBox control at
design time by clicking the **Browse** button from the Properties window to set the Image
property. Figure 19.7 shows how you can select an image directly from resources.

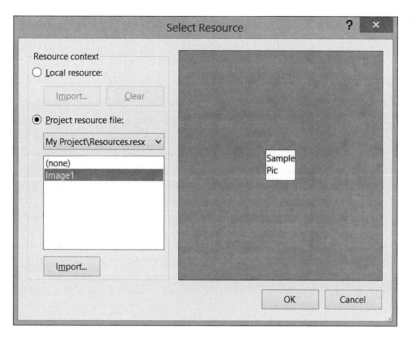

FIGURE 19.7   Assigning an image to a PictureBox picking from resources.

The same is true for icons: You can create and draw a new icon with the Visual Studio Designer and then assign it to a Windows Forms Icon property. For audio files, you can add only .Wav files to ensure that they are automatically recognized as audio files. Such files are then mapped as System.IO.UnmanagedMemoryStream objects and can be played via My.Computer as follows:

```
My.Computer.Audio.Play(My.Resources.
                       AnAudioFile,
                       AudioPlayMode.WaitToComplete)
```

You can also add files other than text, pictures, icons, and audio. When Visual Studio cannot recognize a file type, it returns it from resources by byte array (System.Byte()), so you should implement code to analyze the particular resource. Visual Studio also creates a project-level folder named Resources where it stores resource files. Another interesting thing is to understand how resources are defined in code. Each time you add a resource via the designer, the IDE generates a Visual Basic property for it. For example, the following code shows how the new .jpeg image is mapped in code:

```
Friend ReadOnly Property MyCustomImage() As System.Drawing.Bitmap
    Get
        Dim obj As Object = ResourceManager.
                         GetObject("MyCustomImage", resourceCulture)
        Return CType(obj, System.Drawing.Bitmap)
    End Get
End Property
```

And this is how the first string resource is mapped:

```
Friend ReadOnly Property TestString() As String
    Get
        Return ResourceManager.
              GetString("TestString", resourceCulture)
    End Get
End Property
```

The `ResourceManager` class provides methods for retrieving resources according to the specified culture that by default is the system one. Such properties are available in the Resources.designer.vb file that should never be edited manually.

Getting Resources by Name in Code

Sometimes you need to access resources by name in code. This can be accomplished via the Reflection, which is discussed in Chapter 44. The following code provides an example:

```
'Returns the specified resource of type String
'usage:
'Dim myRes As String = GetResourceByName("TestString")
Function GetResourceByName(resourceName As String) As String
    'An example for [Application Name].[Resource File]
    'is the current app:
    'MyNamespace.Resources.resx
    Dim rm As New ResourceManager("[Application Name].[Resource File]",
                                  Assembly.GetExecutingAssembly)

    Return rm.GetString(resourceName)
End Function
```

In this case the method returns resources of type `String`, but you can implement methods that return a different type.

My.User

`My.User` is a property that allows getting information on the user who logged in to the Windows operating system and that is running the application. Such a property is of type `Microsoft.VisualBasic.ApplicationServices.User` and is a wrapper of this last mentioned one, meaning that you can invoke both and obtain the same results. Utilizing `My.User` is straightforward because it offers just a few but easy-to-understand members, as summarized in Table 19.2.

TABLE 19.2   `My.User` Members

Member	Type	Description
CurrentPrincipal	Property	Retrieves information on the current user based on the System.Security.Principal implementation for a role-based security
InitializeWithWindowsUser	Method	Associates the application with the current principal that logged into Windows
Name	Property	A string that stores the name of the currently logged user
IsAuthenticated	Property	A Boolean value representing if the current user is authenticated
IsInRole	Method	Returns True if the current user belongs to the specified role

Listing 19.1 shows how you can get information on the current user that runs the application. Notice how an invocation to `InitializeWithWindowsUser` is required to associate the current user to the application.

LISTING 19.1   Using `My.User` to Get Information on the Current User

```
Module Module1

    Sub Main()
        MyUserInformation()
        Console.ReadLine()
    End Sub


    Sub MyUserInformation()
        My.User.InitializeWithWindowsUser()
        Console.WriteLine("Current user is: {0}", My.User.Name)
        Console.WriteLine("User is authenticated: {0}", My.User.IsAuthenticated)
        Console.WriteLine("Application is running as Administrator: {0}",
                        My.User.IsInRole("BUILTIN\Administrators"))
        Console.WriteLine(My.User.CurrentPrincipal.
                        Identity.AuthenticationType.ToString)
    End Sub

End Module
```

The code shown in Listing 19.1 produces, on my machine, the following output:

```
Current user is: DELSOLELAPTOP\Alessandro
User is authenticated: True
Application is running as Administrator: False
NTLM
```

Notice how the username is provided as "Computer name\user name" and also how the role for the `IsInRole` method requires the name of the machine. (BUILTIN is a default value for all machines.) The authentication type is determined via the `CurrentPrincipal.Identity.AuthenticationType` property. Here, `Identity` is a `System.Security.Principal.IIdentity` object that provides information about a user, considering the role-based security system in the .NET Framework (for more information, check the MSDN documentation). With a few lines of code, you can get information about the current user without the need of dealing with classes and members from the `Microsoft.VisualBasic.ApplicationServices.User` object.

My.WebServices

When you have in your application references to web services, you can easily reach members provided by the proxy classes using `My.WebServices`. For example, if you have a proxy class named `DataAccess` exposing a `GetCustomers` method, you can write the following line:

```
My.WebServices.DataAccess.GetCustomers()
```

This is a rapid way for invoking members from referenced web services (as long as they are in the same solution of your application).

Extending My

One of the most interesting features of the `My` namespace is that it is extensible with custom members. You can both extend `My` at the root level or extend existing members such as `Application` and `Computer`. The first goal of this section is to show how you can extend `My` at the higher level, implementing functionalities for working with collections, such as a property that allows converting from a generic collection into an `ObservableCollection(Of T)`. You need to mimic how Visual Basic 2015 handles the `My` namespace, so first add a new module to the project and name it **MyCollectionsUtils**. Each member you want to be added to `My` must start with the **My** letters; this is the reason for using the `MyCollectionsUtils` identifier. The compiler can then distinguish that this member belongs to `My` if you enclose it within such a namespace. Add a reference to the WindowsBase.dll assembly (not required in WPF applications) and then write the code shown in Listing 19.2.

LISTING 19.2   Extending `My` at Root Level

```
Imports System.Collections.ObjectModel

Namespace My

    <Global.Microsoft.VisualBasic.HideModuleName(),
     Global.System.Diagnostics.DebuggerNonUserCode()>
    Module MyCollectionsUtils
```

```
        Private helper As New _
               ThreadSafeObjectProvider(Of ObservableCollectionHelper)

        Friend ReadOnly Property CollectionsUtils _
              As ObservableCollectionHelper
           Get
               Return helper.GetInstance
               helper = Nothing
           End Get
        End Property
     End Module

End Namespace

Class ObservableCollectionHelper

   Public Function ConvertToObservableCollection(Of T) _
                      (collection As ICollection(Of T)) _
                      As ObservableCollection(Of T)
        Return New ObservableCollection(Of T)(collection)
   End Function
End Class
```

FRIEND VISIBILITY

Module's members are marked as `Friend` to reproduce the default Visual Basic behavior.

There are some tasks to perform after examining Listing 19.2. First, notice how the `ObservableCollectionHelper` class exposes a public method that effectively converts an `ICollection(Of T)` into a new `ObservableCollection`. Also notice how there is the need to explicitly provide a `Namespace My..End Namespace` declaration, which encloses custom members for `My`. The `MyCollectionsUtils` module exposes members that are effectively accessible via `My`. To replicate the VB default behavior, the module is marked as `System.Diagnostics.NonUserCode` so that the debugger does not step into such code (if you instead need debugger support, remove this attribute) and as `Microsoft.VisualBasic.HideModuleName` that prevents the module name to be shown by IntelliSense when invoking your custom members. Then notice how the helper field is of type `ThreadSafeObjectProvider(Of T)`. According to the Microsoft documentation, this is a best practice because it ensures that each thread invoking `My.CollectionsUtils` has access to a separate instance. The read-only property `CollectionsUtils` then wraps the `ObservableCollectionHelper.ConvertToObservableCollection` method being exposed through the `GetInstance` invocation. When you have created your extension, you can use it in a simple way. The following code shows how you can convert a `List(Of Integer)` into an `ObservableCollection` using your custom `My.CollectionsUtils` member:

19

```
Dim someInts As New List(Of Integer) From {1, 2, 3}

Dim obs As ObservableCollection(Of Integer) =

        My.CollectionsUtils.ConvertToObservableCollection(someInts)

For Each number As Integer In obs
    Console.WriteLine(number)
Next
```

After seeing how you can extend My at the root level, let's now see how you can customize existing members.

Extending My.Application and My.Computer

Extending existing members such as Application and Computer is straightforward because both are implemented as partial classes, so you can add your own partial classes without the need of editing auto-generated code. Previous considerations remain unchanged, meaning that your partial classes' names need to start with My (such as MyApplication and MyComputer) and that both must be enclosed within an explicit declaration of a Namespace My..End Namespace code block. For example, imagine you want to extend My.Application with a method that associates a file extension with your application so that each time you double-click a file with that particular extension it will be opened by your application. Listing 19.3 accomplishes this (notice that if you run Windows Vista, Windows 7, or Windows 8.x you need to start Visual Studio with administrative rights).

LISTING 19.3   Extending My.Application

```
Imports Microsoft.Win32

Namespace My

    Partial Friend Class MyApplication

        Public Function AssociateExtension(extension As String,
                                           mimeType As String) As Boolean
            Try
                'Creates a registry entry for the extension
                My.Computer.Registry.ClassesRoot.
                CreateSubKey(extension).SetValue("",
                mimeType, RegistryValueKind.String)

                'Creates a registry entry for the Mime type
                'Environment.GetCommandLineArgs(0) returns
                'the executable name for Console applications
                My.Computer.Registry.ClassesRoot.
                CreateSubKey(mimeType & "\shell\open\command").
```

```
            SetValue("", Environment.GetCommandLineArgs(0) & " ""%1"" ",
            RegistryValueKind.String)

            Return True
        Catch ex As Exception
            Return False
        End Try
    End Function
    End Class
End Namespace
```

Notice how the `MyApplication` class is marked as `Partial Friend`. This is required to match the definition provided by Visual Basic to `My.Application`. Now you can use the extension as you normally would do with `My.Application`. The following is an example:

```
Dim succeeded As Boolean =
    My.Application.AssociateExtension(".ale",
    "AlessandroDelSole/document")
```

Extending `My.Computer` works similarly. For example, you could implement a property that returns the MIME type for the specified filename. Code in Listing 19.4 demonstrates this.

LISTING 19.4   Extending `My.Computer`

```
Imports Microsoft.Win32

Namespace My
    Partial Friend Class MyComputer

        Public ReadOnly Property MimeType(fileName As String) As String
            Get
                Return getMimeType(fileName)
            End Get
        End Property

        Private Function getMimeType(fileName As String) As String

            Dim mimeType As String = String.Empty

            Dim fileExtension = System.IO.Path.
                            GetExtension(fileName).ToLower()
            Dim registryKey = Registry.ClassesRoot.
                            OpenSubKey(fileExtension)

            If registryKey IsNot Nothing And _
```

19

```
                           registryKey.GetValue("Content Type") _
                           IsNot Nothing Then

            mimeType = registryKey.
                           GetValue("Content Type").ToString
        Else
            imeType = ""
        End If
        Return mimeType
    End Function


    End Class
End Namespace
```

You still need to mark the class as Partial Friend by enclosing it within the My namespace declaration. At this point, you can use your extension as usual—for example, to retrieve the MIME type of a text file:

```
Dim mimeType As String = My.Computer.MimeType("Testfile.txt")
```

Of course, you are not limited to extending Application and Computer; you can also extend Settings and Resources.

Extending My.Resources and My.Settings

Extending My.Resources and My.Settings is also possible, although with a few differences. Resources is a namespace, so you need to declare it as follows:

```
Namespace My.Resources
    Friend Module MyResources
        'Your code here
    End Module
End Namespace
```

Generally, you do not need custom extensions to Resources; you could decide to offer alternative localized versions of some contents. Extending My.Settings works more similarly to Application and Computer, but you do not need to provide custom extensions here because the Visual Studio 2015 Designer provides a graphical environment for performing all operations you need and selecting all available .NET types.

My in Different Applications

Now that you know how My can be customized, you can easily understand why different kinds of Visual Basic applications have their own customizations, provided by the IDE. For example, Windows Presentation Foundation applications provide a My.Windows property that allows access to windows' instances, as follows:

```
'Get the instance of the Main window
 Dim aWindows As Window = My.Windows.MainWindow
```

This is mainly due to the support offered in code by the My namespace to the Application Framework feature. This feature enables you to execute special tasks at the beginning and at the end of the application lifetime, such as showing splash screens or establishing what form is the main application form normally. In Windows Forms applications the application framework is enabled by default, and you can get in touch with it by opening My Project and selecting the **Application** tab, as shown in Figure 19.8.

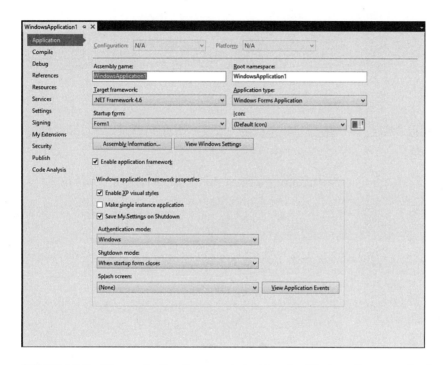

FIGURE 19.8   The application framework designer for Windows Forms applications.

Enabling the application framework allows you to visually manage features with no lines of code, although you are allowed to customize the related auto-generated code. For example, the following line manually establishes that My.Settings has to be saved when the application shuts down:

```
My.Application.SaveMySettingsOnExit = True
```

The following line shows how you instead can set the minimum number of milliseconds for a splash screen to be shown:

```
My.Application.MinimumSplashScreenDisplayTime = 1000
```

19

For WPF applications the application framework is slightly different, as shown in Figure 19.9.

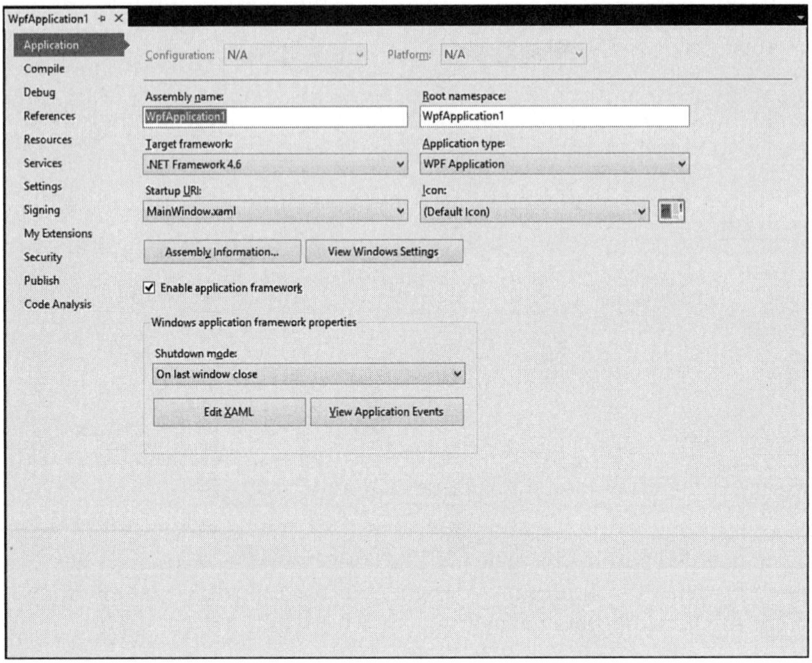

FIGURE 19.9   The application framework for WPF applications.

The following lines show how you can take advantage of `My.Application` in WPF to retrieve some information:

```
'The main Window XAML's uri
Dim startup As String = My.Application.StartupUri.ToString


'Main Window
Dim mainWindow As Window = My.Application.MainWindow


'Application resources
Dim appResources As ResourceDictionary = My.Application.Resources
```

All members are self-explanatory, so IntelliSense can be a great friend to you in this situation, too. In both Windows Forms and WPF applications, the **View Application Events** button redirects you to the appropriate file for defining application events (Application. xaml.vb in WPF and Application.Designer.vb in Win Forms). For web applications, Silverlight applications do not support the My namespace, and ASP.NET applications do not offer the `My.Application` and `My.WebServices` members; they instead expose the `My.Response` and `My.Request` properties that respectively wrap members from `System.Web.HttpResponse` and `System.Web.HttpRequest`.

Understanding Application Events

Applications that provide support for the application framework can be also managed with application events. This is the typical case of client applications such as Windows Forms and WPF applications. Windows Forms applications provide the following events:

- ▶ `NetworkAvailabilityChanged`, which is raised when the network becomes available or the connection is no longer available

- ▶ `ShutDown`, which is raised when the application shuts down

- ▶ `Startup`, which is raised when the application starts

- ▶ `StartupNextInstance`, which is raised when another instance of the application starts up

- ▶ `UnhandledException`, which is raised when the application encounters an unhandled exception during tasks that involve the application framework

Application events are handled within the code file that implements `My.Application` customizations, which by default is Application.designer.vb. The following example shows how you can intercept the network state change:

```
Private Sub MyApplication_NetworkAvailabilityChanged(sender As Object,
                                e As Microsoft.VisualBasic.
                                Devices.
                                NetworkAvailableEventArgs) _
                                Handles
                                Me.NetworkAvailabilityChanged

    If e.IsNetworkAvailable = False Then
        'Network no longer available
    Else
        'Network available
    End If
End Sub
```

In WPF applications you have more events that you can handle. First, application events in WPF are handled in the Application.xaml.vb file. You have the following events available:

- ▶ `Activated`, which is raised when the application gets the foreground focus

- ▶ `Deactivated`, which is raised when the application loses the foreground focus

▶ `DispatcherUnhandledException`, which is raised when the Dispatcher object encounters an unhandled exception

▶ `Exit`, which is raised when the application shuts down

▶ `LoadCompleted`, `Navigated`, `Navigating`, `NavigationFailed`, `NavigationProgress`, and `NavigationStopped`, which are raised in case of navigation applications, which is self-explanatory if you think of navigation between pages

▶ `Startup`, which is raised when the application starts up and specifies the main UI object

▶ `FragmentNavigation`, which is raised when navigating to a specific XAML Uri

▶ `SessionEnding`, which is raised when the user logs off from Windows or is shutting down the system

The following example shows how you can intercept the `SessionEnding` event and decide to back up your work if the `e.ReasonSessionEnding` property has value `ReasonSessionEnding.Shutdown`:

```
Private Sub Application_SessionEnding(sender As Object,
                                      e As _
                                      SessionEndingCancelEventArgs) _
                                      Handles Me.SessionEnding

    If e.ReasonSessionEnding = ReasonSessionEnding.Shutdown Then
        'Backup your files here
    End If
End Sub
```

Application events provide a great way for getting information on what happens behind the scenes of the application lifetime.

Summary

The `My` namespace is a unique feature of Visual Basic language that offers lots of shortcuts to most common operations. It was first made available in VB 2005. In this chapter you saw how you can interact with your application with `My.Application` and how you can perform operations on your system with `My.Computer`, including file operations, Registry operations, and clipboard operations. You then got information about an important feature provided by `My.Settings`, which has the capability to save and load user preferences using the Visual Studio Designer and managed code; this is a convenient way if compared to old initialization files. Next you learned about `My.Resources`, a special place for embedding files in your executable, typically for Console and Windows Forms applications. Finally, you got in touch with one of the most important features in `My`: the ability to extend the namespace with custom members, both at root level and existing members.

CHAPTER 20

Advanced Language Features

Back in 2008, the .NET Framework 3.5 introduced revolutionary technologies such as LINQ. Because of its complex infrastructure, all .NET languages required new keywords, syntaxes, and constructs to interact with LINQ but that could be successfully used in lots of other scenarios. Visual Basic 2010 introduced even more features to make the coding experience better, and now Visual Basic 2015 not only continues to support those language features but also has support for new things like debugging lambda expressions. Most of the language features discussed in this chapter are important for the comprehension of the next chapters, so it is recommended that you pay particular attention to the topics presented here.

Local Type Inference

Local type inference is a language feature that allows you to omit specifying the data type of a local variable even if `Option Strict` is set to `On`. The Visual Basic compiler can deduce (*infer*) the most appropriate data type depending on the variable's usage. The easiest way to understand and hopefully appreciate local type inference is to provide a code example. Consider the following code and pay attention to the comments:

```
Sub Main()
    'The compiler infers String
    Dim oneString = "Hello Visual Basic 2015!"

    'The compiler infers Integer
    Dim oneInt = 324

    'The compiler infers Double
```

```
    Dim oneDbl = 123.456

    'The compiler infers Boolean

    Dim oneBool = True
End Sub
```

As you can see, the code doesn't specify the type for all variables because the compiler can infer the most appropriate data type according to the usage of a variable. To ensure that the VB compiler inferred the correct type, pass the mouse pointer over the variable declaration to retrieve information via a useful tooltip, as shown in Figure 20.1.

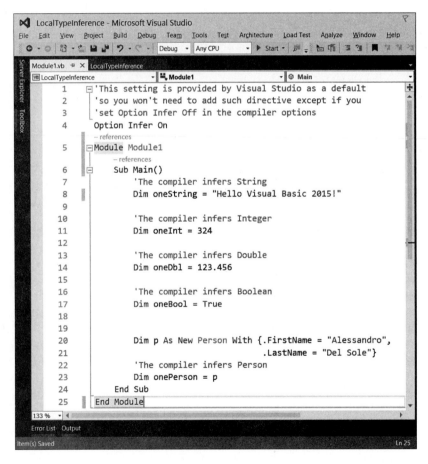

FIGURE 20.1   A tooltip indicates which type the Visual Basic compiler inferred to local variables.

BEHIND THE SCENES OF LOCAL TYPE INFERENCE

Types' inference is determined via the dominant type algorithm. This was described perfectly (and is still valid) in the Visual Basic 11.0 language specifications document, available at http://www.microsoft.com/en-us/download/details.aspx?id=15039.

The local type inference also works with custom types, as demonstrated by the following example:

```
Dim p As New Person With {.FirstName = "Alessandro",
                          .LastName = "Del Sole"}
'The compiler infers Person
Dim onePerson = p
```

You can also use local type inference within loops or in any other circumstance you like:

```
'The compiler infers System.Diagnostic.Process
For Each proc In Process.GetProcesses
    Console.WriteLine(proc.ProcessName)
Next
```

Option Infer Directive

To enable or disable local type inference, the Visual Basic grammar provides the `Option Infer` directive. `Option Infer On` enables inference, whereas `Option Infer Off` disables it. You do not need to explicitly provide an `Option Infer` directive because it is offered at the project level by Visual Studio. By default, `Option Infer` is `On`. If you want to change the default settings for the current project, open My Project and then switch to the **Compile** tab. There you can find the Visual Basic compiler options, including `Option Infer`. If you instead want to change settings for each new project, select the **Options** command from the Tools menu. When the Options dialog box appears, move to the **Projects and Solutions** tab and select the **VB defaults** item, as shown in Figure 20.2.

20

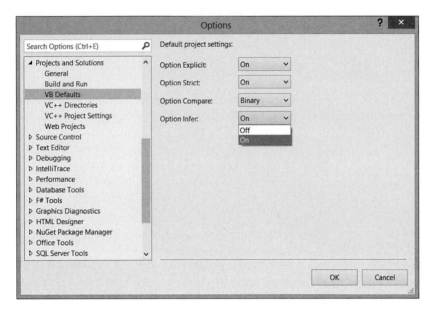

FIGURE 20.2   Changing the default behavior for `Option Infer`.

You then need to add an `Option Infer On` directive if you want to switch back to local type inference.

Local Type Inference Scope

The word *local* in the local type inference definition has a special meaning. Local type inference works only with local variables defined within code blocks and does not work with class-level declarations. For example, consider the following code:

```
Class Person

    Property LastName As String
    Property FirstName As String

    Function FullName() As String
        'Local variable: local type inference works
        Dim completeName = Me.LastName & " " & Me.FirstName
        Return completeName
    End Function
End Class
```

Local type inference affects the `completeName` local variable, which is enclosed within a method. Now consider the following code:

```
'Both Option Strict and Option Infer are On
Class Person
```

```
'Local type inference does not work with
'class level variables. An error will be
'thrown.
Private completeName
```

The preceding code will not be compiled because local type inference does not affect class-level declarations; therefore, the Visual Basic compiler throws an error if `Option Strict` is `On`. If `Option Strict` is `Off`, the `completeName` class-level variable will be considered of type `Object` but still won't be affected by local type inference. So be aware of this possible situation. The conclusion is that you always need to explicitly provide a type for class-level variables, whereas you can omit the specification with local variables.

WHY LOCAL TYPE INFERENCE?

If you are an old-school developer, you will probably be surprised and perhaps unhappy by local type inference because you have always written your code to be as explicit as possible. You will not be obliged to declare types by taking advantage of local type inference except when you need to generate *anonymous types*, which are discussed later in this chapter. Also, in Visual Basic 2015, local type inference is very useful with the null-conditional operator because it prevents you from needing to provide the appropriate type, especially with nullable value types. I always use (and suggest) the local type inference because it's straightforward and avoids the need of worrying about types while still providing type safety, especially with different kinds of query result when working with LINQ. I often use this feature in the rest of the book.

Array Literals

The array literals feature works like the local type inference but is specific to arrays. It was first introduced in Visual Basic 2010. Consider this array of strings declaration as you would write it in Visual Basic 2008:

```
Dim anArrayOfStrings() As String = {"One", "Two", "Three"}
```

In Visual Basic 2015 you can write it as follows:

```
'The compiler infers String()
Dim anArrayOfStrings = {"One", "Two", "Three"}
```

According to the preceding code, you are still required to place only a couple of parentheses, but you can omit the type that is correctly inferred by the compiler as you can easily verify by passing the mouse pointer over the variable declaration. Of course, array literals work with value types, too, as shown here:

```
'The compiler infers Double
Dim anArrayOfDouble = {1.23, 2.34, 3.45}
'The compiler infers Integer
Dim anArrayOfInteger = {4, 3, 2, 1}
```

Array literals also support mixed arrays. For example, the following array is inferred as an array of `Object`:

```
'Does not work with Option Strict On
Dim mixedArray = {1.23, "One point Twentythree"}
```

The preceding code will not be compiled if `Option Strict` is `On`, and the compiler will show a message saying that the type cannot be inferred, which is a situation that can be resolved explicitly by assigning the type to the array. You could therefore explicitly declare the array as `Dim mixedArray() As Object`, but you need to be careful in this because mixed arrays could lead to errors.

Multidimensional and Jagged Arrays

Array literals also affect multidimensional and jagged arrays. The following line of code shows how you can declare a multidimensional array of integers by taking advantage of array literals:

```
Dim multiIntArray = {{4, 3}, {2, 1}}
```

In this case, you do not need to add parentheses. The Visual Basic compiler infers the type as follows:

```
Dim multiIntArray(,) As Integer = {{4, 3}, {2, 1}}
```

Figure 20.3 shows how you can check the inferred type by passing the mouse pointer over the declaration, getting a descriptive tooltip.

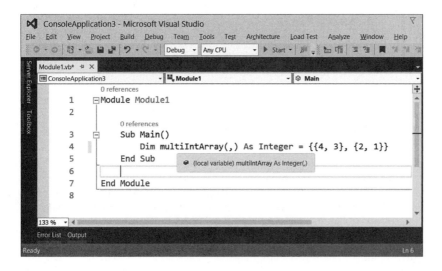

FIGURE 20.3   Type inference for a multidimensional array.

Array literals work similarly on a jagged array. For example, you can write a jagged array of strings as follows:

```
Dim jaggedStringArray = {({"One", "Two"}),
                         ({"Three", "Four"})}
```

This is the same as writing:

```
Dim jaggedStringArray()() As String = {({"One", "Two"}),
                                       ({"Three", "Four"})}
```

And the same as for multidimensional arrays in which the code editor can provide help on type inference, as shown in Figure 20.4.

Array literals can help in writing more elegant and shorter code.

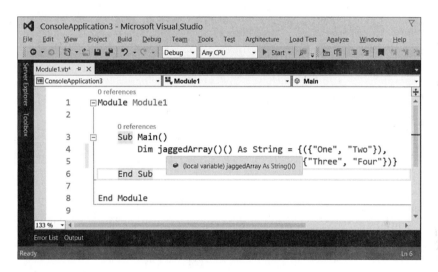

FIGURE 20.4   Type inference for a jagged array.

Extension Methods

Extension methods are a feature that Visual Basic 2015 inherits from its predecessors. As for other features discussed in this chapter, their main purpose is being used with LINQ, although they can also be useful in hundreds of scenarios. Extension methods are special methods that can extend the data type they are applied to. The most important thing is that you can extend existing types even if you do not have the source code and without the need to rebuild class libraries that expose types you go to extend, and this is important. For example, you can extend .NET built-in types, as you see in this section, although you do not have .NET source code.

20

We now discuss extension methods in two different perspectives: learning to use exist-ing extension methods exposed by .NET built-in types and implementing and exporting custom extension methods. The first code example retrieves the list of processes running on the system and makes use of an extension method named `ToList`:

```
Dim processList = Process.GetProcesses.ToList
```

`ToList` converts an array or an `IEnumerable` collection into a strongly typed `List(Of T)`, in this case into a `List(Of Process)` (notice how the assignment works with local type inference). Extension methods are easily recognizable within IntelliSense because they are characterized by the usual method icon plus a blue down arrow, as shown in Figure 20.5.

They are also recognizable because the method definition is marked as `<Extension>` as you can see from the descriptive tooltip shown in Figure 20.5, but this will also be discussed in creating custom methods. The next example uses the `AsEnumerable` method for converting an array of `Process` into an `IEnumerable(Of Process)`:

```
Dim processEnumerable As IEnumerable(Of Process) =
                    Process.GetProcesses.AsEnumerable
```

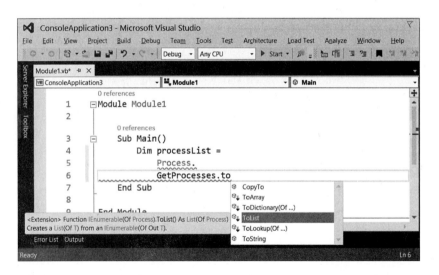

FIGURE 20.5   Recognizing extension methods within IntelliSense.

Extension methods can execute hundreds of tasks, so it is not easy to provide a general summarization, especially because they can be customized according to your needs. At a higher level, .NET built-in extension methods accomplish three main objectives: convert-ing types into other types, data filtering, and parsing. The most common built-in .NET extension methods are provided by the `System.Linq.Enumerable` class and are summarized in Table 20.1.

TABLE 20.1   Built-in Extension Methods

Method	Description
`Aggregate`	Accumulates items of a sequence.
`All`	Checks whether elements within a sequence satisfy a condition.
`Any`	Checks whether any elements within a sequence satisfy a condition.
`AsEnumerable`	Converts a sequence of elements into an `IEnumerable(Of T)`.
`Average`	Retrieves the result of the average calculation from the members of a sequence.
`Cast`	Performs the conversion from an `IEnumerable(Of T)` into the specified type. It is used explicitly when the compiler cannot infer the appropriate type.
`Concat`	Returns the concatenation of two sequences.
`Contains`	Checks if a sequence contains the specified item.
`Count`	Returns the number of items in a sequence.
`DefaultIfEmpty`	Returns the elements of the specified sequence or the type parameter's default value in a singleton collection if the sequence is empty.
`Distinct`	Ensures that no duplicates are retrieved from a sequence or removes duplicates from a sequence.
`ElementAt`	Obtains the object in the sequence at the specified index.
`ElementAtOrDefault`	Like `ElementAt` but returns a default value if the index is wrong.
`Except`	Given two sequences, creates a new sequence with elements from the first sequence that are not also in the second one.
`First`	Gets the first element of a sequence.
`FirstOrDefault`	Like `First` but returns a default value if the first element is not what you are searching for.
`GroupBy`	Given a criteria, groups elements of a sequence into another sequence.
`GroupJoin`	Given a criteria, joins elements from two sequences into one sequence.
`Intersect`	Creates a sequence with common elements from two sequences.
`Join`	Joins elements from two sequences based on specific criteria, such as equality.
`Last`	Retrieves the last item in a sequence.
`LastOrDefault`	Like `Last` but returns a default value if the specified instance is not found.
`LongCount`	Returns the number of items in a sequence under the form of `Long` (`System.Int64`) type.
`Max`	Retrieves the highest value in a sequence.
`Min`	Retrieves the minimum value in a sequence.
`OfType`	Filters an `IEnumerable` collection according to the specified type.
`OrderBy`	Orders elements in a sequence using the specified criteria.

20

Method	Description
OrderByDescending	Orders elements in a sequence using the specified criteria in a descending order.
Reverse	Reverses the order of items in a sequence.
Select	Puts an item into a sequence for queries.
SelectMany	Puts more than one item into a sequence for queries.
SequenceEquals	Determines whether two sequences are equal by comparing the elements by using the default equality comparer for their type or using a specified comparer.
Single	Returns the only item from a sequence that matches the specified criteria.
SingleOrDefault	Like Single but returns a default value if the specified item could not be found.
Skip	When creating a new sequence, skips the specified number of items and returns the remaining items from the starting sequence.
SkipWhile	Like Skip but only while the specified condition is satisfied.
Sum	In a sequence of numeric values, returns the sum of numbers.
Take	Returns the specified number of items starting from the beginning of a sequence.
TakeWhile	Like Take but only while the specified condition is satisfied.
ThenBy	After invoking OrderBy, provides the ability of a subsequent ordering operation.
ThenByDescending	After invoking OrderBy, provides the ability of a subsequent ordering operation in a descending way.
ToArray	Converts an IEnumerable(Of T) into an array.
ToDictionary	Converts an IEnumerable(Of T) into a Dictionary(Of T, T).
ToList	Converts an IEnumerable(Of T) into a List(Of T).
ToLookup	Converts an IEnumerable(Of T) into a LookUp(Of TSource, TKey).
Union	Creates a new sequence with unique elements from two sequences.
Where	Filters a sequence according to the specified criteria.

ARGUMENTS AS LAMBDAS

In most cases you use lambda expressions as arguments for extension methods. Lambda expressions are discussed later in this book; therefore, examples where lambdas are not used are provided.

In the next part of this book, which is dedicated to data access with LINQ, you see how extension methods are used for filtering, ordering, and parsing data. The following code snippet shows an example of filtering data using the `Where` extension method:

```
'A real app example would use
'a lambda expression instead of a delegate
Dim filteredProcessList = Process.GetProcesses.
    Where(AddressOf EvaluateProcess).ToList

Private Function EvaluateProcess(ByVal p As Process) As Boolean
    If p.ProcessName.ToLowerInvariant.StartsWith("e") Then Return True
End Function
```

The preceding code adds `Process` objects to a list only if the process name starts with the letter e. The evaluation is performed through a delegate; although in this chapter you learn how to accomplish this using the lambda expression. Table 20.1 cannot be exhaustive because the .NET Framework offers other extension methods specific to some development areas that are eventually discussed in the appropriate chapters. IntelliSense provides help about extension methods not covered here. By reading Table 20.1, you can also understand that extension methods from `System.Linq.Enumerable` work on or return results from a sequence of elements. This notion is important because you use such methods against a number of different collections (that is, sequences of elements of a particular type), especially when working with LINQ.

EXTENSION METHODS BEHAVIOR

Although extension methods behave as instance methods, the Visual Basic compiler translates them into static methods. This is because extension methods are defined within modules (or static classes if created in Visual C#).

Coding Custom Extension Methods

One of the most interesting things when talking about extension methods is that you can create your custom extensions. This provides great power and flexibility to development because you can extend existing types with new functionalities, even if you do not have the source code for the type you want to extend. There are a set of rules and best practices to follow in coding custom extension methods; the first considerations are the following:

▶ In Visual Basic, extension methods can be defined only within modules because they are considered as shared methods by the compiler.

▶ Only `Function` and `Sub` methods can be coded as extensions. Properties and other members cannot work as extensions.

▶ Methods must be decorated with the `System.Runtime.CompilerServices.Extension` attribute. Decorating modules with the same attribute is also legal but not required.

▶ Extension methods can be overloaded.

20

▶ Extension methods can extend reference types, value types, delegates, arrays, interfaces, and generic parameters but cannot extend `System.Object` to avoid late binding problems.

▶ They must receive at least an argument. The first argument is always the type that the extension method goes to extend.

For example, imagine you want to provide a custom extension method that converts an `IEnumerable(Of T)` into an `ObservableCollection(Of T)` The `ObservableCollection` is a special collection exposed by the `System.Collections.ObjectModel` namespace, which is usually used in WPF and Windows Store applications. The code in Listing 20.1 shows how this can be implemented.

LISTING 20.1   Implementing Custom Extension Methods

```
Imports System.Runtime.CompilerServices
Imports System.Collections.ObjectModel

<Extension()> Module Extensions
    <Extension()> Function ToObservableCollection(Of T) _
                        (ByVal List As IEnumerable(Of T)) _
                        As ObservableCollection(Of T)
        Try
            Return New ObservableCollection(Of T)(List)
        Catch ex As Exception
            Throw
        End Try
    End Function

End Module
```

The code in Listing 20.1 is simple. Because the `ObservableCollection` is generic, the `ToObservableCollection` extension method is also generic and goes to extend the generic `IEnumerable` type, which is the method argument. The constructor of `ObservableCollection` provides an overload that accepts an `IEnumerable` to populate the new collection and then returns an instance of the collection starting from the `IEnumerable` data. Using the new method is straightforward:

```
Dim processCollection = Process.GetProcesses.ToObservableCollection
```

Now suppose you want to extend the `string` type to provide an extension method that can check whether a string is a valid email address. In such a situation the best check can be performed using regular expressions. The following code shows how you can implement this extension method:

```
'Requires an Imports System.Text.RegularExpressions statement
<Extension()> Function IsValidEMail(ByVal EMailAddress As String) _
```

```
            As Boolean
    Dim validateMail As String = _
    "^([\w-\.]+)@((\[[0-9]{1,3}\.[0-9]{1,3}\.)" & _
    "|(([\w-]+\.)+))([a-zA-z]{2,4}|[0-9]{1,3})(\]?)$"

    Return Regex.IsMatch(EMailAddress, _
                        validateMail)

End Function
```

The goal is not to focus on the comparison pattern via regular expressions, which is complex. Just notice how the result of the comparison (`Regex.IsMatch`) is returned by the method that extends `String` because such type is the first (and only) argument in the method. You can then use the method as follows:

```
Dim email As String = "Alessandro.delsole@visual-basic.it"
If email.IsValidEMail Then
    Console.WriteLine("Valid address")
Else
    Console.WriteLine("Invalid address")
End If
```

You may remember that extension methods are shared methods but behave as instance members; this is the reason the new method is available on the email instance and not on the String type.

Overloading Extension Methods

Extension methods support the overloading technique and follow general rules already described in Chapter 7, "Class Fundamentals," especially that overloads cannot differ only because of their return types but must differ in their signatures.

Exporting Extension Methods

You can create libraries of custom extension methods and make them reusable from other languages. This could be useful if you need to offer your extension methods to other applications written in different programming languages. To accomplish this, you need to be aware of a couple of things. First, the module defining extensions must be explicitly marked as `Public`, and the same is true for methods. Second, you need to write a public sealed class with an empty private constructor because the Common Runtime Language (CLR) provides access to extension methods through this class, to grant interoperability between languages. Listing 20.2 shows a complete example.

LISTING 20.2   Building an Extension Methods Library

```
Imports System.Runtime.CompilerServices
Imports System.Collections.ObjectModel
Imports System.Text.RegularExpressions
```

```vbnet
<Extension()> Public Module Extensions
    <Extension()> Public Function ToObservableCollection(Of T) _
                        (ByVal List As IEnumerable(Of T)) _
                        As ObservableCollection(Of T)
        Try
            Return New ObservableCollection(Of T)(List)
        Catch ex As Exception
            Throw
        End Try
    End Function

    <Extension()> Public Function IsValidEMail(ByVal EMailAddress As String) _
            As Boolean
        Dim validateMail As String = _
        "^([\w-\.]+)@((\[[0-9]{1,3}\.[0-9]{1,3}\.)" & _
        "|(([\w-]+\.)+))([a-zA-z]{2,4}|[0-9]{1,3})(\]?)$"

        Return Regex.IsMatch(EMailAddress, _
                            validateMail)

    End Function
End Module

Public NotInheritable Class MyCustomExtensions

    Private Sub New()

    End Sub
End Class
```

Creating a public sealed class is necessary because modules are a specific feature of Visual
Basic; therefore, such a class is the bridge between our code and other languages. By
compiling the code shown in Listing 20.2 as a class library, .NET languages can take
advantage of your extension methods.

EXPORTING EXTENSION METHODS TIPS

Exporting extension methods requires a little bit of attention. For example, extending
types in which you do not own the source code can be dangerous because it may lead to
conflicts if, in the future, the original author adds extensions with the same name. Instead
consider encapsulating extensions within specific namespaces. Microsoft created a document containing a series of best practices that can be found at the following address:
http://msdn.microsoft.com/en-us/library/bb384936(VS.110).aspx

Anonymous Types

As their name implies, *anonymous types* are .NET objects that have no previously defined type in the .NET Framework or your code and can be generated on-the-fly. They were first introduced with .NET Framework 3.5, and their main purpose is collecting data from LINQ queries. You prefer named types to anonymous types outside particular LINQ scenarios; however, it's important to understand how anonymous types work. Declaring an anonymous type is straightforward, as shown in the following code snippet:

```
Dim anonymous = New With {.FirstName = "Alessandro",
                          .LastName = "Del Sole",
                          .Email = "",
                          .Age = 37}
```

As you can see, no name for the new type is specified, and a new instance is created just invoking the `New With` statement. Creating an anonymous type takes advantage of two previously described features, object initializers and local type inference. Object initializers are necessary because anonymous types must be generated in one line, so they do need such a particular feature. Local type inference is fundamental because you have no other way for declaring a new type as an anonymous type, meaning that only the compiler can do it via local type inference. This is the reason declaring an anonymous type cannot be accomplished using the `As` clause. For example, the following code throws an error and will not be compiled:

```
'Throws an error: "the keyword does not name a type"
Dim anonymous As New With {.FirstName = "Alessandro",
                           .LastName = "Del Sole",
                           .Age = 37}
```

Local type inference is also necessary for another reason. As you can see, you can assign but not declare properties when declaring an anonymous type. (`FirstName`, `LastName`, `Age`, and `Email` are all properties for the new anonymous type that are both implemented and assigned.) Therefore, the compiler needs a way to understand the type of a property and then implement one for you, and this is only possible due to the local type inference. In the preceding example, for the `FirstName`, `LastName`, and `Email` properties, the compiler infers the `String` type, whereas for the `Age` property it infers the `Integer` type. When you have an anonymous type, you can use it like any other .NET type. The following code provides an example:

```
'Property assignment
anonymous.Email = "alessandro.delsole@visual-basic.it"
'Property reading
Console.WriteLine("{0} {1}, of age: {2}",
                  anonymous.FirstName,
                  anonymous.LastName,
                  anonymous.Age.ToString)
```

As previously mentioned, you can work with an anonymous type like with any other .NET type. The difference is that anonymous types do not have names. Such types can also implement read-only properties. This can be accomplished using the `Key` keyword with a property name, as demonstrated here:

```
'The Age property is read-only and can
'be assigned only when creating an instance
Dim anonymousWithReadOnly = New With {.FirstName = "Alessandro",
                                      .LastName = "Del Sole",
                                      Key .Age = 37}
```

In this example, the `Age` property is treated as read-only and thus can be assigned only when creating an instance of the anonymous type. You probably wonder why anonymous types can be useful. You get more practical examples in Part IV, "Data Access with ADO.NET and LINQ."

Relaxed Delegates

When you code methods that are pointed to by delegates, your methods must respect the delegate's signature. An exception to this rule is when your method has parameters that are not used and therefore can be omitted. Such a feature is known as *relaxed delegates*. The simplest example to help you understand relaxed delegates is to create a WPF application. After you've created your application, drag a **Button** control from the toolbox onto the main window's surface. Double-click the new button to activate the code editor so that Visual Studio generates an event handler stub for you and type the following code:

```
Private Sub Button1_Click(ByVal sender As Object,
                          ByVal e As RoutedEventArgs) _
                          Handles Button1.Click
    MessageBox.Show("It works!")
End Sub
```

As you can see, the method body shows a text message but does not make use of both sender and e arguments received by the event handler (which is a method pointed by a delegate). Because of this, Visual Basic allows an exception to the method signature rule, and therefore the preceding method can be rewritten as follows:

```
'Relaxed delegate
Private Sub Button1_Click() Handles Button1.Click
    MessageBox.Show("It works! - relaxed version")
End Sub
```

The code still works correctly because the compiler can identify the preceding method as a relaxed delegate. This feature can be useful especially in enhancing code readability. In addition, relaxed delegates can be used in other scenarios, as shown in the following code, where comments provide explanations:

```
' Relaxed delegates can drop the return type of the lambda
Dim lambdaReturnType As Action = Function() 1

' Relaxed delegates can drop the parameters of the delegate
Dim delegateParameters As Action(Of Integer) = Sub() Console.WriteLine()

' Relaxed delegates can do widening conversions
' from a lambda's return type to delegate return type
Dim lambdaToDelegate As Func(Of Integer?) = Function() 1

' Delegate relaxation can do widening conversions from
' delegate parameter type to lambda parameter type
Dim delegateParamType As Action(Of Integer) =
    Sub(i As Integer?) Console.WriteLine(i)
```

Lambda Expressions

Lambda expressions have existed in .NET development since Visual Basic 2008. Because of their flexibility, they are one of the most important additions to .NET programming languages. The main purpose of lambda expressions, as for other language features, is related to LINQ, as you see in the next chapters. They can also be successfully used in many programming scenarios. Lambda expressions in Visual Basic are anonymous methods that can be generated on-the-fly within a line of code and can replace the use of delegates. The easiest explanation of lambdas is that you can use a lambda wherever you need a delegate.

UNDERSTANDING LAMBDA EXPRESSIONS

Lambda expressions are powerful, but they are probably not easy to understand at first. Because of this, several steps of explanations are provided before describing their common usage, although this might seem unnecessary.

You create lambda expressions using the `Function` keyword. When used for lambda expressions, this keyword returns a `System.Func(Of T, TResult)` (with overloads) delegate that encapsulates a method that receives one or more arguments of type `T` and returns a result of type `TResult`. `System.Func` is defined within the `System.Core.dll` assembly and can accept as many `T` arguments for as many parameters that are required by the anonymous method. The last argument of a `System.Func` type is always the return type of a lambda. For example, the following line of code creates a lambda expression that accepts two `Double` values and returns another `Double` constituted by the multiplication of the first two numbers:

```
Dim f As Func(Of Double, Double, Double) = Function(x, y) x * y
```

As you can see, the `Function` keyword does not take any method name. It just receives two arguments, and the result is implemented after the last parenthesis. Such a lambda expression returns a `System.Func(Of Double, Double, Double)` in which the first two doubles correspond to the lambda's arguments, whereas the third one corresponds to the lambda's result type. You can then invoke the obtained delegate to perform a calculation, as in the following line:

```
'Returns 12
Console.WriteLine(f(3, 4))
```

Of course, this is not the only way to invoke the result of a lambda expression, but it is an important starting point. The code provides a lambda instead of declaring an explicit delegate. Now consider the following code that rewrites the previously shown lambda expression:

```
Function Multiply(ByVal x As Double, ByVal y As Double) As Double
    Return x * y
End Function
Dim f As New Func(Of Double, Double, Double)(AddressOf Multiply)


'Returns 12
Console.WriteLine(f(3, 4))
```

As you can see, this second code explicitly creates a method that performs the required calculation that is then passed to the constructor of the `System.Func`. Invoking the delegate can then produce the same result. The difference is that using a lambda expression brought major elegance and dynamicity to our code. `System.Func` can receive up to 16 arguments; independently from how many arguments you need, remember that the last one is always the return value. Another common scenario is a lambda expression that evaluates an expression and returns a Boolean value. To demonstrate this, we can recall the `IsValidEMail` extension method that was described in the "Extension Methods" section to construct complex code. Listing 20.3 shows how you can invoke extension methods for a lambda expression to evaluate whether a string is a valid email address, getting back True or False as a result.

LISTING 20.3   Complex Coding with Lambda Expressions

```
Module TestLambda

    Sub ComplexEvaluation()
        Dim checkString As Func(Of String, Boolean) = Function(s) s.IsValidEMail
        Console.WriteLine(checkString("alessandro.delsole@visual-basic.it"))
    End Sub
End Module


<Extension()> Module Extensions
    <Extension()> Public Function IsValidEMail(ByVal EMailAddress As String) _
            As Boolean
        Dim validateMail As String = _
```

```
        "^([\w-\.]+)@((\[[0-9]{1,3}\.[0-9]{1,3}\.)" & _
        "|(([\w-]+\.)+))([a-zA-z]{2,4}|[0-9]{1,3})(\]?)$"

        Return Regex.IsMatch(EMailAddress, _
                             validateMail)
    End Function
End Module
```

If you look at Listing 20.3, you notice that the checkString delegate takes a String to evaluate and returns Boolean. Such an evaluation is performed invoking the IsValidEMail extension method.

OKAY, BUT WHY LAMBDAS?

You might wonder why you need lambda expressions instead of invoking methods. The reason is code robustness offered by delegates, as you will remember from Chapter 15, "Delegates and Events." Therefore if you decide to use delegates, using lambda expressions is a good idea while it becomes a necessity if you access data with LINQ.

You often use lambda expressions as arguments for extension methods. The following code shows how you can order the names of running processes on your machine, including only names starting with the letter *e*:

```
Dim processes = Process.GetProcesses.
                OrderBy(Function(p) p.ProcessName).
                Where(Function(p) p.ProcessName.ToLowerInvariant.
                StartsWith("e"))
```

The OrderBy extension method receives a lambda expression as an argument that takes an object of type System.Diagnostics.Process and orders the collection by the process name, whereas the Where extension method still receives a lambda as an argument pointing to the same Process instance and that returns True if the process name starts with the letter e. To get a complete idea of how the lambda works, the best way is rewriting code without using the lambda. The following code demonstrates this concept; and the first lambda remains to provide an idea of how code can be improved using such a feature:

```
'An explicit method that evaluates the expression
Private Function EvaluateProcess(ByVal p As Process) As Boolean
    If p.ProcessName.ToLowerInvariant.StartsWith("e") Then
        Return True
    Else
        Return False
    End If
End Function
    Dim processes = Process.GetProcesses.
                    OrderBy(Function(p) p.ProcessName).
                    Where(AddressOf EvaluateProcess)
```

20

As you can see, avoiding the usage of lambda expressions requires you to implement a method that respects the signature of the `System.Func` delegate and that performs the required evaluations. Such a method is then pointed via the `AddressOf` keyword. You can easily understand how lambda expressions facilitate writing code and make code clearer, especially if you compare the `OrderBy` method that still gets a lambda expression. For the sake of completeness, it's important to understand that lambda expressions improve the coding experience, but the Visual Basic compiler still translates them the old-fashioned way, as explained later in the "Lexical Closures" section. All the examples provided until now take advantage of the local type inference feature and leave to the VB compiler the work of inferring the appropriate types. The next section discusses this characteristic.

Type Inference and Lambda Expressions

At a higher level, lambda expressions fully support local type inference so that the Visual Basic compiler can decide for you the appropriate data type. For lambdas, there is something more to say. Type inference is determined by how you write your code. Consider the first lambda expression at the beginning of this section:

```
Dim f As Func(Of Double, Double, Double) = Function(x, y) x * y
```

In the preceding code, local type inference affects both arguments and the result of the `Function` statement. The compiler can infer `Double` to the `x` and `y` parameters and therefore can determine `Double` as the result type. This is possible only because we explicitly provided types in the delegate declaration, that is, `Func(Of Double, Double, Double)`. Because a local type inference is determined by the compiler using the *dominant algorithm*, something must be explicitly typed. For a better understanding, rewrite the preceding code as follows:

```
'The compiler infers Object
Dim f = Function(x, y) x * y
```

In this case because no type is specified anywhere, the compiler infers `Object` for the `f` variable, but in this special case it also throws an exception because operands are not supported by an `Object`. Thus, the code will not be compiled if `Option Strict` is `On`. If you set `Option Strict Off`, you can take advantage of late binding. In such a scenario both the result and the arguments will be treated as `Object` at compile time, but at runtime the CLR can infer the appropriate type depending on the argument received by the expression. The other scenario is when the type result is omitted but arguments' types are provided. The following code demonstrates this:

```
Dim f = Function(x As Double, y As Double) x * y
```

In this case the result type for the f variable is not specified, but arguments have been explicitly typed so that the compiler can infer the correct result type.

Multiline Lambdas

With multiline lambdas, you have the ability to write complete anonymous delegates within a line of code, as demonstrated in the following snippet:

```
Console.WriteLine("Enter a number:")
Dim number = CDbl(Console.ReadLine)

Dim result = Function(n As Double)
                If n < 0 Then
                    Return 0
                Else
                    Return n + 1
                End If
             End Function

Console.WriteLine(result(number))
```

In this particular case, the compiler can infer the `System.Func(Of Double, Double)` result type because the n argument is of type `Double`. Within the method body, you can perform required evaluations, and you can also explicitly specify the return type (take a look at the first lambda example) to get control over the `System.Func` result. Another example is for multiline lambdas without variable declarations, as in the following code:

```
Dim processes = Process.GetProcesses.
                Where(Function(p)
                        Try
                            'Returns True
                            p.ProcessName.ToLowerInvariant.
                            StartsWith("e")
                        Catch ex As Exception
                            Return False
                        End Try
                      End Function)
```

This code performs the same operations described in the "Lambda Expressions" section, but now you have the ability to write more complex code, for example, if you need to provide error handling infrastructures as previously shown.

Sub Lambdas

So far you have seen lambda expressions that were represented only by functions that could return a value and that were realized via the `Function` keyword. You can also use *Sub lambdas* that C# developers know as *anonymous methods*. This feature lets you use the `Sub` keyword instead of the `Function` one so that you can write lambda expressions that do not return a value. The following code demonstrates this:

```
Dim collection As New List(Of String) From {"Alessandro",
                            "Del Sole",
                            alessandro.delsole@visual-basic.it"}
```

```
collection.ForEach(Sub(element) Console.WriteLine(element))
```

The preceding code iterates a `List(Of String)` collection and sends to the Console window the result of the iteration. A `Sub` lambda is used because here no return value is required.

Array.ForEach AND List(Of T).ForEach

The `System.Array` and the `System.Collections.Generic.List(Of T)` classes offer a `ForEach` method that allows performing loops similarly to the `For..Each` statement described in Chapter 4, "Data Types and Expressions." The difference is that you can take advantage of lambda expressions and eventually of delegates to iterate elements.

Consider that trying to replace `Sub` with `Function` causes an error. (That makes sense because `Console.WriteLine` does not return values while `Function` does.) Like `Function`, arguments' types within `Sub` can be inferred by the compiler. In this case the element is of type `String` because it represents a single element in a `List(Of String)` collection. You can use `Sub` lambdas each time a `System.Action(Of T)` is required, opposite to the `System.Func(Of T, T)` required by `Function`. `System.Action(Of T)` is a delegate that represents a method accepting just one argument and that returns no value. `Sub` lambdas can also be implemented as multiline lambdas. The following code shows a multiline implementation of the previous code, where a simple validation is performed onto every string in the collection:

```
' "collection" has the same previous implementation
collection.ForEach(Sub(element)
                Try
                    If String.IsNullOrEmpty(element) = False Then
                        Console.WriteLine(element)
                    Else
                        Console.
                        WriteLine("Cannot print empty strings")
                    End If
                Catch ex As Exception

                End Try
            End Sub)
```

In this way you can also implement complex expressions, although they do not return a value.

> **LAMBDA EXPRESSIONS AND OBJECT LIFETIME**
>
> When methods end their job, local variables get out of scope and therefore are subject to garbage collection. By the way, lambda expressions within methods hold references to local variables unless you explicitly release resources related to the lambda. Consider this when planning objects' lifetime management.

Lexical Closures

To provide support for lambda expressions, the Visual Basic compiler implements a background feature known as *lexical closures*. Before going into the explanation, remember that you will not use closures in your code because they are typically generated for compiler use only. However, it's important to know what they are and what they do. Lexical closures allow access to the same class-level variable to multiple functions and procedures. A code example provides a better explanation. Consider the following code, in which the Divide method takes advantage of a lambda expression to calculate the division between two numbers:

```
Class ClosureDemo

    Sub Divide(ByVal value As Double)
        Dim x = value
        Dim calculate = Function(y As Double) x / y
        Dim result = calculate(10)
    End Sub
End Class
```

Because both the Divide method and its lambda expression have access to the x local variable, the compiler internally rewrites the preceding code in a more logical way that looks like the following:

```
Class _Closure$__1

    Public x As Double

    Function _Lambda$__1(ByVal y As Double) As Double
        Return x * y
    End Function
End Class

Class ClosureDemo

    Sub Divide(ByVal value As Double)
        Dim closureVariable_A_8 As New _
```

```
        _Closure$__1
    _Closure$__1.closureVariable_A_8 = value

    Dim calculate As Func(Of Double, Double) _
    = AddressOf _Closure$__1._Lambda$__1
    Dim result = calculate(10)


    End Sub
End Class
```

Identifiers are not easy to understand, but they are generated by the compiler that is the only one responsible for their handling. The lexical closure feature creates a new public class with a public field related to the variable having common access. It also generated a separate method for performing the division that is explicitly accessed as a delegate (and here you will remember that lambdas can be used every time you need a delegate) from the Divide method. In conclusion, lexical closures provide a way for a logical organization of the code that provides behind-the-scenes support for lambda expressions but, as stated at the beginning of this section, they are exclusively the responsibility of the Visual Basic compiler.

Debugging Lambda Expressions

The Visual Studio 2015 IDE introduces support for using lambda expressions in the Watch and Immediate windows; the developer community has been asking for this for many years. Now you can actually debug both lambdas and LINQ queries, and in this chapter you see how to debug a lambda and then, in other chapters in Part IV, you see how to debug a query; you'll notice that debugging works the same in many cases. To understand how this new feature works, consider the following method, which simply creates a list of some first names, of type String:

```
Sub GenerateStrings()
    Dim myList As New List(Of String) From {"Alessandro", "Antonio", "Diego",
        "Renato"}
End Sub
```

Say that you want to debug a lambda expression that extracts only those names whose first letter is *A*. To do this, you place a breakpoint on the line of code that contains the myList variable declaration and run the code by pressing F5. (Of course, you have to place an invocation to the GenerateStrings method somewhere, such as the Main method.) When the debugger breaks the execution on the specified line of code, right-click myList and then select **Add Watch**. The Watch 1 window now contains the selected variable. Next, you press F11 to execute the line of code and populate the myList variable. At this point, in the Watch 1 window, place your cursor on the line after the myList variable and start typing the following expression:

```
myList.Where(Function(N) N.StartsWith("A"))
```

You will notice that as you type, IntelliSense helps you work with the selected variable (see Figure 20.6).

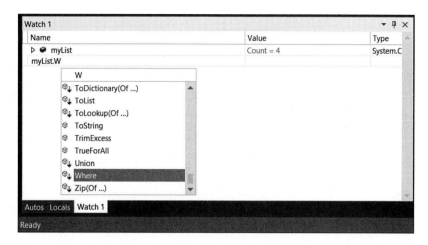

FIGURE 20.6   IntelliSense helps you as you debug lambda expressions.

Once you have written your expression and press **Enter**, the debugger evaluates it, and you can easily see the evaluation result, as shown in Figure 20.7.

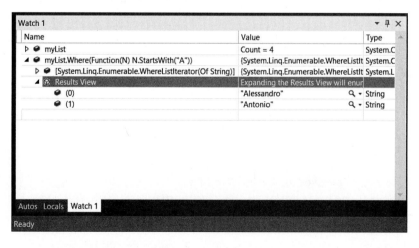

FIGURE 20.7   Evaluating lambda expressions.

This is a very useful feature because it allows you to check whether an expression works as expected before you move it to your code. You can similarly evaluate LINQ queries, and you can also perform evaluations in the Immediate window by taking advantage of IntelliSense.

Generic Variance

The concept of generic variance was introduced in Visual Basic 2010 and is divided into two areas: covariance and contra variance. This concept is related to inheritance versus generics and generic collections; a couple of examples are provided next for a better explanation.

Covariance

Covariance enables you to assign strongly typed collections (such as `List`) of derived classes to `IEnumerable` collections of abstract classes. The code in Listing 20.4 shows how covariance works.

LISTING 20.4   Covariance in Visual Basic 2015

```
Module Covariance

    Sub Main()

        'Using collection initializers
        Dim stringsCollection As New List(Of String) _
                            From {"Understanding ", "covariance ", "in VB 2015"}

        'This code is now legal
        Dim variance As IEnumerable(Of Object) = stringsCollection

        For Each s In variance
            Console.WriteLine(s)
        Next

        Console.ReadLine()
    End Sub
End Module
```

If you examine Listing 20.4, you see that the variance variable is generic of type `IEnumerable(Of Object)` and receives the assignment of a generic `List(Of String)` content, in which `Object` is the base class of `String`. Until Visual Basic 2008, this code was illegal and would therefore report a compile exception. Starting with Visual Basic 2010, this code is legal but works only with `IEnumerable(Of T)` collections. If you try to replace `IEnumerable(Of Object)` with `List(Of Object)`, the compiler still throws an error suggesting that you use an `IEnumerable`. By the way, you assigned a collection of `String` to a collection of `Object`, and this is how covariance works. The `For..Each` loop correctly recognizes items in the `IEnumerable` as `String` and therefore produces the following, simple output:

Understanding
covariance
in VB 2015

Contra Variance

Contra variance works the opposite of covariance: From a derived class, you can take advantage of an abstract class or of a base class. To understand how contra variance works, the best example is to create a client application in which two events of the same control are handled by the same event handler. For this, create a new Windows Presentation Foundation application and write the following XAML code to define a simple `Button` control:

```
<Button Content="Button" Height="50" Name="Button1" Width="150" />
```

CREATING WPF APPLICATIONS

If you are not familiar with WPF applications, you notice one important thing when creating such projects: The designer provides a graphical editor and the code editor for the XAML code (which is XML-styled). You can write the previous snippet within the XAML code editor or drag a `Button` control from the toolbox onto the Window, which is not a problem. You can also notice, in Solution Explorer, the presence of the code-behind file that has an .xaml.vb extension. There you can write the code shown next. Chapter 28, "Creating WPF Applications," discusses WPF applications in detail.

Like other controls, the `Button` control exposes several events. For example, let's consider the `MouseDoubleClick` event and the `KeyUp` event and decide that it would be a good idea to handle both events writing a unique event handler. To accomplish this, you can take advantage of contra variance. Consider the following code, which explicitly declares handlers for events:

```
Public Sub New()

    ' This call is required by the Windows Form Designer.
    InitializeComponent()

    ' Explicitly specify handlers for events
    AddHandler Button1.KeyUp, AddressOf CommonHandler
    AddHandler Button1.MouseDoubleClick, AddressOf CommonHandler
End Sub
```

Both events point to the same delegate, which is implemented as follows:

```
Private Sub CommonHandler(ByVal sender As Object,
                          ByVal e As EventArgs)
    MessageBox.Show("You did it!")
End Sub
```

20

The `KeyUp` event should be handled by a delegate that receives a `System.Windows.Input.KeyEventArgs` argument, whereas the `MouseDoubleClick` should be handled by a delegate that receives a `System.Windows.Input.MouseButtonEventArgs` argument. Because both objects inherit from `System.EventArgs`, you can provide a unique delegate that receives an argument of such type and that can handle both events. If you now try to run the application, you see that the message box is correctly shown if you either double-click the button or press a key when the button has the focus. The advantage of contra variance is that you can use abstract classes to handle the behavior of derived classes.

Summary

In this chapter, you got the most out of some advanced language features that provide both special support for the LINQ technology and improvements to your coding experience. Local type inference enables developers to avoid specifying types in local variables assignment because the Visual Basic compiler automatically provides the most appropriate one. Array literals extend local type inference to arrays. Extension methods allow extending existing objects, even if you do not own the source code (such as in case of the .NET Framework) with custom methods. Anonymous types enable you to generate on-the-fly no-name types that you often use within LINQ queries. Relaxed delegates provide the ability to write code smarter and faster because you are authorized to not respect delegates' signatures if you do not use arguments. Lambda expressions strengthen your code by introducing anonymous delegates that can be generated on-the-fly, improving your code quality and efficiency. Sub lambdas can be used to handle anonymous delegates that do not return a value. In addition, Visual Studio now lets you debug lambda expressions. Generic covariance and contra variance provide further control over generic `IEnumerable` collections when you work with inheritance.

CHAPTER 21

Introducing ADO.NET and DataSets

Working with data is one of the primary tasks that an application must accomplish. Over the years, the .NET Framework has evolved, offering various kinds of data access platforms, but, at a higher level, the way you work with data is based only on two ways: connected or disconnected modes. For the disconnected mode, DataSets still play an important role today because many developers build or maintain applications based on DataSets—and maybe you are one of them. But times change, and technology advances. New data platforms, such as the ADO.NET Entity Framework and LINQ to SQL, have been introduced to the .NET world, and the classic approach is becoming obsolete. If you think of Windows Store and Windows Phone applications, you cannot use DataSets. You instead use LINQ. Of course, in some situations you can still take advantage of the old approach (such as the connected mode), and this is left to your strategy. Because of these considerations, the purpose of this chapter is to provide a quick recap on connected mode and disconnected mode with DataSets, especially for maintenance of existing applications. This book focuses on what is new in data access with LINQ in the following chapters. Basically, you get information that can put you on the right track for comparing and appreciating the power of LINQ.

System Requirements

This chapter and the next ones are all about data. For this reason, you need to set up a development environment for testing code that works with data. Microsoft Visual Studio 2015 ships with an edition of SQL Server 2014 called Local DB. This is a reduced edition of SQL Server Express, which is dedicated to developers who need to test data on their development machines. However, some compatibility issues exist with Local DB when using the old Data Readers. Even though it is appropriate on a development machine, it does not completely allow simulating a real-world database engine. For this reason, the current chapter and the next ones require you to install Microsoft SQL Server 2014 Express Edition, which is still available for free. You can download it from http://msdn.microsoft.com/en-us/evalcenter/ dn434042.aspx. After you have downloaded, installed, and configured SQL Server 2014 Express, you are required to install the famous Northwind sample database, which is also available for free at http://archive.msdn.com/Northwind. You will need to open the InstNwnd.sql file in Visual Studio 2015 and execute the script against the specified SQL Server instance.

Introducing ADO.NET

ADO.NET is the .NET Framework area that provides the capability to access data from databases, and can be thought of as the .NET version of ActiveX Data Objects (ADO), which was the data access technology prior to .NET, based on the COM architecture. ADO.NET can be observed from two perspectives, known as connected and disconnected modes. It can access data from different data sources thanks to data providers. In the next sections, you learn about providers and connection modes and how you can access data in a connected environment.

After completing these procedures, a recap on DataSets is offered before discussing LINQ in the next chapter.

Data Providers

Data providers are .NET objects that allow the .NET Framework to speak with data sources. Data sources are generally databases, such as SQL Server, Oracle, and Access, but also include Microsoft Excel spreadsheets. The .NET Framework includes several built-in data providers exposed by the `System.Data` namespace. Table 21.1 summarizes built-in data providers.

TABLE 21.1   .NET Data Providers

Provider	Namespace
SQL Server	`System.Data.SqlClient`
OleDb	`System.Data.OleDb`
ODBC	`System.Data.Odbc`
Oracle	`System.Data.Oracle` (requires reference to the System.Data.Oracle.dll assembly)
EntityClient	`System.Data.EntityClient` (allows data access with the ADO.NET Entity Framework, which is covered in Chapter 26, "Introducing ADO.NET Entity Framework")

These are the most common providers, but several companies provided their own, such as MySQL or PostgreSQL. Notice how the OleDb provider is available to provide support for data sources such as Microsoft Access databases or Excel spreadsheets. In this book, for this chapter and the ones dedicated to LINQ, Visual Basic topics using the SQL Server provider are covered. There are obviously some differences when writing code for each provider; however, you also find several similarities in connecting to data sources and manipulating data. Such operations are discussed in the next sections.

Connection Modes

ADO.NET provides support for both connected and disconnected modes. The big difference between the two modes is that in a connected mode, you explicitly open and close connections against a data source so that you can work with data. This is something you accomplish with the `Connection`, `DataReader`, and `Command` objects. In a disconnected environment, you work against in-memory data that is later persisted to the underlying data source. This is achieved with DataSets, although you see starting from Chapter 24, "LINQ to SQL," how such an approach is the same in LINQ to ADO.NET. I'm sure that you already worked with both modes in your developer experience, so here's just a quick recap so that you appreciate the difference between what you learn in this chapter and what you learn studying LINQ.

Understanding Connections and Data Readers

To establish a connection to a database, you need to create an instance of the `SqlConnection` class by passing the connection string as an argument. Then you invoke the `Open` method to open the connection so you can perform your data operations. Finally, you invoke `Close` to close the connection. The following code, which requires an `Imports System.Data.SqlClient` directive, demonstrates how you establish a connection to the Northwind database:

```
Using myConnection As New _
    SqlConnection("Data Source=SERVERNAME\SQLEXPRESS;
Initial Catalog=Northwind;" &
"Integrated Security=True;MultipleActiveResultSets=True")
    myConnection.Open()

End Using
```

Utilizing a `Using..End Using` block ensures that the connection will be correctly released without the need of invoking `Close`. You have to replace SERVERNAME with the name of the SQL Server to which you are connecting.

Inserting Data

To perform an insert operation, you create an instance of the `SqlCommand` class by passing the SQL instructions that perform the actual insertion. The constructor also requires the connection to be specified. The following code demonstrates this:

```
Using myConnection As New  _
        SqlConnection("Data Source=SERVERNAME\SQLEXPRESS;
Initial Catalog=Northwind;" &
"Integrated Security=True;MultipleActiveResultSets=True")

        myConnection.Open()

    Using addCustomer As New SqlCommand("INSERT INTO CUSTOMERS(CompanyName, "&
                                        "CustomerID) VALUES (@COMPANYNAME,
                                        @CUSTOMERID)",
                                        myConnection)
        addCustomer.Parameters.AddWithValue("@COMPANYNAME", "Del Sole")
        addCustomer.Parameters.AddWithValue("@CUSTOMERID", "DELSO")
        addCustomer.ExecuteNonQuery()
    End Using
End Using
```

Notice how you can provide parameterized query strings specifying values with the
`SqlCommand.Parameters.AddWithValue` method. The code adds a new customer to the
Customers table in the database, specifying two fields, `CompanyName`, and `CustomerID`. The
`ExecuteNonQuery` method enables the execution of a Transact-SQL operation instead of a
simple query.

Updating Data

Updating data works similarly to inserting, in that you write the same code, changing the
SQL instructions in the query string. The following code provides an example affecting
the previously added customer:

```
Using updateCustomer As New _
        SqlCommand("UPDATE CUSTOMERS SET " &
        "COMPANYNAME=@NAME WHERE
        CUSTOMERID=@ID",
        myConnection)
        updateCustomer.Parameters.
        AddWithValue("@NAME", "Alessandro Del Sole")
        updateCustomer.Parameters.
        AddWithValue("@ID", "DELSO")
        updateCustomer.ExecuteNonQuery()
End Using
```

So, you simply use an `Update` SQL instruction.

Deleting Data

Deletion works the same as other operations, differing only when it comes to the SQL
code that uses a `Delete` statement. The following code demonstrates this:

```
Using deleteCustomer As New _
      SqlCommand("DELETE FROM WHERE CUSTOMERID=@ID",
      myConnection)
      deleteCustomer.Parameters.AddWithValue("@ID", "DELSO")
      deleteCustomer.ExecuteNonQuery()
End Using
```

Querying Data

Querying data is the last operation; it is important because it demonstrates a fundamental object: the `SqlDataReader`. The object enables the retrieval of a series of rows from the specified database object. The following code demonstrates how you can retrieve a series of customers:

```
Using myConnection As New   _
      SqlConnection("Data Source=SERVERNAME\SQLEXPRESS;
Initial Catalog=Northwind;" &
"Integrated Security=True;MultipleActiveResultSets=True")

    myConnection.Open()

    Using queryCustomers As New SqlCommand("SELECT * FROM CUSTOMERS",
                                        myConnection)

        Dim reader As SqlDataReader = queryCustomers.ExecuteReader()

        While reader.Read
            Console.WriteLine("Customer: {0}", reader("CompanyName"))
        End While

    End Using
End Using
```

The query string contains a projection statement that enables the querying of data. The `ExecuteReader` method sends the reading query string to the data source and retrieves the desired information. Now that you have recalled the ways for working with data in a connected mode, it is time to recall the disconnected mode and DataSets.

Introducing DataSets

A `DataSet` is basically an in-memory database that lets you work in a disconnected mode. Being disconnected means that first a connection is open, data is read from the data source and pushed to the `DataSet`, and finally the connection is closed and you work against in-memory data stored by the `DataSet`. DataSets introduced a first attempt of typed programming against in-memory data, a concept that has been unleashed in the modern data access layers such as LINQ to SQL and ADO.NET Entity Framework. Now you get a quick recap on DataSets with Visual Basic before facing LINQ.

Creating DataSets

You create DataSets starting from a database and adding a new data source to your project. This is accomplished by clicking the **Add New Data Source** command from the Project menu in Visual Studio 2015. This launches the Data Source Configuration Wizard where you choose the Database source, as shown in Figure 21.1.

When you proceed, you are prompted to specify whether you want to create a DataSet or an Entity Data Model. Select **DataSet** and click **Next**. At this point, you are prompted to specify the database connection. For example, with the Northwind database available on SQL Server, your connection looks similar to the one shown in Figure 21.2, which represents what I have on my machine.

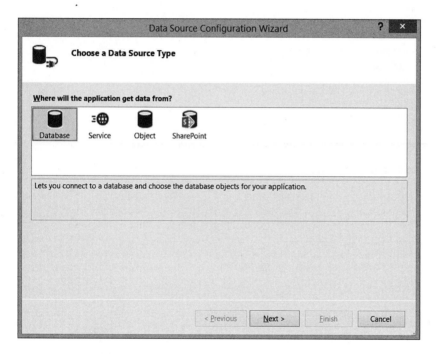

FIGURE 21.1   The first step of the Data Source Configuration Wizard.

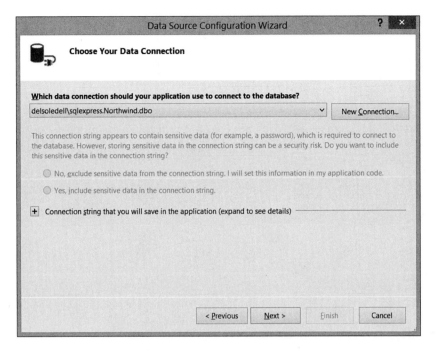

FIGURE 21.2   Specifying the database connection.

Next, you are prompted to specify the database objects you want to be represented by the
new DataSet. Choose the number of tables you like, but be sure that the Products table
is also selected, to complete the next code examples. When the wizard completes,
Visual Studio generates a DataSet that you can manage via the designer, represented in
Figure 21.3.

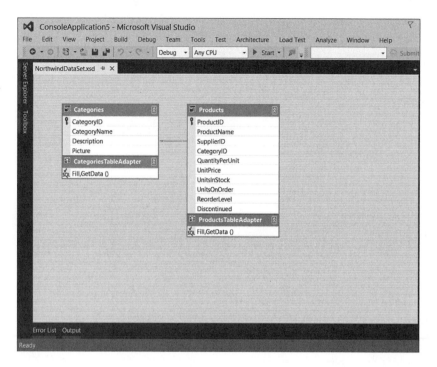

FIGURE 21.3   The DataSet designer.

The designer shows how database objects have been mapped into the `DataSet`. Each table is represented by a `DataTable` object. Each record in a table is represented by a `DataRow` object, and each field is a property having its own data type. DataSets use Data Adapters to read and write data. A Data Adapter is actually a bridge between the data source and the DataSet. Each `DataTable` works with a specific adapter; with more than one adapter, an object must take care of all of them, which is the job of the `TableAdapterManager`. If you work with Windows Forms and WPF applications, Visual Studio generates all adapters for you. For Console applications, as in the following example, you must perform a few steps manually. When you have your DataSet, you need an instance of the DataSet and of table adapters:

```
'DataSet here is also the project name
Imports DataSet.NorthwindDataSetTableAdapters
...
    Dim WithEvents NWindDataSet As New NorthwindDataSet
    Dim WithEvents ProductsTblAdapter As New ProductsTableAdapter
    Dim WithEvents TblAdapterManager As New TableAdapterManager
```

Then you populate the DataSet's object by invoking the adapter `Fill` method. In the meantime, you also assign a `TableAdapterManager` if you have more than one adapter:

```
ProductsTblAdapter.Fill(NWindDataSet.Products)
TblAdapterManager.ProductsTableAdapter = ProductsTblAdapter
```

The next paragraphs recap the insert/update/delete operations. For the moment, remember that you can save back changes to your data source by invoking the adapter's Update method as follows:

```
ProductsTblAdapter.Update(NWindDataSet.Products)
```

Inserting Data

Each DataTable exposes a NewTableRow method, where Table is the name of the DataTable. In the example of the Products table, the method is named NewProductsRow. This method returns a new instance of the ProductRow object that you can fill with your information. Finally, you invoke the AddProductsRow method to send your data to the DataSet. Of course, each table has a corresponding Add method. The following code demonstrates how you can insert a new product:

```
'Insert
Dim row As NorthwindDataSet.ProductsRow = NWindDataSet.
                                    Products.NewProductsRow
row.ProductName = "Italian spaghetti"
row.Discontinued = False

NWindDataSet.Products.AddProductsRow(row)
ProductsTblAdapter.Update(NWindDataSet.Products)
```

Generally, when performing create/read/update/delete (CRUD) operations, you work against rows.

Updating Data

To update a row, you first retrieve the instance of the corresponding DataRow so that you can perform manipulations. Then you can update your data. The following snippet demonstrates this:

```
'Update
Dim getRow As NorthwindDataSet.ProductsRow
getRow = NWindDataSet.Products.FindByProductID(1)

getRow.Discontinued = True
ProductsTblAdapter.Update(NWindDataSet.Products)
```

Notice how the instance has been retrieved via the FindByProductID method. When you create a DataSet, Visual Studio generates a FindByXXX method that allows you to retrieve the instance of the specified row.

Deleting Data

Deleting a row is simple. You get the instance of the row and then invoke the `DataRow.Delete` method. The following code demonstrates this:

```
'Delete
Dim delRow As NorthwindDataSet.ProductsRow
delRow = NWindDataSet.Products.FindByProductID(1)
delRow.Delete()


ProductsTblAdapter.Update(NWindDataSet.Products)
```

To delete an object, you could also invoke the `TableAdapter.Delete` method. However, this would require the complete specification of the row's properties.

Querying Data

You query data from DataSets by writing query strings. This is the old approach, though; in Visual Basic 2015 a more convenient way is to use LINQ to DataSets, which is covered in Chapter 25, "LINQ to DataSets."

Summary

ADO.NET is the .NET Framework area providing the data access infrastructure for data access. With ADO.NET, you access data in two modes: connected and disconnected. For the connected mode, you create `Connection` objects to establish a connection, `Command` objects to send SQL query strings to the data source, and `DataReader` for fetching data; finally, you close the `Connection` object. In a disconnected environment, you take advantage of DataSets that are in-memory representations of databases and where each table is a `DataTable` object, each record is a `DataRow` object, and `TableAdapter` objects act like a bridge between the database and the `DataSet`. You perform CRUD operations invoking the `Add`, `Delete`, `Update`, and `New` methods of `DataTable` objects, although a better technique for querying data is offered by LINQ to DataSets in Chapter 25. After this brief recap on the old-fashioned data access techniques, you are ready to start a new journey through the LINQ technology.

CHAPTER 22

Introducing LINQ

Developers create applications that in most cases need to access data sources and manipulate data. Over the years, hundreds of data sources and file formats saw the light, and each of them has its own specifications, requirements, and language syntaxes. Whenever an application requires accessing data from a database or parsing a structured file, in most cases manipulation commands are supplied as strings, making it difficult to reveal bugs at compile time. LINQ solves all these problems in one solution, changing how developers write code and improving productivity. This chapter provides an overview of this revolutionary technology that is reprised and discussed in detail in the next chapters.

What Is LINQ?

The LINQ project has been the most important new feature in the .NET Framework 3.5, affecting both Visual Basic 2008 and Visual C# 3.0. LINQ stands for **Language INtegrated Query** and is a project Microsoft began developing in 2003. The first beta versions saw the light in 2005 and eventually became part of the Common Language Runtime (CLR) with .NET 3.5 and later versions. As its name implies, LINQ is a technology that allows querying data directly from the programming language. LINQ is very important and revolutionary because most real-world applications need to access data by querying, filtering, and manipulating that data. The word data has several meanings. In the modern computer world, there are hundreds of different data sources, such as databases, XML documents, Microsoft Excel spreadsheets, web services, in-memory collections, and so on. And each of these kinds of data sources can be further differentiated. For example, there is not just one kind of database; there are lots of databases, such as Microsoft SQL Server, Microsoft Access, Oracle, MySQL, and so on. Each of these databases has its own infrastructure, its own administrative tools, and its own syntax. As you can imagine, developers need to adopt different programming techniques and syntaxes according to the specific data source they are working on, and this can be complex. Accessing an XML document is completely different from accessing a SQL Server database; therefore, there is the need for specific types and members for accessing such data sources, and one is different from the other one. So, the first thing that Microsoft considered is related to the plethora of programming techniques to adopt depending on the data source. The next part of this discussion is related to practical limitations of the programming techniques before LINQ came in. For example, consider accessing a SQL Server database with DataSets. Although powerful, this technique has several limitations that can be summarized as follows:

▶ You need to know both the SQL Server syntax and the Visual Basic/Visual C# syntax. Although preferable, this is not always possible, and in some cases it can lead to confusion.

▶ SQL queries are passed to the compiler as strings. This means that if you write a bad query (for example, because of a typo), this will not be visible at compile time but only when your application runs. IntelliSense support is not provided when writing SQL syntax; therefore, typos can easily occur. The same is true for possibly bad query logical implementations. Both scenarios should be avoided, but often they can be subtle bugs to identify.

▶ In most cases the developer will not also deeply know the database structure if she is not also an administrator. This means that she cannot necessarily know which data types are exposed by the database, although it is always a preferable situation.

Now consider querying in-memory collections of .NET objects. Before LINQ, you could only write long and complex For and For..Each loops or conditional code blocks (such as If..Then or Select..Case) to access collections. The last example is related to XML documents: Before LINQ, you had two ways of manipulating XML files. You could treat them as text files, which is very inefficient, or you could recur to the System.Xml namespace, which makes things difficult when you need to simply read and write a document. All these considerations caused Microsoft to develop LINQ; so again we ask the question, "What is LINQ?" The answer is the following: LINQ provides a unified programming model that allows accessing, querying, filtering, and manipulating different kinds of data sources, such as databases, XML documents, and in-memory collections, using the same programming techniques independently from the data source. This is accomplished via special keywords of typical SQL derivation that are integrated into .NET languages and that allow working in a completely object-oriented way. Developers can take advantage of a new syntax that offers the following returns:

▶ The same techniques can be applied to different kinds of data sources.

▶ Because querying data is performed via new keywords integrated in the language, this enables you to work in a strongly typed way, meaning that eventual errors can be found at compile time. This keeps you from having to spend a large amount of time investigating problems at runtime.

▶ Full IntelliSense support.

LINQ syntax is powerful, as you see in this chapter and in the following ones, and it can deeply change how you write your code.

LINQ IN THIS BOOK

LINQ is a big technology and has lots of features, so discussing the technology in deep detail would require another dedicated book. What you find in this book is first the Visual Basic syntax for LINQ. Second, you learn how to use LINQ for querying and manipulating data, which is the real purpose of LINQ. You will not find dedicated scenarios such as LINQ in WPF, LINQ in Windows Store apps, and so on. Just keep in mind that you can bind LINQ queries to every user control that supports the `IEnumerable` interface or convert LINQ queries into writable collections (which is shown here) to both present and edit data via the user interface (UI). For example, you can directly assign (or first convert to a collection) a LINQ query to a Windows Forms `BindingSource` control, a WPF `CollectionViewSource`, or an ASP.NET `DataGrid`.

LINQ Examples

To understand why LINQ is revolutionary, the best way is to begin with some code examples. In the next chapters, you see a huge quantity of code snippets, but this chapter offers basic queries to provide a high-level comprehension. Imagine you have a `Person` class exposing the `FirstName`, `LastName`, and `Age` properties. Then, imagine you have a collection of `Person` objects, of type `List(Of Person)`, called `People`. Last, imagine you want to extract from the collection all `Person` instances whose `LastName` property begins with the letter D. This scenario is performed via the following code snippet that uses a LINQ query:

```
' "People" is of type List(Of Person)
Dim peopleQuery = From pers In People
                  Where pers.LastName.StartsWith("D")
                  Order By pers.Age Descending
                  Select pers
```

This form of code is known as *query expression* because it extracts from a data source only a subset of data according to specific criteria. Notice how query expressions are performed using some keywords that recall the SQL syntax, such as `From`, `Where`, `Order By`, and `Select`. Such keywords are also known as *clauses*, and the Visual Basic grammar offers a large set of clauses that is examined in detail in the next chapters. The first consideration is that, while typing code, IntelliSense speeds up your coding experience, providing the usual appropriate suggestions. This is due to the integration of clauses with the language. Second, because clauses are part of the language, you can take advantage of the background compiler that determines whether a query expression fails before running the application. Now let's examine what the query does. The `From` clause specifies the data source to be queried, in this case a collection of `Person` objects, which allows specifying a condition that is considered if evaluated to `True`. In the previous example, each `Person` instance is taken into consideration only if its `LastName` property begins with the letter D. The `Order By` clause allows sorting the result of the query depending on the specified criteria; here it's the value of the `Age` property in descending order. The `Select` clause extracts objects and pulls them into a new `IEnumerable(Of Person)` collection that is the type for the `peopleQuery` variable. Although this type has not been explicitly assigned, local type inference is used, and the Visual Basic compiler automatically infers the appropriate type as the query result. Another interesting consideration is that queries are now strongly typed. You are not writing queries as strings because you work with reserved keywords and .NET objects, and therefore your code can take advantage of the Common Language Runtime (CLR) control, allowing better results at both compile time and at runtime. Working in a strongly typed way is one of the greatest LINQ features thanks to its integration with the CLR.

IMPLICIT LINE CONTINUATION

Unlike Visual Basic 2008 and starting from Visual Basic 2010, you can omit the underscore (_) character within LINQ queries as demonstrated by the previous code.

The same result can be obtained by querying a data source with extension methods. The following code demonstrates this:

```
Dim peopleQuery2 = people.Where(Function(pers) pers.LastName.
                        StartsWith("D")).OrderBy(Function(pers) pers.Age).
                        Select(Function(pers) pers)
```

The .NET Framework offers extension methods that replicate Visual Basic and Visual C# reserved keywords and that receives lambda expressions as arguments pointing to the data source.

Language Support

In Chapter 20, "Advanced Language Features," you got an overview of some advanced language features in the Visual Basic 2015 language. Some of those features were already introduced with Visual Basic 2008 and have the purpose of providing support for LINQ. Particularly, the language support to LINQ is realized via the following features:

► Local type inference

► Anonymous types

► Lambda expressions

► Extension methods

The addition of keywords such as `From`, `Where`, and `Select` complete the language support for this revolutionary technology. In the next chapters, you see LINQ in action and learn how to use all the language features and the dedicated keywords.

Understanding Providers

The .NET Framework 4.6 provides the ability of using LINQ against six built-in kinds of data sources, which are summarized in Table 22.1.

TABLE 22.1   LINQ Standard Providers

Provider Name	Description
LINQ to Objects	Allows querying in-memory collections of .NET objects
LINQ to DataSets	Allows querying data stored within DataSets
LINQ to SQL	Allows querying and manipulating data from an SQL Server database via a specific object relational mapping engine
LINQ to XML	Allows querying and manipulating XML documents
LINQ to Entities	Allows querying data exposed by an Entity Data Model (see ADO.NET Entity Framework for details)
Parallel LINQ	An implementation that allows querying data using the Task Parallel Library

A specific LINQ implementation exists, according to the data source (objects, datasets, SQL databases, and XML documents). Such implementations are known as *standard providers*. Due to their importance, each provider is covered in a specific chapter (but Parallel LINQ is covered in Chapter 41, "Parallel Programming and Parallel LINQ," because it requires some concepts about the parallel programming first). LINQ implementation is also referred to as providers or standard providers. There could be situations in which you need to use a custom data source and would like to take advantage of the LINQ syntax. Luckily, LINQ is also extensible with custom providers that can allow access to any kind of data source; this is possible due to its particular infrastructure. (A deep discussion on LINQ infrastructure is out of the scope here, and you might want to consider a specific publication, while the focus is on the Visual Basic language for LINQ.) Custom implementations such as LINQ to CSV, LINQ to Windows Desktop Search, and LINQ to NHibernate give a good idea about the power of this technology.

EXTENDING LINQ

The following document in the MSDN Library can help you get started with extending LINQ with a custom provider: http://msdn.microsoft.com/en-us/library/bb546158(v=vs.110).aspx.

Overview of LINQ Architecture

Providing detailed information on the LINQ architecture is out of the scope of this book. Getting a high-level overview can help you understand how LINQ works. Basically, LINQ is the last layer of a series, as shown in Figure 22.1.

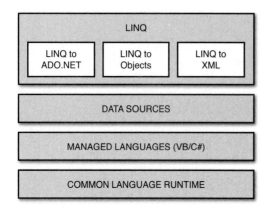

FIGURE 22.1   LINQ is at the top of a layered infrastructure.

At the bottom is the Common Language Runtime that provides the runtime infrastructure for LINQ. The next layer is constituted by the managed languages that offer support to LINQ with special reserved keywords and features. The next layer is all about data and is represented by the data sources LINQ allows querying. The last layer is LINQ itself with its standard providers. You may or may not love architectures built on several layers, but LINQ has one big advantage, particularly when working with databases: It will do all the work behind the scenes for sending the SQL commands to the data source and avoid the need for you to perform it manually. This also offers several high-level classes and members for accessing data in a completely object-oriented way. You see practical demonstrations of this discussion in the appropriate chapters.

Summary

In this chapter you got a brief overview of Language INtegrated Query, which is discussed in more depth in the next chapters. You learned what LINQ is and how it can improve querying data sources thanks to integrated reserved keywords and taking advantage of a strongly typed approach. You got an overview of the built-in LINQ providers and information on the specific language support for LINQ. Now you are ready to delve into LINQ in the next chapters.

LINQ to Objects

L INQ changes the way you write code. This is some-thing that you will often hear when talking about LINQ. It provides the ability to query different data sources and take advantage of the same syntax, background compiler, IntelliSense, and Common Language Runtime (CLR) control with its intuitive programming model. LINQ's syntax is so straightforward that you become familiar with the technology quickly. In this chapter you learn about LINQ to Objects, which is the starting point of every LINQ discussion. You see how easy querying .NET objects, such as in-memory collections, is. In the next chapters, you'll find out how you can use the same approach against differ-ent data sources and LINQ providers. Take your time to read this chapter; it's important, especially the second part, which is about standard query operators. It explains concepts that pervade every LINQ provider and will not be explained again in other chapters, except where expressly required.

Introducing LINQ to Objects

The previous chapter provided an overview of the LINQ technology, and you learned that it provides a unified programming model for querying various types of data sources using the same syntax constructs. You got a few examples of LINQ syntax, but now you'll get to see LINQ in action in different scenarios and with more examples. This chapter is about LINQ to Objects, which is the stan-dard provider for querying in-memory objects. This defini-tion considers collections, arrays, and any other object that implements the `IEnumerable` or `IEnumerable(Of T)` inter-face (or interfaces deriving from them). LINQ to Objects can be considered as the root of LINQ providers, and it's important to understand how it works because the approach is essentially the same in accessing databases and XML documents. This chapter focuses on code more than on introducing the provider with annoying discussions, so let's start.

Querying in Memory Objects

LINQ to Object's purpose is querying in-memory collections in a strongly typed fashion using recently added keywords that recall SQL instructions syntax and that are now integrated in the Visual Basic language. This enables the compiler to manage your actions at compile time. Before querying data, you need a data source. For example, imagine you have the following `Product` class that represents some food products of your company:

```
Class Product
    Property ProductID As Integer
    Property ProductName As String
    Property UnitPrice As Decimal
    Property UnitsInStock As Integer
    Property Discontinued As Boolean
End Class
```

CODING TIP: USING OBJECT INITIALIZERS

In this chapter and the next ones dedicated to LINQ, you notice that in most cases classes do not implement an explicit constructor. You see the advantages of object initializers in both normal code and in LINQ query expressions, which is the reason custom classes have no explicit constructors. This is not a mandatory rule; instead it is an approach specific to LINQ that you need to be familiar with.

At this point consider the following products, as a demonstration:

```
Dim prod1 As New Product With {.ProductID = 0,
                               .ProductName = "Pasta",
                               .UnitPrice = 0.5D,
                               .UnitsInStock = 10,
                               .Discontinued = False}

Dim prod2 As New Product With {.ProductID = 1,
                               .ProductName = "Mozzarella",
                               .UnitPrice = 1D,
                               .UnitsInStock = 50,
                               .Discontinued = False}

Dim prod3 As New Product With {.ProductID = 2,
                               .ProductName = "Crabs",
                               .UnitPrice = 7D,
```

```
                          .UnitsInStock = 20,
                          .Discontinued = True}

Dim prod4 As New Product With {.ProductID = 3,
                               .ProductName = "Tofu",
                               .UnitPrice = 3.5D,
                               .UnitsInStock = 40,
                               .Discontinued = False}
```

The code is simple; it just creates several instances of the Product class populating its properties with some food names and characteristics. Usually, you collect instances of your products in a typed collection. The following code accomplishes this, taking advantage of collection initializers:

```
Dim products As New List(Of Product) From {prod1,
                                            prod2,
                                            prod3,
                                            prod4}
```

Because the List(Of T) collection implements IEnumerable(Of T), it can be queried with LINQ. The following query shows how you can retrieve all non-discontinued products in which the UnitsInStock property value is greater than 10:

```
Dim query = From prod In products
            Where prod.UnitsInStock > 10 _
            AndAlso prod.Discontinued = False
            Order By prod.UnitPrice
            Select prod
```

CODING TIP: IMPLICIT LINE CONTINUATION

In LINQ queries, you can take advantage of the feature known as *implicit line continuation* that avoids the need of writing the underscore character at the end of a line. An exception in LINQ queries is when you use logical operators, as in the preceding code snippet, in which the underscore is required. The code provides an easy view of this necessity. As an alternative, you can place the logical operator (And, in the example) on the preceding line to avoid the underscore.

This kind of LINQ query is also known as *query expression*. The From keyword points to the data source; the prod identifier represents one product in the products list. The Where keyword allows filtering data in which the specified condition is evaluated to True; the Order By keywords allow sorting data according to the specified property. Select pushes each item that matches the specified Where conditions into an IEnumerable(Of T) result. Notice how local type inference avoids the need of specifying the query result type that is inferred by the compiler as IEnumerable(Of Product). Later in this chapter you will see why type inference is important in LINQ queries for anonymous types' collections. At this point, you can work with the result of your query; for example, you can iterate the preceding `query` variable to get information on the retrieved products:

```
For Each prod In query
    Console.WriteLine("Product name: {prod.
    ProductName}, Unit price: {prod.UnitPrice}")
Next
```

This code produces on your screen a list of products that are not discontinued and where there is a minimum of 11 units in stock. For your convenience, Listing 23.1 shows the complete code for this example, providing a function that returns the query result via the `Return` instruction. Iteration is executed later within the caller.

LISTING 23.1   Querying In-Memory Collections with LINQ

```
Module Module1

    Sub Main()

        Dim result = QueryingObjectsDemo1()

        For Each prod In result
            Console.WriteLine("Product name: {0}, Unit price: {1}",
                            prod.ProductName, prod.UnitPrice)
        Next
        Console.Readline()
    End Sub

    Function QueryingObjectsDemo1() As IEnumerable(Of Product)

        Dim prod1 As New Product With {.ProductID = 0,
                                .ProductName = "Pasta",
                                .UnitPrice = 0.5D,
                                .UnitsInStock = 10,
                                .Discontinued = False}

        Dim prod2 As New Product With {.ProductID = 1,
                                .ProductName = "Mozzarella",
                                .UnitPrice = 1D,
                                .UnitsInStock = 50,
                                .Discontinued = False}

        Dim prod3 As New Product With {.ProductID = 2,
                                .ProductName = "Crabs",
                                .UnitPrice = 7D,
                                .UnitsInStock = 20,
                                .Discontinued = True}
```

```
        Dim prod4 As New Product With {.ProductID = 3,
                                      .ProductName = "Tofu",
                                      .UnitPrice = 3.5D,
                                      .UnitsInStock = 40,
                                      .Discontinued = False}

        Dim products As New List(Of Product) From {prod1,
                                                  prod2,
                                                  prod3,
                                                  prod4}

        Dim query = From prod In products
                    Where prod.UnitsInStock > 10 _
                    And prod.Discontinued = False
                    Order By prod.UnitPrice
                    Select prod

        Return query
    End Function
End Module

Class Product
    Property ProductID As Integer
    Property ProductName As String
    Property UnitPrice As Decimal
    Property UnitsInStock As Integer
    Property Discontinued As Boolean
End Class
```

If you run the code in Listing 23.1, you get the following result:

```
Product name: Mozzarella, Unit price: 1
Product name: Tofu, Unit price: 3.5
```

Such a result contains only those products that are not discontinued and that are available in more than 11 units. You can perform complex queries with LINQ to Objects.

The following example provides a LINQ to Objects representation of what you get with relational databases and LINQ to SQL or LINQ to Entities. Consider the following class that must be added to the project:

```
Class ShippingPlan
    Property ProductID As Integer
    Property ShipDate As Date
End Class
```

The purpose of the `ShippingPlan` is storing the ship date for each product, represented by an ID. Both the `ShippingPlan` and `Product` classes expose a `ProductID` property that provides a basic relationship. Now consider the following code that creates four instances of the `ShippingPlan` class, one for each product and a collection of items:

```
Dim shipPlan1 As New ShippingPlan With {.ProductID = 0,
                                        .ShipDate = #2015-1-1#}
Dim shipPlan2 As New ShippingPlan With {.ProductID = 1,
                                        .ShipDate = #2015-2-1#}
Dim shipPlan3 As New ShippingPlan With {.ProductID = 2,
                                        .ShipDate = #2015-3-1#}
Dim shipPlan4 As New ShippingPlan With {.ProductID = 3,
                                        .ShipDate = #2015-4-1#}
Dim shipPlans As New List(Of ShippingPlan) From {
                                        shipPlan1,
                                        shipPlan2,
                                        shipPlan3,
                                        shipPlan4}
```

At this point, the goal is to retrieve a list of product names and the related ship date. This can be accomplished as follows:

```
Dim queryPlans = From prod In products
    Join plan In shipPlans On plan.ProductID Equals prod.ProductID
    Select New With {.ProductName = prod.ProductName,
                     .ShipDate = plan.ShipDate}
```

As you can see, the `Join` clause enables the joining of data from two different data sources having in common one property. This works similarly to the JOIN SQL instruction. Notice how you can take advantage of anonymous types to generate a new type on-the-fly that stores only the necessary information, without the need of creating a custom class for handling that information. The problem is now another one. If you need to use such a query result within a method body, no problem. The compiler can distinguish which members and how many members an anonymous type exposes so that you can use these members in a strongly typed way. The problem is when you need to return a query result that is the result of a function. You cannot declare a function as an `IEnumerable(Of anonymous type)`, so you should return a nongeneric `IEnumerable`, which returns an `IEnumerable(Of Object)`. Therefore, you cannot invoke members from anonymous types except if you recur to late binding. This makes sense because anonymous types' members have visibility only within the parent member that defines them. To solve this problem, you need to define a custom class holding query results. For example, consider the following class:

```
Class CustomProduct
    Property ProductName As String
    Property ShipDate As Date
End Class
```

It stores information from both `Product` and `ShippingPlan` classes. Now consider the following query:

```
Dim queryPlans = From prod In products
    Join plan In shipPlans On plan.ProductID Equals prod.ProductID
    Select New CustomProduct With {.ProductName = prod.ProductName,
                        .ShipDate = plan.ShipDate}
```

It creates an instance of the `CustomProduct` class each time an object matching the condition is encountered. In this way, you can return the query result as the result of a function returning `IEnumerable(Of CustomProduct)`. This scenario is represented for your convenience in Listing 23.2.

LISTING 23.2   Complex LINQ to Objects Queries

```
Function QueryObjectsDemo2() As IEnumerable(Of CustomProduct)
    Dim prod1 As New Product With {.ProductID = 0,
                        .ProductName = "Pasta",
                        .UnitPrice = 0.5D,
                        .UnitsInStock = 10,
                        .Discontinued = False}

    Dim prod2 As New Product With {.ProductID = 1,
                            .ProductName = "Mozzarella",
                            .UnitPrice = 1D,
                            .UnitsInStock = 50,
                            .Discontinued = False}

    Dim prod3 As New Product With {.ProductID = 2,
                            .ProductName = "Crabs",
                            .UnitPrice = 7D,
                            .UnitsInStock = 20,
                            .Discontinued = True}

    Dim prod4 As New Product With {.ProductID = 3,
                            .ProductName = "Tofu",
                            .UnitPrice = 3.5D,
                            .UnitsInStock = 40,
                            .Discontinued = False}

    Dim products As New List(Of Product) From {prod1,
                                prod2,
                                prod3,
                                prod4}

    Dim shipPlan1 As New ShippingPlan With {.ProductID = 0,
                                .ShipDate = #2015-1-1#}
```

```
        Dim shipPlan2 As New ShippingPlan With {.ProductID = 1,
                                                .ShipDate = #2015-2-1#}
        Dim shipPlan3 As New ShippingPlan With {.ProductID = 2,
                                                .ShipDate = #2015-3-1#}
        Dim shipPlan4 As New ShippingPlan With {.ProductID = 3,
                                                .ShipDate = #2015-4-1#}

        Dim shipPlans As New List(Of ShippingPlan) From {
                                                    shipPlan1,
                                                    shipPlan2,
                                                    shipPlan3,
                                                    shipPlan4}

        Dim queryPlans = From prod In products
                         Join plan In shipPlans On _
                         plan.ProductID Equals prod.ProductID
                         Select New CustomProduct _
                         With {.ProductName = prod.ProductName,
                               .ShipDate = plan.ShipDate}
        Return queryPlans
    End Function
    Sub QueryPlans()
        Dim plans = QueryObjectsDemo2()
        For Each plan In plans
            Console.WriteLine("Product name: {0} will be shipped on {1}",
                        plan.ProductName, plan.ShipDate)
        Next
        Console.ReadLine()
    End Sub


'If you invoke the QueryPlans method, you get the following output:
'Product name: Pasta will be shipped on 01/01/2015
'Product name: Mozzarella will be shipped on 02/01/2015
'Product name: Crabs will be shipped on 03/01/2015
'Product name: Tofu will be shipped on 04/01/2015
```

You would obtain the same result with anonymous types if the iteration were performed within the method body and not outside the method itself. This approach is always useful and becomes necessary in scenarios such as LINQ to XML on Windows Phone applications. LINQ to Objects offers a large number of operators, known as *standard query operators*; these are discussed in this chapter. An important thing you need to consider is that you can also perform LINQ queries via extension methods. Language keywords for LINQ have extension methods counterparts that can be used with lambda expressions for performing queries. The following snippet provides an example of how the previous query expression can be rewritten invoking extension methods:

```
Dim query = products.Where(Function(p) p.UnitsInStock > 10 And _
            p.Discontinued = False).
            OrderBy(Function(p) p.UnitPrice).
            Select(Function(p) p)
```

Notice how extension methods are instance methods of the data source you are querying. Each method requires a lambda expression that returns instances of the `Product` class, letting you perform the required tasks. Before studying operators, there is an important concept that you must understand; it's related to the actual moment when queries are executed.

Understanding Deferred Execution

When the Common Language Runtime (CLR) encounters a LINQ query, the query is not executed immediately. LINQ queries are executed only when they are effectively used. This concept is known as *deferred execution* and is part of all LINQ providers you encounter, both standard and custom ones. For example, consider the query that is an example in the previous discussion:

```
Dim query = From prod In products
            Where prod.UnitsInStock > 10 _
            And prod.Discontinued = False
            Order By prod.UnitPrice
            Select prod
```

This query is not executed until you effectively use its result.

For example, iterations cause the query to be executed:

```
'The query is executed here, the Enumerator is invoked
For Each prod In query
    Console.WriteLine("Product name: {0}, Unit price: {1}",
                    prod.ProductName, prod.UnitPrice)
Next
```

Another example of query execution is when you just invoke a member of the result as in the following example:

```
Console.WriteLine(query.Count)
```

You can also force queries to be executed when declared, invoking methods on the query itself. For example, converting a query result into a collection causes the query to be executed, as demonstrated here:

```
Dim query = (From prod In products
             Where prod.UnitsInStock > 10 _
             And prod.Discontinued = False
             Order By prod.UnitPrice
             Select prod).ToList 'the query is executed here
```

This is also important at debugging time. For example, consider the case where you have a query and want to examine its result while debugging, taking advantage of Visual Studio's DataTips. If you place a breakpoint on the line of code immediately after the query and then pass the mouse pointer over the variable that receives the query result, the DataTips feature pops up a message saying that the variable is an in-memory query and that clicking to expand the result processes the collection. This is shown in Figure 23.1.

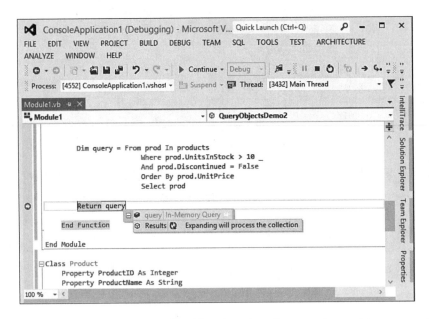

FIGURE 23.1   Visual Studio DataTips show how the query has not been executed yet.

At this point, the debugger executes the query in memory. When executed, you can inspect the query result before it is passed to the next code. DataTips enable you to examine every item in the collection. Figure 23.2 demonstrates this.

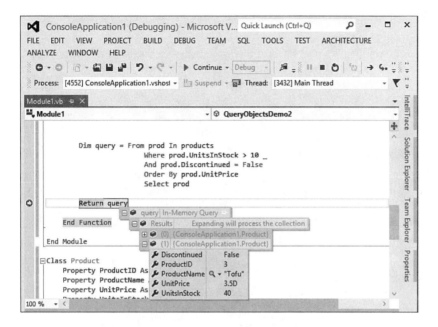

FIGURE 23.2   The debugger executes the query so that you can inspect its result.

The preceding discussion is also valid if you are adding query result variables to the Watch window. Also, Visual Basic 2015 allows you to write and evaluate custom LINQ queries as well as lambda expressions in the Watch and Immediate windows, as you saw in Chapter 20, "Advanced Language Features."

Deferred execution is a key topic in LINQ development, and you always need to keep in mind how it works to avoid problems in architecting your code.

Introducing Standard Query Operators

Querying objects with LINQ (as much as XML documents and ADO.NET models) is accomplished via the standard query operators that are a set of Visual Basic keywords allowing performing both simple and complex tasks within LINQ queries. This chapter covers standard query operators illustrating their purpose. For this, remember that this topic is important because you need operators in other LINQ providers as well. You can also notice that standard query operators have extension methods counterparts that you can use as well.

CODING TIPS

The following examples consistently use local type inference and array literals. They dramatically speed up writing LINQ queries, and therefore using such a feature is something that you should try in practical examples. Nothing prevents you from using old-fashioned coding techniques, but showing the power of Visual Basic 2015 is one of this book's purposes. Also, examples of the new null-propagating operator is provided.

Projection Operators

LINQ query expressions extract values from data sources and then push results into a sequence of elements. This operation of pushing items into a sequence is known as *projection*. Select is the projection operator for LINQ queries. Continuing the example of products shown in the previous section, the following query creates a new sequence containing all product names:

```
Dim productNames = From prod In products
                   Select prod.ProductName
```

The query result is now an IEnumerable(Of String). If you need to create a sequence of objects, you can select each single item as follows:

```
Dim productSequence = From prod In products
                      Select prod
```

This returns an IEnumerable(Of Product). You can also pick more than one member for an item:

```
Dim productSequence = From prod In products
                      Select prod.ProductID, prod.ProductName
```

This returns an IEnumerable(Of Anonymous type). Of course, for an anonymous type, you can use the extended syntax that also allows specifying custom properties names:

```
Dim productSequence = From prod In products
                      Select ID = prod.ProductID,
                      Name = prod.ProductName
```

This is the equivalent of the following:

```
Dim productSequence = From prod In products
                      Select New With {.ID = prod.ProductID,
                      .Name = prod.ProductName}
```

An extension counterpart exists for Select, which is the Select extension method that receives a lambda expression as an argument that allows specifying the object or member that must be projected into the sequence and that works like this:

```
'IEnumerable(Of String)
Dim prodSequence = products.Select(Function(p) p.ProductName)
```

Query expressions can require more complex projections, especially if you work on different sources. Another projection operator known as `SelectMany` is an extension method, but it can be performed in expressions, too. To continue with the next examples, refer to the "Querying in Memory Objects" section and retake the `ShippingPlan` and `Product` classes and code that populates new collections of such objects. After you've done this, consider the following query:

```
Dim query = From prod In products
            From ship In shipPlans
            Where prod.ProductID = ship.ProductID
            Select prod.ProductName, ship.ShipDate
```

With nested `From` clauses, you can query different data sources, and the `Select` clause picks data from both collections, acting as `SelectMany` that has an extension method counterpart that accepts lambda expressions as arguments pointing to the desired data sources.

Restriction Operators

LINQ offers an operator named `Where` that allows filtering query results according to the specified condition. For example, continuing with the previous examples of a collection of products, the following code returns only non-discontinued products:

```
Dim query = From prod In products
            Where prod.Discontinued = False
            Select prod
```

The same result can be accomplished by invoking a same-named extension method that works as follows:

```
Dim result = products.Where(Function(p) p.Discontinued = False). _
            Select(Function(p) p)
```

`Where` supports lots of operators on the line that are summarized in Table 23.1.

TABLE 23.1   Operators Supported by `Where`

Operator	Description
<, >	Major and minor operators that return `True` if the value is smaller or greater than the other one, respectively
=, <>	Equality and inequality operators for value types comparisons
Is	Returns `True` if the comparison between two objects succeeds
IsNot	Returns `True` if the comparison between two objects does not succeed
And	Allows specifying two conditions and returns `True` if both conditions are true
AndAlso	Allows specifying two conditions and returns `True` if both conditions are true; but if the first one is `False` the second one is skipped

Operator	Description
Or	Allows specifying two conditions and returns True if at least one of the conditions is evaluated to True
OrElse	Allows specifying two conditions and returns True if both conditions are True
Like	Compares a string to a pattern and returns True if the string matches the pattern
Mod	Returns the remainder of a division between numbers

The following code provides a more complex example of filtering using Where and logical operators to retrieve the list of executable files that have been accessed within two dates:

```
Dim fileList = From item In My.Computer.FileSystem.
                            GetDirectoryInfo("C:\").GetFiles
              Where item.LastAccessTime < Date.Today _
              AndAlso item.LastAccessTime > New Date(2014, 9, 10) _
              AndAlso item.FullName Like "*.exe"
              Select item
```

The preceding code uses AndAlso to ensure that the three conditions are True. Using AndAlso short-circuiting offers the benefit of making evaluations more efficient in one line. Notice how Like is used to provide a pattern comparison with the filename. You find a lot of examples about Where in this book, so let's discuss other operators.

Aggregation Operators

Aggregation operators allow performing simple mathematic calculations on a sequence's items using the Aggregate and Into clauses. The combination of such clauses can affect the following methods:

▶ Sum, which returns the sum of values of the specified property for each item in the collection

▶ Average, which returns the average calculation of values of the specified property for each item in the collection

▶ Count and LongCount, which return the number of items within a collection, respectively as Integer and Long types

▶ Min, which returns the lowest value for the specified sequence

▶ Max, which returns the highest value for the specified sequence

For example, you can get the sum of unit prices for your products as follows:

```
'Returns the sum of product unit prices
Dim totalAmount = Aggregate prod In products
                  Into Sum(prod.UnitPrice)
```

You need to specify the object property that must be affected by the calculation (`UnitPrice` in this example) and that also works the same way in other aggregation operators. The following code shows how you can retrieve the average price:

```
'Returns the average price
Dim averagePrice = Aggregate prod In products
                Into Average(prod.UnitPrice)
```

The following snippet shows how you can retrieve the number of products in both `Integer` and `Long` formats:

```
'Returns the number of products
Dim numberOfItems = Aggregate prod In products
                Into Count()
```

```
'Returns the number of products as Long
Dim longNumberOfItems = Aggregate prod In products
                Into LongCount()
```

The following code shows how you can retrieve the lowest and highest prices for your products:

```
'Returns the lowest value for the specified
'sequence
Dim minimumPrice = Aggregate prod In products
                Into Min(prod.UnitPrice)
```

```
'Returns the highest value for the specified
'sequence
Dim maximumPrice = Aggregate prod In products
                Into Max(prod.UnitPrice)
```

All the preceding aggregation operators have extension method counterparts that work similarly. For example, you can compute the minimum unit price as follows:

```
Dim minimum = products.Min(Function(p) p.UnitPrice)
```

Such extension methods require you to specify a lambda expression pointing to the member you want to be part of the calculation. Other extension methods work the same way.

NOTE

When using aggregation operators, you do not get back an `IEnumerable(Of T)` type. You instead get a single value type.

Understanding the `Let` Keyword

The Visual Basic syntax offers a keyword named `Let` that can be used for defining temporary identifiers within query expressions. The following code shows how you can query Windows Forms controls to get a sequence of text boxes:

```
Dim query = From ctrl In Me.Controls _
            Where TypeOf (ctrl) Is TextBox _
            Let txtBox = DirectCast(ctrl, TextBox) _
            Select txtBox.Name
```

The `Let` keyword enables the defining of a temporary identifier so that you can perform multiple operations on each item of the sequence and then invoke the item by its temporary identifier.

Conversion Operators

LINQ query results are returned as `IEnumerable(Of T)` (or `IQueryable(Of T)`, as you see in the next chapters), but you often need to convert this type into a most appropriate one. For example, query results cannot be edited unless you convert them into a typed collection. To do this, LINQ offers some extension methods whose job is converting query results into other .NET types such as arrays or collections. Let's consider the `Products` collection of the previous section's examples and first perform a query expression that retrieves all products that are not discontinued:

```
Dim query = From prod In products
            Where prod.Discontinued = False
            Select prod
```

The result of this query is `IEnumerable(Of Product)`. The result can easily be converted into other .NET types. First, you can convert it into an array of `Product` invoking the `ToArray` extension method:

```
'Returns Product()
Dim productArray = query.ToArray
```

Similarly, you can convert the query result into a `List(Of T)` invoking `ToList`. The following code returns a `List(Of Product)` collection:

```
'Returns List(Of Product)
Dim productList = query.ToList
```

You can perform a more complex conversion with `ToDictionary` and `ToLookup`. `ToDictionary` generates a `Dictionary(Of TKey, TValue)` and receives only an argument that, via a lambda expression, specifies the key for the dictionary. The value part of the key/value pair is always the type of the query (`Product` in this example). This is an example:

```
'Returns Dictionary(Of Integer, Product)
Dim productDictionary = query.ToDictionary(Function(p) _
                                           p.ProductID)
```

Because the value is a typed object, the `Value` property of each `KeyValuePair` in the `Dictionary` is an instance of your type; therefore, you can access members from `Value`. The following snippet demonstrates this:

```
For Each prod In productDictionary
    Console.WriteLine("Product ID: {0}, name: {1}", prod.Key,
                      prod.Value.ProductName)
Next
```

The next operator is `ToLookup` that returns an `ILookup(Of TKey, TElement)`, where `TKey` indicates a key similarly to a `Dictionary` and `TElement` represents a sequence of elements. Such a type can be used in mapping one-to-many relationships between an object. Continuing the example of the `Product` class, you can provide an elegant way for getting the product name based on the ID. Consider the following code snippet that returns an `ILookup(Of Integer, String)`:

```
Dim productLookup = query.ToLookup(Function(p) p.ProductID, _
                                   Function(p) p.ProductName & " has " & _
                                   p.UnitsInStock & " units in stock")
```

We can now query the products sequence based on the `ProductID` property and extract data such as product name and units in stock. Because of the particular structure of `ILookup`, a nested `For..Each` loop is required and works like the following:

```
For Each prod In productLookup
    Console.WriteLine("Product ID: {0}", prod.Key)

    For Each item In prod
        Console.WriteLine("    {0}", item)
    Next
Next
```

`Prod` is of type `IGrouping(Of Integer, String)`, a type that characterizes a single item in an `ILookup`. If you run this code, you get the following result:

```
Product ID: 0
    Pasta has 10 units in stock
Product ID: 1
    Mozzarella has 50 units in stock
Product ID: 3
    Tofu has 40 units in stock
```

23

Opposite from operators that convert into typed collections or arrays, two methods convert from typed collections into IEnumerable or IQueryable. They are named AsEnumerable and AsQueryable, and their usage is pretty simple:

```
Dim newList As New List(Of Product)
'Populate your collection here..


Dim anEnumerable = newList.AsEnumerable
Dim aQueryable = newList.AsQueryable
```

Another operator filters a sequence and retrieves only items of the specified type, generating a new sequence of that type. It is named OfType and is considered a conversion operator. The following code provides an example in which from an array of mixed types only Integer types are extracted and pushed into an IEnumerable(Of Integer):

```
Dim mixed() As Object = {"String1", 1, "String2", 2}
Dim onlyInt = mixed.OfType(Of Integer)()
```

This is the equivalent of using the TypeOf operator in a query expression. The following query returns the same result:

```
Dim onlyInt = From item In mixed
              Where TypeOf item Is Integer
              Select CInt(item)
```

It is not uncommon to need to immediately convert a query result into a collection, so you can invoke conversion operators directly in the expression as follows:

```
Dim query = (From prod In products
             Where prod.Discontinued = False
             Select prod).ToList
```

Remember that invoking conversion operators causes the query to be executed.

Generation Operators

Most of LINQ members are offered by the System.Enumerable class. This also exposes two shared methods, Range and Repeat, which provide the capability to generate sequences of elements. Range allows generating a sequence of integer numbers, as shown in the following code:

```
'The sequence will contain 100 numbers
'The first number is 40
Dim numbers = Enumerable.Range(40, 100)
```

It returns IEnumerable(Of Integer), so you can then query the generated sequence using LINQ. Repeat enables you to generate a sequence where the specified item repeats the given number of times. Repeat is generic in that you need to specify the item's type first.

For example, the following code generates a sequence of 10 Boolean values and `True` is repeated 10 times:

```
Dim stringSequence = Enumerable.Repeat(Of Boolean)(True, 10)
```

Repeat returns `IEnumerable(Of T)`, where `T` is the type specified for the method itself.

Ordering Operators

Ordering operators allow sorting query results according to the given condition. Within LINQ queries, this is accomplished via the `Order By` clause. This clause allows ordering query results in both ascending and descending order, where ascending is the default. The following example sorts the query result so that products are ordered from the one that has the lowest unit price to the one having the highest unit price:

```
Dim query = From prod In products
            Order By prod.UnitPrice
            Select prod
```

To get a result ordered from the highest value to the lowest, you use the `Descending` keyword as follows:

```
Dim queryDescending = From prod In products
                      Order By prod.UnitPrice Descending
                      Select prod
```

This can shape the query result opposite of the first example. You can also provide more than one `Order By` clause to get subsequent ordering options. Using extension methods provides a bit more granularity in ordering results. For example, you can use the `OrderBy` and `ThenBy` extension methods for providing multiple ordering options, as demonstrated in the following code:

```
Dim query = products.OrderBy(Function(p) p.UnitPrice).ThenBy(Function(p)
➥p.ProductName)
```

As usual, both methods take lambdas as arguments. In addition, the `OrderByDescending` and `ThenByDescending` extension methods order the result from the highest value to the lowest. The last ordering method is `Reverse` that reverses the query result and that you can use as follows:

```
Dim revertedQuery = query.Reverse()
```

Set Operators

Set operators let you remove duplicates and merge sequences and exclude specified elements. For instance, you could have duplicate items within a sequence or collection; you can remove duplicates using the `Distinct` operator. The following provides an example on a simple array of integers:

```
Dim someInt = {1, 2, 3, 3, 2, 4}
'Returns {1, 2, 3, 4}
Dim result = From number In someInt Distinct
             Select number
```

The result is a new `IEnumberable(Of Integer)`. In real scenarios, you could find this operator useful in LINQ to SQL or the Entity Framework for searching duplicate records in a database table. The next operator is `Union`, which is an extension method and merges two sequences into a new one, excluding duplicates. The following is an example:

```
Dim someInt = {1, 2, 3, 4}
Dim otherInt = {4, 5, 2, 1}


Dim result = someInt.Union(otherInt)
```

The preceding code returns an `IEnumerable(Of Integer)` containing 1, 2, 3, 4, 5. The first items in the new sequences are those from the collection or array that you invoke `Union` on. In the preceding example, only 5 from the second array is taken because other items are duplicates. Next operator is `Intersect`, which is another extension method. This method creates a new sequence with elements that two other sequences have in common. The following code demonstrates this:

```
Dim someInt = {1, 2, 3, 4}
Dim otherInt = {1, 2, 5, 6}


Dim result = someInt.Intersect(otherInt)
```

The new sequence is an `IEnumerable(Of Integer)` containing only 1 and 2 because they are the only values that both original sequences have in common. The last set operator is `Except` that generates a new sequence taking only those values that two sequences do not have in common. The following code is an example, which then requires a further explanation:

```
Dim someInt = {1, 2, 3, 4}
Dim otherInt = {1, 2, 5, 6}
Dim result = someInt.Except(otherInt)
```

Surprisingly, this code returns a new `IEnumerable(Of Integer)` containing only 3 and 4, although 5 and 6 also are values that the two sequences do not have in common. This is because the comparison is executed only on the sequence that you invoke `Except` on, and therefore all other values are excluded.

Grouping Operators

The grouping concept is something that you already know if you ever worked with data. Given a products collection, dividing products into categories would provide a better organization of information. For example, consider the following `Category` class:

```
Class Category
    Property CategoryID As Integer
    Property CategoryName As String
End Class
```

Now consider the following review of the `Product` class, with a new `CategoryID` property:

```
Class Product
    Property ProductID As Integer
    Property ProductName As String
    Property UnitPrice As Decimal
    Property UnitsInStock As Integer
    Property Discontinued As Boolean
    Property CategoryID As Integer
End Class
```

At this point you can write code that creates instances of both classes and populates appropriate collections, as in the following snippet:

```
Sub GroupByDemo()

    Dim cat1 As New Category With {.CategoryID = 1,
                                   .CategoryName = "Food"}

    Dim cat2 As New Category With {.CategoryID = 2,
                                   .CategoryName = "Beverages"}

    Dim categories As New List(Of Category) From {cat1,
                                                  cat2}

    Dim prod1 As New Product With {.ProductID = 0,
                                   .ProductName = "Pasta",
                                   .UnitPrice = 0.5D,
                                   .UnitsInStock = 10,
                                   .Discontinued = False,
                                   .CategoryID = 1}

    Dim prod2 As New Product With {.ProductID = 1,
                                   .ProductName = "Wine",
                                   .UnitPrice = 1D,
                                   .UnitsInStock = 50,
                                   .Discontinued = False,
                                   .CategoryID = 2}
```

23

```
Dim prod3 As New Product With {.ProductID = 2,
                               .ProductName = "Water",
                               .UnitPrice = 0.5D,
                               .UnitsInStock = 20,
                               .Discontinued = False,
                               .CategoryID = 2}

Dim prod4 As New Product With {.ProductID = 3,
                               .ProductName = "Tofu",
                               .UnitPrice = 3.5D,
                               .UnitsInStock = 40,
                               .Discontinued = True,
                               .CategoryID = 1}

Dim products As New List(Of Product) From {prod1,
                                           prod2,
                                           prod3,
                                           prod4}
```

To make things easier to understand, only two categories have been created. Notice also how each product now belongs to a specific category. To group foods into the Food category and beverages into the Beverages category, you use the Group By operator. This is the closing code of the preceding method, which is explained just after you write it:

```
Dim query = From prod In products
            Group prod By ID = prod.CategoryID
            Into Group
            Select CategoryID = ID,
                   ProductsList = Group

' "prod" is inferred as anonymous type
For Each prod In query
    Console.WriteLine("Category {0}", prod.CategoryID)

    ' "p" is inferred as Product
    For Each p In prod.ProductsList
        Console.WriteLine("    Product {0}, Discontinued: {1}",
                          p.ProductName, p.Discontinued)
    Next
Next
End Sub
```

The code produces the following result:

```
Category 1
    Product Pasta, Discontinued: False
    Product Tofu, Discontinued: True
```

```
Category 2
    Product Wine, Discontinued: False
    Product Water, Discontinued: False
```

Group By requires you to specify a key for grouping. This key is a property of the type composing the collection you are querying. The result of the grouping is sent to a new IEnumerable(Of T) sequence represented by the Into Group statement. Finally, you invoke Select to pick up the key and items grouped according to the key; the projection generates an IEnumerable(Of anonymous type). Notice how you need a nested For..Each loop. This is because each item in the query result is composed of two objects: the key and a sequence of object (in this case sequence of Product) grouped based on the key. The same result can be accomplished using extension methods' counterpart that works like this:

```
Dim query = products.GroupBy(Function(prod) prod.CategoryID,
                             Function(prod) prod.ProductName)
```

Union Operators

You often need to create sequences or collections with items taken from different data sources. If you consider the example in the previous "Grouping Operators" section, it would be interesting to create a collection of objects in which the category name is also available so that the result can be more human-readable. This is possible in LINQ using union operators (not to be confused with the union Set operator keyword), which perform operations that you know as *joining*. To complete the following steps, recall the previously provided implementation of the Product and Category classes and the code that populates new collections of products and categories. The goal of the first example is to create a new sequence of products in which the category name is also available. This can be accomplished as follows:

```
Dim query = From prod In products
            Join cat In categories On _
            prod.CategoryID Equals cat.CategoryID
            Select CategoryName = cat.CategoryName,
                   ProductName = prod.ProductName
```

The code is quite simple to understand. Both products and categories collections are queried, and a new sequence is generated to keep products and categories whose CategoryID is equal. This is accomplished via the Join keyword in which the On operator requires the condition to be evaluated as True. Notice that Join does not accept the equality operator (=), but it does require the Equals keyword. In this case the query result is an IEnumerable(Of Anonymous type). You could, however, create a helper class exposing properties to store the result. You can then iterate the result to get information on your products, as in the following snippet:

23

```
For Each obj In query
    Console.WriteLine("Category: {0}, Product name: {1}",
                        obj.CategoryName, obj.ProductName)
Next
```

The code produces the following output:

```
Category: Food, Product name: Pasta
Category: Beverages, Product name: Wine
Category: Beverages, Product name: Water
Category: Food, Product name: Tofu
```

This is the simplest joining example and is known as *Cross Join*, but you are not limited to this. For example, you might want to group items based on the specified key, which is known as *Group Join*. This allows you to rewrite the same example of the previous paragraph but taking advantage of joining can get the category name. This is accomplished as follows:

```
Dim query = From cat In categories
            Group Join prod In products On _
            prod.CategoryID Equals cat.CategoryID
            Into Group
            Select NewCategory = cat,
                   NewProducts = Group
```

Notice that now the main data source is `Categories`. The result of this query is generating a new sequence in which groups of categories store groups of products. This is notable if you take a look at the `Select` clause, which picks sequences instead of single objects or properties. The following iteration provides a deeper idea on how you access information from the query result:

```
For Each obj In query
    Console.WriteLine("Category: {0}", obj.NewCategory.CategoryName)

    For Each prod In obj.NewProducts
        Console.WriteLine("   Product name: {0}, Discontinued: {1}",
                            prod.ProductName, prod.Discontinued)
    Next
Next
```

Such nested iteration produces the following output:

```
Category: Food
    Product name: Pasta, Discontinued: False
    Product name: Tofu, Discontinued: True
Category: Beverages
    Product name: Wine, Discontinued: False
    Product name: Water, Discontinued: False
```

The *Cross Join with Group Join* technique is similar. The following code shows how you can perform a cross group join to provide a simplified version of the previous query result:

```
Dim query = From cat In categories
            Group Join prod In products On _
            prod.CategoryID Equals cat.CategoryID
            Into Group
            From p In Group
            Select CategoryName = cat.CategoryName,
                   ProductName = p.ProductName
```

Notice that by providing a nested `From` clause pointing to the group, you can easily select what you need from both sequences, such as the category name and the product name. The result, which is still a sequence of anonymous types, can be iterated as follows:

```
For Each item In query
    Console.WriteLine("Product {0} belongs to {1}",
                      item.ProductName,
                      item.CategoryName)
Next
```

It produces the following output:

```
Product Pasta belongs to Food
Product Tofu belongs to Food
Product Wine belongs to Beverages
Product Water belongs to Beverages
```

The last union operator is known as *Left Outer Join*. It is similar to the cross group join, but it differs in that you can provide a default value in case no item is available for the specified key. Consider the following code:

```
Dim query = From cat In categories
            Group Join prod In products On _
            prod.CategoryID Equals cat.CategoryID
            Into Group
            From p In Group.DefaultIfEmpty
            Select CategoryName = cat.CategoryName,
                   ProductName = If(p IsNot Nothing,
                   p.ProductName, "No available product")
```

Notice the invocation of the `Group.DefaultIfEmpty` extension method that is used with the `If` ternary operator to provide a default value. You can then retrieve information from the query result as in the cross group join sample.

Equality Operators

You might want to compare two sequences to check whether they are perfectly equal. The SequenceEqual extension method allows performing this kind of comparison. It compares whether a sequence is equal considering both items and the items order within a sequence, returning a Boolean value. The following code returns True because both sequences contain the same items in the same order:

```
Dim first = {"Visual", "Basic", "2015"}
Dim second = {"Visual", "Basic", "2015"}
'Returns True
Dim comparison = first.SequenceEqual(second)
```

The following code returns instead False because, although both sequences contain the same items, they are ordered differently:

```
Dim first = {"Visual", "Basic", "2015"}
Dim second = {"Visual", "2015", "Basic"}
'Returns False
Dim comparison = first.SequenceEqual(second)
```

Quantifiers

LINQ offers two interesting extension methods for sequences, Any and All. Any checks whether at least one item in the sequence satisfies the specified condition. For example, the following code checks whether at least one product name contains the letters "of":

```
Dim result = products.Any(Function(p) p.ProductName.Contains("of"))
```

The method receives a lambda as an argument that specifies the condition and returns True if the condition is matched. All checks whether all members in a sequence match the specified condition. For example, the following code checks whether all products are discontinued:

```
Dim result = products.All(Function(p) p.Discontinued = True)
```

As previously noted, the lambda argument specifies the condition to be matched. Both Any and All work well with the null-propagating operator, which allows you to detect whether a collection is null before their invocations, as demonstrated in the following snippet:

```
Dim result = products?.Any(Function(p) p.ProductName.Contains("of"))
Dim result = products?.All(Function(p) p.Discontinued = True)
```

In the preceding code, both methods are invoked only if products is not Nothing. You can also combine the ?. and If operators to check whether a collection is not null and not empty, as in the following code:

```
If products?.Any Then
    'Products is not null and not empty
End If
```

IMPROVING CODE PERFORMANCE WITH Any

Very often you will need to know if a collection contains at least one element (that is, not empty). A common error is using the following syntax:

```
If myCollection.Count > 0 Then ...
```

This had to be used prior to LINQ (and lots of Visual Basic 6 users migrating to .NET use that), but with LINQ you can write:

```
If myCollection.Any Then...
```

The difference is huge: if you use Count, the runtime will move the iterator through all the elements in the collection. But if you use Any, the runtime will move the iterator just one position, which is enough to return True or False. This dramatically increases performance, especially if the collection has hundreds or thousands of elements.

Concatenation Operators

Sequences (that is, IEnumerable(Of T) objects) expose a method named Concat that enables the creation of a new sequence containing items from two sequences. The following code shows an example in which a new sequence of strings is created from two existing arrays of strings:

```
Dim firstSequence = {"One", "Two", "Three"}
Dim secondSequence = {"Four", "Five", "Six"}

Dim concatSequence = firstSequence.Concat(secondSequence)
```

The result produced by this code is that the concatSequence variable contains the following items: "One", "Two", "Three", "Four", "Five", and "Six". The first items in the new sequence are taken from the one you invoke the Concat method on. You can also use the null-propagating operator to check whether the first sequence is null before performing the concatenation, as demonstrated in the following code:

```
Dim concatSequence = firstSequence?.Concat(secondSequence)
```

Elements Operators

Some extension methods enable you to get the instance of a specified item in a sequence. The first one is Single, and it gets the instance of only the item that matches the specified condition. The following code gets the instance of the only product whose product name is Mozzarella:

```
Try
    Dim uniqueElement = products.Single(Function(p) p.
                                    ProductName = "Mozzarella")

Catch ex As InvalidOperationException
    'The item does not exist
End Try
```

`Single` takes a lambda expression as an argument in which you can specify the condition that the item must match. It returns an `InvalidOperationException` if the item does not exist in the sequence (or if more than one element matches the condition). As an alternative, you can invoke `SingleOrDefault`, which returns a default value if the item does not exist instead of throwing an exception. The following code returns `Nothing` because the product name does not exist:

```
Dim uniqueElement = products.SingleOrDefault(Function(p) p.
                        ProductName = "Mozzarell")
```

The next method is `First`. It can return either the first item in a sequence or the first item that matches a condition. You can use it as follows:

```
'Gets the first product in the list
Dim firstAbsolute = products.First

Try
    'Gets the first product where product name starts with P
    Dim firstElement = products.First(Function(p) p.ProductName.
                                    StartsWith("P"))
Catch ex As InvalidOperationException
    'No item available
End Try
```

The previous example is self-explanatory: If multiple products have their names starting with the letter *P*, `First` returns just the first one in the sequence or throws an `InvalidOperationException` if no item is available. Additionally, a `FirstOrDefault` method returns a default value, such as `Nothing`, if no item is available. `Last` and `LastOrDefault` return the last item in a sequence and that work like the preceding illustrated ones. You can also use the null-propagating operator for checking whether a collection is null before invoking element operators. The following code provides an example:

```
'Return Nothing if no product name starts with P
Dim firstElement = products?.First(Function(p) p.ProductName.
                                    StartsWith("P"))
'Return Nothing if no product name matches "Mozzarella"
Dim uniqueElement = products?.Single(Function(p) p.
                                ProductName = "Mozzarella")
```

Partitioning Operators

Partitioning operators enable you to use a technique known as *paging*, which is common in data access scenarios. There are two main operators in LINQ: Skip and Take. Skip avoids selecting the specified number of elements, and Take puts the specified number of elements into a sequence. The code in Listing 23.3 shows an example of paging implementation using the two operators.

LISTING 23.3   Implementing a Basic Paging Technique

```
Module Partitioning

    Private pageCount As Integer
    Private Products As List(Of Product)

    Sub PopulateProducts()
        Dim prod1 As New Product With {.ProductID = 0,
                                       .ProductName = "Pasta",
                                       .UnitPrice = 0.5D,
                                       .UnitsInStock = 10,
                                       .Discontinued = False}

        Dim prod2 As New Product With {.ProductID = 1,
                                       .ProductName = "Mozzarella",
                                       .UnitPrice = 1D,
                                       .UnitsInStock = 50,
                                       .Discontinued = False}

        Dim prod3 As New Product With {.ProductID = 2,
                                       .ProductName = "Crabs",
                                       .UnitPrice = 7D,
                                       .UnitsInStock = 20,
                                       .Discontinued = True}

        Dim prod4 As New Product With {.ProductID = 3,
                                       .ProductName = "Tofu",
                                       .UnitPrice = 3.5D,
                                       .UnitsInStock = 40,
                                       .Discontinued = False}

        Products = New List(Of Product) From {prod1,
                                              prod2,
                                              prod3,
                                              prod4}
    End Sub
```

```
    Function QueryProducts() As IEnumerable(Of Product)

        Dim query As IEnumerable(Of Product)
        query = From prod In Products
                Order By prod.ProductID
                Skip pageCount Take 10

        'In real applications ensure that query is not null
        Return query
    End Function
End Module
```

The private field pageCount acts as a counter. According to its value, the query skips the number of elements already visited, represented by the value of pageCount. If no elements were visited, the query skips nothing. The code invoking QueryProducts increases or decreases the pageCount value by 10 units depending on whether you want to move forward or backward to the collection items.

Summary

In this chapter, you got a high-level overview of LINQ key concepts. In this particular discussion, you got information about LINQ to Objects as the built-in provider for querying in-memory collections. Specific sections showed LINQ in action via specific Visual Basic keywords that recall the SQL syntax, such as From, Select, Where, and Join. You can build LINQ queries while writing Visual Basic code, taking advantage of the background compiler, IntelliSense, and CLR control. Such queries written in the code editor are known as *query expressions*. Query expressions return an IEnumerable(Of T) but are not executed immediately. According to the key concept of deferred execution, LINQ queries are executed only when they are effectively utilized. This is something that you find in subsequent LINQ providers. With LINQ, you can build complex query expressions to query your data sources via the standard query operators, which were covered in the last part of the chapter. LINQ to Objects is the basis of LINQ, and most of the concepts shown in this chapter will be revisited in the next ones.

CHAPTER 24

LINQ to SQL

How many times did you face runtime errors when sending SQL instructions to your databases for querying or manipulating data? Your answer is probably "several times." Sending SQL instructions in the form of strings has been, for years, the way of accessing data in the .NET development, but one of the main disadvantages was the lack of compile time control over your actions. Experienced developers can also remember when they had to work against databases in a connected environment taking care of everything that happened. LINQ to SQL solves several of these issues, providing both a disconnected way for working with data, where data is mapped into an object model that you work with until you decide to save back data, and a strongly typed programming fashion that improves your productivity by checking queries and CRUD operations at compile time. In this chapter you explore the most important LINQ to SQL functionalities, learning the basics of data access with such technology.

PREFER THE ADO.NET ENTITY FRAMEWORK

Although powerful, Microsoft is no longer investing in LINQ to SQL (but it is supported), and it should not be used in new projects. We discuss it because it is still a standard LINQ provider, because it offers concepts that you will reuse later, and because you might have existing code relying on this provider (including Windows Phone 7.x apps). You are encouraged to use the ADO.NET Entity Framework and LINQ to Entities in new desktop or web applications and explore additional options for your mobile apps, such as the Entity Framework 7.

Introducing LINQ to SQL

LINQ to SQL is an object relational mapping engine for Microsoft SQL Server databases. In has been the first built-in LINQ provider for SQL Server when LINQ first shipped in the .NET Framework 3.5, offering not only the capability of querying data (as instead LINQ to DataSet is limited to) but also a complete infrastructure for manipulating data, including connections, queries, and *CRUD* (Create/Read/Update/Delete) operations. LINQ to SQL is another layer in the data access architecture, but it is responsible for everything starting from opening the connection until closing. One of the advantages from LINQ to SQL is that you will query your data using the usual LINQ syntax thanks to the unified programming model offered by the technology. But this is not the only advantage. Being an object relational mapping engine makes LINQ to SQL mapping databases' tables and relationships into .NET objects. This allows working in a disconnected way and in a totally strongly typed fashion so that you can get all the advantages of the CLR management. Each table from the database is mapped into a .NET class, whereas relationships are mapped into .NET properties, providing something known as *abstraction*. This enables you to work against a conceptual model instead of against the database, and you will work with objects until you finish your edits that will be persisted to the underlying data source only when effectively required. This provides several advantages: First, you work with strongly typed objects, and everything is managed by the Common Language Runtime (CLR). Second, you do not work connected to the database, so your original data will be secure until you send changes after validations. According to the LINQ terminology, classes mapping tables are called *entities*. A group of entities is referred to as an *entity set*. Relationships are instead called *associations*. You access LINQ to SQL features by creating specific classes that are described in next section.

LINQ INTERNALS

This is a language-focused book, so discussing LINQ to SQL internals and architecture is not possible. A discussion of this kind would probably require a specific book. Here you will instead learn of manipulating and querying data with LINQ to SQL and the Visual Basic language, getting the fundamental information about architecture when necessary.

Prerequisites and Requirements for This Book

This chapter assumes that you have installed Microsoft SQL Server 2014, at least the Express Edition, or possibly the "With Tools" version that also includes SQL Server

Management Studio Express. If you did not install it yet, you can download it from here: http://www.microsoft.com/express/sql/default.aspx.

If you installed SQL Server Management Studio (Express or higher), it is a good idea to attach the Northwind database to the SQL Server instance so you can simulate a production environment.

Understanding LINQ to SQL Classes

To access SQL Server databases with LINQ to SQL, you need a LINQ to SQL class. This kind of class is generated by Visual Studio when you select members for the new object model and contains all the Visual Basic code that represents tables, columns, and relationships. Adding a LINQ to SQL class is also necessary to enable the Visual Studio OR/M Designer for LINQ to SQL. To understand what these sentences mean, follow these preliminary steps:

▶ Create a new project for the Console and name it **LinqToSql**.

▶ Establish a connection to the Northwind database either via the Server Explorer tool window or via the new SQL Server Object Explorer tool window.

▶ In Solution Explorer, right-click the project name and select **Add, New Item**. When the Add New Item dialog box appears move to the Data folder and select the **LINQ to SQL Classes** item, replacing the default name with **Northwind.dbml**. Figure 24.1 shows this scenario.

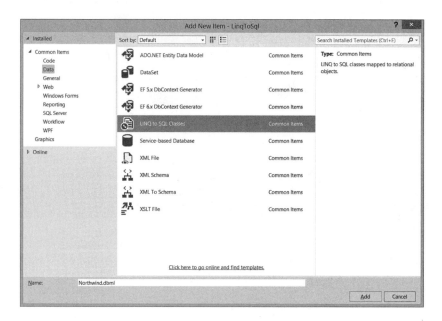

FIGURE 24.1   Adding a new LINQ to SQL class to the project.

When you click **Add**, after a few seconds the Visual Studio 2015 IDE shows the LINQ to SQL Object Relational Designer that appears empty, as shown in Figure 24.2.

The designer provides a brief description of its job, requiring you to pick items from either the Server Explorer window or from the toolbox. You need to pick tables from the Northwind database, passing them to Visual Studio to start the mapping process. Look at Figure 24.3 and then expand Server Explorer (or SQL Server Object Explorer) to show the Northwind database structure; then expand the Tables folder.

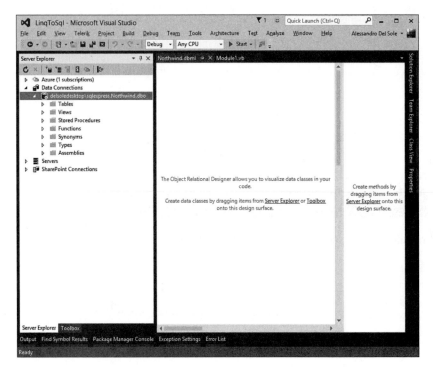

FIGURE 24.2   The LINQ to SQL designer popping up for the first time.

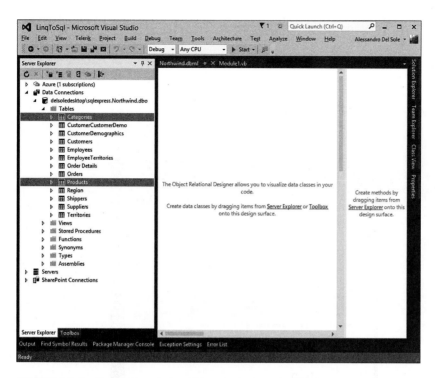

FIGURE 24.3   Preparing to pick tables from the Northwind database.

Now keep the Ctrl key pressed and click both the **Categories** and **Products** tables. Our goal is to provide an example of a master-details relationship. When selected, drag the tables onto the designer surface until you get the result shown in Figure 24.4.

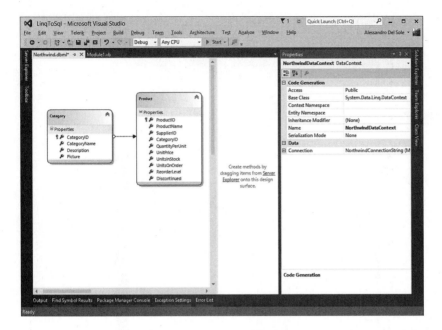

FIGURE 24.4   The LINQ to SQL designer is now populated.

At this point, you need to consider a few things. Visual Studio generated a diagram that is the representation of Visual Basic code. This diagram contains the definition of two entities, `Category` and `Product`. Each of them is mapped to Visual Basic classes with the same name. If you inspect the diagram, you notice that both classes expose properties. Each property maps a column within the table in the database. Figure 24.4 also shows the Properties window opened to show you a new, important concept, the `System.Data.Linq.DataContext` class. Every LINQ to SQL object model defines a class that inherits from `DataContext` and which is the main entry point of a LINQ to SQL class. It is, in other words, an object-oriented reference to the database. It is responsible for the following:

- ▶ Opening and closing connections

- ▶ Handling relationships between entities

- ▶ Keeping track, with a single instance, of all changes applied to entities during all the object model lifetimes

- ▶ Translating Visual Basic code into the appropriate SQL instructions

- ▶ Managing entities' lifetimes, no matter how long

Visual Studio generates a new `DataContext` class by forming its name and concatenating the database name with the `DataContext` phrase. So in our example, the class is named `NorthwindDataContext`. This class, as you can see in Figure 24.4, exposes some properties including the connection string, base class, and access modifier.

INHERITANCE AND SERIALIZATION

Although this chapter also covers advanced LINQ to SQL features, some things are beyond the scope in this language-focused book, such as inheritance and serialization of data contexts. Such features are better described in the MSDN documentation at the following address: http://msdn.microsoft.com/en-us/library/bb386976(v=vs110).aspx

Now click the `Category` item in the designer that represents an entity described in Figure 24.5 within the Properties window.

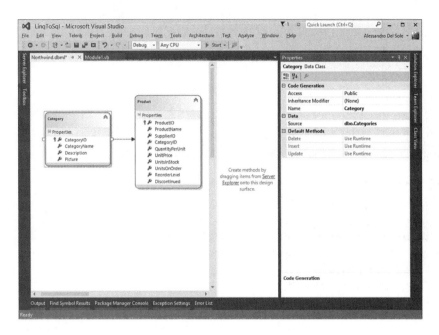

FIGURE 24.5   Examining the `Category` class.

It is interesting to understand that such a class has public access that requires code (Use Runtime definition) to support Insert/Update/Delete operations. The `Source` property also tells us what the source table in the database is. Now click on the arrow that establishes the relationship. Figure 24.6 shows how the Properties window describes such an object.

Notice how a one-to-many relationship is represented. The Child property shows the "many" part of the one-to-many relationship, whereas the Parent property shows the "one" part of the relationship.

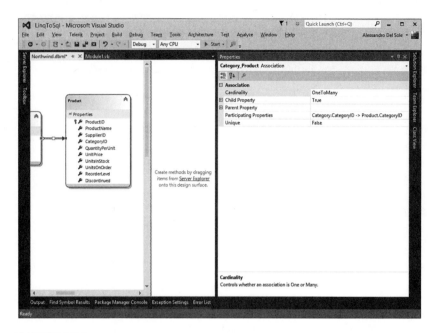

FIGURE 24.6   Examining associations.

RELATIONSHIPS

LINQ to SQL does not support many-to-many relationships. For this purpose, you should use the ADO.NET Entity Framework.

Now that you have a clearer idea about LINQ to SQL classes in a graphical way, it's time to understand the architecture. This kind of a class is referred via a .dbml file that groups nested files. To see nested files, you need to activate the **View All Files** view in Solution Explorer. The first nested file has a .dbml.layout extension and contains the XML definition for the class diagram that you just saw in the Visual Studio Designer. All edits, including Visual Studio-generated items, are performed onto the designer and then reflected into a .designer.vb file (in our example, Northwind.designer.vb). This file is fundamental because it stores code definitions for the `DataContext`, entities, and associations classes. Understanding how this file is defined is important, although you should never edit it manually. Listing 24.1 shows the definition of the `NorthwindDataContext` class.

LISTING 24.1   The `NorthwindDataContext` Class Definition

```
<Global.System.Data.Linq.Mapping.DatabaseAttribute(Name:="Northwind")> _
Partial Public Class NorthwindDataContext
    Inherits System.Data.Linq.DataContext

    Private Shared mappingSource As System.Data.Linq.Mapping.MappingSource = _
```

```
                        New AttributeMappingSource()

Partial Private Sub OnCreated()
End Sub
Partial Private Sub InsertCategory(instance As Category)
End Sub
Partial Private Sub UpdateCategory(instance As Category)
End Sub
Partial Private Sub DeleteCategory(instance As Category)
End Sub
Partial Private Sub InsertProduct(instance As Product)
End Sub
Partial Private Sub UpdateProduct(instance As Product)
End Sub
Partial Private Sub DeleteProduct(instance As Product)
End Sub


Public Sub New()
    MyBase.New(Global.LinqToSql.My.MySettings.Default.
            NorthwindConnectionString, mappingSource)
    OnCreated
End Sub


Public Sub New(connection As String)
    MyBase.New(connection, mappingSource)
    OnCreated
End Sub


Public Sub New(connection As System.Data.IDbConnection)
    MyBase.New(connection, mappingSource)
    OnCreated
End Sub


 Public Sub New(connection As String,
            mappingSource As System.Data.Linq.
            Mapping.MappingSource)
    MyBase.New(connection, mappingSource)
    OnCreated()
End Sub


Public Sub New(connection As System.Data.IDbConnection,
            mappingSource As System.Data.Linq.
            Mapping.MappingSource)
    MyBase.New(connection, mappingSource)
    OnCreated()
End Sub
```

24

```
Public ReadOnly Property Categories() As System.Data.Linq.Table(Of Category)
    Get
        Return Me.GetTable(Of Category)
    End Get
End Property
Public ReadOnly Property Products() As System.Data.Linq.Table(Of Product)
    Get
        Return Me.GetTable(Of Product)
    End Get
End Property
End Class
```

The class is marked with the `DataBase` attribute and inherits from `DataContext`, meaning
that it has to be a managed reference to the database. The constructor provides several
overloads, most of them accepting a connection string if you do not want it to be stored
in the configuration file (which is the default generation). Two properties are important,
`Categories` and `Products` of type `System.Data.Linq.Table(Of T)`. This type offers a
.NET representation of a database table. The `GetTable` method invoked within properties creates `Table(Of T)` objects based on entities. Notice how several partial methods
for Insert/Update/Delete operations are defined and can be extended later. Similar to
the `DataContext` class, both `Product` and `Category` classes have a Visual Basic definition within the same file. As a unified example, Listing 24.2 shows the definition of the
`Category` class.

LISTING 24.2   The `Category` Class Definition

```
<Global.System.Data.Linq.Mapping.TableAttribute(Name:="dbo.Categories")> _
Partial Public Class Category
    Implements System.ComponentModel.INotifyPropertyChanging,
            System.ComponentModel.INotifyPropertyChanged

    Private Shared emptyChangingEventArgs As PropertyChangingEventArgs = _
                New PropertyChangingEventArgs(String.Empty)

    Private _CategoryID As Integer

    Private _CategoryName As String

    Private _Description As String

    Private _Picture As System.Data.Linq.Binary

    Private _Products As EntitySet(Of Product)

    Partial Private Sub OnLoaded()
    End Sub
```

```vb.net
Partial Private Sub OnValidate(action As System.Data.Linq.ChangeAction)
End Sub
Partial Private Sub OnCreated()
End Sub
Partial Private Sub OnCategoryIDChanging(value As Integer)
End Sub
Partial Private Sub OnCategoryIDChanged()
End Sub
Partial Private Sub OnCategoryNameChanging(value As String)
End Sub
Partial Private Sub OnCategoryNameChanged()
End Sub
Partial Private Sub OnDescriptionChanging(value As String)
End Sub
Partial Private Sub OnDescriptionChanged()
End Sub
Partial Private Sub OnPictureChanging(value As System.Data.Linq.Binary)
End Sub
Partial Private Sub OnPictureChanged()
End Sub


Public Sub New()
    MyBase.New
    Me._Products = New EntitySet(Of Product)(AddressOf Me.attach_Products, _
                                    AddressOf Me.detach_Products)
    OnCreated
End Sub


<Global.System.Data.Linq.Mapping.ColumnAttribute(Storage:="_CategoryID", _
    AutoSync:=AutoSync.OnInsert, DbType:="Int NOT NULL IDENTITY", _
    IsPrimaryKey:=True, IsDbGenerated:=True)> _
Public Property CategoryID() As Integer
    Get
        Return Me._CategoryID
    End Get
    Set(ByVal value As Integer)
        If ((Me._CategoryID = Value) _
           = False) Then
            Me.OnCategoryIDChanging(Value)
            Me.SendPropertyChanging()
            Me._CategoryID = Value
            Me.SendPropertyChanged("CategoryID")
            Me.OnCategoryIDChanged()
        End If
    End Set
End Property
```

```vb
<Global.System.Data.Linq.Mapping.ColumnAttribute(Storage:="_CategoryName",
        DbType:="NVarChar(15) NOT NULL", CanBeNull:=False)> _
Public Property CategoryName() As String
    Get
        Return Me._CategoryName
    End Get
    Set(value As String)
        If (String.Equals(Me._CategoryName, Value) = False) Then
            Me.OnCategoryNameChanging(Value)
            Me.SendPropertyChanging()
            Me._CategoryName = Value
            Me.SendPropertyChanged("CategoryName")
            Me.OnCategoryNameChanged()
        End If
    End Set
End Property


<Global.System.Data.Linq.Mapping.ColumnAttribute(Storage:="_Description",
        DbType:="NText", UpdateCheck:=UpdateCheck.Never)> _
Public Property Description() As String
    Get
        Return Me._Description
    End Get
    Set(value As String)
        If (String.Equals(Me._Description, Value) = False) Then
            Me.OnDescriptionChanging(Value)
            Me.SendPropertyChanging()
            Me._Description = Value
            Me.SendPropertyChanged("Description")
            Me.OnDescriptionChanged()
        End If
    End Set
End Property


<Global.System.Data.Linq.Mapping.ColumnAttribute(Storage:="_Picture",
        DbType:="Image", UpdateCheck:=UpdateCheck.Never)> _
Public Property Picture() As System.Data.Linq.Binary
    Get
        Return Me._Picture
    End Get
    Set(value As System.Data.Linq.Binary)
        If (Object.Equals(Me._Picture, Value) = False) Then
            Me.OnPictureChanging(Value)
            Me.SendPropertyChanging()
            Me._Picture = Value
            Me.SendPropertyChanged("Picture")
            Me.OnPictureChanged()
```

```vb
            End If
        End Set
    End Property


    <Global.System.Data.Linq.Mapping.AssociationAttribute(Name:="Category_Product", _
            Storage:="_Products", ThisKey:="CategoryID", OtherKey:="CategoryID")> _
    Public Property Products() As EntitySet(Of Product)
        Get
            Return Me._Products
        End Get
        Set(value As EntitySet(Of Product))
            Me._Products.Assign(Value)
        End Set
    End Property


    Public Event PropertyChanging As PropertyChangingEventHandler Implements _
            System.ComponentModel.INotifyPropertyChanging.PropertyChanging


    Public Event PropertyChanged As PropertyChangedEventHandler Implements _
            System.ComponentModel.INotifyPropertyChanged.PropertyChanged


    Protected Overridable Sub SendPropertyChanging()
        If ((Me.PropertyChangingEvent Is Nothing)  _
                = false) Then
            RaiseEvent PropertyChanging(Me, emptyChangingEventArgs)
        End If
    End Sub


    Protected Overridable Sub SendPropertyChanged(ByVal propertyName As [String])
        If ((Me.PropertyChangedEvent Is Nothing)  _
                = false) Then
            RaiseEvent PropertyChanged(Me, _
                                New PropertyChangedEventArgs(propertyName))
        End If
    End Sub


    Private Sub attach_Products(ByVal entity As Product)
        Me.SendPropertyChanging
        entity.Category = Me
    End Sub


    Private Sub detach_Products(ByVal entity As Product)
        Me.SendPropertyChanging
        entity.Category = Nothing
    End Sub
End Class
```

The class is marked with the `System.Data.Linq.TableAttribute` attribute, meaning that it has to represent a database table. It implements both the `INotifyPropertyChanging` and `INotifyPropertyChanged` interfaces to provide the ability of notifying the user interface of changes about entities. It then defines partial methods that you can extend and customize when a particular event occurs. (This is covered when discussing data validation.) Each property is decorated with the `System.Data.Linq.Mapping.ColumnAttribute` that represents a column within a database table. This attribute takes some arguments that are self-explanatory. The most important of them are `Storage`, which points to a private field used as a data repository, and `DbType`, which contains the original SQL Server data type for the column. It is worth mentioning that Visual Basic provides an appropriate type mapping according to the related SQL data type. A primary key requires two other attributes, `IsPrimaryKey = True` and `AutoSync`. The second one establishes that it has to be auto-incremented and synchronized when a new item is added. In the end, notice how Set properties members perform a series of actions, such as raising events related to the beginning of property editing, storing the new value, and finally raising events related to the property set completion. This is auto-generated code from Visual Studio, and you should never change it manually. You are instead encouraged to use the LINQ to SQL designer that reflects changes in code. The last file for a LINQ to SQL class has a .dbml layout extension and is just related to the diagram layout. Now that you are a little bit more familiar with LINQ to SQL classes, you can begin querying data with LINQ to SQL.

Querying Data with LINQ to SQL

Before you begin querying data with LINQ to SQL, you need to instantiate the `DataContext` class. Continuing with the Console application example started in the previous section, you can declare such an instance at the module level as follows:

```
Private northwind As New NorthwindDataContext
```

REAL-WORLD LINQ: CLASS-LEVEL DECLARATION

In this example, the instance is declared at the module level because a Console application is covered. In most cases, you work with client applications such as WPF or Windows Forms; therefore, the instance will be generated at the class level. Also, in my client applications, I used to follow this approach: I'd provide a class-level declaration of the `DataContext` but instantiate the object within the constructor. This allows handling exceptions that could occur at runtime while attempting to connect to the database, other than performing other initialization actions.

Declaring a single instance at the module or class level allows one `DataContext` to manage entities for all the object model lifetimes. When you create such an instance, the `DataContext` connects to the database and provides required abstraction so that you can work against the object model instead of working against the database. The `DataContext` class's constructor also accepts a connection string if you want it to be hard-coded instead of storing it within a configuration file. You have different alternatives for querying data.

For example, you might want to retrieve the complete list of products that is accomplished as follows:

```
'Returns Table(Of Product)
Dim allProduct = northwind.Products
```

This code returns a `System.Data.Linq.Table (Of Product)` that is an object inheriting from `IQueryable(Of T)` and that represents a database table. `IQueryable (Of T)` is the general type returned by LINQ to SQL queries and inherits from `IEnumerable (Of T)` but also offers some more members specific for data manipulation. Although this type can be directly bound to user interface controls for presenting data as much as `IEnumerable`, it does not support data editing. A `Table(Of T)` instead supports adding, removing, and saving objects. To perform LINQ queries using filtering, ordering, and projection operators, you use the LINQ keywords and the same programming techniques provided by the unified programming model of this technology. A little difference from LINQ to Objects is that LINQ to SQL queries return an `IQueryable(Of T)` instead of `IEnumerable(Of T)`. For example, the following LINQ query returns the list of products in which the unit price is greater than 10:

```
'Returns IQueryable(Of Product)
Dim queryByPrice = From prod In northwind.Products
                   Where prod.UnitPrice > 10
                   Select prod
```

You can also convert a query into an ordered collection such as the `List(Of T)` using extension methods:

```
'Returns List(Of Product)
Dim queryByPrice = (From prod In northwind.Products
                    Where prod.UnitPrice > 10
                    Select prod).ToList
```

Remember that *LINQ queries are effectively executed only when used*; therefore, the first example does not run the query until you invoke something on it. The second query is instead executed immediately because of the `ToList` invocation. For example, the following iteration would cause the first query to be executed when the enumerator is invoked:

```
'Returns IQueryable(Of Product)
Dim queryByPrice = From prod In northwind.Products
                   Where prod.UnitPrice > 10
                   Select prod

'Query is executed now
For Each prod In queryByPrice
    Console.WriteLine(prod.ProductName)
Next
```

24

This iteration shows the list of product names. You can also perform more complex queries that are probably what you will do in your real applications. The following method queries products for the specified category, given the category name taking only products that are not discontinued, finally ordering the result by the number of units in stock for product:

```
Function QueryByCategoryName(categoryName As String) _
        As List(Of Product)

    Dim query = From categories In northwind.Categories
                Where categories.CategoryName = categoryName
                Join prod In northwind.Products
                On prod.CategoryID Equals categories.CategoryID
                Where prod.Discontinued = False
                Order By prod.UnitsInStock
                Select prod

    Return query.ToList
End Function
```

You can invoke the method and iterate the result as follows:

```
Dim productsList = QueryByCategoryName("Seafood")

For Each prod In productsList
    Console.WriteLine("Product name: {0}, unit price: {1}",
                      prod.ProductName,
                      prod.UnitPrice)
Next
```

The preceding code produces the following result:

```
Product name: Rogede sild, unit price: 9.5000
Product name: Nord-Ost Matjeshering, unit price: 24.8900
Product name: Gravad lax, unit price: 26.0000
Product name: Konbu, unit price: 6.0000
Product name: Ikura, unit price: 31.0000
Product name: Carnarvon Tigers, unit price: 62.5000
Product name: Escargots de Bourgogne, unit price: 13.2500
Product name: Jack's New England Clam Chowder, unit price: 9.6500
Product name: Spegesild, unit price: 12.0000
Product name: Röd Kaviar, unit price: 15.0000
Product name: Inlagd Sill, unit price: 19.0000
Product name: Boston Crab Meat, unit price: 18.4000
```

In other cases, you need to data-bind your result to user interface controls. If you work with Windows Forms applications, a good idea is returning a `System.ComponentModel.BindingList(Of T)` that is a collection specific for data-binding. So the preceding method could be rewritten as follows:

```
Function QueryByCategoryName(categoryName As String) _
        As System.ComponentModel.BindingList(Of Product)

    Dim query = From categories In northwind.Categories
                Where categories.CategoryName = categoryName
                Join prod In northwind.Products
                On prod.CategoryID Equals categories.CategoryID
                Where prod.Discontinued = False
                Order By prod.UnitsInStock
                Select prod

    Return New System.ComponentModel.
                BindingList(Of Product)(query.ToList)
End Function
```

Similarly, for WPF applications you would return an `ObservableCollection(Of T)`:

```
Function QueryByCategoryName(categoryName As String) _
        As System.ObjectModel.ObservableCollection(Of Product)

    Dim query = From categories In northwind.Categories
                Where categories.CategoryName = categoryName
                Join prod In northwind.Products
                On prod.CategoryID Equals categories.CategoryID
                Where prod.Discontinued = False
                Order By prod.UnitsInStock
                Select prod

    Return New System.ObjectModel.ObservableCollection(query)
End Function
```

IMPORTANT NOTE ON LINQ TO SQL QUERIES

When performing LINQ to SQL queries (and LINQ to Entities queries in the next chapter), they can execute only members that have a corresponding type or function in SQL Server and the SQL syntax; otherwise, an exception will be thrown. For example, try to invoke the `ToLowerInvariant` method on the `categories.CategoryName` statement within the Where clause in the previous method. The Visual Basic compiler correctly compiles the code because the .NET Framework correctly recognizes all members. But SQL Server does not have a function that does the same, so a `NotSupportedException` will be thrown at runtime. Therefore, always ensure that .NET members you invoke have a counterpart in SQL Server. Keep in mind this rule also for the next chapter.

You could also take advantage of anonymous types for collecting data from different tables into a unique collection. The following code obtains a list of products for the given category name, picking up some information:

```
Dim customQuery = From prod In northwind.Products
                  Join cat In northwind.Categories On
                  prod.CategoryID Equals cat.CategoryID
                  Order By cat.CategoryID
                  Select New With {.CategoryName = cat.CategoryName,
                                   .ProductName = _
                                   prod.ProductName,
                                   .UnitPrice = prod.UnitPrice,
                                   .Discontinued = _
                                   prod.Discontinued}
```

This query, when executed, returns an `IQueryable(Of Anonymous type)`. As you already know, lists of anonymous types can be iterated or also bound to user interface controls for presenting data but cannot be edited. If you need to create custom objects from query results, such as collecting data from different tables, you first need to implement a class that groups all required data as properties. Consider the following class:

```
Class CustomObject
    Property CategoryName As String
    Property ProductName As String
    Property UnitPrice As Decimal?
    Property Discontinued As Boolean?
End Class--
```

Now you can rewrite the preceding query as follows, changing the Select clause allowing generating a new `CustomObject` instance:

```
Dim customQuery = From prod In northwind.Products
                  Join cat In northwind.Categories On
                  prod.CategoryID Equals cat.CategoryID
                  Order By cat.CategoryID
                  Select New CustomObject _
                        With {.CategoryName = cat.CategoryName,
                              .ProductName = prod.ProductName,
                              .UnitPrice = prod.UnitPrice,
                              .Discontinued = prod.Discontinued}
```

Now the query returns an `IQueryable(Of CustomObject)`. You can convert it into a typed collection according to your needs or iterate it as in the following example:

```
For Each obj In customQuery
    Console.WriteLine("Category name: {0}, Product name: {1},
                       Unit price: {2}, Discontinued: {3}",
                       obj.CategoryName, obj.ProductName,
                       obj.UnitPrice, obj.Discontinued)
Next
```

Providing this approach instead of working against anonymous types can allow you to bind your collections to user interface controls and provide two-way data binding, or simpler, can provide the ability of programmatically coding Insert/Update/Delete operations as explained in the next section.

Insert/Update/Delete Operations with LINQ

LINQ to SQL is not just querying data but is also a complete infrastructure for data manipulation. This means that you can perform Insert/Update/Delete operations against your object model using LINQ. Let's discuss first how a new entity can be added to an entity set.

Inserting Entities

You instantiate a new entity as any other .NET class and then set its properties. The following code shows how you can add a new `Product` to the `Products` entity set. Notice how the method receives the belonging category as an argument, which is required for setting the one-to-many relationship:

```
Sub AddProduct(categoryReference As Category)
    Dim aProduct As New Product

    aProduct.ProductName = "Italian spaghetti"
    aProduct.Discontinued = False
    aProduct.QuantityPerUnit = "10"
    aProduct.UnitPrice = 0.4D

    'Setting the relationship
    aProduct.Category = categoryReference

    'Adding the new product to the object model
    northwind.Products.InsertOnSubmit(aProduct)
End Sub
```

You set property values as you would in any other .NET class. Here you have to pay attention to add a non-null value to non-nullable members. In the previous example, `QuantityPerUnit` is a non-nullable and therefore must be assigned with a valid string. You can then omit assigning nullable members. LINQ to SQL can provide auto-increment functionalities on primary keys that in the original SQL Server database implement such a feature. In this example, `ProductID` is not assigned because it is an auto-incrementable primary key. You set a one-to-many relationship assigning the property referring to the other part of the relationship (`Category` in the preceding example) with the instance of the entity that completes the relationship. When this is performed, you invoke the `InsertOnSubmit` method on the instance of the entity set that receives the new entity (respectively `Products` and `Product` in our example). This method saves the new data into the object model, but it does not send data to the underlying database until you invoke the `SubmitChanges` method, as follows:

```
Sub SaveChanges()
    Try
        northwind.SubmitChanges()

    Catch ex As SqlClient.SqlException

    Catch ex As Exception

    End Try
End Sub
```

This saves data to the database. If something fails, you need to handle a `SqlClient.SqlException` exception. Now add an invocation to the custom `SaveChanges` method after the `InsertOnSubmit` one. At this point you can invoke the custom `AddProduct` method for programmatically adding a new product that must be bound to a specific category because of the one-to-many relationship. Working with a Console application, you can add such an invocation within the `Main` method. The following code demonstrates this:

```
Dim cerealsCategory As Category = _
    northwind.Categories.Single(Function(cat) _
    cat.CategoryName = "Grains/Cereals")

AddProduct(cerealsCategory)
```

You need the instance of the category you want to pass to the method. To accomplish this, you can invoke the `Single` extension method on the categories' collection to get the unique category with the specified name, taking advantage of a lambda expression. As an alternative, you can directly pass a lambda as an argument as follows:

```
AddProduct(northwind.Categories.
        Single(Function(cat) cat.CategoryName = "Grains/Cereals"))
```

Both solutions accomplish the same result.

GETTING INSTANCES IN CLIENT APPLICATIONS

In client applications such as Windows Forms, WPF, or Silverlight, getting an instance of an entity is even simpler. You just need to retrieve the current element of the data control (for example, `ComboBox`, `DataGrid`, or `DataGridView`) or, even better, the current selected item in the data source bridge control, such as `BindingSource` or `CollectionViewSource`.

If you run this code and everything works fine, your new product is added to the `Products` table of the `Northwind` database when the `DataContext.SubmitChanges` method is invoked and a relationship with the `Grains/Cereals` category is also set. You can easily verify this by opening Server Explorer and then expanding the Northwind Tables folder; then right-click the **Products** table and select **Show Table Data**. (If you have a local copy of the Northwind database instead, you need to double-click the database copy available in the Bin\Debug or Bin\Release folder to open it in Server Explorer.) As an alternative, you can open the new SQL Server Object Explorer tool window, expand the Northwind database, and then right-click the **Products** table and select **View data**. Figure 24.7 reproduces the scenario, showing also the new product, this time in SQL Server Object Explorer.

One thing that you need to remember is to check whether an entity already exists to prevent malicious runtime exceptions. To accomplish this, you can take advantage of the `Single` extension method that throws an exception if the specified entity does not exist; therefore, it can be added. The `AddProduct` method can be rewritten as follows (see comments in code):

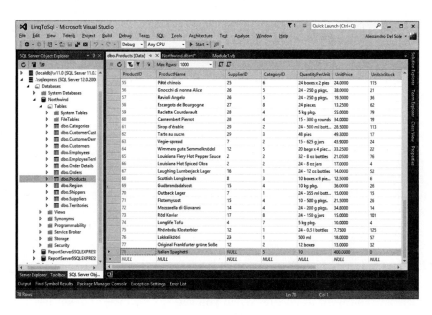

FIGURE 24.7   Checking that the new product has been correctly saved to the database.

```
Sub AddProduct(categoryReference As Category)
    Try
        Dim productCheck = northwind.Products.
                        Single(Function(prod) _
                        prod.ProductName = "Italian spaghetti")
        productCheck = Nothing

        'the Product does not exist, so add it
    Catch ex As InvalidOperationException
        Dim aProduct As New Product

        aProduct.ProductName = "Italian spaghetti"
        aProduct.Discontinued = False
        aProduct.QuantityPerUnit = "10"

    aProduct.UnitPrice = 0.4D
        aProduct.CategoryID = categoryReference.CategoryID

        'Setting the relationship
        aProduct.Category = categoryReference

        'Adding the new product to the object model
        northwind.Products.InsertOnSubmit(aProduct)
        SaveChanges()

    End Try
End Sub
```

Now that you know how to create and save data, it's also important to understand how updates can be performed.

ADDING MULTIPLE ENTITIES

Because the `DataContext` can handle all CRUD operations during an application's lifetime, you can add all entities you need and send them to the underlying database with a unique `DataContext.SubmitChanges` invocation. Alternatively, instead of making an `InsertOnSubmit` invocation for each new entity, you can also send a unique insertion invoking the `InsertAllOnSubmit` method.

Updating Entities

Updating existing entities is even easier than adding new ones. First, you need to obtain the instance of the entity you want to update. When you get the instance, you edit its properties and then invoke the `DataContext.SubmitChanges` method. The following code provides an example:

```
Sub UpdateProduct(ByVal productInstance As Product)

    'Throws an exception if a null value is passed
    If productInstance Is Nothing Then
        Throw New NullReferenceException
    Else
        With productInstance
            .ProductName = "Italian Linguine"
            .UnitsInStock = 100
        End With
    End If

    SaveChanges()
End Sub
```

This method requires an instance of the `Product` entity to be updated. To get an instance of the desired product, you can still take advantage of a lambda, but this time exception handling is reverted, as you can see from the fol!owing snippet:

```
Try
    UpdateProduct(northwind.Products.
                    Single(Function(prod) prod.
                    ProductName = "Italian spaghetti"))

    'The specified product does not exist
Catch ex As InvalidOperationException

End Try
```

When the `NorthwindDataContext.SubmitChanges` method is invoked, data is updated to the underlying database. Notice that you can update multiple entities and the `SubmitChanges` method sends changes all at once. You can easily check for correct updates following the steps shown in the previous paragraph and summarized in Figure 24.7.

Deleting Entities

Deleting an entity works similarly to update, at least for retrieving the entity instance. Deletion is performed by invoking the `DeleteOnSubmit` method, which works opposite to the `InsertOnSubmit`. The following is an example, which also checks whether the entity exists:

```
Sub DeleteProduct(productInstance As Product)

    If productInstance Is Nothing Then
        Throw New NullReferenceException
    Else
```

```
    northwind.Products.DeleteOnSubmit(productInstance)
    SaveChanges()
  End If
End Sub
```

Remember how the custom `SaveChanges` method invokes the `NorthwindDataContext.SubmitChanges` one. The following code shows invoking the previous method for performing a product deletion:

```
Try
    DeleteProduct(northwind.Products.
                    Single(Function(prod) prod.
                    ProductName = "Italian spaghetti"))

    'The specified product does not exist
Catch ex As InvalidOperationException
End Try
```

Similarly to `InsertAllOnSubmit`, you can also invoke `DeleteAllOnSubmit` to remove multiple entities from the object model.

> **NULL CHECKS**
>
> You can use the null-propagating operator `?.` to determine whether an object is null when updating or deleting entities.

Mapping Stored Procedures

LINQ to SQL allows mapping stored procedures from the SQL Server database into a .NET method that you can use within your object model and that is managed by the running instance of the `DataContext`. In this way, you do not lose the advantage of stored procedures when working with LINQ. To map a stored procedure, go back to the Visual Studio Designer for LINQ to SQL and ensure that the Methods pane is opened on the right side of the designer; then open Server Explorer, expand the database structure, and expand the Stored Procedures folder. After you've done this, drag the stored procedure you need onto the Methods pane. Figure 24.8 shows how to accomplish this against the Northwind database of the current example.

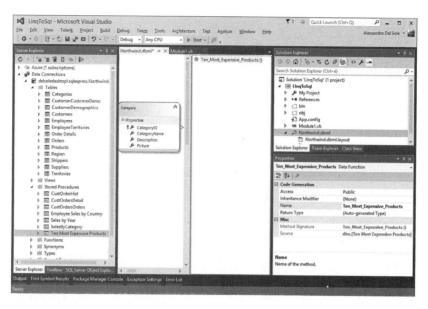

FIGURE 24.8   Mapping a stored procedure to a .NET method in LINQ to SQL.

Notice also how the Properties window shows method properties, such as access qualifier and signature. The **Return type** property is set as auto-generated because the result is
determined according to the stored procedure type. Some procedures return a single result
value, and therefore the returned type is ISingleResult(Of T). Other ones can return
multiple result values, and therefore the returned type is IMultipleResult(Of T). Behind
the scenes, a stored procedure is mapped into a method, but such a method also requires a
support class mapping types used by the stored procedure. The following code is excerpted
from the Northwind.designer.vb file and shows the class definition:

```
Partial Public Class Ten_Most_Expensive_ProductsResult

    Private _TenMostExpensiveProducts As String

    Private _UnitPrice As System.Nullable(Of Decimal)

    Public Sub New()
        MyBase.New
    End Sub

    <Global.System.Data.Linq.Mapping.
            ColumnAttribute(Storage:="_TenMostExpensiveProducts",
            DbType:="NVarChar(40) NOT NULL", CanBeNull:=False)> _
    Public Property TenMostExpensiveProducts() As String
        Get
            Return Me._TenMostExpensiveProducts
```

```
        End Get
        Set(ByVal value As String)
            If (String.Equals(Me._TenMostExpensiveProducts, value) = False)
            Then
                 Me._TenMostExpensiveProducts = value
            End If
        End Set
    End Property


    <Global.System.Data.Linq.Mapping.ColumnAttribute(Storage:="_UnitPrice",
        DbType:="Money")> _
    Public Property UnitPrice() As System.Nullable(Of Decimal)
        Get
            Return Me._UnitPrice
        End Get
        Set(ByVal value As System.Nullable(Of Decimal))
            If (Me._UnitPrice.Equals(Value) = False) Then
                Me._UnitPrice = Value
            End If
        End Set
    End Property
End Class
```

The class works like other auto-generated classes in that it sets or returns values taken from the data source. The method that actually performs the action is mapped as follows within the `NorthwindDataContext` class definition:

```
<Global.System.Data.Linq.Mapping.
        FunctionAttribute(Name:="dbo.[Ten Most Expensive Products]")> _
Public Function Ten_Most_Expensive_Products() As _
        ISingleResult(Of Ten_Most_Expensive_ProductsResult)
    Dim result As IExecuteResult = Me.ExecuteMethodCall(Me,
                                    CType(MethodInfo.GetCurrentMethod,
                                    MethodInfo))
    Return CType(result.ReturnValue,
                ISingleResult(Of Ten_Most_Expensive_ProductsResult))
End Function
```

The `System.Data.Linq.Mapping.FunctionAttribute` attribute decorates the method signature with the original stored procedure name. As you can see, this particular method returns an `ISingleResult(Of T)`, and invocation to the stored procedure is performed via reflection. Invoking in code, a stored procedure is as simple as in other methods usage. The following code takes an `ISingleResult(Of T)`:

```
'Gets the list of the ten most expensive
'products from the Products table
Dim result = northwind.Ten_Most_Expensive_Products
```

You can then iterate the result to get a list of the products as in the following example:

```
For Each r In result
    Console.WriteLine(r.UnitPrice)
Next
```

This simple iteration produces the following result:

```
263,5000
123,7900
97,0000
81,0000
62,5000
55,0000
53,0000
49,3000
46,0000
45,6000
```

Notice that an `ISingleResult` can be iterated only once; otherwise, you get an `InvalidOperationException`. If you plan to access this result multiple times, the only way is to convert the result into a generic collection such as the `List(Of T)`. The following code converts the stored procedure result into a `List`, making possible iterations more than once:

```
'Gets the list of the ten most expensive
'products from the Products table into
'a List(Of T)
Dim result = northwind.Ten_Most_Expensive_Products.ToList
```

Also notice that converting to `IQueryable(Of T)` will not allow the result to be accessed more than once.

Using the Log

LINQ to SQL sends SQL instructions each time it has to perform an operation on our demand. This is accomplished via its complex infrastructure that relies on the .NET Framework. By the way, as a developer you may be interested in understanding what really happens behind the scenes and in getting information about the real SQL instructions sent to SQL Server. Luckily, you can use a SQL log that allows showing SQL instructions. You need to set the `DataContext.Log` property as follows, before taking actions you want to inspect:

```
northwind.Log = Console.Out
```

If you want to monitor everything happening, add the preceding code after the creation of the `DataContext` instance. If you apply this code before running the first example shown in the "Insert/Update/Delete Operations with LINQ" section, you get the result shown in Figure 24.9.

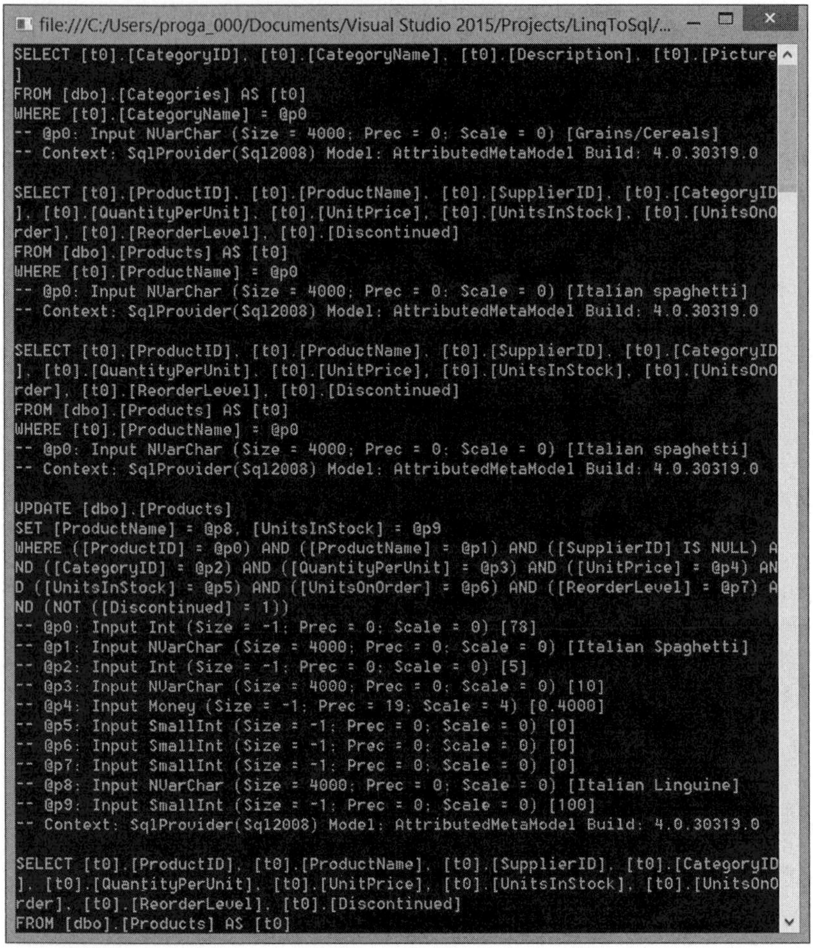

```
file:///C:/Users/proga_000/Documents/Visual Studio 2015/Projects/LinqToSql/...
SELECT [t0].[CategoryID], [t0].[CategoryName], [t0].[Description], [t0].[Picture
]
FROM [dbo].[Categories] AS [t0]
WHERE [t0].[CategoryName] = @p0
-- @p0: Input NVarChar (Size = 4000; Prec = 0; Scale = 0) [Grains/Cereals]
-- Context: SqlProvider(Sql2008) Model: AttributedMetaModel Build: 4.0.30319.0

SELECT [t0].[ProductID], [t0].[ProductName], [t0].[SupplierID], [t0].[CategoryID
], [t0].[QuantityPerUnit], [t0].[UnitPrice], [t0].[UnitsInStock], [t0].[UnitsOnO
rder], [t0].[ReorderLevel], [t0].[Discontinued]
FROM [dbo].[Products] AS [t0]
WHERE [t0].[ProductName] = @p0
-- @p0: Input NVarChar (Size = 4000; Prec = 0; Scale = 0) [Italian spaghetti]
-- Context: SqlProvider(Sql2008) Model: AttributedMetaModel Build: 4.0.30319.0

SELECT [t0].[ProductID], [t0].[ProductName], [t0].[SupplierID], [t0].[CategoryID
], [t0].[QuantityPerUnit], [t0].[UnitPrice], [t0].[UnitsInStock], [t0].[UnitsOnO
rder], [t0].[ReorderLevel], [t0].[Discontinued]
FROM [dbo].[Products] AS [t0]
WHERE [t0].[ProductName] = @p0
-- @p0: Input NVarChar (Size = 4000; Prec = 0; Scale = 0) [Italian spaghetti]
-- Context: SqlProvider(Sql2008) Model: AttributedMetaModel Build: 4.0.30319.0

UPDATE [dbo].[Products]
SET [ProductName] = @p8, [UnitsInStock] = @p9
WHERE ([ProductID] = @p0) AND ([ProductName] = @p1) AND ([SupplierID] IS NULL) A
ND ([CategoryID] = @p2) AND ([QuantityPerUnit] = @p3) AND ([UnitPrice] = @p4) AN
D ([UnitsInStock] = @p5) AND ([UnitsOnOrder] = @p6) AND ([ReorderLevel] = @p7) A
ND (NOT ([Discontinued] = 1))
-- @p0: Input Int (Size = -1; Prec = 0; Scale = 0) [78]
-- @p1: Input NVarChar (Size = 4000; Prec = 0; Scale = 0) [Italian Spaghetti]
-- @p2: Input Int (Size = -1; Prec = 0; Scale = 0) [5]
-- @p3: Input NVarChar (Size = 4000; Prec = 0; Scale = 0) [10]
-- @p4: Input Money (Size = -1; Prec = 19; Scale = 4) [0.4000]
-- @p5: Input SmallInt (Size = -1; Prec = 0; Scale = 0) [0]
-- @p6: Input SmallInt (Size = -1; Prec = 0; Scale = 0) [0]
-- @p7: Input SmallInt (Size = -1; Prec = 0; Scale = 0) [0]
-- @p8: Input NVarChar (Size = 4000; Prec = 0; Scale = 0) [Italian Linguine]
-- @p9: Input SmallInt (Size = -1; Prec = 0; Scale = 0) [100]
-- Context: SqlProvider(Sql2008) Model: AttributedMetaModel Build: 4.0.30319.0

SELECT [t0].[ProductID], [t0].[ProductName], [t0].[SupplierID], [t0].[CategoryID
], [t0].[QuantityPerUnit], [t0].[UnitPrice], [t0].[UnitsInStock], [t0].[UnitsOnO
rder], [t0].[ReorderLevel], [t0].[Discontinued]
FROM [dbo].[Products] AS [t0]
```

FIGURE 24.9   Showing the LINQ to SQL log result.

As you can see, this is useful because you get an idea about the actual SQL instructions sent by LINQ to SQL to SQL Server. The DataContext.Log property is of type System. IO.TextWriter; therefore, you can assign it with a stream pointing to a file on disk if you want the SQL output to be redirected to a file instead of the Console window.

Advanced LINQ to SQL

While you become familiar with LINQ to SQL, you understand how it allows performing usual data operations in a strongly typed way. Because of this, you also see the need to perform other operations that you are used to making in classical data development, such as data validation and handling optimistic concurrency. The next section describes this but also something more.

Custom Validations

Validating data is one of the most important activities in every data access system, so LINQ to SQL provides its own methodologies, too. To accomplish data validation, you can take advantage of partial methods. You might remember that in Chapter 20, "Advanced Language Features," you got a practical example of partial methods when discussing LINQ to SQL. Validation rules are useful in LINQ to SQL for two main reasons: The first one is that they enable you to understand whether supplied data is compliant to your requirements; the second one is that they allow you to check whether supplied data has a SQL Server type counterpart. The following code example demonstrates both examples. Imagine you want to add a new product to the object model and then save changes to the database, as you already did following the steps in the first part of the previous section. If you take a look at the `QuantityPerUnit` property—for example, recurring to the Visual Studio Designer—you notice that it is mapped to a `string` .NET type, but its SQL Server counterpart type is `NVarChar(20)`, meaning that the content of the property is a string that must not be longer than 20 characters; otherwise, saving changes to SQL Server will be unsuccessful. To provide validation rules, the first step is to add a partial class. With that said, right-click the project name in Solution Explorer, then select **Add New Class**, and, when requested, supply the new class name, for example **Product.vb**. When the new class is added to the project, add the `Partial` keyword as follows:

```
Partial Public Class Product

End Class
```

At this point you can implement a partial method that performs validation. Because partial methods' signatures are defined within the Northwind.designer.vb code file, here you can implement the full method body as follows:

```
Private Sub OnQuantityPerUnitChanging(value As String)
    If value.Length > 20 Then Throw New _
        ArgumentException _
        ("Quantity per unit must be no longer than 20 characters")
End Sub
```

Notice that you have to handle methods whose names end with `Changing`, which maps an event that is raised before changes are sent to the object model. The code checks for the length of the supplied value, and if it does not match the `NVarChar(20)` type of SQL Server, it throws an `ArgumentException`. To understand how it works, consider the following code that creates a new product and then attempts to write changes:

```
Sub AddProduct(ByVal categoryReference As Category)
    Try
        Dim productCheck = northwind.Products.
                        Single(Function(prod) _
                        prod.ProductName = "Italian spaghetti")
        productCheck = Nothing
```

```
                    'the Product does not exist, so add it
        Catch ex As InvalidOperationException

            Try
                Dim aProduct As New Product

                aProduct.ProductName = "Italian spaghetti"
                aProduct.Discontinued = False

                'The string is 22 characters long
                aProduct.QuantityPerUnit = "1000000000000000000000"
                aProduct.UnitPrice = 0.4D
                aProduct.CategoryID = categoryReference.CategoryID

                'Setting the relationship
                aProduct.Category = categoryReference

                'Adding the new product to the object model
                northwind.Products.InsertOnSubmit(aProduct)
                SaveChanges()

            Catch e As ArgumentException
                Console.WriteLine(e.Message.ToString)
                Exit Try
            Catch e As Exception

            End Try
        End Try
    End Sub
```

Notice how a nested `Try..End Try` block has been provided to handle eventual
`ArgumentNullException` errors coming from validation. You can still invoke the
`AddProduct` method in the previous section as follows:

```
AddProduct(northwind.Categories.
          Single(Function(cat) cat.CategoryName = "Grains/Cereals"))
```

If you now try to run the code, you get an error message advising that the
`QuantityPerUnit` content cannot be longer than 20 characters. In this way, you can
control the content of your data but also ensure that data matches the related SQL Server
type. By using this technique, you can perform validation on each data you want.

DATA VALIDATION AND THE UI

One common scenario is implementing the IDataErrorInfo interface in partial classes so that its members can send notifications to the user interface. Windows Forms and WPF applications can take advantage of notifications for presenting error messages in ways different from a simple messages box. The official documentation for the interface is available here: http://msdn.microsoft.com/en-us/library/system.componentmodel. idataerrorinfo(VS.110).aspx.

Handling Optimistic Concurrency

Optimistic concurrency is a scenario in which multiple clients send changes to the database simultaneously. LINQ to SQL allows resolving optimistic concurrency with the DataContext.ChangeConflicts.ResolveAll method. Such method receives an argument that is an enumeration of type System.Data.Linq.RefreshMode and allows resolving the exception with one of the enumeration members summarized in Table 24.1.

TABLE 24.1   RefreshMode Enumeration Members

Member	Description
KeepCurrentValues	If any changes, keeps original values in the database
KeepChanges	If any changes, keeps changes but other values are updated with original database values
OverwriteCurrentValues	Overrides all current values with original values from database

The following is an example of handling optimistic concurrency, providing a revisited version of the previously utilized SaveChanges custom method:

```
Sub SaveChanges()
    Try
        northwind.SubmitChanges()

    Catch ex As System.Data.Linq.ChangeConflictException

        northwind.ChangeConflicts.ResolveAll(Data.Linq.RefreshMode.
                                KeepCurrentValues)
        northwind.SubmitChanges()
    Catch ex As SqlClient.SqlException

    Catch ex As Exception

    End Try
End Sub
```

Notice first how a `ChangeConflictException` is handled. Here the `ChangeConflicts.`
`ResolveAll` method is required to resolve concurrency. The `KeepCurrentValues` argument
allows keeping original values in the database. Also notice how a subsequent invocation
to `SubmitChanges` is made. This is necessary because the first invocation caused the exception; therefore, another execution must be attempted.

Using SQL Syntax Against Entities

LINQ to SQL also allows writing SQL code against entities so that you can still take advantage of the object model if you prefer the old-fashioned way of manipulating data. The
`DataContext` class offers an instance method named `ExecuteQuery(Of T)` that allows
sending SQL instructions in string form. For example, the following code retrieves a list of
products for the `Grain/Cereals` category, ordered by product name:

```
Sub DirectSqlDemo()

    Dim products = northwind.
        ExecuteQuery(Of Product)("SELECT * FROM PRODUCTS WHERE " & _
                            "CATEGORYID='5' ORDER BY PRODUCTNAME")

    For Each prod In products
        Console.WriteLine(prod.ProductName)
    Next
End Sub
```

`ExecuteQuery(Of T)` returns an `IEnumerable(Of T)` that you can then treat as you like,
according to LINQ specifications. You can also send SQL instructions directly to the database, invoking the `ExecuteCommand` method. This method returns no value and allows
performing Insert/Update/Delete operations against the data. For example, the following
code updates the product name of a product:

```
northwind.ExecuteCommand("UPDATE PRODUCTS SET " & _
        "PRODUCTNAME='Italian mozzarella' WHERE PRODUCTID='72'")
```

If you then want to check that everything work correctly, get the instance of the product
and get information:

```
Dim updatedProduct = _
    northwind.Products.First(Function(prod) prod.ProductID = 72)


'Returns "Italian mozzarella"
Console.WriteLine(updatedProduct.ProductName)
```

Remember: Sending SQL instructions can prevent you from taking advantage of compile-
time checking offered by the LINQ syntax and exposes your code to possible runtime
errors. Be aware of this.

Summary

LINQ to SQL is a built-in object relational mapping engine for Microsoft SQL Server databases. The engine maps database information such as tables and columns into .NET objects such as classes and properties, enabling you to work in a disconnected fashion against an object model rather than against the database. Mapped classes are known as entities. Adding LINQ to SQL classes to your projects can provide the ability of using LINQ for both querying entities and performing CRUD operations via specific methods offered by the `DataContext` class. This is responsible for managing the connection and entities during an application's lifetime, including keeping track of changes that can be submitted to the database in one shot. LINQ to SQL also offers a trace log to understand which SQL instructions were sent to the database and provides the ability of handling optimistic concurrency as much as validating data by taking advantage of partial methods. Finally, you can still write your queries the old-fashioned way by sending SQL instructions directly to the data source.

24

LINQ to DataSets

For many years DataSets have been the main data access technology for .NET developers, including Visual Basic programmers. Although the most recent versions of the .NET Framework introduced new object relational mapping technologies such as LINQ to SQL and ADO.NET Entity Framework, DataSets are still very diffused, especially in older applications. Because of this, Microsoft produced a LINQ standard provider that is specific for querying DataSets: *LINQ to DataSets*. In this chapter you do not find information on manipulating DataSets (refer to Chapter 21, "Introducing ADO.NET and DataSets"); instead you learn to query existing DataSets using LINQ, and you become familiar with some peculiarities of this provider that are not available in the previous ones. Of course, you should consider working with LINQ to DataSets only for simplifying your code when maintaining older applications; you are definitely strongly discouraged from using DataSets in new projects, as they are neither the present nor the future in accessing data with .NET-based development platforms.

Querying DataSets with LINQ

LINQ to DataSets is the standard LINQ provider for querying DataSets and is offered by the `System.DataSet.DataSetExtensions` namespace. Querying means that LINQ can only get information for DataSets but not for manipulating them. If you need to add, remove, replace, or persist data versus DataSets, you need to use old-fashioned techniques. Instead you can improve getting information using LINQ. You typically use DataSets in Windows client applications such as Windows Forms and WPF. This chapter shows you code within a Console application for demonstration purposes. To complete the proposed examples, follow these steps:

► Create a new Console application and name the project **LinqToDataSets**.

► Establish a connection to the Northwind database via the **Server Explorer** window.

► Add a new DataSet including the `Customers`, `Orders`, and `Order Details` tables.

When done, you need to manually write some code that populates the DataSet. Usually such tasks are performed by Visual Studio if you generate a DataSet within Windows Forms or WPF applications; however, in this case you need to do it. Write the following code that declares three `TableAdapter` objects and populates them with data coming from tables:

```
Imports LinqToDataSets.NorthwindDataSetTableAdapters

Module Module1

    Dim NwindDataSet As New NorthwindDataSet

    Dim NorthwindDataSetCustomersTableAdapter As CustomersTableAdapter _
        = New CustomersTableAdapter()
    Dim NorthwindDataSetOrdersTableAdapter As OrdersTableAdapter _
        = New OrdersTableAdapter()
    Dim NorthwindDataSetOrderDetailsTableAdapter As _
        Order_DetailsTableAdapter _
        = New Order_DetailsTableAdapter

    Sub Main()
        NorthwindDataSetCustomersTableAdapter.Fill(NwindDataSet.Customers)
        NorthwindDataSetOrdersTableAdapter.Fill(NwindDataSet.Orders)
        NorthwindDataSetOrderDetailsTableAdapter.
                    Fill(NwindDataSet.Order_Details)
    End Sub
End Module
```

Now you are ready to query your DataSet with LINQ. LINQ syntax is the same as for other providers but with a few exceptions:

► LINQ queries `DataTable` objects, each representing a table in the database.

► LINQ to DataSets queries return `EnumerableRowCollection(Of DataRow)` instead of `IEnumerable(Of T)` (or `IQueryable(Of T)`), in which `DataRow` is the base class for strongly typed rows. The only exception is when you create anonymous types within queries. In such situations, queries return `IEnumerable(Of Anonymous type)`.

You can use LINQ to retrieve a list of objects. For example, consider the following code that retrieves the list of orders for the specified customer:

```
Private Sub QueryOrders(ByVal CustomerID As String)

    Dim query = From ord In NwindDataSet.Orders
             Where ord.CustomerID = CustomerID
             Select ord
End Sub
```

As you can see, the syntax is the same as other providers. The query variable type is inferred by the compiler as `EnumerableRowCollection(Of OrdersRow)`. There is a particular difference: The query result is not directly usable if you want to provide the ability of editing data. As it is, the query can only be presented; you need first to convert it into a `DataView` using the `AsDataView` extension method. The following code rewrites the preceding query, providing the ability of binding data to a control:

```
Dim query = (From ord In NwindDataSet.Orders
          Where ord.CustomerID = CustomerID
          Select ord).AsDataView
```

When you invoke `AsDataView`, you can bind a LINQ query to any user control that supports data binding, such as the Windows Forms `BindingSource`. Don't invoke `AsDataView` if you simply need to get information without the need of manipulating data (for example, with a `For.. Each` loop). You can use other query operators to get different information; the following code shows how you can get the number of orders made by the specified customer using the `Aggregate` clause:

```
Private Function QueryOrders(CustomerID As String) As Integer

    Dim ordersByCustomer = Aggregate ord In NwindDataSet.Orders
                        Where ord.CustomerID = CustomerID
                        Into Count()

    Return ordersByCustomer
End Function
```

STANDARD QUERY OPERATORS

LINQ to DataSets allows the querying of DataSets using standard query operators offered by LINQ to Objects; because of this, the chapter does not explore standard operators. It also provides some additions discussed in the next section.

Building Complex Queries with Anonymous Types

Same as you would do with other LINQ providers, you can build complex queries taking advantage of anonymous types in LINQ to DataSets. The following code shows how you can join information from the `Orders` and `Order_Details` tables retrieving information on order details for each order made by the given customer. Projection is accomplished by generating anonymous types:

```
Private Sub QueryOrderDetails(CustomerID As String)

    Dim query = From ord In NwindDataSet.Orders
                Where ord.CustomerID = CustomerID
                Join det In NwindDataSet.Order_Details
                On det.OrderID Equals ord.OrderID
                Select New With {.OrderID = ord.OrderID,
                                 .OrderDate = ord.OrderDate,
                                 .ShippedDate = ord.ShippedDate,
                                 .ShipCity = ord.ShipCity,
                                 .ProductID = det.ProductID,
                                 .Quantity = det.Quantity,
                                 .UnitPrice = det.UnitPrice}
End Sub
```

The query variable is of type `IEnumerable(Of Anonymous type)`, which is different from normal queries. Remember that `IEnumerable` results cannot be edited; therefore, you are limited to presenting data through specific controls such as `BindingSource`. In LINQ to DataSets `IEnumerable(Of Anonymous type)`, queries do not support `AsDataView`; therefore, you should consider creating a new `DataTable`, which is shown in the first example of the next section.

LINQ to DataSets' Extension Methods

As a specific provider for DataSets, LINQ to DataSets exposes some special extension methods generally required when converting from data rows collections into other objects. In this section you get an overview of methods and their usage.

Understanding `CopyToDataTable`

Tables from databases are represented within DataSets via `DataTable` objects. You can create custom tables in code using a special extension method named `CopyToDataTable`, which can convert from `EnumerableRowCollection (Of T)` into a new `DataTable`. Imagine you want to create a subset of orders from the `Orders` table and that you want to create a new table with this subset of information. The following code accomplishes this:

```
Dim query = (From ord In NwindDataSet.Orders
             Where String.IsNullOrEmpty(ord.ShipCountry) = False
             Select ord).CopyToDataTable
query.TableName = "FilteredOrders"
NwindDataSet.Tables.Add(query)
```

The query retrieves only the orders where the `ShipCountry` property contains something and creates a new `DataTable` with this piece of information. The query variable's type is `DataTable`; therefore, you can treat this new object as you would versus a classical table as demonstrated by assigning the `TableName` property and by the addition of the new table to the DataSet. You can also create custom tables with more granularities by taking advantage of anonymous types. For example, imagine you want to create a table that wraps information from both the `Orders` and `Order_Details` tables. You need to manually create a new table, add columns, perform the query, and then add rows. The following code demonstrates this:

```
Private Function CreateCustomTable() As DataTable

    'Create a new table
    Dim customTable As New DataTable("Custom_orders")

    'Add columns
    With customTable
        With .Columns
            .Add("OrderID", GetType(Integer))
            .Add("Quantity", GetType(Short))
            .Add("UnitPrice", GetType(Decimal))
        End With
    End With

    'Retrieve data from different sources
    Dim query2 = From ord In NwindDataSet.Orders,
                     det In NwindDataSet.Order_Details
                 Where det.Quantity > 50
                 Select New With {.OrderID = ord.OrderID,
                                  .Quantity = det.Quantity,
                                  .UnitPrice = det.UnitPrice}

    'Add rows
    For Each item In query2
        customTable.Rows.Add(New Object() {item.OrderID,
                                           item.Quantity,
                                           item.UnitPrice})
    Next

    Return customTable
End Function
```

Notice how the new table is created in code and how columns are added. The `Columns.Add` method allows specifying the type (via the `GetType` keyword) for each column. Suppose you just want to retrieve the `OrderID`, `Quantity`, and `UnitPrice` information only for those products whose quantity is greater than 50. The LINQ query returns an `IEnumerable(Of Anonymous types)`. Because of this, you need to iterate the collection and instantiate a new array of `Object` for each row, containing the specified information. When you have the new table populated, you can add it to the DataSet and use it as any other table.

25

Understanding `Field(Of T)` and `SetField(Of T)`

The `Field` generic extension method allows retrieving a strongly typed form for all values from a given column within a table. `Field` receives as an argument the column name or the column index and then tries to convert values in a column into the specified type. Because of this, when using `Field` you should also predict some exceptions, such as `InvalidCastException` that can occur if the conversion fails, `NullReferenceException` if `Field` attempts to access a non-`Nullable` null value, and `IndexOutOfRangeException` if you pass an invalid index for the column. The following code retrieves all strongly typed versions of orders' data:

```
Private Sub FieldDemo()

    Try
        Dim query = From ord In NwindDataSet.Orders
                    Where ord.Field(Of Date)("ShippedDate") < Date.Today
                    Select New With {
                            .OrderID = ord.
                                    Field(Of Integer)("OrderID"),
                            .OrderDate = ord.
                                    Field(Of Date)("OrderDate"),
                            .ShipCountry = ord.
                                    Field(Of String) _
                                    ("ShipCountry")

    Catch ex As InvalidCastException
        'Conversion failed

    Catch ex As NullReferenceException
        'Attempt to access to a non nullable
        'null object

    Catch ex As IndexOutOfRangeException
        'Wrong index

    Catch ex As Exception

    End Try
End Sub
```

In addition, a `SetField` method enables you to put a strongly typed value into the specified field, and that works like this:

```
ord.SetField(Of Date)("OrderDate",Date.Today)
```

Summary

Although Microsoft is making lots of investments in much more modern technologies such as ADO.NET Entity Framework, DataSets are a data source that you can find in tons of applications. Because of this, the .NET Framework provides the LINQ to DataSets provider to enable the querying of DataSets via the LINQ syntax. Datasets are particular; therefore, there are specific extension methods that you can use versus DataSets, such as `CopyToDataTable` that generates a new `DataTable` from a LINQ query and `Field` that allows getting strongly typed information from columns. In this chapter you got an overview of how LINQ works over DataSets, and how you can use retrieved information in your applications.

25

Introducing ADO.NET Entity Framework

Most applications require accessing data. This is a sentence that you already read in this book and probably in many other places, but it is so important. Before the .NET Framework 3.5, developers had to access data using DataSets or they were required to work directly against the database; then they had a new opportunity with LINQ to SQL. This was revolutionary because it proposes a conceptual object model that enables you to work with managed objects, being responsible for whatever is necessary in managing also the underlying database. But it has some limitations. It supports only SQL Server databases; it does not support many-to-many relationships; and it does not provide support for modeling data before creating a database. To provide a modern data platform based on the idea of the conceptual object model, Microsoft created the ADO. NET Entity Framework that was first introduced as a library in .NET Framework 3.5 SP 1 and that has become part of the .NET Framework since version 4.0. In this chapter you get started with the Entity Framework by learning to perform the most common operations on data and understanding the basics of such a platform, also learning some new APIs that change the way data models are generated and that make code much cleaner and simpler.

Introducing Entity Framework

ADO.NET Entity Framework, also referred to as Entity Framework (EF), is a modern data platform included in .NET Framework 4.6. .NET 4.6 and Visual Studio 2015 have built-in support for Entity Framework 5 and 6. It is an object-relational mapping engine, but it is powerful, absolutely more flexible and powerful than LINQ to SQL. It enables you to create conceptual object models, known as Entity Data Models (EDMs), that provide a high level of abstraction from the underlying data source. Abstraction means that tables and tables' columns within a database are mapped into .NET classes and properties, meaning that you do not work against the database but with .NET objects that represent the database so that you can take advantage of manipulating .NET objects under the Common Language Runtime (CLR) control, with IntelliSense support and live compiler analysis. You do not need to have knowledge of the database infrastructure, although this is always suggested because the Entity Framework is responsible for communications between the object model and the data source. It provides the entire necessary infrastructure so that you can focus only on writing code for manipulating and querying data. Working with an abstractive object model means taking advantage of all the .NET Framework's power and all available Visual Studio instrumentation. The .NET Framework 4.6 supports the so-called Code First approach, which enables you coding your model independently from the database, that can be generated later. Visual Studio 2015 generates Entity Data Models based on Code First's APIs. In the next section, you start with the EF by understanding Entity Data Models and the new classes provided by the .NET Framework 4.6. In the second part of this chapter, you will see how to code your data models.

Understanding Entity Data Models

The best way to understand EDMs is to create one. First, create a new Visual Basic project for the Console and name it **EntityFramework**. Save the new project immediately, so that all references required by the EF are updated. The next steps require the Northwind database that you installed in Chapter 21, "Introducing ADO.NET and DataSets." Right-click on the project name in Solution Explorer and select **Add New Item**. When the Add New Item dialog box appears, move to the Data Node, select the **ADO.NET Entity Data Model** item template, and name it **Northwind**, as shown in Figure 26.1.

When you click **Add**, the Entity Data Model Wizard starts. In the first screen you need to specify the source for the EDM. In Visual Studio 2015, you have several options to start with:

▶ EF Designer from Database, which allows you to create an EDM with design tools based on an existing database.

▶ Empty EF Designer Model, which you choose if you want to model a custom EDM from scratch. This approach is also known as *database first*.

▶ Empty Code First Model, which you use to write a model with the Code First approach, starting from zero.

▶ Code First from Database, which generates a data model using the Code First approach, based on an existing database.

For now, select the **EF Designer from Database** option, as shown in Figure 26.2.

The next screen is important because it requires the specification of the database. You can click **New Connection** or select one of the favorite connections from the appropriate combo box. Figure 26.3 shows how on my machine the connection points to Northwind as it is available on SQL Server.

Notice how the connection string is represented in the dialog box. Also notice that this is not the usual connection string because it contains metadata information that will be clearer when the EDMs' infrastructure is explained. You decide whether to save the string in the configuration file. Next, you specify which version of the Entity Framework you want to use. Available options are 6.x and 5.0. Note that for EF 6, you do not see a specific version number but instead get 6.x because you could start with the most recent version you have installed on your machine and then manage the desired Runtime via NuGet packages. Samples in this chapter require version 6 or higher, so you should select 6.x now.

ENTITY FRAMEWORK 7

Microsoft is working on Entity Framework 7, which is available as a preview release at this writing. Entity Framework 7 will be a great addition to your toolbox because, among other things, it will support ASP.NET 5 Core and Windows Store/Windows Phone apps. However, we do not know when the final version of EF 7 will be released to the public. For this reason, this chapter focuses on the latest stable version (6.1.2). However, you are encouraged to check out the ADO.NET Team blog for announcements and additional resources about EF 7. You can find it at http://blogs.msdn.com/b/adonet/.

The next step is crucial because you have to select what database objects you want to be mapped into the EDM. Figure 26.4 shows the dialog box.

FIGURE 26.1   Adding a new Entity Data Model.

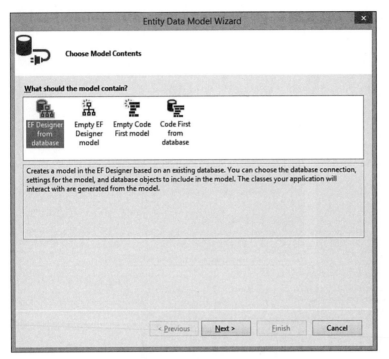

FIGURE 26.2   Creating an EDM from an existing database.

FIGURE 26.3   Choosing the database and connection settings.

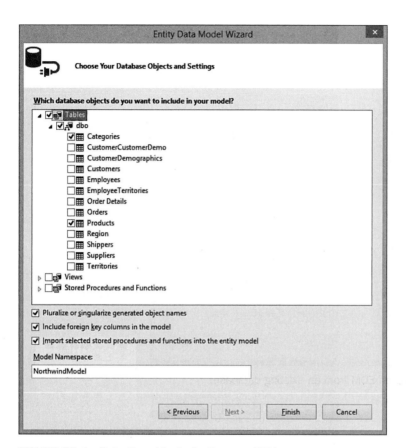

FIGURE 26.4   Selecting objects for the new EDM.

FOREIGN KEY COLUMNS SUPPORT

The ADO.NET Entity Framework supports mapping foreign keys from the database into the model. This is the reason you find a check box in the Entity Data Model wizard, as shown in Figure 26.4. Select the check box to add the foreign key's support.

Also notice how you are required to specify a model namespace. This is important because the namespace stores Visual Basic definitions for objects that are mapped to database objects, which are explained later. You can write your own or leave the default identifier unchanged. At the moment, just choose the Categories and Products tables and then Click Finish. After a few moments, when Visual Studio generates the code for the object model, the EDM Designer opens as shown in Figure 26.5. Visual Studio also adds references to the EntityFramework.dll and EntityFramework.SqlServer.dll assemblies.

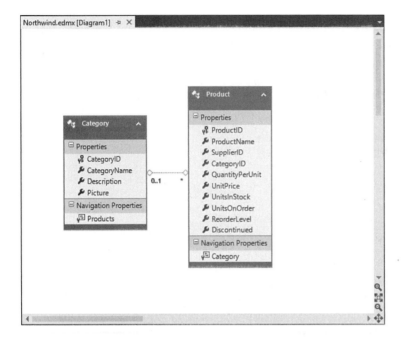

FIGURE 26.5   The EDM Designer for Visual Studio.

The object model available in the Visual Studio designer is, behind the scenes, defined by a new XML document that is the schema for the Entity Data Model. This XML file is the one with the .edmx extension, in our case Northwind.edmx. The schema is divided into three sections that are summarized in Table 26.1.

TABLE 26.1   Sections of the Entity Data Model

Section Name	Description
Conceptual Schema Definition Language	Defines entities, relationships, and inheritance. .NET classes are generated based on this section.
Store Schema Definition Language	Provides a representation of the original database.
Mapping Specification Language	Maps entities as they are defined in the CSDL against db objects as they are defined in the SSDL.

To understand how an EDM is composed, in Solution Explorer right-click the Northwind. edmx file; then select **Open With**, and when the Open With dialog box appears, double-click the **XML editor** option. At this point, Visual Studio shows the content of the EDM as an XML file instead of the designer. The file contains three sections as described in Table 26.1. Listing 26.1 shows the CSDL definition (which is actually the second section in the XML file).

LISTING 26.1   Conceptual Schema Definition Language

```
<edmx:ConceptualModels>
  <Schema Namespace="NorthwindModel" Alias="Self"
   annotation:UseStrongSpatialTypes="false"
   xmlns:annotation="http://schemas.microsoft.com/ado/2009/02/edm/annotation"
        xmlns:customannotation="http://schemas.
➥microsoft.com/ado/2013/11/edm/customannotation"
        xmlns="http://schemas.microsoft.com/ado/2009/11/edm">
    <EntityType Name="Category">
      <Key>
        <PropertyRef Name="CategoryID" />
      </Key>
      <Property Name="CategoryID" Type="Int32" Nullable="false"
              annotation:StoreGeneratedPattern="Identity" />
      <Property Name="CategoryName" Type="String"
              MaxLength="15" FixedLength="false"
              Unicode="true" Nullable="false" />
      <Property Name="Description" Type="String"
              MaxLength="Max" FixedLength="false"
              Unicode="true" />
      <Property Name="Picture" Type="Binary"
              MaxLength="Max" FixedLength="false" />
      <NavigationProperty Name="Products"
                        Relationship="Self.FK_Products_Categories"
                        FromRole="Categories" ToRole="Products" />
    </EntityType>
    <EntityType Name="Product">
      <Key>
        <PropertyRef Name="ProductID" />
      </Key>
      <Property Name="ProductID" Type="Int32" Nullable="false"
              annotation:StoreGeneratedPattern="Identity" />
      <Property Name="ProductName" Type="String"
              MaxLength="40" FixedLength="false"
              Unicode="true" Nullable="false" />
      <Property Name="SupplierID" Type="Int32" />
      <Property Name="CategoryID" Type="Int32" />
      <Property Name="QuantityPerUnit" Type="String" MaxLength="20"
              FixedLength="false" Unicode="true" />
      <Property Name="UnitPrice" Type="Decimal" Precision="19" Scale="4" />
      <Property Name="UnitsInStock" Type="Int16" />
      <Property Name="UnitsOnOrder" Type="Int16" />
      <Property Name="ReorderLevel" Type="Int16" />
      <Property Name="Discontinued" Type="Boolean" Nullable="false" />
      <NavigationProperty Name="Category"
       Relationship="Self.FK_Products_Categories"
```

26

```
                        FromRole="Products" ToRole="Categories" />
    </EntityType>
    <Association Name="FK_Products_Categories">
      <End Role="Categories" Type="Self.Category" Multiplicity="0..1" />
      <End Role="Products" Type="Self.Product" Multiplicity="*" />
      <ReferentialConstraint>
        <Principal Role="Categories">
          <PropertyRef Name="CategoryID" />
        </Principal>
        <Dependent Role="Products">
          <PropertyRef Name="CategoryID" />
        </Dependent>
      </ReferentialConstraint>
    </Association>
    <EntityContainer Name="NorthwindEntities"
     annotation:LazyLoadingEnabled="true">
      <EntitySet Name="Categories" EntityType="Self.Category" />
      <EntitySet Name="Products" EntityType="Self.Product" />
      <AssociationSet Name="FK_Products_Categories"
       Association="Self.FK_Products_Categories">
        <End Role="Categories" EntitySet="Categories" />
        <End Role="Products" EntitySet="Products" />
      </AssociationSet>
    </EntityContainer>
  </Schema>
 </edmx:ConceptualModels>
```

Entities (EntityType) are defined along with scalar properties (Property), relationships
(Association), entity sets (EntitySet), and a container named NorthwindEntities. The
next section that we consider is the SSDL, which is constituted by the XML markup code
shown in Listing 26.2 and which is actually the first section in the XML file.

LISTING 26.2   The Store Schema Definition Language

```
  <edmx:StorageModels>
    <Schema Namespace="NorthwindModel.Store" Provider="System.Data.SqlClient"
          ProviderManifestToken="2012" Alias="Self"
          xmlns:store="http://schemas.microsoft.com/
ado/2007/12/edm/EntityStoreSchemaGenerator"
          xmlns:customannotation="http://schemas.microsoft.com/
ado/2013/11/edm/customannotation"
          xmlns="http://schemas.microsoft.com/ado/2009/11/edm/ssdl">
      <EntityType Name="Categories">
        <Key>
          <PropertyRef Name="CategoryID" />
        </Key>
```

```xml
    <Property Name="CategoryID" Type="int" StoreGeneratedPattern="Identity"
            Nullable="false" />
    <Property Name="CategoryName" Type="nvarchar" MaxLength="15"
            Nullable="false" />
    <Property Name="Description" Type="ntext" />
    <Property Name="Picture" Type="image" />
  </EntityType>
  <EntityType Name="Products">
    <Key>
      <PropertyRef Name="ProductID" />
    </Key>
    <Property Name="ProductID" Type="int" StoreGeneratedPattern="Identity"
            Nullable="false" />
    <Property Name="ProductName"
     Type="nvarchar" MaxLength="40" Nullable="false" />
    <Property Name="SupplierID" Type="int" />
    <Property Name="CategoryID" Type="int" />
    <Property Name="QuantityPerUnit" Type="nvarchar" MaxLength="20" />
    <Property Name="UnitPrice" Type="money" />
    <Property Name="UnitsInStock" Type="smallint" />
    <Property Name="UnitsOnOrder" Type="smallint" />
    <Property Name="ReorderLevel" Type="smallint" />
    <Property Name="Discontinued" Type="bit" Nullable="false" />
  </EntityType>
  <Association Name="FK_Products_Categories">
    <End Role="Categories" Type="Self.Categories" Multiplicity="0..1" />
    <End Role="Products" Type="Self.Products" Multiplicity="*" />
    <ReferentialConstraint>
      <Principal Role="Categories">
        <PropertyRef Name="CategoryID" />
      </Principal>
      <Dependent Role="Products">
        <PropertyRef Name="CategoryID" />
      </Dependent>
    </ReferentialConstraint>
  </Association>
  <EntityContainer Name="NorthwindModelStoreContainer">
    <EntitySet Name="Categories" EntityType="Self.Categories"
            Schema="dbo" store:Type="Tables" />
    <EntitySet Name="Products" EntityType="Self.Products"
            Schema="dbo" store:Type="Tables" />
    <AssociationSet Name="FK_Products_Categories"
                Association="Self.FK_Products_Categories">
      <End Role="Categories" EntitySet="Categories" />
      <End Role="Products" EntitySet="Products" />
    </AssociationSet>
```

26

```
    </EntityContainer>
  </Schema>
</edmx:StorageModels>
```

This schema is similar to the previous schema, except that it represents the database structure, as you can see from type definition within `Property` elements. The last schema is the Mapping Definition Language that is illustrated in Listing 26.3.

LISTING 26.3   Mapping Definition Language

```
  <edmx:Mappings>
<Mapping Space="C-S"
 xmlns="http://schemas.microsoft.com/ado/2009/11/mapping/cs">
  <EntityContainerMapping
    StorageEntityContainer="NorthwindModelStoreContainer"
                          CdmEntityContainer="NorthwindEntities">
    <EntitySetMapping Name="Categories">
      <EntityTypeMapping TypeName="NorthwindModel.Category">
        <MappingFragment StoreEntitySet="Categories">
          <ScalarProperty Name="CategoryID" ColumnName="CategoryID" />
          <ScalarProperty Name="CategoryName" ColumnName="CategoryName" />
          <ScalarProperty Name="Description" ColumnName="Description" />
          <ScalarProperty Name="Picture" ColumnName="Picture" />
        </MappingFragment>
      </EntityTypeMapping>
    </EntitySetMapping>
    <EntitySetMapping Name="Products">
      <EntityTypeMapping TypeName="NorthwindModel.Product">
        <MappingFragment StoreEntitySet="Products">
          <ScalarProperty Name="ProductID" ColumnName="ProductID" />
          <ScalarProperty Name="ProductName" ColumnName="ProductName" />
          <ScalarProperty Name="SupplierID" ColumnName="SupplierID" />
          <ScalarProperty Name="CategoryID" ColumnName="CategoryID" />
          <ScalarProperty Name="QuantityPerUnit"
           ColumnName="QuantityPerUnit" />
          <ScalarProperty Name="UnitPrice" ColumnName="UnitPrice" />
          <ScalarProperty Name="UnitsInStock" ColumnName="UnitsInStock" />
          <ScalarProperty Name="UnitsOnOrder" ColumnName="UnitsOnOrder" />
          <ScalarProperty Name="ReorderLevel" ColumnName="ReorderLevel" />
          <ScalarProperty Name="Discontinued" ColumnName="Discontinued" />
        </MappingFragment>
      </EntityTypeMapping>
    </EntitySetMapping>
  </EntityContainerMapping>
  </Mapping>
</edmx:Mappings>
```

The content of the MDL is quite simple, in that each `ScalarProperty` represents an entity's property and establishes mapping between the property and the related column name in the database table.

Understanding the `DbContext` Class: The Visual Basic Mapping

Schemas in the Entity Data Model have a Visual Basic counterpart that enables you to write code to work against entities. To understand this, enable the **View All Files** view in Solution Explorer and expand the **Northwind.edmx** file. You will see two files with a .tt extension, Northwind.Context.tt and Northwind.tt. Files with a .tt extension are templates that Visual Studio uses for code generation and that are useful to the IDE to generate classes that allow developers to interact with the object model. Regardless of their content, which you are not required to understand for this chapter, start expanding the Northwind.Context.tt file, which contains another file called Northwind.Context.vb. Similar to the `DataContext` class in LINQ to SQL, the ADO.NET Entity Framework provides a class named `System.Data.Entity.DbContext`. This class, also referred to as the object context, is also the basis of the Code First pattern; It acts as a reference to the Entity Data Model and encapsulates the entities' definition so that you can work with entities. It is also responsible for opening and closing connections, persisting data, keeping track of changes, and persisting data back to the database. `DbContext` is just the base class (as the `DataContext` is in LINQ to SQL) that every entity data model inherits from. Listing 26.4 shows how the object context is defined in our specific scenario.

LISTING 26.4   `DbContext` Definition

```
Imports System
Imports System.Data.Entity
Imports System.Data.Entity.Infrastructure

Partial Public Class NorthwindEntities
    Inherits DbContext

    Public Sub New()
        MyBase.New("name=NorthwindEntities")
    End Sub

    Protected Overrides Sub OnModelCreating(modelBuilder As DbModelBuilder)
        Throw New UnintentionalCodeFirstException()
    End Sub

    Public Property Categories() As DbSet(Of Category)
    Public Property Products() As DbSet(Of Product)
End Class
```

The code is easy to understand. There is only one constructor that creates an instance of the object model. Next, notice the `Categories` and `Products` properties: `DbSet(Of`

Category) and DbSet(Of Product). A System.Data.Entity.DbSet(Of T) represents an entity set and provides several methods and members for manipulating entities, such as the Add or Remove methods. Properties of type DbSet handle references to a series of objects. Such objects are defined in separate code files, one for each entity, all nested inside the Northwind.tt file. For the sake of simplicity, Listing 26.5 shows only the definition of the Category class in the Category.vb file whereas the Product class is left out, being substantially defined using the same concepts.

LISTING 26.5   The Category Entity Definition

```
Imports System
Imports System.Collections.Generic

Partial Public Class Category
    Public Property CategoryID As Integer
    Public Property CategoryName As String
    Public Property Description As String
    Public Property Picture As Byte()

    Public Overridable Property Products As _
            ICollection(Of Product) = New HashSet(Of Product)
End Class
```

Each entity class represents a database object, but differently from the previous versions of the Entity Framework, the entity definition is now made of only a few lines of code and relies on the Plain Old CLR Object (POCO) definition. This means that there is no platform-specific code, but normal classes that you could use not only inside an object model definition. You can easily compare the example shown in the previous edition of this book with the current example to see how much cleaner the code now is.

Navigation Properties in Code

Finally, notice how those things named Navigation Properties in the EDM are also defined within entity classes. A navigation property is a .NET property of type ICollection(Of T), in the case of the "many" part of the relationship, or of the entity type that the current entity is associated with for the "one" part of the relationship (in the case of the Product entity, the navigation property is of type Category). Navigation properties typically represent foreign keys in the database.

Now that you have a clearer idea of what Visual Basic requires behind the scenes, you are ready to understand the usage of some interesting design-time tools.

Entity Designer Tool Windows

When the EDM designer is active, you notice that some new tool windows appear in the IDE. The first one is the Mapping Details tool window, which shows how database objects are mapped to .NET types. Figure 26.6 shows the Mapping Details window.

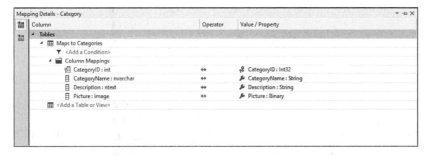

FIGURE 26.6   The Mapping Details tool window.

As you can see in Figure 26.6, on the left side of the window, you can find the original SQL definition and on the right side of the window, you can find the .NET type utilized to map SQL types into the EDM. You can manually edit such mapping, but the suggestion is you leave unchanged what the IDE proposes by default unless you understand that a bad mapping from SQL to .NET has been performed. The second tool is the Model Browser, which provides a hierarchical graphical view of the object model so that you can easily browse both the conceptual model and the store model. Figure 26.7 shows the tool window.

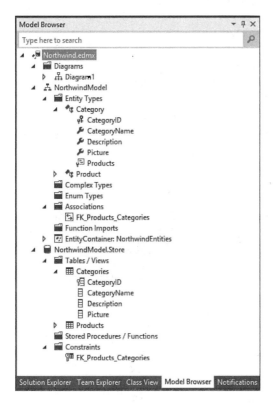

FIGURE 26.7   The Model Browser tool window.

Such a tool window also simplifies performing operations on the entity data model, such as updating the model itself, as explained later in this chapter with regard to stored procedures. Other than these tool windows, you can take advantage of the Properties window for getting information on the objects that compose the entity data model. For example, if you click the blank space in the designer, the Properties window shows high-level information on the EDM, such as the database schema name, the entity container name (that is, the object context), or the model namespace. Figure 26.8 provides an overview.

Similarly, you can get information on the entities' definition by clicking the desired entity name in the designer. Figure 26.9 represents the Properties window showing information about the `Category` entity.

The window shows information about the class implementation, such as the class name, the inheritance level, or the access level other than the related entity set container name. If you instead try to click a navigation property, the Properties window provides information on how relationships are handled. For example, the name of the foreign key, the return type, and multiplicity type is shown in a human-readable fashion, as demonstrated in Figure 26.10.

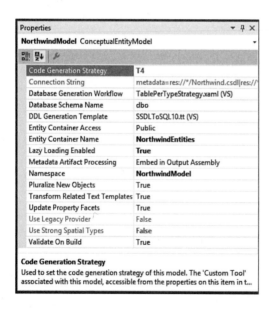

FIGURE 26.8   Getting model information via the Properties window.

FIGURE 26.9   Getting entity information with the Properties window.

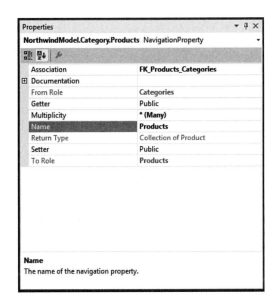

FIGURE 26.10   Getting information on navigation properties with the Properties window.

Useful information can also be retrieved on relationships. If you click the association line that conjuncts entities in the designer, the Properties window not only shows how the relationship is defined, but also enables you to choose custom behavior when deleting entities (for example, Cascade). Of course, this must be supported (or just enabled) in the underlying database. In the case of SQL Server databases, you can modify associations' behaviors using SQL Server Management Studio. Figure 26.11 shows such a scenario.

The last use of the Properties window is getting and setting values for scalar properties. For example, click the `QuantityPerUnit` property in the `Product` entity. Figure 26.12 shows how the Properties window displays.

Properties are self-explanatory, and you can get more information by clicking the property you are interested in; the tool window will be updated with information. Consider two properties: `Entity Key`, which establishes whether the scalar property represents a primary key, and `StoreGeneratedPattern`, which provides the ability to autogenerate the column in the database during insert and update operations. This tooling is particularly useful because here you can manually change the entities' behavior without the need to edit the autogenerated Visual Basic code; this job belongs to Visual Studio and you should always let it do this for you.

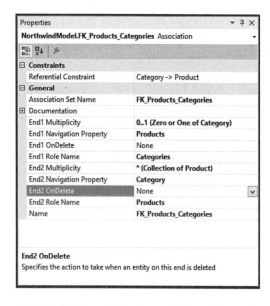

FIGURE 26.11   Getting associations information via the Properties window.

FIGURE 26.12   Getting information on scalar properties.

Insert/Update/Delete Operations for Entities

The ADO.NET Entity Framework offers a complete infrastructure for manipulating data, meaning that it offers the ability to add, update, and remove data to and from the object model and subsequently from the database. Let's discover these features.

Instantiating the `DbContext`

The first task you need to accomplish when working with the ADO.NET Entity Framework in code is to get an instance of the `DbContext` class. At the beginning of this chapter you were told to create a new Visual Basic project for the Console, so let's continue on this path. At module level (or class level, in most common scenarios), declare a variable of type `NorthwindEntities` that represents our object context as follows:

```
Private northwindContext As NorthwindEntities
```

Within the `Sub Main` (or in the constructor if you work with classes), create the actual instance:

```
Sub Main()
    Try
        northwindContext = New NorthwindEntities
    Catch ex As SqlClient.SqlException
        'Handle a SqlException here...
    Catch ex As Exception
```

```
            'Handle general exceptions here...


        End Try

End Sub
```

Notice how a `System.Data.SqlClient.SqlException` general exception is handled in case of problems.

When you have the object context instance, you can read and write data on your object model.

Adding Entities

Adding entities against an entity data model requires you to pass the instance of the entity to the `Add` method exposed by the entity set. For example, in our demonstration scenario we have a `Products` entity set exposing an `Add` method. The following code shows how you can programmatically create a new product and add it to the object model:

```
Sub AddProduct(ByVal categoryReference As Category)
    Try

        Dim check = northwindContext.Products.
                Single(Function(p) p.
                ProductName = "Italian spaghetti")

    Catch ex As InvalidOperationException

        Try
            Dim prod As New Product
            With prod
                .ProductName = "Italian spaghetti"
                .QuantityPerUnit = "10 packs"
                .Discontinued = True
                .SupplierID = 4
                .UnitPrice = 0.5D
                .UnitsInStock = 100
```

```
                .UnitsOnOrder = 50

                .Category = categoryReference
            End With

            northwindContext.Products.Add (prod)
            northwindContext.SaveChanges()

        Catch e As Exception
    'Exception handling when saving changes
        End Try

    Catch ex As Exception
        'Handle general exceptions here
    End Try
End Sub
```

First, the code checks whether the product already exists based on the specified condition. This is accomplished by invoking the `Single` extension method. It is something that you already saw in LINQ to SQL and is not discussed thoroughly here. Notice how you set properties for the new product. The custom method receives a `Category` instance as an argument. This is necessary for setting a one-to-many relationship between the new product and the desired category. Setting the relationship just requires you to assign the `Category` property with the category instance. When done, you invoke the `northwindContext.Products.Add` method by passing the new product and then invoke the `SaveChanges` method for sending changes to the database.

TRACKING CHANGES

Remember that the `DbContext` instance can keep track of changes during the application lifetime, so its `SaveChanges` method will persist all pending changes.

In Chapter 24, "LINQ to SQL," you saw how to use Visual Studio to inspect the database for checking if changes were correctly submitted to the database. The good news is that the same technique can be also used when working with EDMs.

Deleting Entities

Deleting entities is also a simple task. You first need to get the instance of the entity you want to remove and then invoke the `DbSet(Of T).Remove` method. The following code shows how to get the instance of the specified product and then to remove it first from the model and then from the database:

```
Sub DeleteProduct()

    Try
        Dim check = northwindContext.Products.
```

26

```
                   Single(Function(p) p.
                   ProductName = "Italian spaghetti")

        northwindContext.Products.Remove(check)
        northwindContext.SaveChanges()

        'Does not exist
     Catch ex As InvalidOperationException

     End Try
End Sub
```

Same as in previous code, we take advantage of the `Single` method that throws an `InvalidOperationException` if the object does not exist.

DELETING ENTITIES WITH RELATIONSHIPS

In this chapter you see simplified examples focusing on the technology. In some situations you need to delete entities with relationships; for example, imagine you have an `Order` class with associated `OrderDetails`. When you delete the order, you probably want to remove associated details. To accomplish this, you need to work at the database level and enable it to cascade the deletion. For SQL Server databases, you can accomplish this within SQL Server Management Studio, changing properties for the foreign key related to the relationship.

Updating Entities

Updating entities is a little bit different from adding and deleting in that there is no Update method in either the `DbContext` or the `DbSet` classes. You get the instance of the object you want to update, change its properties, and then invoke `SaveChanges`. The following code demonstrates this:

```
Sub UpdateProduct()

     Try
          Dim check = northwindContext.Products.
                   Single(Function(p) p.
                   ProductName = "Italian spaghetti")

          check.Discontinued = True
          check.UnitsInStock = 30
          northwindContext.SaveChanges()

          'Product does not exist
     Catch ex As InvalidOperationException
```

```
    Catch ex As UpdateException
    End Try
End Sub
```

Just remember to check whether the product exists before trying an update. Notice also how a `System.Data.Entity.Core.UpdateException` is caught; this is thrown when there is some problem in sending updates to the data source.

Handling Optimistic Concurrency

Of course, the ADO.NET Entity Framework provides the ability to handle optimistic concurrency exceptions. You need to intercept eventual `System.Data.Entity.Infrastructure.DbUpdateConcurrencyException` instances. When intercepted, you need to determine what entries were not updated in the database by using the `Entries` property of the exception instance and make an appropriate decision. The following code revisits the `UpdateProduct` custom method described in the "Updating Entities" subsection, providing the first example:

```
Sub UpdateProduct()

    Try
        Dim check = northwindContext.Products.
                Single(Function(p) p.
                ProductName = "Italian spaghetti")

        check.Discontinued = True
        check.UnitsInStock = 30
        northwindContext.SaveChanges()

        'Product does not exist
    Catch ex As InvalidOperationException

        'Handle optimistic concurrency
    Catch ex As DbUpdateConcurrencyException
        ex.Entries.Single.Reload()
    Catch ex As UpdateException
    End Try
End Sub
```

If a `DbUpdateConcurrencyException` is thrown, you can invoke the `Reload` method on the instance of the entity that was not updated and reload original values from the database, overwriting the current entity values. This is the first possible way to solve concurrency blocks and is known as *database wins*. The second possibility is known as *client wins* and is the opposite, which means that you can force to overwrite database values with the current entity's values. This requires a particular technique, which will set the original values for the entity with values from the database.

The following code demonstrates this:

```
Catch ex As DbUpdateConcurrencyException
    Dim entry = ex.Entries.Single
    entry.OriginalValues.SetValues(entry.GetDatabaseValues)
```

The `OriginalValues.SetValues` method takes an argument of type `DbPropertyValues`, which is a collection of properties for an entity. The `GetDatabaseValues` returns a collection of current properties from the database. What you have to keep in mind when working with optimistic concurrency is that you handle the `Entries` property and retrieve the instance of the entity that could not be updated; of course there are additional techniques that the MSDN documentation describes in more detail at: http://msdn.microsoft.com/en-us/data/jj592904.aspx.

NOTE ABOUT CURRENT AND ORIGINAL VALUES

When an entity is attached to the object context, the Entity Framework keeps track of two values for each property: The current value that is the current value of the property in the entity. The original value is instead the value that the property had when the entity was queried from the database or attached to the context. The MSDN documentation shows additional ways to work with entity properties at http://msdn.microsoft.com/en-us/data/jj592677.

Of course, in this book it is not possible to reproduce a real concurrency scenario, but now you know what the main objects are for handling this situation.

Validating Data

Data validation involves decorating entities and their properties with some attributes from the `System.ComponentModel.DataAnnotations` and `System.ComponentModel.DataAnnotations.Schema` namespaces (from the System.ComponentModel.DataAnnotations.dll assembly). Each attribute provides additional information or validation rules to types. This is not new: if you have developed Silverlight applications with WCF RIA Services in the past, you used data annotations frequently. The following code demonstrates how to add some validation rules to the `Product` entity using data annotations:

```
Imports System.ComponentModel.DataAnnotations

Partial Public Class Product
    Public Property ProductID As Integer
    'The product name length must be at least 5 and no more than 15 characters
    'A custom error message is provided
    <StringLength(15, ErrorMessage:="String length not within the expected range",
        ErrorMessageResourceName:=Nothing,
        ErrorMessageResourceType:=Nothing,
        MinimumLength:=5)> Public Property ProductName As String
```

```
    <Required> Public Property SupplierID As Nullable(Of Integer)
    Public Property CategoryID As Nullable(Of Integer)
    'QuantityPerUnit is now a mandatory field, minimum length is 4
    <Required>Public Property QuantityPerUnit As String
    Public Property UnitPrice As Nullable(Of Decimal)
    Public Property UnitsInStock As Nullable(Of Short)
    Public Property UnitsOnOrder As Nullable(Of Short)
    Public Property ReorderLevel As Nullable(Of Short)
    Public Property Discontinued As Boolean

    Public Overridable Property Category As Category

End Class
```

The `Required` attribute marks a property as mandatory, so the user must supply a value
for it. The `StringLength` attribute allows specifying a minimum and a maximum length
for a string, including a custom error message and resources. Notice that all values are
optional except the first argument, which is the maximum length. Useful attributes are
also `MaxLength` and `MinLength` which instead determine the maximum and the minimum
length of an array of `String` respectively. The validation mechanism can run in two ways.
The first way is automatic and is when the runtime executes the `DbContext.SaveChanges`
method. This causes the runtime to check if an entity adheres to validation rules; if not, a
`DbEntityValidationException` is thrown. The second way is checking for validation errors
programmatically, before attempting to save changes. You can check for all validation
errors in the current object context, or you can check a single entity or a single property.
The following code demonstrates how to check for any validation errors in the model
instance by invoking the `DbContext.GetValidationErrors` method:

```
If northwindContext.GetValidationErrors.Any Then
    'There is at least one validation error
End If
```

This method returns a collection of `DbEntityValidationResult` objects, each containing
detailed information on the error. You can also validate a single entity on demand, by
invoking the `DbEntityEntry.GetValidationResult` method on the specified entity like in
the following code:

```
'Validate an entity
Dim result As DbEntityValidationResult = _
        northwindContext.Entry(prod).GetValidationResult
For Each validationError In result.ValidationErrors
    Console.WriteLine("Property {0} raised the following message: {1}",
                    validationError.PropertyName,
                    validationError.ErrorMessage)
Next
```

The method returns an object of type `DbEntityValidationResult`, whose `ValidationErrors` property contains a list of validation errors pending on the specified entity instance. Notice that such an instance must be attached to the current context. Each error is represented by an instance of the `DbValidationError` class, which exposes two properties: `PropertyName` and `ErrorMessage`; the first property stores the name of the entity property that raised the validation error, whereas the second one contains a descriptive error message. Finally you can validate a single property of an entity, like in the following example:

```
'Validate a single property
Dim productNameProperty As DbPropertyEntry = _
    northwindContext.Entry(prod).Property(Function(p) p.ProductName)
For Each validationError In productNameProperty.GetValidationErrors
    Console.WriteLine("Property {0} raised the following message: {1}",
                    validationError.PropertyName,
                    validationError.ErrorMessage)
 Next
```

You first retrieve the property you want to validate via the `DbEntityEntry.Property` method. You need to pass the property name you want to validate and this can be done by passing the property name as a string or via a lambda expression, like in the above code, which takes advantage of the background compiler and IntelliSense to determine the property name correctly. `GetValidationErrors` and its results remain the same as in the previous example. Actually the `System.ComponentModel.DataAnnotations` namespace provides additional attributes that are instead useful when using the Code First approach to create the model and to generate the database. These are discussed in the section called "Introducing Data Annotations" later in this chapter.

Querying EDMs with LINQ to Entities

LINQ to Entities is the standard LINQ provider for querying entities within an Entity Data Model. You use the same LINQ syntax for querying entities, too, so you will not encounter particular difficulties.

> **USING STANDARD QUERY OPERATORS**
>
> LINQ to Entities supports standard query operators described in Chapter 23, "LINQ to Objects," to perform complex query expressions.

The one big difference is about eager loading, which is explained after showing the code. As in LINQ to SQL, LINQ to Entities queries return an `IQueryable(Of T)`, unless you convert the result into a different type using extension methods at the end of the query. The following code returns the list of products for the specified category, taking only those products that are not discontinued and sorting the result by unit price:

```vb
Sub LINQtoEntitiesDemo(ByVal CategoryName As String)

    Dim query = From prod In northwindContext.Products.
                Include("Category")
                Where prod.Category.CategoryName = CategoryName _
                And prod.Discontinued = False
                Order By prod.UnitPrice
                Select prod

    Console.WriteLine("Category: {0}",
                      CategoryName)

    For Each prod In query
        Console.WriteLine("Product name: {0}, Unit price: {1:c}",
                          prod.ProductName, prod.UnitPrice)
    Next
End Sub
```

As you can see, the LINQ syntax works similarly to other LINQ providers except that here the `Include` method has been invoked on the entity set instance. This method requires an argument of type `String`, which is the name of the navigation property mapped to the entity being queried, that is, the name of the entity set with which the queried entity has a relationship. `Include` performs that technique known as *eager loading* that enables you to load related entities. This is necessary if you want to perform comparisons as in the preceding example, where an evaluation must be done on the category name to which the current product belongs. In other words, if you do not invoke `Include`, you will have available only `Products` information but not `Categories` information while you need this to perform the comparison. You can take advantage of standard query operators described in Chapter 23 to accomplish complex LINQ queries against entities as well. You can also use iterators for efficient code in long running query operations. For instance, you can rewrite the last code example as follows:

```vb
Sub LINQtoEntitiesDemo(ByVal CategoryName As String)
    Console.WriteLine("Category: {0}",
                      CategoryName)

    For Each prod In GetProducts(CategoryName)
        Console.WriteLine("Product name: {0}, Unit price: {1:c}",
                          prod.ProductName, prod.UnitPrice)
    Next
End Sub

Iterator Function GetProducts(categoryName As String) As IEnumerable(Of Product)
    Dim query = From prod In northwindContext.Products.
        Include("Category")
        Where prod.Category.CategoryName = categoryName _
        And prod.Discontinued = False
        Order By prod.UnitPrice
```

26

```
        Select prod


    For Each prod In query
        Yield prod
    Next
End Function
```

Querying EDMs with Entity SQL

LINQ to Entities is not the only way to query data exposed by EDMs. An important alternative named Entity SQL enables you to query entity data models by providing both the ability to send SQL instructions to the data source and to treat query results as managed entities. To accomplish this, the DbSet class exposes a method named SqlQuery that queries the EDM via the specified set of SQL instructions. The following example shows how you can retrieve a list of products for the Grains/Cereals category in Northwind, sorting the result by the product name:

```
Sub EntitySQLDemo()
    Try
      Dim grainProducts = northwindContext.Products.
      SqlQuery("SELECT * FROM PRODUCTS WHERE " & _
               "CATEGORYID='5' ORDER BY PRODUCTNAME")
    Catch ex As EntitySqlException
        Console.WriteLine("An error occurred in column: {0}",
                          ex.Column.ToString)
    Catch ex As Exception
        Console.WriteLine(ex.ToString)
    End Try
End Sub
```

SqlQuery returns a DbSqlQuery object that represents a strongly typed query against entities. As with any other LINQ query, Entity SQL queries are executed when they are effectively used, for example in For..Each loops, when converting to collections. By default, entities returned by the method are tracked by the instance of the DbContext class. You can change this by invoking the AsNoTracking method on the returned collection.

Mapping Stored Procedures

The Entity Framework enables you to import stored procedures from a SQL Server database into the object model and Visual Studio 2015 makes thing easy. In this section you learn to add stored procedure mappings to the entity data model. To accomplish this, first open the Visual Studio designer by double-clicking the Northwind.edmx file in Solution Explorer. When ready, right-click the designer and select the **Update Model from**

Database command. This launches again the wizard that enables you to select database objects not included yet in the entity data model. Now, expand the Stored Procedures item and select the **Ten Most Expensive Products** stored procedure, as shown in Figure 26.13.

FIGURE 26.13   Adding a stored procedure to the EDM.

You can follow these steps to add database objects to the EDM if you did not do it before. This operation provides mappings for the stored procedure. The mapping lets the stored procedure be mapped into a .NET method that returns a value; therefore, you need to know which kind of value such methods must return. To accomplish this, open either the Server Explorer or the SQL Server Object Explorer tool window, expand the Northwind database structure, and then expand the Stored Procedures folder (if you use the SQL Object Explorer this folder is under Programmability); finally double-click the **Ten Most Expensive Products** stored procedure. Now the Visual Studio 2015 IDE shows the SQL instructions for the previously selected stored procedure, as shown in Figure 26.14.

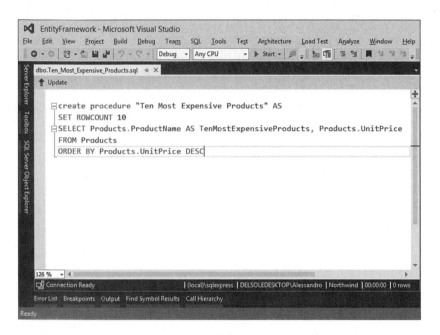

FIGURE 26.14 Examining SQL instructions for the stored procedure.

SCRIPT FILES

When Visual Studio shows SQL code for database objects, it also generates a .sql script file that can be saved for your later reuse. The SQL code editor points in fact to a newly generated script file that contains the code you see on screen.

Examining the SQL code, you can see that the stored procedure returns a list of product names. Now switch back to the EDM designer so that the Model Browser tool window becomes active. Inside the window expand the NorthwindModel, Function Imports item. You will notice the presence of an element called `Ten_Most_Expensive_Product` (see Figure 26.15 for a reference). This is nothing but a .NET method that Visual Studio 2015 has automatically generated to map the requested stored procedure. Because it is a method that returns a set of records, it must also have a return type. Visual Studio 2015 automatically generated a complex type (which means neither a scalar type like `String`, `Integer`, and so on, nor an entity type like `Product` or `Category`, but a specific type that includes information from specific columns) called `Ten_Most_Expensive_Product_Result`, as you can see by expanding the NorthwindModel, Complex Types node in the Model Browser (see Figure 26.15).

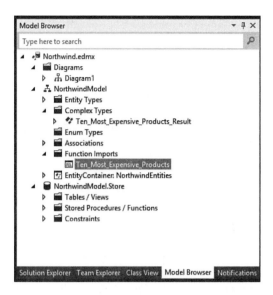

FIGURE 26.15   The method mapping the stored procedure and its return type.

The `Ten_Most_Expensive_Products_Result` complex type is a class exposing two auto-generated properties, one called `TenMostExpensiveProducts` of type `String` that stores the product name and one called `UnitPrice` of type `Nullable(Of Decimal)`. You are now ready to invoke your stored procedure as a .NET method being part of the entity data model, exposed by the `NorthwindEntities` class. For example, if you want to retrieve the list of the ten most-expensive products, you can write something like this:

```
For Each prod In northwindContext.Ten_Most_Expensive_Products
'Print the names of the ten most expensive products
    Console.WriteLine(prod.TenMostExpensiveProducts)
Next
```

Behind the scenes, mapping a stored procedure is something that Visual Basic accomplishes by adding the following invocation to the `ExecuteFunction(Of T)` method to the `NorthwindEntities` class definition:

```
Public Overridable Function Ten_Most_Expensive_Products() As _
    ObjectResult(Of Ten_Most_Expensive_Products_Result)
    Return DirectCast(Me, IObjectContextAdapter).
        ObjectContext.ExecuteFunction(Of Ten_Most_Expensive_Products_Result) _
        ("Ten_Most_Expensive_Products")
End Function
```

By completing this, you have the basic knowledge for working with the ADO.NET Entity Framework; you can learn more from the MSDN documentation.

MODIFYING AUTO-GENERATED FUNCTION IMPORTS AND COMPLEX TYPES

You might want to make some edits over autogenerated function imports or complex types. In the Model Browser window you can right-click the function import name (such as `Ten_Most_Expensive_Products` of the current example) and then select Properties in the pop-up menu. The Properties window will provide an opportunity of changing the function name and of editing the complex type as well, by clicking the buttons with three dots near the Return Type property. This enables the Edit Function Import dialog box, where you can rename the function and assign a new complex type as the return type. To accomplish this, you first need to click **Get Column Information** and then **Create New Complex Type**.

Introducing the Code First Approach

So far, you have seen how the Entity Framework enables you to create applications that access data based on a model-centric approach, in which an abstraction layer enables you to map to .NET objects an existing database (Database First), via convenient tools and designers. Back in Visual Studio 2010, Microsoft also introduced the so-called Model First approach, which enables you to generate an empty model without having a database; here you design your entities and associations in the Entity Framework designer and can finally generate a database with the Generate Database from Model command that is available when you right-click the designer. You can easily experiment with Model First on your own by selecting the Empty Model option when adding a new Entity Data Model. Both approaches are well made and can take advantage of a convenient designer, but they have the following limitations:

▶ Database First requires an existing database. You can still model your entities in the designer, but you must be sure of the perfect correspondence between a managed environment (the Entity Framework) and the data store (SQL Server).

▶ Model First enables you to model your entities in a convenient designer, but this can be difficult and tiring when the model gets complex.

▶ Both have dependencies on the EDMX file.

To make things faster and to avoid dependencies, Microsoft introduced a new approach called Code First with Entity Framework 4.3.1 and that is still available in most recent versions. As its name implies, with Code First you model your data only writing code; the IntelliSense and the power of the Visual Studio's code editor will help you write your entities quickly and all the power of the Entity Framework will remain unchanged. In Visual Studio 2015 you have two options for generating a data model based on Code First: generating an empty model or generating a model based on an existing database. In this chapter you will learn how to start from an empty model, which is better for learning purposes. Therefore, create a new Console application called CodeFirst and add to it a new ADO.NET Entity Data Model called BookStore (see Figure 26.1 for an example), which must be based on the Empty Code First Model option (see Figure 26.2). Visual Studio generates a very simple `Northwind` class, which inherits from `DbContext`. Listing 26.6 shows the content of this class.

LISTING 26.6   The Northwind Model Class

```
Imports System.Data.Entity
Imports System.Linq


Public Class BookStore
    Inherits DbContext

    ' Your context has been configured to use a 'BookStore'
    ' connection string from your application's
    ' configuration file (App.config or Web.config).
    ' By default, this connection string
    ' targets the 'CodeFirst.BookStore' database on your LocalDb instance.
    '
    ' If you wish to target a different database and/or database
    ' provider, modify the 'BookStore'
    ' connection string in the application configuration file.
    Public Sub New()
        MyBase.New("name=BookStore")
    End Sub


    ' Add a DbSet for each entity type that you want to include in your model.
    ' For more information on configuring and using a Code First model,
    ' see http:'go.microsoft.com/fwlink/?LinkId=390109.
    ' Public Overridable Property MyEntities() As DbSet(Of MyEntity)
End Class
```

The class needs some manual edits, but you first need to define your data model.

Coding Your Model

As you learned previously, with the Code First approach you define entities and associations in code. Let's provide a simple example, in which you implement business objects like an Author class and a Book class representing two entities. Listing 26.7 shows how to define both entities.

LISTING 26.7   Coding Two Entities in Code First

```
Public Class Author
    Public Property AuthorId As Integer
    Public Property FirstName As String
    Public Property LastName As String


    Public Property Books As ICollection(Of Book)
End Class


Public Class Book
```

```
    Public Property BookId As Integer
    Public Property Title As String
    Public Property Author As Author
    Public Property ISBN As String
    Public Property Price As Decimal
End Class
```

There is nothing difficult in Listing 26.7 because it is a normal class definition and you are probably now remembering the definition of the `Product` and `Category` classes generated by Visual Studio in the example about the Northwind database. Notice how the `Author` class exposes a `Books` property of type `ICollection(Of Book)`. The `ICollection(Of T)` type is typical in Code First to represent a navigation property for the "many" part of a one-to-many relationship. This example is in fact simulating a one-to-many relationship in which an author has multiple books. In real-world applications, you should implement a many-to-many relationship for a scenario like this (because multiple authors can write many books), but for making it easier to understand how Code First works, a one-to-many is enough. The next step is editing the context class. Add the following properties to the `BookStore` class:

```
Public Property Books As DbSet(Of Book)
Public Property Authors As DbSet(Of Author)
```

The `BookStore` class inherits from `DbContext` all the necessary infrastructure for working with data, plus it exposes two properties of type `DbSet(Of T)`, each representing a collection of entities as defined in Listing 26.7. So now you have a basic model definition (that will be extended later). Before using the model and entities, you need to supply a connection string to the database. Because Code First's main goal is simplicity, the connection string must be supplied in the simplest form possible. The new connection string must be added in the `ConnectionStrings` section of the application configuration file, so open App.config in the code editor (when adding the Entity Framework package, Visual Studio 2015 automatically adds the configuration file if not found). By convention, the name of the new connection string should match the name of the context class, which in this example is `BookStore`. This is not mandatory but is a good practice. As explained in the comments inside the `BookStore` class definition, Visual Studio 2015 adds a default connection string definition, which points to the `LocalDb` instance.

WHAT IS `LocalDb`?

`LocalDb` is a SQL Server execution mode expressly dedicated to software developers. It includes a minimal set of files required to start an instance of SQL Server on a development machine. This is not the same as SQL Server Express Edition, and it has some limitations. You should have installed SQL Server Express when reading the previous chapters, so you are encouraged to use it instead of `LocalDb`. For further information about this execution mode, see http://msdn.microsoft.com/en-us/library/hh510202.aspx.

This is the auto-generated connection string:

```
<connectionStrings>
  <add name="BookStore"
   connectionString="data source=(LocalDb)\MSSQLLocalDB;initial
   catalog=CodeFirst.BookStore;integrated
   security=True;MultipleActiveResultSets=True;App=EntityFramework"
   providerName="System.Data.SqlClient" />
</connectionStrings>
```

LocalDb is optimal for testing purpose on a development machine, but it is not appropriate for simulating a real-world situation. For this reason, change the connection string in order to use SQL Server Express Edition:

```
  <add name="BookStore"
      connectionString="data source=.\SQLEXPRESS;initial
      catalog=BookStore;integrated security=True;
      MultipleActiveResultSets=True;
      App=EntityFramework" providerName="System.Data.SqlClient" />
</connectionStrings>
```

Inside the connectionString attribute, you must first specify the server name and the name of the database that will be used. In this case replace CodeFirst.BookStore with BookStore. Both the model and the connection string are ready, so you can now perform operations against data.

Generating the Database and Executing Data Operations

So far, you have created your data model in code, but you do not have a database yet. The power of Code First is that the Entity Framework checks whether the database exists and, if not, it automatically creates one for you with the name specified in the connection string, without writing a single line of code. After the database is ready, data operations can be performed. The goal is now to generate some Author and Book entities and populate the database. This is an Insert operation. The DbSet(Of T) class is a collection, and therefore it exposes Add and Remove methods for adding and removing entity instances—that is, data into and from the database. You will use the same techniques learned previously with EDMs. Listing 26.8 demonstrates how to add a new author and two books per that author; finally the code demonstrates how you still use LINQ to Entities for querying the data model.

LISTING 26.8   Querying the Model and Executing Insert Operations

```
Sub Main()
    Using db As New BookStore
        Dim _author As New Author With {.FirstName = "Alessandro",
                                        .LastName = "Del Sole"}
        db.Authors.Add(_author)
```

26

```
            Dim LSBook As New Book With {.Title = "Visual Basic LightSwitch Unleashed",
                                         .Author = _author,
                                         .ISBN = "978-0672335532",
                                         .Price = 31.49D}
        db.Books.Add(LSBook)

            Dim VB2012Book As New Book With {.Title = "Visual Basic " _
                                             + " 2012 Unleashed",
                                             .Author = _author,
                                             .ISBN = " 978-0672336317",
                                             .Price = 31.49D}
        db.Books.Add(VB2012Book)

        db.SaveChanges()

        Dim authorInstance = db.Authors.
            Single(Function(a) a.LastName = "Del Sole")
        Console.WriteLine(authorInstance.FirstName + " " + authorInstance.LastName)

        For Each item In authorInstance.Books
            Console.WriteLine("    published ""{0}"", ISBN: {1}",
                              item.Title,
                              item.ISBN)
        Next

    End Using
    Console.ReadLine()
End Sub
```

Notice in Listing 26.8 how you perform Insert operations by generating new entity
instances and sending such instances to the model with the Add method of the desired
collection. In this particular example, you use the Single extension method to retrieve the
specified Author instance and then iterate the Books collection. If you run the code, you
will get the result shown in Figure 26.16.

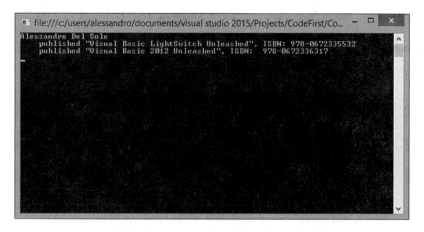

FIGURE 26.16   Adding and querying data against the database.

It is really interesting to see how data has been sent somewhere, even if you did not create a database. As you were told previously, the Entity Framework created the database for you at the moment in which the code started and determined that the database did not exist yet. You can either use Server Explorer or SQL Server Object Explorer to see how the database was created and attached to the instance of the server that was specified in the connection string. Figure 26.17 shows how the database appears in SQL Server Object Explorer.

FIGURE 26.17   The structure of the autogenerated database, with data.

If you expand the structure of the database, you can see how Books and Authors tables have been created based on our Code First approach, including columns and keys for relationships. You can also show the tables' content (see Figure 26.17) to demonstrate that the code has sent data to the database correctly.

THE MAGIC OF CONVENTIONS

You might wonder how Entity Framework was also capable of generating primary keys if you did not decorate the code in any manner. The Author entity has an AuthorId property, and the Book entity has a BookId property; both property names contain the Id suffix. By convention, Entity Framework considers an entity property, named Id or containing the Id suffix or prefix as the primary key. Similarly, EF behaves for foreign keys. The relationship between Author and Books is defined via an ICollection object whose generic type is an entity. Based on this, it generates the appropriate keys.

You have seen how convenient the Code First approach is for working with data, but it has some limitations as it is. For example, you cannot specify some primary validation rules or you cannot customize the mapping to meet specific database requirements. Fortunately, the EF 6 provides two ways to make this possible: Data Annotations and the Fluent APIs.

Introducing Data Annotations

Data Annotations consists in decorating entities and their properties with some attributes from the System.ComponentModel.DataAnnotations and System.ComponentModel.Data-Annotations.Schema namespaces (from the System.ComponentModel.DataAnnotations.dll assembly, which is automatically referenced when you create a Code First–based model). You already saw a particular usage of data annotations when talking about data validation previously, but you can also provide additional information to types, not just validation rules. The following code demonstrates how to rewrite the Book entity using data annotations:

```
Imports System.ComponentModel.DataAnnotations
Imports System.ComponentModel.DataAnnotations.Schema
<Table("OneBook")>
Public Class Book
    'Primary key
    <Key> Public Property BookNumber As Integer

    'Forced to be mandatory,
    'minimum length is 20 characters,
    'maximum length is 150
    <Required> <MinLength(20)> <StringLength(150)>
    Public Property Title As String

    'Determine the name of the foreign key
    'for the relationship
```

```
<ForeignKey("Books_Author")> Public Property Author As Author

'Force the type in SQL Server to be 'char(10)'
<Column(TypeName:="char"), StringLength(10)> Public Property ISBN As String

'Force the type in SQL Server to be 'money'
<Column(TypeName:="money")> Public Property Price As Decimal
End Class
```

By reading the comments in the code, you can understand how attributes enable you to better customizations over the model and, consequently, over the database. For instance, using the `Table` attribute to mark the class will cause the database to contain a table called `OneBook` instead of `Book`, but in your code you will still use `Book`. The `Key` attribute marks a property as a primary key and is useful if you do not want to use a conventional name (that is, containing the `Id` literal). It is worth mentioning that you can force the mapping of a .NET type into a SQL type in the data store by using the `Column` attribute and then specifying the SQL type, like for `ISBN` and `Price` properties in the previous code. Table 26.2 summarizes the most common data annotations attributes.

TABLE 26.2   Data Annotations Attributes

Attribute	Description
Table	Enables you to specify the table name in the database.
Key	Enables you to specify the name of the primary key, based on the property that is decorated with the attribute.
Required	Marks a property as non-nullable. This is particularly useful with reference types, like `String`, since value types are non-nullable by default unless you define them as nullable using the `Nullable(Of T)` syntax or the question mark after the type name.
StringLength	Specifies the maximum length for a string.
MinLength, MaxLength	Enable you to specify the minimum and maximum length of a string, respectively (`MaxLength` is equivalent to `StringLength`).
ForeignKey	Enables you to specify the name for a navigation property representing a relationship.
Column	Enables you to specify the SQL Server data type that will be used to map the property's .NET type.

Using Data Annotations will not change the way the Entity Framework checks for the database existence and creation if not found. Data Annotations are very useful but rely on a huge amount of attributes. You have an alternative for manipulating entities without using attributes, based on the Fluent APIs.

Handling Changes on the Database Schema

If you use the Code First approach and let the Entity Framework generate the database for you the first time you run the code that defines your model, the next time you make edits to your model you might also need to re-create your database. This is a common situation at development time and of course should never occur with production data. The reason is that the database schema could no longer match the model in some situations like adding/removing relationships, changing table definitions, and so on. In fact it might happen that you encounter an InvalidOperationException if you attempt to let EF access the database after breaking changes in your model, which means you need to re-create the database. You can delete the database manually—for example, using Server Explorer or SQL Server Object Explorer in Visual Studio 2015—but you can also take advantage of the Database class that Entity Framework provides to decide in code how and when the database should be re-created. You have two options. The first option is re-creating the database every time you run the code; the second option is re-creating the database only when some differences exist between the database and classes that constitute the model. To accomplish this, you use the Database.SetInitializer shared method. The following code snippet demonstrates both options:

```
Imports System.Data.Entity
'Recreate the database only in case of changes
'between the model and the database schema
Database.SetInitializer(New DropCreateDatabaseIfModelChanges(Of BookStore))

'Always recreate the database
Database.SetInitializer(New DropCreateDatabaseAlways(Of BookStore))
```

The method's parameter can be either a new instance of the DropCreateDatabaseIfModelChanges class or a new instance of the DropCreateDatabaseAlways class. Both are generic classes, and the type parameter is the name of the context class.

The line of code that establishes how to re-create the database must come before the initialization of the context class. **Remember to remove the line of code when the application goes to production.** There is another class called CreateDatabaseIfNotExists, which is the default behavior and that you can omit.

CODE FIRST MIGRATIONS

The ADO.NET Entity Framework Team at Microsoft realized that making changes on the model and then sending those changes to the database schema is in most cases a complex task. For this reason, they are offering a migration mechanism called Code First Migrations that is available via NuGet and that is explained in the MSDN Library at http://msdn.microsoft.com/en-us/data/jj591621.

Introducing the Fluent APIs

There is an interesting alternative for customizing the model mapping in code, based on the Fluent APIs. As the name implies, this technique enables customizations only writing fluent code, without additional attributes or external mapping files. To use the Fluent APIs, you need to override the OnModelCreating method in the context class and, inside the method body, apply edits via lambda expressions. The following code demonstrates how to rewrite the `BookStore` and `Book` classes using fluent code:

```vbnet
Public Class BookStore
    Inherits DbContext

    Public Property Books As DbSet(Of Book)
    Public Property Authors As DbSet(Of Author)

    Protected Overrides Sub OnModelCreating(modelBuilder As DbModelBuilder)
        'Define the primary key
        modelBuilder.Entity(Of Book).HasKey(Function(b) b.BookNumber)

        'Define a one-to-many relationship
        modelBuilder.Entity(Of Book).HasRequired(Function(b) b.Author).WithMany()

        modelBuilder.Entity(Of Book)() _
            .Property(Function(b) b.Title).
            IsRequired.HasMaxLength(150)

        modelBuilder.Entity(Of Book)() _
            .Property(Function(b) b.ISBN).HasColumnType("char").
            HasMaxLength(10).IsFixedLength()

        modelBuilder.Entity(Of Book)() _
            .Property(Function(b) b.Price).
            HasColumnType("money")
    End Sub
End Class
```

Following is a list of interesting notes:

▶ The method's argument is an instance of the `DbModelBuilder` class, which is responsible to translate .NET code into a database schema.

▶ The generic `Entity(Of T)` method of the `DbModelBuilder` class takes the entity you want to edit as the type parameter.

▶ `Entity(Of T)` exposes a method called `Property`, whose argument is a lambda expression in which you specify the entity property you want to edit.

▶ You can set the primary key using the `HasKey` method, passing to the lambda expression the property that you want to be the primary key.

▶ You can set foreign keys using the `HasRequired` method, passing to the lambda expression the type that you want to be the other part of the relationship. You specify `WithMany` to create a one-to-many relationship (see the previous example).

26

▶ You can use multiple mapping methods over the specified properties, method names are self-explanatory, and IntelliSense helps you choose the appropriate methods.

The same rules for the database recreation apply to the Fluent APIs.

Additional Fluent Methods

Because the goal of the Fluent APIs is making it possible to write cleaner code, the Entity Framework provides specific members that make data manipulation easier. All members are exposed by the `DbSet(Of T)` class. The `Find` method enables you to retrieve the specific entity instance based on its primary key:

```
Dim anAuthor = db.Authors.Find(1)
```

The `Local` property enables you to work against in-memory data, which is the data currently stored in the model (except for those objects marked for deletion) without querying the database again:

```
Dim myBooks = From aBook In db.Books.Local
              Select aBook
              Order By aBook.Price Descending
```

The `Include` method, that you saw against EDMs, in Code First offers a generic implementation so that you no longer need to type the name of the entity. You use it with a lambda expression like this:

```
Dim myBooks = db.Authors.Include(Function(b) b.Books)
```

Finally, the `Load` extension method immediately executes a query against the database, avoiding the deferred execution. This is the equivalent of writing code to use a query at least once to make its result available. You use it like this:

```
db.Authors.Load()
```

All these members provide additional efficient ways to work with data in the Code First approach. You can also use the Object Browser and IntelliSense to see other members exposed by the `DbContext` and `DbSet` classes, and you will discover that most of them have a similar behavior of counterparts exposed by `ObjectContext` and `ObjectSet` classes that you met when talking about Entity Data Models. This makes migrating from one approach to another definitely easier.

MORE ABOUT CODE FIRST IN ENTITY FRAMEWORK

This chapter provided an overview of Code First, so you might want to check out the Data Developer Center at http://msdn.microsoft.com/en-us/data/aa937723, where you can find additional information and learning resources about Entity Framework and related development techniques.

Summary

In this chapter you got a high-level overview of ADO.NET Entity Framework in .NET 4.6, also known as EF 6. Entity Framework is a modern data platform providing a high abstraction layer from the database that enables you to work with a conceptual model instead of working directly with the data source. Database objects are mapped to the .NET equivalent into an Entity Data Model object model. Entities are a key concept in the EF and are classes representing database tables, as much as scalar properties represent tables' columns and navigation properties represent relationship. The DbContext class is responsible for managing the EDM lifetime, including the execution of Insert/Update/Delete operations that can be performed by invoking specific methods from entities. Querying data is instead accomplished via LINQ to Entities, a specific LINQ provider for the EF, and Entity SQL. You also saw how Visual Studio 2015 makes it easier to map stored procedures to the object model. Finally, you got started with the new Code First approach, which requires you to write some more code but which also enables you to maintain cleaner code and provides more controls over the generated data model.

26

CHAPTER 27

Manipulating XML Documents with LINQ and XML Literals

With the growing diffusion of the Internet during the years, one of the most common needs has been establishing standards for information exchange across computers in different parts of the world. For such an exchange, the XML file format was introduced to provide a unified standard that was specific to structured data. Because of its flexibility, the XML file format became popular among developers, and the .NET Framework has always offered a built-in way for manipulating XML documents: the `System.Xml` namespace. With the advent of LINQ in Visual Basic 2008, things have been improved. Although the `System.Xml` namespace still exists for several reasons, a more efficient way of manipulating XML documents is available in Visual Basic due to important features such as LINQ to XML and XML literals that are also integrated into the language syntax. In this chapter you learn about manipulating XML documents using LINQ to XML and XML literals, and you discover how much more powerful this opportunity is when compared to the `System.Xml` namespace.

KNOWLEDGE OF XML

The goal of this chapter is not explaining XML syntax and document structure, so you are required to be familiar with XML syntax and implementation.

Introducing LINQ to XML

LINQ to XML is the standard LINQ provider for reading, creating, and manipulating XML documents with the .NET languages starting from Visual Basic 2008 and Visual C# 3.0. Such a provider is implemented in the System.Xml.Linq.dll assembly and supports all operators available in LINQ to Objects with a few differences due to the XML document structure and other specific language features. The good news is that you can take advantage of the unified programming model offered by LINQ to perform XML manipulations via the classical LINQ syntax that you already know. Visual Basic 2015, like its predecessors, offers particular syntax paradigms for LINQ to XML that are also described in this chapter. You first learn how to create and manipulate XML documents using managed objects; in the second part of this chapter, you become skillful with XML literals that can allow you to write code more quickly and cleanly.

The `System.Xml.Linq` Namespace

The `System.Xml.Linq` namespace exposes objects for creating, reading, and manipulating XML documents. All objects inherit from `System.Xml.Linq.XObject`. Table 27.1 summarizes and describes available objects.

TABLE 27.1　Objects Available in the `System.Xml.Linq` Namespace

Object	Description
XDocument	Represents an entire XML document
XElement	Represents an XML element with attributes
XAttribute	Represents an XML attribute
XComment	Represents a comment within an XML document
XDeclaration	Represents the XML declaration, including version number and encoding
XNode	Represents an XML node which is made of an XML element and children elements
XName	Provides a name to an XML element or attribute
XCData	Represents a CData section
XText	Represents a text node
XContainer	Represents a container for node
XNamespace	Declares an XML namespace
XDocumentType	Represents a Document Type Definition (DTD) typically for XML schemas

You create an XML document declaring an instance of the XDocument class:

```
Dim myDocument As New XDocument
```

When you have the instance, you can add all acceptable objects mentioned in Table 27.1. The first required element is the XML declaration that can be added as follows and that is mandatory:

```
myDocument.Declaration = New XDeclaration("1.0", "utf-8", "no")
```

If you want to add comments to your XML documents, you can create as many instances of the XComment class for as many comments as you need to add:

```
myDocument.Add(New XComment("My first Xml document with LINQ"))
```

The next step is creating a first-level XElement that stores nested XElement objects:

```
Dim mainElement As New XElement("Contacts")
```

Now you can create nested elements and specify some attributes, as demonstrated in the following code:

```
'An Xml element with attributes
Dim firstNestedElement As New XElement("Contact")
Dim attribute1 As New XAttribute("LastName", "Del Sole")
Dim attribute2 As New XAttribute("FirstName", "Alessandro")
Dim attribute3 As New XAttribute("Age", "37")
firstNestedElement.Add(attribute1)
firstNestedElement.Add(attribute2)
firstNestedElement.Add(attribute3)

Dim secondNestedElement As New XElement("Contact")
Dim attribute4 As New XAttribute("LastName", "White")
Dim attribute5 As New XAttribute("FirstName", "Robert")
Dim attribute6 As New XAttribute("Age", "40")
secondNestedElement.Add(attribute4)
secondNestedElement.Add(attribute5)
secondNestedElement.Add(attribute6)

'In-line initialization with an array of XAttribute
Dim thirdNestedElement As New XElement("Contact", New XAttribute() {
                                New XAttribute("LastName", "Red"),
                                New XAttribute("FirstName", "Stephen"),
                                New XAttribute("Age", "41")})
```

When you create an XAttribute you need to invoke the XElement.Add instance method to assign the new attribute. Creating elements and assigning attributes is a simple task because classes are self-explanatory, and IntelliSense helps you understand which arguments the constructors need. But if you take a look at the last instance, you can see that things can become difficult, especially if you think that you could create an array of XElement with nested XElement definitions, with nested XAttribute definitions. You see

27

later in this chapter how XML literals make things easier; for now let's focus on fundamentals. The next step is to add all nested XElement objects to the main XElement as
follows:

```
With mainElement
    Add(firstNestedElement)
    Add(secondNestedElement)
    Add(thirdNestedElement)
End With
```

mainElement now stores a sequence of XML elements that must be added to the document
as follows:

```
myDocument.Add(mainElement)
```

In the end, you can save your XML document to disk by invoking the Save method:

```
myDocument.Save("C:\Contacts.xml")
```

This method has several overloads that also enable the specifying of a stream instead of
a string of file options for controlling formatting. If you just want to check your result,
invoke XDocument.ToString as follows:

```
Console.WriteLine(myDocument.ToString)
```

This line of code allows you to see how your document is formed. The output follows:

```
<!--My first Xml document with LINQ-->
<Contacts>
  <Contact LastName="Del Sole" FirstName="Alessandro" Age="37" />
  <Contact LastName="White" FirstName="Robert" Age="40" />
  <Contact LastName="Red" FirstName="Stephen" Age="41" />
</Contacts>
```

Creating an XML document with the System.Xml.Linq namespace is more intuitive than
the older System.Xml namespace, but things can go better as you see later. At the moment
you need to know how to load and parse existing documents.

Loading and Parsing Existing XML Documents

To load an existing XML document, you invoke the shared XDocument.Load method as
follows:

```
Dim myDocument = XDocument.Load("C:\Contacts.xml")
```

You can get a new instance of XDocument and get access to its members via numerous
methods and properties that the class offers. Table 27.2 summarizes the most important
members.

TABLE 27.2   Most Important Members of the `XDocument` Class

Member	Type	Description
`AddAfterSelf`	Method	Adds the specified content just after the node whose instance is invoking the method itself
`AddBeforeSelf`	Method	Adds the specified content just before the node whose instance is invoking the method itself
`AddFirst`	Method	Adds the specified content as the first node in the document
`ReplaceWith`	Method	Replaces the node whose instance is invoking the method with the specified content
`Root`	Property	Returns the root `XElement`
`Remove`	Method	Removes the node from its parents
`RemoveNodes`	Method	Removes children nodes from the object instance that is invoking the method
`Element`	Method	Retrieves an `XElement` instance of the specified XML element
`Descendants`	Method	Returns an `IEnumerable(Of XElement)` collection of descendant `XElement` objects

`FirstNode/`
`LastNode/`
`NextNode/`
`PreviousNode`
	Properties	Return the instance of the node which position is indicated by the property name

Notice that both `XDocument` and `XElement` classes expose methods in Table 27.2, and `XElement` can also load and save XML content as much as `XDocument`. Both `XDocument` and `XElement` classes also allow parsing strings containing XML representation to get an appropriate object. This is accomplished invoking the `Parse` method as in the following example:

```
Dim document As String = "<?xml version=""1.0""?>" & Environment.NewLine & _
                "    <Contacts>" & Environment.NewLine & _
                "    <Contact FirstName=""Alessandro"" Last
                    Name=""Del Sole"" Age=""37""/>" & _
                Environment.NewLine & _
                "    <Contact FirstName=""Robert"" Last
                    Name=""White"" Age=""40""/>" & _
                Environment.NewLine & _
                "  </Contacts>"

Dim resultingDocument As XDocument = XDocument.Parse(document)
resultingDocument.Save("C:\Contacts.xml")
```

This can be useful if you need to get a real XML document from a simple string.

27

Querying XML Documents with LINQ

You can take advantage of the LINQ syntax for querying XML documents. Consider the following XML file:

```
<Contacts>
  <Contact LastName="Del Sole" FirstName="Alessandro" Age="37" />
  <Contact LastName="White" FirstName="Robert" Age="40" />
  <Contact LastName="Red" FirstName="Stephen" Age="41" />
</Contacts>
```

Now imagine you want to get a list of last names for people with an age greater than or equal to 40. This can be accomplished by the following query:

```
Dim query = From element In myDocument.Descendants("Contact")
            Where Integer.Parse(element.Attribute("Age").Value) >= 40
            Select element.Attribute("LastName").Value
```

The `Descendants` method returns an `IEnumerable(Of XElement)` and stores all `XElement` objects whose `XName` is the one specified as the argument. To get the value of an attribute about comparisons as in our situation, you invoke the `XElement.Attribute()`. `Value` property that contains the actual value of the `xAttribute` instance whose name is specified within `Attribute("")`. Notice how an explicit conversion is required from `String` to `Integer` to perform an evaluation on numbers. The preceding query returns an `IEnumerable(Of String)`. If you need to generate custom results, you can take advantage of anonymous types as in the following query that get only the `LastName` and `Age` values:

```
Dim query = From element In myDocument.Descendants("Contact")
            Let age = Integer.Parse(element.Attribute("Age").Value)
            Where age >= 40
            Select New With {.LastName = element.
                                        Attribute("LastName").Value,
                    Age = age}
```

The preceding query returns `IEnumerable(Of anonymous type)`. Notice how the `Let` keyword is used to provide a temporary identifier that can be used both for performing a comparison and for assignment to the anonymous type's `Age` property. With the exception of anonymous types, as you remember from the LINQ to Objects discussion, you can bind results of LINQ to XML queries directly to user interface controls, such as the `BindingSource` in Windows Forms or the `CollectionViewSource` in WPF. By the way, remember that, if you do not select just one attribute per element (which would return an `IEnumerable(Of String)`), this would work as collections of `XElement`; therefore, it is not the best approach because you need to work against your business objects and not against `XElement` instances. Just to provide a simple example, if you need an iteration over your query, iterating an `IEnumerable(Of XElement)` would not probably make much sense; though it instead would with a `List(Of Contact)`. The appropriate approach is creating a class that maps each element within the XML document. For example, consider the following simplified implementation of the `Contact` class:

```
Class Contact
    Property FirstName As String
    Property LastName As String
    Property Age As Integer
End Class
```

At this point, you can write a LINQ query that generates a collection of `Contact` and that can be both mapped to a user interface control and that can be edited:

```
'Returns a List(Of Contact)
Dim contactCollection = (From element In myDocument.Descendants("Contact")
                    Let age = Integer.Parse(element.
                                              Attribute("Age").Value)
                    Select New Contact With {.FirstName = element.

                                Attribute("FirstName").Value,
                                LastName = element.

                                Attribute("LastName").Value,
                                Age = age}).ToList
```

Now you have a `List(Of Contact)` that can be both used for presenting data or for editing. On the contrary, you could create an XML document starting from a collection of objects, but this is something you see in a more efficient way in the discussion of XML literals in the next section.

Writing XML Markup in VB with XML Literals

The `System.Xml.Linq` namespace is powerful. Manipulating complex XML documents that store a lot of data can lead to writing less elegant and more complex code. Luckily, the Visual Basic language provides a powerful feature for manipulating XML documents, known as *XML literals*. You can write XML markup together with the Visual Basic code. The following code provides an example:

```
'The compiler infers XDocument
Dim Contacts = <?xml version="1.0"?>
        <Contacts>
            <Contact LastName="Del Sole"
                FirstName="Alessandro"
                Age="37"
                email="alessandro.delsole@visual-basic.it"/>
            <!-- Fantasy name-->
            <Contact LastName="White"
                FirstName="Robert"
                Age="45"
                email="address1@something.com"/>
        </Contacts>
```

This means that you can write entire XML documents integrating XML markup and Visual Basic code. Here IntelliSense features are less powerful than in the classic Visual Studio XML editor, but they are good enough to provide syntax colorization and code indentation. Figure 27.1 shows what the preceding code looks like in the Visual Basic code editor.

```
XmlLiterals.vb*  ⊕ ✕
[VB] LinqToXml                    ▾  ┗ XmlLiterals                  ▾  ⊙ LiteralsDemo                 ▾
            0 references
    1    ⊟ Module XmlLiterals
    2
            0 references
    3    ⊟     Sub LiteralsDemo()
    4              'The Compiler infers XDocument
    5    ⊟         Dim Contacts = <?xml version="1.0"?>
    6    ⊟                        <Contacts>
    7                                <Contact LastName="Del Sole"
    8                                    FirstName="Alessandro"
    9                                    Age="35"
   10                                    email="alessandro.delsole@visual-basic.it"/>
   11                                <!-- Fantasy name-->
   12                                <Contact LastName="White"
   13                                    FirstName="Robert"
   14                                    Age="45"
   15                                    email="address1@something.com"/>
   16                             </Contacts>
   17          End Sub  .
   18    End Module
   19
126 %  ▾ ◀                                                                          ▶
```

FIGURE 27.1   XML literals in the Visual Basic code editor.

Just think that you can paste from the clipboard the content of long and complex XML documents, such as Microsoft Excel workbooks or Open XML documents, and take advantage of XML literals. The Visual Basic compiler can then map XML nodes to the appropriate .NET type. In the previous example, `Contacts` and `Contact` are mapped to `XElement` objects, whereas properties of each `Contact` element are mapped to `XAttribute` objects. The previous example also takes advantage of local type inference. In such a scenario, the Visual Basic compiler infers the `XDocument` type for the `Contacts` variable. This is because the XML markup contains the XML declaration. If you do not specify such a declaration, the XML markup is mapped to an `XElement`, as in the following code:

```
'The compiler infers XElement
Dim Contacts = <Contacts>
                <Contact LastName="Del Sole"
                    FirstName="Alessandro"
                    Age="37"
                    email="alessandro.delsole@visual-basic.it"/>
            </Contacts>
```

If you do not want to use local type inference, you need to pay attention to which type the XML markup is mapped. For example, both the following code snippets throw an `InvalidCastException`:

```
'Throws an InvalidCastException
'Cannot assign to XElement markup that
'ships with the Xml declaration
Dim Contacts As XElement = <?xml version="1.0"?>
                        <Contacts>
                            <Contact LastName="Del Sole"
                                FirstName="Alessandro"
                                Age="37"
                                email="alessandro.delsole@visual-basic.it"/>
                                    <!-- Fantasy name-->
                            <Contact LastName="White"
                                FirstName="Robert"
                                Age="45"
                                email="address1@something.com"/>
                        </Contacts>
'Throws an InvalidCastException
'Cannot assign to XDocument markup that
'does not have the Xml declaration
Dim Contacts As XDocument = <Contacts>
                            <Contact LastName="Del Sole"
                                FirstName="Alessandro"
                                Age="37"
                                email="alessandro.delsole@visual-basic.it"/>
                            <!-- Fantasy name-->
                            <Contact LastName="White"
                                FirstName="Robert"
                                Age="45"
                                email="address1@something.com"/>
                        </Contacts>
```

XML literals are powerful because they allow you to write more elegant code and provide a view of your XML documents as you would get within an XML editor. This is much better than generating nodes, elements, and attributes the old-fashioned way. The preceding code has one limitation: It is hard-coded, meaning that values have been added manually. This would be a big limitation because you often need to dynamically generate XML documents (for example, generating elements for each member within a data source). Luckily, XML literals make this easier, providing the ability to embed local variables' values and LINQ queries within the XML markup, as shown in the next section.

BEHIND THE SCENES

The Visual Basic compiler parses XML documents, elements, and attributes written with XML literals into the appropriate .NET types, such as XDocument, XElement, and XAttribute. Comments are included in such a mapping and converted into XComment objects and so on. Please refer to Table 27.1 for available objects.

LINQ Queries with XML Literals

XML literals provide an alternative syntax for LINQ to XML queries in Visual Basic code. Let's look at the first XML document used in "The `System.Xml.Linq` Namespace" section again, which looks like the following but with a slight modification:

```
<?xml version="1.0" encoding="utf-8"?>
<Contacts>
  <Contact FirstName="Alessandro"
        LastName="Del Sole"
        Age="37"
        Email="alessandro.delsole@visual-basic.it">
  </Contact>
  <!--The following are fantasy names-->
  <Contact FirstName="Stephen"
        LastName="Red"
        Age="40"
        Email="address1@something.com">
  </Contact>
  <Contact FirstName="Robert"
        LastName="White"
        Age="41"
        Email="address2@something.com">
  </Contact>
  <Contact FirstName="Luke"
        LastName="Green"
        Age="42"
        Email="address3@something.com">
  </Contact>
  <Person FirstName="Alessandro"
        LastName="Del Sole">
  </Person>
</Contacts>
```

There is a `Person` element that we want to be excluded. The goal is querying all `Contact` elements whose age is greater than or equal to 40. Instead of recurring to the classical syntax, you can write the following code:

```
Dim doc = XDocument.Load("Contacts.xml")

Dim query = From cont In doc.<Contacts>.<Contact>
            Where Integer.Parse(cont.@Age) >= 40
            Select cont
```

The preceding code uses new symbols for querying documents known as *XML Axis Properties*. Table 27.3 summarizes XML axis.

TABLE 27.3   XML Axis

Symbol	Description
...<>	XML Axis Descendants Property. Returns all descendant elements of the XML document named as the identifier enclosed within the symbols.
.<>	XML Axis Child Property. Returns children of an `XElement` or `XDocument`.
.@	XML Axis Attribute Property. Returns the value of an attribute within an XML element.

The preceding query can be described by this sentence: "Process all Contacts' children `Contact` elements." The difference with the XML Axis Descendants Properties can be explained with another example. Consider the following document that is just a revalidation of the previous one:

```
<?xml version="1.0" encoding="utf-8"?>
<Contacts>
  <Contact>
    <FirstName>Alessandro</FirstName>
    <LastName>Del Sole</LastName>
    <Age>37</Age>
    <Email>alessandro.delsole@visual-basic.it</Email>
  </Contact>
  <Contact>
    <FirstName>Stephen</FirstName>
    <LastName>Red</LastName>
    <Age>40</Age>
    <Email>address1@something.com</Email>
  </Contact>
  <Person>
    <FirstName>Robert</FirstName>
    <LastName>White</LastName>
  </Person>
</Contacts>
```

Now each `Contact` element has sub-elements. If you wanted to get a collection of all `LastName` elements for all elements, you could use the XML Axis Descendants property as follows:

```
'Returns a collection of all <LastName></LastName>
'elements within the document
Dim onlyLastNames = From cont In doc...<LastName>
```

It's worth mentioning that such a query also includes results from the `Person` element because it exposes a `LastName` attribute. So if you need to filter results depending on the root element, you should invoke the Axis Descendants property. Notice also how in both the previous code examples an explicit conversion is required when you need a comparison against non-String data. In this particular case the comparison is done against an integer number (40); therefore, you can invoke the `Integer.Parse` method because you expect that the `Age` attribute contains the string representation of a number. XML Axis properties provide a simplified and cleaner way for querying XML documents. Just remember that, as discussed in the previous section, *you will need helper classes for mapping each XElement content into a .NET type* to provide data-binding features to your code.

WHY `Option Strict On` IS IMPORTANT

One of the last code snippets had an explicit conversion using `Integer.Parse`. If you set `Option Strict On` and forget to perform such a conversion, the compiler throws an exception requiring you to perform an appropriate conversion, which is always good. If you instead set `Option Strict Off`, no conversion is required at compile time, but in all cases you encounter errors at runtime except if you assign the value of an attribute to a `String` variable. You should always keep `Option Strict On`.

The Null-Propagating Operator and XML Literals

In Visual Basic 2015, XML literals support the null-propagating operator `?..` You can use this operator in `?...<>`, `?.<>`, and `?.@` expressions. For instance, the following code returns the email address for the first contact in a list only if the `Contacts` collection is not null, then if there is at least a `Contact` XML node (that is `Contact` is not null), and then if the first contact in the list is not null:

```
Dim x = Contacts?...<Contact>?.First?.@Email
```

Notice that you cannot use this syntax in a LINQ query. For example, the following code would result in an `ArgumentNullException` because the `From` clause requires a non-null collection:

```
'Throws an ArgumentNullException
Dim list = From cont In contacts?...<Contact>
           Select cont
```

Compared to other LINQ scenarios, in LINQ to XML, you will probably have fewer chances to use the null-propagating operator. However, it is important for you to know that this option is available and what the correct syntax is.

Understanding Embedded Expressions

With embedded expressions, you can include local variables or perform dynamic queries within XML literals. Let's look again at the first example about XML literals, where an XML document contains a couple of contacts. Imagine you want to generate a contact starting from some variables (that you could populate at runtime with different values) instead of hard-coding the last name, first name, and age. This can be accomplished as follows:

```
'All with type inference
Dim FirstName = "Alessandro"
```

```
Dim LastName = "Del Sole"
Dim Age = 37


Dim Contacts = <?xml version="1.0"?>
            <Contacts>
                <Contact LastName=<%= LastName %>
                    FirstName=<%= FirstName %>
                    Age=<%= Age %>
                    email="alessandro.delsole@visual-basic.it"/>
                <!-- Fantasy name-->
                <Contact LastName="White"
                    FirstName="Robert"
                    Age="45"
                    email="address1@something.com"/>
            </Contacts>
```

Although the second contact in the list is equal to the first example, the first contact is generated with embedded expressions. You create an embedded expression including an expression within <%= and => symbols. While you write the expression after the opening tag, IntelliSense works to improve your coding experience. In this way, you can create elements dynamically. But this code works just for one element. What if you need to dynamically generate as many elements for as many items stored within a collection or within a database table? Imagine you have a Contact class that is implemented as follows:

```
Class Contact
    Property FirstName As String
    Property LastName As String
    Property Age As Integer
    Property EmailAddress As String
End Class
```

Now imagine that within a method body you create a collection of Contact. For demo purposes, four instances of the Contact class are created and then pushed into a new collection:

```
Dim firstContact As New Contact With {.FirstName = "Alessandro",
            LastName = "Del Sole",
            EmailAddress = "alessandro.delsole@visual-basic.it",
            Age = 37}


'Now fantasy names
Dim secondContact As New Contact With {.FirstName = "Stephen",
            LastName = "Red",
            EmailAddress = "address1@something.com",
            Age = 40}
Dim thirdContact As New Contact With {.FirstName = "Robert",
            LastName = "White",
```

27

```
                  EmailAddress = "address2@something.com",
                  Age = 41}
Dim fourthContact As New Contact With {.FirstName = "Luke",
                  LastName = "Green",
                  EmailAddress = "address3@something.com",
                  Age = 42}


Dim people As New List(Of Contact) From {
                  firstContact,
                  secondContact,
                  thirdContact,
                  fourthContact}
```

Our goal is to generate an XML document that contains all the preceding created contacts as XML nodes. This is accomplished by the following code:

```
Dim newDocument = <?xml version="1.0"?>
                  <Contacts>
                      <%= From cont In people
                          Where cont.Age > 37
                          Select <Contact
                                     FirstName=<%= cont.FirstName %>
                                     LastName=<%= cont.LastName %>
                                     Age=<%= cont.Age %>
                                     Email=<%= cont.EmailAddress %>>
                                 </Contact>
                      %>
                  </Contacts>


newDocument.Save("C:\Contacts.xml")
```

Embedding an expression means that you can also embed a LINQ query. Notice how the query is part of the first embedded expression and how the Select clause allows the creation of a new XElement object using XML literals where nested embedded expressions can provide advantage of local variables. The previous code can produce the following result (remember that only people with an age greater than 37 have been included):

```
<Contacts>
  <Contact FirstName="Stephen" LastName="Red" Age="40"
      Email="address1@something.com"></Contact>
  <Contact FirstName="Robert" LastName="White" Age="41"
      Email="address2@something.com"></Contact>
  <Contact FirstName="Luke" LastName="Green" Age="42"
      Email="address3@something.com"></Contact>
</Contacts>
```

Using XML literals and embedded expressions, you dynamically created an XML document that can contain an infinite number of elements. This example was related to a simple generic collection, but you can easily understand what kinds of results you can reach if you need to generate XML documents from database tables. If you work with LINQ to SQL or with ADO.NET Entity Framework, the code remains the same; the only exception is that the data source in the `From` clause is the `DataContext` instance for LINQ to SQL or the `DbContext` class in the ADO.NET Entity Framework.

> **NOTE**
>
> XML literals can map any kind of XML markup. For example, you can dynamically generate WPF controls writing XAML code that Visual Basic recognizes as XML and that can be assigned to `XElement` objects. Another useful example is a Microsoft Excel workbook saved as XML format that can be entirely pasted into the Visual Basic editor. Other than writing cleaner code, the ability to wrap any XML content is probably the best feature of XML literals.

Iterators and XML Literals

Iterators can be used inside XML literals code blocks. Specifically, you can use the anonymous iterators (or iterator lambdas). The following code shows how to use an anonymous iterator to retrieve only the `LastName` property for each item in the `People` collection created previously and creates an XML document where each contact has only the `LastName` attribute:

```
Dim doc = <?xml version="1.0"?>
        <Contacts>
            <%= (Iterator Function()
                    For Each person In people
                        Yield person
                    Next
                End Function)().
                Select(Function(c) <Contact LastName=<%= c.LastName %>>
                                    </Contact>) %>
        </Contacts>
```

By using the iterator lambda you can write more responsive code, whose result can be elaborated while the rest of processing is still in progress.

Summary

The .NET Framework offers a special LINQ provider named LINQ to XML that enables working with XML documents. Via the `System.Xml.Linq` namespace, this provider allows creating and manipulating XML documents in an efficient way. Classes such as `XDocument`, `XElement`, `XAttribute`, `XComment`, and `XDeclaration` are self-explanatory and allow easy generation of XML documents. To query XML documents, you just write LINQ queries using the unified syntax that you already know, with a few additions such as the `Descendants` or `Attribute` property. Although efficient, `System.Xml.Linq` can be confusing when XML documents become larger. Luckily, Visual Basic provides the XML literals feature that enables the writing of XML markup code directly into the VB code editor. To make things real, with embedded expressions you can generate documents putting local variables, expressions, and LINQ queries within XML literals so that you can generate XML documents dynamically.

CHAPTER 28

Creating WPF Applications

Over the years, the requirement for high-quality applications has dramatically increased. Modern technologies enable users to perform even more complex tasks; technology and computers are a significant part of users' lives. Computer applications need to respond to such requests. The user experience is something that cannot be disregarded anymore, even if an application works perfectly on data access. The more complex the task an application can perform, the more important is the need of an interactive user interface that enables the user to easily perform tasks through the application. And this is something that is strictly related to different kinds of applications: business applications, home applications, and multimedia and entertainment applications. Universal Windows apps are the most recent examples of great user interfaces. For many years, .NET developers could build user interfaces based on the Windows Forms, which has been a good and important framework for creating user experiences with the .NET technology. Windows Forms has big limitations, especially if you need to create dynamic interfaces or complex data-bindings. Also, .NET Framework 4.0 signaled the last point in which some real enhancements have been added to Windows Forms and .NET 4.6 just adds an option for auto-resizing some controls, but Microsoft stopped investing in that platform, even if it's still supported. With the purpose of providing a unified programming model for building advanced user interfaces, being suitable for combining data access, dynamic interfaces, multimedia, and documents capabilities, Microsoft created the Windows Presentation Foundation technology (WPF), which dramatically increases developer productivity and offers a great environment for styling the application layout by a professional designer. WPF combines in one framework all you need to build new generation applications. If you are an experienced WPF developer, maybe this chapter is just a quick recap for you. If you are new to WPF, this and the following chapters give you the basics for beginning to build modern applications with Visual Basic 2015.

What Is WPF?

Windows Presentation Foundation (WPF) is the premier framework from Microsoft for building user interfaces in desktop applications for Windows 8.x, Windows 7, and Windows Vista. WPF is not intended to be a replacement for Windows Forms; it can be considered as a revolutionary alternative for building rich client applications. Windows Presentation Foundation offers several advantages that make user interface development straight-forward. First, it is built on the top of the Microsoft DirectX graphic libraries, meaning that WPF applications can embed audio, videos, pictures, animations, and 3D graphics, all in a .NET-oriented fashion, with few lines of code. You can create rich client applications while continuing to write Visual Basic code as you are already used to doing. WPF takes advantage of the GPU support of a graphics card, but it is also fully compatible with software rendering and can fall back on that when a GPU is not available (although it is actually expensive in terms of performance). Second, WPF has a powerful data-binding engine that makes it easier to build data-oriented applications. Third, it provides a separation layer between the developer and the designer so that professional designers can completely restyle the application's layout with specific tools, improving what the developer built. WPF completely changes the way you think of your user interfaces but does not change the way you write Visual Basic code. WPF has some big differences with Windows Forms in its architecture; therefore, you need a different approach to some problems. As an example, WPF handles events via the routed events that are completely different from the event infrastructure in Windows Forms. You can handle events in WPF the same way you do in Windows Forms. The way you write code is the same, on the top of different technologies. WPF has been the first platform using the XAML markup language for declaring the user interface; XAML was later brought to Silverlight, Windows Phone, and Windows 8.x Store apps (with some small differences due to their different contexts). This means that all the investments you made (or you are ready to make) in learning WPF are also valid in a number of other development platforms; by using the same programming approach you can quickly be productive against different platforms and scenarios. This should be enough to convince you why learning WPF is so important.

PERSONAL SUGGESTIONS ON APPROACHING WPF

I have delivered several technical speeches and trainings on Windows Presentation Foundation, and one thing I've noticed is that lots of developers do not approach WPF correctly. This is because the Internet is full of impressive demo applications with enhanced user interfaces and graphical experience, and lots of presentation demos are built to show advanced WPF topics. Seeing a 3D application with animations is surely impressive, but it can be quite frustrating if you try to reproduce it after a few days' experience with WPF. Because of this, often developers do not continue studying WPF. The best approach is instead to understand what one needs to work with WPF even if the UI is not so impressive. When you know how user controls work and how they are built, you can easily search within the MSDN library to make them nicer.

Improvements in WPF 4.6

If you already have experience with WPF, you might be interested in getting some hints about improvements in the new version. Visual Studio 2015 inherits from Visual Studio 2013 some important improvements to the XAML code editor, such as support for IntelliSense with data binding and resources. The XAML code editor in Visual Studio 2015 also offers the Peek Definition functionality, which you saw in Chapter 2, "The Visual Studio 2015 IDE for Visual Basic." Microsoft has also been very busy improving general WPF performance and support for modern hardware and touch devices. Controls such as `TextBox` and `ComboBox` have been improved to support common touch gestures and stylus input. In addition, Visual Studio 2015 introduces new diagnostic tools to WPF, such as Live Visual Tree, a user interface debugger, and the Timeline tool, which allows you to diagnose performance and understand how the application consumes resources. The Timeline tool is discussed in Chapter 51, "Code Analysis: The .NET Compiler Platform and Tools," because it can be used against Windows 8.1 Store apps, too.

In the next sections you learn the foundations of WPF and learn about specific features of this interesting technology.

> **NOTE**
>
> This is a language-oriented book; therefore, covering every aspect of the WPF technology is not possible. If you want to learn more about the WPF technology, consider *Windows Presentation Foundation Unleashed* from Sams Publishing.

Introducing the WPF Architecture

WPF relies on a layered architecture that is represented in Figure 28.1. The first layer is the Windows operating system. The second layer is constituted by the combination of two communicating layers: User32, which is the part of the operating system responsible for exchanging messages with applications, and the DirectX libraries, which are the real power of WPF. .NET 4.6 improves the WPF Runtime in order to support the most recent version of the DirectX libraries. The next layer is named Milcore and is written in unmanaged code. It is responsible for integrating the unmanaged area of the architecture with the managed architecture that starts from the next layer, the Common Language Runtime (CLR), which is the root of every managed activity or layer. The PresentationCore is the first WPF layer that is responsible for implementing several important features such as the XAML language (covered later) or the integration with media contents. The next layer is the PresentationFramework, which is fundamental because it exposes all namespaces and classes that developers can take advantage of for building applications (and that are also utilized by Visual Studio when generating new projects).

28

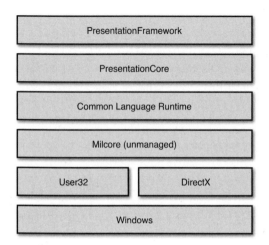

FIGURE 28.1   Windows Presentation Foundation architecture.

PresentationFramework exposes namespaces and classes through a complex hierarchy of inheritance, in which the root class is System.Object. The hierarchy provides the infrastructure for the user interface elements. This hierarchy is composed of the following list of classes, where each class inherits from the previous one:

▶ System.Object

▶ System.Threading.DispatcherObject

▶ System.Windows.DependencyObject

▶ System.Windows.Media.Visual

▶ System.Windows.UIElement

▶ System.Windows.FrameworkElement

▶ System.Windows.Controls.Control

The System.Threading.DispatcherObject is responsible for threading and messages that WPF relies on. The dispatcher takes advantage of the User32 messages for performing cross-thread calls. The WPF architecture is also based on a complex properties infrastructure that in most cases replaces methods and events. This is because a property-based architecture is preferable for showing contents of UI controls and because they better integrate with other development models. To provide this infrastructure, the WPF architecture exposes the System.Windows.DependencyObject class that implements a common set of properties for derived objects. The main capability of this class is keeping track of property changes so that bound objects can automatically update their statuses according to those changes. `System.Windows.Media.Visual` is responsible for the graphic rendering of all elements belonging to the user interface, under the form of a tree (known as Visual Tree that is covered later). `System.Windows.UIElement` adds other functionalities to the infrastructure, such as the capability to receive input from the user and other overridable members. `System.Windows.FrameworkElement` is important, exposing special features of WPF such as objects lifetime, styles, animations, and the data-binding engine. The last class is `System.Windows.Controls.Control`, which is the base class for WPF user controls and that adds further functionalities that empower base controls and custom user controls. Now that you have a basic knowledge of the WPF architecture, it is time to create the first application.

Building WPF Applications with Visual Studio 2015

You create WPF applications in Visual Studio 2015 by selecting one of the available project templates. WPF project templates are available in the Windows Desktop section of the New Project window, as shown in Figure 28.2, and are summarized in Table 28.1 (for your convenience, the list of project templates in Figure 28.2 has been restricted to WPF ones by using the search box, as the figure itself demonstrates).

TABLE 28.1   WPF Project Templates

Template	Description
WPF Application	Allows creating a WPF desktop application for Windows
WPF Browser Application	Allows creating a WPF application that can be run within a web browser
WPF User Control Library	Allows creating WPF user controls
WPF Custom Control Library	Allows redefining WPF controls at code level

This chapter shows you WPF in action with a desktop Windows application.

NOTE

If you have installed the Visual Studio 2015 SDK, you will also see a project template called WPF Toolbox Control, which allows you to package, deploy, and install WPF controls to the IDE's toolbox. (This is beyond the scope of this book.)

Select the **WPF application** template and name the new project **WPFDemo_Chapter28**. After a few seconds, the IDE shows the code editor, so in Solution Explorer double-click the **MainWindow.xaml** file so you access the designer, as shown in Figure 28.3.

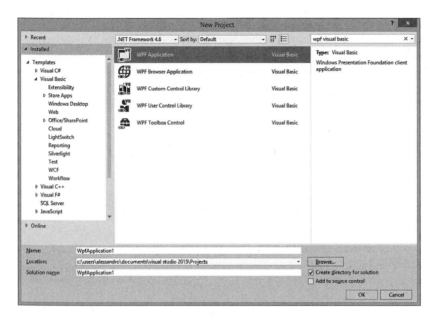

FIGURE 28.2　Available project templates for WPF applications.

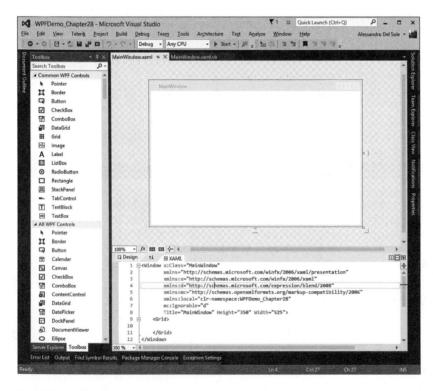

FIGURE 28.3　The IDE is ready on a new WPF project.

As you can see, things are a little different from a Windows Forms project. In the upper part of the IDE, you can see the designer showing the main window of the new application. On the left side is the Toolbox; this is a tool that you already understand and that contains specific WPF controls. In the lower part of the IDE is a special code editor for the *eXtensible Application Markup Language* (XAML, pronounced as *ZAMEL*) that you must know as a WPF developer. The next section describes XAML and explains how it works. In Solution Explorer, you can see a file with the .xaml extension. Each .xaml file can represent a window, control (or set of controls), or set of resources. For each .xaml file there is a Visual Basic code-behind file (with a .xaml.vb extension) that you can access by expanding the filename. The reason for this separation between the .xaml file and the .xaml.vb file is part of a key concept in the WPF development, which is the separation of roles between developers and designers that is described better in the next section.

MY PROJECT

WPF applications enable you to take advantage of the My Project designer similarly to other kinds of client applications. If you examine the window, you see these similarities, and you also see how different options are self-explanatory.

Understanding the eXtensible Application Markup Language

In Windows Presentation Foundation applications, the user interface is defined via the *eXtensible Application Markup Language* (*XAML*), which is a markup language that allows defining the interface in a declarative mode and that derives from the XML language. This markup language is revolutionary because it allows the separation of the roles of designers and developers. Professional designers can style the application's layout by using specific tools that allow generating and editing XAML without the need of knowing the programming fundamentals, leaving unchanged the code that empowers the application.

NOTE ON DESIGNER TOOLS

Designers typically use professional tools such as Microsoft Blend for Visual Studio 2015 (which ships together with Visual Studio) for styling WPF and, more generally, XAML-based applications. Because this book's focus is developer-oriented, the usage of Blend for manipulating XAML is not covered, whereas the focus is on what you do need to know as a developer from within Visual Studio 2015.

This discussion provides an explanation that for each .xaml file there is a VB code-behind file. The .xaml file contains XAML code that defines the user interface, whereas the .xaml.vb code-behind file contains Visual Basic code that makes the user interface alive with the rest of the application. XAML logic is simple: Each XML element represents a user control, and each XML attribute represents a property to a control. Because of the special XML syntax, XAML refers to a specific XML schema for WPF controls.

XAML AND WINDOWS STORE APPS

You need to learn how XAML works if you are also interested in developing mobile applications for Windows 10, Windows Phone 8.1, and Windows 8.1. As explained in Chapter 36, "Building Universal Apps for Windows 10," developing apps for Windows 10 with VB is also based on XAML for the UI side.

Now take a look at Listing 28.1 that contains the code generated by Visual Studio 2015 when a new project is created.

LISTING 28.1   XAML Default Code for a WPF Project

```xml
<Window x:Class="MainWindow"
        xmlns="http://schemas.microsoft.com/winfx/2006/xaml/presentation"
        xmlns:x="http://schemas.microsoft.com/winfx/2006/xaml"
        xmlns:d="http://schemas.microsoft.com/expression/blend/2008"
        xmlns:mc="http://schemas.openxmlformats.org/markup-compatibility/2006"
        xmlns:local="clr-namespace:WPFDemo_Chapter28"
        mc:Ignorable="d"
        Title="MainWindow" Height="350" Width="525">
    <Grid>

    </Grid>
</Window>
```

In WPF applications, every window is wrapped by a `System.Windows.Window` control. The root element in the XAML code is a `Window` element. The `x:Class` attribute (which is actually a property) points to the Visual Basic class that handles the Window on the runtime side. The `Title` property contains text shown on the window's title bar. `Width` and `Height` are self-explanatory properties that define the window's size. Also notice how XML schemas are imported via `xmlns` tags. These schemas have two purposes: enabling IntelliSense in the XAML code editor and ensuring that only valid elements are used in the XAML code.

IMPORTED NAMESPACES

The XAML editor in Visual Studio 2015 automatically imports a `local` namespace that points to the current assembly. This new behavior is very useful because it is very common to point to the current assembly (for example, to use classes that it exposes, like converters). This way, you no longer need to add the namespace manually.

`Grid` is one of the WPF *panels*. Unlike Windows Forms, user controls in WPF are arranged within panels; the last part of this chapter introduces them in more detail. Now you understand better what was explained at the beginning of this section: In XAML every element (except for resources) represents a control with properties (attributes). XAML offers a hierarchical organization of controls. For example, a `Window` can contain one or more panels that can contain other panels that can contain controls, and so on. This hierarchical logic is versatile because it enables great customizations of the interface, as you see in this chapter and subsequent ones. As previously stated, the XAML editor fully supports IntelliSense. You can check this out by writing code, as demonstrated in Figure 28.4.

You are not obliged to manually type XAML code to design your user interface. Every time you drag a control from the Toolbox onto the designer, Visual Studio generates the related XAML code for you and you can assign event handlers in the Properties window. In some circumstances manually editing the XAML code is a good task to fix a control's position. Moreover, although initially writing XAML can seem annoying, when you understand its hierarchical logic, it becomes straightforward, also due to IntelliSense. What you perform manually writing XAML can be accomplished with the design tools.

FIGURE 28.4   The XAML code editor fully supports IntelliSense.

Declaring and Using Controls with the Designer and XAML

To add controls to the user interface, you have two possibilities: dragging controls from the Toolbox onto the designer surface or manually writing XAML. For a better under-standing, you first learn how to drag from the Toolbox. With the Toolbox open, click the **Button** control and drag it onto the designer. When you release it, the IDE should look like Figure 28.5.

28

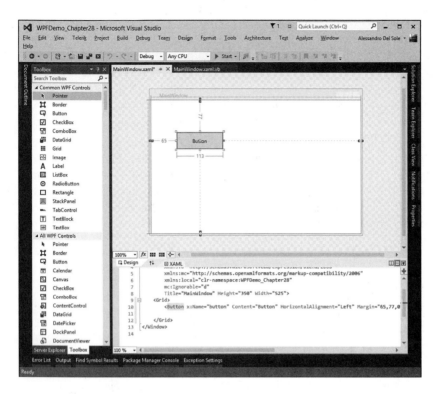

FIGURE 28.5   Dragging controls and generating XAML.

As you can see from Figure 28.5, Visual Studio also generates the XAML code for the controls you add to the UI. For the new button, this is the XAML code generated:

```
<Button Content="Button" Height="39"
        HorizontalAlignment="Left"
        Margin="25,62,0,0" Name="Button1"
        VerticalAlignment="Top" Width="113" />
```

Confirming that each control is represented as an XML element, the most interesting properties here are Name, which assigns an identifier to the control, and Content, which stores the control's content. To manage your controls you now have two choices: editing its XAML code or using the Properties window, which is represented in Figure 28.6.

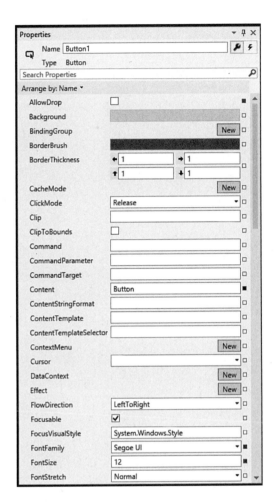

FIGURE 28.6   Managing controls with the Properties window.

28

If you are not familiar with WPF, probably you can find lots of properties that you do not know yet. You can learn most of these properties in this book and in your further studies; what is important here is to understand how the designer can control the UI members. The Properties window for WPF controls also offers a special tab that you can enable by clicking the **Events** button (in the upper side of the tool window); that enables associating event handlers to each event exposed by that specific control (see Figure 28.7). Obviously, event handlers are written in Visual Basic code; the next section explains how you handle events.

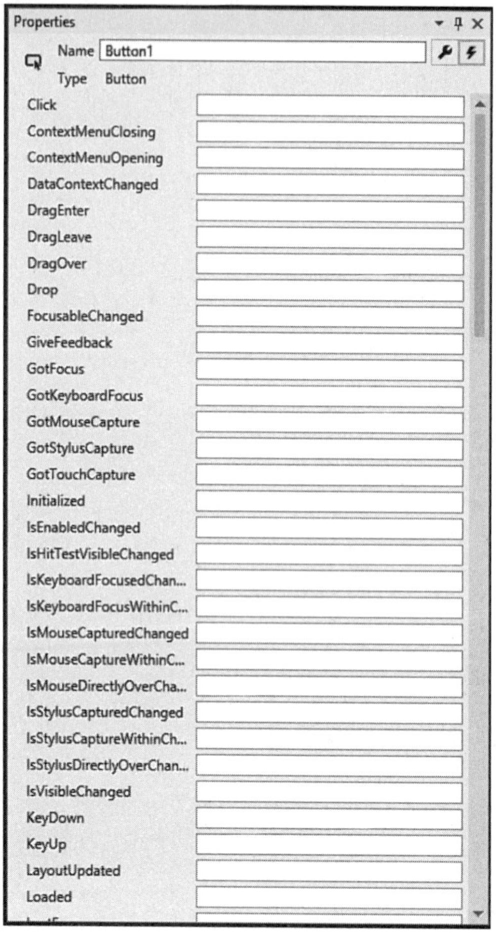

FIGURE 28.7   The Properties window enables the selecting of event handlers.

Declarative and Imperative Modes

Writing (or letting Visual Studio generate) XAML code is known as *declarative mode*. This is because XAML allows declaring elements required by the user interface but does not allow them taking actions. By the way, an important statement is that with Visual Basic (or Visual C# as well) you can do anything you do in XAML, meaning that you can declare user interface elements in Visual Basic code and add them to the user interface at runtime. Moreover, managing controls with Visual Basic allows them taking actions. This is the *imperative mode*. For a better explanation, consider the following XAML code that declares a simple button:

```
<Button Content="Button" Height="30"
        Name="Button1"
        Width="100"/>
```

The same thing can be also accomplished in Visual Basic. The following code demonstrates this:

```
Dim Button1 As New Button
With Button1
    Width = 100
    Height = 30
    Content = "Button1"
End With
Me.Grid1.Children.Add(Button1)
```

The difference is that in Visual Basic you need to explicitly add your control to a panel in the user interface.

Understanding Visual Tree and Logical Tree

When talking about WPF applications, you will often hear about the Logical Tree and the Visual Tree. The Logical Tree is a tree representation of the .NET classes for user interface controls. Consider the following XAML code:

```
<Window>
    <StackPanel Orientation="Horizontal" Margin="5">
        <TextBlock Text="Sample controls" Margin="5"/>
        <Button Content="Test button" Margin="5"/>
    </StackPanel>
</Window>
```

This code uses .NET objects within a hierarchical structure that can be reconfigured in a Logical Tree, as shown in Figure 28.8.

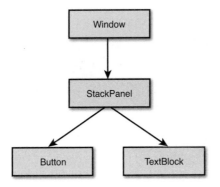

FIGURE 28.8   The Logical Tree provides a hierarchical view of the UI elements.

You can investigate the Logical Tree in a more convenient way, with the Document Outline tool window (you find it in **View, Other Windows**) that provides a hierarchical view of the interface (see Figure 28.9).

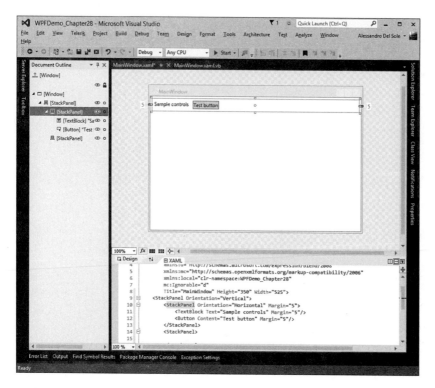

FIGURE 28.9   Investigating the Logical Tree with the Document Outline tool.

The Visual Tree is a more complex concept that is important. As explained in the next chapters, WPF controls are the result of the aggregation of primitive elements, and they can be completely redefined with control templates. For example, a default `Button` is made of `Chrome`, `ContentPresenter`, and `TextBlock` controls. The combination of these elements creates a `Visual`, which represents a visual element in the user interface. The Visual Tree is thus the representation of all the visual elements in the UI that are rendered to the screen, plus their components. Consider the following simple XAML:

```
<StackPanel Orientation="Horizontal" Margin="5">
    <Button Content="Test button" Margin="5"/>
</StackPanel>
```

The visual tree representation is reported in Figure 28.10.

Understanding the Visual Tree is important for understanding another key concept in the WPF development: routed events. These are described just after introducing how you handle events in WPF.

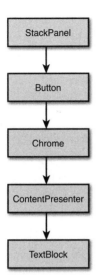

FIGURE 28.10   The Visual Tree representation for UI elements.

Handling Events in WPF

You handle events in WPF the same way you do in other kinds of applications: You code a Visual Basic event handler and associate the handler to a control event. What actually changes is the way you assign the handler to the event. For example, you can assign an event handler to a control event directly within the XAML code editor. To accomplish this, you type the name of the event you want to handle (events are recognizable within IntelliSense with the Lightning icon) and then press **Tab** when IntelliSense shows the <New Event Handler> pop-up command (see Figure 28.11 for details).

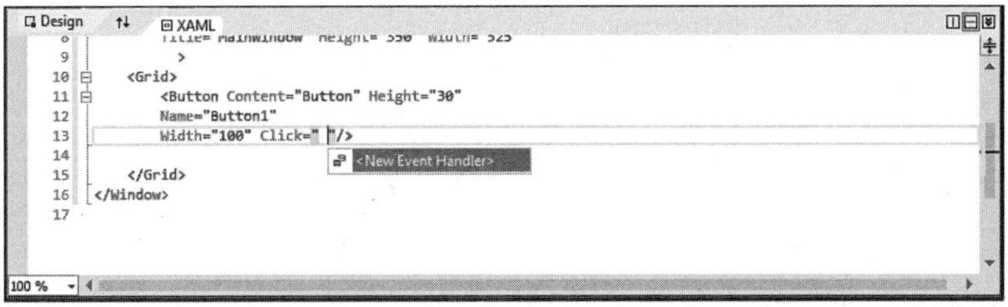

```
 Design  ↑↓   XAML
   8            Title= MainWindow  Height= 350  Width= 525
   9          >
  10       <Grid>
  11          <Button Content="Button" Height="30"
  12             Name="Button1"
  13             Width="100" Click=" "/>
  14                         <New Event Handler>
  15       </Grid>
  16   </Window>
  17
100 %
```

FIGURE 28.11   Generating a new event handler with IntelliSense.

This generates an event handler stub in your code-behind file. Continuing the example of the previous button, Visual Studio first assigns a new identifier to the *Click* event in XAML, which looks like this:

```
Click="Button1_Click"
```

As you can see, the IDE generates the event handler's identifier considering the control's name. Now right-click the event handler's name and select the **Go to Definition** command from the pop-up menu. This redirects to the Visual Basic event handler generated for you, which looks like this:

```
Private Sub Button1_Click(ByVal sender As System.Object,
                          ByVal e As System.Windows.RoutedEventArgs)


End Sub
```

It is worth mentioning two aspects. The first one is that the event handler signature requires an argument of type `RoutedEventArgs`. WPF introduces the concept of routed events that is covered in the next section. The second one is that in this case there is no `Handles` clause. This is because the IDE added an `AddHandler` instruction behind the scenes in the Window1.g.vb file (which is generated at compile time). Notice that such a filename depends on the current `Window` name, in this case `Window1`. As an alternative, you can specify the `Handles` clause the same way you would do in other kinds of applications. However, in this case you must not specify the event handler in XAML, to avoid an event being caught twice. You can also double-click a control in the designer to generate an event handler for the default event. For instance, say a button's default event is `Click`, so double-clicking a button in the designer generates an event handler stub for handling the `Click` event. The default event for a `TextBox` control is `TextChanged`, so double-clicking a text box generates an event handler stub for the `TextChanged` event, and so on. When you add event handlers by double-clicking `controls`, such handlers use the `Handles` clause on the method name. As previously mentioned, the last alternative is to assign an existing event handler to a control's event with the Properties window.

A More Thorough Discussion: Introducing the Routed Events

WPF introduces a revolutionary way to generate and handle events, known as *routed events*. When a user's interface element generates an event, the event passes along through the entire Visual Tree, rethrowing the event for each element in the tree. The WPF runtime can then understand what element first generated the event that is the actual handled event. Event handlers whose job is managing a routed event must include an object of type `System.Windows.RoutedEventArgs` in their signature. For a better understanding, consider the following basic XAML code that implements three buttons:

```
<StackPanel Button.Click="OnClick">
    <Button Width="100" Height="30"
            Content="Button One" Name="Button1" />
    <Button Width="100" Height="30"
            Content="Button Two" Name="Button2" />
    <Button Width="100" Height="30"
            Content="Button Three" Name="Button3" />
</StackPanel>
```

Notice how no event handler is specified for buttons, whereas a unique handler is specified within the `StackPanel` definition taking advantage of the `Button.Click` attached event. This enables the establishing of one event handler for each button in the `StackPanel`'s children. In the code-behind file, write the following handler:

```
Private Sub OnClick(ByVal sender As Object, ByVal e As RoutedEventArgs)

    Dim element As FrameworkElement = CType(e.Source,
                                            FrameworkElement)

    Select Case element.Name
        Case Is = "Button1"
            MessageBox.Show("You clicked Button1")
        Case Is = "Button2"
            MessageBox.Show("You clicked Button2")
        Case Is = "Button3"
            MessageBox.Show("You clicked Button3")
    End Select
End Sub
```

Thanks to routed events, you can write just one common handler. To get the instance of the element that actually generated the event, you need to convert the `e.Source` property (which is of type `Object`) into the appropriate type. In this case the conversion could be with a `Button` type, but `FrameworkElement` is utilized to include various kinds of elements or controls. This is because with routed events you can intercept events from each element in the Visual Tree (such as the `ContentPresenter` for buttons), thus not only user controls.

Introducing Routing Strategies: Direct, Tunneling, and Bubbling

Routed events are implemented according to three modes, known as *routing strategies*. Strategies are implemented by the `System.Windows.RoutingStrategy` enumeration and can be summarized as follows:

▶ **Direct**—The event is generated directly against the target object. This is what usually happens in other kinds of .NET applications, such as Windows Forms, and is the most uncommon strategy in WPF.

▶ **Tunnel**—In the tunneling strategy, an event is generated from the root object and passes through the entire Visual Tree until getting to the target object.

▶ **Bubble**—The bubbling strategy is opposite to the tunneling one, meaning that an event starts from the target object and passes back through the Visual Tree.

In most cases, such as the preceding code example, you face tunneling routed events or bubbling ones. Offering a thorough discussion on routed events is beyond the scope of this chapter; you can refer to the MSDN official page that you can find at http://msdn.microsoft.com/en-us/library/ms742806(VS.110).aspx.

28

Arranging Controls with Panels

WPF changes the way you arrange controls on the user interface. This is because one goal of WPF is to provide the ability to create dynamic interfaces that can be rearranged according to the user's preferences or when the user resizes the interface. Because of this, WPF controls are arranged within special containers, known as panels. WPF provides several panels, each allowing different arrangement possibilities. This is different from Windows Forms, where you place controls on the user interface, but the controls are not flexible. Although some types of panels are available, Windows Forms panels are not as versatile as WPF panels. In this section you learn about WPF panels and how you use them to arrange controls. The most important thing that you have to keep in mind is that WPF controls have a hierarchical logic; therefore, you can nest multiple panels to create complex user experiences. Panels are all exposed by the `System.Windows.Controls` namespace from the PresentationFramework.dll assembly.

The `Grid` Panel

The `Grid` is one of the easiest panels to understand in WPF. It allows creating tables, with rows and columns. In this way you can define cells and each cell can contain a control or another panel storing nested controls. The `Grid` is versatile in that you can just divide it into rows or into columns or both. The following code defines a `Grid` that is divided into two rows and two columns:

```
<Grid>
    <Grid.RowDefinitions>
        <RowDefinition />
        <RowDefinition />
    </Grid.RowDefinitions>
    <Grid.ColumnDefinitions>
        <ColumnDefinition />
        <ColumnDefinition />
    </Grid.ColumnDefinitions>

</Grid>
```

`RowDefinitions` is a collection of `RowDefinition` objects, and the same is true for `ColumnDefinitions` and `ColumnDefinition`. Each item represents a row or a column within the `Grid` respectively. You can also specify a `Width` or a `Height` property to delimit row and column dimensions; if you do not specify anything, both rows and columns are dimensioned at the maximum size available, and when resizing the parent container, rows and columns are automatically rearranged. The preceding code creates a table with four cells. The Visual Studio 2015 Designer offers a convenient way for designing rows and columns. When the cursor is within the `Grid` definition in the XAML code editor or when the `Grid` has the focus in the designer, you use the `Rows` and `Columns` properties in the Properties window. Figure 28.12 shows how you add columns to the `Grid` and how you can set properties for each column. Adding rows works exactly the same.

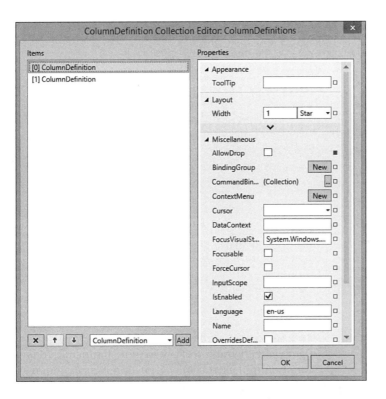

FIGURE 28.12   Adding columns with design tools.

To place controls in the Grid, you specify the row and column position. The following code places two buttons, the first one in the upper-left cell and the second one in the upper-right cell:

```
<Button Width="100" Height="50" Grid.Column="0"
        Grid.Row="0" Name="Button1" Content="First button"/>
<Button Width="100" Height="50" Grid.Column="1"
        Grid.Row="0" Name="Button2" Content="Second button"/>
```

To place controls, you select the column via the Grid.Column property, whose index is zero-based, meaning that 0 is the first column from the left. This kind of property is known as *attached property* and allows setting a property of a parent container from within the current object. Specifying the row works similarly, in that you assign the row via the Grid.Row attached property. The property's index is also zero-based, meaning that 0 represents the first row from the top. You can place nested containers within a cell or a single row or column. The following code shows how to nest a grid with children control into a single cell:

```
<Grid Grid.Row="1" Grid.Column="0">
    <Grid.ColumnDefinitions>
        <ColumnDefinition />
```

28

```
        <ColumnDefinition />
    </Grid.ColumnDefinitions>
    <Grid.RowDefinitions>
        <RowDefinition />
        <RowDefinition />
    </Grid.RowDefinitions>

    <Button Width="50" Height="50" Grid.Column="0"
        Grid.Row="0" Name="Button3" Content="Button3"/>
    <Button Width="50" Height="50" Grid.Column="1"
        Grid.Row="0" Name="Button4" Content="Button4"/>
</Grid>
```

If you run the code shown in this section, you get the result shown in Figure 28.13. This should give you an idea on how controls can be placed within a `Grid`.

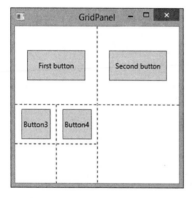

FIGURE 28.13   Arranging controls within a `Grid`.

SHOWING GRID LINES

Grid lines are not shown by default. To make them visible, add a `ShowGridLines` property to the `Grid` element and set its value to `True`.

PERSONAL SUGGESTION

Each time you study a WPF container, try to resize the application windows or controls so that you can get a good idea of how panels work.

The `StackPanel` Panel

The `StackPanel` panel allows placing controls near each other, as in a stack that can be arranged both horizontally and vertically. As with other containers, the `StackPanel` can contain nested panels. The following code shows how you can arrange controls horizontally and vertically. The root `StackPanel` contains two nested panels:

```
<StackPanel Orientation="Vertical">
    <StackPanel Orientation="Horizontal" Margin="5">
        <TextBlock Text="Sample controls" Margin="5"/>
        <Button Content="Test button" Margin="5"/>
    </StackPanel>

    <StackPanel Orientation="Vertical" Margin="5">
        <TextBlock Text="Sample controls" Margin="5"/>
        <Button Content="Test button" Margin="5"/>
    </StackPanel>
</StackPanel>
```

The `Orientation` property can be set as `Horizontal` or `Vertical`, and this influences the final layout. One of the main benefits of XAML code is that element names and properties are self-explanatory, and this is the case of `StackPanel`'s properties, too. Remember that controls within a `StackPanel` are automatically resized according to the orientation. If you do not like this behavior, you need to specify `Width` and `Height` properties. If you run this code, you get the result shown in Figure 28.14.

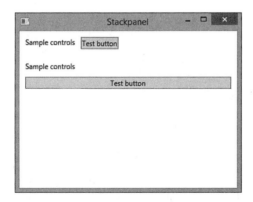

FIGURE 28.14   Arranging controls within `StackPanel`s.

If you want to provide a dynamic user interface, you need to take care of some considerations. If you do not provide static `Width` and `Height` values, your controls will be resized along with the `StackPanel`, which also automatically adapts to its parent container.

Alternatively, controls arranged within a `StackPanel` are not resized, but they have the limitation of being hidden when decreasing the parent's container size, as better represented in Figure 28.15.

If you predict that your application will encounter such a situation, you should implement a `WrapPanel` panel, which is covered in the next subsection.

FIGURE 28.15   Resizing fixed controls within a `StackPanel` causes them to be hidden.

The `WrapPanel` Panel

The `WrapPanel` container works like `StackPanel`, but it differs in that it can rearrange controls on multiple lines in the interface so that they are never hidden. Figures 28.16 and 28.17 show how the `WrapPanel` enables the rearranging of controls when resizing the parent container (a `Window`, in our examples).

FIGURE 28.16   `WrapPanel` arranges controls similarly to the `StackPanel`.

FIGURE 28.17 `WrapPanel` rearranges controls dynamically making them always visible, as if they were implemented line-by-line.

In code terms, the panel is represented by a `WrapPanel` element in XAML. The following code reproduces what you saw in the previous figures:

```
<WrapPanel>
    <TextBlock Text="WrapPanel test" Margin="5"/>
    <Button Width="140" Height="30" Content="Test Button"
            Margin="5"/>
    <TextBlock Text="Second test" Margin="5"/>
</WrapPanel>
```

The `VirtualizingStackPanel` Control

In some situations you need to show a big number of elements in your user interface. This is the case of the `DataGrid` or `ListBox` controls, which can display hundreds of elements within a single control. This would heavily affect the application performances if you were using a classic `StackPanel`, which would show all the available items. The `VirtualizingStackPanel` control offers a valid alternative that can calculate how many items can appear in a particular moment and then arranges controls according to the calculation result. You do not need to implement the `VirtualizingStackPanel` manually (it is the default item template of data controls) but, if you need to, you write the following definition:

```
<VirtualizingStackPanel>
    <!--Nest controls here...-->
</VirtualizingStackPanel>
```

This kind of panel works like the `StackPanel`, with the previously described difference.

The `Canvas` Panel

Most WPF containers allow the dynamic rearrangement of controls within the user interface. This is useful when you want your user to adjust interface settings, but it can

28

complicate things when you need to place controls in a fixed, unchangeable place (as happens in Windows Forms). To accomplish this, you use the `Canvas` container, which allows absolute placement, meaning that it allows specifying the position of nested controls. When you place controls into a `Canvas` container, you specify the absolute position with some attached properties: `Canvas.Left`, `Canvas.Top`, `Canvas.Right`, and `Canvas.Bottom`. The following code shows how you place a button that never changes its position in the user interface, thanks to the `Canvas.Left` and `Canvas.Top` attached properties:

```
<Canvas>
    <Button Width="100" Height="50" Content="Test Button"
            Canvas.Left="30" Canvas.Top="50"/>
</Canvas>
```

The `DockPanel` Panel

The `DockPanel` container has some similarities with the `StackPanel` in that it allows arranging child controls near each other. The main difference in `DockPanel` is that child controls are docked to the panel sides according to the direction you specify, and they are docked to each other and you can establish the position and size for each child control. The most common usage of the `DockPanel` panel is creating interfaces for placing menus and toolbars. The following example shows how you can dock multiple toolbars and their buttons within a `DockPanel`:

```
<DockPanel VerticalAlignment="Top"
           LastChildFill="True">
    <ToolBar DockPanel.Dock="Top"
             Name="MainToolbar" >
        <Button Content="First Button"/>
        <Button Content="Second Button"/>
    </ToolBar>

    <ToolBar DockPanel.Dock="Top"
             Name="NextToolbar" >
        <Button Content="First Button"/>
        <Button Content="Second Button"/>
    </ToolBar>
</DockPanel>
```

You set the `DockPanel` orientation by specifying either the `VerticalAlignment` property or `HorizontalAlignment`. The `LastChildFill` is a property that indicates whether child controls must completely fill the available blank space in the container. Notice how within child controls (such as the Toolbars) you specify the docking position by taking advantage of an attached property named `DockPanel.Dock`, whose value indicates where the control must be docked within the `DockPanel`. This is because child controls are not limited to being docked into one side of the `panel` but can be docked into any of the four sides. The preceding code produces the result shown in Figure 28.18.

FIGURE 28.18 Docking controls within a `DockPanel`.

The `ViewBox` Panel

The `ViewBox` panel allows adapting nested controls to its size, including the content of controls. For example, consider the following code:

```
<Viewbox>
    <Button Width="150" Height="75">
        ViewBoxed button
    </Button>
</Viewbox>
```

You immediately notice how the button's text is expanded to best fit the button size. This also happens if you decrease or increase the window size, as demonstrated in Figure 28.19.

FIGURE 28.19 The `ViewBox` panel in action.

In a few words, the `ViewBox` allows resizing controls and their content.

28

Managing Windows

WPF allows managing windows similarly to Windows Forms, although there are some obvious differences, such as the fact that WPF windows can be considered as the root container for all other child panels when arranging UI elements. Whatever way you decide to apply windows properties, at design time such properties are addressed in XAML code, but you are also allowed to set them at runtime in Visual Basic code. Available properties enable the establishing of the window startup position, its resize mode, its appearance on the task bar, and so on. Table 28.2 summarizes the most important available properties.

TABLE 28.2   `Window`'s Properties

Name	Description
`Title`	Specifies text for the window title bar
`WindowStartupLocation`	Specifies the position for the window when it is first loaded (can be `Manual`, `CenterScreen`, or `CenterOwner`)
`WindowState`	Specifies the window state when loaded (can be `Normal`, `Maximized`, or `Minimized`)
`WindowStyle`	Specifies the window layout style (`None`, `SingleBorderWindow`, `ThreeDBorderWindow`, or `ToolWindow`)
`TopMost`	Makes the window always visible on top
`ShowInTaskBar`	Makes the window title visible in the operating system task bar
`Background`	Allows specifying a brush for the background color (see Chapter 30, "Brushes, Styles, Templates, and Animations in WPF")
`BorderBrush`	Specifies a color or brush for the Window border
`BorderThickness`	Specifies how thick the border is

You can take advantage of the Properties tool window for setting the previously mentioned properties at design time. The following XAML code snippet shows how you can set some window properties:

```
<!-- The following code sets the Window as Maximized,
    its startup position at the center of the screen,
    its style as a Window with 3D borders and keeps it
    always on top. It also replaces the default title-->
<Window x:Class="MainWindow"
    xmlns="http://schemas.microsoft.com/winfx/2006/xaml/presentation"
    xmlns:x="http://schemas.microsoft.com/winfx/2006/xaml"
    Title="Chapter 28 demonstration" Height="240" Width="500"
    WindowStartupLocation="CenterScreen"
    WindowState="Maximized" WindowStyle="ThreeDBorderWindow"
    Topmost="True">
</Window>
```

This is what you do at design time. The same result can be accomplished in managed code as follows:

```
'Me is the current Window
With Me
    Title = "Chapter 31 demonstration"
    WindowStartupLocation = WindowStartupLocation.
                            CenterScreen
    WindowState = WindowState.
                  Maximized
    WindowStyle = WindowStyle.
                  ThreeDBorderWindow
    Topmost = True
End With
```

To add more `Window` objects to your project you select the **Project**, **Add Window** command and assign the filename in the New Item dialog box. Remember that every Window in the project inherits from `System.Windows.Window`. When you have multiple windows in your project, you can also establish which of them must be the startup object. To accomplish this, go to My Project and select the new window in the Startup URI combo box. Figure 28.20 shows how to accomplish this.

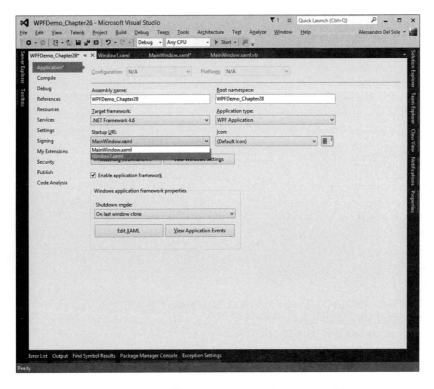

FIGURE 28.20   Selecting a different `Window` as the startup object.

The window is specified via the related XAML file address (Uri).

Instantiating Windows at Runtime

Creating and displaying windows at runtime is a common task in every client application. To do this, you create an instance of a `System.Windows.Window` and then invoke the `Show` or `ShowDialog` methods, depending on whether the `Window` must be considered a modal dialog box. The following Visual Basic code demonstrates how you create and show a new `Window`:

```
Dim aWindow As New Window
'Set your Window properties here...
aWindow.ShowDialog()
'....
aWindow.Close()
```

In the preceding code, a new Window is generated from scratch, so this requires specifying all properties. In most cases you can instead create and show instances of existing windows that you implemented at design time; for this, in the above code you just replace Window with the name of your custom window. This works the same as Windows Forms, although all the backend technology is completely different. This approach helps you when moving your Windows Forms applications to WPF.

Introducing the Application Object

As for Windows Forms, WPF also provides an `Application` class that allows interacting with your application instance. The class exposes several methods and properties that allow the getting or assigning of settings available within My Project. First, you need to get the instance of the running application. You accomplish this by assigning the `Application.Current` property to a variable as follows:

```
Dim myApp As Application = CType(Application.Current, Application)
```

When you get the instance of the application, you can get or set required information. The following code shows how you can retrieve the startup Uri (which corresponds to the startup object referred to in a XAML file), the main application window, and assembly information:

```
'Gets the startup object under the form of a XAML file
Dim startupObject As Uri = myApp.StartupUri

'Gets (but also allows setting) the application main window
Dim mainWindow As Window = myApp.MainWindow

'Get assembly information
With myApp.Info
    Dim companyName As String = .CompanyName
    Dim appName As String = .ProductName

    'get other info here...
End With
```

The `Application` class does not directly expose a `Close` method as instead happens in Windows Forms. If you want to programmatically shut down your application, you invoke the `Current.ShutDown` shared method as follows:

```
Application.Current.Shutdown()
```

Table 28.3 summarizes the most important members of the `Application` class.

TABLE 28.3   Application Class's Most Important Members

Member	Type	Description
Current	Property	Returns the instance of the running application.
Dispatcher	Property	Returns the instance of the `Dispatcher` for the current application. The `Dispatcher` is responsible for managing threads.
FindResource	Method	Searches for the specified resource (which is at XAML level).
Info	Property	Returns a collection of assembly information.
LoadComponent	Method	Loads a XAML file from the specified Uri and then converts the resulting object into an instance that is added to the application.
Main	Method	The application entry point.
MainWindow	Property	Returns the instance of the Window object that is first run at startup.
Resources	Property	Returns a collection of resources.
Run	Method	Runs a WPF application.
Shutdown	Method	Shuts down the application.
ShutdownMode	Property	Gets or sets how an application must shut down.
StartupUri	Property	Returns the Uri of the XAML file that is loaded at startup.
Windows	Property	Returns a collection of `Window` objects that have been instantiated in the application.

28

TIP

Chapter 19, "The `My` Namespace," discussed the `My` namespace. WPF applications provide a special extension of `My` that allows interacting with the application by invoking the `My.Application` property.

The `Application` class is also important for another reason: It contains the entry point (that is, the `Sub Main`) that effectively runs your application and is the place where you control application events, such as the startup or the shutdown. This class is implemented as a partial class. In Solution Explorer, you can find the Application.xaml file that can store application-level resources; the file has a code-behind counterpart named Application.xaml.vb where you can write code that influences the entire application instead of single elements of the user interface. The following code shows how you can handle the `Startup` and `Exit` events that represent the initial and final moments of the application lifetime:

```vbnet
Class Application

    ' Application-level events, such as Startup, Exit,
    ' and DispatcherUnhandledException
    ' can be handled in this file.

    Private Sub Application_Startup(ByVal sender As Object,
                                    ByVal e As System.Windows.
                                                StartupEventArgs) _
                                    Handles Me.Startup
        MessageBox.Show("Application is starting up")
    End Sub

    Private Sub Application_Exit(ByVal sender As Object,
                                 ByVal e As System.Windows.ExitEventArgs) _
                                 Handles Me.Exit
        MessageBox.Show("Application is closing")
    End Sub
End Class
```

You use the `Application` class for controlling specific moments in the lifetime; when you instead need to set application properties, the best choice is opening the My Project designer.

Brief Overview of WPF Browser Applications

Since the first version of WPF, developers have been allowed to build applications that can run within a web browser, such as Microsoft Internet Explorer or Mozilla Firefox. This kind of application is named WPF Browser Applications (formerly known as Xaml Browser Applications) or XBAP. Several differences exist between a client application and an XBAP; first, Browser Applications can only be executed online (from the Internet or an intranet). Second, they are executed with the limitations of the Internet Zone of the .NET Framework's Code Access Security rules. Because of this, Browser Applications cannot perform several tasks. The main advantage is instead that, keeping in mind the previously mentioned limitations, you can use the same programming model.

AVOID BROWSER APPLICATIONS

WPF Browser Applications are not intended to be Web applications. You should use ASP. NET to build Web applications instead of Browser Applications. These are kept for compatibility reasons, but situations where you should use them are limited. If your company needs an online application with WPF capabilities but with a small number of functionalities, Browser Applications could do well, but ASP.NET 4.6 and ASP.NET Core 5 provide a full-featured environment for each kind of Web application.

You create an application of this kind by selecting the **WPF Browser Application** project template from the New Project window. Then, create a new Browser Application naming the project **WpfBrowserApplication_Chapter28**. When the project is ready, you soon notice another difference from classic WPF applications. In the XAML code editor, you can see how the root object is now a `Page` instead of a `Window`. This is required for applications to work within a web browser. The second difference is the presence of a strong name file (with .pfx extension) in Solution Explorer. This is required because of the CAS rules. At this point you can implement some features to see the application in action. The goal of the example is to create an application that can validate an email address showing the validation result. Listing 28.2 shows the user interface implementation, which is simple.

LISTING 28.2   Defining the XBAP's Interface

```
<Page x:Class="Page1"
    xmlns="http://schemas.microsoft.com/winfx/2006/xaml/presentation"
    xmlns:x="http://schemas.microsoft.com/winfx/2006/xaml"
    xmlns:mc="http://schemas.openxmlformats.org/markup-compatibility/2006"
    xmlns:d="http://schemas.microsoft.com/expression/blend/2008"
    mc:Ignorable="d"
    d:DesignHeight="300" d:DesignWidth="300"
    Title="Page1">
    <StackPanel>
        <Label Content="Enter the e-mail address to validate:" Margin="5"/>
        <TextBox Name="MailTextBox" Margin="5"/>
        <Button Width="100" Height="30" Content="Validate" Margin="5"
            Name="Button1" />
    </StackPanel>
</Page>
```

On the Visual Basic side, you need to implement a method that validates the user input and an event handler for the button's `Click` event. Code in Listing 28.3 shows how to accomplish this.

LISTING 28.3   Providing Actions for the XAML Browser Application

```
Imports System.Text.RegularExpressions

Class Page1

    Private Sub Button1_Click(ByVal sender As System.Object,
                        ByVal e As System.Windows.RoutedEventArgs) _
                        Handles Button1.Click

        If String.IsNullOrEmpty(Me.MailTextBox.Text) = True Then Exit Sub
```

28

```
        MessageBox.Show("Is a valid address: " & IsValidEMail(Me.MailTextBox.Text))

    End Sub

    Function IsValidEMail(ByVal EMailAddress As String) _
            As Boolean
        Dim validateMail As String = _
        "^([\w-\.]+)@((\[[0-9]{1,3}\.[0-9]{1,3}\.)" & _
        "|(([\w-]+\.)+))([a-zA-z]{2,4}|[0-9]{1,3})(\]?)$"

        Return Regex.IsMatch(EMailAddress, _
                        validateMail)

    End Function
End Class
```

Notice how you handle a routed event the same way you would in a Windows application. The IsValidEmail method is already explained in this book; it uses regular expressions for validation. If you run the application, you get the result shown in Figure 28.21.

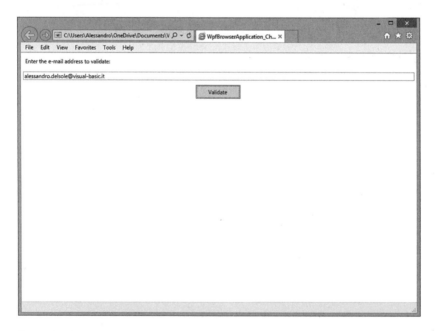

FIGURE 28.21   The WPF Browser Application running in the default web browser.

When the application is launched from the Visual Studio debugger, the default web
browser is launched and points to the application.

XBAP DEPLOYMENT

Deploying an XBAP is a task that you should perform through ClickOnce. This technology, which is covered in Chapter 50, "Deploying Applications with ClickOnce," is perfect for this purpose because it can deploy the application to a web server, manage CAS settings, and deploy an application as "online" (a required scenario for XBAPs). Finally, ClickOnce cannot install assemblies to the GAC, and thus you can be sure that the target machine will not be affected.

Live Visual Tree

Visual Studio 2015 introduces a new interesting tool for WPF debugging, called Live Visual Tree. With this tool, you can analyze the whole visual tree of a WPF application running in debug mode and see real-time property values for each object. This tool starts automatically when you press **F5** to debug a WPF application. Figure 28.22 shows an example.

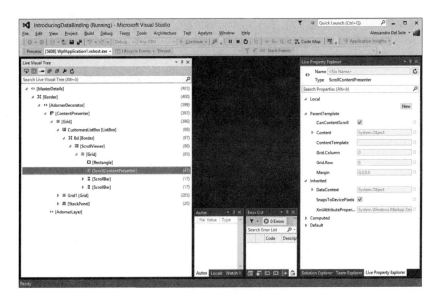

FIGURE 28.22   Live Visual Tree and Live Property Explorer.

Live Visual Tree is basically a tool window (on the left side of the IDE, as shown in Figure 28.22) that allows you to browse the current window's visual tree. When you select any item in the visual tree, the Live Property Explorer tool window (on the right side of the IDE) shows real-time property values for the selected object. This is particularly useful for inspecting application execution when the user interface's behavior may vary depending on user choices or when some objects change their property values at runtime.

Live Visual Tree is all about the user interface composition and does not allow you to analyze performance. If you need to analyze how your application spends its time, you can use the new Diagnostic Tools described in Chapter 51.

Summary

In this chapter you took a first look at the Windows Presentation Foundation technology. You saw what WPF is and how it is architected. You then saw how to create your first WPF application with Visual Studio 2015, getting a high-level introduction of the XAML markup language and the interaction with managed code. For the architecture, you learned about some concepts such as the Logical Tree and the Visual Tree. For the Visual Tree, understanding this led you to another key concept: routed events. These events enable the generating of cascade events through the hierarchical structure of the user interface. After this, you made a contact with WPF, understanding how you arrange controls within panels, getting also a first overview of all available panels. Last, you saw another kind of client application in action with WPF: Browser Applications. You saw how this kind of application can run within a web browser, although with some limitations due to their nature. With these basics, you are now ready to take some more control over WPF. This is the goal of the next chapters.

CHAPTER 29

WPF Common Controls

Being a technology for Windows desktop applications, Windows Presentation Foundation offers built-in controls that you can immediately use in your applications to build rich user interfaces. You can also build your own custom controls. WPF 4.6 offers a good standard toolbox, provided by the System.Windows.Controls namespace. If you are new to WPF and you come from the Windows Forms experience, you can certainly find differences in controls implementation between the two technologies, but, fortunately, you will feel at home because of the names. Look for WPF controls that are counterparts to Windows Forms interface elements. In this chapter you first learn some important features in WPF controls; next, you take a tour through the most common user controls so you can start building your user interface.

Introducing WPF Controls Features

Before using WPF controls, you need to understand some behaviors. In Chapter 28, "Creating WPF Applications," you learned that UI elements, including controls, are declared in XAML code. You also saw how to assign a name to controls to interact with them in Visual Basic code. XAML allows you to declare and implement controls even if you do not assign a name. For example, the following Button declaration is legal:

```
<Button Width="100" Height="50" Click="OnClick"/>
```

The control declared in this way works normally as you would expect, also raising click events that you can handle in managed code. This is possible because of the particular WPF architecture part that implements routed events discussed in Chapter 28. When an unnamed control raises an event, the event passes through the entire Visual Tree, and the WPF runtime can intercept the event independently from the control name. Providing a name therefore is useful when you need to assign properties in managed code or when you want to assign an event handler to a specific visual element. Another interesting feature is that WPF controls are defined as *lookless*. This means that WPF controls are classes that expose a series of properties defining the behavior of controls while the look is assigned via a *template*. When you drag a WPF control from the toolbox to the designer, the control takes advantage of a standard template that defines its layout, but templates can be completely customized or overridden with the so-called *control templates*. Chapter 30, "Brushes, Styles, Templates, and Animations in WPF," provides more examples and explanations, but you need to understand the concept before examining common controls. Basing controls' layout on templates enables roles separation between developers and designers and is the reason Microsoft created a tool such as Blend for Visual Studio 2015. Another fundamental feature in WPF control is that it can contain almost any visual elements. This is possible with the `ContentControl` item, which is the subject of the next section.

WPF CONTROLS AND WINRT CONTROLS

Understanding WPF controls is useful for Windows Store app development, too. In most cases, controls described here have a counterpart in Windows Store apps, and this is why a similar discussion is not provided in Chapter 36, "Building Universal Apps for Windows 10."

Understanding the `ContentControl`

One of the biggest presentation benefits in WPF is the capability for controls to show more than simple text. Particularly, all controls exposing a `Content` property can nest complex visual elements to offer special effects with or without text. For example, consider the following button whose content is just text:

```
<Button Name="Button1" Width="100" Height="100" Content="Click me!"/>
```

The `Content` property can be declared in a hierarchical fashion so that you can take advantage of the XAML logic for nesting complex elements. The following example shows how you can replace the button text with a movie:

```
<Button Name="Button1" Width="100" Height="100">
    <Button.Content>
        <MediaElement Source="MyVideo.wmv" LoadedBehavior="Play"/>
    </Button.Content>
</Button>
```

At this point your button plays a video instead of showing the `Click me!` text. This is possible because of a special element named `ContentControl` that provides the capability to embed complex visual elements within controls offering the `Content` property.

It is an invisible element, but its presence is noticeable when you can get these results. Another example is nesting multiple elements within a panel as the child element of the ContentControl. The following example shows how you can embed text and video together:

```
<Button Name="Button1" Width="100" Height="100">
   <Button.Content>
    <StackPanel>
       <MediaElement LoadedBehavior="Play"
                      Source="MyVideo.wmv"/>
       <TextBlock Text="Click me!"/>
    </StackPanel>
   </Button.Content>
</Button>
```

It is fundamental to understand the existence of the ContentControl because even the most classic controls can be enriched with complex visual elements with a couple lines of code.

Understanding Common Controls

In this section you learn about the most common controls in Windows Presentation Foundation. In most cases, XAML implementation is provided because this is the place where you define your user interface; remember that everything you do in XAML is reproducible in Visual Basic code for runtime handling (refer to Chapter 28).

The Border Control

Consider the Border control as a special container that draws a border around the child control, with the specified color, thickness, and corner radius. The following XAML code draws a red border with a depth of 3 around a rectangle:

```
<Border BorderBrush="Red" BorderThickness="3"
       CornerRadius="8">
   <Rectangle Height="100"/>
</Border>
```

Changes are immediately visible in the Visual Studio designer. Notice that the Border can nest just one child element, so if you want to add multiple visual elements, you need to encapsulate them within a container such as the Grid or StackPanel. Figure 29.1 shows the result of the preceding code.

SPECIFYING DIFFERENT BRUSHES

In the preceding code the BorderBrush is assigned with a SolidColorBrush (Red), but according to the hierarchical logic of XAML, you could set it with a different brush, such as LinearGradientBrush.

29

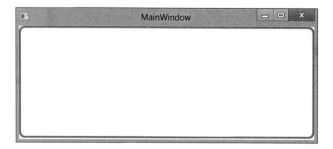

FIGURE 29.1   Drawing a border.

The `Button` Control

In Chapter 28 you saw some `Button` examples in action, so this chapter does not cover this control again.

Showing Dates with the `Calendar` Control

The `Calendar` control shows a calendar where you can select a particular day in the specified month and year. The following XAML code defines a calendar with a custom border and a `TextBox` that contains the selected date to be assigned programmatically:

```
<StackPanel Orientation="Horizontal">
    <Calendar Name="Calendar1" Margin="5"
        BorderBrush="Blue" BorderThickness="3"
        SelectedDatesChanged="Calendar1_SelectedDatesChanged">
    </Calendar>
    <TextBox Name="TextBox1" Margin="5" Height="30" Width="200"/>
</StackPanel>
```

The `SelectedDatesChanged` event is raised when the user clicks a different date. The following is instead the event handler that gets the instance of the calendar and sends the selected date to the text box:

```
Private Sub Calendar1_SelectedDatesChanged(ByVal sender As Object,
                                   ByVal e As Windows.Controls.
                                   SelectionChangedEventArgs)

    Dim currentCalendar = CType(sender, Calendar)
    Me.TextBox1.Text = currentCalendar.SelectedDate.Value.ToString

End Sub
```

Figure 29.2 shows the result of our work.

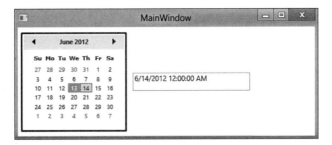

FIGURE 29.2   Implementing a `Calendar` control.

You can also programmatically assign the `SelectedDate` property with an object of type `Date` to change the date shown in the `Calendar` control with a different one.

Item Selection with the `CheckBox` Control

The WPF `CheckBox` control works like any other same-named controls in other technologies. Take a look at the following XAML code:

```
<CheckBox Name="Check1" Content="I will do this"
          Margin="5" Checked="Check1_Checked"
          Unchecked="Check1_Unchecked"/>
```

The `CheckBox`'s text is set via the `Content` property. Setting `Content` also means that you can fill the control with visual elements other than text. It exposes two events, `Checked` and `Unchecked`, that are raised when you place or remove the flag from the control and that can be handled as follows:

```
Private Sub Check1_Checked(ByVal sender As System.Object,
                           ByVal e As System.Windows.RoutedEventArgs)
    MessageBox.Show("Checked")
End Sub

Private Sub Check1_Unchecked(ByVal sender As Object,
                             ByVal e As System.Windows.RoutedEventArgs)
    MessageBox.Show("Unchecked")
End Sub
```

Finally, you invoke the `IsChecked` Boolean property for verifying whether the control is checked. Figure 29.3 shows the control.

29

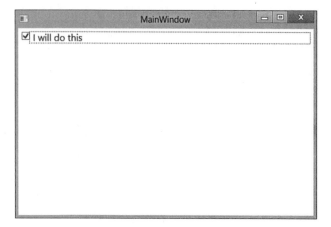

FIGURE 29.3   Implementing a `CheckBox`.

Selecting Values from a List with the `ComboBox` Control

The WPF `ComboBox` also works the same as in other technologies. The following XAML snippet shows how you implement a sample `ComboBox` showing a list of hypothetical customers:

```
<ComboBox Name="CustomerNamesCombo"
          Width="200" Height="30"
          SelectionChanged="CustomerNamesCombo_SelectionChanged">
    <ComboBox.Items>
        <ComboBoxItem Content="Alessandro"/>
        <ComboBoxItem Content="Brook"/>
    </ComboBox.Items>
</ComboBox>
```

Each item in the control is represented by a `ComboBoxItem` object whose `Content` property sets the item's content that can be also something different from text. (For example, you might embed a video through a `MediaElement` control.) The `SelectionChanged` event is raised when the user selects an item.

DESIGNER TOOLS FOR ADDING ITEMS

You can add items to a `ComboBox` by clicking the button on the Items property in the Properties window. This displays a dialog box where you can take advantage of the Visual Studio designer tools.

This control is powerful because it also supports data-binding. The next example renames the `ComboBox` into `ProcessNamesCombo`, setting the `ItemsSource` property as follows:

```
<ComboBox Name="ProcessNamesCombo"
         Width="200" Height="30" ItemsSource="{Binding}"
         SelectionChanged="CustomerNamesCombo_SelectionChanged">
```

This ensures that items will be populated at runtime via data-binding. The following Visual Basic code shows how you populate the ComboBox via a LINQ query with the list of running processes' names:

```
Private Sub MainWindow_Loaded(ByVal sender As Object,
                             ByVal e As RoutedEventArgs) _
                             Handles Me.Loaded
    Dim procList = From proc In Process.GetProcesses
              Select proc.ProcessName

    'Assuming the Combo's name is now ProcessNamesCombo
    Me.ProcessNamesCombo.ItemsSource = procList
End Sub
```

If you want to handle items selection, you write an event handler such as the following:

```
Private Sub CustomerNamesCombo_SelectionChanged(ByVal sender As Object,
                             ByVal e As SelectionChangedEventArgs)

    Dim selectedProcess = CType(CType(sender, ComboBox).SelectedItem,
                          String)

    MessageBox.Show("You selected " & selectedProcess)
End Sub
```

You need to get the instance of the selected item (ComboBox.SelectedItem) and then convert it into the appropriate type, which in this case is String. If you bounded a list of Process objects, instead of their names, conversion would return Process. You would need to add a DisplayMemberPath attribute on the XAML side pointing to the property you wanted to show (for example, ProcessName). Figure 29.4 shows the result of the data-bound ComboBox. In the .NET Framework 4.6, the ComboBox control has been improved with a more reliable stylus input for touch screen devices.

Presenting Tabular Data with the DataGrid Control

The DataGrid control enables you to present and edit tabular data. A complete example is available in Chapter 32, "Introducing Data-Binding."

29

FIGURE 29.4   Binding a `ComboBox` to a list of objects.

Selecting Dates with the `DatePicker` Control

The `DatePicker` control shows a pop-up calendar where you can pick a date; the date is then bound to a text box placed near the control. The `DatePicker` is used in data-binding techniques (see Chapter 32). The following XAML code shows how you can implement a `DatePicker`; the selection, which is mapped by the `SelectedDate` property of type `Date`, is then bound to a second, external text box to demonstrate how the value can be consumed by other user controls:

```
<StackPanel Orientation="Horizontal">
    <DatePicker Name="DatePicker1" Margin="5"
            SelectedDateChanged="DatePicker1_SelectedDateChanged" />
    <TextBox Name="TextBox2" Margin="5"
            Text="{Binding ElementName=DatePicker1,
                        Path=SelectedDate}"
            Height="30" Width="200"/>

</StackPanel>
```

Figure 29.5 shows how the `DatePicker` appears.

The `DatePicker` exposes an event called `SelectedDateChanged` that is raised when the user selects another date. The following event handler shows an example of handling the event:

```
Private Sub DatePicker1_SelectedDateChanged(ByVal sender As Object,
                                    ByVal e As _
                                    SelectionChangedEventArgs)

    'Use the "e" object to access the DatePicker control
    '(Source represents
    'the instance)
    MessageBox.Show("The new date is " & CType(e.Source,
            DatePicker).SelectedDate.
            Value.ToLongDateString)
End Sub
```

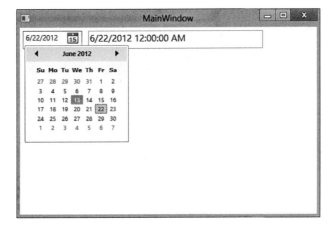

FIGURE 29.5   Implementing a `DatePicker`.

Viewing XPS Documents with the `DocumentViewer` Control

The `DocumentViewer` control enables viewing flow documents. A complete example is available in Chapter 31, "Manipulating Media and Documents."

Drawing Shapes: The `Ellipse`

The `Ellipse` element is not properly a user control because it is actually a geometric shape. It is useful to understand how the element works because you can use it when creating your custom control templates. The following XAML code declares an `Ellipse`:

```
<Ellipse Width="150" Height="80" Stroke="Red"
        StrokeThickness="3" Fill="Orange"/>
```

The most important properties are `Width` and `Height` that define dimensions. `Stroke` defines the color that surrounds the ellipse, and `StrokeThickness` is a value indicating the stroke depth. As with other geometric shapes, `Ellipse` background can be assigned via the `Fill` property. Figure 29.6 shows the drawn ellipse.

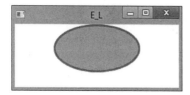

FIGURE 29.6   Drawing and filling an ellipse.

Organizing Controls with the `Expander`

The `Expander` control is a special kind of control container that can be expanded or collapsed and that is useful for organizing your controls. The following is an example of `Expander` with nested controls:

```
<Expander Name="Expander1" Header="Expand to view controls"
          Background="LightBlue">
    <StackPanel>
        <ComboBox Name="Combo1" Margin="10">
            <!-- Add your items here...-->
        </ComboBox>
        <ListBox Name="List1" Margin="10">
            <!-- Add your items here...-->
        </ListBox>
    </StackPanel>
</Expander>
```

You must use a panel, as in the preceding example, if you want to add multiple visual elements because the `Expander`'s `Content` property supports just one element. You access members by invoking their names as if they were not nested inside the `Expander`. Figure 29.7 shows the `Expander` in action.

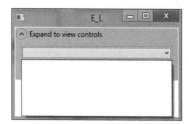

FIGURE 29.7   Implementing the `Expander` and nesting controls.

Viewing HTML Contents with `Frame`

The `Frame` control enables showing Html contents, including web pages. The most basic usage is assigning its `Source` property with an `Uri`, as in the following example:

```
<Frame Source="http://msdn.com/vstudio" />
```

Figure 29.8 shows how the website appears in the `Frame` control.

FIGURE 29.8   Opening a website with a `Frame` control.

This control exposes a `Navigate` method that enables programmatically browsing HTML contents and/or web pages as in the following snippet:

```
Frame1.Navigate(New Uri("Http://msdn.com/vstudio"))
```

You can also point to an html file on disk; just remember that each content name must be converted into `Uri`.

USING `WebBrowser`

Later this chapter discusses the `WebBrowser` control that provides better functionalities for browsing web pages. Frame should be considered as an HTML document viewer more than a real browsing control.

29

Organizing Controls with the `GroupBox` Control

The WPF `GroupBox` control has the same purpose for same named controls in other technologies, offering a container with a header and a border for grouping nested controls. The following code shows how you can implement a `GroupBox`, assigning its headers and nesting controls:

```
<GroupBox Name="Group1" Margin="5">
    <GroupBox.Header>
        <TextBlock Text="Set your options"/>
    </GroupBox.Header>
    <StackPanel Margin="10">
        <CheckBox Name="Check3" Content="Set a single option"/>
        <RadioButton Name="Radio3" Content="Use this"/>
        <RadioButton Name="Radio4" Content="Use that"/>
    </StackPanel>
</GroupBox>
```

Figure 29.9 shows the output of this code.

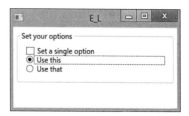

FIGURE 29.9   Grouping controls with a `GroupBox`.

Notice that in this example the `Header` property is defined in the hierarchical fashion, meaning that you can add to the header complex visual elements other than simple text. For example, you can add a `StackPanel` nesting an image with text.

Displaying Images with the `Image` Control

The `Image` control enables presenting images. A complete example is available in Chapter 31.

Displaying Text Messages with the `Label` Control

The `Label` control shows a text message, as in the following code example:

```
<Label Name="Label1" Content="A sample value"/>
```

WPF offers the `TextBlock` control that provides deeper customizations features for text, so you should use the one covered in more detail later in this chapter.

Presenting Data with the `ListBox` Control

The `ListBox` control enables listing a series of items. The good news is that you are not limited to text items but can also add complex items. Each item is represented by a `ListBoxItem` object, nested in the `ListBox`. The following example shows how you can declare a `ListBox` in XAML code:

```
<ListBox Name="ListBox1">
    <ListBoxItem Content="Item 1"/>
    <ListBoxItem Content="Item 2"/>
    <!-- Creating a complex item,
        with text and picture -->
    <ListBoxItem>
        <ListBoxItem.Content>
            <StackPanel>
                <TextBlock Text="Item 3 with image"/>
                <Image Source="MyImage.jpg" />
            </StackPanel>
        </ListBoxItem.Content>
    </ListBoxItem>
</ListBox>
```

A `ListBox` is populated at runtime via data-binding. These concepts are the same as illustrated for the `ComboBox` control, so take a look there for a recap. To accomplish data-binding, specify the `ItemsSource` markup extension as follows:

```
<ListBox Name="ListBox1" ItemsSource="{Binding}"/>
```

Then in Visual Basic code, you assign the `ItemsSource` property with a data-source as demonstrated in the following LINQ query that returns a list of names about running processes:

```
Dim procList = From proc In Process.GetProcesses
               Select proc.ProcessName

Me.ListBox1.ItemsSource = procList
```

You access items in the `ListBox` via some properties such as the following:

▶ `SelectedItem`, of type `Object`, which returns the instance of the selected item in the `ListBox`. The returned object must be converted into the appropriate type.

▶ `Items`, which returns a read-only collection of items in the control.

In Chapter 32 you see a more extensive example of data-binding using the `ListBox`. Figure 29.10 shows the result for the data-bound implementation.

DATA-BINDING

The `ListBox` control is intended for presenting data, even if you can customize items' template with `TextBox` controls. For two-way data-binding, use the `DataGrid` control described in Chapter 32.

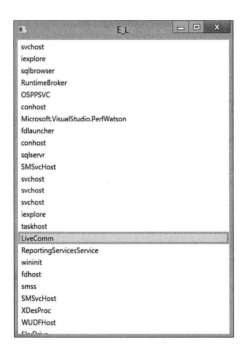

FIGURE 29.10   A data-bound `ListBox`.

Presenting Data with the `ListView` Control

The `ListView` control offers a higher customization level if compared to the `ListBox` and can also be used for receiving user input other than just presenting data. Same as for the `ListBox`, you might want to consider the `DataGrid` control for advanced data-binding techniques. To present a series of items, the `ListView` can be declared the same way as the `ListBox`. Things are better when you instead use this control with columns, such as in a grid. Consider the following XAML code that declares a `ListView` data-bound to the list of running processes:

```
<ListView Name="ListView1" ItemsSource="{Binding}">
    <ListView.View>
        <GridView>
            <GridViewColumn Header="Process ID">
                <GridViewColumn.CellTemplate>
                    <DataTemplate>
                        <TextBlock Text="{Binding Path=Id}"/>
                    </DataTemplate>
                </GridViewColumn.CellTemplate>
            </GridViewColumn>
            <GridViewColumn Header="Process name">
                <GridViewColumn.CellTemplate>
                    <DataTemplate>
                        <TextBlock
                        Text="{Binding Path=ProcessName}"/>
                    </DataTemplate>
                </GridViewColumn.CellTemplate>
            </GridViewColumn>

        </GridView>
    </ListView.View>
</ListView>
```

The `View` property establishes how the control will look. The `GridView` creates a nested grid with column definitions. Each `GridViewColumn` represents a single column where you can customize cells by defining the `CellTemplate` item. A `DataTemplate` item is nested that actually stores one or more visual elements that show how each object in the `ListView` appears. See Chapter 32 for more details on data-binding; at the moment consider that the `Binding Path` extension points to the specified property of the associated data source. Then you assign the `ItemsSource` property, as in the following Visual Basic code that retrieves the list of running processes:

```
Me.ListView1.ItemsSource = Process.GetProcesses.AsEnumerable
```

This populates the `ListView` that just shows two properties from the data source. Figure 29.11 shows the result of the code.

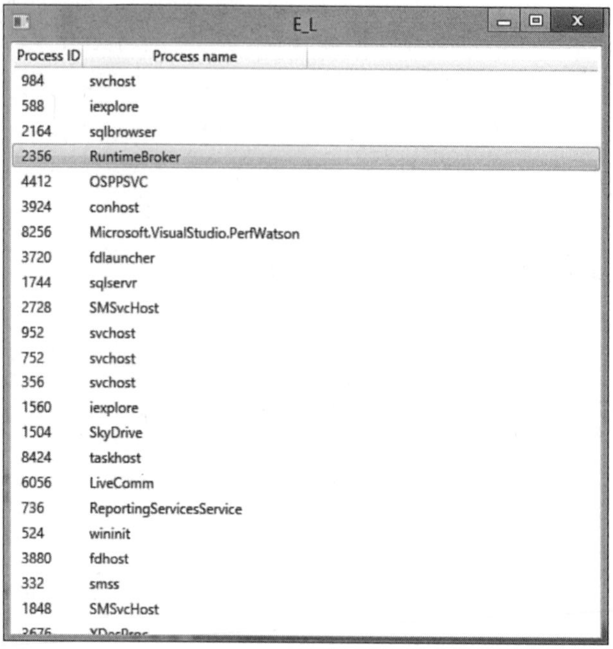

FIGURE 29.11   The result for the data-bound `ListView`.

Playing Audio and Video with the `MediaElement` Control

The `MediaElement` control enables playing multimedia files. A complete example is available in Chapter 31.

Building Effective User Interfaces with the `Menu` Control

WPF still enables creating user interfaces based on menus via the `Menu` control. You nest inside the `Menu` control many `MenuItem` objects and as many commands as you need; you can also nest `MenuItem` objects into other `MenuItems` to create submenus. Menus in WPF are highly customizable because you can specify background and foreground colors, add images and other visual elements, and set different fonts for specific menu items. The following example shows how to accomplish this:

```
<DockPanel LastChildFill="True" VerticalAlignment="Top">
    <Menu DockPanel.Dock="Top">

        <MenuItem Header="First menu" IsEnabled="True"
                DockPanel.Dock="Top">

            <MenuItem Header="_TestMenu"/>
            <Separator/>
            <MenuItem IsEnabled="True" Name="Copy"
                    Click="Copy_Click">
```

```
                      <MenuItem.Header>_Copy</MenuItem.Header>
                </MenuItem>
                <MenuItem IsEnabled="True" Name="Paste"
                        Click="Paste_Click"
                        ToolTip="Paste your text">
                    <MenuItem.Header>_Paste</MenuItem.Header>
                </MenuItem>
                <Separator />

            <MenuItem Name="FontMenuItem" Header="Item with another font"
                FontFamily="Tahoma" FontSize="16" FontStyle="Italic"
                FontWeight="Bold"
                />
        </MenuItem>

        <MenuItem Header="Second menu" DockPanel.Dock="Top"
                Background="Blue" Foreground="White">

            <!--<MenuItem Header="Item with bitmap image">
                <MenuItem.Icon>

                    <Image Source="Images/MyImage.png" />
                </MenuItem.Icon>
            </MenuItem>-->

            <MenuItem Header="Checkable item" IsCheckable="True"
                    IsChecked="True" />
            <MenuItem Header="Disabled item" IsEnabled="False"
                    Name="DisabledMenuItem"/>

        </MenuItem>
    </Menu>
</DockPanel>
```

You can set a lot of properties within menus. Table 29.1 summarizes the most important ones that were used in the preceding code.

TABLE 29.1   Most Common Properties in Menu and MenuItems

Property	Description
Header	Sets the content of the item
IsEnabled	Sets the item enabled or disabled (True or False)
Name	Assigns an identifier so that you can interact in VB code
Tooltip	Provides a description over the item when the mouse passes over
IsCheckable	Sets the item to be flagged via a check box
Icon	Sets the menu item's icon

29

By assigning the `Click` property for each `MenuItem`, you can handle the click event, as in the following code snippet:

```
Private Sub Copy_Click(ByVal sender As System.Object,
                       ByVal e As System.Windows.RoutedEventArgs)
    MessageBox.Show("You clicked Copy")
End Sub

Private Sub Paste_Click(ByVal sender As System.Object,
                        ByVal e As System.Windows.RoutedEventArgs)
    MessageBox.Show("You clicked Paste")
End Sub
```

Notice that the main `Menu` item is placed inside a `DockPanel` container that provides better arrangement for this kind of control. Figure 29.12 shows the result of the menu implementation.

Entering Passwords with the `PasswordBox` Control

The `PasswordBox` control is a special text box intended for entering passwords and that automatically hides characters. The following code snippet shows an example:

```
<StackPanel Orientation="Horizontal">
    <PasswordBox Name="PasswordBox1" Margin="5"
                 Width="150" MaxLength="20"
                 PasswordChar="*"/>
    <Button Name="PasswordButton" Width="100" Height="30"
            Margin="5" Content="Check password"
            Click="PasswordButton_Click"/>
</StackPanel>
```

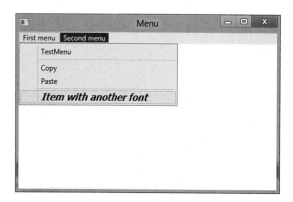

FIGURE 29.12   Implementing menus and submenus.

By default, characters are hidden with a dot, but you can replace it via the `PasswordChar` property (optional). The `MaxLength` property limits the password length (optional). Such control exposes the `Password` property of type `String` that is the entered password, as demonstrated by the following code:

```
Private Sub PasswordButton_Click(ByVal sender As Object,
                                 ByVal e As RoutedEventArgs)
    Dim myPassword = "TestPassword"
    If PasswordBox1.Password = myPassword Then
        MessageBox.Show("Password matches")
    Else
        MessageBox.Show("Password does not match")
    End If
End Sub
```

Figure 29.13 shows the result of the code.

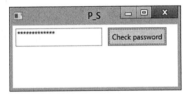

FIGURE 29.13   Implementing a `PasswordBox`.

The main event in the `PasswordBox` is `PasswordChanged` that is raised when the control's content changes.

Showing the Progress of an Operation with the `ProgressBar` Control

The `ProgressBar` control requires you to set some start properties, such as `Minimum`, `Maximum`, and `Value`. Then you can increase the value at runtime. The following XAML code declares a `ProgressBar`:

```
<ProgressBar Name="ProgressBar1" Height="30"
             Value="0"
             Minimum="0" Maximum="10000"/>
```

To update the progress value, a good approach is making this asynchronously. This can be accomplished by invoking the `Dispatcher`, which is the WPF object responsible for managing threads. This points to the `ProgressBar.SetValue` to update the progress value. So the first step is to create a custom delegate that matches `SetValue`'s signature:

```
Private Delegate Sub updateDelegate(ByVal depProperty As    _
            System.Windows.DependencyProperty, _
            ByVal value As Object)
```

The next step is to provide code that updates the progress value. This is just a demonstration loop that invokes the dispatcher while increasing the progress value:

```
Private Sub HandleProgressBar()
    Dim value As Double = ProgressBar1.Value

    Dim updateProgressBar As New _
        updateDelegate(AddressOf _
                            ProgressBar1.SetValue)

    Do Until ProgressBar1.Value = ProgressBar1.Maximum
        value += 1

        Dispatcher.Invoke(updateProgressBar, _
            System.Windows.Threading.DispatcherPriority.Background, _
            New Object() {ProgressBar.ValueProperty, value})
    Loop
End Sub
```

The `Dispatcher.Invoke` method invokes the delegate, which does nothing but invoke `ProgressBar.SetValue`. The other interesting argument is an array of `Object` storing the dependency property to be updated (`ProgressBar.ValueProperty`), which will be reflected onto `Value`, and its value. Figure 29.14 shows the result of the code.

FIGURE 29.14   The `ProgressBar` value increasing.

USING `Dispatcher.InvokeAsync`

The previous version of WPF, 4.5, introduced some new methods for the `Dispatcher` class. It is worth mentioning `InvokeAsync`. Different from `Invoke`, which you saw in the previous example and which works synchronously, `InvokeAsync` executes the specified thread asynchronously on the thread the Dispatcher is associated with.

Accepting User Choices with the `RadioButton` Control

The `RadioButton` control works similarly to the `CheckBox`, differing in that this enables one choice among several alternatives, but it exposes the same properties. The following XAML code declares two `RadioButton` controls:

```
<StackPanel>
    <RadioButton Name="Radio1" Content="First option"/>
    <RadioButton Name="Radio2" Content="Second option"/>
</StackPanel>
```

Each instance exposes the `IsChecked` property and the `Checked` and `Unchecked` events. For this, take a look back at the `CheckBox` discussion. Figure 29.15 shows how the controls look.

FIGURE 29.15   Adding `RadioButton` selection.

Drawing Shapes: The `Rectangle`

The `Rectangle` element is another common geometric shape that you can utilize in custom control templates. Drawing a rectangle is easy, as demonstrated in the following code example:

```
<Rectangle Width="150" Height="50"
           Fill="Orange" Stroke="Red"
           StrokeThickness="3"/>
```

You define its dimensions, specifying `Stroke` and `StrokeThickness` as for the ellipse (optional). Figure 29.16 shows how the object is drawn.

29

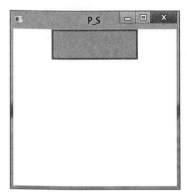

FIGURE 29.16   Drawing a rectangle.

`Rectangle` also has the `RadiusX` and `RadiusY` properties that you can assign to round corners.

Editing Text with the `RichTextBox` Control

WPF offers a `RichTextBox` control that works differently from Windows Forms and requires you to understand flow documents. This topic will be discussed in Chapter 31.

Extended View with the `ScrollBar` Control

You can implement scrollbars with the `ScrollBar` control. The following code provides an example:

```
<ScrollBar Name="Scroll1" Maximum="100" Minimum="0"
           Value="50" Scroll="Scroll1_Scroll"/>
```

The implementation is simple because you just have to provide the `Minimum`, `Maximum`, and current `Value`. The `Scroll` event is instead raised when the selector position changes. The event handler is then implemented as follows:

```
Private Sub Scroll1_Scroll(ByVal sender As System.Object,
                           ByVal e As Primitives.
                           ScrollEventArgs)

End Sub
```

WPF offers a more versatile control, named `ScrollViewer`, as described in the next section.

Scrolling the Visual Tree with the `ScrollViewer` Control

The `ScrollViewer` element enables scrolling its entire content with both horizontal and vertical scrollbars. This can be easily understood directly at design time. Type the following XAML code:

```
<ScrollViewer VerticalScrollBarVisibility="Auto"
              HorizontalScrollBarVisibility="Auto">
    <StackPanel>
        <TextBlock Width="1000"/>
        <TextBlock Height="2000"/>
    </StackPanel>
</ScrollViewer>
```

You notice that, because of the big width and height values, the `ScrollViewer` provides both scrollbars, as demonstrated in Figure 29.17.

FIGURE 29.17   Implementing a `ScrollViewer`.

This control is useful when you need to arrange multiple elements in a fixed fashion and still want to provide the ability of scrolling them within the window.

Separating Visual Elements with the `Separator` Control

The `Separator` control is used for drawing a separation line between visual elements. An example is provided earlier in this chapter, in the section "Building Effective User Interfaces with the `Menu` Control."

Value Selection with the `Slider` Control

The `Slider` control provides a selector you can use to set a particular value that is bound to another control. Chapter 31 provides an example binding a `Slider` to a `MediaElement` for controlling the volume; however, at the moment consider the following code:

```
<Slider Name="Slider1"

        Maximum="10" Minimum="0" Value="5"
        AutoToolTipPlacement="BottomRight"
        TickPlacement="TopLeft" TickFrequency="1"
        />
```

29

```
<TextBlock Text="{Binding ElementName=Slider1,
          Path=Value}"/>
```

A `Slider` requires a `Minimum` and `Maximum` value, whereas `Value` is the current selected value. You can place ToolTips reporting the value (`AutoToolTipPlacement`) that specify the position (`TopLeft` or `BottomRight`). Moreover, you can place ticks so that visualization is clearer and decide how many ticks to place (`TickFrequency`). For example, the preceding code can produce 10 ticks (1 per possible value). The `TextBlock` shows the value of the slider via data-binding, which is the preferred way of binding a `Slider` value to another control. This object raises a `ValueChanged` event when the user moves the selector to another value. Figure 29.18 shows the result of the preceding code.

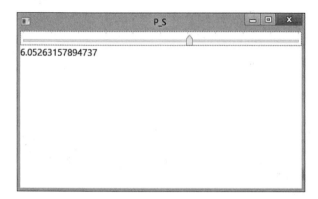

FIGURE 29.18   Setting values with a `Slider`.

Displaying Information with the `StatusBar` Control

WPF enables you to place status bars at the bottom of a `Window`. This is accomplished by declaring a `StatusBar` object that nests `StatusBarItems` elements. The good news is that you are not limited to adding text to a `StatusBar` because you can add several kinds of visual elements. The following example shows adding text and a `ProgressBar` into a `StatusBar`:

```
<StatusBar>
    <StatusBarItem Name="Item1" Content="Ready"/>
    <StatusBarItem Name="Item2">
        <ProgressBar Name="Progress1"
            Minimum="0" Maximum="200" Value="50"
            Width="50" Height="15" />
    </StatusBarItem>
</StatusBar>
```

Figure 29.19 shows the result of the preceding code. You access members in the bar at the Visual Basic level via their identifiers.

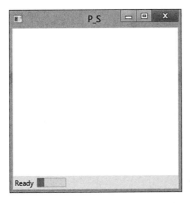

FIGURE 29.19   A `StatusBar` with nested controls.

Organizing User Interfaces with the `TabControl` Control

The `TabControl` enables you to split an area into tabs. Each tab is represented by a `TabItem` object, and tabs are enclosed within a `TabControl.TabItems` collection. The following code demonstrates how you can implement a `TabControl` with both standard and customized tabs:

```
<TabControl>
    <TabControl.Items>
        <TabItem Header="Tab1">
            <!-- Nest your controls here.. -->
        </TabItem>
        <TabItem Foreground="Blue"
                Background="Orange">
            <TabItem.Header>
                <StackPanel Orientation="Horizontal">
                    <TextBlock Text="Tab2"/>
                    <!-- Replace with a valid image -->
                    <Image Source="MyImage.jpg"/>
                </StackPanel>
            </TabItem.Header>
        </TabItem>
    </TabControl.Items>
</TabControl>
```

You set the tab header content assigning the `Header` property for each `TabItem` and then nest controls within the element. Notice how you can customize tabs by setting `Foreground` and `Background` and declaring the `Header` in a hierarchical fashion to place multiple elements. Figure 29.20 shows the `TabControl` implementation.

FIGURE 29.20   Implementing a `TabControl`.

You can also customize the header with text and an image, as you can check in the comment placed in the code. Then you access nested controls via their names as you would do in any other situation.

Presenting Text with the `TextBlock` Control

The `TextBlock` control enables showing text messages. Its purpose is similar to the `Label`'s purpose, but it differs in that `TextBlock` offers deeper control over text customization. The following example demonstrates how you can present customized text using the `TextBlock`:

```
<TextBlock Name="TextBlock1" FontFamily="Tahoma"
          FontSize="20" FontStyle="Italic"
          FontWeight="Bold"
          Text="Sample text with TextBlock">
    <TextBlock.Foreground>
        <LinearGradientBrush>
            <GradientStop Offset="0" Color="Blue"/>
            <GradientStop Offset="0.5" Color="Violet"/>
            <GradientStop Offset="1" Color="Green"/>
        </LinearGradientBrush>
    </TextBlock.Foreground>
</TextBlock>
```

Font properties are of particular interest. `FontFamily` indicates the font name, `FontStyle` indicates whether the font is normal or oblique, and `FontWeight` sets the font depth. IntelliSense enables easy selections for available members on each of the previously mentioned properties. Figure 29.21 shows the result of the preceding code.

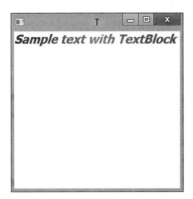

FIGURE 29.21   Drawing a `TextBlock`.

Because of its flexibility, the `TextBlock` control is often used in custom control templates that require customizing text. You can also set the `TextBlock` text at runtime by assigning the `Text` property.

Entering Text with the `TextBox` Control

Another typical control that is also provided by WPF is the `TextBox`. You declare one as follows:

```
<TextBox Name="TextBox1"
         TextChanged="TextBox1_TextChanged"/>
```

The most common event is `TextChanged` that is raised when the text is modified and that can be handled as follows:

```
Private Sub TextBox1_TextChanged(ByVal sender As System.Object,
                                 ByVal e As System.Windows.Controls.
                                 TextChangedEventArgs)

End Sub
```

The `e` object of type `TextChangedEventArgs` offers a `Changes` collection property that can be iterated to get a list of changes that affect the control's content. The `TextBox` control provides support for undo actions (that is, Ctrl+Z) and a `SelectedText` property that enables you to easily retrieve in VB code the currently selected text in the control. Also, the `TextBox` control has been improved in this release to better support touch gestures on mobile devices. In fact, you can now select a word with a double-tap gesture.

Offering Commands with the `ToolBar` Control

The `ToolBar` control enables you to create toolbars for your WPF applications. You can add multiple `ToolBar` objects within a `ToolBarTray` object. The following XAML code shows how you can define a simple toolbar; you have to replace image files with valid ones:

```
<ToolBarTray>
    <ToolBar>
        <Button Name="NewButton"
                Click="NewButton_Click">
            <Image Source=NewDocument.png" />
        </Button>
        <Button Name="OpenButton"
                Click="OpenButton_Click">
            <Image Source="OpenFolder.png" />
        </Button>
        <Button Name="SaveButton"
                Click="SaveButton_Click">
            <Image Source="Save.png" />
        </Button>
    </ToolBar>
</ToolBarTray>
```

Notice how the code implements primitive Button controls that you can manage in Visual Basic code with classic event handlers for the Click event. Following this logic, you can place additional ToolBar objects inside the ToolBarTray. Figure 29.22 shows the ToolBar.

FIGURE 29.22   Implementing a ToolBar.

Presenting Hierarchical Data with the TreeView Control

The TreeView is another important control, and WPF provides its own implementation that exposes a TreeView.Items collection where you nest nodes. Each node is represented by a TreeViewItem object. You can build complex items as in the following example:

```
<TreeView Name="TreeView1">
    <TreeView.Items>
```

```xml
            <TreeViewItem Header="Root Node" Name="RootNode"
                        Tag="Information for this node">
             <TreeViewItem Header="Node0" Name="Node0"/>
             <TreeViewItem Header="Node1" Name="Node1">
                 <TreeViewItem Header="SubNode"
                             Name="SubNode"/>
             </TreeViewItem>
           </TreeViewItem>
        </TreeView.Items>
</TreeView>
```

The text in the node is specified with the `Header` property, while you can assign additional information with the `Tag` property. Assigning the `Name` property is also useful because you can interact with nodes in managed code. To add nodes at runtime, you create an instance of the `TreeViewItem` class and then add it to the specified node as demonstrated here:

```vb
Dim nt As New TreeViewItem
With nt
    .Header = "New sub node"
    .Tag = "Runtime added"
End With

Node0.Items.Add(nt)
```

Figure 29.23 shows the result for all the preceding code.

FIGURE 29.23   Implementing and populating a `TreeView`.

The `TreeView` can also be populated via data-binding with the `ItemsSource` property; it exposes the `SelectedItem` property, exactly as it happens for the `ComboBox` and `ListBox` controls. Thus, you can apply the same techniques.

29

Accessing the Web with the `WebBrowser` Control

The `WebBrowser` control provides specific functionalities for browsing websites. You add it to the user interface by declaring a `WebBrowser` element as follows:

```
<WebBrowser Name="Browser1"/>
```

Then you can control the `WebBrowser` behavior from Visual Basic code; the following are methods exposed by the `WebBrowser` allowing navigation:

```
'Open the specified website
Browser1.Navigate(New Uri("Http://msdn.com/vstudio"))
'Back to the previous page
Browser1.GoBack()
'Forward to the next page
Browser1.GoForward()
'Refresh the page
Browser1.Refresh()
```

The `WebBrowser` also exposes some events; the most important is `LoadCompleted`, which is raised when the control completes loading a web page. This can be handled to get useful information on the visited website, as in the following code snippet:

```
Private Sub Browser1_LoadCompleted(ByVal sender As Object,
                         ByVal e As NavigationEventArgs) _
                         Handles Browser1.Navigated
    MessageBox.Show(e.Uri.ToString)
End Sub
```

The object of type `NavigationEventArgs` provides properties that retrieve information such as the website URL or the `WebResponse` instance.

Windows Forms Interoperability with the `WindowsFormsHost` Control

The `WindowsFormsHost` control enables interoperability with the Windows Forms technology and provides a way for hosting Win Forms user controls within a WPF application.

INTEROPERABILITY TIPS

I often answer questions in online forums about WPF, and one of the most common questions is about interoperability between Windows Forms and WPF, especially for developers who are moving their applications to WPF. So many architectural differences exist between the two technologies that interoperability is not a task that I suggest. You should use interoperability only when there is no other way of rewriting a WPF version of a Windows Form control, which is improbable.

To host a Windows Forms control, you drag the `WindowsFormsHost` element from the Toolbox onto the Window surface. The next step is adding a reference to the System.Windows.Forms.dll assembly. If you want to host Windows Forms controls built in the

.NET Framework, you need to add an XML namespace declaration at the Window level; the following line of XAML code demonstrates this:

```
xmlns:wf="clr-namespace:System.Windows.Forms;assembly=System.Windows.Forms"
```

At this point, you can nest the desired control inside the WindowsFormsHost declaration, as in the following example that adds a System.Windows.Forms.PictureBox:

```
<WindowsFormsHost Height="100"
                  Name="WindowsFormsHost1"
                  Width="200">
    <wf:PictureBox x:Name="Picture1"/>
</WindowsFormsHost>
```

Notice that you need to provide the x:Name attribute to make the control reachable from the Visual Basic code. Now you can interact with the PictureBox as you would in any other Windows Forms application by invoking its identifier, as demonstrated in the following code snippets, where the code loads an image file and assigns it to the PictureBox. This particular example also requires a reference to the System.Drawing.dll assembly:

```
'This is Windows Forms code inside a WPF application
Me.Picture1.Image = System.Drawing.Image.
                    FromFile("C:\Picture.jpg")
```

This technique works with custom user controls as well; you just need to add an XML namespace reference pointing to the appropriate assembly exposing the custom user control (including the current project). Then you can use the control itself.

Using Common Dialogs

In WPF 4.6, as well as its predecessors, common dialogs are wrappers of Win32 dialogs. They are exposed by the Microsoft.Win32 namespace and are OpenFileDialog and SaveFileDialog. (WPF also provides a PrintDialog control exposed by the System.Windows.Controls namespace.) The following code demonstrates how you instantiate both dialogs:

```
'Instantiating an OpenFileDialog
Dim od As New Microsoft.Win29.OpenFileDialog
With od
    .Title = "Your title here..."
    .Filter = "All files|*.*"
    .ShowReadOnly = True

    If .ShowDialog = True Then
        Dim fileName As String = .FileName
    End If
```

29

```
End With

'Instantiating a SaveFileDialog
Dim sd As New Microsoft.Win29.SaveFileDialog
With sd
    .Title = "Your title here..."
    .InitialDirectory = "."
    .Filter = "All files|*.*"
    If .ShowDialog = True Then
        Dim fileName As String = .FileName
    End If
End With
```

Notice that the ShowDialog method returns a Nullable(Of Boolean), in which True means that the user clicks **OK**, False when she clicks **Cancel**, and Nothing when she closes the dialog.

Summary

In this chapter you got an overview of WPF's most commonly used controls, which you can use in your client applications, understanding how they can be both implemented in XAML or VB code. Also, this chapter covered some particular aspects about them, such as their so-called lookless implementation, understanding why they can also be nameless because of routed events. You also got information about some improvements introduced with the .NET Framework 4.6, such as enhanced touch support on controls like TextBox and ComboBox.

CHAPTER 30

Brushes, Styles, Templates, and Animations in WPF

Building rich user experiences has become an important business. Functionalities are no longer the only requirement, even in business applications, because an attractive user interface (UI) also plays a fundamental role. Windows Presentation Foundation (WPF) offers the ideal platform for enriching the user interface with interactive content, such as animations, media files, dynamic documents, and graphical effects. WPF is also the ideal platform for building graphics manipulation applications, in which geometry or 3D graphics can run. Before you learn such important features, it is important to know about some graphics fundamentals so that you can enrich visual elements. It is worth mentioning that one of the biggest benefits of WPF is that you can take complete control over UI elements' customization. You can fill them with impressive gradients; you can completely rewrite their layout while keeping their behavior safe; and you can animate them along the UI, ensuring that they will still work as you expect. The goal of this chapter is to illustrate customization so that you can make your UI more and more attractive.

Introducing Brushes

At one time or another, you have probably wanted to fill your UI controls with interesting background textures or gradients or set a particular color, maybe as the background or the foreground. In WPF, you fill visual elements with brushes. WPF defines several kinds of brushes, all deriving from `System.Windows.Media.Brush`. The following list summarizes available brushes:

▶ `SolidColorBrush` enables you to fill a graphical object with a single color. Colors are exposed as static properties from the `System.Windows.Media.Colors` class.

▶ `LinearGradientBrush` enables you to fill a graphical object with a linear gradient composed of multiple colors.

▶ `RadialGradientBrush` is similar to `LinearGradientBrush`, but the gradient is circular.

▶ `ImageBrush` enables you to fill a graphical object with a picture.

▶ `DrawingBrush` enables you to fill a graphical object with geometrical shapes or pen drawings.

▶ `SelectionBrush` enables you to define the highlighting color when selecting text in specific controls.

▶ `CaretBrush` enables you to define the mouse pointer color in particular controls. Actually, `CaretBrush` is a property exposed by controls such as `TextBox` and `RichTextBox`, which accept Brush objects.

▶ `VisualBrush` enables you to fill a graphical object with the content of another element in the user interface.

▶ `BitmapCacheBrush` enables you to cache a visual element instead of rendering it again and is useful when you need to recall the same visual elements multiple times.

You can apply brushes to properties in visual elements exposing a `Background`, `Foreground`, or `Fill` property, such as user controls and geometrical shapes. In the next sections, you learn to fill your UI elements with the previously listed brushes. Before providing examples, let's create a new WPF project with Visual Basic 2015. Divide the default `Grid` into eight rows and adjust `Window`'s size as follows:

```
<Window x:Class="MainWindow"
    xmlns="http://schemas.microsoft.com/winfx/2006/xaml/presentation"
    xmlns:x="http://schemas.microsoft.com/winfx/2006/xaml"
    Title="MainWindow" Height="550" Width="550">
    <Grid>
```

```
        <Grid.RowDefinitions>
            <RowDefinition />
            <RowDefinition />
            <RowDefinition />
            <RowDefinition />
            <RowDefinition />
            <RowDefinition />
            <RowDefinition />
            <RowDefinition />
        </Grid.RowDefinitions>
    </Grid>
</Window>
```

ABBREVIATING LINES OF CODE

To make lines of code shorter, add an `Imports System.Windows.Media` directive in the Visual Basic code behind the file.

Applying a `SolidColorBrush`

The `System.Windows.Media.SolidColorBrush` object enables you to fill an object with a single color. The color is applied to the `Fill` property of geometric shapes and to the `Background` or `Foreground` properties in UI controls. The following code demonstrates how to apply a `SolidColorBrush`:

```
<Rectangle Grid.Row="0" Width="200" Margin="5">
    <Rectangle.Fill>
        <SolidColorBrush Color="Red"/>
    </Rectangle.Fill>
</Rectangle>
```

The `Color` property receives a value of type `System.Windows.Media.Color`. Colors are exposed by the `System.Windows.Media.Colors` class as shared properties. The result of this color brush is shown in Figure 30.1.

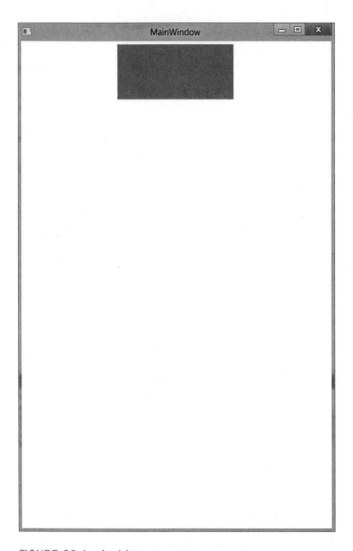

FIGURE 30.1   Applying a `SolidColorBrush`.

Applying a color at runtime in Visual Basic code is also a simple task. The following snippet shows how you can set it within the code-behind file:

```
Dim rect As New Rectangle

Dim scb As New SolidColorBrush(Colors.Red)
rect.Fill = scb
```

Applying a `LinearGradientBrush`

A `LinearGradientBrush` enables you to apply a gradient color to fill a visual element. Valid targets are the `Fill` property for geometric shapes—Background and Foreground properties for user controls. The following code draws a `Rectangle` and demonstrates that the gradient is applied both as background color (`Fill` property) and as foreground (`Stroke`):

```
<Rectangle Grid.Row="1" Width="200" Margin="5" Name="GradientRectangle"
                StrokeThickness="3">
    <Rectangle.Fill>
        <LinearGradientBrush StartPoint="0,0" EndPoint="0,1">
            <GradientStop Offset="0" Color="Orange"/>
            <GradientStop Offset="0.5" Color="Red"/>
            <GradientStop Offset="0.9" Color="Yellow"/>
        </LinearGradientBrush>
    </Rectangle.Fill>
    <Rectangle.Stroke>
        <LinearGradientBrush StartPoint="0,0" EndPoint="0,1">
            <GradientStop Offset="0" Color="Blue"/>
            <GradientStop Offset="0.5" Color="Green"/>
            <GradientStop Offset="0.9" Color="Violet"/>
        </LinearGradientBrush>
    </Rectangle.Stroke>
</Rectangle>
```

First, it is worth mentioning that the `StrokeThickness` property of `Rectangle` specifies the shape's border size. Each color in the gradient is represented by a `GradientStop` element. Its `Offset` property requires a value from 0 to 1 and specifies the color position in the gradient, whereas the color property accepts the color name or the color hexadecimal representation. Also notice how the `StartPoint` and `EndPoint` properties in the `LinearGradientBrush` enable you to influence the gradient direction. Figure 30.2 shows the result of the preceding code.

You can define a `LinearGradientBrush` in Visual Basic code for runtime appliance. This is accomplished by the following code:

```
Dim lgb As New LinearGradientBrush
lgb.GradientStops.Add(New GradientStop With {.Offset = 0,
                                   Color = Colors.Red})
lgb.GradientStops.Add(New GradientStop With {.Offset = 0,
                                   Color = Colors.Yellow})
lgb.GradientStops.Add(New GradientStop With {.Offset = 0,
                                   Color = Colors.Orange})
'rect is a Rectangle instance
rect.Fill = lgb
```

30

FIGURE 30.2   Applying a `LinearGradientBrush`.

Notice how you add instances of the `GradientStop` class to the `GradientStops` collection. Each `GradientStop` requires both `Offset` (of type `Double`) and `Color` (of type `System. Windows.Media.Color`) properties to be set. `Colors` are exposed by the `System.Windows. Media.Colors` class as shared properties.

Applying a `RadialGradientBrush`

The `RadialGradientBrush` brush works exactly like the `LinearGradientBrush`, except that it creates a circular gradient. The following code shows how you can apply such a brush to an `Ellipse`:

```
<Ellipse Width="100" Margin="5" Grid.Row="2" Stroke="Black"
        StrokeThickness="2" >
    <Ellipse.Fill>
        <RadialGradientBrush>
                <GradientStop Offset="0" Color="Blue"/>
                <GradientStop Offset="0.5" Color="Green"/>
                <GradientStop Offset="0.9" Color="Violet"/>
        </RadialGradientBrush>
    </Ellipse.Fill>
</Ellipse>
```

You are not limited to the `Ellipse` shape, but for demo purposes it is the one that best fits the example. Figure 30.3 shows the result of the brush applied.

The Visual Basic code for applying the brush at runtime is similar to the one for the linear gradient. The following code snippet provides an example:

```
Dim ragb As New RadialGradientBrush
ragb.GradientStops.Add(New GradientStop With {.Offset = 0,
                                        Color = Colors.Red})
ragb.GradientStops.Add(New GradientStop With {.Offset = 0,
                                        Color = Colors.Yellow})
ragb.GradientStops.Add(New GradientStop With {.Offset = 0,
                                        Color = Colors.Orange})
rect.Fill = ragb
```

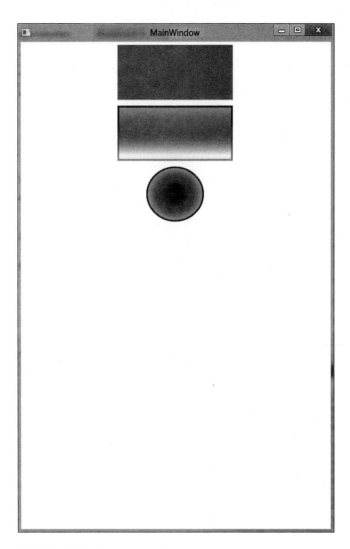

FIGURE 30.3   The result of the `RadialGradientBrush`.

Applying an `ImageBrush`

You can fill a visual element with an image file by using the `ImageBrush` brush. This object is useful even if you want to fill text with image textures. The following code snippet shows how to apply an `ImageBrush` as a button background and as the text foreground color:

```
<StackPanel Grid.Row="3" Orientation="Horizontal">
    <Button Width="100" Margin="5" Content="Hello!"
        Foreground="Yellow">
        <Button.Background>
            <ImageBrush Opacity="0.5"
                ImageSource=
            "/StylesBrushesTemplatesAnimations;component/Images/Avatar.jpg" />
        </Button.Background>
    </Button>

    <TextBlock Margin="5"
            FontFamily="Segoe UI" FontSize="40" Text="Hello!"
            FontWeight="Bold" >
        <TextBlock.Foreground>
            <ImageBrush ImageSource=
            "/StylesBrushesTemplatesAnimations;component/Images/Avatar.jpg"/>
        </TextBlock.Foreground>
    </TextBlock>
</StackPanel>
```

> **NOTE**
>
> In the previous code, the Avatar.jpg file is just a sample picture of me. I suppose you might prefer to replace my face with one of your favorite pictures!

The image is specified by assigning the ImageSource property with the image's Uniform Resource Identifier (URI). The previous code produces the result shown in Figure 30.4 (see the last row).

30

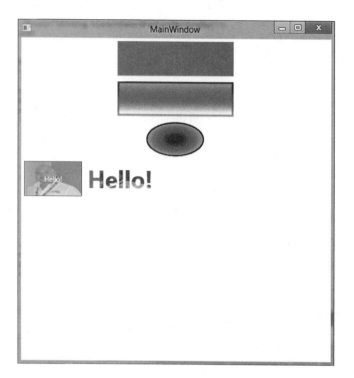

FIGURE 30.4   Applying an ImageBrush as the background and foreground color.

If you want to add your images to the application resources so that you can easily refer to them when applying the ImageBrush, follow these steps:

1. Write the ImageBrush element in the XAML code editor.

2. Add image files to the project (Project, Add Existing Item).

3. In the XAML code editor, select the previously added ImageBrush object and then press F4 to open the Properties window.

4. Select the ImageSource property and expand the drop-down box, as shown in Figure 30.5. Pick up the desired picture that will be assigned to the selected brush. When added, its address will be assigned to the ImageProperty in the XAML code under the form of a packed Uri.

Applying an ImageBrush in Visual Basic code is also a simple task, demonstrated by the following code snippet:

```vb
Dim myButton As New Button
Dim imgb As New ImageBrush
imgb.ImageSource = New BitmapImage _
    (New _
    Uri("/StylesBrushesTemplatesAnimations;component/Images/Avatar.jpg",
    UriKind.Relative))
myButton.Background = imgb
```

FIGURE 30.5   Selecting an image with the designer tools.

Notice how, in Visual Basic code, you specify the image by creating first an instance of the `BitmapImage` class whose constructor receives an argument of type `Uri` pointing to the actual image file.

30

Applying `SelectionBrush` and `CaretBrush`

WPF 4.6 offers two special objects, `SelectionBrush` and `CaretBrush`, which are properties of type `System.Windows.Media.Brush` and that accept brushes to be assigned to them. The first one enables you to apply a brush to the highlighting color when selecting text, whereas the second one applies a brush to the mouse caret within the control. Controls that can receive application of these brushes are `TextBox` and `PasswordBox`. `SelectionBrush` can also be applied to `FlowDocumentPageViewer`, `FlowDocumentReader`, and `FlowDocumentScrollViewer`. You apply both brushes as child nodes of the desired control. The following code demonstrates how to apply a linear gradient color for both the highlighting selection color and the caret color:

```
<TextBox Grid.Row="4" Margin="5"
        FontSize="20" FontWeight="Bold"
        Name="TextBox1">
    <TextBox.SelectionBrush>
        <LinearGradientBrush>
            <GradientStop Offset="0" Color="Chartreuse"/>
            <GradientStop Offset="0.5" Color="Violet"/>
            <GradientStop Offset="1" Color="Blue"/>
        </LinearGradientBrush>
    </TextBox.SelectionBrush>

    <TextBox.CaretBrush>
        <LinearGradientBrush>
            <GradientStop Offset="0" Color="Red"/>
            <GradientStop Offset="0.5" Color="Yellow"/>
            <GradientStop Offset="1" Color="Orange"/>
        </LinearGradientBrush>
    </TextBox.CaretBrush>
</TextBox>
```

Figure 30.6 shows the result of this code, although the caret gradient is not visible at this point, but you will see there are no problems on your screen.

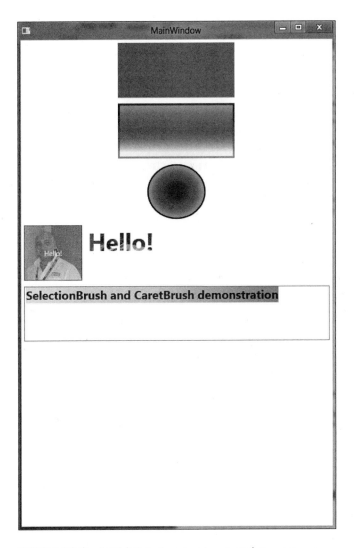

FIGURE 30.6   Applying `SelectionBrush` and `CaretBrush`.

You can apply different kinds of brushes, such as `ImageBrush` or `VisualBrush`, as described in the next section.

Applying a `VisualBrush`

The `VisualBrush` enables you to fill an object with the content of another visual element in the user interface. For example, you could set a button's background with the content of a `MediaElement` that is playing a video. Applying a `VisualBrush` is simple, in that you just need to assign its `Visual` property with the name of the visual element you want to bind. The following code example shows how you can assign another visual element currently in the user interface as the background of a button:

```
<Button Width="100" Margin="5" Grid.Row="5">
    <Button.Background>
        <VisualBrush Visual="{Binding ElementName=GradientRectangle}"/>
    </Button.Background>
</Button>
```

The requirement is that the source visual element has a `Name` property set. You assign the visual element with the `Binding` markup extension, whose `ElementName` property points to the actual visual element. You learn more about the `Binding` extension in Chapter 32, "Introducing Data-Binding." The previous example produces the result shown in Figure 30.7.

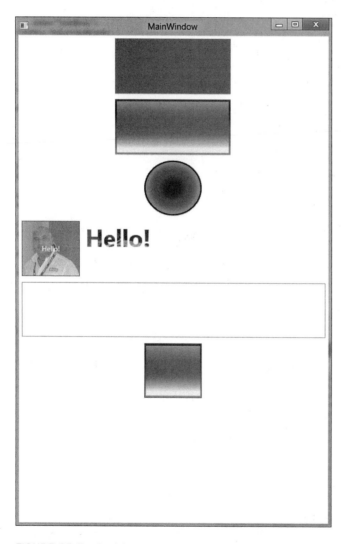

FIGURE 30.7   Applying a `VisualBrush`.

The button's background typically is not a color but is a rectangle with all its properties. So, if you make modifications to the binding source, the changes will be reflected into the `VisualBrush`. This is the real power of this brush. For example, try to use a `TextBox` as the source element; when you write in the `TextBox`, your text will be reflected into the `VisualBrush`.

Applying a `DrawingBrush`

The `DrawingBrush` brush enables you to paint an area with a so called *drawing*. A drawing, according to the MSDN documentation, can be a shape, an image, a video, text, or another item and is an instance of the `System.Windows.Media.Drawing` class. The following code sample fills a rectangle with a `DrawingBrush` defining a drawing where two ellipses intersect each other:

```xml
<Rectangle Width="100"
           Grid.Row="6">
    <Rectangle.Fill>
        <DrawingBrush>
            <DrawingBrush.Drawing>
                <GeometryDrawing>
                    <GeometryDrawing.Brush>
                        <LinearGradientBrush>
                            <GradientStop Offset="0" Color="Blue"/>
                            <GradientStop Offset="0.7" Color="LightBlue"/>
                        </LinearGradientBrush>
                    </GeometryDrawing.Brush>
                    <GeometryDrawing.Geometry>
                        <GeometryGroup>
                            <EllipseGeometry RadiusX="0.1" RadiusY="0.5"
                                             Center="0.5,0.5" />
                            <EllipseGeometry RadiusX="0.5" RadiusY="0.1"
                                             Center="0.5,0.5" />
                        </GeometryGroup>
                    </GeometryDrawing.Geometry>
                </GeometryDrawing>
            </DrawingBrush.Drawing>
        </DrawingBrush>
    </Rectangle.Fill>
</Rectangle>
```

Other than the brush, it is interesting here how ellipses are declared via `EllipseGeometry` objects that are the geometric representation of ellipses and are enclosed within a `GeometryGroup` that can group different kinds of geometric representations, such as `LineGeometry` or `RectangleGeometry`. (These classes derive from `System.Windows.Media.Geometry`, for your further studies.) Figure 30.8 shows the result of the previous snippet.

30

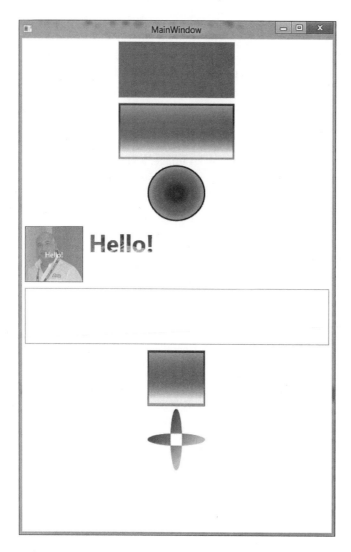

FIGURE 30.8   Applying a DrawingBrush.

Applying a BitmapCacheBrush

WPF 4.6 has the concept of *cached composition*, which was introduced back in WPF 4 and that lets you store a visual element to a cache so that redrawing an element is faster and provides better performance instead of rendering the graphic element each time it needs to be used. Among the others, with cached composition you can cache images to apply as a brush. This is accomplished by first declaring a BitmapCache object that establishes the rules for caching the desired object and then by applying a `BitmapCacheBrush` to the visual element. The following code demonstrates how to apply a `BitmapCacheBrush` as the background of two `TextBlock` controls, by using cached composition (comments in the code will help you understand better):

```xml
<StackPanel Grid.Row="7">
    <StackPanel.Resources>
        <!-- an image pointing to the previously added
             resource -->
        <Image x:Key="cachedImage"
Source="/StylesBrushesTemplatesAnimations;component/Images/Avatar.jpg">
            <!-- supposing we'll use the same image multiple
                 times, we can cache it instead of
                 rendering each time -->
            <Image.CacheMode>
                <!-- RenderAtScale = 1 means that it is cached
                     at its actual size (no zoom) -->
                <BitmapCache RenderAtScale="1"
                             EnableClearType="False"
                             SnapsToDevicePixels="False"/>
            </Image.CacheMode>
        </Image>
        <!-- Applying the cached image as a brush -->
        <BitmapCacheBrush x:Key="cachedBrush"
            Target="{StaticResource cachedImage}"/>
    </StackPanel.Resources>

    <TextBlock Text="Text one..." FontSize="24"
               Height="60" Foreground="Blue"
               FontWeight="Bold"
               Background="{StaticResource cachedBrush}"/>
    <TextBlock Text="Text two..." FontSize="24"
               Height="60" Foreground="Green"
               FontWeight="Bold"
               Background="{StaticResource cachedBrush}"/>
</StackPanel>
```

The `BitmapCache.RenderAtScale` property establishes when the visual element has to be cached. If assigned with 1, as in the preceding example, the visual element is cached at its natural size. For example, you could assign such a property with 2 in case you want to cache the visual element only when it is zoomed at the double of its size. The `BitmapCache.EnableClearType` property lets you decide whether you want to apply Clear Type precision to the visual elements, but it is useful only with text. The `BitmapCache.SnapsToDevicePixels` property should be assigned with `True` when you need precise pixel-alignment and takes the same value of the `EnableClearType` property. Finally, notice how the `BitmapCacheBrush` object points to the image via the `Target` property and how it is applied to `TextBlock` controls via the `Background` property pointing to the new resource. The preceding code produces the result shown in Figure 30.9. Now that you know about WPF brushes, you are ready to get an overview of another great feature: styles.

Introducing Styles

One of the biggest benefits of WPF user controls is that their layout is completely customizable. As explained further in the "Introducing Control Templates" section, you can completely redefine their layout and behavior using templates. In some situations, you have multiple controls of the same type and want them to have the same properties. For example, you might want to implement three buttons, with each button having the same width, height, and font as the other ones. To avoid the need of applying the same properties for each control, which can be annoying if you have dozens of controls, you can define a *style*. A style is an instance of the `System.Windows.Style` class and enables you to define a set of common properties for the specified type of control. Styles are defined within the `Resources` section of a `Window`, of panels, or at the application level (Application.xaml file). Each style must have an identifier assigned via the `x:Key` attribute and is applied to controls assigning their `Style` property. The code in Listing 30.1 defines a style for buttons and applies the style to three buttons in the interface.

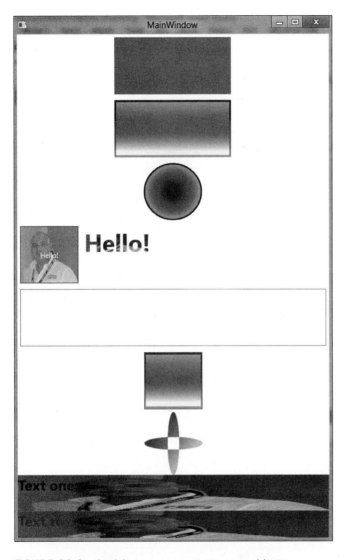

FIGURE 30.9   Applying `BitmapCachedBrush` objects.

LISTING 30.1   Defining and Assigning a Style for Buttons

```
<Window x:Class="Styles"
    xmlns="http://schemas.microsoft.com/winfx/2006/xaml/presentation"
    xmlns:x="http://schemas.microsoft.com/winfx/2006/xaml"
    Title="Styles" Height="300" Width="300">
    <StackPanel>
        <StackPanel.Resources>
            <Style x:Key="ButtonStyle" TargetType="Button">
```

```
                <Setter Property="Width" Value="100"/>
                <Setter Property="Height" Value="40"/>
                <Setter Property="Foreground" Value="Blue"/>
                <Setter Property="FontFamily" Value="Verdana"/>
                <Setter Property="Margin" Value="5"/>
                <Setter Property="Background">
                    <Setter.Value>
                        <LinearGradientBrush>
                            <GradientStop Offset="0.2" Color="Orange"/>
                            <GradientStop Offset="0.8" Color="Red"/>
                        </LinearGradientBrush>
                    </Setter.Value>
                </Setter>
            </Style>
        </StackPanel.Resources>

        <Button Style="{StaticResource ButtonStyle}" Content="Hello!"/>
        <Button Style="{StaticResource ButtonStyle}" Content="Another styled"/>
        <Button Style="{StaticResource ButtonStyle}" Content="Button three"/>
    </StackPanel>
</Window>
```

Understanding the scope of styles is important. In the code example, the style is defined
at the panel level, meaning that buttons outside the panel cannot get the style applied.
Notice how the TargetType property enables you to specify the target control type. If it's
not specified, WPF assumes FrameworkElement as the target. Properties are specified via
Setter elements. Each setter requires the target Property specification and its value. You
can also define a complex value by splitting its definition to create a Setter.Value node,
which can store multiple lines of XAML code. This was shown in Listing 30.1, where the
technique is used to define a LinearGradientBrush gradient. Finally, notice how the new
style is assigned to buttons setting the Style property, pointing to the style identifier via
an XAML markup extension named StaticResource.

StaticResource AND DynamicResource

In different situations you can often find controls pointing to resources via
StaticResource or DynamicResource markup extensions. The difference is that a
StaticResource is something defined in the XAML that will not change during the
application lifetime. It will be assigned only once, even before its actual point of use.
A DynamicResource instead is assigned when its value is required and if its content
changes during the application lifetime, its changes are reflected to the caller.

Running the code can produce the interesting result shown in Figure 30.10.

On the Visual Basic side, you create and apply a style as in the following code snippet:

```
Dim buttonStyle As New Style
'Need to specify the System.Type
buttonStyle.TargetType = GetType(Button)
'The Setter.Property member is assigned with a dependency property exposed
'by the System.Type
buttonStyle.Setters.Add(New Setter With {.Property = Button.WidthProperty,
                                         Value = "100"})

Button1.Style = buttonStyle
```

FIGURE 30.10   Styling multiple controls of the same type with Styles.

This can be particularly useful if you need to generate a style at runtime, although you define styles at design time. Therefore, declaring and applying them via XAML is the most preferable way (so that designers can eventually take advantage of XAML for their work).

Styles Inheritance

You can define a style that inherits from another one to extend it with new settings. This is accomplished by specifying the BasedOn property as follows:

```
<Style x:Key="InheritedStyle" TargetType="Button"
       BasedOn="{StaticResource ButtonStyle}">
    <Setter Property="FontWeight" Value="ExtraBold"/>
</Style>
```

If you now assign this new style to a button, it can take all the style properties of the base style plus the FontWeight value.

Understanding Triggers

Until now, you saw how styles can be applied to controls without condition. This is useful, but it is more useful for deciding when to apply a style. The easiest example is to consider a button: You apply a background color that you might want to change when the button gets focus; this behavior should be replicated for each button in the UI via styles. To conditionally apply styles, you use *triggers*. A trigger essentially represents a condition that enables you to apply a particular style when the condition is evaluated as True. Triggers are defined within a Style.Triggers collection, and each of them requires you to specify the property affected by the condition and a Boolean value (True or False) that determines when the trigger has to be executed. The code in Listing 30.2 retakes the first style example, adding a trigger condition in the final part of the code.

LISTING 30.2   Applying a Single Trigger Condition

```
<Style x:Key="ButtonStyle" TargetType="Button">
    <Setter Property="Width" Value="100"/>
    <Setter Property="Height" Value="40"/>
    <Setter Property="Foreground" Value="Blue"/>
    <Setter Property="FontFamily" Value="Verdana"/>
    <Setter Property="Margin" Value="5"/>
    <Setter Property="Background">
        <Setter.Value>
            <LinearGradientBrush>
                <GradientStop Offset="0.2" Color="Orange"/>
                <GradientStop Offset="0.8" Color="Red"/>
            </LinearGradientBrush>
        </Setter.Value>
    </Setter>

    <Style.Triggers>
        <Trigger Property="IsFocused" Value="True">
            <Setter Property="Background">
                <Setter.Value>
                    <LinearGradientBrush>
                        <GradientStop Offset="0.2" Color="Red"/>
                        <GradientStop Offset="0.8" Color="Yellow"/>
                    </LinearGradientBrush>
                </Setter.Value>
            </Setter>
        </Trigger>
    </Style.Triggers>
</Style>
```

Applying the trigger described in code can cause buttons to have a different background color when they get focus, which happens after you click. In this example, you applied a style according to just one condition, but sometimes multiple conditions have to be evaluated. For instance, continuing the Button control discussion, you could decide to apply a style when the control gets focus and also when the button is enabled. This can be accomplished using a MultiTrigger object. A MultiTrigger can contain multiple condition specifications and as many setters for as many properties as you want to apply in the style.

The following code snippet demonstrates how to declare a `MultiTrigger` for the preceding implemented style:

```
<Style.Triggers>
    <MultiTrigger>
        <MultiTrigger.Conditions>
            <Condition Property="IsFocused" Value="True"/>
            <Condition Property="IsEnabled" Value="True"/>
        </MultiTrigger.Conditions>
        <Setter Property="Background">
            <Setter.Value>
                <LinearGradientBrush>
                    <GradientStop Offset="0.2" Color="Red"/>
                    <GradientStop Offset="0.8" Color="Yellow"/>
                </LinearGradientBrush>
            </Setter.Value>
        </Setter>
    </MultiTrigger>
</Style.Triggers>
```

In this case the new background is applied only when both conditions are evaluated as True.

Introducing Control Templates

WPF controls have a particular structure, in which the layout system is separated from the behavior. When searching resources about WPF controls, you often find a definition stating that they are *lookless*. This means that WPF controls have no default aspect, whereas they expose a common set of properties that can be assigned for defining the layout and the behavior. This common set is referred to as the *control template*. The WPF system provides a default control template for each available control in the Base Class Library (BCL). You can then override the existing template or create a custom one. Control templates are so versatile because you can completely redesign the control look while keeping its original behavior, but you can also improve the behavior. For example, you can use an `Ellipse` as a control template for a `Button`. The new `Button` will look like an `Ellipse`, but your user can still click it and you can still handle button events.

USE BLEND FOR VISUAL STUDIO 2015

Even if the XAML designer has been enhanced even more in Visual Studio 2015, creating custom control templates can be a hard task to accomplish with the IDE only. This is a developer tool and therefore cannot offer advanced design features as Blend for Visual Studio 2015 does. If you plan to make intensive use of custom control templates, use Blend. Use Visual Studio if your custom templates are basic implementations. In the next examples, you see something easy to implement with Visual Studio, although the logic of control templates is fully implemented.

30

Control templates are implemented as styles, but actually they are not simple styles. The difference between styles and templates is that styles affect existing properties within an existing template, whereas a control template can completely override or replace the properties and layout of a control. Talking in code terms, a control template is defined within a `Style` definition, setting the `Template` property and assigning the `Value` of this property. The code in Listing 30.3 shows how to utilize an `Ellipse` as the control template for buttons, where the background gradient color changes when the button is pressed or when the mouse pointer flies over it.

LISTING 30.3   Building a Control Template

```
<Window.Resources>
    <Style x:Key="ButtonStyle1" TargetType="{x:Type Button}">
        <Setter Property="Template">
            <Setter.Value>
                <ControlTemplate TargetType="{x:Type Button}">
                    <Grid>
                        <Ellipse x:Name="ellipse" Stroke="Black">
                            <Ellipse.Fill>
                                <LinearGradientBrush EndPoint="0.5,1"
                                                     StartPoint="0.5,0">
                                    <GradientStop Color="Black" Offset="0"/>
                                    <GradientStop Color="White" Offset="1"/>
                                </LinearGradientBrush>
                            </Ellipse.Fill>
                        </Ellipse>
                        <ContentPresenter HorizontalAlignment=
                         "{TemplateBinding HorizontalContentAlignment}"
                         VerticalAlignment=
                         "{TemplateBinding VerticalContentAlignment}"
                         SnapsToDevicePixels=
                         "{TemplateBinding SnapsToDevicePixels}"
                         RecognizesAccessKey="True"/>
                    </Grid>
                    <ControlTemplate.Triggers>
                        <Trigger Property="IsFocused" Value="True"/>
                        <Trigger Property="IsDefaulted" Value="True"/>
                        <Trigger Property="IsMouseOver" Value="True">
                            <Setter Property="Fill" TargetName="ellipse">
                                <Setter.Value>
                                    <LinearGradientBrush EndPoint="0.5,1"
                                                         StartPoint="0.5,0">
                                        <GradientStop Color="White" Offset="0"/>
                                        <GradientStop Color="Black" Offset="1"/>
                                    </LinearGradientBrush>
                                </Setter.Value>
```

```
                                    </Setter>
                            </Trigger>
                            <Trigger Property="IsPressed" Value="True">
                                <Setter Property="Fill" TargetName="ellipse">
                                    <Setter.Value>
                                        <LinearGradientBrush EndPoint="0.5,1"
                                                            StartPoint="0.5,0">
                                            <GradientStop Color="#FF4F4F4F"
                                                        Offset="0"/>
                                            <GradientStop Color="#FF515050"
                                                        Offset="1"/>
                                            <GradientStop Color="White"
                                                        Offset="0.483"/>
                                        </LinearGradientBrush>
                                    </Setter.Value>
                                </Setter>
                            </Trigger>
                            <Trigger Property="IsEnabled" Value="False"/>
                        </ControlTemplate.Triggers>
                    </ControlTemplate>
                </Setter.Value>
            </Setter>
        </Style>
</Window.Resources>
```

TIP: RESTYLING WINDOWS

Control templates are not limited to user controls, but they can be successfully implemented for completely restyling `Window` objects layout so that you can create custom windows while still taking advantage of their behavior. The template's `TargetType` is therefore `Window`.

If you look at the code, you can notice how the button default aspect is replaced by an `Ellipse` within the `ControlTemplate` value of the `Template` property. Probably some concepts you learned about styles help you understand what is happening. Triggers enable you to change the background color according to specific mouse actions. Don't forget to add the `ContentPresenter` element in your custom templates because it enables you to show text or other UI elements within your control. Control templates are assigned to controls using the `DynamicResource` markup extension. The following XAML line assigns the previous custom control template to a button:

```
<Button Click="Button_Click" Name="Button1"
        Style="{DynamicResource ButtonStyle1}"
        Width="100" Height="80" Content="Button"/>
```

30

Changes will be automatically reflected at design time. You can also assign an event handler for the `Click` event to ensure that everything is working fine:

```
Private Sub Button_Click(sender As System.Object,
                         e As System.Windows.RoutedEventArgs)
    MessageBox.Show("You clicked!")
End Sub
```

Figure 30.11 shows how the button looks within the running application when the mouse pointer passes over it.

FIGURE 30.11   The custom control template designs a button as an ellipse.

RECOMMENDATION

Control templates enable you to create amazing control layouts, but this is not necessarily a good choice. Remember that users prefer to easily associate a simple control shape to a particular action more than having colored and funny controls that they cannot easily recognize.

Introducing Transformations

Transformations are special objects that modify the appearance of visual elements of type `FrameworkElement`, applying interesting effects such as rotation or translation, keeping unchanged the visual element's functional behavior. For example, with transformations you can rotate a `ListBox` 180°, but it will still work as usual; only the layout changes. Transformations are important to understand if you intend to apply animations to visual elements. Animations are covered in the next section. Keep in mind that when you apply animations, you animate transformation objects that affect visual elements. You apply transformations by adding a `RenderTransform` node for your visual element at the XAML level. This is explained by dividing a `Grid` into four cells, where each cell must contain a `ListBox`. To accomplish this, write the following XAML code that divides the grid and provides a common set of properties for `ListBox` instances via a style:

```
<Grid Name="Grid1">
    <Grid.RowDefinitions>
        <RowDefinition/>
        <RowDefinition/>
    </Grid.RowDefinitions>
    <Grid.ColumnDefinitions>
        <ColumnDefinition/>
        <ColumnDefinition/>
    </Grid.ColumnDefinitions>
    <Grid.Resources>
        <Style x:Key="ListStyle" TargetType="ListBox">
            <Setter Property="Margin" Value="5"/>
            <Setter Property="Width" Value="160"/>
            <Setter Property="Height" Value="160"/>
            <Setter Property="ItemsSource" Value="{Binding}"/>
        </Style>
    </Grid.Resources>
</Grid>
```

At this point, each cell contains a `ListBox`, as explained in the next sections. Before going into that, switch to the code behind file and handle the `Window.Loaded` event as follows:

```
Private Sub Transforms_Loaded(sender As Object,
                    e As System.Windows.RoutedEventArgs) _
                    Handles Me.Loaded

    'Gets a list of names for running processes
    'and populates the Grid.DataContext so that children
    'elements will pick up data from it
    Me.Grid1.DataContext = From proc In Process.GetProcesses
                    Select proc.ProcessName
End Sub
```

The `DataContext` property is the data-source for a given container, and all children controls pick up data from it. In this case, assigning the `Grid1.DataContext` property populates all child `ListBox` controls.

30

CHECKING THE SAMPLES RESULT

For the sake of simplicity, and because the design actions are reflected to the designer, only one figure will be provided about the transformations result. Figure 30.12 shows the complete results. The interesting thing is that `ListBox` controls continue working independently of their skew or position on the screen.

Rotating Visual Elements with `RotateTransform`

`RotateTransform` is a transformation that enables you to rotate a visual element for the specified number of degrees and at the specified position. The following code adds a `ListBox` in the upper-left cell, and it is rotated 180°:

```
<ListBox Name="RotateListBox" Grid.Row="0" Grid.Column="0"
        Style="{StaticResource ListStyle}">
    <ListBox.RenderTransform>
        <RotateTransform Angle="180" CenterX="80" CenterY="80"/>
    </ListBox.RenderTransform>
</ListBox>
```

Notice how the `Angle` property specifies the degrees, whereas `CenterX` and `CenterY` represent the position of rotation. In the preceding example, the rotation comes in at the center of the `ListBox` (both values are the half of `Width` and `Height`). Transformations are automatically reflected to the designer, so you should see the result of what you are doing. Figure 30.12 shows the result of this transformation (see the upper-left cell). Notice also how the control is working normally even if it is in an unusual position.

Dynamically Resizing Visual Elements with `ScaleTransform`

`ScaleTransform` enables you to dynamically resize a control. The following code demonstrates how a `ListBox` can be scaled to different dimensions:

```
<ListBox Name="ScaleListBox" Grid.Row="0" Grid.Column="1"
        Style="{StaticResource ListStyle}">
    <ListBox.RenderTransform>
        <ScaleTransform CenterX="0" CenterY="0" ScaleX="0.6" ScaleY="0.6"/>
    </ListBox.RenderTransform>
</ListBox>
```

Notice how scaling is expressed in percentage with the `ScaleX` and `ScaleY` properties. A value of 0.6 means that the control is scaled to 60% of its original dimensions. A value of 1 means 100% (that is, the original size), whereas a value bigger than 1 enlarges the visual element. Take a look at the upper-right cell in Figure 30.12 to get an idea about the result. With animations, `ScaleTransform` enables you to animate visual elements by making them larger or smaller.

Changing Visual Elements' Angles with `SkewTransform`

`SkewTransform` enables you to skew a visual element for the specified angles on both the X-axis and Y-axis, simulating 3D depth for 2D objects. The following code demonstrates how to apply to a `ListBox` a horizontal skew of 15° and a vertical skew of 30°, where the center point is established by `CenterX` and `CenterY` properties:

```
<ListBox Name="SkewListBox" Grid.Row="1" Grid.Column="0"
        Style="{StaticResource ListStyle}">
    <ListBox.RenderTransform>
        <SkewTransform AngleX="15" AngleY="30" CenterX="50" CenterY="50" />
```

```
        </ListBox.RenderTransform>
</ListBox>
```

Skewing is probably the most impressive transform if you then try to use visual elements and controls, discovering that they work exactly as if they were not transformed. Figure 30.12 shows the result of skewing (see the bottom-left cell).

Dynamically Moving Visual Elements with `TranslateTransform`

`TranslateTransform` enables you to move a visual element from a position to another one in the layout system. This is useful if you want to build animations capable of moving visual elements. The following example shows how you can translate a `ListBox` of 50 points on the X-axis and of 100 points on the Y-axis:

```
<ListBox Name="TranslateListBox" Grid.Row="1" Grid.Column="1"
        Style="{StaticResource ListStyle}">
    <ListBox.RenderTransform>
        <TranslateTransform X="50" Y="100" />
    </ListBox.RenderTransform>
</ListBox>
```

The result of this translation is shown in Figure 30.12 (see the bottom-right cell).

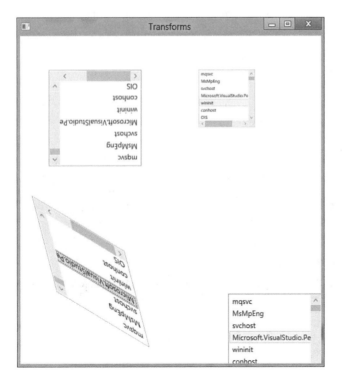

FIGURE 30.12   The result of applying transformations.

30

Applying Multiple Transforms

You can apply multiple transformations by contextually implementing a `TransformGroup` as a nested node of `RenderTransform`. The following code demonstrates how you can both rotate and skew a visual element:

```
<ListBox Name="SkewListBox" Grid.Row="1" Grid.Column="0"
        Style="{StaticResource ListStyle}">
    <ListBox.RenderTransform>
        <TransformGroup>
            <SkewTransform AngleX="15" AngleY="30" CenterX="50"
                            CenterY="50" />
            <RotateTransform Angle="180" CenterX="80" CenterY="80"/>
        </TransformGroup>
    </ListBox.RenderTransform>
</ListBox>
```

A COUPLE IMPORTANT NOTES

Another transformation named `MatrixTransform` is available and enables you to build custom transformations. This is quite a complex object and is beyond of the scope of this book. Visit the official MSDN page at http://msdn.microsoft.com/en-us/library/system. windows.media.matrixtransform(VS.110).aspx.

Next, `RenderTransform` is not the only place for putting transformations. Another node named `LayoutTransform` requires a transformation to be applied before the WPF layout system comes in. This can be useful only when you need the parent of the affected element to adjust the transformed size, but in all other cases use `RenderTransform` because it offers better performance, especially with animations.

Introducing Animations

WPF offers lots of interesting features about graphics and multimedia to provide a great user experience with rich client applications. Animations are one of these features. They enable visual elements (or just some portions of them) to move along the UI or to dynamically change their aspects during the specified interval. Subsequent sections explain how you can apply animations to WPF visual elements. There are different kinds of animations in WPF; this chapter covers the most common of them, `DoubleAnimation` and `ColorAnimation`.

NOTE

A special type of animation based on timelines is available, but it is not easy to implement with Visual Studio. However, it is the easiest animation that you can realize with Blend for Visual Studio 2015. With that said, from a developer perspective, this chapter covers animations based on storyboards.

Animations are cool in that they can be eventually controlled by pausing, removing, stopping, and manually playing and are represented by System.Windows.Media.Animation. Storyboard objects. Each Storyboard can define one or more DoubleAnimation or ColorAnimation that applies to transformations (see the previous section for details). To decide the time when animations need to come in, you define them within the control's triggers specifying an EventTrigger that requires you to specify the event representing the moment for the animation to run. For example, if you want an animation to start when a window is loaded, the EventTrigger points to Window.Loaded. Before providing any code example, add a new window to your current WPF project or create a new project from scratch. When the new window is ready, divide the default Grid into four cells by typing the following XAML:

```
<Grid Name="Grid1">
        <Grid.RowDefinitions>
            <RowDefinition/>
            <RowDefinition/>
        </Grid.RowDefinitions>

        <Grid.ColumnDefinitions>
            <ColumnDefinition/>
            <ColumnDefinition/>
        </Grid.ColumnDefinitions>
</Grid>
```

Applying DoubleAnimation

A DoubleAnimation object enables you to animate the specified transform property; it also enables you to revert the motion, specify the duration, and specify whether the animation needs to be repeated unlimitedly. The first example animates an image, applying the animation to a SkewTransform and to a ScaleTransform contextually. The code in Listing 30.4 shows how to accomplish this.

LISTING 30.4   Applying a DoubleAnimation to an Image

```
        <Image Grid.Row="0" Grid.Column="0" Name="Image1"
Source="/StylesBrushesTemplatesAnimations;component/Images/Avatar.jpg">

            <Image.RenderTransform>
                <TransformGroup>
                    <SkewTransform x:Name="SkewImage"/>
                    <ScaleTransform x:Name="ScaleImage"/>
                </TransformGroup>
            </Image.RenderTransform>

            <Image.Triggers>
                <EventTrigger RoutedEvent="Image.Loaded">
                    <EventTrigger.Actions>
```

30

```
                    <BeginStoryboard>
                        <Storyboard>
                            <DoubleAnimation Storyboard.TargetName="SkewImage"
                                Storyboard.TargetProperty="AngleY"
                                            From="0" To="15" Duration="0:0:3"
                                            AutoReverse="True"
                                            RepeatBehavior="Forever" />
                            <DoubleAnimation Storyboard.TargetName="ScaleImage"
                                Storyboard.TargetProperty="ScaleX"
                                From="1" To="0.3" Duration="0:0:3"
                                            AutoReverse="True"
                                            RepeatBehavior="Forever" />
                            <DoubleAnimation Storyboard.TargetName="ScaleImage"
                                Storyboard.TargetProperty="ScaleY"
                                From="1" To="0.3" Duration="0:0:3"
                                            AutoReverse="True"
                                            RepeatBehavior="Forever" />
                        </Storyboard>
                    </BeginStoryboard>
                </EventTrigger.Actions>
            </EventTrigger>

        </Image.Triggers>
    </Image>
```

The code first applies to transformations. They are empty, with no properties set, therefore with no changes to the Image. But they have a name so that they can be referred to from the storyboard. The `EventTrigger` within triggers specifies the `Image.Loaded` routed event, which establishes that the animation will run when the image is loaded. The `BeginStoryboard` object is a container for children `Storyboard` objects. In the code example there is just one Storyboard that contains multiple `DoubleAnimation` objects. Notice how each `DoubleAnimation` refers to a transformation via the `Storyboard.TargetName` attached property and to the particular transformation's property via the `Storyboard.TargetProperty` attached property. `From` and `To` specify the starting and finish points of the animation, respectively. In the case of the `SkewTransform`, they specify the angle degrees, whereas in the case of the `ScaleTransform` they specify the scaling percentage. `Duration` is a property for specifying how many hours:minutes:seconds the animation will last; `AutoReverse` specifies whether the animation has to be repeated back, and `RepeatBehavior` specifies how long the animation will last (`Forever` is self-explanatory). At this point, run the application to have your image skewed and scaled via the animation. Refer to Figure 30.13 to see an approximate result. (Figures cannot show animations running!) Next, the code example about `DoubleAnimation` is applied to a `TextBlock` object for animating text. In this case you see the conjunction of a `RotateTransform` and `SkewTransform`. The code in Listing 30.5 provides the previously mentioned example.

LISTING 30.5   Applying `DoubleAnimation` to a `TextBlock`

```
<TextBlock Grid.Row="0" Grid.Column="1" Text="Animated Text" FontSize="24"
        FontFamily="Verdana" FontWeight="Bold"
        HorizontalAlignment="Center"
        VerticalAlignment="Center" RenderTransformOrigin="0.5 0.5">

<TextBlock.Foreground>
  <LinearGradientBrush>
    <GradientStop Offset="0" Color="Red" />
    <GradientStop Offset="0.5" Color="Yellow" />
    <GradientStop Offset="1" Color="Orange"/>
  </LinearGradientBrush>
</TextBlock.Foreground>

<TextBlock.RenderTransform>
    <TransformGroup>
        <RotateTransform x:Name="RotateText" />
        <SkewTransform x:Name="SkewText"/>
    </TransformGroup>
</TextBlock.RenderTransform>

<TextBlock.Triggers>
  <EventTrigger RoutedEvent="TextBlock.Loaded">
    <BeginStoryboard>
      <Storyboard Name="TextAnimation">
        <DoubleAnimation Storyboard.TargetName="RotateText"
                    Storyboard.TargetProperty="Angle"
                    From="0" To="360" Duration="0:0:5"
                    RepeatBehavior="Forever" />

        <DoubleAnimation Storyboard.TargetName="SkewText"
                    AutoReverse="True"
                    Storyboard.TargetProperty="AngleX"
                    From="0" To="45" Duration="0:0:5"
                    RepeatBehavior="Forever" />

      </Storyboard>
    </BeginStoryboard>
  </EventTrigger>
</TextBlock.Triggers>
</TextBlock>
```

The logic is the same, with the `EventTrigger` and transformations. The first
`DoubleAnimation` is applied to a `RotateTransform` that affects rotation degrees. Run the
code to get an idea of the result and refer to Figure 30.13 for a graphical representation.

Applying `ColorAnimation`

A `ColorAnimation` enables you to animate colors within a brush, such as
`LinearGradientBrush` and `RadialGradientBrush`. A color is replaced with another one
passing through a gradient. The next example is a little bit particular because it will be
applied to a `DataGrid` control to demonstrate that business controls can receive animations. The `DataGrid` exposes an `AlternatingRowBackground` property that enables you to
specify a different color for alternating rows. The goal of the example is animating colors
in the background of such rows. For this, code in Listing 30.6 shows how to apply the
described color animation.

LISTING 30.6   Applying a `ColorAnimation`

```
<DataGrid Name="CustomerDataGrid" AutoGenerateColumns="True"
        Grid.Row="1" Grid.Column="1" Margin="5">
    <DataGrid.AlternatingRowBackground>
        <LinearGradientBrush EndPoint="0.5,1" StartPoint="0.5,0">
            <GradientStop Color="Black" Offset="0" />
            <GradientStop Color="Black" Offset="1" />
            <GradientStop Color="White" Offset="0.4" />
            <GradientStop Color="White" Offset="0.6" />
        </LinearGradientBrush>
    </DataGrid.AlternatingRowBackground>
    <DataGrid.Triggers>
        <EventTrigger RoutedEvent="DataGrid.Loaded">
            <EventTrigger.Actions>
                <BeginStoryboard>
                    <Storyboard>
                        <ColorAnimation From="Black" To="Violet"
                                    Duration="0:0:2"
                                    Storyboard.TargetProperty=
                            "AlternatingRowBackground.GradientStops[0].Color"
                                    AutoReverse="True"
                                    RepeatBehavior="Forever"/>
                        <ColorAnimation From="Black" To="Chartreuse"
                                    Duration="0:0:2"
                                    AutoReverse="True"
                                    RepeatBehavior="Forever"
                                    Storyboard.TargetProperty=
                            "AlternatingRowBackground.GradientStops[3].Color"/>
                    </Storyboard>
                </BeginStoryboard>
            </EventTrigger.Actions>
        </EventTrigger>
    </DataGrid.Triggers>
</DataGrid>
```

As you can see, this type of animation works like `DoubleAnimation` except that `From` and `To` require you to specify the source and target colors. When referring to a `GradientStop`, you enclose its index within square parentheses. (Remember that the index is zero-based.) To complete the example, you need to populate the `DataGrid` with some data. Switch to the code behind file and write the code in Listing 30.7, which defines a `Customer` class, creates some instances of the class, and creates a `List(Of Customer)` collection that is the data source.

LISTING 30.7   Populating the `DataGrid`

```
Public Class Animations

    Private Sub Animations_Loaded(sender As Object,
                             e As System.Windows.RoutedEventArgs) _
                             Handles Me.Loaded

        Dim cust1 As New Customer With {.Address = "7Th street",
                .CompanyName = "Del Sole",
                .ContactName = "Alessandro Del Sole"}
        Dim cust2 As New Customer With {.Address = "5Th street",
                CompanyName = "Fictitious Red & White",
                ContactName = "Robert White"}

        Dim custList As New List(Of Customer) From {cust1, cust2}
        Me.CustomerDataGrid.ItemsSource = custList
    End Sub
End Class

Public Class Customer
    Public Property CompanyName As String
    Public Property Address As String
    Public Property ContactName As String
End Class
```

Run the application. You get the result represented in Figure 30.13.

Working with Animation Events

Storyboard objects expose events that can help you get control over the animations. The first step is assigning a name to the desired storyboard, as in the following example:

```
<Storyboard Name="ImageStoryBoard">
```

After you assign a name to the `Storyboard`, you can handle events summarized in Table 30.1.

30

FIGURE 30.13   The result of applied animations.

TABLE 30.1   Storyboard Events

Event	Occurs When
Completed	The animation completes.
Changed	An object is modified.
CurrentGlobalSpeedInvalidated	The time progress rate changes.
CurrentStateInvalidated	The CurrentState property of the animation clock changes.
CurrentTimeInvalidated	The CurrentTime property of the animation clock changes.
RemoveRequested	The animation clock is removed.

You handle the Completed event to make an action when an animation completes, as in the following code snippet:

```
Private Sub ImageStoryBoard_Completed(sender As Object,
                            e As System.EventArgs) _
                        Handles ImageStoryBoard.Completed
```

```
                'Write code for the animation completion
End Sub
```

Notice how animations do not throw routed events, whereas they raise standard events. `Storyboard` objects also expose some methods that enable controlling the animation in code, such as `Begin`, `Stop`, `Pause`, `Seek`, and `Resume`, which are all self-explanatory. Moreover, some animations explained through XAML can be set in Visual Basic code, as in the following code snippet:

```
With ImageStoryBoard
      AutoReverse = True
      RepeatBehavior = System.Windows.Media.Animation.
                       RepeatBehavior.Forever
      Duration = New TimeSpan(0, 0, 5)
End With
```

Animations can also be applied to 3D graphics that are beyond the scope of this book but that you can explore through the MSDN documentation.

Creating Animations with Visual Basic

Maybe you understood that XAML is the best way for creating, customizing, and managing visual elements. Writing VB code is something that you should practice only when there is an effective need to apply effects at runtime. This can also be the case of animations. The code in Listing 30.8 shows how to create at runtime a new button and how to apply an animation that increases and decreases the button's height. The code is not difficult to understand when you have a clear idea of the sequence of elements required within an animation.

LISTING 30.8   Creating an Animation in VB Code

```
Public Class Animations
      Private myAnimation As Animation.DoubleAnimation
      Private WithEvents aButton As Button
      Private heightAnimationStoryboard As Animation.Storyboard

      Private Sub CreateRuntimeAnimation()

          'An instance of a new Button
          aButton = New Button With {.Width = 150, .Height = 50,
                                 Content = "Runtime button",
                                 Name = "RuntimeButton"}

          'Associates the button's name to the Window names collection
          '(required at runtime)
          Me.RegisterName(aButton.Name, aButton)
```

30

```
    'Adds the Button to the Grid at the given row/column
    Grid.SetColumn(aButton, 0)
    Grid.SetRow(aButton, 1)
    Grid1.Children.Add(aButton)

    'Creates a new DoubleAnimation, with properties
    myAnimation = New Animation.DoubleAnimation
    With myAnimation
        AutoReverse = True
        'From and To are Nullable(Of Double)
        From = 50
        To = 15
        RepeatBehavior = Animation.RepeatBehavior.Forever
        Duration = New TimeSpan(0, 0, 3)
    End With

    'Sets the target control via its name
    Animation.Storyboard.SetTargetName(myAnimation, aButton.Name)
    'Sets the target property
    Animation.Storyboard.SetTargetProperty(myAnimation,
                                    New PropertyPath(Button.
                                            HeightProperty))

    'Create a new storyboard instance and adds the animation
    'to the storyboard's collection of animations
    heightAnimationStoryboard = New Animation.Storyboard
    heightAnimationStoryboard.Children.Add(myAnimation)
End Sub

'Starts the animation when the button is loaded
Private Sub aButton_Loaded(sender As Object, e As RoutedEventArgs) _
                    Handles aButton.Loaded
    heightAnimationStoryboard.Begin(aButton)
End Sub
End Class
```

The one thing you have to pay attention to is registering the button name because, otherwise, it will not be accessible at runtime by the animation. Another thing that is worth mentioning regards how you set the storyboard target property. This is accomplished via the `StoryBoard.SetTargetProperty` shared method that requires the animation instance and a `PropertyPath` instance that receives a dependency property as an argument. Figure 30.14 represents a particular moment of the animation running.

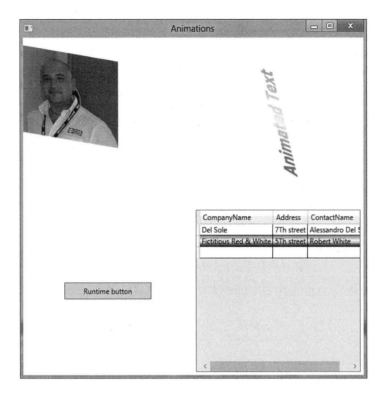

FIGURE 30.14   The application runs the Visual Basic-generated animation.

Summary

Windows Presentation Foundation offers great benefits for customizing user interface elements. In this chapter you got a high-level overview of the modes allowed for customizing elements and for making them more interesting to the final user. First, you got information about brushes and saw how many brushes are offered by WPF and how you can apply them for coloring or filling visual elements. Next, you learned about styles, understanding how you can use them for setting a common set of properties for the specified control type. Subsequently, you got an overview of control templates, learning how you can completely redefine the graphical aspect of a user control while keeping its behavior safe. You also got information on transformations, learning how they can dynamically change controls' appearance. Finally, you took a tour of animations, seeing how you can enrich your user interface with cool animations that take advantage of transformations. The next chapter discusses other important features of WPF: the ability to create dynamic documents and manage media contents.

30

Manipulating Media and Documents

Windows Presentation Foundation (WPF) offers native controls for working with media content and manipulating documents. This last topic is also important because documents are one of the most common requirements in modern applications, and WPF provides a way for creating and managing documents that can be dynamically arranged to offer a better user experience. In this chapter you learn how to use media contents to enrich your applications and to manipulate dynamic documents through built-in controls exposed by the .NET Framework.

Viewing Images

You use the `System.Windows.Controls.Image` control to show images. To see how the control works, create a new WPF project that will be used for all examples in this chapter and name it **DocumentsAndMedia.** When ready, drag an `Image` control from the toolbox onto the new `Window;` then set its dimensions as you like. To view an image, you need to set the `Source` property that points to a URI, but you might want to add some images to your project first. As for any other kind of project, it is a good idea to organize contents into subfolders based on their types. So, in Solution Explorer create a new project subfolder called Images. Right-click this folder and then select **Add, Existing Item**. When the dialog box appears, select the number of image files you want to be added to the project. At this point, select the `Image` control either in the XAML designer or in the XAML code editor and open the Properties window by pressing **F4**. Select the Source property and expand the drop-down box for this property (see Figure 31.1). Here you can pick up an image from a list of image files and the image will be assigned to the `Image` control.

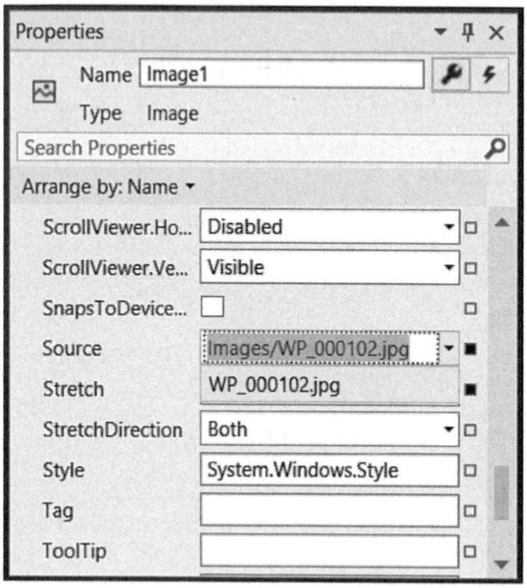

FIGURE 31.1   Adding images to the project.

Visual Studio automatically sets the `Source` property in XAML, taking advantage of the packed URI, as demonstrated by the following line of XAML code:

```
<Image Source="Images/IMG006.jpg"
  Stretch="Fill" Name="Image1" />
```

The `Stretch` property enables you to establish how pictures will be tiled inside the `Image` control. `Fill`, which is the default value, dynamically adapts the picture to fill the entire `Image` control, but when you resize the control you can lose the original aspect ratio. If you instead use `Uniform`, you can keep the aspect ratio and dynamically adapt the picture. While setting `UniformToFill`, the picture will work like `Uniform` except that it will clip the source image so that the layout will be based on the `Image` control size. If you assign the `Stretch` property with `None`, the source image will be shown in its original size. Figure 31.2 shows how the image looks with `Stretch` set as `Fill`. You can also assign the `Source` property at runtime from Visual Basic code so you can provide users the capability to select different pictures. Unlike the XAML code, in VB you need to first create an instance of the `BitmapImage` class and assign some of its properties as follows:

```
Private Sub LoadPicture(fileName As String)

    Dim img As New BitmapImage
    With img
            .BeginInit()
            .BaseUri = New Uri("MyPicture.jpg")
            .EndInit()
End With
        Image1.Source = img
End Sub
```

FIGURE 31.2   Showing images with the `Image` control.

You invoke `BeginInit` to start editing; then you set `BaseUri` pointing to the desired file and finally invoke `EndInit` to finish editing. When you perform these steps, you can assign the new instance to the `Image.Source` property.

Playing Media

Windows Presentation Foundation enables you to easily reproduce media files, such as audio and videos, through the `System.Windows.Controls.MediaElement` control. This enables reproducing, among others, all media contents supported by the Windows Media Player application, such as .wmv, .wma, .avi, and .mp3 files. This section shows you how to build a simple media player using `MediaElement` and Visual Basic 2015. Now add a new `Window` to an existing project, setting this as the main window. The goal of the next example is to implement a media player and buttons for controlling media reproduction. Code in Listing 31.1 declares the user interface (UI).

LISTING 31.1   Defining the User Interface for a Simple Media Player

```
<Window x:Class="PlayingMedia"
    xmlns="http://schemas.microsoft.com/winfx/2006/xaml/presentation"
    xmlns:x="http://schemas.microsoft.com/winfx/2006/xaml"
    Title="PlayingMedia" Height="300" Width="600">
    <Grid>
        <Grid.RowDefinitions>
```

```
            <RowDefinition />
            <RowDefinition Height="50" />
        </Grid.RowDefinitions>
        <MediaElement Name="Media1" Grid.Row="0" LoadedBehavior="Manual"
                Volume="{Binding ElementName=VolumeSlider, Path=Value}"
                MediaFailed="Media1_MediaFailed"
                MediaEnded="Media1_MediaEnded"/>

        <StackPanel Orientation="Horizontal" Grid.Row="1">
            <Button Name="PlayButton" Width="70" Height="40"
                Margin="5" Click="PlayButton_Click"
                Content="Play"/>

        <Button Name="PauseButton" Width="70" Height="40"
            Margin="5" Click="PauseButton_Click"
            Content="Pause"/>

        <Button Name="StopButton" Width="70" Height="40"
            Margin="5" Click="StopButton_Click"
            Content="Stop"/>

        <Button Name="BrowseButton" Width="40" Height="40"
            Margin="5" Content="..."
            Click="BrowseButton_Click"/>

        <Slider Name="VolumeSlider" Width="80" Margin="5"
                Minimum="0" Maximum="1" Value="0.5"
                TickFrequency="0.1"
                AutoToolTipPlacement="TopLeft"
                TickPlacement="BottomRight"
                ToolTip="Adjust volume"/>
        </StackPanel>
    </Grid>
</Window>
```

The MediaElement control has no look, so when you place it onto the user interface, it has a dark gray background and border, although you can replace this with your custom background and border. The LoadedBehavior property enables you to establish how the media file needs to be reproduced. For example, Play means that the associated video will be automatically played when the control is loaded; Manual means that playing will be started via Visual Basic code at the specified moment. (IntelliSense can help you to choose the most appropriate self-explanatory option.) You associate a media file to the MediaElement by assigning the Source property, but this is not mandatory because you can accomplish this later in code. The Volume property enables you to adjust reproduction volume, and its range is between 0 and 1. In this example the Volume value is bound to the `VolumeSlider.Value` property. The control also offers some events such as `MediaFailed` and `MediaEnded` that are raised when an error occurs when attempting to open the media file and when the reproduction completes, respectively. The `MediaElement` control also provides some methods for controlling reproduction in code, such as `Play`, `Pause`, and `Stop`. The code in Listing 31.2 shows how to implement the features and how to enable media selection from disk.

LISTING 31.2   Controlling the MediaElement in Code

```
Public Class PlayingMedia

    Dim sourceMedia As String = String.Empty

    Private Sub Media1_MediaEnded(sender As System.Object,
            e As System.Windows.
            RoutedEventArgs)
        'Playing completed
    End Sub

    Private Sub Media1_MediaFailed(sender As System.Object,
            e As System.Windows.
            ExceptionRoutedEventArgs)
        MessageBox.Show(e.ErrorException.Message)
    End Sub

    Private Sub PlayButton_Click(sender As System.Object,
            e As System.Windows.RoutedEventArgs)
        If String.IsNullOrEmpty(Me.sourceMedia) = False Then
            Me.Media1.Play()
        End If
    End Sub

    Private Sub PauseButton_Click(sender As System.Object,
            e As System.Windows.RoutedEventArgs)
        If String.IsNullOrEmpty(Me.sourceMedia) = False Then
            Me.Media1.Pause()
        End If
    End Sub

    Private Sub StopButton_Click(sender As System.Object,
            e As System.Windows.RoutedEventArgs)
        If String.IsNullOrEmpty(Me.sourceMedia) = False Then
            Me.Media1.Stop()
        End If
    End Sub
```

```
    Private Sub BrowseButton_Click(sender As System.Object,
            e As System.Windows.RoutedEventArgs)
        Dim dialog As New Microsoft.Win32.OpenFileDialog

        With dialog
            .Title = "Select a media file"
            .Filter = "Avi & Wmv|*.avi;*.wmv|Audio|*.wma;*.mp3|All files|*.*"
            If .ShowDialog = True Then
            Me.sourceMedia = .FileName
            Me.Media1.Source = New Uri(sourceMedia,
                UriKind.RelativeOrAbsolute)
            End If
        End With
    End Sub
End Class
```

Notice how the `MediaFailed` event handler shows an error message in case an exception is thrown and how the media file is assigned under the form of a URI to the `MediaElement`. `Source` property. This also means that you can assign a URI such as a web address to play media content stored on a website. Now you can run the application, click the **Browse** button to select your media content, and click **Play**. Figure 31.3 shows the application playing a video. The `MediaElement` control also offers a `Position` property (of type `TimeSpan`) that provides the capability to seek the desired position within the media content.

FIGURE 31.3   The sample application playing a video.

Manipulating Documents

One of the most important requirements in modern applications is the ability to manage documents. WPF offers the `System.Windows.Documents` namespace that exposes objects so you can create flexible and dynamic documents that can adapt their layouts dynamically to the user interface. These kinds of documents use the Clear Type technology and are hosted inside `FlowDocument` objects. A `FlowDocument` is composed of `Paragraph` objects where you can place and format your text. Paragraphs are powerful because they enable you to add figures, bulleted lists, fully functional hyperlinks, and text formatting. To present and browse a flow document, you need to add a `FlowDocumentReader` control to the user interface. Flexibility and dynamicity are just two benefits of flow documents. Another cool feature in flow documents is that users can interact with documents as if they were reading a book, so they can add annotations and highlights that can be stored to disk for later reuse. Annotations are provided by the `System.Windows.Annotations` namespace that needs to be imported at the XAML level. The goals of the next code example are

▶ Illustrating how you can create flow documents

▶ Illustrating how you can add and format text within flow documents

▶ Implementing features for adding annotations to documents and saving them to disk

Add a new `Window` to the current one, setting it as the startup page. When ready, write the XAML code shown in Listing 31.3 that implements the UI side of the application. The code is explained at the end of the listing.

> **NOTE**
>
> The content of the sample flow document is just an excerpt of the content of Chapter 28, "Creating WPF Applications," which is provided as an example, but you can replace it with a more complete text of your own.

LISTING 31.3   Implementing Flow Documents

```
<Window x:Class="ManipulatingDocuments"
    xmlns="http://schemas.microsoft.com/winfx/2006/xaml/presentation"
    xmlns:x="http://schemas.microsoft.com/winfx/2006/xaml"
    xmlns:ann="clr-namespace:System.Windows.Annotations;assembly=
➡PresentationFramework"
    Title="ManipulatingDocuments" Height="480" Width="600">
    <Grid>
        <Grid.RowDefinitions>
            <RowDefinition />
            <RowDefinition Height="40"/>
        </Grid.RowDefinitions>
```

```xml
      <StackPanel Grid.Row="1" Orientation="Horizontal">
      <StackPanel.Resources>
          <Style x:Key="ButtonStyle" TargetType="Button">
  <Setter Property="Width" Value="100"/>
  <Setter Property="Height" Value="30"/>
  <Setter Property="Margin" Value="5"/>
</Style>
</StackPanel.Resources>

      <Button Command="ann:AnnotationService.CreateTextStickyNoteCommand"
      CommandTarget="{Binding ElementName=FlowReader1}"
      Style="{StaticResource ButtonStyle}">
      Add note</Button>
    <Separator/>
    <Button Command="ann:AnnotationService.CreateInkStickyNoteCommand"
       CommandTarget="{Binding ElementName=FlowReader1}"
       Style="{StaticResource ButtonStyle}">
    Add Ink
    </Button>
    <Separator/>
    <Button Command="ann:AnnotationService.DeleteStickyNotesCommand"
          CommandTarget="{Binding ElementName=FlowReader1}"
          Style="{StaticResource ButtonStyle}">
          Remove note
    </Button>
    <Separator/>
    <Button Command="ann:AnnotationService.CreateHighlightCommand"
          CommandTarget="{Binding ElementName=FlowReader1}"
          Style="{StaticResource ButtonStyle}">
        Highlight
  </Button>
  <Separator/>
  <Button Command="ann:AnnotationService.ClearHighlightsCommand"
          CommandTarget="{Binding ElementName=FlowReader1}"
          Style="{StaticResource ButtonStyle}">
          Remove highlight
  </Button>
  </StackPanel>

  <FlowDocumentReader Grid.Row="0" BorderThickness="2" Name="FlowReader1">
      <FlowDocument Name="myDocument"
      TextAlignment="Justify"
      IsOptimalParagraphEnabled="True"
      IsHyphenationEnabled="True"
      IsColumnWidthFlexible="True"
      ColumnWidth="300"
```

```
        ColumnGap="20">
          <Paragraph FontSize="36" FontWeight="Bold"
          FontStyle="Oblique">Chapter 28</Paragraph>
      <Paragraph FontSize="24" FontWeight="Bold">Introducing
          WPF</Paragraph>
      <Paragraph>
                    Windows Presentation Foundation relies on a layered architecture
                    that is represented in Figure 28.1. The first layer is the
                    Windows operating system. The second layer is constituted by the
                    combination of two communicating layers:
                    User32, which is the part of the operating system responsible
                    for exchanging messages with applications, and the DirectX
                    libraries which are the real power of WPF.
                     <!-- Add other text here.... -->
                     <Figure Width="300">
                        <BlockUIContainer>
                        <StackPanel>
                      <!--Replace the image file with a valid one-->
                        <Image
            Source="/DocumentsAndMedia;component/Images/28fig01.tif"
                            Width="200"
                            Height="300"
                            Stretch="Fill" />
                            <Separator></Separator>
                            <TextBlock VerticalAlignment="Center"
                            Width="220" TextWrapping="Wrap"
                            FontSize="10" FontStyle="Italic">
                            Figure 28.1 - WPF architecture
      </TextBlock>
     </StackPanel>
    </BlockUIContainer>
                    </Figure>
                    <Bold>PresentationFramework</Bold> exposes namespaces
                    and classes
                    through a complex hierarchy of inheritance,
                    where the root class is System.Object.
                    Such hierarchy provides the infrastructure for the user
                    interface elements.
                    This hierarchy is composed by the following list of classes,
                    where each class inherits from the previous one:
            </Paragraph>
            <List>
                <ListItem>
                    <Paragraph
                    FontFamily="Courier New">System.Object</Paragraph>
                </ListItem>
```

```
        <ListItem>
            <Paragraph
            FontFamily="Courier New">
            System.Threading.DispatcherObject</Paragraph>
        </ListItem>
        <ListItem>
            <Paragraph FontFamily="Courier New">
            System.Windows.DependencyObject</Paragraph>
        </ListItem>
        <ListItem>
            <Paragraph
            FontFamily="Courier New">
            System.Windows.Media.Visual</Paragraph>
        </ListItem>
    </List>
        <Paragraph>
        The
        <Hyperlink
        NavigateUri="http://msdn.microsoft.com/en-
        us/library/ms750441(VS.110).aspx
        #System_Threading_DispatcherObject">
        System.Threading.DispatcherObject</Hyperlink>
    is responsible for threading and messages which
    WPF relies on. The dispatcher takes advantage
    of the User32 messages for performing
    cross thread calls.
        </Paragraph>
    </FlowDocument>
    </FlowDocumentReader>
 </Grid>
</Window>
```

Let's begin by illustrating the `FlowDocumentReader` control. It provides a container for flow documents and automatically implements buttons for browsing multiple-page documents and controlling documents' layout, as you see later in Figure 31.4. The `FlowDocument` object instead contains the document and exposes some interesting properties. The previous code uses the most important ones. `TextAlignment` enables specifying how the text must be aligned within the document and can have one of the following values: `Center`, `Right`, `Left`, or `Justify`. `IsOptimalParagraph` set as `True` enables paragraph layout optimization. `IsHyphenationEnable` set as `True` enables word hyphenation in the document. `IsColumnWidthFlexible` set as `True` means that the value of the `ColumnWidth` property is not fixed. This last property takes place when you enable the document view by columns. The `ColumnGap` property indicates the spacing between columns. A complete list of properties is available in the MSDN Library: http://msdn.microsoft.com/en-us/library/system. windows.documents.flowdocument.aspx. For the document content, notice the following techniques:

▶ You divide the content into multiple Paragraph objects to provide different paragraph formatting.

▶ You can add inline formatting. For example, the following line contains bold formatting within a paragraph:

```
<Bold>PresentationFramework</Bold> exposes namespaces and classes
```

▶ You can also add fully functional hyperlinks as in the following sample line:

```
<Hyperlink
 NavigateUri="http://msdn.microsoft.com/en-
us/library/ms750441(VS.110).aspx#System_Threading_DispatcherObject">
        System.Threading.DispatcherObject</Hyperlink>
```

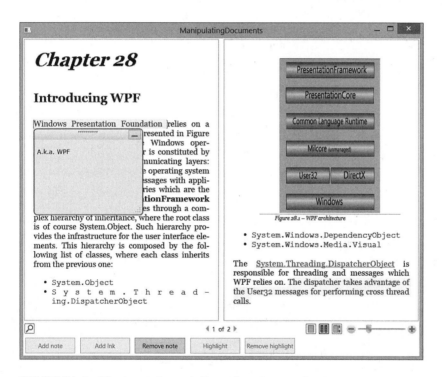

FIGURE 31.4   Viewing and annotating a flow document.

The sample document also shows how to implement bulleted lists via a `List` object that contains `ListItem` elements. It is interesting how flow documents also support figure insertion via a `Figure` element that contains a `BlockUIContainer` object nesting an `Image` control that stores the figure and a `TextBlock` control describing the figure. Each paragraph and subparagraph can be customized by setting font properties different from other paragraphs.

Switching the discussion to buttons implementation, instead of handling `Click` events, the code uses a technique known as *commanding* that takes advantage of built-in commands associated to specific actions. Each button is associated to one of the built-in actions for the annotation service via the `Command` property and points to the flow document as the target of the action (`CommandTarget`). At this point, you need to write code that enables the annotation service at the application startup so that the user can annotate or highlight text and then save annotations to disk for later reuse. The annotation service relies on the `System.Windows.Annotations` namespace that provides an `AnnotationService` class whose instance enables you to edit the document. Next, the `System.Windows.Annotations.Storage` namespace provides objects for storing annotations to XML files for later reuse. The code in Listing 31.4 shows how to implement the annotation service with Visual Basic. The code must be written to the code-behind file for the current window and contains comments for better reading.

LISTING 31.4   Implementing the Annotation Service

```vb
Imports System.Windows.Annotations
Imports System.Windows.Annotations.Storage
Imports System.IO


Public Class ManipulatingDocuments

    Dim annotationStream As FileStream

    Private Sub ManipulatingDocuments_Initialized(sender As Object,
                e As System.EventArgs) _
                Handles Me.Initialized

        'Gets the instance of the AnnotationService pointing to the FlowDocument
        Dim annotationServ As AnnotationService = _
            AnnotationService.GetService(FlowReader1)

        'Declares a store for annotations
        Dim annotationArchive As AnnotationStore

        'If no annotation service already exists for
        'the current flow document...
        If annotationServ Is Nothing Then
            '...creates a new service
            ' and a new store to an Xml file
            annotationStream = New FileStream("annotations.xml",
                        FileMode.OpenOrCreate)
            annotationServ = New AnnotationService(FlowReader1)

            'Gets the instance of the stream
            annotationArchive = New XmlStreamStore(annotationStream)
```

```
            'Enables the document
            annotationServ.Enable(annotationArchive)
        End If
    End Sub

    Private Sub ManipulatingDocuments_Closed(sender As Object,
            e As System.EventArgs) _
            Handles Me.Closed
        Dim annotationServ As AnnotationService = _
        AnnotationService.GetService(FlowReader1)

        'If an instance of the annotation
        'service is available
        If annotationServ IsNot Nothing And _
            annotationServ.IsEnabled Then

            'shuts down the service
            'and releases resources
            annotationServ.Store.Flush()
            annotationServ.Disable()
            annotationStream.Close()
        End If
    End Sub
End Class
```

The annotation service startup is placed inside the `Window.Initialized` event handler, whereas the annotation service shutdown is placed inside the `Window.Closed` event handler. Now run the demo application by pressing **F5**. As you can see on the screen, if you resize the window, the flow document content is automatically and dynamically adapted to the window's layout. Moreover, you can decide, using the appropriate controls on the `FlowDocumentReader`, how the document has to be viewed (for example, if one or two pages appear on the window or with zoom enabled). The best way for getting a feel about how this works is to resize the window. Figure 31.4 shows how the application looks, including an example of annotation.

APPLYING ANNOTATIONS AND HIGHLIGHT

You apply annotations or highlights by selecting the desired text and then clicking one of the related buttons. You write the annotation text just after clicking the green box. Annotations are editable when reloaded.

You can also add ink annotations to your documents. Figure 31.5 shows how ink annotations look and how text is exposed with fonts other than the standard one. Also notice how the hyperlink is correctly highlighted and functional so that if you click it, you will be redirected to the related web page associated via the `NavigateUri` property in the XAML code.

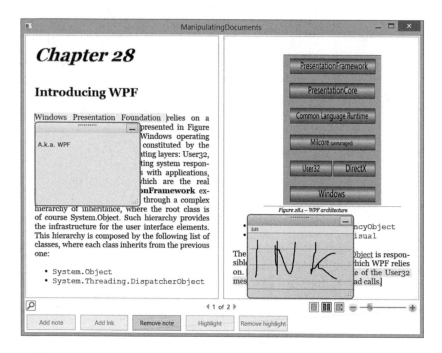

FIGURE 31.5   Adding ink notes and viewing formatted text.

Annotations are automatically stored into an XML file, as implemented in code. Remember to resize the window to understand the flexibility of flow documents and of the `FlowDocumentReader` control.

Understanding the `RichTextBox` Control

WPF offers a `RichTextBox` control that works as you would expect for some aspects, thus enabling advanced formatting and image support. However, it differs from other technologies in that this control stores its content as a flow document. This is the reason for discussing this control in the current chapter. In XAML code the control definition looks like this:

```
<RichTextBox Name="RichTextBox1">
    <!-- add your flow document here -->
</RichTextBox>
```

You could nest within the control the flow document shown in the previous section to get a fully editable document or write your text into the control, where such text takes standard formatting settings. You can also load an existing file into the `RichTextBox`, which requires some lines of code. The following method shows how to load a document as text:

```
Private Sub LoadDocument(fileName As String)

    Dim range As TextRange

    If File.Exists(fileName) Then
        range = New TextRange(RichTextBox1.Document.ContentStart,
            RichTextBox1.Document.ContentEnd)

        Using documentStream As New FileStream(fileName,
                FileMode.
                OpenOrCreate)
            range.Load(documentStream,
                System.Windows.DataFormats.Text)
        End Using
    End If
End Sub
```

The TextRange class represents the text area, and the code takes the entire area from start to end. Then the code invokes the TextRange.Load method to open the specified stream and converts the file content into a System.Windows.DataFormats.Text format that is acceptable for the RichTextBox. Notice that the previous example loads a text document that is then converted into XAML by the runtime. You can also load contents from XAML files using the DataFormats.Xaml option. To save the document content, you need to invoke the TextRange.Save method. The following method shows an example:

```
Private Sub SaveDocument(fileName As String)
    Dim range As New TextRange(Me.RichTextBox1.Document.ContentStart,
            Me.RichTextBox1.Document.ContentEnd)

    Using documentStream As New FileStream(fileName,
            FileMode.Create)
        range.Save(documentStream, DataFormats.Xaml)
    End Using

End Sub
```

In this case the document content is saved under the form of XAML content, but you can still use the Text option to save such content as text, although this can cause a loss of formatting settings due to the restrictive conversion.

Implementing Spell Check

The RichTextBox control provides built-in spell check support. This can be enabled by setting the SpellCheck.IsEnabled property as follows:

```
<RichTextBox Name="RichTextBox1" SpellCheck.IsEnabled="True">
```

When enabled, when the user types unrecognized words in the English language the words are highlighted in red. By right-clicking the highlighted word, a list of valid alternatives is suggested, similar to what happens in applications such as Microsoft Word. Figure 31.6 shows how the spell check feature can help users fix typos in their documents.

FIGURE 31.6   The built-in spell check feature helps users fix typos.

Viewing XPS Documents

Starting from Windows Vista, Microsoft introduced a new file format known as XPS that is a portable file format for documents and is useful because you can share documents without having installed the application that generated that type of document because you need a viewer. WPF offers full support for XPS documents, also offering a `DocumentViewer` control that enables developers to embed XPS viewing functionalities in their applications. Support for XPS documents is provided by the ReachFramework. dll assembly (so you need to add a reference) that exposes the `System.Windows.Xps.Packaging` namespace. For code, you drag the `DocumentViewer` control from the toolbox onto the `Window` surface so that the generated XAML looks like the following:

```
<DocumentViewer Name="DocumentViewer1" />
```

At design time, this control offers a number of buttons for adjusting the document layout, zooming, and printing. XPS documents are fixed documents, unlike flow documents, so you need to create an instance of the `XpsDocument` class and get a fixed sequence of sheets to be assigned to the `Document` property of the viewer. This is demonstrated in the following code snippet that enables loading and presenting an XPS document:

```
Dim documentName As String = "C:\MyDoc.xps"
Dim xpsDoc As XpsDocument

xpsDoc = New XpsDocument(documentName, IO.FileAccess.ReadWrite)
DocumentViewer1.Document = xpsDoc.GetFixedDocumentSequence
```

Figure 31.7 shows a sample XPS document opened in the `DocumentViewer` control.

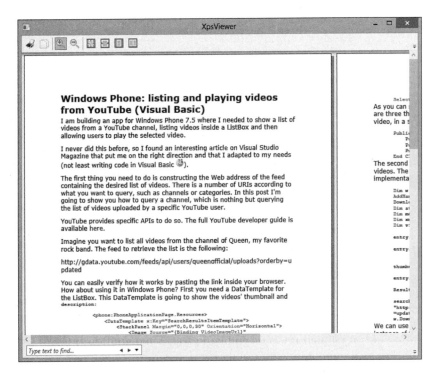

FIGURE 31.7   Viewing XPS documents through the DocumentViewer control.

So with a few steps, you can embed XPS functionalities in your applications.

Summary

This chapter was an overview about manipulating media and documents in WPF 4.6. You saw how you can present pictures with the Image control and how to reproduce media contents, such as videos and audio, through the MediaElement control, which also exposes events that you can intercept to understand the state of reproduction. Then flow documents and the FlowDocumentReader and RichTextBox controls were covered, examining how documents can be produced for dynamic arrangement within the user interface. Finally, the chapter discussed WPF support for XPS documents through the DocumentViewer control and the XpsDocument class.

CHAPTER **32**

Introducing
Data-Binding

Many developers erroneously used to think of Windows
Presentation Foundation (WPF) as just a multimedia platform, especially when the first versions came out. WPF is
instead a complete framework for rich client applications
development, including datacentric applications. This technology offers a powerful data-binding engine, and version
4.6 provides the ideal environment for building great business applications. This chapter provides a high-level introduction to the data-binding in WPF 4.6 with Visual Basic
2015, discussing the most important .NET objects that you
can explore in further studies by applying WPF-specific
patterns such as Model-View-View Model (MVVM).

SYSTEM REQUIREMENTS

Code examples are provided that require the Northwind
database to be installed and made available on SQL
Server 2014 Express or higher. You should already have
done this if you read the chapters about LINQ.

In this case, this note is just a quick reminder.

Introducing the Data-Binding
in WPF

Windows Presentation Foundation offers a powerful
data-binding engine, held by the `System.Windows.Data`
namespace, which makes binding data to the user interface (UI) and receiving input from the user even simpler.
At a higher level, you perform data-binding between a
user control and a data source making use of the `Binding`
markup extension, which a lot of controls enable. It is
worth mentioning that in WPF, a data source can be a

collection of .NET objects but also a property from another user control. The following examples show you both scenarios. Particularly, you receive an explanation of the
`DataGrid` control for tabular data representations and the `ObservableCollection(Of T)` in
action for binding to a collection. Before going on, create a new WPF project with Visual
Basic and name it `IntroducingDataBinding`. When the code editor is ready, write the
following XAML code that divides the root `Grid` into two columns and adds some controls
that will be necessary for the next examples:

```xaml
<Grid Name="Grid1">
    <Grid.ColumnDefinitions>
        <ColumnDefinition Width="200" />
        <ColumnDefinition />
    </Grid.ColumnDefinitions>

    <StackPanel Grid.Column="0">
        <TextBox Name="ValueTextBox"
            Margin="5"/>

        <Slider Name="ValueSlider" Margin="5"
            Minimum="0" Maximum="10"/>
    </StackPanel>
    <StackPanel Grid.Column="1">
        <DataGrid Name="DataGrid1"
            Height="150"/>
        <TextBox Margin="5" Foreground="Red"
            Name="LogBox"
            Height="100"/>
    </StackPanel>
</Grid>
```

Utilized user controls now have no other properties than the ones necessary for defining
their layout, which are set in code in the next sections.

Binding UI Elements with the `Binding` Markup Extension

You perform data-binding between a user control and a data source via the `Binding` XAML
markup extension. Such an extension requires specifying two properties: `ElementName`,
which is the source item name, and `Path`, which is the property containing the actual
data to bind and whose name must be exposed by the object assigned to `ElementName`.
The following example, in which you have to substitute to the first `TextBox` in the earlier
example, shows how to bind the context of a `TextBox` to the value of a `Slider` control so
that when the user moves the selector, the slider value is reflected into the `TextBox`:

```xaml
<TextBox Text="{Binding ElementName=ValueSlider,
        Path=Value}"
    Name="ValueTextBox"
    Margin="5"/>
```

Binding has to be applied to the property that will present bound data, in this case Text. If you now run the application and move the selector on the slider, you see how its value is reflected as the TextBox.Text content, as demonstrated in Figure 32.1.

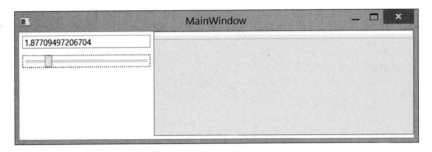

FIGURE 32.1   Binding a control's property to another control's content.

This is the most basic data-binding example and can be considered as the one-way mode because the binding is performed only from the data-source (the Slider.Value property) to the UI control (the TextBox). In fact, the data-binding does not return a value from the TextBox to the Slider. To accomplish this, which means updating the Slider value according to the TextBox content, you need the two-way data-binding that enables binding from and to the data source. You apply for two-way data-binding by adding the Mode=TwoWay assignment within the Binding markup extension. The following code demonstrates this:

```
<TextBox Text="{Binding ElementName=ValueSlider,
            Path=Value, Mode=TwoWay}"
        Name="ValueTextBox"
        Margin="5"/>

<Slider Name="ValueSlider" Margin="5"
        Minimum="0" Maximum="10"
        Value="{Binding ElementName=ValueTextBox,
        Path=Text, Mode=TwoWay}"/>
```

Notice how both controls need to set binding on the two-way mode so that they can reflect each other's value. If you run the application, you can see how the slider's selector value is updated according to the text box content. One-way and two-way are not the only allowed modes. Table 32.1 summarizes available data-binding modes in WPF, exposed by the System.Windows.Data.BindingMode enumeration.

TABLE 32.1   Available Data-Binding Modes

Mode	Description
OneWay	The data-binding is performed only from the data source to the UI. Changes on the data source are reflected to the UI, but not vice versa.

Mode	Description
TwoWay	The data-binding is performed from the data source to the UI, and vice versa. Changes on the data source are reflected to the UI and changes via the UI are reflected to the data source.
OneWayToSource	Changes on the UI are reflected to the data source, but not vice versa. This is the opposite of OneWay.
OneTime	The data-binding is performed from the data source to the UI only once. When performed, changes are ignored and the UI is not updated. This is useful for presenting data, where you are sure that you will not update the data source.
Default	Applies the most convenient mode according to the user control. For example, the TextBox supports the two-way mode and thus this is the default mode. When you do not specify a different mode, this is the default.

Creating Bindings with Visual Basic

In case you need to create data-binding expressions at runtime, you need to write some Visual Basic code. You need an instance of the System.Windows.Data.Binding class setting some of its property and then pass such instance to the target control. The following snippet reproduces the data-binding expression described in the previous section, this time utilizing Visual Basic code:

```
Dim bind As New Binding
 'Instead of ElementName, use Source assigning the control
bind.Source = ValueSlider
bind.Path = New PropertyPath("Value")
bind.Mode = BindingMode.TwoWay
 'You set the binding considering a dependency property
Me.ValueTextBox.SetBinding(TextBox.TextProperty, bind)
```

Until now you saw the most basic data-binding technique that can be useful when you need to make controls depend on other controls' properties. In the next section you will see data-binding techniques against data sources based on .NET collections.

Understanding the DataGrid and the ObservableCollection

In most cases you perform data-binding operations against .NET collections, even when fetching data from databases. WPF offers a different binding mechanism, such as user controls like the new DataGrid, the ListView, or the ListBox; you can bind specific data to single controls like TextBox (for example, when building master-details representations). In this book, you get an example of how to take advantage of the DataGrid control, which offers a convenient and fast way for tabular data. The goal of the next example is binding a collection of objects to a DataGrid enabling you to insert/update/delete operations onto the collection. First, add a new implementation of the Person class to the project as follows:

```
Public Class Person

    Public Property FirstName As String
    Public Property LastName As String
    Public Property Age As Integer

End Class
```

Now add a new `People` class, which inherits from `ObservableCollection(Of Person)` as follows:

```
Imports System.Collections.ObjectModel

Public Class People
    Inherits ObservableCollection(Of Person)

End Class
```

This new collection is the data source for binding to the `DataGrid`. Now go to the VB code behind the file for the main window. You need to declare a variable of type `People` and handle the `Window_Loaded` event to instantiate some `Person` objects to populate the collection. The following code accomplishes this:

```
Private WithEvents source As People

Private Sub MainWindow_Loaded(sender As Object,
            e As System.Windows.
            RoutedEventArgs) Handles Me.Loaded

    Dim personA As New Person With {.FirstName = "Alessandro",
            .LastName = "Del Sole",
            .Age = 37}
    'fantasy name
    Dim personB As New Person With {.FirstName = "Robert",
            .LastName = "White",
            .Age = 40}

    source = New People
    source.Add(personA)
    source.Add(personB)
    Me.Grid1.DataContext = source

    'If you plan to data-bind only the DataGrid:
    'Me.DataGrid1.ItemsSource = source
End Sub
```

You easily created an instance of the People collection with collection initializers. The most important thing here is the assignment of the Grid.DataContext property. As a general rule, DataContext is a property that points to a data source, and all children controls within the panel that exposes the DataContext property will populate by picking up data from this property. This also means that DataContext has scope; for example, the Window.DataContext property can share data to all controls in the user interface, whereas the DataContext from a particular panel can share data only with controls nested in that particular panel. In the previous code example, only controls nested in the Grid (including thus the DataGrid) can populate picking data from the DataContext. This is not mandatory. If you have a single control that you want to bind, you do not need to assign the DataContext, but you can assign the specific control data property. For instance, the DataGrid control exposes an ItemsSource property (like ListView and ListBox) that populates the control. Data-binding to user interface controls in WPF is possible thanks to the implementation of the INotifyPropertyChanged interface. Controls can reflect changes from data sources that implement that interface. The ObservableCollection(Of T) generic collection also implements behind the scenes and therefore can notify the user interface of changes so that it can be refreshed automatically. This is the reason the example uses such a collection. This specialized collection is also interesting because it enables you to get information on what changed on data. It exposes a CollectionChanged event that offers an argument of type NotifyCollectionEventArgs that offers some useful information. For example, it enables intercepting when an item is added or removed or retrieving a collection of added items. Continuing with the example, suppose you want to create a sort of log to write a message each time an item is added or removed from the source collection. This is useful for demonstrating that the collection is effectively updated with changes performed through the user interface. The second TextBox in the user interface of the sample application is the place where log messages will be put. According to this, consider the following code snippet that provides an event handler for the CollectionChanged event:

```
'Requires an Imports System.Collections.Specialized directive
Private Sub
source_CollectionChanged(sender As Object,
            e As _
            NotifyCollectionChangedEventArgs) _
            Handles source.CollectionChanged

    Me.LogBox.Text += e.Action.ToString & Environment.NewLine
End Sub
```

The code sends to the text box the current value of the System.Collection.Specialized. NotifyCollectionChangedAction enumeration, which can be one of the following: Add, Remove, Move, Replace, or Reset. If you perform multiple CRUD operations on an ObservableCollection instance, you might also be interested in the NewItems and OldItems properties. They represent a collection of items added to the data source and a collection of items affected by a remove, replace, or move operation, respectively. Before running the application, it is necessary to perform a couple of operations on the DataGrid at the XAML level; therefore, switch back to the XAML code editor. Extend the `DataGrid` declaration as follows:

```
<DataGrid Name="DataGrid1"
          AutoGenerateColumns="True"
          AlternatingRowBackground="LightGreen"
          ItemsSource="{Binding}"
          Height="150"/>
```

First, the `DataGrid` automatically generates columns for you according to each property exposed by a single item (`Person`) in the bound collection (`People`). Second, the `ItemsSource`, which populates the control, is set to `Binding` with no arguments, meaning that the data-binding will be performed at runtime. Notice how the `AlternatingRowBackground` property enables specifying a color (which you can eventually replace with a brush) for the background in alternating rows. Now run the application. You get the result shown in Figure 32.2.

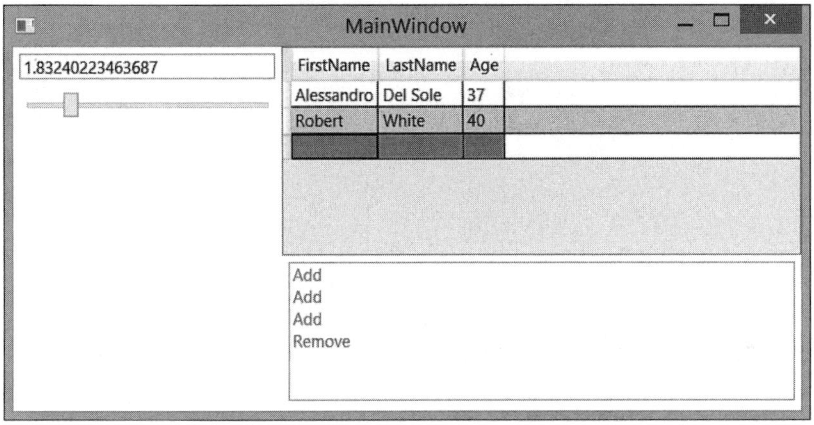

FIGURE 32.2   The data-bound `DataGrid` enables you to present and manipulate data.

DataGrid **BINDING TIPS**

Different from controls such as the `ListView` and the `ListBox`, the `DataGrid` enables you to bind any collection implementing `IList` or `IBindingList`. This is because such control requires a place for editing, other than presenting. So remember this requirement when you try to bind the result of LINQ queries to a `DataGrid`, which requires conversion into a generic collection. For LINQ, if you try to bind LINQ to XML, query results also remember to create a class for holding objects, just like the `Person` class and `People` collection instead of directly binding the query result.

If you play with the `DataGrid`, you can easily understand how it enables adding, removing, and editing items. The log text box stores messages each time you perform an operation, confirming that the underlying collection is actually affected by changes performed through the user interface. You can then plan to implement some code for saving your data. The `DataGrid` exposes other interesting properties:

- ▶ `.SelectedItem`, which returns the instance of the selected object in the control

- ▶ `.CurrentCell`, which returns the content of the selected cell

- ▶ `.CanUserAddRows` and `CanUserRemoveRows`, which provide (or not) the user the ability of adding and deleting rows, respectively

- ▶ `.CanUserReorderColumns`, `CanUserResizeColumns`, `CanUserSortColumns`, which provide (or not) the ability of changing the order of resizing and sorting columns

- ▶ `.CanUserResizeRows`, which provides (or not) the ability of resizing rows

- ▶ `.RowStyle`, which enables you to override the style for rows

So far, you've seen simple data-binding tasks, although the last code example provides a good way for understanding the mechanism. WPF data-binding is even more complex and the .NET Framework offers specific objects that are important in more articulate scenarios. The next section describes such objects taking advantage of new Visual Studio features.

Discussing the Drag and Drop Data-Binding

Visual Studio 2015 retakes from its predecessor the feature of the drag and drop data-binding, something that was already available in Windows Forms for many years. The drag and drop data-binding enables developers to quickly build data forms in WPF by dragging items from the Data Sources window, and Visual Studio will generate all the XAML code for you, including master-details scenarios. This section explains how you can take advantage of the WPF drag and drop data-binding to easily build data forms, explaining the meaning and behavior of the auto-generated code. This section also relies on many concepts described in Chapter 26, "Introducing ADO.NET Entity Framework," such as `DbContext` and `DbSet` classes, so refer to that chapter if you have any doubts.

TIP

The drag and drop data-binding has some limitations, and in many cases you need to put your hands over the auto-generated code or write your own data-binding code from scratch. This new technique offers several advantages: The result is completely customizable, as in the style of WPF applications; second, if you are new to data-binding in WPF, it enables you to understand how things work against a more complex data-source (such as an EDM or a DataSet). Finally, it also provides the ability of separating the data-source from the user interface, although this is something that you will probably need to edit according to your application logic.

To complete the next code examples, follow these steps:

1. Create a new WPF project for Visual Basic.

2. Add a new Entity Data Model based on the Northwind sample database, ensuring that you include the `Customers` and `Orders` tables. If you need a recap, take a look at Chapter 26.

After this brief introduction, it is time to understand how easy building data forms is with WPF 4.6.

Creating Tabular Data Forms

The goal of the next example is to show how simple it is to create tabular data representations, also taking a look at necessary objects for performing data-binding in code. To accomplish this, first divide the default Grid into two columns as follows:

```
<Grid>
    <Grid.ColumnDefinitions>
        <ColumnDefinition Width="200"/>
        <ColumnDefinition/>
    </Grid.ColumnDefinitions>
</Grid>
```

Next, add a `ListBox` control either by dragging it from the Toolbox or by writing the following code (for better layout purposes, ensure that you place it in the left column):

```
<ListBox Name="CustomersListBox"
        Grid.Column="0"/>
```

This `ListBox` stores a list of customers' names that will be added shortly. Now follow these steps:

1. Open the Data Sources window by clicking **Shift+Alt+D**.

2. Click **Add New Data Source**.

3. When the Data Source Configuration Wizard starts, select **Object** and then click **Next**.

4. Expand your project's name and its root namespace, select both the `Customer` and `Order` entities, and click **Finish**.

The Data Sources window now looks as shown in Figure 32.3.

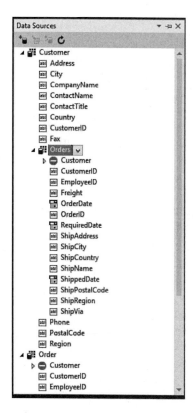

FIGURE 32.3   The Data Sources window lists entities from the EDM.

The default icon near each entity name indicates that data will be represented as tabular, but you can replace this representation with a list view or with a details view by selecting the appropriate value from the combo box on the right side of each entity name. (At the moment, leave the default selection unchanged.) Now, expand the Customers entity (as shown in Figure 32.3) and select the CompanyName item; then drag it onto the ListBox and release the mouse. When you release the mouse, you will not notice anything new on the designer surface, but look at what happened in the XAML code editor:

```
<Window.Resources>
    <CollectionViewSource x:Key="CustomersViewSource"
            d:DesignSource=
              "{d:DesignInstance my:Customer,
                CreateList=True}" />
</Window.Resources>
<Grid DataContext="{StaticResource CustomersViewSource}">
    <Grid.ColumnDefinitions>
        <ColumnDefinition Width="200"/>
        <ColumnDefinition/>
    </Grid.ColumnDefinitions>
```

```
<ListBox Name="CustomersListBox"
    Grid.Column="0" DisplayMemberPath="CompanyName"
    ItemsSource="{Binding}" />
</Grid>
```

Visual Studio generates some code, both XAML and Visual Basic, each time you perform some drag and drop action. For now, it generated a `CollectionViewSource` object within the window's resources. You can compare the WPF `CollectionViewSource` to the Windows Forms' `BindingSource` control, which acts like a bridge between the underlying data collection and the user interface. The code states that such `CollectionViewSource` is populated via a list (`CreateList=True`) of `Customer` instances. This statement is accomplished via the `d:DesignInstance` custom markup extension, exposed by the d XML namespace that points to Microsoft Expression Blend schema for WPF. This is useful because it provides resources for design-time data-binding. Notice also how Visual Studio added a `DataContext` property for the default `Grid`, whose source is the previously described `CollectionViewSource`. In this way, all child controls will populate by picking data from the `CollectionViewSource`. You can get an example of this by taking a look at the `ListBox` overridden definition: It is populated with data-binding (`ItemsSource` property) and shows just the value of the `CompanyName` property (`DisplayMemberPath`) for each item in the bound collection. Now drag onto the form the `Orders` item from the Data Sources window, ensuring that you drag the one nested within `Customers`. When dragged and dropped, the result should look like Figure 32.4.

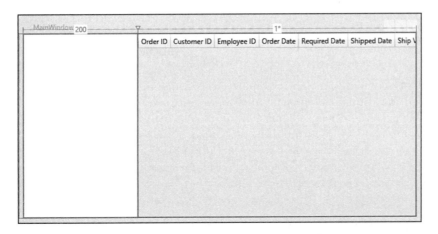

FIGURE 32.4   The result of the drag and drop operations in the Visual Studio designer.

First, notice how the new `DataGrid` control enables you to build tabular data representations. By dragging the data source, Visual Studio generated all the necessary items for you. If you now take a look at the XAML code editor, you will first notice a second `CollectionViewSource` referring to the `Orders` data:

```
<CollectionViewSource x:Key="CustomerOrdersViewSource"
        Source="{Binding Path=Orders,
        Source={StaticResource CustomersViewSource}}" />
```

Notice how the source for the data-binding is the Orders collection from the previously generated CustomersViewSource object of type CollectionViewSource. Next, Visual Studio also generated markup code for the DataGrid. For this, it did not take advantage of columns auto-generation; it instead created specific columns for each property in the bound collection. This enables the IDE to also generate custom cell templates that can show data with the appropriate control. The following is the XAML code for the DataGrid:

```
<DataGrid AutoGenerateColumns="False"
      EnableRowVirtualization="True"
      Grid.Column="1"
      ItemsSource="{Binding
      Source={StaticResource CustomerOrdersViewSource}}"
      Name="OrdersDataGrid"
      RowDetailsVisibilityMode="VisibleWhenSelected">
   <DataGrid.Columns>
    <DataGridTextColumn x:Name="OrderIDColumn"
        Binding="{Binding Path=OrderID}"
        Header="Order ID"
        Width="SizeToHeader" />
    <DataGridTextColumn x:Name="CustomerIDColumn"
        Binding="{Binding Path=CustomerID}"
        Header="Customer ID"
        Width="SizeToHeader" />
    <DataGridTextColumn x:Name="EmployeeIDColumn"
        Binding="{Binding Path=EmployeeID}"
        Header="Employee ID"
        Width="SizeToHeader" />
    <DataGridTemplateColumn x:Name="OrderDateColumn"
        Header="Order Date"
        Width="SizeToHeader">
    <DataGridTemplateColumn.CellTemplate>
     <DataTemplate>
      <DatePicker
         SelectedDate="{Binding Path=OrderDate}" />
     </DataTemplate>
    </DataGridTemplateColumn.CellTemplate>
   </DataGridTemplateColumn>
   <DataGridTemplateColumn x:Name="RequiredDateColumn"
        Header="Required Date"
        Width="SizeToHeader">
     <DataGridTemplateColumn.CellTemplate>
        <DataTemplate>
          <DatePicker
```

```xml
              SelectedDate="{Binding Path=RequiredDate}" />
    </DataTemplate>
    </DataGridTemplateColumn.CellTemplate>
 </DataGridTemplateColumn>
 <DataGridTemplateColumn x:Name="ShippedDateColumn"
        Header="Shipped Date"
        Width="SizeToHeader">
    <DataGridTemplateColumn.CellTemplate>
  <DataTemplate>
  <DatePicker
  SelectedDate="{Binding Path=ShippedDate}" />
 </DataTemplate>
 </DataGridTemplateColumn.CellTemplate>
</DataGridTemplateColumn>
<DataGridTextColumn x:Name="ShipViaColumn"
        Binding="{Binding Path=ShipVia}"
        Header="Ship Via"
        Width="SizeToHeader" />
   <DataGridTextColumn x:Name="FreightColumn"
        Binding="{Binding Path=Freight}"
        Header="Freight"
        Width="SizeToHeader" />
   <DataGridTextColumn x:Name="ShipNameColumn"
        Binding="{Binding Path=ShipName}"
        Header="Ship Name"
        Width="SizeToHeader" />
    <DataGridTextColumn x:Name="ShipAddressColumn"
        Binding="{Binding Path=ShipAddress}"
        Header="Ship Address"
        Width="SizeToHeader" />
    <DataGridTextColumn x:Name="ShipCityColumn"
        Binding="{Binding Path=ShipCity}"
        Header="Ship City"
        Width="SizeToHeader" />
    <DataGridTextColumn x:Name="ShipRegionColumn"
        Binding="{Binding Path=ShipRegion}"
        Header="Ship Region"
        Width="SizeToHeader" />
    <DataGridTextColumn x:Name="ShipPostalCodeColumn"
        Binding="{Binding Path=ShipPostalCode}"
        Header="Ship Postal Code"
        Width="SizeToHeader" />
    <DataGridTextColumn x:Name="ShipCountryColumn"
        Binding="{Binding Path=ShipCountry}"
        Header="Ship Country"
        Width="SizeToHeader" />
```

32

```
    </DataGrid.Columns>
</DataGrid>
```

The `DataGrid` data source is set via the `ItemsSource` property pointing to the `CustomersOrdersViewSource` object, which includes information from both `Customers` and related `Orders`. The rest of the code is quite simple to understand. Each column has a cell template, which is of type `DataGridTextColumn` for text fields. Other built-in types are `DataGridHyperLinkColumn` for displaying hyperlinks, `DataGridCheckBoxColumn` for displaying Boolean values with a check box control, and `DataGridComboBoxColumn` for selecting items from within a combo box. It is worth mentioning that for data types, the `DataGrid` has no default counterpart. Visual Studio generates a custom cell template with `DataGridTemplateColumn` objects. In this case the custom template has been generated for embedding `DatePicker` controls for setting and displaying dates within cells.

DESIGNING COLUMNS

The IDE provides a convenient way for designing columns with the designer instrumentation. Select the `DataGrid` and in the Properties window, click **Columns**. Figure 32.5 shows how you can edit existing columns or add new ones, also setting data-binding at design time.

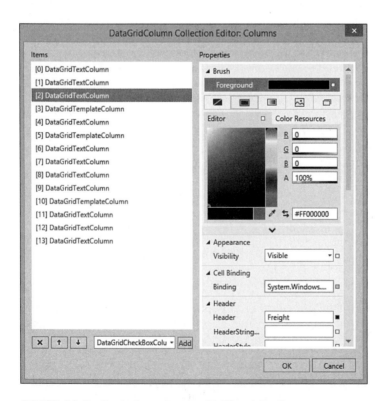

FIGURE 32.5   Designing columns with Visual Studio.

This is not enough, of course, in that some Visual Basic code is also required for fetching data and assigning the data to the user interface for presenting. If you now open the code behind file for the current `Window`, you will see that Visual Basic has generated the following code:

```
Class MainWindow
    Private Sub Window_Loaded(sender As Object, e As RoutedEventArgs) _
        Handles MyBase.Loaded

        Dim CustomerViewSource As System.Windows.Data.CollectionViewSource =
            CType(Me.FindResource("CustomerViewSource"),
            System.Windows.Data.CollectionViewSource)
        'Load data by setting the CollectionViewSource.Source property:
        'CustomerViewSource.Source = [generic data source]

    End Sub
End Class
```

Unlike its predecessor, Visual Basic 2015 gives you a very basic implementation, where the auto-generated code only provides a `CollectionViewSource` declaration, matching the same object in the `Window`'s resources. So it is totally up to you to write the code that populates the user interface with data. You might start by writing a method that gets the list of customers and associated orders, like the following:

```
Private northwindEntities As NorthwindEntities
'Requires:
'Imports System.Collections.ObjectModel
'Imports System.Data.Entity
Private Function GetCustomersQuery() _
    As ObservableCollection(Of Customer)

    'Load the collection of customers
    'This include associated orders
    northwindEntities.Customers.Load()

    'Return the collection of customers
    Return northwindEntities.Customers.Local
End Function
```

The method loads the collection of customers exposed by the `NorthwindEntities` object, which inherits from `DbContext`. Such a collection inherits from the `DbSet` class. Then it returns the fetched data via the `Local` property. This is of type `ObservableCollection(Of Customer)`, and it is the optimal type for data-binding. It is worth mentioning that the `Load` method invoked on a data collection also returns associated items, in this case a collection of orders per customer.

LoadAsync METHOD

The DbSet class exposes a LoadAsync method that works asynchronously. This is useful but requires you to have knowledge of the async/await pattern, which is described in Chapter 42, "Asynchronous Programming." After reading that chapter, you will be able to take advantage of LoadAsync.

Then you have to write code that instantiates the NorthwindEntities object and that assigns data to the user interface. This is done in the Window.Loaded event handler. Listing 32.1 shows the full code for this example.

LISTING 32.1   The VB Auto-Generated Code for the Drag and Drop Data-Binding

```vb
Imports System.Collections.ObjectModel
Imports System.Data.Entity


Class MainWindow

    Private northwindEntities As NorthwindEntities
    'Requires:
    'Imports System.Collections.ObjectModel
    'Imports System.Data.Entity
    Private Function GetCustomersQuery() _
        As ObservableCollection(Of Customer)

        'Load the collection of customers
        'This include associated orders
        northwindEntities.Customers.Load()

        'Return the collection of customers
        Return northwindEntities.Customers.Local
    End Function

    Private Sub Window_Loaded(sender As Object, e As RoutedEventArgs) _
        Handles MyBase.Loaded

        Me.northwindEntities = New NorthwindEntities()
        'Load data into Customers. You can modify this code as needed.
        Dim CustomersViewSource As CollectionViewSource =
            CType(Me.FindResource("CustomerViewSource"),
            CollectionViewSource)

        CustomersViewSource.Source = GetCustomersQuery()
    End Sub
End Class
```

When the window is loaded, other than the `DbContext` instance, notice how the code retrieves the instance of the `CustomersViewSource` (of type `CollectionViewSource`) via the `FindResource` method, which enables searching for a resource declared in XAML. This instance will finally receive the executed query so that its result will be reflected to the user interface. The process is the following: The query fetches data; data is assigned to a `CollectionViewSource` instance; because this instance is bound to a UI control (such as the `DataGrid`), fetched data is reflected to the UI, and vice versa. This is also because the `DataGrid` control provides support for the two-way data-binding, and is also allowed by the `ObservableCollection(Of T)` class.

Before testing the application, you need an additional step. When the Entity Framework generates model classes, it assigns the `HashSet(Of T)` type to collections in the *many* part of a *one-to-many* relationship. Unfortunately, `HashSet(Of T)` does not support editing items, and this assignment would result in runtime exceptions when attempting to edit items in data-bound controls. In the example, the `Customer` class has an `Orders` property of type `HashSet(Of Order)`; you must replace this with a different collection type, such as `List` or, better in WPF, `ObservableCollection`. To accomplish this, follow these steps:

1. In Solution Explorer, enable the Show All Files view and then expand the Northwind.edmx file.

2. Expand the Northwind.tt file and then double-click the Customer.vb file to make it visible in the code editor.

3. Locate the `Orders` property and replace `New HashSet(Of Order)` with `New ObservableCollection(Of Order)`.

At this point, you can run the application to see the result shown in Figure 32.6.

With a few mouse clicks and some manual edits, you can build an application that can present tabular data. You can click inside the `DataGrid` for editing existing data or for adding new rows. If you want to save data to the underlying database, you should implement a control, such as a `Button`, whose `Click` event handler invokes the `DbContext.SaveChanges` or `DbContext.SaveChangesAsync` method, and you are done. But you see this example in the next section, which is interesting but that requires a little bit of manual work.

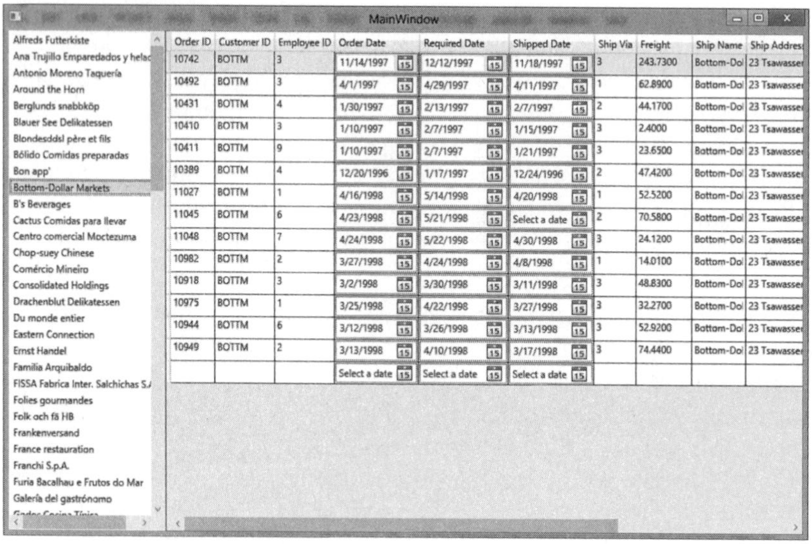

FIGURE 32.6   The tabular data application running.

Creating Master-Details Forms

Similarly to what already happened in Windows Forms, creating master-details forms in WPF 4.6 is also straightforward. This also enables you to understand other important concepts for the data-binding. Add a new window to the current project and name it **MasterDetails**. Divide the default `Grid` into four cells, so that you can also add special buttons, as follows:

```
<Grid>
    <Grid.ColumnDefinitions>
    <ColumnDefinition Width="200"/>
    <ColumnDefinition/>
    </Grid.ColumnDefinitions>
    <Grid.RowDefinitions>
        <RowDefinition/>
        <RowDefinition Height="50"/>
    </Grid.RowDefinitions>
</Grid>
```

Repeat the step of adding a `ListBox` and binding the customer's `CompanyName` property, just as in the first part of the previous subsection. Ensure that the `ListBox` is placed in the upper-left column. Visual Studio 2015 generates exactly the same XAML code of the previous example for you. Now go to the Data Sources window, select the **Orders** item nested within **Customers**; then from the combo box, select **Details**. Next, drag **Orders** onto the upper-right cell of the window. Figure 32.7 shows the result of this operation.

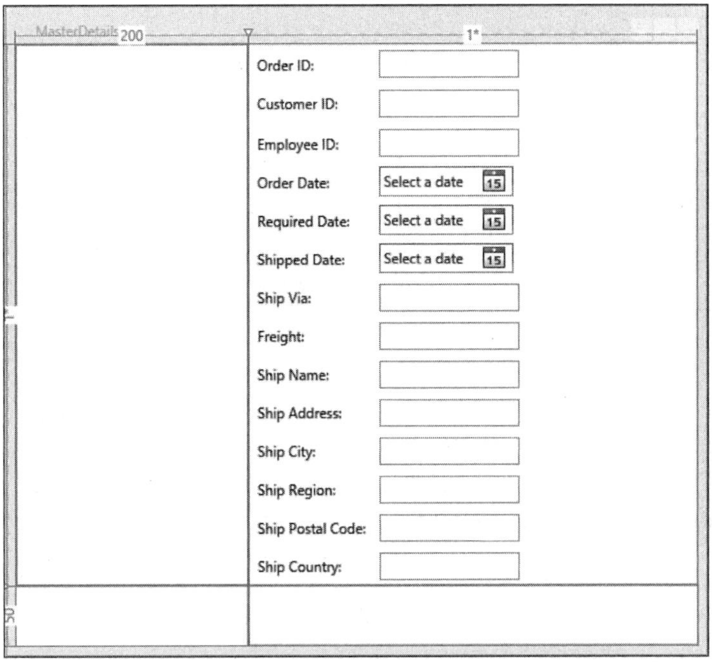

FIGURE 32.7   The result of the master-details drag and drop.

Notice how Visual Studio generated a series of controls, which are couples of Label/ TextBlock. Also notice how the IDE can recognize the bound data type and add the appropriate controls. For example, for dates, it adds to the form some DatePicker controls. Instead of a DataGrid, the auto-generated XAML code contains a new Grid with a series of children controls. Listing 32.2 shows an excerpt of the content of the new Grid.

LISTING 32.2   Excerpt of the Auto-Generated XAML Code for Details

```
<Grid DataContext="{StaticResource CustomerOrdersViewSource}"
    Grid.Column="1"
    Grid.Row="0" Name="Grid1" >
  <Grid.ColumnDefinitions>
    <ColumnDefinition Width="Auto" />
    <ColumnDefinition Width="Auto" />
  </Grid.ColumnDefinitions>
  <Grid.RowDefinitions>
    <RowDefinition Height="Auto" />
    <RowDefinition Height="Auto" />
    <RowDefinition Height="Auto" />
    <RowDefinition Height="Auto" />
    <RowDefinition Height="Auto" />
    <RowDefinition Height="Auto" />
    <RowDefinition Height="Auto" />
```

```
        <RowDefinition Height="Auto" />
        <RowDefinition Height="Auto" />
        <RowDefinition Height="Auto" />
        <RowDefinition Height="Auto" />
        <RowDefinition Height="Auto" />
        <RowDefinition Height="Auto" />
        <RowDefinition Height="Auto" />
    </Grid.RowDefinitions>
    <Label Content="Order ID:" Grid.Column="0" Grid.Row="0"
        HorizontalAlignment="Left" Margin="3"
        VerticalAlignment="Center" />
    <TextBox Grid.Column="1" Grid.Row="0" Height="23"
        HorizontalAlignment="Left" Margin="3" Name="OrderIDTextBox"
        Text="{Binding Path=OrderID}"
        VerticalAlignment="Center" Width="120" />
    <Label Content="Customer ID:" Grid.Column="0" Grid.Row="1"
        HorizontalAlignment="Left" Margin="3"
        VerticalAlignment="Center" />
    <TextBox Grid.Column="1" Grid.Row="1" Height="23"
        HorizontalAlignment="Left" Margin="3" Name="CustomerIDTextBox"
        Text="{Binding Path=CustomerID}"
        VerticalAlignment="Center" Width="120" />
    <Label Content="Employee ID:" Grid.Column="0" Grid.Row="2"
        HorizontalAlignment="Left" Margin="3"
        VerticalAlignment="Center" />
    <TextBox Grid.Column="1" Grid.Row="2" Height="23"
        HorizontalAlignment="Left"
        Margin="3" Name="EmployeeIDTextBox"
        Text="{Binding Path=EmployeeID}"
        VerticalAlignment="Center" Width="120" />
    <Label Content="Order Date:" Grid.Column="0" Grid.Row="3"
        HorizontalAlignment="Left" Margin="3"
        VerticalAlignment="Center" />
    <DatePicker Grid.Column="1" Grid.Row="3" Height="25"
        HorizontalAlignment="Left" Margin="3"
        Name="OrderDateDatePicker"
        SelectedDate="{Binding Path=OrderDate}"
        VerticalAlignment="Center" Width="115" />
    <!--Following other controls... -->
</Grid>
```

The code implements pairs of labels/text. For dates, you can notice the presence of
`DatePicker` controls whose `SelectedDate` property is bound to the date property from
the data source. If you take a look at the Visual Basic auto-generated code, you see no
differences with the one shown in the first example. Now there is some other work to do.

Building a master-details form requires providing controls for navigating, adding, deleting, and saving items. Now, you need to add the following XAML code, which implements some buttons whose meanings should be self-explanatory:

```xaml
<StackPanel Grid.Row="1" Grid.Column="1" Orientation="Horizontal">
    <StackPanel.Resources>
      <Style TargetType="Button" x:Key="ButtonStyle">
        <Setter Property="Width" Value="80"/>
        <Setter Property="Height" Value="40"/>
        <Setter Property="Margin" Value="5"/>
    </Style>
  </StackPanel.Resources>
  <Button Style="{StaticResource ButtonStyle}" Content="Save"
      Name="SaveButton" Click="SaveButton_Click"/>
  <Button Style="{StaticResource ButtonStyle}" Content="Add"
      Name="AddButton" Click="AddButton_Click"/>
  <Button Style="{StaticResource ButtonStyle}" Content="Delete"
      Name="DeleteButton" Click="DeleteButton_Click"/>
  <Button Style="{StaticResource ButtonStyle}" Content="Next"
      Name="NextButton" Click="NextButton_Click"/>
  <Button Style="{StaticResource ButtonStyle}" Content="Back"
      Name="BackButton" Click="BackButton_Click"/>
</StackPanel>
```

Now switch to the Visual Basic code. To fetch data and assign the data to the user interface, you can simply reuse the same code written for the previous example:

```vbnet
Private northwindEntities As NorthwindEntities
Private Sub Window_Loaded(sender As Object, e As RoutedEventArgs) _
    Handles MyBase.Loaded

    Me.northwindEntities = New NorthwindEntities

    Dim CustomerViewSource As CollectionViewSource =
        CType(Me.FindResource("CustomerViewSource"),
        CollectionViewSource)
    'Load data by setting the CollectionViewSource.Source property:
    CustomerViewSource.Source = GetCustomersQuery()

End Sub
Private Function GetCustomersQuery() _
    As ObservableCollection(Of Customer)

    'Load the collection of customers
    'This include associated orders
    northwindEntities.Customers.Load()
```

```
    'Return the collection of customers
    Return northwindEntities.Customers.Local
End Function
```

Now you need to handle buttons. The first button that can be handled is the SaveButton. The Click event handler is the following:

```
Private Sub SaveButton_Click(sender As System.Object,
       e As System.Windows.
       RoutedEventArgs)
    'Handle your logic here, such as exceptions
    'and optimistic concurrency
    Try
        Me.northwindEntities.SaveChanges()
    Catch ex As Exception

    End Try
End Sub
```

The second task is moving to class level the CollectionViewSource objects declarations so that you can invoke them within event handlers. They actually are enclosed in the Window_Loaded event handler and thus have no external visibility. Moreover, you also need to manually declare and get the instance of the CustomersOrdersCollectionViewSource object because the application needs to provide the ability of adding and removing items only to the Orders collection. (Performing this on CustomersViewSource would affect Customers, too.) The code in Listing 32.3 summarizes the edits that you need to do manually at this point.

LISTING 32.3   Moving CollectionViewSource Declarations at the Class Level

```
Private CustomerViewSource As CollectionViewSource
Private CustomerOrdersViewSource As CollectionViewSource

Private Sub Window_Loaded(sender As Object, e As RoutedEventArgs) _
    Handles MyBase.Loaded

    Me.northwindEntities = New NorthwindEntities

    CustomerViewSource = CType(Me.FindResource("CustomerViewSource"),
        CollectionViewSource)

    CustomerOrdersViewSource = CType(Me.
            FindResource("CustomerOrdersViewSource"),
        CollectionViewSource)

    CustomerViewSource.Source = GetCustomersQuery()
End Sub
```

The next buttons require explaining other concepts, which the next sections cover.

Understanding Views and Binding Lists

`CollectionViewSource` objects expose an interesting property named `View`. It provides the ability of filtering, sorting, and navigating through a bound collection of items. To understand how a view works, the best example in our scenario is handling the `Next` and `Back` buttons. The following code snippet shows how easy it is to navigate back and forward through items:

```
Private Sub NextButton_Click(sender As System.Object,
        e As System.Windows.RoutedEventArgs)
  If Me.CustomerOrdersViewSource.View.CurrentPosition < _
    CType(Me.CustomerOrdersViewSource.View, CollectionView).
    Count - 1 Then
  Me.CustomerOrdersViewSource.View.MoveCurrentToNext()
  End If
End Sub

Private Sub BackButton_Click(sender As System.Object,
        e As System.Windows.RoutedEventArgs)
  If Me.CustomerOrdersViewSource.View.CurrentPosition > 0 Then
    Me.CustomerOrdersViewSource.View.MoveCurrentToPrevious()
  End If
End Sub
```

The code calculates the position and enables moving back or forward only if there are any other items that can be navigated. Notice how the `CustomerOrdersViewSource.View` property exposes the `Count` property, representing the current position being examined in the collection. Methods such as `MoveCurrentToNext` and `MoveCurrentToPrevious` enable moving back and forward to another item. Other interesting members from views are self-explanatory and are summarized in Table 32.2.

TABLE 32.2   Views' Most Common Members

Member	Type	Description
CanSort	Property	Returns a Boolean value indicating whether the collection can be sorted.
CanFilter	Property	Returns a Boolean value indicating whether the collection can be filtered.
CanGroup	Property	Returns a Boolean value indicating whether the collection can be grouped.
MoveCurrentTo	Method	Sets the specified item as the current item in the collection.
MoveCurrentToFirst	Method	Sets the first item in the collection as the current item.

Member	Type	Description
MoveCurrentToLast	Method	Sets the last item in the collection as the current item.
MoveCurrentToNext	Method	Sets the next item in the collection as the current item.
MoveCurrentToPrevious	Method	Sets the previous item in the collection as the current item.
CurrentItem	Property	Returns the instance of the current item in the collection. Because it is of type Object, it must be converted into the appropriate type.
CurrentPosition	Property	Returns an index corresponding to the current item in the collection.

To retrieve the items count, a CType operator converts from CollectionViewSource.View into a CollectionView object. This last one represents a single view, and the conversion is required because Option Strict is On and the View property is of type ICollectionView. Views from CollectionViewSource objects are straightforward because they also support data-binding but have several limitations. As you can see from Table 32.2, no member is exposed for adding, editing, or removing items in the underlying data collection. To provide the ability of CRUD operations, the best approach is utilizing a System.Window. Data.ListCollectionView, which also offers a reference to data collections but provides more capabilities. At class level, declare the following variables:

```
Private WithEvents CustomerView As ListCollectionView
Private CustomerOrdersView As ListCollectionView
```

Now, in the Window_Loaded event handler, add the following lines as the last lines of code in the method:

```
Me.CustomerView = CType(Me.CustomerViewSource.View, _
        ListCollectionView)
Me.CustomerOrdersView = CType(Me.CustomerOrdersViewSource.View, _
        ListCollectionView)
```

This converts views references to two ListCollectionView objects. Now with these you can perform insert/update/delete operations to the underlying collection, which is picked up from the CollectionViewSource associations and is data-bound to the ListCollectionView, too. To understand how this works, write the following handler for the Click event about the Add button so that you can provide the capability of adding a new order:

```
Private Sub AddButton_Click(sender As System.Object, _
        e As System.Windows.RoutedEventArgs)
    'A new order
    Dim newOrder As Order
```

```
    'Adds a new order to the view and assigns the instance
    'to the newly declared order
    newOrder = CType(Me.CustomerOrdersView.AddNew(), Order)

    'If I need to assign properties to newOrder before
    'it is sent to the collection, then this is the place

    'Sends the new order to the view
    Me.CustomerOrdersView.CommitNew()
End Sub
```

The AddNew method adds an instance of the specified object type to the view, and the addition is automatically reflected to the bound user interface controls. The CType conversion is required because the method returns Object; therefore, converting to the appropriate type returns the effective instance of the order. This is not actually required, but it is useful if you want to set some default properties before the object is sent to the underlying collection. Notice that this code submits the new item to the underlying collection, but the new object will not persist to the underlying database until you invoke the DbContext.SaveChanges method. Removing items works similarly, in that you retrieve the current object instance and invoke one of the enabled methods. The following event handler for the Delete button demonstrates this:

```
Private Sub DeleteButton_Click(sender As System.Object,
         e As System.Windows.
         RoutedEventArgs)
    If Me.CustomerOrdersView.CurrentPosition > -1 Then

        Dim result = MessageBox.Show("Are you sure?",
                "", MessageBoxButton.YesNo)
    If result = MessageBoxResult.Yes Then
        Me.CustomerOrdersView.
        RemoveAt(Me.CustomerOrdersView.CurrentPosition)
    Else
        Exit Sub
      End If
    End If
End Sub
```

In this case you can use RemoveAt to remove the item at the current position, but you can also invoke Remove, which requires the instance of the current object. RemoveAt requires fewer lines of code. Before running the application, there is one thing that you need to take care of: The ListCollectionView content needs to be refreshed each time you move to another item in the master part of the master-details relationships. Considering our code example, you need to remember the ListCollectionView referred to orders each time you select a different customer. To accomplish this, you handle the CurrentChanged event in the master part of the relationship, as demonstrated by the following code:

```
Private Sub CustomerView_CurrentChanged(sender As Object,
        e As System.EventArgs) _
        Handles CustomerView.CurrentChanged
    Me.CustomersOrdersView = CType(Me.CustomerOrdersViewSource.View,
        ListCollectionView)
End Sub
```

The preceding event handler is invoked when you click a different customer in the user
interface and refreshes the CustomerOrdersView (of type ListCollectionView) object
pointing to the actual orders collection referred by the underlying CollectionViewSource.
That keeps the data-binding alive. Now you can run the application and get the result
summarized in Figure 32.8.

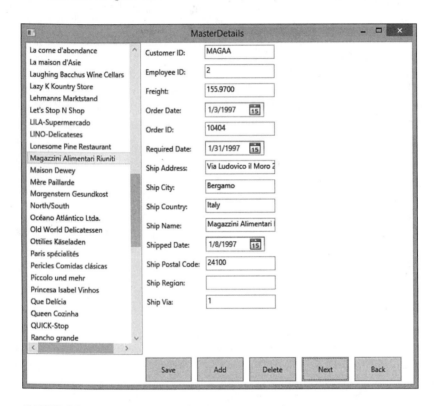

FIGURE 32.8   The master-details application running.

BINDING TO DATASETS

The drag and drop data-binding works the same with DataSets, and you can still take
advantage of CollectionViewSource and ListCollectionView objects. The code
remains the same as the previously shown examples, whereas the difference is where you
need to persist data to the database or fetch data, where you can use DataSet methods
and LINQ to DataSets, respectively.

You can now play with additional controls such as Add, Delete, Next, and Back. When you are done, try to save changes to ensure that new or edited data is correctly persisted to the database. This sample application can be enhanced in several other ways. For example, you can implement entities validation or show details for a single order using LINQ. These topics are beyond the scope of an introductory chapter about data-binding, but you can further explore them with the help of the MSDN documentation. Particularly, you are encouraged to read this blog post by Beth Massi from Microsoft, where she discusses WPF validation on entities: http://blogs.msdn.com/bethmassi/archive/2009/07/07/ implementing-validation-in-wpf-on-entity-framework-entities.aspx. Although the blog post targets the .NET Framework 3.5 SP 1, this technique is convenient on .NET 4.6, too.

Implementing String Formatters and Value Converters

The need to represent strings in a more appropriate format when binding data to the user interface is not uncommon. For example, you might want to present money values or percentages. In WPF, you can accomplish this in two modes: string formatters and the IValueConverter interface. This section describes both, showing how they can be used for better presentation purposes.

Implementing String Formatters

You can apply string formats directly in the XAML Binding markup extension that performs data-binding. This enables you to express a particular value type in a more convenient string format. For a better understanding, consider Figure 32.8. Notice how the Freight field is shown as a decimal number. However, you probably want to display it with your currency symbol. Locate the XAML code that implements the Freight textbox and apply the StringFormat property as shown in the following code snippet:

```
<TextBox Grid.Column="1" Grid.Row="7" Height="23"
        HorizontalAlignment="Left" Margin="3"
        Name="FreightTextBox"
        Text="{Binding Path=Freight, StringFormat=c}"
        VerticalAlignment="Center" Width="120" />
```

The BindingBase.StringFormat property is applied within the Binding markup extension and requires the specification of the formatter. Figure 32.9 shows how the Freight field is now represented with a currency symbol.

Table 32.3 summarizes the most common StringFormat values.

TABLE 32.3   Most Common Formatters' Values

Value	Description
c or C	Represents a value as a string with currency symbol.
p or P	Formats a value as a string with percentage representation.
D	Formats a date value as an extended string representation (for example, Monday, 21 October 2009).
d	Formats a date value as a short string representation (for example, 10/21/2009).

Value	Description
F	Provides a string representation of a decimal number with floating point. It is followed by a number that establishes how many numbers follow the floating point (for example, 3.14 can be represented by F2).
E	Scientific formatting.
X	Hexadecimal formatting.
G	General.

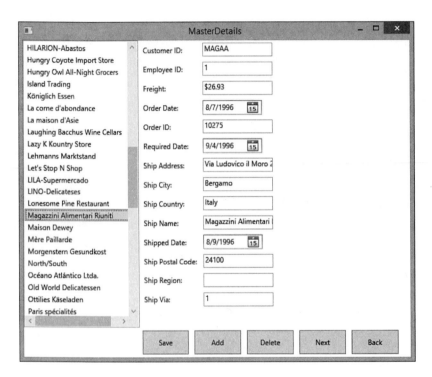

FIGURE 32.9   Representing strings with `StringFormat`.

The good news is that string formatters also provide converting the user input. For the `Freight` example, if you type a value into the field, it is represented as a currency in the user interface, but it is correctly saved to the data source according to the required type. `StringFormat` also enables string formatting as it happens in Visual Basic code. Consider the following code:

```
<TextBox Name="FreightTextBox"
       Text="{Binding Path=Freight, StringFormat=Amount: {0:c}}"/>
```

In the preceding code, the `Amount` word takes the place of 0 at runtime. So the result will be `Amount: $1.21`. There is another useful technique known as *multibinding*. The following code demonstrates how you can apply multiple formatters with `MultiBinding`:

```
<!--Applies date and currency formatting-->
<TextBlock>
  <TextBlock.Text>
    <MultiBinding StringFormat="Order date: {0:D}, Cost: {1:C}">
      <Binding Path="OrderDate"/>
      <Binding Path="OrderPrice"/>
    </MultiBinding>
  </TextBlock.Text>
</TextBlock>
```

Several user controls, such as `Button` and `Label`, also offer a `ContentStringFormat` property that enables you to apply formatting to the control's content the same way as `StringFormat` works. The following is an example:

```
<Label ContentStringFormat="C" Content="200"/>
```

Similarly, controls such as `ListView`, `ListBox`, and `DataGrid` offer the `HeaderStringFormat` and `ItemStringFormat` properties that enable you to format the header content for columns and items in the list, respectively. String formatters are straightforward, but in some situations you need more extensive control over value representation, especially when you need to actually convert from one data type to another. This is where `IValueConverter` comes in.

Implementing the `IValueConverter` Interface

Sometimes default conversions provided by string formatters are not enough, especially if you have to implement your custom logic when converting from the user input into another type. With `IValueConverter`, you can implement your custom logic getting control over the conversion process from and to the data source. To follow the next steps, create a new class and name it `CustomConverter`. When the new class is ready, implement the `IValueConverter` interface. The resulting code will be the following:

```
Public Class CustomConverter
    Implements IValueConverter

    Public Function Convert(value As Object,
            targetType As System.Type,
            parameter As Object,
            culture As
            System.Globalization.CultureInfo) _
            As Object Implements _
            System.Windows.Data.IValueConverter.Convert

    End Function
```

```
    Public Function ConvertBack(value As Object,
            targetType As System.Type,
            parameter As Object,
            culture As System.Globalization.
            CultureInfo) As Object _
            Implements _
            System.Windows.Data.IValueConverter.
            ConvertBack


    End Function
End Class
```

The interface implementation requires two methods, Convert and ConvertBack. The first one manages data when applying from the data source to the user interface, and the second one manages the conversion when getting back from the user interface to the data source. The most important argument in the Convert method is parameter, which represents how data must be converted. Such data is stored by the value argument. Implementing Convert is quite easy, in that you need to format value as a string according to parameter's establishment. This can be accomplished taking advantage of the current culture. The following is the standard Convert implementation:

```
Public Function Convert(value As Object,
        targetType As System.Type,
        parameter As Object,
        culture As _
        System.Globalization.CultureInfo) _
        As Object Implements System.Windows.Data.
        IValueConverter.Convert

    If parameter IsNot Nothing Then
        Return String.Format(culture, parameter.ToString, value)
    End If

    Return value
End Function
```

This ensures that on the XAML side a valid converter property (reflected by parameter), which is described later, has been provided and that it is not null. In this case the method returns the string representation of the value according to the system culture. If no converter is specified, the method returns the value. ConvertBack is a little bit more complex because it has to convert strings (that is, the user input) into a more appropriate type. The goal of this example is providing conversion from String to Decimal, for money fields. The following code snippet implements the method (see comments for explanations):

```vbnet
Public Function ConvertBack(value As Object,
        targetType As System.Type,
        parameter As Object,
        culture As System.Globalization.
        CultureInfo) As Object _
        Implements System.Windows.Data.
        IValueConverter.ConvertBack

    'If the type to send back to the source is Decimal or Decimal?
    If targetType Is GetType(Decimal) OrElse targetType _
        Is GetType(Nullable(Of Decimal)) Then

      Dim resultMoney As Decimal = Nothing

        'Checks if the input is not null
        If Decimal.TryParse(CStr(value), resultMoney) = True Then
        'in such case, it is returned
    Return CDec(value)
      'if it is empty, returns Nothing
    ElseIf value.ToString = String.Empty Then
        Return Nothing
    Else
        'If it is not empty but invalid,
        'returns a default value
        Return 0D
        End If
    End If

    Return value
End Function
```

It is worth mentioning that you need to provide conversion for nullable types, as in the preceding code, if you work against an Entity Data Model (EDM). If your user interface presents data but does not receive input from the user, you can implement ConvertBack by putting a Throw New NotImplementedException as the method body. The MSDN official documentation suggests an interesting best practice when implementing custom converters. This requires applying the ValueConversion attributes to the class; this attribute enables you to specify data types involved in the conversion, as in the following line that has to be applied to the CustomConverter class:

```
<ValueConversion(GetType(String), GetType(Decimal))>
```

The first attribute's argument is the type you need to convert from, and the second one is the type you need to convert to. Custom converters must be applied at XAML level. This requires first adding an XML namespace pointing to the current assembly that defines the class. For the previous example, add the following namespace declaration within the

`Window` element definition, taking care to replace the `IntroducingDataBinding` name with the name of your assembly (IntelliSense will help you choose):

```
xmlns:local="clr-namespace:IntroducingDataBinding"
```

When you have a reference to the assembly, which can be useful for utilizing other classes at the XAML level, you need to declare a new resource that points to the custom converter. Within the `Window.Resources` element, add the following line:

```
<local:CustomConverter x:Key="customConverter"/>
```

Now that the converter has an identifier and can be used at the XAML level, you pass it to the bound property you want to convert. For example, suppose you want to format and convert the `Freight` property from the `Order` class. The following code demonstrates how to apply the converter:

```
<TextBox Grid.Column="1" Grid.Row="7" Height="23"
         HorizontalAlignment="Left" Margin="3"
         Name="FreightTextBox"
         Text="{Binding Path=Freight,
            Converter={StaticResource customConverter},
            ConverterParameter='\{0:c\}'}"
    VerticalAlignment="Center" Width="120" />
```

You pass the converter identifier to the `Converter` property of the `Binding` markup extension. The `ConverterParameter` receives the conversion value, which are the same in Table 32.3. If you run the application, you get the result shown in Figure 32.9; the difference is that with custom converters, you can control how the conversion and formatting processes behave.

Summary

The data-binding is a key concept in every kind of application, and this is true for WPF, too. In the first part of this chapter, you learned how to apply data-binding to simple controls with the `Binding` markup extension in XAML code, to bind some properties to the value of other controls or to a .NET data source. For this, you got an overview of the `DataGrid` control and of the `ObservableCollection(Of T)` generic class (which you already studied), this time applied to WPF. You found out how the `DataGrid` supports the two-way data-binding also due to the underlying support for the technique offered by the `ObservableCollection`. The second part of the chapter covered the drag and drop data-binding and how easily you can create data forms. After this discussion, the `StringFormat` and `IValueConverter` objects were presented for formatting and converting objects to and from `String`. There is much more to say about data access in WPF, but it is beyond the scope here. The next chapter is the last one on WPF and is related to another important topic: localization.

CHAPTER 33

Localizing Applications

Limiting applications' user interfaces (UIs) to just one language means limiting your business. If you want to increase the possibilities of your applications being sold worldwide, you need to consider creating user interfaces that support multiple languages and the culture specifications of your users. Of course, you can give users the option to select the desired language or provide localized interfaces for a particular country, but the main concept is that localization is a common requirement in modern applications. The .NET Framework helps developers in localizing applications with several kinds of resources. In this chapter, you learn how to localize desktop applications and explore Windows Forms and WPF applications to understand the fundamentals of localization in both technologies. Even if you only focus on WPF applications, you are strongly encouraged to read the Windows Forms section first, which describes steps that are common to WPF and that will not be explained twice.

AVAILABLE TECHNIQUES

Localizing applications is something that you can accomplish in several ways in both Windows Forms and WPF. This chapter discusses the most commonly used techniques, just remember that they are not the only ones.

Introducing .NET Localization

The .NET Framework provides the infrastructure for application localization via the `System.Globalization` namespace. The most important class in this namespace is the `CultureInfo` class that allows getting or setting information on the current application culture or on new custom settings. This class works with the `System.Threading.Thread.CurrentThread` class that provides access to the thread representing your executable and that exposes the `CurrentCulture` and `CurrentUICulture` properties you can assign with a `CultureInfo` object. The following code demonstrates how to get information on the current thread culture and how to set a new `CultureInfo`:

```
'Requires an Imports System.Globalization directive

'Gets the current culture and shows information
Dim culture As CultureInfo = System.Threading.Thread.
        CurrentThread.CurrentCulture
Console.WriteLine(culture.DisplayName)

'Creates an instance of the CUltureInfo class
'based on the Italian culture and sets it as
'the current culture
Dim customCulture As New CultureInfo("it-IT")
System.Threading.Thread.CurrentThread.
    CurrentCulture = customCulture
```

The `CultureInfo` class provides lots of properties that enable applications to adhere to the required culture specifications. For example, `DisplayName` shows the name of the culture as it appears on the system, `DateTimeFormat` specifies the appropriate format for date and time in the specified culture, and `NumberFormat` provides specifications on how numbers and percentages need to be formatted in the specified culture. In this chapter you learn how to localize smart client applications, thus Windows Forms and WPF.

Introducing the Multilingual App Toolkit

Localizing applications is often not an easy task, and it requires many manual steps. Also, different development platforms require different ways of implementing localization. To make things far easier, Microsoft has developed the Multilingual App Toolkit (MAT), a free and easy-to-use tool that integrates into Visual Studio 2015 and offers a unified way of localizing applications, regardless of the development platform you are working on. In fact, with this toolkit, you can localize Windows Forms, WPF, and even Windows Store apps by using the same steps and techniques. The MAT allows you to add a number of languages and provides automatic translations for each language.

In the rest of the chapter, you will see the MAT in action against Windows Forms and WPF applications. Before going on, you need to download and install the MAT from the Visual Studio Gallery, at https://visualstudiogallery.msdn.microsoft.com/6dab9154-a7e1-46e4-bbfa-18b5e81df520. Remember that Visual Studio 2015 supports version 4.0 or higher.

Windows Forms Localization

> **WHY WINDOWS FORMS?**
>
> As for other code examples provided throughout the book, even if Windows Forms is no longer explained, localization is discussed because such a platform is still popular and common to have to maintain in the industry.

If you are an experienced Windows Forms developer, maybe you already faced the localization problem with this technology. There are different ways for localizing a Windows Forms application, but basically all of them rely on managed resources. The MAT that you previously installed makes it really easy to localize an application. An example is the best way for providing explanations; the goal of this example is to localize a Windows Forms application in both English and Italian. Run Visual Studio 2015, create a new Windows Forms project with Visual Basic 2015, and name it **WindowsFormsLocalization**. Follow these steps:

1. Drag a `Button` from the toolbox onto the new form surface.

2. Drag a `Label` from the toolbox onto the new form surface.

3. Open My Project and then click **Assembly Information** in the Application tab. In the Neutral Language field select **English (United States)**. Finally, click **OK** and save the project.

4. Select **Tools, Multilingual App Toolkit, Enable Selection** to enable the project for localization with the MAT.

5. Build the project and enable the **Show All Files** view in Solution Explorer.

6. Expand My Project and then double-click the Resources.resx file. In the resource editor, add two new strings: `LocalizedButton`, with value `Localized button`, and `LocalizedLabel`, with value `Localized label`.

Now in Solution Explorer, right-click the project name and select **Multilingual App Toolkit, Add Translation Languages**. In the Translation Languages dialog (see Figure 33.1) select **Italian**.

You can add as many languages as you like. Also, for each language, you can select specific cultures. For instance, if you expand Italian, you can select Italian (Italy), with culture it-IT, and Italian (Switzerland) with culture it-CH. For now just select **Italian** and click **OK**. Visual Studio 2015 generates a new resource file called Resources.it.resx. Generally speaking, Visual Studio will generate a new resource file for each culture you select. In addition, Visual Studio will generate an .xlf file for each language in the MultilingualResources folder. The filename includes the project name, the language/culture couple, and the .xlf file extension. This extension represents the XLIFF (XML Localization Interchange File Format) format, which is an industry standard for file translations. Each .xlf file contains translations of strings added to the Resources.resx file. The very good news is that you do not need to translate manually either the Resource.it.resx file or the WindowsFormsLocalization.it.xlf files because the IDE does this work for you.

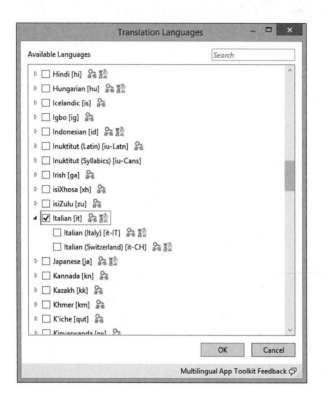

FIGURE 33.1   Adding translation languages.

In Solution Explorer, right-click the WindowsFormsLocalization.it.xlf file and select **Multilingual App Toolkit, Generate Machine Translations**. Visual Studio will connect to the Internet and take advantage of the Microsoft Translator Services for automatic translations. At this point, you can rebuild the project and answer **Yes** if Visual Studio asks you to reload the Resources.it.resx file. Then you can open this file in the resource designer and see that both strings were localized properly (see Figure 33.2).

It is very important that you change Access Modifier for both Resources.resx and Resources.it.resx to Public; otherwise, your code will not be able to consume those resources. The MAT also ships with a convenient visual editor that you can launch by double-clicking an .xlf file and then selecting **Open With, Multilingual Editor**. The multilingual editor allows great control over translations, in that it allows you to edit strings, review translations, add comments, and set a translation state—for example, Needs Reviews or Translated. Figure 33.3 shows the editor over the WindowsFormsLocalization. it.xlf file.

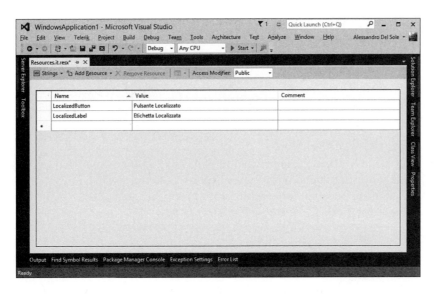

FIGURE 33.2 Visual Studio 2015 automatically translated resource strings.

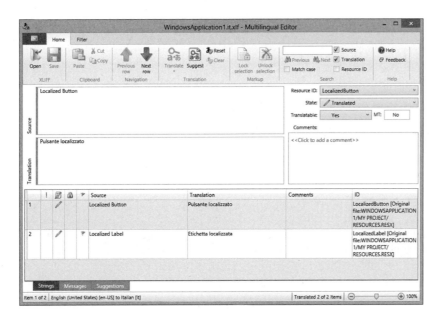

FIGURE 33.3 The multilingual editor in action.

When you are satisfied with the translation, change the state of each string from **Needs Review** to **Signed Off**. The last step is to assign the translated resources to the proper controls and the desired culture to the UI thread. You can do this in Visual Basic code—for example, when the application starts up or when the current window loads:

```
Private Sub Form1_Load(sender As Object, e As EventArgs) Handles MyBase.Load
    Threading.Thread.CurrentThread.
            CurrentCulture = New Globalization.CultureInfo("it")
    Threading.Thread.CurrentThread.
            CurrentUICulture = New Globalization.CultureInfo("it")
    Me.Button1.Text = My.Resources.LocalizedButton
    Me.Label1.Text = My.Resources.LocalizedLabel
End Sub
```

The code assigns to the current thread the new culture information that will be retrieved from the .xlf file and that must match your language/culture selection (see Figure 33.1). Figure 33.4 shows how the application looks with localized controls.

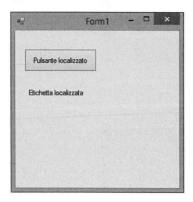

FIGURE 33.4   The localized Windows Forms application in action.

WPF Localization

In the past, localizing a WPF was a tricky task. In fact, you had different alternatives, some of them based on command-line tools, manual generation of satellite assemblies, and manual translation of each resource string. You also had to deal with BAML (Binary Application Markup Language), an intermediate file format for linked resources. With the MAT, all these problems have been solved, and you can take advantage of translation automation and visual tools, with a unified approach that is common to multiple platforms. This section explains how easy it is to localize a WPF application with the MAT in a few steps.

Localizing a WPF Application

Say that you want to create a localized version for the Italian culture of a WPF application based on English as the primary culture. Create a new WPF project with Visual Basic and name it as **WpfLocalization**, and add the code shown in Listing 33.1 on the XAML side. The goal is to provide a WPF counterpart of the Windows Forms example shown in the previous section.

LISTING 33.1 Preparing the User Interface Before Localization

```
<Window x:Class="MainWindow"
    xmlns="http://schemas.microsoft.com/winfx/2006/xaml/presentation"
    xmlns:x="http://schemas.microsoft.com/winfx/2006/xaml"
    Title="MainWindow" Height="350" Width="525">
    <StackPanel>
        <Button Name="Button1" Width="100" Margin="5"
            Height="40" Content="Localized button"/>
        <TextBlock Text="Localized text"
            Margin="5"
            Name="TextBlock1"/>
    </StackPanel>
</Window>
```

Now repeat exactly the same steps described for the Windows Forms sample, from specifying the English (United States) neutral language to marking translations as completed in the multilingual editor. The only change you might want to make is to add a string called `LocalizedText` instead of `LocalizedLabel`, with the value `Localized text`. Then add the following XML namespace alias at the `Window` declaration level:

```
xmlns:properties="clr-namespace:WpfLocalization.My.Resources"
```

Because you might want to take advantage of binding XAML properties to resource strings, you need this XML namespace alias to reach your resources. Now replace the `Button` and `TextBlock` definitions as follows:

```
<Button Name="Button1" Width="100" Margin="5"
    Height="40" Content="{x:Static properties:Resources.LocalizedButton}"/>
<TextBlock Text="{x:Static properties:Resources.LocalizedButton}"
    Margin="5"
    Name="TextBlock1"/>
```

Notice that you use the `x:Static` markup extension to point to resource strings, which are actually shared public properties. At this point, you need to assign the new culture to the current UI thread. This can be done in the `Application`'s class constructor, or in the `Window.Loaded` event handler for the main window, as follows:

```
Private Sub MainWindow_Loaded(sender As Object, e As RoutedEventArgs) _
        Handles Me.Loaded
    Threading.Thread.CurrentThread.
            CurrentCulture = New Globalization.CultureInfo("it")
    Threading.Thread.CurrentThread.
            CurrentUICulture = New Globalization.CultureInfo("it")
End Sub
```

If you now run the application by pressing **F5**, you will be able to see how the UI elements have been localized properly, as shown in Figure 33.5.

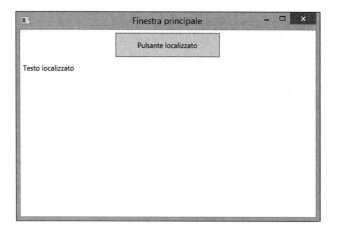

FIGURE 33.5   The localized WPF application in action.

Summary

This chapter covered localization. First, you got information on how the .NET Framework provides objects for application localization at a general level. Next, the discussion focused on the Multilingual App Toolkit and the unified approach it provides to localizing both Windows Forms and WPF applications taking advantage of automatic translation services.

CHAPTER 34

Building and Publishing ASP.NET Web Applications

Many of the most common activities in everyday life are often performed via the Internet and websites. You book a flight via airline companies' websites; you buy tickets for the theater via ticketing websites; and you can pay your bills via your bank's website. Also, most companies (and probably yours, too) have local networks running internal web applications for several kinds of purposes, such as office automation, storing data, and so on. Being a complete technology, the .NET Framework offers its own web platform for developing websites based on .NET, which is named ASP.NET. This is an engine for websites running on the server side, which enables building robust web applications using managed code. Even though several technologies came out in the past years for building web applications, including Microsoft platforms, this is still the most valid choice. In this chapter you start with the ASP.NET programming model and build web applications with Visual Basic 2015, also leveraging some of the new features typical of ASP.NET 4.6. Discussing ASP.NET in detail would probably require more than one specific book. The latest version also brings so many new features that summarizing them all would be certainly beyond the scope of this chapter. Also, this chapter does not discuss ASP.NET 5 Core, the open source stack for the web. For additional information about ASP.NET 4.6 and ASP.NET 5 Core, see http://www.asp.net.

Introducing the ASP.NET Model

So far, we've discussed several kinds of client applications, such as Console, Windows Forms, and WPF. For this last technology, the discussion was deeper because WPF is the premier technology for building desktop clients. Developing web applications for ASP.NET with Visual Basic 2015 is different. If you are a web developer, this chapter will probably just be an overview of some new features introduced by .NET 4.6. However, if you are new to ASP.NET, although you can find lots of similarities with the client world in writing managed code and creating applications, the code in the web environment runs differently. So you need to understand where the code is running and why scaling applications is fundamental; therefore, you also need to understand the concept of the stateless nature of the Web so you can handle it in your applications. This is discussed next.

Platforms and APIs

You develop ASP.NET web applications using the following platforms and APIs:

- ▶ **Web Forms**—This allows you to build web applications using common techniques based on drag and drop, controls, design surface, and an event-driven model. Web Forms has existed since the first version of ASP.NET.

- ▶ **MVC (Model-View-Controller)**—The MVC provides a pattern-based way of building web applications that makes possible clean separation between data, UI, and logic. The MVC is very powerful and modern, and it allows great control and more granularity in the application architecture.

- ▶ **Web API**—This framework enables developers to easily build HTTP services that are available to a wide range of clients, such as browsers and mobile devices. In .NET 4.6 and Visual Studio 2015, Web API also serves the OData platform, as discussed in Chapter 38, "Implementing and Consuming OData Services."

Whatever platform you choose, in Visual Studio 2015, the ASP.NET platform leverages all the power of the .NET Compiler Platform. Also, MVC and Web API have been moved into a unified programming model. Another important factor is that Visual Studio no longer includes the whole .NET Framework's BCL for creating an ASP.NET project; in fact, ASP.NET now allows you to reference and use only the libraries your application effectively needs.

When you create a new project, Visual Studio adds a minimum set of assemblies. Then, as you develop the application and use either the toolbox or other platform-specific instrumentation, it downloads the required assemblies from NuGet. This approach, known as *composable stack*, allows you to create web applications that are also optimized to be deployed to Microsoft Azure more easily.

After explaining the basis of the ASP.NET model, this chapter will provide an example based on Web Forms. Don't forget to bookmark the official ASP.NET website (www.asp.net) for more detailed information.

Understanding Page Requests

When you create a web application, the application will be hosted on a web server. This is the place where your Visual Basic compiled code actually resides. When the code is executed, the ASP.NET engine renders it as HTML so it can be consumed on the client side by a web browser such as Internet Explorer or Firefox, which can interpret Hypertext Markup Language (HTML) and display web pages. When you type a website address into your browser, it sends a web page request. This is then translated into an address that searches for the server hosting the requested page. When the server receives the request, the installed web server software catches the request and, if this is about an ASP.NET web page, passes the request to the ASP.NET engine so this can render the result as HTML and return it to the calling browser. Samples of web server software include Internet Information Services (IIS) and IIS Express. Visual Studio 2015 ships with its own web server, IIS Express. This enables you to simulate a web server environment on the development machine for testing applications. Visual Studio allows you to select a different web server, such as the local IIS, in the project's properties.

One key point is that you do not only write HTML markup; instead, you also write Visual Basic code that is compiled into an assembly residing on the server. So the ASP.NET engine sends requests to your code for processing and then returns the processing result as HTML that can be consumed by client browsers. All these operations are fine, but there is a problem: In a desktop environment, you have one user running one instance of the application that works against its set of data and information; even if you have hundreds of database records to load, the application will be responsive in most cases. The same is not true for web applications if you think that one web application hosted on a server could potentially receive hundreds of concurrent requests. Therefore, elaborating hundreds of data requests concurrently can cause a bottleneck with hard performance problems. Fortunately, ASP.NET provides a mechanism for scalability that lets the application solve performance problems the best way possible.

Scalability and Performance

Scalability is the capability of an application to serve requests well without getting too slow or crashing when the amount of work increases. As described before, in a single-user environment such as desktop applications, scalability is a recommended plus but not a requirement. But it is a requirement in a web environment, where multiple requests can come to a web page. Because you do not want your application to get too slow or to crash when a large number of simultaneous requests come in, you instead want requests to be served in a small amount of time. So, you need to be aware of scalability and performance. Luckily, ASP.NET has its own mechanism that serves for application scalability. Think of desktop applications for a moment: in such environment all the work is in memory, when you load data into variables. Variables are instances of managed objects that you release when no more are needed so that the garbage collection process frees up unused resources. In a web environment, this is not possible because the application resides on one server and serving a large number of requests would soon lead to out-of-memory errors. Thus, the mechanism of state management must be necessarily different. The following is the list of operations that occur against the code when ASP.NET receives a request:

1. ASP.NET creates an instance of the Page object, which is the web counterpart of Form and Window.

2. Because Page is a managed object, when ASP.NET processes the request, it releases the reference of the page instance.

3. The Garbage Collection process clears from the managed heap all objects that no longer have any reference, including released Page objects.

This is cool because, when an object completes its work, it is soon removed from memory, and this improves scalability. The problem is that if the object is no longer available, then data exposed by that object is also no longer available. This means that if the same user sends another request to the same page (that is, creating a new instance of the Page object), the page will result empty. This occurs frequently, if you think of web pages that require filling in some fields before they make available other controls that require the page to be reloaded. So, this is the reason ASP.NET needs a different state management, which is provided by the Application and Session state objects that will be discussed later.

Another problem that travels hand-in-hand with scalability is performance. Each time you send a page request, you have to wait a few seconds. This is normal because sending the request takes time and waiting for the server to respond also takes time. Plus, elaborating complex data requires additional time because the number of bytes to transfer is increased. With complex web applications, performance can become a problem, but fortunately ASP.NET includes everything an application needs to stay performant. You will now get started in getting some skills on ASP.NET. The first step in acquiring such skills is starting to create your first web project with VB 2015.

Available Project Templates

The previous version of the IDE, Visual Studio 2013, introduced *One ASP.NET*. With One ASP.NET, there is basically only one project template for building ASP.NET web applications, and you can select frameworks and libraries for them to use. To create a new project, you still invoke the New Project dialog via File, New Project, but in Visual Studio 2015 you see only the ASP.NET Web Application template, as shown in Figure 34.1.

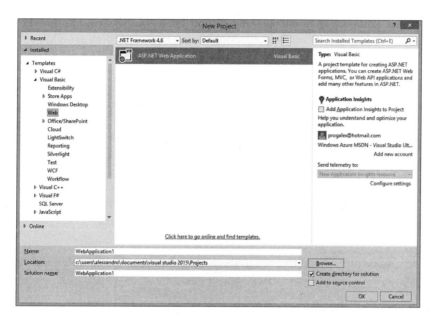

FIGURE 34.1   The Web application project template available with VB 2015.

After you give the project a name and click **OK**, you will be asked to specify what kind of UI framework, libraries, and authentication mode you want to use. Figure 34.2 shows where you do this.

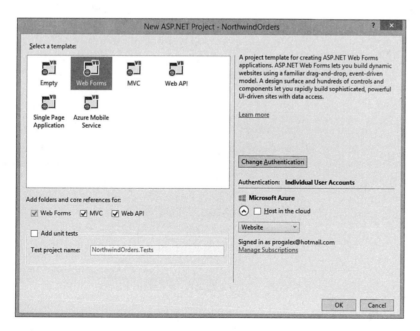

FIGURE 34.2   Selecting frameworks, libraries, and authentication mode.

For each available template, the dialog shows a very detailed description. You can mix multiple frameworks and APIs in each template, which means including Web Forms, MVC, and Web APIs models in one application. The default authentication mode is based on individual user accounts, but you can choose a different mode, such as Windows or anonymous authentication, by simply clicking the Change Authentication button. Later in this chapter, you will build a complete working example using the ASP.NET Web Forms Application template, which provides a skeleton of a web application with preconfigured pages. For the first experiments, create a new project based on the **Empty** template and ensure that the **Web Forms** option is checked. This generates a new empty project, where the first thing you have to do is add some pages. Pages in ASP.NET are represented by web forms.

Web Forms and Master Pages

ASP.NET web applications are made of pages. These can be standalone pages or ones providing common elements for each page. Standalone pages are known as *web forms*, while the other kind is known as a *master page*.

Web Forms

A web form represents a page in ASP.NET (a file with an .aspx extension) and is composed of markup code known as Extensible Hypertext Markup Language (XHTML) and of a code-behind part made of Visual Basic code. (XHTML is intended as an enhancement of classic HTML.) The concept is similar to the WPF development where the XAML code is for the user interface and the Visual Basic code makes the UI alive. The same is true for web forms, but the difference is that the UI is provided via XHTML code. The XHTML code in a web form contains markup for page layout, user controls, and eventually scripts. Each web application needs at least a Default.aspx page, so right-click the project name in Solution Explorer and select **Add New Item**. In the Add New Item dialog box, select the Web Form template, name it **Default.aspx**, and then click **OK**. When ready, the new page is made of some XHTML code. The following is the basic code of a web form, including a `Label` control for demonstrating some concepts:

```
<%@ Page Language="vb" AutoEventWireup="false"
        CodeBehind="Default.aspx.vb"
        Inherits="webApplication1._Default" %>


<!DOCTYPE html PUBLIC "-//W3C//DTD XHTML 1.0 Transitional//EN"
        "http://www.w3.org/TR/xhtml1/DTD/xhtml1-transitional.dtd">


<html xmlns="http://www.w3.org/1999/xhtml">
<head runat="server">
    <title></title>
</head>
<body>
    <form id="form1" runat="server">
    <div>
```

```
        <asp:Label ID="Label1" runat="server" Text="Label"></asp:Label>
    </div>
    </form>
</body>
</html>
```

The most important thing you need to remember is that code is executed on the server, so it is fundamentally adding a `runat="server"` attribute for each control; otherwise, it will not be correctly consumed by client browsers.

STYLING TIPS

ASP.NET enables you to style and apply themes to web forms via Cascade Style Sheets (CSS) files. A simpler way of styling controls is by selecting the `AutoFormat` option that's available when you click the smart tag.

Notice how the markup code contains classic HTML items that will be correctly rendered to client browsers. Each web form has a code-behind file, which you can find in Solution Explorer by enabling the Show All Files view and then expanding the desired web page file. When you double-click the Visual Basic code-behind file on a new web form, you can see that it is nothing but a class providing an event handler for the `Page.Load` event. As explained in the next subsection, a web form has a lifetime that is established by events.

Page Lifetime and Page Events

Each page has a lifetime that you need to understand so you can ensure changes you made through a postback are not ignored or overwritten. Page lifetime is articulated in events, each of them representing a particular moment. Although starting from ASP.NET 2.0 the `Page` class offers a bigger number of events, the most important are the following:

▶ `Init`, which is where the page initializes controls

▶ `Load`, which is when the page is loaded and you can play with controls

▶ `PreRender`, which occurs just before the page is rendered as HTML

Cached and Postback Events

Earlier in this chapter you learned that the biggest difference between the ASP.NET programming model and the client one is that in the ASP.NET development you cannot keep objects in memory and that, for scalability purposes, a page is reloaded each time you need to process some data. Reloading a page happens when you interact with controls on the page. Such controls raise events depending on the actions you took on them. These actions are divided into two categories: cached events and postback events. *Cached* events occur on controls that do not require an immediate page reload. The typical example is the `TextBox` control in which a `TextChanged` event is raised every time you edit the text but the page is not reloaded at each edit. *Postback* events occur on controls that cause an immediate page reload, such as `Button` and `ComboBox`. This is convenient because you expect immediate data processing when you click the `Button` or select a combo box item.

Cached events will also be elaborated at the page reload. Reloading a page means destroying the instance of the current page and then creating a new instance of the current page. This is good because you avoid overhead when working with big amounts of data, but the problem is that all objects and values held by the previous instance are lost, so you need a mechanism for restoring the original object values. This mechanism is typically the `ViewState` object that is covered later in more details; at the moment look at how you store an object value (such as the text stored in a `TextBox`) inside the `ViewState` before the page is reloaded at the `Button` click:

```
Protected Sub Page_Load(sender As Object,
        e As System.EventArgs) _
        Handles Me.Load
    If Not Page.IsPostBack Then
        Me.TextBox1.Text = CStr(Me.ViewState("MyText"))
    End If
End Sub

Protected Sub Button1_Click(sender As Object,
        e As EventArgs) _
        Handles Button1.Click
    Me.ViewState("MyText") = Me.TextBox1.Text
End Sub
```

The only situation when a postback event does not occur is when you open the website, meaning that the page is loaded for the first time. You can check whether the page is being loaded for the first time in the `Page_Load` event handler, where you read the value of the `Page.IsPostBack` property. If true, you can retrieve the content of the `ViewState` property to restore the original values.

> **TIP**
>
> If you use the `ComboBox control`, remember to set its `AutoPostBack` property as `True` so that it will cause a postback each time you select an item, when such behavior is desired.

Considering cached and postback events, the following is the updated list for the page lifetime:

1. Init

2. Load

3. Cached events

4. Postback events

5. PreRender

ASP.NET Controls

ASP.NET offers both server and HTML controls. Server controls run on the server side and emulate or are built upon existing HTML tags, but they provide more advanced features and usability. They also are object-oriented controls and support events, whereas HTML controls don't. Generally, HTML controls are more and more limited if compared to ASP.NET controls, although they can be still processed on the server by adding the usual `runat="server"` tag. The next sections list the most common controls from both types.

Server Controls

Server controls are typically user interface objects that users can use when running a web application on clients. You can notice that in most cases, ASP.NET server controls are counterparts of HTML controls but provide a fully object-oriented development environment and full support for managed code. Table 34.1 summarizes the most common server controls.

TABLE 34.1   Most Common Server Controls

Control	Description
AdRotator	Shows a series of advertisements.
BulletedList	Shows a bulleted list of items.
Button	A button that can be clicked.
Calendar	Provides a monthly calendar.
CheckBox	A check box control for Boolean check state.
CheckBoxList	A group of multiselection check boxes.
DataList	A drop-down list with database data.
DetailsView	Can show a single record of data.
DropDownList	A drop-down list enabling single selection.
FileUpload	Provides the capability of uploading files. ASP.NET 4.5 introduced the possibility of uploading multiple files in web browsers that support HTML5.
GridView	Enables tabular data representations.
HiddenField	Keeps data that will be hidden in the UI.
HyperLink	A hyperlink to open other websites.
Image	Shows a picture.
ImageButton	A button containing a picture instead of text.
ImageMap	Enables creating image regions that can be clicked.
Label	Enables presenting static text.
LinkButton	A button with hyperlink functionalities.
ListBox	Enables scrolling a list of items.
MultiView	Provides the capability of creating tabbed user interfaces.
Panel	A container for other controls.

Control	Description
RadioButton	A button with single option choice.
RadioButtonList	A group of radio button controls.
RangeValidator	Checks if the specified entry is between upper and lower bounds.
RequiredFieldValidator	Checks for the existence of an entry.
Substitution	A control that does not enable storing its content in cache.
Table	Enables presenting data within tables.
TextBox	A control that accepts text. Starting with ASP.NET 4.5, its `TextMode` property supports HTML5's input types like `email` and `datetime`.
View	One item in a `Multiview` control.
Wizard	Enables creating wizards.
Xml	Provides combination between Xml and XSLT objects.

All the controls in Table 34.1 are then rendered as their HTML equivalent so they can be consumed by web browsers.

> **NOTE**
>
> Server controls are not the only ones available. If you take a look at the Visual Studio toolbox, you notice the presence of different tabs. Remaining controls are typically data controls used for data-binding or navigation, validation, and login controls that will not necessarily be placed on the user interface.

HTML Controls

HTML controls in ASP.NET are representations of their classic HTML. Also, ASP.NET 4.6 is optimized to support HTML5. Table 34.2 summarizes the most common among available HTML controls.

> **WHAT IS HTML5?**
>
> You have probably heard a lot about HTML5 in recent years, so you might be wondering what HTML5 actually is. It is the fifth version of the standard specifications of HTML, and it introduces some new rules that browsers will respect with particular regard to videos, audios, geolocation, JavaScript support for animation, media contents, and an information storage system called Web Storage that enables the local storing of more information than with cookies. Visual Studio 2015 and ASP.NET 4.6 support HTML5 in a number of ways, including IntelliSense improvements for JavaScript code and control enhancements. Your approach as a web developer will not change; you will only have new features and more powerful applications as web browsers will fully support the new HTML standard. Take a look at the World Wide Web Consortium (W3C) for updates about the HTML5 standard at http://www.w3.org/html.

TABLE 34.2   HTML Controls

Control	Description
HtmlAnchor	Allows accessing the `<a>` HTML element on the server
HtmlButton	A button that can be clicked
HtmlForm	A form control
HtmlGenericControl	An element that cannot be mapped to any specific HTML control
Image	A control showing a picture
HtmlInputButton	Expects input via a button
HtmlInputCheckBox	Expects input via a Checkbox
HtmlInputFile	Expects input from a file
HtmlInputHidden	Hides its content
HtmlInputImage	Expects an image as the input
HtmlInputRadioButton	Expects input via a RadioButton
HtmlInputText	Expects input via some text
HtmlTable	Represents a table
HtmlTableCell	Represents a cell within a table
HtmlTableRow	Represents a row within a table
HtmlTextArea	Represents an area of text

The main difference between HTML controls and their ASP.NET counterparts is that ASP. NET versions can be accessed on the server side with managed code by adding an ID attribute and the `runat="server"` attribute, although HTML controls actually work on the server side. It is worth mentioning that, with ASP.NET 4.6, those HTML controls having a URL property support `runat="server"`.

Handling Events

Due to the code-behind logic, handling events in ASP.NET applications looks similar to what you saw with WPF. This means that a user control is implemented on the XHTML side and an event handler in the Visual Basic side.

HANDLING EVENTS TIP

If you need to catch events from objects that are not user controls, such as business objects or collections, you just write the event handler in Visual Basic code the usual way.

For example, consider the following XHTML code that provides a Button and a Label:

```
<form id="form1" runat="server">
<div>
    <asp:Button ID="Button1" runat="server" Text="Button"/>
    <asp:Label ID="Label1" runat="server"></asp:Label>
```

```
</div>
</form>
```

You can handle the `Button.Click` as usual—for example, with the following code that writes a message to the `Label`:

```
Protected Sub Button1_Click(sender As Object,
        e As EventArgs) Handles Button1.Click
    Me.Label1.Text = "You clicked!"
End Sub
```

Notice that you can also specify the event handler in the XHTML code, avoiding the `Handles` clause on the VB side, exactly as in WPF. The `Click` event handler is specified with the `OnClick` attribute:

```
<asp:Button ID="Button1" runat="server" Text="Button"
OnClick="Button1_Click" />
```

And then you write the event handler without `Handles`:

```
Protected Sub Button1_Click(sender As Object,
        e As EventArgs)
    Me.Label1.Text = "You clicked!"
End Sub
```

Understanding State Management

As you read at the beginning of this chapter, ASP.NET applications have to manage their states in a different way than client applications. State is managed via some special objects: `Application`, `Cache`, `Context`, `Session`, and `ViewState`. All of them work with the `Object` type, and you use them like dictionaries because they accept key/value pairs. The next subsections explain this and provide examples.

The `Application` State

One of the most common situations with websites is that you have many people using the website concurrently. If you want to hold shared information across all the application instances, you use the `Application` state. The following is an example:

```
Application("SharedKey") = "Shared value"

Dim sharedString As String = CStr(Application("SharedKey"))
```

Notice the key/value semantics and how you need to perform an explicit conversion from `Object` to `String`. You will not use `Application` often because each application instance runs on a separate thread that could modify the information and therefore could corrupt the values, too.

The `Cache` **State**

The ASP.NET `Cache` has the same scope of `Application`, meaning that both can be accessed by all page requests. The primary difference is that `Cache` enables holding information in memory, which avoids the need of re-creating and retrieving objects. This is good if you want to maintain updatable objects but could cause overhead (always considering that the bigger the amount of data to transfer, the lower the performance) because it requires memory. So, it should be used only when needed or when you ensure that performance is acceptable. The following is an example of storing and retrieving information with `Cache`:

```
Cache("MyUpdatableDataKey") = "My updatable data"
Dim myUpdatableData As String = CStr(Cache("MyUpdatableDataKey"))
```

In addition, an alternative way for adding objects to the cache is the `Cache.Add` method. It provides the ability of setting advanced settings for the object, as demonstrated in this code:

```
Protected Sub Page_Load(sender As Object,
        e As System.EventArgs) _
        Handles Me.Load

    Dim callBack As New CacheItemRemovedCallback( _
        AddressOf Cache_ItemRemoved)

    'Sets the key, adds the data, sets the CacheDependency,
    'sets the expiration mode, expiration time, priority
    'and delegate to invoke when the item is removed
    Cache.Add("MyUpdatableDataKey", "My updatable data", Nothing,
        Cache.NoAbsoluteExpiration, New TimeSpan(0, 0, 45),
        CacheItemPriority.High, callBack)

    'Removes the item
    Cache.Remove("MyUpdatableDataKey")
End Sub

Private Sub Cache_ItemRemoved(key As String,
        item As Object,
        reason As CacheItemRemovedReason)
    'The item has been removed
End Sub
```

The most interesting settings are the expiration mode and the priority. The first one can be `Cache.NoAbsoluteExpiration` (like in the preceding code), which means that the data will always be available during the page lifetime `Cache.SlidingExpiration`, on the other hand, means that the data will be removed after it is not accessed for the specified amount of time. Priority is also important in case you have lots of objects in memory and ASP.NET is about to encounter out-of-memory problems. At this point, ASP.NET begins evicting items according to their priority. (An object with lower priority is evicted before another one with high priority.)

The `Context` State

You use the `Context` state when you want to hold state only for the lifetime of a single request. This is useful when you need to have information in memory for a long period of time and need to ensure that keeping such information does not affect scalability. This is an example:

```
Context.Items("MyStringKey") = "My string value"
Dim contextString As String = CStr(Context.Items("MyStringKey"))
```

The context information is accessed at the page level and will not be available again on the next request.

Using Cookies for Saving Information

Cookies are pieces of information that a user's browser can hold and that can have a maximum size of 4 Kbytes. Each time the browser opens your web application, it recalls all cookies provided by the website. The following are examples of writing and reading cookies:

```
'Write a cookie
Dim aCookie As New HttpCookie("MyCookie")
aCookie.Value = "Information to store"
aCookie.Expires = New DateTime(10, 10, 2010)
Response.Cookies.Add(aCookie)


'Read a cookie
Dim getCookie As HttpCookie = Request.Cookies("MyCookie")
Dim cookieVale As String = getCookie.Value
```

Notice that the `Expires` property of type `Date` is required to specify that the cookie information will no longer be valid after that date, whereas the `Value` property is of type `String` so that you can store information without conversions.

The `Session` State

ASP.NET provides the ability of holding per-user information via the `Session` object. When a user opens the website, ASP.NET creates a cookie with a session identifier and then manages the session for that user based on the ID. The only issue is that you have no way of knowing when the user leaves the website, so a `Session` state expires after 20 minutes as a default. The following is an example:

```
Session("MyKey") = "User level information"
Dim userInfo As String = CStr(Session("MyKey"))
```

The `ViewState` State

To provide support for the work that a page needs to do in its lifetime, ASP.NET provides a mechanism known as `ViewState`. It provides the infrastructure that serializes values for each control in the page. For example, when a page is rendered, a control has a particular value. When this value changes, and such change raises an event, ASP.NET makes a comparison between the `ViewState` and form variables so that it can update the control value. (The `TextBox` control with its `TextChanged` event is the most common example.) Such a mechanism is available behind the scenes, but you can also use the `ViewState` by yourself. The following is an example that makes an object available at page level:

```
ViewState("MyPageDataKey") = "Page-level information"
Dim myPageData As String = CStr(ViewState("MyPageDataKey"))
```

Making this information available at the page level means also making it available when the page is posted back, but that decreases performance because the size of bytes to transfer is bigger. Excluding the user controls necessary to your web form, you should use `ViewState` for your needs with care.

Creating a Web Application with VB 2015 with Data Access and Pages

Visual Basic 2015 makes it easy to create web applications with navigation capabilities because the Web Forms template provides a master page implementation with default pages and designer tools for adding further elements. If you want to create a data-centric web application, the .NET Framework 4.6 offers specific controls that enable you to supply a data source and data-binding capabilities with a few mouse clicks. This section shows you how to reach this objective.

WEB FORMS AND MVC SCAFFOLDING

Visual Studio 2013 and later allow you to mix Web Forms and MVC libraries and take advantage of *scaffolding*. With scaffolding, Visual Studio generates a number of controller classes and views (that is, data-bound pages) based on a data model. Originally, scaffolding was available to MVC only, but with Visual Studio 2013 and later, you can include MVC libraries in a Web Forms app and use scaffolding. This provides more granularity and greater control over both the business logic and the user interface, but it requires some knowledge of MVC. For this reason, this chapter explains how to create a Web Forms application with data-bound pages using a classic approach. If you want to discover more about MVC and scaffolding, visit www.asp.net.

Select **File**, **New Project** and from the web projects folder, select the **ASP.NET Web Application** template; name the new project **NorthwindOrders** and then click **OK**. In the New ASP.NET Project dialog, select the Web Forms template and click **OK**. When the project is available in Solution Explorer, notice the presence of some web pages (Default. aspx and About.aspx) and of the master page (the Site.Master file). Now click the **Site. Master** file. You now see the simplest example of a master page, as shown in Figure 34.3.

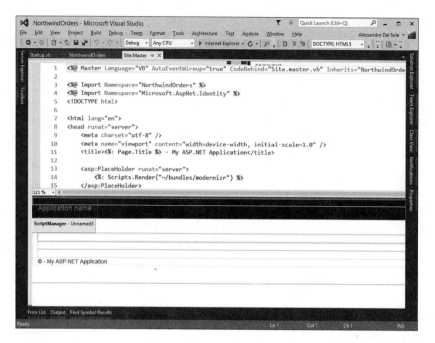

FIGURE 34.3   The default master page for the new web application.

Master Pages

A master page is a special page with .master extension, which provides a template containing a set of common elements for each page in the application. A master page typically contains elements such as headers, footers, and navigation elements so that you can implement a number of elements that each page can contain all at once. Visual Studio provides a specific item template for creating a master page, but the simplest way to understand how it works is to examine a basic one. When you create a new project using the ASP.NET Web Forms Application template, such as in the current example, the IDE adds a master page for you. As you can see, Visual Studio implements by default some links for navigating between pages, such as Home, Contact, and About. Such links have related web pages in the project, which are Default.aspx, Contact.aspx, and About.aspx. Also notice the Login link that points to a Login.aspx page stored in the Account folder, which also contains other auto-generated pages for registering to the web application and for password management. The most basic code for designing a master page is the following:

```
<%@ Master Language="VB" AutoEventWireup="true"
CodeBehind="Site.master.vb"
Inherits="NorthwindOrders.SiteMaster" %>

<%@ Import Namespace="NorthwindOrders" %>
<%@ Import Namespace="Microsoft.AspNet.Identity" %>
```

```
<!DOCTYPE html>

<html lang="en">
<head runat="server">
    <meta charset="utf-8" />
    <meta name="viewport" content="width=device-width, initial-scale=1.0" />
    <title><%: Page.Title %> - My ASP.NET Application</title>

    <asp:PlaceHolder runat="server">
        <%: Scripts.Render("~/bundles/modernizr") %>
    </asp:PlaceHolder>

    <webopt:bundlereference runat="server" path="~/Content/css" />
    <link href="~/favicon.ico" rel="shortcut icon" type="image/x-icon" />

</head>
<body>
    <form runat="server">
        <asp:ScriptManager runat="server">
            <Scripts>
                <%--To learn more about bundling scripts in ScriptManager see
                    http://go.microsoft.com/fwlink/?LinkID=301884 --%>
                <%--Framework Scripts--%>
                <asp:ScriptReference Name="MsAjaxBundle" />
                <asp:ScriptReference Name="jquery" />
                <asp:ScriptReference Name="bootstrap" />
                <asp:ScriptReference Name="respond" />
                <asp:ScriptReference Name="WebForms.js"
                Assembly="System.Web" Path="~/Scripts/WebForms/WebForms.js" />
                <asp:ScriptReference Name="WebUIValidation.js"
                 Assembly="System.Web"
                Path="~/Scripts/WebForms/WebUIValidation.js" />
                <asp:ScriptReference Name="MenuStandards.js" Assembly="System.Web"
                Path="~/Scripts/WebForms/MenuStandards.js" />
                <asp:ScriptReference Name="GridView.js" Assembly="System.Web"
                Path="~/Scripts/WebForms/GridView.js" />
                <asp:ScriptReference Name="DetailsView.js" Assembly="System.Web"
                Path="~/Scripts/WebForms/DetailsView.js" />
                <asp:ScriptReference Name="TreeView.js" Assembly="System.Web"
                Path="~/Scripts/WebForms/TreeView.js" />
                <asp:ScriptReference Name="WebParts.js" Assembly="System.Web"
                Path="~/Scripts/WebForms/WebParts.js" />
                <asp:ScriptReference Name="Focus.js" Assembly="System.Web"
                Path="~/Scripts/WebForms/Focus.js" />
                <asp:ScriptReference Name="WebFormsBundle" />
                <%--Site Scripts--%>
```

34

```
        </Scripts>
    </asp:ScriptManager>

    <div class="navbar navbar-inverse navbar-fixed-top">
        <div class="container">
            <div class="navbar-header">
                <button type="button" class="navbar-toggle"
                 data-toggle="collapse"
                    data-target=".navbar-collapse">
                    <span class="icon-bar"></span>
                    <span class="icon-bar"></span>
                    <span class="icon-bar"></span>
                </button>
                <a class="navbar-brand" runat="server"
                  href="~/">Application name</a>
            </div>
            <div class="navbar-collapse collapse">
                <ul class="nav navbar-nav">
                    <li><a runat="server" href="~/">Home</a></li>
                    <li><a runat="server" href="~/About">About</a></li>
                    <li><a runat="server" href="~/Contact">Contact</a></li>
                </ul>
                <asp:LoginView runat="server" ViewStateMode="Disabled">
                    <AnonymousTemplate>
                        <ul class="nav navbar-nav navbar-right">
                            <li><a runat="server"
                                href="~/Account/Register">Register</a></li>
                            <li><a runat="server"
                                href="~/Account/Login">Log in</a></li>
                        </ul>
                    </AnonymousTemplate>
                    <LoggedInTemplate>
                        <ul class="nav navbar-nav navbar-right">
                            <li><a runat="server" href="~/Account/Manage"
                                title="Manage your account">Hello,

                                <%: Context.User.Identity.
                                    GetUserName()  %>!</a></li>
                            <li>
                                <asp:LoginStatus runat="server"
                                  LogoutAction="Redirect" LogoutText="Log off"
                                  LogoutPageUrl="~/" OnLoggingOut="Unnamed_
                                  LoggingOut" />
                            </li>
                        </ul>
                    </LoggedInTemplate>
```

```
                </asp:LoginView>
            </div>
        </div>
    </div>
    <div class="container body-content">
        <asp:ContentPlaceHolder ID="MainContent" runat="server">
        </asp:ContentPlaceHolder>
        <hr />
        <footer>
            <p>&copy; <%: DateTime.Now.Year %> - My ASP.NET Application</p>
        </footer>
    </div>
  </form>
</body>
</html>
```

It is worth mentioning that Visual Studio 2015 also adds an optimized master page for mobile devices, called Site.Mobile.Master. Simply double-click it to investigate its content. The goal of the sample application is fetching the list of orders from the Northwind database, showing the list in a `GridView` control (with editing capabilities), and adding navigation features to the master page. So, in the next section you see how to add the data source and data-bound controls. ASP.NET 4.6 takes from its predecessor some features for working with data, and at the end of this discussion you will also get some hints about strongly typed data controls *and* model binding.

Adding the Data Model

The first thing to add in the web project is the data source. This can be of different kinds, such as POCO objects and Entity Data Models. The example will be based on the Entity Framework, thus you should add a new entity data model named Northwind.edmx and add to the model the Orders table from the database. Such steps have been described a lot of times in this book (refer to Chapter 26, "Introducing ADO.NET Entity Framework," for a full discussion), so they will not be shown again in detail. When you have the data, you need a place for presenting and editing the data, so you need a new web form.

Adding a New Web Form

To add a new web form to the project, right-click the project name in Solution Explorer and select **Add New Item**. When the same-named dialog box appears, click the **Web** folder. Among all available items, you see options to add a Web Form (which is just a web page) or a Web Form Using Master Page. This second template is useful if you want to show the new page within a master page, unlike the first template which is instead for free pages. Select the second template so that we can link the new page to the master page, and name the new page **Orders.aspx** (see Figure 34.4); then click **OK**.

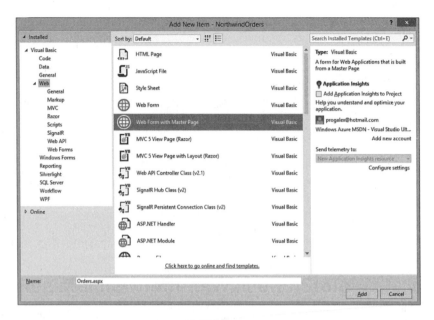

FIGURE 34.4   Adding a new web form using a master page.

At this point, Visual Studio asks you to indicate a master page from the project to link the new web form. In this case, you can choose between the normal and the mobile-optimized master pages. Select the Site.Master one, as shown in Figure 34.5.

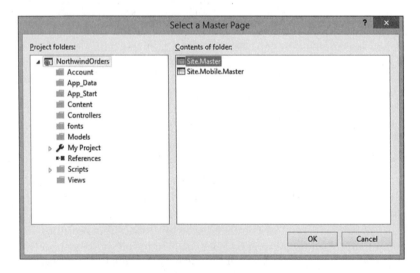

FIGURE 34.5   Specifying the master page to be associated to the new web form.

If you now double-click the **Orders.aspx** page, you get a new empty page linked to the master page, thus having navigation features. Now that we have a page, we can bind it to the data source.

Adding Data Controls

ASP.NET 4.6 offers a number of data controls that can be used to bind a data source to user controls and that act like a bridge. In particular, a control called `EntityDataSource` enables binding an entity data model to a graphic control.

ENABLING THE DESIGNER

By default, Visual Studio splits the workspace into two areas, one showing the HTML code for the pages and one the design surface. To enable the Visual Studio designer full view, click the **Design** button. Click **Source** if you only want to see the markup code, or **Split** to return to the default view.

In Visual Studio 2015, you can configure the control and bind it to a data source without writing a single line of code only if you use Entity Framework 5 via a very convenient wizard. If you instead use Entity Framework 6, you must perform some steps manually. Because the latter is the most recent version available, this section explains the second scenario.

You need to download a specific version of the `EntityDataSource` control for Entity Frame-work 6. You can easily accomplish this via the NuGet package manager, so right-click your project in Solution Explorer, select Manage NuGet Packages, and then search for the `Microsoft.AspNet.EntityDataSource` package, as shown in Figure 34.6. Finally, click **Install**.

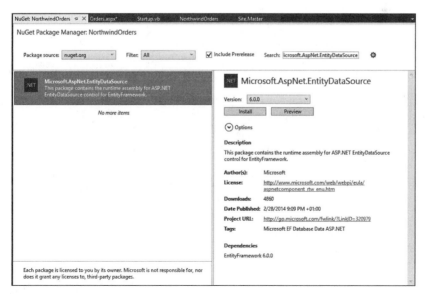

FIGURE 34.6   Downloading and installing the latest `EntityDataSource` control.

To use the control, you must add a prefix tag in the Web.config file, within the `controls` item, as follows:

```
<controls>
  <add tagPrefix="ef" assembly="Microsoft.AspNet.EntityDataSource"
      namespace="Microsoft.AspNet.EntityDataSource" />
</controls>
```

You can now declare an instance of the control in the Orders.aspx page, like this:

```
<ef:entitydatasource ID="EntityDataSource1" runat="server"
    ConnectionString="name=NorthwindEntities"
    DefaultContainerName="NorthwindEntities"
    EntitySetName="Orders"
</ef:entitydatasource>
```

Notice that the control must point to the appropriate connection string, whose name you saw when you generated the Entity Data Model and that is available in Web.config. Also, you must supply the context class name (`DefaultContainerName`) and the entity set (`EntitySetName`)—in this case, the list of orders. The `EntityDataSource` control is a bridge between data and user interface, so if you want to be able to edit, delete, and sort data, you must enable some self-explanatory properties, as follows:

```
<ef:entitydatasource ID="EntityDataSource1" runat="server"
    ConnectionString="name=NorthwindEntities"
    DefaultContainerName="NorthwindEntities"
    EntitySetName="Orders" AutoGenerateOrderByClause="True"
    AutoGenerateWhereClause="True" EnableDelete="True"
    EnableInsert="True"
    EnableUpdate="True">
</ef:entitydatasource>
```

You can now use any data-bound control, like `ListView` or `GridView`. You can either write the markup or drag'n'drop the control from the toolbox. The following code demonstrates how to declare a `GridView` bound to the specified `EntityDataSource`:

```
<asp:GridView ID="GridView1" runat="server"
    DataSourceID="EntityDataSource1" AllowPaging="True"
    AllowSorting="True" AutoGenerateDeleteButton="True"
    AutoGenerateEditButton="True"
    PageSize="20" >
</asp:GridView>
```

In this code you can see some optional properties, each enabling a particular scenario, such as paging, sorting, and options to edit and delete items in the collection. The `GridView` control can auto-generate columns by default, but in this case the designer is not very useful. If you want to have a visual representation of your grid, you should disable auto-generation and manually write column definitions as follows:

```
<asp:GridView ID="GridView1" runat="server" AllowPaging="True"
    AllowSorting="True"
    AutoGenerateColumns="False"
    AllowCustomPaging="true"
    PageSize="20"
    AutoGenerateEditButton="true" AutoGenerateDeleteButton="true"
    DataKeyNames="OrderID"
    DataSourceID="EntityDataSource1">
    <Columns>
        <asp:CommandField ShowSelectButton="True" />
        <asp:BoundField DataField="OrderID" HeaderText="OrderID" ReadOnly="True"
    SortExpression="OrderID" />
        <asp:BoundField DataField="CustomerID" HeaderText="CustomerID"
    SortExpression="CustomerID" />
        <asp:BoundField DataField="EmployeeID" HeaderText="EmployeeID"
    SortExpression="EmployeeID" />
        <asp:BoundField DataField="OrderDate" HeaderText="OrderDate"
    SortExpression="OrderDate" />
        <asp:BoundField DataField="RequiredDate" HeaderText="RequiredDate"
    SortExpression="RequiredDate" />
        <asp:BoundField DataField="ShippedDate" HeaderText="ShippedDate"
    SortExpression="ShippedDate" />
        <asp:BoundField DataField="ShipVia" HeaderText="ShipVia"
    SortExpression="ShipVia" />
        <asp:BoundField DataField="Freight" HeaderText="Freight"
    SortExpression="Freight" />
        <asp:BoundField DataField="ShipName" HeaderText="ShipName"
    SortExpression="ShipName" />
        <asp:BoundField DataField="ShipAddress" HeaderText="ShipAddress"
    SortExpression="ShipAddress" />
        <asp:BoundField DataField="ShipCity" HeaderText="ShipCity"
    SortExpression="ShipCity" />
        <asp:BoundField DataField="ShipRegion" HeaderText="ShipRegion"
    SortExpression="ShipRegion" />
        <asp:BoundField DataField="ShipPostalCode" HeaderText="ShipPostalCode"
    SortExpression="ShipPostalCode" />
        <asp:BoundField DataField="ShipCountry" HeaderText="ShipCountry"
    SortExpression="ShipCountry" />
    </Columns>
</asp:GridView>
```

If you now look at the designer, you see a perfect visual representation of your grid, as shown in Figure 34.7.

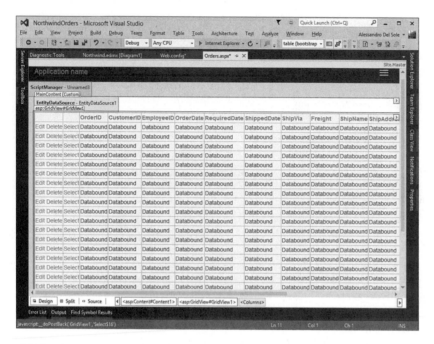

FIGURE 34.7   The design-time representation of the GridView control.

The page is ready for showing and editing orders from the database. Another couple features for filtering data are shown next so that you can better understand how powerful ASP.NET is.

RUNTIME DATA-BINDING TIP

Most of ASP.NET data controls expose a `DataSource` property that can be assigned at runtime with a custom data source, such as a `List(Of T)`. When assigned this property, you invoke the control's `DataBind` method to perform the binding.

Adding Filtering Capabilities

It would be interesting having filtering capabilities; for example, you could implement a filter that enables fetching all orders with the `ShipCity` property value that starts with the specified text. Thus, in the toolbox double-click a `TextBox` and a `Button`. These controls will be automatically placed onto the page (they will be placed at the top if that is where the cursor is in the designer). Now replace the `Name` property value of the `TextBox` with `FilterTextBox`. In the `Button` properties, change the `Id` value with `FilterButton` and the `Text` property with `Filter`. To provide filtering capabilities over the data source, ASP.NET offers the `QueryExtender` control that you can find within data controls in the toolbox. Add it to the page and then assign its `TargetControlID` property with `EntityDataSource1`, which is the name of the data control to be queried or filtered. Now you need to specify an expression for filtering; these kinds of expressions are known as *search expressions*.

ASP.NET offers more than one search expression, but the simplest and most appropriate for our purposes is `SearchExpression`. This object requires the specification of the search type and of the columns to be interrogated, but this is not sufficient. A `ControlParameter` element needs to be nested so you can specify the control where the search criteria are inserted (in our case the textbox) and the .NET type involved in the expression. Talking in code terms, you need to manually write the following code inside the `QueryExtender`:

```
<asp:QueryExtender ID="QueryExtender1" runat="server"
    TargetControlID="EntityDataSource1">
    <asp:SearchExpression DataFields="ShipCity" SearchType="StartsWith">
        <asp:ControlParameter ControlID="FilterTextBox" Type="String" />
    </asp:SearchExpression>
</asp:QueryExtender>
```

The only Visual Basic code we need to write is the event handler for the `Page.Loaded` event to check the `PostBack` state. This is accomplished by writing the following code in the Orders.aspx.vb code file:

```
Protected Sub Page_Load(sender As Object,
        e As System.EventArgs) _
        Handles Me.Load
    If Not Page.IsPostBack Then
        FilterTextBox.Text = ""
    End If
End Sub
```

This is all you need. Before running the sample web application, let's make the new web form reachable from the master page.

Adding Navigation Controls

Open the master page in the designer. You see the availability of two buttons named Home, About, and Contact. These are menu items inside a Menu control that point to the associated web form. If you split the view so that the source code is visible, you can easily add menu items inside `ul` elements. The following XHTML code demonstrates how to add a new button pointing to the Orders.aspx page, after the existing buttons:

```
<div class="navbar-collapse collapse">
    <ul class="nav navbar-nav">
        <li><a runat="server" href="~/">Home</a></li>
        <li><a runat="server" href="~/About">About</a></li>
        <li><a runat="server" href="~/Contact">Contact</a></li>
                <li><a runat="server" href="~/Orders">Orders</a></li>
        </ul>
```

As you can see, the `href` tag holds a relative URI that points to the page, while the `a` element contains the description of the button.

Running the Application

You can run the demo application by pressing **F5**. Figure 34.8 shows the Orders page, with a list of orders filtered according to the given search criteria. Also notice how paging features have been correctly implemented. Finally, try clicking the page buttons that provide navigation capabilities.

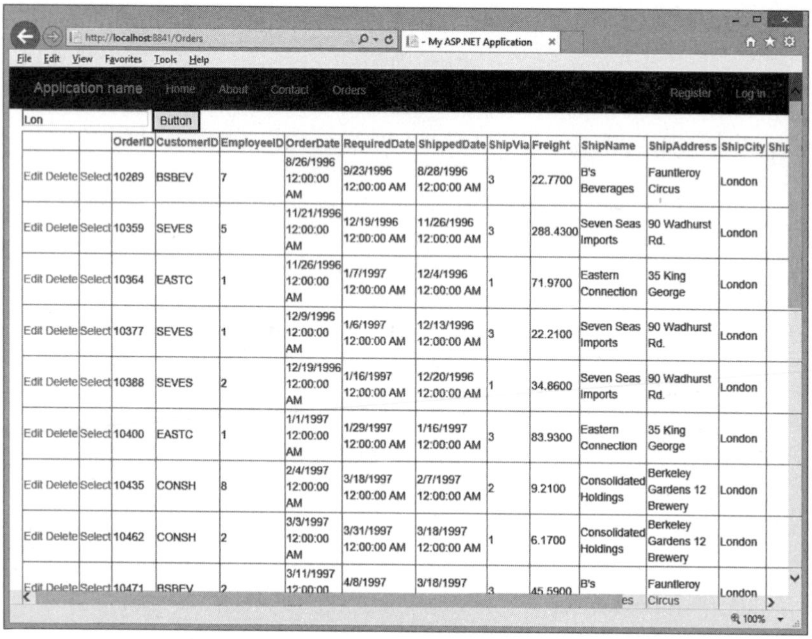

FIGURE 34.8   The sample web application running.

Strongly Typed Data Controls and Model Binding

In the real world, you often need to perform data-binding at runtime. For example, if you have a `GridView` control like in the previous sample application, you can perform runtime binding by assigning the `DataSource` property and then invoking the `DataBind` method explicitly like this:

```
Me.GridView1.DataSource = northwind.Orders
Me.GridView1.DataBind()
```

ASP.NET 4.6 inherits some goodies from its predecessor to help you write both declarative and runtime data-binding code, offering strongly typed data controls and model binding.

Strongly Typed Data Controls

When data-binding at runtime, it is useful to specify the type of the data to which the control is bound. Visual Studio 2015 allows this via *strongly typed data controls*. You can specify the type by assigning the new `ItemType` property with the data type. (Notice that during the assignment, IntelliSense will help you choose among the available types with a convenient drop-down list.) Next, you use an `Item` expression as in the following code, which uses a `FormView` control that allows you to show an object's details:

```
<asp:FormView ID="FormView1" runat="server" ItemType="NorthwindOrders.Order">
    <ItemTemplate>
        <li>
            Order ID: <%# Item.OrderID%><br />
            Ship City: <%# Item.ShipCity%><br />
        </li>
    </ItemTemplate>
</asp:FormView>
```

When you type the dot after `Item`, you will see that IntelliSense lists all available members from the selected object type. This will avoid a lot of runtime errors due to bad writing and will use both IntelliSense and the background compiler so that errors will be immediately shown in the Errors tool window at compile time.

Model Binding

ASP.NET 4.6 extends web forms data controls with the model binding, which enables you to work with code-focused models like EDMs or Code First. You assign the `SelectMethod` property of data controls with the name of a method that returns a collection of objects, so you will no longer need to invoke `DataBind` explicitly. Let's see an example with a `GridView` that shows a reduced number of columns from the `Orders` table from the Northwind database:

```
<asp:GridView ID="GridView1" runat="server" AutoGenerateColumns="false"
    ItemType="NorthwindOrders.Order" SelectMethod="GetOrders">
    <Columns>
        <asp:BoundField DataField="OrderDate" HeaderText="OrderDate"
    SortExpression="OrderDate" />
        <asp:BoundField DataField="RequiredDate" HeaderText="RequiredDate"
    SortExpression="RequiredDate" />
        <asp:BoundField DataField="ShippedDate" HeaderText="ShippedDate"
    SortExpression="ShippedDate" />
        <asp:BoundField DataField="ShipVia" HeaderText="ShipVia"
    SortExpression="ShipVia" />
        <asp:BoundField DataField="Freight" HeaderText="Freight"
    SortExpression="Freight" />
    </Columns>
</asp:GridView>
```

You first use the strongly typed approach described previously by assigning the `ItemType` property. Then you specify a query method that returns the collection of data for the `SelectMethod` property. This method must be defined in the page's code-behind and must return an `IQueryable` or `IQueryable(Of T)`. In our case, the method can be defined as follows:

```
Public Function GetOrders() As IQueryable(Of Order)
    'Where 'northwind' is an instance of the EDM
    Return northwind.Orders
End Function
```

Because query methods return IQueryable or its generic flavor, you can either write LINQ queries or set the GridView's properties (or other data controls' properties) to allow filtering and sorting options. The following imperative code demonstrates how to execute a LINQ query to return a filtered and ordered collection of orders:

```
Public Function GetOrders() As IQueryable(Of Order)
    'Where 'northwind' is an instance of the EDM
    Dim query = From ord In northwind.Orders
        Where ord.OrderDate < Date.Today
        Order By ord.ShipCity
    Select ord
    Return query
End Function
```

With this code, the GridView will hold data-binding to the filtered and sorted collection without the need of invoking DataBind explicitly. Similarly, you can work directly on the XHTML code. The following snippet demonstrates how to enable paging and sorting directly on the GridView definition:

```
<asp:GridView ID="GridView1" runat="server" AutoGenerateColumns="false"
    ItemType="NorthwindOrders.Order" DataKeyNames="OrderID"
    AllowPaging="true" PageSize="100" AllowSorting="true"
    SelectMethod="GetOrders">
    <Columns>
        <asp:BoundField DataField="OrderDate" HeaderText="OrderDate"
        SortExpression="OrderDate" />
        <asp:BoundField DataField="RequiredDate" HeaderText="RequiredDate"
        SortExpression="RequiredDate" />
        <asp:BoundField DataField="ShippedDate" HeaderText="ShippedDate"
        SortExpression="ShippedDate" />
        <asp:BoundField DataField="ShipVia" HeaderText="ShipVia"
        SortExpression="ShipVia" />
        <asp:BoundField DataField="Freight" HeaderText="Freight"
        SortExpression="Freight" />
    </Columns>
</asp:GridView>
```

Notice how you enable paging by setting AllowPaging with true and by specifying the number of items per page with PageSize. Sorting is enabled by setting AllowSorting with true and with DataKeyNames, which contains the column(s) name used for sorting. Model binding also enables you to update data other than read-only query operations. For this purpose, you assign the UpdateMethod property on the data control. If you do not create a method first and choose the option to generate a new method via IntelliSense, Visual Studio will create a method stub (with a lot of useful comments) that you will have to change to make your changes to the selected object. For example, the following method has been generated by choosing the new method option with IntelliSense and demonstrates how to retrieve the instance of the selected order and how to send changes to the data source:

```vb
' The id parameter name should match the DataKeyNames value set on the control
Public Sub GridView1_UpdateItem(id As Integer)
    Dim item As NorthwindOrders.Order = northwind.Orders.
        FirstOrDefault(Function(o) o.OrderID = id)
    ' Load the item here, e.g. item = MyDataLayer.Find(id)
    If item Is Nothing Then
      ' The item wasn't found
      ModelState.AddModelError("",
        String.Format("Item with id {0} was not found", id))
      Return
    End If


    'Make your changes:
    item.ShipVia = 1


    'Update your model:
    TryUpdateModel(item)
    If ModelState.IsValid Then
      ' Save changes here, e.g. MyDataLayer.SaveChanges()
        northwind.SaveChanges()
    End If
End Sub
```

If you now assign `UpdateMethod="GridView1_UpdateItem"` on the `GridView`, this will always use the specified method to perform edits on the selected object.

Forcing Login for Security

The sample web application that was illustrated in the previous section has one important limitation: It can be accessed by anonymous users who can access important data. If your application just presents information, anonymous access is typically fine. But if your application has the purpose of managing data or restricted information, you need to force users to log in with their own credentials, such as a username and password. Together with One ASP.NET, Microsoft introduced into ASP.NET a new security model called ASP. NET Identity. It provides an improved way to manage security and simplifies the way users access sensitive information by generating proper login pages and the necessary code when creating a project. ASP.NET Identity is beyond the scope in this chapter, but you can find further information at http://www.asp.net/identity/overview/getting-started/ introduction-to-aspnet-identity.

In this section you will learn how to force users to log in before they can access sensitive data. The easiest way is to write some markup in the Web.config file, but of course you can control identity in managed code with more granularity. For instance, suppose you want to force users to log in before they can access the Orders page. This can be accomplished by adding the following markup in the Web.config file, under the `configuration` root node:

```
<location path="Orders.aspx">
  <system.web>
    <authorization>
      <deny users="?"/>
    </authorization>
  </system.web>
</location>
```

The `location` tag indicates the page the user must log in to. Nested in other tags, the `deny` tag with the `users` property set with ? means that users will be denied access to the Orders page unless they log in. To demonstrate how this works, press **F5** to start the application for debugging. If you now attempt to access the Orders page, you will be redirected to the login page, as you can see in Figure 34.9.

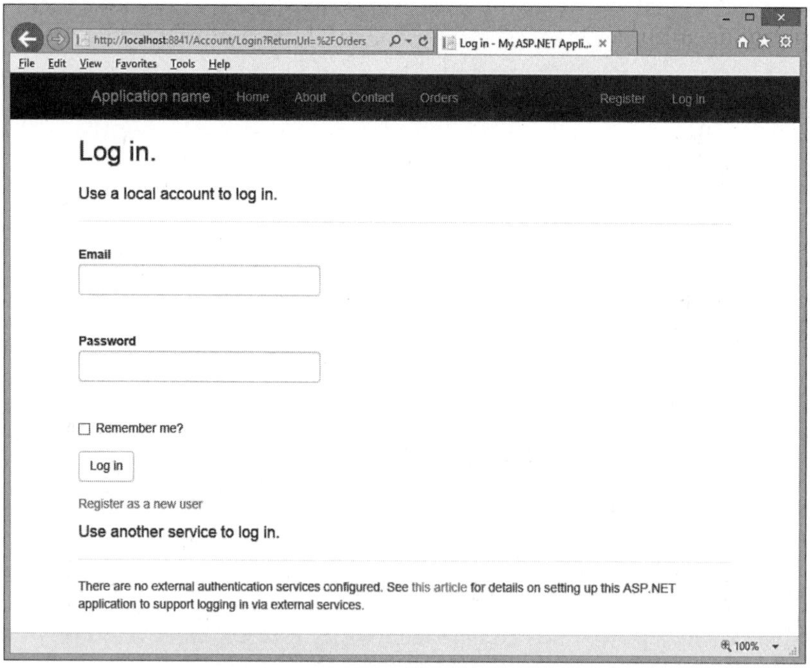

FIGURE 34.9   Forcing users to log in.

If you are a use, at this point, you must register with your email address and password, so click **Register as a New User**. Figure 34.10 provides an example.

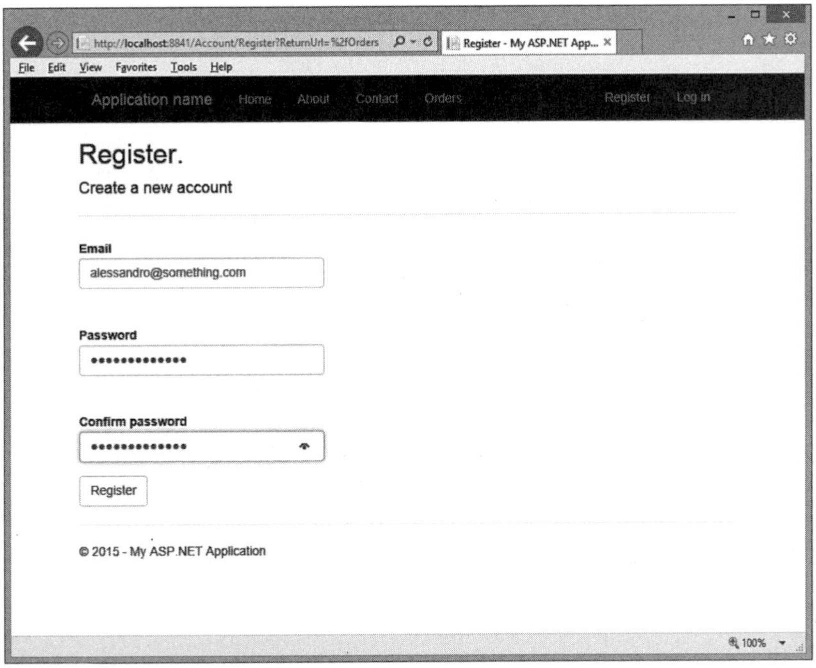

FIGURE 34.10   Registering as a new user.

Notice that the ASP.NET Identity model requires password enforcement, so you need to specify at least one non-digit character. When you're done, click **Register**. At this point, you will be able to access the Orders page. To understand how this works for users who are already registered, click **Log Off** in the upper-right corner on the page and then click **Orders**. You must enter your credentials, so provide your email address and password, and you will be able to access that sensitive information.

Of course, this is a basic security implementation, but there is more to Windows authentication, including roles. The official site, http://www.asp.net/identity, provides information about additional scenarios.

WHERE IS THE ASP.NET ADMINISTRATION TOOL?

If you have experience with previous versions of Visual Studio, or if you read previous editions of this book, you might know about the ASP.NET Administration Tool. This tool is no longer available in Visual Studio 2015 out of the box because it was strictly related to the ASP.NET Development Server (known as "Cassini"), which has been replaced by IIS Express. Therefore, this book no longer discusses that tool. However, you can still enable the ASP.NET Configuration Tool with some manual tricks explained in this MSDN blog post: http://bit.ly/1yhB3zz. Because this tool is not part of the Visual Studio 2015 instrumentation, we don't discuss it further here.

Publishing ASP.NET Web Applications

To make your web application reachable by other users, you need to deploy it to a host web server, either on the Internet or on a local area network, such as your company's network. ASP.NET 4.6 and Visual Studio 2015, as in the previous version, make the deployment experience for web applications even simpler, via a special tool named MSDeploy. They also introduce better integration with Microsoft Azure for simplified deployment, but this is discussed in Chapter 35, "Building and Deploying Applications for Microsoft Azure." In this section you learn how to publish an ASP.NET 4.6 application using a number of available options.

Deployment Overview

Deploying a web application can be accomplished directly from within Visual Studio 2015, as it was for its predecessors. You can publish a web application to the following destinations:

▶ A web server with Internet Information Services 7 or higher installed

▶ A website on Microsoft Azure

▶ An FTP site

▶ The local file system

▶ The local Internet Information Services

Visual Studio 2015 retakes some important changes brought by versions 2012 and 2010, which made the deployment experience different but certainly better as you discover in a few moments.

The 1-Click Deployment

Visual Studio 2015 retakes and follows the logic of deployment simplification with *1-Click deployment* introduced by its predecessor. What does it mean?

It means that you supply the required information such as web address and credentials; then you just click once on a button and Visual Studio will do the rest of the work for you, independently from the destination type. The reason for this important new way to deploy web applications is the presence of a tool named MSDeploy, which is described later and that can deploy articulated web applications. For now, let's begin to see how you can deploy web applications to FTP sites and IIS servers with the 1-Click deployment. As a general rule, to publish a web application, you can right-click the project name in Solution Explorer and select **Publish**. This opens the Publish Web dialog, shown in Figure 34.11.

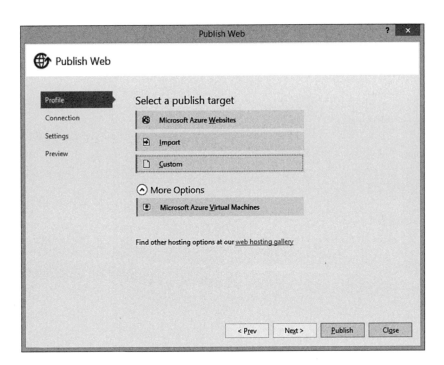

FIGURE 34.11   The Publish Web dialog.

This is the where you first decide whether the deployment target is Microsoft Azure or another hosting option. Microsoft Azure is discussed in Chapter 35, so now you will discover other available opportunities.

Classic Publishing

Visual Studio 2015 still provides the capability of publishing web applications the usual way, so it supports direct deployment to FTP sites, websites with FrontPage extensions enabled, the file system, and the local Internet Information Services, although some innovations are available in the graphical user interface of the deployment window. For example, you might want to deploy the NorthwindOrders web application, created before, to an FTP site. In Solution Explorer, right-click the project name and then click **Publish**. This launches the Publish Web dialog box (refer to Figure 34.11), where you must specify a new profile or import an existing one. Assuming you do not have an existing profile, click **Custom**. At this point, you will be prompted to enter a name for the new profile, for example, **MyFirstProfile**. The Connection tab is now enabled and you will have to specify settings for the new profile. Select **FTP** in the Publish Method combo box. Figure 34.12 shows the dialog box.

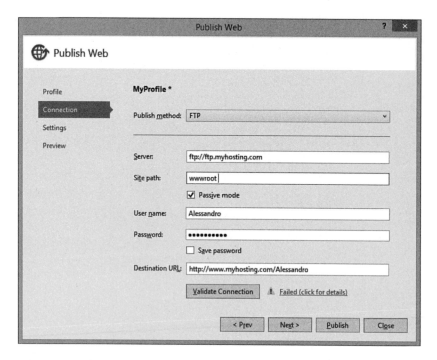

FIGURE 34.12   Publishing a web application to an FTP site.

Click **Publish** so that Visual Studio 2015 publishes your web application to the specified FTP, or click Validate Connection if you want to be sure that supplied credentials
can establish a successful connection. If you click Settings on the left side of the dialog
box before publishing, you will be able to specify which project configuration will be
published (Debug, Release, or any other available configuration) and whether files of a
previous version of the application will be erased on the target machine when publishing
the new one.

PROVIDERS' FIREWALL

Several Internet service providers or hosts enable firewalls to avoid unrecognized incoming
connections. If you want to publish web applications to a website or FTP site, you need to
ensure that the host's firewall accepts connections from Visual Studio 2015.

Another example is publishing the application to IIS, which can be also particularly useful
for testing purposes. You accomplish this by setting the File System option in the Publish
Method combo box and then typing the IIS instance address, as demonstrated in Figure
34.13. Publishing to the local IIS requires Visual Studio 2015 to be launched with administrative privileges and does not allow publishing the database schema, which must be
deployed separately.

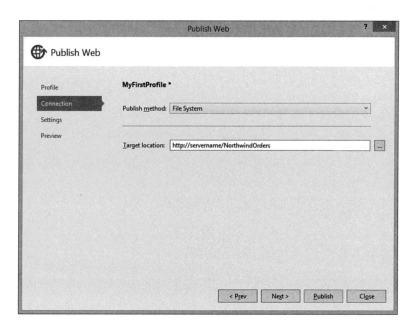

FIGURE 34.13   Publishing the web application to Internet Information Services.

You can click the Browse button (the one with three dots) to select an existing web folder or create a new one inside IIS.

MSDeploy Publish

One of the most interesting features in deploying web applications is the Microsoft Web Deployment Tool, also known as MSDeploy. It is a command-line tool included in the .NET Framework 4.6 and can build advanced deployment scripts. MSDeploy is an advanced tool in that it can

- ▶ Publish web applications and their settings

- ▶ Deploy SQL Server databases

- ▶ Direct advanced deployment to Internet Information Services web servers

- ▶ Publish GAC, COM, and Registry settings

MSDeploy is a complex tool, and writing the appropriate command lines can be annoying. Fortunately, Visual Studio 2015 enables you to publish web applications via MSDeploy through the Publish Web dialog box, as demonstrated later. Before getting into that, you need to know how web applications are packaged before deployment.

Understanding Packages

When you deploy a web application via MSDeploy, the application is first packaged into one archive that makes deployment easier. The package contains all the required information about the host web server and files and settings required by the application. You set package information in the Package/Publish Web tab of My Project, as shown in Figure 34.14.

Here you can find default settings for the local IIS, but you can place settings provided by the system administrator of the target machine. The package contains the following elements:

▶ The package containing the application and settings

▶ The destination manifest, which contains information on how to reach the target server

▶ The command-line script that will be passed to MSDeploy

When you have specified your package's settings, you are ready to deploy it with MSDeploy.

PRECOMPILING APPLICATIONS

ASP.NET 4.6 enables you to precompile a web application by selecting the **Precompile the application before publishing** box in the package properties (see Figure 34.14). With this option enabled, Visual Studio precompiles the application and merges all the site's content when you publish it. You can control a number of options by clicking the Advanced button that becomes available after the option is selected, such as merging all the site's content into one or multiple assemblies.

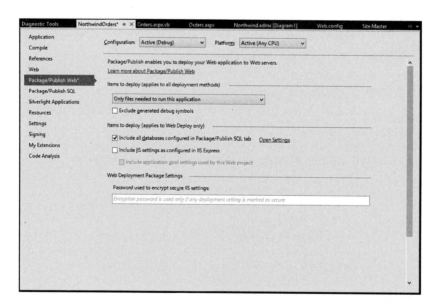

FIGURE 34.14   Setting options for packaging web applications for deployment.

Web Deploy with MSDeploy

Visual Studio 2015 provides the opportunity to deploy web applications with MSDeploy through its instrumentation in two alternative ways:

▶ Direct publishing to a web server

▶ Generation of a package that can be manually installed later on the server

In this chapter we examine both options, starting by the direct publishing. To publish a web application directly to a web server, right-click the project name in Solution Explorer and then click **Publish**. When the **Publish** Web dialog box appears, select the **Web Deploy** option from the Publish Method combo box in the Connection tab. Figure 34.15 shows the dialog box.

You need to provide some settings to deploy the web application with MSDeploy, and most of them are given to you by the Administrator of the target server. Table 34.3 summarizes the required settings.

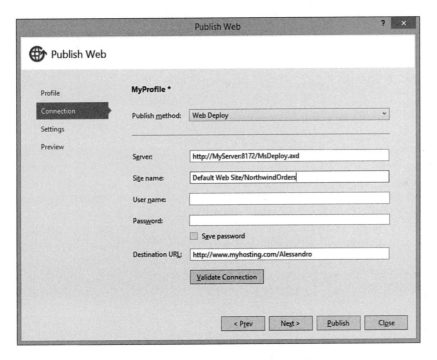

FIGURE 34.15   Setting options for the MSDeploy publish.

TABLE 34.3   Required Settings for MSDeploy Publish

Option	Tab	Description
Service URL	Connection	The URL of the MSDeploy service provided by the host or administrator. If you are publishing to your local IIS on the development machine for testing purposes, enter http://localhost; otherwise, see Figure 34.15 for an example of how the URL should be composed.
Site/Application	Connection	The name of the site and application on the target IIS. Here you can include subfolders.
Destination URL	Connection	The target URL of the web application after it is deployed
Username/Password	Connection	Credentials required to access the target IIS, provided by the server administrator.
Configuration	Settings	The project output you want to deploy based on the configuration (Debug, Release).
File Publish Options	Settings	Enables you to remove files that are no longer part of the deployment when publishing a new version, to precompile code, and to exclude the App_Data folder.
Databases	Settings	This is a group of connection strings and can vary depending on how many database connections you have in your project. Specify the appropriate connection string for each database (see Figure 34.16 for an example).

If you choose to validate your credentials, Visual Studio will also check whether a valid certificate is available. Also, if you want to see how many files will be deployed to the web server, select the Preview tab in the Publish Web dialog box. This is especially useful when you are updating an existing application and want to see which files are going to be replaced with new versions. When you provide all required settings, click **Publish** to get your application deployed to the web server with MSDeploy, remembering that this tool provides the opportunity to deploy additional requirements such as SQL Server databases and GAC settings.

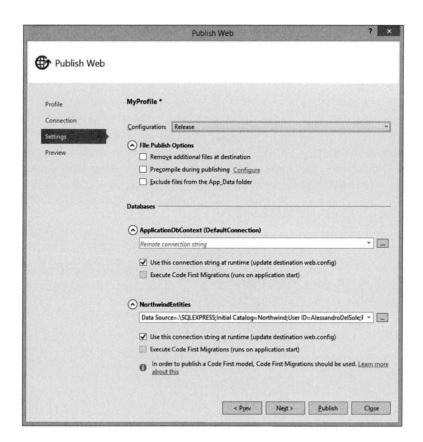

FIGURE 34.16   Specifying database connections.

Packaging Web Applications for Manual Installation

MSDN REFERENCES

The goal of this chapter is explaining how to publish web applications from a developer perspective, so here you learn how to generate packages. However, in this section we are assuming that the installation is made by another person such as the server administrator. For this reason (and because explaining the process in detail would be beyond the scope of this book), here you learn how to generate a package. You will be invited to read the appropriate MSDN documentation to understand how to perform a manual installation of the package on the server.

The steps described in the previous paragraph enable you to automate the generation of a package that is automatically deployed to a web server. This is convenient but presents a couple of problems:

▶ You must have administrative privileges on the server to which you are deploying the application.

▶ The server administrator might need to customize the installation process because of some company's policies.

For this reason, Visual Studio allows you to generate a package as a .zip file that can be later installed manually on the server by another person. To accomplish this, you select the Web Deploy Package option in the Connection tab of the Publish Web dialog box and then specify some basic information that can be edited during the installation process. Figure 34.17 shows how you specify the target folder for the .zip package and the destination on the server.

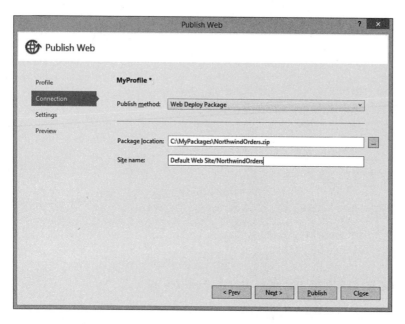

FIGURE 34.17   Specifying settings for manual package generation.

The Settings tab works like in the Web Deploy option. When you click Publish, Visual Studio generates several files into the folder that you specified, but the most important of them are the .zip package and a .deploy.cmd file (whose name starts with the application's name). These enable you to install the package locally or remotely. So, now you have two options for installing the package onto the web server:

▶ Launch the .deploy.cmd file. The MSDN documentation has specific explanations about this at http://msdn.microsoft.com/en-us/ff356104(v=vs.110).aspx.

▶ Import the package through the Internet Information Services Manager, which must be enabled on the server. Further information can be found at www.iis.net/learn/publish/using-web-deploy/import-a-package-through-iis-manager.

With both options, administrators can control the package installation and make the appropriate decisions based on the company's policies.

Summary

This chapter provides an overview of the ASP.NET technology and how you can build websites based on it. You read about important concepts on the ASP.NET model and how it maintains the application state; then you learned how to create a web application with Visual Basic 2015. You learned what web forms are and how the logic is divided into XHTML code for the user interface side and Visual Basic code for performing executive tasks. You took a look at available user controls, both server and HTML controls; then you put your hands on a sample web application to manage data exposed from an Entity Data Model. You learned the steps necessary to configure security for websites implementing login credentials. Finally, the chapter discussed how to deploy ASP.NET web applications in both the classic fashion and the one based on the Microsoft Web Deployment tool. Now you know how to use the 1-Click publish deployment system for quickly deploying your web applications directly from Visual Studio 2015.

34

CHAPTER 35

Building and Deploying Applications for Microsoft Azure

Maintaining servers and data centers has costs and requires a company to have people specifically working on maintenance and administration. To reduce costs, a new way of thinking about data and web applications working on data is *cloud computing*. The idea of cloud computing is that you eliminate physical servers and data centers from your company's location and deploy your web applications to servers that are elsewhere in the world and maintained by another company, using network connections for accessing your data. Microsoft has been working hard since 2008 on its own cloud computing platform, known as Microsoft Azure, which is now a mature platform. This platform is composed of several services, such as applications hosted on a 64-bit operating system, SQL Server data access, and .NET services. A deep discussion on Azure would certainly require an entire book; in this chapter you learn what Microsoft Azure is and how you can build and deploy Visual Basic web applications to Azure using Visual Studio 2015; further discussions on the numerous offered services are available in the MSDN official documentation.

Overview of the Microsoft Azure Platform

Microsoft Azure is the cloud computing platform from Microsoft. It offers an infrastructure for scaling applications on the Internet where services and applications are hosted on Microsoft data centers. With Microsoft Azure, you do not need physical servers in your company because data and applications are hosted by Microsoft servers. Microsoft

Azure is the perfect platform for new companies because it allows quick time-to-market opportunities; in fact, you can make a web application available on the Internet in a few minutes. Windows Azure is instead just a part of the Azure Platform and is a 64-bit operating system providing the runtime and the environment for hosting your applications and the platform's services and for managing the applications' lifecycle. It is essentially based on Windows Server 2012. You are not limited to .NET applications; you can host PHP, Java, and other kinds of web applications on Azure as well. Also, you can use Azure to host mobile services for mobile apps, including iOS and Android apps. In this chapter, though, you learn only about .NET. One of the biggest benefits in developing for Microsoft Azure is that you can keep your existing skills in developing ASP.NET and WCF services with just slight modifications due to the platform infrastructure, still utilizing Visual Studio 2015 as the development environment. The goal of this chapter is introducing you to developing and deploying your Visual Basic applications to the Azure platform. In-depth discussions are not possible here, although it is important to understand how you use Visual Studio 2015 to build and deploy Visual Basic applications. The Microsoft Azure platform offers several services other than the Windows Azure operating system, which include, among the others, the following:

▶ **App Service**—This new service includes all you need to build both mobile and web applications with tools that fully integrate with Visual Studio. It is available for several programming languages, both within and outside the .NET family, such as PHP, Java, and Python. With App Service, Microsoft Azure offers a service hosting space that runs applications and a Storage Account service where you can place data. Also, App Service provides an easy way to create backends for your mobile apps. Finally, it provides support for integrating Microsoft BizTalk services hosted on the cloud.

▶ **Cloud Services**—This includes SQL Database (formerly known as SQL Azure), a full relation database engine based on SQL and APIs to connect public cloud networks with private networks.

▶ **Virtual Machines**—An environment to easily migrate existing Windows or Linux virtual machines to Microsoft Azure without the need of changing existing code, it also enables you to connect an on-premise network to virtual machines running on the cloud.

▶ **Active Directory and Authentication Services**—A convenient way to manage users, roles, and permissions in your Azure-hosted web applications.

▶ **Media Services**—This allows you to host media content in the cloud and provides support for media streaming.

▶ **Azure Marketplace**—An online store with applications, add-ons, and data sets preconfigured for Microsoft Azure.

▶ **Cloud Storage**—A place to store files and data (see the following bulleted list).

Cloud Storage, which is enabled when you create your account, includes the following areas:

▶ **Blob Storage**—Here, you can place files and streams that you can reach via HTTP and HTTPS addresses.

▶ **Tables Storage**—Here, you can organize unstructured data within tables.

▶ **Local Storage**—The space on the disk in the virtual machine hosting your Microsoft Azure applications that your code can access for your needs.

▶ **Azure Drives**—Virtual VHD disks that your code running on the virtual machine can mount and that are backed by a blob.

▶ **Queues Storage**—Service for sending and receiving messages on the network.

The Blob Storage is particularly useful when you need to store some files, which can be of any kind, to use in your applications. The Azure platform offers many other services, which you will learn about when you access the Management Portal discussed shortly. However, don't forget to bookmark the official Microsoft page Microsoft, http://azure. microsoft.com, where you can find all the necessary information on the Azure platform, its services, and application development. The Microsoft Azure Developer Center contains hundreds of learning resources about all the previously mentioned services. You can find it at http://azure.microsoft.com/en-us/documentation/. This chapter explains the tools necessary for building and deploying web applications to Azure, but before getting your hands dirty writing code, it is important to mention how you can register to the Microsoft Azure Platform.

Registering for Microsoft Azure

To deploy hosted applications to Microsoft Azure, you first need to register and get an account. Microsoft Azure and related services are paid services, and you pay only for resources that you actually consume, which is the biggest benefit of a cloud-based solution (pay-as-you-go). Fortunately, you can request a 30-day free trial and decide to purchase a subscription later. You can request your free trial at http://azure.microsoft.com/en-us/ pricing/free-trial/. At the expiration of the trial period, if you are interested in Microsoft cloud computing and in purchasing services, ensure you read this page about pricing first: http://azure.microsoft.com/en-us/pricing/purchase-options/. Only if you decide to pay for cloud computing services, follow the instructions provided in the Azure's website. Note that you can enable a spending limit on your subscription; this wallet-saving feature will make services unavailable if you consume all the available resources for your plan.

Assuming you have chosen either a trial subscription or a paid subscription, you need to log in with a valid Microsoft Account (formerly Windows Live ID). After you've logged in, follow the instructions shown to get your tokens. You will also receive an email with instructions to follow to activate your token on Microsoft Azure. Only when you are a registered user can you visit the Microsoft Azure Management Portal that is located at https://manage.windowsazure.com. Your new account will give you access to all of the available services listed above.

Later in this chapter you see how to manage applications within the Microsoft Azure Management Portal. Before going into that, you need to enable Visual Studio 2015 for cloud development.

Downloading and Installing Tools for Visual Studio

Visual Studio 2015 is the premier development environment for Microsoft Azure. To enable the IDE, you need to download and install Microsoft Azure SDK for .NET and Visual Studio 2015. At this writing, the latest SDK available is version 2.5.1. You can find it at http://azure.microsoft.com/en-us/downloads/. Download the installer and follow the instructions to target Visual Studio 2015. Installing the SDK will make available on your machine some tools for Visual Studio that enable you to create and manage projects the usual way, as well as the Microsoft Azure SDK. The Microsoft Azure SDK is composed by the Compute Emulator, a tool that locally reproduces the hosting services on the cloud and that is required for running your applications locally; the Storage Emulator, which reproduces locally the environment for publishing blobs, queues, and messages; project templates for Visual Studio 2015; tools that integrate with the IDE and extend some built-in features; and the documentation. The Microsoft Azure SDK also contains sample applications with full source code for further studies. Also be sure to periodically check out the official Cloud Computing tools team blog from Microsoft, available at http://blogs.msdn.com/cloud/.

Introducing the Management Portal

The Management Portal is where you create and manage Azure services. You access the Management Portal at https://mange.windowsazure.com. Once you log in with your Microsoft Account, you will find a list of available services on the left side of the page. For each service, you have an option of creating and managing items. Figure 35.1 shows an example based on my subscription (with some information hidden for privacy reasons).

FIGURE 35.1   A first look at the Azure Management Portal.

For each service, you have an option of managing existing resources and creating new items. Figure 35.2 shows an example based on a new web application.

FIGURE 35.2   Quick creation of a new web app.

As a general rule, for any item you create, you should choose the data center location closest to your location. This will reduce the resources you consume to send and receive data over the Internet.

In this chapter you will use the Management Portal only to create a new database server, and then you will perform all the required operations directly within Visual Studio or via other client tools. This chapter will show a sample ASP.NET web application that connects to a cloud-based Northwind database and that runs in the cloud. Because migrating an existing database is a very common scenario, you will learn how to accomplish this situation rather than create a new database from scratch.

Creating a SQL Azure Database

Microsoft Azure can host infinite types of applications, not just data-centric ones. When building data-centric applications with Visual Basic, you have different options for working with a database. You can model an existing database, or you can create a database and data model from scratch. Visual Studio 2015 supports both scenarios when working with Azure, and you can take advantage of existing techniques learned in previous chapters. As you will see later in this chapter, Visual Studio 2015 provides automated database deployment for you. Creating empty databases and data models is left to you as an exercise; this chapter explains how to create a database server in the cloud and how to migrate an existing SQL Server database.

You need a database server, so in the Management Portal select **SQL Databases** (refer to Figure 35.1). Then click **Server**, and then click the **Add** button at the bottom of the page. As you can see in Figure 35.3, you have to specify your administrator credentials and a region (remember that you should select the one closest to your location).

FIGURE 35.3   Creating a database server.

After your confirmation, the database server will be created in a few minutes and will be shown in the list of database servers (see Figure 35.4). Take note of the new server's name because you will need it soon.

FIGURE 35.4   The list of database servers.

Now you need a database. Your SQL database server in the cloud is very close to a classic SQL Server environment, so you have different options for creating and managing databases:

▶ **In the Management Portal**—In the Server page list, you can click Databases and then the New button to design a new database from scratch.

▶ **From SQL Server Management Studio**—This very popular tool for developers and database administrators can connect to a SQL cloud database server and perform the same operations it would do on-premise, including creating databases and executing scripts.

▶ **From Visual Studio 2015**—The SQL Server Object Explorer tool window can work against a SQL cloud database server exactly as it does against an on-premise server. Also, Visual Studio can create a new database when you create an ASP.NET application for Azure.

▶ **From SQL Azure Migration Wizard**—This free, open source tool from Microsoft enables developers to migrate existing SQL Server databases to the cloud.

Before creating a database, you need to consider the database connection. A database server on Azure can be reached via the Internet with the following address: *servername.database*.windows.net, where *servername* is the name of the server you created before.

You also need to consider SQL scripts. Even if they are very similar, cloud-based databases have some differences from on-premise SQL Server databases. For instance, tables of SQL databases in the cloud must have clustered indexes. A full list of differences is available at https://msdn.microsoft.com/en-us/library/azure/ee336281.aspx.

If you have not practiced much with SQL databases before, a better option is to script databases with proper tools. For the current example, you will migrate the Northwind database from your development SQL Express instance to your new cloud database server. To accomplish this, you need to download the Microsoft SQL Azure Migration Wizard, available at https://sqlazuremw.codeplex.com/. Choose the version that matches your SQL Server Express Edition version. The tool does not need to be installed, so you can simply extract the archive content into a new folder on disk and then launch SQLAzureMW.exe.

The first wizard dialog requires you to specify a target server and a task. Select **Azure SQL Database** as the target and select the **Analyze/Migrate Database** option, as shown in Figure 35.5.

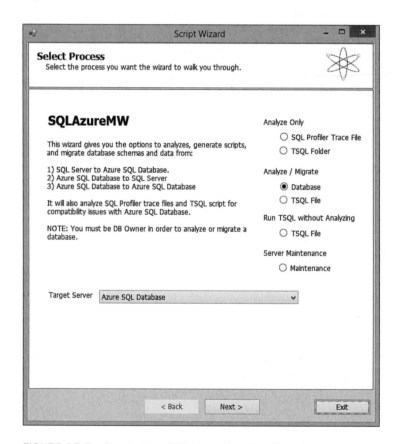

FIGURE 35.5   Starting the SQL Azure Migration Wizard.

In the next dialog, called Select Source, you will specify the source database, so select the Northwind database on your SQL Express instance and then click **Next**. The next dialog, Choose Objects, allows you to specify database objects that you want to migrate, including stored procedures, tables, and views. Leave the default selection of scripting all database objects. Notice that, by default, only the database schema is scripted. If you want to include data, click **Advanced** and then change the value for **Script Table/Data** to **Table Schema with Data**. This is a good choice for the current example because it gives you sample data to consume. When you're ready, click **Next**. At this point, you see a summary of objects that will be scripted, and when you click **Next**, the tool will generate a full Transact-SQL script for you. When the generation completes, the tool shows a summary, as well as the edits required to make the database acceptable by Microsoft Azure (see Figure 35.6.)

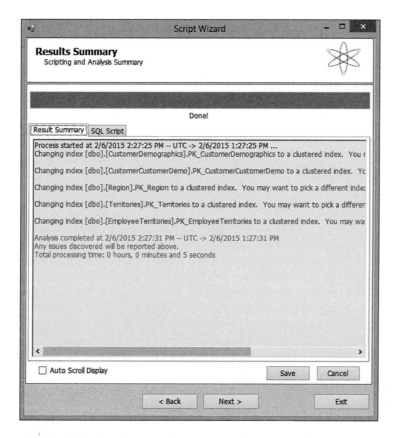

FIGURE 35.6   Script generation summary before migration.

Click **Next**. At this point you have to specify information about the target server, in particular the target server name (based on the address described previously), and credentials. Figure 35.7 shows how to accomplish this.

FIGURE 35.7   Connecting to the target cloud server.

Once connected, you can either pick up an existing (empty) database or create a new one. You don't have any existing databases yet, so click **Create Database**. In the Create Database dialog (see Figure 35.8), you can specify the database name, which will be Northwind for consistency with the example, and you can select the service tier. The service tier you choose depends on how much you're willing to pay for space and resources, so this is left to your choice. The example shows the Basic tier selected. When you're ready, click **Create Database**.

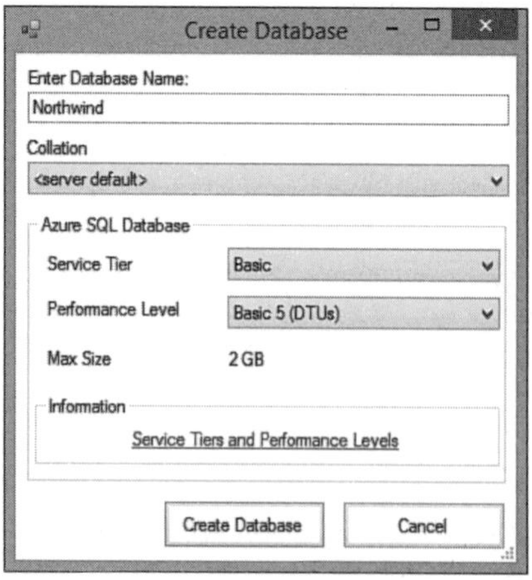

FIGURE 35.8   Creating a new cloud database.

When the process completes, you see the new database in the list of SQL databases in the Management Portal (refer to Figure 35.1). You can manage your database with an online design portal that you can enable by clicking **Manage**. (The details of this are beyond of the scope of this chapter.) Now that you have your cloud database, you can start building an ASP.NET application.

Creating an ASP.NET Application for the Cloud

Visual Studio 2015 and the Azure SDK offer a number of specific project templates for cloud-hosted applications. To see available project templates, in Visual Studio 2015 select **File, New Project** and then select the **Cloud** node in the New Project dialog, as shown in Figure 35.9.

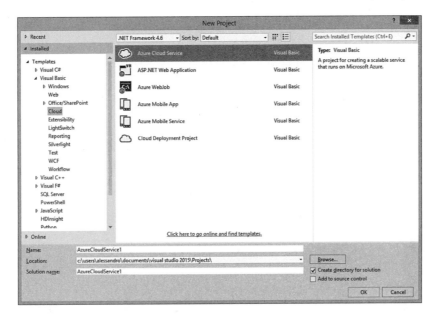

FIGURE 35.9   Available project templates for Azure.

These are the available templates:

▶ **Azure Cloud Service**—This project template allows you to create scalable services that run on Azure, based on web roles and worker roles. You'll get information on both of these at the end of this chapter. This is the most complex template, and it allows you to integrate with the local storage and compute emulators.

▶ **ASP.NET Web Application**—This is the same template you saw in Chapter 34, "Building and Publishing ASP.NET Web Applications."

▶ **Azure WebJob**—This project template allows you to create programs that run on the Windows Azure operating system, such as background tasks.

▶ **Azure Mobile App**—This project template allows you to create ASP.NET mobile backends for Microsoft Azure Mobile apps.

▶ **Azure Mobile Service**—This project template allows you to create ASP.NET mobile backends for the Microsoft Azure Mobile Services building block.

▶ **Cloud Deployment Project**—This project template makes it easier to provision resources and environments for your cloud applications, including a deployment project and SQL database generation.

For more on the available project templates, see the .NET Azure documentation, which you can find at http://azure.microsoft.com/en-us/develop/net. For this chapter, select the ASP.NET Web Application template and call the project NorthwindUnleashed. When you click **OK**, the New ASP.NET Project dialog allows you to specify templates and APIs. You already saw this dialog in action in Chapter 34. Notice in this case that the **Host in the Cloud** option is enabled by default (see Figure 35.10.)

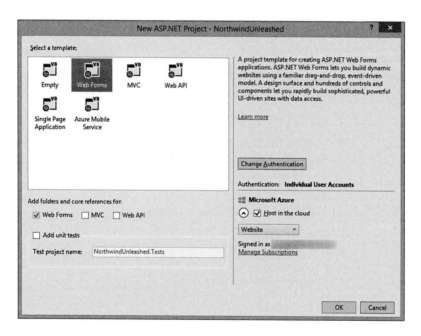

FIGURE 35.10   The new ASP.NET project is cloud-enabled.

When you click **OK**, Visual Studio shows the Configure Microsoft Azure Website dialog (see Figure 35.11) and asks you to supply the following information:

▶ **Site name**—This is the unique name for your website. This is very important because it's the first part of the full application's web address, in the form of *sitename*.azurewebsites.net. By default, Visual Studio uses the project name as the site name. The IDE notifies you about whether the name is available.

▶ **Region**—This is the location for the datacenter that will host your application and must be the location closest to you.

▶ **Database server**—You can specify a database server if you want to create a brand-new database for your application. If you already have a database, you do not need to specify a server. Because you already have the Northwind database in the cloud, select **No Database**.

▶ **Database username and Database password**—These selections are required only when you provide a database server. They must be administrator credentials, used to connect to the database server and create the database.

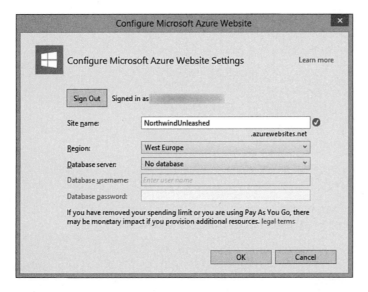

FIGURE 35.11   Creating a new Azure website for your application.

At this point, you should re-create the same application you built in the "Creating a Web Application with VB 2015 with Data Access and Pages" section of Chapter 34, but this time you do not want to implement login, so you should stop before the "Forcing Login for Security" information. When you are at the point of creating the Entity Data Model, you will connect to the Northwind database in the cloud rather than to the one on your local machine. Figure 35.12 demonstrates this (with the server name hidden for privacy).

FIGURE 35.12   Connecting to a database in the cloud.

When you finish building the example, you can test it locally by pressing **F5**. You should get the same result as in Chapter 34 except that now your data is in the cloud.

In this section, you re-created an existing example in order to see how existing ASP.NET applications can be moved to the Azure environment. The next section, about publishing, will makes this concept even clearer.

Deploying Applications to Microsoft Azure

Deploying to Microsoft Azure involves the Web Deploy option and requires the same steps shown for publishing an ASP.NET application to other hosts, as you saw in Chapter 34. Visual Studio 2015 dramatically simplifies the deployment process by supplying all the required information automatically. To understand how it works, in Solution Explorer right-click **Publish** to open the Publish Web dialog. In this dialog, you should see that the Web Deploy option is enabled and all the connection information has been automatically added by the IDE (see Figure 35.13). You do not need to make any changes.

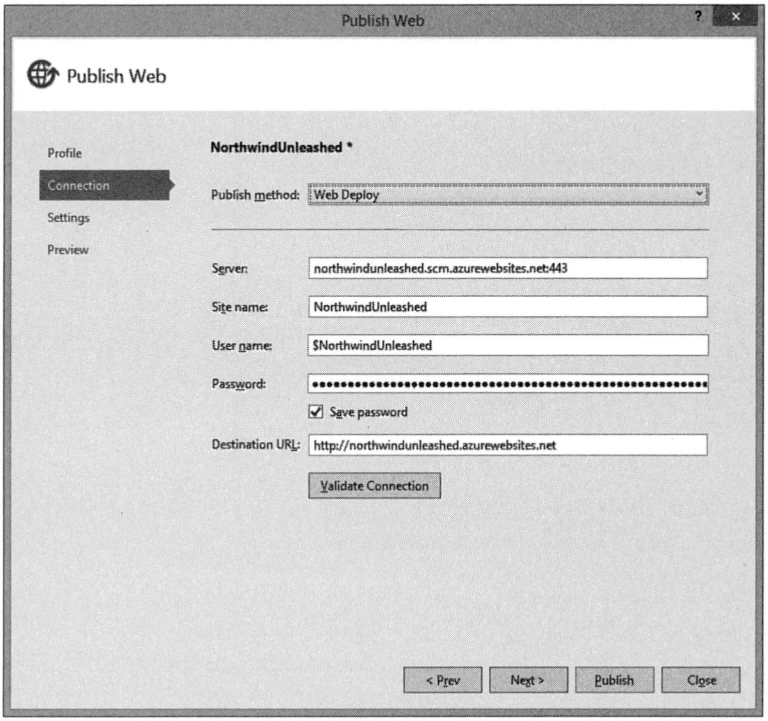

FIGURE 35.13   Automatic configuration for deployment.

If you click Settings, you can see that Visual Studio also automatically supplies the appropriate connection strings (see Figure 35.14).

When you're ready, simply click **Publish**. Visual Studio will be busy publishing your application for a few minutes. You can follow the publishing progress details in the Web Publish Activity tool window, as shown in Figure 35.15. It should be enabled by default; if it is not, you can get it be selecting **View, Other Windows, Web Publish Activity**.

FIGURE 35.14   Automatic connection settings.

FIGURE 35.15   The Web Publish Activity window.

When Visual Studio finishes the publishing process, it automatically starts your cloud-based applications inside your default web browser, as shown in Figure 35.16.

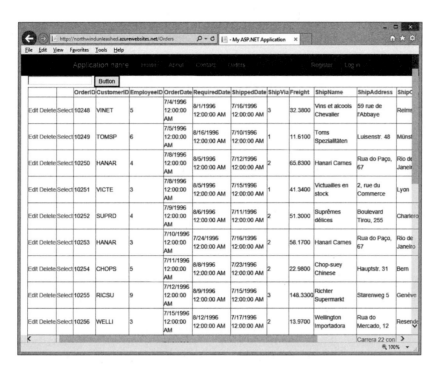

FIGURE 35.16   Your ASP.NET application, running in the cloud.

With a very few steps, you have been able to publish your application to a production environment without having your own server and infrastructure; this is probably the biggest benefit of Azure websites.

Unlike in Chapter 34, here you do not force users to log in. There are many differences with authenticating users on Azure services, and understanding them requires knowledge of services like Active Directory. If you want to implement authentication, you should read the official documentation for Azure Active Directory, available at http://azure. microsoft.com/en-us/documentation/services/active-directory/.

DELETE YOUR TEST CLOUD SERVICES!

Do not forget to completely delete any cloud services, databases, and storage accounts that you no longer use to avoid paying for them. Remember that you are charged for services that are stopped but have not been deleted. The only way to avoid paying extra money is to delete services, which you can do in the Management Portal.

A Step Further: Web Roles and Worker Roles

A key concept in Microsoft Azure development is the *role*, which is typically a single component running in the Azure environment and built in managed code. Roles can be of two types: web roles and worker roles. A *web* role is an ASP.NET web application or a WCF service. You might think of *worker* roles as services running behind the scenes—for example, running in the cloud in the case of Windows services. An Azure solution can have multiple roles and multiple instances of one role; moreover, you can configure roles as required. So web roles and worker roles can leverage all Azure services.

Working with roles has an important advantage: Visual Studio allows you to simulate the Microsoft Azure platform locally, via the Microsoft Azure Debugging Environment, which includes the Compute Emulator and Storage Emulator that you can reach from the Windows System Tray when debugging the application. The Compute Emulator allows you to understand how your services consume resources on a local emulator, whereas the Storage Emulator reproduces locally the Azure's Cloud Storage service for development purposes.

To implement roles, in the New Project dialog you select the **Azure Cloud Service** project template (refer to Figure 35.9). Notice that, at this writing, this project template does not support .NET 4.6, so you will have to test roles against .NET 4.5. When you create a new cloud service, the New Microsoft Azure Cloud Service dialog appears. In this dialog, you select one or more roles for your solution. Figure 35.17 shows the available roles.

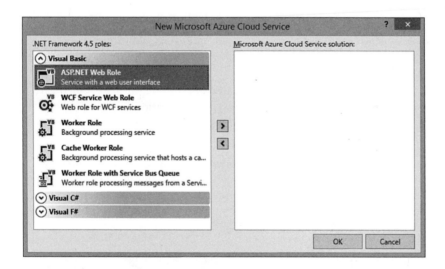

FIGURE 35.17   Available roles for cloud services.

Whatever roles you add to a solution, Visual Studio generates web/worker role projects and a service project where you can configure role properties. To access role configuration, in Solution Explorer, locate the folder called Roles, under the service project name. Double-click a role name so that a special implementation of the My Project designer pops up. Figure 35.18 shows what you see onscreen at this point.

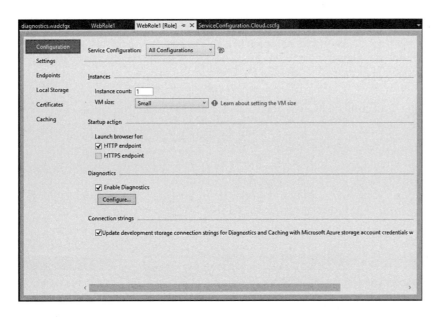

FIGURE 35.18   Configuring role options.

The **Configuration** tab enables you to set options for your roles: in the cloud, locally, or both. The environment is selected via the Service Configuration field. The **Instance Count** field enables you to set how many instances of the role are permitted, and **VM Size** enables you to specify the size of the virtual machine hosting your service. The size and power of virtual machines have changed over the years and will probably continue to evolve as time goes on, so you should take a look at the official website for detailed information: http://azure.microsoft.com/en-us/pricing/calculator/?scenario=virtual-machines.

Keep in mind that a small virtual machine is a good choice if you have an MSDN subscription with Microsoft Azure benefits included. The aforementioned options are very important because they enable you to make an application more or less scalable with simple configuration changes. The Startup Action group enables you to specify whether debugging should be launched via an HTTP or HTTPS endpoint (which must be defined in the Endpoints tab). In the Settings tab, you can define settings that you can access via the Microsoft Azure SDK Runtime API. In the Endpoints tab, you can define endpoints for your application; you can retrieve endpoints in the Management Portal. Applying for an HTTPS endpoint also requires a valid SSL certificate. You add certificates to your deployment via the Certificates tab. The Local Storage tab enables you to configure the local file system storage resources for each instance. All the preceding options and settings are reflected into the ServiceConfiguration.cscfg and ServiceDefinition.csdef files that you can see in Solution Explorer and that are XML representations of settings.

ADDING MULTIPLE ROLES AND 64-BIT CONSIDERATIONS

You can add multiple web roles and worker roles by right-clicking the Roles folder in Solution Explorer. Another consideration that you need to keep in mind is that Microsoft Azure is a 64-bit operating system, so take care if you plan to invoke unmanaged code that might fail.

The Certificates tab allows you to configure certificate installation for the instance of the currently selected role; certificates must be uploaded to Microsoft Azure using the Management Portal. Finally, the Caching tab enables in-memory caching for multiple instances of the role for faster data access. From a programming perspective, with roles you write code the usual way. Web roles and worker roles provide an infrastructure that better integrates with the Azure services, and it is worth considering them when you become more expert with the Azure platform.

TRY WEBJOBS

Azure WebJobs allows you to execute programs in the cloud in a simpler and smarter way than with worker roles. On the other hand, worker roles allow more granularity of control and more careful fine-tuning. You might want to check out WebJobs and see whether it satisfies your needs better than worker roles.

Additional Tools

Visual Studio 2015 provides additional integrated tools that you can use to interact with your Microsoft Azure subscription and services. The Server Explorer tool window allows you to connect to your subscription services, as shown in Figure 35.19.

Server Explorer provides shortcuts to common tasks for each service and is not intended to be a replacement for the Management Portal. For instance, in Server Explorer you cannot delete a website, but you can stop it. Also, you cannot delete a database but you have shortcuts to open a database in SQL Server Object Explorer or to open the database management page on the Web. When you install the Azure SDK 2.5.1, Server Explorer is extended with the Storage Explorer instrumentation, which allows you to browse and manage your cloud storage, both locally and in the cloud. You can simply right-click a storage account to create a container (that is, a folder) and then upload files or data (blobs) to the container. Figure 35.20 shows an example.

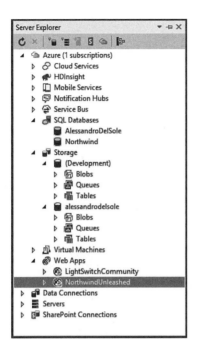

FIGURE 35.19   Server Explorer allows you to connect to your Azure services.

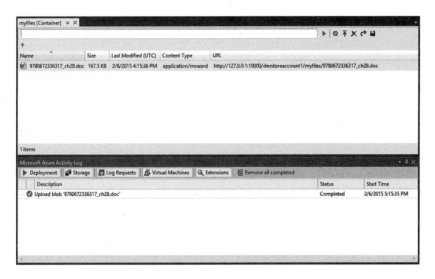

FIGURE 35.20   Managing cloud storage accounts from within Visual Studio.

35

DELETE YOUR TEST CLOUD SERVICES!

If you want a more powerful client application to manage your storage services than the Management Portal, you can download a free trial of the popular Cloud Storage Studio from Cerebrata, which is a professional WPF application that manages not only blobs, but also tables and queues. It also enables you to manage permissions, show analytics, and handle multiple accounts. Download a trial at http://www.cerebrata.com/products/CloudStorageStudio.

Summary

The Microsoft Azure platform is Microsoft's cloud computing platform. It includes several services, such as the Windows Azure operating system, a SQL database, websites, and application building blocks. Windows Azure is a 64-bit operating system enabling web applications to be hosted and running in a cloud environment. To develop applications for the cloud, you use Visual Studio 2015, which must be enabled by installing the appropriate tools. After you install these tools and register for the Microsoft Azure services, you can begin developing and deploying applications. You can create ASP.NET web applications or WCF services that can be deployed to Azure. You can test your applications locally before deployment, due to the presence of the Microsoft Azure Debugging Environment that includes tools for locally running applications with the same environment that is on the cloud. This tooling is installed together with the Microsoft Azure SDK for .NET and Visual Studio 2015. To publish a web application to the Azure platform, you use Visual Studio instrumentation; then you can still use the IDE or the Microsoft Azure Management Portal to edit, configure, and maintain your applications and data in the cloud.

CHAPTER 36

Building Universal Apps for Windows 10

Today people want and need to stay connected more than ever before. They also do more dynamic jobs and often need to check for work emails, browse the Internet, and run business tools when traveling or otherwise out of the office. Mobile devices, including smartphones and tablets, have become personal assistants, with calendars, appointments, and applications (also known as *apps*) that can solve an infinite number of problems and even provide personal entertainment. Smartphones and tablets play a fundamental role in everyday life for both business and personal purposes. In addition, the Internet of Things (IoT) is becoming more important every day. More and more, we are using apps to remotely control hardware, devices, and even electronic appliances. Microsoft is releasing a new offering for modern devices: Windows 10.

In this chapter you learn how to build universal Windows apps. You can develop such an app and then run it on all devices running Windows 10, such as desktop PCs, tablets, mobile phones, Xbox One consoles, and IoT hardware. You will see how easy it is to build these apps if you already have knowledge of XAML. Building universal apps can be an important business opportunity, and Visual Basic offers all the power you need to build awesome apps. Universal Windows apps are also known as Windows Store apps, and this chapter uses these terms interchangeably.

SOFTWARE USED IN THIS CHAPTER

This chapter was written based on Windows 10 Technical Preview (build 10074) and
Visual Studio 2015 Release Candidate, both announced and released at the Microsoft
Build 2015 conference in late April 2015. Both of these technologies may have changed
by the time they're released to the general public as RTM, final versions. By the way, this
chapter assumes that you have installed Windows 10 (at least the Technical Preview with
build number 10074 or later) and Visual Studio 2015. You can create a virtual machine
running Windows 10 instead of installing the new system onto your production machine.
(However, in that case, you cannot use emulators, which also run as virtual machines on
Hyper-V.)

Introducing Universal Windows Apps

As you know, operating systems for mobile devices allow you to download applications
from a virtual marketplace, typically referred to as a *store*. In the past, Windows Phone
and Windows 8 had two different stores, which presented a huge limitation: If a paid app
was available to both Windows Phone and Windows 8, a user had to pay twice to have
same application on two different devices. With Windows 8.1 and Windows Phone 8.1,
Microsoft made an important step forward: It unified the Windows Phone Store and the
Windows Store into one store, called the Windows Store, providing users a way to pay
for an app once and use it on all devices running the aforementioned operating systems.
With this store unification, Microsoft created the **universal Windows apps** experience
(also known as **universal apps**). With universal apps, a user pays for an app once but can
download it on all her devices running Windows 8.1 and Windows Phone 8.1. From a
developer perspective, Windows Phone 8.1 and Windows 8.1 share a common Runtime,
known as Windows Runtime, but they actually are two different operating systems.
Sharing a common Runtime means that developers can write code once and build apps
that run on both operating systems. Before this, you had to build apps for Windows
Phone and Windows 8 separately, using different APIs and coding techniques. In addition, you had to build two different packages, one for Windows Phone 8.1 and one for
Windows 8.1. Visual Studio 2013 Update 2 (and higher) made this easier by providing
a specific project template for C# and allowing you to create portable libraries in Visual
Basic to share code, XAML resources, and assets.

In Windows 10, things are much more amazing: With previous operating systems, the
concept of universal apps typically focused on the customer experience, whereas from a
development perspective, you had to build two different packages, also using different
APIs in some cases. In Windows 10, you build one binary package that will run on every
device running the operating system, including desktop PCs, tablets, mobile phones, Xbox
One console, HoloLens (the holographic computer from Microsoft), and IoT devices, such
as the Raspberry Pi 2 board. So, with Windows 10, a universal app is not only a customer-
focused concept but also a development-focused concept. Visual Basic 2015 fully supports
building apps for Windows 10 with specific project templates that you learn about in this
chapter. Building a single binary that runs on every Windows 10 device is possible because
of the Universal Windows Platform, described in the next section.

Introducing the Universal Windows Platform

Windows 10 is basically available in two versions: one for desktop PCs, and one for devices. You will often hear references to Windows 10 for desktop and Windows 10 for mobile. From a technical point of view, Windows 10 converges desktop and mobile versions of the same operating system; in fact, there is a guaranteed core APIs layer across devices. This common core is known as the **Universal Windows Platform (UWP)**. This core includes a number of ready-to-use APIs that enable developers to build apps that automatically adapt to the device they run on, making it easier to create consistent and flexible experiences. In particular, the Windows 10 core includes the following:

- ▶ **An adaptive user experience (UX)**—This enables an app's user interface to fluidly adapt at runtime, based on the device capabilities and on the way the user is interacting with the app itself. This adaptive experience includes new controls, like `SplitView` and the `RelativePanel`, which adapt their appearance for different types of devices, layouts, and device orientations.

- ▶ **Natural user input**—Windows 10 provides APIs that better support a more human way of interacting with an app, such as natural speech (including **Cortana**, the built-in personal assistant), improved touch gestures, and inking.

- ▶ **Cloud-based services**—Windows 10 offers services like Windows Notification Services, Windows Credential Locker, and roaming data services. Many services in Windows 10 heavily rely on Microsoft Azure to provide a great development experience; for example, Application Insights allows you to get complex telemetry information for your apps.

In addition, the common core includes the following set of APIs:

- ▶ **Multimedia**—You can easily manage multimedia contents such as videos, music, pictures, and built-in cameras.

- ▶ **I/O**—You can easily access local files and synced OneDrive folders.

- ▶ **Networking**—Apps that need an Internet connection can easily perform tasks over the network. Also, the developer has many options for informing users about costs in case they are using a metered connection. There are also APIs for roaming content across devices.

- ▶ **Notifications**—You can easily manage live tiles, toast notifications, and push notifications. Notifications can also be scheduled for information updates at specified time intervals.

- ▶ **Security**—Universal apps support the latest authentication techniques to provide users the best experience possible, especially with sensitive information.

36

All the aforementioned APIs have converged into a single Windows SDK, which is automatically referenced when you create a new universal Windows app project. However, there are situations in which you need to write platform-specific code, such as for a mobile phone (as discussed later in this chapter). In such cases, you can easily take advantage of the **Microsoft Desktop Extension SDK for Universal App Platform**, the **Microsoft Mobile Extension SDK for Universal App Platform**, and the **Microsoft IoT Extension SDK for Universal App Platform**, depending on whether you want to use APIs that are specific to the desktop, mobile devices, or IoT devices. All these options are available in the Reference Manager dialog.

The Universal Windows Platform relies on .NET Core as the base framework and on the .NET Native compiler. With .NET Native, a universal app is compiled into native code and performs much faster than a classic .NET application.

In summary, with Windows 10, you build an app once, you publish it to one store, and because of the common core, the app will run on any Windows 10 device.

Registering with the Windows Store

To publish an application to the Windows Store, no matter if it is free or paid, you must be a registered developer. Registering is a paid service unless you have an MSDN subscription, which entitles you to claim a complimentary developer account. You should register only if you are really sure that you will be publishing apps to the Windows Store; otherwise, you should not register but should instead use the developer tools for local testing with the device emulators.

This chapter describes application development based on the device emulators, so you do not need to register with the Store. Only the last part of this chapter describes the submission process, which requires a developer account, but you can read it without registering. (For detailed information on the registration process and on pricing, see https://msdn. microsoft.com/library/windows/apps/bg124287.aspx.)

Installing the Developer Tools

To provide programmers the best development experience possible, Microsoft provides the appropriate software development kits (SDKs) with the Visual Studio 2015 installer. SDKs contain libraries, project templates, certification toolkits, and device emulators that you use to test apps locally. When you install Visual Studio 2015, make sure you select the Windows 10 SDK and Windows 10 Emulators elements. If you did not, you can perform an installation repair via the Control Panel, Programs and Features tool.

For additional tools and SDKs, see http://dev.windows.com/en-us/develop/downloads. You are also encouraged to download the Universal Windows Apps Sample Pack with source code, which covers all the possible areas in developing universal apps and is available for free at https://github.com/Microsoft/Windows-universal-samples.

Creating Apps with Visual Basic

WHAT YOU FIND IN THIS CHAPTER AND WHAT YOU DON'T

Developing universal Windows apps is very exciting and interesting, but explaining the whole process would require an entire book. For this reason, the goal of this chapter is to teach you the basics of building apps with Visual Basic, providing information on the most common topics. Here you learn how to create and debug an app, how to write XAML and VB code, how to call APIs for common tasks and local storage, and how to customize and prepare an app for publication. You will not find topics like live tiles, sensors, push notifications, or location services. Once you understand the basics provided in this chapter, all those other topics will be easier to study through the resources available in the Windows Developer Center, at http://dev.windows.com.

The application programming model for universal Windows apps is based on .NET Core 5 and .NET Native; it takes advantage of all the power of Visual Studio and the integrated tools, including IntelliSense. You can build universal Windows apps with either XAML and managed languages (VB/C#) or HTML5 and JavaScript. This chapter focuses on the XAML/Visual Basic pair. Using this approach provides a tremendous benefit because many of your existing skills with technologies like WPF will still be valid, with some obvious differences and restrictions due to the specific platform. Also, most of .NET programming concepts and the language syntax are totally available. What you actually have to learn is how to interact with devices' functionalities and how to manage the application lifetime. This chapter cannot cover every possible opportunity in building universal Windows apps, but it is a good "getting started" guide.

You start coding a universal app for Windows 10 via a Visual Basic project, as usual. This chapter shows how to create a sample universal app that downloads the RSS feed from Microsoft's Channel9 website and presents a list of available videos. For each video, the sample app will show the preview page and will provide an option of playing the video directly inside the app. You will learn about many concepts such as local settings, folders, toast notifications, media playing, and the navigation framework, plus you'll get an introduction to the asynchronous pattern that will be discussed in more technical detail in Chapter 42, "Asynchronous Programming."

To start, in Visual Studio 2015 select **File, New Project**. In the New Project dialog that appears, locate the Visual Basic, Windows, Windows Universal node and select the **Blank App (Windows Universal)** template. Call the new solution UniversalReader, as shown in Figure 36.1, and click **OK**.

FIGURE 36.1   Creating a blank application.

AVAILABLE PROJECT TEMPLATES

Three project templates are available: Blank App, which allows you to develop a universal app; Class Library (Windows Universal), which allows you to create reusable class libraries for universal apps; and Windows Runtime Component (Windows Universal), which allows you to create a managed Windows Runtime component, regardless of the programming language in which the apps are written.

When the new project is ready, you will see the XAML designer and the XAML code editor, as you already saw in WPF. In this case, instead of working with a `Window` object, you work with a `Page` object. Because a universal app can run on multiple devices with different sizes, the designer allows you to easily preview how your pages will adapt to different factors via a convenient combo box on the left side of the screen (see Figure 36.2). From this combo box, you can select different device factors to see how the layout will automatically adapt to the selected device. By default, the selected device factor is **5" Phone (1920 x 1080) 300% scale**, but you can choose between factors targeting desktop PCs, tablets, IoT devices, and even the new Surface Hub collaboration device.

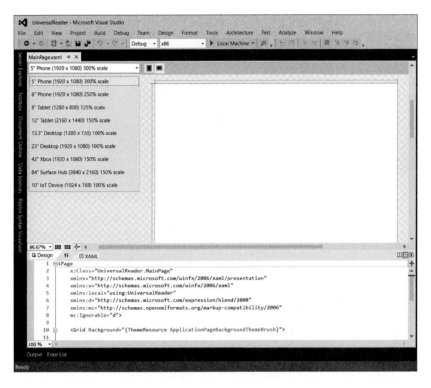

FIGURE 36.2   Selecting a size factor to preview how the UI adapts to devices.

Notice the two buttons that allow you to select the page orientation (landscape or portrait), so that you can have a more precise idea at design time of how the app's user interface will look.

Expand the References node in Solution Explorer, and you see two important components: **.NET for Windows Store apps** and **Windows Universal** (see Figure 36.3). The first component represents the .NET Core's core libraries, and the second one represents the Universal Windows Platform's APIs.

FIGURE 36.3   Auto-referenced components for a universal app.

Now that you have seen what a universal app project consists of, it is time to write code and create your very first app for Windows 10.

Implementing a Data Model

At this point, you need to implement a class representing a single item in the RSS feed. Add a new folder called Model to the project and then to this folder add a class called FeedItem, whose code looks like this:

```
Public Class FeedItem
    Public Property Title As String
    Public Property Url As String
    Public Property Thumbnail As String
    Public Property Video As String
    Public Property DateRecorded As String
    Public Property Speaker As String

    Public Shared FeedUrl As String = _
            "http://channel9.msdn.com/Tags/visual+basic/RSS"
End Class
```

The code is very simple, and the properties are self-explanatory. It is worth mentioning that the Video property stores the name of an .mp4 video, the app will be able to play, and DateRecorded is of type String because it will be formatted a custom way.

The next step is to implement code that downloads the RSS feed and that returns content in a way that can be data-bound to the user interface. Before getting your hands dirty on some code, you need to understand a few considerations. When building universal apps, you need to keep in mind perceived performance. If a page had to download the RSS feed content every time, it would need to use an Internet connection and make the user wait. Instead, you can download the RSS feed content only the first time, store the information on disk, and allow users to refresh information from the Internet on demand. Also, downloading information from the Internet can be a long-running operation, but mobile apps must always stay responsive. For this reason, universal Windows apps execute most operations asynchronously, by typically implementing the Async/Await pattern, which is discussed in detail in Chapter 42. Here's what you need to know for now:

▶ Asynchronous code is executed in methods marked with the Async modifier.

▶ Asynchronous method names end with the Async literal by convention.

▶ Asynchronous methods return Task(Of T), where T is the actual type used.

▶ Asynchronous methods require the Await operator within their body. The Await operator waits for an asynchronous operation to complete before returning the result. In the meantime, the user interface takes control back until the asynchronous operation completes and stays responsive.

Now you're ready to add a new class called UniversalReader to the Model folder. Then you can add the following Imports directives, keeping in mind that XML namespaces are required for LINQ queries and that other namespaces are discussed elsewhere:

```
Imports System.Net.Http
Imports System.Runtime.Serialization
Imports Windows.Networking.Connectivity
Imports Windows.Storage
Imports <xmlns:media="http://search.yahoo.com/mrss/">
Imports <xmlns:dc="http://purl.org/dc/elements/1.1/">
```

Internet Connection, Local Files, and Folders

The first method you implement in the new class performs a number of tasks:

▶ Checks whether an Internet connection is available. This is a requirement in applications that work over the Internet and is accomplished with objects from the Windows.Networking.Connectivity namespace.

▶ Checks whether a data file containing serialized feed items exists. If so, this file is deleted. The Windows.Storage namespace exposes objects for working with folders and files.

▶ Downloads the RSS feed content and generates a new collection based on a LINQ query.

▶ Invokes a separate method to serialize the downloaded content and returns the generated collection to the caller (a page in the app).

ABOUT SERIALIZATION

Serialization is the process of saving the state of an object, and deserialization is the opposite. Serialization is discussed in more details in Chapter 39, "Serialization," but for now it is enough for you to know what this term means.

The following code declares a class-level, shared `client` variable of type `HttpClient` and implements the `RefreshFeedAsync` method:

```vb
Private Shared client As HttpClient
Public Shared Async Function RefreshFeedAsync() As _
    Task(Of ObservableCollection(Of FeedItem))

    'Get the current Internet profile.
    'Return Nothing if not connected
    Dim internetConnectionProfile As ConnectionProfile =
        NetworkInformation.GetInternetConnectionProfile

    'If not connected...
    If internetConnectionProfile Is Nothing Then
        Return Nothing
    End If

    Try
        'Get the current app's local folder
        Dim localFolder As StorageFolder =
            ApplicationData.Current.LocalFolder
        'Get the instance of the data file
        Dim fileInstance As StorageFile =
            Await localFolder.GetFileAsync("FeedData.bin")

        'Delete the file
        If fileInstance IsNot Nothing Then _
            Await fileInstance.DeleteAsync
    Catch
        'File not found, just ignore
    End Try

    'Download the RSS feed content
    client = New HttpClient()
    Dim fullFeed = Await client.
                GetStringAsync(FeedItem.FeedUrl)

    'Convert to XDocument
    Dim doc = XDocument.Parse(fullFeed)
```

```
        Dim query = From item In doc...<item>
                Let videos = item...<media:content>.
                    Where(Function(vid) vid.@url.ToLower.
                    Contains("mp4"))
                Let videoDate =
                    Date.Parse(item.<pubDate>.Value,
                    Globalization.CultureInfo.
                    InvariantCulture).ToString
                Select New FeedItem With {
                    .Title = item.<title>.Value,
                    .Speaker = item.<dc:creator>.Value,
                    .Url = item.<link>.Value,
                    .Thumbnail = item...<media:thumbnail>.
                    LastOrDefault?.@url,
                    .Video = videos.
                    LastOrDefault?.@url,
                    .DateRecorded = $"Recorded on {videoDate}"}

        Dim result As New _
                ObservableCollection(Of FeedItem)(query)

        'Serialize the collection
        Await SaveFeedAsync(result)
        Return result
End Function
```

`NetworkInformation.GetInternetConnectionProfile` returns an object of type `ConnectionProfile`, which contains information about the current network connection. If the device is not connected, the method returns `Nothing`. If the device is connected, the `ConnectionProfile` object allows retrieval of information, including the detection of a metered connection. This can be useful if your apps need to exchange much information over the Internet so that you can inform users to check their data plan first. The code shows the most basic usage, which simply allows you to detect whether an Internet connection is available, but you might want to check the MSDN documentation for further details: https://msdn.microsoft.com/library/windows/apps/windows.networking.connectivity.connectionprofile.aspx. The goal of the sample app is to improve perceived performance by storing the RSS feed content in a data file and downloading the content again on demand. To accomplish this, the code first gets the instance of the app's folder via the `ApplicationData.Current.LocalFolder` property, of type `Windows.Storage.StorageFolder`. Other available folders are `TemporaryFolder` and `RoamingFolder`; the latter is used to roam app information across devices.

Once you have a reference to the app folder, you need to get a reference to the data file. This is accomplished via the `StorageFolder.GetFileAsync` method, which returns an object of type `Windows.Storage.StorageFile`. If the method returns `Nothing`, it means the file does not exist; on the other hand, if an instance of StorageFile is returned, it means that the file already exists and so it can be deleted before downloading RSS content again.

The next piece of code creates an instance of the System.Net.Http.HttpClient class, which provides an easy way to retrieve content via HTTP. In particular, the GetStringAsync method sends a GET request to the specified URL and downloads the related content in the form of a string object. In this case, it downloads the specified RSS feed content from the Channel9 website. Then a LINQ query returns an IEnumerable(Of FeedItem); this query result is converted into an ObservableCollection(Of FeedItem), a more proper collection for data-binding. Finally, the code invokes another method called SaveFeedAsync, which is responsible for serializing the collection into a data file.

The easiest way to implement serialization and deserialization is to use the JSON format. In Windows 10 apps, you can take advantage of a simple, free library called Newtonsoft. Json. To use it in your project, select **Tools, NuGet Package Manager, Package Manager Console**. When the NuGet Package Manager console appears, type the following command:

```
Install-Package Newtonsoft.Json
```

This library offers the JsonConvert class, which exposes shared methods like SerializeObject and DeserializeObject, which make it simple to serialize and deserialize an object. The code for the method is as follows:

```
'Requires an Imports Newtonsoft.Json directive
Public Shared Async _
     Function SaveFeedAsync(feedData As _
     ObservableCollection(Of FeedItem)) As Task
   Try
      'Serialize the data into an in-memory stream
      Dim sessionData = JsonConvert.SerializeObject(feedData)
      'Create a data file
      Dim folder As StorageFolder =
          ApplicationData.Current.LocalFolder
      Dim newFile = Await folder.
          CreateFileAsync("FeedData.bin",
                        CreationCollisionOption.ReplaceExisting)

      'Write the serialized object into the file
      Await FileIO.WriteTextAsync(newFile, sessionData)

   Catch ex As HttpRequestException
       'handle connection exceptions here...
   Catch ex As Exception
       'handle exceptions here...
   End Try
End Function
```

The `JsonConvert.Serialize` method converts the specified type into a string that can be serialized. Then the code gets a reference to the app's folder and creates a new data file, called FeedData.bin, replacing an existing version. This is accomplished via the `StorageFolder.CreateFileAsync` method and the `CreationCollisionOption.ReplaceExisting` option. (IntelliSense will help you discover other available creation options.) The result of `CreateFileAsync` is an object of type `StorageFile`. Then the code invokes the `FileIO.WriteTextAsync` method, which writes the specified string (the serialized `sessionData` object) into the specified `StorageFile` instance. You then need a method that reads the data file and that performs deserialization. This method, called `LoadFeedAsync`, looks like this:

```
Public Shared Async Function LoadFeedAsync() As _
    Task(Of ObservableCollection(Of FeedItem))

    Try
        Dim file = Await ApplicationData.
                Current.LocalFolder.GetFileAsync("FeedData.bin")
        Dim data = JsonConvert.
            DeserializeObject(Of ObservableCollection(Of FeedItem)) _
            (Await FileIO.ReadTextAsync(file))


        Return data

    Catch ex As Exception
        Return Nothing
    End Try
End Function
End Class
```

This is a very important method because the caller will decide whether to download the RSS feed content from the Internet or bind existing data based on its result. The code gets a reference to the data file and deserializes its content via the `JsonConverter.DeserializeObject` method. This has two overloads, one non-generic and one generic; the generic one, which is used in the current example, automatically converts the string retrieved from the file into the appropriate type, `ObservableCollection(Of FeedItem)`. Based on the availability of existing data, the caller code will decide where to take the RSS feed content. The caller is the last method you implement in the class and is called `GetFeedAsync`. Following is the code for this method:

```
Public Shared Async Function GetFeedAsync() As _
        Task(Of ObservableCollection(Of FeedItem))

    Dim data = Await LoadFeedAsync()
    'No existing feed data
    If data Is Nothing Then
```

```
        'Download the RSS feed from the Internet
        Dim result = Await RefreshFeedAsync()
        If result IsNot Nothing Then
            'Return the downloaded feed
            Return result
        Else
            'Encountered problems, return Nothing
            Return Nothing
        End If
    Else
        'Existing feed data
        Return data
    End If
End Function
```

As you can see, depending on the result of the invocation to LoadFeedAsync, this method decides whether to download the RSS feed from the Internet or return existing data to the user interface. The caller of LoadFeedAsync will be a page, but before you design the user interface with pages, you need to define a template for presenting information.

Defining a Data Template

So far you have written code that downloads RSS content, using an instance of the FeedItem class. As you learned for WPF, in XAML-based development platforms, presenting data requires you to define a data template. In this case, you need to define one to represent every instance of the FeedItem class. In the App.xaml code file, add the following definition:

```xml
<Application
    x:Class="UniversalReader.App"
    xmlns="http://schemas.microsoft.com/winfx/2006/xaml/presentation"
    xmlns:x="http://schemas.microsoft.com/winfx/2006/xaml"
    xmlns:local="using:UniversalReader"
    RequestedTheme="Light">

    <Application.Resources>
        <DataTemplate x:Key="FeedTemplate">
            <Border BorderBrush="Black" Margin="5"
                BorderThickness="2" Tag="{Binding Url}">
                <StackPanel>
                    <Image Source="{Binding Thumbnail}"/>
                    <TextBlock Text="{Binding Title}" TextWrapping="Wrap"
                        FontWeight="Bold"/>
                    <TextBlock Text="{Binding DateRecorded}"/>
                    <TextBlock Text="{Binding Speaker}" Foreground="Red"/>
                </StackPanel>
            </Border>
```

```
            </DataTemplate>
        </Application.Resources>
</Application>
```

This XAML code defines a simple `DataTemplate` object called `FeedTemplate`, which provides a way to present every single item in the RSS feed by including a thumbnail, the content's title, the recording date, and the author name. Notice that relevant properties are bound to appropriate controls, including an `Image` control that will display a thumbnail for each video.

Understanding Pages, the App Bar, and Navigation

In WPF you have windows and `Window` objects. In universal Windows apps you have pages and `Page` objects from the `Windows.UI.XAML.Controls` namespace. With pages, you still define the user interface with XAML markup, and for each page, there is a Visual Basic code-behind file. In a universal app, a page can automatically adapt its layout to the device. The startup page (MainPage.xaml) is responsible for presenting the RSS feed content to the user. To accomplish this, the page uses the data template defined previously in App.xaml. Following is the XAML code for the described requirements:

```
<Grid Background="{ThemeResource ApplicationPageBackgroundThemeBrush}">
    <Grid.RowDefinitions>
        <RowDefinition Height="30"/>
        <RowDefinition/>
    </Grid.RowDefinitions>
    <ProgressBar Name="Progress1"
                 Visibility="Collapsed"/>
        <ListView Name="FeedView"
                  Grid.Row="1"
              IsItemClickEnabled="True"
              ItemClick="FeedView_ItemClick"
              ItemsSource="{Binding}"
              ItemTemplate="{StaticResource FeedTemplate}">
        </ListView>
</Grid>
```

The `ProgressBar` control is hidden at startup (`Visibility="Collapsed"`) and will be enabled only when the app is downloading the RSS feed content from the Internet. Finally, the `ListView` control uses the shared data template to present information. Notice how `IsItemClickEnabled` allows users to click (or tap) an item, and the `ItemClick` event allows the user to take appropriate actions that you see in the code-behind file.

Now switch to the code-behind file. The startup code for the page is typically written by overriding the `OnNavigatedTo` method. In the current example, the code needs to set the logo image taken from shared assets, and then it downloads (or binds existing) data from the RSS feed. The following code demonstrates this:

```
Protected Overrides Async Sub OnNavigatedTo(e As NavigationEventArgs)
    Me.Progress1.Visibility = Visibility.Visible
    Me.Progress1.IsIndeterminate = True
    Try
        DataContext = Await UniversalReader.GetFeedAsync()
        If DataContext Is Nothing Then
            Dim dlg As New Windows.UI.Popups.
            MessageDialog("Check your Internet connection")
            Await dlg.ShowAsync
        End If
    Catch ex As Exception
        Debug.WriteLine(ex.Message)
    Finally
        Me.Progress1.IsIndeterminate = False
        Me.Progress1.Visibility = Visibility.Collapsed
    End Try
End Sub
```

The code first makes the progress bar visible, with the `Indeterminate` state set to `True`. This gives users the perception that the operation is running. Next, the code invokes the `UniversalReader.GetFeedAsync` method and assigns its result to the page's `DataContext`. If the result is `Nothing`, the code assumes that the aforementioned method was unable to retrieve the RSS feed content and shows an error message via the `Windows.UI.Popups.MessageDialog` object. If the result is not null, the resulting `ObservableCollection(Of FeedItem)` is assigned to the `DataContext`, and the user interface presents items based on the specified data template. Eventually, the code stops and hides the progress bar.

The current page still needs two features: an option to refresh content on demand and an option to open the full feed item in a separate page. Let's start with the first requirement. Unlike in Windows desktop applications (WPF, Windows Forms, Win32), where you have menus, universal Windows apps have an application bar (or app bar), which is where you implement buttons and commands. The application bar can be placed at the top or bottom of a page. The guidelines recommend offering buttons and commands in the bottom app bar and limiting the top app bar to situations in which you must offer advanced navigation capabilities (for example, allowing users to select among multiple open documents). You implement the app bar with either the `Page.BottomAppBar` object or `Page.TopAppBar` object, depending on the position. Then you add a `CommandBar` object, which reserves space for the app bar on the user interface. The `CommandBar` can be divided into `PrimaryCommands` and `SecondaryCommands`. Primary commands appear as buttons with icons, whereas secondary command appear as labels. Figure 36.4 shows an example of how primary and secondary commands appear on a tablet and on a phone.

FIGURE 36.4   App bar, primary commands, and secondary commands on devices.

36

Every button in the app bar is represented by an `AppBarButton` object. To help you better understand this, the next example implements only one button in the command bar. This button allows the user to refresh the RSS feed content from the Internet and is represented by the following XAML code:

```
<Page.BottomAppBar>
    <CommandBar>
        <CommandBar.PrimaryCommands>
            <AppBarButton Name="RefreshButton"
                          Icon="Refresh"
                          Label="Refresh"
                          Click="RefreshButton_Click"/>
        </CommandBar.PrimaryCommands>
    </CommandBar>
</Page.BottomAppBar>
```

An `AppBarButton`'s behavior is very close to that of a normal button. It is worth mentioning two properties: `Label`, which shows the given text under the button, and `Icon`, which allows picking up one of the many built-in icons that you can easily associate to the button's action. The possible choices are self-explanatory, and IntelliSense will show a list of available icons as you type. The `Click` event handler for the button invokes the `UniversalReader.RefreshFeedAsync` method directly, forcing you to download the RSS content from the Internet:

```
Private Async Sub RefreshButton_Click(sender As Object,
                                      e As RoutedEventArgs)
    Me.Progress1.Visibility = Visibility.Visible
    Me.Progress1.IsIndeterminate = True
```

```
    Me.DataContext = Await UniversalReader.RefreshFeedAsync

    Me.Progress1.IsIndeterminate = False
    Me.Progress1.Visibility = Visibility.Collapsed
End Sub
```

You will implement additional app bars in new pages that you will be constructing shortly.

Now we'll switch gears and talk about navigation. In most cases, an app needs to show several pages. The Universal Windows Platform provides a built-in navigation framework that makes navigating between pages easier. Continuing the previous example, suppose you want to show the full web page for the selected feed item in a separate page, without opening an instance of the web browser. (This is actually a practice that you should always prefer, according to the guidelines.) To make this happen, select **Project, Add New Item**, and in the Add New Item dialog that appears, select the **BlankPage** template (see Figure 36.5.) Call the new page BrowserPage.xaml and click **OK**.

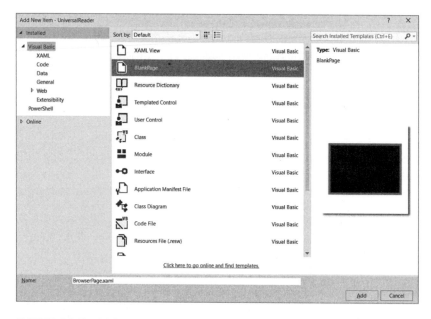

FIGURE 36.5   Adding a new page.

You can add a `ProgressBar` control and a `WebView`. The latter allows you to present HTML contents within apps and is a good choice for displaying a web page. This is the first code snippet:

```
<Grid Background="{ThemeResource ApplicationPageBackgroundThemeBrush}">
    <Grid.RowDefinitions>
        <RowDefinition Height="30"/>
```

```
        <RowDefinition/>
    </Grid.RowDefinitions>
    <ProgressBar Name="Progress1"
                 Visibility="Collapsed"/>
    <WebView Name="FeedWebView"
             Grid.Row="1"/>
</Grid>
```

The `WebView` control exposes a property called `Source`, of type `System.Uri`, which you simply assign with the URI of the content you want to show. This is done later, in code-behind.

Suppose you want to give users the opportunity to play the selected feed's video inside another page and share the web page with other apps. You need some commands, and therefore an app bar. The following code demonstrates this:

```
<Page.BottomAppBar>
    <CommandBar>
        <CommandBar.PrimaryCommands>
            <AppBarButton Icon="Play"
                          Label="Play"
                          Name="PlayButton"
                          Click="PlayButton_Click"/>
            <AppBarButton Icon="ReShare"
                          Label="Share"
                          Name="ShareButton"
                          Click="ShareButton_Click"/>
        </CommandBar.PrimaryCommands>
        <CommandBar.SecondaryCommands>
            <AppBarButton Icon="Back"
                          Label="Back"
                          Name="BackButton"
                          Click="BackButton_Click"/>
        </CommandBar.SecondaryCommands>
    </CommandBar>
</Page.BottomAppBar>
```

Notice that this code also implements a button that allows the user to navigate to the previous page. However, note that this implementation is provided just to demonstrate how navigation works in a universal Windows app because Windows Phone devices already have a built-in Back button, and the system automatically implements a Back button in apps running on either the desktop (in the taskbar) or a tablet (in the title bar).

Sharing contents and playing media require more detailed explanation, but before we get into that, you must first discover how to land on the current page from the startup page. To understand this, go back to the MainPage.xaml file. Recall that the `ListView` control has an `ItemClick` event that you must still handle. The following code demonstrates how to handle the event in the case of the sample app:

```
Private Sub FeedView_ItemClick(sender As Object,
                                    e As ItemClickEventArgs)
    Dim item As FeedItem = CType(e.ClickedItem, FeedItem)
    Frame.Navigate(GetType(BrowserPage), item)
End Sub
```

The second argument of the method signature is an object of type `ItemClickEventArgs`. The most important property for this object is `ClickedItem`, which represents the selected item in the list and is of type `Object` and therefore needs to be converted into a more appropriate type (`FeedItem` in the current example). The next line of code invokes the `Frame.Navigate` method. `Frame` is a property of the `Page` class and offers methods for moving between pages. `Navigate` opens the specified page by passing the type name of the page (`GetType(BrowserPage)`) and, optionally, an argument that the destination page will be able to handle. In this case, the argument passed to the destination page is the instance of the selected `FeedItem` object. This will be received in the BrowserPage.xaml page. More specifically, you can retrieve the navigation argument in the `OnNavigatedTo` method as follows:

```
Private currentFeed As FeedItem

Protected Overrides Sub OnNavigatedTo(e As NavigationEventArgs)
    Me.currentFeed = CType(e.Parameter, FeedItem)
    Me.FeedWebView.Source = New Uri(Me.currentFeed.Url)
End Sub
```

This method receives an argument of type `NavigationEventArgs`, whose `Parameter` property contains data sent from the calling page. You need to convert the property content into the most appropriate type—in this case, `FeedItem`. Next, you assign the `WebView.Source` property with the item's URI.

At this point, you must implement code for going back to the previous page. This is accomplished by handling the `BackButton.Click` event as follows:

```
Private Sub BackButton_Click(sender As Object, e As RoutedEventArgs)
    If Frame.CanGoBack Then
        Frame.GoBack()
    End If
End Sub
```

The `Frame` class exposes a lot of members, but (other than `Navigate`) the most important of them are the `GoBack` and `GoForward` methods and the `CanGoBack` and `CanGoForward` properties. The latter are of type `Boolean` and return `True` if the app can navigate to another page.

In addition, because you implemented a `ProgressBar`, you must handle its behavior. You might want to make it visible and indeterminate while content is loaded and hide it once the operation completes. The `WebView` exposes, among other things, two interesting events: `ContentLoading`, which is raised when the control starts loading the web content, and `LoadCompleted`, which is raised at completion. You can simply change the progress bar's appearance by handling both events as follows:

```
Private Sub FeedWebView_ContentLoading(sender As WebView,
                        args As WebViewContentLoadingEventArgs) _
                                    Handles FeedWebView.ContentLoading
    Me.Progress1.Visibility = Visibility.Visible
    Me.Progress1.IsIndeterminate = True
End Sub

Private Sub FeedWebView_LoadCompleted(sender As Object,
                        e As NavigationEventArgs) _
                                    Handles FeedWebView.LoadCompleted
    Me.Progress1.IsIndeterminate = False
    Me.Progress1.Visibility = Visibility.Collapsed
End Sub
```

So far you have done a lot of work, but you still need to do more. When you created the `BrowserPage` page, you implemented a button for sharing the page's content to other applications. This is accomplished via the so-called *share contract*, which is the topic of the next subsection.

Handling Hardware-Specific Tasks

There are many situations in which a universal Windows app must check whether it is running on specific hardware. For instance, Windows Phone devices have the Camera button, which starts up the built-in camera. If you write an app that allows the user to take pictures, you need to handle the action of pressing the Camera button. To solve this kind of problem, you first need to reference the proper device SDK; then you need to detect in code whether hardware-specific APIs are available, such as events related to the Camera button; finally, you handle the hardware-specific task as needed. Continuing the discussion of the Camera button, the first thing you want to do is enable the Microsoft Mobile Extension SDK for Universal App Platform, available in the Windows Universal, Extensions node of the Reference Manager dialog, as shown in Figure 36.6.

36

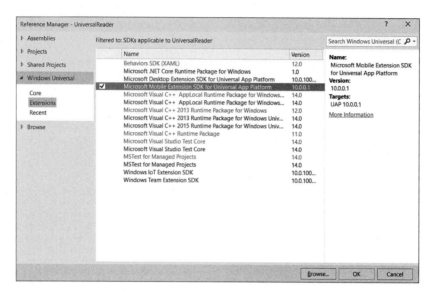

FIGURE 36.6   Referencing the mobile SDK.

The next step is to check whether the Windows Phone hardware APIs are available and supply an event handler for the Camera button's `CameraPressed` event. The following code demonstrates this:

```
If Metadata.ApiInformation.
    IsTypePresent("Windows.Phone.UI.Input.HardwareButtons") Then
        AddHandler HardwareButtons.CameraPressed,
        AddressOf HardwareButtons_CameraPressed
End If


Private Sub HardwareButtons_CameraPressed(sender As Object,
                                e As CameraPressedEventArgs)
    'Your logic here...
End Sub
```

The `IsTypePresent` method from `Windows.Foundation.Metadata.ApiInformation` allows you to detect whether the app is using libraries that expose the specified APIs—in this case, the `Windows.Phone.UI.Input.HardwareButtons` class. If this API is available, the code registers an event handler for the `CameraPressed` event, which is raised when the user taps the Camera button on a Windows Phone device.

The preceding discussion and code have no relationship with the current sample application, but this is definitely something you need to know in order to properly handle application behavior on different physical devices.

Sharing Content

Universal Windows apps can share content with other apps, via specific parts of the system's user interface. In order to share or receive content, you must implement a *share contract*. With it, your app can integrate with built-in features of the operating systems that provide the infrastructure to send and receive contents. If an app shares content, it is referred to as the *share source*; if it receives content, it is referred to as the *share target*. This chapter explains how to implement a share source scenario by providing the option to share the link of the web page shown in the `BrowserPage` page with other apps.

Objects that are required to share contents are exposed by the `Windows.ApplicationModel.DataTransfer` namespace. More specifically, you work with the `DataTransferManager` class. This allows integration with the operating system's sharing features. You need to handle its `DataRequested` event, which is raised when the user invokes the sharing UI. Consider this code:

```
Private dataManager As DataTransferManager
Private Sub RegisterForShare()
    Me.dataManager = DataTransferManager.GetForCurrentView
    AddHandler dataManager.DataRequested, AddressOf dataManager_DataRequested
End Sub
```

The `DataTransferManager.GetForCurrentView` shared method gets the instance of the `DataTransferManager` class associated with the current page, and its result is stored inside a private field. The code then subscribes to the `DataRequested` event, which is raised when the user invokes the sharing UI. The preceding method must be called at page startup, so you should write it as the first line of code in the `OnNavigatedTo` method (or in the page constructor). As a developer, you decide what to share. You can share text, links, images, HTTP contents, and files. In this case, the sample app will share the link of the currently open web page, plus a title and a description. The following event handler demonstrates this:

```
Private Sub dataManager_DataRequested(sender As DataTransferManager,
                                      args As DataRequestedEventArgs)
    Dim request As DataRequest = args.Request
    request.Data.Properties.Title = currentFeed.Title
    request.Data.Properties.Description = currentFeed.DateRecorded
    request.Data.SetWebLink(New Uri(currentFeed.Url))
End Sub
```

The `DataRequest` class represents data that will be shared. Its `Data` property exposes a subproperty called `Properties`, which contains actual information for sharing, such as `Title` and `Description` properties. You specify the type of content via self-explanatory methods from the `Data` property, each representing a specific content type, such as `SetBitmap`, `SetText`, `SetRtf`, `SetHtmlFormat`, and `SetWebLink`. (The full list is available via IntelliSense.) The sample code invokes `SetWebLink` to share a web address—in this case, the `FeedItem.Url` property. The final step is to launch the operating system's UI for sharing content, which is done in the `ShareButton` control's code. This is the code for the `ShareButton.Click` event handler:

```
Private Sub ShareButton_Click(sender As Object, e As RoutedEventArgs)
    DataTransferManager.ShowShareUI()
End Sub
```

You need to handle one last button, called `PlayButton`. This is discussed in the next subsection, where you'll learn about toast notifications.

Raising Toast Notifications

Windows apps provide support for many kinds of notifications, such as updatable live tiles, scheduled notifications, and toast notifications. These are the simplest notifications available, and this section provides an overview of them.

A toast notification is a small, nonblocking popup that informs the user that something has happened. You use the `Windows.UI.Notifications` namespace and the `ToastNotificationManager` class to create toast notifications. For example, you can notify users that an operation has completed, or you can show error messages. Examples of toast notifications in Windows 10 for phones are incoming text messages and new wireless connections found. An example of a toast notification in Windows 10 for desktop is the popup that appears when you connect a USB device to your machine.

The sample app you're building in this chapter should raise a toast notification if the user attempts to play a video but no associated media is available. In fact, some RSS feed items might contain information but no links to any videos. To understand how this can be done in code, consider the following event handler for the `PlayButton.Click` event:

```
Private Sub PlayButton_Click(sender As Object, e As RoutedEventArgs)
    If Me.currentFeed.Video IsNot Nothing Then
        Frame.Navigate(GetType(PlayerPage), currentFeed.Video)
    Else
        'Get a text template
        Dim toastXml = ToastNotificationManager.
            GetTemplateContent(ToastTemplateType.ToastText01)

        'Specify the text message
        Dim elements = toastXml.
            GetElementsByTagName("text")
        For Each node As IXmlNode In elements
            node.InnerText =
                String.Format("No media available for this item")
        Next

        'Raise a new notification
        Dim notification As New ToastNotification(toastXml)
        ToastNotificationManager.
```

```
            CreateToastNotifier().Show(notification)
    End If
End Sub
```

If the current `FeedItem.Video` property is not null, the code navigates to a new page called `PlayerPage` (which you will construct shortly). If it is null, the code raises a toast notification showing an error message.

Toast notifications can rely on several templates. Some contain only text, some contain text and images, and some contain text, images, and audio. You select the template via the `ToastNotificationManager.GetTemplateContent` method, whose argument is a value from the `ToastTemplateType` enumeration. IntelliSense provides the full list of value names, and you can easily tell if they are about text only or text and image templates. The `ToastText01` template is all about text. `GetTemplateContent` returns an object of type `XmlDocument`. Some templates allow you to store multiple text messages, so you have to iterate the collection of nodes containing text (`GetElementsByTagName("text")`) and assign the desired message to each node; with the current template, only one message is assigned. Once you have set text messages, you create an instance of the `ToastNotification` class, passing the template to the constructor. Then you invoke the `ToastNotificationManager.CreateToastNotifier` method to enable notifications on the current code and then the `ToastNotifier.Show` method, whose constructor receives the `ToastNotification` instance as an argument. You will see toast notifications working in a few minutes.

Playing Media

You need to add a very last page for the sample application, called PlayerPage.xaml, still using the BlankPage template. This page offers a very basic media player, using the `MediaElement` control (which you also saw in WPF) and some buttons in the app bar. Following is the XAML code for the page:

```xml
<Grid Background="{ThemeResource ApplicationPageBackgroundThemeBrush}">
    <MediaElement Name="Player1" AutoPlay="True"/>
</Grid>
<Page.BottomAppBar>
    <CommandBar>
        <CommandBar.PrimaryCommands>
            <AppBarButton Icon="Play" Label="Play" Name="PlayButton"
             Click="PlayButton_Click"/>
            <AppBarButton Icon="Stop" Label="Stop" Name="StopButton"
             Click="StopButton_Click"/>
            <AppBarButton Icon="Pause" Label="Pause" Name="PauseButton"
             Click="PauseButton_Click"/>
        </CommandBar.PrimaryCommands>
        <CommandBar.SecondaryCommands>
            <AppBarButton Icon="Back" Label="Back" Name="BackButton"
             Click="BackButton_Click"/>
```

36

```
    </CommandBar.SecondaryCommands>
  </CommandBar>
</Page.BottomAppBar>
```

The page's code-behind is also very simple. Notice how the page parameter is converted into a URI and assigned to the `MediaElement.Source` property:

```
Imports Windows.UI.Xaml.Navigation
Public NotInheritable Class PlayerPage
    Inherits Page
    Protected Overrides Sub OnNavigatedTo(e As NavigationEventArgs)
        Me.Player1.Source = New Uri(CStr(e.Parameter))
    End Sub

    Private Sub BackButton_Click(sender As Object, e As RoutedEventArgs)
        If Frame.CanGoBack Then
            Frame.GoBack()
        End If
    End Sub

    Private Sub PlayButton_Click(sender As Object, e As RoutedEventArgs)
        Me.Player1.Play()
    End Sub

    Private Sub StopButton_Click(sender As Object, e As RoutedEventArgs)
        Me.Player1.Stop()
    End Sub

    Private Sub PauseButton_Click(sender As Object, e As RoutedEventArgs)
        Me.Player1.Pause()
    End Sub
End Class
```

You have already done most of the work on this app. You just need to edit the application manifest, and then you will be ready to test your first universal app on your development machine.

Customizing the Application Manifest

The application manifest (or app manifest) is where you provide information and capabilities about your apps. It is basically an XML file that you can edit via a convenient designer. Unfortunately, at this writing, with Visual Studio 2015 Release Candidate, such a designer has not been implemented yet, but it will be available when Visual Studio 2015 is released. However, if you have ever worked with Windows Store and Windows Phone apps with Visual Studio 2013, you know what the manifest designer is and what it looks like; the designer in Visual Studio 2015 will be very close to that previous version.

The application manifest basically contains information about the app identity, the author's identity, visual assets (logos), hardware requirements, and permissions the app needs to access some of the device's features. If you want to build apps that access specific device features, such as the location sensor, you must edit the app manifest and enable the required features. To understand how the app manifest is made, double-click the Package.appxmanifest file in Solution Explorer. Listing 36.1 shows the app manifest for the current sample application, which is a very basic manifest implementation.

LISTING 36.1   Understanding the App Manifest

```
<?xml version="1.0" encoding="utf-8"?>

<Package
  xmlns="http://schemas.microsoft.com/appx/manifest/foundation/windows10"
  xmlns:mp="http://schemas.microsoft.com/appx/2014/phone/manifest"
  xmlns:uap="http://schemas.microsoft.com/appx/manifest/uap/windows10"
  IgnorableNamespaces="uap mp">

  <Identity
    Name="a98a356d-daeb-4516-a9cd-31f97d00f67f"
    Publisher="CN=alessandrodelsole"
    Version="1.0.0.0" />

  <mp:PhoneIdentity
      PhoneProductId="a98a356d-daeb-4516-a9cd-31f97d00f67f"
      PhonePublisherId="00000000-0000-0000-0000-000000000000"/>

  <Properties>
    <DisplayName>UniversalReader</DisplayName>
    <PublisherDisplayName>alessandrodelsole</PublisherDisplayName>
    <Logo>Assets\StoreLogo.png</Logo>
  </Properties>

  <Dependencies>
    <TargetDeviceFamily Name="Windows.Universal"
     MinVersion="10.0.10069.0"
     MaxVersionTested="10.0.10069.0" />
  </Dependencies>

  <Resources>
    <Resource Language="x-generate"/>
  </Resources>

  <Applications>
    <Application Id="App"
      Executable="$targetnametoken$.exe"
```

36

```
          EntryPoint="UniversalReader.App">
          <uap:VisualElements
            DisplayName="UniversalReader"
            Square150x150Logo="Assets\Logo.png"
            Square44x44Logo="Assets\SmallLogo.png"
            Description="UniversalReader"
            BackgroundColor="#464646">
            <uap:SplashScreen Image="Assets\SplashScreen.png" />
          </uap:VisualElements>
        </Application>
      </Applications>

  <Capabilities>
    <Capability Name="internetClient" />
  </Capabilities>
</Package>
```

If you walk through the XML markup code for the app manifest, you can see the following major nodes:

▶ **Package**—This is the root XML node that comprises all the information and requirements for the current app.

▶ **Identity**—This node uniquely identifies the app package and is intended to provide information to the Windows Store. The easiest and best way to supply the proper identity values is to select **Project, Store, Associate App with the Store**. (This command is currently disabled because the Windows Store for universal Windows app is not open yet, but when Visual Studio 2015 is released and the Windows 10 Store is open, this command will automatically set the required identity values emitted by the Windows Store.) You are strongly encouraged to use this option instead of supplying values manually.

▶ **Properties**—This node contains user-friendly information about the app, such as the display name, the publisher name, and the app logo.

▶ `Dependencies`—This node contains a list of `TargetDeviceFamily` elements, each referencing a code base specific for a device type. The default code base is `Windows.Universal`, but it might be the Windows SDK Extension for desktop, or for IoT, or for mobile.

▶ **Applications**—This node contains a collection of `Application` element, each representing an app in the package. Then every `Application` element contains information such as the display name, the splash screen image, and the app logo in different sizes.

▶ **Capabilities**—This node is very important because it's where you specify hardware requirements and features that an app needs to access. It can contain many `Capability` and `DeviceCapability` elements. `Capability` elements apply to common programming scenarios, such as accessing special folders (Music, Pictures, SD cards), accessing the Internet, and so on. `DeviceCapability` elements apply to hardware features such as sensors. By default, the app manifest defines a capability called `internetClient`, which allows an app to browse the Internet.

`BackgroundColor` PROPERTY

In the Windows 10 developer tools targeting the build used to write this chapter, the `BackgroundColor` property in the manifest is set with the `#464646` value, which is a dark gray color. In future releases, this value will be replaced with `Transparent` so that the app's icons pick up the proper system theme color.

Editing the app manifest may be required even when you're testing an app on your development machine. For instance, if your app needs to use the location sensor to detect the device geolocation coordinates, you must declare a `DeviceCapability` element, as in the following code:

```
<Capabilities>
  <Capability Name="internetClient" />
  <DeviceCapability Name="location"/>
</Capabilities>
```

Many capabilities are available through the `uap` XML alias, which is declared in the `Package` root element of the manifest. For instance, if your app needs to store information onto a removable SD card, you need the following capability:

```
<uap:Capability Name="removableStorage" />
```

As another example, if your app needs to access the contacts list on your device, you need to declare the following capability:

```
<uap:Capability Name="contacts" />
```

Supplying the proper capabilities is important for running, debugging, and testing the application; because capabilities will be listed in the Windows Store's page for your app, users will be able to decide whether to download your app based on its requirements and based on features it needs to access.

For the sample application you've been building in this chapter, you do not need to edit any capabilities because the app just downloads syndicated content from the Internet, and the required capability (`internetClient`) is enabled by default. (Remember to add a privacy policy URL in the app submission page in the Windows Store, though, or certification will fail.) However, you are strongly encouraged to read the package manifest schema reference, available at https://msdn.microsoft.com/en-us/library/windows/apps/br211473. aspx, even if you will use the Visual Studio 2015 manifest designer. Until RTM, the documentation will allow you to properly set your app capabilities and requirements.

Starting and Debugging Universal Windows Apps

You've done a lot of work in this chapter, and now you are finally ready to test the sample app locally. All the instrumentation that Visual Studio offers for debugging Visual Basic applications can be used with universal Windows apps as well. For example, you can use breakpoints, DataTips, and tool windows for debugging.

Everything you learned about in Chapter 5, "Debugging Visual Basic 2015 Applications," is still valid with universal Windows apps. The real difference is how you execute apps for debugging and testing. In fact, you can either test and debug your apps on the local development machine, on local device emulators, or on physical devices. However, if you want to test apps on a Windows Phone physical device, this must be *developer unlocked*, which means it can be used for development purposes only if the associated Microsoft account has been registered as a developer account. The standard Visual Studio toolbar contains a combo box that enables you to specify the execution environment (see Figure 36.7).

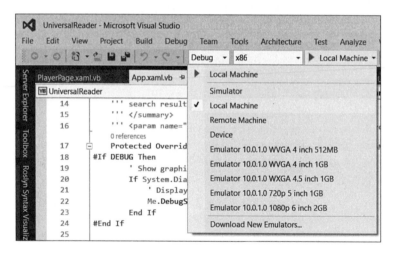

FIGURE 36.7   Selecting the target environment for testing apps.

You can select among the local machine, a physical device, the Windows Simulator (which represents a tablet running Windows 10), and several phone emulators with different screen sizes and memory capacities. These choices allow you to test your app on different devices, emulators, and screen factors.

ARM CONFIGURATION

The preceding discussion applies to x64 and x86 configurations. If you select the ARM configuration, you can test your app only on a physical device, locally or remotely.

You can connect a physical device to your machine for debugging, and you can also take advantage of remote debugging. You can do this over a wireless connection but need to install some tools on the target machine. To prepare for remote debugging, see this page of the MSDN library: http://bit.ly/1KeslI5.

Unlike with Windows Phone, where you can select among different emulators, the Windows simulator provides an option to select different screen resolutions. Start with selecting the Windows simulator, then press **F5**. The sample app downloads content from the RSS feed and presents that information onscreen, as shown in Figure 36.8.

FIGURE 36.8   The sample app on the Windows simulator.

If you tap an item, the full page is shown in a separate page, as shown in Figure 36.9, where you can also see the app bar.

FIGURE 36.9   Showing a full web page in-app.

If you tap the Play button, another page opens and plays the video. The app bar allows the user to control the media or go back to the previous page (see Figure 36.10).

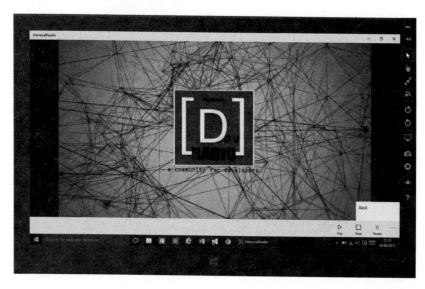

FIGURE 36.10   Playing a video.

If you go back to the startup page, you see that the list of items is not downloaded again because it has been stored locally. This provides better perceived performance and avoids the need to download content from the Internet every time the app is launched or resumed, which is a best practice especially with metered connections.

Now stop debugging and select one of the Windows Phone emulators as the target and then press **F5** again. The selected emulator starts up and loads the application, as shown in Figure 36.11.

FIGURE 36.11   The sample app on a Windows Phone device.

Similarly, if you tap an item, the app shows the full related web page, as shown in Figure 36.12.

FIGURE 36.12   Showing a full web page on Windows Phone.

Finally, you can play a video as you did on the Windows Simulator, as shown in Figure 36.13.

FIGURE 36.13   Playing a video on Windows Phone.

By writing code once and sharing resources, you have been able to generate an app that runs on different devices. Notice that on Windows Phone devices, playing videos is better when the device's orientation is landscape.

Desktop Mode and Tablet Mode

The concept of adaptive user interfaces in Windows 10 is not simply related to building apps but also applies to the system as whole. In fact, you can select the **Tablet Mode** (in the Notification center), and Windows 10 rearranges the user interface in a way that is more appropriate and touch-friendly on tablet devices. Then you can revert to the Desktop mode by disabling **Tablet Mode** in the Notification center. This is very important to understand because universal Windows apps have different appearances depending on the selected mode. For instance, when the Tablet mode is disabled (thus the UI is optimized for the desktop), a universal app appears in the so-called windowed mode, which means that the app looks like a classic window. In the previous section, figures show the sample universal Windows app in the windowed mode, but Figure 36.14 provides a larger view.

36

FIGURE 36.14   A universal Windows app running in Desktop mode.

When the system is running in Desktop mode, the user interface for windowed apps is optimized for the desktop and for using the mouse and keyboard. When the system is running in Tablet mode, the app user interface is optimized for touch gestures and the onscreen keyboard, and it has the typical appearance of a Windows Store app, as in Windows 8 and 8.1. Figure 36.15 shows the current sample app running in Tablet mode.

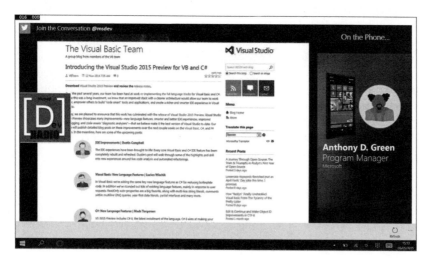

FIGURE 36.15   A universal Windows app running in Tablet mode.

TESTING ADAPTIVE UI AND SCREEN FACTORS

Remember to test your app in both the Desktop and Tablet modes so that you can be sure that the user interface correctly adapts to different screen factors and accepts user input properly, with either physical devices or touch gestures.

Understanding .NET Core for Windows 10

As you might recall from Chapter 1, "Introducing .NET 2015," and from the initial discussions in this chapter, universal Windows apps rely on .NET Core, which means that an app package ships with the set of libraries it actually needs instead of having references to a full framework. To demonstrate this, in Solution Explorer right-click the project name and then select **Open Folder in File Explorer** to open the Windows File Explorer on the project folder. Now open the bin subfolder. Here you will find one subfolder per configuration, such as x86, x64, and ARM. Open the x86 subfolder and then the Debug one (assuming that you started debugging the application with the Debug configuration selected). Among other things, this contains a subfolder called AppX, which contains the app package and all the required files. If you open the AppX subfolder, you will see the app package file (in this case, UniversalReader.exe) and a number of .dll files, each containing types used by the application. WinMetadata contains a file called Windows.winmd, which contains metadata for the Windows APIs that an app may call.

Creating and Testing App Packages

Once you have finished developing and debugging an app, you might want to prepare to submit it to the Windows Store. Submitting an app means generating application packages. Application packages are .appx files that you can easily generate from Visual Studio by selecting **Project, Store, Create App Packages**. By following a very simple wizard, you can get your packages ready in a few seconds. When the wizard completes (see Figure 36.16), it asks if you want to launch the Windows App Certification Kit, a tool that performs some automated tests to detect common issues.

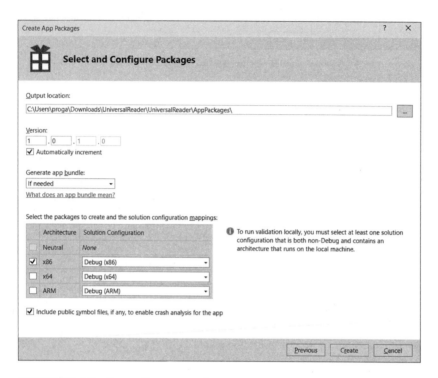

FIGURE 36.16   Generating app packages.

Executing this tool is a best practice and will save you time by solving problems before you submit an app to the Windows Store. Once you have generated and tested packages, you are ready to submit your apps to the Windows Store.

Submitting Apps to the Store

APPLICATION CERTIFICATION REQUIREMENTS

Before you submit an app to the Windows Store, you must be sure that it adheres to the certification policies. You should bookmark the certification requirements page on MSDN because it will be one of your closest friends for avoiding rejections: https://msdn. microsoft.com/en-us/library/windows/apps/dn764944.aspx.

When you have finished developing and testing an app, it is time to submit it to the Windows Store so that other users will be able to download (and possibly buy) your app on their devices. To submit an app, you need to access the Developer Center at http:// dev.windows.com and sign in with your registered Microsoft account. At this writing, the Windows Store is not available yet to Windows 10 universal apps, but it is available for Windows 8.1 and Windows Phone 8.1, so a thorough discussion on publishing a universal Windows app to the Windows Store is not possible yet. However, there are some common steps in publishing apps to the Windows Store:

1. Reserve the app name.

2. Specify the selling details, such as the app price or in-app purchases.

3. Specify an age rating.

4. Upload the app package.

5. Provide a number of screenshots.

Once you have completed all the required steps, the app is submitted for certification. When Microsoft finishes reviewing the app, it will send you an email, telling you whether the app was successfully certified and published or if it failed certification. If your app fails, Microsoft will also attach a document to help you identify the problem and fix it. If your app passes, it will be listed in the Windows Store as soon as it passes the certification.

Summary

The upcoming release of Windows 10 is unifying the development experience for PCs, tablets, phones, Xbox One, HoloLens, and IoT devices based on the Universal Windows Platform. It is also unifying the user experience with adaptive user interfaces and only one Windows Store. To support this unification, Microsoft has created tools for Visual Studio 2015 that allow you to build, debug, and test universal Windows apps. With universal Windows apps, you code once, and your app works on every device running Windows 10. You can also provide users an optimized Windows Store experience, allowing them to purchase an app (or single in-app functionalities) once and have it available on all their devices.

This chapter provided an overview of universal app development by showing how to create an RSS feed reader that downloads and presents contents, shows web pages, and plays videos on every Windows 10 device. This chapter also marks the end of this book's discussions about client applications. In the next chapter, you start learning about implementing distributed services over networks with Visual Basic 2015.

36

CHAPTER 37

Creating and Consuming WCF Services

During the last several years, many technologies were developed for distributed applications that communicate over networks. The idea is that client applications can exchange information with a service via a network protocol such as Hypertext Transport Protocol (HTTP) or Transmission Control Protocol (TCP), just to mention some. Among these technologies there are SOAP (an XML-based information exchange system), Microsoft Messaging Queue (a message-based system), the well-known web services, and the .NET Remoting (which connects applications based on the .NET Framework). Although powerful, all these technologies have one limitation: Two or more applications can connect only if all of them rely on the same technology. Just for clarification, an application based on MSMQ cannot communicate with another one based on SOAP. To avoid this limitation, Microsoft created the Windows Communication Foundation (WCF) technology that was first introduced with the .NET Framework 3.0. It is a unified programming model for distributed applications. With WCF, developers can write code for exchanging data and information between services and clients without worrying about how data is transmitted because this is the job of the .NET Framework. WCF is another large technology, and covering every single aspect would require an entire book; therefore, in this chapter you learn about implementing, configuring, hosting, and consuming WCF services with Visual Basic 2015.

Introducing Windows Communication Foundation

WCF is a technology that enables data and information exchange between services and clients through messages. The service exposes information through the network and is nothing but a .NET assembly. Then the client receives that information and can send back other information or data. In this section, you learn how data exchange between the service and clients works before creating your first WCF service. This is important because you need to know some fundamentals about WCF infrastructure before putting your hands on the code. If you ever developed .NET Web Services (.asmx), you'll notice several similarities with WCF, at least in the implementation. However, several things under the hood make WCF more powerful. Moreover, although web services are obviously still allowed and supported in .NET Framework 4.6, WCF is the main technology for data exchange through networks and is intended to be a replacement of web services, even though WCF provides fully integrated support with client and web applications, such as WPF and Silverlight.

WCF AND .NET 2015

As you learned in Chapter 1, "Introducing .NET 2015," Microsoft has embraced open source, and the .NET Framework is part of a huge process in which some development platforms have been moved to open source. Windows Communication Foundation is currently divided into two pieces: the server-side stack, which is part of .NET 4.6 and is not open source, and the client-side stack, which is now part of .NET Core and is open source. From a practical point of view, this does not affect the way you use the platform, so both the explanations and the sample code in this chapter do not need to worry about this change. But it is important to know how things are moving.

Understanding Endpoints

A WCF service is a .NET assembly (in the form of dll) relying on the `System.ServiceModel` namespace and exposing objects and members like any other class library. Thus, client applications can invoke members and use objects exposed by services. Behind the scenes, this happens through message exchanges. Client and services exchange messages through *endpoints*. An endpoint is the place where client and service meet and is where both applications exchange their information, so it can be considered like a communication port. Each WCF service offers at least one endpoint; multiple endpoints serve as communication ports for different data types (for example, .NET objects and messages). But every endpoint needs to be configured with some other information to be a functional place for meeting the needs of service and clients. The configuration is provided by the `Address`, `Binding`, and `Contract` as explained in the next section.

Address, Binding, Contract: The ABC of WCF

When a client application attempts to reach a service, it needs to know some information for finding the service and for data exchange. The service exposes such information via the ABC, which represents the *Address*, *Binding*, and *Contract* properties in the service. The *Address* is the physical URI where the service is running. For example, on the local machine the Address could be http://localhost/MyService.svc or http://www.something. com/MyService.svc if the service is running on the Internet. The *Binding* property is a complex object and is responsible for

▶ Establishing how service and clients communicate (with a `Behavior` object)

▶ Establishing which protocol and credentials must be used within the communication

▶ Handling data transmission to the target (via a `Channel` object), converting data into an acceptable format, and transmitting data via the specified protocol (such as HTTP, HTTPS, and so on)

The *Contract* is probably the most significant item in the ABC. It establishes what data can be exchanged and which .NET objects/members are exposed by the service and that the client must accept; this is defined as platform-independent because clients will just accept the contract without worrying about the code that implemented objects on the server side. If you think of classic managed class libraries, when you add a reference to a class library, you want to use its members, but in most cases you will not worry about the code that implemented those members. With WCF, it is the same thing. For code, a contract is a .NET interface that defines public members available from the service to clients. Such an interface is then implemented by a class that actually makes members available to the external world. All these concepts will be explained in code. There are different contract types in WCF, but the most important are summarized in Table 37.1.

TABLE 37.1 WCF Contracts

Contract	Description
`ServiceContract`	Provides the service skeleton and defines methods that will be available to the public
`DataContract`	Defines classes that will be available to the public as data objects
`MessageContract`	Used to exchange data with SOAP-based applications and serializes data into SOAP messages

As you see in the next section, contracts are applied with special .NET attributes. The good news about the ABC is that all information is typically stored inside the configuration file and therefore can be edited with any text editor by system and network administrators, too, without the need of recompiling the source code. This makes services administration simpler. At this point, you are ready to create your first WCF service with Visual Basic 2015.

Implementing WCF Services

Visual Studio 2015 offers some project templates for creating WCF projects. Table 37.2 lists them all.

TABLE 37.2   WCF Project Templates

Template	Description
WCF Service Application	Used for creating a self-hosted WCF service
WCF Service Library	Used for creating a WCF service to be manually hosted and configured
WCF Workflow Service Application	Enables you to create a WCF service with integration with Workflow Foundation
WCF Syndication Library	Generates a WCF service enabled for RSS syndication

This book covers the WCF Service Application template, which is useful because it provides service self-hosting. A WCF service cannot be run or consumed as a standalone and must be hosted inside a .NET application. Host applications can be of several types: Console applications, Internet Information Services (including the Express edition), and ASP.NET Development Server are all valid host applications. The WCF Service Application template provides hosting inside the Internet Information Services (IIS) Express development server. IIS Express is a lightweight version of the famous IIS web server and is typically used on development machines for testing purposes. In Visual Studio 2015, IIS Express is the default setting for WCF services, but you can also use a local IIS server or an external host (see Figure 37.6 later in this chapter to locate the host selection). Select the **File, New Project** command, and in the **New Project** dialog box, select the **WCF Service Application** template, as shown in Figure 37.1. Name the new project **BookService** and then click **OK**.

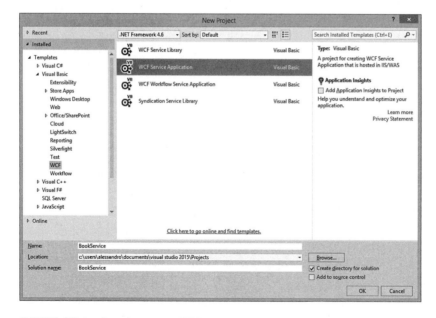

FIGURE 37.1   Creating a new WCF project.

The goal of the example is to offer a way for validating books' information, such as ISBN code, title, and author. The service exposes a `Book` class representing a single book and a method named `ValidateBook` that provides the validation logic. Before writing custom code, you should take a look at the autogenerated code to understand what WCF needs. Visual Studio 2015 generated a web project visible in Solution Explorer. The new project contains the following files:

- ▶ IService1.vb, which defines the contract interface

- ▶ Service1.svc.vb (nested into Service1.svc as a code-behind file), which defines the class that implements the contract

- ▶ Service1.svc, which is the actual service that exposes data and that is to be consumed by clients

- ▶ Web.config, which provides definitions for the ABC

NOTE ON THE WEB.CONFIG FILE

Starting with the .NET Framework 4.0 and Visual Studio 2010, the Web.config file no longer contains a WCF metadata definition in case you use the default settings because they are considered as implicit. This is important with regard to the current example. If you decide to implement custom settings instead, the Web.config stores the metadata definition. Because configuration files in client applications reflect Web.config files from services, later in this chapter you see the client-side metadata definition mapping the implicit metadata of the current sample service.

Let's take a look at the IService1.vb file, reported in Listing 37.1, which defines a couple of contracts.

LISTING 37.1   Autogenerated Contracts

```
' NOTE: You can use the "Rename" command on the "Refactor" menu
' to change the interface name "IService1" in both code and
' config file together.
<ServiceContract()>
Public Interface IService1

    <OperationContract()>
    Function GetData(value As Integer) As String

    <OperationContract()>
    Function GetDataUsingDataContract(composite As _
                            CompositeType) As CompositeType

    ' TODO: Add your service operations here

End Interface
```

```
' Use a data contract as illustrated in the sample below
' to add composite types to service operations.
<DataContract()>
Public Class CompositeType

    <DataMember()>
    Public Property BoolValue() As Boolean

    <DataMember()>
    Public Property StringValue() As String
End Class
```

The `IService1` interface is decorated with the `ServiceContract` attribute, meaning that it establishes which members the service defines and makes available to the public. The interface defines two methods, both decorated with the `OperationContract` attribute. This attribute makes methods visible to the external world and consumable by clients. You need to remember that, in WCF, marking a method as `Public` is not sufficient to make it available to clients; it needs to be marked as `OperationContract` to be visible. Methods exposed by WCF services are also known as *service operations*. Notice how the `GetDataUsingDataContract` method receives an argument of type `CompositeType`. This type is a custom class declared as `DataContract`, so the WCF service can exchange data of this type. Members from this class also need to be marked as `DataMember` to be visible to the external world. As for service operations, marking a member as `Public` is not sufficient; you need to decorate members with the `DataMember` attribute. The `Service1` class shows an example of implementing the contract and the logic for service operations. Listing 37.2 shows the autogenerated sample code.

LISTING 37.2   Autogenerated Contracts Implementation

```
' NOTE: You can use the "Rename" command on the "Refactor" menu to
' change the class name "Service1" in code, svc and config file together.
Public Class Service1
    Implements IService1

    Public Sub New()
    End Sub

    Public Function GetData(value As Integer) As String _
                Implements IService1.GetData
        Return String.Format("You entered: {0}", value)
    End Function

    Public Function GetDataUsingDataContract(composite As CompositeType) As   _
                CompositeType Implements IService1.GetDataUsingDataContract
```

```
        If composite Is Nothing Then
            Throw New ArgumentNullException("composite")
        End If
        If composite.BoolValue Then
            composite.StringValue &= "Suffix"
        End If
        Return composite
    End Function
End Class
```

The class implements the contract interface and provides logic for service operations working like any other .NET class. The content of the .svc file is discussed later; for now let's make some edits to the code replacing the autogenerated one with custom implementation.

Implementing Custom Logic for the WCF Service

Rename the IService1.vb file to **IBookService.vb**; then switch to the code editor. Right-click the `IService1` identifier and select **Rename**. Next, provide the new `IBookService` identifier and click **OK**. Visual Studio will prompt for confirmation and will rename the instances in code as well. This is important to update all references inside the project to the interface, including references inside the .svc file. Now delete the code for the `CompositeType` class and replace the entire code with the one shown in Listing 37.3.

LISTING 37.3 Implementing Custom Contracts

```
<ServiceContract()>
Public Interface IBookService

    <OperationContract()>
    Function ValidateBook(bookToValidate As Book) As String

End Interface

<DataContract()>
Public Class Book

    <DataMember()>
    Public Property Title As String

    <DataMember()>
    Public Property ISBN As String

    <DataMember()>
    Public Property Author As String
```

37

```
    <DataMember()>
    Public Property DatePublished As Date?
End Class
```

The `IBookService` contract defines a `ValidateBook` method that will be invoked for validating a book. A single book is represented by the `Book` class, which exposes four self-explanatory properties. Now switch to the `Service1` class and, following the steps described before, rename the `Service1` identifier into `BookService`. Then replace the auto-generated code with the one shown in Listing 37.4.

LISTING 37.4   Implementing the Service Logic

```
Imports System.Text.RegularExpressions
Public Class BookService
    Implements IBookService

    Private Const isbnPattern As String = _
    "ISBN(?:-13)?:?\x20*(?=.{17}$)97(?:8|9)([ -])\d{1,5}\1\d{1,7}\1\d{1,6}\1\d$"

    Public Function ValidateBook(bookToValidate As Book) As _
                String Implements IBookService.ValidateBook

        Dim isValidIsbn As Boolean = Regex.IsMatch(String.Concat("ISBN-13: ",
                                        bookToValidate.ISBN),
                                        isbnPattern)

        If isValidIsbn = False Then
            Return "Invalid ISBN"
        End If

        Dim isValidAuthor As Boolean = String.IsNullOrEmpty(bookToValidate.Author)
        If isValidAuthor = True Then
            Return "Author not specified"
        End If

        Dim isValidTitle As Boolean = String.IsNullOrEmpty(bookToValidate.Title)
        If isValidTitle = True Then
            Return "Title not specified"
        End If

        If bookToValidate.DatePublished Is Nothing Then
            Return "Book data is valid but date published was not specified"
        End If
```

```
        Return "Valid book"
    End Function
End Class
```

The code for the `ValidateBook` method is simple. It uses a regular expression for checking whether the ISBN code is valid and then checks for valid properties in the Book class instance that must be validated.

NOTE ON THE REGULAR EXPRESSION PATTERN

The regular expression pattern for checking ISBNs is from the RegExLibrary website at the following address: http://regexlib.com/REDetails.aspx?regexp_id=1748. A lot of patterns for validating ISBNs are available; the one used in this book is just an example. You can replace it with a different one.

Now right-click the **BookService.svc** file in Solution Explorer, and select **View in Browser**. In a few seconds, the WCF service will be hosted by the ASP.NET Development Server and will run inside the web browser, as demonstrated in Figure 37.2.

This test is required to ensure that the service works correctly. Notice how information is provided on how consuming the service is. The web page shows information explaining that you should invoke the **SvcUtil.exe** command-line tool pointing to the WSDL metadata of the service.

WHAT IS WSDL?

Web-service Definition Language (WSDL) is a standard format and is an XML representation of how a web service works (including WCF services), describing document information and procedure information, including endpoints and messages. WSDL explains how a service must work, for example, how information has to be transmitted, which protocol must be used, and how it interacts in scenarios such as REST and SOAP. Such information is known as *service metadata* and in WCF it plays an important role.

SvcUtil is described in the next section. Click the link available near SvcUtil.exe. By doing so, you access metadata offered by the WCF service, including contracts and members, as reported in Figure 37.3.

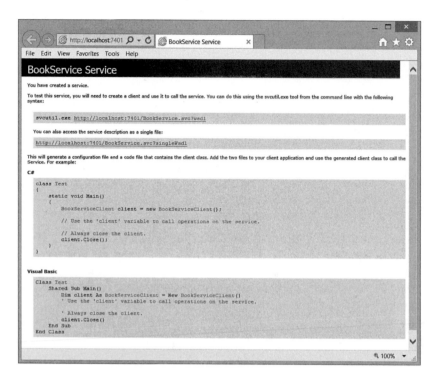

FIGURE 37.2   The WCF service has been hosted by the IIS Express Development Server and is now running.

Client applications invoke service members passing through the service metadata. The next section explains how you invoke service members through a proxy class, but before going into that, let's take a look at the BookService.svc file.

EXPOSING GENERICS IN WCF

Because WCF services metadata are exposed via WSDL, some issues with generics are not supported by this. You might want to read this blog post by MVP Jeff Barnes, which provides explanations and workarounds: http://bit.ly/4CzGv3.

Right-click this file and select **View Markup**. The XHTML code for this file is the following:

```
<%@ ServiceHost Language="VB" Debug="true"
        Service="BookService.BookService" CodeBehind="BookService.svc.vb" %>
```

FIGURE 37.3   Exploring the service's metadata.

This file defines the service entry point. It states that the `BookService` class is the service entry point because it defines the real logic that implements the contract. There is some other information such as the programming language used and the code-behind the file, but the `Service` tag is absolutely the most important. After this overview of the service implementation, it's time to consume the service from a client application.

EXPOSING ENTITY DATA MODELS AND LINQ TO SQL CLASSES

WCF services are also used to expose Entity Data Models (EDM) and LINQ to SQL classes via serialization. Entities and their members in EDMs are marked by default with the `DataContract` and `DataMember` attributes, respectively. LINQ to SQL classes, on the other hand, have to be enabled for serialization by setting the `Serialization Mode` property of the `DataContext` class as `Unidirectional` and then marking entities with `DataContract`. In Chapter 38, "Implementing and Consuming OData Services," you learn about OData Services, which provide an easy implementation of WCF services by exposing data models without the need of making such customizations manually. Thus, you should create custom WCF services for exposing data models only when you need to handle special scenarios that require implementing different business logic than the one offered by OData Services.

Consuming WCF Services

Clients can easily consume WCF services by adding a service reference directly from Visual Studio 2015. In the next example, you create a simple Console client application for validating ISBNs by invoking objects from the WCF service implemented in the previous section.

Creating the Client and Adding a Service Reference

Add a new Console project to the current solution and name it **BookClient**. The first step you have to accomplish is adding a service reference to the WCF service. Right-click the new project name in Solution Explorer and select **Add Service Reference**.

ADD SERVICE REFERENCE AND ADD CONNECTED SERVICE

Visual Studio 2015 allows you to add references to several sources. Some of these (such as Microsoft Azure services) can be reached via the command Add Connected Service. At this writing, the command to use for WCF is still Add Service Reference, but it might be transitioned to Add Connected Service in future releases, so look for that if you do not find Add Service Reference any longer.

This brings up the Add Service Reference dialog box, where you need to enter the full web address of your service. If the service you want to add a reference to is available in the current solution, as in the current example, click **Discover**. The service appears in the dialog box, as shown in Figure 37.4.

Click the service name on the left to enable the development server to correctly host the service and discover its members. At this point, the dialog box lists available contracts (`IBookService` in this case) and their members. Replace the Namespace identifier with `BookServiceReference`.

FIGURE 37.4   The Add Service Reference dialog box enables you to add a reference to a WCF service.

Understanding the Proxy Class

The WCF service is exposed through the network via a WSDL. To consume objects and data exposed by the WSDL, the client needs a proxy class that is responsible for translating WSDL information into managed code that you can reuse. This is accomplished via a command-line tool named SvcUtil.exe, which is part of the .NET Framework. Fortunately, you do not need to run SvcUtil manually because Visual Studio will do the work for you. When you click **OK** from the Add Service Reference dialog box, Visual Studio invokes SvcUtil and generates a proxy class. In Solution Explorer, a new folder named Service references appears. This folder contains all service references and, for the current example, stores a new item named BookServiceReference. This new item provides all the metadata information required to consume the service and especially the proxy class. Click the **Show All Files** button in Solution Explorer and expand the **Reference.svcmap** file; then double-click the **Reference.vb** file. This code file exposes the BookServiceReference namespace to provide client-side code for accessing members exposed from the service. This namespace exposes client-side implementations of the Book class and the IBookService interface. The most important class exposed by the namespace is named BookServiceClient and is the actual proxy class, which inherits from System.ServiceModel.ClientBase and is responsible for connecting to the service and closing the connection. It is also responsible for exposing service members such as the ValidateBook that was implemented on the service side. The namespace also exposes the IBookServiceChannel interface that inherits from IClientChannel, which provides members for the request/reply infrastructure required by WCF services. You instantiate the proxy class to establish a connection with the WCF service, and you interact with the proxy class for accessing members from the service, as explained in the next section.

Invoking Members from the Service

To invoke service members, you need to create an instance of the proxy class, which in our example is named BookClient.BookServiceReference.BookServiceClient. Creating an instance of the class can establish a connection to the WCF service and give you access to public members. Continuing with the previous example, the client application could have an instance of the Book class and invoke the ValidateBook method for checking whether the Book instance is correct according to our needs. The code in Listing 37.5 shows how to accomplish this.

LISTING 37.5   Instantiating the Proxy Class and Invoking Service Members

```
Imports BookClient.BookServiceReference

Module Module1

    Sub Main()
        'Creates an instance of the proxy class
        'and automatically establishes a connection
        'to the service
        Dim client As New BookServiceClient

        'A new book
        'Note that the RegEx pattern requires to write the ISBN in the form
        'provided below, so like: 000-0-0000-0000-0 including the minus
        'character
        Dim myBook As New Book
        With myBook
            .Author = "Alessandro Del Sole"
            .Title = "Visual Studio LightSwitch Unleashed"
            .ISBN = "978-0-6723-3553-2"
            .DatePublished = Date.Today
        End With

        'Invokes the ValidateBook method from
        'the service
```

```
        Console.WriteLine(client.ValidateBook(myBook))
        Console.WriteLine("Done")
        Console.ReadLine()
        client.Close()

    End Sub
End Module
```

In the client you can invoke all public members from the service, where *public* means functions decorated with the `OperationContract` attribute and data classes decorated with the `DataContract` attribute. Running the code in Listing 37.5 produces the result shown in Figure 37.5, but you can try to change the ISBN code to check how the application works with different values.

FIGURE 37.5   The client application validated a book.

Remember to close the connection to the service invoking the `Close` method on the proxy class. This ensures that the service will be shut down.

Understanding the Configuration File

When you add a proxy class to your WCF service, Visual Studio also updates the configuration file to provide information on how to reach and interact with the service. The most important information is stored in the `System.ServiceModel` section of the **app.config** file. Listing 37.6 shows the most interesting excerpt.

LISTING 37.6   Configuration Settings for the Client

```xml
<?xml version="1.0" encoding="utf-8" ?>
<configuration>
    <startup>
        <supportedRuntime version="v4.0" sku=".NETFramework,Version=v4.5" />
    </startup>
    <system.serviceModel>
        <bindings>
            <basicHttpBinding>
                <binding name="BasicHttpBinding_IBookService" />
            </basicHttpBinding>
        </bindings>
        <client>
            <endpoint address="http://localhost:18315/BookService.svc"
                    binding="basicHttpBinding"
                    bindingConfiguration="BasicHttpBinding_IBookService"
                    contract="BookServiceReference.IBookService"
                    name="BasicHttpBinding_IBookService" />
        </client>
    </system.serviceModel>
</configuration>
```

The app.config file maps the related nodes in the Web.config file from the service. This is important to remember in case you want to implement a custom configuration different from the default one. The bindings node defines how data and information are transferred. The `basicHttpBinding` binding is the simplest way and uses HTTP and Text or XML as the encoding format. WCF offers lots of other bindings specific for particular needs, such as secured communications or peer-to-peer applications. Table 37.3 summarizes built-in bindings.

TABLE 37.3   WCF Built-in Bindings

Binding	Description
BasicHttpBinding	Used for ASP.NET-based web services. It uses the HTTP protocol and text or XML for messages encoding.
WSHttpBinding	Used for secured communications in non-duplex service contracts.
WSDualHttpBinding	Used for secured communications in duplex service contracts including SOAP.
WSFederationHttpBinding	Used for secured communications according to the WS-Federation protocol that provides an easy authentication and authorization system within a federation.
NetTcpBinding	Used for secured communications between WCF applications distributed across multiple machines.

Binding	Description
NetNamedPipeBinding	Used for secured communications between WCF applications on the same machine.
NetMsmqBinding	Used for messaging communications between WCF applications.
NetPeerTcpBinding	Used for peer-to-peer applications.
MsmqIntegrationBinding	Used for communications between WCF applications and MSMQ applications across multiple machines.
BasicHttpContextBinding	Similar to BasicHttpBinding but with the capability of enabling cookies.
NetTcpContextBinding	Used for communications between WCF applications that need to use SOAP headers for data exchange across multiple machines.
WebHttpBinding	Used for WCF services exposed via endpoints requiring HTTP requests instead of SOAP endpoints.
WSHttpContextBinding	Similar to WsHttpBinding with the ability of enabling SOAP headers for information exchange.

In addition to built-in bindings, WCF enables defining custom bindings, but this is beyond the scope of this chapter.

IMPLEMENTING SECURE BINDINGS ON BOTH SERVICE AND CLIENTS

The current code example uses, on both the service side and client side, the basicHttp-Binding, which is the simplest binding available. Using a different binding depends on the particular scenario you need to work on. Because of this, look at the official MSDN documentation related to built-in bindings, which also provides examples and explanations on when each binding should be used. The documentation is located at the following address: http://msdn.microsoft.com/en-us/library/ms730879(v=vs.110).aspx.

37

You can also customize timeouts by specifying the closeTimeout, openTimeout, send-Timeout, and receiveTimeOut properties; you could change the maximum size for data exchange by setting maxBufferSize and maxReceivedMessageSize. These two are important because you might be required to increase the default size in case your application transfers large amounts of data. Now take a look at the client node. This defines the endpoint's ABC, such as the address pointing to the physical URI of the service, the binding transport protocol, and the contract interface (BookServiceReference. IBookService). Notice that when moving the service to production, the address URI must be replaced with the Internet/intranet address of your service. This can be accomplished by replacing the address item in the configuration file without the need of rebuilding the application.

Handling Exceptions in WCF

WCF applications can throw communication exceptions that both services and clients need to handle. Typically, the most common exception in the WCF development is the `System.ServiceModel.FaultException`; it offers a generic, strongly typed flavor and a nongeneric one. The exception needs to first be handled in the WCF service, but the nongeneric implementation is less useful than the generic one because it provides less detailed information. Because of this, it is now important to consider how to handle the `FaultException(Of T)`. Replace the `ValidateBook` method definition in the `IBookService` interface as follows:

```
<OperationContract()> <FaultContract(GetType(Book))>
Function ValidateBook(bookToValidate As Book) As String
```

The `FaultContract` attribute receives the type that might encounter processing errors during the invocation of the service operation. This can enable the `FaultException` to throw detailed SOAP information for that type. To accomplish this, replace the `ValidateBook` method implementation in the `BookService` class with the following:

```
Public Function ValidateBook(bookToValidate As Book) As _
            String Implements IBookService.ValidateBook

    Try
        Dim isValidIsbn As Boolean = Regex.IsMatch(String.
                            Concat("ISBN-13: ",
                            bookToValidate.ISBN), isbnPattern)

        If isValidIsbn = False Then
            Return "Invalid ISBN"
        End If

        Dim isValidAuthor As Boolean = _
            String.IsNullOrEmpty(bookToValidate.Author)
        If isValidAuthor = True Then
            Return "Author not specified"
        End If

        Dim isValidTitle As Boolean = _
            String.IsNullOrEmpty(bookToValidate.Title)
        If isValidTitle = True Then
            Return "Title not specified"
        End If
```

```
        If bookToValidate.DatePublished Is Nothing Then
            Return _
            "Book data is valid but date published was not specified"
        End If

        Return "Valid book"

    Catch ex As FaultException(Of Book)
        Throw New FaultException(Of Book)(bookToValidate,
                                    ex.Reason, ex.Code)
    Catch ex As Exception
        Throw
    End Try
End Function
```

The intercepted `FaultException` is rethrown to the caller specifying the instance of the `Book` class that caused the error, a `Reason` property that contains a SOAP description of the problem, and a `Code` property that returns a machine-readable identifier used for understanding the problem. With these pieces of information, client applications can understand what the problem was during the communication.

Hosting WCF Services in Internet Information Services and Microsoft Azure

Host applications for WCF services can be of various kinds. Besides IIS Express, you can host services inside managed applications, Windows services, and Internet Information Services as well. In most cases, you will need to deploy to IIS, so that scenario is covered here. To host your WCF service in IIS on your development machine, follow these steps:

1. Restart Visual Studio 2015 under administrator privileges.

2. Go to the My Project designer for the WCF service project and select the **Web** tab.

3. Select the **Local IIS** option and specify, if required, a different directory; then rerun the WCF service (see Figure 37.6).

37

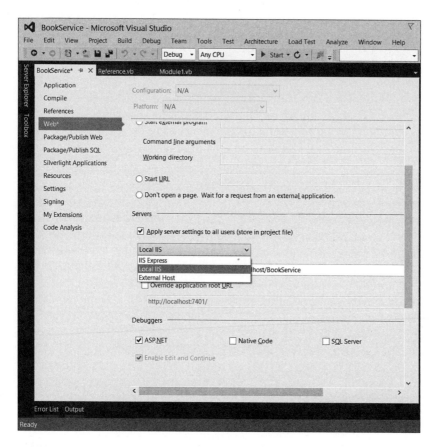

FIGURE 37.6   Setting IIS as the deployment web server.

Visual Studio will request your permission for creating and configuring a virtual directory on IIS, so you just need to accept it. When this is done, remember to replace the endpoint address in the client application configuration file with the new service URI. To publish a WCF service to a production machine, you can take advantage of the Web Publish dialog discussed in Chapter 34, "Building and Publishing ASP.NET Web Applications." From here, you can choose to easily deploy your service to an on-premise IIS server or to an Azure website. In this case, unlike with ASP.NET applications, you need an existing website.

Configuring Services with the Configuration Editor

WCF services enable high-level customizations over their configuration. This task can be complex if you consider that there are hundreds of options that you should translate into XML. Fortunately, the .NET Framework offers a graphical tool called WCF Service Configuration Editor that you can also launch from the Tools menu in Visual Studio. In this section, you see how this tool can be used to enable tracing for WCF services. Tracing is useful because it lets you record into log file (with .svclog extension) events occurring during the WCF service running time. When launched, open the Web.config file for your service. When ready, click the **Diagnostics** folder on the left and then click the **Enable Tracing** command under the Tracing title on the right (see Figure 37.7).

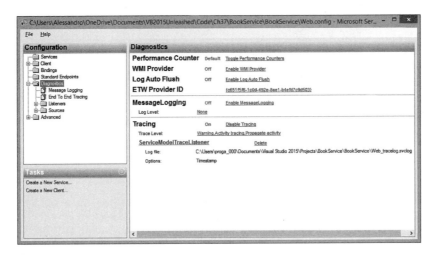

FIGURE 37.7   Enabling tracing for WCF services.

By default, tracing records messages classified at least as warnings. To modify this behavior, click the **Trace Level** link. If you click the **ServiceModelTraceListener** link, you can also specify additional information to be tracked, such as the process ID, the call stack, and the Thread ID. To view the log of recorded information, you need to run the Service Trace Viewer tool located in the C:\Program Files (x86)\Microsoft SDKs\Windows\ v10.0A\bin\NETFX 4.6 Tools folder on 64-bit machines (or C:\Program Files\Microsoft SDKs\Windows\v10.0A\bin\NETFX 4.6 Tools on 32-bit systems). When the tool is running, open the .svclog file, which usually resides in the service folder. Figure 37.8 shows an example of log analysis. The tool provides tons of information about every event occurring at the service level and is helpful if you encounter any problems.

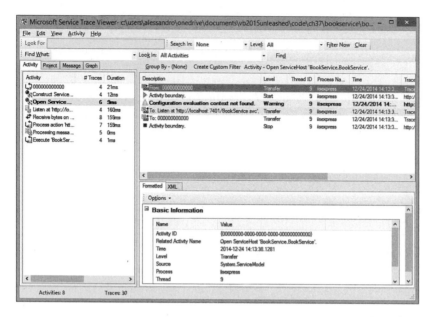

FIGURE 37.8   The Service Trace Viewer tool in action.

Summary

Windows Communication Foundation is a unified programming model for distributed applications that share information across networks. In this chapter, you got an introductory overview and then learned the basics about metadata. You learned that WCF services expose endpoints to be accessible from clients and that each endpoint exposes the ABC (Address-Binding-Contract). The contract is a .NET interface (marked with the ServiceContract attribute) that establishes service operations that can be consumed by clients. Services expose information and data through a class that implements the contract, which is the main entry point in the service. WCF services can also expose objects marked with the DataContract attribute and that represent data that services and clients can exchange. Next, you found out how to consume WCF services from clients by adding service references and creating proxy classes to access service members. The last part of this chapter provided an overview of exceptions handling and configurations with specific tools such as the Configuration Editor and the Service Trace Viewer.

CHAPTER 38

Implementing and Consuming OData Services

The growth of networks such as the Internet or local intranets increased the need to implement infrastructures for data exchange between companies or among users. Windows Communication Foundation (WCF) introduced an important unified programming model for information exchange over networks, but implementing a custom logic is not always an easy task. To share and consume data more easily, you can leverage the Open Data Protocol (OData), a very popular standard that offers a unified programming model based on HTTP requests and that, from a .NET perspective, you implement via ASP.NET and consume via specific client libraries. With OData you can easily propagate various kinds of data sources based on the .NET Framework. In this chapter you get started building data-oriented applications with OData, .NET Framework, and Visual Basic 2015.

What Are OData Services?

With OData services you expose data through networks, such as the Internet or a local intranet. Clients work with data by sending HTTP requests to the service and get back the appropriate response. Requests are based on the Open Data Protocol, which provides a standardized way to query and manipulate data. OData uses ATOM (that is, XML) and JavaScript Object Notation (JSON, a text-based format used in AJAX applications) serialization modes, and it can be used in an infinite number of scenarios because it is based on a pure web approach rather than on a specific technology. OData exposes data as resources that can be reached via URIs. Clients access and update data by using standard HTTP verbs such as GET, PUT, POST, and DELETE.

OData exposes resources as *feeds* and implements the entity-relationship conventions of the Entity Data Models (EDMs) so that data services can expose entity sets and related data under the form of resources that are related by associations. OData services can propagate through networks several types of data sources—not only entity data models but also in-memory collections that can be consumed by several kinds of client applications, both Windows and web. These include WPF, Windows Forms, Windows Store apps, and ASP.NET Web Forms or MVC.

If you have already had experience with OData, you might need to know about some important changes. The OData protocol was originally created by Microsoft but now is held by the Oasis consortium (www.oasis-open.org), whose goal is to promote open standards in the IT world. The official specifications for the OData protocol are available at https://www.oasis-open.org/standards#odatav4.0. You should rely on this page only and disregard any other information source. OData's current version is 4.0, usually referred to as OData v4. OData v4 has many important changes compared to v3.

From a development perspective, Microsoft is gradually discontinuing the well-known WCF Data Services platform in favor of the most recent ASP.NET Web API. This framework makes it easy to build HTTP, REST-enabled services that can be available to a plethora of clients. These services allow better integration with ASP.NET Web applications, are more powerful, and allow great control over data access via controllers. Today ASP.NET Web APIs support both OData v3 and OData v4, but this chapter focuses on OData v4. To make this possible, Microsoft created specific libraries for both the server side and the client side.

In this chapter you will get started building an OData service with Visual Basic 2015 and then learn how to consume data exposed by the service from a client application. Finally, you will discover interesting business logic customizations using Web APIs.

Creating an OData Endpoint

The first thing you need to do in order to expose data through a network is build an OData service. Clients will be able to reach this service via an endpoint, and it will allow them to perform HTTP requests via a URL. The OData service is exposed by an ASP.NET application, with Web API enabled. In Visual Studio 2015, select **File, New Project** and then select the **ASP.NET Web Application** template (see Figure 38.1.) Name the new project **OrderService** and click **OK**.

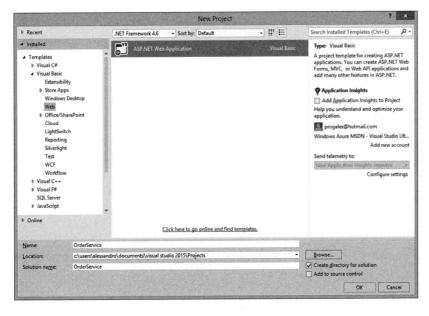

FIGURE 38.1   Creating a new web application for hosting an OData service.

When the New ASP.NET Project dialog appears, select the **Empty** template and ensure that
the **Web API** check box is selected, as shown in Figure 38.2.

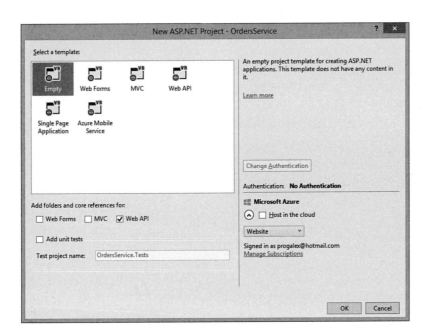

FIGURE 38.2   Selecting proper templates for the OData service.

You can embed an OData service within a more complex ASP.NET web application, but for the sake of simplicity, here you use the Empty template. Now you need to enable the new web application to support OData. Select **Tools, NuGet Package Manager, Package Manager Console** to activate the NuGet Console. NuGet is discussed in more detail in Chapter 52, "Advanced IDE Features." In the Console, type the following line:

```
Install-package Microsoft.AspNet.OData
```

This command downloads libraries that enable your application to support OData on the server side. Specifically, the libraries are Microsoft.OData.Core (which provides the core infrastructure for OData services), Microsoft.OData.Edm (which allows you to expose entity data models through OData-ready objects), Microsoft.Spatial (which allows you to represent geospatial objects as primitive types), and NewtonSoft.Json (which provides support for JSON serialization).

Adding a Data Model

The next step is to add a data model. In this example, you will add an Entity Data Model, but you are not limited to this scenario. You can also write custom business objects and then use specific classes (described shortly) to represent your business objects as EDMs. Using an existing database is a very common scenario, but you must be aware of possible incompatibilities between object types. For instance, OData v4 does not support the System.DateTime object; instead, it supports System.DateTimeOffset. For this reason, and because your data models will map your objects in the data store, in your SQL Server database, you must change the type for objects designed as datetime to datetimeoffset(7). For the current example, open the SQL Server Object Explorer tool window, connect to the Northwind database, and expand the tables until you see the Orders table. Right-click it and then select **View Design**. When the designer appears, replace the datetime type with datetimeoffset(7), as shown in Figure 38.3.

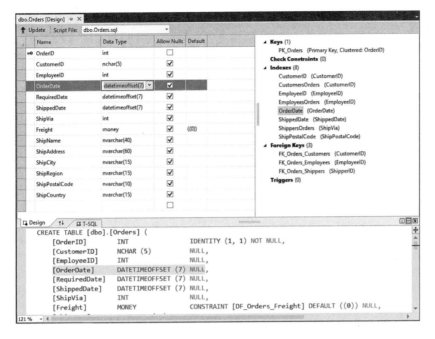

FIGURE 38.3   Replacing a `datetime` type with `datetimeoffset`.

Notice the following:

▶ You are making this change because you are working on a sample project. In real-world scenarios, you should design your databases and tables based on the actual requirements before building data-oriented applications.

▶ In case Visual Studio refuses to save changes because the table is dropped and re-created, you should use SQL Server Management Studio instead and disable the option **Prevent Saving Changes That Require Table Re-creation**.

Once you have made the proper replacement, right-click the project name in Solution Explorer and then select **Add, New Item**. In the Add New Item dialog, click the **Data** node and select the **ADO.NET Entity Data Model** template (see Figure 38.4). Name the new model Northwind and click OK.

FIGURE 38.4   Adding a new entity data model.

When the Entity Data Model Wizard starts, select the **Code First from Database** option (see Figure 38.5).

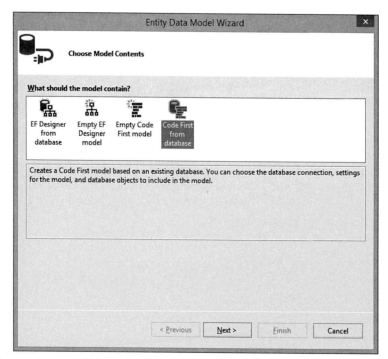

FIGURE 38.5   Selecting the Code First approach.

The Code First approach is the most appropriate when working with Web API because it allows you to better fine-tune the data model according to the OData requirements. In the next dialogs, you need to select the Northwind database and the Customers and Orders tables. To do this, you follow the same steps you already learned in previous chapters for creating an EDM. Visual Studio generates a new context class and two business objects, called `Customer` and `Order`, respectively. Listing 38.1 shows the context class definition.

LISTING 38.1   Context Class Definition

```
Imports System.Data.Entity

Partial Public Class Northwind
    Inherits DbContext

    Public Sub New()
        MyBase.New("name=Northwind")
    End Sub

    Public Overridable Property Customers As DbSet(Of Customer)
    Public Overridable Property Orders As DbSet(Of Order)

    Protected Overrides Sub OnModelCreating(ByVal modelBuilder As DbModelBuilder)
        modelBuilder.Entity(Of Customer)() _
            .Property(Function(e) e.CustomerID) _
            .IsFixedLength()

        modelBuilder.Entity(Of Order)() _
            .Property(Function(e) e.CustomerID) _
            .IsFixedLength()

        modelBuilder.Entity(Of Order)() _
            .Property(Function(e) e.Freight) _
            .HasPrecision(19, 4)
    End Sub
End Class
```

In the context class, note the `Customers` and `Orders` collection properties, of type `DbSet`. Listing 38.2 and Listing 38.3, respectively, show the `Customer` and `Order` object definitions.

LISTING 38.2   Customer Class

```
Imports System.ComponentModel.DataAnnotations

Partial Public Class Customer
    Public Sub New()
        Orders = New HashSet(Of Order)()
```

38

```vb
        End Sub

        <StringLength(5)>
        Public Property CustomerID As String

        <Required>
        <StringLength(40)>
        Public Property CompanyName As String

        <StringLength(30)>
        Public Property ContactName As String

        <StringLength(30)>
        Public Property ContactTitle As String

        <StringLength(60)>
        Public Property Address As String

        <StringLength(15)>
        Public Property City As String

        <StringLength(15)>
        Public Property Region As String

        <StringLength(10)>
        Public Property PostalCode As String

        <StringLength(15)>
        Public Property Country As String

        <StringLength(24)>
        Public Property Phone As String

        <StringLength(24)>
        Public Property Fax As String

        Public Overridable Property Orders As ICollection(Of Order)
End Class
```

LISTING 38.3 Order Class

```vb
Imports System.ComponentModel.DataAnnotations
Imports System.ComponentModel.DataAnnotations.Schema

Partial Public Class Order
```

```
    Public Property OrderID As Integer

    <StringLength(5)>
    Public Property CustomerID As String

    Public Property EmployeeID As Integer?

    Public Property OrderDate As DateTimeOffset?

    Public Property RequiredDate As DateTimeOffset?

    Public Property ShippedDate As DateTimeOffset?

    Public Property ShipVia As Integer?

    <Column(TypeName:="money")>
    Public Property Freight As Decimal?

    <StringLength(40)>
    Public Property ShipName As String

    <StringLength(60)>
    Public Property ShipAddress As String

    <StringLength(15)>
    Public Property ShipCity As String

    <StringLength(15)>
    Public Property ShipRegion As String

    <StringLength(10)>
    Public Property ShipPostalCode As String

    <StringLength(15)>
    Public Property ShipCountry As String

    Public Overridable Property Customer As Customer
End Class
```

This implementation allows you to represent a one-to-many relationship, where one customer can have many orders. The Customer class has a property Orders of type ICollection(Of Order), which contains the list of orders per customer. The Orders class has a Customer property of type Customer, which handles a reference to the related customer. Notice that the Order class correctly maps the datetimeoffset(7) SQL type with the System.DateTimeOffset .NET type. Also notice that most properties have been decorated with attributes from the `System.ComponentModel.Annotations` namespace; such attributes typically express validation rules (such as `Required` and `StringLength`) and additional mapping information (such as `Column`). Next, you will build the project in order to update all references in your code.

Enabling Code First Migration

To work with the Web API, you need to implement the Code First Migrations tool. Code First Migrations is very useful when you work on a new data model that changes frequently when you develop a new application. It basically allows you to update a database with only changes you made to the data model, which means you don't need to drop and re-create the database every time; this ensures that your data model and the database are in sync. Even though you are working with an existing, well-designed database in this case, you must enable Code First Migrations. To do this, in the Package Manager Console type the following line:

```
Enable-migrations
```

This adds a new `Configuration` class to the project, which is responsible for syncing the model with the database. Investigating code migration is not the focus of this chapter, but you can refer to the following article in the Data Development Center from MSDN for more information: https://msdn.microsoft.com/en-us/data/jj591621.aspx.

Registering the OData Service

When you create any Web API service, Visual Studio 2015 generates a file called WebApiConfig.vb, which is located in the App_Start folder. By default, the code in this file defines a template for routing HTTP requests to web pages in the application. This works fine in a Web API normal service, but it must be changed when working with an OData service. For this reason, replace the default code with the following:

```
Imports System.Web.Http
Imports System.Web.OData.Builder
Imports System.Web.OData.Extensions

Public Module WebApiConfig
    Public Sub Register(ByVal config As HttpConfiguration)
        Dim builder As New ODataConventionModelBuilder()
        builder.EntitySet(Of Customer)("Customers")
        builder.EntitySet(Of Order)("Orders")
        config.MapODataServiceRoute("northwind", Nothing, builder.GetEdmModel())
    End Sub
End Module
```

The `ODataConventionModelBuilder` class allows you to build an object model based on the EDM, according to the OData protocol specifications. The `EntitySet` generic method allows you to represent entity sets based on the specified business object instance, and its argument contains the plural name for the entity set. The `HttpConfiguration`.

`MapODataServiceRoute` method specifies routing rules for the OData service. More specifically, the first argument represents the name of the service as it will be used with HTTP requests; the second argument optionally contains a route prefix, which is not necessary in this case, so it is set as `Nothing`; the third argument is an object of type `Microsoft.OData.Edm.IEdmModel` and represents the object model generated based on the EDM. The object model is generated by invoking the `GetEdmModel` method on the current `ODataConventionModelBuilder` instance. Once you have registered the service with this code, clients know how to reach it via HTTP.

Adding Controllers

Controllers are classes that expose members which perform actions against data. In a Web API–enabled OData service, controllers expose methods that clients (including web browsers) invoke in order to send HTTP requests to the service. Visual Studio 2015 makes it easier to generate controllers for your entities by doing most of the work for you. You need to generate one controller for each entity in the data model. In Solution Explorer, right-click the Controllers folder and then select **Add, New Scaffolded Item**. When the Add Scaffold dialog appears, select the **Web API 2 Controller with Actions, Using Entity Framework** template (see Figure 38.6) and then click **Add**.

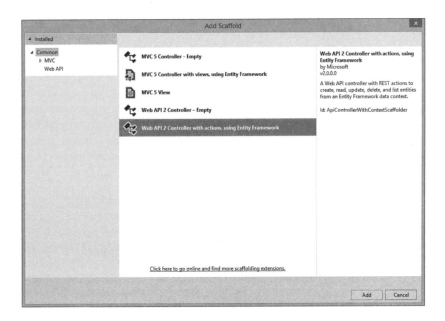

FIGURE 38.6   Adding a new scaffolded item.

At this point, the Add Controller dialog appears. Here you have to specify the entity that the controller will be generated for, as well as the context class. The controller name will be auto-generated based on the entity name. Select the `Customer` entity and the `Northwind` context class and then select the **Use Async Controller Actions** option, as shown in Figure 38.7.

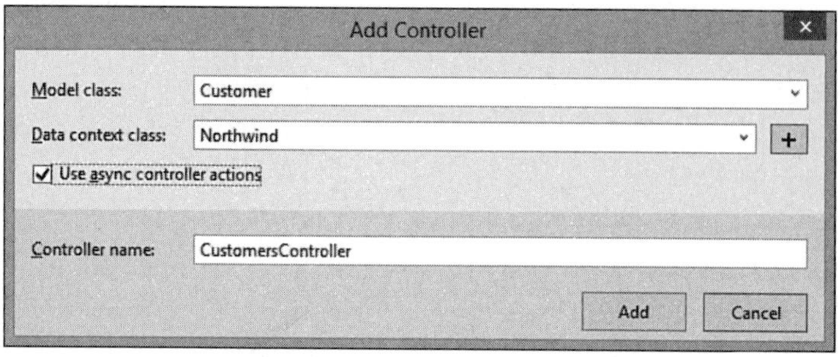

FIGURE 38.7   Specifying controller options.

When you click **OK**, a new `CustomerController` class is generated. Before we discuss the controller's details, you should repeat the same steps with the `Order` entity so that a controller called `OrderController` is also generated.

By default, controllers inherit from the `System.Web.Http.ApiController` class, and they expose auto-generated methods that interact with the data model for querying and manipulating data. However, you need to make some edits in order to make controllers work with the OData protocol. For each controller, you first need to add an `Imports System.Web.OData` directive. Next, you need to replace inheritance for each controller from `ApiController` to `ODataController`. `ODataController` still inherits from `ApiController` and is required because the latter has built-in support for JSON serialization and deserialization, and this is how OData v4 exchanges information. You then need to modify method definitions for both queries and CRUD operations.

Implementing Queries

Every auto-generated method name recalls an HTTP action; for instance, the `CustomerController` class has `GetCustomers` to return the list of customers, `PostCustomer` to add a new customer, `PutCustomer` to edit an existing customer instance, and so on. This works in a classic Web API scenario, but an OData service requires method names to exactly match HTTP verbs. In addition, you need to change method bodies that include code that is specific to Web API and not to OData.

The first thing you change is the `Get` action. You see two methods, `GetCustomers` (which returns the full list of customers) and `GetCustomer` (which returns a single customer instance). Both names must be replaced with `Get`, which matches the same-named HTTP verb. The following code demonstrates this:

```
<EnableQuery> Public Async Function [Get]() As Task(Of List(Of Customer))
    Return Await db.Customers.ToListAsync
End Function
```

```
<EnableQuery>
Public Function [Get](<FromODataUri> key As String) _
      As SingleResult(Of Customer)
    Dim result = db.Customers.Where(Function(c) c.CustomerID = key)
    Return SingleResult.Create(result)
End Function
```

The first method has been decorated with the `EnableQuery` attribute to make it visible to clients. It has also been rewritten using the asynchronous pattern, which is discussed more thoroughly in Chapter 42, "Asynchronous Programming," and Chapter 36, "Building Universal Apps for Windows 10." It simply returns the full list of customers, but you can edit the query as much as you like. The second method takes a single customer based on its ID—that is, the `CustomerID` property of type `String`. Notice how the `<FromODataUri>` attribute is applied to the method argument. This allows you to convert the ID passed by clients into the appropriate OData format. The method returns an object of type `System. Web.Http.SingleResult`, which represents an `IQueryable` object that contains zero or one entities and is specifically designed to work with OData services. In this case, such an object contains a single customer instance. Similarly, you replace query methods in the `OrdersController` class as follows:

```
<EnableQuery> Public Async Function [Get]() As Task(Of List(Of Order))
    Return Await db.Orders.ToListAsync
End Function

<EnableQuery>
Public Function [Get](<FromODataUri> key As Integer) As _
      SingleResult(Of Order)
    Dim result = db.Orders.Where(Function(o) o.OrderID = key)
    Return SingleResult.Create(result)
End Function
```

Implementing CRUD Operations

The next step is to implement CRUD operations. For queries, methods in the OData service must match HTTP verbs. Adding a new object through an OData service is done via the POST verb. So you need to replace the `PostCustomer` method with the following:

```
<ResponseType(GetType(Customer))>
Async Function Post(ByVal customer As Customer) _
      As Task(Of IHttpActionResult)
    If Not ModelState.IsValid Then
        Return BadRequest(ModelState)
    End If

    db.Customers.Add(customer)

    Try
```

```
        Await db.SaveChangesAsync()
    Catch ex As DbUpdateException
        If (CustomerExists(customer.CustomerID)) Then
            Return Conflict()
        Else
            Throw
        End If
    End Try


    Return Created(customer)
End Function
```

The code is pretty simple. It checks whether the object model is in a valid state via the `ApiController.ModelState.IsValid` property. If the state is invalid, it invokes the `ApiController.BadRequest` method, passing the `ModelState` instance, so that the caller gets back an error. If it is valid, the code adds the object instance to the entity set and saves changes. Exception handling returns a conflict error if an object with the same ID exists; otherwise, it rethrows the exception.

Deleting an object is accomplished via the DELETE verb, which is mapped by the `Delete` method. Replace `DeleteCustomer` with the following:

```
<ResponseType(GetType(Customer))>
Async Function Delete(<FromODataUri> ByVal id As String) As _
    Task(Of IHttpActionResult)
    Dim customer As Customer = Await db.Customers.FindAsync(id)
    If IsNothing(customer) Then
        Return NotFound()
    End If


    db.Customers.Remove(customer)
    Await db.SaveChangesAsync()


    Return StatusCode(HttpStatusCode.NoContent)
End Function
```

Notice how the method identifies the object via the `id` method argument, which is decorated with the `FromODataUri` attribute. The code first checks whether the object instance exists. If it does not, it invokes the `NotFound` method, which basically returns a "404 – Not Found" error to clients. If the object instance is available, the object is removed from the collection, and changes are saved. Methods like `Delete`, `Put`, and `Patch` must return an HTTP status code. This is accomplished by invoking the `ApiController.StatusCode` method and passing the `HttpStatusCode.NoContent` value. `HttpStatusCode` is an enumeration that contains a number of values, each representing HTTP status code numbers. IntelliSense will show the full list and the status code for each value in the enumeration.

Updating entities is accomplished via two HTTP verbs, PUT and PATCH. The first replaces an entity as a whole, whereas the second method allows you to replace only specific edits made to an entity. Auto-generated controllers do not have a definition for the Patch method, so you should supply one. The following is the code for the Put and Patch methods:

```vb
<ResponseType(GetType(Void))> <EnableQuery>
Async Function Put(<FromODataUri> ByVal id As String,
                   ByVal customer As Customer) As _
                   Task(Of IHttpActionResult)

    If Not ModelState.IsValid Then
        Return BadRequest(ModelState)
    End If
    If id <> customer.CustomerID Then
        Return BadRequest()
    End If
    db.Entry(customer).State = EntityState.Modified
    Try
        Await db.SaveChangesAsync()
    Catch generatedExceptionName As DbUpdateConcurrencyException
        If Not CustomerExists(id) Then
            Return NotFound()
        Else
            Throw
        End If
    End Try
    Return Updated(customer)
End Function


<ResponseType(GetType(Void))>
Public Async Function Patch(<FromODataUri> key As String,
                            Customer As Delta(Of Customer)) _
                            As Task(Of IHttpActionResult)
    If Not ModelState.IsValid Then
        Return BadRequest(ModelState)
    End If
    Dim entity = Await db.Customers.FindAsync(key)
    If entity Is Nothing Then
        Return NotFound()
    End If
    Customer.Patch(entity)
    Try
        Await db.SaveChangesAsync()
    Catch generatedExceptionName As DbUpdateConcurrencyException
        If Not CustomerExists(key) Then
```

```
            Return NotFound()
        Else
            Throw
        End If
    End Try
    Return Updated(entity)
End Function
```

The behavior of `Put` and `Patch` is very similar, as they first check for a valid model state
and then they find the object instance via its ID. The main difference is that `Put` method
sets the entity instance's state as `EntityState.Modified`, to make the service understand
that it has been changed. This is not done in `Patch` because the instance is represented
by an object of type `Delta(Of T)` (see the method signature), a class that tracks specific
changes for the given entity; this avoids the need of considering an entity to be modified
as a whole. Both methods then save changes and return a "404 – Not Found" if the object
does not exist or a successful result via the `ODataController.Updated` method. Listing 38.4
shows the edits that you must perform on the `OrderController` class (but does not show
other auto-generated methods).

LISTING 38.4   `OrderController` Class

```
Public Class OrdersController
    Inherits ODataController

    Private db As New Northwind

    ' GET: api/Orders
    <EnableQuery> Public Async Function [Get]() As Task(Of List(Of Order))
        Return Await db.Orders.ToListAsync
    End Function

    ' GET: api/Orders/5
    <EnableQuery>
    Public Function [Get](<FromODataUri> key As Integer) As _
            SingleResult(Of Order)
        Dim result = db.Orders.Where(Function(o) o.OrderID = key)
        Return SingleResult.Create(result)
    End Function

    ' PUT: api/Orders/5
    <ResponseType(GetType(Void))>
    Async Function Put(<FromODataUri> ByVal id As Integer,
        ByVal order As Order) As Task(Of IHttpActionResult)
        If Not ModelState.IsValid Then
            Return BadRequest(ModelState)
        End If
```

```vbnet
        If Not id = order.OrderID Then
            Return BadRequest()
        End If

        db.Entry(order).State = EntityState.Modified

        Try
            Await db.SaveChangesAsync()
        Catch ex As DbUpdateConcurrencyException
            If Not (OrderExists(id)) Then
                Return NotFound()
            Else
                Throw
            End If
        End Try

        Return Updated(order)
    End Function

    <ResponseType(GetType(Void))>
    Public Async Function Patch(<FromODataUri> key As Integer,
                            order As Delta(Of Order)) _
                            As Task(Of IHttpActionResult)
        If Not ModelState.IsValid Then
            Return BadRequest(ModelState)
        End If
        Dim entity = Await db.Orders.FindAsync(key)
        If entity Is Nothing Then
            Return NotFound()
        End If
        order.Patch(entity)
        Try
            Await db.SaveChangesAsync()
        Catch generatedExceptionName As DbUpdateConcurrencyException
            If Not OrderExists(key) Then
                Return NotFound()
            Else
                Throw
            End If
        End Try
        Return Updated(entity)
    End Function

    ' POST: api/Orders
    <ResponseType(GetType(Order))>
```

38

```vbnet
Async Function Post(ByVal order As Order) _
      As Task(Of IHttpActionResult)
    If Not ModelState.IsValid Then
        Return BadRequest(ModelState)
    End If

    db.Orders.Add(order)
    Try
        Await db.SaveChangesAsync()
    Catch ex As DbUpdateException
        If (OrderExists(order.OrderID)) Then
            Return Conflict()
        Else
            Throw
        End If
    End Try

    Return Created(order)
End Function

' DELETE: api/Orders/5
<ResponseType(GetType(Order))>
Async Function Delete(<FromODataUri> ByVal id As Integer) _
    As Task(Of IHttpActionResult)
    Dim order As Order = Await db.Orders.FindAsync(id)
    If IsNothing(order) Then
        Return NotFound()
    End If

    db.Orders.Remove(order)
    Await db.SaveChangesAsync()

    Return StatusCode(HttpStatusCode.NoContent)
End Function
End Class
```

Handling Relationships Between Entities

In the current example, the Customer and Order entities have a one-to-many relationship in which one customer can have many orders. In OData terminology, relationships are referred to as *references*. References are automatically managed by the .NET Framework, except when you create a new object and you must add a relationship, or when you update a relationship on an existing object. These situations are respectively represented by POST and PUT verbs. Suppose you want to handle situations in which you add new orders or update existing orders. In the `OrdersController` class, you need to add the following method (pay attention to the comments):

```
<AcceptVerbs("POST", "PUT")>
Public Async Function CreateRef(<FromODataUri> key As Integer,
        navigationProperty As String,
        <FromBody> link As Uri) As Task(Of IHttpActionResult)
    'Get the instance of an order
    Dim order = Await db.Orders.
        SingleOrDefaultAsync(Function(o) o.OrderID = key)

    'If null, return Not Found
    If order Is Nothing Then
        Return NotFound()
    End If

    'Find the navigation property
    Select Case navigationProperty
        'If Customer...
        Case "Customer"
            'Get the value of related Customer's CustomerID
            Dim relatedKey = GetKeyFromUri(Of String)(Request, link)
            'Get the Customer instance based on the CustomerID
            Dim customer = Await db.Customers.
                SingleOrDefaultAsync(Function(c) c.CustomerID = relatedKey)
            If customer Is Nothing Then
                Return NotFound()
            End If

            'Assign the customer instance to the Order.Customer property
            'This establishes a relationship
            order.Customer = customer
            Exit Select
        Case Else

            Return StatusCode(HttpStatusCode.NotImplemented)
    End Select
    Await db.SaveChangesAsync()
    Return StatusCode(HttpStatusCode.NoContent)
End Function
```

Notice how the `CreateRef` method is decorated with the `AcceptVerbs` attribute, which specifies HTTP verbs supported by the method. The code invokes another method, called `GetKeyFromUri`, which is responsible for retrieving an entity's ID from its URI:

```
Public Shared Function GetKeyFromUri(Of TKey)(request As HttpRequestMessage,
                            uri As Uri) As TKey
```

```
    If uri Is Nothing Then
        Throw New ArgumentNullException("uri")
    End If

    Dim urlHelper = If(request.GetUrlHelper(),
        New UrlHelper(request))

    Dim serviceRoot As String = urlHelper.
        CreateODataLink(request.ODataProperties().RouteName,
                        request.ODataProperties().PathHandler,
        New List(Of ODataPathSegment)())
    Dim odataPath = request.ODataProperties().
        PathHandler.Parse(request.ODataProperties().Model,
                          serviceRoot, uri.LocalPath)

    Dim keySegment = odataPath.Segments.
        OfType(Of KeyValuePathSegment)().FirstOrDefault()
    If keySegment Is Nothing Then
        Throw New InvalidOperationException("The link does not contain a key.")
    End If

    Dim value = ODataUriUtils.
        ConvertFromUriLiteral(keySegment.Value, ODataVersion.V4)
    Return value
End Function
```

This method invokes objects from the OData library to get the entity path (`UrlHelper.CreateODataLink`), split the URI path into segments (`HttpRequestMessage.ODataProperties.PathHandler.Parse`), find the segment that contains the key, and convert the key into the proper type and version of the OData protocol (`ODataUriUtils.ConvertFromUriLiteral`).

Publishing an OData Endpoint

Before you can consume an OData endpoint, you need to publish it to a web server. For debugging purposes, it is okay to use Internet Information Services Express, which is the default option in Visual Studio 2015. For production, you can choose either a local server or Microsoft Azure. Because in this case you have created an ASP.NET application, to publish your OData endpoint, you simply follow what you learned in Chapter 34, "Building and Publishing ASP.NET Applications," about deployment. For the current example, leave unchanged the IIS Express option, which is good for debugging on the development machine. The next steps are about showing the JSON representation for your data model. If you plan to use Microsoft Internet Explorer for your testing, ensure that you first follow these steps:

1. Open the Windows Registry Editor (Regedit.exe).

2. Locate the HKEY_CLASSES_ROOT\MIME\Database\Content Type key.

3. Search for the application/JSON key. If not available, right-click **Content Type**, select **New, Key**, and create one.

4. Add a String value named **CLSID**, with value of **{25336920-03F9-11cf-8FD0-00AA00686F13}**.

5. Add a DWord value named **Encoding**, with value of **80000**.

Figure 38.8 shows how the Registry Editor looks like at this point.

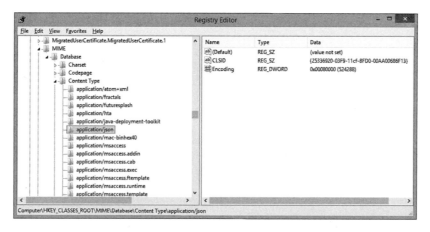

FIGURE 38.8   Setting registry values to show JSON values in Internet Explorer.

These edits are required because, by default, Internet Explorer does not show JSON representations, and it instead proposes to download JSON objects as text files. No changes are required if you instead plan to use Mozilla Firefox or Google Chrome. At this point, press **Ctrl+F5** to start the IIS Express development server and the OData endpoint with no debugger attached, so that the service will keep running even if you need to go back to Visual Studio and go on with development. Figure 38.9 shows how the web browser displays the JSON representation of the endpoint's URL and available entities.

38

FIGURE 38.9   Displaying JSON representations of endpoint and entity definitions.

Querying Data via HTTP Requests

Before you create .NET client applications, it is important to understand how HTTP requests can query and manipulate data over an OData service. When you have your service running inside your favorite web browser, you can manually type some requests. After all, a web browser is a 100% client. The first request you write is to show metadata. Metadata contain an XML representation of your data model, including full entity definition and additional objects, such as functions (described later in this chapter). You invoke the service metadata with the following syntax:

```
http://servername/servicename/$metadata
```

In the current example, the OData service is the only endpoint contained in the web application, so you can omit the *servicename* name. If the sample service is running on port 18407 of IIS Express, your request will be:

```
http://localhost:18407/$metadata
```

Figure 38.10 shows the XML metadata representation.

```
<?xml version="1.0" encoding="UTF-8"?>
- <edmx:Edmx xmlns:edmx="http://docs.oasis-open.org/odata/ns/edmx" Version="4.0">
    - <edmx:DataServices>
        - <Schema xmlns="http://docs.oasis-open.org/odata/ns/edm"
          Namespace="OrderService">
            - <EntityType Name="Customer">
                - <Key>
                    <PropertyRef Name="CustomerID"/>
                </Key>
                <Property Name="CustomerID" Nullable="false" Type="Edm.String"/>
                <Property Name="CompanyName" Nullable="false" Type="Edm.String"/>
                <Property Name="ContactName" Type="Edm.String"/>
                <Property Name="ContactTitle" Type="Edm.String"/>
                <Property Name="Address" Type="Edm.String"/>
                <Property Name="City" Type="Edm.String"/>
                <Property Name="Region" Type="Edm.String"/>
                <Property Name="PostalCode" Type="Edm.String"/>
                <Property Name="Country" Type="Edm.String"/>
                <Property Name="Phone" Type="Edm.String"/>
                <Property Name="Fax" Type="Edm.String"/>
                <NavigationProperty Name="Orders" Type="Collection(OrderService.Order)"/>
            </EntityType>
            - <EntityType Name="Order">
                - <Key>
                    <PropertyRef Name="OrderID"/>
                </Key>
                <Property Name="OrderID" Nullable="false" Type="Edm.Int32"/>
                <Property Name="CustomerID" Type="Edm.String"/>
                <Property Name="EmployeeID" Type="Edm.Int32"/>
                <Property Name="OrderDate" Type="Edm.DateTimeOffset"/>
                <Property Name="RequiredDate" Type="Edm.DateTimeOffset"/>
                <Property Name="ShippedDate" Type="Edm.DateTimeOffset"/>
                <Property Name="ShipVia" Type="Edm.Int32"/>
                <Property Name="Freight" Type="Edm.Decimal"/>
                <Property Name="ShipName" Type="Edm.String"/>
                <Property Name="ShipAddress" Type="Edm.String"/>
                <Property Name="ShipCity" Type="Edm.String"/>
                <Property Name="ShipRegion" Type="Edm.String"/>
                <Property Name="ShipPostalCode" Type="Edm.String"/>
                <Property Name="ShipCountry" Type="Edm.String"/>
                - <NavigationProperty Name="Customer" Type="OrderService.Customer">
                    <ReferentialConstraint ReferencedProperty="CustomerID"
                      Property="CustomerID"/>
                </NavigationProperty>
            </EntityType>
```

FIGURE 38.10   Metadata representation of entities.

Now suppose you want to query the full list of customers. This can be accomplished with the following request:

```
http://localhost:18407/Customers
```

This request invokes the Get method exposed by the CustomersController class in your service. Notice that requests are case-sensitive and must match the entity set names you registered in the Register method of the WebApiConfig module, so Customers is different from customers. Figure 38.11 shows the JSON representation for the Customers entity set.

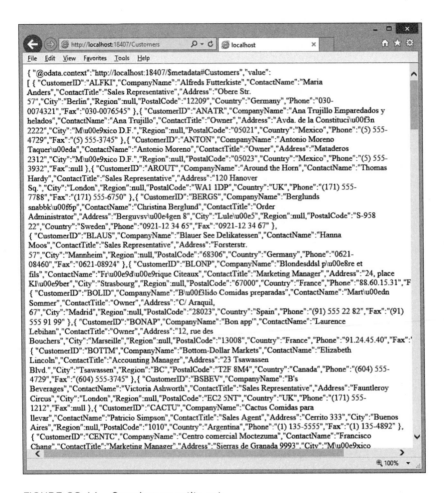

FIGURE 38.11   Querying an entity set.

If you wanted to show only one specific customer, your request would look like the following:

```
http://localhost:18407/Customers('ALFKI')
```

This request would produce the result shown in Figure 38.12.

Your query string must include the ID for your entity, which is typically the primary key. If an entity has related objects, you can easily write a request like the following, which returns orders for the specified customer:

```
http://localhost:18407/Customers('ALFKI')?$expand=Orders
```

The ?$expand query option allows you to return a collection of related entities. Figure 38.13 shows the JSON representation for the preceding request.

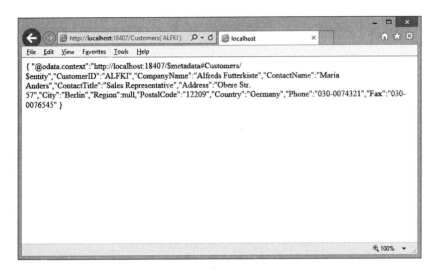

FIGURE 38.12   Querying a single entity.

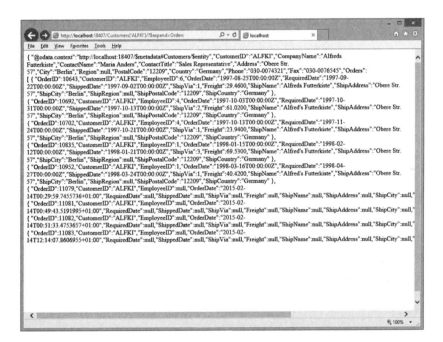

FIGURE 38.13   Querying a single entity with a relationship.

You can also filter an entity set by using the `$filter` query options. The following request, for example, retrieves the list of customers residing in London:

```
http://localhost:18407/Customers?$filter=City eq 'London'
```

Where eq stands for *equals*. This request returns the result shown in Figure 38.14.

FIGURE 38.14   Filtering an entity set.

You can combine multiple query options by using the & symbol, as in the following example, which takes the first 100 entities ($top) and sorts the list by city ($orderby):

http://localhost:18407/Customers?$top=100&$orderby=City

Query options are very powerful and allow complex HTTP requests, including paging. The full list of query options in OData v4 is available at http://docs.oasis-open.org/odata/odata/v4.0/odata-v4.0-part2-url-conventions.html. Now that you have a clearer idea of how an OData service receives and addresses HTTP requests, you are ready to build a .NET client application.

Consuming OData Services

Any .NET client application can consume an OData service like the sample service you built previously. To make this happen, you must use special client libraries for OData. Microsoft offers the Microsoft.OData.Client library as a NuGet package, which allows you to query and manipulate data over an OData v4 service. Microsoft has also created an extension for Visual Studio called OData Client Code Generator, which simplifies the generation of proxy classes to interact with data models exposed by an OData service. Unfortunately, this tools is only available for the Visual C# programming language, so you need to perform some more manual work. The next subsections explain how to consume the preceding OData service from a Console .NET client application. You will implement query and CRUD operations in a way that will be reusable in different clients.

Creating a Client Application

The goal of the next example is to show how you can perform read/insert/update/delete operations against an OData service from a client. Add a new Console project to the current solution and name it **ClientApp**. Next, in the Package Manager Console type the following instruction:

```
Install-package Microsoft.OData.Client
```

This installs the required libraries for clients, including the following assemblies:

- ▶ Microsoft.OData.Client.dll

- ▶ Microsoft.OData.Core.dll

- ▶ Microsoft.OData.Edm.dll

- ▶ Microsoft.Spatial.dll

You have to map entities on the client application. This is an easy step because you just need to copy the `Customer` and `Order` class definitions from the OData service. For a perfect mapping, add a reference to the System.ComponentModel.DataAnnotations.dll assembly. Then copy the class definitions for both entities, as summarized in Listing 38.5.

LISTING 38.5   `Customer` and `Order` Classes for Data Mapping

```
Imports System.ComponentModel.DataAnnotations
Imports System.ComponentModel.DataAnnotations.Schema

Public Class Customer
    Public Sub New()
        Orders = New HashSet(Of Order)()
    End Sub

    <StringLength(5)>
    Public Property CustomerID As String

    <Required>
    <StringLength(40)>
    Public Property CompanyName As String

    <StringLength(30)>
    Public Property ContactName As String

    <StringLength(30)>
    Public Property ContactTitle As String
```

38

```vbnet
        <StringLength(60)>
        Public Property Address As String

        <StringLength(15)>
        Public Property City As String

        <StringLength(15)>
        Public Property Region As String

        <StringLength(10)>
        Public Property PostalCode As String

        <StringLength(15)>
        Public Property Country As String

        <StringLength(24)>
        Public Property Phone As String

        <StringLength(24)>
        Public Property Fax As String

        Public Overridable Property Orders As ICollection(Of Order)
End Class
Public Class Order
        Public Property OrderID As Integer

        <StringLength(5)>
        Public Property CustomerID As String

        Public Property EmployeeID As Integer?

        Public Property OrderDate As DateTimeOffset?

        Public Property RequiredDate As DateTimeOffset?

        Public Property ShippedDate As DateTimeOffset?

        Public Property ShipVia As Integer?

        <Column(TypeName:="money")>
        Public Property Freight As Decimal?

        <StringLength(40)>
        Public Property ShipName As String
```

```
<StringLength(60)>
Public Property ShipAddress As String

<StringLength(15)>
Public Property ShipCity As String

<StringLength(15)>
Public Property ShipRegion As String

<StringLength(10)>
Public Property ShipPostalCode As String

<StringLength(15)>
Public Property ShipCountry As String

Public Overridable Property Customer As Customer
End Class
```

Now you need a way to interact with the OData service from a .NET perspective. The `Microsoft.OData.Client.DataServiceContext` class can be used for this purpose, since it represents the runtime context for the OData service in a managed way. This class exposes methods for querying and manipulating data, for invoking service functions, and for representing the most common query options. Since you cannot take advantage of code generation tools that only work in C# (and are not available to Visual Studio 2015 at this writing), you need to manually get a reference to the data model exposed by the OData service and convert the result into an in-memory Entity Data Model that the OData client library can understand. Start by creating a new class called `MyDataServiceClient`, which inherits from `DataServiceContext`, like the following:

```
Imports System.Net
Imports Microsoft.OData.Client
Imports Microsoft.OData.Edm

Public Class MyDataServiceClient
    Inherits DataServiceContext
End Class
```

Now take a look at the class's constructor:

```
Public Sub New(serviceRoot As Uri)
    MyBase.New(serviceRoot)
    Me.Format.LoadServiceModel = AddressOf Me.LoadServiceModel
    Me.Format.UseJson()
End Sub
```

It receives the service URI as the argument, and then it invokes the `DataServiceContext.Format.LoadServiceModel` method to get a reference to the data model from the OData service, via a delegate called `LoadServiceModel`, which you will implement shortly. The `UseJson` method invocation is instead required to specify the proper serialization and deserialization format for the data model. The following code defines the `LoadServiceModel` delegate:

```
Private Function LoadServiceModel() As IEdmModel
    'If no model exists in memory
    If model Is Nothing Then
        'Get the service metadata's Uri
        'e.g. http://localhost:18470/$metadata
        Dim metadataUri = Me.GetMetadataUri()

        'Create an HTTP request to the metadata's Uri
        'in order to get a representation for the data model
        Dim request = WebRequest.CreateHttp(metadataUri)

        'Wait for a response
        Using response = request.GetResponse()
            'Translate the response into an in-memory stream
            Using stream = response.GetResponseStream()
                'Convert the stream into an XML representation
                Using reader = System.Xml.XmlReader.Create(stream)
                    'Parse the XML representation of the data model
                    'into an Entity Data Model that can be utilized
                    'by OData client libraries
                    model = Csdl.EdmxReader.Parse(reader)
                End Using
            End Using
        End Using
    End If


    Return model
End Function
```

This method works directly against the service's metadata and converts the result into a proper Entity Data Model, using objects from the `Microsoft.OData.Edm` namespace (see the comments in the code). The next step is to expose the query results. The following two properties return the full list of customers and the full list of orders, respectively:

```
Public ReadOnly Property Customers As DataServiceQuery(Of Customer)
    Get
        Return CreateQuery(Of Customer)("Customers").
            Expand("Orders")
    End Get
End Property
```

```
Public ReadOnly Property Orders As DataServiceQuery(Of Order)
    Get
        Return CreateQuery(Of Order)("Orders")
    End Get
End Property
```

In its most basic usage, `CreateQuery(Of T)` is a generic method that returns an entity set of the specified type, and the result is of type `DataServiceQuery(Of T)`. This type allows you to perform additional operations over data, such as expand related entities. This is the case with the `Customers` property, which returns the `Customers` entity set and related `Orders`. You can specify additional query options via the `AddQueryOption` method. The following code demonstrates how to take the first five orders and sort by order data:

```
Return CreateQuery(Of Order)("Orders").
AddQueryOption("$top", "5").
AddQueryOption("$orderby", "OrderDate")
```

The first argument for `AddQueryOption` is one of the available query options, whereas the second argument is the value. The OData library automatically translates the method invocation into the proper HTTP requests and returns the result as `DataServiceQuery(Of T)`. Now that you have queries, you can finally consume the service.

Accessing and Querying Data

In order to access and manipulate data, you need to get a reference to the OData service by creating an instance of the `DataServiceContext` class—in this case the `MyDataServiceClient` implementation—and pass the service's URI as the argument for the constructor. In the `Main` method of your module, write the following code:

```
Module Module1

    Sub Main()
        Dim client As New MyDataServiceClient(New Uri("http://localhost:18407"))
    End Sub
End Module
```

Once you have a reference to the OData service, you can perform queries and other operations. For instance, you can easily retrieve the full list of customers and the full list of orders per customer with the following code:

```
For Each cust In client.Customers
    Console.WriteLine(cust.CompanyName)
    For Each ord In cust.Orders
        Console.WriteLine("      " + ord.OrderDate.ToString)
    Next
Next
```

Figure 38.15 shows the result of this code.

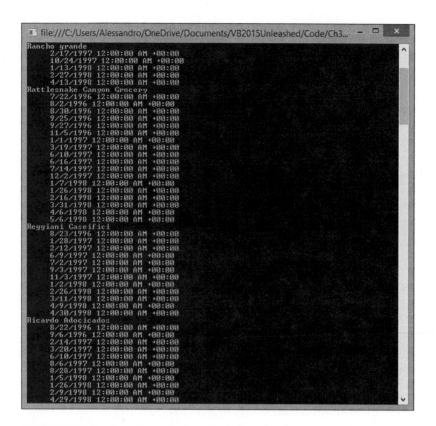

FIGURE 38.15   Querying data from the OData service.

Queries return `DataServiceQuery(Of T)`, which implements the `IEnumerable(Of T)` interface, and thus the queries support LINQ queries. As an example, the following query demonstrates how to select the `CompanyName` and `City` properties from customers residing in Italy:

```
Dim query = From cust In client.Customers
            Where cust.Country = "Italy"
            Select cust.CompanyName, cust.City
```

As another example, the following code demonstrates how to retrieve a specific instance of the `Customer` class with extension methods and lambda expressions and how to write a LINQ query to retrieve orders that have not shipped yet:

```
Dim aCustomer = client.Customers.Where(Function(c)
    c.CustomerID = "ALFKI").FirstOrDefault
Dim query = From ord In aCustomer.Orders
            Where ord.ShippedDate.HasValue = False
            Select ord
```

```
Console.
WriteLine("Orders not shipped yet for customer " & _
aCustomer.CompanyName)
For Each order In query
    Console.WriteLine(order.OrderID)
Next
```

You can definitely use all the available LINQ standard query operators to write complex queries. Refer to Chapter 23, "LINQ to Objects," for a more thorough discussion about LINQ standard query operators.

Performing CRUD Operations

The `DataServiceContext` class is responsible for tracking entities and changes made to entity instances. Changes are kept in memory until they are persisted to the data store with an explicit invocation to the `SaveChanges` method. To manipulate data, `DataServiceContext` exposes methods for executing create/read/update/delete (CRUD) operations. Specifically, it exposes the following methods:

▶ `AddObject` adds an instance of a business object into the data model through the OData service. It invokes the POST HTTP method.

▶ `DeleteObject` removes the specified instance of a business object from the data model. It invokes the DELETE HTTP verb.

▶ `UpdateObject` updates an existing instance of a business object in the data model. It invokes the PUT HTTP verb.

The following code demonstrates how to add a new `Order` object and specify a relationship to a specific `Customer` instance:

```
Console.WriteLine("Adding new order...")
Dim aCustomer = client.Customers.Where(Function(c)
    c.CustomerID = "ALFKI").FirstOrDefault
Dim newOrder As New Order With {.CustomerID = "ALFKI",
    .Customer = aCustomer,
    .OrderDate = DateTimeOffset.Now, .ShipCountry = "Italy"}

client.AddObject("Orders", newOrder)
client.SaveChanges()
```

The relationship is established by assigning the navigation property (`Order.Customer`) with the `Customer` instance. The `AddObject` method has two arguments. The first argument is the name for the entity set that will receive the new object instance, and the second argument is the instance itself. Similarly, you can update an existing object by retrieving the instance, update properties of interest, and then invoke `UpdateObject`. The following code demonstrates this:

```
Console.WriteLine("Updating order...")
Dim existingOrder = client.Orders.Where(Function(o)
    o.OrderID = "11081").FirstOrDefault
If existingOrder IsNot Nothing Then
    existingOrder.ShippedDate = DateTimeOffset.Now
    client.UpdateObject(existingOrder)
    client.SaveChanges()
End If
Console.WriteLine("Updating done.")
```

`UpdateObject` takes only one argument, which is the object instance. You delete an object by invoking `DeleteObject` and passing the object instance as the only argument. The following code provides an example based on the preceding `existingOrder` instance:

```
Console.WriteLine("Deleting order...")
client.DeleteObject(existingOrder)
client.SaveChanges()
Console.WriteLine("Deleting done.")
```

Because `DataServiceContext` tracks entities, you do not need to invoke `SaveChanges` at every operation. You can invoke it once to save changes in a batch. Remember that `DataServiceContext`'s methods follow some rules in the data store. For instance, you cannot delete an object if it has existing related objects unless you explicitly set a cascade rule for deletion in the database.

Implementing and Consuming Functions

OData services can expose functions. A *function* executes server-side operations and returns a result to the client. A function must be registered in the service configuration and must be implemented in the controller class that refers to the entity that the function works on. For example, suppose you want to execute a server-side query that returns the most recent order and that returns the result to caller clients. The function will work with the `Order` entity, and so it will be placed in the `OrdersController` class. In this controller, write the following code:

```
<HttpGet> <EnableQuery>
Public Function MostRecentOrder() As IHttpActionResult
    Dim maxDate = db.Orders.Max(Function(o) o.OrderDate)
    Dim query = db.Orders.Where(Function(o)
        o.OrderDate = maxDate).FirstOrDefault.OrderID


    Return Ok(query)
End Function
```

The method simply checks for the most recent `OrderDate` value with the `Max` extension method and then checks what `Order` object matches that value taking the `OrderID` integer value. Finally, it returns this value through an `IHttpActionResult` object, which creates a response of type `HttpResponseMessage` (which can be interpreted by web browsers and client libraries). Notice that the method is decorated with the `HttpGet` and `EnableQuery` methods. This is required to make clients invoke the function via a GET request. The next step is to register the function, so open the `WebApiConfig` module and add the following lines of code before the `MapODataServiceRoute` invocation:

```
builder.Namespace = "OrderService"
builder.EntityType(Of Order)().Collection.Function("MostRecentOrder").
        Returns(Of Integer)()
```

In order to invoke functions, you must first define a namespace via the `ODataConventionModelBuilder.Namespace` property. Defining a namespace is required in OData because clients invoke functions with their fully qualified name. Functions can be executed against a single entity or an entity set. You first invoke the generic method `EntityType(Of T)`, where `T` is the entity type. Then you invoke the `Function` method directly if the function works against a single entity, or you invoke `Function` on the `Collection` property if the function works against an entity set. The argument for `Function` is the function name. In the current example, the function determines the most recent order from an entity set, so `Function` is invoked over `Collection`. The final part of the function implementation is the `Returns(Of T)` method, where `T` is the return type, in this case `Integer`, which is the type for the `OrderID` property that the function will send back to callers. To invoke a function, clients must send an HTTP request like the following:

```
http://localhost:18470/OrderService.MostRecentOrder
```

As you can see, the request contains the namespace, a dot, and the function name. Notice that IIS might block requests containing the dot symbol; if this happens, you can replace the content for the `handlers` section in the Web.config file with the following:

```
<system.webServer>
    <clear/>
    <add name="ExtensionlessUrlHandler-Integrated-4.0" path="/*"
        verb="*" type="System.Web.Handlers.TransferRequestHandler"
        preCondition="integratedMode,runtimeVersionv4.0" />
    </handlers>
</system.webServer>
```

From the client perspective, functions must be invoked using the `DataServiceContext.Execute(Of T)` method, where `T` is the type for the expected function result. For the current example, extend the `MyDataServiceClient` class with the following property, which maps the `MostRecentOrder` function:

```
Public ReadOnly Property MostRecentOrder As Integer
    Get
        Dim query As Integer = Execute(Of Integer)
            (New Uri("/Orders/OrderService.MostRecentOrder",
            UriKind.Relative)).FirstOrDefault
```

38

```
        Return query
    End Get
End Property
```

`Execute` takes the function's URI as the argument. The URI requires you to specify the entity set name, the namespace, a dot, and the function name, and it must be a relative URI. Using the function result is very easy at this point. Your client code could simply invoke it like this:

```
Console.WriteLine(client.MostRecentOrder)
```

In addition to functions, OData v4 has actions. An *action* executes an operation on the server side, but it make changes to entities or entity sets. For example, the following action changes the `ShippedDate` property for the specified order to the current date:

```
<HttpPost> <EnableQuery>
Public Async Function ChangeShippedDate(<FromODataUri> OrderID As _
    Integer) As Task(Of IHttpActionResult)
    If Not ModelState.IsValid Then
        Return BadRequest()
    End If

    Dim order As Order = db.Orders.Where(Function(o)
        o.OrderID = OrderID).FirstOrDefault
    If IsNothing(order) Then
        Return NotFound()
    End If

    order.ShippedDate = DateTimeOffset.Now
    Await db.SaveChangesAsync()

    Return StatusCode(HttpStatusCode.NoContent)
End Function
```

Actions must be registered similarly to functions. The following code demonstrates how to register the `ChangeShippedDate` action in the `WebApiConfig` module:

```
builder.EntityType(Of Order).Action("ChangeShippedDate")
```

Like functions, actions can be executed against a single entity or entity sets. From the client perspective, you still invoke actions via the `DataServiceContext.Execute(Of T)` method. Functions and actions can have complex implementations, plus they can be bound to an entity (as in the preceding examples) or unbound. For a full description, read the following article on the ASP.NET website: http://www.asp.net/web-api/overview/odata-support-in-aspnet-web-api/odata-v4/odata-actions-and-functions.

Summary

OData services constitute an important data platform and offer a standardized way to expose data through networks supporting HTTP requests such as GET, POST, PUT, and DELETE. In this chapter you got a high-level overview of OData services; you first learned about implementing services and how they can be easily created within ASP. NET web applications by using Web API and OData libraries. Services running within a web browser can then be queried via HTTP requests (URI). Next, you saw how to consume OData services from client applications and perform CRUD operations using the DataServiceContext class that exposes appropriate members for such kinds of operations. Finally, you learned how to implement functions and actions for best results on the server side.

CHAPTER 39

Serialization

Most real-world applications need to store, exchange, and transfer data. Due to its special nature, the .NET Framework stores data into objects and can exchange data via objects. If you need to store data only for your application, you have a lot of alternatives. The problem is when you need to exchange and transfer data with other applications. In other words, you need to think of how your objects are represented and decide whether you need to convert them into a different format. This is because another application cannot understand objects in their pure state; therefore, how information is persisted needs to be standardized. Serialization enables you to save your object's state to disk and then re-create the object according to the specified format. With serialization, you store your data and transfer data to other applications that can re-create the information. For example, say you have an application that needs to store and transfer data to another application through a network. With the .NET Framework, you serialize your data (that is, save the result of the serialization process to a stream), transfer your data to the target application, and wait for the target application to deserialize (that is, re-create the object starting from the serialized information) your data and use it. In this chapter, you learn to implement serialization in your applications, understanding what decisions you should make if you need to transfer data to non-.NET and non-Windows applications, too.

Objects Serialization

Serializing .NET objects is the easiest serialization mode. In this particular scenario, you need a file stream where you have to place data and a formatter establishing the serialization mode. When you have the formatter instance, you invoke the `Serialize` method. The `System.Runtime.Serialization.Formatters` namespace provides two sub namespaces, `Binary` and `Soap`. They expose `BinaryFormatter` and `SoapFormatter`, respectively. The first one serializes objects in a binary way. It is efficient, but you should use it only if you are sure that your objects will be deserialized by .NET applications because such binary format is not universal. If you instead want to be sure that your objects can be shared across various applications and platforms, you should use the `SoapFormatter` that produces an XML-based result that is useful when working with SOAP web services.

Binary Serialization

The following example shows how you can serialize a typed collection of strings into a file on disk using the `BinaryFormatter` class:

```
Dim stringSeries As New List(Of String) From
                   {"Serialization", "demo",
                    "with VB"}

Dim targetFile As New _
    FileStream("C:\temp\SerializedData.dat",
               FileMode.Create)
Dim formatter As New BinaryFormatter

formatter.Serialize(targetFile, stringSeries)
targetFile.Close()
formatter = Nothing
```

> **NOTE**
>
> The previous code example requires `Imports System.IO` and `Imports System.Runtime.Serialization.Formatters.Binary` directives.

The code creates a new file named `SerializedData.dat` and puts the result of the binary serialization in the file. If you examine the content of the file with the Windows Notepad, you can obtain a result similar to what is shown in Figure 39.1.

You don't need to know how your objects are serialized, but it is interesting to understand the type of information placed into the target file, such as the serialized type, assembly information, and the actual data. To deserialize a binary file, you invoke the `BinaryFormatter.Deserialize` method, as shown in the following code, which you write immediately after the preceding example:

```
Dim sourceFile As New FileStream("C:\temp\SerializedData.dat",
                            FileMode.Open)

formatter = New BinaryFormatter
Dim data = CType(formatter.Deserialize(sourceFile),
            List(Of String))

sourceFile.Close()
formatter = Nothing

'Iterates the result
For Each item In data
    Console.WriteLine(item)
Next
```

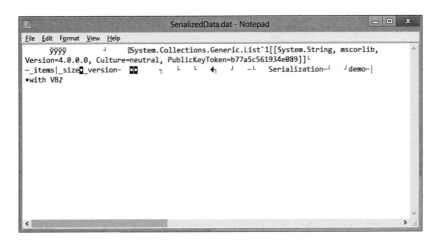

FIGURE 39.1   Examining the result of the serialization process.

Notice that Deserialize returns Object; therefore, the result needs to be converted into the appropriate type that you expect. If you run the preceding code, you see on your screen how the strings from the collection are correctly listed. This kind of serialization is also straightforward because it enables serializing entire object graphs. Moreover, you can use this technique against user interface controls in Windows Forms and WPF applications to persist the state of your interface objects that can be later re-created.

HANDLING SERIALIZATION EXCEPTIONS

Remember to perform serialization and deserialization operations within a Try..Catch block and implement code for handling the SerializationException exception that provides information on serialization/deserialization errors.

Creating Objects Deep Copies with Serialization

Chapter 4, "Data Types and Expressions," illustrated how to create objects' copies implementing the `ICloneable` interface and how you can clone an object with the `MemberWiseClone` method. Such scenarios have a big limitation: They cannot create copies of an entire object graph. Luckily, binary serialization can instead serialize entire object graphs and thus can be used to create complete deep copies of objects. The code in Listing 39.1 shows how to accomplish this by implementing a generic method.

LISTING 39.1   Implementing Deep Copy with Serialization

```
Imports System.Runtime.Serialization
Imports System.Runtime.Serialization.Formatters.Binary
Imports System.IO

Public Class CreateDeepCopy

    Public Shared Function Clone(Of T)(objectToClone As T) As T

        'If the source object is null, returns the current
        'object (as a default)
        If Object.ReferenceEquals(objectToClone, Nothing) Then
            Return objectToClone
        End If

        'Creates a new formatter whose behavior is for cloning purposes
        Dim formatter As New BinaryFormatter(Nothing,
                                    New StreamingContext(
                                        StreamingContextStates.Clone))
        'Serializes to a memory stream
        Dim ms As New MemoryStream
        Using ms
            formatter.Serialize(ms, objectToClone)

            'Gets back to the first stream byte
            ms.Seek(0, SeekOrigin.Begin)
            'Deserializes the object graph to a new T object
            Return CType(formatter.Deserialize(ms), T)
        End Using
    End Function
End Class
```

Because you are not limited to file streams, taking advantage of a memory stream is good in such a scenario. You invoke the preceding method as follows:

```
Dim result As Object = CreateDeepCopy.Clone(objectToClone)
```

You could also implement extension methods for providing deep copy to all types.

SOAP Serialization

SOAP serialization works similarly to binary serialization. First, you need to add a reference to the `System.Runtime.Serialization.Formatters.Soap.dll` assembly. Then you add an `Imports System.Runtime.Serialization.Formatters.Soap` directive. Then you can serialize and deserialize your objects. To continue the example of the typed collection shown in the previous section, write the following code to accomplish serialization with the SOAP formatter:

```
'Requires an Imports System.Runtime.Serialization.Formatters.Soap directive
Dim stringToSerialize As String = "Serialization demo with VB"

Dim targetFile As New FileStream("C:\temp\SerializedData.xml",
                                 FileMode.Create)

Dim formatter As New SoapFormatter
formatter.Serialize(targetFile, stringToSerialize)
targetFile.Close()
formatter = Nothing
```

There is no difference in the syntax for the SOAP formatter if compared to the binary one.

TIP ON GENERIC COLLECTIONS

The `SoapFormatter` class does not enable you to serialize generic collections. This is why a simpler example against a single string is provided.

You can still examine the result of the serialization process with the Windows Notepad. Figure 39.2 shows how the target file stores information in a XML fashion.

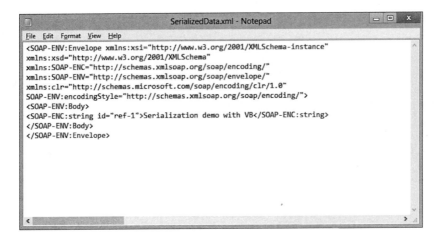

FIGURE 39.2   Examining the result of the SOAP serialization process.

Typically, the SOAP serialization is intended to be used when working with SOAP web services. If you want to serialize objects in a pure XML mode, you can take advantage of XML serialization, which is described in the "XML Serialization" section later in this chapter.

Providing Serialization for Custom Objects

You can make your custom objects serializable so that you can apply the previously described techniques for persisting and re-creating objects' state. To be serializable, a class (or structure) must be decorated with the `Serializable` attribute. This is the most basic scenario and is represented by the following implementation of the `Person` class:

```
Imports System.Runtime.Serialization


<Serializable()>
Public Class Person
    Public Property FirstName As String
    Public Property LastName As String
    Public Property Age As Integer
    Public Property Address As String
End Class
```

If you do not need to get control over the serialization process, this is all you need. By the way, there can be certain situations that you need to handle. For instance, you might want to disable serialization for a member that could become obsolete if too much time passes between serialization and deserialization. Continuing the `Person` class example, suppose you decide to disable serialization for the `Age` member because between serialization and deserialization the represented person might be older than the moment when serialization occurred. To accomplish this, you apply the `NonSerialized` attribute. The big problem here is that this is a field-level attribute; therefore, it cannot be applied to properties. In such situations using auto-implemented properties is not possible, so you must write them the old-fashioned way. The following code shows how you can prevent the `Age` member from being serialized:

```
<NonSerialized()> Private _age As Integer
Public Property Age As Integer
    Get
        Return _age
    End Get
    Set(value As Integer)
        _age = value
    End Set
End Property
```

The subsequent problem is that you need a way for assigning a valid value to nonserialized members when deserialization occurs. The most common technique is implementing the `IDeserializationCallBack` interface that exposes an `OnDeserialization` method where you can place your initialization code. The following is the revisited code for the `Person` class according to the last edits:

```
Imports System.Runtime.Serialization

<Serializable()>
Public Class Person
    Implements IDeserializationCallback


    Public Property FirstName As String
    Public Property LastName As String

    <NonSerialized()> Private _age As Integer
    Public Property Age As Integer
        Get
            Return _age
        End Get
        Set(value As Integer)
            _age = value
        End Set
    End Property

    Public Sub OnDeserialization(sender As Object) Implements _
            System.Runtime.Serialization.IDeserializationCallback.
            OnDeserialization
        'Specify the new age
        Me.Age = 32
    End Sub
End Class
```

When the deserialization process invokes the `OnDeserialization` method, members that were not serialized can be correctly initialized anyway. Another consideration that you need to take care of is versioning. When you upgrade your application to a new version, you might also want to apply some changes to your classes, such as by adding new members. This is fine but can result in problems if the previous version of your application attempts to deserialize an object produced by the new version. To solve this problem, you can mark a member as `OptionalField`. In this way, the deserialization process is not affected by new members and both `BinaryFormatter` and `SoapFormatter` will not throw exceptions if they encounter new members during the process. Because the `OptionalField` attribute works at field level, this is another situation in which you cannot take advantage of auto-implemented properties. The following code shows how you can mark the `Address` member in the `Person` class as optional:

```
<OptionalField()> Private _address As String
Public Property Address As String
```

39

```
    Get
        Return _address
    End Get
    Set(value As String)
        _address = value
    End Set
End Property
```

The member is still involved in the serialization process, but if a previous version of the application attempts to perform deserialization, it will not throw exceptions when it encounters this new member that was not expected.

NonSerialized Events

Visual Basic 2015, as well as its predecessor, offers a feature known as *NonSerialized Events*. You can decorate an event with the NonSerialized attribute in custom serialization. A common scenario for applying this technique is when you work on classes that implement the INotifyPropertyChanged interface because it is more important to serialize data and not an event that just notifies the user interface of changes on data. The following code shows an example about NonSerialized events inside a class that implements INotifyPropertyChanged:

```
<Serializable()>
Public Class Customer
    Implements INotifyPropertyChanged

    <NonSerialized()>
    Public Event PropertyChanged(
            sender As Object,
            e As System.ComponentModel.PropertyChangedEventArgs) _
            Implements System.ComponentModel.
                    INotifyPropertyChanged.PropertyChanged

    Protected Sub OnPropertyChanged(strPropertyName As String)
        If Me.PropertyChangedEvent IsNot Nothing Then
            RaiseEvent PropertyChanged(Me,
                    New PropertyChangedEventArgs(strPropertyName))
        End If
    End Sub
End Sub
```

XML Serialization

One of the main goals of serialization is to provide a way for exchanging data with other applications so that such applications can re-create objects' state. If you want to share your objects with non-.NET applications or with applications running on different platforms, a convenient way for serializing objects is provided by the XML serialization. As you know, XML is a standard international file format for data exchange. XML files are text files organized according to a hierarchical structure and thus can be manipulated in whatever platforms and applications you want. XML serialization provides two great benefits: absolute interoperability and background compatibility. If you upgrade or modify your applications, XML format remains the same. Opposite to such benefits, XML serialization has two limitations: It cannot serialize object graphs (therefore single objects) and cannot serialize private members. XML serialization is performed by using objects exposed by the `System.Xml.Serialization` namespace. You can use the `XmlSerializer` class that requires a `System.IO.Stream` object for outputting serialized data and the data itself. The following code shows how you can serialize a typed collection of strings using XML serialization:

```
Dim stringSeries As New List(Of String) From
    {"Serialization", "demo",
     "with VB"}

Dim targetFile As New FileStream("C:\temp\SerializedData.xml",
                              FileMode.Create)
Dim formatter As New XmlSerializer(GetType(List(Of String)))

formatter.Serialize(targetFile, stringSeries)
targetFile.Close()
formatter = Nothing
```

The `XmlSerializer` constructor requires the specification of the data type you are going to serialize, which is accomplished via the `GetType` operator. To serialize data, you invoke the `XmlSerializer.Serialize` method. As you can see, there are no big differences with other serialization techniques shown in the previous section. To check how your data was serialized, you can open the SerializedData.xml file. You can accomplish this with an XML editor or with a web browser instead of Notepad. Figure 39.3 shows the serialization result within Internet Explorer.

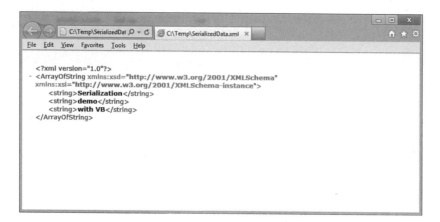

FIGURE 39.3   The XML serialization result shown in Internet Explorer.

Notice how the newly obtained file has a perfect XML structure and therefore can be shared with other applications having the ability to perform XML deserialization. To deserialize your data, you invoke the `XmlSerializer.Deserialize` method, as shown in the following code:

```
Dim sourceFile As New FileStream("C:\temp\SerializedData.xml",
                            FileMode.Open)

formatter = New XmlSerializer(GetType(List(Of String)))
Dim data = CType(formatter.Deserialize(sourceFile),
            List(Of String))

sourceFile.Close()
formatter = Nothing

'Iterates the result
For Each item In data
    Console.WriteLine(item)
Next
```

Customizing XML Serialization

Consider the following implementation of the `Person` class:

```
Public Class Person
    Public Property FirstName As String
    Public Property LastName As String
    Public Property Age As Integer
End Class
```

When you serialize an instance of that `Person` class, you would obtain an XML representation similar to the following:

```
<?xml version="1.0" ?>
<Person xmlns:xsi="http://www.w3.org/2001/XMLSchema-instance"
        xmlns:xsd="http://www.w3.org/2001/XMLSchema">
  <FirstName>Alessandro</FirstName>
  <LastName>Del Sole</LastName>
  <Age>37</Age>
</Person>
```

The `System.Xml.Serialization` namespace offers attributes for controlling output of the XML serialization to affect the target file. For example, consider the following code:

```
Imports System.Xml.Serialization

<XmlRoot("Contact")> Public Class Person
    <XmlIgnore()> Public Property FirstName As String
    Public Property LastName As String
    <XmlAttribute()> Public Property Age As Integer
End Class
```

When an instance is serialized, the output looks like the following:

```
<?xml version="1.0" ?>
<Contact xmlns:xsi="http://www.w3.org/2001/XMLSchema-instance"
         xmlns:xsd="http://www.w3.org/2001/XMLSchema"
         Age="37">
  <LastName>Del Sole</LastName>
</Contact>
```

The `XmlRoot` attribute changed the name of the root element from `Person` to `Contact`. The `XmlIgnore` attribute prevented a property from being serialized, and the `XmlAttribute` attribute treated the specified member as an XML attribute instead of an XML element. You can find the complete attributes list in the dedicated page of the MSDN Library at http://msdn.microsoft.com/en-us/library/system.xml.serialization.xmlattributes(v=vs.110). aspx. The reason you should get a reference on the Internet is that XML serialization is a settled concept for most developers, whereas .NET Framework 4.6 provides a more interesting way for XML serialization, known as XAML serialization, which is covered later in this chapter and that is more important to learn.

Custom Serialization

In most cases, the .NET built-in serialization engine is good enough. But if it does not meet your particular needs, you can override the serialization process with custom serialization. This means implementing the `ISerializable` interface that requires the implementation of the `GetObjectData` method. Such a method is important because it is invoked during serialization. A custom implementation of the class constructor must also be provided. You have to first reproduce at least what built-in formatters do during serialization. The code in Listing 39.2 shows how to provide custom serialization for the `Person` class.

LISTING 39.2   Providing Custom Serialization

```
Imports System.Runtime.Serialization
Imports System.Security.Permissions

<Serializable()>
Public Class Person
    Implements ISerializable

    Public Overridable Property FirstName As String
    Public Overridable Property LastName As String
    Public Overridable Property Age As Integer

    <SecurityPermission(SecurityAction.Demand,
                        SerializationFormatter:=True)>
    Protected Sub GetObjectData(info As System.Runtime.Serialization.
                                        SerializationInfo,
                        context As System.Runtime.Serialization.
                                        StreamingContext) _
                        Implements System.Runtime.
                        Serialization.ISerializable.
                                        GetObjectData

        info.AddValue("First name", Me.FirstName)
        info.AddValue("Last name", Me.LastName)
        info.AddValue("Age", Me.Age)
    End Sub


    'At deserialization time
    Protected Sub New(info As SerializationInfo,
                    context As StreamingContext)
        MyBase.New()
        Me.FirstName = info.GetString("First name")
        Me.LastName = info.GetString("Last name")
        Me.Age = info.GetInt32("Age")
    End Sub
End Class
```

The `GetObjectData` method is invoked when you pass an object to the `Serialize` method of a formatter and require an information argument of type `SerializationInfo`. This class stores all the information needed for serialization. It exposes an `AddValue` method that stores data and a value utilized for recognizing data. Notice that the information is retrieved by the special constructor implementation invoked at deserialization time via `GetXXX` methods, where `xxx` corresponds to .NET types such as `Integer`, `Boolean`, `Short`, and so on. Also, `GetObjectData` is decorated with the `SecurityPermission` attribute demanding for permissions about the serialization formatter. This is necessary because the permission is allowed only to full-trusted code, thus intranet and Internet zones are not allowed. Both `GetObjectData` and the constructor are `Protected` so that derived classes can still take advantage of them but are prevented from being public. If you are sure that your class will not be inherited, `GetObjectData` can also be Private.

INHERITANCE TIP

When you create a class that inherits from another class where `ISerializable` is implemented, if you add new members, you can also provide a new implementation of both `GetObjectData` and the constructor.

Implementing `ISerializable` is not the only way for controlling serialization. You can control serialization events, too.

Serialization Events

The serialization process raises four events, which are summarized in Table 39.1.

TABLE 39.1   Serialization Events

Event	Description
`OnSerializing`	Occurs just before serialization begins
`OnSerialized`	Occurs just after serialization completes
`OnDeserializing`	Occurs just before deserialization begins
`OnDeserialized`	Occurs just after deserialization completes

Serialization events are handled differently than classic events are. There is an attribute for each event that you can handle as follows:

```
'Invoke this method before
'serialization begins
<OnSerializing()>
Private Sub FirstMethod()

End Sub


'Invoke this method after
'serialization completes
<OnSerialized()>
Private Sub SecondMethod()
```

```
End Sub

'Invoke this method before
'deserialization begins
<OnDeserializing()>
Private Sub ThirdMethod()

End Sub

'Invoke this method after
'deserialization completes
<OnDeserialized()>
Private Sub FourthMethod()

End Sub
```

The runtime takes care of invoking the specified method according to the moment represented by each attribute. In this way, you can provide additional actions based on serialization events.

Serialization with XAML

This book has five chapters dedicated to the Windows Presentation Foundation technology, due to its importance in modern application development. You learned what XAML is and how you use it to define applications' user interface. XAML offers other advantages that can be taken in completely different scenarios; one of these is serialization. The System.Xaml.dll assembly implements the system.Xaml namespace. It offers the XamlServices class, whose purpose is providing members for reading and writing XAML in serialization scenarios. Because XAML is substantially XML code that adheres to specific schemas, serialization output will be under XML format. The good news is that you are not limited in using XAML serialization only in WPF applications. You need to add a reference to System.Xaml.dll. To understand how it works, create a new Console project with Visual Basic and add the required reference. The goal of the code example is to understand how entire objects' graphs can be serialized with this technique. Consider the following implementation of the Person class:

```
Public Class Person
    Public Property FirstName As String
    Public Property LastName As String
    Public Property Age As Integer
    Public Property Friends As List(Of Person)
End Class
```

Other than the usual properties, it exposes a Friends property of type List(Of Person). This enables you to create a simple object graph. Now consider the following code that creates two instances of the Person class that populates the Friends property of the main Person instance that you serialize:

```
Dim oneFriend As New Person With {.LastName = "White",
                                  .FirstName = "Robert", .Age = 35}
Dim anotherFriend As New Person With {.LastName = "Red",
                                      .FirstName = "Stephen", .Age = 42}

Dim p As New Person With {.LastName = "Del Sole", .FirstName = "Alessandro",
                          .Age = 37,
                          .Friends = New List(Of Person) _
                                  From {oneFriend, anotherFriend}}
```

Using objects and collection initializers makes this operation straightforward. To serialize an object graph, you invoke the `XamlServices.Save` shared method that requires an output stream and the object to be serialized. The following code snippet demonstrates this:

```
Imports System.IO, System.Xaml
'...
Using target As New FileStream("C:\Temp\Person.xaml", FileMode.Create)
    XamlServices.Save(target, p)
End Using
```

SERIALIZING GENERIC COLLECTIONS

When you serialize generic collections, especially custom ones, ensure that they implement the `IList` or `IDictionary` interfaces; otherwise, the serialization process might not work correctly.

The previously described serialization process produces the following output:

```
<Person Age="37"
    FirstName="Alessandro"
    LastName="Del Sole"
    xmlns="clr-namespace:XamlSerialization;assembly=XamlSerialization"
    xmlns:scg="clr-namespace:System.Collections.Generic;
               assembly=mscorlib"
    xmlns:x="http://schemas.microsoft.com/winfx/2006/xaml">

  <Person.Friends>
    <scg:List x:TypeArguments="Person" Capacity="4">
      <Person Friends="{x:Null}" Age="35" FirstName="Robert"
              LastName="White" />
      <Person Friends="{x:Null}" Age="42" FirstName="Stephen"
              LastName="Red" />
    </scg:List>
  </Person.Friends>
</Person>
```

39

This technique is efficient and makes output readable. As usual in XAML files, the XAML schema is pointed to via the x namespace. The scg namespace points to the System. Collections.Generic .NET namespace, required for deserializing the content as a generic collection. Additionally, the Person.Friends element defines subsequent Person elements storing information on child Person classes being part of the Friends property. Finally, the Friends property for nested Person elements is null. (We did not define child elements for the property.) Deserializing such content is also straightforward. To accomplish this, you invoke the XamlServices.Load shared method by converting its result into the appropriate type. The following code shows how deserialization works, iterating the final result for demonstrating that deserialization was correctly performed:

```
Using source As New FileStream("C:\temp\person.xaml", FileMode.Open)
    Dim result As Person = CType(XamlServices.Load(source), Person)

    'Shows:
    'White
    'Green
    For Each p In result.Friends
        Console.WriteLine(p.LastName)
    Next
    Console.ReadLine()
End Using
```

XAML serialization can be used in different situations, such as persisting the state of WPF controls but also serializing entire .NET objects graphs.

Serialization in Windows Communication Foundation

In some situations serialization is required for persisting state of objects from WCF services. Starting with .NET Framework 3.0, you can serialize objects exposed by WCF services using the DataContractSerializer class (which inherits from XmlObjectSerializer). The usage of such a class is not so different from other serialization classes. The only need is that you must mark your serializable classes either with the Serializable or with the DataContract attribute and, in this case, their members with the DataMember attribute. To see how this works in code, create a new WCF service project within Visual Studio 2015 (refer to Chapter 37, "Creating and Consuming WCF Services," for a recap) and name it **WcfPersonService**. Rename the default IService1 interface to IPersonService; then rename the default Service1 class to PersonService. The new service exposes a special implementation of the Person class. Listing 39.3 shows the complete code for the WCF sample service.

LISTING 39.3   Exposing Serializable Objects from WCF Services

```
<ServiceContract()>
Public Interface IPersonService

    <OperationContract()>
```

```vb
        Function GetPersonFullName(onePerson As Person) As String
End Interface

<DataContract()>
Public Class Person

    <DataMember()>
    Public Property FirstName As String

    <DataMember()>
    Public Property LastName As String
End Class
Public Class PersonService
    Implements IPersonService

    Public Function GetPersonFullName(onePerson As Person) As String _
                Implements IPersonService.GetPersonFullName

        Dim fullName As New Text.StringBuilder
        fullName.Append(onePerson.FirstName)
        fullName.Append(" ")
        fullName.Append(onePerson.LastName)
        Return fullName.ToString
    End Function
End Class
```

Notice how you decorate the `Person` class and its members with the `DataContract` and `DataMember` attributes, respectively. Now create a new Console project for testing the WCF service and serialization. Name the new project as **TestWcfSerialization**; then add a service reference to the WcfPersonService project (refer to Chapter 37 for a recap). This adds a reference to the WCF service creating a proxy class in Visual Basic. All you need to do now is to get the instance of the service client and invoke the `DataContractSerializer` class that requires a stream for putting serialized data to. The code in Listing 39.4 shows both serialization and deserialization processes.

LISTING 39.4   Performing WCF Serialization

```vb
Imports TestWcfSerialization.PersonServiceReference
Imports System.IO
Imports System.Runtime.Serialization

Module Module1

    Sub Main()

        Dim client As New PersonServiceClient
```

```
        Dim p As New Person With {.FirstName = "Alessandro",
                                  .LastName = "Del Sole"}

        Dim target As New FileStream("C:\Temp\WcfSerialized.xml", FileMode.Create)
        Dim serializer As New DataContractSerializer(GetType(Person))
        serializer.WriteObject(target, p)
        target.Close()
        serializer = Nothing

        Console.ReadLine()
        Dim source As New FileStream("C:\Temp\WcfSerialized.xml", FileMode.Open)
        serializer = New DataContractSerializer(GetType(Person))

        Dim result As Person = CType(serializer.ReadObject(source), Person)

        Console.WriteLine(result.LastName)
        Console.ReadLine()
    End Sub
End Module
```

In this code, you invoke the `WriteObject` instance method for persisting data. The method requires the file stream instance and the data instance as arguments. `WriteObject` can also serialize an entire object graph, similarly to the binary standard serialization. Data is also serialized to XML format. To deserialize objects, you invoke the `ReadObject` instance method converting the result into the appropriate type. Serialization in WCF can cause special exceptions: `InvalidDataContractException`, which is thrown when the data contract on the service side is badly implemented, and `System.ServiceModel.QuotaExceededException`, which is thrown when serialization attempts to write a number of objects greater than the allowed number. Such a number is represented by the `DataContractSerializer.MaxItemsInObjectsGraph` property, and the default value is `Integer.MaxValue`. The following snippet shows how you catch the previously mentioned exceptions:

```
Try
    serializer.WriteObject(target, p)
Catch ex As InvalidDataContractException
    'Data contract on the service side is wrong
Catch ex As QuotaExceededException
    'Maximum number of serializable object exceeded
Finally
    target.Close()
    serializer = Nothing
End Try
```

If you wonder when you would need WCF serialization, there can be several answers to your question. The most common scenarios are when you have WCF services exposing

LINQ to SQL models or Entity Data Models. Data exchange from and to clients is performed via WCF serialization. This requires a little bit of work in LINQ to SQL, whereas Entity Data Models (EDMs) are serialization-enabled, which is covered in the "Serialization in the ADO.NET Entity Framework" section.

JSON Serialization

The .NET languages support the JavaScript Object Notation (JSON) serialization, offered by the `System.Runtime.Serialization.Json` namespace. It is particularly useful when you need to serialize objects as JavaScript-compliant and is used in WCF and ASP.NET Ajax applications. Conceptually, JSON serialization works like the WCF serialization illustrated previously. The only difference is that you use a `DataContractJsonSerializer` class that works as in the following code snippet:

```
Dim target As New FileStream("C:\Temp\WcfSerialized.xml", FileMode.Create)
Dim jsonSerializer As New DataContractJsonSerializer(GetType(Person))
jsonSerializer.WriteObject(target, p)
```

To deserialize objects, you invoke the `DataContractJsonSerializer.ReadObject` method and convert the result into the appropriate type.

Serialization in the ADO.NET Entity Framework

You can easily serialize objects exposed by an Entity Data Model generated by the ADO.NET Entity Framework. In Visual Studio 2015, this process is different than in previous versions because all available options to generate data models (EF Designer or Code First) now produce Plain Old CLR Objects (POCO). For this reason, in both cases, you simply use the `Serializable` attribute and techniques described in the section "Providing Serialization for Custom Objects," earlier in this chapter. This is because POCO objects are platform independent and thus are custom business objects, like the ones described previously. You can easily check this by investigating the code-behind files for EDMs. Using POCO enables binary and XML serialization for entities also in WCF scenarios. To understand how this works, create a new Console project and add a new EDM wrapping the Northwind database (refer to Chapter 26, "Introducing ADO.NET Entity Framework," for a review), including only the `Customers` and `Orders` tables.

In Solution Explorer, enable the Show All Files view and then expand the Northwind.edmx file and then the Northwind.tt item. At this point, open both the Customer.vb and Order.vb code files and apply a `Serializable` attribute to both class definitions, as follows:

```
<Serializable>
Partial Public Class Customer

    ...


End Class
<Serializable>
Partial Public Class Order
```

. . .

```
End Class
```

Then you can use formatters as you did in the objects' serialization with no differences. The code in Listing 39.5 shows how to accomplish this.

LISTING 39.5   Serializing Entities from an Entity Data Model

```
Imports System.Runtime.Serialization.Formatters.Binary
Imports System.IO

Module Module1
    Sub Main()
        Using northwind As New NorthwindEntities
            'Retrieves the first order, as an example
            Dim anOrder As Order = northwind.Orders.Include("Customer").First

            'Same as classic objects serialization
            Dim formatter As New BinaryFormatter
            Using stream As New FileStream("C:\temp\EFSerialization.dat",
                            FileMode.Create)
                formatter.Serialize(stream, anOrder)
            End Using

            Dim newOrder As Order
            Using source As New FileStream("C:\temp\EFSerialization.dat",
                            FileMode.Open)
                newOrder = CType(formatter.Deserialize(source), Order)
            End Using
        End Using

        Console.ReadLine()
    End Sub
End Module
```

If you need to retrieve data via a WCF service, you use a DataContractSerializer by using serialization in WCF scenarios as described earlier in this chapter. Listing 39.5 shows an example of binary serialization, but you can also take advantage of other techniques described in this chapter as well.

Summary

Serialization is the capability to save objects' state to disk (or memory) and to re-create the states later. The .NET Framework offers several serialization techniques, all provided by the System.Runtime.Serialization namespace. You can perform binary serialization via the `BinaryFormatter` class or SOAP serialization (XML-based mode for SOAP web services) via the `SoapFormatter` class. In both cases you need an output stream and then invoke the `Serialize` method for performing serialization. `Deserialize`, on the other hand, is for performing deserialization. Another common technique is the XML serialization that creates XML documents starting from your objects, which is useful if you need to exchange your data with non-.NET applications or with non-Windows applications, due to the standard format of this kind of document. If you need deep control over the serialization process, you implement the `ISerializable` interface that requires the implementation of the `GetObjectData`, where you can customize the behavior of the process other than handling serialization events. The .NET Framework 4.6 also offers WCF serialization, which uses the `DataContractSerializer` class or the XAML serialization that is performed via the `XamlServices` class. Finally, you can serialize entities from an Entity Data Model using all the preceding techniques so that you can easily exchange (or save the state of) your data without changing the programming model.

CHAPTER 40

Processes and Multithreading

In our everyday lives, we all do a number of things such as go to work, have appointments, and visit with friends or family; we are all very busy, of course. Sometimes we can do two things simultaneously, such as speaking on the phone while writing something on a piece of paper, but in most cases we do just one thing at a time. After all, there is only one of us. It would be great if we could share our things to do with other people so that multiple people could do the same work concurrently. We would be less tired and would have more time for relaxing or being with our families. In the computers' world, a similar problem exists. You can compare a real person to an application. If an application has to complete hard and long work totally alone, it can cause overhead on the system and take more time. Moreover, recent hardware architectures (such as multicore processors) would remain unexploited. So it would be useful to have the ability to split the work of an application among multiple parts that could work concurrently. This is where threading comes in with the .NET Framework development. With *threading*, you can create multiple threads of work to perform multiple tasks concurrently so that your applications can take advantage of optimized performance and resources. But threading is not the only way you request actions. In many circumstances, you need to launch external executables and possibly hold a reference to them in your code, so you also often work with processes. In this chapter, you take a look at how the .NET Framework enables you to manage processes and how you can split operations across multiple threads, both created manually and provided by the .NET thread pool.

Managing Processes

You use the `System.Diagnostics.Process` class to manage processes on your machine.

This class offers both shared and instance members so that you can launch an external process but also get a reference to one or more processes. The following code shows how to launch an external process via the shared implementation of the `Start` method:

```
Process.Start("Notepad.exe")
```

Any call to the `Process.Start` method will return a `Process` object. You can also specify arguments for the process by specifying the second parameter for the method as follows:

```
Process.Start("Notepad.exe", "C:\aFile.txt")
```

One of the most important features of the `Start` method is that you can also supply the username, password, and domain for launching a process:

```
Process.Start("Notepad.exe", "C:\aFile.txt",
              "Alessandro", Password, "\\MYDOMAIN")
```

Notice that the password is necessarily an instance of the `System.Security.SecureString` class, so see the MSDN documentation about this. The `Process` class also has an instance behavior that enables you to get a reference to a process instance. This is useful when you want to programmatically control a process. With regard to this, you first need an instance of the `ProcessStartInfo` class that can store process execution information. The class exposes lots of properties, but the most important are summarized in the following code snippet:

```
Dim procInfo As New ProcessStartInfo
With procInfo
    .FileName = "Notepad.exe"
    .Arguments = "aFile.txt"
    .WorkingDirectory = "C:\"
    .WindowStyle = ProcessWindowStyle.Maximized
    .ErrorDialog = True
End With
```

Particularly, the `ErrorDialog` property makes the `Process` instance display an error dialog box if the process cannot be started regularly. When you have done this, you create an instance of the `Process` class and assign its `StartInfo` property; finally, you invoke `Start` as demonstrated in the following code:

```
Dim proc As New Process
proc.StartInfo = procInfo
proc.Start()

'Alternative syntax:
'Dim proc As Process = Process.Start(procInfo)
```

Approaching processes in this fashion is helpful if you need to programmatically control processes. For example, you can wait until a process exits for the specified number of milliseconds as follows:

```
'Waits for two seconds
proc.WaitForExit(2000)
```

To close a process, you write the following code:

```
proc.Close()
```

Finally, you can kill unresponsive processes by invoking the `Kill` method as follows:

```
proc.Kill()
```

The `Process` class also exposes the `EnableRaisingEvents` Boolean property, which enables you to set whether the runtime should raise the `Exited` event when the process terminates. Such an event is raised if either the process terminates normally or an invocation to the `Kill` method occurs. So far, you have learned how to launch processes, but the `Process` class is also useful when you need to get information on running processes, as discussed in the next subsection.

Querying Existing Processes

You can easily get information on running processes through some methods from the `Process` class that provide the ability of getting process instances. For example, `GetProcesses` returns an array of `Process` objects, each one representing a running process. `GetProcessById` and `GetProcessByName` return information on the specified process given the identification number or name, whereas `GetCurrentProcess` returns an instance of the `Process` class representing the current process. Then the `Process` class exposes a lot of useful properties for retrieving information. Each of them should be self-explanatory, such as `ProcessName`, `Id`, `ExitCode`, `Handle`, and `HasExited`. However, other advanced information properties are available, such as `PageMemorySize` or `VirtualMemorySize`, which return the memory size associated with the process on the page memory and the virtual memory, respectively. The Visual Studio's Object Browser and IntelliSense can help you with the rest of the available properties. At the moment, let's focus on how you can get information on running processes. The coolest way of getting process information is by using LINQ to Objects. The following query, and subsequent `For..Each` loop, demonstrates how to retrieve a list of names of running processes:

```
Dim processesList = From p In Process.GetProcesses
                    Select p.ProcessName


For Each procName In processesList
    Console.WriteLine(procName)
Next
```

40

Introducing Multithreading

A *thread* is a unit of work. The logic of threading-based programming is performing multiple operations concurrently so that a big operation can be split across multiple threads. The .NET Framework 4.6 offers support for multithreading via the `System.Threading` namespace. But .NET 4.6 also takes from its predecessor an important library, which is discussed in Chapter 41, "Parallel Programming and Parallel LINQ." It provides support for the parallel computing. For this reason, this chapter provides summary information on the multithreading approach so that in the next chapter you get more detailed information on the task-based programming. After reading Chapter 41, approaching another important language feature in Visual Basic 2015 will be easier. This is discussed in Chapter 42, "Asynchronous Programming."

Imports DIRECTIVES

The code examples shown in this chapter require an `Imports System.Threading` directive.

Creating Threads

You create a new thread for performing an operation with an instance of the `System.Threading.Thread` class. The constructor of this class requires you to also specify an instance of the `System.Threading.ThreadStart` delegate that points to a method that can actually do the work. Then you invoke the `Thread.Start` instance method. The following code snippet demonstrates how you can create a new thread:

```
Private Sub simpleThread()
    Dim newThread As New Thread(New ThreadStart(AddressOf _
                                        executeSimpleThread))
    newThread.Start()
End Sub

Private Sub executeSimpleThread()
    Console.WriteLine("Running a separate thread")
End Sub
```

To actually start the new thread, you invoke the method that encapsulates the thread instance, which in this case is `simpleThread`.

Creating Threads with Lambda Expressions

You might recall from Chapter 20, "Advanced Language Features," that lambda expressions can be used anywhere you need a delegate. This is also true in threading-based programming. The following code snippet demonstrates how you can use statement lambdas instead of providing an explicit delegate:

```
Private Sub lambdaThread()
    Dim newThread As New Thread(New _
```

```
                    ThreadStart(Sub()
                                Console.WriteLine("Thread with lambda")
                            End Sub))
    newThread.Start()
End Sub
```

Now you can invoke the `lambdaThread` method to run a secondary thread, and with one method you reach the same objective of the previous code where two methods were implemented.

Passing Parameters

In many cases, you might need to pass data to new threads. You can do this by creating an instance of the `ParameterizedThreadStart` delegate, which requires an argument of type `Object` that you can use for sharing your data. The following code demonstrates how you create a thread with parameters:

```
Private Sub threadWithParameters(parameter As Object)
    Dim newThread As New Thread(New _
                        ParameterizedThreadStart(AddressOf _
                        executeThreadWithParameters))
    newThread.Start(parameter)
End Sub
```

Notice how the `Thread.Start` method has an overload that takes the specified parameter as the data. Because such data is of type `Object`, you need to convert it into the most appropriate format. The following code demonstrates how to implement a method to which the delegate refers and how to convert the data into a hypothetical string:

```
Private Sub executeThreadWithParameters(anArgument As Object)
    Dim aString = CType(anArgument, String)
    Console.WriteLine(aString)
End Sub
```

You can use lambda expressions if you do not want to provide an explicit delegate in this kind of scenario.

Understanding the .NET Thread Pool

In the previous section, you saw how simple it is to create and run a new thread. When you have one or two threads, things are also easy for performance. But if you decide to split a process or an application across several concurrent threads, the previous approach can cause performance and resources overhead. So, you should manually search for the best configuration to fine-tune system resource consumption with your threads. Your application can run on different configurations in terms of available memory, processors, and general resources, so it is difficult to predict how many threads you can launch concurrently on target machines without affecting performance and causing overhead.

40

Fortunately, the .NET Framework maintains its own set of threads that you can also reuse for your purposes instead of writing code for creating and running new threads, ensuring that only the specified number of threads will be executed concurrently, all controlled by the Framework. The set is named *thread pool*, and you access it via the `System.Threading.ThreadPool` class. This class offers static methods for assigning tasks to threads in the box because the thread pool has a predefined number of available threads, which can be increased if doing so would get work done more quickly. If they are all busy doing something else, the new task is put into a queue and is executed when a thread completes its work. To take advantage of threads in the thread pool, you invoke the `System.Threading.ThreadPool.QueueUserWorkItem` method, as demonstrated in the following code:

```
Sub QueueWork()

    ThreadPool.QueueUserWorkItem(New WaitCallback(AddressOf FirstWorkItem))
    ThreadPool.QueueUserWorkItem(New WaitCallback(AddressOf SecondWorkItem))
    ThreadPool.QueueUserWorkItem(New WaitCallback(Sub()
                                                      Console.
                                                      WriteLine _
                                                      ("Third work item")
                                                  End Sub))

End Sub


Private Sub FirstWorkItem(state As Object)
    Console.WriteLine("First work item")
End Sub
Private Sub SecondWorkItem(state As Object)
    Console.WriteLine("Second work item")
End Sub
```

With `QueueUserWorkItem` you ask the runtime to put the specified task in the execution queue so that it will be executed when a thread in the thread pool is available. The `WaitCallBack` delegate allows passing state information and requires referred methods to have an argument of type `Object` in their signatures. Notice how you can still use lambdas to supply the desired action.

Getting and Setting Information in the Thread Pool

You can query information on the thread pool by invoking the `ThreadPool.GetMaxThreads`, `ThreadPool.GetMinThreads`, and `ThreadPool.GetAvailableThreads` methods. `GetMaxThreads` return the maximum number of concurrent threads that are held by the thread pool; `GetMinThreads` return the number of idle threads that are maintained waiting for the first new task being requested; and `GetAvailableThreads` returns the number of available threads. Whichever you use, they all return two values: the number of worker threads and the number of completion threads. Worker threads are units of execution, whereas completion threads are asynchronous I/O operations. The following code demonstrates how you get information on available threads:

```
Sub PoolInfo()
    Dim workerThreads As Integer
    Dim completionPortThreads As Integer

    ThreadPool.GetAvailableThreads(workerThreads,
                           completionPortThreads)
    Console.WriteLine("Available threads: {0}, async I/O: {1}",
                    workerThreads, completionPortThreads)
    Console.ReadLine()
End Sub
```

The `workerThreads` and `completionPortThreads` arguments are passed by reference; this is why you need variables for storing values. Similarly, you can use `SetMaxThreads` and `SetMinThreads` to establish the maximum number of requests held by the thread pool and the minimum number of idle threads. The following line is an example:

```
ThreadPool.SetMaxThreads(2000, 1500)
```

CHANGING DEFAULT VALUES

You should take care when editing the default values for the thread pool. You should do it only when you have a deep knowledge of how many resources will be consumed on the machine and of the system resources so that edits will not be negative for the target system. Default values in the thread pool are high enough, but you can check this out by invoking `GetMaxThreads`.

Threads Synchronization

So far, you have learned how to create and run new threads of execution to split big operations across multiple threads. This is useful, but there is a problem: Imagine that you have multiple threads accessing the same data source simultaneously: What happens to the data source, and how are threads handled to avoid errors? This is a problem that is solved with thread synchronization. The idea is that, when a thread accesses a resource, this resource is locked until the required operations are completed to prevent other threads from accessing that resource. Visual Basic and the .NET Framework provide keywords and objects, respectively, to accomplish threads synchronization, as covered in the next subsections.

The `SyncLock..End SyncLock` Statement

The Visual Basic language offers the `SyncLock..End SyncLock` statement, which is the place where you can grant access to the specified resource to only one thread per time. For example, imagine you have a class where you define a list of customers and a method for adding a new customer to the list, as demonstrated by the following code snippet:

```
Private customers As New List(Of String)

Sub AddCustomer(customerName As String)

    SyncLock Me
        customers.Add(customerName)
    End SyncLock
End Sub
```

The preceding code locks the entire enclosing class, preventing other threads from accessing the instance until the requested operation completes. Locking an entire class is not always the best idea because it can be expensive in terms of resources and performance and other threads cannot also access other members. Unfortunately, you cannot directly lock the resource; the MSDN documentation in fact states that you need to declare a *lock object* that you can use as follows:

```
Private customers As New List(Of String)
Private lockObject As New Object()

Sub AddCustomer(customerName As String)

    SyncLock lockObject
        customers.Add(customerName)
    End SyncLock
End Sub
```

The lock object is typically a `System.Object`. Using an object like this can ensure that the code block executed within `SyncLock..End SyncLock` will not be accessible by other threads. Another approach is using `GetType` instead of the lock object, pointing to the current type where the synchronization lock is defined. The following code demonstrates this:

```
Class Customers
    Inherits List(Of String)

    Public Sub AddCustomer(customerName As String)
        SyncLock GetType(Customers)
            Me.Add(customerName)
        End SyncLock
    End Sub
End Class
```

The `SyncLock..End SyncLock` statement is typical of Visual Basic language grammar. By the way, the statement is translated behind the scenes into invocations to the `System.Threading.Monitor` class, as described in the next section.

Synchronization with the `Monitor` Class

The `System.Threading.Monitor` class is the support object for the `SyncLock..End SyncLock` statement, and the compiler translates `SyncLock` blocks into invocations to the `Monitor` class. You use it as follows:

```
Sub AddCustomer(customerName As String)
    Dim result As Boolean

    Try
        Monitor.Enter(lockObject, result)
        customers.Add(customerName)
    Catch ex As Exception
    Finally
        If result Then Monitor.Exit(lockObject)
    End Try
End Sub
```

> **TIP**
>
> `Monitor.Enter` has an overload that takes a second argument of type `Boolean`, passed by reference, indicating whether the lock was taken.

`Monitor.Enter` locks the object; `Monitor.Exit` unlocks it. It is fundamental to place `Monitor.Exit` in the `Finally` part of the `Try..Catch` block so that resources will be unlocked anyway. At this point, you might wonder why you should use `Monitor` instead of `SyncLock..End SyncLock` because they produce the same result. The difference is that `Monitor` also exposes additional members, such as the `TryEnter` method that supports timeout, as demonstrated here:

```
Monitor.TryEnter(lockObject, 3000, result)
```

This code attempts to obtain the lock on the specified object for three seconds before terminating.

Read/Write Locks

A frequent scenario is when you have a shared resource that multiple reader threads need to access. In a scenario like this, you probably want to grant writing permissions just to a single thread to avoid concurrency problems. The .NET Framework provides the `System.Threading.ReaderWriterLockSlim` class, which provides a lock enabled for multiple threads reading and exclusive access for writing.

> **`ReaderWriterLock` CLASS**
>
> The .NET Framework still provides the `ReaderWriterLock` class, as in its previous versions, but it is complex and used to handle particular multithreading scenarios. Instead, as its name implies, the `ReaderWriterLockSlim` class is a lightweight object for reading and writing locks.

An instance of this class is declared as a shared field and is used to invoke both methods for reading and writing. The following code demonstrates how you enable a writer lock:

```
Private Shared rw As New ReaderWriterLockSlim

Sub AddCustomer(customerName As String)
    Try

        rw.EnterWriteLock()
        customers.Add(customerName)
    Catch ex As Exception
    Finally
        rw.ExitWriteLock()
    End TrThe
End Sub
```

This ensures that only one thread can write to the customers' collection. The next code snippet shows instead how you can enable a reader lock:

```
Sub GetInformation()
    Try
        rw.EnterReadLock()
        Console.WriteLine(customers.Count.ToString)
    Catch ex As Exception
    Finally
        rw.ExitReadLock()
    End Try
End Sub
```

`ReaderWriterLockSlim` is an object you should use if you expect more readers than writers; in other cases you should consider custom synchronization locks implementations.

Summary

This chapter covered processes management and multithreading with Visual Basic 2015. First, you saw how to utilize the `System.Diagnostics.Process` class for launching and managing external process from your applications, including programmatic access to processes. Next, you got an overview of threads and the `System.Threading.Thread` class, understanding how a thread is a single unit of execution and seeing how you create and run threads both programmatically and inside the .NET's thread pool. In the final part of this chapter, you learned about synchronization locks, which are necessary so that multiple threads access the same resources concurrently. For this, remember the `SyncLock..End SyncLock` VB statement and the `Monitor` class. Understanding threads is particularly important in the .NET programming, especially to understand how the Runtime can the application execution. But from the point of view of writing responsive applications, the .NET Framework offers more modern patterns: parallel computing and asynchronous programming. Without a knowledge of threading, it would be difficult to understand how both work. They are discussed in the next chapters.

CHAPTER 41

Parallel Programming and Parallel LINQ

Modern computers ship with multicore architectures, meaning that they have more than one processor. The simplest home computer has at least dual-core architecture, so you surely have a machine with multiple processors. Managed applications do their work using only one processor. This makes things easier, but with this approach you do not unleash all the system resources. The reason is that all elaborations rely on a single processor that is overcharged and will take more time. Having the possibility of scaling the application execution over all available processors instead is a technique that would improve how system resources are consumed and would speed up the application execution. The reason is simple: Instead of having only one processor doing the work, you have all the available processors doing the work concurrently. Scaling applications across multiple processors is known as *parallel computing*, which is not something new in the programming world. The word *parallel* means that multiple tasks are executed concurrently, in parallel. The .NET Framework 4.6 includes a special library dedicated to parallel computing for the Microsoft platform. This library is called the Task Parallel Library. It includes a specific implementation of Language Integrated Query, known as Parallel LINQ. In this chapter you learn what the library is, how it is structured, and how you can use it for writing parallel code in your applications starting from basic concepts up to writing parallel queries with LINQ and passing through interesting objects such as the concurrent collections.

Introducing Parallel Computing

The .NET Framework 4.6 (as well as its predecessor) provides support for parallel computing through the Task Parallel Library (TPL), which is a set of Application Programming Interfaces (APIs) offered by specific extensions of the System.Threading.dll assembly. The reference to this assembly is included by default when creating new projects, so you do not need to add one manually. The TPL is reachable via the `System.Threading` and `System.Threading.Tasks` namespaces that provide objects for scaling work execution over multiple processors. You write small units of work known as *tasks*. Tasks are scheduled for execution by the TPL's Task Scheduler, which is responsible for executing tasks according to available threads. This is possible because the Task Scheduler is integrated with the .NET thread pool. The good news is that the .NET Framework can automatically use all available processors on the target machines without the need to recompile code.

> **NOTE**
>
> Parallel computing makes it easier to scale applications over multiple processors, but it remains something complex in terms of concepts. This is because you will face some threading concepts, such as synchronization locks, deadlocks, and so on. Therefore, you should have at least a basic knowledge of threading issues before writing parallel code. Another important consideration is figuring out when you should use parallel computing. The answer is not easy because you are the only one who knows how your applications consume resources. The general rule is that parallel computing gives the best advantage when you have intensive processing scenarios. In simpler elaborations, parallel computing is not necessarily the best choice and can cause performance loss. Use it when your applications require hard CPU loops.

Most of the parallel APIs are available through the `System.Threading.Tasks.Task` and `System.Threading.Tasks.Parallel` classes. The first one is described in detail later; now you learn about the most important classes for parallelism.

Introducing Parallel Classes

Parallelism in the .NET Framework 4.6 is possible due to a number of classes, some responsible for maintaining the architecture of the TPL and some for performing operations in a concurrent fashion. The following subsection provides a brief coverage of the most important classes, describing their purpose.

The `Parallel` Class

The `System.Threading.Tasks.Parallel` class is one of the most important classes in parallel computing because it provides shared methods for running concurrent tasks and for executing parallel loops. In this chapter, you can find several examples of usage of this class; for now, you just need to know that it provides the `Invoke`, `For`, and `ForEach` shared methods. The first one enables running multiple tasks concurrently, and the other ones enable you to execute loops in parallel.

The `TaskScheduler` Class

The `System.Threading.Tasks.TaskScheduler` class is responsible for the low-level work of sending tasks to the thread queue. This means that when you start a new concurrent task, the task is sent to the scheduler that checks for thread availability in the .NET thread pool. If a thread is available, the task is pushed into the thread and executed. You do not interact with the task scheduler. (The class exposes some members that you can use to understand the task's state.) The first property is `Current`, which retrieves the instance of the running task scheduler. This is required to access information. For example, you can understand the concurrency level by reading the `MaximumConcurrencyLevel` property as follows:

```
Console.WriteLine("The maximum concurrency level is {0}",
                TaskScheduler.Current.MaximumConcurrencyLevel)
```

There are also some protected methods that can be used to force tasks execution (such as `QueueTask` and `TryDequeue`), but these are accessible if you want to create your own custom task scheduler, which is beyond the scope of this chapter.

The `TaskFactory` Class

The `System.Threading.Tasks.TaskFactory` class provides support for generating and running new tasks and is exposed as a shared property of the `Task` class, as explained in the next section. The most important member is the `StartNew` method, which enables creating a new task and automatically starting it.

The `ParallelOptions` Class

The `System.Threading.Tasks.ParallelOptions` class provides a way for setting options on tasks creation. Specifically, it provides properties for setting task cancellation properties (`CancellationToken`), the instance of the scheduler (`TaskScheduler`), and the maximum number of threads that a task is split across (`MaxDegreeOfParallelism`).

Understanding and Using Tasks

The parallel computing in the .NET Framework development relies on the concept of tasks. This section is therefore about the core of the parallel computing, and you learn to use tasks for scaling units of work across multiple threads and processors.

READ THIS SECTION CAREFULLY

This section is particularly important not only with regard to the current chapter, but also because the concept of tasks returns in Chapter 42, "Asynchronous Programming." For this reason it is very important that you carefully read the concepts about tasks; you will reuse them in the next chapter.

What Is a Task?

In the Task Parallel Library and parallel computing with the .NET Framework, the basic and most important concept is the *task*, which represents an asynchronous operation. Tasks typically represent delegates that are queued to the thread pool for execution. The thread pool can automatically determine and adjust the number of threads via automatic load balancing to maximize performances. In this way, tasks are generally lightweight and independent, and they can run concurrently, thus making it easier to enable efficient parallelism. In terms of code, a task is nothing but an instance of the `System.Threading.Tasks.Task` class that holds a reference to a delegate, pointing to a method that does some work. The power of the `Task` class relies on the deep control you have over the execution of work items via a rich set of APIs that support cancellation, scheduling, cancellation, exception handling, and more. You have two alternatives for executing operations with tasks: The first one is calling the `Parallel.Invoke` method; the second one is manually creating and managing instances of the `Task` class. The following subsections cover both scenarios.

Running Tasks with `Parallel.Invoke`

The first way of running tasks in parallel is calling the `Parallel.Invoke` shared method. This method can receive an array of `System.Action` objects as parameters, so each `Action` is translated by the runtime into a task. If possible, tasks are executed in parallel. The following example demonstrates how to perform three calculations concurrently:

```
'Requires an Imports System.Threading.Tasks directive

    Dim angle As Double = 150
    Dim sineResult As Double
    Dim cosineResult As Double
    Dim tangentResult As Double

    Parallel.Invoke(Sub()
                        Console.WriteLine(Thread.CurrentThread.
                                ManagedThreadId)
                        Dim radians As Double = angle * Math.PI / 180
                        sineResult = Math.Sin(radians)
                    End Sub,
                    Sub()
                        Console.WriteLine(Thread.CurrentThread.
                                ManagedThreadId)
                        Dim radians As Double = angle * Math.PI / 180
                        cosineResult = Math.Cos(radians)
                    End Sub,
                    Sub()
                        Console.WriteLine(Thread.CurrentThread.
                                ManagedThreadId)
                        Dim radians As Double = angle * Math.PI / 180
```

```
            tangentResult = Math.Tan(radians)
        End Sub)
```

In the example, the code uses statement lambdas; each of them is translated into a task by the runtime that is also responsible for creating and scheduling threads and for scaling tasks across all available processors. If you run the code, you can see how the tasks run within separate threads, automatically created for you by the TPL. As an alternative, you can supply AddressOf clauses pointing to methods performing the required operations, instead of using statement lambdas. Although this approach is useful when you need to run tasks in parallel the fastest way, it does not enable you to take control over tasks themselves. This is something that requires explicit instances of the Task class, as explained in the next subsection.

Creating, Running, and Managing Tasks: The Task Class

The System.Threading.Tasks.Task class represents the unit of work in the parallel computing based on .NET Framework. Differently from calling Parallel.Invoke, when you create an instance of the Task class, you get deep control over the task itself, such as starting, stopping, waiting for completion, and cancelling. The constructor of the class requires you to supply a delegate or a lambda expression to provide a method containing the code to be executed within the task. The following code demonstrates how you create a new task and then start it:

```
Dim simpleTask As New Task(Sub()
                               'Do your work here...
                           End Sub)


simpleTask.Start()
```

You supply the constructor with a lambda expression or with a delegate and then invoke the Start instance method. A much simpler way to create and start a task is by using its Run method, which is more readable and avoids common pitfalls such as creating but not starting a task. You use Task.Run like this:

```
Dim simpleTask = Task.Run(Sub()
                              'Do your work here...
                          End Sub)
```

The Task class also exposes a Factory property of type TaskFactory that offers members for interacting with tasks. For example, you can use this property for creating and starting a new task all in one as follows:

```
Dim factoryTask = Task.Factory.StartNew(Sub()
                                            'Do your work here
                                        End Sub)
```

This has the same result as the first code snippet. The logic is that you can create instances of the `Task` class, each with some code that will be executed in parallel. Generally speaking, you should prefer `Task.Run` and use `Task.Factory.StartNew` only when you need advanced task configuration options.

GETTING THE THREAD ID

When you launch a new task, the task is executed within a managed thread. If you want to get information on the thread, in the code for the task you can access it via the `System.Threading.Thread.CurrentThread` shared property. For example, the `CurrentThread.ManagedThreadId` property will return the thread ID that is hosting the task.

Creating Tasks That Return Values

The `Task` class also has a generic counterpart that you can use for creating tasks that return a value. Consider the following code snippet that creates a task returning a value of type `Double`, which is the result of calculating the tangent of an angle:

```
Dim taskWithResult = Task(Of Double).
    Factory.StartNew(Function()
                        Dim radians As Double _
                            = 120 * Math.PI / 180
                        Dim tan As Double = _
                            Math.Tan(radians)
                        Return tan
                    End Function)
```

You use a `Function`, which represents a `System.Func(Of T)`, so that you can return a value from your operation. The result is accessed via the `Task.Result` property, in this case `taskWithResult.Result`. In the preceding example, the `Result` property contains the result of the tangent calculation. The problem is that the start value on which the calculation is performed is hard-coded. If you want to pass a value as an argument, you need to approach the problem differently. The following code demonstrates how to implement a method that receives an argument that can be reached from within the new task:

```
Private Function CalcTan(ByVal angle As Double) As Double

    Dim t = Task(Of Double).Factory.
        StartNew(Function()
                    Dim radians As Double = angle * Math.PI / 180
                    tangentResult = Math.Tan(radians)
                    Return tangentResult
                End Function)
    Return t.Result
End Function
```

The result of the calculation is returned from the task. This result is wrapped by the `Task.Result` instance property, which is then returned as the method result.

Waiting for Tasks to Complete

You can explicitly wait for a task to complete by invoking the `Task.Wait` method. The following code waits until the task completes:

```
Dim simpleTask = Task.Factory.StartNew(Sub()

                                        'Do your work here
                                    End Sub)

simpleTask.Wait()
```

You can alternatively pass a number of milliseconds to the `Wait` method so that you can also check for a timeout. The following code demonstrates this:

```
simpleTask.Wait(1000)
If simpleTask.IsCompleted Then
    'completed
Else
    'timeout
End If
```

Notice how the `IsCompleted` property enables you to check whether the task is marked as completed by the runtime. `Wait` has to be enclosed inside a `Try..Catch` block because the method asks the runtime to complete a task that could raise any exceptions. This is an example:

```
Try
    simpleTask.Wait(1000)
    If simpleTask.IsCompleted Then
        'completed
    Else
        'timeout
    End If

    'parallel exception
Catch ex As AggregateException
End Try
```

Exception Handling

Handling exceptions is a crucial topic in parallel programming. The problem is that multiple tasks that run concurrently could raise more than one exception concurrently, and you need to understand what the actual problem is. The .NET Framework 4.6 offers the `System.AggregateException` class that wraps all exceptions that occurred concurrently into one instance. Such class then exposes, over classic properties, an `InnerExceptions` collection that you can iterate for checking which exceptions occurred. The following code demonstrates how you catch an `AggregateException` and how you iterate the instance, starting two tasks that attempt to access two files that do not exist:

```vbnet
Dim aTask = Task.Run(Sub()
                         'this file does not exist, throw an exception
                         Dim file1 =
                         My.Computer.FileSystem.
                         ReadAllText("C:\MyFile.txt")
                     End Sub)
Dim bTask = Task.Run(Sub()
                         'this file does not exist, throw an exception
                         Dim file2 =
                         My.Computer.FileSystem.
                         ReadAllText("C:\MyFile2.txt")
                     End Sub)
Try
    Task.WaitAll(aTask, bTask)
Catch ex As AggregateException
    For Each fault In ex.InnerExceptions
        If TypeOf (fault) Is InvalidOperationException Then
            'Handle the exception here..
        ElseIf TypeOf (fault) Is NullReferenceException Then
            'Handle the exception here..
        ElseIf TypeOf (fault) Is IO.FileNotFoundException Then
            'Handle the exception here..
        End If
    Next
Catch ex As Exception

End Try
```

Notice how the code invokes `Task.WaitAll`, a method that accepts an array of `Task(Of T)` as an argument and that waits for all the specified tasks to complete. Each item in `InnerExceptions` is an exception that you can verify with `TypeOf`. Another problem is when you have tasks that run nested tasks that throw exceptions. In this case you can use the `AggregateException.Flatten` method, which wraps exceptions thrown by nested tasks into the parent instance. The following code demonstrates how to accomplish this:

```vbnet
Dim aTask = Task.Run(Sub()
                         'this file does not exist, throw an exception
                         Dim file1 =
                         My.Computer.FileSystem.
                         ReadAllText("C:\MyFile.txt")
                     End Sub)
Dim bTask = Task.Run(Sub()
                         'this file does not exist, throw an exception
                         Dim file2 =
```

```
                    My.Computer.FileSystem.
                    ReadAllText("C:\MyFile2.txt")
                End Sub)
Try
    Task.WaitAll(aTask, bTask)
Catch ex As AggregateException
    For Each fault In ex.Flatten.InnerExceptions
        If TypeOf (fault) Is InvalidOperationException Then
            'Handle the exception here..
        ElseIf TypeOf (fault) Is NullReferenceException Then
            'Handle the exception here..
        ElseIf TypeOf (fault) Is IO.FileNotFoundException Then
            'Handle the exception here..
        End If
    Next
Catch ex As Exception

End Try
```

`Flatten` returns an instance of the `AggregateException` storing inner exceptions that included errors coming from nested tasks.

Canceling Tasks

In some situations you want to cancel task execution. To programmatically cancel a task, you need to enable tasks for cancellation, which requires some lines of code. You need an instance of the `System.Threading.CancellationTokenSource` class; this instance tells a `System.Threading.CancellationToken` that it should be canceled. The `CancellationToken` class provides notifications for cancellation. The following lines declare both objects:

```
Dim tokenSource As New CancellationTokenSource()
Dim token As CancellationToken = tokenSource.Token
```

SETTING TIME FOR CANCELLATION

The .NET Framework 4.6 enables you to create an instance of the `Cancellation-TokenSource` class and specify on such an instance how much time will have to pass before a cancellation occurs:

```
Dim tokenSource As New CancellationTokenSource(TimeSpan.FromSeconds(5))
```

You specify a `TimeSpan` value directly in the constructor.

Then you can start a new task using an overload of the `TaskFactory.StartNew` method that takes the cancellation token as an argument. The following line accomplishes this:

```
Dim aTask = Task.Factory.StartNew(Sub() DoSomething(token))
```

You still pass a delegate as an argument; in the preceding example the delegate takes an argument of type `CancellationToken` that is useful for checking the state of cancellation during the task execution. The following code snippet provides the implementation of the `DoSomething` method, in a demonstrative way:

```
Sub DoSomething(cancelToken As CancellationToken)

    For i As Integer = 0 To 1000
        cancelToken.ThrowIfCancellationRequested()

        'Simulates some work
        Thread.Sleep(10000)
    Next

End Sub
```

The `ThrowIfCancellationRequested` method throws an `OperationCanceledException` to communicate to the caller that the task was canceled. The method internally checks whether cancellation was requested over the current task. In the preceding code snippet, the `Thread.Sleep` method simulates some work inside a loop. Notice how checking for cancellation is performed at each iteration so that an exception can be thrown if the task is actually canceled. The next step is to request cancellation in the main code. This is accomplished by invoking the `CancellationTokenSource.Cancel` method, as demonstrated in the following code:

```
tokenSource.Cancel()

Try
    aTask.Wait()
Catch ex As AggregateException
    'Handle concurrent exceptions here...
Catch ex As Exception

End Try
```

DISABLE "JUST MY CODE"

The `OperationCanceledException` is correctly thrown if the Just My Code is disabled (refer to Chapter 5, "Debugging Visual Basic 2015 Applications," for details on Just My Code). If it is enabled, the compiler sends a message saying that an `OperationCanceledException` was unhandled by user code. This is benign, so you can go on running your code by repressing F5.

The `Barrier` Class

The `System.Threading` namespace in .NET 4.6 exposes a class named `Barrier`. The goal of this class is bringing a number of tasks that work concurrently to a common point before taking further steps. Tasks work across multiple phases and signal that they arrived at the barrier, waiting for all other tasks to arrive. The constructor of the class offers several overloads, but all have the number of tasks participating in the concurrent work in common. You can also specify the action to take after they arrive at the common point (that is, they reach the barrier and complete the current phase). Notice that the same instance of the `Barrier` class can be used multiple times, for representing multiple phases. The following code demonstrates how three tasks reach the barrier after their work, signaling the work completion and waiting for other tasks to finish:

```
Sub BarrierDemo()
    ' Create a barrier with three participants
    ' The Sub lambda provides an action that will be taken
    ' at the end of the phase
    Dim myBarrier As New Barrier(3,
                         Sub(b)
                             Console.
                             WriteLine("Barrier has been " & _
                             "reached (phase number: {0})",
                             b.CurrentPhaseNumber)
                         End Sub)

    ' This is the sample work made by all participant tasks
    Dim myaction As Action =
        Sub()
            For i = 1 To 3
                Dim threadId As Integer =
                    Thread.CurrentThread.ManagedThreadId
                Console.WriteLine("Thread {0} before wait.", threadId)

                'Waits for other tasks to arrive at this same point:
                myBarrier.SignalAndWait()
                Console.WriteLine("Thread {0} after wait.", threadId)
            Next
        End Sub

    ' Starts three tasks, representing the three participants
    Parallel.Invoke(myAction, myAction, myAction)

    ' Once done, disposes the Barrier.
    myBarrier.Dispose()
End Sub
```

The code performs these steps:

1. Creates an instance of the `Barrier` class adding three participants and specifying the action to take when the barrier is reached.

2. Declares a common job for the three tasks (the `myAction` object), which perform an iteration against running threads simulating some work. When each task completes the work, the `Barrier.SignalAndWait` method is invoked. This tells the runtime to wait for other tasks to complete their work before going to the next phase.

3. Launches the three concurrent tasks and disposes of the `myBarrier` object at the appropriate time.

The code also reuses the same `Barrier` instance to work across multiple phases. Such a class also exposes interesting members, such as these:

▶ `AddParticipant` and `AddParticipants` enable you to add one or the specified number of participant tasks to the barrier, respectively.

▶ `RemoveParticipant` and `RemoveParticipants` enable you to remove one or the specified number of participant tasks from the barrier, respectively.

▶ `CurrentPhaseNumber` property of type `Long` returns the current phase number.

▶ `ParticipantCount` property of type `Integer` returns the number of tasks involved in the operation.

▶ `ParticipantsRemaining` property of type `Integer` returns the number of tasks that have not invoked the `SignalAndWait` method yet.

A `Barrier` represents a single phase in the process; multiple instances of the same `Barrier` class, like in the preceding code, represent multiple phases.

Parallel Loops

The Task Parallel Library offers the ability of scaling loops such as `For` and `For Each`. This is possible due to the implementation of the shared `Parallel.For` and `Parallel.ForEach` methods. Both methods can use a multicore architecture for the parallel execution of loops, as explained in next subsections. Now create a new Console application with Visual Basic. The goal of the next example is to simulate an intensive processing for demonstrating the advantage of parallel loops and demonstrating how the Task Parallel Library is responsible for managing threads for you. With that said, write the following code:

```
'Requires an Imports System.Threading directive

    Private Sub SimulateProcessing()
        Threading.Thread.SpinWait(80000000)
    End Sub

    Private Function GetThreadId() As String
```

```
        Return "Thread ID: " + Thread.CurrentThread.
                        ManagedThreadId.ToString
    End Function
```

TIP

The `Thread.SpinWait` method tells a thread that it has to wait for the specified number of iterations to be completed. You might often find this method in the code samples about parallel computing with the .NET Framework.

The `SimulateProcessing` method just simulates and performs intensive processing against fictitious data. `GetThreadId` can help demonstrate the TPL influence on threads management. Now in the `Sub Main` of the main module, write the following code that takes a `StopWatch` object for measuring elapsed time:

```
Dim sw As New Stopwatch
sw.Start()
'This comment will be replaced by
'the method executing the loop
sw.Stop()
Console.WriteLine("Elapsed: {0}", sw.Elapsed)
Console.ReadLine()
```

This code helps to measure time in both classic and parallel loops as explained soon.

NOTE

Remember that parallel loops get the most out in particular circumstances such as intensive processing. If you need to iterate a collection without heavy CPU business, parallel loops will probably not be helpful, and you should use classic loops. Choose parallel loops only when your processing is intensive enough to require the work of all the processors on your machine.

`Parallel.For` Loop

Writing a parallel `For` loop is an easy task, although it is important to remember that you can use parallelism against intensive and time-consuming operations. Imagine you want to invoke the code defined at the beginning of this section for a finite number of times to simulate an intensive processing. This is how you would do it with a classic `For` loop:

```
Sub ClassicForTest()
    For i = 0 To 15
        Console.WriteLine(i.ToString + GetThreadId())
        SimulateProcessing()
    Next
End Sub
```

Nothing new here; the code writes the thread identifier at each step and simulates an intensive processing. If you run the code, you get the result shown in Figure 41.1, where you can see how all the work relies on a single thread and how the loop result is ordered.

The next code snippet is how you write a parallel loop that accomplishes the same thing:

```
'Requires an Imports System.Threading.Tasks directive
    Sub ParallelForTest()
        Parallel.For(0, 16, Sub(i)
                        Console.WriteLine(i.ToString &
                        GetThreadId())
                        SimulateProcessing()
                    End Sub)
    End Sub
```

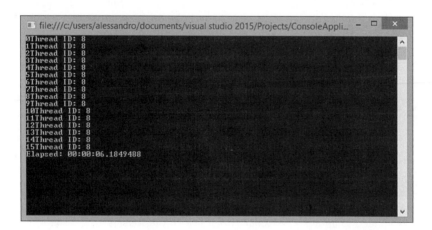

FIGURE 41.1   Running a classic `For` loop to demonstrate single threading.

`Parallel.For` receives three arguments: The first one is the "from" part of the `For` loop, the second one is the "to" part of the `For` loop (and it is exclusive to the loop), and the third is the action to take at each step. Such action is represented by a `System.Action(Of Integer)` that you write under the form of a statement lambda that takes a variable (`i` in the previous example) representing the loop counter. To provide a simpler explanation, the `Sub..End Sub` block in the statement lambda of the parallel loop contains the same code of the `For..Next` block in the classic loop. If you run the code, you can see how things change, as shown in Figure 41.2.

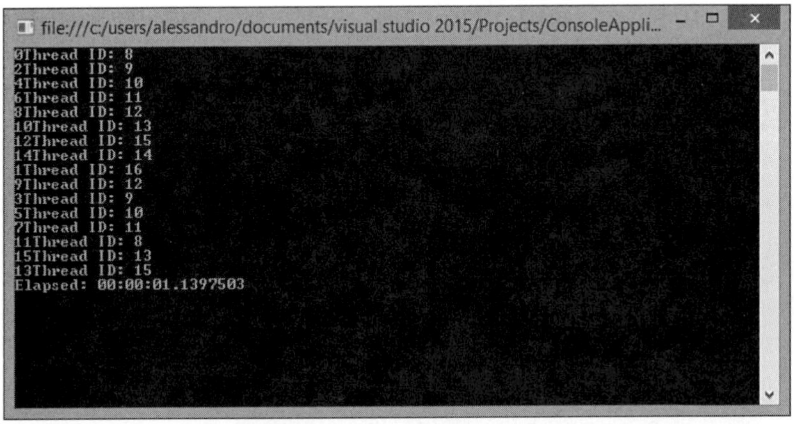

FIGURE 41.2   The parallel loop runs multiple threads and takes less time.

You immediately notice two things: The first one is that `Parallel.For` automatically splits the loop execution across multiple threads, differently from the classic loop in which the execution relied on a single thread. Multiple threads are shared across the multicore architecture of your machine, thus speeding up the loop. The second thing you notice is the speed of execution. Using a parallel loop, running the previous example on my machine took about 5 seconds less than the classic loop. Because the loop execution is split across multiple threads, such threads run in parallel. This means that maintaining a sequential execution order is not possible with `Parallel.For` loops. As you can see from Figure 41.2, the iterations are not executed sequentially, and this is appropriate because it means that multiple operations are executed concurrently, which is the purpose of the TPL. Just be aware of this when architecting your code.

Parallel.ForEach **Loop**

Similarly to `For` loops, the `Parallel` class offers an implementation of `For..Each` loops for iterating items within a collection in parallel. Using the methods shown at the beginning of this section for retrieving thread information, simulate intensive processing and the measuring of elapsed time. Imagine you want to retrieve the list of image files in the user-level Pictures folder simulating an intensive processing over each filename. This task can be accomplished via a classic `For..Each` loop as follows:

```
Sub ClassicForEachTest()
    Dim allFiles = IO.Directory.
        EnumerateFiles("C:\users\alessandro\pictures")

    For Each fileName In allFiles
        Console.WriteLine(fileName & GetThreadId())
        SimulateProcessing()
    Next
End Sub
```

The intensive processing simulation still relies on a single thread and on a single processor; thus, it will be expensive in terms of time and system resources. Figure 41.3 shows the result of the loop.

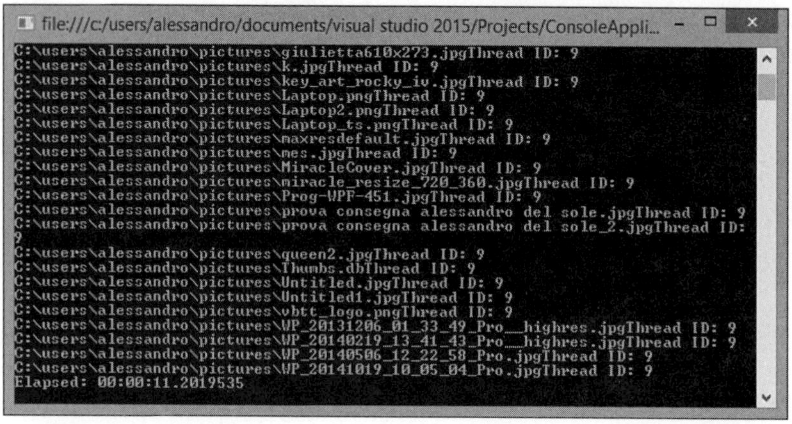

FIGURE 41.3   Iterating items in a collection under intensive processing is expensive with a classic `For..Each` loop.

Fortunately, the Task Parallel Library enables you to iterate items in a collection concurrently. This is accomplished with the `Parallel.ForEach` method, which is demonstrated in the following code:

```
Sub ParallelForEachTest()

    Dim allFiles = IO.Directory.
                EnumerateFiles("C:\users\alessandro\pictures")
    Parallel.ForEach(Of String)(allFiles, Sub(fileName)
                                    Console.WriteLine( _
                                    fileName & GetThreadId())
                                    SimulateProcessing()
                               End Sub)
End Sub
```

`Parallel.ForEach` is generic and therefore requires specifying the type of items in the collection. In most cases, the generic type argument can be inferred. In this case the collection is an `IEnumerable(Of String)`, so `ForEach` takes `(Of String)` as the generic parameter. Talking about arguments, the first one is the collection to iterate, whereas the second one is an `Action(Of T)`. Therefore, it's a reference to a delegate or a statement lambda like in the preceding example, representing the action to take over each item in the collection. If you run the code snippet, you get the result shown in Figure 41.4.

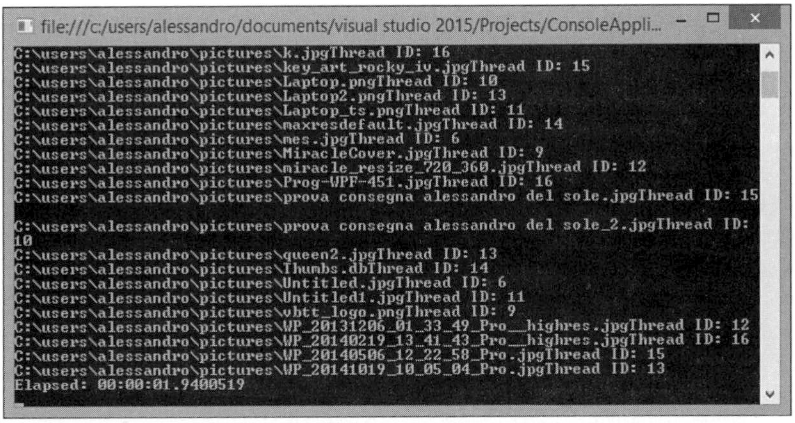

FIGURE 41.4   Performing a `Parallel.ForEach` loop speeds up intensive processing over items in the collection.

The difference is evident. The parallel loop completes processing in almost 10 seconds less than the classic loop on my machine; this is because the parallel loop automatically runs multiple threads for splitting the operation across multiple units of work. Specifically, it takes full advantage of the multicore processor's architecture of the running machine to take the most from system resources.

Partitioning Best Practices

When a `Parallel.ForEach` loop (and PLINQ queries as well) processes an `IEnumerable`, the runtime uses a default partitioning scheme that involves chunking. This means that every time a thread goes back to the `IEnumerable` to fetch more items, the thread can take multiple items at a time. This provides optimal performances but involves buffering items, which is not always an appropriate approach for some situations. For instance, if you think of data going over networks, you might prefer to process a single data item as soon as it is received rather than waiting for multiple items to be received and processed concurrently. The .NET Framework 4.6 offers an enumeration called `System.Collections.Concurrent.EnumerablePartitionerOptions` that enables you to specify whether the runtime should not use the default partitioning scheme and, consequently, avoid the buffering. The following code provides an example with the `Parallel.ForEach` loop that you saw previously:

```
'With no buffering
Parallel.ForEach(Of String)(Partitioner.Create(allFiles,
        EnumerablePartitionerOptions.NoBuffering),
                Sub()
                    Console.WriteLine(fileName + GetThreadId())
                    SimulateProcessing()
                End Sub)
```

You invoke the `Create` shared method of the `System.Collections.Concurrent.Partitioner` class to specify both the `IEnumerable` source and the partitioning scheme. `PartitionerOptions` has two values: `NoBuffering`, which avoids buffering, and `None` which is the default partitioning scheme (and that you can eventually avoid, using the normal syntax described earlier in this chapter, in the "`Parallel.ForEach` Loop" section).

The `ParallelLoopState` Class

The `System.Threading.Tasks.ParallelLoopState` enables you to get information on the state of parallel loops such as `Parallel.For` and `Parallel.ForEach`. For example, you can find out whether a loop has been stopped via the Boolean property `IsStopped` or whether the loop threw an exception via the `IsExceptional` property. Moreover, you can stop a loop with the `Break` and `Stop` methods. The first one requests the runtime to stop the loop execution when possible, but including the current iteration. `Stop` does the same but excludes the current iteration. You need to pass a variable of type `ParallelLoopState` to the delegate invoked for the loop or let the compiler infer the type as in the following example:

```
'The compiler infers ParallelLoopState
'for the loopState identifier
Parallel.For(0, 16, Sub(i, loopState)
                    Console.WriteLine(i.ToString + _
                        GetThreadId())
                    SimulateProcessing()

                    If loopState.IsExceptional Then
                        'an exception occurred
                    End If

                    'Breaks the loop at the 10th iteration
                    If i = 10 Then
                        loopState.Break()
                    End If
                End Sub)
```

Debugging Tools for Parallel Tasks

Visual Studio 2015 offers two useful tool windows that you can use for debugging purposes when working on both parallel tasks and loops. To understand how such tooling works, consider the following code that creates and starts three tasks:

```
Sub CreateSomeTaks()
    Dim taskA = Task.Factory.StartNew(Sub() Console.WriteLine("Task A"))
    Dim taskB = Task.Factory.StartNew(Sub() Console.WriteLine("Task B"))
    Dim taskC = Task.Factory.StartNew(Sub() Console.WriteLine("Task C"))
End Sub
```

Place a breakpoint on the End Sub statement and run the code. Because the tasks work in parallel, some of them may be running at this point and others may not be. To understand what is happening, you can open the Tasks tool window (select **Debug, Windows, Tasks** if it's not already visible). This window shows the state of each task, as represented in Figure 41.5.

	ID	Status	Start Time (sec)	Duration (sec)	Location	Task	
✓	1	ⓘ Scheduled	0,000	1,270	[Scheduled and waiting to run]	Task: _Lambda$_2	
✓	2	ⓘ Scheduled	0,000	1,270	[Scheduled and waiting to run]	Task: _Lambda$_4	
✓	3	ⓘ Scheduled	0,000	1,270	[Scheduled and waiting to run]	Task: _Lambda$_6	

FIGURE 41.5   The Tasks tool window.

Among the other information, such a window shows the task ID, the status (that is, if it is running, scheduled, waiting, dead-locked, or completed), the delegate that is making the actual job (in the Task column), and the actual thread that refers to the task. Next, you can use the **Parallel Stacks** tool window (which can be enabled via Debug, Windows, Parallel Stacks) that shows the call stack for threads and their relationships. Figure 41.6 shows an example.

For each thread the window shows information that you can investigate by right-clicking each row.

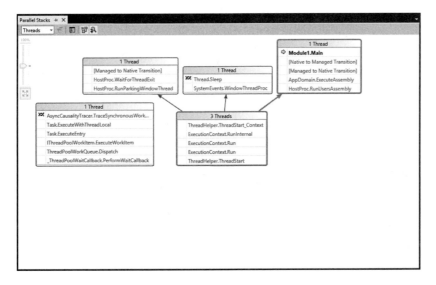

FIGURE 41.6   The Parallel Stacks window.

Concurrent Collections

Parallel computing relies on multithreading, although with some particular specifications for taking advantage of multicore architectures. The real problem is when you need to work with collections because in a multithreaded environment, multiple threads could access a collection attempting to make edits that need to be controlled. The .NET Framework 4.6 retakes from its predecessor a number of *thread-safe* concurrent collections, exposed by the System.Collections.Concurrent namespace, which is useful in parallel computing with .NET Framework because they grant concurrent access to their members from threads.

> **WHAT DOES *THREAD-SAFE* MEAN?**
>
> A collection is *thread-safe* when it remains correct despite any number of threads invoking its members concurrently.

Table 41.1 summarizes concurrent collections in .NET 4.6.

TABLE 41.1   Available Concurrent Collections

Collection	Description
ConcurrentBag(Of T)	Represents an unordered collection of items
ConcurrentQueue(Of T)	Represents a concurrent FIFO collection
ConcurrentStack(Of T)	Represents a concurrent LIFO collection
ConcurrentDictionary(Of TKey, TValue)	Represents a concurrent Dictionary(Of TKey, TValue)
BlockingCollection(Of T)	A thread-safe collection with bounding and blocking capabilities against threads

The first four listed collections are essentially thread-safe implementations of generic collections you already learned in Chapter 16, "Working with Collections and Iterators." BlockingCollection is a little bit more complex but interesting.

ConcurrentBag(Of T)

The ConcurrentBag(Of T) is the most basic concurrent collection, in that it is just an unordered collection of items. The following code demonstrates how you use it for adding, iterating, counting, and removing items:

```
'Creating an instance
Dim cb As New ConcurrentBag(Of String)

'Adding some items
cb.Add("String one")
cb.Add("String two")
cb.Add("String three")
```

```
'Showing items count
Console.WriteLine(cb.Count)

'Listing items in the collection
For Each item In cb
    Console.WriteLine(item)
Next

'Removing an item
Dim anItem As String = String.Empty
cb.TryTake(anItem)
Console.WriteLine(anItem)
```

You add items to the collection by invoking the `Add` method. The `Count` property gets the number of items in the collection, and the `IsEmpty` property tells you whether the collection is empty. To remove an item, you invoke `TryTake`, which takes the first item, assigns it to the result variable (in this case `anItem`), and then removes it from the collection. It returns `True` if removing succeeds; otherwise, it returns `False`. Keep in mind that this collection offers no order for items; therefore, iteration results are completely random.

ConcurrentQueue(Of T)

The `ConcurrentQueue(Of T)` collection is just a thread-safe implementation of the `Queue(Of T)` collection, so it takes the logic of FIFO (first in, first out), where the first element in the collection is the first to be removed. The following code shows an example:

```
'Creating an instance
Dim cq As New ConcurrentQueue(Of Integer)

'Adding items
cq.Enqueue(1)
cq.Enqueue(2)

'Removing an item from the queue
Dim item As Integer
cq.TryDequeue(item)
Console.WriteLine(item)

'Returns "1":
Console.WriteLine(cq.Count)
```

The main difference with `Queue` is how items are removed from the queue. In this concurrent implementation, you invoke `TryDequeue`, which passes the removed item to a result variable by reference. The method returns `True` in case of success; otherwise, it returns `False`. Still the `Count` property returns the number of items in the queue.

ConcurrentStack(Of T)

ConcurrentStack(Of T) is the thread-safe implementation of the Stack(Of T) generic collection and works according to the LIFO (last in, first out) logic. The following code shows an example of using this collection:

```
'Creating an instance
Dim cs As New ConcurrentStack(Of Integer)

'Adding an item
cs.Push(1)
'Adding an array
cs.PushRange(New Integer() {10, 5, 10, 20})


Dim items() As Integer = New Integer(3) {}

'Removing an array
cs.TryPopRange(items, 0, 4)

'Iterating the array
Array.ForEach(Of Integer)(items, Sub(i)
                                     Console.WriteLine(i)
                                 End Sub)

'Removing an item
Dim anItem As Integer
cs.TryPop(anItem)
Console.WriteLine(anItem)
```

The big difference between this collection and its thread-unsafe counterpart is that you can also add an array of items invoking PushRange, but you still invoke Push to add a single item. To remove an array from the stack, you invoke TryPopRange, which takes three arguments: the target array that will store the removed items, the start index, and the number of items to remove. Both PushRange and TryPopRange return a Boolean value indicating whether they succeeded. The Array.ForEach loop in the preceding code is just an example for demonstrating how the array was actually removed from the collection. Finally, you invoke TryPop for removing an item from the stack; this item is then assigned to a result variable, passed by reference.

ConcurrentDictionary(Of TKey, TValue)

The ConcurrentDictionary collection has the same purpose as its thread-unsafe counterpart, but it differs in how methods work. All methods for adding, retrieving, and removing items return a Boolean value indicating success or failure, and their names all start with Try. The following code shows an example:

```
'Where String is for names and Integer for ages
Dim cd As New ConcurrentDictionary(Of String, Integer)

Dim result As Boolean

'Adding some items
result = cd.TryAdd("Alessandro", 37)
result = cd.TryAdd("Nadia", 31)
result = cd.TryAdd("Robert", 38)

'Removing an item
result = cd.TryRemove("Nadia", 31)

'Getting a value for the specified key
Dim value As Integer
result = cd.TryGetValue("Alessandro", value)

Console.WriteLine(value)
```

The logic of the collection is then the same as `Dictionary`, so refer to this one for details.

BlockingCollection(Of T)

The `BlockingCollection(Of T)` is a special concurrent collection. At the highest level such a collection has two characteristics. The first is that if a thread attempts to retrieve items from the collection while it is empty, the thread is blocked until some items are added to the collection. The second one is that if a thread attempts to add items to the collection, but this has reached the maximum number of items possible; the thread is blocked until some space is freed in the collection. Another interesting feature is completion. You can mark the collection as complete so that no other items can be added. This is accomplished via the `CompleteAdding` instance method. After you invoke this method, if a thread attempts to add items, an `InvalidOperationException` is thrown. The following code shows how to create a `BlockingCollection` for strings:

```
Dim bc As New BlockingCollection(Of String)

bc.Add("First")
bc.Add("Second")
bc.Add("Third")
bc.Add("Fourth")

'Marks the collection as complete
bc.CompleteAdding()

'Returns an exception
'bc.Add("Fifth")
```

```
'Removes an item from the collection (FIFO)
Dim result = bc.Take()
Console.WriteLine(result)
```

You add items invoking the `Add` method, and you mark the collection complete with `CompleteAdding`. To remove an item, you invoke `Take`. This method removes the first item added to the collection, according to the FIFO approach. This is because the `BlockingCollection` is not actually a storage collection, though it creates a `ConcurrentQueue` behind the scenes, adding blocking logic to this one. The class also exposes some properties:

▶ `BoundedCapacity` returns the bounded capacity for the collection. You can provide the capacity via the constructor. If not, the property returns `-1` as the value indicating that it's a growing collection.

▶ `IsCompleted` indicates whether the collection has been marked with `CompleteAdding`, and it is also empty.

▶ `IsAddingCompleted` indicates whether the collection has been marked with `CompleteAdding`.

The class has other interesting characteristics. For example, the beginning of the discussion explained why it is considered blocking. By the way, it also offers methods whose names all begin with `Try`, such as `TryAdd` and `TryTake`, which provides overloads that enable doing their respective work without being blocked. The last feature of the `BlockingCollection` is a number of static methods that you can use for adding and removing items to and from multiple `BlockingCollection` instances simultaneously, both blocking and nonblocking. These methods are `AddToAny`, `TakeFromAny`, `TryAddToAny`, and `TryTakeFromAny`. The following code shows an example of adding a string to multiple instances of the collection:

```
Dim collection1 As New BlockingCollection(Of String)
Dim collection2 As New BlockingCollection(Of String)

Dim colls(1) As BlockingCollection(Of String)
colls(0) = collection1
colls(1) = collection2

BlockingCollection(Of String).AddToAny(colls, "anItem")
```

All the mentioned methods take an array of collections; this is the reason for the code implementation as previously illustrated.

Introducing Parallel LINQ

Parallel LINQ, also known as *PLINQ*, is a special LINQ implementation provided by .NET Framework 4.6 that enables developers to query data using the LINQ syntax but uses multicore and multiprocessor architectures that have support by the Task Parallel Library.

Creating "parallel" queries is an easy task, although there are some architectural differences with classic LINQ (or more with classic programming). These are discussed during this chapter. To create a parallel query, you just need to invoke the `AsParallel` extension method onto the data source you are querying. The following code provides an example:

```
Dim range = Enumerable.Range(0, 1000)


'Just add "AsParallel"
Dim query = From num In range.AsParallel
            Where (IsOdd(num))
            Select num
```

You can use Parallel LINQ and the Task Parallel Library only in particular scenarios, such as intensive calculations or large amounts of data. Because of this, to give you an idea of how PLINQ can improve performance, the code presented in this chapter simulates intensive work on easier code so that you can focus on PLINQ instead of other code.

Simulating an Intensive Work

Parallel LINQ provides benefits when you work in extreme situations such as intensive works or large amounts of data. In different situations, PLINQ is not necessarily better than classic LINQ. To understand how PLINQ works, first you need to write code that simulates an intensive work. After creating a new Console project, write the following method that determines whether a number is odd but suspends the current thread for several milliseconds by invoking the `System.Threading.Thread.SpinWait` shared method:

```
'Checks if a number is odd
Private Function IsOdd(ByVal number As Integer) As Boolean
    'Simulate an intensive work
    System.Threading.Thread.SpinWait(1000000)
    Return (number Mod 2) <> 0
End Function
```

Now that you have an intensive work, you are ready to compare both the classic and parallel LINQ queries.

Measuring Performances of a Classic LINQ Query

The goal of this paragraph is to explain how you can execute a classic LINQ query over intensive processing and measure its performance in milliseconds. Consider the following code:

```
Private Sub ClassicLinqQuery()
    Dim range = Enumerable.Range(0, 1000)

    Dim query = From num In range
                Where (IsOdd(num))
                Select num
```

```
'Measuring performance
Dim sw As Stopwatch = Stopwatch.StartNew

'Linq query is executed when invoking Count
Console.WriteLine("Total odd numbers: " + query.Count.ToString)
sw.Stop()
Console.WriteLine(sw.ElapsedMilliseconds.ToString)
Console.ReadLine()
End Sub
```

Given a range of predefined numbers (`Enumerable.Range`), the code looks for odd numbers and collects them into an `IEnumerable(Of Integer)`. To measure performance, you can use the `Stopwatch` class that starts a counter (`Stopwatch.StartNew`). Because, as you already know, LINQ queries are executed when you use them; such a query is executed when the code invokes the `Count` property to show how many odd numbers are stored within the query variable. When done, the counter is stopped so that you can get the number of milliseconds needed to perform the query itself. By the way, measuring time is not enough. The real goal is to understand how the CPU is used and how a LINQ query impacts performance. To accomplish this, on Windows 8/8.1 right-click the **Windows Task Bar** and start the **Task Manager**. Then click the **Performance** tab, and then click the **Open Resource Monitor**. This provides a way for looking at the CPU usage while running your code. If you are running Windows 7 or Windows Vista with Service Pack 2, you will not need to open any resource monitor because the Task Manager provides all you need in the main window (just select the Always on Top option for a better view). The previous code, which can be run by invoking the `ClassicLinqQuery` from the `Main` method, produces the following result on my dual-core machine:

```
Total odd numbers: 500
3667
```

This means that executing a query versus the intensive processing took about 3 1/2 seconds. The other interesting thing is about the CPU usage. Figure 41.7 shows that during the processing, the CPU was used for a medium percentage of resources. Obviously, this percentage can vary depending on the machine and on the running processes and applications.

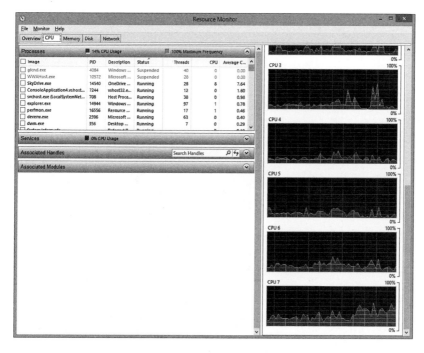

FIGURE 41.7   CPU usage during a classic LINQ query.

That CPU usage was not full is not necessarily good because it means that all the work relies on a single thread and is considered as if it were running on a single processor. Therefore, an overload of work exists for only some resources while other resources are free. To scale the work over multiple threads and multiple processors, a Parallel LINQ query is more efficient.

Measuring Performances of a PLINQ Query

To create a parallel query, you need to invoke the `AsParallel` extension method for the data source you want to query. Copy the method shown in the previous paragraph and rename it as `PLinqQuery`; then change the first line of the query as follows:

```
Dim query = From num In range.AsParallel
```

Different from a LINQ query, `AsParallel` returns a `ParallelQuery(Of T)` that is exposed by the `System.Linq` namespace and that is specific for PLINQ. However, it works as an `IEnumerable(Of T)` but enables you to scale data over multicore processors. Now edit `Sub Main` so that it invokes the `PLinqQuery` method and runs the code again. Figure 41.8 shows what you should see when the application is processing data.

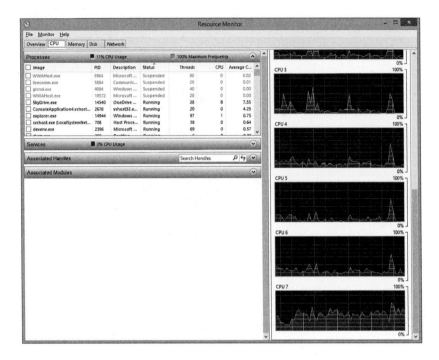

FIGURE 41.8   CPU usage during a Parallel LINQ query.

It is worth noticing how all processors are being used, which is demonstrated by the peaks of CPU usage. Processing was scaled along all available processors. On my quad-core machine, the previous code produces the following result:

```
Total odd numbers: 500
842
```

The PLINQ query took less than one second, which is much less than the classic LINQ query result. So, PLINQ can dramatically improve your code performance, although there are some other considerations, as discussed in the next paragraphs.

CONVERTING TO SEQUENTIAL QUERIES

PLINQ queries are evaluated in parallel, meaning that they use multicore architectures, also thanks to the `ParallelQuery(Of T)` class. If you want to convert such a result into an `IEnumerable (Of T)` and provide sequential evaluation of the query, you can invoke the `AsSequential` extension method from the query result variable.

Ordering Sequences

One of the most important consequences of Parallel LINQ (and, more generally, of parallel computing) is that processing is not done sequentially as it would happen on single-threaded code. This is because multiple threads run concurrently. To understand this, the following is an excerpt from the iteration on the result of the parallel query:

```
295
315
297
317
299
319
```

You would probably expect something like the following instead, which is produced by the classic LINQ query:

```
295
296
297
298
299
300
```

If you need to work in sequential order but do not want to lose the capabilities of PLINQ query, you can invoke the `AsOrdered` extension method that preserves the sequential order of the result, as demonstrated by the following code snippet:

```
Dim query = From num In range.AsParallel.AsOrdered
```

If you now run the code again, you get an ordered set of odd numbers.

`AsParallel` and Binary Operators

In some situations you use operators that take two data sources; among such operators, there are the following binary operators: `Join`, `GroupJoin`, `Except`, `Concat`, `Intersect`, `Union`, `Zip`, and `SequenceEqual`. To use parallelism with binary operators on two data sources, you need to invoke `AsParallel` on both collections, as demonstrated by the following code:

```
Dim result = firstSource.AsParallel.Except(secondSource.AsParallel)
```

The following code still works, but it won't use parallelism:

```
Dim result = firstSource.AsParallel.Except(secondSource)
```

Using `ParallelEnumerable`

The `System.Linq` namespace for .NET 4.6 provides the `ParallelEnumerable` class, which is the parallel counterpart of `Enumerable` and provides extension methods specific to parallelism, such as `AsParallel`. You can use `ParallelEnumerable` members instead of invoking `AsParallel` because both return a `ParallelQuery(Of T)`. For example, the PLINQ query in the first example could be rewritten as follows:

```
Dim range = ParallelEnumerable.Range(0, 1000)

'Just add "AsParallel"
Dim query = From num In range
            Where (IsOdd(num))
            Select num
```

In this case the range variable is of type `ParallelEnumerable(Of Integer)`, and therefore you do not need to invoke `AsParallel`. Some differences in how data is handled do exist, which can often lead `AsParallel` to be faster. Explaining in detail the `ParallelEnumerable` architecture is beyond the scope in this introductory chapter, but if you are curious you can take a look at this blog post from the Task Parallel Library Team, which is still valid today: http://blogs.msdn.com/pfxteam/archive/2007/12/02/6558579.aspx.

Controlling PLINQ Queries

PLINQ offers additional extension methods and features to provide more control over tasks that run queries, all exposed by the `System.Linq.ParallelEnumerable` class. In this section you get an overview of extension methods and learn how you can control your PLINQ queries.

Setting the Maximum Tasks Number

As explained previously in this chapter, the Task Parallel Library relies on tasks instead of threads, although working with tasks means scaling processing over multiple threads. You can specify the maximum number of tasks that can execute a thread by invoking the `WithDegreeOfParallelism` extension method and passing the number as an argument. The following code demonstrates how you can get the list of running processes with a PLINQ query that runs a maximum of three concurrent tasks:

```
Dim processes = Process.GetProcesses.
                AsParallel.WithDegreeOfParallelism(3)
```

Forcing Parallelism in Every Query

Not all code can benefit from parallelism and PLINQ. Such technology is intelligent enough to determine whether a query can benefit from PLINQ according to its *shape*. The shape of a query consists of the operator it requires and algorithm or delegates that are involved. PLINQ analyzes the shape and can determine where to apply a parallel algorithm. You can force a query to be completely parallelized, regardless of its shape, by invoking the `WithExecutionMode` extension methods that receive an argument of type `ParallelExecutionMode` that is an enumeration exposing two self-explanatory members: `ForceParallelism` and `Default`. The following code demonstrates how you can force a query to be completely parallelized:

```
Dim processes = Process.GetProcesses.
                AsParallel.WithExecutionMode( _
                ParallelExecutionMode.ForceParallelism)
```

Merge Options

PLINQ automatically partitions query sources so that it can use multiple threads that can work on each part concurrently. You can control how parts are handled by invoking the `WithMergeOptions` method that receives an argument of type `ParallelMergeOptions`. Such enumeration provides the following specifications:

▶ `NotBuffered` returns elements composing the result as soon as they are available

▶ `FullyBuffered` returns the complete result, meaning that query operations are buffered until every one has been completed

▶ `AutoBuffered` leaves to the compiler to choose the best buffering method in that particular situation

You invoke `WithMergeOptions` as follows:

```
Dim processes = Process.GetProcesses.
                AsParallel.WithMergeOptions( _
                ParallelMergeOptions.FullyBuffered)
```

With the exception of the `ForAll` method that is always `NotBuffered` and `OrderBy` that is always `FullyBuffered`, other extension methods/operators can support all merge options. The full list of operators is described in the following page of the MSDN Library: http:// msdn.microsoft.com/en-us/library/dd547137(v=vs.110).aspx.

Canceling PLINQ Queries

If you need to provide a way for canceling a PLINQ query, you can invoke the `WithCancellation` method. You first need to implement a method to be invoked when you need to cancel the query. The method receives a `CancellationTokenSource` argument (which sends notices that a query must be canceled) and can be implemented as follows:

```
Dim cs As New CancellationTokenSource

Private Sub DoCancel(ByVal cs As CancellationTokenSource)
    'Ensures that query is cancelled when executing
    Thread.Sleep(500)
    cs.Cancel()
End Sub
```

When you have a method of this kind, you need to start a new task by pointing to this method as follows:

```
Tasks.Task.Factory.StartNew(Sub()
                                DoCancel(cs)
                            End Sub)
```

When a PLINQ query is canceled, an `OperationCanceledException` is thrown so that you can handle cancellation, as demonstrated in the following code snippet:

```
Private Sub CancellationDemo()
    Try

        Dim processes = Process.GetProcesses.
                            AsParallel.WithCancellation(cs.Token)

    Catch ex As OperationCanceledException
        Console.WriteLine(ex.Message)
    Catch ex As Exception

    End Try
End Sub
```

To cancel a query, invoke the `DoCancel` method.

Handling Exceptions

In single-core scenarios, LINQ queries are executed sequentially. This means that if your code encounters an exception, the exception is at a specific point, and the code can handle it normally. In multicore scenarios, multiple exceptions could occur because more threads are running on multiple processors concurrently. Because of this, PLINQ uses the `AggregateException` class, which is specific for exceptions within parallelism and has already been discussed in this chapter. With PLINQ, you might find useful two members: `Flatten` is a method that turns it into a single exception, and `InnerExceptions` is a property storing a collection of `InnerException` objects. Each represents one of the occurred exceptions.

DISABLE "JUST MY CODE"

As you did for Task Parallel Library samples shown previously, to correctly catch an `AggregateException` you need to disable the Just My Code debugging in the debug options; otherwise, the code execution will break on the query and will not enable you to investigate the exception.

Consider the following code, in which an array of strings stores some null values and causes `NullReferenceException` at runtime:

```
Private Sub HandlingExceptions()
    Dim strings() As String = New String() {"Test",
                                             Nothing,
                                             Nothing,
                                             "Test"}

    'Just add "AsParallel"
    Try
        Dim query = strings.AsParallel.
                        Where(Function(s) s.StartsWith("T")).
```

```
            Select(Function(s) s)
        For Each item In query
            Console.WriteLine(item)
        Next

    Catch ex As AggregateException

        For Each problem In ex.InnerExceptions
            Console.WriteLine(problem.ToString)
        Next

    Catch ex As Exception

    Finally
        Console.ReadLine()
    End Try
End Sub
```

In a single-core scenario, a single `NullReferenceException` is caught and handled the first time the code encounters the error. In multicore scenarios, an `AggregateException` could happen due to multiple threads running on multiple processors; therefore, you cannot control where and how many exceptions can be thrown. Consequently, the `AggregateException` stores information on such exceptions. The previous code shows how you can iterate the `InnerExceptions` property.

Summary

Parallel computing enables you to use multicore architectures for scaling operation execution across all available processors on the machine. In this chapter, you learned how parallel computing in .NET Framework 4.6 relies on the concept of task; for this, you learned how to create and run tasks via the `System.Threading.Tasks.Task` class to generate units of work for running tasks in parallel. You also learned how to handle concurrent exceptions and request tasks cancellation. Another important topic in parallel computing is loops. Here you learned how the `Parallel.For` and `Parallel.ForEach` loops enable multithreaded iterations that are scaled across all available processors. Next, you took a tour inside the concurrent collections in .NET Framework 4.6, a set of thread-safe collections you can use to share information across tasks. Finally, you got information about a specific LINQ implementation known as Parallel LINQ that enables you to scale query executions over multiple threads and processors so that you can get the benefits in improving performances of your code. Specifically, you learned how to invoke the `AsParallel` method for creating parallelized queries and comparing them to classic LINQ queries. You also saw how to control queries forcing parallelism, implementing cancellation, setting the maximum number of tasks, and handling the `AggregateException` exception.

CHAPTER 42

Asynchronous Programming

When you go to the restaurant, there are waiters and waitresses ready to serve your table. A waiter takes your order, brings the order to the kitchen, goes to serve another table, and then comes back to your table to bring you your meals. While waiting for you to finish, the waiter does similar operations for other patrons. So, the waiter does not stand at your table from when you arrive until you finish your meal before going to serve another table; if he did, the restaurant would need to hire one waiter per table to avoid the block of their activity, which is not practical. If you compare this real-world description with computer programming, the waiter is some code in your application. If this code must perform a long-running operation and you write such a code in the user interface (UI) thread or, more generally, in one thread, your code will act like a waiter that waits from the start to the end of the meal on a table and cannot do anything else in the meantime, thereby blocking the application activity. This is what happens when you write code in a synchronous approach; synchronous code performs one task at a time and the next task starts only when the previous one completes. To avoid blocking the application, you can use multithreading and instances of the Thread class, described in Chapter 40, "Processes and Multithreading." With multithreading, you can write code that performs a long-running operation on a separate thread and keep the application responsive. Threading is a way to write asynchronous code that developers have been using for a long time, along with two patterns: the Event-based Asynchronous Pattern and the Asynchronous Programming Model. But actually, asynchrony does not necessarily mean running on a background thread. Instead, it means that a task is executed in different moments. Threading is one way to achieve asynchrony, but it is quite complex and not always the best choice. For this reason, back in .NET 4.5 Microsoft introduced new libraries and new keywords to the Visual Basic and Visual C# languages to make asynchronous calls easy. In this chapter, you get an overview of both the Event-based Asynchronous Pattern and the Asynchronous Programming Model; then you learn about the Asynchronous Pattern, which is without a doubt one of the most important features in Visual Basic language. You will see how easily you can now write modern and responsive applications via asynchronous code.

Overview of Asynchrony

Modern applications often need to perform complex computations or access resources through a network. Complex computations can become very long, a network resource might not be available, or the application might not scale well on the server. If the code that performs this kind of operation is running in the same thread as the caller, the thread gets blocked until all operations complete. If such a thread is the UI thread, the user interface becomes unresponsive and can no longer accept the user input until all operations have been completed. This type of approach is called *synchronous* because only one operation at a time is executed until all the processes are completed.

Having an unresponsive user interface is not acceptable in modern applications, so this is the place where asynchrony comes in. Asynchrony enables you to execute some pieces of code in a different thread or context, so that the caller thread never blocks. If this is the UI thread, the user interface remains responsive even if other operations are running. The other thread (or context) then tells the caller thread that an operation completed, regardless of the successful or unsuccessful result. The .NET Framework has been offering, for a long time, two thread-based approaches to asynchrony called *Event-based Asynchrony* and *Asynchronous Programming Model* in which you launch operations in a different thread and get notification of their completion via delegates. As you saw in Chapter 41, "Parallel Programming and Parallel LINQ," the .NET Framework 4.0 introduced the Task Parallel Library and the concept of parallelism. TPL makes it easier to create applications capable of scaling long-running operations across all the available processors. TPL also makes applications faster and more responsive while executing complex tasks concurrently, but this all about concurrency, which is not the same as asynchrony. In this chapter, you first learn about the Event-based Asynchrony and the Asynchronous Programming Model to get started with the important concepts; then you start putting your hands on the possibilities offered by the .NET Framework 4.6. By doing so, it will be easier for you to compare the old way to the new way and understand why you should migrate your exiting code to use the new patterns.

The Old-Fashioned Way: Event-Based Asynchrony

More often than not, applications need to perform multiple tasks at one time, while still remaining responsive to user interaction. One of the possibilities offered by the .NET Framework since the early days is the *Event-based Asynchronous Pattern* (EAP). A class that adheres to this pattern implements a number of methods whose names terminate with the

`Async` suffix and that execute some work on a different thread. Such methods mirror their synchronous counterparts, which instead block the caller thread. Also, for each of these asynchronous methods, there is an event whose name terminates with the `Completed` suffix and that is raised when the asynchronous operation completes. This way, the caller gets notification of the completion. Because the user might want to cancel an asynchronous operation at a certain point, classes adhering to the EAP must also implement methods whose names terminate with `CancelAsync`, each related to one of the asynchronous methods that actually performs the requested work. When such work is completed, a delegate will handle the operation result before control is sent back to the caller; this delegate is also known as *callback*. This pattern also requires classes to support cancellation and progress reporting. To understand how EAP works, let's consider a simple example based on the `System.Net.WebClient` class, which enables you to access networks from client applications. Consider the following code:

```
Sub Main()
    Dim client As New System.Net.WebClient
    AddHandler client.DownloadStringCompleted,
            AddressOf client_DownloadStringCompleted

    client.DownloadStringAsync(New Uri("http://msdn.microsoft.com"))
End Sub
```

A new instance of the `WebClient` class is created. To receive notification of completion, you must subscribe the `DownloadStringCompleted` event (assuming you will download a string, but other methods and related events are available) and supply a delegate that will be invoked when the event is raised. After you have subscribed the event, you can then invoke the desired method; in the current example, it's the `WebClient.DownloadStringAsync` method that downloads contents from the specified URL as a string. If you write other lines of code after the invocation of `DownloadStringAsync`, these are not necessarily executed after the download operation has completed as it would instead happen in synchronous code. So, if you need to manipulate the result of an asynchronous operation, you must do it inside the callback, which is the delegate invoked after the completion event is raised. The following code provides an example:

```
Private Sub client_DownloadStringCompleted(sender As Object,
                                e As DownloadStringCompletedEventArgs)
    If e.Error Is Nothing Then
        Console.WriteLine(XDocument.Parse(e.Result).ToString)
        Console.WriteLine("Done")
    End If
End Sub
```

As you can see, the `DownloadStringCompletedEventArgs` class contains information about the result of the asynchronous operation. Usually, a specific class inherits from `System.EventArgs` and stores the result of an asynchronous operation, one per asynchronous method. You can check for errors, and if everything is successful, you can then work with the `e.Result` property that contains the actual result of the task. Classes that adhere to the EAP also enable you to report the progress of an asynchronous operation by exposing a `ProgressChanged` event. Continuing the previous example, the `WebClient` class exposes an event called `ProgressChanged` and a class called `DownloadProgressChangedEventArgs` that stores information about the operation progress. To handle such an event, you must first subscribe it like this:

```
AddHandler client.DownloadProgressChanged,
          AddressOf client_DownloadProgressChanged
```

You then handle the `ProgressChanged` event to report progress:

```
Private Sub client_DownloadProgressChanged(sender As Object,
                                      e As DownloadProgressChangedEventArgs)
    Console.WriteLine(e.ProgressPercentage)
    'Use e.BytesReceived for the number of bytes received in progress
    'Use e.TotalBytesToReceive to get the total bytes to be downloaded
End Sub
```

You can eventually use lambda expressions and statement lambdas as anonymous delegates, as demonstrated in the following code:

```
Private Sub Download()
    Dim client As New WebClient
    AddHandler client.DownloadStringCompleted,
            Sub(sender, e)
                If e.Error Is Nothing Then
                    Console.WriteLine(XDocument.
                                    Parse(e.Result).
                                    ToString)
                End If
            End Sub

    client.DownloadStringAsync(New Uri("http://msdn.microsoft.com"))
End Sub
```

The EAP has been very popular among developers for years because the way you write code is similar to how you handle events of the user interface. This certainly makes the asynchronous approach simpler. Later in this chapter, when comparing EAP to the new `Async` pattern, you will better understand why the old way can lead to confusion and become very complex to handle.

The Old-Fashioned Way: The Asynchronous Programming Model

The Asynchronous Programming Model (APM) is still based on threading. In this model, an operation is launched on a separated thread via a method whose name starts with `Begin` (e.g., `BeginWrite`). A method like this must accept, among its parameters, an argument of type `IAsyncResult`. This is a special type used to store the result and the state of an asynchronous operation. The most important members of this interface are two properties: `AsyncState` (of type `Object`), which represents the result of the operation under the form of either a primitive or a composite type, and `IsCompleted` (of type `Boolean`), which returns if the operation actually completed. As another parameter, these methods must receive a delegate that will be executed when the asynchronous operation is completed. Within this delegate, you will be able to analyze the result of the asynchronous operation, but you will also need to explicitly end the asynchronous operation by invoking a method whose name starts with `End` (e.g., `EndWrite`). Some classes in the .NET Framework are built to be APM-ready, such as `Stream` and its derived classes. So, to demonstrate how APM works, a good example can be based on the `FileStream` class. The following code demonstrates how to write some bytes to a stream asynchronously and how the callback receives information from the caller with `IAsyncResult`.

```
Private Sub OpenStreamAsync()
    Dim someBytes(1000) As Byte
    Dim randomGenerator As New Random()
    'Generate a random sequence of bytes
    randomGenerator.NextBytes(someBytes)

    Using fs As New FileStream("Somedata.dat", FileMode.Create, FileAccess.Write)
        Dim result As IAsyncResult =
            fs.BeginWrite(someBytes, 0, someBytes.Length,
                    AddressOf fs_EndWrite, fs)
    End Using

End Sub


Private Sub fs_EndWrite(result As IAsyncResult)
    Dim stream As FileStream = CType(result.AsyncState, FileStream)
    stream.EndWrite(result)
    'Additional work goes here...
End Sub
```

The `IAsyncResult.AsyncState` property contains the actual data sent from the caller and must be explicitly converted into the type that you need to work with; in this case, the stream. The reason is that you also must explicitly invoke the `EndWrite` method that finalizes the asynchronous operation. You can also pass custom objects as the `IAsyncResult` argument for the callback, to pass more complex and detailed information that you might need to elaborate when the task completes.

The Modern Way: The `Async` Pattern

Visual Basic 2012 introduced a new pattern that solves some problems related to threading and enables you to write better and cleaner code. It does this with two keywords: `Async` and `Await`. `Async` is a modifier you use to mark methods that run asynchronous operations. Await is an operator that gets a placeholder for the result of an asynchronous operation and waits for the result, which will be sent back at a later time while other operations are executed. This enables you to keep the caller thread responsive. For a first understanding of how this pattern works, let's take a look at the following function that downloads the content of a website as a string, returning the result as an XDocument that can be manipulated with LINQ:

```
Function DownloadSite() As XDocument
    Dim client As New System.Net.WebClient
    Dim content As String =
        client.DownloadString("http://www.microsoft.com")

    Dim document As XDocument = XDocument.Parse(content)
    Return document
End Function
```

This code is pretty easy because it creates an instance of the WebClient class, then downloads the content of the specified website, and finally returns the XML document converted through XDocument.Parse. This code is synchronous, meaning that the caller thread will remain blocked until all the operations in the method body are completed. If the caller thread is the UI thread, the user interface will remain blocked. Figure 42.1 shows a graphical representation of how a synchronous call works.

UI Thread

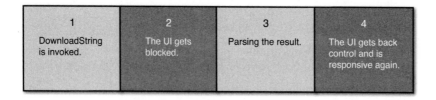

1	2	3	4
DownloadString is invoked.	The UI gets blocked.	Parsing the result.	The UI gets back control and is responsive again.

FIGURE 42.1   Representation of a synchronous call.

This is how you can rewrite the previous code using the Async pattern:

```
Async Function DownloadSiteAsync() As Task(Of XDocument)
    Dim client As New System.Net.WebClient
    Dim content As String =
        Await client.DownloadStringTaskAsync("http://www.microsoft.com")

    Dim document As XDocument = XDocument.Parse(content)

    Return document
End Function
```

`Await` AS A RESERVED KEYWORD

The `Await` keyword is not a reserved word everywhere in the code. It is a reserved word when it appears inside a method or lambda marked with the `Async` modifier and only if it appears after that modifier. In all other cases, it is not a reserved word.

This code is asynchronous, so it will never block the caller thread because not all the code is executed at the same time. Figure 42.2 shows a representation of an asynchronous call.

UI Thread

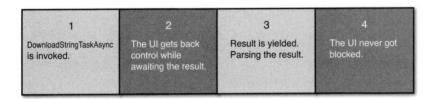

FIGURE 42.2   Representation of an asynchronous call.

THE STORY OF THREADS WITH `Async/Await`

The `Async` pattern relies on the concept of `Task` described in the previous chapter. For this reason, asynchronous code written with `Async/Await` does not necessarily run on a separate thread. In fact, it is represented by an instance of the `Task` class. Because one thread can run multiple `Task` instances, it is normal that asynchronous code can run in the same caller thread, such as the UI thread.

The following is a list of important considerations that will be discussed in the next section:

▶ A method that runs asynchronous code must be marked with the `Async` modifier. When the compiler encounters this modifier, it expects an Await expression inside the method body.

▶ Methods marked with `Async` are also referred to as *asynchronous methods*.

▶ By convention, names of asynchronous methods must end with the `Async` suffix.

▶ Asynchronous methods must return a `Task` (if they return no value) or a `Task(Of T)`, where T is the type that you would return with synchronous methods. See the previous `XDocument` example.

▶ Asynchronous methods support the standard access modifiers (such as `Private`, `Public`, and so on), but they cannot be iterator methods at the same time, so the `Iterator` modifier cannot be used along with `Async`.

▶ The `Main` method of an application can never be asynchronous. Notice that if you mark the `Main` method as asynchronous and write asynchronous calls in its body, the background compiler will not report any warnings or exceptions. It will report an error when you compile or try to run the code.

▶ Any method that returns a `Task` or `Task(Of T)` can be used along with `Await` ("awaitable").

▶ The `Await` expression puts a placeholder for the result of the invoked task. The result will be returned later at some time, making the application remain responsive. However, the next code will actually run when the result has been returned. This is because the compiler ideally splits the method into two parts; the second part is nothing but a callback that is executed when the awaited task notifies the caller of its completion.

▶ Although you should return a `Task` or `Task(Of T)`, the compiler automatically infers the task-based type even if you return the original type. The second code snippet in the previous example demonstrates how the `Return` statement returns `XDocument` but the compiler automatically returns `Task(Of XDocument)`.

Although these first important considerations might sound confusing, you will soon appreciate the benefits of using the `Async` pattern. It enables you to avoid multithreading and explicit callbacks, enabling you to write much easier and cleaner code. In the next section, you get started with the `Async` pattern with a practical example so that all the concepts described so far will be explained better.

Where Do I Use `Async`?

The `Async` libraries are in the .NET Framework 4.6, so you can use the pattern in whatever technology uses .NET 4.6. WPF, Windows Forms, ASP.NET, and even Windows Store apps. These are all technologies that can leverage the power of these libraries.

In other words, you have no limits in using the new pattern and should always use this new way to asynchrony.

`Async` AND WINDOWS 8.X STORE APPS

There is another important reason beyond the availability of the `Async` pattern in .NET languages now: developing Windows 8.x Store Apps. Windows 8.x Apps require you to write most of the code asynchronously, and using old techniques would make developing apps really difficult. Instead, with the `Async` pattern, coding for Windows 8.x is much faster, easier, and cleaner. Because the user interface of Windows 8.x apps must always be responsive with no exceptions, using the `Async` pattern is very common. Also, the unification of the programming model with the Windows Phone 8.1 platform made the `Async` pattern natively available in these kinds of apps. This is another reason to read this chapter with particular attention.

When and Why to Use `Async/Await` and Comparisons with the TPL

Using the `Async` pattern enables you to write applications that are more responsive and that perform better, but you will not use it everywhere. In fact, there are specific situations in which `Async` has benefits. As a general rule, `Async`'s main purpose is to keep the UI responsive while tasks running in the UI thread might become potentially blocking. You use `Async` in the following scenarios:

▶ Potentially blocking tasks running in the user interface thread

▶ Image processing

▶ I/O operations (disk, networking, web access)

▶ Working with sockets

Using `Async` and `Await` differs from parallel programming because the purpose is not to have pieces of code that run concurrently; instead, the purpose is keeping the user interface responsive. In parallel programming, you have code that is CPU-consuming, so you use `Task` instances to split the execution of your code into multiple units of work. Thus, most of the code is executed at the same time by using a multicore architecture. In `Async`, instead, you do not have CPU-consuming code. You might have potentially blocking tasks, though, so your goal is to keep the UI thread free. This is possible because the result of an `Await` expression is delayed and control is yielded to the caller while waiting.

Getting Started with `Async/Await`

In this section you see the `Async` pattern with an example based on retrieving information from the Internet. You will build a WPF application that downloads RSS feeds information from the Web, simulating a long-running process over a network. You first, though, create an application that works synchronously; then you see how to implement the Event-based Asynchronous Pattern described at the beginning of this chapter. Finally, you learn how things change in a third example built using the new `Async` and `Await` keywords.

The Synchronous Approach

Create a new WPF project with Visual Basic 2015 and .NET Framework 4.6. The application will consume the Visual Basic RSS feed exposed by the Microsoft's Channel9 website, with particular regard to the list of published videos. Each item in the feed has a large number of properties, but for the sake of simplicity only the most important will be presented in the application's UI. So, the first thing you need to do is create a class that represents a single video described in the feed. Listing 42.1 demonstrates how to implement a class called `Video`.

LISTING 42.1   Representing a Single Video

```
Public Class Video
    Public Property Title As String
    Public Property Url As String
```

```
    Public Property Thumbnail As String
    Public Property DateRecorded As String
    Public Property Speaker As String

    Public Shared FeedUrl As String = _
        "http://channel9.msdn.com/Tags/visual+basic/RSS"
End Class
```

Notice that all the properties are of type `String` just to represent values as they exactly come from the feed. Also, a shared field contains the feed URL. Now open the MainWindow.xaml file, to prepare the application's user interface. The goal is to show the videos' thumbnails and summary information and to provide the ability to click a thumbnail to open the video in its original location. The `ListBox` control is a good choice to display a collection of items. This will be placed inside the default `Grid` panel. Each item in the `ListBox` will be presented via a custom template made of a Border and a `StackPanel` that contains an `Image` control (for the video thumbnail) and a number of `TextBlock` controls that are bound to properties of the `Video` class. Listing 42.2 shows the full code for the main window.

LISTING 42.2   Implementing the Application's User Interface

```
<Window x:Class="MainWindow"
    xmlns="http://schemas.microsoft.com/winfx/2006/xaml/presentation"
    xmlns:x="http://schemas.microsoft.com/winfx/2006/xaml"
    Title="MainWindow" Height="350" Width="525">
    <Grid>
        <ListBox Name="VideoBox" ItemsSource="{Binding}"
                ScrollViewer.HorizontalScrollBarVisibility="Disabled">
            <ListBox.ItemsPanel>
                <ItemsPanelTemplate>
                    <WrapPanel VirtualizingPanel.IsVirtualizing="True"/>
                </ItemsPanelTemplate>
            </ListBox.ItemsPanel>
            <ListBox.ItemTemplate>
                <DataTemplate>
                    <Border BorderBrush="Black" Margin="5"
                            BorderThickness="2" Tag={Binding Url}
                            MouseLeftButtonUp="Border_MouseLeftButtonUp_1"
                            Width="200" Height="220">
                        <StackPanel>
                            <Image Source="{Binding Thumbnail}"
                                    Width="160" Height="120" />
                            <TextBlock Text="{Binding Title}" TextWrapping="Wrap"
                                    Grid.Row="1"/>
                            <TextBlock Text="{Binding DateRecorded}" Grid.Row="2"/>
                            <TextBlock Text="{Binding Speaker}" Grid.Row="3"/>
```

```
                    </StackPanel>
                </Border>
            </DataTemplate>
        </ListBox.ItemTemplate>
    </ListBox>
</Grid>
</Window>
```

42

It is worth mentioning that the code replaces the default items container (a
`VirtualizingStackPanel`) with a `WrapPanel` container so that items are not forced to be
presented on one line horizontally. This requires disabling the horizontal scrollbar on the
`ListBox` (`ScrollViewer.HorizontalScrollBarVisibility="Disabled"`) and changing the
`ListBox.ItemsPanel` content with the `WrapPanel`. Also notice how the `Border.Tag` property is bound to the `Url` property of the `Video` class. This enables you to store the video's
URL and click the Border at runtime to open the video in its original location. Now switch
to the code-behind file. The first thing you must do is add a number of `Imports` directives,
some for importing XML namespaces needed to map information from the RSS feed and
some for working with additional .NET classes:

```
Imports System.Net
Imports <xmlns:media="http://search.yahoo.com/mrss/">
Imports <xmlns:dc="http://purl.org/dc/elements/1.1/">
```

The next step is implementing a method that queries the RSS feed returning the list of
videos. In this first implementation, you will use a synchronous approach, which will
block the user interface when the application is running:

```
Private Function QueryVideos() As IEnumerable(Of Video)
    Dim client As New WebClient

    Dim data As String = client.DownloadString(New Uri(Video.FeedUrl))

    Dim doc As XDocument = XDocument.Parse(data)
        Dim query = From video In doc...<item>
                    Select New Video With {
                        .Title = video.<title>.Value,
                        .Speaker = video.<dc:creator>.Value,
                        .Url = video.<link>.Value,
                        .Thumbnail = video...<media:thumbnail>.
                        FirstOrDefault?.@url,
                        .DateRecorded = String.Concat("Recorded on ",
                        Date.Parse(video.<pubDate>.Value,
                        Globalization.CultureInfo.InvariantCulture).
                        ToShortDateString) }

    Return query
End Function
```

The code is simple. An instance of the WebClient class, which provides simplified access to networked resources, is created and the invocation of its DownloadString method downloads the entire content of the feed under the form of a String object. Notice that this is the point at which the user interface gets blocked. In fact, it will need to wait for DownloadString to complete the operation before returning to be responsive. After the feed has been downloaded, it is converted into an object of type XDocument and a LINQ query enables you to retrieve all the needed information (refer to Chapter 27, "Manipulating XML Documents with LINQ and XML Literals," for further information on LINQ to XML). Finally, a method called LoadVideos will run the query and assign the result to the Window's DataContext; such a method will be invoked at startup. You can change this type of implementation, but it will be more useful later when making comparisons with the asynchronous implementation. The following code demonstrates this, plus the event handler for the MouseLeftButtonUp event of the Border control, where you launch the video in its original web page:

```
Private Sub LoadVideos()
    Me.DataContext = QueryVideos()
End Sub


Private Sub MainWindow_Loaded(sender As Object,
                            e As RoutedEventArgs) Handles Me.Loaded
    LoadVideos()
End Sub


Private Sub Border_MouseLeftButtonUp_1(sender As Object,
                                    e As MouseButtonEventArgs)
    'Tag is of type Object so an explicit conversion to String is required
    Dim instance = CType(sender, Border)
    Process.Start(CStr(instance.Tag))
End Sub
```

You can now run the application. Figure 42.3 shows the result of the query over the video feed.

FIGURE 42.3   Loading an RSS feed the synchronous way.

The application works as expected, but the real problem with this approach is that the user cannot interact with the interface while the query is running. The reason is that the query's code is running in the UI thread, so the user interface is busy with the query and does not accept any interaction. This can be easily demonstrated by attempting to move the window while the query is running because you will not be able to move it elsewhere. This has other implications: you cannot refresh controls that display the status of the task because they would be refreshed only when the query completes. Also, you cannot enable users to cancel the operation because you would need a button that the user would never be able to click.

Event-Based Asynchrony and Callbacks

A much better approach is moving the long-running operation into a separate thread, so that the UI can remain responsive while the other thread executes the operation. Lots of classes in the .NET Framework, especially those whose job is interacting with the Web and with networks-expose event-based asynchrony through methods that launch and execute an operation on a separate thread and raise an event when it is completed, passing the result to the caller via a callback. The `WebClient` class has an asynchronous counterpart of `DownloadString`, called `DownloadStringAsync`, that you can use to execute the code on a separate thread and wait for the query result via a callback. The following code demonstrates how to accomplish this (do not worry if you notice something wrong because an explanation is provided in moments):

```vbnet
Private Function QueryVideos() As IEnumerable(Of Video)
    Dim client As New WebClient
    Dim query As IEnumerable(Of Video)

    AddHandler client.DownloadStringCompleted, Sub(sender, e)
                                                   If e.Error IsNot Nothing Then
                                                       'Error handling logic here..
                                                   End If

                                                   Dim doc = _
                                                       XDocument.Parse(e.Result)
                                                   Dim query = From video
                                                            In doc...<item>
                                                            Select _
                                                            New Video With {
                                                     .Title =
                                                     video.<title>.Value,
                                                     .Speaker =
                                                     video.<dc:creator>.
                                                     Value,
                                                     .Url = video.<link>.Value,
                                                     .Thumbnail =
                                                     video...<media:thumbnail>.
                                                     FirstOrDefault?.@url,
                                                     .DateRecorded =
                                                     String.Concat("Recorded on ",
                                                     Date.Parse(video.
                                                     <pubDate>.Value,
                                                     Globalization.CultureInfo.
                                                     InvariantCulture).
                                                     ToShortDateString)}
                                               End Sub

    client.DownloadStringAsync(New Uri(Video.FeedUrl))
    Return query
End Function
```

The code specifies a statement lambda as an event handler for the DownloadString-Completed event, instead of declaring a separate delegate and pointing to this via an AddressOf clause. The e object is of type DownloadStringCompletedEventArgs and contains the result of the operation. The problem in this code is that the Return statement does not work because it is attempting to return a result that has not been produced yet. On the other side, you cannot write something like this:

```
Private Function QueryVideos() As IEnumerable(Of Video)
    Dim client As New WebClient
    Dim query As IEnumerable(Of Video)

    AddHandler client.DownloadStringCompleted, Sub(sender, e)
                                        If e.Error IsNot Nothing Then
                                            'Error handling logic here..
                                        End If

                                        Dim doc = _
                                            XDocument.Parse(e.Result)
                                        Dim query = From ...
                                        Return query


                                    End Sub

    client.DownloadStringAsync(New Uri(Video.FeedUrl))
End Function
```

This code does not work because you cannot return a result from a `Sub` and because it should be returned from the outer method, not the inner. In conclusion, `Return` statements do not work well with event-based asynchrony. The solution at this point is returning the result via a callback and an `Action(Of T)` object. So the appropriate implementation of the `QueryVideos` method in this approach is the following:

```
Private Sub QueryVideos(listOfVideos As Action(Of IEnumerable(Of Video),
                                        Exception))
    Dim client As New WebClient
    AddHandler client.DownloadStringCompleted, Sub(sender, e)
                                        If e.Error IsNot Nothing Then
                                            listOfVideos(Nothing,
                                                        e.Error)
                                            Return
                                        End If

                                        Dim doc = _
                                            XDocument.Parse(e.Result)
                                        Dim query =
                                            From video In doc...<item>
                                            Select New Video With {
                                            .Title =
                                            video.<title>.Value,
                                            .Speaker =
                                            video.<dc:creator>.
                                            Value,
                                            .Url = video.<link>.Value,
```

```
                                                    .Thumbnail =
                                                    video...<media:thumbnail>.
                                                    FirstOrDefault?.@url,
                                                    .DateRecorded =
                                                    String.Concat("Recorded on ",
                                                    Date.Parse(video.
                                                    <pubDate>.Value,
                                                    Globalization.CultureInfo.
                                                    InvariantCulture).
                                                    ToShortDateString)}
                                            listOfVideos(query, Nothing)
                                    End Sub

        Try
            client.DownloadStringAsync(New Uri(Video.FeedUrl))
        Catch ex As Exception
            listOfVideos(Nothing, ex)
        End Try
    End Sub
```

The previous code does the following:

1. Holds the list of videos from the RSS feed in an `Action(Of IEnumerable(Of Video), Exception)` object. The `Exception` instance here is useful to determine whether an error occurred during the query execution.

2. If the query completes successfully, the query result is passed to the `Action` object (that is, the callback).

3. If an exception occurs during the query execution (see the first `If` block inside the statement lambda), the callback receives `Nothing` as the first parameter because the collection of items was not retrieved successfully and the exception instance as the second parameter.

4. If an exception occurs immediately when the web request is made, the callback still receives `Nothing` and the exception instance. This is at the `Try..Catch` block level.

So using a callback here has been necessary for two reasons: sending the query result back to the caller correctly and handling two exception scenarios. But you are not done yet. In fact, you have to completely rewrite the `LoadVideos` method to hold the result of the callback and determine whether the operation completed successfully before assigning the query result to the Window's `DataContext`. The following code demonstrates this:

```
Private Sub LoadVideos()
    Dim action As Action(Of IEnumerable(Of Video),
                            Exception) = Nothing
    action =
        Sub(videos, ex)
```

```
            If ex IsNot Nothing Then
                MessageBox.Show(ex.Message)
                Return
            End If

            If (videos.Any) Then
                Me.DataContext = videos
            Else
                QueryVideos(action)
            End If
        End Sub
    QueryVideos(action)
End Sub
```

As you can see, the code is not easy, unless you are an expert. There is an invocation to the previous implementation of `QueryVideos`, passing the instance of the callback. When the result is sent back, the statement lambda first checks for exceptions and, if not, takes the query result as the data source. If you now run the application again, you will get the same result shown in Figure 42.3; however, this time the user interface is responsive and the user can interact with it. But reaching this objective had costs. You had to completely rewrite method implementations and write code that is complex and difficult to read and to extend. So, the multithreading in this situation has not been very helpful. This is the point in which the `Async/Await` pattern comes in to make things simple.

Asynchrony with `Async/Await`

The `Async/Await` pattern has the goal of simplifying the way developers write asynchronous code. You will learn a lot about the underlying infrastructure, but before digging into that, it is important for you to see how your code can be much cleaner and readable. Let's start by modifying the `QueryVideos` method to make some important considerations:

```
Private Async Function QueryVideosAsync() As _
        Task(Of IEnumerable(Of Video))
    Dim client As New WebClient

    Dim data = Await client.DownloadStringTaskAsync(New Uri(Video.FeedUrl))

    Dim doc = XDocument.Parse(data)

    Dim query = From video In doc...<item>
                Select New Video With {
                    .Title = video.<title>.Value,
                    .Speaker = video.<dc:creator>.Value,
                    .Url = video.<link>.Value,
                    .Thumbnail = video...<media:thumbnail>.
                    FirstOrDefault?.@url,
                    .DateRecorded = String.Concat("Recorded on ",
```

```
                    Date.Parse(video.<pubDate>.Value,
                        Globalization.CultureInfo.InvariantCulture).
                    ToShortDateString)}

        Return query
End Function
```

Asynchronous methods must be decorated with the `Async` modifier. When the compiler encounters this modifier, it expects that the method body contains one or more `Await` statements. If not, it reports a warning saying that the method will be treated as synchronous, suggesting that the `Async` modifier should be removed. `Async` methods must return an object of type `Task`. If the method returns a value (`Function`), then it must return a `Task(Of T)` where `T` is the actual result type. Otherwise, if the method returns no value, both following syntaxes are allowed:

```
Async Function TestAsync() As Task
    'You can avoid Return statements, the compiler assumes returning no values
End Function

Async Sub TestAsync()
    '...
End Sub
```

The difference between the two implementations is that the first one can be called inside another method with `Await`, but the second one cannot (because it does not need to be awaited). A typical example of the second syntax is about event handlers: they can be asynchronous and can use `Await`, but no other method will wait for their result. By convention, the suffix of asynchronous methods is the `Async` literal. This is why `QueryVideos` has been renamed into `QueryVideosAsync`. An exception is represented by asynchronous methods already existing in previous versions of the .NET Framework, based on the EAP, whose name already ends with `Async`. In this case `Async` is replaced with `TaskAsync`. For instance (as you discover in moments), the `DownloadStringAsync` method in the `WebClient` class has a new counterpart called `DownloadStringTaskAsync`. Any method that returns a `Task` or `Task(Of T)` can be used with `Await`. With `Await`, a task is started but the control flow is immediately returned to the caller. The result of the task will not be returned immediately, but later and only when the task completes. But because the control flow immediately returns to the caller, the caller remains responsive. `Await` can be thought as of a placeholder for the task's result, which will be available after the awaited task completes. In the previous `QueryVideosAsync` method, `Await` starts the `WebClient.DownloadStringTaskAsync` method and literally waits for its result but, while waiting, the control flow does not move to `DownloadStringAsyncTask`, while it remains in the caller. Because in the current example the code is running in the UI thread, the user interface remains responsive because the requested task is being executed asynchronously.

In other words, what `Await` actually does is sign up the rest of the method as a callback on the task, returning immediately. When the task that is being awaited completes, it will invoke the callback and will resume the execution from the exact point it was left.

After the operation has been completed, the rest of the code can elaborate the result. With this kind of approach, your method looks much simpler, like the first synchronous version, but it is running asynchronously with only three edits (the `Async` modifier, `Task(Of T)` as the return type, and the `Await` operator).

WHY THE `Task` TYPE?

In Chapter 41 you learned a lot about the `Task` class and saw how this can run CPU-intensive work on a separate thread, but it also can represent an I/O operation such as a network request. For this reason, the `Task` class is the natural choice as the result type for asynchronous operations using `Async/Await`.

Continuing considerations on the previous method, take a look at the final `Return` statement. It is returning an `IEnumerable(Of Video)`, but actually the method's signature requires returning a `Task(Of IEnumerable(Of Video))`. This is possible because the compiler automatically makes `Return` statements to return a `Task`-based version of their result even if they do not. As a result, you will not get confused because you will write the same code but the compiler will take care of converting the return type into the appropriate type. This also makes migration of synchronous code to asynchronous easier. Technically speaking, the compiler synthesizes a new `Task(Of T)` object at the first `Await` in the method. This `Task(Of T)` object is returned to the caller at the first `Await`. Later on, when it encounters a `Return` statement, the compiler causes that already-existing `Task(Of T)` object to transition from a "not yet completed" state into the "completed with result" state. Continuing the migration of the code example to the `Async/Await` pattern, you now need a few edits to the `LoadVideos` method. The following code demonstrates this:

```
Private Async Function LoadVideosAsync() As Task
    Me.DataContext = Await QueryVideosAsync()
End Sub
```

The method is now called `LoadVideoAsync` and marked with the `Async` modifier. The reason is that it contains an `Await` expression that invokes the `QueryVideosAsync` method. The result of this invocation is taken as the main window's data source. Finally, you have to edit the `MainWindow_Loaded` event handler and make it asynchronous like this:

```
Private Async Sub MainWindow_Loaded(sender As Object,
                              e As RoutedEventArgs) Handles Me.Loaded
    Await LoadVideosAsync()
End Sub
```

If you now run the application, you will still get a responsive user interface that you can interact with while the long-running task (the query) is executing, but you have achieved this by modifying existing code with very few edits.

How `Async` and `Await` Work Behind the Scenes

Behind the scenes of the ease of the `Async` pattern, the compiler does incredible work to make the magic possible. When you make an asynchronous call by using `Await`, that invocation starts a new instance of the `Task` class. As you know from Chapter 41, one thread can contain multiple `Task` instances. So you might have the asynchronous operation running in the same thread but on a new `Task`. Internally, it's as if the compiler could split an asynchronous method in two parts, a method and its callback. If you consider the `QueryVideosAsync` shown previously, you could imagine a method defined until the invocation of `Await`. The next part of the method is moved into a callback that is invoked after the awaited operation is completed. This has two benefits. The first benefit is that it ensures that code that needs to manipulate the result of an awaited operation will work with the actual result, which has been returned after completion of the task (this is in fact the moment in which the callback is invoked). Second, such callback is invoked in the same calling thread, which avoids the need of managing threads manually or using the `Dispatcher` class in technologies like WPF or Silverlight. Figure 42.4 gives you an ideal representation of how the asynchronous method has been split.

```
Private Async Function QueryVideosAsync() As _
        Task(Of IEnumerable(Of Video))
    Dim client As New WebClient

    Dim data = Await client.DownloadStringTaskAsync(New Uri(Video.
                                                        FeedUrl))

    Dim doc = XDocument.Parse(data)
```

```
    Dim query = From video In doc...<item>
                Select New Video With {
                    .Title = video.<title>.Value,
                    .Speaker = video.<dc:creator>.Value,
                    .Url = video.<link>.Value,
                    .Thumbnail = video...<media:thumbnail>.
                    FirstOrDefault?.@url,
                    .DateRecorded = String.Concat("Recorded on ",
                    Date.Parse(video.<pubDate>.Value,
                        Globalization.CultureInfo.InvariantCulture).
                    ToShortDateString)}

    Return query
End Function
```

FIGURE 42.4   An asynchronous method is split into two ideal parts; the second is a callback.

Beyond considerations like the ones about threading, it is interesting to analyze the code the compiler generated to make asynchrony so efficient in Visual Basic 2015. For this exercise, you need a decompiler tool such as .NET Reflector from Red-Gate, which is available as a free trial from https://www.red-gate.com/products/dotnet-development/reflector/. If you open the compiled .exe file with a tool like this, you can see that the implementation of asynchronous methods is completely different from the one you wrote and that the compiler generated several structures that implement a state machine that supports asynchrony. Figure 42.5 shows the QueryVideosAsync real implementation.

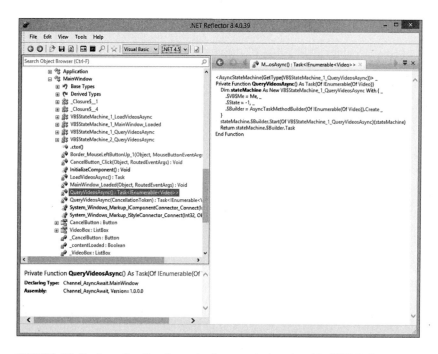

FIGURE 42.5   Investigating the actual generated code with .NET Reflector.

For your convenience, the following is the auto-generated code for QueryVideosAsync:

```
<AsyncStateMachine(GetType(VB$StateMachine_1_QueryVideosAsync))> _
Private Function QueryVideosAsync() As Task(Of IEnumerable(Of Video))
    Dim stateMachine As New VB$StateMachine_1_QueryVideosAsync With { _
        .$VB$Me = Me, _
        .$State = -1, _
        .$Builder = AsyncTaskMethodBuilder(Of IEnumerable(Of Video)).Create _
    }
    stateMachine.$Builder.
    Start(Of VB$StateMachine_1_QueryVideosAsync)(stateMachine)
    Return stateMachine.$Builder.Task
End Function
```

You do not need to know the code in detail because this implementation is purely internal; however, the real code relies on the AsyncTaskMethodBuilder class, which creates an instance of an asynchronous method and requires specifying a state machine that controls the execution of the asynchronous task (which is returned once completed). For each asynchronous method, the compiler generated an object representing the state

machine. For instance, the compiler generated an object called VB$StateMachine_1_
QueryVideosAsync that represents the state machine that controls the execution of
the QueryVideosAsync method. Listing 42.3 contains the code of the aforementioned
structure.

LISTING 42.3   Internal Implementation of a State Machine for Async Methods

```
<CompilerGenerated> _
Private NotInheritable Class VB$StateMachine_1_QueryVideosAsync
    Implements IAsyncStateMachine
    ' Methods
    Public Sub New()
    <CompilerGenerated> _
    Friend Sub MoveNext() Implements IAsyncStateMachine.MoveNext
    <DebuggerNonUserCode> _
    Private Sub SetStateMachine(stateMachine As IAsyncStateMachine) _
            Implements IAsyncStateMachine.SetStateMachine

    ' Fields
    Friend $A0 As TaskAwaiter(Of String)
    Public $Builder As AsyncTaskMethodBuilder(Of IEnumerable(Of Video))
    Public $State As Integer
    Friend $VB$Me As MainWindow
    Friend $VB$ResumableLocal_client$0 As WebClient
    Friend $VB$ResumableLocal_data$1 As String
    Friend $VB$ResumableLocal_doc$2 As XDocument
    Friend $VB$ResumableLocal_query$3 As IEnumerable(Of Video)
End Class
```

The code in Listing 42.3 is certainly complex, and you are not required to know how it
works under the hood, but focus for a moment on the MoveNext method. This method is
responsible of the asynchronous execution of tasks; depending on the state of the task,
it resumes the execution at the appropriate point. You can see how the compiler translates the Await keyword into an instance of the TaskAwaiter structure, which is assigned
with the result of the invocation to the Task.GetAwaiter method (both are for compiler-
use only). If you compare the result of this analysis with the ease of usage of the Async
pattern, it is obvious that the compiler does tremendous work to translate that simplicity
into a very efficient asynchronous mechanism.

Documentation and Examples of the Async Pattern

Microsoft offers a lot of useful resources to developers who want to start coding the new
way. The following list summarizes several resources that you are strongly encouraged to
visit to make your learning of Async complete:

▶ **Visual Studio Asynchronous Programming:** The official developer center for Async.
Here you can find documentation, downloads, instructional videos, and more on

language specifications. It is available at http://msdn.microsoft.com/en-us/vstudio/async.aspx.

▶ **101 Async Samples:** An online page that contains a huge number of code examples based on Async for both Visual Basic and Visual C#. You can find samples at http://www.wischik.com/lu/AsyncSilverlight/AsyncSamples.html.

▶ **Sample code:** Available on the MSDN Code Gallery (http://code.msdn.microsoft.com).

Do not leave out of your bookmarks the root page of the .NET Framework 4.5 and 4.6 documentation (http://msdn.microsoft.com/en-us/library/w0x726c2).

Exception Handling in `Async`

Another great benefit of using the `Async` pattern is that exception handling is done the usual way. In fact, if an awaited method throws an exception, this can be naturally handled within a `Try..Catch..Finally` block. The following code provides an example:

```
Private Async Sub DownloadSomethingAsync()
    Dim client As New System.Net.WebClient
    Try
        Dim result = Await client.
            DownloadStringTaskAsync("http://msdn.com/vbasic")
    Catch ex As Exception
        Console.WriteLine(ex.Message)
    Finally
        Console.WriteLine("Operation completed.")
    End Try
End Sub
```

As you can see, there is no difference in handling exceptions inside asynchronous methods compared to classic synchronous methods. This makes code migration easier.

Implementing Task-Based Asynchrony

As you remember from Chapter 41, the `Task` class provides methods and other members that enable you to execute CPU-intensive work, by splitting code across all the available processors so that most of the code is executed concurrently, when possible. Such members of the `Task` class return instances of the `Task` class itself, and therefore can be used along with `Await`. This possibility has some advantages:

▶ You can execute synchronous code on a separate thread more easily.

▶ You can run multiple tasks concurrently and wait for them to complete before making further manipulations.

▶ You can use `Await` with CPU-consuming code.

This approach is known as Task-Based Asynchrony, and in this section you learn how to get the most out of it.

Switching Threads

In Chapter 40 you learned how to write code that can run on a separate thread, how to create new threads manually, and how to use the Thread Pool managed by the .NET Framework. With this approach, you run a portion of synchronous code in a separate thread, thus keeping the caller thread-free from an intensive and potentially blocking work. In the .NET Framework 4.6, you have additional alternatives to reach the same objective but writing simpler code. The Task.Run method enables you to run a new task asynchronously, queuing such a task into a thread in the Thread Pool. The result is returned as Task handle for the intensive work, so that you can use Await to wait for the result. Task.Run takes as the first argument a delegate that defines the work that will be executed in the background thread. Such a delegate can be represented either by a method that you point to via the AddressOf clause or by lambdas. In the latter case, the delegate can be a System.Action represented by a statement lambda or a System.Func(Of T) represented by a lambda expression. The following example demonstrates how synchronous code is easily executed in a separate thread by invoking Task.Run:

```
Private Async Sub RunIntensiveWorkAsync()
    'This runs on the UI thread
    Console.WriteLine("Starting...")

    'This runs on a Thread Pool thread
    Dim result As Integer = Await Task.Run(Function()
                                               Dim workResult As Integer = _
                                                   SimulateIntensiveWork()
                                               Return workResult
                                           End Function)

    'This runs again on the UI thread
    Console.WriteLine("Finished")
    Console.ReadLine()
End Sub

Private Function SimulateIntensiveWork() As Integer
    Dim delay As Integer = 5000
    Threading.Thread.Sleep(delay)
    Return delay
End Function
```

While the result of Task.Run is being awaited, the control is immediately returned to the user interface, which remains responsive in the Console window. All the Console.WriteLine and Console.ReadLine statements are executed on the UI thread, whereas the simulated CPU-consuming code runs on the separate thread. Task.Run schedules a new task exactly as `Task.Factory.StartNew` does; you saw this method in Chapter 41. So, this code has the same effect as using `Task.Run`:

```
Dim result As Integer = Await Task.Factory.StartNew(Function()
                                       Dim workResult _
                                       As Integer = _
                                           SimulateIntensiveWork()
                                       Return workResult
                                   End Function)
```

In summary, `Task.Run` lets you easily execute intensive computations on a separate thread, taking all the benefits of `Await`.

Using Combinators

The `Task` class has other interesting usages, such as managing concurrent operations. This is possible because of two methods, `Task.WhenAll` and `Task.WhenAny`, also known as *combinators*. `Task.WhenAll` creates a task that will complete when all the supplied tasks complete; `Task.WhenAny` creates a task that will complete when at least one of the supplied tasks completes. For example, imagine you want to download multiple RSS feeds information from a website. Instead of using `Await` against individual tasks to complete, you can use `Task.WhenAll` to continue only after all tasks have completed. The following code provides an example of concurrent download of RSS feeds from the Microsoft Channel 9 feed used previously:

```
Private Async Sub DownloadAllFeedsAsync()
    Dim feeds As New List(Of Uri) From
        {New Uri("http://channel9.msdn.com/Tags/windows+8/RSS"),
         New Uri("http://channel9.msdn.com/Tags/windows+phone"),
         New Uri("http://channel9.msdn.com/Tags/visual+basic/RSS")}

    'This task completes when all of the requests complete
    Dim feedCompleted As IEnumerable(Of String) = _
                                    Await Task.
                                    WhenAll(From feed In feeds
                                    Select New System.Net.WebClient().
                                    DownloadStringTaskAsync(feed))

    'Additional work here...
End Sub
```

This code creates a collection of tasks by sending a `DownloadStringTaskAsync` request for each feed address in the list of feeds. The task completes (and thus the result of awaiting `WhenAll` is returned) only when all three feeds have been downloaded, meaning that the complete download result will not be available if only one or two feeds have been downloaded. `WhenAny` works differently because it creates a task that completes when any of the tasks in a collection of tasks completes. The following code demonstrates how to rewrite the previous example using `WhenAny`:

```
Private Async Sub DownloadFeedsAsync()
    Dim feeds As New List(Of Uri) From
        {New Uri("http://channel9.msdn.com/Tags/windows+8/RSS"),
         New Uri("http://channel9.msdn.com/Tags/windows+phone"),
         New Uri("http://channel9.msdn.com/Tags/visual+basic/RSS")}

    'This task completes when any of the requests complete
    Dim feedCompleted As Task(Of String) = Await Task.WhenAny(From feed In feeds
                                           Select New System.Net.WebClient().
                                           DownloadStringTaskAsync(feed))

    'Additional work here...
End Sub
```

In this case a single result will be yielded because the task will be completed when any of the tasks completes. You can also wait for a list of tasks defined as explicit asynchronous methods, like in the following example:

```
Public Async Sub WhenAnyRedundancyAsync()

    Dim messages As New List(Of Task(Of String)) From
        {
            GetMessage1Async(),
            GetMessage2Async(),
            GetMessage3Async()
        }
    Dim message = Await Task.WhenAny(messages)
    Console.WriteLine(message.Result)
    Console.ReadLine()
End Sub


Public Async Function GetMessage1Async() As Task(Of String)
    Await Task.Delay(700)
    Return "Hi VB guys!"
End Function


Public Async Function GetMessage2Async() As Task(Of String)
    Await Task.Delay(600)
    Return "Hi C# guys!"
End Function


Public Async Function GetMessage3Async() As Task(Of String)
    Await Task.Delay(500)
    Return "Hi F# guys!"
End Function
```

Here you have three asynchronous methods, each returning a string. The code builds a list of tasks including each asynchronous method in the list. `Task.WhenAny` receives the instance of the collection of tasks as an argument and completes when one of the three methods completes. In this example, you are also seeing for the first time the `Task.Delay` method. This is the asynchronous equivalent of `Thread.Sleep`, but while the latter blocks the thread for the specified number of milliseconds, with `Task.Delay` the thread remains responsive.

ADDITIONAL SAMPLES ON `WhenAny`

The 101 `Async` Samples include a couple of interesting examples of different usages of `WhenAny`, such as interleaving one request at a time and limiting the number of concurrent downloads. You find them under the Combinators node of the samples page mentioned at the beginning of the chapter.

Cancellation and Progress

Because the `Async` pattern relies on the `Task` class, implementing cancellation is something similar to what you have already studied back in Chapter 41, thus the `CancellationTokenSource` and `CancellationToken` classes are used. In this section you see how to implement cancellation both for asynchronous methods and for `Task.Run` operations. Next, you learn how to report the progress of an operation, which is common in asynchronous programming and improves the user experience.

Implementing Cancellation

Let's look at the WPF sample application created in the section "Getting Started with `Async/Await`." Imagine you want to give users the ability of cancelling the download of the RSS feed from the Microsoft Channel9 website. First, make a slight modification to the user interface so that the main `Grid` is divided into two rows, and in the first row add a `Button` like this:

```
<Grid.RowDefinitions>
    <RowDefinition Height="40"/>
    <RowDefinition/>
</Grid.RowDefinitions>
<Button Width="120" Height="30" Name="CancelButton"
        Content="Cancel"/>
```

Do not forget to add the `Grid.Row="1"` property assignment for the `ListBox` control. Double-click the new button so that you can quickly access the code editor. Declare a new `CancellationTokenSource` object that will listen for cancellation requests. The event handler for the new button's `Click` event will invoke the `Cancel` method on the instance of the `CancellationTokenSource`:

```
Private tokenSource As CancellationTokenSource

Private Sub CancelButton_Click(sender As Object, e As RoutedEventArgs) _
    Handles CancelButton.Click
    'If Me.tokenSource IsNot Nothing Then
    '    Me.tokenSource.Cancel()
    'End If
    Me.tokenSource?.Cancel()
End Sub
```

The user can now request cancellation by clicking this button. Next, you need to make a couple of edits to the `QueryVideosAsync` method created previously. The first edit is making this method receive a `CancellationToken` object as an argument. This object will handle cancellation requests during the method execution. The second edit requires replacing the `WebClient` class with a new class called `HttpClient`. The reason for this change is that the `WebClient`'s asynchronous methods no longer support cancellation as in the first previews of the `Async` library, although asynchronous methods in `System.Net.Http.HttpClient` do. Among the others, this class exposes a method called `GetAsync` that retrieves contents from the specified URL and receives the cancellation token as the second argument. The result is returned under the form of a `System.Net.Http.HttpResponseMessage` class. As the name implies, this class represents an HTTP response message including the status of the operation and the retrieved data. The data is represented by a property called `Content`, which exposes methods to convert data into a stream (`ReadAsStreamAsync`), into an array of bytes (`ReadAsByteArrayAsync`), and into a string (`ReadAsStringAsync`). Other than changing the code to use `HttpClient` and to receive the cancellation token, you only need to handle the `OperationCanceledException`, which is raised after the cancellation request is received by the asynchronous method. The following code demonstrates the `QueryVideosAsync` method:

```
'The following implementation with HttpClient supports Cancellation
Private Async Function QueryVideosAsync(token As CancellationToken) As  _
        Task(Of IEnumerable(Of Video))
    Try
        Dim client As New HttpClient

        'Get the feed content as an HttpResponseMessage
        Dim data = Await client.GetAsync(New Uri(Video.FeedUrl), token)

        'Parse the content into a String
        Dim actualData = Await data.Content.ReadAsStringAsync

        Dim doc = XDocument.Parse(actualData)

        Dim query = From video In doc...<item>
                Select New Video With {
                .Title = video.<title>.Value,
                .Speaker = video.<dc:creator>.Value,
                .Url = video.<link>.Value,
```

```
        .Thumbnail = video...<media:thumbnail>.
            FirstOrDefault?.@url,
        .DateRecorded = String.Concat("Recorded on ",
            Date.Parse(video.<pubDate>.Value,
            Globalization.CultureInfo.InvariantCulture).
            ToShortDateString)}


    Return query
Catch ex As OperationCanceledException
    MessageBox.Show("Operation was canceled by the user.")
    Return Nothing
Catch ex As Exception
    MessageBox.Show(ex.Message)
    Return Nothing
End Try
End Function
```

The very last edit to the application is changing the LoadVideosAsync method to launch the query passing a cancellation token:

```
Private Async Function LoadVideosAsync() As Task
    Me.tokenSource = New CancellationTokenSource

    Me.DataContext = Await QueryVideosAsync(Me.tokenSource.Token)
End Function
```

If you now run the application, not only will the user interface remain responsive, but you will be also able to click the Cancel button to stop the query execution. Notice that in a synchronous approach, implementing cancellation has no benefits. In fact, if on one side writing code to support cancellation is legal, on the other side the user would never have a chance to click a button because the UI thread would be blocked until the completion of the task. Similarly, you can add cancellation to tasks running in a separate thread and started with Task.Run. By continuing the example shown previously about this method, you can first rewrite the SimulateIntensiveWork method as follows:

```
Private Function SimulateIntensiveWork(token As CancellationToken) _
        As Integer
    Dim delay As Integer = 5000
    Threading.Thread.Sleep(delay)

    token.ThrowIfCancellationRequested()

    Return delay
End Function
```

You should be familiar with this approach because it has been discussed in Chapter 41. The method receives the cancellation token and checks for cancellation requests. If any exist, it throws an `OperationCanceledException`. Next, you add support for cancellation by passing an instance of the `CancellationTokenSource` class to the method invocation inside `Task.Run`:

```
Private cancellationToken As CancellationTokenSource

Private Async Sub RunIntensiveWorkAsync()
    cancellationToken = New CancellationTokenSource
    'This runs on the UI thread
    Console.WriteLine("Starting...")

    Try
        'This runs on a Thread Pool thread
        Dim result As Integer = Await Task.Run(Function()
                                                   Dim workResult As Integer = _
                                                   SimulateIntensiveWork( _
                                                   cancellationToken.Token)
                                                   Return workResult
                                               End Function)

        'This runs again on the UI thread
        Console.WriteLine("Finished")
    Catch ex As OperationCanceledException
        Console.WriteLine("Canceled by the user.")
    Catch ex As Exception

    End Try
    Console.ReadLine()
End Sub
```

To request cancellation, you should call the `cancellationToken.Cancel` method. At that point, the request is intercepted and an `OperationCanceledException` is thrown.

Reporting Progress

Reporting the progress of an asynchronous method execution is a common requirement. There is a pattern that you can use and that makes things easier. This pattern relies on the `System.IProgress(Of T)` interface and the `System.Progress(Of T)` class, which expose a `ProgressChanged` event that must be raised when the asynchronous operation is in progress. To provide an example that is easy to understand, imagine you still want to download the content of some feeds from the Microsoft Channel9 website and refresh the progress every time a site has been downloaded completely. The current example is based on a Console application. Consider the following code:

```
Private progress As Progress(Of Integer)
Private counter As Integer = 0
```

```
Sub Main()
    Try
        progress = New Progress(Of Integer)
        AddHandler progress.ProgressChanged, Sub(sender, e)
                                                 Console.
                                                 WriteLine _
                                                 ("Download progress: " & _
                                                 CStr(e))
                                             End Sub

        DownloadAllFeedsAsync(progress)

    Catch ex As Exception
        Console.WriteLine(ex.Message)
    Finally
        Console.ReadLine()
    End Try
End Sub
```

You first declare an object of type `Progress(Of Integer)` and a counter. The first object
will receive the progress value when the `ProgressChanged` event is raised. In this case,
the code uses the `Integer` type to pass a simple number, but you can pass more complex
information with a different or custom type. Then the code specifies a handler for the
`ProgressChanged` event, with type inference for the lambda's parameters. `Sender` is always
`Object`, whereas `e` is of the same type as the generic type you assigned to `Progress`. So, in
this case it is of type `Integer`. Here you are working in a Console application and are thus
displaying the value as a text message. But in real-world applications, this is the value that
you could assign to a `ProgressBar` control to report the progress in the user interface. The
instance of the `Progress` class must be passed to the asynchronous method that performs
the required tasks. The `Progress` class has just one method called `Report`; you invoke it
after an `Await` invocation. The following code demonstrates how to report the progress of
downloading a number of feeds:

```
Private Async Sub DownloadAllFeedsAsync(currentProgress As IProgress(Of Integer))
    Dim client As New System.Net.WebClient

    Dim feeds As New List(Of Uri) From
        {New Uri("http://channel9.msdn.com/Tags/windows+8/RSS"),
         New Uri("http://channel9.msdn.com/Tags/windows+phone"),
         New Uri("http://channel9.msdn.com/Tags/visual+basic/RSS")}
    For Each URL In feeds
        Await client.DownloadStringTaskAsync(URL)
        counter += 1
        If currentProgress IsNot Nothing Then currentProgress.Report(counter)
    Next
End Sub
```

`Report` receives as an argument an object of the same type that you assigned as the generic argument of the `Progress` class declaration in this case a counter of type `Integer` that is incremented every time a feed is downloaded. If you run this code, every time a feed is returned, the progress is also shown in the user interface, as demonstrated in Figure 42.6.

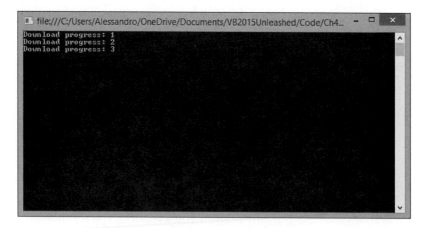

FIGURE 42.6   Reporting the progress of an asynchronous method.

This pattern makes reporting the progress of a task and in real-world applications, such as WPF and Windows apps, easy. It also makes updating controls like the `ProgressBar` incredibly simple by assigning to such controls the value stored in the instance of the `Progress` class.

Asynchronous Lambda Expressions

Methods can be asynchronous, but so can lambda expressions. To be asynchronous, a lambda must have the `Async` modifier and must return `Task` or `Task(Of T)`, but it cannot accept `ByRef` arguments and cannot be an iterator function. A lambda can be asynchronous when its code uses the `Await` operator to wait for a `Task` result. An example of asynchronous lambdas is with event handlers. For instance, you might need to wait for the result of a task when an event is raised, as in the following code snippet that handles a button's `Click`:

```
AddHandler Me.Button1.Click, Async Sub(sender, e)
                          Await DoSomeWorkAsync
                  End Sub
```

You do not need an asynchronous lambda if the work you are going to execute does not return a `Task`. Another typical usage of asynchronous lambdas is with `Task.Run`. The following code shows the same example described when introducing `Task.Run`, but now the lambda that starts the intensive work is marked with `Async` and the method that actually performs intensive computations returns a `Task` so that it can be awaited:

```
Private Async Sub RunIntensiveWorkAsync()
    cancellationToken = New CancellationTokenSource
    'This runs on the UI thread
    Console.WriteLine("Starting...")

    Try
        'This runs on a Thread Pool thread
        Dim result As Integer = Await Task.Run(Async Function()
                                                   Dim workResult As Integer = _
                                                   Await _
                                                   SimulateIntensiveWorkAsync()
                                                   Return workResult
                                               End Function)
        'This runs again on the UI thread
        Console.WriteLine("Finished")
    Catch ex As OperationCanceledException
        Console.WriteLine("Canceled by the user.")
    Catch ex As Exception

    End Try
    Console.ReadLine()
End Sub

Private Async Function SimulateIntensiveWorkAsync() As Task(Of Integer)
    Dim delay As Integer = 1000
    Await Task.Delay(delay)
    Return delay
End Function
```

This code simulates CPU-intensive work inside an asynchronous method. However, this is not best practice and should be avoided when possible. Here it is shown for demonstration purposes only. For additional tips about asynchronous methods, visit http://channel9.msdn.com/Series/Three-Essential-Tips-for-Async/Async-Library-Methods-Shouldn-t-Lie.

Asynchronous I/O File Operations in .NET 4.6

Before .NET Framework 4.5, you could perform asynchronous operations over files and streams by using the Asynchronous Programming Model and methods such as `Stream.BeginRead` and `Stream.EndRead`. This kind of approach can be good, but it has the limitations described in the section "Getting Started with `Async`/`Await`" in this chapter. With .NET Framework 4.5 and after, asynchronous I/O operations can be simplified by using the `Async` pattern and by implementing asynchronous versions of methods that work with files and stream to avoid blocking the main thread. Such methods are exposed by the

`Stream`, `FileStream`, `MemoryStream`, `TextReader`, and `TextWriter` classes that you saw in action back in Chapter 18, "Manipulating Files and Streams." Table 42.1 summarizes the available asynchronous methods.

TABLE 42.1   Asynchronous Methods for Stream Classes

Method	Description	Return Type
ReadAsync	Reads a sequence of bytes from a stream and advances the position by the number of bytes read, with an asynchronous approach	Task(Of Integer)
WriteAsync	Writes a sequence of bytes to a stream, with an asynchronous approach	Task
FlushAsync	Clears buffers associated with the stream sending buffered data to the stream, using asynchrony	Task
CopyToAsync	Asynchronously copies a number of bytes from a stream to another	Task
ReadLineAsync	Reads a line of characters using asynchrony and returns a string	Task(Of String)
ReadToEndAsync	Asynchronously reads all characters from the current position to the end of the stream, and returns one string	Task(Of String)

To see some of these methods in action, create a new WPF project. The user interface of this sample application will have to look like Figure 42.7.

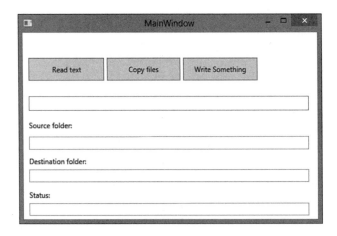

FIGURE 42.7   The user interface of the new sample application.

That said, add the following controls in the designer:

1. Three buttons, named `ReadTextButton`, `CopyButton`, and `WriteButton`. Then, set their `Content` properties with `Read text`, `Copy files`, and `Write Something`, respectively.

2. Four `TextBox` controls, named `ReadTextBox`, `SourceTextBox`, `DestinationTextBox`, and `StatusTextBox`.

3. Three `TextBlock` controls. You do not need to specify a name, but make sure their `Text` property is set with Source folder, Destination folder, and Status, respectively.

The first example uses the `StreamReader` class to read a text file asynchronously. The event handler for the `ReadTextButton.Click` event looks like this:

```
Private Async Sub ReadTextButton_Click(sender As Object,
                                   e As RoutedEventArgs) _
                                   Handles ReadTextButton.Click
    Using reader As New StreamReader("TextFile1.txt")
        Me.ReadTextBox.Text = Await reader.ReadToEndAsync
    End Using

End Sub
```

You mark the event handler with `Async`, and because this method will not be awaited by any other methods, it does not need to return a `Task`. Therefore, it can be defined as a `Sub`. Notice how you use `Await` together with the `ReadToEndAsync` method, while the rest of the implementation is made the usual way. The next example is about copying streams asynchronously. The following code shows the implementation of the `CopyButton.Click` event handler:

```
Private Async Sub CopyButton_Click(sender As Object,
                               e As RoutedEventArgs) _
                               Handles CopyButton.Click
    If Me.SourceTextBox.Text = "" Then
        MessageBox.Show("Please specify the source folder")
        Exit Sub
    End If

    If Me.DestinationTextBox.Text = "" Then
        MessageBox.Show("Please specify the target folder")
        Exit Sub
    End If

    For Each fileName As String In Directory.
        EnumerateFiles(Me.SourceTextBox.Text)
```

```
        Using SourceStream As FileStream = File.Open(fileName, FileMode.Open)
            Using DestinationStream As FileStream =
                File.Create(String.Concat(Me.DestinationTextBox.Text,
                                          fileName.
                                          Substring(fileName.LastIndexOf("\"c))))
                Await SourceStream.CopyToAsync(DestinationStream)
                Me.StatusTextBox.Text = "Copied " + DestinationStream.Name
            End Using
        End Using
    Next

End Sub
```

In particular, the code enumerates the content of the source folder and for each file it opens a stream for reading and another one for writing into the target folder. Await enables you to execute asynchronously the operation with the asynchronous method called CopyToAsync. It is worth mentioning that, with this approach, you can refresh the user interface with useful information, like showing the name of the last copied file. In a synchronous approach, this would not be possible because the UI would be blocked until the completion of the operation. The last example demonstrates how to write some text into a file asynchronously. This is the event handler for the WriteButton.Click event:

```
Private Async Sub WriteButton_Click(sender As Object,
                                    e As RoutedEventArgs) Handles WriteButton.Click
    Dim uniencoding As UnicodeEncoding = New UnicodeEncoding()
    Dim filename As String =
        "c:\temp\AsyncWriteDemo.txt"

    Dim result As Byte() = uniencoding.GetBytes("Demo for Async I/O")

    Using SourceStream As FileStream = File.Open(filename, FileMode.OpenOrCreate)
        SourceStream.Seek(0, SeekOrigin.End)
        Await SourceStream.WriteAsync(result, 0, result.Length)
    End Using

End Sub
```

In this particular example, the code is written exactly like in the synchronous counter-part, except for the Async modifier and the Await statement that invokes the WriteAsync method (instead of running Write). By using the Async pattern, writing applications that work with streams and remain responsive has become dramatically simpler.

IMPLEMENTING CUSTOM AWAITERS

By using the Task-based asynchrony, you can work with instances of the `Task` class and use `Await` when waiting for their results. Using `Task.Run` and combinators will usually avoid the need to create custom types that can be used along with `Await`. However, in some situations you might want to define your own awaitable types. Reasons for making this can be various for example, performing some work over a control in the user interface from within a background thread. To accomplish this, you define a `Structure` or `Class` that implements the `INotifyCompletion` interface to expose a method called `OnCompleted`; then you need a method called `GetAwaiter`. The MSDN documentation does not provide enough information about building custom types that can be used with Await, but fortunately a blog post series by Lucian Wischik from Microsoft shows how to create one. You can find it at http://blogs.msdn.com/b/lucian/archive/2012/11/28/how-to-await-a-storyboard-and-other-things.aspx. There is also another blog post from the Stephen Toub, in which he discusses how to implement a custom awaitable type to perform asynchronous operations with sockets; you can find it at http://blogs.msdn.com/b/pfxteam/archive/2011/12/15/10248293.aspx.

Debugging Tasks

Visual Studio 2015 allows you to collect information about asynchronous tasks with the Tasks window. This is not a new tool; it has been available since Visual Studio 2012, but only for the Task Parallel Library. It now provides support for the `Async/Await` pattern in Visual Studio 2013 and requires Windows 8 or higher. To understand how it works, place a breakpoint on the `QueryVideosAsync` method in the sample WPF application and press **F5**. When the breakpoint is hit, select **Debug**, **Windows**, **Tasks** and press **F11** to step into the code. As you step into asynchronous method calls, the Tasks window shows information on each task, as shown in Figure 42.8.

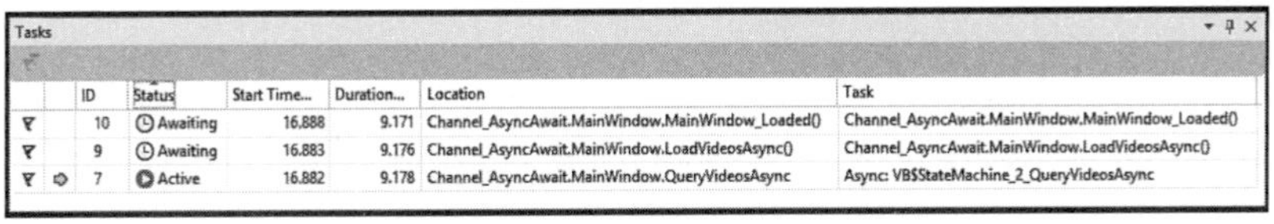

		ID	Status	Start Time...	Duration...	Location	Task
▼		10	Awaiting	16.888	9.171	Channel_AsyncAwait.MainWindow.MainWindow_Loaded()	Channel_AsyncAwait.MainWindow.MainWindow_Loaded()
▼		9	Awaiting	16.883	9.176	Channel_AsyncAwait.MainWindow.LoadVideosAsync()	Channel_AsyncAwait.MainWindow.LoadVideosAsync()
▼	⟳	7	Active	16.882	9.178	Channel_AsyncAwait.MainWindow.QueryVideosAsync	Async: VBSStateMachine_2_QueryVideosAsync

FIGURE 42.8   The Tasks window.

As you can see, the Tasks window shows what task is active and what other tasks are awaiting the completion of the active task. It shows the duration, the method that started the asynchronous task (in the Location column), and the actual running task, such as a state machine (in the Task column). If you hover over the values in the ID column, you will also get additional information about the task execution order. This very useful tool helps you understand the execution flow of your asynchronous code.

Summary

Building applications that remain responsive whatever task they are executing is something that developers must take care of, especially from the user interface perspective. This chapter explained how to use asynchrony to build responsive applications by first discussing old-style programming models such as the Event-based Asynchronous Pattern and the Asynchronous Programming Model. Both provide techniques to write asynchronous code that runs on separate threads. However, both have some limitations, such as code complexity, issues in returning information to caller threads or functions, and managing errors effectively. Visual Basic 2015 offers the asynchronous pattern based on the `Async` and `Await` keywords, which enable you to keep the UI thread free and write code that is similar to the synchronous approach and is much easier to read and maintain. You invoke an asynchronous task, and then its result is returned some time later, but the control is immediately returned to the caller. When the result is available, an implicit callback enables you to consume the result of the asynchronous operation effectively. The `Async` pattern relies on the concept of task and on the `Task` class, which means that asynchrony easily includes support for cancellation, progress, anonymous delegates, and concurrent operations. The .NET Framework 4.6 itself exposes built-in classes that use the new `Async` pattern for making asynchronous I/O operations much easier with particular regard to streams and network requests. The `Async` pattern and the `Async/Await` keywords can be used across multiple platforms and presentation technologies.

CHAPTER 43

Working with Assemblies

IN THIS CHAPTER

▶ Assembly Overview

▶ Understanding Application Domains

▶ Security Model in .NET 4.6

So many times in this book, and of course in many other .NET resources, you find the word *assembly* associating it to managed executable files such as .NET applications and libraries. You need to know some key concepts about assemblies to understand how they actually work, what kind of information they offer, and how you can avoid bad surprises when executing them. In this chapter, you first get an overview of assemblies' structure and base concepts; then you learn about advanced concepts that can help you understand their context of execution.

Assembly Overview

Assemblies can be discussed with two points of view: a physical one and a logical one. From the physical point of view, an assembly is an .exe or .dll file containing executable modules and resources. From a logical point of view, an assembly is the smallest unit for deploying .NET applications that also provides version information and enables code reuse. Chapter 44, "Reflection," discusses how, from the physical perspective, an assembly is a container of Intermediate Language code, metadata, and resources. This chapter focuses the discussion on the logical perspective so that you can understand some other purposes of this unit of work. In some cases, details of some of the topics have been previously discussed, but for your convenience they are summarized in this chapter.

.NET NATIVE AND WINDOWS 10

When you write an app for Windows 10 and compile it using the Release configuration, the .NET Native compiler is used. This compiler repackages all the managed EXEs or DLLs in your app together into a single native DLL. Finally, to speed up the app's startup process, the compiler writes a small native executable that calls it.

Information Stored Within Assemblies

An assembly doesn't necessarily coincide with a standalone application. In many cases, assemblies are also compiled class libraries. Independently from what kind of assembly you are working with, it exposes the following information:

▶ **Types**—Through the IL code necessary to the application execution, assemblies can expose reusable types that can be consumed by other assemblies. This is the reason assemblies are considered the smallest unit for code reuse.

▶ **Version**—Assemblies contain version information, and all modules within the assembly have the same version; this is important to the Common Language Runtime (CLR) that can distinguish between assemblies with the same name but with different version numbers without registration.

▶ **Scope**—Assemblies provide the scope of exposed types, establishing whether they can be externally visible. This is accomplished in code by Visual Basic qualifiers such as `Public`, `Friend`, and `Private`.

Assembly Location

To understand where assemblies are located, you must consider that they are generally divided into *private assemblies* and *shared assemblies*. Private assemblies are standalone assemblies or assemblies that reside exclusively in the same folder of the application that holds a reference. This is a common scenario and makes the deployment easier because you just need to distribute the content of the application folder (known as *XCopy deployment*). Every application holding a reference to a private assembly needs to have a copy of the assembly inside its folder. This means that if you have 10 applications referencing the assembly, you will also have 10 copies of the assembly. Shared assemblies are instead files with a digital signature that can be installed to a particular location known as the Global Assembly Cache. It allows having a single shared copy of the assembly only if this comes from a trusted publisher. The Global Assembly Cache (GAC) is an important topic that Chapter 48, "Understanding the Global Assembly Cache," addresses, so read it for further details.

BINDING, Codebase, PROBING

When one assembly is referenced by another one, the .NET runtime needs to link them. This process is known as *binding* and is performed based on the assembly version, culture information, and strong name if available. When the runtime resolves binding, it searches for the physical assembly. This search process is known as *probing*. Because a signed assembly also has signature information that is kept when you add a reference, search is first performed in the GAC. If the assembly is not found there, the runtime searches for it, looping through the application folder and subfolders until it's found. If you plan to place assemblies to locations different from the GAC and the application folder, you can place a `codeBase` suggestion in the application configuration file to tell the runtime where the required assembly will be found.

Signing Assemblies

To mark your assemblies as trusted, you need to add a digital signature known as a *strong name*. This becomes mandatory if you want to install an assembly to the GAC. Chapter 48 also provides a thorough discussion on signing assemblies with a strong name.

Assembly Information and Attributes

As you saw in various parts of the book, assemblies contain information that can make them recognizable from the external world, such as name, version, author, and copyright information. All these items are part of the assembly metadata and are injected to the assembly by adding some attribute declarations to the AssemblyInfo.vb file through instances of the Assembly attribute. Such attributes are covered in Chapter 3, "The Anatomy of a Visual Basic Project," particularly in Listing 3.3, which shows how to map properties assigned via the My Project Designer. Now that you know more about assemblies' contents and purposes, let's see where the CLR executes these complex units of work.

Understanding Application Domains

An *application domain* is a unit of isolation for executing managed code. For a better understanding, let's make a comparison with the Win32 world. In Win32, you have processes. Each process is isolated from other processes by the system so that a process cannot interfere with other processes or with resources required by such processes. This prevents process corruption and unexpected crashes. In .NET Framework architecture, the idea of isolation is provided by application domains, so an application domain is the place where an assembly runs isolated from other assemblies; when an application is started, the CLR creates one application domain for it. Although a Win32 process can host multiple application domains, when an assembly is executing within an application domain, it cannot interfere with other assemblies within different application domains. However, application domains can communicate with each other. One assembly can create multiple application domains (which are handled by the CLR) and run separate assemblies within such domains, as the next section explains.

Creating Application Domains and Executing Assemblies

You have two ways for executing assemblies inside application domains: getting the instance of the default application domain for the running assembly (that is, your application) and creating a new application domain. The System.AppDomain class provides a shared property named CurrentDomain, of type System.AppDomain, which represents the instance of the current application domain. You get the instance and then execute the assembly as follows:

```
Dim currentDomain As AppDomain = AppDomain.CurrentDomain
currentDomain.ExecuteAssembly("AnotherApp.exe")
```

The `AppDomain` class exposes an instance `ExecuteAssembly` method that enables executing the specified assembly within an application domain. Executing an assembly in the current application domain is not a good idea because you cannot unload the assembly when the execution has completed. Because of this, a better approach is to create a new application domain. For now, let's see how you can get information on application domains:

```
'Shows the AppDomain friendly name
Console.WriteLine(currentDomain.FriendlyName)
'Shows the AppDomain id within the process
Console.WriteLine(currentDomain.Id)
'Shows the working directory for the running
'assembly within the AppDomain
Console.WriteLine(currentDomain.BaseDirectory)
'Returns True if the code is classified as
'fully-trusted
Console.WriteLine(currentDomain.IsFullyTrusted)
```

You can interrogate some properties for retrieving application domain information. The `AppDomain` class offers a number of other advanced properties that are not covered here. A useful resource for finding information related to `AppDomain` properties is the MSDN Library: http://msdn.microsoft.com/en-us/library/system.appdomain(v=vs.110).aspx. Now it's time to understand how you can create new application domains and execute assemblies. You invoke the `AppDomain.CreateDomain` static method and then invoke `ExecuteAssembly`.

AppDomain.Load

The `AppDomain` class exposes a `Load` method that also enables you to load an assembly. According to the official MSDN documentation, usage of this method should always be restricted to COM interoperability scenarios. So always use `ExecuteAssembly` instead.

Also remember to unload the application domain after loaded assemblies have completed their work. The following code provides an example:

```
Dim secondDomain As AppDomain = AppDomain.
    CreateDomain("secondDomain")

Try
    secondDomain.ExecuteAssembly("MyApp.exe")
Catch ex As AppDomainUnloadedException
    Console.WriteLine("The AppDomain was already unloaded")
Catch ex As Exception
Finally
    Try
        AppDomain.Unload(secondDomain)
    Catch ex As CannotUnloadAppDomainException
```

```
        Console.Write("Unable to unload the AppDomain")
    End Try
End Try
```

The CLR throws an `AppDomainUnloadedException` if the code attempts to access an already unloaded application domain. As you can see from the code, you unload an application domain by invoking the `AppDomain.Unload` shared method that takes the application domain instance as an argument. If the application domain cannot be unloaded, a `CannotUnloadAppDomainException` is thrown. The `AppDomain.CreateDomain` method offers several overloads. One of them enables you to take an argument of type `AppDomainSetup`. It is a special object that gives you the opportunity to set some application domain properties. The following code provides an example:

```
Dim domainSetup As New AppDomainSetup
With domainSetup
    'Sets the current directory for the AppDomain
    .ApplicationBase = Environment.CurrentDirectory
    'Sets the application name
    .ApplicationName = "App domain demo"
    'Allows assembly binding redirection
    .DisallowBindingRedirects = False
    'Disallows code download from assemblies
    'via http
    .DisallowCodeDownload = True
    'Assigns a config file to the new app domain,
    'in this case the app.config of the current domain
    .ConfigurationFile = AppDomain.CurrentDomain.
                    SetupInformation.ConfigurationFile
End With

Dim thirdDomain As AppDomain = AppDomain.
    CreateDomain("thirdDomain", Nothing, domainSetup)
```

Notice that the second argument is of type `System.Security.Policy.Evidence` and is useful if you want to assign specific security policies to the application domain. In this demonstrative code, this is not accomplished. For this particular topic, application domains are important for security policies that you apply to your code. In the next section, you learn about the managed security model in the .NET Framework 4.6.

CREATING AND EXECUTING DYNAMIC CODE AT RUNTIME

In the next chapter, you learn about reflection and how you can create assemblies and code at runtime. When you have a dynamically created assembly with custom code, you can execute the assembly within an application domain with the same techniques shown in this section.

Security Model in .NET 4.6

Assemblies contain code that is executed when you run the application. As for the operating system and for any development environment, code is executed according to security rules that prevent the code from unauthorized access to system resources. The .NET Framework 4.6 retakes a new security model introduced by version 4.0, highly simplified if compared to the previous Code Access Security platform. The code will still be classified as fully trusted and partially trusted. Full trust means that the code has elevated permissions for accessing resources, whereas partial trust means that the code is restricted by the permissions it has. The security model provided by the CLR is now easier to understand and to implement, differently from what Code Access Security was in the past.

The following are the major changes in the security model introduced by .NET 4.0 and still available in .NET 4.6:

▶ Code Access Security policies and machine-wide security policies are now turned off by default.

The *transparency model* has been enforced and applied to the .NET Framework and managed applications. The transparency model can separate code that runs as part of the application (transparent code) and code that runs as part of the .NET infrastructure (critical code). As a result, critical code can access privileged resources, such as native code, but transparent code can access only resources allowed by the specified permissions set and cannot invoke or inherit from critical code. With the transparency model, groups of code are isolated based on privileges. Such privileges are divided into full-trust and partial-trust in the sandboxed model. The following is a list of the most important points that you have to care about with the security model in .NET 4.6:

▶ The enforcement of the transparency model is also why the .NET Framework configuration tool is no longer available for setting CAS policies.

▶ The *sandboxed model* enables you to run code in a restricted environment that grants code the only permissions it actually requires, and the natural place for the model is the application domains described in the previous section.

▶ Desktop applications always run as fully trusted. This is also true for applications started from Windows Explorer, a command prompt, and a network share.

▶ Permissions are still a central part in security, but some security actions from the `System.Security.Permission.SecurityAction` class have been deprecated. They are `Deny`, `RequestMinimum`, `RequestOptional`, and `RequestRefuse`.

▶ You can expose partially trusted assemblies via the `AllowPartiallyTrustedCallers` attribute.

▶ To enable constraints on types that can be used as evidence objects, .NET Framework 4.6 has the `System.Security.Policy.EvidenceBase` base class that must be inherited from all objects that want to be candidates as evidence.

TRANSPARENCY MODEL

The transparency model is not new in the .NET Framework; it was first introduced with version 2.0 as a mechanism for validating code efficiency. In .NET 4, it has been revisited (this is the reason it is also known as Level 2) and provides an enforcement mechanism for code separation.

The next sections provide explanations and code examples about security features in .NET Framework 4.6 with Visual Basic 2015.

Implementing and Requiring Permissions

With the exceptions described in the previous bulleted list for deprecated security actions, applying permissions in the new security model is similar to the previous versions of the .NET Framework. This means that you can leverage permissions from the `System.Security.Permissions` namespace, such as `FileIOPermission`, `UIPermission`, `IsolatedStoragePermission`, and `EnvironmentPermission`. The following code demonstrates how you use the declarative syntax for implementing a class that requires the caller code having the `FileIOPermission` to execute. Such a class simply implements a method that returns an `XDocument` from a text file:

```
'The caller code will need the FileIOPermission permission
'with unrestricted access otherwise it will fail
<FileIOPermission(Security.Permissions.SecurityAction.Demand,
                Unrestricted:=True)>
Class XmlParse

    Shared Function String2Xml(ByVal fileName As String) As XDocument
```

```
        'Expects an Xml-formatted string
        Return XDocument.Parse(fileName)
    End Function
End Class
```

You can also use the imperative syntax, which looks like this:

```
Dim fp As New FileIOPermission(PermissionState.Unrestricted)
Try
    fp.Demand()


Catch ex As Security.SecurityException


End Try
```

You create an instance of the required permission and then invoke Demand for checking whether the application has that level of permissions. If not, a System.Security. SecurityException is thrown.

The Transparency Level 2

By default, when you create a new application, it relies on security rules provided by the Transparency Level 2 of .NET Framework 4.6. The level name has this form to allow distinction from the old transparency level of previous .NET versions (known as Transparency Level 1). So the Transparency Level 2 security rules are applied implicitly, but a better idea is applying them explicitly by applying the System.Security. SecurityRules attribute that can be added at the assembly level as follows:

```
<Assembly: SecurityRules(Security.SecurityRuleSet.Level2)>
```

Applying the attribute explicitly is appropriate for code reading and future maintenance and avoids confusion. This level of enforcement brings into the .NET Framework some new ways of thinking about security policies. Most rely on the concept of *host*, where this means an environment is responsible for executing applications; ClickOnce, ASP.NET, and Internet Explorer are host examples. For code trust, applications that are not hosted, such as programs launched from a command prompt, from Windows Explorer, or from a shared network path, now run as full-trust. Instead, hosted or sandboxed applications still run according to host-based policies and run as partial-trust. For hosted and sandboxed applications, they are considered as *transparent* because they run with the limited permissions set granted by the sandbox. This means that you will no longer need to check for permissions when running partially trusted code because transparent applications run with the permissions set granted by the sandbox, so your only preoccupation should be targeting the sandbox permissions set and to not write code requiring the full-trust policy. It is important to mention that the transparency mechanism can separate code that is part of the .NET infrastructure (and that thus requires high privileges such as invoking native code), which is called *critical code*, and code that is part of the application, also known as *transparent code.* The idea behind the scenes is separating groups of code based on privileges. When working with sandboxes, such privileges are of two types: fully trusted, which is the unrestricted level, and partially trusted, which is the level restricted to the permission set established in the sandbox.

DESKTOP APPLICATIONS

With the Transparency Level 2 enabled, desktop applications run as full-trust.

The `System.Security.SecurityRules` attribute is not the only one that you can apply for establishing permissions rules. There are other attributes available, summarized in Table 43.1.

TABLE 43.1   Security Attributes

Attribute	Description
SecurityTransparent	Specifies that the code is transparent, meaning that it can be accessed by partially trusted code, that it cannot allow access to protected resources, and that it cannot cause an elevation of privileges. All types and members are transparent.
SecurityCritical	Code introduced by types exposed from the assembly is considered as security-critical, meaning that it can perform operations that require an elevation of privileges, whereas all other code is transparent. Methods overridden from abstract classes or implemented via an interface must be also explicitly marked with the attribute.
SecuritySafeCritical	Specifies that types expose critical code but allows access from partially trusted assemblies.

If you do not specify any attribute other than `SecurityRules`, for fully trusted assemblies the runtime considers all code as security-critical and thus callable only from fully trusted code, except where this could cause inheritance violations. If the assembly is instead partially trusted, specifying no attribute other than `SecurityRules` will make the runtime consider types and members as transparent by default, but they can be security-critical or security-safe-critical. For further detail on inheritance in the transparency model and on attributes listed in Table 43.1, visit the following page in the MSDN Library: http://msdn.microsoft.com/en-us/library/dd233102(v=vs.110).aspx. This is the reason it is opportune to explicitly provide the most appropriate attribute. The following is an example of applying both the `SecurityRules` and `SecurityTransparent` attributes:

```
<Assembly: SecurityRules(Security.SecurityRuleSet.Level2)>
<Assembly: SecurityTransparent()>
Class Foo
End Class
```

TIPS ON `SecurityTransparent`

Transparency enforcements are handled by the Just-in-Time compiler and not by the CLR infrastructure. This means that if you apply the `SecurityTransparent` attribute to an assembly, the assembly cannot call transparent and security-safe-critical types and members independently from the permissions set (including full-trust). In such a scenario, if the code attempts to access a security-critical type or member, a `MethodAccessException` will be thrown.

Sandboxing

You can execute partially trusted code within a sandbox that runs with the specified permissions set. Code, including assemblies, executed within the sandbox will be also granted to just the specified permissions set. To create and run a sandbox, you need an instance of the `AppDomain` class. The example here creates a sandbox for running an external assembly given the `LocalIntranet` zone's permissions. Before showing the sandbox example, follow these steps:

1. Create a new Console application and name the new project as **ExternalApp**.

2. In the `Main` method, add a `Console.Writeline` statement for showing whatever text message you like.

3. Build the project; then create a new folder named C:\MyApps and copy the newly generated **ExternalApp.exe** into C:\MyApps.

Such steps are required to have a simple external assembly to run inside the security sandbox. Now close the **ExternalApp** project and create a new Console project, naming it **SandBox**. The goal is to create a sandbox with `LocalIntranet` permission and run an external assembly inside the sandbox so that this external application will also be granted the same permissions. When ready, first add the following `Imports` directives:

```
Imports System.Security
Imports System.Security.Policy
Imports System.Reflection
```

Now move inside the `Main` method. The first thing you need is an `Evidence` object that you assign with the required permissions set, as demonstrated by the following code:

```
Dim ev As New Evidence()
ev.AddHostEvidence(New Zone(SecurityZone.Intranet))
```

When you have the `Evidence` instance, you can get a sandbox with the specified permissions as demonstrated by the following line:

```
Dim permSet As PermissionSet = SecurityManager.GetStandardSandbox(ev)
```

The `SecurityManager.GetStandardSandbox` returns a sandbox limited to the specified permissions. This sandbox will be used later when running the external assembly. As an alternative, you can set your own permissions and create your custom permissions set using the `PermissionSet` object as follows:

```
Dim permSet As New PermissionSet(Permissions.PermissionState.None)
permSet.AddPermission( _
        New SecurityPermission(SecurityPermissionFlag.Execution))
permSet.AddPermission(New UIPermission(PermissionState.Unrestricted))
```

At this point, you can put your hands on application domains. The first thing to do is create an instance of the `AppDomainSetup` class for specifying the working directory of the external assembly:

```
Dim ads As New AppDomainSetup()
ads.ApplicationBase = "C:\MyApps"
```

Next, you need to set the host `Evidence` and then create the `AppDomain`, passing the security information; then you'll invoke `AppDomain.ExecuteAssembly` to run the sandboxed assembly:

```
Dim hostEvidence As New Evidence()
Dim sandbox As AppDomain = AppDomain.
    CreateDomain("Sandboxed Domain", hostEvidence, ads, permSet, Nothing)

sandbox.ExecuteAssemblyByName("ExternalApp")
```

The `AppDomain.CreateDomain` method has an overload that enables you to create an application domain with a permissions set. Because the application domain has security permissions, an instance of the `Evidence` class is required to tell the runtime that the assembly will be affected by such permissions. Other arguments are the `AppDomainSetup` instance and the permissions set under which the external assembly is going to be run. The last null argument can be replaced with a reference to the strong name, in case you want to add it to the full trust list. This would first require the current application to be signed with a strong name (covered in Chapter 48) and then by getting a reference to the strong name via the `System.Security.Policy.StrongName` class as shown in the following line:

```
Dim fullTrustAssembly As StrongName = Assembly.
    GetExecutingAssembly.Evidence.GetHostEvidence(Of StrongName)()
```

The `Assembly.Evidence.GetHostEvidence(Of StrongName)` method returns the reference to the strong name. (The `System.Assembly` class is discussed in Chapter 44.) Finally, you pass the strong name reference to `AppDomain.CreateDomain` as follows:

```
Dim sandbox As AppDomain = AppDomain.
    CreateDomain("Sandboxed Domain", hostEvidence, ads,
                permSet, fullTrustAssembly)
```

Listing 43.1 shows the complete code example for your convenience.

LISTING 43.1   Running a Sandboxed Assembly

```vb
Imports System.Security
Imports System.Security.Policy
Imports System.Reflection

Module Module1

    Sub Main()
        Dim ev As New Evidence()
        ev.AddHostEvidence(New Zone(SecurityZone.Intranet))

        Dim permSet As PermissionSet = SecurityManager.GetStandardSandbox(ev)

        Dim ads As New AppDomainSetup()
        ads.ApplicationBase = "C:\MyApps"

        Dim hostEvidence As New Evidence()
        Dim sandbox As AppDomain = AppDomain.
            CreateDomain("Sandboxed Domain", hostEvidence, ads,
                        permSet, Nothing)

        'The assembly runs in a LocalIntranet sandboxed environment
        sandbox.ExecuteAssemblyByName("ExternalApp")
    End Sub
End Module
```

SANDBOX COMPLEXITY

Working with sandboxes can include complex scenarios. Particularly, you might have the need to execute not-trusted code from an external assembly with customized permissions sets. This also requires advanced application domains concepts. Fortunately, the MSDN Library provides an interesting walk-through covering these scenarios, available at http://msdn.microsoft.com/en-us/library/bb763046(v=vs.110).aspx. This is also useful to get a practical example about implementing the `MarshalByRefObject` for dynamic code execution within application domains.

Conditional APTCA

You can allow an assembly to be called by partially trusted code by applying the `System.Security.AllowPartiallyTrustedCallers` attribute at the assembly level. This can be accomplished as follows:

```vb
Imports System.Security
```

```vb
<Assembly: AllowPartiallyTrustedCallers()>
```

Without this attribute, only full-trusted code can call the assembly. Different from versions prior to 4.0, in the .NET Framework 4.x this attribute no longer requires an assembly to be signed with a strong name, and its presence involves all the security functions present in the code in the security checks.

Migrating from Old CAS-Based Code

If you move your existing code to .NET Framework 4.x and used Code Access Security policies, you might be advised with a message saying that CAS is obsolete. In these situations, you can add a specific section to the application configuration file, which allows legacy policies that look like this:

```
<configuration>
  <runtime>
    <NetFx40_LegacySecurityPolicy enabled="true"/>
  </runtime>
</configuration>
```

Of course, you always need to check whether legacy policies are appropriate in the particular scenario you are facing. You are encouraged to read the MSDN documentation about CAS migration, available at http://msdn.microsoft.com/en-us/library/ee191568(v=vs.110).aspx.

Summary

Understanding how assemblies work and how they can be managed is a key topic in .NET development. In this chapter, you first got an overview of assemblies, including their structure; their locations; and the type of information they share, such as code and metadata. Next, the discussion focused on application domains and the `System.AppDomain` class, which provides units of isolation for executing assemblies. Finally, you got an overview of the security model available in .NET Framework 4.x, starting from discussing the transparency level and the sandboxed model to analyzing specific code examples.

CHAPTER 44

Reflection

There are situations in which you need to implement logic for performing some tasks depending on user choices. This kind of a situation is not uncommon. The problem is when you cannot predetermine the code required for executing actions depending on user input. Think of code generators: These tools know how to generate code but cannot predetermine which code has to be generated until the users specify their requirements. Also think of assemblies external from your application. In some cases you might want to use types from an external assembly; in other cases you might just want to get information on types provided by the assembly; and in still other cases you might want to reach members with limited scope visibility that you could not reach by adding a reference. Reflection is a key part in the .NET Framework that enables you to accomplish all these mentioned scenarios. In this chapter, you learn to use reflection to both inspect assemblies and types and to generate and consume code on-the-fly. Also, in the final part of the chapter you learn about an interesting feature known as Caller Information. It enables you to retrieve information that in the past was available only via advanced reflection techniques and that is now easier to get.

Introducing Reflection

Reflection is an important part of the .NET Framework and provides the capability for interrogating assemblies' metadata and collecting information on types exposed by assemblies. Reflection also enables you to invoke code from external assemblies and generate code on-the-fly. You can take advantage of reflection by using objects exposed by the `System.Reflection` namespace. It can be particularly useful when you need to generate code according to some user input or when you are in late bound scenarios where making decisions on which code must be invoked (or generated) is something determined at runtime. Before putting your hands on code, it is necessary to get an overview of how assemblies are structured so that you can have a better understanding of the type of information you can investigate with the reflection.

Understanding Assemblies' Metadata

As you know, when you build an executable with Visual Basic, you build a .NET assembly. An assembly is a container of metadata and code. Metadata is information that the Common Language Runtime (CLR) uses in correctly loading and running the assembly. Figure 44.1 represents how an assembly is structured.

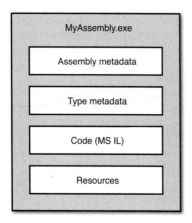

FIGURE 44.1   How an assembly is structured.

The Assembly Metadata, also known as *assembly manifest*, provides assembly information such as the name, version, culture, copyright information, and signature. The Type Metadata contains information on types defined within the assembly, such as class names and names of class members, including their parameters. The Code part is the actual Intermediate Language code that will be executed when the assembly is loaded. The Resources block contains all resources required by the assembly, such as images, icons, and strings. Additionally, types within an assembly can be grouped into multiple modules. A module is a container of types, whereas an assembly is a container of modules. With reflection, you can inspect metadata and code from an assembly using Visual Basic code, including assembly information.

Preparing a Sample Assembly

Before showing reflection capabilities, a good idea is to prepare an appropriate code example. First, create a new class library project and name it **People**. The goal of the library is to expose a special implementation of the `Person` class, with interfaces and enumeration implementations for a better demonstration on reflection. When ready, write the code in Listing 44.1, which is quite simple.

LISTING 44.1   Preparing Code for Reflection

```
Imports System.Text

Public Enum Genders
    Male = 0
    Female = 1
End Enum

Public Interface IPerson
    Property FirstName As String
    Property LastName As String
    Property Age As Integer
    Property Gender As Genders
    Event InstanceCreated()
    Function BuildFullName() As String
End Interface

Public Class Person
    Implements IPerson

    Public Property FirstName As String Implements IPerson.FirstName
    Public Property Gender As Genders Implements IPerson.Gender
    Public Property LastName As String Implements IPerson.LastName
    Public Property Age As Integer Implements IPerson.Age
    Public Event InstanceCreated() Implements IPerson.InstanceCreated

    Public Overridable Function BuildFullName() As String _
                Implements IPerson.BuildFullName

        Dim fullName As New StringBuilder
```

```
        fullName.Append(LastName)
        fullName.Append(" ")
        fullName.Append(FirstName)
        fullName.Append(", ")
        fullName.Append(Gender.ToString)
        fullName.Append(", of age ")
        fullName.Append(Age.ToString)
        Return fullName.ToString
    End Function
End Class
```

Build the project; then add a new Console project to the current solution. Finally, add a reference to the People class library so that, just for demo purposes, you can load the assembly for reflection without specifying the full path.

Getting Assembly Information

You get assembly metadata information by creating an instance of the `System.Reflection.Assembly` class. This class provides both static and instance members for accessing assembly information. Typically, you use one of the methods summarized in Table 44.1 to load an assembly for getting information.

TABLE 44.1   Methods for Loading an Assembly

Method	Description
GetAssembly	Loads an assembly containing the specified type
GetCallingAssembly	Gets the assembly that stores the code that invoked the current method
GetExecutingAssembly	Returns the instance of the current assembly
GetEntryAssembly	Returns the instance of the assembly that ran the current process
Load	Loads the specified assembly into the current application domain
LoadFile	Loads the specified assembly from the specified path
LoadFrom	Loads the specified assembly into the current application domain, given the specified path
ReflectionOnlyLoad	Like `Load`, but limits you to only reflection inspection and not code execution
ReflectionOnlyLoadFrom	Like `LoadFrom`, but limits you to only reflection inspection and not code execution

When you get the instance of the assembly you want to inspect, you can access information via some useful properties. The code in Listing 44.2 shows how to accomplish this. (See comments for explanations.)

LISTING 44.2   Inspecting Assembly Information

```
Imports System.Reflection

Module GettingAsmInfo

    Sub Main()
        'Infers System.Reflection.Assembly
        Dim asm = Assembly.ReflectionOnlyLoadFrom("People.dll")

        With asm
            'Gets the full assembly name with
            'version and culture
            Console.WriteLine("Assembly name:")
            Console.WriteLine(.FullName)
            'Gets whether the assembly is fully trusted
            Console.WriteLine("Is full-trust: {0}", .IsFullyTrusted)
            'Gets the assembly entry point. If empty, the
            'constructor is the entry point
            Console.WriteLine("The entry point method is: {0}", .EntryPoint)
            'Gets the .NET version that the
            'assembly was built upon
            Console.WriteLine("Image runtime version: {0}", .ImageRuntimeVersion)
            'Gets whether the assembly was loaded from
            'the GAC
            Console.WriteLine("Loaded from the GAC: {0}", .GlobalAssemblyCache)
            'Gets the assembly location
            Console.WriteLine("Assembly path: {0}", .Location)

            'Gets an array of modules loaded
            'by the assembly
            Console.WriteLine("Loaded modules: ")
            For Each item As System.Reflection.Module _
                In .GetLoadedModules
                Console.WriteLine("   {0}", item.Name)
            Next
        End With
        Console.ReadLine()
    End Sub
End Module
```

Notice how the code uses the `ReflectionOnlyLoadFrom` method to enable only inspection without code execution capabilities. If you run the preceding code, you get the following result:

```
Assembly name:
People, Version=1.0.0.0, Culture=neutral, PublicKeyToken=null
Is full-trust: True
The entry point method is:
Image runtime version: v4.0.30319
Loaded from the GAC: False
Assembly path: C:\Users\Alessandro\documents\visual studio
2012\Projects\Reflection\Reflection\bin\Debug\People.dll
Loaded modules:
     People.dll
```

The `Assembly.GetModules` method returns an array of modules loaded by the instance of the assembly. Other interesting methods are `GetExportedTypes`, which returns an array of publicly visible types, and `GetFiles`, which returns an array of `FileStream` objects, each representing a file in the assembly's resources. Inspecting assembly information is just the first level of reflection. The next step is inspecting types.

Reflecting Types

Reflection enables retrieving information on programs, including modules, types, and type members defined within an assembly. For example, you might want to enumerate all types and type members defined in the People.dll assembly. Take a look at the following code:

```
Dim asm = Assembly.LoadFrom("People.dll")

Console.WriteLine("Enumerating types:")
For Each t In asm.GetTypes
    Console.WriteLine("Type name: {0}", t.ToString)

    Console.WriteLine(" Constructors:")
    For Each constructor In t.GetConstructors
        Console.WriteLine("     " + constructor.ToString)
    Next

    Console.WriteLine(" Methods:")
    For Each method In t.GetMethods
        Console.WriteLine("     " + method.ToString)
    Next

    Console.WriteLine(" Properties:")
    For Each [property] In t.GetProperties
        Console.WriteLine("     " + [property].ToString)
```

```
    Next

    Console.WriteLine(" Fields:")
    For Each field In t.GetFields
        Console.WriteLine("      " + field.ToString)
    Next

    Console.WriteLine(" Events:")
    For Each [event] In t.GetEvents
        Console.WriteLine("      " + [event].ToString)
    Next
Next
```

You still get the instance of the desired assembly; then you can iterate types (or modules if preferred). The `Assembly.GetTypes` method returns an array of `System.Type` objects defined in the assembly that you can iterate for detailed information. The `System.Type` class exposes several `GetX` methods, in which `x` can stand for `Constructors`, `Properties`, `Methods`, `Fields`, and `Events`. Each of these methods returns an `XInfo` class instance, such as `MethodInfo`, `PropertyInfo`, `FieldInfo`, and so on. Each class exposes interesting properties about the inspected member for further information such as `IsPrivate`, `IsPublic`, or `IsStatic`.

> **USING** `Tostring`
>
> Each `XInfo` class also exposes a `Name` property that returns the name of the member. In this case, `ToString` was used instead of the name to return the full member signature.

Also, the `System.Type` class offers some useful properties enabling you to understand what kind of type you are inspecting such as `IsClass`, `IsInterface`, or `IsEnum`. The `Namespace` property enables you to get the namespace exposing the inspected type. Notice that the preceding code inspects all types defined in the specified assembly, including the ones that are usually part of My Project. Also notice that reflection considers properties' getters and setters such as methods that thus will be listed within this category. For a better understanding, the following is an excerpt of the output produced by the previously illustrated code:

```
Enumerating types:
Type name: People.Genders
 Constructors:
 Methods:
    Boolean Equals(System.Object)
    Int32 GetHashCode()
    System.String ToString()
    System.String ToString(System.String, System.IFormatProvider)
    Int32 CompareTo(System.Object)
    System.String ToString(System.String)
    System.String ToString(System.IFormatProvider)
```

```
    Boolean HasFlag(System.Enum)
    System.TypeCode GetTypeCode()
    System.Type GetType()
 Properties:
 Fields:
    Int32 value__
    People.Genders Male
    People.Genders Female
 Events:
Type name: People.IPerson
 Constructors:
 Methods:
    System.String get_FirstName()
    Void set_FirstName(System.String)
    System.String get_LastName()
    Void set_LastName(System.String)
    Int32 get_Age()
    Void set_Age(Int32)
    People.Genders get_Gender()
    Void set_Gender(People.Genders)
    System.String BuildFullName()
    Void add_InstanceCreated(InstanceCreatedEventHandler)
    Void remove_InstanceCreated(InstanceCreatedEventHandler)
 Properties:
    System.String FirstName
    System.String LastName
    Int32 Age
    People.Genders Gender
 Fields:
 Events:
    InstanceCreatedEventHandler InstanceCreated
Type name: People.Person
 Constructors:
    Void .ctor()
 Methods:
    System.String get_FirstName()
    Void set_FirstName(System.String)
    People.Genders get_Gender()
    Void set_Gender(People.Genders)
    System.String get_LastName()
    Void set_LastName(System.String)
    Int32 get_Age()
    Void set_Age(Int32)
    Void add_InstanceCreated(InstanceCreatedEventHandler)
    Void remove_InstanceCreated(InstanceCreatedEventHandler)
    System.String BuildFullName()
```

```
    System.String ToString()
    Boolean Equals(System.Object)
    Int32 GetHashCode()
    System.Type GetType()
 Properties:
    System.String FirstName
    People.Genders Gender
    System.String LastName
    Int32 Age
 Fields:
 Events:
    InstanceCreatedEventHandler InstanceCreated
Type name: People.My.Resources.Resources
 Constructors:
 Methods:
    System.String ToString()
    Boolean Equals(System.Object)
    Int32 GetHashCode()
    System.Type GetType()
 Properties:
 Fields:
 Events:
Type name: People.My.MySettings
 Constructors:
    Void .ctor()
 Methods:
    People.My.MySettings get_Default()
    System.Configuration.SettingsContext get_Context()
    System.Configuration.SettingsPropertyCollection get_Properties()
    System.Configuration.SettingsPropertyValueCollection get_PropertyValues()
    System.Configuration.SettingsProviderCollection get_Providers()
    System.String get_SettingsKey()
    Void set_SettingsKey(System.String)
    Void add_PropertyChanged(System.ComponentModel.PropertyChangedEventHandler)

    Void remove_PropertyChanged(System.ComponentModel.
            PropertyChangedEventHandler)
    Void add_SettingChanging(System.Configuration.SettingChangingEventHandler)
    Void remove_SettingChanging(System.Configuration.
    SettingChangingEventHandler)
    Void add_SettingsLoaded(System.Configuration.SettingsLoadedEventHandler)
    Void remove_SettingsLoaded(System.Configuration.SettingsLoadedEventHandler)

    Void add_SettingsSaving(System.Configuration.SettingsSavingEventHandler)
    Void remove_SettingsSaving(System.Configuration.SettingsSavingEventHandler)
```

44

```
    System.Object GetPreviousVersion(System.String)
    Void Reload()
    Void Reset()
    Void Save()
    System.Object get_Item(System.String)
    Void set_Item(System.String, System.Object)
    Void Upgrade()
    Void Initialize(System.Configuration.SettingsContext, System.Configuration.
SettingsPropertyCollection, System.Configuration.SettingsProviderCollection)
    Boolean get_IsSynchronized()
    System.String ToString()
    Boolean Equals(System.Object)
    Int32 GetHashCode()
    System.Type GetType()
  Properties:
    People.My.MySettings Default
    System.Configuration.SettingsContext Context
    System.Configuration.SettingsPropertyCollection Properties
    System.Configuration.SettingsPropertyValueCollection PropertyValues
    System.Configuration.SettingsProviderCollection Providers
    System.String SettingsKey
    System.Object Item [System.String]
    Boolean IsSynchronized
  Fields:
  Events:
    System.ComponentModel.PropertyChangedEventHandler PropertyChanged
    System.Configuration.SettingChangingEventHandler SettingChanging
    System.Configuration.SettingsLoadedEventHandler SettingsLoaded
    System.Configuration.SettingsSavingEventHandler SettingsSaving
Type name: People.My.MySettingsProperty
  Constructors:
  Methods:
    System.String ToString()
    Boolean Equals(System.Object)
    Int32 GetHashCode()
    System.Type GetType()
  Properties:
  Fields:
  Events:
Type name: People.My.MyApplication
  Constructors:
    Void .ctor()
  Methods:
    System.String GetEnvironmentVariable(System.String)
    Microsoft.VisualBasic.Logging.Log get_Log()
    Microsoft.VisualBasic.ApplicationServices.AssemblyInfo get_Info()
```

```
        System.Globalization.CultureInfo get_Culture()
        System.Globalization.CultureInfo get_UICulture()
        Void ChangeCulture(System.String)
        Void ChangeUICulture(System.String)
        System.String ToString()
        Boolean Equals(System.Object)
        Int32 GetHashCode()
        System.Type GetType()
    Properties:
        Microsoft.VisualBasic.Logging.Log Log
        Microsoft.VisualBasic.ApplicationServices.AssemblyInfo Info
        System.Globalization.CultureInfo Culture
        System.Globalization.CultureInfo UICulture
    Fields:
    Events:
Type name: People.My.MyComputer
    Constructors:
        Void .ctor()
    Methods:
        Microsoft.VisualBasic.Devices.Audio get_Audio()
        Microsoft.VisualBasic.MyServices.ClipboardProxy get_Clipboard()
        Microsoft.VisualBasic.Devices.Ports get_Ports()
        Microsoft.VisualBasic.Devices.Mouse get_Mouse()
        Microsoft.VisualBasic.Devices.Keyboard get_Keyboard()
        System.Windows.Forms.Screen get_Screen()
        Microsoft.VisualBasic.Devices.Clock get_Clock()
        Microsoft.VisualBasic.MyServices.FileSystemProxy get_FileSystem()
        Microsoft.VisualBasic.Devices.ComputerInfo get_Info()
        Microsoft.VisualBasic.Devices.Network get_Network()
        System.String get_Name()
        Microsoft.VisualBasic.MyServices.RegistryProxy get_Registry()
        System.String ToString()
        Boolean Equals(System.Object)
        Int32 GetHashCode()
        System.Type GetType()
    Properties:
        Microsoft.VisualBasic.Devices.Audio Audio
        Microsoft.VisualBasic.MyServices.ClipboardProxy Clipboard
        Microsoft.VisualBasic.Devices.Ports Ports
        Microsoft.VisualBasic.Devices.Mouse Mouse
        Microsoft.VisualBasic.Devices.Keyboard Keyboard
        System.Windows.Forms.Screen Screen
        Microsoft.VisualBasic.Devices.Clock Clock
        Microsoft.VisualBasic.MyServices.FileSystemProxy FileSystem
        Microsoft.VisualBasic.Devices.ComputerInfo Info
        Microsoft.VisualBasic.Devices.Network Network
```

44

```
     System.String Name
     Microsoft.VisualBasic.MyServices.RegistryProxy Registry
 Fields:
 Events:
Type name: People.My.MyProject
 Constructors:
 Methods:
     System.String ToString()
     Boolean Equals(System.Object)
     Int32 GetHashCode()
     System.Type GetType()
 Properties:
 Fields:
 Events:
Type name: People.IPerson+InstanceCreatedEventHandler
 Constructors:
     Void .ctor(System.Object, IntPtr)
 Methods:
     System.IAsyncResult BeginInvoke(System.AsyncCallback, System.Object)
     Void EndInvoke(System.IAsyncResult)
     Void Invoke()
     Void GetObjectData(System.Runtime.Serialization.SerializationInfo,
         System.Runtime.Serialization.StreamingContext)
     Boolean Equals(System.Object)
     System.Delegate[] GetInvocationList()
     Int32 GetHashCode()
     System.Object DynamicInvoke(System.Object[])
     System.Reflection.MethodInfo get_Method()
     System.Object get_Target()
     System.Object Clone()
     System.String ToString()
     System.Type GetType()
 Properties:
     System.Reflection.MethodInfo Method
     System.Object Target
 Fields:
 Events:
Type name: People.My.MyProject+MyWebServices
 Constructors:
     Void .ctor()
 Methods:
     Boolean Equals(System.Object)
     Int32 GetHashCode()
     System.String ToString()
     System.Type GetType()
 Properties:
```

```
  Fields:
  Events:
Type name: People.My.MyProject+ThreadSafeObjectProvider`1[T]
  Constructors:
      Void .ctor()
  Methods:
      System.String ToString()
      Boolean Equals(System.Object)
      Int32 GetHashCode()
      System.Type GetType()
  Properties:
  Fields:
  Events:
```

Notice also how `EventHandler` types, generated behind the scenes when you implement a simple event, are inspected and illustrated. Also notice how the members' signature recalls the Intermediate Language syntax.

Reflecting a Single Type

Reflecting all types within an assembly can be useful, but in most cases you will probably be interested in reflecting a single type. To accomplish this, you need the instance of a `System.Type`. Then you need to invoke members described in the previous section. For example, imagine you want to inspect members from the `Person` class. You first get the type instance, and then you can perform reflection as demonstrated by the following code:

```
Dim myType As Type = (New People.Person).GetType

Console.WriteLine(" Methods:")
For Each method In myType.GetMethods
    Console.WriteLine("      " + method.ToString)
Next

Console.WriteLine(" Properties:")
For Each [property] In myType.GetProperties
    Console.WriteLine("      " + [property].ToString)
Next

Console.WriteLine(" Fields:")
For Each field In myType.GetFields
    Console.WriteLine("      " + field.ToString)
Next

Console.WriteLine(" Events:")
For Each [event] In myType.GetEvents
    Console.WriteLine("      " + [event].ToString)
Next
```

44

The preceding code produces the following result:

```
Methods:
     System.String get_FirstName()
     Void set_FirstName(System.String)
     People.Genders get_Gender()
     Void set_Gender(People.Genders)
     System.String get_LastName()
     Void set_LastName(System.String)
     Int32 get_Age()
     Void set_Age(Int32)
     Void add_InstanceCreated(InstanceCreatedEventHandler)
     Void remove_InstanceCreated(InstanceCreatedEventHandler)
     System.String BuildFullName()
     System.String ToString()
     Boolean Equals(System.Object)
     Int32 GetHashCode()
     System.Type GetType()
 Properties:
     System.String FirstName
     People.Genders Gender
     System.String LastName
     Int32 Age
 Fields:
 Events:
     InstanceCreatedEventHandler InstanceCreated
```

For more details, the MSDN documentation on the `System.Reflection` namespace and the `System.Type` class are a good source of information on available members.

REFLECTION SECURITY CONSIDERATIONS

Reflection is both a key topic and a powerful tool in the .NET developer toolbox. By the way, you had the opportunity to understand how fragile your code is in security terms because, with a few lines of code, anyone can see types and members exposed by the assembly. Because preventing reflection is not possible, if you want to protect your code, you need to use an obfuscation tool such as Preemptive Dotfuscator (which ships with Visual Studio 2015) that can add more effective protection.

Invoking Code Dynamically

Reflection also enables you to execute dynamic code, meaning that you can pick up types defined within an assembly, creating instances and invoking types from Visual Basic code without having a reference to that assembly. For example, imagine you want to load the People.dll assembly and create and populate an instance of the `Person` class, as shown in Listing 44.3.

LISTING 44.3   Creating and Running Dynamic Code

```vb
Imports System.Reflection
Module DynamicCode

    Sub DynCode()
        Dim asm = Assembly.LoadFrom("People.dll")

        'Gets the type definition
        Dim personType = asm.GetType("People.Person")

        'Gets the LastName property definition
        Dim lastNameProperty As PropertyInfo = personType.
                                        GetProperty("LastName")
        'Gets a reference to the property setter
        Dim lastNamePropSet As MethodInfo = lastNameProperty.
                                    GetSetMethod

        Dim firstNameProperty As PropertyInfo = personType.
                                        GetProperty("FirstName")
        Dim firstNamePropSet As MethodInfo = firstNameProperty.
                                    GetSetMethod

        Dim ageProperty As PropertyInfo = personType.GetProperty("Age")
        Dim agePropSet As MethodInfo = ageProperty.GetSetMethod

        'Creates an instance of the Person class
        Dim newPerson As Object = _
            Activator.CreateInstance(personType)

        'Each method is invoked upon the new type instance
        lastNamePropSet.Invoke(newPerson, New Object() {"Del Sole"})
        firstNamePropSet.Invoke(newPerson, New Object() {"Alessandro"})
        agePropSet.Invoke(newPerson, New Object() {37})

        'Gets the BuildFullName method from the Person class
        Dim buildFullNameMethod = personType.GetMethod("BuildFullName")

        'The method returns String but Invoke returns Object, so
        'a conversion is required
        Dim result As String = CStr(buildFullNameMethod.
                            Invoke(newPerson, Nothing))

        Console.WriteLine(result)
        Console.ReadLine()
    End Sub
End Module
```

44

When you have the type instance, you invoke the `GetProperty` method to get a reference of the desired property. This returns a `PropertyInfo` object. To set the property value, you need a reference to the setter method that is obtained via the `GetSetMethod` and that returns a `MethodInfo` object. (If you also want the ability to get a property value, you need to instead invoke `GetGetMethod` the same way.) When you have all the properties, you need an instance of the class. This can be obtained by calling the `Activator.CreateInstance` method, which takes the type instance as the argument.

The `System.Activator` class contains members for creating code locally or retrieving code from a remote location. Having an instance of the class is required before you set properties because it is against the instance that property setters will be invoked. To actually run the property setter, you call the `MethodInfo.Invoke` instance method; the first argument is the type instance, and the second argument is an array of items of type `Object`, each to be used as a property value. In our case, each property in the `Person` class accepts just one value, so each array can store just one item. Similarly, you can get reference to methods by invoking `GetMethod` on the type instance, as it happens in Listing 44.3, to get a reference to the `Person.BuildFullName` method. When you call `Invoke` to run the method, you can pass `Nothing` as the second argument if the original method does not require parameters. The code produces the following result:

```
Del Sole Alessandro, Male of Age: 37
```

After seeing how you can call dynamic code provided by an existing assembly, let's now see how to create code at runtime.

SECURITY NOTE

In many cases, you can also invoke members marked as private or with limited visibility. Although this can seem exciting, be careful. If you invoke a private member but you are not completely sure about its purpose, you expose your code to potentially uncontrollable dangers.

Generating Code at Runtime with `Reflection.Emit`

The `System.Reflection.Emit` namespace provides objects for generating assemblies, types, and type members at runtime. You need to perform the following operations sequentially:

1. Create an in-memory assembly within the current application domain with an instance of the `AssemblyBuilder` class.
2. Create a module for containing types via an instance of the `ModuleBuilder` class.
3. Create types with instances of the `TypeBuilder` class.
4. Add members to the `TypeBuilder` via `XBuilder` objects, such as `MethodBuilder`, `FieldBuilder`, and `PropertyBuilder`.
5. Save the assembly to disk if required.

The code in Listing 44.4 demonstrates how to dynamically create a simple implementation of the `Person` class with one property and one method.

LISTING 44.4   Generating Code at Runtime

```
Imports System.Reflection
Imports System.Reflection.Emit

Module CreatingCode

    Sub CreateAssembly()

        'Creates assembly name and properties
        Dim asmName As New AssemblyName("People")
        asmName.Version = New Version("1.0.0")
        asmName.CultureInfo = New Globalization.CultureInfo("en-US")

        'Gets the current application domain
        Dim currentAppDomain As AppDomain = AppDomain.CurrentDomain

        'Creates a new in-memory assembly in the current application domain
        'providing execution and saving capabilities
        Dim asmBuilder As AssemblyBuilder = currentAppDomain.
                                DefineDynamicAssembly(asmName,
                                AssemblyBuilderAccess.RunAndSave)

        'Creates a module for containing types
        Dim modBuilder As ModuleBuilder = _
            asmBuilder.DefineDynamicModule("PersonModule",
                                "People.dll")

        'Creates a type, specifically a Public Class
        Dim tyBuilder As TypeBuilder = _
            modBuilder.DefineType("Person",
                            TypeAttributes.Public _
                            Or TypeAttributes.Class)
        'Defines a default empty constructor
        Dim ctorBuilder As ConstructorBuilder = _
            tyBuilder.DefineDefaultConstructor(MethodAttributes.Public)

        'Defines a field for storing a property value
        Dim fldBuilder As FieldBuilder = _
            tyBuilder.DefineField("_lastName",
                            GetType(String),
                            FieldAttributes.Private)
```

```vb
'Defines a property of type String
Dim propBuilder As PropertyBuilder = _
    tyBuilder.DefineProperty("LastName",
                                PropertyAttributes.None, GetType(String),
                                Type.EmptyTypes)

'Defines a series of attributes for both getter and setter
Dim propMethodAttributes As MethodAttributes = _
    MethodAttributes.Public Or
    MethodAttributes.SpecialName Or
    MethodAttributes.HideBySig

'Defines the getter method for the property
Dim propGetMethod As MethodBuilder = _
    tyBuilder.DefineMethod("get_LastName",
                                propMethodAttributes,
                                GetType(String),
                                Type.EmptyTypes)

'Generates IL code for returning the field value
Dim propGetMethodIL As ILGenerator = propGetMethod.GetILGenerator
propGetMethodIL.Emit(OpCodes.Ldarg_0)
propGetMethodIL.Emit(OpCodes.Ldfld, fldBuilder)
propGetMethodIL.Emit(OpCodes.Ret)

'Defines the setter method for the property
Dim propSetMethod As MethodBuilder = _
    tyBuilder.DefineMethod("set_LastName",
                                propMethodAttributes,
                                GetType(String),
                                Type.EmptyTypes)

'Generates the IL code for setting the field value
Dim propSetMethodIL As ILGenerator = propSetMethod.GetILGenerator
propSetMethodIL.Emit(OpCodes.Ldarg_0)
propSetMethodIL.Emit(OpCodes.Ldarg_1)
propSetMethodIL.Emit(OpCodes.Stfld, fldBuilder)
propSetMethodIL.Emit(OpCodes.Ret)

'Assigns getter and setter to the property
propBuilder.SetGetMethod(propGetMethod)
propBuilder.SetSetMethod(propSetMethod)

'Defines a public method that returns String
Dim methBuilder As MethodBuilder = _
    tyBuilder.DefineMethod("BuildFullName",
```

```
                    MethodAttributes.Public,
                    GetType(String),
                    Type.EmptyTypes)

        'Method body cannot be empty, so just return
        Dim methodILGen As ILGenerator = methBuilder.GetILGenerator
        methodILGen.EmitWriteLine("Method implementation needed")
        methodILGen.Emit(OpCodes.Ret)

        'Creates an instance of the type
        Dim pers As Type = tyBuilder.CreateType

        'Enumerates members for demo purposes
        For Each member In pers.GetMembers
            Console.WriteLine("Member name: {0}", member.Name)
        Next

        'Saves the assembly to disk
        asmBuilder.Save("People.dll")
        Console.ReadLine()
    End Sub
End Module
```

After you create an `AssemblyName` for assigning assembly properties and get the instance of the current application domain, you use the `AppDomain.DefineDynamicAssembly` method to generate an in-memory assembly. The method returns an instance of the `AssemblyBuilder` class and receives the `AssemblyName` instance and a value from the `AssemblyBuilderAccess` enumeration that establishes the access level for reflection. `RunAndSave` enables you to execute and save the assembly, but you can also limit reflection with the `ReflectionOnly` value.

The next step is creating an instance of the `ModuleBuilder` class that can act as a container of types. This is accomplished by invoking the `AssemblyBuilder.DefineDynamicModule` method that requires you to specify the module name and the filename. (This one should be the same as for `AssemblyName` if you want metadata to be merged into a single assembly.) When you have a module, you can put your types into it. For each type, you need to create an instance of the `TypeBuilder` class, which you accomplish by invoking the `ModuleBuilder.DefineType` method that receives the type name and qualifiers as arguments. Qualifiers are one or more values from the `TypeAttributes` enumeration; in the current example, `Public` and `Class` values are assigned to the new type to create a new class with public visibility. The `TypeBuilder` class provides lots of methods for adding members, such as constructors, field, properties, and methods. For constructors, the code demonstrates how to add a public, empty, and default constructor by invoking the `TypeBuilder.DefineDefaultConstructor`, but you can supply constructor overloads via the `DefineConstructor` method.

To implement properties, you first need to supply fields. These are implemented via the `TypeBuilder.DefineField` method that requires three arguments: the field name; the type (retrieved via `GetType`); and qualifiers, which are determined with values from the `FieldAttributes` enumeration. Similarly, you implement properties by invoking the `TypeBuilder.DefineProperty` method, but this is not enough because you also need to explicitly generate the getter and setter methods for each property. These are special methods that require providing some properties defined within the `propMethodAttributes` variable that takes values from the `MethodAttributes` enumeration. When you establish method attributes, you create two `MethodBuilder` instances. Such a class generates each kind of method, including special ones. You just supply the method name, the attributes, the return type, and an array of type parameters. The actual problem is how you implement method bodies. As a general rule, methods implemented via reflection cannot have an empty method body, so you must provide some Intermediate Language code to populate the method body. This is accomplished by invoking methods from the `ILGenerator` class that enable injecting IL code to the method. Consider the following snippet, excerpted from Listing 44.4:

```
'Generates IL code for returning the field value
Dim propGetMethodIL As ILGenerator = propGetMethod.GetILGenerator
propGetMethodIL.Emit(OpCodes.Ldarg_0)
propGetMethodIL.Emit(OpCodes.Ldfld, fldBuilder)
propGetMethodIL.Emit(OpCodes.Ret)
```

The `MethodBuilder.GetILGenerator` method returns an instance of the `ILGenerator` class. Then you invoke the `Emit` method to execute IL code. In the preceding snippet, the IL code returns the value of the `fldBuilder` variable, pushes the value onto the stack, and then returns. Actions to execute via the IL are taken via shared fields from the `OpCodes` class, each related to an IL instruction.

NOTE ON OpCodes

Reflection is powerful, but because you need to know the MS Intermediate Language in detail before implementing dynamic code, and because this would be beyond the scope in this book, you should look at the appropriate MSDN documentation at http://msdn. microsoft.com/en-us/library/8ffc3x75(v=vs.110).aspx.

When you provide the method body for getters and setters, you add them to the related properties via the `PropertyBuilder.SetGetMethod` and `PropertyBuilder.SetSetMethod` methods. Similarly, you implement any other method, and the sample code demonstrates this by providing a simple method body that invokes `EmitWriteLine`. This is a method that sends to the assembly the appropriate IL code for writing a message to the Console window. Finally, you invoke `AssemblyBuilder.Save` to save the assembly to disk. More than running the code, you can ensure that everything works by inspecting the assembly with a reflection tool such as Microsoft IL Disassembler. Figure 44.2 shows how the assembly looks if opened with ILDasm, demonstrating the correct result of our work.

Typically, you will use code generators instead of reflection to generate code on-the-fly because in that case you do not need to know about Intermediate Language. After you define your types on-the-fly, you can consume them using the techniques described in the "Invoking Code Dynamically" section.

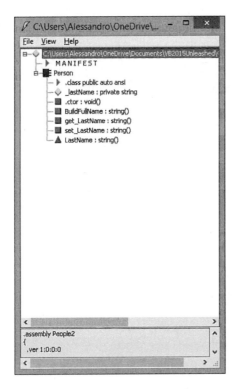

FIGURE 44.2   The assembly created at runtime opened in IL Disassembler.

CODE GENERATION WITH THE .NET COMPILER PLATFORM

In Chapter 51, "Code Analysis: The .NET Compiler Platform and Tools," you learn the basics of code generation with the new .NET Compiler Platform APIs. In that chapter you do not generate external assemblies but you learn how to take advantage of more modern APIs for generating code. With the .NET Compiler Platform, you work over language syntax trees and are not required to have knowledge of the Intermediate Language. If you plan to build code-generation tools, you should definitely take a deeper look at the .NET Compiler Platform and the code-generation APIs, including the `Microsoft.CodeAnalysis.Compilation` class and its `Emit` method. The .NET Compiler Platform documentation, which you are encouraged to read after Chapter 51, is available at https://github.com/dotnet/roslyn, and the reference for `Compilation` is available at http://source.roslyn.io/#Microsoft.CodeAnalysis/Compilation.

Late Binding Concepts

Late binding is a particular programming technique that you use to resolve types at runtime and dynamic loading, which is accomplished by assigning objects to variable of type Object. For a better understanding, consider its counterpart, the early binding. This happens at compile time where the compiler checks that argument types utilized to invoke methods match their signatures. An example is the background compiler that provides real-time checks for types used in code, thanks to early binding. On the contrary, late binding requires you to specify the function signatures. Moreover, you must ensure that the code uses the correct types. This means that binding requirements, such as binary files to load or methods to invoke, is long delayed, in many cases until before the method is invoked. Reflection frequently uses late binding because in many cases you work with objects of type Object, and this requires late resolution for invoking appropriate members. The following example, although not related to reflection, demonstrates how to invoke members from objects declared as Object that are instead of different types, but this is determined late at runtime:

```
' This code creates an instance of Microsoft Excel and adds a new WorkBook.
' Requires Option Strict Off
Sub LateBindingDemo()
    Dim xlsApp As Object
    Dim xlsBook As Object
    xlsApp = CreateObject("Excel.Application")
    xlsBook = xlsApp.Workbooks.Add
End Sub
```

> **Option Strict Off BEST PRACTICES**
>
> Because in many situations turning Option Strict to Off can be very dangerous, if you need to work with late binding, you should consider moving the code that requires such a technique to a separate code file and just mark this code file with Option Strict Off, instead of setting it Off at the project level.

As you can see, invoking members from Object in late binding is different because the compiler cannot predetermine whether members exist and you don't have IntelliSense support. But if the actual type defines members that you are attempting to invoke, they will be correctly bound at runtime. Just remember that late binding requires an Option Strict Off directive, and that should be used carefully.

Caller Information

Reflection is very powerful and enables you to retrieve every possible bit of information from an assembly and types defined in the assembly, including at runtime. However, you might want to catch some information, typically to log some activities, which would be difficult to retrieve via reflection, at least with an easy approach. The .NET Framework 4.6

makes this easier by offering a set of attributes called *caller information*. This is the list of new attributes exposed by the `System.Runtime.CompilerServices` namespace:

▶ `CallerFilePath` returns the name of the file where a specific code block is being executed

▶ `CallerLineNumber` returns the line number for the code that has been executed

▶ `CallerMemberName` returns the name of a member that has received some changes

In the past, you could retrieve the same information with advanced reflection techniques, which would also require a full trust context and the inclusion of debug symbol files in the assembly. With caller information, you can retrieve such information easily and without the full trust and debug symbol restrictions because they are available through types exposed directly by the .NET Framework. To use caller information, you must declare methods that receive optional parameters decorated with the attribute that you need. For a better understanding, let's consider an example. Listing 44.5 demonstrates how to implement a method that writes a log about some information entered by the user.

LISTING 44.5   Writing a Log with Caller Information

```
Imports System.Runtime.CompilerServices
Module Module1

    Sub Main()
        'Wait for the user input
        Console.WriteLine("Type something: ")
        Dim input = Console.ReadLine

        'show what the user entered:
        Console.WriteLine("You entered: {0}", input)

        WriteLog()
        Console.ReadLine()
    End Sub

    'Declare optional arguments. These are decorated
    'with CallerFilePath and CallerLineNumber attributes
    Private Sub WriteLog(<CallerFilePath()> Optional file As String = Nothing,
                         <CallerLineNumber()> Optional line As Integer = 0)
        Console.WriteLine("File: {0}", file)
        Console.WriteLine("Line number: {0}", line)
    End Sub

End Module
```

44

In this code, the `WriteLog` method receives optional arguments, decorated with the `CallerFilePath` (of type `String`) and the `CallerLineNumber` (of type `Integer`) attributes, respectively. Marking these arguments as optional is mandatory. When you invoke the method, you pass no arguments because the runtime will automatically supply the required information. Figure 44.3 demonstrates how the application shows the name of the file in which the code is executed and the line number.

In this case, line number 12 is the invocation to `WriteLog`. This means you will invoke a method with caller information definition at the exact point in which you want to track the line number. The last attribute, `CallerMemberName`, is only used together with the `INotifyPropertyChanged` interface. As you might know, the `INotifyPropertyChanged` interface is used in WPF, Windows Phone, and Windows Store apps to let the runtime know that some change occurred on the value of a property. `CallerMemberName` makes it easier to understand which property has changed. Consider the special implementation of the `Person` class shown in Listing 44.6.

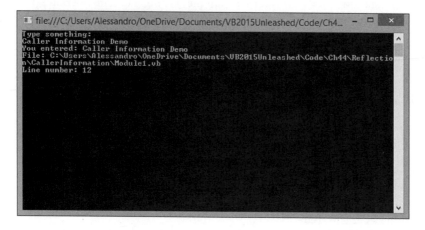

FIGURE 44.3   Retrieving the filename and line number for the executed code.

LISTING 44.6   Using `CallerMemberName` to Retrieve Property Changes

```
Imports System.ComponentModel
Imports System.Runtime.CompilerServices

Public Class Person
    Implements INotifyPropertyChanged

    Private _fullName As String
    Public Property FullName As String
        Get
            Return _fullName
```

```
        End Get
        Set(value As String)
            Me._fullName = value
            NotifyChange(_fullName, value)
        End Set
    End Property


    Public Event PropertyChanged(sender As Object, e As PropertyChangedEventArgs) _
        Implements INotifyPropertyChanged.PropertyChanged


    Private Sub NotifyChange(Of T As IEquatable(Of T))(
                                            ByRef v1 As T, v2 As T,
                                            <CallerMemberName()>
                                            Optional prop As String =
➥Nothing)
        If v1 IsNot Nothing AndAlso v1.Equals(v2) Then Return
        If v1 Is Nothing AndAlso v2 Is Nothing Then Return
        v1 = v2
        RaiseEvent PropertyChanged(Me, New PropertyChangedEventArgs(prop))
    End Sub
End Class
```

Inside the `Set` method of the `FullName` property definition, the `PropertyChanged` event is not raised directly. Instead, the code invokes a separate method called `NotifyChange` that has an optional argument of type `String`, decorated with the `CallerMemberName` attribute. Such an argument will be populated at runtime with the name of the property that is being changed. To understand how it works, declare an instance of the `Person` class like this:

```
Dim p As New Person With {.FullName = "Alessandro Del Sole"}
```

Next, place a breakpoint on this line by pressing **F9**; then run the code. When the debugger encounters the breakpoint, pass the mouse pointer over the `prop` variable declared as the optional parameter in `NotifyChanges`. You will see how such a variable contains the name of the property (`FullName` in the example) that has been changed when the class has been instantiated.

Summary

This chapter covered one of the most important topics in the .NET development, reflection. You saw what reflection is and how assemblies are structured. Talking in code terms, you then saw how to interrogate assembly information and how to reflect types to inspect types and type members exposed by an entire assembly or by a single type. Next, dynamically invoking code from an external assembly without the need of having a reference to that assembly was explained. You then learned how to take advantage of the `System.Reflection.Emit` namespace to create an assembly, types, and members at runtime. Finally, you learned about caller information, which enables you to retrieve information such as the name of the file where a code block is executed, the line number, and the name of a property that has been changed, through three special attributes in the .NET Framework 4.6.

Coding Attributes

Executables produced by .NET languages are different from Win32 executables. Other than the Intermediate Language (IL), they store additional information on types defined in the assembly, on members, and on data. The information is referred to as *metadata*. Assemblies' metadata also contains information about *attributes*, which are declarative programming elements that enable annotating types with custom information and that can condition types' behavior according to the information provided. They are pieces of information for types and therefore are part of the application metadata. You can find attributes in a lot of different scenarios in .NET development. For example, you saw attributes in Chapter 26, "Introducing ADO.NET Entity Framework," when discussing how the Entity Framework defines entities. Chapter 39, "Serialization," discussed serialization and the `Serializable` attribute. In this chapter, you reach two objectives. First, you get information on applying attributes, which is a specific recap of information you should already know. The second objective is to learn to create custom attributes and provide additional information to your applications by using metadata.

Applying Attributes

You have seen a lot of examples about applying attributes. This section provides explanation about applying attributes. When applying an attribute to your own type or member, you enclose the attribute name between angle brackets, as in the following example:

```
<Serializable()>
Public Class Person

End Class
```

In this case, the `Serializable` attribute is parameterless (and in this case you can omit round parentheses).

When you apply an attribute, your object is *decorated* with that attribute. Another common description utilized when applying attributes is that an object is *marked*. Referring to the previous example, you can say that the `Person` class is decorated with the `Serializable` attribute or that it is marked as `Serializable`. Attributes can receive arguments. The following example shows how to pass arguments to the `CLSCompliant` attribute:

```
<CLSCompliant(True)>
Public Class Person

End Class
```

Attributes' arguments are separated by commas according to the number of arguments required. As explained when discussing custom attributes, optional parameters are also allowed. You apply multiple attributes and separate them with commas or write each attribute after the other one. Both the following modes are perfectly legal:

```
<Serializable()>
<CLSCompliant(True)>
Public Class Person

End Class
```

```
<Serializable(), CLSCompliant(True)>
Public Class Person

End Class
```

IMPLICIT-LINE CONTINUATION

In the first code snippet, notice how attributes no longer require the underscore character when written on multiple lines. This is one of the allowed scenarios for the implicit-line continuation features in Visual Basic starting from version 2010.

Attributes can be applied to the following programming elements:

▶ Classes

▶ Structures

▶ Methods (including constructors)

▶ Fields

▶ Properties

▶ Interfaces

▶ Delegates and events

▶ Parameters and return values

▶ Enumerations

As mentioned at the beginning of this chapter, attributes are information that is stored in the assembly metadata. Figure 45.1 represents how such information is stored within the assembly, including type information and member information.

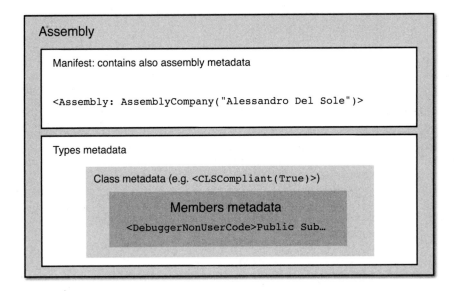

FIGURE 45.1   Attribute information stored in the assembly metadata.

Considering the representation shown in Figure 45.1, you might notice the description about assembly metadata. You can apply attributes at the assembly level, in the `AssemblyInformation.vb` file. Assembly-level attributes are set at design time with the My Project window's tabs (refer to Chapter 3, "The Anatomy of a Visual Basic Project," and Chapter 19, "The `My` Namespace," for details). This means that each application property has a related assembly-level attribute. There is just one attribute named Assembly that requires the specification of nested attributes setting particular properties. For example, the following attributes' specifications set the title, description, and company name properties for the application:

```
<Assembly: AssemblyTitle("CodingAttribute")>
<Assembly: AssemblyDescription("Demo for Chapter 45")>
<Assembly: AssemblyCompany("Alessandro Del Sole")>
```

In the preceding code, `Assembly` is the main attribute, and `AssemblyTitle`, `AssemblyDescription`, and `AssemblyCompany` are other attributes that are nested into the

Assembly declaration. Examining AssemblyInfo.vb you can see available assembly-level attributes, and you discover how each attribute is related to an application property settable in My Project. So far, you have seen how to apply existing attributes, but these special objects provide great flexibility over your object development and provide the ability to deeply enhance your types, especially if you create custom attributes, as you will better understand in the next section.

Coding Custom Attributes

A *custom* attribute is a class that inherits, directly or indirectly, from System.Attribute. When coding custom attributes, the class name should end with the Attribute word. This is not mandatory but, besides being required by Microsoft's Common Language Specification (CLS), it provides a better way for identifying attributes in code. When applying attributes, you can shorten the attribute names by excluding the Attribute word. For example, imagine you have a Document class representing a simple text document. You might want to provide further information on the document, such as the author, reviewer, or last edit date. This information can be provided and stored in the assembly metadata using a custom attribute. Code in Listing 45.1 shows the implementation of a custom attribute that exposes document properties, which is explained next.

LISTING 45.1   Writing a Custom Attribute

```
<AttributeUsage(AttributeTargets.Class Or AttributeTargets.Property)>
Public Class DocumentPropertiesAttribute
    Inherits Attribute

    'Attributes can be inherited
    'therefore private fields are Protected
    Protected _author As String
    Protected _reviewer As String

    Public Overridable ReadOnly Property Author As String
        Get
            Return Me._author
        End Get
    End Property

    Public Overridable ReadOnly Property Reviewer As String
        Get
            Return Me._reviewer
        End Get
    End Property

    Public Overridable Property LastEdit As String
```

```
    Public Sub New(author As String, reviewer As String)
        Me._author = author
        Me._reviewer = reviewer
        Me._lastEdit = CStr(Date.Today)
    End Sub
End Class
```

In Visual Basic, every custom attribute is a class with `Public` or `Friend` access level and decorated with the `AttributeUsage` attribute that enables you to specify which programming elements can be targeted by the custom attribute. Programming elements are specified via the `System.AttributeTargets` enumeration; the enumeration exposes a number of elements, each of them self-explanatory about the targeted programming element. For example, `AttributeTargets.Class` enables you to apply the attribute to reference types, and `AttributeTargets.Methods` enables you to apply the attribute to methods. IntelliSense shows the full list of the enumeration members, which is straightforward. An available member for each element is described in the previous section for targetable programming elements. `AttributeTargets` members support bitwise operators so that you combine multiple targets using `Or`. Actual metadata is exposed to the external world via properties that can be either read-only or read/write. Attributes can receive arguments, although this is not mandatory. For arguments, it is important to understand how you can ask for required parameters and optional ones. This is not something that you define as you would usually do in other programming elements such as methods. Required parameters are specified in the class constructor. Continuing with the example of Listing 45.1, our custom attribute requires the specification of the author and the reviewer of the document, and the last edit date is optional and is still available via a specific property. Optional parameters initialization is not required; in the mentioned example a default value for the `LastEdit` property is supplied. As explained in the next subsection, optional arguments are invoked with named parameters.

TYPES FOR ATTRIBUTE PARAMETERS

You should have noticed that the `LastEdit` property in the custom attribute is of type `String` instead of type `Date`. There are some limitations in the applicable data types for attributes parameters. For example, `Decimal` and `Date` are not supported (like structured types as well). Supported types are instead numeric types (`Bytes`, `Short`, `Integer`, `Long`, `Single`, and `Double`), string types (`String` and `Char`), enumerations, and the `Boolean` type. Take care of these limitations because they can result in exceptions when passing arguments.

There are several other ways to customize attributes, but before discovering them, here's how to apply custom attributes to complete the discussion on parameters.

Applying Custom Attributes

The previous subsection discussed the definition of a custom attribute for assigning metadata to a class representing a basic text document. The code in Listing 45.2 implements the related `Document` class that is decorated with the `DocumentPropertiesAttribute`.

LISTING 45.2   Applying Custom Attributes

```
<DocumentProperties("Alessandro Del Sole",
                    "Robert White",
                    LastEdit:="12/31/2014")>
Public Class Document

    Public Property Text As String

    Public ReadOnly Property Length As Integer
        Get
            Return Text.Length
        End Get
    End Property

    <DocumentProperties("Alessandro Del Sole",
                        "Stephen Green")>
    Public Property DocumentName As String

    Public Sub SaveDocument(fileName As String)
        '...
    End Sub

    Public Sub LoadDocument(filneName As String)
        '...
    End Sub
End Class
```

When you apply an attribute, you can shorten its name by excluding the `Attribute` word in the identifier. For example, `DocumentPropertiesAttribute` can be shortened to `DocumentProperties`. The Visual Basic compiler correctly recognizes the identifier of an attribute. Then you must provide required arguments, respecting the data type. Such arguments are defined in the constructor of the attribute definition (see the previous subsection). If you want to also specify an optional argument, such as the `LastEdit` one in the previous example, you need to perform it via a named parameter. Named parameters are literals followed by the `:=` symbols and by information of the required type. This is the only way to provide optional arguments. Notice also how the custom attribute is applied at both class and property level; this is allowed by the attribute definition. Attributes are therefore useful for providing additional information that will be stored in the assembly metadata, to custom objects. Attributes are flexible for other reasons that are covered in the next sections.

Applying Attributes Multiple Times

According to the particular nature of your custom attributes, you can decide whether multiple instances can be applied to programming elements. This is accomplished by setting the `AllowMultiple` property as `True` in the `AttributeUsage`. The following is an example:

```
<AttributeUsage(AttributeTargets.Class Or AttributeTargets.Property,
                AllowMultiple:=True)>
Public Class DocumentPropertiesAttribute
    Inherits Attribute
```

`AllowMultiple` is optional and thus is invoked as a named parameter. The following is an example of how you apply multiple instances of an attribute:

```
<DocumentProperties("Alessandro Del Sole",
                    "Stephen Green")>
<DocumentProperties("Alessandro", "Stephen",
                    LastEdit:="07/10/2014")>
Public Property DocumentName As String
```

In the particular example of the `DocumentProperties` attribute, multiple instances probably do not make much sense, but this is the way to apply them.

Using `CObj` in Attribute Arguments

Previous versions of Visual Basic did not allow use of the `CObj` conversion function in attribute arguments. Visual Basic 2015 fixes this issue. For instance, suppose you extend the `DocumentPropertiesAttribute` class with the following `Metadata` property of type `Object` and accept an argument of the same type in the constructor:

```
Protected _metaData As Object
Public Overridable Property Metadata As Object
    Get
        Return Me._metaData
    End Get
    Set(value As Object)
        Me._metaData = value
    End Set
End Property
Public Sub New(author As String, reviewer As String, metaData As Object)
    Me._author = author
    Me._reviewer = reviewer
    Me._LastEdit = CStr(Date.Today)
    Me._metaData = metaData
End Sub
```

In Visual Basic 2015, you can now write the following decoration:

```
<DocumentProperties("Alessandro Del Sole",
                    "Robert White",
                    CObj("Good version!"), LastEdit:="12/31/2014")>
```

```
Public Class Document
End Class
```

You can now use CObj to convert some information into Object when applying an attribute. This was not possible in previous versions of the language because the result of CObj was not recognized as a constant even though it actually is.

Defining Inheritance

In some situations you create classes that inherit from other classes that are decorated with attributes. Attribute inheritance is not automatic in that you can establish whether your attributes are inheritable. You establish this behavior by setting the Inherited property at AttributeUsage level. By default, if you do not explicitly set Inherited, it is considered as True. The following example shows how you enable attribute inheritance:

```
'Attribute is also inherited

<AttributeUsage(AttributeTargets.Class Or AttributeTargets.Property,
                Inherited:=True)>
Public Class DocumentPropertiesAttribute
```

The following snippet shows instead how to make an attribute not inheritable:

```
'Attribute is not inherited
<AttributeUsage(AttributeTargets.Class Or AttributeTargets.Property,
                Inherited:=False)>
Public Class DocumentPropertiesAttribute
```

Inheritance is enabled by default because, if a base class is decorated with attributes, derived classes probably also need them. Because of this, you should be careful when disabling inheritance. The code in Listing 45.3 shows an example of declaring two attributes with inheritance definitions and how a derived type is influenced by attribute inheritance.

LISTING 45.3   Conditioning Attribute Inheritance

```
<AttributeUsage(AttributeTargets.Class Or AttributeTargets.Method,
                Inherited:=False)>
Public Class FirstAttribute
    Inherits Attribute


    'Implement your code here..
End Class


<AttributeUsage(AttributeTargets.Class Or AttributeTargets.Method)>
Public Class SecondAttribute
    Inherits Attribute
```

```
    'Implement your code here..
End Class

Public Class Person
    Public Property LastName As String
    Public Property FirstName As String

    'The base class takes both attributes
    <First(), Second()> Public Overridable Function FullName() As String
        Return String.Concat(LastName, " ", FirstName)
    End Function
End Class

Public Class Contact
    Inherits Person

    'This derived class takes only the Second attribute
    'because First is marked as Inherited:=False
    Public Overrides Function FullName() As String
        Return MyBase.FullName()
    End Function
End Class
```

45

Notice how the `FullName` method in the `Contact` class inherits just the `Second` attribute appliance, but the `First` attribute is not applied because of inheritance settings.

Reflecting Attributes

Attributes are about applications' metadata. Because of this, you can use reflection (refer to Chapter 44, "Reflection," for details) to check whether a type recurs to custom attributes and investigate metadata (that is, application information). To accomplish this, you invoke the `System.Reflection.MemberInfo.GetCustomAttributes` and `System. Reflection.Attributes.GetCustomAttributes` shared methods. The first one returns all attributes applied to the specified type; the second one returns an array of custom attributes applied to an assembly, a type or its members, and method parameters. The following is the most basic example for retrieving information about attributes applied to members of the `Document` class:

```
'Requires an Imports System.Reflection directive

    Public Sub GetMyAttributes()
        'About members in the Document class
        Dim info As System.Reflection.MemberInfo = GetType(Document)
        'Retrieves an array of attributes
        Dim attributesList() As Object = info.GetCustomAttributes(True)
```

```
        'Enumerates applied attributes
        For i As Integer = 0 To attributesList.Length - 1
            Console.WriteLine(attributesList(i))
        Next (i)
    End Sub
```

The following example is a little bit more complex and shows how you can perform actions on each attribute instance through `Attribute.GetCustomAttributes`:

```
Public Sub GetMyAttributesComplex()
    Dim typeToInvestigate As Type = GetType(Document)

    ' Get the type information for the DocumentName property.
    Dim member_Info As PropertyInfo =
        typeToInvestigate.GetProperty("DocumentName")
    If Not (member_Info Is Nothing) Then

        'Iterate through all the attributes of the property.
        Dim attr As Attribute
        For Each attr In Attribute.GetCustomAttributes(member_Info)
            ' Check for the DocumentPropertiesAttribute attribute.
            If attr.GetType().
                Equals(GetType(DocumentPropertiesAttribute)) Then
                    Console.WriteLine("Author: {0}", CType(attr,
                                DocumentPropertiesAttribute).Author)

            'Additional ElseIf conditions here for other attributes..
            End If
        Next attr
    End If
End Sub
```

In this particular scenario, the code is used to iterate applied attributes. Do not forget the simplicity of Caller Information described in the previous chapter, which enables you to retrieve specific information on the current assembly without iterating the assembly's attributes.

Summary

Attributes provide great flexibility in .NET development by giving you the ability to decorate your types and members with custom additional information that is stored in the assembly metadata. All custom attributes are public classes deriving from `System.Attribute` and can be applied to various programming elements, such as assemblies, classes, modules, methods, properties, and so on. When you code custom attributes, the Visual Basic language requires you to decorate them with the `AttributeUsage` attribute that provides specifications on targeted elements. When defining custom attributes, you can provide both required and optional parameters; the first ones are established in the constructor. All parameters refer to attribute information that is exposed to the external world via properties. Remember that you need to provide a named parameter when invoking optional arguments. You can also decide to make your attributes inheritable (`Inherited` property) and to make them applicable more than once (`AllowMultiple`). Finally, you can investigate assemblies' and types' attributes via Reflection.

45

CHAPTER 46

Platform Invokes and Interoperability with the COM Architecture

The .NET Framework 4.6 Base Class Library offers tons of objects and methods for covering almost everything in modern application development. In most cases, objects and methods are managed wrappers of the Windows Application Programming Interface (API) so you can use them in the managed environment of the Common Language Runtime (CLR). In some situations you might need to access some operating system functionalities that have not been wrapped yet by the .NET Framework, or you might have legacy code exposed by Component Object Model (COM) objects, such as type libraries. Both the .NET Framework and Visual Basic still enable interoperability with the COM architecture, and in this chapter you see how to reach these objectives.

THE WINDOWS 8.X STORY

As you know, the Windows Runtime (WinRT) in Windows 8.x is based on COM and exposes objects in a way that is known to .NET developers, making such objects appear as if they were managed. Some functionality, such as low-level audio-playing APIs, is only exposed via COM. WinRT is a wrapper of COM objects, so if you want to build applications that use COM interoperability you might consider interacting with WinRT rather than writing using the old model. You will certainly use techniques described in this chapter if your applications will also run on Windows 7 and Windows Vista, not only Windows 8.x. If you can't predict the target audience of your application, follow this chapter. If your desktop application will only run on Windows 8.x, spend a little time getting deeper knowledge of interaction between .NET and WinRT.

Importing and Using COM Objects

The .NET Framework 4.6, like previous versions, offers support for interoperability with the COM architecture via an engine named *Runtime Callable Wrapper*, which is the infrastructure that provides a communication bridge between .NET and COM. It is also responsible for type marshaling and handling events. Because of this engine, you can import COM objects and use them in your managed applications. You can import two kinds of COM components: type libraries and ActiveX components. Importing COM components is accomplished via two command-line tools: **TlbImp.exe**, which is required to import a type library, and **AxImp.exe**, which is required for importing ActiveX controls. This chapter does not discuss how to invoke such tools from the command line, but you do find out how to import COM components from within Visual Studio so that the IDE can do the work for you. The next example shows how to import an ActiveX control into the Visual Studio toolbox and use the control in code.

Importing COM Components into Visual Studio

In this chapter, you learn how to use COM components in a WPF application. The reason you should use WPF is that it is the only technology you should use to create modern desktop applications, even if it requires some more work when compared to Windows Forms. Also, the goal of this chapter is illustrating a very common scenario, which is having the ability of displaying PDF documents. Before going on, make sure you install the Adobe Reader program (www.adobe.com), which includes an ActiveX control to display PDF documents and that will be used in our example. You can replace the Adobe Reader with different software that has an ActiveX control, such as Foxit Reader.

.NET AND PDF FILES

Throughout the years, many libraries and controls to work with PDFs have been built in managed code—on .NET for .NET. If you need to work with PDF documents, you are strongly encouraged to use one of these free or paid components. Showing the Adobe Reader ActiveX control is a good choice for instructional purposes and because it is one of the most popular programs in the world. However, in real-world scenarios, you should instead use pure .NET components.

At this point, create a new WPF project with Visual Basic. In Windows Forms, you can use COM components directly on `Form` objects, but in WPF you cannot. So the first thing you have to do is add a new Windows Forms user control to the WPF project; this enables you to host COM objects in WPF. To accomplish this, select **Project, Add New Item** and select the **User Control** item template in the Windows Forms category. Name the new user control as **PDFControl.vb**. Figure 46.1 demonstrates this.

Ensure the user control is visible in the designer and then open the Visual Studio toolbox. When done, right-click the toolbox and select **Choose Items**. This launches the same-named dialog box that you already know because of adding .NET controls to the toolbox. Select the **COM** tab and search for the **Adobe PDF Reader** item, as shown in Figure 46.2.

When you click **OK**, Visual Studio generates two files for you:

- ▶ **Interop.AcroPDFLib.dll**—A CLR wrapper for using COM objects exposed by the Adobe Reader type library in a .NET fashion.

- ▶ **AxInterop.AcroPDFLib.dll**—A Windows Forms proxy that provides the infrastructure required for hosting the control in your forms. You now might better understand why you needed a Windows Forms user control to host a COM component.

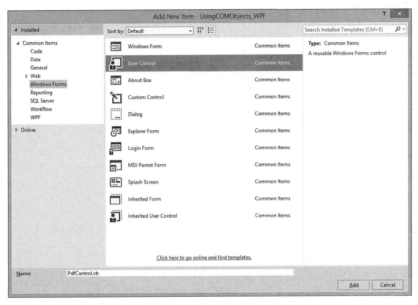

FIGURE 46.1   Adding a Windows Forms user control to the WPF project.

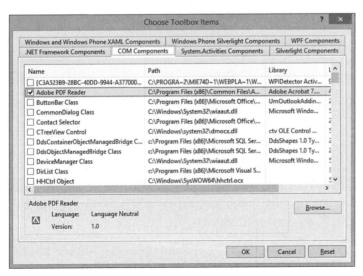

FIGURE 46.2   Choosing a COM component to add to the toolbox.

At this point, the Adobe Reader ActiveX control is available inside the toolbox. Now drag the PDF control over the Windows Forms user control form and resize it as you like. Visual Studio then generates some code for you to declare the control and enables you to use it. If you expand the PDFControl.vb file and double-click the AxAcroPDF1 item, you find the following initialization code for the ActiveX control:

```
'NOTE: The following procedure is required by the Windows Form Designer
'It can be modified using the Windows Form Designer.
'Do not modify it using the code editor.
<System.Diagnostics.DebuggerStepThrough()> _
Private Sub InitializeComponent()
    Dim resources As System.ComponentModel.ComponentResourceManager = _
        New System.ComponentModel.ComponentResourceManager(GetType(PDFControl))
    Me.AxAcroPDF1 = New AxAcroPDFLib.AxAcroPDF()
    CType(Me.AxAcroPDF1, System.ComponentModel.ISupportInitialize).BeginInit()
    Me.SuspendLayout()
    '
    'AxAcroPDF1
    '
    Me.AxAcroPDF1.Enabled = True
    Me.AxAcroPDF1.Location = New System.Drawing.Point(-15, -15)
    Me.AxAcroPDF1.Name = "AxAcroPDF1"
    Me.AxAcroPDF1.OcxState = CType(resources.GetObject("AxAcroPDF1.OcxState"),
                        System.Windows.Forms.AxHost.State)
    Me.AxAcroPDF1.Size = New System.Drawing.Size(192, 192)
    Me.AxAcroPDF1.TabIndex = 0
    '
    'PDFControl
    '
    Me.AutoScaleDimensions = New System.Drawing.SizeF(6.0!, 13.0!)
    Me.AutoScaleMode = System.Windows.Forms.AutoScaleMode.Font
    Me.Controls.Add(Me.AxAcroPDF1)
    Me.Name = "PDFControl"
    CType(Me.AxAcroPDF1, System.ComponentModel.ISupportInitialize).EndInit()
    Me.ResumeLayout(False)

End Sub
Friend WithEvents AxAcroPDF1 As AxAcroPDFLib.AxAcroPDF
```

AxHost CLASS

ActiveX controls are wrapped by the System.Windows.Forms.AxHost class that enables you to treat COM components as you would .NET objects.

Now you can work with the ActiveX control in a managed way, as illustrated in the next subsection.

Using COM Objects in Code

When you have an instance of the ActiveX control, or of a type library, you can access its members like any other .NET object, thus invoking methods, assigning properties, or handling events. The following code loads and shows the specified document in the Adobe's viewer:

```
Private Sub PDFControl_Load(sender As Object, e As EventArgs) Handles Me.Load
    Me.AxAcroPDF1.LoadFile("C:\Users\Alessandro\Documents\TestDoc.pdf")
End Sub
```

You can also handle events if available, as demonstrated by the following code snippet:

```
Private Sub AxAcroPDF1_OnError(sender As Object, e As EventArgs) Handles_
➥AxAcroPDF1.OnError
    MessageBox.Show("An error has occurred while loading the document")
End Sub
```

In this particular case, the `OnError` event is raised when an error occurs while opening the PDF file. At a more general level, wrapping an ActiveX control enables you to import different kinds of members, including events.

Catching Exceptions

When you implement `Try..Catch..End Try` blocks, you can intercept and handle only CLS-compliant exceptions, that is, exceptions inheriting from `System.Exception`. Exceptions wrapped by the COM import tools are not CLS-compliant, so a classic `Try` block would fail. To intercept exceptions coming from wrapped objects, the .NET Framework offers the `System.Runtime.CompilerServices.RuntimeWrappedException`. It can be used for error handling when working with wrappers. The following code shows an example:

```
Try
    Me.AxAcroPDF1.LoadFile("C:\Users\Alessandro\Documents\TestDoc.pdf")

Catch ex As RuntimeWrappedException

Catch ex As Exception

End Try
```

Other than the usual exception properties, this class exposes a `WrappedException` property, of type `Object`, which represents the problem that occurred.

Releasing COM Objects

You should always explicitly release objects that wrap COM components so that the associated resources are also released. You accomplish this by invoking the `System.Runtime.`

`InteropServices.Marshal.ReleaseCOMObject` method. It is worth noting that calling this method does not explicitly free all resources but decreases the reference count on the COM object, and when the count hits 0, the resources are freed. Continuing with the previous example, you release the `AxAcroPDF1` object as follows:

```
System.Runtime.InteropServices.Marshal.ReleaseComObject(AxAcroPDF1)
```

This is important because COM objects treat system resources differently from .NET objects; therefore, an explicit release is required.

Calling COM Objects from WPF

Now that you have completed all the required steps to wrap a COM component into a Windows Forms user control, you need a way to use such a control in WPF. As you learned in Chapter 29, "WPF Common Controls," you use a `WindowsFormsHost` control to embed Windows Forms contents inside a WPF window or user control. So, double-click the MainWindow.xaml file in Solution Explorer. Then, when the main window of the application is available in the designer, drag the `WindowsFormsHost` control from the toolbox onto the window. Remove all auto-generated property values and assign a name, so that the `WindowsFormsHost` definition looks like this:

```
<WindowsFormsHost Name="FormsHost1" />
```

The next step is assigning an instance of the `PDFControl` user control as the child content of the `WindowsFormsHost`. This is done in the code-behind file, like in the following code:

```
Public Sub New()

    ' This call is required by the designer.
    InitializeComponent()

    ' Add any initialization after the InitializeComponent() call.
    Dim pdfViewer As New PDFControl
    Me.FormsHost1.Child = pdfViewer
End Sub
```

If you now run the sample application, you will be able to see how the specified PDF document is shown inside the application's main window. You do this by using COM interoperability.

DEPLOYMENT TIPS

When you deploy an application that works with COM interop, you must ensure you also include both the auto-generated AxInterop.XXX.dll and the Interop.XXX.dll files. You should also include the ActiveX control or the type library that your application has a reference to, but in some cases this is not possible for copyright reasons. For instance, the sample discussed in this chapter uses the Adobe Reader's ActiveX control, which is not redistributable. Thus, clients must install the Adobe Reader on their machines and then your application will handle a reference to the ActiveX.

Exposing .NET Objects to the COM World

Although in modern world applications this practice occurs less frequently than in the past, you can expose .NET objects to the COM world. For example, a VB 6 application can consume an object like this. To demonstrate how you accomplish this export, create a new class library and rename Class1.vb to Contact.vb. The first thing you need to do to enable a class to be called from COM is provide COM interoperability support. Now open **My Project** and select the **Compile** tab. Flag the **Register for COM Interop** item at the bottom of the page, as shown in Figure 46.3.

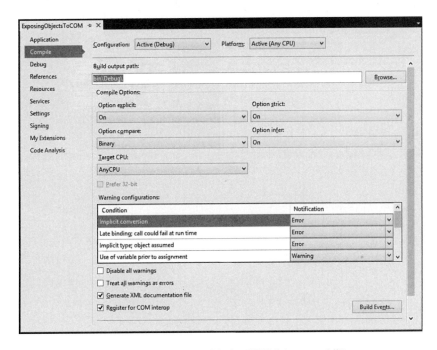

FIGURE 46.3   Registering an assembly for COM Interoperability.

This operation tells Visual Studio that it needs to register the COM component on build and adds the following line of code in AssemblyInfo.vb so that it makes it visible to COM:

```
<Assembly: ComVisible(True)>
```

CLASS REQUIREMENTS FOR COM EXPOSURE

Any class that you want to expose to COM has the following requirements: It must have a public, empty, parameterless constructor; any member, including types, to be exposed must be `Public` (no other modifiers are allowed) and it cannot include abstract classes. (This is just because they cannot be consumed.)

The ComVisible attribute establishes the visibility level and granularity not only at assembly level, but also for classes and class members. The default for this attribute is True, so you need to explicitly set classes and members for False where you do not want them to be exposed. Next, implement the Contact class as follows:

```
Public Class COMContact

    Public Property FirstName As String
    Public Property LastName As String
    Public Property Email As String
    Public Property BirthDay As Date


    Public Sub New()


    End Sub
End Class
```

Now you can decide the visibility level for each member in the class by decorating the class and its members with the System.Runtime.InteropServices.ComVisible attribute. The following code demonstrates how to make COM-visible only some members from the Contact class:

```
Imports System.Runtime.InteropServices

<ComVisible(True)>
Public Class COMContact

    <ComVisible(True)>
    Public Property FirstName As String
    <ComVisible(True)>
    Public Property LastName As String
    <ComVisible(False)>
    Public Property Email As String

    <ComVisible(False)>
    Public Property BirthDay As Date

    Public Sub New()

    End Sub
End Class
```

A public, empty constructor is required for COM-visible objects. You must mark the class as ComVisible(True) to expose it correctly. The only exception is when the class you marked as false gets inherited into a new class marked as true, then the members in the base class will be exposed through the inherited class unless the individual members of the base class were also marked ComVisible(False). The next step should be to register the COM component after the build process. Fortunately, on the development machine, Visual Studio 2015 does the work for you. (This requires the IDE to be launched with elevated privileges.) Therefore, compile the project to have a class library that is consumable from the COM architecture.

WHAT HAPPENS BEHIND THE SCENES?

When you build a class library exposed to COM, Visual Studio first invokes the Visual Basic compiler (vbc.exe) with the /t switch pointing to the executable name; next it launches the type library exporter utility (TlbExp.exe). The conjunction of both tools can build a COM-enabled library.

P/Invokes and Unmanaged Code

One of the biggest benefits of the .NET Framework is that the technology is a bridge between you and the Windows operating system and is responsible for managing a lot of system features (such as memory management). This reduces the risk of bad system resources management that could lead the system to unwanted crashes or problems. This is the reason (as you might recall from Chapter 1, "Introducing .NET 2015") that .NET programming is also known as *managed*. The .NET Framework Base Class Library (BCL) exposes managed wrappers for most of the Windows API system so that you do not need to manually handle system resources. It also enables you to reap all the benefits of the CLR. By the way, in some situations you still need to access the Windows API (for example, when there is not a .NET counterpart of an API function), and thus you need to work with *unmanaged code*. Unmanaged code is all code not controlled by the .NET Framework and that requires you to manually handle system resources. When you work with unmanaged code, you commonly invoke Windows API functions; such invocations are also known as *Platform Invokes* or, simpler, *P/Invokes*. This section covers both situations, starting with P/Invokes.

NOTE ON UNMANAGED CODE

You should always avoid unmanaged code. The .NET Framework 4.6 offers an infinite number of managed objects and methods for performing almost everything. Using unmanaged code means working directly against the operating system and its resources, and if your code does not perfectly handle resources, it can lead to problems. Moreover, when performing unmanaged calls, you need to be certain that they work or exist on all versions of the Windows operating system you plan to support for your application. Always search through the Base Class Library to ensure that a .NET counterpart for the Windows API already exists. It probably does.

Understanding P/Invokes

Calls to Windows API functions are known as Platform Invokes or P/Invokes. The Visual Basic programming language offers two ways of performing platform invokes:

▶ `Declare` keyword

▶ `System.Runtime.InteropServices.DllImport` attribute

The `Declare` keyword has a behavior similar to what happened in Visual Basic 6, and it has been kept for compatibility; however, you should always use the `DllImport` attribute because this is the one way recognized by the Common Language Specification. Now you can see how to declare a P/Invoke. The next example considers the `PathIsUrl` function, from the Shlwapi.dll system library, which checks whether the specified is a URL and returns a value according to the result. This is with the `Declare` keyword:

```
Declare Function PathIsUrl Lib "shlwapi.dll" Alias _
        "PathIsURLA" (ByVal path As String) As Integer
```

MATCHING NUMERIC TYPES

Keep in mind the difference in numeric types between the Windows API system and the .NET common types system because Windows APIs return `Long`; however, when you perform P/Invokes, you must use the .NET counterpart `Integer`. The same is true for `Integer` in the Windows API, which is mapped by `Short` in .NET. Similarly, remember to use the `IntPtr` structure for declarations that require a handle (or a pointer) of type `Integer`.

As you can see, the API declaration looks similar to what you used to write in VB 6. The following is how you declare the API function via the `DllImport` attribute:

```
'Requires an
'Imports System.Runtime.InteropServices directive
<DllImport("shlwapi.dll", entrypoint:="PathIsURLA")>
Shared Function PathIsURL(ByVal path As String) As System.Int32
End Function
```

Among its many options, the most important in `DllImport` are the library name and the `entrypoint` parameter that indicates the function name. It is important to remember that P/Invokes must be declared as `Shared` because they cannot be exposed as instance methods; the only exception to this rule is when you declare a function within a module. When declared, you can consume P/Invokes like any other method (always remembering that you are not passing through the CLR), as demonstrated here:

```
Dim testUrl As String = "http://www.visual-basic.it"
Dim result As Integer = PathIsURL(testUrl)
```

Both `Declare` and `DllImport` lead to the same result, but from now only `DllImport` is used.

Encapsulating P/Invokes

Encapsulating P/Invokes in classes is a programming best practice and makes your code clearer and more meaningful. Continuing the previous example, you could create a new class and declare inside the class the `PathIsUrl` function, marking it as `Shared` so that it can be consumed by other objects. You need to consider one more thing. If you plan to wrap Windows API functions in reusable class libraries, the best approach is to provide CLS-compliant libraries and API calls. For this reason, the discussion now focuses on how you can encapsulate P/Invokes following the rules of the Common Language Specification (CLS). The first rule is to create a class that stores only P/Invokes declarations. Such a class must be visible only within the assembly, must implement a private empty constructor, and will expose only shared members. The following is an example related to the `PathIsUri` function:

```
Friend Class NativeMethods
    <DllImport("shlwapi.dll", entrypoint:="PathIsURLA")>
    Shared Function PathIsURL(ByVal path As String) As System.Int32
    End Function

    Private Sub New()

    End Sub
End Class
```

The class is marked with `Friend` to make it visible only within the assembly. A CLS-compliant class for exposing P/Invokes declarations can have only one of the following names:

- ▶ `NativeMethods` is used on the development machine and indicates that the class has no particular security and permissions requirements

- ▶ `SafeNativeMethods` is used outside the development machine and indicates that the class and methods have no particular security and permissions requirements

- ▶ `UnsafeNativeMethods` is used to explain to other developers that the caller needs to demand permissions to execute the code (demanding permissions for one of the classes exposed by the `System.Security.Permissions` namespace)

To expose P/Invokes to the external call, you need a wrapper class. The following class demonstrates how you can expose the `NativeMethods.PathIsUrl` function in a programmatically correct approach:

```
Public Class UsefulMethods

    Public Shared Function CheckIfPathIsUrl(ByVal path As String) _
            As Integer
        Return NativeMethods.PathIsURL(path)
    End Function

End Class
```

46

Finally, you can consume the preceding code as follows (for example, adding a reference to the class library):

```
Dim testUrl As String = "http://www.visual-basic.it"
Dim result As Integer = UsefulMethods.CheckIfPathIsUrl(testUrl)
```

Working with unmanaged code is not only performing P/Invokes. There are some other important concepts about error handling and type marshaling, as explained in the next sections.

Converting Types to Unmanaged

When you work with P/Invokes, you might need to pass custom types as function arguments. If such types are .NET types, the most important thing is converting primitives into types that are acceptable by the COM/Win32 architecture. The `System.Runtime.InteropServices` namespace exposes the `MarshalAs` attribute that can be applied to fields and method arguments to convert the object into the most appropriate COM counterpart. The following sample implementation of the `Person` class demonstrates how to apply `MarshalAs`:

```vb
Imports System.Runtime.InteropServices

Public Class Person

    <MarshalAs(UnmanagedType.LPStr)>
    Private _firstName As String
    <MarshalAs(UnmanagedType.SysInt)>
    Private _age As Integer

    Public Property FirstName As String
        Get
            Return _firstName
        End Get
        Set(ByVal value As String)
            _firstName = value
        End Set
    End Property

    Public Property Age As Integer
        Get
            Return _age
        End Get
        Set(ByVal value As Integer)
            _age = value
        End Set
    End Property
```

```
    Sub ConvertParameter(<MarshalAs(UnmanagedType.LPStr)> _
                          ByVal name As String)
    End Sub
End Class
```

The attribute receives a value from the `UnmanagedType` enumeration. IntelliSense offers great help about members in this enumeration, showing the full members list and explaining what each member is bound to convert. You can check this out as an exercise.

The `StructLayout` Attribute

An important aspect of unmanaged programming is how you handle types, especially when such types are passed as P/Invoke arguments. Unlike P/Invokes, types representing counterparts from the Windows API pass through the CLR and, as a general rule, you should provide the CLR the best way for handling them to keep performance high. When you write a class or a structure, you give members a particular order that should have a meaning for you. In other words, if the `Person` class exposes `FirstName` and `Age` as properties, keeping this order should have a reason, which is dictated only by some kind of logic. With the `System.Runtime.InteropServices.StructLayout` attribute, you can tell the CLR how it can handle type members; it enables you to decide if it has to respect a particular order or if it can handle type members the best way it can according to performances. The `StructLayout` attribute's constructor offers three alternatives:

▶ `StructLayout.Auto` causes the CLR to handle type members in its preferred order.

▶ `StructLayout.Sequential` causes the CLR to handle type members preserving the order provided by the developer in the type implementation.

▶ `StructLayout.Explicit` causes the CLR to handle type members according to the order established by the developer, using memory offsets.

By default, if `StructLayout` is not specified, the CLR assumes `Auto` for reference types and `Sequential` for structures. For example, consider the COMRECT structure from the Windows API, which represents four points. This is how you write it in Visual Basic, making it available to unmanaged code:

```
<StructLayout(LayoutKind.Sequential)>
Public Structure COMRECT

    Public Left As Integer
    Public Top As Integer
    Public Right As Integer
    Public Bottom As Integer


    Shared Sub New()


    End Sub
```

46

```
Public Sub New(ByVal left As Integer,
               ByVal top As Integer,
               ByVal right As Integer,
               ByVal bottom As Integer)

    Me.Left = left
    Me.Top = top
    Me.Right = right
    Me.Bottom = bottom
End Sub
End Structure
```

TIPS ON DEFAULT OPTIONS

StructLayout must be applied explicitly if your assembly needs to be CLS-compliant. This happens because you have two choices, Sequential and Explicit. For classes, though, this is not necessary because they are always considered as Auto. Because of this, this section describes only structures.

This is how you can apply StructLayout.Explicit instead, providing memory offsets:

```
<StructLayout(LayoutKind.Explicit)>
Public Structure COMRECT

    <FieldOffset(0)> Public Left As Integer
    <FieldOffset(4)> Public Top As Integer
    <FieldOffset(8)> Public Right As Integer
    <FieldOffset(12)> Public Bottom As Integer

    Shared Sub New()

    End Sub

    Public Sub New(ByVal left As Integer,
                   ByVal top As Integer,
                   ByVal right As Integer,
                   ByVal bottom As Integer)

        Me.Left = left
        Me.Top = top
        Me.Right = right
        Me.Bottom = bottom
    End Sub
End Structure
```

The `FieldOffset` attribute specifies the memory offset for each field. In this case the structure provides fields of type `Integer`, so each offset is 4 bytes.

The `VBFixedString` Attribute

The `VBFixedString` attribute can be applied to structure members of type `String`, to delimit the string length because by default string length is variable. Such delimitation is established in bytes instead of characters. This attribute is required in some API calls. The following is an example:

```
Public Structure Contact
'Both fields are limited to 10 bytes size
    <VBFixedString(10)> Public LastName As String
    <VBFixedString(10)> Public Email As String
End Structure
```

Notice that the `VBFixedString` can be applied to fields but is not valid for properties.

Handling Exceptions

Functions from Windows API return a numeric value as their results (called `HRESULT`), for telling the caller whether the function succeeded or failed. You can handle exceptions coming from the P/Invokes world with a classic `Try..Catch` block, and then the .NET Framework can wrap unmanaged errors that have a .NET counterpart into managed exceptions. For instance, if a Windows API invocation causes an out-of-memory error, the .NET Framework maps such error as an `OutOfMemoryException` that you can embrace within a normal `Try..Catch` block. It is reasonable that not all unmanaged errors can have a managed counterpart, due to differences in COM and .NET architectures. To solve this, .NET provides the `System.Runtime.InteropServices.SEHException`, in which `SEH` stands for *Structured Exception Handling*. It maps all unmanaged exceptions that .NET cannot map. The exception is useful because it exposes an `ErrorCode` property that stores the `HRESULT` sent from P/Invokes. You use it like this:

```
Try
    'Add your P/Invoke here..
Catch ex As SEHException
    Console.WriteLine(ex.ErrorCode.ToString)
Catch ex As Exception

End Try
```

TIP

The `SEHException` does not provide many exception details, unlike managed exceptions, but it is the most appropriate exception for error handling in a `Try..Catch` block within unmanaged code.

There is also an alternative, which requires some explanation. P/Invokes raise Win32 errors calling themselves the `SetLastError` native method that is different from how exceptions are thrown in the CLR. In the earlier days, you could call the `GetLastError` method to retrieve the error code, but this is not the best choice because it can refer to managed exceptions rather than Win32 exceptions. A better, although not the ultimate, approach can be provided by invoking the `System.Runtime.InteropServices.Marshal.GetLastWin32Error` method, which can intercept the last error coming from a Win32 call. To make this work, first you need to set the `SetLastError` property in the `DllImport` attribute as `True`; then you can invoke the method. The following code shows an example of the `Beep` function, which returns a numeric value as the result:

```
<DllImport("kernel32.dll", entrypoint:="Beep", SetLastError:=True)>
Public Shared Function Beep(ByVal frequency As UInteger,
                            ByVal duration As UInteger) As Integer
End Function
```

```
    Dim beepResult = NativeMethods.Beep(100, 100)
    If beepResult = 0 Then
        Console.WriteLine(Marshal.GetLastWin32Error())
    End If
```

Here you need to know first which values can return a particular function. `Beep` returns zero if it does not succeed. So, after a check on the result value, the `Marshal.GetLastWin32Error` method is invoked to understand the error code.

References to the Win32 API Calls

Developers can reference the MSDN documentation or the Windows SDK to get detailed information on the Windows API functions and their signatures. The following are resources available on the Internet for your reference:

▶ MSDN reference: http://msdn.microsoft.com/en-us/library/aa383749(VS.85).aspx

▶ Windows SDK: https://msdn.microsoft.com/en-us/windows/desktop/bg162891.aspx

▶ PInvoke.net website: http://www.pinvoke.net

Summary

The .NET technology can definitely interoperate with the COM legacy architecture and components. In the first part of the chapter, you saw how to import COM components into managed applications, understanding how Visual Studio generates .NET wrappers to interact with COM. Next, you got information on how to create and expose .NET libraries to COM, utilizing the Visual Studio instrumentation and applying the `ComVisible` attribute to classes and class members to grant visibility granularity. In the last part of the chapter, you saw how to call and run unmanaged code, with particular regard to Platform Invokes and types conversions for working directly against the Windows operating system.

CHAPTER 47

Documenting Source Code with XML Comments

One of the most common programming rules states that documenting the source code is fundamental. This is the truth, but you have to think about the way source code is commented. Classical comments are useful to explain what code does so that you can easily remember how your code works if you need to reuse it after a long time, or they can help other developers to understand your code. But this is not the only way of documenting code in .NET development. A sophisticated environment such as Visual Studio offers the IntelliSense technology that speeds up the way you write code and shows instructions on how you use objects and members. This is possible because of special kinds of comments that you can add to your code, known as *XML comments*. Such comments enable you to write the source code documentation, explain objects' and members' behavior, and provide descriptions and examples that can be displayed by IntelliSense. But that is not all. Documenting code with XML comments is particularly important if you develop reusable compiled libraries and enables you to automate the process of building compiled documentation files (such as .chm files) in a similar way to the MSDN documentation. In this chapter, you learn to use XML comments to provide simple and complex source code documentation, also learning how to build compiled documentation.

Understanding XML Comments

XML comments are not new in Visual Basic 2015; they were first natively introduced with Visual Basic 2005. (In versions prior to 2005, XML comments were possible only via third-party add-ins.) Visual Basic 2015 brings some improvements to comments that are discussed throughout this chapter. To understand why XML comments are an essential topic, let's take a look at a method invocation within the code editor. Figure 47.1 shows how IntelliSense appears on an uncommented method.

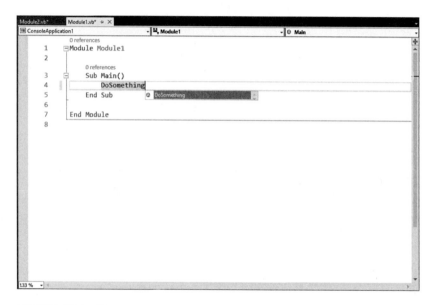

FIGURE 47.1   Uncommented members make IntelliSense incapable of displaying useful information.

As you can see from Figure 47.1, IntelliSense will correctly display, but it will just show the method name in a tooltip, without providing information on the method usage. This is because the method was not commented with XML comments. Now take a look at Figure 47.2. It shows how IntelliSense can provide information if the method was commented with XML comments.

The difference is evident. Objects and members decorated with XML comments can provide full explanation on their usage. This works in the code editor when IntelliSense displays with both source files and with compiled assemblies. As mentioned at the beginning of this chapter, providing XML comments is useful not only for IntelliSense, but also when you investigate objects in the Object Browser or for automating the process of build-ing compiled documentation for your libraries. Because of this, adding XML comments to your code is necessary in most cases, especially if you develop reusable assemblies. In the next sections, you learn practical techniques for commenting the source code and getting the most out of XML comments with Visual Basic.

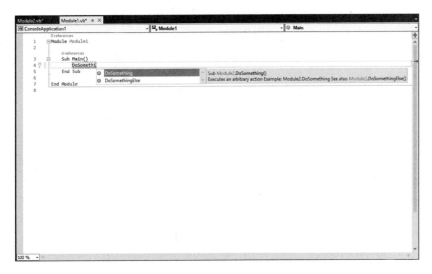

FIGURE 47.2   Commented members are well described when IntelliSense displays in the code editor.

Enabling XML Comments

When Visual Studio builds the project output, it also creates an XML document storing all XML comments. The XML document constitutes the actual code documentation. In Visual Studio 2015, XML comments are enabled by default. Before reading this chapter, ensure that XML comments are enabled in your project. To accomplish this, open **My Project**; select the **Compile** tab and, if it's not checked, check the **Generate XML Documentation file** box. See Figure 47.3 for details.

Behind the scenes, this requires the Visual Basic compiler to be launched by Visual Studio with the /doc option, which makes the compiler also generate the XML documentation. At this point, you are ready to implement XML comments in your Visual Basic code.

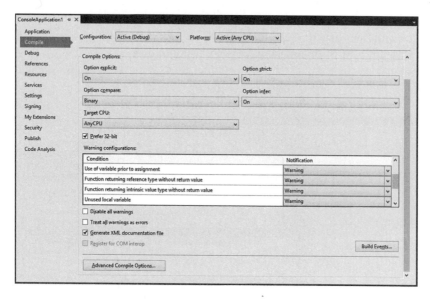

FIGURE 47.3   Enabling XML comments.

Implementing XML Comments

XML comments have a double purpose. The first one is enabling additional help within IntelliSense when you write code. The second one is generating an XML file storing information that can be built into a compiled documentation file, such as the .chm format that also enables navigation between documented items. In this section, you learn to implement XML comments and learn the various tags and why they are important, although in some cases they might not seem to be. Before implementing comments, create a new Console application and implement a `Person` class as follows:

```
Public Class Person

    Public Overridable Property FirstName As String
    Public Overridable Property LastName As String
    Public Overridable Property Age As Integer

    Public Overridable Function GetFullName() As String
        Dim fn As New Text.StringBuilder
        fn.Append(Me.FirstName)
        fn.Append(" ")
        fn.Append(Me.LastName)
        Return fn.ToString
    End Function
End Class
```

The `Person` class will be the base for our experiments. You implement an XML comment by typing three apostrophes. The Visual Studio code editor adds a comment skeleton to your code that first looks like the following example:

```
''' <summary>
'''
''' </summary>
''' <returns></returns>
Public Overridable Function GetFullName() As String
    Dim fn As New Text.StringBuilder
    fn.Append(Me.FirstName)
    fn.Append(" ")
    fn.Append(Me.LastName)
    Return fn.ToString
End Function
```

As you can see, these comments have typical XML structure according to the `<tag> </tag>` syntax. The `summary` XML tag enables describing what an object (or member) does. The description will be also available within IntelliSense. The `returns` tag specifies the type returned by the member (being a method or a property); if the member is a method that does not return a value, Visual Studio will not add the `returns` tag. You can also take advantage the `remarks` tag, which enables you to provide additional information on what you already specified in the summary; the information will also be displayed in the Object Browser (but not in IntelliSense). In Visual Basic 2015, `remarks` no longer appears automatically, so you must write it explicitly. You should populate comments as follows:

```
''' <summary>
''' Gets the complete person's name
''' </summary>
''' <returns>String</returns>
''' <remarks>This method returns the complete person's name</remarks>
Public Overridable Function GetFullName() As String
    Dim fn As New Text.StringBuilder
    fn.Append(Me.FirstName)
    fn.Append(" ")
    fn.Append(Me.LastName)
    Return fn.ToString
End Function
```

Now go to the `Main` method in your Console application, and write the following code that instantiates and populates the Person class:

```
Dim p As New Person With {.FirstName = "Alessandro", .LastName = "Del Sole",
                          .Age = 37}

Dim fullName As String = p.GetFullName
```

When typing code, IntelliSense provides information on the GetFullName method according to the XML comment's content. This is represented in Figure 47.4.

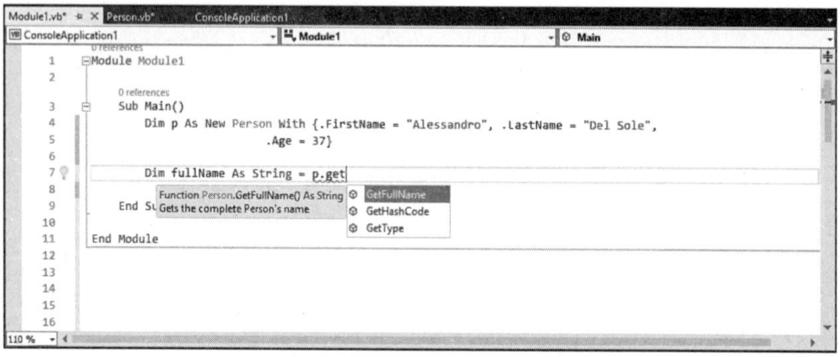

FIGURE 47.4   IntelliSense shows the information provided by the XML comments.

As you can see, IntelliSense shows the content of the summary tag, but it does not show the content of the returns and remarks tags. This makes sense in that IntelliSense's tooltips are the fastest way for getting help. If you instead open the Object Browser on the Person class, you get a result that looks similar to Figure 47.5 (additional information appearing in the window is covered shortly). You obtain the same detailed information if you build a compiled documentation file, as described later in this chapter. The one shown before is the most basic implementation of XML comments. This great Visual Basic feature enables you to define complex documentation over your code, which can be particularly useful due to the integration with the Visual Studio environment.

SCOPE

XML comments can be applied to both public and private objects and members.

Defining Complex Code Documentation

The MSDN documentation says that the Visual Basic compiler can parse any valid XML tag. The MSDN also recommends a series of tags that are specific to the code documentation. Table 47.1 summarizes the recommended tags.

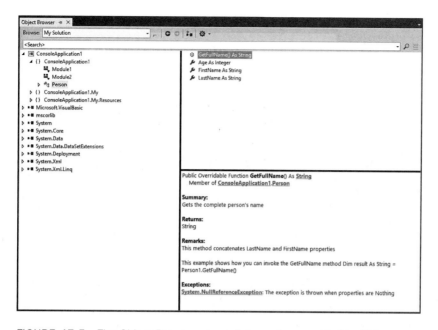

FIGURE 47.5   The Object Browser shows information provided by XML comments.

TABLE 47.1   Recommended Tags for XML Comments

Tag	Description
c	Identifies a code element
cref	Creates a cross reference to another documented object
code	Provides a code snippet about the code usage
example	Provides a description about how code can be used
exception	Enables you to specify the exception that your member could throw
include	Points to an external XML file containing documentation for the code
list	Enables you to generate a bulleted, numbered, or tabled list
para	Enables you to formatting its content as a paragraph
param	Defines a parameter that can be referenced by paramref
paramref	Enables you to format a word as a parameter defined via param
permission	Specifies the Code Access Security permission required by the commented member
remarks	Provides additional notes on your code
returns	Specifies the .NET type returned by your member
see	Provides a link to another member

47

Tag	Description
seealso	Adds a member in the See Also section of the compiled documentation
summary	Provides a description about a member; also shown within IntelliSense
typeparam	Provides type parameter name and description when declaring generic types
value	Describes the value of a member (for example, a property)

CASE-SENSITIVITY

Tags within XML comments are case-sensitive and lowercase. Take note of this to ensure that the Visual Basic compiler correctly recognizes tags.

NOTE ON COMPLEX DOCUMENTATION

You can appreciate complex documentation generated with XML comments only when building compiled help files. This is because within IntelliSense or in the Object Browser, only a few tags' contents will be shown. For example, XML comments enable you to build bulleted lists or specify links to other documentation regarding different code. All this cannot be shown in IntelliSense, but it makes a lot of sense in a help file or a help system built on HTML pages. If you are interested in only building documentation for Visual Studio internal usage, you can theoretically limit XML comments to the basic implementations.

Let's go back to the `Person` class and provide an XML comment for the `FirstName` property. The XML comment must look like this:

```
''' <summary>
''' Contains the person's first name
''' </summary>
''' <value>Person's first name</value>
''' <returns>String</returns>
''' <remarks></remarks>
Public Overridable Property FirstName As String
```

Here there is a new tag, `value`. The `summary` tag describes a property, and `value` describes the property's value. Do the same thing on the `LastName` property, specifying the appropriate description, similarly to `FirstName`. Other tags can be added in a straightforward way, thanks to the always present IntelliSense. Figure 47.6 shows how IntelliSense provides available XML tags, according to the particular context where they have to be added.

FIGURE 47.6   IntelliSense helps you select XML tags according to the particular context.

Referring to Code Elements

XML comments enable references to other code elements with specific tags. The first one is `c` that identifies the element within angle bracket as code. To show an example, rewrite XML comments for the `GetFullName` method as follows:

```
''' <summary>
''' Gets the complete person's name
''' </summary>
''' <returns>String</returns>
''' <remarks>This method concatenates <c>LastName</c> and
''' <c>FirstName</c> properties</remarks>
Public Overridable Function GetFullName() As String
    Dim fn As New Text.StringBuilder
    fn.Append(Me.FirstName)
    fn.Append(" ")
    fn.Append(Me.LastName)
    Return fn.ToString
End Function
```

Notice how the `c` tag embraces both the `LastName` and `FirstName` properties, communicating to the compiler that both tags represent a code element. It is enclosed and nested within a remarks tag (IntelliSense can be helpful in choosing the allowed tags). This is not the only way of referring to code; you can provide an entire code example that will be

47

included in your documentation. To accomplish this, you first declare a sample tag, which contains the sample description and then a code tag that contains a code snippet demonstrating the member purpose. Edit the preceding XML comment as follows:

```
''' <summary>
''' Gets the complete person's name
''' </summary>
''' <returns>String</returns>
''' <remarks>This method concatenates <c>LastName</c> and
''' <c>FirstName</c> properties
''' <example>This example shows how you can invoke
''' the <c>GetFullName</c> method
''' <code>
''' Dim result As String = Person1.GetFullName()
''' </code>
''' </example>
''' </remarks>
Public Overridable Function GetFullName() As String
```

This is useful because your documentation also shows examples of your libraries.

WHY DON'T I SEE THEM?

Code, c, and example tags provide documentation that is not available within IntelliSense. It is, however, available within the generated XML file; thus you can appreciate them when building an HTML-based or compiled documentation or within the Object Browser.

XML comments enable you to easily refer to and document members' arguments. For a better understanding, write the following overload of the GetFullName method that accepts a Title argument:

```
Public Overridable Function GetFullName(Title As String) As String

    If String.IsNullOrEmpty(Title) = True Then Throw New _
                                        ArgumentNullException

    Dim fn As New Text.StringBuilder
    fn.Append(Title)
    fn.Append(" ")
    fn.Append(Me.FirstName)
    fn.Append(" ")
    fn.Append(Me.LastName)
    Return fn.ToString
End Function
```

Now add an XML comment. It looks like this:

```
''' <summary>
''' Gets the complete person's name
''' </summary>
''' <param name="Title"></param>
''' <returns>String</returns>
''' <remarks></remarks>
Public Overridable Function GetFullName(Title As String) As String
```

The `param` tag enables you to refer to a member's argument, specified by the name attribute. If you try to type the name on your own, IntelliSense helps you choose the argument. XML comments also enable you to specify an exception that your member could encounter, according to the actions it takes. For example, the `GetFullName` method could throw a `NullReferenceException` if the `Title` argument is an empty or null string. For this, you use an `exception` tag to specify the exception. The tag is used with `cref`. This one is straightforward in that it enables you to point a reference to a .NET object using IntelliSense. The following tag (which must be added before the method definition) specifies which exception can be thrown:

```
''' <exception cref="ArgumentNullException">
''' The exception that is thrown when <paramref name="Title"/> is Nothing
''' </exception>
''' <returns>String</returns>
''' <remarks></remarks>
Public Overridable Function GetFullName(Title As String) As String
```

When typing `cref`, the IntelliSense window shows all the available objects. You pick the exception you are interested in. This speeds up the way you write your comment, also ensuring that you type a valid object name. You can also specify the description for the exception. The good news about `cref` is that it creates a cross-reference to the documentation related to the pointed object. For instance, when you create a compiled documentation file based on the XML comments, `cref` enables you to redirect to another page showing information on the pointed object. You can also refer to the argument by specifying the `paramref` tag within a descriptive text, which requires a name attribute pointing to the argument. `paramref` also takes advantages of IntelliSense.

If you have experience with previous versions of Visual Basic, you will notice some improvements to both `cref` and `paramref` in Visual Basic 2015. First, objects referred to with `cref` and `paramref` are now colorized properly, whereas in previous versions they were represented in gray. You can also see ToolTips by simply hovering over them, as you do in the code editor. Most importantly, they now have full IntelliSense support, which means you can right-click objects and use Go to Definition or Find All References. You can also enable the light bulb and quick actions to perform refactorings (such as simplifying fully qualified names). If you rename a member that is referenced within an XML comment, that reference is also automatically updated to match the new name. Finally, if you have a method with several overloads, you can now refer to each one unambiguously because IntelliSense quickly helps you choose the appropriate one, as demonstrated in Figure 47.7.

47

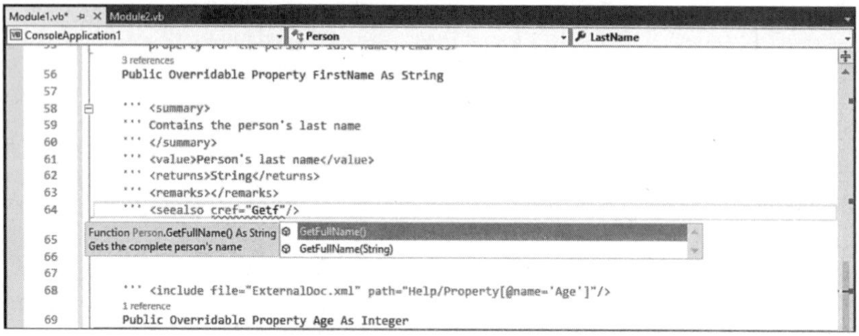

FIGURE 47.7   Unambiguous method selection in VB 2015.

All these improvements make it easier to reference types and members in your XML comments, providing a more productive and efficient environment.

Referring to an External Documentation File

The Visual Basic compiler can link documentation to your code from an external XML document. To do this, you use the `include` tag. The tag requires a file attribute that points to the external document and a path attribute that points to the position in the document providing documentation for the given member. The following code sets external documentation for the `Age` property:

```
''' <include file="ExternalDoc.xml" path="Help/Property[@name='Age']"/>
Public Overridable Property Age As Integer
```

To understand how the path tag works, here is the XML representation of the external document:

```
<?xml version="1.0" encoding="utf-8" ?>
<Help>
  <Property name="Age">
    <summary>Returns how old a person is</summary>
    <returns>Integer</returns>
  </Property>
  <!-- Other properties...-->
  <Property>

  </Property>
</Help>
```

Creating Lists

Documentation often requires bulleted and numbered lists or tables, as in any other kind of document. Luckily, XML comments enable you to easily build lists. You do this with the `list` tag that requires a `type` attribute specifying whether the list is a bulleted or numbered list or a two-column table. The following example shows how to build a numbered list on the `Person` class documentation:

```
''' <summary>
''' Represents a human being
''' </summary>
''' <remarks>
''' <list type="number">
''' <item><description>Instantiate the class</description></item>
''' <item><description>Populate its properties</description></item>
''' <item><description>Eventually retrieve the full
''' name</description></item>
''' </list>
''' </remarks>
Public Class Person
....
End Class
```

The type attribute can have one of the following values: `bullet` (bulleted list), `number` (numbered list), or `table` (two-column table). Notice how each item in the list is represented by an item tag that requires a nested description tag providing the actual description. If you want to provide a table, each item must contain a term tag and a description tag as in the following example:

```
''' <item><term>Action one</term></item>
''' <item><description>Instantiate the class</description></item>
```

The item's content will be also shown in IntelliSense and the Object Browser, but it will be formatted as a list only in the compiled documentation.

Documenting Permissions Requirements

Sometimes your objects expose members that require special permissions to access system resources. You can provide documentation about required permissions by adding a permission tag with `cref`, pointing to the desired .NET permission. The following example shows how to comment the `GetFullName` method with the `UIPermission` requirement:

```
''' <permission cref="System.Security.Permissions.UIPermission"/>
Public Overridable Function GetFullName() As String
```

Of course, you can specify multiple permissions by adding multiple permission tags.

Specifying Links to Other Resources

When documenting the code, it is not unusual to provide links to other members. XML comments enable you to do this by specifying `see` and `seealso` tags. The `see` tag enables you to specify a link to another member's documentation from within the description text. The `seealso` tag does the same, but it differs in that the link to the other member appears in the *See Also* section of the compiled page. The following example demonstrates this on the `FirstName` property providing a link to `LastName`:

```
''' <remarks>Use the <see cref="LastName"/>
''' property for the person's last name</remarks>
Public Overridable Property FirstName As String
```

If you want the link to be shown in the See Also section, replace see with seealso.

XML Comments and Generics

When you define your custom generics, you can use XML comments to describe the type parameter. This is accomplished via the typeparam tag, as shown in the following code snippet:

```
''' <summary>
''' A test class
''' </summary>
''' <typeparam name="T">
''' A type parameter that must implement IEnumerable
''' </typeparam>
''' <remarks></remarks>
Public Class TestGenerics(Of T As IEnumerable)

End Class
```

The Visual Basic compiler automatically recognizes the generic implementation and thus adds for you the typeparam tag when adding the XML comment.

Generating Compiled Help Files

When you document your source code with XML comments, you might want to generate compiled help files that you can distribute together with your libraries. Compiled help files are .chm files that can be easily opened with the Windows integrated Help Viewer. The .chm file format is the most appropriate in such situations because it is a standalone and does not require additional applications. A number of third-party (paid) tools can generate .chm files starting from XML comments. The following are some popular tools:

▶ Help + Manual from EC Software (http://www.ec-software.com)

▶ FAR from Helpware (http://www.helpwaregroup.com/products/far)

▶ HelpNDoc (http://www.helpndoc.com)

These tools are very good in that they enable you to generate multiple output formats, not only .chm files.

Summary

This chapter covered how to use XML comments instead of classic comments. With XML comments, you specify tags that identify an element in the code as a special formatted element in the generated documentation file. Such a file is an XML document that enables IntelliSense documentation for your own code and constitutes the source for automating building compiled help files that accompany your libraries as the documentation. This chapter also provided information about new productivity features introduced for some XML tags in Visual Basic 2015. To automate the help-generation process, you were informed about the existence of tools produced by third-party vendors.

47

Understanding the Global Assembly Cache

The Visual Studio IDE is a great place to create applications, but in most cases, you need to deploy them to your customers. The .NET Framework offers a nice infrastructure for making this possible, but you need to know some concepts about the infrastructure before effectively deploying applications. Often you can create libraries and reference those libraries, or third-party libraries, other than the .NET Framework base libraries in your projects. These libraries need to be deployed together with your application, but the .NET deployment model for assemblies works differently from the COM model. The goal of this chapter is to illustrate how .NET base libraries are organized, why you can be sure to find them on a target machine, and how you deploy your own libraries or third-party libraries that your applications work with. This information is important if you consider deploying an application is not only deploying the executable, but also all libraries required by the application. This is the reason you need to read this chapter before discovering the deploying modes offered by the .NET Framework and Visual Studio 2015.

The Dll Hell Problem

One of the biggest problems of the COM programming model is the *Dll hell*. COM components (such as ActiveX controls or type libraries) need to be registered so the system knows where to find them even if they are not available in the application directory. The problem is when you have different versions of the component installed on the same machine. Registration can be painful, and there are often many problems in making an application recognize the correct version of the component. In many cases, an application will not work correctly. This is the reason the situation is called Dll hell. Since version 1.0, the .NET Framework provides a brilliant way to solve this big problem by introducing assemblies and the *global assembly cache* (GAC). Before discussing the GAC, it is important to understand how assemblies can be deployed and recognized by applications and why they solve the Dll hell problem. To accomplish this, the discussion first focuses on the most basic mode for deploying assemblies: XCopy deployment.

XCopy Deployment

If you have been an MS-DOS person, you will remember the `XCopy` command. It enabled you to copy entire directory trees, including files and subdirectories, from one location to another. In honor of this command, the most basic deployment technique in the .NET Framework is XCopy deployment. The reason for this name is that a .NET application can work when the executable and the assemblies referenced by the executable all reside in the same folder. According to this, you can deploy an application by copying its folder. This approach has a huge implication: If an application folder contains a copy of required assemblies, these are isolated from one another and do not require registration anymore. Because they are no longer required to be registered, multiple versions of an assembly can reside on the same machine avoiding the big problem of the Dll hell.

BASE CLASS LIBRARY ASSEMBLIES

The preceding discussion is not valid when talking about the Base Class Library assemblies being part of the .NET Framework and cannot be included in the application folder. They stay in the GAC, as covered in next section.

When you compile your project, Visual Studio generates a Bin subfolder within the project folder. Bin contains Debug and Release subfolders (referring to default build configurations). Both folders contain the executable and referenced assemblies. You can perform an XCopy deployment by distributing the content of the Release folder, and your application will work. XCopy deployment is something you have to know to understand how things work. In a business environment, you will deploy your applications with professional installers, such as InstallShield for Windows Installer and ClickOnce, which are discussed in the next two chapters. Another consideration about XCopy deployment is that every application keeps its own copy of referenced assemblies. This means if you have ten applications referring to the same assembly, you will have ten copies of the assembly. This is good in that assemblies will not interfere with each other, especially in the case of different versions. However, it can be annoying if you have ten copies of the same version of your assembly. A solution to this is provided by the global assembly cache, which solves other problems and is the subject of the following section.

The Global Assembly Cache

The .NET Framework consists of hundreds of libraries and tools. Most libraries implement the Base Class Library. The BCL's assemblies are located in GAC. This is the reason you can be sure a .NET application requiring only base assemblies can correctly work on a target machine that has the .NET Framework installed. The GAC can be considered as a repository of shared assemblies. This means that an application can have a reference to an assembly available in the GAC instead of bringing its own copy of the assembly as happens in the XCopy deployment. The GAC is a folder in the system and is located at C:\Windows\Assembly. Because of the particular nature of this folder, its representation within Windows Explorer is a little bit different from other folders. Figure 48.1 shows how the GAC is represented in Windows Explorer.

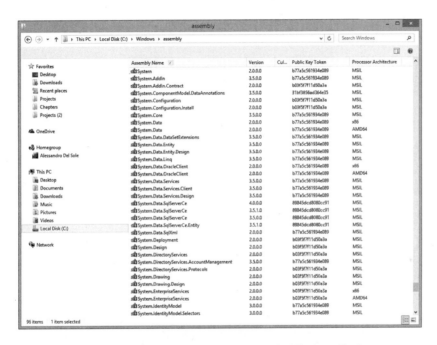

FIGURE 48.1   The global assembly cache shown in Windows Explorer.

You might notice from Figure 48.1 how the GAC lists installed the assemblies, version number, public key token, and target processor architecture. The public key token is a unique identifier, which identifies the assembly within the .NET infrastructure. If the assembly targets a specific culture, this information is also shown. You can easily notice how different versions of the same assembly can be available in the GAC. (For example, check the `System.Data.SqlServerCe.dll` assembly.) This is important because it means the GAC is responsible for handling different versions of the same assembly, solving the versioning and registration problems.

Installing and Uninstalling Assemblies

A common way for referring to assemblies available in the GAC is saying they are installed into the GAC. (Installing an assembly to the GAC means making the assembly recognizable by the GAC and by the .NET Framework while the physical file stays in its original location.) Suppose you have an assembly named C:\MyAssemblies\MyLibrary.dll and you want to install this assembly into the GAC. The installation procedure adds to the GAC metadata information for the assembly but does not copy the file to the GAC; instead, MyLibrary.Dll remains in C:\MyAssemblies. Installing and uninstalling assemblies to and from the GAC is a step you have to divide in two parts: development time and real deployment time. At development time, you have two opportunities for installing assemblies to the GAC. The first way is invoking the **GacUtil.exe** command-line tool passing the /i option and the assembly name. The following is a command-line example for installing an assembly:

```
GacUtil.exe /i C:\MyAssemblies\MyLibrary.dll
```

You uninstall an assembly from the GAC by passing the /u option to GacUtil, as in the following command line:

```
GacUtil.exe /u C:\MyAssemblies\MyLibrary.dll
```

The second way for installing assemblies is dragging them to Windows Explorer opened to the GAC folder. To uninstall one or more assemblies, right-click the assembly name and select **Uninstall**.

INSTALLING AND UNINSTALLING REQUIRE ELEVATED PRIVILEGES

Administrators using an Access Control List can protect the Global Assembly Cache folder. If this is your situation, remember that installing and uninstalling assemblies to the GAC requires elevated privileges. If you are using Windows Vista, Windows 7, or Windows 8.x, you will be required to run the command prompt or Windows Explorer with administrator privileges before attempting to install or uninstall assemblies.

Both ways can be useful at development time, but they cannot be absolutely indicated at deployment time for several reasons. The most important reason is that both ways have no reference counting and it is not appropriate to require your user to manually manipulate the GAC with Windows Explorer. Because of this, you should always choose professional installation systems, such as InstallShield for Windows Installer, that install and uninstall assemblies without troubles. The next chapter discusses setup and deployment projects for Windows Installer, covering GAC situations. ClickOnce has some limitations from this point of view because it does not allow installing assemblies to the GAC, which is important to consider when deciding the deployment strategy. In addition, installing assemblies to the global assembly cache has a huge requirement: You can only install assemblies signed with a strong name.

Signing Assemblies with Strong Names

A strong name is a signature added to assemblies to provide uniqueness and represents the assembly's identity. It is composed by the assembly name, version, culture, public key, and digital signature. The public key is generated from the related private key, which is stored in the assembly manifest.

SECURITY ISSUES

To avoid security issues, strong-named assemblies can only use type from other strong-named assemblies (such as the Base Class Library assemblies).

You have two modes for signing an assembly with a strong name. The first is invoking command-line tools such as Sn.exe and Al.exe. But because most of your developer life is spent within Visual Studio, the second mode is offered by the IDE. To add a strong name to your assembly, you first open **My Project** and then select the **Signing** tab where you flag the **Sign the Assembly** check box as shown in Figure 48.2.

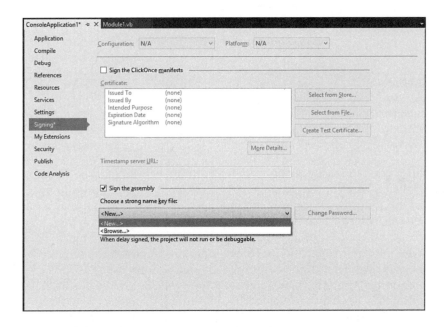

FIGURE 48.2   Adding a strong name to the project.

You can either add a new strong name or import an existing one. To add a new strong name, click the <**New...**> item in the combo box (see Figure 48.2). You will be prompted for specifying the filename and a password. This generates a .pfx file that is added to the project and is visible in Solution Explorer. For instance, in the Create Strong Name Key dialog box, type **MyStrongName** as the filename and **MyStrongName** as the password. Figure 48.3 shows how to accomplish this.

Specifying a password is not mandatory. If you do not provide a password, Visual Studio generates an .snk file instead of a .pfx one. Specifying a password is strongly recommended.

FIGURE 48.3   Providing name and password for the new strong name.

KEEP YOUR PASSWORD

Take note of the password you assign to strong names. It will be required every time you open the project from another computer different from the one where you first added the strong name.

In Visual Studio 2015, you can specify an encryption algorithm, between **sha256RA** and **sha1RSA**. Both calculate a hash for the input data, which is the signature. The first one produces a 256 bit hash, the second one a 160 bit hash. The default selection is sha256RA and you can leave it unchanged. Remember that strong names are not the equivalent of certificates (such as Authenticode) that provide security trust, other than uniqueness, according to .NET security requirements. Finally, strong names can be applied to assemblies with the delay signing technique (see the Delay sign option in the MyProject Signing tab). In a few words, this technique writes only the public key in the executable and requires the private key be passed at a later stage, preventing the project from being compiled, debugged, and run from within Visual Studio. Because of this you need to skip the signature verification (e.g., running the Sn.exe tool passing the -Vr option). It is worth noting that you can disable signing enforcement on a machine even at the specific assembly signature level in the event you need to delay sign, but still want to debug. This topic is not covered in more detail because of its particular nature. You can get more information in the official MSDN documentation at http://msdn.microsoft.com/en-us/library/t07a3dye(VS.110).aspx.

CLS-COMPLIANT ASSEMBLIES

Signing assemblies with strong names is mandatory in case you want them to be CLS-compliant.

Top Reasons for Installing (or Not) Assemblies to the GAC

As a rule, installing assemblies to the GAC is something that should be restricted only to particular scenarios. Situations when you want to take advantage of the GAC can be summarized as follows:

▶ **Multiple applications referencing the same assemblies**—In this case, it can be convenient to have a single copy of assemblies in the GAC instead of providing several copies in the application folder.

▶ **Versioning**—The GAC can maintain different versions of the same assembly. This problem is solved by the XCopy deployment, but your company can have a deployment strategy that prefers the GAC.

▶ **Security**—The GAC can be managed by system administrators for controlling permissions using the Access Control List. If you need this control, installing assemblies to the GAC is a good choice.

In all other cases, you should refrain from installing assemblies to the GAC. Remember that this procedure affects the .NET Framework and any mistake can be fatal.

Summary

This chapter discussed important concepts you need to know before deploying .NET applications. You saw how the .NET Framework solves the Dll Hell problem by avoiding the need of component registration and allowing the XCopy deployment. Then you saw what the global assembly cache is and how you can manage it for sharing assemblies among multiple applications. In addition, you got information on strong names and on how to apply them to your assemblies so these can be installed to the GAC. Finally, you understood how to configure Windows Registry for making custom assemblies in the GAC visible from the Add Reference dialog box in Visual Studio. All this information is important to understand how you deploy libraries, controls, and assemblies together with your executables. Now that you know this, you are ready to deploy your applications with Visual Studio tools.

48

CHAPTER 49

Setup and Deployment Projects with InstallShield for Visual Studio

When you deliver your application to your customers, you do not tell them it supports the XCopy deployment and you do not provide technical explanations on how .NET applications work. This is because modern applications require a convenient setup procedure that can install them in a professional fashion, put files in the appropriate places, create shortcuts in the Windows user interface, check for system requirements, and perform components registration. The users are just required to select the target folder and what options in your applications they want to be installed on their machine. Creating a user-friendly setup procedure is something that increases professionalism and gives customers the first good impression of your work. The .NET-based applications, like the ones you create with Visual Basic 2015, can be deployed in several modes. One of these is taking advantage of the Windows Installer engine that provides great flexibility over installation requirements and takes the maximum from integration with the operating system. Like Visual Studio 2012 and Visual Studio 2013, Visual Studio 2015 does not offer out of the box the Setup & Deployment projects that were available until version 2010; instead, it brings into the development environment a professional tool for creating setup projects based on Windows Installer: InstallShield Limited Edition (LE). This has an important consequence: Existing Setup & Deployment projects built with Visual Studio 2010 and earlier versions are no longer supported and cannot be opened in Visual Studio 2015 directly. Fortunately, InstallShield LE has an option that allows you to convert old projects into InstallShield projects.

SUPPORTING VISUAL STUDIO INSTALLER PROJECTS

Microsoft has created an extension for Visual Studio that brings back the old Visual Studio Installer project templates. At this writing, this extension is only available for Visual Studio 2012 and 2013, but Microsoft plans to make it available for Visual Studio 2015. If you used to work with this project types in the past, you might want to check out the extension's page: https://visualstudiogallery.msdn.microsoft.com/9abe329c-9bba-44a1-be59-0fbf6151054d. This chapter does not discuss this extension because InstallShield LE is the tool included in Visual Studio 2015, whereas installing the external extension is an optional choice.

In this chapter, you will learn how to create a setup project for Windows Installer using InstallShield and Visual Studio 2015 so you can deploy your Visual Basic applications in the most professional way possible. Even though you now use InstallShield, this still relies on the Windows Installer engine and generates MSI packages. For this reason, an overview of Windows Installer can be useful, especially if you do not have technical experience with an installation engine.

ABOUT WINDOWS STORE APPS

Windows Store Apps have their own specific mechanism for installation via the Windows Store, so they cannot be installed with Windows Installer or ClickOnce.

Windows Installer Overview

Windows Installer is the Microsoft technology for deploying applications. This technology has been part of the Windows operating system for many years and can be considered as an engine for installing .msi packages. An .msi package, or installer package, contains all files to be installed with your application and other important information including shortcuts, icons, license agreements, other redistributable packages, and key/values to be written to the Windows Registry.

Windows Installer is the most powerful technology for deploying .NET applications with Visual Studio 2015. This is because Windows Installer has few limitations, whereas it brings many benefits. Windows Installer makes it difficult to provide updates, so if you plan to release frequent updates for your applications, you should consider ClickOnce, which is discussed in the next chapter. You should choose Windows Installer as the deployment system for your application if you meet one or more of the following requirements:

- ▶ Adding values to the Windows Registry

- ▶ Customizing installation folders

- ▶ Installing assemblies to the global assembly cache or installing and registering COM components

- ▶ Installing Windows services and peripheral drivers

- ▶ Executing custom actions and specifying launch conditions

- ▶ Managing ODBC components

- ▶ Creating custom shortcuts in the Windows user interface

- ▶ Elevated permissions and deeper interaction with the user

In scenarios different from the ones listed, you might consider ClickOnce. Visual Studio 2015 is the perfect environment for creating projects that can build Windows Installer packages that install your applications on target machines the most appropriate way. In the next section, you can see how to accomplish this.

Introducing InstallShield

InstallShield is software for creating Windows Installer packages. It has been very popular for many years because it has been the first fully-featured environment for building complete MSI packages via a very powerful instrumentation. Other tools existed in the past for creating Windows Installer packages, but InstallShield has always been a step ahead. InstallShield is produced by Flexera (www.flexera.com) and is available both as a standalone environment and as an add-on for Visual Studio 2015. In fact, this is not the first time that InstallShield enters Visual Studio's life. InstallShield LE existed for Visual Studio 2010 and Visual Studio 2012.

Obtaining Your Copy of InstallShield LE

InstallShield is not available by default in Visual Studio 2015, so you need to download it separately. The easiest way to request InstallShield is going in Visual Studio and selecting **File, New Project**. When the New Project dialog box appears, expand the Other Project Types node and select **Setup and Deployment**. At this point, you will see an item called **Enable InstallShield Limited Edition**, as demonstrated in Figure 49.1.

49

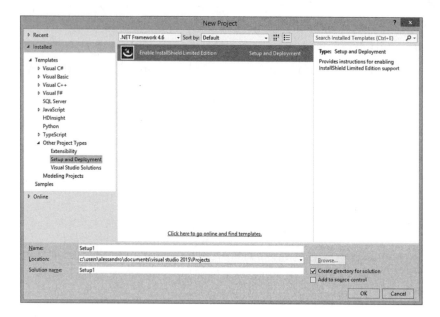

FIGURE 49.1   Enabling InstallShield LE.

At this point, an HTML document already residing on your machine will open. Follow the instructions to download a copy of InstallShield LE and store the activation key that is sent to you via email. This is important for activating InstallShield at the first project. Once you have downloaded your copy, close Visual Studio 2015 and launch the installation of InstallShield. When the installation completes, restart Visual Studio 2015.

Creating a Setup Project

The goal of this chapter is to demonstrate how you create a setup project for a Windows client application. First, create a new WPF project with Visual Basic and name it DeploymentDemo. This project just serves as the demo application to be deployed. When the new project is ready, right-click the solution name in Solution Explorer and select **Add, New Project**. In the New Project dialog box, select the **Other Project Types, Setup and Deployment, InstallShield Limited Edition** templates subfolder and select the **InstallShield Limited Edition Project** template, as shown in Figure 49.2. Name the new project SetupExample and click OK.

FIGURE 49.2   Adding a new setup project to the solution.

When you click OK, Visual Studio generates a new InstallShield project. Notice that during the creation of the very first project you will be prompted to enter the activation code you received via email. When the project is ready, you will see the InstallShield Project Assistant, which is where you start creating your setup package (see Figure 49.3).

AVAILABILITY OF CERTAIN FEATURES

If you look at Solution Explorer, you will see that the InstallShield project offers a number of shortcuts and features. Not all of them are available in the Limited Edition for Visual Studio 2015. Some of them are available only in paid versions. So this section explains how to build a setup project by using the Project Assistant instead of selecting features in Solution Explorer because this might lead to confusion.

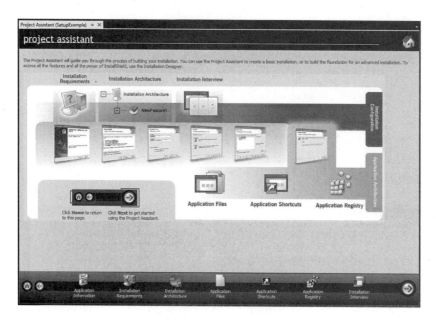

FIGURE 49.3   The InstallShield's Project Assistant.

At the bottom of the Project Assistant you can find a toolbar that provides a number of shortcuts you should follow from the left to the right, so you can start from supplying all the required information and finish with the package generation process. Now you will get an overview of all the available shortcuts to create a sample MSI package for the current project.

Application Information

The Application Information group allows specifying general information for the installation package such as the software's producer name, application version, and producer's website. You can specify a custom icon for the installer by clicking the Browse button. Figure 49.4 shows an example.

You can change the target directory for the installed application. The default is set based on the company name and application name under the form of C:\Program Files\ *CompanyName\ApplicationName*. You can change the target directory by selecting the **Edit the Default Installation Location** hyperlink on the left side of the Project Assistant. InstallShield assigns the target directory value to a variable called INSTALLDIR and is used by the Windows Installer engine to determine the target folder. After setting the Application Information, it is time to set prerequisites.

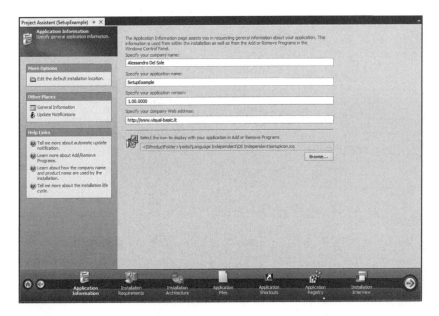

FIGURE 49.4   Specifying general application information for the package.

Installation Requirements

Installation Requirements include the specification of the Windows operating system that the application is going to target and those packages or runtime components that must be installed together with the application so it correctly works. As you can see from Figure 49.5, the Installation Requirement group is divided into two parts. The first part allows specifying the target operating systems, whereas the second part (at the bottom) allows specifying prerequisites like specific versions of the .NET Framework or other components (for example, Adobe Reader, SQL Server, and so on). The .NET Framework 4.6 is included by default and it is not available in the list.

Remember that the .NET Framework 4.6 is not supported on Windows XP and Windows Server 2003 so unselect these operating systems if you are deploying applications based on version 4.6 of .NET. Regarding runtime components and prerequisites, you can configure additional options for every single component. You can do this by clicking the Requirements shortcut on the left. This will open the Requirements designer where you can specify hardware requirements and customize installation messages. Figure 49.6 shows the Requirements designer and demonstrates an example about SQL Server 2008 R2. You can click the Edit the Message button to customize the text message that will show if a prerequisite is not found on the target machine.

49

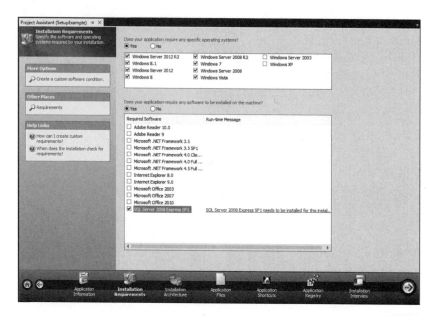

FIGURE 49.5   Configuring Installation Requirements.

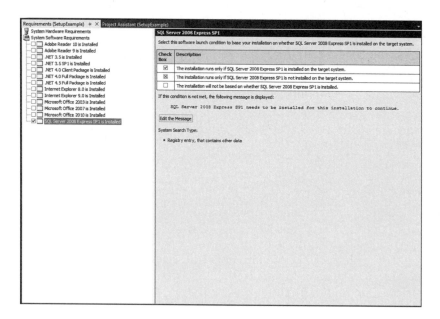

FIGURE 49.6   The Requirements designer.

When you click the Edit the Message button, the Text and Message designer opens. There you will be able to customize predefined values that are stored inside tables of the MSI package. You can finally create a custom software condition, by clicking the same-named shortcut on the left side of the Project Assistant. A custom software condition allows proceeding with the installation only if the specified item is found on the target machine. The installer can search for files, folders, registry keys, and INI file values. Clicking the Custom Software Condition shortcut will launch the System Search Wizard, an easy-to-use tool where you can specify what item will be searched in a convenient step-by-step procedure. This tool is not discussed in further detail because common scenarios are already predetermined in the default settings. The discussion will move to the Application Files group to specify what files of the application will be deployed onto the target machine. You will see the Installation Architecture group first, but this is not available for InstallShield Limited Edition.

Application Files

You can manage files to be installed with your package in the Application Files group. The first thing you have to add is the primary output of the main project, DeploymentDemo in our case. To accomplish this you click **Add Project Outputs** and in the Visual Studio Output Selector dialog box select **Primary Output**, as demonstrated in Figure 49.7.

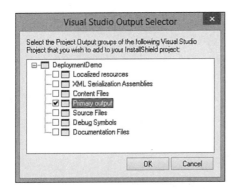

FIGURE 49.7   Adding the primary output to the installation package.

The primary output represents only the main .exe file, but InstallShield will check for dependencies at build time only in editions higher than the LE so you will have to add referenced assemblies manually with the Limited Edition. After you specify the primary output, this is added to the designer (as shown in Figure 49.8).

You can then click the **Add Files** button, which can be used to include any other kind of required files into your package (including dependencies). You can use the **Add Folder** button to include an entire folder tree. It is worth mentioning that in case your solution contains multiple projects, you can choose the primary output for each project in the Visual Studio Output Selector dialog box. This is useful if you have several assemblies you want to deploy. Finally, you are not limited to the executable file but you can include other items like debug symbols, source code files, documentation, etc. Application files are added by default to the target folder under Program Files. If you select a different folder in the directory tree on the left, then selected files will be installed to the newly selected folder. You can add custom and special folders by right-clicking the root item of the directory tree (Destination Computer) and add a new folder. For instance, if you want to add an assembly that will be installed to the global assembly cache you can follow these steps:

1. Right-click **Destination Computer**.

2. Select **Show Predefined Folder** and then **[GlobalAssemblyCache]**.

3. Select the **GAC** folder in the directory tree and add assemblies to this folder.

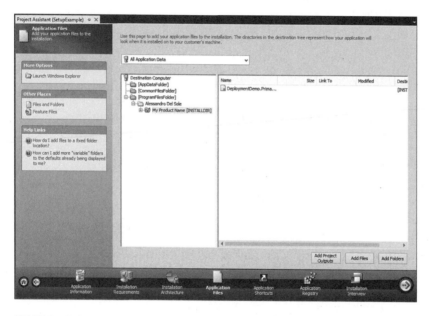

FIGURE 49.8   The Application Files group shows target folders and files.

This action is very useful to install files to specific locations, other than application files to the INSTALLDIR directory.

DRAGGING FILES TO THE PACKAGE

If you click the Files and Folders shortcut on the left side of the Project Assistant, Visual Studio will open the Files and Folders designer that shows a view of files and directories on your computer and in the current solution you can easily drag and release onto the application files list.

Assuming you have added all the required application files, or at least the primary output, it is time to specify shortcuts the user will click to launch your application.

Application Shortcuts

Users launch applications via shortcuts. These are normally available on the Desktop, in the Windows Start menu, or within groups in the applications list in the case of Windows 8.x. With InstallShield LE you create shortcuts in the Application Shortcuts group. The first thing to do is to click the **New** button. When the Browse for a Destination File dialog box is ready, you have to browse the folders structure and locate the file that will be reachable via the new shortcut, such as the main .exe file. Figure 49.9 shows an example of how to create a shortcut for the DeploymentDemo sample application.

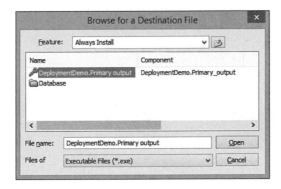

FIGURE 49.9   Creating a new shortcut.

After you click **Open**, a new shortcut called Built is available in the Project Assistant. Click **Rename** to replace the default name with a more meaningful one. You can decide to add a shortcut to the destination Desktop and Start menu (in Windows 8 this will add the shortcut to the applications list). Figure 49.10 shows how the Project Assistant appears at this point, with a renamed shortcut.

Repeat the same operation to add multiple shortcuts in case you have different files you want users to be able to reach easily.

SHORTCUTS HIERARCHY

You can click the **Shortcuts** hyperlink on the left to open the Shortcuts designer where you will be able to get a hierarchical view of shortcuts inside the desktop and the Start menu representations. This is useful to manage shortcuts in a graphical fashion.

You can create a file extension definition so files with the specified extension can be opened or manipulated with your application. Once you have your extension definition, this can be associated to shortcuts. To create an extension definition, follow these steps:

1. Click the **File Extensions** shortcut on the left.

2. When the designer appears, right-click **File Extensions** and select **New Extension**.

3. Specify the extension and then add settings in the properties pane on the right.

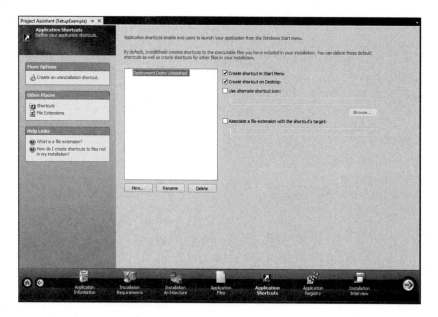

FIGURE 49.10   Specifying shortcut details.

Follow the instructions to specify the **Command** that will be executed by your application when it gets associated to the file extension and in the **File** property specify your application's primary output. If you do not specify any command, Open is assumed by default, which means files with the given extension will be always opened with your application (unless the user changes this setting manually). Figure 49.11 shows an example.

You can specify command line arguments (Arguments) and an icon for the extension (Icon). If you now go back to the Shortcuts group in the Project Assistant, you will see that the new extension has been associated to the selected shortcut. The next step is setting registry keys and values.

Application Registry

One of the biggest benefits in deploying applications with Windows Installer is that you can add keys and values to the Windows Registry on the target machine. You create keys, subkeys, and values by selecting the **Application Registry** in the Project Assistant and then right-click the desired root key. Finally, add the required key or value. Figure 49.12 shows how to accomplish this.

Values are then visible on the right side of the editor. In this way, you have complete control over the Registry so your application can immediately store information onto the target system. The last part of the Project Assistant is all about the user interface of the installer.

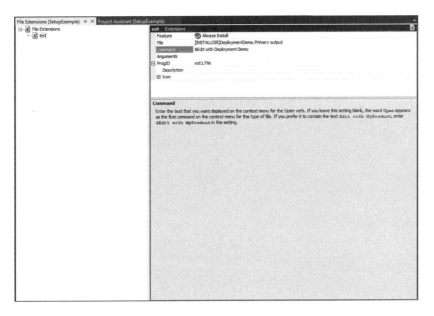

FIGURE 49.11   Creating an extension definition and specifying settings.

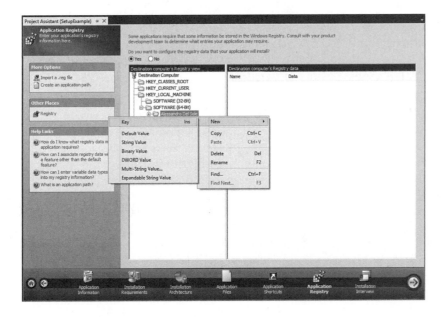

FIGURE 49.12   Adding keys and values to the target Windows registry.

Installation Interview

In the Installation Interview group, you can customize the way users interact with your installation package. Figure 49.13 shows an example.

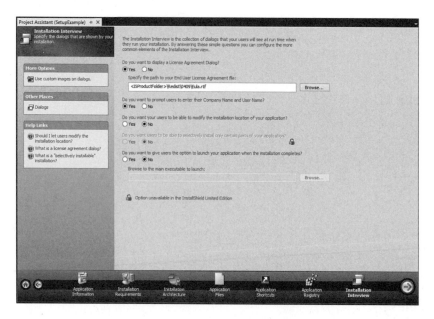

FIGURE 49.13   Customizing the user interface of the installation package.

You can specify an End User License Agreement under the form of a Rich Text Format (RTF) file. You can allow users to change the default installation folder, ask them to launch the application after the installation completes, and provide an opportunity of entering user and company name. Features adorned with a locker are not available in the Limited Edition. Because InstallShield provides default banners and bitmaps for MSI packages, you can replace these with custom ones that will be shown when the installer runs. To accomplish this, click the **Use custom images on dialogs** shortcut and supply the necessary bitmaps. In addition, you can specify a different number of dialogs for your package, each providing a different kind of information. You select dialogs for your package by clicking the **Dialogs** hyperlink. This will launch the Dialogs designer where you can select among the available dialogs and specify properties for each dialog box, as demonstrated in Figure 49.14.

As you can see, you can select a theme and specify banner bitmaps directly from this designer.

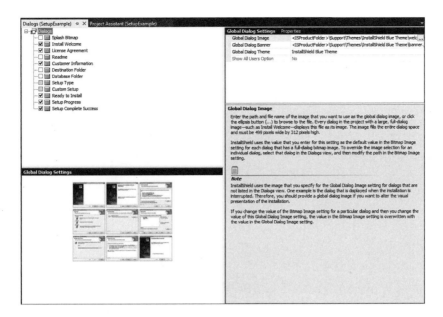

FIGURE 49.14   Specifying dialogs for the installation packages.

Specifying Environment Variables

InstallShield LE allows creating Windows environment variables when the application is installed. To accomplish this, in Solution Explorer double-click the Environment Variables element to open the appropriate designer. When ready, right-click the **Environment Variables** root item and then select **Add Environment Variable**. Enter a name for the variable and then specify the value and other self-explanatory properties on the right. See Figure 49.15.

Environment variables are typically used when applications need special kinds of interaction with the operating system. You will not need this editor if this is not your case.

Configuring the Setup Project

You can supply additional configuration settings for your Windows Installer package by selecting the General Information item in Solution Explorer. This will open the same-named designer and enable you to set a number of package's properties. All the available properties affect layout, messages, and target folders when launching the installer. Figure 49.16 shows an example of how you can set properties.

Properties are self-explanatory, but you can click each of them to get a description at the bottom of the window.

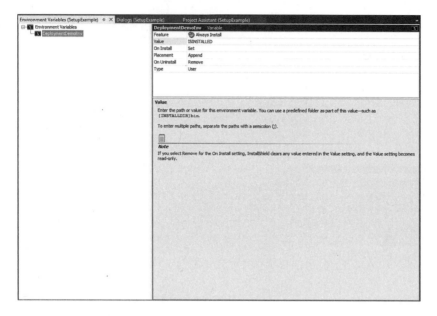

FIGURE 49.15   Adding environment variables.

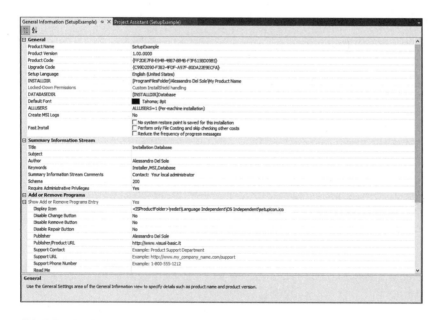

FIGURE 49.16   Setting additional package properties.

Building and Deploying the Windows Installer Package

To create your Windows Installer distributable package, right-click the setup project name in Solution Explorer and select **Build**. As an alternative, you can choose the appropriate **Build** command from the Build menu. This generates a bootstrapper named Setup.exe and the Windows Installer package with an .msi extension, which in our case is named SetupExample.msi. The output will be available in the Express project subfolder that contains files you need to distribute to your customers for installing your application. They run the Setup.exe bootstrapper that correctly starts the Windows Installer package.

CUSTOMIZING RELEASES

InstallShield can generate different kinds of distribution media, such as a single image, DVD-ROM, or CD-ROM. To customize how the installation packages are generated, click the **Releases** item in Solution Explorer.

Summary

This chapter covered how to create setup projects for Windows Installer in Visual Studio 2015 using InstallShield LE. First, you read about the reasons you should choose a technique. Then you saw how to generate a setup project with InstallShield Limited Edition. Next, the discussion focused on configuring and customizing your project with special integrated editors. Finally, you learned how to build and deploy your Windows Installer package.

49

Deploying Applications with ClickOnce

Sometimes customers want simple installations for applications they purchase. They do not want to step through complex guided procedures with several dialog boxes and lots of options. They want to make just two or three mouse clicks and nothing more. To accomplish this particular scenario, Microsoft created ClickOnce, the one-click deployment technology for .NET Framework applications. ClickOnce is useful for installations that are just a few steps, but it is the easiest way for bringing automatic updating capabilities to your applications. In this chapter, you will learn about deploying client applications with ClickOnce and discover some new features.

Introducing ClickOnce

ClickOnce is the deployment technology offered by all Visual Studio editions, and it enables you to create distribution procedures for Windows client applications in a simple way, according to *one-click deployment* logic. The idea behind ClickOnce is that the final user will have the ability to install an application with a minimum number of mouse clicks and interactions, even if the user does not have administrative rights on the machine. This technology was first introduced with .NET Framework 2.0 and Visual Studio 2005 and has been improved over the years. Further improvements were introduced in .NET 4.0 and Visual Studio 2010, and Visual Studio 2015 retakes them all. ClickOnce enables you to publish the deployment package to file system folders, FTP servers, and HTTP servers and can make applications available online, offline, or both. Before illustrating how you publish deployment packages with ClickOnce, it is important to understand how it works and when you should use it.

How ClickOnce Handles Applications

Different from the Windows Installer engine, which is integrated in the operating system, ClickOnce is integrated with the .NET Framework. Applications deployed via ClickOnce run in a security sandbox that is fully managed by the .NET Framework. This provides great flexibility because the .NET Framework can apply managed trust rules to ClickOnce-deployed applications and provide the infrastructure for automating application updates. For example, thanks to the .NET integration, developers can write code to programmatically check for updates or to access the deployment system. However, ClickOnce does have some limitations for Windows Installer. The next section explains these limitations and provides information on when you should use ClickOnce for your deployments.

When to Use ClickOnce

ClickOnce is a powerful technology and is useful when you need to deploy applications that require a minimum amount of interaction from the user. ClickOnce is appropriate in the following scenarios:

▶ You want to provide your application with the capability of being frequently updated without writing a single line of code.

▶ Your application makes use of third-party components that are not required to be installed into the global assembly cache.

▶ You want your application to be installed by nonadministrative users.

▶ You want to deploy add-ins for Microsoft Office.

▶ Your installation process does not require you to customize the target system other than creating shortcuts.

ClickOnce does have limitations you must consider when choosing the most appropriate deployment system:

▶ You cannot install assemblies to the global assembly cache.

▶ ClickOnce does not enable writing values to the Windows Registry.

▶ It does not enable deep installation customization.

▶ It does not let you choose the target folder for the application on the target machine. This is because, as ClickOnce is integrated with the .NET Framework, applications run inside a security sandbox managed by .NET which has its own folders.

If you need to perform just one of these customizations, ClickOnce is not appropriate, and you need to recur to Windows Installer by creating InstallShield projects for Visual Studio 2015 (as explained in the previous chapter). At this point, you will learn how to deploy applications with ClickOnce.

NOTE ON CLIENT APPLICATIONS

With the growth of WPF applications, ClickOnce has been erroneously considered as a technology for deploying these kinds of applications. This is true in part, meaning that ClickOnce is not limited to WPF applications, whereas it can deploy all kinds of Windows client applications, including Windows Forms and Console applications.

Deploying Applications with ClickOnce

To deploy an application with ClickOnce, you have three options: the Publish command in the Build menu, right-clicking the project in Solution Explorer, and selecting Publish or the Publish Now button in the ClickOnce configuration page within My Project. For now, focus on the first option. (The second option is covered in the next section.)

Create a new WPF project with Visual Basic and name it **ClickOnceDemo**. There is no need to write code for the application because a base for our example is enough. To deploy an application with ClickOnce, follow these steps:

1. Click **Build, Publish**. Visual Studio launches the Publish Wizard. Figure 50.1 shows the first dialog box of the wizard, in which you need to specify the location where the application will be published. Notice how the dialog box explains available possibilities, such as disk path, network shared path, or FTP server. Visual Studio 2015 no longer supports publishing to a web server directly, so in this case, you should first publish the application to a disk path and then upload files manually. You can change the target type and location by clicking **Browse**. For the current example, you will publish the sample application to a shared network path, which is a very common real-world situation. The shared folder will be called AppPublish. To create a network shared path, on either a web server or the local machine, you simply create a new folder, right-click its name, click **Properties**, and then access the Sharing tab in the Properties dialog. To understand how publishing works, you should grant yourself full access permissions so that you will be able to fine-tune permissions according to your needs.

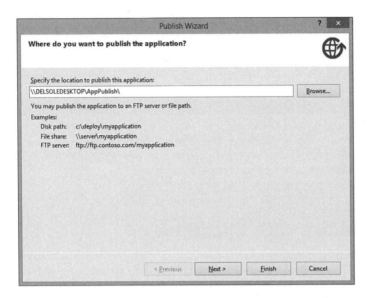

FIGURE 50.1   Choosing the target location for the ClickOnce deployment.

PUBLISHING TO FILE SYSTEM

Publish the application to a local folder on the file system if you want to deploy the application on supported media such as CD-ROM or zipped archives. This option can make the application available only offline.

PUBLISHING TO MICROSOFT AZURE

Although ClickOnce does not support direct publishing to a web server, you can publish your ClickOnce application to Microsoft Azure via App Service. In this way, you can quickly publish a ClickOnce application if you do not have your own server. This option requires some manual steps, including publishing your files to the BLOB storage. If you want to take advantage of this, have a look at this article from Jake Ginnivan: http://jake.ginnivan.net/clickonce-from-azure-blob-storage/.

2. Click **Next**. The second dialog box of the wizard lets you specify how users will install the application. Available options are **From a Web Site**, which you choose if you manually publish your files to a web server, **From a UNC Path or File Share**, which you choose in this case, and **From a CD-ROM or DVD-ROM**, which you choose if you publish the application to the local file system. Figure 50.2 shows how you provide information for the file share option. Remember to replace the server name with yours.

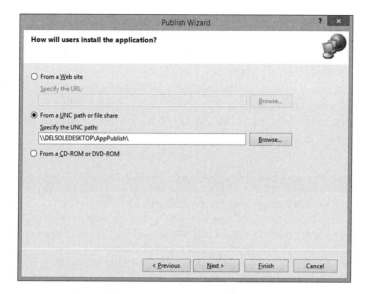

FIGURE 50.2   Specifying where the application will be available.

3. Click **Next**. The third dialog box of the wizard lets you specify if the application will be available offline. In this case, the .NET Framework creates a shortcut in the Start menu for launching the application and another one in the Add/Remove Programs tool for enabling uninstalling the application. Figure 50.3 shows how you set this option. This is all the information Visual Studio needs to create a ClickOnce deployment.

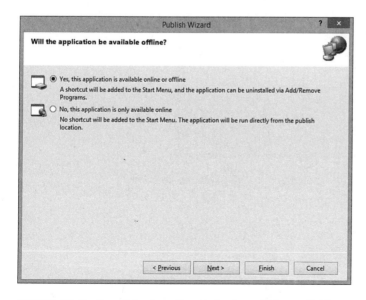

FIGURE 50.3   Specifying how the application will be available.

4. Click **Next**. You will see the last dialog box of the wizard showing the deployment information summary (see Figure 50.4).

5. Click **Finish**. Visual Studio generates all the required files and folders inside the *ServerName*\AppPublish shared folder. (These files and folders are described in more detail in the next section.) By default, Visual Studio generates a Publish.htm web page from which users can install the application. This page is very useful if you need to send users a convenient installation link. Figure 50.5 shows the page created for this sample application.

TIPS ON THE PUBLISH.HTM WEB PAGE

Being a simple HTML page, the default Publish.htm can be edited to accomplish your particular needs or just to provide a different appearance. In this case, the web page address points to the specified shared network path, but if you publish the application onto a real server, you probably publish the application files via an FTP account; users will be able later to install the application from a web address similar to the following: www.something.com/ClickOnceDemo/publish.htm.

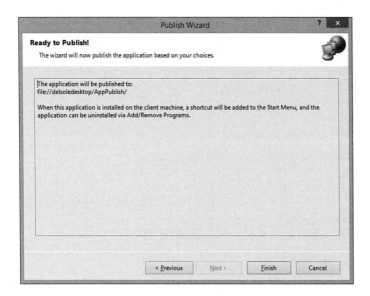

FIGURE 50.4   Collecting summary information for the ClickOnce deployment.

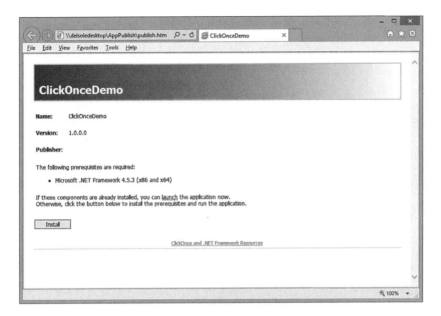

FIGURE 50.5   The web page from which the application will be downloaded.

Now click **Install**. The Web page launches a bootstrapper called Setup.exe, and you need to give this file permission to run. When the installer starts, a security warning informs you that the application is downloading from a shared network path with other information about the publisher, as shown in Figure 50.6.

FIGURE 50.6   ClickOnce shows a security warning asking confirmation before installing the application and providing information on the application's publisher and source.

Because you are the publisher and you trust yourself, click **Install**. This installs the application on your system, and a shortcut will be added to the Start menu. (If you have Windows 8.x, you will find the application in the list of installed programs.) To remove the application open the **Control Panel, Programs and Features** tool, and then select the application from the list.

Understanding the Structure of a ClickOnce Deployment

The publish process, whatever target you select, generates a subfolder containing the following elements:

▶ A bootstrapper file named Setup.exe, which launches the installation.

▶ The application manifest, which contains information on how the application has to be run in the ClickOnce context. The application manifest is a file with an .application extension, and the .NET Framework also allows you to launch the installation by double-clicking this file.

▶ The Publish.htm file (only if the application has been published to an FTP space or shared network path).

▶ A subfolder containing the actual application and related files. This subfolder has a version number that is recognized by the .NET Framework when the application finds updates.

If you publish the application to the file system for deploying to supported media such as a CD-ROM, you just need to copy to the media the content of the publish folder.

TIP

Unless you specify a publish folder, the deployment package is published to Bin\Debug\ Publish or Bin\Release\Publish depending on the selected configuration.

Configuring ClickOnce

You can customize your ClickOnce deployment by setting its property page in My Project. Click the **Publish** tab to activate the ClickOnce options designer represented in Figure 50.7.

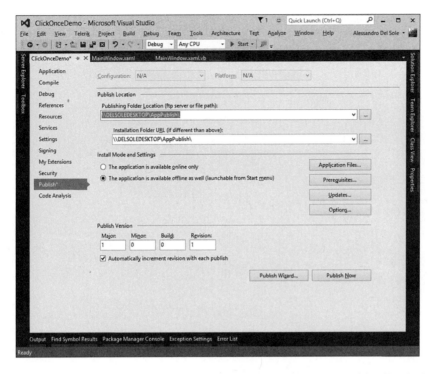

FIGURE 50.7   The ClickOnce properties designer enables customizing the deployment.

The upper part of the designer shows properties you already set with the Publish Wizard. The Publish Version group enables you to specify the deployment version that is important for allowing automatic updates. Automatically incrementing the revision number is a convenient way for allowing installed applications to check for updates. Just remember that the publish version is just a ClickOnce-related version and does not affect the application version. Now let's take a look at the other available options.

Application Files

By clicking the **Application Files** button, you can view or specify files that need to be included in the deployment package. If you want some required files included in the deployment package (such as documents or databases), you need to set their Build Action property as **Content**. Visual Studio can automatically classify files according to their role in the project, so this is something you rarely need to perform manually.

50

Prerequisites

Prerequisites are those files the application needs to work correctly. An example of this is runtime components such as the .NET Framework or third-party controls, which the installer installs on the target machine before the application is installed. Visual Studio can detect the appropriate prerequisites and select them for you, but there are situations in which you need to perform this manually. An example of this is when you need to install third-party components. Figure 50.8 shows the Prerequisites dialog box.

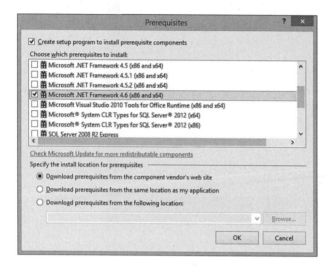

FIGURE 50.8   Selecting prerequisites for your applications.

If you use third-party components, ensure the producer made available a redistributable package you can include in the deployment prerequisites. The .NET Framework will always be included as a prerequisite because ClickOnce cannot predict if on the target machine the .NET Framework is already available.

Custom Prerequisites

Visual Studio 2015 does not provide a built-in functionality for packaging custom prerequisites. To accomplish this particular need, follow the instructions described in this page of the MSDN Library: http://msdn.microsoft.com/en-us/library/ms165429(v=vs.120).aspx.

Publishing Application Updates

One of the most important features in ClickOnce (and one of the reasons why you should use it) is the capability of updating applications without writing code to accomplish this. The idea is that you publish a new version of the application and when you run the old version, it checks for updates and automatically upgrades to the new version. Automatic updates are not available for applications published to the file system. To enable automatic updates, click the **Updates** button and then in the Application Updates dialog box, check **The Application Should Check for Updates** check box, as shown in Figure 50.9.

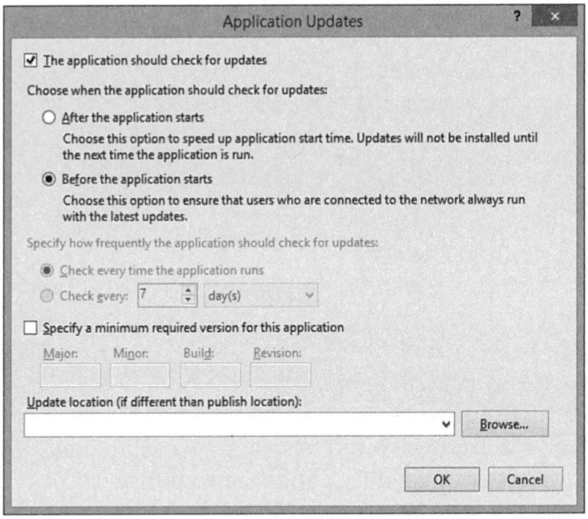

FIGURE 50.9   Enabling automatic updates.

You can decide whether the application will be updated before it starts (default option) so users always run the latest updates or if it will be updated after it starts, but in this case changes will be applied only at the next start. You can specify how frequently the application has to check for updates. The default setting is that the application checks for updates each time it runs. Otherwise, you can specify a time interval expressed in days, hours, or minutes. (This option is available only if you decide to update the application after it starts.)

TESTING UPDATES

When you enable updates and you want to ensure this feature works correctly, perform any kind of modification to the application (such as adding a button). Then publish it again. Finally, run the application and check that the new version downloaded and installed.

Options

When you click the **Options** button, you have access to additional features. For instance, you can edit the Description part in the deployment manifest so you can set a full description for your installation. Figure 50.10 shows an example of how you can specify information.

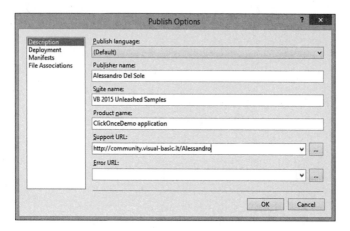

FIGURE 50.10   Setting description options for the deployment package.

Consider that the Publisher name will be used to create a root shortcuts folder in the Start menu, whereas the Suite name value will be used to create a shortcuts subfolder for the current application. The Deployment option enables you to set some aspects of the publish process. Figure 50.11 shows an example for setting these options. You can decide if the Publish.htm web page has to be created and shown, if the wizard generates an Autorun.inf file for automatic CD start, or if the deployment will use the .deploy extension. Pay attention to this particular option. Unless you uncheck this check box, the application files will be deployed with the addition of the .deploy extension, which might cause errors if your application attempts to access external files. If this is your case, disable the extension and deploy the application again. The Manifest option lets you establish how application URLs must be treated, but more particularly, it enables you to set if a desktop shortcut needs to be created for your application (see Figure 50.12).

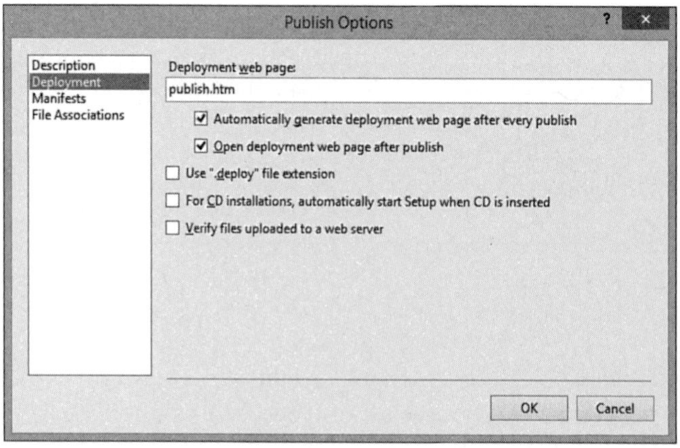

FIGURE 50.11   Setting deployment options.

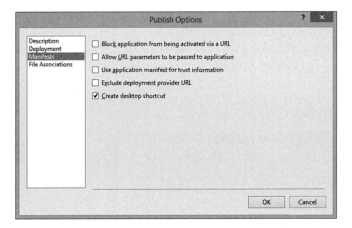

FIGURE 50.12   Setting manifest options.

Another useful option is the File Associations that is the only Registry customization allowed to ClickOnce. This enables you to assign a file extension to your executable.

Security Considerations

Depending on how an application is deployed or what system resources it needs to have access to, it will be considered under the Full Trust or the Partial Trust rules of .NET Framework Code Access Security. For example, an application that needs to access the Registry or other system resources needs to be full-trusted, but this is not a good idea if your application will be deployed via the Internet, which should instead be partial-trusted. You set the trust level for your ClickOnce deployments in the My Project, Security tab (see Figure 50.13).

The ClickOnce manifest can be signed with Full Trust or Partial Trust. This second option is divided into the Internet and intranet zones. You can choose the most appropriate for you or even create a custom configuration by editing the application manifest file (Edit Permissions XML button).

Providing Certificates

To make ClickOnce deployments the most trustable possible, you should use a certificate. If you look at Solution Explorer after you publish the application, you notice that Visual Studio has signed the assembly with a .pfx strong name. This is good in local test scenarios, but the most convenient way (although not mandatory) for providing security information to customers is adding an Authenticode certificate, especially if your application is deployed via the Internet. Visual Studio adds a test certificate, as demonstrated in Figure 50.14, which shows the Signing tab in My Project. The test certificate is intended for local

50

testing purposes only and should never be used in real-life deployment, in which you will prefer an Authenticode certificate you can purchase from the specific authorities. After you add a valid certificate, to sign the ClickOnce manifest, full and trusted information will be shown to your customers when they download and install the application.

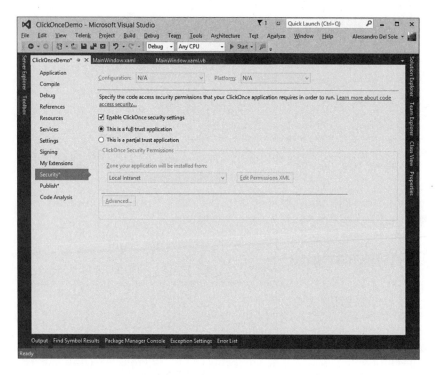

FIGURE 50.13   Specifying security settings for the ClickOnce deployment.

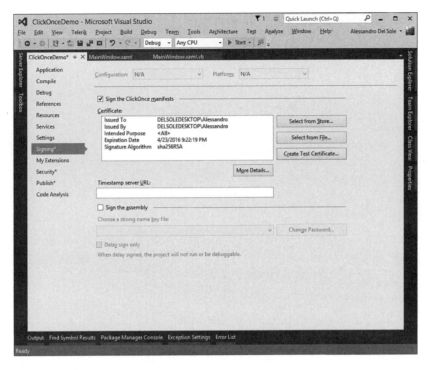

FIGURE 50.14   Signing the ClickOnce manifest.

Programmatically Accessing ClickOnce

As pointed out at the beginning of this chapter, ClickOnce is handled by the .NET Framework, but more precisely it is part of the .NET Framework. This means it can be accessed via managed code. The .NET Framework exposes the `System.Deployment` namespace that offers a managed way for interacting with ClickOnce. The subnamespace `System.Deployment.Application` and the `System.Deployment.Application.ApplicationDeployment` class are the most useful items because they offer objects that enable developers to programmatically access ClickOnce information from an application. The `ApplicationDeployment` class exposes a shared `CurrentDeployment` property that enables access to interesting information on the current application deployment. The following code demonstrates how you can use the property to retrieve information on the current deployment:

```
Private Sub GetClickOnceInformation()
    'Checks if the application has been deployed with ClickOnce
    If ApplicationDeployment.IsNetworkDeployed = True Then

        'Retrieves the data folder for this application
        Dim dataFolder As String = ApplicationDeployment.
                        CurrentDeployment.DataDirectory
```

50

```
      'Retrieves the path where updates will be
      'downloaded from
      Dim updatesPath As Uri = ApplicationDeployment.
                          CurrentDeployment.UpdateLocation
      'Gets the version number for updates
      Dim updateVersion = ApplicationDeployment.
                          CurrentDeployment.UpdatedVersion
      'Determines the last time that updates were checked for
      Dim lastUpdate As Date = ApplicationDeployment.
                          CurrentDeployment.TimeOfLastUpdateCheck

    End If
End Sub
```

You can programmatically check and download updates. This can be useful if you do not want the application to be automatically updated but you still want to provide the user the ability of updating the application manually. The following code demonstrates this:

```
Private Sub ApplicationUpdate()

    Dim isUpdateAvailable As Boolean = _
        ApplicationDeployment.CurrentDeployment.CheckForUpdate

    If isUpdateAvailable = True Then
        ApplicationDeployment.CurrentDeployment.Update()
    End If
End Sub
```

Both methods offer an asynchronous counterpart (`CheckForUpdateAsync` and `UpdateAsync`) that can be used as well.

Registration-Free COM

One of the biggest benefits from ClickOnce is users do not have administrator permissions that can install applications. Note that there are situations in which an application is deployed together with some COM libraries, but this can be a problem because these libraries need to be registered and a non-administrator user does not have the appropriate permissions for this. Fortunately, with ClickOnce you can take advantage of a technique known as Registration-Free COM, which refers to a COM library visible to the application only without the need of registration. You need to right-click the library name in Solution Explorer, References and select Properties. Finally, set the Isolated property as True (see Figure 50.15). When you build the project, Visual Studio generates a manifest file that provides the actual state of isolation of the library. Listing 50.1 shows a sample manifest file.

FIGURE 50.15   Isolating the library for Registration-Free COM.

LISTING 50.1   Sample Manifest for Registration-Free COM

```
<?xml version="1.0" encoding="utf-8"?>
<assembly xsi:schemaLocation="urn:schemas-microsoft-com:asm.v1 assembly.adaptive.
➥xsd"
          manifestVersion="1.0" xmlns:asmv1="urn:schemas-microsoft-com:asm.v1"
          xmlns:asmv2="urn:schemas-microsoft-com:asm.v2"
          xmlns:asmv3="urn:schemas-microsoft-com:asm.v3"
          xmlns:dsig="http://www.w3.org/2000/09/xmldsig#"
          xmlns:co.v1="urn:schemas-microsoft-com:clickonce.v1"
          xmlns:co.v2="urn:schemas-microsoft-com:clickonce.v2"
          xmlns="urn:schemas-microsoft-com:asm.v1"
          xmlns:xsi="http://www.w3.org/2001/XMLSchema-instance">
  <assemblyIdentity name="Native.MyCOMLibrary" version="1.0.0.0" type="win32" />
  <file name="wmp.dll" asmv2:size="11406336">
    <hash xmlns="urn:schemas-microsoft-com:asm.v2">
      <dsig:Transforms>
        <dsig:Transform
```

50

```
            Algorithm="urn:schemas-microsoft-com:HashTransforms.Identity" />
      </dsig:Transforms>
      <dsig:DigestMethod Algorithm="http://www.w3.org/2000/09/xmldsig#sha256" />
      <dsig:DigestValue> kaMt4lcikbZvNzRrAtbzkM6mAlQQ5fm56Jj8Ed6xmOk=
➡</dsig:DigestValue>
    </hash>
    <typelib tlbid="{6bf52a50-394a-11d3-b153-00c04f79faa6}"
          version="1.0" helpdir="" resourceid="0" flags="HASDISKIMAGE" />
    <comClass clsid="{6bf52a52-394a-11d3-b153-00c04f79faa6}"
              threadingModel="Apartment"
              tlbid="{6bf52a50-394a-11d3-b153-00c04f79faa6}"
              progid="WMPlayer.OCX.7"
              description="Windows Media Player ActiveX Control" />
  </file>
</assembly>
```

The manifest file is part of the setup process, so you need to include it in your ClickOnce
deployment (Visual Studio takes care of this for you). If you are interested in understanding how the Registration-Free COM technique works, you can read a specific article in the
MSDN Magazine available at http://msdn.microsoft.com/en-us/magazine/cc188708.aspx.

Summary

This chapter described how to build deployment packages with ClickOnce, the one-
click deployment technology included in the .NET Framework. You saw how to use the
Publish Wizard to create a setup procedure in a few steps. Then you learned how you can
configure the deployment options with the Visual Studio designer, including allowing
automatic updates and adding publisher information. You then stepped through security
considerations required so that you can understand what happens on the target machines.
Finally, the discussion focused on how to programmatically interact with ClickOnce
by writing Visual Basic code taking advantage of the System.Deployment.Application.
ApplicationDeployment class.

CHAPTER 51

Code Analysis: The .NET Compiler Platform and Tools

Writing code is just one part of the developer life. There are so many other aspects to consider in producing high-quality applications. For example, if you produce reusable .NET class libraries, you must ensure that your code is compliant with Common Language Specification, and this requires deep analysis. Another key aspect is performance. If you produce a great application with the most desired functionalities but with poor performance, perhaps your customer will prefer a faster and less-consuming application even if this has a minor number of features. Also, you need to analyze your code for issues and refactor for better maintainability. Visual Studio 2015 offers a number of integrated tools to analyze performance and improve the quality of your applications. In addition, the Visual Basic compiler is now built on top of the .NET Compiler Platform, which provides rich, live code analysis as you type and helps you find code issues and refactor your code in a more maintainable way. This is a key chapter in this book because it describes the most important new additions to the developer tools. In fact, in this chapter you discover how to build your own live analysis and refactoring tools with .NET Compiler Platform, and you learn how to leverage all the power of the new Diagnostic Tools, an incredible tool that deeply analyzes how your application spends time during its entire life cycle.

Live Code Analysis with the .NET Compiler Platform

In the past, you could only analyze your code for issues with static, build-time code analysis based on the Microsoft coding design rules and language-specific rules. This approach has the following limitations:

▶ You have to first build a project to get notified about code issues.

▶ Coding rules are targeted to solve problems developer had with older versions of the .NET Framework.

▶ It is difficult to extend coding rules with domain-specific analysis.

In Chapter 6, "Errors, Exceptions, and Code Refactoring," you learned that Visual Studio 2015 allows you to detect and fix code issues via the light bulb and quick actions. As in the past, the Visual Basic compiler still performs live code analysis as you type; it still highlights errors and warnings with colored squiggles under a code issue and suggests one or more ways to fix each issue via a very convenient preview. As a recap, Figure 51.1 shows how you fix an error about a not-yet-defined interface, and Figure 51.2 shows how you can refactor a method body by introducing an inline temporary variable.

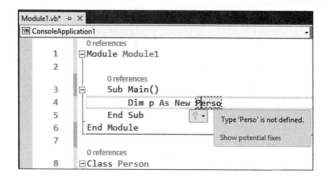

FIGURE 51.1   The light bulb shows potential fixes for your code, with a preview.

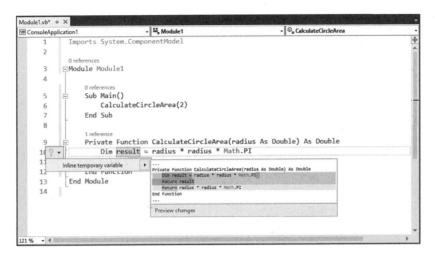

FIGURE 51.2   Refactoring a method body.

The huge differences between Visual Basic 2015 and earlier versions are that now live code analysis is built on the .NET Compiler Platform, it is not limited to a few rules coded at Microsoft, and it has been opened up to everyone. Live analysis in Visual Basic 2015 is based on two kinds of components: *analyzers* and *code refactorings*. As their names imply, an analyzer detects errors and code issues, and it suggests potential fixes via the light bulb; a code refactoring allows you to rewrite a piece of code in a more maintainable way. The Visual Basic and C# compilers expose the analysis APIs, so that these can be consumed by developer tools, including Visual Studio 2015. With the .NET Compiler Platform, developer tools can analyze the syntax and semantics of a single code file, a project, or an entire solution. The very good news is that you can build custom analyzers and code refactorings that integrate with the light bulbs and that offer custom quick actions. This means you can write an infinite number of domain-specific live analysis tools that you can easily share with other developers either as NuGet packages or as Visual Studio extensions, and it takes just a few lines of code and limited effort. For example, if your business is producing reusable class libraries or controls, you can also produce analyzers that help other developers get the most out of your products.

Of course, the .NET Compiler Platform is not limited to analyzers and code refactorings. In fact, it also provides the basis for many features in the Visual Studio 2015 IDE, including code editor features, expression evaluators, language services, visualizers, and much more. This chapter provides a high-level overview of the most important feature and biggest benefits in the .NET Compiler Platform for you as a developer. Do not forget to check for additional documentation and examples at http://github.com/dotnet/roslyn.

Before you learn how to build custom analyzers and refactorings, you must understand how the .NET Compiler Platform is organized and what layers and objects make it possible to interact with code and compilers with limited effort.

Getting Started with the .NET Compiler Platform

The .NET Compiler Platform has two main layers of APIs, which empower features like code fixes and refactorings: the Compiler APIs and the Workspaces APIs. Some of these APIs empower some of Visual Studio 2015's features and tools, including (but not limited to) the source code compilation process. Figure 51.3 shows this layered architecture.

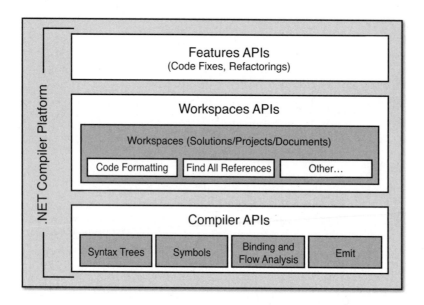

FIGURE 51.3   Layered architecture of the .NET Compiler Platform.

The Compiler APIs layer represents the object model related to syntactic and semantic information exposed at each phase of the compiler pipeline. It also includes an immutable snapshot of a single invocation of a compiler; this immutable snapshot includes assembly references, source code files, and compiler options.

Visual Basic and C# languages have distinct compiler APIs, which are very similar but tailored to each language. This layer includes the Diagnostic APIs, which you work with in this chapter. The Diagnostic APIs are extensible APIs that allow compilers to analyze everything in your code, from syntax to semantics, to produce errors, warnings, squiggles, and related diagnostics for each code issue. This extensible set of APIs integrates naturally with tools such as MSBuild and Visual Studio 2015.

SCRIPTING API

According to the official documentation, at this writing, the .NET Compiler Platform team at Microsoft is working on a Scripting APIs layer that allows you to compile and execute code snippets and accumulate a runtime execution context. At the moment, this layer is available on GitHub at http://source.roslyn.io, but it will not ship as part of .NET Compiler Platform 1.0.

The second layer is the Workspaces APIs, which is a fundamental layer for performing code analysis. It exposes an object model that represents and organizes all the information available in a solution; this model provides direct access to the compiler's object model without requiring you to parse source code files or configure compile options and dependencies. In addition, this layer implements a common set of APIs that offer code analysis and refactorings for tools like Find All References, code generation, and code formatting in Visual Studio 2015.

Assemblies and Namespaces

Most objects you use to build analyzers and code refactorings are exposed by the Microsoft.CodeAnalysis.dll and Microsoft.CodeAnalysis.VisualBasic.dll assemblies, as well as from the `Microsoft.CodeAnalysis` and `Microsoft.CodeAnalysis.VisualBasic` namespaces. Additional libraries, namespaces, and objects are mentioned throughout this chapter. If you are interested in discovering more about assemblies, namespaces, and type definitions in the .NET Compiler Platform, you can browse the Reference Source online, available at http://source.roslyn.io, which also provides the source code for compilers and the other APIs.

Understanding Syntax

The Compiler APIs layer exposes the lexical and syntactic structure of source code through *syntax trees*. These are very important because they allow tools, such as Visual Studio, to process the syntactic structure of the source code in a project; in addition, they allow you to rearrange the code in a managed way without working against pure text. They serve as the basis for compilation, code analysis, refactoring, and code generation, and they constitute the main entry point to identify and categorize the many structural elements of a language. Syntax trees represent everything the compiler finds in the source code—including lexical constructs, white spaces, comments, and syntax tokens—exactly as typed. This also means a syntax tree can be round-tripped back to the text it was parsed from, so you can use syntax trees to create the equivalent text.

Syntax trees are also important for another reason: You can edit and replace a syntax tree with a new tree without editing the actual text. Syntax trees have an important characteristic: They are immutable. This means that after you get an instance of a syntax tree, it never changes, and if you want to edit a syntax tree, you actually create a new one based on the existing tree. This provides thread-safety and allows multiple developers to interact with the same syntax tree without locking or duplication problems. Immutability is a key concept in the .NET Compiler Platform, and you will get more details when creating custom analyzers later in this chapter. Syntax trees are made of syntax nodes, syntax tokens, and syntax trivia, and the best way to get started with them is to use the Syntax Visualizer tool.

Investigating Syntax with the Syntax Visualizer

To familiarize yourself with syntax in the .NET Compiler Platform, you can use an important tool known as Syntax Visualizer. In Visual Studio 2015, select **Tools, Extensions and Updates**. In the Extensions and Updates dialog (see Figure 51.4), search online for the .NET Compiler Platform Syntax Visualizer tool and install it.

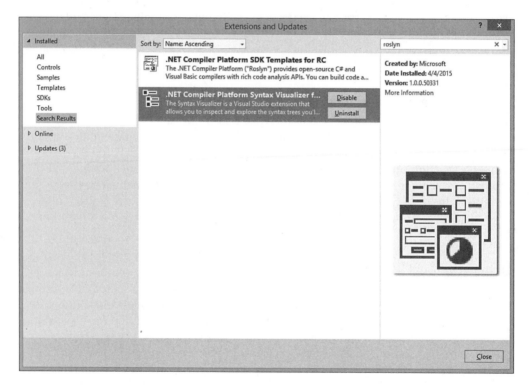

FIGURE 51.4   Installing the .NET Compiler Platform Syntax Visualizer.

Once it is installed, create a new Console project with Visual Basic. Then select **View, Other Windows, Roslyn Syntax Visualizer**. This tool window has two areas. The upper area, called Syntax Tree, provides a hierarchical view of the syntax tree for the current code file (see Figure 51.5), and the view is updated as you click anywhere in the code or as you type. Every element has a different color, according to its meaning: Blue represents a syntax node, green represents a syntax token, maroon represents a trivia (either leading or trailing), and pink highlight represents code that has diagnostics (such as errors or warnings). You can see this information at any time by clicking Legend. This chapter often refers to *diagnostics* to mean either errors or warnings or both.

Roslyn Syntax Visualizer
Syntax Tree
Legend
CompilationUnit [0..110)
ModuleBlock [0..108)
ModuleStatement [0..14)
ModuleKeyword [0..6)
Trail: WhitespaceTrivi
IdentifierToken [7..14)
SubBlock [22..94)
SubStatement [22..32)
SubKeyword [22..25)
IdentifierToken [26..30)
ParameterList [30..32)
LocalDeclarationStatement [42..81)
DimKeyword [42..45)
VariableDeclarator [46..81)
ModifiedIdentifier [46..53)
IdentifierToken [46..53)
Trail: WhitespaceTrivia [53..54)
SimpleAsClause [54..63)
EqualsValue [64..81)
EndSubStatement [87..94)
EndModuleStatement [98..108)
EndOfFileToken [110..110)
Blue SyntaxNode
Green SyntaxToken
Lead:Maroon Leading SyntaxTrivia
Trail:Maroon Trailing SyntaxTrivia
Pink Has Diagnostics

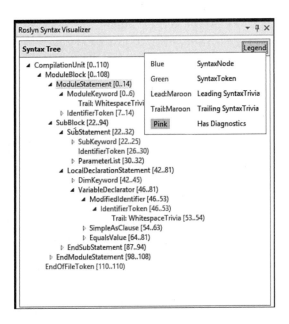

FIGURE 51.5 Browsing the syntax tree with the Syntax Visualizer.

The lower area of the Syntax Visualizer is called Properties and shows properties for the selected item in the syntax tree. Figure 51.6 shows an example.

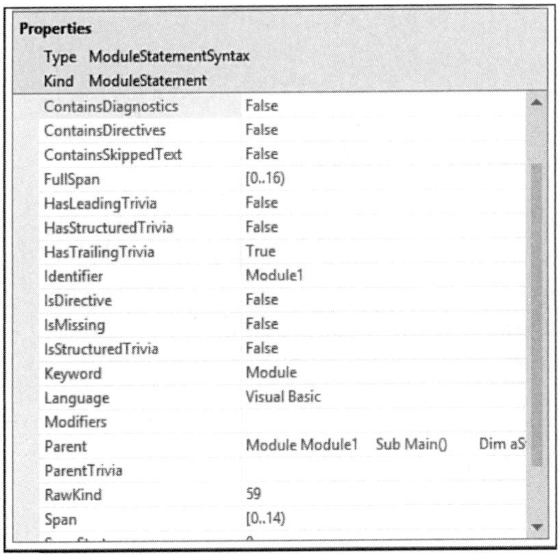

Properties
Type ModuleStatementSyntax
Kind ModuleStatement
ContainsDiagnostics False
ContainsDirectives False
ContainsSkippedText False
FullSpan [0..16)
HasLeadingTrivia False
HasStructuredTrivia False
HasTrailingTrivia True
Identifier Module1
IsDirective False
IsMissing False
IsStructuredTrivia False
Keyword Module
Language Visual Basic
Modifiers
Parent Module Module1 Sub Main() Dim aS
ParentTrivia
RawKind 59
Span [0..14)

FIGURE 51.6 Visualizing properties for syntax nodes, tokens, and trivia.

You can also use the Properties area to understand the type and the kind of each element in the tree, such as syntax nodes, syntax tokens, and syntax trivia. When you build analyzers and code refactorings later in this chapter, you will get more detailed information and will use the Syntax Visualizer many times. You should take some time to browse the Syntax Visualizer to see how your code is represented, including when you write new code, which you will do many times in this chapter.

Now it is time for a more thorough discussion about syntax elements in the .NET Compiler Platform.

Syntax Nodes

Syntax nodes are primary elements in the syntax trees. They represent constructs such as statements, declarations, clauses, and expressions. Each syntax node has a corresponding class that derives from `Microsoft.CodeAnalysis.SyntaxNode`. Syntax nodes always have other child nodes and tokens. A syntax node exposes a `Parent` property, which allows you to access the parent node, which is immutable. You have three options for accessing a syntax node's child nodes:

▶ You can access named properties specific to each node type. For example `ClassStatementSyntax` has both `ClassKeyword` and `Identifier` properties. This option usually returns children with a more specific type than other methods, which generically return `SyntaxNode`.

▶ You can use the `ChildNodes` method, which returns a sequential list of nested syntax nodes, but it does not contain syntax tokens.

▶ You can use the `Descendant` methods, such as `DescendantNodes`, `DescendantTokens`, and `DescendantTrivia`. Each respectively returns a list of nodes, tokens, and trivia that exist in the subnode.

You very often work with syntax nodes when building analyzers and code refactorings.

Syntax Tokens

Syntax tokens include keywords, identifiers, literals, and punctuation, and they are never parents of other syntax nodes or syntax tokens. A syntax token is represented by an instance of the `SyntaxToken` structure and is therefore a value type. `SyntaxToken` exposes the `Value` property of type `Object`, which returns the raw value of the object it represents, whereas the `ValueText` property of type `String` returns the result of invoking `ToString()` on `Value`. To understand the difference, consider a value of 16: `Value` always contains 16, whereas `ValueText` can either contain 16 or `&H10` or `&O20` for different representations. These three tokens have different text but the same value (16).

Syntax Trivia

Syntax trivia refers to portions of source text that are typically insignificant to understanding the code, such as white spaces, end-of-line terminators, preprocessing directives, and comments (including XML comments). They are not included in the syntax tree as child nodes, but they actually exist in the syntax tree to maintain full fidelity with the source text. In fact, when you generate a new syntax tree from an existing one, you must include trivia. A trivia is represented by the `SyntaxTrivia` structure (still a value type), and you can investigate a node's trivia with the `LeadingTrivia` and `TrailingTrivia` collections.

Spans

Syntax nodes, syntax tokens, and syntax trivia know their positions in the source text and the number of characters they consist of. These types of information are referred to as *spans* and are represented by the `TextSpan` object. Syntax nodes expose the `Span` and `FullSpan` properties, both based on `TextSpan`. The `Span` property represents the text span from the start of the first token in the syntax node's subtree to the end of the last token, and it does not include the span of any trivia. `FullSpan` is like `Span`, but it includes the span of trivia. Detecting the code position with spans is very important to understand where error/warning squiggles must be placed in the code when writing analyzers.

Kinds

Kinds identify the exact syntax elements you are working with. They are expressed via the `Kind` extension method, of type `Integer`, that each node, token, or trivia exposes. Visual Basic has the `SyntaxKind` enumeration with integer values that represent all possible nodes, tokens, and trivia. With `Kind`, it is easier to disambiguate syntax node types that share the same node class.

Understanding Semantics

Syntax trees describe all the declarations and logic in the source code, and they help you understand the syntactic and lexical structure of a code file. However, there is more to a program than just syntax. The semantics of a program—that is, the way the language rules are applied to produce meaningful results—are necessary to get a complete picture. For example, depending on the context, it is possible that exactly the same textual representation could reference a method or property of an object returned by a local variable, field, or property; invoke shared members; or qualify a type or namespace.

The .NET Compiler Platform includes the Compilation, Symbol, and Semantic model types.

Compilation

A compilation is an object of type `Microsoft.CodeAnalysis.Compilation` that represents everything needed to compile a Visual Basic program, such as source code files, assembly references, and compiler options (similar to a project in Visual Studio). It makes it easier to get detailed information about elements in the source code because everything needed in the process is in one place. The compilation also represents each declared type, member, or variable as a symbol and contains several methods that help find and relate symbols that have been declared in the source code or imported from an external assembly. A compilation is also immutable, which means you can create a new compilation based on an existing one and supply the required changes.

Symbols

Every namespace, type, type member, parameter, or local variable—both from the source text and from an external assembly—is represented by a *symbol*, which also includes metadata and information on other referenced symbols. The Compilation type offers a number of methods and properties for finding symbols. These offer a common representation of namespaces, types, and members via objects that derive from ISymbol, each with methods and properties tailored for a given symbol type. For instance, method symbols are of type IMethodSymbol.

Symbols are so important in the .NET Compiler Platform that even the Syntax Visualizer tool provides a way to get a visual symbol representation. In fact, you can right-click an element in the syntax tree and select **View Symbol (if any)**. Symbol information is then presented in the Properties area of the tool window. Figure 51.7 shows an example based on the symbol for a submethod.

FIGURE 51.7 Visualizing symbol information for a method.

Symbols are not available for syntax tokens and trivia. As you get more familiar with the .NET Compiler Platform, you will better understand how symbol information can save you a lot of time. You will see a practical example of symbols in one of the upcoming sample analyzers.

Semantic Model

The semantic model is represented by an object of type `Microsoft.CodeAnalysis.SemanticModel`, and it provides all the semantic information for a source code file. For example, the semantic model lets you know what symbols are referenced at a specific location, all diagnostics (errors and warnings), and the result types for any expressions. It also includes APIs for data and control flow analysis so that you can perform tasks like retrieving variables captured or written in a given span of text or detecting whether a line of code is reachable through normal program execution. There is a separate `SemanticModel` for each syntax tree in a compilation.

Understanding Workspaces

A workspace is a representation of a solution, as a collection of projects, where each project has a collection of documents. A document typically represents a source code file. A solution is an immutable model of projects and documents and is represented by the `Microsoft.CodeAnalysis.Solution` object; projects and documents are represented by the `Microsoft.CodeAnalysis.Project` and `Microsoft.CodeAnalysis.Document` objects, respectively. You can select the workspace to analyze and then get the semantic model and syntax trees via methods like `GetSemanticModelAsync` and `GetSyntaxTreeAsync`.

Now that you have gotten an overview of the main points of interest in the .NET Compiler Platform, it is time to start building analyzers and learning additional concepts while writing code.

Building Analyzers

An analyzer detects domain-specific errors and code issues as you type, and it suggests proper fixes with the light bulb. Building an analyzer requires specific project templates, so to start you need to install the following additional software:

- ▶ Visual Studio 2015 SDK, available at http://www.visualstudio.com/en-us/downloads

- ▶ .NET Compiler Platform SDK templates, which you can download via the Extensions and Updates dialog in Visual Studio

Once these are installed, you will find three specific project templates in the Extensibility node of the New Project dialog (see Figure 51.8):

- ▶ **Stand-Alone Code Analysis Tool**—This allows you to create a code analysis command line application, but it is not covered in this chapter because it is for more advanced scenarios and does not fit well in explaining how to integrate custom analysis logic into Visual Studio.

- ▶ **Analyzer with Code Fix (NuGet + VSIX)**—This allows you to create an analyzer with one or more code fixes, and it includes all you need to share your analyzer via either a NuGet package or a VSIX package for Visual Studio.

- ▶ **Code Refactoring (VSIX)**—This template allows you to create a custom code refactoring that integrates with the light bulb.

FIGURE 51.8   Project templates for the .NET Compiler Platform.

Next, you will build two different analyzers, and then you learn how to build a code refactoring.

Your First Analyzer: Replacing `List(Of T)` with `ObservableCollection(Of T)`

As you know, in some situations, using a `List(Of T)` collection is not the best choice. For instance, in XAML-based development platforms, such as WPF and Windows Store apps, using `ObservableCollection(Of T)` is the recommended choice because it supports change notification on data-binding. Therefore, the new analyzer you will build next will detect whether the code instantiates a `List(Of T)`, squiggle the declaration with a green warning, and suggest a fix to replace that object with an `ObservableCollection(Of T)`.

Create a new project of type Analyzer with Code Fix (see Figure 51.8) and name it ObservableCollectionAnalyzer. The selected template provides an analyzer skeleton whose instructional purpose is to detect and fix lowercase letters in the names of types. Explore the auto-generated code is left to you as an exercise because in this section you start with analysis from scratch.

You need to use Solution Explorer to explore the solution, which contains three projects. The first project is a portable class library that implements the analyzer; it is called ObservableCollectionAnalyzer (Portable.) This project contains two code files: DiagnosticAnalyzer.vb, which implements the analysis logic and raises the desired errors or warnings, and CodeFixProvider.vb, where you implement code fixes that will integrate with the light bulb.

CODE FILENAMES

Both DiagnosticAnalyzer.vb and CodeFixProvider.vb are conventional names that the project template generates for you. You can rename the code files to make it easier to understand what analyzers and fixes they provide, and this is something you will do if you add multiple analyzers in one library.

The second project is a test project (ObservableCollectionAnalyzer.test) that contains unit tests to test your analyzer in a separate environment. This is not discussed in this chapter because it requires knowledge of unit testing, which is explained in Chapter 53, "Testing Code with Unit Tests and Test-Driven Development," and because it is not relevant at this point.

The third project is a VSIX package that allows you to deploy your analyzer to Visual Studio with a .Vsix installer. This project must always be the startup project because it will be used to test the analyzer in the experimental instance of Visual Studio 2015. Before implementing the analysis logic, you must understand what syntax nodes you are going to analyze. To accomplish this, you need the Syntax Visualizer tool discussed earlier. Open another instance of Visual Studio 2015, create a new Console project, and write the `Main` method as follows:

```
Sub Main()
    Dim newList As New List(Of String)
End Sub
```

Select `New List(Of String)`, which is what the analyzer wants to recognize as a code issue. As you can see from Figure 51.9, the Syntax Visualizer tool shows that it corresponds to a syntax node of type `ObjectCreationExpression`. The Properties area of the Syntax Visualizer shows that it is represented by an object of type `ObjectCreationExpressionSyntax`. You do not need to investigate the entire syntax tree to discover all the `ObjectCreationExpression` elements and then iterate through each of them to discover whether it is a declaration of a new `List(Of T)` instance. This is because the syntax tree provides very fast and easy ways to directly reach only the elements you actually need. Open the DiagnosticAnalyzer.vb code file and consider the following code:

```
<DiagnosticAnalyzer(LanguageNames.VisualBasic)>
Public Class ObservableCollectionAnalyzerAnalyzer
    Inherits DiagnosticAnalyzer

    Public Const DiagnosticId = "ObservableCollectionAnalyzer"
    ' You can change these strings in the Resources.resx file.
    ' If you do not want your analyzer to be localize-able,
    ' you can use regular strings for Title and MessageFormat.
    Friend Shared ReadOnly Title As LocalizableString =
        New LocalizableResourceString(NameOf(My.Resources.AnalyzerTitle),
                                      My.Resources.ResourceManager,
                                      GetType(My.Resources.Resources))
```

```
Friend Shared ReadOnly MessageFormat As LocalizableString =
    New LocalizableResourceString(NameOf(My.Resources.AnalyzerMessageFormat),
                                  My.Resources.ResourceManager,
                                  GetType(My.Resources.Resources))
Friend Shared ReadOnly Description As LocalizableString =
    New LocalizableResourceString(NameOf(My.Resources.AnalyzerDescription),
                                  My.Resources.ResourceManager,
                                  GetType(My.Resources.Resources))
Friend Const Category = "Naming"

Friend Shared Rule As New DiagnosticDescriptor(DiagnosticId,
                                               Title, MessageFormat,
                                               Category,
                                               DiagnosticSeverity.Warning,
                                               isEnabledByDefault:=True)


Public Overrides ReadOnly Property SupportedDiagnostics _
        As ImmutableArray(Of DiagnosticDescriptor)
    Get
        Return ImmutableArray.Create(Rule)
    End Get
End Property

Public Overrides Sub Initialize(context As AnalysisContext)
    ' TODO: Consider registering other actions
    ' that act on syntax instead of or in addition to symbols
    context.RegisterSymbolAction(AddressOf AnalyzeSymbol, SymbolKind.NamedType)
End Sub
```

Every analyzer class must be decorated with the `DiagnosticAnalyzer` attribute, which specifies the target language. Every analyzer class inherits from `Microsoft.CodeAnalysis.Diagnostics.DiagnosticAnalyzer`. This abstract class provides the common infrastructure for analyzers, based on the `SupportedDiagnostics` property and `Initialize` method. The `DiagnosticId`, `Title`, `MessageFormat`, `Description`, and `Category` fields determine the information that the analyzer sends to Visual Studio and that will be shown in the Error List window and in the light bulb. The default implementation provides support for localization, which involves storing string values in the Resources.resx file for the project, which you access by selecting **My Project, Resources**.

Notice that `NameOf` is used to get the corresponding constant value. For the sake of simplicity, suppose that the analyzer is available in English only and replace the default definitions with the following:

```
Public Const DiagnosticId = "WPF001"
Friend Shared Readonly Title As String = "List(Of T) in WPF"
Friend Shared Readonly MessageFormat As String = "WPF warning: {0}"
Friend Shared ReadOnly Description As String = _
```

```
"Detects invalid usages of List(Of T) in a WPF app"
Friend Const Category = "Syntax"
```

It is possible to replace field values with regular strings. The values of `DiagnosticId` and `MessageFormat` are displayed in the Error List window when the code issue is detected. The shared Rule field returns a `DiagnosticDescriptor`. This type describes an analyzer to Visual Studio via the preceding string values, plus it allows you to specify whether the diagnostics must be enabled by default and the severity of the diagnostics with a value from the `DiagnosticSeverity` enumeration. Available values are `Warning` (default), `Error`, `Info`, and `Hidden`. Remember that if the severity for your diagnostics is set to `Error`, the project will not be compiled until the code issue is fixed. `Warning` and `Info`, instead, do not prevent the project from being compiled.

The diagnostic descriptor is exposed to Visual Studio via the `SupportedDiagnostics` property. This tells Visual Studio how many diagnostics are in the analyzer and returns an immutable array with one element (`ImmutableArray.Create`). In this case, the analyzer offers only one diagnostic, so there is nothing to change. But if your analyzer offers multiple diagnostics, you should generate multiple descriptors and return them from `SupportedDiagnostics`.

The `Initialize` method is the main entry point of the analyzer. Here you register a set of actions to respond to compiler events, such as finding syntax nodes or declaring a new symbol (as in this case). To register an action, you invoke one of the available methods from the context object, of type `Microsoft.CodeAnalysis.Diagnostics.AnalysisContext`, which represents the context for initializing an analyzer. Table 51.1 shows available methods for registering actions.

TABLE 51.1   Methods for Registering Actions

Method	Description
RegisterSyntaxNodeAction	Registers an action to be executed at the completion of the semantic analysis of a syntax node.
RegisterSyntaxTreeAction	Registers an action to be executed after a code file is parsed.
RegisterSymbolAction	Registers an action to be executed at completion of the semantic analysis over an object deriving from `ISymbol`.
RegisterSemanticModelAction	Registers an action to be executed after a code document is parsed, in the context of the semantic model for the document.
RegisterCompilationStartAction	Registers an action to be executed when compilation starts.
RegisterCompilationEndAction	Registers an action to be executed when compilation completes.

Method	Description
RegisterCodeBlockStartAction	Registers an action to be executed at the start of the semantic analysis of a method body or of an expression that is outside a method body.
RegisterCodeBlockEndAction	Registers an action to be executed at the end of the semantic analysis of a method body or of an expression that is outside a method body.

It is important to choose the proper method for registering actions, and the choice you make depends on the type of element you want to analyze. The Syntax Visualizer tool tells you that you want to analyze objects of type ObjectCreationExpressionSyntax, which indirectly inherit from SyntaxNode, so the method of your choice in this example is RegisterSyntaxNodeAction. The first argument for this method is a delegate that performs the actual analysis and exactly the kind of syntax node via the SyntaxKind enumeration. Rewrite the Initialize method as follows:

```
Public Overrides Sub Initialize(context As AnalysisContext)
    context.RegisterSyntaxNodeAction(AddressOf AnalyzeCollection,
                            SyntaxKind.ObjectCreationExpression)

End Sub
```

Determining the correct value for SyntaxKind is very easy: The Properties area of the Syntax Visualizer shows the Kind value that corresponds to the value you have to pick up from the enumeration. Now delete the AnalyzeSymbol method, which you do not need, and create a new AnalyzeCollection method with the following definition:

```
Private Sub AnalyzeCollection(context as SyntaxNodeAnalysisContext)
End Sub
```

This is where you actually implement the analysis logic. The first thing to do is cast the syntax node into the appropriate node type, as follows:

```
Dim creationExpression = TryCast(context.Node, ObjectCreationExpressionSyntax)
If creationExpression Is Nothing Then Return
```

The SyntaxNodeAnalysisContext represents the analysis context for a syntax node, and its Node property represents the actual syntax node to be analyzed. The code converts the node type into ObjectCreationExpressionSyntax, which is the one the analysis logic is based on. If the conversion fails, it is not a node of the type you want to analyze, so the process ends here. Once you have an instance of the syntax node, you need a way to determine that it declares a new List(Of T). With the help of the Syntax Visualizer, you can see the list of properties for the `ObjectCreationExpressionSyntax` object, and you can see that a good way to understand what you need is to consider the `Type` property, which contains the full generic type declaration. So the second test you can run is the following:

```
If creationExpression.Type.ToString.StartsWith("List(Of") = False Then
    Return
Else
End If
```

The code simply checks whether the string representation for the `Type` property starts with the desired type name. If not, it means that it is not a syntax node you want to analyze, and so it returns. If instead the result is `True`, you have to create a new diagnostic with the specified rules, as follows:

```
If creationExpression.Type.ToString.StartsWith("List(Of") = False Then
    Return
Else
    Dim diagn = Diagnostic.Create(Rule, creationExpression.GetLocation,
            "Consider using ObservableCollection instead of List")
    context.ReportDiagnostic(diagn)
End If
```

The `Diagnostic.Create` method creates a new diagnostic for the current syntax node, using the rules defined in the `Rule` property. It also specifies the location for the squiggle, which you can retrieve via the `GetLocation` method of the syntax node instance. Finally, you send the diagnostic information to Visual Studio with the `ReportDiagnostic` method from the `SyntaxNodeAnalysisContext` class instance, which is `context` in this case. This is enough to detect the code issue.

Now you press **F5** to start the experimental instance of Visual Studio; the analyzer package will be deployed to the experimental instance and will be running inside an isolated environment that does not affect the development environment. When the experimental instance is running, create a new WPF project with Visual Basic and declare a new `List(Of String)` object wherever you like. Figure 51.9 shows how both the code editor and the Error List window show a warning based on the analyzer.

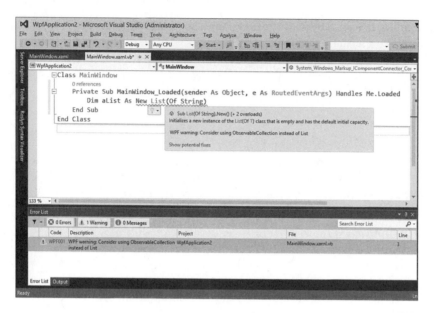

FIGURE 51.9   The analyzer shows a warning on the specified code issue.

CREATING ANALYZERS EFFICIENTLY

The secret to creating analyzers efficiently is implementing small tests, one at a time, instead of making deep syntax node investigations. In the preceding example, the code performs two small tests: It first checks whether the syntax node is of the proper type, and if not, it returns; then it checks whether the type is a generic list, which is another small test. When you take this approach, your analyzers will not impose excessive performance overhead on the coding experience.

Listing 51.1 shows the full code for the DiagnosticAnalyzer.vb file.

LISTING 51.1   Writing an Analyzer

```vb
<DiagnosticAnalyzer(LanguageNames.VisualBasic)>
Public Class ObservableCollectionAnalyzerAnalyzer
    Inherits DiagnosticAnalyzer

    Public Const DiagnosticId = "WPF001"
    Friend Const Title = "List(Of T) in WPF"
    Friend Const MessageFormat = "WPF warning: {0}"
    Friend Shared ReadOnly Description As String = _
    "Detects invalid usages of List(Of T) in a WPF app"
    Friend Const Category = "Syntax"
```

```vbnet
Friend Shared Rule As New DiagnosticDescriptor(DiagnosticId, Title,
                                       MessageFormat, Category,
                                       DiagnosticSeverity.Warning,
                                       isEnabledByDefault:=True,
                                       description:=Description)

Public Overrides ReadOnly Property SupportedDiagnostics As _
        ImmutableArray(Of DiagnosticDescriptor)
    Get
        Return ImmutableArray.Create(Rule)
    End Get
End Property

Public Overrides Sub Initialize(context As AnalysisContext)
    context.RegisterSyntaxNodeAction(AddressOf AnalyzeCollection,
                                SyntaxKind.ObjectCreationExpression)

End Sub

Private Sub AnalyzeCollection(context As SyntaxNodeAnalysisContext)
    'Check WPF
    If context.SemanticModel.Compilation.
        GetTypeByMetadataName("System.Windows.Navigation.JournalEntry") _
        Is Nothing Then Return

    Dim creationExpression =
        TryCast(context.Node, ObjectCreationExpressionSyntax)
    If creationExpression Is Nothing Then Return

    If creationExpression?.Type.ToString.StartsWith("List(Of") = False Then
        Return
    Else
        Dim diagn = Diagnostic.Create(Rule, creationExpression.GetLocation,
                    "Consider using ObservableCollection instead of List")
        context.ReportDiagnostic(diagn)
    End If

End Sub
End Class
```

Now the analyzer detects and highlights a code issue, but it needs to suggest potential fixes that will be listed in the light bulb. This is done in the CodeFixProvider.vb code file. In this file, you can find the definition for the ObservableCollectionAnalyzerCodeFixProvider class, which inherits from Microsoft. CodeAnalysis.CodeFixes.CodeFixProvider. This abstract class provides a common infrastructure for code fixes, and it has three methods: `FixableDiagnosticIds`, `GetAllFixProvider`, and `RegisterCodeFixesAsync`. The first method returns an immutable array with one element, representing the diagnostic ID with which it is associated and that can be fixed with the current class. The second method defines a way to provide fixes, which you can select from the `FixAllProvider` class. Following is the relevant code for this:

```
Imports Microsoft.CodeAnalysis.CodeGeneration
Imports Microsoft.CodeAnalysis.Formatting
Imports Microsoft.CodeAnalysis.Rename


<ExportCodeFixProvider("ObservableCollectionAnalyzerCodeFixProvider",
 LanguageNames.VisualBasic), [Shared]>
Public Class ObservableCollectionAnalyzerCodeFixProvider
    Inherits CodeFixProvider

    Public NotOverridable Overrides Function FixableDiagnosticIds() _
        As ImmutableArray(Of String)
        Return ImmutableArray.
        Create(ObservableCollectionAnalyzerAnalyzer.DiagnosticId)
    End Function

    Public NotOverridable Overrides Function GetFixAllProvider() As FixAllProvider
        Return WellKnownFixAllProviders.BatchFixer
    End Function
```

Notice how the class is decorated with the `ExportCodeFixProvider` attribute, which basically makes the code fix visible to the IDE. It requires you to specify the name and the supported languages. The `CodeFixProvider` base class also requires you to implement a method called `RegisterCodeFixesAsync`, which is where you implement your logic. You need to delete the auto-generated `MakeUppercaseAsync` method, which is not required, and replace the `RegisterCodeFixesAsync` definition with the following (see the comments for details):

```
Public NotOverridable Overrides Async Function _
    RegisterCodeFixesAsync(context As CodeFixContext) As Task
    'Get the root syntax node for the current document
    Dim root = Await context.Document.
        GetSyntaxRootAsync(context.CancellationToken).ConfigureAwait(False)

    'Get a reference to the diagnostic (warning squiggle) to fix
    Dim diagnostic = context.Diagnostics.First()
    'Get the location for the diagnostic
    Dim diagnosticSpan = diagnostic.Location.SourceSpan

    'Find the syntax node on the squiggle span
    Dim node = root.FindNode(context.Span)
```

```
' Register a code action that will invoke the fix.
context.RegisterCodeFix(
    CodeAction.Create("Replace List(Of T) with ObservableCollection(Of T)",
                Function(c) ReplaceListAsync(context.
                Document, node, c)), diagnostic)
End Function
```

The method argument is a structure of type CodeFixContext, which represents the context for code fixes, made of syntax nodes that have diagnostics. The code finds the root syntax node for the document (see the root declaration), and then it gets a reference to the diagnostic to fix. The code then uses the diagnostic.Location.SourceSpan property, which returns the location in the source code for the diagnostic. Next, it retrieves the syntax node that you must fix. The last step in the method is to register an action that will be displayed in the light bulb and that will invoke the fix. This is accomplished with the CodeFixContent.RegisterCodeFix method; this invokes the Microsoft.CodeAnalysis. CodeActions.CodeAction.Create method, passing the text message to show in the light bulb, a delegate that will perform the fix, and the diagnostic instance. For the current example, this delegate is called ReplaceListAsync, and its signature is the following:

```
Private Async Function ReplaceListAsync(document As Document,
                node As SyntaxNode,
                cancellationToken As CancellationToken) _
                        As Task(Of Document)
```

This function receives three arguments: the document instance, the syntax node that must be fixed, and a cancellation token. The document instance is required because you will create a new document from the existing one, replacing the old syntax node with the fixed node. In a code fix provider, you typically do not need to repeat tests you made in the analyzer class because the code fix provider receives the expected nodes. You can start writing the code fix with the following lines:

```
Dim root = Await document.GetSyntaxRootAsync
Dim objectCreationNode = CType(node, ObjectCreationExpressionSyntax)
```

The Document.GetSyntaxRootAsync method returns an instance of the syntax node for the document. The second line converts the passed syntax node instance into an ObjectCreationExpressionSyntax node, which is where you want to apply the code fix. To understand the next step, you must use the Syntax Visualizer. If you expand the ObjectCreationExpression node for the instance of the List(Of String) you wrote previously in a separate project, you will see that the generic type is represented with a GenericName element, mapped with a GenericNameSyntax object, which represents the collection's name (List); this also has a descendant node called TypeArgumentList, mapped with a TypeArgumentListSyntax object, which represents the generic type parameter for the collection ((Of String)). So your goal is to generate a new GenericNameSyntax for ObservableCollection and retrieve the existing TypeArgumentListSyntax. This is accomplished with the following code:

```
'Get the GenericNameSyntax
Dim nodes = objectCreationNode.DescendantNodes(node.Span)
Dim genericNameNode = CType(nodes.First, GenericNameSyntax)
Dim newGenericNameNode = SyntaxFactory.GenericName("ObservableCollection",
                                   genericNameNode.TypeArgumentList)
```

Since you saw that the `GenericName` element is the first descendant node for the `ObjectCreationExpression`, you can cast the first descendant node into a `GenericNameSyntax` object. The result is assigned to the `genericNameNode` variable, which represents an immutable generic name. To create a new generic name, you use the `SyntaxFactory.GenericName` method. The `SyntaxFactory` class exposes many methods to create new elements in a syntax node, and you will work with it very often. It is not possible here to summarize all available methods from the class, but you will get additional examples in the following subsections, and you can use IntelliSense to discover what it offers. The `SyntaxFactory.GenericName` method generates a new `GenericName` node with a new name, but with the existing type parameters taken from the immutable node's `TypeArgumentList` object.

Now that you have a new `GenericName`, you must create a new syntax node for it. Before you do this, you must consider that the `ObservableCollection` type requires an `Imports System.Collections.ObjectModel` directive, and you cannot assume that the user already added it; if you fix the collection issue, you must also ensure that the user does not need additional code fixes. Adding an `Imports` directive is possible, but it is a little trickier for you at this point. As an easier alternative, you can edit the new `GenericName` with its fully qualified name. The `SyntaxFactory` class has a `QualifiedName` method that returns a qualified name, but it requires you to specify additional tokens. The most recent APIs in the .NET Compiler Platform offer an additional opportunity with the `Microsoft.CodeAnalysis.Editing.SyntaxGenerator` class. This class allows you to generate syntax nodes that are language specific but that are semantically similar between languages. You get an instance for the current document as follows:

```
Dim generator = SyntaxGenerator.GetGenerator(document)
```

Now you have to generate a fully qualified name that must be bound to the generic name. This is accomplished with the `SyntaxGenerator.QualifiedName` method, whose first argument is the resulting expression from the invocation of `SyntaxGenerator.DottedName`, which produces a qualified name from a string containing dots. The second argument is the syntax node to be bound:

```
Dim boundNode = generator.
    QualifiedName(generator.
    DottedName("System.Collections.ObjectModel"),
          newGenericNameNode)
```

`boundNode` is the new syntax node that must replace the node with issues. The root variable, of type `SyntaxNode`, exposes a `ReplaceNode` method that you invoke as follows:

```
Dim newRoot = root.ReplaceNode(genericNameNode, boundNode)
```

At this point, you must generate a new document that contains the replaced node. The following code demonstrates this:

```
Dim newDocument = document.WithSyntaxRoot(newRoot)
Return newDocument
```

Since the document is an immutable object, you create a new one based on the existing instance and invoke the `WithSyntaxRoot` method, which basically replaces the existing syntax tree. As you get more experienced with the .NET Compiler Platform, you will discover that specialized classes representing syntax nodes, such as `ObjectCreationExpressionSyntax` and `GenericNameSyntax`, have `With*` methods that allow you to create new syntax nodes from an immutable node, replacing the desired information.

Now start the experimental instance of Visual Studio 2015 by pressing **F5** to discover how the code fix works. As you can see from Figure 51.10, the light bulb suggest the potential code fix you implemented, adding the proper qualified name for the new collection.

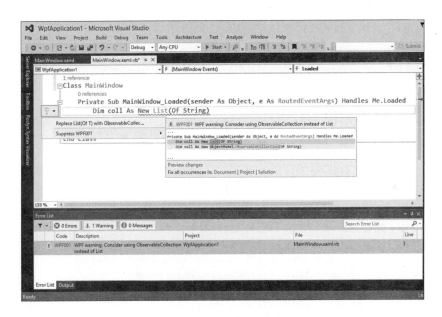

FIGURE 51.10   The code fix appears in the light bulb.

Listing 51.2 shows the full code for the CodeFixProvider.vb file.

LISTING 51.2   Writing a Code Fix Provider

```
Imports System.Collections.Immutable
Imports Microsoft.CodeAnalysis.CodeGeneration
Imports Microsoft.CodeAnalysis.Formatting
Imports Microsoft.CodeAnalysis.Rename
```

```vb
<ExportCodeFixProvider("ObservableCollectionAnalyzerCodeFixProvider",
 LanguageNames.VisualBasic), [Shared]>
Public Class ObservableCollectionAnalyzerCodeFixProvider
    Inherits CodeFixProvider

    Public NotOverridable Overrides Function GetFixableDiagnosticIds() As _
        ImmutableArray(Of String)
        Return ImmutableArray.
        Create(ObservableCollectionAnalyzerAnalyzer.DiagnosticId)
    End Function

    Public NotOverridable Overrides Function GetFixAllProvider() As FixAllProvider
        Return WellKnownFixAllProviders.BatchFixer
    End Function

    Public NotOverridable Overrides Async _
            Function RegisterCodeFixesAsync(context As _
            CodeFixContext) As Task
        'Get the root syntax node for the current document
        Dim root = Await context.Document.
            GetSyntaxRootAsync(context.CancellationToken).ConfigureAwait(False)

        'Get a reference to the diagnostic (warning squiggle) to fix
        Dim diagnostic = context.Diagnostics.First()
        'Get the location for the diagnostic
        Dim diagnosticSpan = diagnostic.Location.SourceSpan

        'Find the syntax node on the squiggle span
        Dim node = root.FindNode(context.Span)

        ' Register a code action that will invoke the fix.
        context.RegisterCodeFix(
            CodeAction.Create("Replace List(Of T) with ObservableCollection(Of T)",
                    Function(c) ReplaceListAsync(context.
                    Document, node, c)), diagnostic)
    End Function

    Private Async Function ReplaceListAsync(document As Document,
                    node As SyntaxNode,
                    cancellationToken As CancellationToken) _
                    As Task(Of Document)

        Dim root = Await document.GetSyntaxRootAsync

        Dim objectCreationNode = CType(node, ObjectCreationExpressionSyntax)
```

```
        'Get the GenericNameSyntax
        Dim nodes = objectCreationNode.DescendantNodes(node.Span)
        Dim genericNameNode = CType(nodes.First, GenericNameSyntax)

        Dim newGenericNameNode = SyntaxFactory.GenericName("ObservableCollection",
                            genericNameNode.TypeArgumentList)


        Dim generator = SyntaxGenerator.GetGenerator(document)


        Dim boundNode = generator.
            QualifiedName(generator.
            DottedName("System.Collections.ObjectModel"),
                    newGenericNameNode)


        Dim newRoot = root.ReplaceNode(genericNameNode, boundNode)
        Dim newDocument = document.WithSyntaxRoot(newRoot)


        Return newDocument
    End Function
End Class
```

With the help of the Syntax Visualizer, you could extend and improve the sample code to suggest fixes for every declaration of List(Of T) and not just new instance declarations, or to find where instances of List(Of T) are assigned to data-bound properties. As it is, the analyzer would search for the specified code issue in every project type, but this is not a good idea; using a List is still an appropriate choice in non-XAML-based development platforms, so you might want to restrict the analyzer to work only in WPF. You can iterate the References or ReferencedAssemblyNames properties for the SemanticModel. Compilation object in your ObservableCollectionAnalyzer class to understand what assemblies have been referenced in the active project, but this is a good choice only in advanced scenarios. Compilation exposes a method called GetTypeByMetadataName, which returns an INamedTypeSymbol object for the specified fully qualified object name. You can use this method against a type that you know exists only in the WPF platform, as in the following code:

```
If context.SemanticModel.Compilation.
    GetTypeByMetadataName("System.Windows.Navigation.JournalEntry") _
    Is Nothing Then Return
```

You know that the System.Windows.Navigation.JournalEntry type only exists in WPF, so if the method returns Nothing, it means that type is not available in the current platform; therefore, the analyzer does not apply to the current project, and it simply returns. The preceding code can be added as the very first small test in the AnalyzeCollection method of the analyzer.

You have successfully completed your very first analyzer. Now you are ready to build a second sample analyzer that involves additional information on the .NET Compiler Platform.

Your Second Analyzer: Live Analysis on Regular Expressions

Regular expressions are widely used to check whether a string matches a specified pattern. For example, you can use regular expressions to check whether a string contains a valid email address. The sample analyzer you'll build next provides live analysis to check whether a string matches the specified pattern. Of course, predicting all possible usages of regular expressions in a custom domain scenario is not possible here, but the code you are going to see will give you additional information, ideas, and understanding of the .NET Compiler Platform. You will see some concepts that you already learned in the previous example, so they will not be discussed again. The analyzer will basically analyze invocations to the `System.Text.RegularExpressions.Regex.IsMatch` method like the following:

```
Dim result = Regex.IsMatch("alessandro@something.com",
                    "[-0-9a-zA-Z.+_]+@[-0-9a-zA-Z.+_]+\.[a-zA-Z]{2,4}")
```

This expression returns `True` because the first argument, an email address, matches the specified pattern. The goal of the analyzer is to check whether the first method argument matches the specified pattern; if it doesn't match, the analyzer must raise a blocking error. With the help of the Syntax Visualizer (see Figure 51.11), you can see that `Regex.IsMatch` is an `InvocationExpression` in the syntax tree, mapped by an `InvocationExpressionSyntax` object, so this is the one you will work with. This object has two descendant nodes, a `SimpleMemberAccessExpression` (mapped by a `MemberAccessExpressionSyntax` object) that represents the `Regex.IsMatch` invocation, and an `ArgumentList` node of type `ArgumentListSyntax`; the latter has some descendant nodes, including two of type `SimpleArgumentSyntax`, each representing a method argument. While you explore these nodes, take a look at the Properties area of the Syntax Visualizer. You will work with these objects and see how powerful the .NET Compiler Platform is.

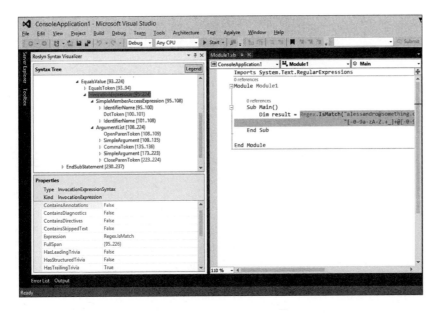

FIGURE 51.11   Understanding syntax nodes for method invocations.

Create a new analyzer project called RegexAnalyzer. In the DiagnosticAnalizer.vb file, change the auto-generated strings and Rule field as follows:

```
Public Const DiagnosticId = "RX001"
Friend Shared ReadOnly Title As String = "Regex error parsing string argument"
Friend Shared ReadOnly MessageFormat As String = "Regex error: {0}"
Friend Shared ReadOnly Description As String = _
"Checks for non-matching regular expressions"
Friend Const Category = "Syntax"
Friend Shared Rule As New DiagnosticDescriptor(DiagnosticId, Title,
                                MessageFormat, Category,
                                DiagnosticSeverity.Error,
                                isEnabledByDefault:=True,
                                description:=Description)
```

Notice that in this case, the diagnostic severity is Error, which means the target project cannot be compiled until the user fixes the code issue. Change the Initialize method as follows:

```
Public Overrides Sub Initialize(context As AnalysisContext)

    context.RegisterSyntaxNodeAction(AddressOf AnalyzeNode,
                                SyntaxKind.InvocationExpression)

End Sub
```

You are registering an action for an `InvocationExpression` syntax kind that corresponds to the `Regex.IsMatch` method invocation. Now you can implement the analysis logic. You will write very small tests to check whether the current syntax node is the one you are interested in. You start by checking whether the current node is of type `MemberAccessExpressionSyntax`:

```
Private Sub AnalyzeNode(context As SyntaxNodeAnalysisContext)
    Dim invocationExpr = TryCast(context.Node,
        InvocationExpressionSyntax)
    If TypeOf (invocationExpr.Expression) _
        IsNot MemberAccessExpressionSyntax Then Return
```

If it is a node of the required type, check whether it contains an invocation to a method called `IsMatch`:

```
Dim memberAccessExpr = DirectCast(invocationExpr.Expression,
    MemberAccessExpressionSyntax)
Dim check1 = memberAccessExpr?.Name.ToString
If memberAccessExpr?.Name.ToString <> "IsMatch" Then Return
```

The `Name` property for the `MemberAccessExpressionSyntax` object contains the name for the method invocation. If it differs from `IsMatch`, then the code returns. As an additional check, ensure that you are analyzing an `IsMatch` method that returns `Boolean`. To determine a method's return type, you need to first get its symbol information. You accomplish this with the following code:

```
Dim memberSymbol = DirectCast(context.SemanticModel.
    GetSymbolInfo(memberAccessExpr).Symbol, IMethodSymbol)
Dim result = memberSymbol.ToString


If Not memberSymbol?.ReturnType.ToString = "Boolean" Then Return
```

You get the symbol information of a node by invoking the `SemanticModel.GetSymbolInfo` method, passing the syntax node as the argument, and then converting the value of its `Symbol` property into a more specialized type; in this case, the result is converted into an `IMethodSymbol` type, which represents the symbol for a method. `IMethodSymbol` exposes a `ReturnType` property that contains the method's return type, which you can convert into the related string representation for comparison. Once you are sure the analyzer is working on the required method, you must get the value for its arguments. The `InvocationExpressionSyntax` instance has a property called `ArgumentList`, of type `ArgumentListSyntax`, that represents a syntax node containing arguments for a method call. You need to check whether the method has two arguments:

```
Dim argumentList = invocationExpr.ArgumentList
If argumentList?.Arguments.Count < 2 Then Return
```

The next step is to get the string value for both arguments so that you can check whether the first string matches the pattern in the second string. The following code snippet returns the value for the first `IsMatch` argument:

```
Dim exprLiteral = DirectCast(argumentList.Arguments(0).GetExpression,
    LiteralExpressionSyntax)
If exprLiteral Is Nothing Then Return
Dim exprLiteralOpt = context.SemanticModel.GetConstantValue(exprLiteral)
Dim stringLiteral = DirectCast(exprLiteralOpt.Value, String)
If stringLiteral Is Nothing Then Return
```

You invoke `GetExpression` on the first argument (with `0` index) in the `Arguments` collection in order to get an `ExpressionSyntax` object that represents the node for the argument. Since the argument is actually a literal, you cast it to a `LiteralExpressionSyntax` object. Then you need to know the value for the constant that the compiler generates to represent the literal at runtime. This is done by invoking the `SemanticModel.GetConstantValue` on the `LiteralExpressionSyntax` instance, which represents the syntax node for a literal. The `Object` returned must be converted into an understandable string, which you get by converting the `Value` property, of type `Object`, into `String`. In this way, the `stringLiteral` variable contains the string in the first `IsMatch` argument. With exactly the same techniques, you can retrieve the string that represents the regular expression pattern contained in the second `IsMatch` argument:

```
Dim regexLiteral = DirectCast(argumentList.Arguments(1).GetExpression,
    LiteralExpressionSyntax)
If regexLiteral Is Nothing Then Return
Dim regexOpt = context.SemanticModel.GetConstantValue(regexLiteral)
Dim patternLiteral = DirectCast(regexOpt.Value, String)
If patternLiteral Is Nothing Then Return
```

Now that you have both strings, you can use `Regex.IsMatch` to check whether they match; if they do not, you create a new diagnostic at the specified location:

```
If System.Text.RegularExpressions.Regex.IsMatch(stringLiteral,
    patternLiteral) = False Then
    Dim diagn = Diagnostic.Create(Rule, exprLiteral.GetLocation,
                "The specified string does not match the regular expression")
    context.ReportDiagnostic(diagn)
End If
```

If you now run the analyzer in the experimental instance of Visual Studio and write a bad regular expression matching, the IDE will show the analysis result as you type. Figure 51.12 shows an example based on a regular expression pattern that validates an email address against a malformed email address.

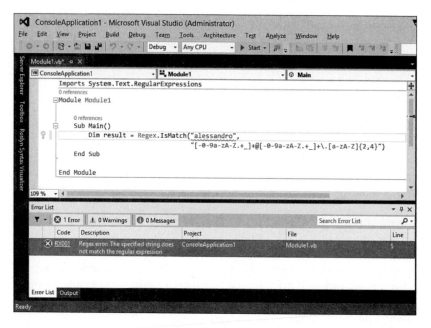

FIGURE 51.12   Live analysis detects errors in the specified regular expression.

Listing 51.3 shows the full code for the analyzer.

LISTING 51.3   An Analyzer to Detect Invalid Regular Expressions

```
<DiagnosticAnalyzer(LanguageNames.VisualBasic)>
Public Class RegexAnalyzerAnalyzer
    Inherits DiagnosticAnalyzer

    Public Const DiagnosticId = "RX001"
    Friend Shared ReadOnly Title As String = "Regex error parsing string argument"
    Friend Shared ReadOnly MessageFormat As String = "Regex error: {0}"
    Friend Shared ReadOnly Description As String = _
    "Checks for non-matching regular expressions"
    Friend Const Category = "Syntax"


    Friend Shared Rule As New DiagnosticDescriptor(DiagnosticId, Title,
                                                   MessageFormat, Category,
                                                   DiagnosticSeverity.Error,
                                                   isEnabledByDefault:=True)

    Public Overrides ReadOnly Property SupportedDiagnostics As _
        ImmutableArray(Of DiagnosticDescriptor)
        Get
```

```vb
            Return ImmutableArray.Create(Rule)
        End Get
    End Property

    Public Overrides Sub Initialize(context As AnalysisContext)

        context.RegisterSyntaxNodeAction(AddressOf AnalyzeNode,
                                SyntaxKind.InvocationExpression)
    End Sub

    Private Sub AnalyzeNode(context As SyntaxNodeAnalysisContext)
        Dim invocationExpr = TryCast(context.Node,
            InvocationExpressionSyntax)
        If TypeOf (invocationExpr.Expression) _
            IsNot MemberAccessExpressionSyntax Then Return

        Dim memberAccessExpr = DirectCast(invocationExpr.Expression,
            MemberAccessExpressionSyntax)
        Dim check1 = memberAccessExpr?.Name.ToString
        If memberAccessExpr?.Name.ToString <> "IsMatch" Then Return

        Dim resultSymbol = context.SemanticModel.
            GetSymbolInfo(memberAccessExpr).Symbol
        If TypeOf (resultSymbol) IsNot IMethodSymbol Then Return

        Dim memberSymbol = DirectCast(context.SemanticModel.
            GetSymbolInfo(memberAccessExpr).Symbol, IMethodSymbol)
        Dim result = memberSymbol.ToString

        If Not memberSymbol?.ReturnType.ToString = "Boolean" Then Return

        Dim argumentList = invocationExpr.ArgumentList
        If argumentList?.Arguments.Count < 2 Then Return

        Dim exprLiteral = DirectCast(argumentList.Arguments(0).GetExpression,
            LiteralExpressionSyntax)
        If exprLiteral Is Nothing Then Return
        Dim exprLiteralOpt = context.SemanticModel.GetConstantValue(exprLiteral)
        Dim stringLiteral = DirectCast(exprLiteralOpt.Value, String)
        If stringLiteral Is Nothing Then Return

        Dim regexLiteral = DirectCast(argumentList.Arguments(1).GetExpression,
            LiteralExpressionSyntax)
        If regexLiteral Is Nothing Then Return
        Dim regexOpt = context.SemanticModel.GetConstantValue(regexLiteral)
        Dim patternLiteral = DirectCast(regexOpt.Value, String)
```

```
        If patternLiteral Is Nothing Then Return

        If System.Text.RegularExpressions.Regex.IsMatch(stringLiteral,
            patternLiteral) = False Then
            Dim diagn = Diagnostic.
                Create(Rule, exprLiteral.GetLocation,
                "The specified string does not match the regular expression")
            context.ReportDiagnostic(diagn)
        End If
    End Sub
End Class
```

The analyzer performs a general-purpose analysis that works with any regular expressions possible, so it is very straightforward. Since you cannot predict fixes for every possible regular expression, a good idea is not to provide a code fix. In fact, when you create an analyzer, you are not obliged to offer code fixes. (The compiler itself has lots of analysis rules that do not provide code fixes.) With this second sample analyzer, you have learned additional concepts about the .NET Compiler Platform, and you are getting a more precise idea of how it empowers built-in features of Visual Studio 2015.

MULTIPLE ANALYZERS IN ONE LIBRARY

You can include multiple analyzers (and code refactorings, too) in a single library. The .NET Compiler Platform SDK also includes item template that you can use to add analyzers, code fixes, and code refactorings to the current project. Just right-click the project name in Solution Explorer and then select **Add, New Item** and choose the desired template in the Extensibility node of the Add New Item dialog.

Building a Code Refactoring

Code refactorings allow you to reorganize portions of code without losing their original behavior. Refactoring code involves, among the other things, simplifying code blocks, making code more readable by introducing inline variables, and removing redundant code. As you learned earlier in the book, Visual Basic gets integrated support for refactoring for the first time in Visual Studio 2015. This support is possible because integrated refactorings are powered by the .NET Compiler Platform. As for analyzers, you can create custom code refactorings that you can share with other developers via NuGet packages or via VSIX packages.

To create a refactoring, you use the Code Refactoring (VSIX) project template, as shown in Figure 51.13.

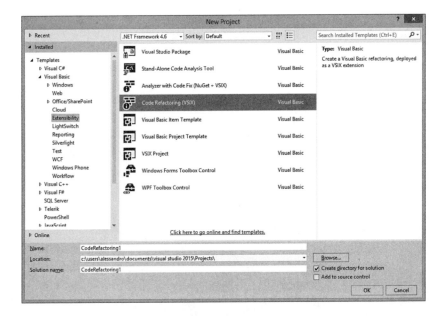

FIGURE 51.13   Creating a custom refactoring.

Creating a refactoring involves many techniques that you've already learned. When it comes to refactoring, the Syntax Visualizer tool is your best friend, helping you understand where to introduce a refactoring and what syntax nodes and objects you need. As a sample refactoring, you will build a tool that checks whether the first letter of an identifier in a private field is an uppercase letter. To understand what you need, in a Console project write the following field definition at the module level:

```
Private OneString As String, OneInt, TwoInt As Integer
```

FIELD DECLARATIONS WITH MULTIPLE TYPES

Remember that any field declaration can contain a number of identifiers and that these can represent different types. It is very important to keep this in mind when you write refactorings that target fields. This is why the current example declares a filed with many identifiers and different types.

Open the Syntax Visualizer. As you can see from Figure 51.14, a field is represented by the FieldDeclaration syntax node and mapped by a FieldDeclarationSyntax.

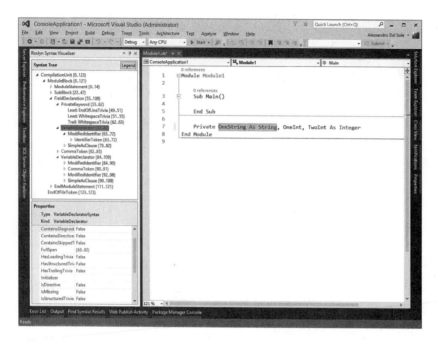

FIGURE 51.14   Using the Syntax Visualizer to understand the structure of a field.

Every `FieldDeclaration` has one `VariableDeclarator` element per identifier/type pair.
The `VariableDeclarator` element is mapped by a `VariableDeclaratorSyntax` object.
Every `VariableDeclarator` element has a `ModifiedIdentifier` element that represents the variable identifier, mapped by a `ModifiedIdentifierSyntax` object. There
are additional elements, such as `SimpleAsClause`, which represents the `As` keyword, or
`PredefinedType`, which represents a built-in type in the .NET Framework. Your goal is
to check the first letter for each variable identifier, so you do not need too many syntax
nodes. In fact, you need to find `FieldDeclaration` elements, their `VariableDeclarator`
nodes, and the `ModifiedIdentifier` nodes. Therefore, create a new project based on the
Code Refactoring template and name it PrivateFieldCodeRefactoring. When the project
is ready, you can see that it includes just one code file, called CodeRefactoringProvider.
vb. The auto-generated class inherits from `Microsoft.CodeAnalysis.CodeRefactorings.`
`CodeRefactoringProvider`, which offers the proper infrastructure to build a code refactoring via the `ComputeRefactoringAsync` method. This is where you write your refactoring
logic. Before writing any logic, add the following simple method, which returns a new
string in which the first letter is lowercase:

```
Private Function ConvertName(oldName As String) As String
    Return Char.ToLowerInvariant(oldName(0)) + oldName.Substring(1)
End Function
```

Now move inside `ComputeRefactoringAsync` and delete all of its auto-generated content.
You need to check whether the current syntax node is of type `FieldDeclarationSyntax`

and whether its modifier is `Private`; in fact, you want to avoid refactoring a `Public`, `Protected`, or `Protected Friend` field because these allow their first letter to be uppercase. This is accomplished with the following code:

```
Public NotOverridable Overrides Async Function _
    ComputeRefactoringsAsync(context As CodeRefactoringContext) As Task

    Dim root = Await context.Document.
        GetSyntaxRootAsync(context.CancellationToken).ConfigureAwait(False)

    ' Find the node at the selection.
    Dim node = root.FindNode(context.Span)

    Dim fieldDecl = TryCast(node, FieldDeclarationSyntax)
    If fieldDecl Is Nothing Or fieldDecl.Modifiers.
        ToFullString.Contains("Private") = False Then
        Return
    End If
```

Notice that the `FieldDeclarationSyntax` object exposes a property called `Modifiers`, of type `SyntaxTokenList`, which can be used to detect the visibility of the current field. Next, you can check whether at least one identifier in the field declaration should be refactored. Take a look at this code:

```
Dim mustRegisterAction As Boolean

For Each declarator In fieldDecl.Declarators
    ' If at least one starting character is
    ' upper case, must register an action
    If declarator.Names.Any(Function(d) _
                Char.IsUpper(d.Identifier.Value.ToString(0))) Then
        mustRegisterAction = True
    Else
        mustRegisterAction = False
    End If
Next
```

`FieldDeclarationSyntax` exposes a property called `Declarators`, of type `SeparatedSyntaxList(Of VariableDeclaratorSyntax)`, which contains the list of `VariableDeclarator` elements in the field. Each exposes the `Names` property, of type `SeparatedSyntaxList(Of ModifiedIdentifierSyntax)`, which contains the list of identifiers in the `VariableDeclarator`. So the code iterates each `VariableDeclarator`, and if at least one variable name starts with a lowercase letter, sets to `True` a Boolean variable that determines whether an action must be registered for refactoring the current field. The `ModifiedIdentifierSyntax` type exposes the `Identifier` property, which represents the actual variable identifier. You will work with it later; for now its `Value` property is used to detect the form of the first letter in its string representation. If at least one identifier matches the condition, you register an action for the current syntax node as follows:

```
If mustRegisterAction = False Then
    Return
Else
    Dim action = CodeAction.Create("Make first char lower case",
                        Function(c) RenameFieldAsync(context.
                        Document, fieldDecl, c))

    ' Register this code action.
    context.RegisterRefactoring(action)
End If
```

You create an action by invoking the `Create` method from the `Microsoft.CodeAnalysis.CodeActions.CodeAction` class; arguments are the text shown in the light bulb and a delegate that performs the refactoring. In this case the delegate, as for analyzers, receives the current document instance, the current syntax node, and a cancellation token as its arguments. The `RenameFieldAsync` method starts by getting an instance of the semantic model and an instance of the syntax root for the current document, which is something you already saw with analyzers:

```
Private Async Function RenameFieldAsync(document As Document,
                fieldDeclaration As FieldDeclarationSyntax,
                cancellationToken As CancellationToken) _
                As Task(Of Document)

    Dim semanticModel = Await document.
        GetSemanticModelAsync(cancellationToken).
        ConfigureAwait(False)

    Dim root = Await document.GetSyntaxRootAsync
```

The logic of your action requires iterating variable declarators in the current field; for each declarator, you need to generate new identifiers for variables whose name starts with an uppercase letter. Finally, you have to generate new declarators and a new document based on the supplied changes. Start by storing the collection of existing variable declarators and declaring two collections of `ModifiedIdentifierSyntax` and `VariableDeclaratorSyntax` objects, as follows:

```
Dim oldDeclarators = fieldDeclaration.Declarators
Dim listOfNewModifiedIdentifiers As _
    New SeparatedSyntaxList(Of ModifiedIdentifierSyntax)
Dim listOfNewModifiedDeclarators As _
    New SeparatedSyntaxList(Of VariableDeclaratorSyntax)
```

The next step is to iterate the collection of variable declarators and their names in order to generate new ModifiedIdentifierSyntax objects with new names. The following code demonstrates this (be sure to read the comments):

```
'Iterate the declarators collection
For Each declarator In oldDeclarators
    'For each variable name in the declarator...
    For Each modifiedIdentifier In declarator.Names
        'Get a new proper name
        Dim tempString = ConvertName(modifiedIdentifier.ToFullString)

        'Generate a new ModifiedIdentifierSyntax based on
        'the previous one's properties but with a new Identifier
        Dim newModifiedIdentifier As ModifiedIdentifierSyntax =
            modifiedIdentifier.
            WithIdentifier(SyntaxFactory.ParseToken(tempString)).
            WithTrailingTrivia(modifiedIdentifier.GetTrailingTrivia)

        'Add the new element to the collection
        listOfNewModifiedIdentifiers =
            listOfNewModifiedIdentifiers.Add(newModifiedIdentifier)
    Next
    'Store a new variable declarator with new
    'variable names
    listOfNewModifiedDeclarators =
        listOfNewModifiedDeclarators.Add(declarator.
        WithNames(listOfNewModifiedIdentifiers))

    'Clear the list before next iteration
    listOfNewModifiedIdentifiers = Nothing
    listOfNewModifiedIdentifiers = New _
        SeparatedSyntaxList(Of ModifiedIdentifierSyntax)
Next
```

Once you have a list of new VariableDeclaratorSyntax objects, you can generate a new FieldDeclarationSyntax like this:

```
Dim newField = fieldDeclaration.
    WithDeclarators(listOfNewModifiedDeclarators)
```

The FieldDeclarationSyntax.WithDeclarators method allows you to specify the variable declarators for the field instance. As you did with analyzers, you generate a new syntax node and replace the old FieldDeclarationSyntax node with the newly created one:

```
Dim newRoot As SyntaxNode =
    root.ReplaceNode(fieldDeclaration, newField)
```

```
Dim newDocument =
    document.WithSyntaxRoot(newRoot)

Return newDocument
End Function
```

You can now press **F5** to start the experimental instance and test your code refactoring. If you right-click the field declaration and select **Quick Actions**, you will be able to see a preview of how the code is going to be refactored, as shown in Figure 51.15.

FIGURE 51.15   The custom code refactoring is working in the Visual Studio's light bulb.

Listing 51.4 shows the full code for the custom refactoring.

LISTING 51.4   Implementing a Custom Refactoring

```
<ExportCodeRefactoringProvider(PrivateFieldCodeRefactoringCodeRefactoringProvider.
                        RefactoringId,
                        LanguageNames.VisualBasic), [Shared]>
Friend Class PrivateFieldCodeRefactoringCodeRefactoringProvider
    Inherits CodeRefactoringProvider

    Public Const RefactoringId As String = "PrivateFieldCodeRefactoring"

    Public NotOverridable Overrides Async Function _
        ComputeRefactoringsAsync(context As CodeRefactoringContext) As Task
```

```
    Dim root = Await context.Document.
        GetSyntaxRootAsync(context.CancellationToken).ConfigureAwait(False)

    ' Find the node at the selection.
    Dim node = root.FindNode(context.Span)

    Dim fieldDecl = TryCast(node, FieldDeclarationSyntax)
    If fieldDecl Is Nothing Or fieldDecl.Modifiers.
        ToFullString.Contains("Private") = False Then
        Return
    End If

    Dim mustRegisterAction As Boolean

    For Each declarator In fieldDecl.Declarators
        'If at least one starting character is
        'upper case, must register an action
        If declarator.Names.Any(Function(d) _
                                Char.
                                IsUpper(d.Identifier.
                                Value.ToString(0))) Then
            mustRegisterAction = True
        Else
            mustRegisterAction = False
        End If
    Next

    If mustRegisterAction = False Then
        Return
    Else
        Dim action = CodeAction.Create("Make first char lower case",
                                Function(c) RenameFieldAsync(context.
                                Document, fieldDecl, c))

        ' Register this code action.
        context.RegisterRefactoring(action)
    End If
End Function

Private Async Function RenameFieldAsync(document As Document,
                        fieldDeclaration As FieldDeclarationSyntax,
                        cancellationToken As CancellationToken) _
                        As Task(Of Document)

    Dim semanticModel = Await document.
        GetSemanticModelAsync(cancellationToken).
```

```vb
    ConfigureAwait(False)

Dim root = Await document.GetSyntaxRootAsync

Dim oldDeclarators = fieldDeclaration.Declarators
Dim listOfNewModifiedIdentifiers As _
    New SeparatedSyntaxList(Of ModifiedIdentifierSyntax)
Dim listOfNewModifiedDeclarators As _
    New SeparatedSyntaxList(Of VariableDeclaratorSyntax)

'Iterate the declarators collection
For Each declarator In oldDeclarators
    'For each variable name in the declarator...
    For Each modifiedIdentifier In declarator.Names
        'Get a new proper name
        Dim tempString = ConvertName(modifiedIdentifier.ToFullString)

        'Generate a new ModifiedIdentifierSyntax based on
        'the previous one's properties but with a new Identifier
        Dim newModifiedIdentifier As ModifiedIdentifierSyntax =
            modifiedIdentifier.
            WithIdentifier(SyntaxFactory.ParseToken(tempString)).
            WithTrailingTrivia(modifiedIdentifier.GetTrailingTrivia)

        'Add the new element to the collection
        listOfNewModifiedIdentifiers =
            listOfNewModifiedIdentifiers.Add(newModifiedIdentifier)
    Next
    'Store a new variable declarator with new
    'variable names
    listOfNewModifiedDeclarators =
        listOfNewModifiedDeclarators.Add(declarator.
        WithNames(listOfNewModifiedIdentifiers))

    'Clear the list before next iteration
    listOfNewModifiedIdentifiers = Nothing
    listOfNewModifiedIdentifiers = New _
        SeparatedSyntaxList(Of ModifiedIdentifierSyntax)
Next


Dim newField = fieldDeclaration.
    WithDeclarators(listOfNewModifiedDeclarators)
```

```
        Dim newRoot As SyntaxNode =
            root.ReplaceNode(fieldDeclaration, newField)

        Dim newDocument =
            document.WithSyntaxRoot(newRoot)

        Return newDocument
    End Function

    Private Function ConvertName(oldName As String) As String
        Return Char.ToLowerInvariant(oldName(0)) + oldName.Substring(1)
    End Function
End Class
```

Custom refactoring techniques offer additional domain-specific possibilities and can help developers write better code on some platforms or over APIs.

PUBLISHING ANALYZERS AND CODE REFACTORINGS

You have two options for publishing and sharing analyzers with other developers: You can create a NuGet package that can be installed in Visual Studio 2015 with the NuGet Package Manager, or you can generate a VSIX package that can be published to the Visual Studio Gallery and that developers can install via the Extensions and Updates dialog in the IDE. Code refactorings, on the other hand, can be deployed only via VSIX packages. When you test either an analyzer or a code refactoring, you basically deploy a VSIX package to the experimental instance of Visual Studio. In fact, both templates contain a VSIX project template that generates a deployment-ready package. To publish a VSIX package to the Visual Studio Gallery, read the following page: https://msdn. microsoft.com/en-us/library/ff363239.aspx. If you instead want to publish your work to NuGet, you must first get an account at www.nuget.org, and then you must edit the .nuspec file in the project with the package details and upload it to the NuGet publishing page (https://www.nuget.org/packages/upload). Notice that for code refactoring, you instead have to build a NuGet package manually.

FxCop Live Code Analysis

When you develop class libraries that extend or interact with the .NET Framework, you should follow the Framework Design Guidelines (https://msdn.microsoft.com/en-us/library/ms229042(v=vs.110).aspx), which help developers ensure that they write consistent APIs by providing a unified programming model that is independent from the programming language. In some cases, it can be hard to ensure that all your code is compliant with the Framework Design Guidelines, especially when you have large projects with many lines of code. In the past, you could check for guidelines incompatibilities only with build-time analysis offered by integrated tools in the IDE (and actually these tools are still available in Visual Studio 2015 via the Analyze menu) based on the FxCop engine. Now, with the .NET Compiler Platform, Microsoft is offering the same opportunity but with live analysis as you type. This is a tremendous benefit because it allows you to save time. To see live analysis in action, create a new class library and write the following noncompliant code:

```
Public MustInherit Class HelperClass

    Public Sub New()

    End Sub
    Public Enum Sports
        Soccer = 1
        Baseball = 2
        Football = 3
    End Enum

    Public Interface Person

    End Interface
End Class
```

This code violates the following rules:

- ▶ A `MustInherit` class should not have any public constructors.

- ▶ `Enumerations` should have a zero or `None` value.

- ▶ Interface identifiers should begin with the `I` prefix.

- ▶ Assemblies should be marked with the `CLSCompliant` attribute.

To detect and fix these code issues, download and install the `Microsoft.CodeAnalysis.FxCopAnalyzers` package with the NuGet Package Manager. Once it is installed, expand the Analyzers node in Solution Explorer, as shown in Figure 51.16. As you can see, the package adds two analyzers: `Microsoft.CodeAnalysis.FxCopAnalyzers`, which contains analyzers that are not language specific, and `Microsoft.CodeAnalysis.VisualBasic.FxCopAnalyzers`, which is specific to the Visual Basic language. Every analyzer matches a rule in the Microsoft guidelines. Rules are organized into categories, as summarized in Table 51.2.

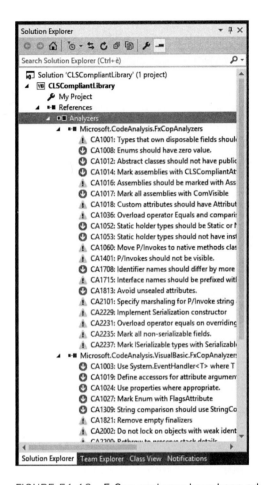

FIGURE 51.16   FxCop analyzers have been added to the project.

TABLE 51.2   Microsoft Code Analysis Rules

Rule Name	Description
Design	Determines whether assemblies contain well-designed objects or if the assembly definition is compliant with the CLR requirements
Globalization	Determines whether globalization techniques are well implemented
Interoperability	Determines whether the code makes correct usage of COM interoperability
Maintainability	Checks for code maintainability according to Microsoft rules
Mobility	Checks for timer and processes correct implementation
Naming	Determines whether all identifiers match the guidelines rules (such as public/private members, method parameters, etc.)

Rule Name	Description
Performance	Checks for unused or inappropriate code for compile time and runtime performances from the CLR perspective
Portability	Determines whether the code is portable for invoked API functions
Reliability	Provides rules for a better interaction with the Garbage Collector
Security	Provides security-related rules sending error messages if types and members are not considered secure
Usage	Determines whether a code block correctly invokes other code

Live FxCop analysis does not require all of the rules to be enabled, but most of them are disabled by default, so before you start live analysis on your code, you must enable the desired rules. To enable rules, right-click Analyzers and then select **Open Rule Set**. When the list of rules appears, in the Group By box select **Analyzer ID** so that you will be able to distinguish between built-in rules and FxCop rules. Next, expand the `Microsoft.CodeAnalysis.FxCopAnalyzers` item and select all the available rules, as shown in Figure 51.17.

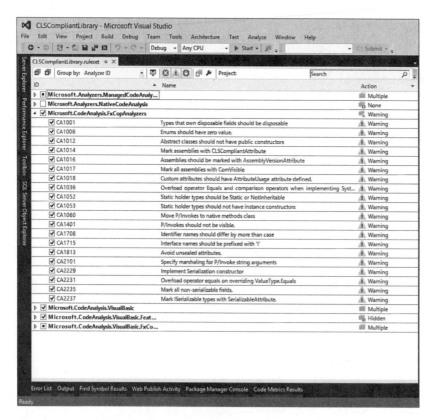

FIGURE 51.17   Selecting FxCop rules for live analysis.

If you now go back to the code editor window for the class created before, you will see several green squiggles, each for a violated rule. The Error List window shows code issues, and you can use the light bulb to fix warnings, exactly as you would do when writing code normally. Figure 51.18 demonstrates this.

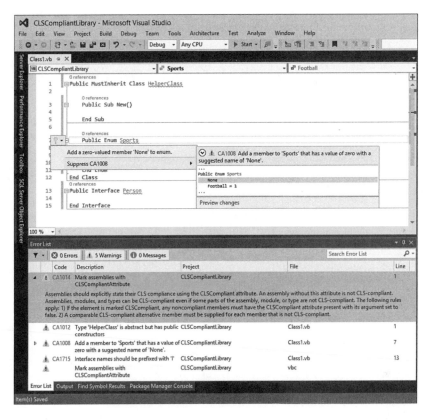

FIGURE 51.18   Fixing FxCop issues with the light bulb and quick actions.

If an issue is not clear, do not forget to check the full message in the Error List window. In this way, you can easily fix FxCop rule violations and write guidelines-compliant code more efficiently.

Calculating Code Metrics

Code Metrics is an interesting tool that analyzes a project or a solution and provides results about the ease of maintainability according to specific indices. To use the tool, select **Analyze, Calculate Code Metrics** or right-click the project name in Solution Explorer and then select the same-named command. The tool calculates code metrics according to the indices summarized in Table 51.3.

TABLE 51.3   Code Metrics Analyzed Indices

Index	Description
Maintainability index	A percentage value indicates ease of maintainability for the selected project or solution. A higher value indicates the project is well structured and easily maintainable.
Cyclomatic complexity	A percentage value indicates complexity of loops, nested loops, and nested conditional blocks, such as nested `For..Next` loops, `Do..Loop` loops, or `If..End If` nested blocks. A higher value indicates you should consider refactoring your code to decrease loop complexity because this leads to difficult maintainability.
Depth of inheritance	Indicates the inheritance level for classes in the project. The result shows the report for the class with the highest inheritance level. A higher value indicates it might be difficult finding problems in a complex inheritance hierarchy.
Class coupling	Calculates how many references to classes there are from method parameters and return values, local variables, and other implementations. A higher value indicates code is difficult to reuse, and you should consider revisiting your code for better maintainability.
Lines of code	Just a statistic value. It returns the number of IL code affected by the analysis.

To understand how it works, in Visual Studio 2015 open the **Channel9_AsyncAwait** sample project described in Chapter 42, "Asynchronous Programming." Next, run the Code Metrics tool by selecting **Analyze**, Calculate Code Metrics **for Solution**. After a few seconds, you get the report shown in Figure 51.19.

Hierarchy ▲	Maintainability Index	Cyclomatic Complexity	Depth of Inheritance	Class Coupling	Lines of Code
▲ 🔲 Async_Await\GettingStarted_plus_cancellation	86	48	9	49	84
▲ { } Channel_AsyncAwait	89	28	9	32	45
▷ ⚙ Application	92	2	3	4	3
▷ ⚙ MainWindow	81	14	9	28	30
▷ ⚙ Video	93	12	1	0	12
▷ { } Channel_AsyncAwait.My	82	20	1	20	39

FIGURE 51.19   Calculating code metrics for the specified project.

As you can see from the report, the project has a maintainability index of 86, which is quite good. Values from 80 to 100 are the best range for maintainability. Visual Studio shows a green symbol if the index is good or a red one if the maintainability index is poor. You can expand the nodes in the **Hierarchy** item to see how the global result is subdivided for each class and for each class member. The global Cyclomatic Complexity index is 48, which is a reasonable number for our kind of project. Depth of Inheritance index is 9, which is also reasonable, meaning one or more class is inheriting from another class that inherits from another one (the third one is `System.Object`). This is an absolutely acceptable value in this particular scenario, especially because it involves a user control that, by its nature, has a deep inheritance hierarchy. The Class Coupling index is a little too high. It is determined by the `MainWindow` class, so this class has a lot of references to other classes. Obviously, not necessarily a high index indicates problems. In this code example, a high value is acceptable because all invocations are required to make the sample work. However, in a reusable class library, a high value should need attention and code refactoring.

EXPORTING TO EXCEL

If you need to elaborate the code metrics results, you can export the analysis report to Microsoft Excel. This can be accomplished with the **Open List in Excel** button on the Code Metrics Result tool window.

Diagnostic Tools and IntelliTrace

Visual Studio 2015 introduces a new excellent debugging tool called Diagnostic Tools, which enables developers to understand how an application is consuming memory and CPU during its life cycle and to investigate debugger events. The Diagnostic Tools includes a Timeline area where you can see where time is spent during the application life cycle; it also has another area where you can investigate debugger events, take memory snapshots at a given time, and see CPU usage. Diagnostic Tools also integrates IntelliTrace, the historical debugger that you know from previous editions of Visual Studio Ultimate (now called Enterprise). In version 2015, IntelliTrace functionalities are no longer offered in a separated tool window but integrated with Diagnostic Tools for a premiere debugging experience.

To understand Diagnostic Tools, open the **Channel9_AsyncAwait** project created in Chapter 42. Start debugging by pressing **F5**. The Diagnostic Tools profiling window appears automatically, displaying live information about memory and CPU utilization during the application life cycle. When the application finishes downloading the RSS feed, close it. The Diagnostic Tools Timeline shows global information about memory and CPU, as you can see in Figure 51.20.

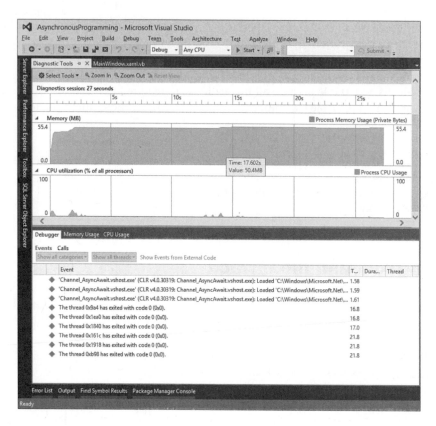

FIGURE 51.20 The Diagnostic Tools Timeline shows memory and CPU information.

If you hover over the graphic with the mouse pointer, you get a ToolTip showing information on both memory consumption and CPU usage for the application process. In the bottom area, you can see information about threads. Now select the Memory Usage tab. You see a button labeled Take Snapshot, which allows you to capture the memory state at a certain point. You can capture multiple snapshots for comparisons. To see how this works, restart the application and take two memory snapshots while the application is running. The first time you take a snapshot, Diagnostic Tools shows the number of object instances in memory and the memory usage, in kilobytes; thereafter, every time you take a snapshot, the tool also shows the difference between the previous count and the current count of object instances and kilobytes used. Figure 51.21 demonstrates this.

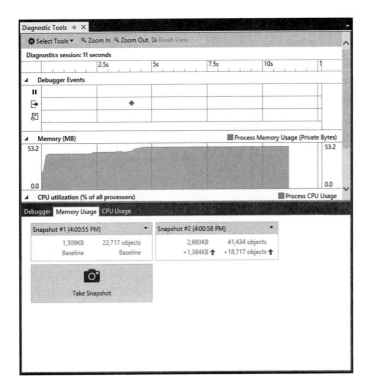

FIGURE 51.21   Summary information for every snapshot.

You can click the object instances count in the latest snapshot to get detailed information about object types, instances, and size in memory in the Heap View window, as shown in Figure 51.22.

Heap View Snapshot #2 ⊕ ✕ Diagnostic Tools

Managed Memory (Channel_AsyncAwait.vshost.exe) Compare to: Snapshot #1 ▾

View Settings ▾ Search

ℹ View Settings have filtered some object types (Just My Code)

Object Type	Count	Count Diff.	Total Size (Bytes)	Total Size Diff. (Bytes)	Inclusive Size (Bytes)	Inclusive Size Diff. (Bytes) ▾
Channel_AsyncAwait.Application	1	0	116	0	1,065,500	+909,284
Channel_AsyncAwait.MainWindow	1	0	916	0	1,064,756	+909,284
List<AutomationPeer>	28	+26	1,540	+1,436	565,632	+565,420
ListBox	1	0	748	0	508,796	+476,476
Enumerable+WhereSelectEnumerableIterator<XElement,...	1	+1	36	+36	416,420	+416,420
XContainer+<GetDescendants>d__a	1	+1	52	+52	416,384	+416,384
XElement	669	+669	111,440	+111,440	414,648	+414,648
Microsoft.XamlDiagnostics.WpfTap.WpfVisualTreeService...	263	+242	9,468	+8,712	351,404	+337,952
List<Microsoft.XamlDiagnostics.WpfTap.WpfVisualTreeSe...	154	+138	6,608	+5,976	334,620	+322,464
ListBoxAutomationPeer	1	0	112	0	285,316	+285,144
ListBoxItemAutomationPeer	25	+25	2,400	+2,400	283,992	+283,992
ArrayList	201	+91	14,652	+8,376	293,792	+275,988
TimerThread+TimerQueue	3	0	60	0	261,512	+261,332
TimerThread+TimerNode	9	+6	360	+240	261,452	+261,332
ConnectionGroup	3	+2	236	+184	259,008	+258,876
Connection	5	+4	21,520	+17,216	258,532	+253,452

Paths to Root | Referenced Types

Object Type	Reference Count	Reference Count Diff. ▾
▲ XElement		
XElement [Cycle Detected]	1,378	+1,378
▲ XAttribute	927	+927
XAttribute [Cycle Detected]	900	+900
XElement [Cycle Detected]	221	+221
▷ XCData	25	+25
▷ XContainer+<GetDescendants>d__a	3	+3

FIGURE 51.22 Detailed information about object instances live at the time of a snapshot.

You can click an object type and get even more detailed information via the Paths to Root tab at the bottom of the window; you can expand nested elements to discover instances of children objects. As its name implies, the Referenced Types tab allows you to get information about types that have been referenced by the currently selected object. With all this detailed information, Visual Studio 2015 offers a convenient way to examine how your applications spend time and to detect what object instances are possibly affecting application performance or using memory improperly. The Diagnostic Tools also allows you to investigate debugger events, including both the debugger and IntelliTrace.

IntelliTrace, also known as the historical debugger, can improve your debugging experience because it can record and navigate every event occurring during the application lifetime, such as events and failures including information on specific threads. IntelliTrace is available only in the Enterprise edition and is fully integrated with the code editor and with the rest of the IDE functionalities, such as Call Stack and Locals tool windows so it can provide a complete debugging environment. The tool is capable of recording (to a file, too) and debugging the following:

▶ Application events, such as user interface events or application exceptions

▶ Playback debugging, which allows deep debugging over specific events occurred before and after a particular code block

▶ Unit test failures

▶ Load test failures and build acceptances test

▶ Manual tests

To understand how you can investigate debugger events, place a breakpoint on the `MessageBox.Show` statement after catching the `OperationCanceledException` exception in the `QueryVideosAsync` method (the one that accepts a `CancellationToken` as an argument). Start debugging with **F5** and press the **Cancel** button in the application. At this point, an `OperationCanceledException` is raised, and the execution breaks on the specified breakpoint. Figure 51.23 shows how the Diagnostic Tools window appears at this point.

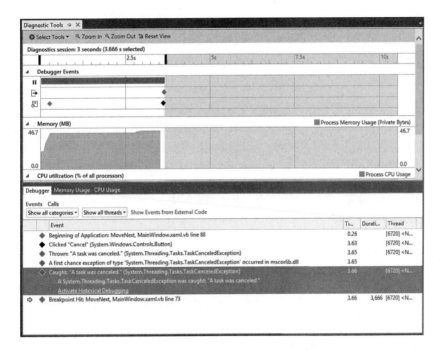

FIGURE 51.23   Investigating debugger events with Diagnostic Tools.

The Debugger Events area in the Timeline shows events raised by the debugger in red, and it shows events raised by IntelliTrace in black. You can hover over the glyph symbols to see a ToolTip describing the event, but most importantly, you can get a detailed list of debugger events in the Debugger tab at the bottom of the window. You can see that IntelliTrace detected a button click, and then the debugger detected an exception. Diagnostic Tools also detected that the exception was caught and that a breakpoint was hit at the specified line.

Now click the **Caught: "A task was canceled."** event. As you can see, there is a hyperlink called Activate Historical Debugging. This enables one of the most important IntelliTrace features, allowing you to resume debugging from a certain point of the application life cycle. If you click that hyperlink, Visual Studio shows the point where the event occurred in the code, highlights the proper line in orange, and allows you to resume the debugger from that point (see Figure 51.24).

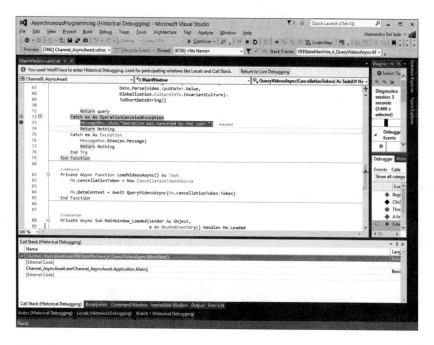

FIGURE 51.24   Historical debugging with IntelliTrace.

Resuming the debugger from a certain point can be very useful for gathering additional information on what caused the application's execution to break. IntelliTrace provides great control over the debugging experience, especially when you enable call information other than trace events in the Options window. (This can affect performance.) Diagnostic Tools can also inspect CPU usage, network usage, and GPU usage, but these are available only when you start an application without debugging—that is, with **Ctrl+F5**. To configure Diagnostic Tools for these scenarios, select **Debug, Start Diagnostic Tools Without Debugging**. You will be able to select more than one diagnostic tool, and you can also change the diagnostic target, which means choosing a different application than the current project, such as a Windows Store app (running or installed), an ASP.NET application, an executable file, or an instance of Internet Explorer on Windows Phone. The place where you select diagnostic tools is called Diagnostic Hub, and it is shown in Figure 51.25.

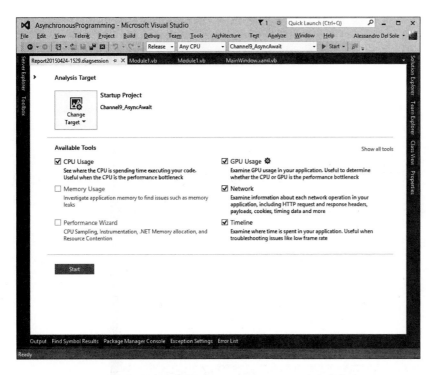

FIGURE 51.25   Selecting multiple diagnostic tools in Diagnostic Hub.

Select the **CPU Usage** and **GPU Usage** tools and then click **Start**. When the application finishes downloading the RSS feed, shut it down. At this point, the Diagnostic Tools window in Visual Studio 2015 shows a tremendous amount of information about both diagnostics, as you can see in Figure 51.26.

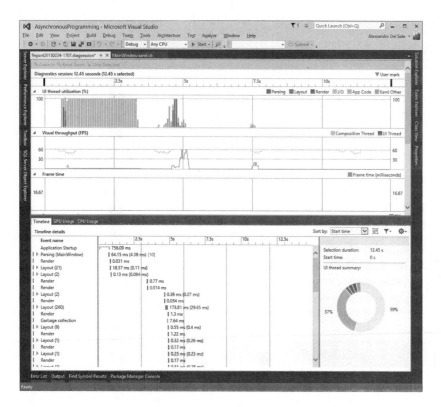

FIGURE 51.26   GPU Usage information in Diagnostic Tools.

The first screen shows the UI thread utilization, with a legend explaining what operations every color refers to. You can investigate frame per seconds and see how much time each operation took to complete in the Timeline tab at the bottom. If you click any element here, Visual Studio shows verbose information on what happened. For example, if you click the garbage collection element, you will get an explanation about why a garbage collection started at that point of the application life cycle. The GPU Usage tab shows more detailed information for a certain interval that you have to select in the UI thread utilization area. The CPU Usage tab (see Figure 51.27) shows detailed information about the CPU usage in percentage, and it helps you understand which code required the CPU resources, including external code.

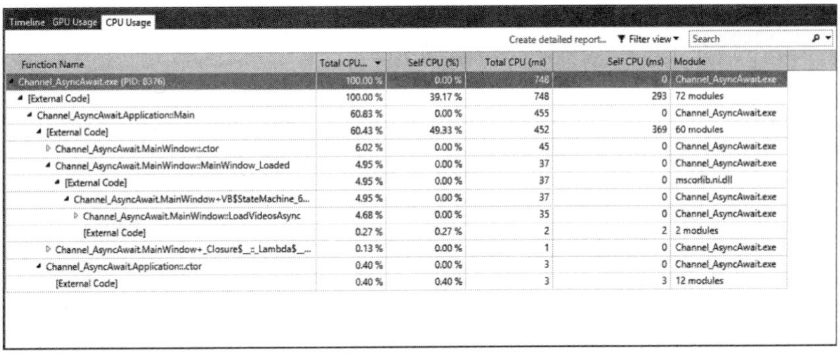

FIGURE 51.27   CPU Usage information in the Diagnostic Tools.

Diagnostic Tools is one of the most important additions to the Visual Studio 2015 development environment, and it really makes the difference between the Enterprise edition and other editions. With this tool, you can carefully investigate what your application does during its life cycle and where and why it spends time and resources. By finding and solving issues you find, you can be sure to create reliable, performant, high-quality applications.

Code Clone Detection

It is common for some applications to be under development for long periods of time. In this kind of situation, you might have millions of lines of code, and you might forget you have already written a procedure or code snippet to solve a particular problem. So you might create a duplicate. Visual Studio 2015 offers a tool called Code Clone Detection, which helps you find code snippets that are equal or very similar. To understand how this new tool works, open the **Channel9_AsyncAwait** project you used before. Then enter the MainWindow.xaml.vb code file and create a copy of the QueryVideosAsync method and rename the copy QueryVideosAsyncCloned. Then select **Analyze, Analyze Solution for Code Clones**. Visual Studio starts searching for cloned code and shows the results in the Code Clone Analysis Result window (see Figure 51.28).

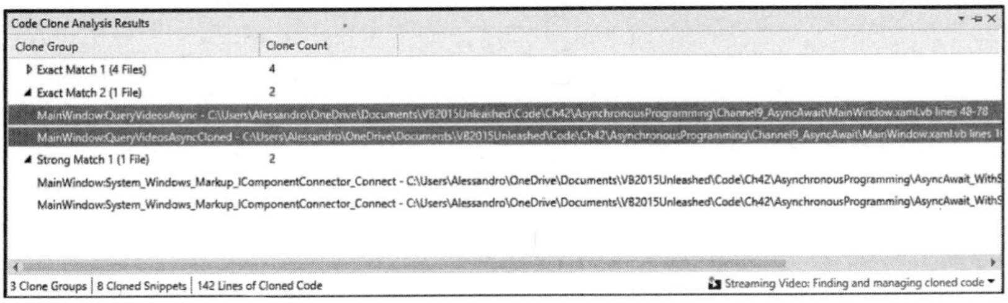

FIGURE 51.28   Finding exact code clones.

Visual Studio groups code clones by their relevance and shows the number of clones for each group, including the line numbers that have been detected as cloned. If you hover the mouse over an item, a ToolTip shows an excerpt of the code. As you can see in Figure 51.28, Visual Studio shows the Exact Match message because clones are exactly the same.

Of course, Visual Studio is powerful enough to identify clones of code snippets, too. To demonstrate this, rename some variables in the `CompileCloned` method and rearrange variable declarations. If you run the Code Clone Detection tool again, you see that Visual Studio still recognizes clones, but this time the message is Strong Match. This means the clones are not exactly the same but are very similar (see Figure 51.29).

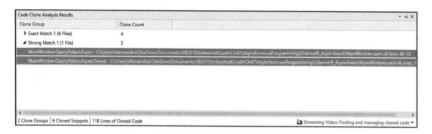

FIGURE 51.29   Finding similar code clones.

If you select two or more clones in the results window and right-click the selection, you can click the **Compare** command to get a visual comparison of code clones. As you can see shown in Figure 51.30, the IDE uses different colors to highlight the lines of code it has recognized as changed compared to the original code. Following is a list of useful information about code detection:

▶ Visual Studio can find clones only longer than 10 lines of code.

▶ It does not analyze type declarations—only methods and properties definitions.

▶ Because code clones often results from copying some code from one location to another one, the tool discovers additions of lines, deletions, and renaming actions.

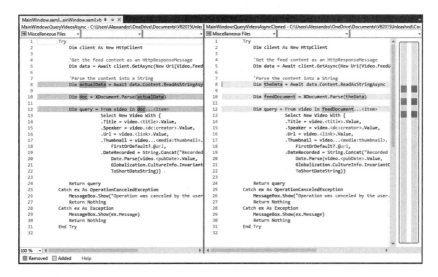

FIGURE 51.30   Comparing code clones.

In this chapter, you saw an example of a code clone inside the same code file, but the tool searches throughout the entire solution. This tool is particularly useful for code refactoring and when updating code due to a long development time.

Summary

This chapter covered some important analysis tools available in Visual Studio 2015. You first got started with the .NET Compiler Platform, discovering how powerful it is for creating live code analyzers and refactorings that integrate with the light bulb. In the process, you got a more precise idea of how the Visual Basic compiler works since it has been reengineered on top of the .NET Compiler Platform. You also learned how to use special analyzers to analyze code for compliance with Microsoft coding rules, which is required especially when you produce reusable class libraries. Then you saw how to check for code maintainability by using the Code Metrics tool. The chapter then focused on the most interesting addition in Visual Studio 2015: the Diagnostic Tools, which now integrates IntelliTrace, the historical debugger. Information was provided on using this tool to understand where the application spends time and consumes resources, keeping track of events and exceptions during the entire application lifetime. Finally, you got an overview of Code Clone Detection, which helps you find duplicate code.

APPENDIX A

Useful Resources and Tools for Visual Basic 2015

The Visual Basic 2015 language is an even more powerful version than its predecessors and enables you to access every feature and technology exposed by .NET Framework 4.6. But the Framework is a large technology, and the language has so many features that remembering everything is almost impossible. So, instead of remembering everything, it is important for you to know where to search for information, resources, and learning material. Moreover, Visual Studio 2015 is a powerful development environment that includes a plethora of tools to make your development experience great. There are some situations in which the IDE does not include particular features that are instead provided by third-party tools. This appendix gives you a number of Visual Basic resources inside the MSDN documentation and websites for you to bookmark in your Favorites. Also, this appendix provides a list of useful tools for you as a Visual Basic developer. They are all free tools, so you can enjoy their functionalities.

Visual Basic Resources in MSDN

Following are learning resources for Visual Basic 2012 inside the MSDN Library and websites:

▶ **The Visual Studio Developer Center–Visual Basic:** The principal website from Microsoft dedicated to Visual Basic: http://msdn.microsoft.com/en-us/vstudio/hh388568.

▶ **Visual Basic "How Do I" videos:** A portal where you can find a lot of videos illustrating programming techniques and usage of Microsoft technologies with Visual Basic: http://msdn.microsoft.com/en-us/vbasic/bb466226.aspx.

▶ **Visual Basic Code Samples:** A sub-list of code samples from the MSDN Code Gallery specifically targeting the Visual Basic language: http://bit.ly/ObAnY6.

▶ **Asynchronous Programming Developer Center:** A specific portal from MSDN where you can find resources about the asynchronous programming patterns and related language syntax. This is available at: http://msdn.microsoft.com/en-us/vstudio/async.aspx.

▶ **CodePlex:** The famous website hosting open source projects (www.codeplex.com) where you can find complete applications written with Visual Basic, including source code.

▶ **Visual Basic MSDN Library:** Probably the most important reference for every Visual Basic developer, where you can find documentation, language reference, walkthroughs and examples: https://msdn.microsoft.com/en-us/library/hh334523.aspx.

▶ **.NET Framework Developer Center:** The principal website for information on all .NET-based Microsoft technologies: https://msdn.microsoft.com/en-us/vstudio/aa496123.

Also don't forget to use search engines, which in most cases will be your best friends. Typically they will return the most accurate results if your search is performed by writing English strings.

Useful Developer Tools for Visual Basic

This section provides a list of free useful tools that will enrich your developer toolbox.

Coding Tools

The following tools can help you improve your productivity in writing better code:

▶ **CodeRush Xpress** from DevExpress is a free Visual Studio add-in that enhances the Visual Studio code editor by providing refactoring tools to write better, more readable, and more efficient code. If you used Refactor! Express in the past, CodeRush is its more powerful successor. You can find it at http://www.devexpress.com/Products/Visual_Studio_Add-in/CodeRushX/.

▶ **Code Snippet Editor** is an open source tool written in Visual Basic for creating and exporting reusable code snippets with advanced functionalities in VB, C#, and XML languages via a comfortable graphical user interface. It is available at http://snippeteditor.codeplex.com.

Networking

One of the most famous tools in networking is **Fiddler**, which is a free Web debugging proxy that can log all http and https traffic between the computer and the Internet. Other than inspecting http traffic, Fiddler can set breakpoints and walk through incoming or outgoing data. You can find it at http://www.fiddler2.com/fiddler2/. Fiddler is particularly useful in debugging WCF services and WCF Data Services, other than requests coming from Web browsers such as Internet Explorer and Firefox.

Data Access

For data access tools, **LINQPad** is very useful. This is a free tool that provides advanced instrumentation for querying data sources and that can generate the necessary code using LINQ. Visual Basic is one of the supported languages. You can find it at http://www. linqpad.net. At the moment in which this appendix is being written, LINQPad supports .NET Framework 4.0 and so can be used with no problems against the new release of Visual Basic.

Miscellaneous

The following tools are not strictly related to a single technology or cannot be classified in other sections:

▶ **Visual Studio Power Tools** is a must-have extension that adds a number of useful coding and management tools to the IDE. It is free and is available from Microsoft on the Visual Studio Gallery.

▶ **JustDecompile** is a free tool from Telerik, capable of exploring .NET assemblies via Reflection. The tool can show the Intermediate Language or offer decompilation results in both Visual Basic and Visual C# of the specified executable. JustDecompile is not only useful for reflecting or decompiling assemblies, but is also particularly useful for inspecting .NET Framework Base Class Libraries and understanding how many things are implemented behind the scenes. You can find it at http://www. telerik.com/justdecompile.aspx.

▶ **Multilingual App Toolkit** is a free extension for Visual Studio that makes it easy to localize WPF and Windows Store applications and also provides an option for adding multiple language translations simultaneously. You can download it from http://bit. ly/1IXo3nR.

▶ **Microsoft Visual Studio Installer Projects** is an extension that adds old-style Setup & Deployment projects for Windows Installer. It is available at https:// visualstudiogallery.msdn.microsoft.com/9abe329c-9bba-44a1-be59-0fbf6151054d/.

Where to Find Additional Tools

If you are interested in enhancing your toolbox with third-party tools, check out the Visual Studio Gallery (http://visualstudiogallery.com) that contains hundreds of useful tools divided into categories. Also visit both the MSDN Code Gallery (http://code.msdn.microsoft.com) and the CodePlex community (http://www.codeplex.com) where you can find hundreds of useful tools, which are free in most cases.

Index

Symbols & Numerics

A

B

C

F

G

P

Q

R

T

X

Y-Z

UNLEASHED

Unleashed takes you beyond the basics, providing an exhaustive, technically sophisticated reference for professionals who need to exploit a technology to its fullest potential. It's the best resource for practical advice from the experts, and the most in-depth coverage of the latest technologies.

informit.com/unleashed

Universal Windows Apps with XAML and C# Unleashed
ISBN-13: 9780672337260

OTHER UNLEASHED TITLES

C# 5.0 Unleashed
ISBN-13: 9780672336904

ASP.NET Dynamic Data Unleashed
ISBN-13: 9780672335655

Microsoft System Center 2012 Unleashed
ISBN-13: 9780672336126

System Center 2012 Configuration Manager (SCCM) Unleashed
ISBN-13: 9780672334375

System Center 2012 R2 Configuration Manager Unleashed: Supplement to System Center 2012 Configuration Manager (SCCM) Unleashed
ISBN-13: 9780672337154

Windows Server 2012 Unleashed
ISBN-13: 9780672336225

Microsoft Exchange Server 2013 Unleashed
ISBN-13: 9780672336119

Microsoft Visual Studio 2015 Unleashed
ISBN-13: 9780672337369

System Center 2012 Operations Manager Unleashed
ISBN-13: 9780672335914

Microsoft Dynamics CRM 2013 Unleashed
ISBN-13: 9780672337031

Microsoft Lync Server 2013 Unleashed
ISBN-13: 9780672336157

Visual Basic 2012 Unleashed
ISBN-13: 9780672336317

Microsoft SQL Server 2014 Unleashed
ISBN-13: 9780672337291

WPF 4.5 Unleashed
ISBN-13: 9780672336973

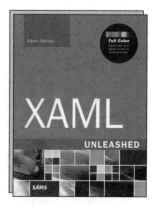

XAML Unleashed
ISBN-13: 9780672337222

SAMS

informit.com/sams